BRITISH RAILWAYS FIRST GENERATION DMUs

BLACKBURN
Way out

BRITISH RAILWAYS FIRST GENERATION DMUs

HUGH LONGWORTH

An imprint of
Ian Allan Publishing

Front cover: With the headcode display covered, a six-car Class 126 formation, with a DMBS(L) leading, passes Cadder Yard on a Glasgow–Edinburgh service. The photograph was taken on 16th May 1971, by which date most such workings on this route where in the hands of Class 27s 'topping and tailing' rakes of Mk 2 stock. *Derek Cross*

Half title: It is the 12th April 1973 at Liverpool Lime Street station. The shafts of sunlight highlight the diesel fumes as a four-car Class 115 DMU struggles up the steep incline heading towards Edge Hill on its way to Manchester. As usual a Class 86 electric locomotive is waiting for departure with a Euston train on Platform 7. This atmospheric picture takes me right back to my teenage years. Growing up in Liverpool this was the departure point for many train spotting trips with Robert Cruickshank and Grahame McCoyd. In later years it was the departure point for travelling to University in London, or waving off my girlfriend (now my wife) Doris to University in Newcastle upon Tyne.

The small batch of high density DMUs based at Allerton to work the Manchester services via Warrington soon became boring at our spotting point at Mossley Hill Station, halfway between home and school. But it was a genuine delight for me to re-acquaint myself with M51852 and M51859 on a visit to Minehead Station on the West Somerset Railway many years later. *D Griffiths*

Previous page: In this scene it is mid-afternoon at Manchester Victoria on the 31st May 1984. On the left Class 104 M53433 waits to work the 16.00 service to Blackburn, while on the right Class 120 M53739 is preparing to depart as the 15.40 to Blackpool North. *B Morrison*

First published 2011

ISBN 978 0 86093 612 1

Published by Oxford Publishing Co

an imprint of Ian Allan Publishing Ltd, Hersham, Surrey, KT12 4RG
Printed in England by Ian Allan Printing Ltd, Hersham, Surrey, KT12 4RG

Code: 1104/C

Distributed in the United States of America and Canada by BookMasters Distribution Services

Visit the Ian Allan Publishing website at www.ianallanpublishing.com

Contents

Preface

I was delighted when my first book (British Railways Steam Locomotives 1948-1968) was received with such enthusiasm.

Now, with encouragement from Peter Waller at Ian Allan, I have the opportunity to turn my attention to a subject of which I have had more personal experience.

I started watching trains in September 1969 when the journey to my new secondary school took me past Mossley Hill Station in the southern suburbs of Liverpool. The North West of England was full of DMUs of many different varieties, and even though spotting locomotives was my first priority, my spotting book was soon filling up with DMU numbers as well. DMU trips were always a joy as they gave us chance to view the line ahead and watch the driver at work. On one trip from Rock Ferry to Chester in a Metropolitan-Cammell DMU, the driver even invited us into his cab to enjoy the journey with him!

I hope you find this book of interest, and I hope you will forgive me for taking the opportunity in a few of the photo captions to go down memory lane.

Hugh Longworth 2010

I'd like to dedicate this book to that small group of friends that met on the wall at Mossley Hill Station, in particular Grahame McCoyd and Robert Cruickshank. From our base at Mossley Hill we planned trips that took us the length and breadth of the country. Thanks for the good times.

I would also like to thank my close friends Tris Reece-Smith and Paul H. Howells for their friendship and support over the past few difficult years, and their encouragement to me to keep going.

But most important is my family – my wife Doris and my daughter Heppy. You might not share my passion for trains, but you have delighted in my enjoyment and shared many fun train times with me. I'm looking forward to many more!

Introduction

This book lists all the Diesel Multiple Unit (DMU) vehicles which were built for British Railways up to 1963. Many units were ordered before the BR Modernisation Plan of 1955, but it was the Modernisation Plan that paved the way for the wholesale introduction of new locomotives and coaching stock to update the railway and replace steam haulage.

By 1963 sufficient vehicles had been built so that, combined with line closures, steam could be completely eradicated by 1968. In fact, the speed of line closures meant that many of the earlier or non-standard units were redundant by the early 1970s, and other units worked on lines for which they were not designed or really suitable.

These units are collectively known as the First Generation units, and there followed a long gap before the first of the Second Generation units were introduced.

Layout of the book

It is my intention in this book to give individual histories for each vehicle, together with a description of the types of units they were formed in, and an indication of their depot allocations. The book covers all first generation units; that is all units built for BR up to 1963. After this date no more units were built for about fifteen years. Although strictly outside the remit of this book the GWR railcars are also listed as they ran at the same period that many of these units were being constructed.

- Part one list the different types of Diesel Multiple Unit in class order.
- Part two lists Diesel Electric Multiple Unit types with details of classes.
- Part three lists DEMU coaches showing the units they belonged to.
- Part four consists of a full listing of individual coaches.
- Part five gives a list of DMU allocations at key points in their history.
- Part six discusses DMU formations and lists formations and unit numbers at key points in their history.
- Appendix 1 gives year-end totals for each class and type.
- Appendix 2 is a numerical list of all BR issued Lot Numbers, with first generation DMUs highlighted.
- Appendix 3 is a numerical list of all the original diagram numbers allocated to DMUs.

Background

Most of the pre-nationalisation railway companies experimented with railcars or multiple units. Steam powered railcars had been seen in the early 20th Century as a way to reduce costs on branch lines. They were never a great success though; combining a steam engine (which was inherently dirty and needed a lot of maintenance) with a coach was not a recipe for success. Electric multiple units were very successful on the electrified lines south of the Thames and in Northern England. It took longer though to produce successful diesel railcars, and the only company to succeed with this before the Second World War was the Great Western Railway.

The GWR worked successfully together with companies involved in the bus and lorry industry to transfer this technology to rail. The combination of a bus type chassis, together with industry-standard diesel engines driving through mechanical transmission proved to be successful. And the GWR did not just develop small branch line rail cars. They had different types of units for suburban, inter-city and parcels use. They had double-ended single cars and single-ended cars which could be run as two- or three-car units. In real terms, only a small number were built; the railway infrastructure was all designed for steam, and the Second World War slowed down development. But they had proved that successful DMUs were a realistic proposition.

It was not long after British Railways was formed in 1948 that thoughts turned back to diesel units. A committee was set up in 1948 to examine future motive power requirements. In 1952 this committee recommended diesel railcars should be developed for local and branch lines which were not scheduled for electrification. It was hoped that this would help avoid closure on many uneconomical steam-operated branches.

There were a number of bus and light railway building companies eager to try out the "bus on rails" approach. The first of these to develop a prototype was BUT which developed a three-car unit (known as the "flying brick" due to its boxy shape). This was successfully trialled on British Railways and was later taken into BR stock.

In 1952 £1.5million was approved for building two-car light alloy DMUs. British Railways built its own "lightweight" units at Derby Works. The first eight two-car units had hydro-mechanical transmission and were coded "red triangle" for coupling, but following units were all built with mechanical pre-selector gear boxes, based on the proven GWR design (coded "yellow diamond"). Private industry got involved, and Metropolitan-Cammell began its long involvement in building DMUs for BR by building some early lightweight sets. All these early units were numbered in the 79xxx series and were not compatible with later "blue square" units.

There was one other type which was numbered in the 79xxx series and this was the first of the Swindon built inter-city units. Designed for work on the Western and Scottish Regions, they soon all migrated north of the border. They were unusual in having two different types of driving cabs – one with a corridor connection and one without – allowing the units to be easily coupled in three or six car sets without losing the through gangway. More units were built to a broadly similar design later; see Class 126.

When the British Railways modernisation plan was announced in 1955 this heralded the end of steam. DMUs were seen as a key part of this, and a mass programme of DMU construction was authorised. Investment was authorised for the construction of 4600 vehicles including single cars, four-wheeled railbuses and DEMUs. Because of the vast scale of the plan it was necessary to get a large number of private builders involved to build around half of the new vehicles, and they were allowed varying degrees of freedom in design matters. This led to a large variety of different DMUs being built, all being numbered in a new 5xxxx series. A number of non-corridor hauled coaches had been built using 5xxxx numbers and they were renumbered in the 4xxxx series to clear the way for these new DMUs.

In general they all followed a standard design. Two engines using mechanical transmission to drive on the bogies was employed in most cases. They were built to the "blue square" coupling code allowing different types of unit to work together. But there were variations. Some units were fitted with hydraulic transmission and others with only one engine.

In every case the units could be fitted into different general categories:

- The most numerous were the low-density units for general use. These were fitted with seats in seating bays with only a couple of doors accessed from vestibules on each vehicle.
- High density units were designed for commuter routes. Each seating bay was accessed by a door each side to allow rapid embarking and disembarking of large numbers of passengers. These were mainly built as non-corridor units but many were later fitted with through corridor connections.
- Cross country units were designed for longer journeys and in general had more seating space. They often included small buffets, but in reality these did not last very long in service, the catering facilities being removed from the vehicles within a few years.
- Inter-city units of several designs were built, which were in essence built to main line coaching stock standards, usually with catering facilities.

British Railways later gave TOPS class numbers to all these later units (see below), and these numbers are used extensively in this book to describe different types of unit.

The Southern Region of British Railways took a different path from other regions. As they already had vast experience in operating electric multiple units, they decided to go for electric transmission for their diesel units. These DEMUs were built with a large diesel engine above the frames, which gave a distinctive sound (they were known as "thumpers" in their later years). In general they operated in fixed units with unit numbers, and as such are listed in a separate section. The coaches were numbered in the 6xxxx series.

One other type of diesel-electric unit which needs to be mentioned is the Blue Pullman units built by Metropolitan-Cammell. Again numbered in the 6xxxx series, full details can be found in the relevant sections.

Coach numbering, classification and mechanical details

When British Railways was formed in 1948 it inherited a large number of coaches from the Big Four pre-nationalisation companies. A decision was made early on not to renumber these coaches, but instead to give them suffix letters to define the original owning company. These were E for ex-LNER vehicles, M for ex-LMS, S for ex-Southern and W for ex-GWR. In addition they carried prefixes to show the region they were allocated to; the same letters with the addition of SC for the newly formed Scottish Region. North Eastern region coaches at first carried the prefix E, then NE in the late 1960s before reverting to E again when the North Eastern Region was amalgamated with the Eastern Region in 1968. Some EMU vehicles working on the Great Eastern electrified lines carried the GE prefix for a while in the 1960s.

Newly built coaches were numbered in a new series without suffixes. The main number series were:

- 1-39999 for corridor fitted hauled stock.
- 40000-59999 for non-corridor hauled stock. This was restricted to the 4xxxx series when the large DMU build programme was announced.

- 50000-59999 for diesel-mechanical units.
- 60000-60999 for diesel-electric units.
- 61000-78999 for electric units.
- 79000-79999 for early DMU vehicles (ordered before the BR Modernisation plan), and four-wheel railcars.
- 80000-99999 for non passenger carrying hauled coaching stock.

Exceptions to these general rules were introduced as time went by.

In the DMU section the number series can be further broken down as follows:

- 50000-52999 Power cars
- 55000-55999 Single units
- 56000-56999 Driving trailer cars
- 59000-59999 Non-driving trailer cars
- 60000-60499 DEMU power cars
- 60500-60799 DEMU non-driving trailer cars
- 60800-60999 DEMU driving trailer cars
- 79000-79699 Early DMU vehicles
- 79700-79997 Four-wheeled railcars
- 79998-79999 Battery electric unit

Again, as time went, on there were exceptions to these rules which will be noted in the book.

In the 1970s BR introduced TOPS (Total Operations Processing System). This computerised system kept track of all rolling stock, and led directly to the renumbering of all locomotives with a class based number system in 1973-74. A decade later, in May 1983, a further refinement of TOPS meant that all rolling stock, locomotives and coaches, needed to carry unique numbers. All items of rolling stock that carried numbers that clashed with locomotives were renumbered. In the DMU section this meant a wholesale renumbering of DMUs in the 50xxx series to 53xxx series to avoid clashing with Class 50 locomotives. The Class 55 Deltics had all been withdrawn by this date so there was no clash in the 55xxx series. All the 56xxx series DMUs were renumbered in the 54xxx series. A few other individual vehicles were later renumbered to avoid clashes with Class 59 and 60 locomotives.

Classification

The introduction of TOPS meant the need to give class numbers to all multiple units. Locomotives were already classified between 01 and 99. In 1968 DMUs received class numbers in the 100-199 series, DEMUs in the 200-299 series, AC EMUs in the 300-399 series, Southern Region DC EMUs in the 400-499 series, and other DC EMUS were numbered in the 501-599 series.

At first each different type of DMU coach (motor coaches, driving trailers and trailers) received a separate class number. For example a three-car Metropolitan-Cammell unit could contain coaches of classes 101/2, 171 and 101/1 (often "/2" was used for second-class only coaches, "/1" was for coaches which included some first-class seats). From January 1979 a simpler system was adopted with one class number for all types, in this case Class 101. These later classes are used in the book, but the earlier class numbers are also shown.

The standard BR coaching classification

British Railways adapted an alphabetic system based on the former LNER system to describe all coaching stock. Each letter used could have more than one meaning (sometimes determined by its position in the code). The main letters used, as applied to DMU coaches, are as follows:

B Brake (guard's) compartment fitted
Battery powered (prefix)
C Composite (contains more than one class of accommodation)
D Driving vehicle (fitted with a drivers cab)
F First Class
H Half-motor (vehicle with one of the two engines removed)
K Corridor vehicle with lavatory
L Lavatory (not used for corridor vehicles which are assumed to have a lavatory)
M Motor (powered) vehicle
O Open (that is, no compartments).
As most diesel mechanical units are open, the O is not included
P Pullman Parlour car
RB Buffet

RK Restaurant Kitchen car
S Second (later Standard) Class
so Semi-open (a mix of compartments and open)
T Trailer (non powered vehicles)

An example would be DMBS, a Driving Motor Brake Second.

Coupling codes

In order to allow different type of unit to operate together, each unit was given a coupling code to show which other units it was compatible with. The symbol was usually painted on the end of the unit above the control cables, but later the blue square was omitted as it became the standard. The full list of coupling codes is as follows:

■ Blue square.	This became the standard coupling code for most units.
♦ Yellow diamond.	This was an early standard, used mainly for vehicles in the 79XXX series.
● White circle.	Used for early Swindon built inter-city units.
▲ Red triangle.	The very first standard class (E79000-7/E79500-7) used this code. After these were withdrawn, the code was reused for Class 127. These originally used a blue star code, but problems arose when these diesel-hydraulics worked with diesel-mechanical units. They were re-coded Red Triangle in January 1969 to avoid coupling these types together.
★ Orange star.	Used for Class 125 diesel-hydraulic units.

Diagram numbers

BR had diagram books giving outline drawings for all types of locomotives, coaches and freight stock. The coaching stock book gave all principle dimensions, weight, seating etc., which would be needed by the operating department. Different types of coaching stock were given a page in the diagram book with pages numbered from 1 up to about 950 although not all numbers were used. DMUs were generally given numbers between 500 and 649 although within this series the numbers seemed to be allocated almost at random. DEMU diagram numbers were in the 650-699 series. See Appendix 3 for a full list.

The small diagrams at the head of each class in this book are reproduced from these diagrams. The diagrams have been tidied up to make then clearer (removing excess dimensional arrows), and have been reproduced at a consistent scale.

One interesting thing to note from a contemporary point of view is the very small amount of space in the units that is designated NS – non smoking. There seems to be no physical separation between smoking and non smoking areas in many cases. It is interesting to see that while the Class 115 Driving Motor Brake seconds used on the Marylebone services (M51861 onwards) contained a section of 32 non-smoking seats (out of 78 seats), the otherwise similar coaches allocated to the Liverpool and Manchester services (M51849 onwards) contained no non-smoking seats at all! The North-South divide?

In about 1980 a new diagram book was introduced. This gives each type of coaching stock a code consisting of two letters and three numbers. These followed logical rules, the rules for DMU vehicles are as follows:

First Letter

D For DMUs the first letter is always D.

Second Letter

B DEMU Driving motor with brake compartment
C DEMU Driving motor
D DEMU Non-driving motor
E DEMU Driving trailer
H DEMU Trailer
P Driving motor
Q Driving motor with brake compartment
R Non-driving motor
S Driving trailer
T Trailer
X Single unit railcar
Z Departmental vehicle

First digit

1 First class
2 Second (later standard) class
3 Composite
5 No passenger accommodation

Second and third digits

Each different design is allocated a different number to give the vehicle a unique design code.

Lot numbers

When BR started designing its own standard coaching stock in 1951 it allocated lot numbers to each batch of coaches that it ordered. The number series started at 30001 and continued right up until the end of BR when the series reached 31146 in 1995. The lot number was carried on a cast oval plate on the sole bar of each coach, together with the coach's builder and build date. These plates are often useful in identifying the origin of coaches, for example in departmental service or preservation. See Appendix 2 for a full list.

Engines

Most vehicles were fitted with two engines fitted below the frames. The most common general types were the AEC and Leyland types of 150bhp. Many AEC engine vehicles were later re-engined with Leyland engines. More powerful engines included the Leyland Albion engine at 230bhp and the eight-cylinder Rolls-Royce engine at 238bhp. The AEC and Leyland engines were marketed by British United Traction (BUT).

Later a number of vehicles ran with only one engine to a vehicle (known as half-motors). These were renumbered in the 78XXX series.

All the Southern Region DEMUs were fitted with one large English Electric 4SRT engine of 500 or 600bhp. These large engines were fitted in their own compartment within the vehicle body.

Transmission

Most diesel mechanical vehicles were fitted with standard transmission consisting of a cardan shaft and freewheel connected to a four-speed epicyclic gearbox, with a further cardan shaft to the final drive. Any other non-standard mechanical or hydraulic transmission is shown in the vehicle heading.

All Southern region units were fitted with electric transmission.

Body Dimensions

Most DMUs were fitted on one of two standard lengths of frame, either 56ft 11in or 63ft 5in. The actual body fitted to these frames could vary by several inches as shown in the class headings.

Classes 201-203 were built for the Hastings line. Narrow tunnels on this line meant that the vehicles were fitted with narrow bodies. Class 207 were also built with a non-standard body width based on their intended area of operation.

Weight

Vehicle weights are shown in the class headings.

Seating

When the first generation DMUs were being built there was still a large demand for first class seats. However, during the 1970s and 1980s many of the services worked no longer required first class. Many units, particularly on the Eastern and Midland regions, had the first class sections downgraded to second, often by simply sewing the armrests into an upright position and removing the branding. Where possible these changes are shown in the heading.

Bibliography

This is a list of some books that I have found helpful and useful as I prepared this book.

- **British Multiple Units: Volume 1 DMUs & DEMUs.** Ashley Butlin. Corlea Publishing.
- **British Rail DMUs & Diesel Railcars: Origins & First Generation Stock.** Brian Morrison. OPC.
- **ABC British Railways Locomotives and Other Motive Power.** Various editions 1955-1987. Ian Allan Publishing.

- **British Railways Locomotives and Coaching stock.** Various editions 1985-2010. Platform 5 Publishing Ltd.
- **The Coaching Stock of British Railways.** 1972, 1974, 1976, 1978, 1980 & 1983/84. P Mallaband and L J Bowles. RCTS.
- **The Railway Observer:** Various editions 1952-2010. RCTS.
- **Departmental Coaching Stock.** 1985, 1987, 1990. Roger Butcher, Peter Fox & Peter Hall. Platform Five Publishing.
- **A Pictorial Record of British Railways Diesel Multiple Units.** Brian Golding. Cheona Publications.
- **British Railways Motive Power Allocations 1948-1968. Part Seven Diesel Railcars & Multiple Units.** Jim Grindlay. Transport Publishing Ltd.
- **British Railway Pictorial: First Generation DMUs.** Kevin Robertson. Ian Allan Publishing.
- **British Railway Pictorial: First-generation DMUs in Colour for the Modeller and Historian.** Stuart Mackay. Ian Allan Publishing.
- **Southern DEMUs.** Michael Welch. Capital Transport.
- **Motive Power Recognition 3: DMUs.** Colin J. Marsden. Ian Allan Publishing.
- **British Rail Fleet Survey 8: Diesel Multiple Units - The First Generation.** Brian Haresnape. Ian Allan Publishing.
- **British Rail Fleet Survey 9: Diesel Multiple Units - The Second Generation and DEMUs.** Brian Haresnape. Ian Allan Publishing.
- **The History of Great Western AEC Diesel Railcars.** Colin Judge. Noodle Books.
- **The British Railcar AEC to HST.** R M Tufnell. David & Charles.

On 25th March 1971 an Ian Allan Excursion formed of an eight-car Pullman set is seen at Basingstoke. This shows the final livery of grey with blue window surrounds, a reversal of the normal BR blue and grey livery

This view shows a Gloucester RCW Class 100 DMU in early blue livery with a small yellow warning panel. The photograph was taken at Hopton on Sea on 29th April 1970 on the final week of service on the line from Lowestoft Central to Yarmouth South Town. *G R Mortimer*

Leith Central is the setting for this view of SC56302 on 7th April 1969. Note the unusual wrapping-round of the yellow front end to include the cab door. This shot clearly shows the distinctive curve of the lower sides on these units. *P R Foster*

Class 100 DMBS M50356 is seen in blue livery at Longsight depot in Manchester on 26th June 1976. *D L Percival*

When this photograph was taken on 29th August 1987, the two cars in this unique unit were the sole survivors of their respective classes. Gloucester RCW Class 100 DMBS M53355 leads Cravens Class 105 DMCL M53812 as they depart from Stockport heading to Stalybridge. *A Dasi-Sutton*

Right: The Eastern region inspection saloon DB975349 and DB975539 was converted from Class 100 DMU carriages E51116 and E56101 respectively. It is seen here on 25th June 1980 at Bishops Stortford after being used to inspect the main line from Liverpool Street. *M L Rogers*

Below: An early view of a Metropolitan-Cammell Class 101 DMU in all over green livery with speed whiskers. SC51465 is seen while working a Fife Coast Service. *P J Sharpe*

When this photograph was taken on 26th February 1967 Class 101 DMBS NE50218 had received a yellow warning panel. It is shown carrying the short-lived NE prefix used for North Eastern Region coaches between 1965 and 1968. The unit is seen at Hexham, where it had been taken after failing at Alston on the Haltwhistle-Alston branch on the previous day. *G Robson*

This official BR photograph taken in July 1974 shows the first refurbished DMU set as it takes part in a tour of the country showing off its features to interested parties. The Class 102 Metropolitan-Cammell three-car unit made up of 51451 (leading), 59545 and 51518 was painted in a distinctive all-white livery with a blue stripe. This was used for all the early refurbished units until replaced by a more practical blue and grey livery. *BR*

Class 101 DMSL (downgraded from DMCL) number E50171 is seen at Middlesbrough as part of a three-car unit on 15th April 1985. *J E Oxley*

Displaying the unit number CH354 a three-car Class 101 unit comprised of 53198, 59302 and 51800 is seen at Manchester Victoria on 25th February 1991. *S Bagwell*

M53333 is seen arriving at Aberystwyth on the 14.42 Shrewsbury to Aberystwyth service on 25th May 1985. I spent many summers on theological study courses at Aberystwyth in the late 1970s and later with my wife in the early 1980s. The usual method of arrival was by train on this long route across Wales from Shrewsbury. This photograph was taken in 1985, the last (and best) summer we spent in Aberystwyth. *J Scrace*

Non-driving trailer cars were much less popular with photographers for obvious reasons. Here is Class 101 TSL SC59305 seen at 62B Dundee in blue livery on 11th August 1971. The non-standard sized SC prefix betrays the fact that this vehicle had been transferred from the Eastern Region a couple of years earlier. *P R Foster*

A Park Royal Class 103 two-car unit is seen working a Rugby-Stafford service between Rugeley (Trent Valley) and Colwich on 5th June 1960. *M Mensing*

This mixed set of DMU stock is seen working the 15.18 service from Wolverhampton High Level to Chester on 6th August 1972. Class 103 DMBS M50398 and Class 101 DTCL M56357 lead a three-car Class 119 Cross-Country unit M51100, M59433 and M51059. *D Earlhither*

A two-car Class 103 unit was converted in 1972 to work as a viaduct inspection unit in Cornwall. Seen at Penzance on 14th April 1974 M50397 (which never carried its allocated number DB975137) is seen with partner DB975228. *D L Percival*

Part 1. DMUs in class order.

This is a list of all the DMU classes, listed in class order. For each class a brief history and description is given. This is followed by a list of all the units in their initial formations with their delivery date and first depot allocation.

TOPS Classes

Class 100

Class 100 was a low density design built by the Gloucester Carriage and Wagon Company. They were built to a "semi-lightweight" design; steel was used in their construction making them heavier than the original Derby Lightweights, but they proved to be longer lasting in service.

Forty twin units were built in two batches. Most were built for use on the Scottish Region but a small batch was allocated to the London Midland Region. However the London Midland Region was in urgent need of its new units so the first Scottish batch was delivered on loan to Longsight in Manchester until its own units were ready.

These units were successful, but were not built in large numbers. Most were transferred away from the Scottish Region by the early seventies and most had been withdrawn by the early eighties.

Several found further use in departmental service. These included E51122 and E56300 which became DB975664 and DB975637 *"The Stourton Saloon"*, the Eastern Region General Manger's Saloon, and E51116 and E56101 which became DB975349 and DB975539 and were used as the Eastern Region Inspection Unit.

Seven cars entered preservation but only four now survive. E56301 was the first of the first generation DMUs to enter preservation, in 1969.

Class 100 Gloucester RC&W

Two-car low density units
DMBS-DTCL

SC50339	SC56094	05/57	9A	Longsight (o/l)
SC50340	SC56095	05/57	9A	Longsight (o/l)
SC50341	SC56096	06/57	9A	Longsight (o/l)
SC50342	SC56097	06/57	9A	Longsight (o/l)
SC50343	SC56098	07/57	9A	Longsight (o/l)
SC50344	SC56099	07/57	9A	Longsight (o/l)
SC50345	SC56100	07/57	9A	Longsight (o/l)
SC50346	SC56101	07/57	9A	Longsight (o/l)
SC50347	SC56102	08/57	9A	Longsight (o/l)
M50348	M56103	08/57	9D	Buxton
M50349	M56104	09/57	5D	Stoke-on-Trent
M50350	M56105	09/57	5D	Stoke-on-Trent
M50351	M56106	09/57	5D	Stoke-on-Trent
M50352	M56107	09/57	5D	Stoke-on-Trent
M50353	M56108	09/57	5D	Stoke-on-Trent
M50354	M56109	09/57	5D	Stoke-on-Trent
M50355	M56110	09/57	6G	Llandudno Junction
M50356	M56111	10/57	9D	Buxton
M50357	M56112	10/57	6G	Llandudno Junction
M50358	M56113	10/57	9A	Longsight

Class 100 Gloucester RC&W

Two-car low density units
DMBS-DTCL

SC51108	SC56300	10/57	64A	Leith Central
SC51109	SC56301	10/57	64A	Leith Central
SC51110	SC56302	10/57	64A	Leith Central
SC51111	SC56303	11/57	64A	Leith Central
SC51112	SC56304	11/57	64A	Leith Central
SC51113	SC56305	11/57	64A	Leith Central
SC51114	SC56306	11/57	64A	Leith Central
SC51115	SC56307	11/57	64A	Leith Central
SC51116	SC56308	12/57	64A	Leith Central
SC51117	SC56309	12/57	64A	Leith Central
SC51118	SC56310	12/57	64A	Leith Central
SC51119	SC56311	01/58	64A	Leith Central
SC51120	SC56312	01/58	64A	Leith Central
SC51121	SC56313	01/58	64A	Leith Central
SC51122	SC56314	01/58	64A	Leith Central
SC51123	SC56315	01/58	64A	Leith Central
SC51124	SC56316	02/58	64A	Leith Central
SC51125	SC56317	02/58	64A	Leith Central
SC51126	SC56318	02/58	64A	Leith Central
SC51127	SC56319	03/58	64A	Leith Central

Class 101

Metropolitan-Cammell of Washwood Heath in Birmingham was the largest private producer of DMUs for BR. The low density units built by Metropolitan-Cammell were some of the most successful and long-lived of the first generation DMUs.

They were derived from the lightweight DMUs which Metropolitan-Cammell had built (in the 79xxx series), and retained the distinctive Metropolitan-Cammell cab design which was first found on those earlier units. They were constructed with a heavier and stronger integral body; the framework and roof panels being made of light alloy while the body ends were made of steel for constructional strength and collision protection.

They were ordered in a variety of different formations for the North Eastern, London Midland and Scottish regions, and later also worked on the Western Region.

They were originally fitted with AEC engines. Other similar units fitted with Leyland engines became Class 102. As many Class 101 units were later fitted with Leyland engines, both classes were combined into Class 101 in 1976.

Being one of the longest-lived classes of DMU, many have survived into preservation.

Class 101 Metropolitan-Cammell

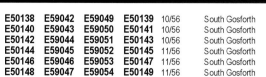

Four-car low density units
DMCL-TSL-TBSL-DMCL

E50138	E59042	E59049	E50139	10/56	South Gosforth
E50140	E59043	E59050	E50141	10/56	South Gosforth
E50142	E59044	E59051	E50143	10/56	South Gosforth
E50144	E59045	E59052	E50145	11/56	South Gosforth
E50146	E59046	E59053	E50147	11/56	South Gosforth
E50148	E59047	E59054	E50149	11/56	South Gosforth
E50150	E59048	E59055	E50151	11/56	South Gosforth

Class 101 Metropolitan-Cammell

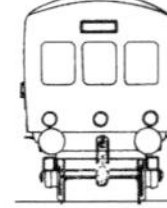

Two-car low density power-twin units
DMBS-DMCL

E50152	E50158	12/56	56G	Bradford Hammerton St
E50153	E50159	12/56	56G	Bradford Hammerton St
E50154	E50160	12/56	56G	Bradford Hammerton St
E50155	E50161	12/56	56G	Bradford Hammerton St
E50156	E50162	01/57	56G	Bradford Hammerton St
E50157	E50163	01/57	56G	Bradford Hammerton St
E50164	E50168	01/57	56G	Bradford Hammerton St
E50165	E50169	01/57	56G	Bradford Hammerton St
E50166	E50170	01/57	56G	Bradford Hammerton St
E50167	E50171	01/57	56G	Bradford Hammerton St

Class 101 Metropolitan-Cammell

Four-car low density units
DMCL-TSL-TBSL-DMCL

E50172	E59060	E59073	E50173	01/57	51A	Darlington
E50174	E59061	E59074	E50175	02/57	51A	Darlington
E50176	E59062	E59075	E50177	02/57	51A	Darlington
E50178	E59063	E59076	E50179	02/57	51A	Darlington
E50180	E59064	E59077	E50181	02/57	51A	Darlington
E50182	E59065	E59078	E50183	03/57	51A	Darlington
E50184	E59066	E59079	E50185	02/57	51A	Darlington
E50186	E59067	E59080	E50187	03/57	51A	Darlington
E50188	E59068	E59081	E50189	03/57	51A	Darlington
E50190	E59069	E59082	E50191	03/57	51A	Darlington
E50192	E59070	E59083	E50193	03/57	51A	Darlington
E50194	E59071	E59084	E50195	04/57	51A	Darlington
E50196	E59072	E59085	E50197	04/57	51A	Darlington

Class 101 Metropolitan-Cammell

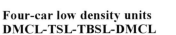

Two-car low density units
DMBS-DTCL

E50198	E56050	04/57	51A	Darlington
E50199	E56051	04/57	51A	Darlington
E50200	E56052	05/57	51A	Darlington
E50201	E56053	05/57	51A	Darlington
E50202	E56054	05/57	51A	Darlington
E50203	E56055	05/57	51A	Darlington
E50204	E56056	05/57	51A	Darlington
E50205	E56057	04/57	51A	Darlington
E50206	E56058	04/57	51A	Darlington
E50207	E56059	05/57	51A	Darlington
E50208	E56060	05/57	51A	Darlington
E50209	E56061	05/57	51A	Darlington
E50210	E56062	05/57	54A	Sunderland
E50211	E56063	05/57	54A	Sunderland
E50212	E56064	06/57	54A	Sunderland
E50213	E56065	06/57	54A	Sunderland
E50214	E56066	06/57	54A	Sunderland
E50215	E56067	07/57	54A	Sunderland
E50216	E56068	07/57	54A	Sunderland
E50217	E56069	07/57	54A	Sunderland
E50218	E56070	07/57	54A	Sunderland
E50219	E56071	07/57	54A	Sunderland
E50220	E56072	07/57	54A	Sunderland
E50221	E56073	08/57	54A	Sunderland
E50222	E56074	06/57	54A	Sunderland
E50223	E56075	06/57	54A	Sunderland
E50224	E56076	06/57	54A	Sunderland
E50225	E56077	06/57	54A	Sunderland
E50226	E56078	07/57	54A	Sunderland
E50227	E56079	07/57	54A	Sunderland
E50228	E56080	07/57	54A	Sunderland
E50229	E56081	07/57	54A	Sunderland
E50230	E56082	08/57	54A	Sunderland
E50231	E56083	08/57	54A	Sunderland
E50232	E56084	08/57	54A	Sunderland
E50233	E56085	09/57	54A	Sunderland

Class 101 Metropolitan-Cammell

Four-car low density units
DMCL-TSL-TBSL-DMCL

E50234	E59086	E59092	E50235	09/57	South Gosforth
E50236	E59087	E59093	E50237	09/57	South Gosforth
E50238	E59088	E59094	E50239	10/57	South Gosforth
E50240	E59089	E59095	E50241	10/57	South Gosforth
E50242	E59090	E59096	E50243	10/57	South Gosforth
E50244	E59091	E59097	E50245	10/57	South Gosforth

Class 101 Metropolitan-Cammell

Two-car low density units
DMBS-DTCL

E50246	E56218	09/57	South Gosforth
E50247	E56219	09/57	South Gosforth
E50248	E56220	09/57	South Gosforth

Class 101 Metropolitan-Cammell

Three-car low density units
DMBS-TSL-DMCL

E50290	E59302	E50745	11/57	56G	Bradford Hammerton St
E50291	E59303	E50746	11/57	51A	Darlington
E50292	E59304	E50747	11/57	51A	Darlington

Class 101 Metropolitan-Cammell

Two-car low density units
DMBS-DTCL

E50293	E56086	12/57	51A	Darlington
E50294	E56087	12/57	51A	Darlington
E50295	E56088	12/57	51A	Darlington
E50296	E56089	12/57	51A	Darlington

Class 101 Metropolitan-Cammell

Three-car low density units
DMBS-TCL-DMCL

M50303	M59114	M50321	02/58	5D	Stoke-on-Trent
M50304	M59115	M50322	02/58	5D	Stoke-on-Trent
M50305	M59116	M50323	02/58	5D	Stoke-on-Trent
M50306	M59117	M50324	02/58	5D	Stoke-on-Trent
M50307	M59118	M50325	02/58	5D	Stoke-on-Trent
M50308	M59119	M50326	03/58	17A	Derby
M50309	M59120	M50327	03/58	17A	Derby
M50310	M59121	M50328	02/58	5B	Crewe South
M50311	M59122	M50329	02/58	5B	Crewe South
M50312	M59123	M50330	03/58	5B	Crewe South
M50313	M59124	M50331	03/58	5B	Crewe South
M50314	M59125	M50332	03/58	5B	Crewe South
M50315	M59126	M50333	03/58	5B	Crewe South
M50316	M59127	M50334	03/58	5B	Crewe South
M50317	M59128	M50335	04/58	3E	Monument Lane
M50318	M59129	M50336	04/58	3E	Monument Lane
M50319	M59130	M50337	04/58	3E	Monument Lane
M50320	M59131	M50338	04/58	3E	Monument Lane

Class 101 Metropolitan-Cammell

Four-car low density units
DMCL-TBSL-TSL-DMCL

E50748	E59112	E59305	E50749	11/57	South Gosforth
E50750	E59113	E59306	E50751	11/57	South Gosforth

Class 101 Metropolitan-Cammell

Two-car low density units
DMBS-DTCL

M51174	M56332	10/58	3C	Walsall Rycroft
M51175	M56333	11/58	3C	Walsall Rycroft
M51176	M56334	11/58	3C	Walsall Rycroft
M51177	M56335	11/58	3C	Walsall Rycroft
M51178	M56336	11/58	3C	Walsall Rycroft
M51179	M56337	11/58	3E	Monument Lane
M51180	M56338	11/58	3E	Monument Lane
M51181	M56339	11/58	3E	Monument Lane
M51182	M56340	11/58	3E	Monument Lane
M51183	M56341	11/58	3E	Monument Lane
M51184	M56342	11/58	3E	Monument Lane
M51185	M56343	11/58	3E	Monument Lane
M51186	M56344	11/58	3E	Monument Lane
M51187	M56345	12/58	3E	Monument Lane
M51188	M56346	12/58	3E	Monument Lane
M51189	M56347	12/58	3C	Walsall Rycroft
M51190	M56348	12/58	3C	Walsall Rycroft
M51191	M56349	12/58	3C	Walsall Rycroft
M51192	M56350	12/58	3C	Walsall Rycroft
M51193	M56351	12/58	3E	Monument Lane
M51194	M56352	12/58	3E	Monument Lane
M51195	M56353	01/59	2D	Coventry
M51196	M56354	01/59	2D	Coventry
M51197	M56355	01/59	26A	Newton Heath
M51198	M56356	01/59	26A	Newton Heath
M51199	M56357	01/59	26A	Newton Heath
M51200	M56358	01/59	26A	Newton Heath
M51201	M56359	01/59	26A	Newton Heath
M51202	M56360	01/59	26A	Newton Heath
M51203	M56361	01/59	26A	Newton Heath
E51204	E56362	07/58	56G	Bradford Hammerton St
E51205	E56363	07/58	56G	Bradford Hammerton St
E51206	E56364	08/58	56G	Bradford Hammerton St
E51207	E56365	08/58	56G	Bradford Hammerton St
E51208	E56366	08/58	53C	Hull Springhead
E51209	E56367	08/58	53C	Hull Springhead
E51210	E56368	09/58	56G	Bradford Hammerton St
E51211	E56369	09/58	56G	Bradford Hammerton St
E51212	E56370	09/58	56G	Bradford Hammerton St
E51213	E56371	09/58	53C	Hull Springhead
E51214	E56372	09/58	53C	Hull Springhead
E51215	E56373	09/58	53C	Hull Springhead
E51216	E56374	09/58	53C	Hull Springhead
E51217	E56375	10/58		South Gosforth
E51218	E56376	10/58		South Gosforth
E51219	E56377	10/58		South Gosforth
E51220	E56378	10/58		South Gosforth
E51221	E56379	10/58		South Gosforth
E51222	E56380	10/58		South Gosforth
E51223	E56381	10/58	53C	Hull Springhead
SC51224	SC56382	05/58	62B	Dundee
SC51225	SC56383	05/58	62B	Dundee
SC51226	SC56384	05/58	62B	Dundee
SC51227	SC56385	05/58	62B	Dundee
SC51228	SC56386	05/58	62B	Dundee
SC51229	SC56387	05/58	62B	Dundee
SC51230	SC56388	05/58	62B	Dundee
SC51231	SC56389	05/58	62B	Dundee
SC51232	SC56390	05/58	62B	Dundee
SC51233	SC56391	05/58	62B	Dundee
SC51234	SC56392	05/58	62B	Dundee
SC51235	SC56393	05/58	62B	Dundee
SC51236	SC56394	05/58	62B	Dundee
SC51237	SC56395	05/58	62B	Dundee
SC51238	SC56396	06/58	62B	Dundee
SC51239	SC56397	06/58	62B	Dundee
SC51240	SC56398	06/58	62B	Dundee
SC51241	SC56399	06/58	62B	Dundee
SC51242	SC56400	06/58	62B	Dundee
SC51243	SC56401	06/58	62B	Dundee
SC51244	SC56402	06/58	62B	Dundee
SC51245	SC56403	06/58	62B	Dundee
SC51246	SC56404	07/58	62B	Dundee
SC51247	SC56405	07/58	62B	Dundee
SC51248	SC56406	07/58	62B	Dundee
SC51249	SC56407	07/58	62B	Dundee
SC51250	SC56408	07/58	62B	Dundee
SC51251	SC56409	07/58	62B	Dundee
SC51252	SC56410	07/58	62B	Dundee
SC51253	SC56411	07/58	62B	Dundee

Class 101 Metropolitan-Cammell

Additional trailer buffet cars
TSLRB

These buffet cars were intended as loose vehicles, to be used as required in the daily rosters. Later they were treated as TSLs with the buffets taken out of use.

E59573	05/60	50B	Neville Hill
E59574	05/60	50B	Neville Hill
E59575	05/60	50B	Neville Hill
E59576	05/60	50B	Neville Hill
E59577	05/60	50B	Neville Hill
E59578	05/60	50B	Neville Hill

Class 102

Some Metropolitan-Cammell units were built with Leyland engines and they became Class 102. In 1976, when many of the AEC fitted members of Class 101 were being refitted with Leyland engines, both classes were amalgamated into Class 101.

Class 102 Metropolitan-Cammell

Two-car low density power-twin units
DMBS-DMCL

E50250	E50260	06/57	51A	Darlington
E50251	E50261	06/57	51A	Darlington
E50252	E50262	07/57	51A	Darlington
E50253	E50263	07/57	51A	Darlington
E50254	E50264	08/57	51A	Darlington
E50255	E50265	09/57	51A	Darlington
E50256	E50266	10/57	51A	Darlington
E50257	E50267	10/57	51A	Darlington
E50258	E50268	10/57	51A	Darlington
E50259	E50269	10/57	51A	Darlington

Class 102 Metropolitan-Cammell

Two-car low density power-twin units
DMBS-DMCL

These were originally ordered as triples but were delivered as power twins.

E51425	E51495	02/59	51A	Darlington
E51426	E51496	02/59	56G	Bradford Hammerton St
E51427	E51497	02/59	51A	Darlington
E51428	E51498	03/59	56G	Bradford Hammerton St
E51429	E51499	03/59	56G	Bradford Hammerton St
E51430	E51500	03/59	51A	Darlington
E51431	E51501	04/59	51A	Darlington
E51432	E51502	04/59	56G	Bradford Hammerton St
E51433	E51503	04/59	51A	Darlington
E51434	E51504	05/59	51A	Darlington

Class 102 Metropolitan-Cammell

Four-car low density units
DMBS-TCL-TCL-DMCL

These were originally ordered as triples but were delivered as quads.

E51435	E59523	E59524	E51505	02/59	53B	Hull Botanic Gardens
E51436	E59525	E59526	E51506	02/59	53B	Hull Botanic Gardens
E51437	E59527	E59528	E51507	03/59	53B	Hull Botanic Gardens
E51438	E59529	E59530	E51508	03/59	53B	Hull Botanic Gardens
E51439	E59531	E59532	E51509	03/59	53B	Hull Botanic Gardens
E51440	E59533	E59534	E51510	03/59	56G	Bradford Hammerton St
E51441	E59535	E59536	E51511	04/59	53B	Hull Botanic Gardens
E51442	E59537	E59538	E51512	04/59		South Gosforth
E51443	E59539	E59540	E51513	04/59	51A	Darlington
E51444	E59541	E59542	E51514	05/59	51A	Darlington

Class 102 Metropolitan-Cammell

Three-car low density units
DMBS-TCL-DMCL

Unit		Date	Shed	Depot
SC51445 SC59543 SC51515		05/59	62A	Thornton Junction
SC51446 SC59544 SC51516		05/59	62A	Thornton Junction
SC51447 SC59545 SC51517		05/59	62A	Thornton Junction
SC51448 SC59546 SC51518		05/59	62A	Thornton Junction
SC51449 SC59547 SC51519		05/59	62A	Thornton Junction
SC51450 SC59548 SC51520		06/59	62A	Thornton Junction
SC51451 SC59549 SC51521		06/59	62A	Thornton Junction
SC51452 SC59550 SC51522		06/59	62A	Thornton Junction
SC51453 SC59551 SC51523		06/59	62A	Thornton Junction
SC51454 SC59552 SC51524		06/59	62A	Thornton Junction
SC51455 SC59553 SC51525		06/59	62A	Thornton Junction
SC51456 SC59554 SC51526		07/59		Leith Central
SC51457 SC59555 SC51527		07/59		Leith Central
SC51458 SC59556 SC51528		07/59		Leith Central
SC51459 SC59557 SC51529		07/59		Leith Central
SC51460 SC59558 SC51530		07/59		Leith Central
SC51461 SC59559 SC51531		08/59		Leith Central
SC51462 SC59560 SC51532		08/59		Leith Central
SC51463 SC59561 SC51533		08/59		Leith Central
SC51464 SC59562 SC51534		08/59		Leith Central
SC51465 SC59563 SC51535		08/59		Leith Central
SC51466 SC59564 SC51536		09/59		Leith Central
SC51467 SC59565 SC51537		09/59		Leith Central
SC51468 SC59566 SC51538		09/59		Leith Central
SC51469 SC59567 SC51539		09/59		Leith Central
SC51470 SC59568 SC51540		09/59		Leith Central

Class 102 Metropolitan-Cammell

Three-car low density units
DMBS-TCL-DMCL

Unit	Date	Shed	Depot
SC51795 SC59686 SC51802	10/59		Leith Central
SC51796 SC59687 SC51803	10/59		Leith Central
SC51797 SC59688 SC51804	11/59	64H	Leith Central
SC51798 SC59689 SC51805	11/59	64H	Leith Central
SC51799 SC59690 SC51806	11/59	64H	Leith Central
SC51800 SC59691 SC51807	12/59	64H	Leith Central
SC51801 SC59692 SC51808	12/59	64H	Leith Central

Class 103

Park Royal built a small number of two-car low density units for the London Midland Region. They were based on BR specifications and closely followed the BR lightweights in design, although they were quite distinctive in appearance.

This was not a particularly successful class. They were constructed from a mixture of steel and light alloy with riveted joints. Engine vibrations combined with the non-standard bodywork gave trouble, which led to their relatively early withdrawal.

They spent most of their life based around the Chester area, although the last four units finished their lives on the Western Region. No vehicles were included in the refurbishment plan, but some survived in departmental service and preservation.

Class 103 Park Royal

Two-car low density units
DMBS-DTCL

Unit	Date	Shed	Depot
M50395 M56150	11/57	6G	Llandudno Junction
M50396 M56151	01/58	6G	Llandudno Junction
M50397 M56152	01/58	6G	Llandudno Junction
M50398 M56153	02/58	6G	Llandudno Junction
M50399 M56154	03/58	6G	Llandudno Junction
M50400 M56155	04/58	6G	Llandudno Junction
M50401 M56156	04/58	3C	Walsall Rycroft
M50402 M56157	05/58	6G	Llandudno Junction
M50403 M56158	05/58	6G	Llandudno Junction
M50404 M56159	05/58	3C	Walsall Rycroft
M50405 M56160	06/58	9A	Longsight
M50406 M56161	06/58	5B	Crewe South
M50407 M56162	07/58	5D	Stoke-on-Trent
M50408 M56163	07/58	5B	Crewe South
M50409 M56164	08/58	5B	Crewe South
M50410 M56165	09/58	3C	Walsall Rycroft
M50411 M56166	09/58	3C	Walsall Rycroft
M50412 M56167	09/58	3C	Walsall Rycroft
M50413 M56168	10/58	3C	Walsall Rycroft
M50414 M56169	10/58	3C	Walsall Rycroft

Class 104

The Birmingham Railway Carriage and Wagon Company of Smethwick was the second-largest private builder of DMUs for BR (after Metropolitan-Cammell). They built a total of 437 vehicles of Classes 104, 110 and 118.

Class 104 consisted of a large number of low-density units for the London Midland and North Eastern Regions. They were supplied in a variety of different formations. They were built from welded steel on short underframes and were fitted with glass-fibre mouldings for the roof ends over the cabs. They were fitted with distinctive cabs fitted with three tall windows.

The class was not selected for refurbishment and they were slowly taken out of service from the early 1980s onwards, the last units surviving into the 1990s.

A number of cars survive in preservation.

Class 104 Birmingham RC&W

Three-car low density units
DMBS-TCL-DMCL

Unit	Date	Shed	Depot
M50420 M59132 M50424	04/57	9A	Longsight
M50421 M59133 M50425	04/57	9A	Longsight
M50422 M59134 M50426	05/57	9A	Longsight
M50423 M59135 M50427	05/57	9A	Longsight

Class 104 Birmingham RC&W

Three-car low density units
DMBS-TCL-DMCL

Unit	Date	Shed	Depot
M50428 M59136 M50480	05/57	9A	Longsight
M50429 M59137 M50481	05/57	9A	Longsight
M50430 M59138 M50482	06/57	9A	Longsight
M50431 M59139 M50483	06/57	9A	Longsight
M50432 M59140 M50484	06/57	9A	Longsight
M50433 M59141 M50485	06/57	9A	Longsight
M50434 M59142 M50486	07/57	5A	Crewe North
M50435 M59143 M50487	07/57	9A	Longsight
M50436 M59144 M50488	07/57	5B	Crewe South
M50437 M59145 M50489	07/57	9A	Longsight
M50438 M59146 M50490	07/57	9A	Longsight
M50439 M59147 M50491	07/57	9A	Longsight
M50440 M59148 M50492	07/57	9A	Longsight
M50441 M59149 M50493	08/57	9D	Buxton
M50442 M59150 M50494	08/57	5D	Stoke-on-Trent
M50443 M59151 M50495	08/57	9D	Buxton
M50444 M59152 M50496	09/57	5B	Crewe South
M50445 M59153 M50497	09/57	5B	Crewe South
M50446 M59154 M50498	09/57	5B	Crewe South
M50447 M59155 M50499	09/57	5B	Crewe South
M50448 M59156 M50500	09/57	5B	Crewe South
M50449 M59157 M50501	10/57	9D	Buxton
M50450 M59158 M50502	10/57	9A	Longsight
M50451 M59159 M50503	10/57	9A	Longsight
M50452 M59160 M50504	10/57	9A	Longsight
M50453 M59161 M50505	10/57	9A	Longsight
M50454 M59162 M50506	10/57	9A	Longsight

M50455	M59163	M50507	10/57	9A	Longsight
M50456	M59164	M50508	11/57	5D	Stoke-on-Trent
M50457	M59165	M50509	11/57	5D	Stoke-on-Trent
M50458	M59166	M50510	11/57	5D	Stoke-on-Trent
M50459	M59167	M50511	11/57	5D	Stoke-on-Trent
M50460	M59168	M50512	11/57	5D	Stoke-on-Trent
M50461	M59169	M50513	11/57	5D	Stoke-on-Trent
M50462	M59170	M50514	12/57	5D	Stoke-on-Trent
M50463	M59171	M50515	12/57	5D	Stoke-on-Trent
M50464	M59172	M50516	12/57	5D	Stoke-on-Trent
M50465	M59173	M50517	12/57	5B	Crewe South
M50466	M59174	M50518	12/57	5B	Crewe South
M50467	M59175	M50519	01/58	5B	Crewe South
M50468	M59176	M50520	01/58	5B	Crewe South
M50469	M59177	M50521	01/58	5B	Crewe South
M50470	M59178	M50522	01/58	5B	Crewe South
M50471	M59179	M50523	01/58	5B	Crewe South
M50472	M59180	M50524	01/58	5B	Crewe South
M50473	M59181	M50525	02/58	5B	Crewe South
M50474	M59182	M50526	02/58	5B	Crewe South
M50475	M59183	M50527	02/58	5B	Crewe South
M50476	M59184	M50528	02/58	5B	Crewe South
M50477	M59185	M50529	02/58	5B	Crewe South
M50478	M59186	M50530	03/58	5B	Crewe South
M50479	M59187	M50531	03/58	5B	Crewe South

Class 104 Birmingham RC&W

Two-car low density units
DMBS-DTCL

M50532	M56175	03/58	5D	Stoke-on-Trent
M50533	M56176	03/58	5D	Stoke-on-Trent
M50534	M56177	04/58	5D	Stoke-on-Trent
M50535	M56178	04/58	5D	Stoke-on-Trent
M50536	M56179	04/58	5B	Crewe South
M50537	M56180	04/58	5B	Crewe South
M50538	M56181	04/58	5B	Crewe South
M50539	M56182	04/58	5B	Crewe South
M50540	M56183	04/58	5B	Crewe South
M50541	M56184	05/58	5B	Crewe South

Class 104 Birmingham RC&W

Four-car low density units
DMCL-TSL-TBSL-DMCL

E50542	E59188	E59209	E50563	06/58	51A	Darlington
E50543	E59189	E59210	E50564	06/58		South Gosforth
E50544	E59190	E59211	E50565	06/58	51A	Darlington
E50545	E59191	E59212	E50566	06/58		South Gosforth
E50546	E59192	E59213	E50567	07/58		South Gosforth
E50547	E59193	E59214	E50568	07/58	53C	Hull Springhead
E50548	E59194	E59215	E50569	07/58	53C	Hull Springhead
E50549	E59195	E59216	E50570	08/58	53C	Hull Springhead
E50550	E59196	E59217	E50571	08/58	53C	Hull Springhead
E50551	E59197	E59218	E50572	09/58	53C	Hull Springhead
E50552	E59198	E59219	E50573	09/58	53C	Hull Springhead
E50553	E59199	E59220	E50574	09/58	53C	Hull Springhead
E50554	E59200	E59221	E50575	09/58	53C	Hull Springhead
E50555	E59201	E59222	E50576	10/58		South Gosforth
E50556	E59202	E59223	E50577	10/58		South Gosforth
E50557	E59203	E59224	E50578	10/58	53C	Hull Springhead
E50558	E59204	E59225	E50579	10/58	53C	Hull Springhead
E50559	E59205	E59226	E50580	11/58	53C	Hull Springhead
E50560	E59206	E59227	E50581	11/58	53C	Hull Springhead
E50561	E59207	E59228	E50582	11/58	53B	Hull Botanic Gardens
E50562	E59208	E59229	E50583	12/58	53B	Hull Botanic Gardens
E50584	E59230	E59240	E50589	01/59	50A	York
E50585	E59231	E59241	E50590	12/58	53B	Hull Botanic Gardens
E50586	E59232	E59242	E50591	01/59	50B	Neville Hill
E50587	E59233	E59243	E50592	01/59		South Gosforth
E50588	E59234	E59244	E50593	03/59	53B	Hull Botanic Gardens

Class 104 Birmingham RC&W

Two-car low density units
DMBS-DTCL

E50594	E56185	05/58	56G	Bradford Hammerton St
E50595	E56186	05/58	56G	Bradford Hammerton St
E50596	E56187	05/58	56G	Bradford Hammerton St
E50597	E56188	05/58	56G	Bradford Hammerton St
E50598	E56189	05/58	56G	Bradford Hammerton St

Class 105

Cravens of Sheffield built 402 passenger carrying DMU vehicles units in a variety of different classes for British Railways. Their standard AEC engined low density units were built for general branch line and local services and were known as Class 105.

They were of all-steel construction, including a fabricated steel underframe which included a built-in fuel tank. They carried the distinctive Cravens front end with two windows giving excellent forward vision. From the side they were identical to Mk I hauled coaching stock, using the same doors and windows. However, some features which were successful in hauled stock (such as door droplights, window toplights and metal luggage racks) soon picked up vibrations in multiple unit stock and produced a distinctive rattle.

They were delivered in two- and three-car formations to the London Midland, Eastern, North Eastern and Scottish regions. The centre cars of the three-car units were later withdrawn, converting them into two-car units.

One car (E50249) was ordered as a replacement car for the Metropolitan-Cammell car E50173, which was withdrawn after an accident in October 1957.

Class 106 was incorporated into Class 105 in 1976. After a trial refurbishment of a few vehicles, no more were refurbished and withdrawal started in the 1980s with only a few vehicles surviving into the 1990s.

Class 105 Cravens

Replacement carriage
DMBS-

Accident replacement

E50249	09/59	51A	Darlington

Class 105 Cravens

Two-car low density units
DMBS-DTCL

E50373	E56128	02/57	53C	Hull Springhead
E50374	E56129	03/57	53C	Hull Springhead
E50375	E56130	03/57	53C	Hull Springhead
E50376	E56131	03/57	53C	Hull Springhead
E50377	E56132	03/57	53C	Hull Springhead
E50378	E56133	04/57	53C	Hull Springhead
E50379	E56134	04/57	53C	Hull Springhead
E50380	E56135	04/57	53C	Hull Springhead
E50381	E56136	05/57	53C	Hull Springhead
E50382	E56137	05/57	53C	Hull Springhead
E50383	E56138	05/57	53C	Hull Springhead
E50384	E56139	05/57	53C	Hull Springhead
E50385	E56140	05/57	53C	Hull Springhead
E50386	E56141	05/57	53C	Hull Springhead
E50387	E56142	06/57	53C	Hull Springhead
E50388	E56143	07/57	53C	Hull Springhead
E50389	E56144	07/57	53C	Hull Springhead

M50390	M56145	07/57	9A	Longsight
M50391	M56146	07/57	9A	Longsight
M50392	M56147	07/57	9A	Longsight
M50393	M56148	08/57	9A	Longsight
M50394	M56149	08/57	9A	Longsight

Class 105 Cravens

Three-car low density units
DMBS-TCL-DMCL

In 1968-70 all the centre trailer cars were removed from service leaving these units as power-twins.

M50752	M59307	M50785	09/57	9A	Longsight
M50753	M59308	M50786	09/57	9A	Longsight
M50754	M59309	M50787	10/57	5B	Crewe South
M50755	M59310	M50788	10/57	5B	Crewe South
M50756	M59311	M50789	10/57	5B	Crewe South
M50757	M59312	M50790	10/57	5B	Crewe South
M50758	M59313	M50791	11/57	5B	Crewe South
M50759	M59314	M50792	11/57	5B	Crewe South
M50760	M59315	M50793	11/57	5B	Crewe South
M50761	M59316	M50794	11/57	5B	Crewe South
M50762	M59317	M50795	12/57	5B	Crewe South
M50763	M59318	M50796	01/58	5B	Crewe South
M50764	M59319	M50797	01/58	5B	Crewe South
M50765	M59320	M50798	01/58	5B	Crewe South
M50766	M59321	M50799	01/58	5B	Crewe South
M50767	M59322	M50800	01/58	5B	Crewe South
M50768	M59323	M50801	02/58	9A	Longsight
M50769	M59324	M50802	02/58	9A	Longsight
M50770	M59325	M50803	03/58	17A	Derby

Class 105 Cravens

Two-car low density power-twin units
DMBS-DMCL

M50771	M50804	02/58	26A	Newton Heath
M50772	M50805	02/58	26A	Newton Heath
M50773	M50806	03/58	26A	Newton Heath
M50774	M50807	03/58	26A	Newton Heath
M50775	M50808	03/58	26A	Newton Heath
M50776	M50809	03/58	26A	Newton Heath
M50777	M50810	03/58	26A	Newton Heath
M50778	M50811	04/58	26A	Newton Heath
M50779	M50812	04/58	26A	Newton Heath
M50780	M50813	04/58	26A	Newton Heath
M50781	M50814	05/58	26A	Newton Heath
M50782	M50815	04/58	26A	Newton Heath
M50783	M50816	05/58	26A	Newton Heath
M50784	M50817	05/58	26A	Newton Heath

Class 105 Cravens

Two-car low density units
DMBS-DTCL

E51254	E56412	05/58	40A	Lincoln
E51255	E56413	05/58	40A	Lincoln
E51256	E56414	06/58	40A	Lincoln
E51257	E56415	06/58	40A	Lincoln
E51258	E56416	06/58	40A	Lincoln
E51259	E56417	06/58	40A	Lincoln
E51260	E56418	06/58	40A	Lincoln
E51261	E56419	06/58	40A	Lincoln
E51262	E56420	06/58	40A	Lincoln
E51263	E56421	07/58	40A	Lincoln
E51264	E56422	07/58	31A	Cambridge
E51265	E56423	07/58	31A	Cambridge
E51266	E56424	07/58	31A	Cambridge
E51267	E56425	07/58	31A	Cambridge
E51268	E56426	07/58	31A	Cambridge
E51269	E56427	08/58	31A	Cambridge
E51270	E56428	08/58	31A	Cambridge
E51271	E56429	08/58	31A	Cambridge
E51272	E56430	09/58	31A	Cambridge
E51273	E56431	09/58	31A	Cambridge
E51274	E56432	09/58	31A	Cambridge
E51275	E56433	09/58	31A	Cambridge
E51276	E56434	09/58	31A	Cambridge
E51277	E56435	09/58	31A	Cambridge
E51278	E56436	09/58	31A	Cambridge
E51279	E56437	09/58	31A	Cambridge
E51280	E56438	09/58	31A	Cambridge
E51281	E56439	10/58	31A	Cambridge
E51282	E56440	10/58	31A	Cambridge
E51283	E56441	10/58	31A	Cambridge
E51284	E56442	10/58	31A	Cambridge
E51285	E56443	10/58	31A	Cambridge
E51286	E56444	11/58	31A	Cambridge
E51287	E56445	11/58	31A	Cambridge
E51288	E56446	11/58	31A	Cambridge
E51289	E56447	11/58	40A	Lincoln
E51290	E56448	11/58	40A	Lincoln
E51291	E56449	11/58	40A	Lincoln
E51292	E56450	12/58	40A	Lincoln
E51293	E56451	12/58	40A	Lincoln
E51294	E56452	12/58	40A	Lincoln
E51295	E56453	12/58	40A	Lincoln
E51296	E56454	12/58	31A	Cambridge
E51297	E56455	01/59	40A	Lincoln
E51298	E56456	01/59	31A	Cambridge
E51299	E56457	01/59	31A	Cambridge
E51300	E56458	01/59	40A	Lincoln
E51301	E56459	01/59	40A	Lincoln

Class 105 Cravens

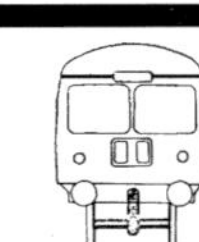

Two-car low density units
DMBS-DTCL

E51471	E56460	02/59	40A	Lincoln
E51472	E56461	02/59	40A	Lincoln
SC51473	SC56462	02/59	61A	Kittybrewster
SC51474	SC56463	02/59	61A	Kittybrewster
SC51475	SC56464	02/59	61A	Kittybrewster
SC51476	SC56465	03/59	61A	Kittybrewster
SC51477	SC56466	03/59	61A	Kittybrewster
SC51478	SC56467	03/59	61A	Kittybrewster
SC51479	SC56468	03/59	61A	Kittybrewster
SC51480	SC56469	03/59	61A	Kittybrewster
SC51481	SC56470	03/59	61A	Kittybrewster
SC51482	SC56471	04/59	61A	Kittybrewster
SC51483	SC56472	04/59	61A	Kittybrewster
SC51484	SC56473	04/59	61A	Kittybrewster
SC51485	SC56474	04/59	61A	Kittybrewster
SC51486	SC56475	04/59	61A	Kittybrewster
SC51487	SC56476	04/59	61A	Kittybrewster
SC51488	SC56477	05/59	61A	Kittybrewster
SC51489	SC56478	05/59	61A	Kittybrewster
SC51490	SC56479	05/59	61A	Kittybrewster
SC51491	SC56480	05/59	61A	Kittybrewster
SC51492	SC56481	05/59	61A	Kittybrewster
SC51493	SC56482	06/59	61A	Kittybrewster
SC51494	SC56483	06/59	66C	Hamilton

Class 106

These were the Leyland engine versions of Class 105, and they were re-classified as Class 105 in 1976.

They were built to work on the rural Midland and Great Northern route, but after the closure of this line they were transferred to work on suburban services out of Kings Cross. They were not really suitable for this route, being fitted with only two side doors per coach and bus-style seating. They ran with up to three or four units coupled together on these services (wasting space in the trains with many unused cabs).

Despite these problems they survived on these services until the Great Northern suburban electrification released them in the late 1970s.

Class 106 Cravens

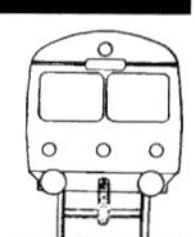

Two-car low density units
DMBS-DTCL

E50359	E56114	08/56	53C	Hull Springhead
E50360	E56115	10/56	53C	Hull Springhead
E50361	E56116	11/56	53C	Hull Springhead
E50362	E56117	11/56	53C	Hull Springhead
E50363	E56118	12/56	53C	Hull Springhead
E50364	E56119	12/56	53C	Hull Springhead
E50365	E56120	01/57	53C	Hull Springhead
E50366	E56121	01/57	53C	Hull Springhead
E50367	E56122	01/57	53C	Hull Springhead
E50368	E56123	01/57	53C	Hull Springhead
E50369	E56124	02/57	53C	Hull Springhead
E50370	E56125	02/57	53C	Hull Springhead
E50371	E56126	02/57	53C	Hull Springhead
E50372	E56127	02/57	53C	Hull Springhead

Class 107

Derby Works followed on from its successful Class 108 design with a heavyweight version of that class. These became known as Class 107. Although built on a short underframe they were considerably heavier and more robust than Class 108.

Twenty-six three-car units were built, and they had a long and successful life, working local services around Glasgow in the Scottish Region.

In 1972 it was planned to merge this class with Class 108, but this did not take place, presumably due to many variations between the types.

These units became popular subjects for preservation.

Class 107 BR Derby

Short heavyweight units
Three-car low density units
DMBS-TSL-DMCL

SC51985	SC59782	SC52011	12/60	66C	Hamilton
SC51986	SC59783	SC52012	12/60	66C	Hamilton
SC51987	SC59784	SC52013	12/60	66C	Hamilton
SC51988	SC59785	SC52014	12/60	66C	Hamilton
SC51989	SC59786	SC52015	12/60	66C	Hamilton
SC51990	SC59787	SC52016	12/60	66C	Hamilton
SC51991	SC59788	SC52017	12/60	66C	Hamilton
SC51992	SC59789	SC52018	12/60	66C	Hamilton
SC51993	SC59790	SC52019	01/61	66C	Hamilton
SC51994	SC59791	SC52020	01/61	66C	Hamilton
SC51995	SC59792	SC52021	01/61	66C	Hamilton
SC51996	SC59793	SC52022	01/61	66C	Hamilton
SC51997	SC59794	SC52023	02/61	66C	Hamilton
SC51998	SC59795	SC52024	02/61	66C	Hamilton
SC51999	SC59796	SC52025	02/61	66C	Hamilton
SC52000	SC59797	SC52026	02/61	66C	Hamilton
SC52001	SC59798	SC52027	02/61	66C	Hamilton
SC52002	SC59799	SC52028	02/61	66C	Hamilton
SC52003	SC59800	SC52029	02/61	66C	Hamilton
SC52004	SC59801	SC52030	03/61	66C	Hamilton
SC52005	SC59802	SC52031	03/61	66C	Hamilton
SC52006	SC59803	SC52032	03/61	66C	Hamilton
SC52007	SC59804	SC52033	04/61	66C	Hamilton
SC52008	SC59805	SC52034	04/61	66C	Hamilton
SC52009	SC59806	SC52035	04/61	66C	Hamilton
SC52010	SC59807	SC52036	06/61	66C	Hamilton

Class 108

British Railways' Derby Works built a large number of low-density units of a variety of formations which became known as Class 108.

Delivered to the London Midland and North Eastern regions for local and general branch line services, they performed well and had long lives. They were of light construction and were generally known as the second "Derby Lightweight" design.

These units were selected for refurbishment and most vehicles remained in traffic until the early 1990s.

Their longevity and the lack of asbestos used in their construction has led to many surviving in preservation.

Class 108 BR Derby

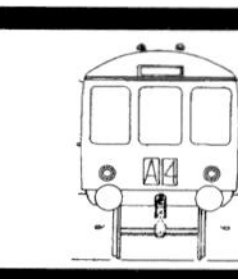

Two-car low density units
DMBS-DTCL

E50599	E56190	07/58	51A	Darlington
E50600	E56191	05/58	53C	Hull Springhead
E50601	E56192	05/58	53C	Hull Springhead
E50602	E56193	05/58	53C	Hull Springhead
E50603	E56194	07/58	51A	Darlington
E50604	E56195	07/58	51A	Darlington
E50605	E56196	06/58	51A	Darlington
E50606	E56197	07/58	53C	Hull Springhead
E50607	E56198	06/58	51A	Darlington
E50608	E56199	07/58	53C	Hull Springhead
E50609	E56200	08/58	56G	Bradford Hammerton St
E50610	E56201	08/58	56G	Bradford Hammerton St
E50611	E56202	08/58	56G	Bradford Hammerton St
E50612	E56203	08/58	56G	Bradford Hammerton St
E50613	E56204	08/58	56G	Bradford Hammerton St
E50614	E56205	07/58	51A	Darlington
E50615	E56206	09/58	56G	Bradford Hammerton St
E50616	E56207	09/58	56G	Bradford Hammerton St
E50617	E56208	08/58	56G	Bradford Hammerton St
E50618	E56209	08/58	56G	Bradford Hammerton St
E50619	E56210	08/58	56G	Bradford Hammerton St

Class 108 BR Derby

Three-car low density units
DMBS-TSL-DMCL

E50620	E59386	E50642	10/58	53C	Hull Springhead
E50621	E59387	E50643	10/58	53C	Hull Springhead
E50622	E59388	E50644	11/58	53C	Hull Springhead
E50623	E59389	E50645	11/58	53C	Hull Springhead
E50624	E59390	E50646	11/58	53B	Hull Botanic Gardens

Class 108 BR Derby

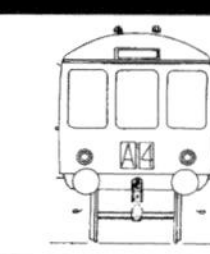

Two-car low density units
DMBS-DTCL

M50625	M56211	12/58	5D	Stoke-on-Trent
M50626	M56212	12/58	18A	Toton
M50627	M56213	12/58	5D	Stoke-on-Trent
M50628	M56214	12/58	5D	Stoke-on-Trent
M50629	M56215	02/59	(s)	Chaddesden

Class 108 BR Derby

Four-car low density units
DMCL-TBSL-TSL-DMCL

E50630	E59245	E59380	E50631	10/58		South Gosforth
E50632	E59246	E59381	E50633	10/58	53C	Hull Springhead
E50634	E59247	E59382	E50635	10/58	53C	Hull Springhead
E50636	E59248	E59383	E50637	10/58		South Gosforth
E50638	E59249	E59384	E50639	10/58		South Gosforth
E50640	E59250	E59385	E50641	10/58		South Gosforth

Class 108 BR Derby

Two-car power-twin low density units DMBS-DMCL

M50924	M51561	10/59		Wrexham Central
M50925	M51562	12/59	6G	Llandudno Junction
M50926	M51563	11/59		Wrexham Central (o/l)
M50927	M51564	11/59	6G	Llandudno Junction
M50928	M51565	11/59	6G	Llandudno Junction
M50929	M51566	11/59	6G	Llandudno Junction
M50930	M51567	12/59	6G	Llandudno Junction
M50931	M51568	12/59	6G	Llandudno Junction
M50932	M51569	12/59	6G	Llandudno Junction
M50933	M51570	01/60	6D	Chester Northgate
M50934	M51571	01/60	6D	Chester Northgate
M50935	M51572	01/60	6D	Chester Northgate

Class 108 BR Derby

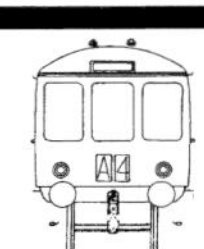

Two-car low density units DMBS-DTCL

Many of these units were stored on delivery pending a decision on initial allocations.

M50938	M56221	01/59	6G	Llandudno Junction
M50939	M56222	01/59	6G	Llandudno Junction
M50940	M56223	01/59	6G	Llandudno Junction
M50941	M56224	01/59	6G	Llandudno Junction
M50942	M56225	01/59	2D	Coventry
M50943	M56226	01/59	2D	Coventry
M50944	M56227	01/59	2D	Coventry
M50945	M56228	01/59	6K	Rhyl
M50946	M56229	01/59	6K	Rhyl
M50947	M56230	02/59	(s)	Warwick
M50948	M56231	02/59	(s)	Warwick
M50949	M56232	02/59	(s)	Warwick
M50950	M56233	02/59	(s)	Warwick
M50951	M56234	02/59	(s)	Warwick
M50952	M56235	02/59	(s)	Warwick
M50953	M56236	02/59	6K	Rhyl (s)
M50954	M56237	03/59	5B	Crewe South
M50955	M56238	03/59	5B	Crewe South
M50956	M56239	03/59	5B	Crewe South
M50957	M56240	03/59	6K	Rhyl (s)
M50958	M56241	04/59	6K	Rhyl (s)
M50959	M56242	04/59	6K	Rhyl (s)
M50960	M56243	04/59	(s)	Chaddesden
M50961	M56244	04/59	(s)	Chaddesden
M50962	M56245	04/59	(s)	Chaddesden
M50963	M56246	06/59	24F	Fleetwood
M50964	M56247	05/59	9E	Buxton
M50965	M56248	05/59	9E	Buxton
M50966	M56249	05/59	9E	Buxton
M50967	M56250	06/59	24F	Fleetwood
M50968	M56251	05/59	24F	Fleetwood
M50969	M56252	06/59	24F	Fleetwood
M50970	M56253	07/59	24F	Fleetwood
M50971	M56254	07/59	24F	Fleetwood
M50972	M56255	07/59	24F	Fleetwood
M50973	M56256	07/59	24F	Fleetwood
M50974	M56257	07/59	24F	Fleetwood
M50975	M56258	08/59	26A	Newton Heath
M50976	M56259	08/59	(s)	Chaddesden
M50977	M56260	08/59	(s)	Chaddesden
M50978	M56261	08/59	26A	Newton Heath
M50979	M56262	08/59	(s)	Chaddesden
M50980	M56263	09/59	26A	Newton Heath
M50981	M56264	09/59	26A	Newton Heath
M50982	M56265	09/59	26A	Newton Heath
M50983	M56266	10/59	26A	Newton Heath
M50984	M56267	10/59	26A	Newton Heath
M50985	M56268	10/59	6G	Llandudno Junction
M50986	M56269	10/59	14E	Bedford (o/l)
M50987	M56270	10/59	14E	Bedford (o/l)

Class 108 BR Derby

Two-car low density units DMBS-DTCL

M51416	M56271	02/60	3C	Walsall Rycroft
M51417	M56272	02/60	3C	Walsall Rycroft
M51418	M56273	02/60	3E	Monument Lane
M51419	M56274	02/60	3E	Monument Lane
M51420	M56275	02/60	14A	Cricklewood
M51421	M56276	03/60	14A	Cricklewood
M51422	M56277	03/60	14A	Cricklewood
M51423	M56278	03/60	26A	Newton Heath
M51424	M56279	03/60	64H	Leith Central (o/l)

Class 108 BR Derby

Two-car low density units DMBS-DTCL

M51901	M56484	03/60		Reddish
M51902	M56485	03/60		Reddish
M51903	M56486	03/60		Reddish
M51904	M56487	03/60		Reddish
M51905	M56488	04/60	18A	Toton
M51906	M56489	04/60	9E	Buxton
M51907	M56490	04/60	18A	Toton
M51908	M56491	04/60	18A	Toton
M51909	M56492	04/60	18A	Toton
M51910	M56493	04/60	18A	Toton
M51911	M56494	04/60	18A	Toton
M51912	M56495	05/60	3C	Walsall Rycroft
M51913	M56496	05/60	18A	Toton
M51914	M56497	05/60	18A	Toton
M51915	M56498	05/60	6G	Llandudno Junction
M51916	M56499	06/60	6G	Llandudno Junction
M51917	M56500	06/60	6G	Llandudno Junction
M51918	M56501	07/60	6G	Llandudno Junction
M51919	M56502	06/60	6G	Llandudno Junction
M51920	M56503	07/60	6G	Llandudno Junction
M51921	M56504	07/60	6G	Llandudno Junction

Class 108 BR Derby

Two-car power-twin low density units DMBS-DMCL

M51922	M52037	07/60	26A	Newton Heath
M51923	M52038	07/60	26A	Newton Heath
M51924	M52039	07/60	26A	Newton Heath
M51925	M52040	08/60	26A	Newton Heath
M51926	M52041	08/60	26A	Newton Heath
M51927	M52042	08/60	26A	Newton Heath
M51928	M52043	10/60	26A	Newton Heath
M51929	M52044	09/60	26A	Newton Heath
M51930	M52045	09/60	26A	Newton Heath
M51931	M52046	09/60	26A	Newton Heath
M51932	M52047	09/60	26A	Newton Heath
M51933	M52048	10/60	26A	Newton Heath
M51934	M52049	10/60	26A	Newton Heath
M51935	M52050	11/60	26A	Newton Heath
M51936	M52051	11/60	26A	Newton Heath
M51937	M52052	10/60	26A	Newton Heath
M51938	M52053	02/61	26A	Newton Heath
M51939	M52054	11/60	26A	Newton Heath
M51940	M52055	11/60	26A	Newton Heath
M51941	M52056	11/60	26A	Newton Heath
M51942	M52057	01/61	26A	Newton Heath
M51943	M52058	12/60	26A	Newton Heath
M51944	M52059	12/60	9E	Buxton
M51945	M52060	01/61	26A	Newton Heath
M51946	M52061	01/61	26A	Newton Heath
M51947	M52062	02/61	26A	Newton Heath
M51948	M52063	02/61	26A	Newton Heath
M51949	M52064	03/61	26A	Newton Heath
M51950	M52065	06/61	26A	Newton Heath

Class 109

Wickham & Co of Ware in Hertfordshire were better known for permanent-way trolley and other lightweight vehicle construction than for coach construction. They developed methods for constructing vehicles with a skeletal body framework which allowed them to dispense with the usual heavy underframe. While this saved a great amount of weight it dramatically increased repair costs for even minor collision damage.

They built five two-car low density units of a highly distinctive design for British Railways. They were quite successful and were fitted with what was considered a flamboyant and extravagant interior. They were put to work on branch line and local services in East Anglia.

Being only five in number they were immediately non-standard, even more so when the manufacturer bought back two units to meet an order for export to the Trinidad Government Railway in 1961.

However, one unit was converted into the Eastern Region General Manager's saloon which ensured its survival long enough to be preserved.

Class 109 Wickham

Two-car low density units
DMBS-DTCL

E50415	E56170	08/57	30A	Stratford
E50416	E56171	10/57	30A	Stratford
E50417	E56172	11/57	30A	Stratford
E50418	E56173	04/58	30A	Stratford
E50419	E56174	08/58	30A	Stratford

Class 110

This class was an updated version of Birmingham RCW's Class 104. They were designed for the arduous Lancashire and Yorkshire route across the Pennines, and were fitted with powerful Rolls-Royce Engines. They became known as the "Calder Valley" units.

They were similar to Class 104, but a four-character headcode box was fitted, together with slanting tops to the front windows which gave them a distinctive appearance.

The three-car low density units were delivered in two batches to work this inter-regional service. The first batch of 20 went to the North Eastern Region and the last 10 to the London Midland Region. Later they were all based on the Eastern Region.

One unit (E51821, E59706 & E51837) was destroyed in a fire at Sowerby Bridge on 13th January 1963.

The class was included in the refurbishment programme. From 1982 they ran as power-twins without their centre trailers, and the last units survived until 1992.

Class 110 Birmingham RC&W

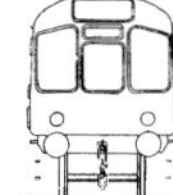

Calder Valley units
Three-car low density units
DMBC-TSL-DMCL

E51809	E59693	E51829	06/61	51A	Darlington
E51810	E59694	E51830	06/61	51A	Darlington
E51811	E59695	E51831	07/61	51A	Darlington
E51812	E59696	E51832	07/61	51A	Darlington
E51813	E59697	E51833	07/61	51A	Darlington
E51814	E59698	E51834	07/61	51A	Darlington
E51815	E59699	E51835	08/61	56G	Bradford Hammerton St
E51816	E59700	E51836	08/61	56G	Bradford Hammerton St
E51817	E59701	E51837	09/61	56G	Bradford Hammerton St
E51818	E59702	E51838	09/61	56G	Bradford Hammerton St
E51819	E59703	E51839	09/61	56G	Bradford Hammerton St
E51820	E59704	E51840	09/61	56G	Bradford Hammerton St
E51821	E59705	E51841	09/61	56G	Bradford Hammerton St
E51822	E59706	E51842	10/61	56G	Bradford Hammerton St
E51823	E59707	E51843	10/61	56G	Bradford Hammerton St
E51824	E59708	E51844	10/61	56G	Bradford Hammerton St
E51825	E59709	E51845	10/61	56G	Bradford Hammerton St
E51826	E59710	E51846	11/61	56G	Bradford Hammerton St
E51827	E59711	E51847	11/61	56G	Bradford Hammerton St
E51828	E59712	E51848	11/61	56G	Bradford Hammerton St

Class 110 Birmingham RC&W

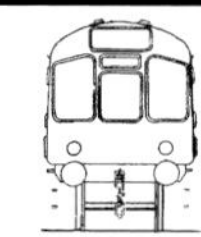

Calder Valley units
Three-car low density units
DMBC-TSL-DMCL

M52066	M59808	M52076	11/61	26A	Newton Heath
M52067	M59809	M52077	11/61	26A	Newton Heath
M52068	M59810	M52078	12/61	26A	Newton Heath
M52069	M59811	M52079	12/61	26A	Newton Heath
M52070	M59812	M52080	12/61	26A	Newton Heath
M52071	M59813	M52081	01/62	26A	Newton Heath
M52072	M59814	M52082	01/62	26A	Newton Heath
M52073	M59815	M52083	01/62	26A	Newton Heath
M52074	M59816	M52084	01/62	26A	Newton Heath
M52075	M59817	M52085	01/62	26A	Newton Heath

Class 111

After the success of their Class 101 units Metropolitan-Cammell produced a higher-powered version. Class 111 units were fitted with 180 hp Rolls Royce engines.

Most of the two- and three-car units were delivered to the North Eastern Region, but four two-car units were for the London Midland Region. The later units were fitted with distinctive four-character headcode boxes mounted above the front cab windows.

In the 1980s the centre cars were removed from the three-car units. In order to reduce maintenance costs, one engine was removed from each of the power cars creating "Half-motors". These were renumbered in the 78xxx number series.

Class 111 Metropolitan-Cammell

Two-car low density units
DMBS-DTCL

M50134	M56090	04/57	9A	Longsight
M50135	M56091	04/57	9A	Longsight
M50136	M56092	04/57	9A	Longsight
M50137	M56093	04/57	9A	Longsight

Class 111 Metropolitan-Cammell

Three-car low density units
DMCL-TSL-DMBS

E50270	E59100	E50280	10/57	56G	Bradford Hammerton St
E50271	E59101	E50281	11/57	56G	Bradford Hammerton St
E50272	E59102	E50282	11/57	56G	Bradford Hammerton St
E50273	E59103	E50283	12/57	56G	Bradford Hammerton St
E50274	E59104	E50284	12/57	56G	Bradford Hammerton St
E50275	E59105	E50285	12/57	56G	Bradford Hammerton St
E50276	E59106	E50286	12/57	56G	Bradford Hammerton St
E50277	E59107	E50287	01/58	56G	Bradford Hammerton St
E50278	E59108	E50288	01/58	56G	Bradford Hammerton St
E50279	E59109	E50289	01/58	56G	Bradford Hammerton St

Class 111 Metropolitan-Cammell

Three-car low density units
DMBS-TSL-DMCL

E51541	E59569	E51551	12/59	56G	Bradford Hammerton St
E51542	E59570	E51552	12/59	56G	Bradford Hammerton St
E51543	E59571	E51553	12/59	56G	Bradford Hammerton St
E51544	E59572	E51554	01/60	56G	Bradford Hammerton St

Class 111 Metropolitan-Cammell

Two-car low density power-twin units
DMBS-DMCL

E51545	E51555	01/60	56G	Bradford Hammerton St
E51546	E51556	01/60	56G	Bradford Hammerton St
E51547	E51557	01/60	56G	Bradford Hammerton St
E51548	E51558	02/60	56G	Bradford Hammerton St
E51549	E51559	02/60	56G	Bradford Hammerton St
E51550	E51560	03/60	56G	Bradford Hammerton St

Class 112

In 1959 Cravens introduced two classes of unusual design, classes 112 and 113. Where all other designs had been fitted with two engines in a power car, these had only one engine fitted per car. It was a powerful 238hp Rolls Royce engine, and all the units were built as power-twins; two power cars in a unit.

Class 112 was fitted with standard mechanical transmission. Twenty-five units were built to this design.

Both classes were designed for the hilly ex-Lancashire and Yorkshire lines in Lancashire, but they were very unsuccessful in this role. They were later tried out working from Cricklewood in London, but with a similar lack of success, and they were all withdrawn before the end of the 1960s.

Class 112 Cravens

Two-car low density power-twin units
DMBS-DMCL

M51681	M51706	10/59	26A	Newton Heath
M51682	M51707	09/59	26A	Newton Heath
M51683	M51708	11/59	26A	Newton Heath
M51684	M51709	08/59	26A	Newton Heath
M51685	M51710	08/59	26A	Newton Heath
M51686	M51711	08/59	26A	Newton Heath
M51687	M51712	08/59	26A	Newton Heath
M51688	M51713	08/59	26A	Newton Heath
M51689	M51714	08/59	26A	Newton Heath
M51690	M51715	08/59	26A	Newton Heath
M51691	M51716	08/59	26A	Newton Heath
M51692	M51717	09/59	26A	Newton Heath
M51693	M51718	09/59	26A	Newton Heath
M51694	M51719	09/59	26A	Newton Heath
M51695	M51720	09/59	26A	Newton Heath
M51696	M51721	09/59	26A	Newton Heath
M51697	M51722	10/59	24A	Accrington
M51698	M51723	10/59	24A	Accrington
M51699	M51724	10/59	24A	Accrington
M51700	M51725	10/59	24A	Accrington
M51701	M51726	10/59	24A	Accrington
M51702	M51727	10/59	24A	Accrington
M51703	M51728	10/59	24A	Accrington
M51704	M51729	10/59	24A	Accrington
M51705	M51730	11/59	24A	Accrington

Class 113

At the same time as Class 112, Cravens built another batch of twenty-five power-twins with the same unusual engine layout, but this time fitted with hydraulic transmission. These were distinguished by a large combined head-code panel and destination indicator on the front end, quite unlike any other units.

If anything these proved even more troublesome than Class 112 and they were prone to catch fire due to overheating of the converter fluid and feeding back to the main fuel tank.

These units suffered the same early demise as Class 112.

Class 113 Cravens

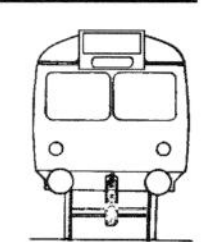

Two-car low density power-twin units
DMBS-DMCL

M51731	M51756	11/59	24A	Accrington
M51732	M51757	11/59	24A	Accrington
M51733	M51758	11/59	24A	Accrington
M51734	M51759	11/59	24A	Accrington
M51735	M51760	12/59	24A	Accrington
M51736	M51761	02/60	24A	Accrington
M51737	M51762	12/59	24A	Accrington
M51738	M51763	12/59	24A	Accrington
M51739	M51764	12/59	24A	Accrington
M51740	M51765	01/60	24A	Accrington
M51741	M51766	01/60	24A	Accrington
M51742	M51767	01/60	24A	Accrington
M51743	M51768	01/60	24A	Accrington
M51744	M51769	01/60	24A	Accrington
M51745	M51770	01/60	26A	Newton Heath
M51746	M51771	02/60	24A	Accrington
M51747	M51772	02/60	24A	Accrington
M51748	M51773	02/60	24A	Accrington
M51749	M51774	02/60	24A	Accrington
M51750	M51775	03/60	24A	Accrington
M51751	M51776	03/60	24A	Accrington
M51752	M51777	03/60	24A	Accrington
M51753	M51778	04/60	24A	Accrington
M51754	M51779	05/60	24A	Accrington
M51755	M51780	07/60	24A	Accrington

Class 114

This was Derby Works' first standard low-density design complete with the standard "Derby" cab, which also became standard on the high-density units built by other manufacturers. They were the first vehicles delivered under the Modernisation Plan proper.

Aluminium construction had proved troublesome and expensive so Derby now opted for steel construction on a long frame, making this a heavyweight design.

Fifty two-car units were built for the Eastern Region and they spent most of their working lives based at Lincoln. They were refurbished under the refurbishment plan and most survived in traffic until 1988-1992.

Most of the class were fitted with high-power Leyland Albion engines. One unit (E50000 and E56000) was fitted with Rolls-Royce engines.

A number of these were used as parcels units towards the end of their lives. Five of these units were rebuilt and were fitted with roller-shutter doors, and renumbered into the parcels unit series.

Class 114 BR Derby

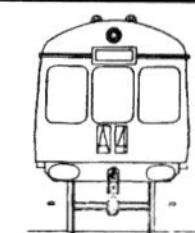

Two-car Low Density units
DMBS-DTCL

E50000	E56000	03/57	40A	Lincoln

Class 114 BR Derby

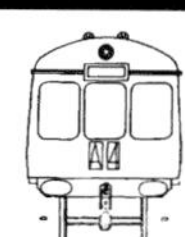

Two-car Low Density units
DMBS-DTCL

E50001	E56001	10/56	40A	Lincoln
E50002	E56002	11/56	40A	Lincoln
E50003	E56003	11/56	40A	Lincoln
E50004	E56004	11/56	40A	Lincoln
E50005	E56005	11/56	40A	Lincoln
E50006	E56006	11/56	40A	Lincoln
E50007	E56007	11/56	40A	Lincoln
E50008	E56008	11/56	40A	Lincoln
E50009	E56009	11/56	40A	Lincoln
E50010	E56010	12/56	40A	Lincoln
E50011	E56011	11/56	40A	Lincoln
E50012	E56012	11/56	40A	Lincoln
E50013	E56013	12/56	40A	Lincoln
E50014	E56014	12/56	40A	Lincoln
E50015	E56015	02/57	40A	Lincoln
E50016	E56016	12/56	40A	Lincoln
E50017	E56017	01/57	40A	Lincoln
E50018	E56018	01/57	40A	Lincoln
E50019	E56019	01/57	40A	Lincoln
E50020	E56020	01/57	40A	Lincoln
E50021	E56021	01/57	40A	Lincoln
E50022	E56022	01/57	40A	Lincoln
E50023	E56023	01/57	40A	Lincoln
E50024	E56024	01/57	40A	Lincoln
E50025	E56025	01/57	40A	Lincoln
E50026	E56026	01/57	40A	Lincoln
E50027	E56027	01/57	40A	Lincoln
E50028	E56028	01/57	40A	Lincoln
E50029	E56029	01/57	40A	Lincoln
E50030	E56030	01/57	40A	Lincoln
E50031	E56031	01/57	40A	Lincoln
E50032	E56032	02/57	40A	Lincoln
E50033	E56033	02/57	40A	Lincoln
E50034	E56034	02/57	40A	Lincoln
E50035	E56035	03/57	40A	Lincoln
E50036	E56036	02/57	40A	Lincoln
E50037	E56037	02/57	40A	Lincoln
E50038	E56038	02/57	40A	Lincoln
E50039	E56039	02/57	40A	Lincoln
E50040	E56040	02/57	40A	Lincoln
E50041	E56041	03/57	40A	Lincoln
E50042	E56042	03/57	40A	Lincoln
E50043	E56043	03/57	40A	Lincoln
E50044	E56044	03/57	40A	Lincoln
E50045	E56045	03/57	40A	Lincoln
E50046	E56046	03/57	40A	Lincoln
E50047	E56047	04/57	40A	Lincoln
E50048	E56048	12/57	40A	Lincoln
E50049	E56049	08/57	40A	Lincoln

Class 115

These four-car long-framed high-density units for outer-suburban services were built at Derby Works. They were fitted with powerful Leyland Albion engines. Two batches (of fifteen and twenty units) were built for the Marylebone services. The remaining small batch of six units was built to work the Liverpool-Manchester services via the CLC route.

Later the Liverpool-Manchester units also worked from Marylebone, and a number of units finished their days working from Tyseley in Birmingham.

These units were similar to the Class 127 units, but had larger windows and better quality furnishings and fittings. They were built without gangway connections, but some were later rebuilt with connecting gangways.

Many cars survive in preservation.

Class 115 BR Derby

Marylebone units
Four-car high density units
DMBS-TS-TCL-DMBS

Many of these units were stored or lent to other depots when new before being delivered to 1D Marylebone.

M51651	M59649	M59664	M51652	03/60	9E	Buxton
M51653	M59650	M59665	M51654	03/60	14A	Cricklewood
M51655	M59651	M59666	M51656	03/60	14A	Cricklewood
M51657	M59652	M59667	M51658	04/60	14A	Cricklewood
M51659	M59653	M59668	M51660	04/60	14A	Cricklewood
M51661	M59654	M59669	M51662	06/60	14A	Cricklewood
M51663	M59655	M59670	M51664	05/60	14A	Cricklewood
M51665	M59656	M59671	M51666	05/60	14A	Cricklewood
M51667	M59657	M59672	M51668	06/60	NER (o/l)	
M51669	M59658	M59673	M51670	06/60	14A	Cricklewood
M51671	M59659	M59674	M51672	06/60	14A	Cricklewood
M51673	M59660	M59675	M51674	05/60	14A	Cricklewood
M51675	M59661	M59676	M51676	05/60	14A	Cricklewood
M51677	M59662	M59677	M51678	06/60	NER (o/l)	
M51679	M59663	M59678	M51680	07/60	NER (o/l)	

Class 115 BR Derby

Liverpool-Manchester units
Four-car high density units
DMBS-TS-TCL-DMBS

These units went on loan to Cricklewood beore being delivered to Allerton.

M51849	M59713	M59719	M51850	02/60	14A	Cricklewood
M51851	M59714	M59720	M51852	02/60	14A	Cricklewood
M51853	M59715	M59721	M51854	02/60	14A	Cricklewood
M51855	M59716	M59722	M51856	02/60	14A	Cricklewood
M51857	M59717	M59723	M51858	02/60	14A	Cricklewood
M51859	M59718	M59724	M51860	03/60	14A	Cricklewood

Class 115 BR Derby

Marylebone units
Four-car high density units
DMBS-TS-TCL-DMBS

Many of these units were stored or lent to other depots when new before being delivered to 1D Marylebone.

M51861	M59725	M59745	M51862	07/60	55H	Neville Hill (o/l)
M51863	M59726	M59746	M51864	07/60	55H	Neville Hill (o/l)
M51865	M59727	M59747	M51866	08/60	(s)	Derby Friargate
M51867	M59728	M59748	M51868	08/60	(s)	Derby Friargate
M51869	M59729	M59749	M51870	08/60	(s)	Derby Friargate
M51871	M59730	M59750	M51872	09/60	(s)	Derby Friargate
M51873	M59731	M59751	M51874	09/60	(s)	Derby Friargate
M51875	M59732	M59752	M51876	09/60	(s)	Derby Friargate
M51877	M59733	M59753	M51878	09/60	(s)	Derby Friargate
M51879	M59734	M59754	M51880	09/60	(s)	Derby Friargate
M51881	M59735	M59755	M51882	09/60	(s)	Derby Friargate
M51883	M59736	M59756	M51884	09/60	(s)	Chaddesden
M51885	M59737	M59757	M51886	09/60	(s)	Chaddesden
M51887	M59738	M59758	M51888	09/60	(s)	Chaddesden
M51889	M59739	M59759	M51890	10/60	(s)	Chaddesden
M51891	M59740	M59760	M51892	10/60	(s)	Chaddesden
M51893	M59741	M59761	M51894	10/60	(s)	Chaddesden
M51895	M59742	M59762	M51896	11/60	(s)	Chaddesden
M51897	M59743	M59763	M51898	11/60	(s)	Chaddesden
M51899	M59744	M59764	M51900	12/60	1E	Bletchley

Class 116

The Western Region ordered a large number of three-car high-density units for its services. The largest order was for these Derby built units.

Although ordered for Western Region services, many were transferred to the London Midland Region by default, when regional boundary changes moved the

GWR lines around Birmingham into London Midland control in 1963. Later unit transfers meant that some units worked on the Scottish and Eastern regions.

They were originally built as non-gangwayed units, and with no toilet facilities, cramped seats and draughty drop-light windows they were very uncomfortable, especially when crowded. The units were included in the refurbishment plan, which improved conditions, and many were later fitted with through gangways within the unit.

Three two-car sets were converted to parcels cars and reclassified as Class 130. They worked with re-wired General Utility Vans (GUVs) to form three-car parcels units.

Class 116 BR Derby

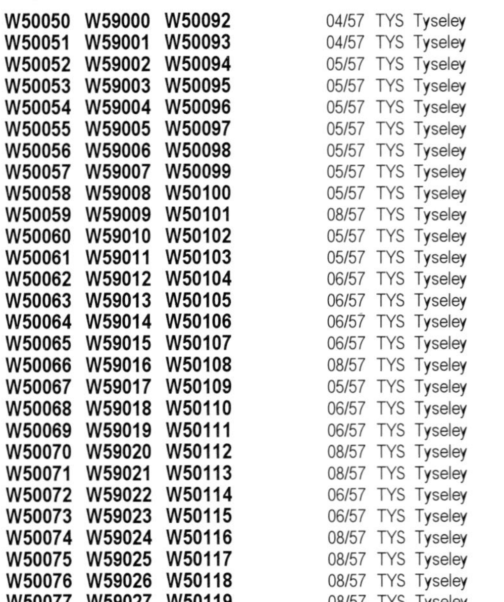

Three-car high density units
DMBS-TC-DMS

W50050	W59000	W50092	04/57	TYS	Tyseley
W50051	W59001	W50093	04/57	TYS	Tyseley
W50052	W59002	W50094	05/57	TYS	Tyseley
W50053	W59003	W50095	05/57	TYS	Tyseley
W50054	W59004	W50096	05/57	TYS	Tyseley
W50055	W59005	W50097	05/57	TYS	Tyseley
W50056	W59006	W50098	05/57	TYS	Tyseley
W50057	W59007	W50099	05/57	TYS	Tyseley
W50058	W59008	W50100	05/57	TYS	Tyseley
W50059	W59009	W50101	08/57	TYS	Tyseley
W50060	W59010	W50102	05/57	TYS	Tyseley
W50061	W59011	W50103	05/57	TYS	Tyseley
W50062	W59012	W50104	06/57	TYS	Tyseley
W50063	W59013	W50105	06/57	TYS	Tyseley
W50064	W59014	W50106	06/57	TYS	Tyseley
W50065	W59015	W50107	06/57	TYS	Tyseley
W50066	W59016	W50108	08/57	TYS	Tyseley
W50067	W59017	W50109	05/57	TYS	Tyseley
W50068	W59018	W50110	06/57	TYS	Tyseley
W50069	W59019	W50111	06/57	TYS	Tyseley
W50070	W59020	W50112	08/57	TYS	Tyseley
W50071	W59021	W50113	08/57	TYS	Tyseley
W50072	W59022	W50114	06/57	TYS	Tyseley
W50073	W59023	W50115	06/57	TYS	Tyseley
W50074	W59024	W50116	08/57	TYS	Tyseley
W50075	W59025	W50117	08/57	TYS	Tyseley
W50076	W59026	W50118	08/57	TYS	Tyseley
W50077	W59027	W50119	08/57	TYS	Tyseley
W50078	W59028	W50120	08/57	TYS	Tyseley
W50079	W59029	W50121	09/57	CAT	Cardiff Cathays
W50080	W59030	W50122	10/57	CAT	Cardiff Cathays
W50081	W59031	W50123	10/57	CAT	Cardiff Cathays

Class 116 BR Derby

Three-car high density units
DMBS-TS-DMS

W50082	W59032	W50124	08/57	CAT	Cardiff Cathays
W50083	W59033	W50125	08/57	CAT	Cardiff Cathays
W50084	W59034	W50126	08/57	CAT	Cardiff Cathays
W50085	W59035	W50127	08/57	CDF	Cardiff Canton
W50086	W59036	W50128	09/57	CDF	Cardiff Canton
W50087	W59037	W50129	09/57	CDF	Cardiff Canton
W50088	W59038	W50130	09/57	CDF	Cardiff Canton
W50089	W59039	W50131	09/57	CDF	Cardiff Canton
W50090	W59040	W50132	09/57	CDF	Cardiff Canton
W50091	W59041	W50133	10/57	CDF	Cardiff Canton

Class 116 BR Derby

Three-car high density units
DMBS-TC-DMS

W50818	W59326	W50871	11/57	CAT	Cardiff Cathays
W50819	W59327	W50872	11/57	CAT	Cardiff Cathays
W50820	W59328	W50873	11/57	CAT	Cardiff Cathays
W50821	W59329	W50874	11/57	CAT	Cardiff Cathays
W50822	W59330	W50875	11/57	CAT	Cardiff Cathays
W50823	W59331	W50876	12/57	CAT	Cardiff Cathays
W50824	W59332	W50877	12/57	CAT	Cardiff Cathays
W50825	W59333	W50878	11/57	CAT	Cardiff Cathays
W50826	W59334	W50879	12/57	CAT	Cardiff Cathays
W50827	W59335	W50880	11/57	CAT	Cardiff Cathays
W50828	W59336	W50881	12/57	CAT	Cardiff Cathays
W50829	W59337	W50882	11/57	CAT	Cardiff Cathays
W50830	W59338	W50883	12/57	CAT	Cardiff Cathays
W50831	W59339	W50884	12/57	CAT	Cardiff Cathays
W50832	W59340	W50885	01/58	CAT	Cardiff Cathays
W50833	W59341	W50886	01/58	CAT	Cardiff Cathays
W50834	W59342	W50887	01/58	CAT	Cardiff Cathays
W50835	W59343	W50888	01/58	CAT	Cardiff Cathays
W50836	W59344	W50889	01/58	CAT	Cardiff Cathays
W50837	W59345	W50890	02/58	CAT	Cardiff Cathays
W50838	W59346	W50891	01/58	CAT	Cardiff Cathays
W50839	W59347	W50892	01/58	CAT	Cardiff Cathays
W50840	W59348	W50893	01/58	CAT	Cardiff Cathays
W50841	W59349	W50894	01/58	CAT	Cardiff Cathays
W50842	W59350	W50895	02/58	CAT	Cardiff Cathays
W50843	W59351	W50896	01/58	CAT	Cardiff Cathays
W50844	W59352	W50897	02/58	CAT	Cardiff Cathays
W50845	W59353	W50898	01/58	CAT	Cardiff Cathays
W50846	W59354	W50899	01/58	CAT	Cardiff Cathays
W50847	W59355	W50900	02/58	CAT	Cardiff Cathays
W50848	W59356	W50901	02/58	CAT	Cardiff Cathays
W50849	W59357	W50902	02/58	CAT	Cardiff Cathays
W50850	W59358	W50903	02/58	CAT	Cardiff Cathays
W50851	W59359	W50904	02/58	CAT	Cardiff Cathays
W50852	W59360	W50905	02/58	CAT	Cardiff Cathays
W50853	W59361	W50906	03/58	CAT	Cardiff Cathays
W50854	W59362	W50907	02/58	CAT	Cardiff Cathays
W50855	W59363	W50908	03/58	CAT	Cardiff Cathays
W50856	W59364	W50909	03/58	CAT	Cardiff Cathays
W50857	W59365	W50910	03/58	CAT	Cardiff Cathays
W50858	W59366	W50911	04/58	CAT	Cardiff Cathays
W50859	W59367	W50912	04/58	CDF	Cardiff Canton
W50860	W59368	W50913	03/58	CDF	Cardiff Canton
W50861	W59369	W50914	04/58	CDF	Cardiff Canton
W50862	W59370	W50915	04/58	CAT	Cardiff Cathays
W50863	W59371	W50916	05/58	CAT	Cardiff Cathays
W50864	W59372	W50917	05/58	CAT	Cardiff Cathays
W50865	W59373	W50918	05/58	CAT	Cardiff Cathays
W50866	W59374	W50919	05/58	CAT	Cardiff Cathays
W50867	W59375	W50920	05/58	CAT	Cardiff Cathays
W50868	W59376	W50921	06/58	CAT	Cardiff Cathays
W50869		W50922	07/58	CAT	Cardiff Cathays
W50870		W50923	07/58	CAT	Cardiff Cathays

Class 116 BR Derby

Three-car high density units
DMBS-TC-DMS

W51128	W59438	W51141	07/58	BL	Bristol
W51129	W59439	W51142	08/58	BL	Bristol
W51130	W59440	W51143	08/58	BL	Bristol
W51131	W59441	W51144	08/58	BL	Bristol
W51132	W59442	W51145	08/58	BL	Bristol
W51133	W59443	W51146	08/58	BL	Bristol
W51134	W59444	W51147	09/58	BL	Bristol
W51135	W59445	W51148	09/58	BL	Bristol
W51136	W59446	W51149	09/58	BL	Bristol
W51137	W59447	W51150	10/58	BL	Bristol
W51138	W59448	W51151	10/58	BL	Bristol
W51139		W51152	10/58	BL	Bristol
W51140		W51153	11/58	BL	Bristol

Class 117

Pressed Steel (part of the British Motor Corporation) built 43 three-car high density units for working the Western Region services out of Paddington. They carried the standard "Derby" type cab as fitted to all the Western Region high density units.

They were similar to the Class 116 units, but had the advantage of toilets within the trailer cars. Because the units were not gangway fitted, most of the passengers could not access the toilets, so to remedy this the Western Region started fitting gangways to all these units.

Most of these units were refurbished. After they were replaced on services out of Paddington by "Thames Turbo" units in 1992 they worked in other areas before final withdrawal.

They proved to be particularly long-lived units, and many of them survive in preservation.

Three units entered service coupled to Class 118 trailers, and remained in this formation for most of their lives.

Class 117 Pressed Steel

Three-car high density units
DMBS-TCL-DMS

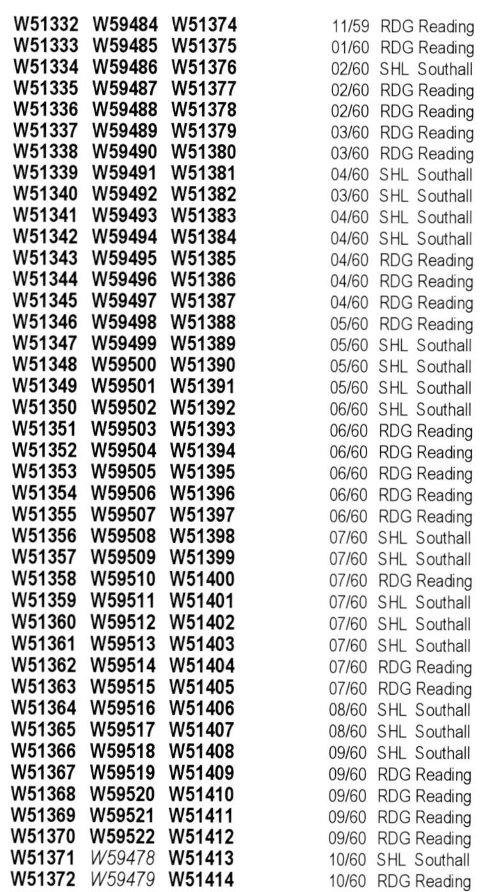

DMBS	TCL	DMS	Date	Depot	
W51332	W59484	W51374	11/59	RDG	Reading
W51333	W59485	W51375	01/60	RDG	Reading
W51334	W59486	W51376	02/60	SHL	Southall
W51335	W59487	W51377	02/60	RDG	Reading
W51336	W59488	W51378	02/60	RDG	Reading
W51337	W59489	W51379	03/60	RDG	Reading
W51338	W59490	W51380	03/60	RDG	Reading
W51339	W59491	W51381	04/60	SHL	Southall
W51340	W59492	W51382	03/60	SHL	Southall
W51341	W59493	W51383	04/60	SHL	Southall
W51342	W59494	W51384	04/60	SHL	Southall
W51343	W59495	W51385	04/60	RDG	Reading
W51344	W59496	W51386	04/60	RDG	Reading
W51345	W59497	W51387	04/60	RDG	Reading
W51346	W59498	W51388	05/60	RDG	Reading
W51347	W59499	W51389	05/60	SHL	Southall
W51348	W59500	W51390	05/60	SHL	Southall
W51349	W59501	W51391	05/60	SHL	Southall
W51350	W59502	W51392	06/60	SHL	Southall
W51351	W59503	W51393	06/60	RDG	Reading
W51352	W59504	W51394	06/60	RDG	Reading
W51353	W59505	W51395	06/60	RDG	Reading
W51354	W59506	W51396	06/60	RDG	Reading
W51355	W59507	W51397	06/60	RDG	Reading
W51356	W59508	W51398	07/60	SHL	Southall
W51357	W59509	W51399	07/60	SHL	Southall
W51358	W59510	W51400	07/60	RDG	Reading
W51359	W59511	W51401	07/60	SHL	Southall
W51360	W59512	W51402	07/60	SHL	Southall
W51361	W59513	W51403	07/60	SHL	Southall
W51362	W59514	W51404	07/60	RDG	Reading
W51363	W59515	W51405	07/60	RDG	Reading
W51364	W59516	W51406	08/60	SHL	Southall
W51365	W59517	W51407	08/60	SHL	Southall
W51366	W59518	W51408	09/60	SHL	Southall
W51367	W59519	W51409	09/60	RDG	Reading
W51368	W59520	W51410	09/60	RDG	Reading
W51369	W59521	W51411	09/60	RDG	Reading
W51370	W59522	W51412	09/60	RDG	Reading
W51371	*W59478*	W51413	10/60	SHL	Southall
W51372	*W59479*	W51414	10/60	RDG	Reading
W51373	*W59480*	W51415	10/60	RDG	Reading

Class 118

The Western Region ordered 15 three-car high density units to exactly the same design as Class 117, from Birmingham RC&W. They were originally based in the West Country.

Three units were delivered as two-car units, leaving three spare trailers. It will be seen by looking at the various orders of three-car units for the Western Region, that the region commonly ordered a different number of trailers to the number of power cars. Perhaps the view was taken that the power cars would be out of service more frequently for maintenance, and the remaining trailers would be swapped about. In the event the Western Region was the one region that kept more stable formations than any other. Several GWR hauled coaches were converted to work with DMUs and filled the gap of missing trailers during the 1960s.

As with the Western Region's other non-gangwayed units, these were fitted with new gangways and new diagram numbers were issued.

Class 118 Birmingham RC&W

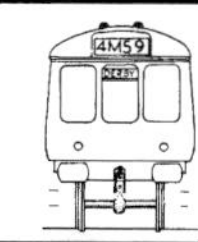

Three-car high density units
DMBS-TCL-DMS

DMBS	TCL	DMS	Date	Depot	
W51302	W59469	W51317	04/60	LA	Laira
W51303	W59470	W51318	04/60	LA	Laira
W51304	W59471	W51319	04/60	LA	Laira
W51305	W59472	W51320	04/60	LA	Laira
W51306	W59473	W51321	05/60	LA	Laira
W51307	W59474	W51322	05/60	LA	Laira
W51308	W59475	W51323	05/60	LA	Laira
W51309	W59476	W51324	05/60	LA	Laira
W51310	W59477	W51325	06/60	LA	Laira
W51311		W51326	06/60	LA	Laira
W51312		W51327	06/60	LA	Laira
W51313		W51328	07/60	LA	Laira
W51314	W59481	W51329	07/60	LA	Laira
W51315	W59482	W51330	07/60	LA	Laira
W51316	W59483	W51331	07/60	LA	Laira
	W59478		06/60	LA	Laira
	W59479		06/60	LA	Laira
	W59480		07/60	LA	Laira

Class 119

The GWR had experience of using diesel railcars on cross-country services, so it was not surprising when it ordered a batch of three-car units for these long distance services.

These units were constructed by the Gloucester Railway Carriage and Wagon Company, and they were fitted with small buffets in the trailer car and large guard's compartments. They were fitted with comfortable seating which was designed to be as good as, if not better than, the locomotive hauled stock they were replacing. They were built to the same design as Class 120 except for being fitted with a standard "Derby" cab.

Some of them ran with Hawksworth composites adapted to run as DMU trailers.

In 1982 some units were used on the Reading-Gatwick Airport service. The disused buffet was converted to luggage space, and together with the large guard's van this made them ideal for this airport connection service.

Class 119 Gloucester RC&W

Cross-country
Three-car units
DMBC-TSLRB-DMSL

DMBC	TSLRB	DMSL	Date	Depot	
W51052		W51080	10/58	BL	Bristol
W51053		W51081	10/58	BL	Bristol
W51054	W59413	W51082	10/58	CDF	Cardiff Canton
W51055	W59414	W51083	10/58	CDF	Cardiff Canton

W51056	**W59415**	**W51084**	11/58	CDF	Cardiff Canton
W51057	**W59416**	**W51085**	11/58	CDF	Cardiff Canton
W51058	**W59417**	**W51086**	12/58	CDF	Cardiff Canton
W51059	**W59418**	**W51087**	12/58	CDF	Cardiff Canton
W51060	**W59419**	**W51088**	01/59	BL	Bristol
W51061	**W59420**	**W51089**	01/59	BL	Bristol
W51062	**W59421**	**W51090**	02/59	BL	Bristol
W51063	**W59422**	**W51091**	02/59	BL	Bristol
W51064	**W59423**	**W51092**	03/59	BL	Bristol
W51065	**W59424**	**W51093**	03/59	BL	Bristol
W51066	**W59425**	**W51094**	04/59	BL	Bristol
W51067	**W59426**	**W51095**	06/59	BL	Bristol
W51068	**W59427**	**W51096**	06/59	BL	Bristol
W51069	**W59428**	**W51097**	06/59	BL	Bristol
W51070	**W59429**	**W51098**	06/59	BL	Bristol
W51071	**W59430**	**W51099**	07/59	TYS	Tyseley
W51072	**W59431**	**W51100**	07/59	TYS	Tyseley
W51073	**W59432**	**W51101**	08/59	CDF	Cardiff Canton
W51074	**W59433**	**W51102**	09/59	CDF	Cardiff Canton
W51075	**W59434**	**W51103**	10/59	RDG	Reading
W51076	**W59435**	**W51104**	10/59	TYS	Tyseley
W51077		**W51105**	12/59	BL	Bristol
W51078	**W59436**	**W51106**	12/59	CDF	Cardiff Canton
W51079	**W59437**	**W51107**	01/60	BL	Bristol

Class 120

Another large batch of three car Cross-Country units was built by BR at Swindon. Internally very similar to Class 119, they had a distinctive cab front fitted with two windows, somewhat reminiscent of Swindon's Inter-city units (Class 126). A small batch of these was delivered to the Scottish Region for use on the Aberdeen to Inverness line.

The last batch of units to be delivered were fitted with distinctive four-character headcodes and were not fitted with buffets.

Beeching cuts meant the closure of many of the lines these units were built for and units often finished up working on services they were not designed for.

Most of the Western Region sets eventually found their way to the London Midland Region. A trial refurbishment was carried out on a few of these cars. However, this turned out to be too expensive which led to their relatively early demise.

Class 120 BR Swindon

Cross-country
Three-car units
DMSL-TSLRB-DMBC

W50647	**W59255**	**W50696**	12/57	03/58	10/57	CDF	Cardiff Canton
W50648	**W59256**	**W50697**	12/57	03/58	10/57	CDF	Cardiff Canton
W50649	**W59257**	**W50698**	01/58	03/58	10/57	CDF	Cardiff Canton
W50650	**W59258**	**W50699**	01/58	03/58	10/57	CDF	Cardiff Canton
W50651	**W59259**	**W50700**	01/58	03/58	10/57	CDF	Cardiff Canton
W50652	**W59260**	**W50701**	01/58	03/58	10/57	CDF	Cardiff Canton
W50653	**W59261**	**W50702**	01/58	03/58	11/57	CDF	Cardiff Canton
W50654	**W59262**	**W50703**	01/58	03/58	11/57	CDF	Cardiff Canton
W50655	**W59263**	**W50704**	02/58	03/58	11/57	CDF	Cardiff Canton
W50656	**W59264**	**W50705**	02/58	03/58	11/57	CDF	Cardiff Canton
W50657	**W59265**	**W50706**	02/58	03/58	11/57	CDF	Cardiff Canton
W50658	**W59266**	**W50707**	02/58	03/58	11/57	CDF	Cardiff Canton
W50659	**W59267**	**W50708**	02/58	03/58	12/57	CDF	Cardiff Canton
W50660	**W59268**	**W50709**	02/58	03/58	12/57	CDF	Cardiff Canton
W50661	**W59269**	**W50710**	03/58	03/58	12/57	CDF	Cardiff Canton
W50662	**W59270**	**W50711**	03/58	03/58	12/57	CDF	Cardiff Canton
W50663	**W59271**	**W50712**	03/58	03/58	01/58	CDF	Cardiff Canton
W50664	**W59272**	**W50713**	03/58	03/58	01/58	CDF	Cardiff Canton
W50665	**W59273**	**W50714**	04/58	05/58	03/58	CDF	Cardiff Canton
W50666	**W59274**	**W50715**	05/58	05/58	03/58	CDF	Cardiff Canton
W50667	**W59275**	**W50716**	05/58	05/58	03/58	CDF	Cardiff Canton
W50668	**W59276**	**W50717**	05/58	05/58	04/58	CDF	Cardiff Canton
W50669	**W59277**	**W50718**	05/58	05/58	04/58	CDF	Cardiff Canton
W50670	**W59278**	**W50719**	05/58	05/58	04/58	CDF	Cardiff Canton
W50671	**W59279**	**W50720**	05/58	05/58	06/58	CDF	Cardiff Canton
W50672	**W59280**	**W50721**	05/58	05/58	06/58	CDF	Cardiff Canton
W50673	**W59281**	**W50722**	05/58	07/58	07/58	CDF	Cardiff Canton
W50674	**W59282**	**W50723**	05/58	07/58	07/58	CDF	Cardiff Canton
W50675	**W59283**	**W50724**	05/58	08/58	08/58	CDF	Cardiff Canton
W50676	**W59284**	**W50725**	06/58	08/58	08/58	CDF	Cardiff Canton
W50677	**W59285**	**W50726**	09/58	09/58	08/58	CDF	Cardiff Canton
W50678	**W59286**	**W50727**	09/58	09/58	08/58	CDF	Cardiff Canton
W50679	**W59287**	**W50728**	09/58	09/58	08/58	CDF	Cardiff Canton
W50680	**W59288**	**W50729**	09/58	09/58	08/58	CDF	Cardiff Canton
W50681	**W59289**	**W50730**	09/58	09/58	08/58	CDF	Cardiff Canton
W50682	**W59290**	**W50731**	09/58	10/58	08/58	CDF	Cardiff Canton
W50683	**W59291**	**W50732**	10/58	10/58	11/58	CDF	Cardiff Canton
W50684	**W59292**	**W50733**	10/58	10/58	11/58	CDF	Cardiff Canton
W50685	**W59293**	**W50734**	10/58	10/58	11/58	CDF	Cardiff Canton
W50686	**W59294**	**W50735**	10/58	10/58	11/58	CDF	Cardiff Canton
W50687	**W59295**	**W50736**	10/58	01/59	11/58	BL	Bristol
W50688	**W59296**	**W50737**	10/58	01/59	12/58	BL	Bristol
W50689	**W59297**	**W50738**	01/59	01/59	12/58	BL	Bristol
W50690	**W59298**	**W50739**	01/59	02/59	12/58	BL	Bristol
W50691	**W59299**	**W50740**	01/59	02/59	12/58	BL	Bristol
W50692	**W59300**	**W50741**	02/59	03/59	12/58	BL	Bristol
W50693	**W59301**	**W50742**	02/59	03/59	12/58	BL	Bristol
W50694		**W50743**	03/59		12/58	BL	Bristol
W50695		**W50744**	03/59		12/58	BL	Bristol

Class 120 BR Swindon

Cross-country
Three-car units
DMBC-TSL-DMSL

W51573	**W59579**	**W51582**	01/61	12/60	04/61	TYS	Tyseley
W51574	**W59580**	**W51583**	01/61	12/60	04/61	TYS	Tyseley
W51575	**W59581**	**W51584**	01/61	12/60	04/61	TYS	Tyseley
W51576	**W59582**	**W51585**	02/61	01/61	04/61	TYS	Tyseley
W51577	**W59583**	**W51586**	02/61	01/61	04/61	TYS	Tyseley
W51578	**W59584**	**W51587**	02/61	03/61	04/61	TYS	Tyseley
W51579	**W59585**	**W51588**	02/61	03/61	05/61	TYS	Tyseley
W51580	**W59586**	**W51589**	02/61	03/61	05/61	TYS	Tyseley
W51581	**W59587**	**W51590**	02/61	03/61	05/61	TYS	Tyseley
	W59588			03/61		TYS	Tyseley

Class 120 BR Swindon

Cross-country
Three-car units
DMBC-TSLRB-DMSL

SC51781	**SC59679**	**SC51788**	11/59	12/59	01/60	61A	Kittybrewster
SC51782	**SC59680**	**SC51789**	11/59	12/59	01/60	61A	Kittybrewster
SC51783	**SC59681**	**SC51790**	11/59	12/59	01/60	61A	Kittybrewster
SC51784	**SC59682**	**SC51791**	12/59	12/59	01/60	61A	Kittybrewster
SC51785	**SC59683**	**SC51792**	12/59	01/60	02/60	61A	Kittybrewster
SC51786	**SC59684**	**SC51793**	12/59	01/60	02/60	61A	Kittybrewster
SC51787	**SC59685**	**SC51794**	12/59	01/60	02/60	61A	Kittybrewster

Class 121

Class 121 was a single-unit version of Pressed Steel's Class 117. The GWR had made much use of single unit railcars, and the Western Region followed in its footsteps. Fifteen of these single cars were built together with ten driving trailers which could run with them. This gave great flexibility in running short branch line trains or extending main line trains.

It was this flexibility which made the power cars extremely useful. They became known as "bubble-cars" and most of them were transferred to departmental services, serving in a variety of roles. In 2010 two of the class were the last of the first generation units still in passenger work on the National Railway. Others still serve in departmental service for Network Rail.

Class 121 Pressed Steel

Single unit railcars
DMBS

W55020	09/60	SHL	Southall

W55021	11/60	SHL	Southall
W55022	11/60	SHL	Southall
W55023	11/60	SHL	Southall
W55024	11/60	SHL	Southall
W55025	11/60	SHL	Southall
W55026	11/60	RDG	Reading
W55027	11/60	SHL	Southall
W55028	12/60	SHL	Southall
W55029	12/60	SHL	Southall
W55030	12/60	RDG	Reading
W55031	12/60	RDG	Reading
W55032	12/60	BL	Bristol
W55033	12/60	BL	Bristol
W55034	01/61	BL	Bristol
W55035	02/61	RDG	Reading

Class 121 Pressed Steel

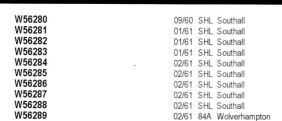

Single unit trailers
DTS-

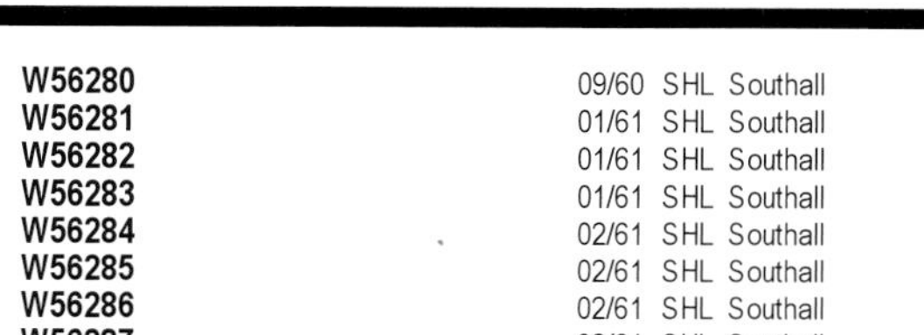

W56280	09/60	SHL	Southall
W56281	01/61	SHL	Southall
W56282	01/61	SHL	Southall
W56283	01/61	SHL	Southall
W56284	02/61	SHL	Southall
W56285	02/61	SHL	Southall
W56286	02/61	SHL	Southall
W56287	02/61	SHL	Southall
W56288	02/61	SHL	Southall
W56289	02/61	84A	Wolverhampton

Class 122

Further single-unit railcars for the Western Region were built by Gloucester RC&W. They were specifically ordered to replace the original GWR railcars. Twenty single cars were built together with nine driving trailers. Although built for the Western, many moved to the London Midland Region and some to Scotland. Three units based in Scotland were rebuilt as parcels units by the removal of their seats and these were reclassified as Class 131.

Again many of these were used in departmental service (some from as early as 1969) and several survive in preservation.

Class 122 Gloucester RC&W

Single unit railcars
DMBS

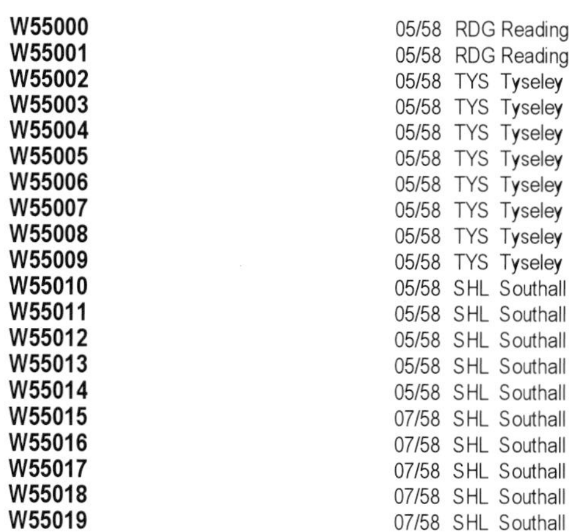

W55000	05/58	RDG	Reading
W55001	05/58	RDG	Reading
W55002	05/58	TYS	Tyseley
W55003	05/58	TYS	Tyseley
W55004	05/58	TYS	Tyseley
W55005	05/58	TYS	Tyseley
W55006	05/58	TYS	Tyseley
W55007	05/58	TYS	Tyseley
W55008	05/58	TYS	Tyseley
W55009	05/58	TYS	Tyseley
W55010	05/58	SHL	Southall
W55011	05/58	SHL	Southall
W55012	05/58	SHL	Southall
W55013	05/58	SHL	Southall
W55014	05/58	SHL	Southall
W55015	07/58	SHL	Southall
W55016	07/58	SHL	Southall
W55017	07/58	SHL	Southall
W55018	07/58	SHL	Southall
W55019	07/58	SHL	Southall

Class 122 Gloucester RC&W

Single unit trailers
DTS-

W56291	06/58	SHL	Southall
W56292	06/58	SHL	Southall
W56293	06/58	SHL	Southall
W56294	06/58	SHL	Southall
W56295	07/58	TYS	Tyseley
W56296	07/58	TYS	Tyseley
W56297	07/58	SHL	Southall
W56298	07/58	SHL	Southall
W56299	07/58	TYS	Tyseley

Class 123

The last new design of first generation DMUs was these Class 123 Inter-city DMUs for the Western Region. They had distinctive gangwayed front ends with wrap-around windscreens. They were based on the Mark I coach design, and were fitted with 230hp Leyland Albion engines. They rode on B4 and B5 type bogies giving an excellent ride and they were particularly well insulated against noise and draughts.

Ten four-car units were built, five of which were fitted with a buffet car. The buffets were removed from service in 1970 leaving a mix of three and four car units. One of the redundant buffets, W59831, was rebuilt as EMU car number E69108 to replace damaged E69105 in AM9 (Class 309) unit number 616.

The units were at first based at Cardiff working Swansea-Birmingham-Derby services with a few turns to Plymouth. In 1965 they transferred to Cardiff-Bristol-Portsmouth services, but after a short while they moved to Reading for use on Paddington-Oxford services

In 1977/8 the whole class moved North to Hull, where they joined with the Class 124 DMUs working the Trans-Pennine services.

None of these units were preserved.

Class 123 BR Swindon

Inter-City units
Four-car units
DMBSL-TCK-TSL-DMSK

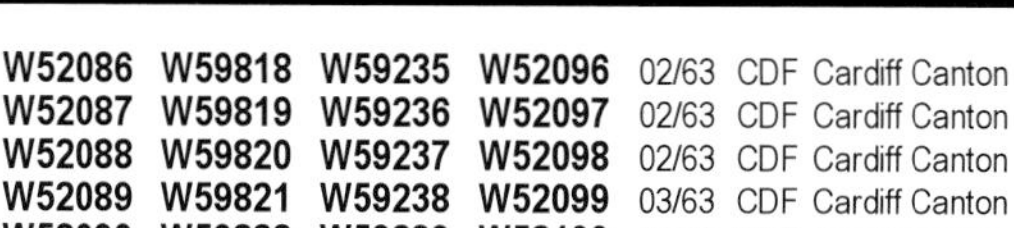

W52086	W59818	W59235	W52096	02/63	CDF	Cardiff Canton
W52087	W59819	W59236	W52097	02/63	CDF	Cardiff Canton
W52088	W59820	W59237	W52098	02/63	CDF	Cardiff Canton
W52089	W59821	W59238	W52099	03/63	CDF	Cardiff Canton
W52090	W59822	W59239	W52100	04/63	CDF	Cardiff Canton

Class 123 BR Swindon

Inter-City units
Four-car units
DMBSL-TCK-TSLRB-DMSK

W52091	W59823	W59828	W52101	05/63	CDF	Cardiff Canton
W52092	W59824	W59829	W52102	05/63	CDF	Cardiff Canton
W52093	W59825	W59830	W52103	06/63	CDF	Cardiff Canton
W52094	W59826	W59831	W52104	06/63	CDF	Cardiff Canton
W52095	W59827	W59832	W52105	06/63	CDF	Cardiff Canton

Class 124

These Inter-city DMUs were specially designed to work the steeply graded Trans-Pennine route. They were fitted with 230hp Leyland Albion engines, two to each power car. They were equipped with four power cars in each six-car set; they were the only DMU class that included non-driving motor cars. They were fitted with distinctive modern-looking non-gangwayed ends with wrap-around windscreens, which turned out to be a maintenance headache.

Enough vehicles for eight and a half six-car units were built but they were never kept in fixed formations.

Over the years they were gradually reduced in size from 6-car units down to 3-car units. When they were running as 4-car units, a number of the non-driving motor cars were rebuilt as trailers and re-numbered.

Unfortunately none of these distinctive units were preserved.

Class 124 BR Swindon
Trans-Pennine
Six-car units
DMC-MBSK-TSL-TFLRB-MBSK-DMC

Not permanent formations

E51951	E51968	E59765	E59774	E51969	E51952	07/60	55H	Neville Hill
E51953	E51970	E59766	E59775	E51971	E51954	08/60	55H	Neville Hill
E51955	E51972	E59767	E59776	E51973	E51956	08/60	55H	Neville Hill
E51957	E51974	E59768	E59777	E51975	E51958	09/60	55H	Neville Hill
E51959	E51976	E59769	E59778	E51977	E51960	09/60	55H	Neville Hill
E51961	E51978	E59770	E59779	E51979	E51962	10/60	55H	Neville Hill
E51963	E51980	E59771	E59780	E51981	E51964	11/60	55H	Neville Hill
E51965	E51982	E59772	E59781	E51983	E51966	12/60	55H	Neville Hill
E51967	E51984	E59773				01/61	55H	Neville Hill

Class 125

This class of twenty three-car high-density suburban units was built by BR at Derby Works for working the Lea Valley line in North East London. They were externally similar to Class 116, but were fitted with hydraulic transmission and 238hp Rolls-Royce Engines. The extra power was needed for the climb out of Liverpool Street to Bethnal Green, particularly when heavily loaded in the evening rush-hour.

They suffered with overheating to their hydraulic transmission and were unreliable in traffic.

After electrification of the Lea Valley route they found work on the suburban services out of Kings Cross, another route with steep climbs at the terminus.

They did not survive long, partly due to their unreliability and partly due to their non-standard "Orange Star" coupling code, and they were all withdrawn by 1977 after electrification of the lines they worked.

None were preserved.

Class 125 BR Derby
Three-car high density units
DMS-TS-DMBS

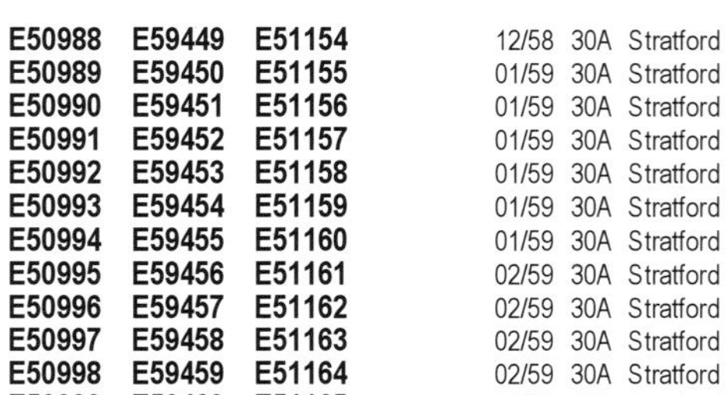

E50988	E59449	E51154	12/58	30A	Stratford
E50989	E59450	E51155	01/59	30A	Stratford
E50990	E59451	E51156	01/59	30A	Stratford
E50991	E59452	E51157	01/59	30A	Stratford
E50992	E59453	E51158	01/59	30A	Stratford
E50993	E59454	E51159	01/59	30A	Stratford
E50994	E59455	E51160	01/59	30A	Stratford
E50995	E59456	E51161	02/59	30A	Stratford
E50996	E59457	E51162	02/59	30A	Stratford
E50997	E59458	E51163	02/59	30A	Stratford
E50998	E59459	E51164	02/59	30A	Stratford
E50999	E59460	E51165	02/59	30A	Stratford
E51000	E59461	E51166	03/59	30A	Stratford
E51001	E59462	E51167	05/59	30A	Stratford
E51002	E59463	E51168	05/59	30A	Stratford
E51003	E59464	E51169	05/59	30A	Stratford
E51004	E59465	E51170	04/59	30A	Stratford
E51005	E59466	E51171	04/59	30A	Stratford
E51006	E59467	E51172	05/59	30A	Stratford
E51007	E59468	E51173	09/59	30A	Stratford

Class 126

These Swindon built Inter-city units were developed from the similar unclassified Swindon units (numbered in the 79xxx series). They were designed to be able to run as three- or six-car units, and they were unique in having two different designs of driving motor cars, one with and one without an end gangway, allowing two three-car units to couple together with a gangway connection throughout the whole set. They were built with the "white star" coupling code to enable them to work with the earlier units.

These units were built to work on services from Glasgow to Ayrshire. Enough vehicles were built to form twenty-one three car units, together with some spares, and a few odd vehicles designed to run with the earlier Inter-city units.

SC51011 was badly damaged and burnt in a collision at Kinning Park on 30th August 1973. It was replace by re-instated Inter-city car SC79168 (SC79165 was also re-instated as a possible replacement, but SC79168 was found to be more suitable).

Class 126 BR Swindon
Inter-City units
Three- and six-car units
DMSL-TFK-DMBSL
DMSL-TCL-DMBSL

Variable Formations

SC50936					11/59	67C	Ayr
SC51008	SC59391	SC51030	04/59	04/59	05/59	67C	Ayr
SC51009	SC59392	SC51031	04/59	04/59	05/59	67C	Ayr
SC51010	SC59393	SC51032	04/59	04/59	05/59	67C	Ayr
SC51011	SC59394	SC51033	04/59	04/59	05/59	67C	Ayr
SC51012	SC59395	SC51034	04/59	06/59	05/59	67C	Ayr
SC51013	SC59396	SC51035	04/59	06/59	05/59	67C	Ayr
SC51014	SC59397	SC51036	08/59	07/59	06/59	67C	Ayr
SC51015	SC59398	SC51037	08/59	07/59	06/59	67C	Ayr
SC51016	SC59399	SC51038	08/59	09/59	06/59	67C	Ayr
SC51017	SC59400	SC51039	08/59	09/59	06/59	67C	Ayr
SC51018	SC59402	SC51040	08/59	04/59	06/59	67C	Ayr
SC51019	SC59403	SC51041	08/59	04/59	06/59	67C	Ayr
SC51020	SC59404	SC51042	08/59	05/59	06/59	67C	Ayr
SC51021	SC59405	SC51043	08/59	05/59	06/59	67C	Ayr
SC51022	SC59406	SC51044	10/59	07/59	09/59	67C	Ayr
SC51023	SC59407	SC51045	10/59	07/59	09/59	67C	Ayr
SC51024	SC59408	SC51046	10/59	08/59	09/59	67C	Ayr
SC51025	SC59409	SC51047	10/59	08/59	09/59	67C	Ayr
SC51026	SC59410	SC51048	10/59	10/59	09/59	67C	Ayr
SC51027	SC59411	SC51049	11/59	10/59	09/59	67C	Ayr
SC51028	SC59412	SC51050	11/59	10/59	09/59	67C	Ayr
SC51029		SC51051	11/59		09/59	67C	Ayr
		SC59098			01/61	64H	Leith Central
		SC59099			01/61	64H	Leith Central

Class 127

Thirty four-car high density suburban units were built by BR at Derby for working the services from St Pancras to Luton and Bedford (the "Bed-pan" line). They were fitted with Rolls-Royce engines and hydraulic transmission. They were designed as a "stop-gap" solution to enable the withdrawal of non-corridor steam hauled services, before the eventual electrification of the line.

This was one of the most intensively worked DMU services in the country. The line was electrified, and should have been complete by 1982, but delays saw these units continue to work with increasing unreliability until the last units were withdrawn in 1984.

Designed to be able to work with standard "Blue Square" DMUs, it was found that a different driving technique was required, especially when changing gear. Early on problems occurred when diesel-mechanical and diesel-hydraulic units worked together and one unit (hydraulic) changed up while the other (mechanical) remained in a lower gear. Not good for the gearbox. For this reason the coupling code changed to Red Triangle in January 1969 to make sure these units were kept apart from others.

In 1985 twenty-two redundant power cars were rebuilt as parcels units, complete with roller shutter doors. They worked from Chester until 1989.

Some trailer cars were refurbished and worked in the West Midlands until 1993.

A number of these units have been preserved.

Class 127 BR Derby
St Pancras units
Four-car high density units
DMBS-TSL-TS-DMBS

Many of these units were stored when new before being delivered to 14A Cricklewood.

M51591	M59589	M59619	M51592	05/59	14A	Cricklewood
M51593	M59590	M59620	M51594	06/59	14A	Cricklewood
M51595	M59591	M59621	M51596	06/59	(s)	Chaddesden
M51597	M59592	M59622	M51598	06/59	(s)	Chaddesden
M51599	M59593	M59623	M51600	06/59	(s)	Chaddesden
M51601	M59594	M59624	M51602	07/59	(s)	Chaddesden
M51603	M59595	M59625	M51604	07/59	(s)	Chaddesden
M51605	M59596	M59626	M51606	08/59	(s)	Chaddesden
M51607	M59597	M59627	M51608	08/59	(s)	Chaddesden
M51609	M59598	M59628	M51610	08/59	(s)	Chaddesden
M51611	M59599	M59629	M51612	08/59	(s)	Chaddesden
M51613	M59600	M59630	M51614	08/59	(s)	Chaddesden
M51615	M59601	M59631	M51616	08/59	(s)	Chaddesden
M51617	M59602	M59632	M51618	09/59	(s)	Chaddesden
M51619	M59603	M59633	M51620	09/59	(s)	Chaddesden
M51621	M59604	M59634	M51622	09/59	(s)	Chaddesden
M51623	M59605	M59635	M51624	09/59	(s)	Chaddesden
M51625	M59606	M59636	M51626	09/59	14A	Cricklewood
M51627	M59607	M59637	M51628	09/59	14A	Cricklewood
M51629	M59608	M59638	M51630	10/59	14A	Cricklewood
M51631	M59609	M59639	M51632	10/59	(s)	Chaddesden
M51633	M59610	M59640	M51634	10/59	(s)	Chaddesden
M51635	M59611	M59641	M51636	10/59	(s)	Derby Friargate
M51637	M59612	M59642	M51638	11/59	(s)	Derby Friargate
M51639	M59613	M59643	M51640	11/59	(s)	Derby Friargate
M51641	M59614	M59644	M51642	11/59	(s)	Derby Friargate
M51643	M59615	M59645	M51644	11/59	(s)	Derby Friargate
M51645	M59616	M59646	M51646	12/59	(s)	Chaddesden
M51647	M59617	M59647	M51648	11/59	(s)	Derby Friargate
M51649	M59618	M59648	M51650	12/59	14A	Cricklewood

Class 128

Ten single-unit parcels cars were built without any passenger seating. Six of them were gangway fitted to allow them to work together, the other four were built without gangway connections. They were purpose-built with three sets of double doors in the body side to provide good access.

Class 128 Gloucester RC&W
Single Unit Parcels Van (Non-gangwayed)
DMPMV

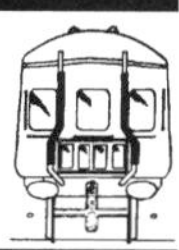

These were ordered for working on the St Pancras suburban services.

M55987	01/60	14A	Cricklewood
M55988	01/60	14A	Cricklewood
M55989	01/60	14A	Cricklewood
M55990	01/60	14A	Cricklewood

Class 128 Gloucester RC&W
Single Unit Parcels Van (Gangwayed)
DMPMV

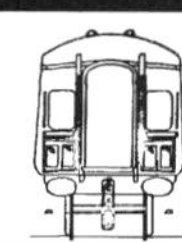

W55991	01/60	SHL	Southall
W55992	02/60	SHL	Southall
W55993	02/60	84D	Leamington Spa
W55994	03/60	TYS	Tyseley
W55995	03/60	TYS	Tyseley
W55996	04/60	TYS	Tyseley

Class 129

Three more parcels cars were built by Cravens. They were originally designed to boost the parcels capacity in Cumberland, working with the Derby lightweight units, hence the Yellow Diamond coupling code. However, by the time they entered service they were no longer needed in Cumberland and spent their lives based on other parts of the London Midland Region, mainly in the Manchester area.

One unit survived in departmental service as a hydraulic transmission testing vehicle, being named "Hydra".

Class 129 Cravens
Single Unit Parcels Van
DMPMV

M55997	07/58	5B	Crewe South
M55998	07/58	5B	Crewe South
M55999	08/58	5B	Crewe South

Class 130

The classification 130 was used for Class 116 units which were converted for parcels use, including removal of all passenger seats. The units were:

W50819	W50872		09/66
W50862	W50915		09/66
W51137	W59447	W51150	12/65

Two GUV parcels vans W86174 and W86572 were rewired to work with these units, to create three car sets when necessary.

Class 131

Three Scottish Region Class 122 single units (SC55013-SC55015) were converted to parcels units by the removal of their seats. They were reclassified 131.

SC55013	09/71
SC55014	09/71
SC55015	09/71

Early Derby Lightweight

The first batch of DMUs built for BR comprised these eight early Derby lightweights. They were built in 1954 for services in the West Riding of Yorkshire.

Derby Works was given the job of design and construction. They made extensive use of light alloys to provide a good power-weight ratio.

The LMS three-car diesel unit of 1938 was used as the prototype for the engines and transmission. They were fitted with Leyland 125hp engines and hydro-mechanical transmissions. These torque convertors were already outdated and these units almost immediately became non-standard as all later units used the proven GWR layout of engines and transmission.

The units were basically used as guinea pigs, testing out ideas for future DMUs, and their upkeep and maintenance was poor. They suffered from problems with their riveted bodies due to engine vibration.

As a result of these problems and their non-standard status they were all withdrawn from service in 1964.

BR Derby

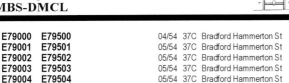

Two-car power twin units
DMBS-DMCL

E79000	E79500	04/54	37C	Bradford Hammerton St
E79001	E79501	05/54	37C	Bradford Hammerton St
E79002	E79502	05/54	37C	Bradford Hammerton St
E79003	E79503	05/54	37C	Bradford Hammerton St
E79004	E79504	05/54	37C	Bradford Hammerton St
E79005	E79505	05/54	37C	Bradford Hammerton St
E79006	E79506	08/54	37C	Bradford Hammerton St
E79007	E79507	09/54	37C	Bradford Hammerton St

Derby Lightweight

Following on from the early Derby Lightweights another batch was built later in 1954. They were fitted with BUT 150hp engines and Wilson four-speed epicyclic gearboxes, exactly the same combination that had been fitted to the earlier GWR railcars.

They were more successful than the earlier Derby lightweights and were built in a variety of one-, two-, and four-car formations for working branch-line and suburban services on the Midland, Eastern and North-Eastern regions. They had the early standard Yellow Diamond coupling code.

They were not considered to need as much power as the early units built for the West Riding so they were built with trailer cars rather than all power cars of the earlier units.

The first batch of 13 units were built for the Maryport and Carlisle route, and later batches went to Tyneside (five units built as four-car units), East Anglia, Lincolnshire and Birmingham. The two single-unit cars were built for use on the Banbury (Merton Street)-Buckingham-Bletchley service.

In 1960 M79649 was rebuilt as an inspection saloon, later becoming DB999510. M79135 was fitted with an experimental Self-Changing Gears automatic four-speed gearbox. M79900 had a new lease of life as RDB975010 "Test Car Iris".

When the Beeching cuts led to a surplus of DMUs these units were chosen for withdrawal from service, due to their non-standard coupling codes.

Some units survived in departmental service and some of these were later preserved.

BR Derby

Two-car units
DMBS-DTCL

M79008	M79600	11/54	12A	Carlisle Upperby
M79009	M79601	01/55	12A	Carlisle Upperby
M79010	M79602	01/55	12A	Carlisle Upperby
M79011	M79603	01/55	12A	Carlisle Upperby
M79012	M79604	01/55	12A	Carlisle Upperby
M79013	M79605	01/55	12A	Carlisle Upperby
M79014	M79606	01/55	12A	Carlisle Upperby
M79015	M79607	12/54	12A	Carlisle Upperby
M79016	M79608	12/54	12A	Carlisle Upperby
M79017	M79609	12/54	12A	Carlisle Upperby
M79018	M79610	01/55	12A	Carlisle Upperby
M79019	M79611	01/55	12A	Carlisle Upperby
M79020	M79612	01/55	12A	Carlisle Upperby

BR Derby

Two-car units
DMBS-DTCL

E79021	E79613	01/55	40A	Lincoln
E79022	E79614	01/55	40A	Lincoln
E79023	E79615	01/55	40A	Lincoln
E79024	E79616	01/55	40A	Lincoln
E79025	E79617	01/55	40A	Lincoln
E79026	E79618	01/55	40A	Lincoln
E79027	E79619	01/55	40A	Lincoln
E79028	E79620	01/55	40A	Lincoln
E79029	E79621	05/55	40A	Lincoln
E79030	E79622	05/55	40A	Lincoln
E79031	E79623	05/55	40A	Lincoln
E79032	E79624	05/55	40A	Lincoln
E79033	E79625	06/55	40A	Lincoln

BR Derby

Two-car units
DMBS-DTCL

E79034	E79250	06/55	32A	Norwich Thorpe
E79035	E79251	06/55	32A	Norwich Thorpe
E79036	E79252	06/55	32A	Norwich Thorpe
E79037	E79253	06/55	32A	Norwich Thorpe
E79038	E79254	06/55	32A	Norwich Thorpe
E79039	E79255	06/55	32A	Norwich Thorpe
E79040	E79256	06/55	32A	Norwich Thorpe
E79041	E79257	06/55	32A	Norwich Thorpe
E79042	E79258	06/55	32A	Norwich Thorpe
E79043	E79259	06/55	32A	Norwich Thorpe
E79044	E79260	08/55	32A	Norwich Thorpe
E79045	E79261	08/55	32A	Norwich Thorpe
E79046	E79262	08/55	32A	Norwich Thorpe

BR Derby

Two-car units
DMBS-DTCL

M79118	M79639	11/55	12A	Carlisle Upperby (o/l)

M79119 M79640	12/55	12A	Carlisle Upperby (o/l)
M79120 M79641	12/55	12A	Carlisle Upperby (o/l)
M79121 M79642	12/55	3E	Monument Lane
M79122 M79643	12/55	3E	Monument Lane
M79123 M79644	12/55	3E	Monument Lane
M79124 M79645	01/56	3E	Monument Lane
M79125 M79646	01/56	3E	Monument Lane
M79126 M79647	01/56	3E	Monument Lane

BR Derby

Two-car units
DMBS-DTCL

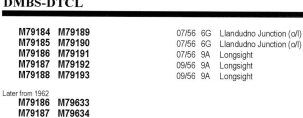

M79127 M79648	02/56	3E	Monument Lane
M79128 M79649	02/56	3E	Monument Lane
M79129 M79650	02/56	3E	Monument Lane
M79130 M79651	03/56	3E	Monument Lane
M79131 M79652	03/56	3E	Monument Lane
M79132 M79653	03/56	3E	Monument Lane
M79133 M79654	03/56	3E	Monument Lane
M79134 M79655	03/56	3E	Monument Lane
M79135 M79656	03/56	6G	Llandudno Junction
M79136 M79657	03/56	6G	Llandudno Junction

BR Derby

Two-car units
DMBS-DTCL

E79137 E79658	03/56		South Gosforth
E79138 E79659	03/56		South Gosforth
E79139 E79660	03/56		South Gosforth
E79140 E79661	03/56		South Gosforth

BR Derby

Two-car units
DMBS-DTCL

M79141 M79662	04/56	3E	Monument Lane
M79142 M79684	07/56	26D	Bury
M79143 M79663	01/56	3E	Monument Lane
M79144 M79664	01/56	3E	Monument Lane
M79145 M79665	02/56	3E	Monument Lane
M79146 M79666	02/56	3E	Monument Lane
M79147 M79667	02/56	3E	Monument Lane
M79148 M79668	02/56	3E	Monument Lane
M79149 M79669	04/56	3E	Monument Lane

BR Derby

Four-car units
DMS-TBSL-TSL-DMC

E79150	E79325	E79400	E79508	09/55	South Gosforth
E79151	E79326	E79401	E79509	09/55	South Gosforth
E79152	E79327	E79402	E79510	09/55	South Gosforth
E79153	E79328	E79403	E79511	09/55	South Gosforth
E79154	E79329	E79404	E79512	09/55	South Gosforth

BR Derby

Two-car units
DMBS-DTCL

M79169 M79670	04/56	3E	Monument Lane
M79170 M79671	05/56	3E	Monument Lane
M79171 M79672	05/56	6G	Llandudno Junction
M79172 M79673	05/56	6G	Llandudno Junction
M79173 M79674	05/56	6G	Llandudno Junction
M79174 M79675	05/56	6G	Llandudno Junction
M79175 M79676	05/56	6G	Llandudno Junction
M79176 M79677	06/56	6G	Llandudno Junction
M79177 M79678	06/56	6G	Llandudno Junction
M79178 M79679	06/56	6G	Llandudno Junction
M79179 M79680	06/56	6G	Llandudno Junction
M79180 M79681	06/56	6G	Llandudno Junction
M79181 M79682	06/56	6G	Llandudno Junction

BR Derby

Two-car power twin units
DMBS-DMCL
DMBS-DTCL

M79184 M79189	07/56	6G	Llandudno Junction (o/l)
M79185 M79190	07/56	6G	Llandudno Junction (o/l)
M79186 M79191	07/56	9A	Longsight
M79187 M79192	09/56	9A	Longsight
M79188 M79193	09/56	9A	Longsight

Later from 1962

M79186 M79633
M79187 M79634
M79188 M79635

BR Derby

DTCL-

M79683	07/56	6G	Llandudno Junction

BR Derby

Single car units
DMBS

M79900	07/56	1E	Bletchley
M79901	08/56	1E	Bletchley

Metropolitan-Cammell

Metropolitan-Cammell was the first private contractor to enter the DMU building field with these 36 twin-car units. Their specification was similar to the Derby lightweights, but they were fitted with the distinctive Metropolitan-Cammell cab that was fitted to all later units. They had the early standard Yellow Diamond coupling code.

Most were originally built for working in East Anglia, but a small batch of seven units was built for the London Midland's Bury-Bacup route.

Their non-standard coupling code led to early withdrawal.

They were distinguishable from the later Metropolitan-Cammell units as they were fitted with cowling below the buffer beam.

Metropolitan-Cammell

Two-car units
DMBS-DTSL

E79047 E79263	01/56	32A	Norwich Thorpe
E79048 E79264	01/56	32A	Norwich Thorpe
E79049 E79265	01/56	32A	Norwich Thorpe
E79050 E79266	01/56	32A	Norwich Thorpe
E79051 E79267	01/56	32A	Norwich Thorpe
E79052 E79268	01/56	32A	Norwich Thorpe
E79053 E79269	02/56	32A	Norwich Thorpe
E79054 E79270	02/56	32A	Norwich Thorpe
E79055 E79271	02/56	32A	Norwich Thorpe
E79056 E79272	02/56	32A	Norwich Thorpe
E79057 E79273	03/56	30A	Stratford

E79058	E79274	03/56	30A	Stratford
E79059	E79275	04/56	40A	Lincoln
E79060	E79276	04/56	40A	Lincoln
E79061	E79277	05/56	40A	Lincoln
E79062	E79278	05/56	40A	Lincoln
E79063	E79279	05/56	40A	Lincoln
E79064	E79280	05/56	40A	Lincoln
E79065	E79281	05/56	32A	Norwich Thorpe
E79066	E79282	05/56	32A	Norwich Thorpe
E79067	E79283	05/56	40A	Lincoln
E79068	E79284	05/56	40A	Lincoln
E79069	E79285	06/56	40A	Lincoln
E79070	E79286	06/56	40A	Lincoln
E79071	E79287	06/56	40A	Lincoln
E79072	E79288	06/56	40A	Lincoln
E79073	E79289	06/56	40A	Lincoln
E79074	E79290	07/56	40A	Lincoln
E79075	E79291	08/56	40A	Lincoln

Metropolitan-Cammell

Two-car units
DMBS-DTCL

M79076	M79626	12/55	26D	Bury
M79077	M79627	12/55	26D	Bury
M79078	M79628	12/55	26D	Bury
M79079	M79629	12/55	26D	Bury
M79080	M79630	12/55	26D	Bury
M79081	M79631	12/55	26D	Bury
M79082	M79632	12/55	26D	Bury

Swindon Inter-City

These Swindon built Inter-city units were designed for Birmingham-Swansea services on the Western Region and the Scottish Region's Glasgow-Edinburgh service. The Western Region units soon joined their sister units in Scotland.

They were the first units to be built on the long (64½ ft) underframes.

The very similar Class 126 was developed from this design. They were designed to be able to run as three- or six-car units, having two different designs of driving motor cars, one with and one without an end gangway, allowing two three-car units to couple together with a gangway connection throughout the whole set.

They were replaced on the Glasgow-Edinburgh Inter-city services by Mk II coaches hauled in push-pull mode by Class 27 diesels in 1972. A few carriages survived, working with the Class 126 units on the Glasgow-Ayr services.

SC79091, SC79093, SC79094, SC79096 and SC79097 were purchased by Lamco in 1972 for use on the Lamco iron-ore railway in Buchanan, Liberia. They were refurbished at Glasgow Works and received full BR blue and grey livery with yellow ends and the slogan "Lamco Inter-city" in normal BR script on the sides.

BR Swindon

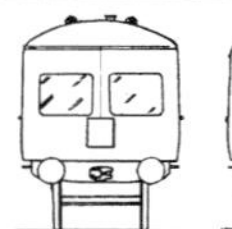
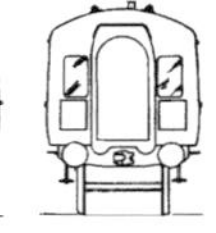

Inter-City units
Three- and six-car units
DMBSL-TFK-DMBSL
DMBSL-TFKRB-DMBSL

Variable Formations

W79083	09/56	64A	Leith Central (o/l)
W79084	09/56	64A	Leith Central (o/l)
W79085	09/56	64A	Leith Central (o/l)
W79086	10/56	64A	Leith Central (o/l)
W79087	10/56	64A	Leith Central (o/l)
W79088	12/56	64A	Leith Central (o/l)
W79089	11/56	64A	Leith Central (o/l)
W79090	11/56	64A	Leith Central (o/l)
W79091	06/57	SDN	Swindon
W79092	06/57	SDN	Swindon
W79093	06/57	SDN	Swindon
W79094	06/57	SDN	Swindon
W79440	06/57	SDN	Swindon
W79441	06/57	SDN	Swindon
W79470	08/56	64A	Leith Central (o/l)
W79471	05/56	64A	Leith Central (o/l)
W79472	05/56	64A	Leith Central (o/l)
W79473	05/56	64A	Leith Central (o/l)

BR Swindon

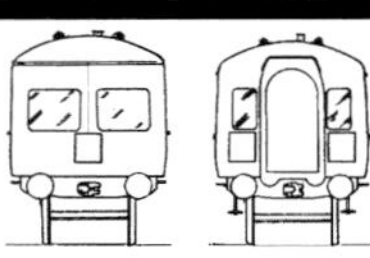

Inter-City units
Three- and six-car units
DMBSL-TFK-DMSL
DMBSL-TFKRB-DMSL

Variable Formations

SC79096	SC79442	SC79095	09/56	02/57	08/56	64A	Leith Central
SC79097	SC79443	SC79155	09/56	03/57	01/57	64A	Leith Central
SC79098	SC79444	SC79156	08/56	03/57	01/57	64A	Leith Central
SC79099	SC79445	SC79157	08/56	04/57	02/57	64A	Leith Central
SC79100	SC79446	SC79158	09/56	04/57	02/57	64A	Leith Central
SC79101	SC79447	SC79159	09/56	04/57	02/57	64A	Leith Central
SC79102	SC79474	SC79160	10/56	08/56	02/57	64A	Leith Central
SC79103	SC79475	SC79161	10/56	09/56	03/57	64A	Leith Central
SC79104	SC79476	SC79162	11/56	09/56	03/57	64A	Leith Central
SC79105	SC79477	SC79163	11/56	09/56	03/57	64A	Leith Central
SC79106	SC79478	SC79164	04/57	10/56	03/57	64A	Leith Central
SC79107	SC79479	SC79165	04/57	10/56	04/57	64A	Leith Central
SC79108	SC79480	SC79166	12/56	11/56	04/57	64A	Leith Central
SC79109	SC79481	SC79167	12/56	11/56	04/57	64A	Leith Central
SC79110	SC79482	SC79168	01/57	12/56	04/57	64A	Leith Central
SC79111			01/57			64A	Leith Central

Four-Wheeled Railbus

British Railways ordered a number of four-wheeled diesel railcars from various manufacturers. These were intended for working on various branch lines where it was felt that their small size and economy of use would allow the branch-lines to work economically and avoid closure. In most cases they simply delayed the closure dates, but several railbuses did perform their planned functions in preservation.

BUT

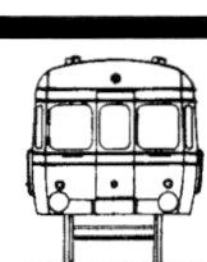

Four-wheeled railbus
One and three-car units
DMS-TS-DMBS

A privately sponsored "ACV demonstration train" was built in 1952. It was a cross between a diesel multiple unit and a railbus. The bodies were manufactured by Park Royal and the units were fitted with BUT's own mass-produced AEC bus engines. They were the first four-wheeled railcars to be introduced in the UK since the end of the 19th Century.

After running trials from Marylebone and on various other lines such as Watford-St. Albans Abbey, Harrow-Belmont and the Allhallows branch in Kent, the three-car unit was purchased in 1954 by the London Midland Region and more were built in 1955 and 1957. They were nicknamed "Flying Bricks" due to their block-like shape.

Not fixed formations

M79740	M79741	M79742	03/54	03/54	03/54		
M79745	M79746	M79743	07/55	08/55	07/55	1C	Watford Junction
	M79747	M79744		08/55	07/55	1C	Watford Junction
M79748	M79749	M79750	08/57	08/57	08/57	1C	Watford Junction

Bristol/Eastern Coach Works

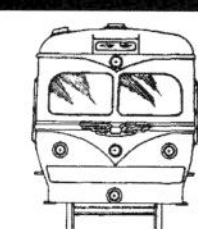

Single-car units
DMBS

Two railbuses were built by Bristol Commercial Vehicles, a subsidiary of the British Aero Engine company, using bodies built by Eastern Coach Works fitted with Gardner engines. They spent their whole lives in Scotland.

SC79958	09/58	60B	Aviemore
SC79959	11/58		Leith Central

Waggon und Maschinenbau

Single-car units
DMBS

Germany was successfully operating a large number of four-wheeled railbuses and BR ordered five to a standard design from the Waggon und Maschinenbau Company of Donauworth. They were built for work on East-Anglian branch lines, but the closure of these branches led them to other pastures. Four of the five survive in preservation.

E79960	04/58	30A	Stratford
E79961	04/58	30A	Stratford
E79962	04/58	31A	Cambridge
E79963	04/58	31A	Cambridge
E79964	04/58	31A	Cambridge

Wickham

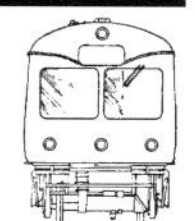

Single-car units
DMBS

D. Wickham Ltd of Hertfordshire built the lightest of the four-wheel railbuses. They used a unique tubular body construction flexibly mounted on a tubular underframe. No buffers were fitted, simply metal bands used as dumb buffers. They spent their short lives based in Scotland.

SC79965	09/58		Leith Central
SC79966	01/59		Leith Central
SC79967	01/59		Leith Central
SC79968	05/59		Leith Central
SC79969	07/59		Leith Central

Park Royal

Single-car units
DMBS

Park Royal built these five units for the London Midland Region. They were constructed with a long overhang at each end of the body and no buffers were fitted, simply metal bands used as dumb buffers.

All five soon were transferred to Scotland working around Alloa, Arrochar and Ayr.

SC79970	02/59		Leith Central
M79971	07/58	15D	Bedford
M79972	07/58	15D	Bedford
M79973	07/58	15D	Bedford
SC79974	11/58		Leith Central

AC Cars

Single-car units
DMBS

These five vehicles were built by Associated Commercial Cars of Thames Ditton in Surrey. W79979 was tested on the Western Region in February 1958 before being taken into stock on the Scottish Region. The Western Region railbuses worked the Kemble to Cirencester and Tetbury branches and later operated from Bodmin and Yeovil. They all later joined SC79979 in Scotland.

Three were preserved, but only two now survive.

W79975	08/58	SDN	Swindon
W79976	09/58	SDN	Swindon
W79977	10/58	SDN	Swindon
W79978	12/58	SDN	Swindon
SC79979	08/58	63A	Perth (South)

Battery electric unit

An experimental two-car battery powered unit was built in 1958, and it was put into service on the Aberdeen-Ballater line in Scotland. Although not a DMU, it was built using standard Derby Lightweight DMU bodies and is therefore included in this book. It was fitted out with Siemens electrical equipment and batteries at Cowlairs.

It was taken into departmental service in October 1967 and has since been preserved.

BR Derby

Battery electric unit Based on Derby Lightweight body
Two-car unit
BDMBS-BDTCL

SC79998 SC79999	03/58	61A	Kittybrewster

In early green livery a Birmingham RCW Class 104 three-car unit led by M50421 is seen at Stockport on a Buxton service. Note the white painted cab roof, a feature which reappeared on some of these units later in their lives. *P J Sharpe*

This photograph shows the view that made the first generation DMUs so popular. Whenever we travelled by DMU we always headed to the front of the train for the best view in the house. Because we could only afford second class tickets it was a shame when the first-class compartment was at the front as in this view of the first-class saloon of a Class 104 unit. This is an official BR photograph taken on 10th July 1957 to illustrate the new three-car trains for Crewe-Stoke-Derby service. *BR*

The end of the line at Buxton. Two Class 104 driving motors (with M53504 nearest the camera) await their return services to Manchester on 31st March 1984. *J C Hillmer*

This evening view taken on 11th November 1980 shows M50531 leading a three-car Class 104 unit at Southport waiting to form the 20.26 service to Manchester Victoria. Many of the North Manchester based Birmingham RCW units carried this distinctive white stripe as part of their livery at this time. It was used to identify units with modified suspension for working the Manchester-Blackpool service. *S J Edge*

The prototype Class 104 "Half motor" conversion M78851 and M78601 wait at Manchester Piccadilly to form the 13.50 service to Rose Hill (Marple) on 4th August 1984. The unit number reads "EXP. DM. 352." presumably standing for Experimental Diesel Multiple-unit set 352. *A Dasi-Sutton*

Top: An early photograph of Cravens Class 105 DMCL M50811 in green livery. *P J Sharpe*

Above: Class 105 DTCL E56430 is seen at Cambridge on 25th July 1976. Do you remember that long hot summer? That was the month I first met my wife, Doris. *D L Percival*

Left: Class 105 DMBS E50373 leads a two-car unit working the Leeds-Harrogate service as it leaves the tunnel at Weeton on 12th June 1976. *G W Morrison*

A two-car Class 105 Cravens DMU comes off the Melton Mowbray line at Syston South Junction while working the 08.52 Cambridge-Birmingham train on 9th June 1984.
W A Sharman

This two-car Cravens unit has been converted to work as a parcels unit. E53364 and E53373 are being serviced in the old DMU shed at Stratford on 3rd February 1987.
B Morrison

On 8th September 1981, Derby Class 107 three-car unit number 107444 with SC52005 leading arrives at Largs on the 12.15 service from Glasgow Central.
L Bertram

On the 28th August 1982 the Branch Line Society ran a rail tour covering freight-only lines in Central Scotland. 107425 is seen here passing Grangemouth MPD. Passenger services were withdrawn on the line from Falkirk to Grangemouth in 1968. *M McDonald*

Right: Class 107 unit 107446 with SC52033 leading is seen here carrying the attractive Strathclyde orange livery. This photograph was taken on 24th May 1985 in the sylvan surroundings of Princess Street Gardens in Edinburgh while working the 10.31 Kirkcaldy-Edinburgh service. *W A Sharman*

Below: It is Good Friday 31st March 1961 and a green liveried Derby Works Class 108 power twin led by M52043 is waiting to leave Liverpool Lime Street with the 3.50pm service to St Helens. *M Mensing*

In the early 1970s a blue liveried Class 108 unit is seen near Widnes on a Liverpool-Warrington stopping service. The unit number AN282 seen displayed on a card in the front window identifies it as one of Allerton depot's power twins. *BR*

Left: Chester has always been a good location to see a wide variety of DMUs. Here on the 1st September 1978 a number of units including members of Class 108 and Class 103 are awaiting departure. *G Pinder*

Below: At Helsby Junction on the 6th May 1982 a blue liveried Class 108 twin unit led by M56213 is seen on a Chester-Manchester Victoria service. The yellow stripe above the windows denotes the first class seating area. *J C Hillmer*

Above: This view is taken inside Lonsight Depot in Manchester on 25th March 1978. A refurbished Class 108 twin unit led by M51905 is wearing the early white livery that refurbished units carried. It is sharing space with a two-car Gloucester RCW Class 100 unit. *J Chalcroft*

Right: On the 22nd July 1978 refurbished Class 108 power twin M52060 and M51945 is seen at Shaw on the Manchester-Oldham-Rochdale line. *L Goddard*

Below: In June 1957 two new Wickham twin units led by E50419 are seen at Kings Lynn on a service to Hunstanton. This is one of the Class 109 units that was sold back to the makers in 1961 to fulfil an export order.

Part 2. DEMU types with details of classes.

The Southern Railway had a long history of electrification, and a lot of experience of electric traction. Therefore it was no surprise that the Southern Region continued this course and the spread of electrification continued under BR. However there were some areas and branches where electrification would not take place in the short term, and the Southern needed DMUs to fill this gap.

Because of their experience with electric traction, the Southern Region took a different course to the other regions. They developed Diesel Electric Multiple Units (DEMUs) using traction motors which were similar to those used on their EMU stock. To provide power they used the proven English Electric 4SRKT engines of 500 or 600hp. These were mounted above the bodywork in the power car. The difference in horsepower was due to the fitting of different sized superchargers. There was exchange of these engines between different types of unit.

This is a list of the formations of Southern DEMUs in unit numerical order. A description of each type is given in the class headers. DEMUs kept stable formations and when alterations were made they are noted in the list. A unit number in italics, with the symbol ⮰ at the end of the line is a reformation of the unit on the previous line. Each unit is followed by a date range which indicates the period that the unit was so formed. When units were renumbered the new number is shown following the symbol ➲. If a unit was reformed on renumbering, the unit number of the new unit which contained the majority of vehicles from the old unit is shown in italics.

A renumbering scheme was announced in January 1984 which would have led to the renumbering of all units as follows:

- Class 201 1001-7 renumbered 101-7
- Class 202 1011-9/31/32 renumbered 201-11
- Class 203 1034-7 renumbered 301-4
- Class 204 1401-4 renumbered 401-4
- Class 205 1101/2/5-20/3-33 renumbered 501-529
- Class 206 1206 renumbered 601
- Class 207 1301-19 renumbered 701-19

However, this re-numbering scheme was not implemented and it was superseded by the 1986 renumbering scheme shown below, which used the TOPS class number as part of the unit number.

The only other type of diesel-electric multiple units were the Blue Pullman trains, listed at the end of this section.

Original number series

Class 201

In the 1950s the Hasting Line was increasing in passenger use and the locomotive hauled stock on the line needed replacing. In 1956 the frames of forty new locomotive-hauled coaches were built at Ashford when a decision was made that they should be built as multiple unit stock instead.

Due to restrictions in the width of some tunnels on the route, the new stock was built to a restricted loading gauge. These units were based on Mark I coach construction with a short 58 ft. underframe and narrow body work. They were known as 6S units (6-car short units). They were fitted with buck-eye couplings throughout. They settled down to work reliably on the line, based at the new depot at St. Leonards.

Three units were disbanded at the end of 1964 to provide stock for working on the Reading-Redhill line (see Class 206).

1007 was substantially damaged in the Hither Green accident of 1967 leading to reformation of the surviving cars.

Class 201 BR Eastleigh
6S 'Hastings Line' units
Six-car 'short' units
DMBSO-TSOL-TFK-TSOL-TSOL-DMBSO

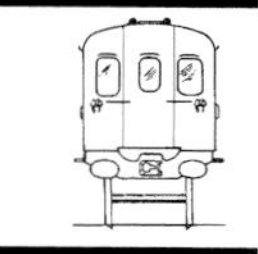

1001	S60000	S60502	S60700	S60501	S60500	S60001	01/57-05/86		
1002	S60002	S60505	S60701	S60504	S60503	S60003	02/57-01/65		
1002	S60002	S60505	S60701	S60504	S60503	S60003	05/79-05/86	*reformed*	⮰
									➲*1067*
1003	S60004	S60508	S60702	S60507	S60506	S60005	02/57-11/64		
1003	S60004	*S60535*	*S60711*	*S60534*	*S60533*	S60005	04/86-04/86	*reformed*	⮰
1004	S60006	S60511	S60703	S60510	S60509	S60007	02/57-01/65		
1004	S60006	*S60509*	*S60718*	S60510	*S60506*	S60007	01/81-03/83	*reformed*	⮰
1004	S60006	*S60506*	S60718	S60510	*S60702*	S60007	04/83-01/85		⮰
1004	S60006	S60506	S60718	S60510	*S60546*	S60007	01/85-04/86		⮰
1005	S60008	S60514	S60704	S60513	S60512	S60009	03/57-04/86		
1006	S60010	S60517	S60705	S60516	S60515	S60011	03/57-04/86		
1007	S60012	S60520	S60706	S60519	S60518	S60013	04/57-01/64		
1007	S60012	S60520	S60706	*S60507*	*S60508*	S60013	11/64-01/68		⮰
1007	S60012	*S60511*	*S60703*	*S60519*	*S60518*	S60013	10/69-04/86		⮰

Class 202

After Class 201 successfully entered service more units were needed to complete the modernisation of the line. Because it was no longer necessary to allow for the length of a locomotive at terminal platforms, standard length bodies could be used to give extra passenger accommodation.

These Class 202 units were known as 6L units (6-car long units).

Class 202 BR Eastleigh

6L 'Hastings Line' units
Six-car 'long' units
DMBSO-TSOL-TFK-TSOL-TSOL-DMBSO

Unit							Dates	Notes
1011	S60014	S60523	S60707	S60522	S60521	S60015	05/57-08/86	➲**203001**
1012	S60016	S60526	S60708	S60525	S60524	S60017	05/57-05/86	
1013	S60018	S60529	S60709	S60528	S60527	S60019	06/57-07/86	➲**202001**
1014	S60020	S60532	S60710	S60531	S60530	S60021	12/57-03/85	
1014	S60020	S60532	S60710	S60531	S60530	*S60031*	03/85-04/86	⇦
1015	S60022	S60535	S60711	S60534	S60533	S60023	12/57-04/86	➲*1003*
1016	S60024	S60538	S60712	S60537	S60536	S60025	01/58-05/86	
1017	S60026	S60541	S60713	S60540	S60539	S60027	02/58-05/86	
1018	S60028	S60544	S60714	S60543	S60542	S60029	02/58-05/86	
1019	S60030	S60547	S60715	S60546	S60545	S60031	03/58-10/84	

Class 203

A final batch of seven units was built to complete the dieselisation of the Hastings line. They included a buffet car in the formation and they were known as 6B units (six-car buffet units).

Too many buffet units were formed for the service requirements and 1031 and 1032 had their buffets replaced in 1964, with 1032 gaining two short trailers. Patronage of the buffets declined over the years and the remaining buffet cars were removed from service in 1980. 1034, 1036 and 1037 ran as five-car units for five years.

Class 203 BR Eastleigh

6B 'Hastings Line' units
Six-car 'buffet' units
DMBSO-TSOL-TFK-TRB-TSOL-DMBSO
DMBSO-TSOL-TFK-TSOL-TSOL-DMBSO
DMBSO-TFK-TFK-TFK-TSOL-DMBSO
DMBSO-TSOL-TFK-TSOL-DMBSO

Unit							Dates	Notes
1031	S60032	S60549	S60716	S60755	S60548	S60033	03/58-01/64	
1031	S60032	S60549	S60716	*S60551*	S60548	S60033	01/64-04/86	⇦
1032	S60034	S60551	S60717	S60750	S60552	S60035	04/58-01/64	
1032	S60034	*S60518*	S60717	*S60519*	S60552	S60035	01/64-10/69	⇦
1032	S60034	*S60701*	S60717	S60519	S60552	S60035	10/69-10/69	⇦
1032	S60034	S60701	S60717	*S60702*	S60552	S60035	10/69-05/79	⇦
1032	S60034	*S60506*	S60717	S60702	S60552	S60035	05/79-11/80	⇦
1032	S60034	*S60554*	S60717	*S60555*	S60552	S60035	01/81-05/86	⇦
1033	S60036	S60554	S60718	S60751	S60555	S60037	04/58-03/80	
1034	S60038	S60550	S60719	S60754	S60557	S60039	04/58-10/80	
1034	S60038	S60550	S60719	S60557	S60039		10/80-11/85	⇦
1034	S60038	S60550	S60719	*S60560*	S60557	S60039	11/85-04/86	⇦
1035	S60040	S60556	S60720	S60752	S60553	S60041	05/58-10/80	
1035	S60040	S60556	S60720	*S60559*	S60553	S60041	10/85-05/86	*reformed* ⇦
1036	S60042	S60559	S60721	S60756	S60558	S60043	05/58-10/80	
1036	S60042	S60559	S60721	S60558	S60043		10/80-10/85	⇦
1037	S60044	S60561	S60722	S60753	S60560	S60045	05/58-10/80	
1037	S60044	S60561	S60722	S60560	S60045		10/80-11/85	⇦

Class 205

Class 205 comprised a number of different two- and three-car units for working various un-electrified lines on the Southern Region. They were fitted with three-link couplers within the sets but had buck-eye couplers at the outer ends of the sets, allowing them to work in multiple with the Hastings line units if required.

1101-1118 were originally two-car units for working in Hampshire (2H units). They were fitted with 500hp engines and they were based at Eastleigh. They proved very successful and this led to an increase in traffic and complaints of overcrowding. In 1959 units 1101-1118 were fitted with a trailer car to create 3H units and their engines were fitted with larger superchargers uprating them to 600hp. In addition four extra three-car units were built to the new specification (1123-1126).

Four more two-car units (1119-1122) were built to work on the Ashford-Hastings line and the Bexhill West and New Romney Branches. They were fitted with 600hp engines, and they were based at St. Leonards.

Finally seven three-car units 1127-1133 were built for the Reading-Salisbury service. They were fitted with larger luggage compartments for this service. They were known as Berkshire units, and were based at Eastleigh

They had a long and successful life. As some of the lines in Hampshire were closed they were transferred to work on other lines, such as the Oxted and Lewes lines.

1111 was refurbished in May 1978.

Many units survive in preservation.

Class 205 BR Eastleigh

2H 'Hampshire' units
Two-car high density units
DMBSO-DTCsoL

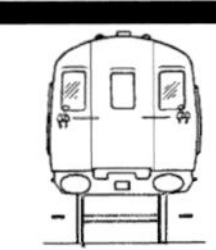

Unit			Dates
1101	S60100	S60800	08/57-10/59
1102	S60101	S60801	08/57-08/59
1103	S60102	S60802	08/57-09/59
1104	S60103	S60803	08/57-09/59
1105	S60104	S60804	08/57-10/59
1106	S60105	S60805	08/57-10/59
1107	S60106	S60806	08/57-09/59
1108	S60107	S60807	09/57-10/59
1109	S60108	S60808	09/57-10/59
1110	S60109	S60809	09/57-10/59
1111	S60110	S60810	09/57-09/59
1112	S60111	S60811	09/57-10/59
1113	S60112	S60812	09/57-10/59
1114	S60113	S60813	10/57-10/59
1115	S60114	S60814	10/57-08/59
1116	S60115	S60815	10/57-10/59
1117	S60116	S60816	10/57-10/59
1118	S60117	S60817	10/57-08/59

Class 205 BR Eastleigh

3H 'Hampshire' units
Three-car high density units
DMBSO-TSO-DTCsoL

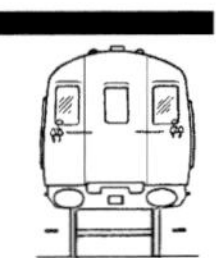

Unit				Dates	Notes
1101	S60100	S60650	S60800	10/59-08/86	➲**205001**
1102	S60101	S60651	S60801	08/59-08/86	➲**205002**
1103	S60102	S60652	S60802	09/59-03/80	➲*1403*
1104	S60103	S60653	S60803	09/59-09/79	➲*1404*
1105	S60104	S60654	S60804	10/59-08/86	➲**205005**
1106	S60105	S60655	S60805	10/59-08/86	➲**205006**
1107	S60106	S60656	S60806	09/59-07/85	
1107	*S60037*	S60656	S60806	07/85-04/86	⇦
1107	*S60022*	S60656	S60806	04/86-09/86	➲**205007** ⇦
1108	S60107	S60657	S60807	10/59-05/74	➲*1121*
1108	*S60120*	S60657	*S60820*	05/74-09/86	➲**205008** ⇦
1109	S60108	S60658	S60808	10/59-06/86	➲**205009**
1110	S60109	S60659	S60809	10/59-08/86	➲**205010**
1111	S60110	S60660	S60810	09/59-08/86	➲**205101**
1112	S60111	S60661	S60811	10/59-08/86	➲**205012**
1113	S60112	S60662	S60812	10/59-04/86	
1114	S60113	S60663	S60813	10/59-08/86	➲**205014**
1115	S60114	S60664	S60814	08/59-08/86	➲**205015**

1116	S60115 S60665 S60815	10/59-09/86	➲**205016**
1117	S60116 S60666 S60816	10/59-05/86	➲**205017**
1118	S60117 S60667 S60817	08/59-07/86	➲**205018**

Class 205 BR Eastleigh

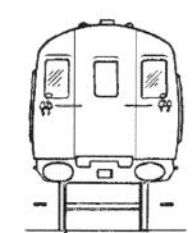

2H (3H) 'Hastings' units
Two (or three) car high density units
DMBSO-DTCsoL
DMBSO-TSO-DTCsoL

1119	S60118 S60818	06/58-03/80	
1119	S60118 *S60653* S60818	03/80-08/86	➲**205019**
1120	S60119 S60819	06/58-03/80	
1120	S60119 *S60652* S60819	03/80-09/86	➲**205020**
1121	S60120 S60820	06/58-05/74	➲*1108*
1121	*S60107 S60807*	05/74-07/79	➲*1402*
1122	S60121 S60821	06/58-02/80	➲*1402*

Class 205 BR Eastleigh

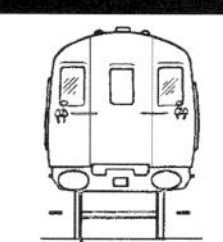

3H 'Hampshire' units
Three-car high density units
DMBSO-TSO-DTCsoL

1123	S60122 S60668 S60822	11/59-09/86	➲**205023**
1124	S60123 S60669 S60823	11/59-06/86	➲**205024**
1125	S60124 S60670 S60824	12/59-10/86	➲**205025**
1126	S60125 S60671 S60825	12/59-10/86	➲**205026**

Class 205 BR Eastleigh

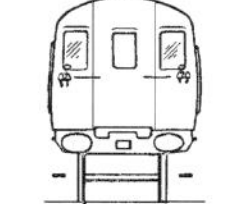

3H 'Berkshire' units
Three-car high density units
DMBSO-TSO-DTCsoL

1127	S60145 S60672 S60826	05/62-08/86	➲**205027**
1128	S60146 S60673 S60827	05/62-05/86	➲**205028**
1129	S60147 S60674 S60828	05/62-05/86	➲**205029**
1130	S60148 S60675 S60829	06/62-09/86	➲**205030**
1131	S60149 S60676 S60830	06/62-08/86	➲**205031**
1132	S60150 S60677 S60831	06/62-06/86	➲**205032**
1133	S60151 S60678 S60832	06/62-07/86	➲**205033**

Class 206

After the success of the Class 205 units in transforming the services they worked, more units were required for the Reading-Redhill line. However money was not available in the economic climate of the time (the height of the Beeching cuts) so the Southern Region came up with a scheme to update the line using redundant rolling stock. Three Class 201 units were found to be surplus to requirements and they were taken out of use. The coaches were reformed with some spare 2EPB EMU driving trailer cars, to provide six three-car units for this service.

The unusual formation with one standard-width EMU car coupled to two narrow Hastings Line gauge coaches led to the units becoming known as "Tadpoles". When conductor-guard operation was introduced on this service the non-corridor compartments in the driving trailer were normally locked and not available for passenger use.

The units were allocated to St. Leonards for maintenance and they performed successfully over the route for fifteen years.

Class 206 BR Eastleigh

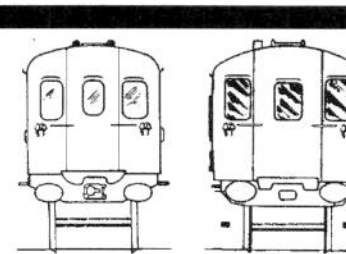

3R 'Reading-Redhill' units
Three-car units
DMBSO-TSOL-DTSso
DMBSO-TFK-DTSso

1201	S60002 S60503 S77500	01/65-05/79	
1202	S60003 S60504 S77503	01/65-05/79	
1203	S60004 S60505 S77507	01/65-05/79	
1204	S60005 S60506 S77508	01/65-05/79	
1205	S60006 S60509 S77509	01/65-01/81	
1206	S60007 S60510 S77510	01/65-11/80	
1206	*S60037 S60702* S77510	11/80-04/83	

Class 207

The final batch of new-build Southern DEMUs was Class 207, nineteen 3D "East Sussex" units designed for working on the Oxted and East Sussex lines. They were based at St. Leonards for maintenance, but were operationally out-based at Tunbridge Wells West. They were similar to the 3H Berkshire units, but restricted tunnels in the Tunbridge Wells area meant that they were built with a body which was three inches narrower than standard.

They were also fitted with a new style of steel-reinforced glass-fibre cab which had rounded corners and recesses for the jumper cables giving a much more modern look. They were fitted with buck-eye couplers throughout.

Class 207 BR Eastleigh

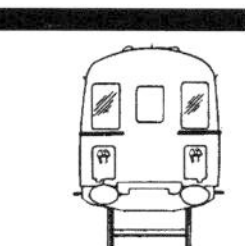

3D 'East Sussex' units
Three-car high density units
DMBSO-TCsoL-DTSO

1301	S60126 S60600 S60900	01/62-07/86	➲**207001**
1302	S60127 S60601 S60901	01/62-08/86	➲**207002**
1303	S60128 S60602 S60902	05/62-08/86	➲**207003**
1304	S60129 S60603 S60903	05/62-08/86	➲**207004**
1305	S60130 S60604 S60904	05/62-06/86	➲**207005**
1306	S60131 S60605 S60905	05/62-10/86	➲**207006**
1307	S60132 S60606 S60906	05/62-06/86	➲**207007**
1308	S60133 S60607 S60907	06/62-07/86	➲**207008**
1309	S60134 S60608 S60908	06/62-11/85	
1309	*S60045* S60608 S60908	11/85-07/86	➲**207009**
1310	S60135 S60609 S60909	06/62-06/86	➲**207010**
1311	S60136 S60610 S60910	06/62-07/86	➲**207011**
1312	S60137 S60611 S60911	07/62-10/86	➲**207012**
1313	S60138 S60612 S60912	07/62-08/86	➲**207013**
1314	S60139 S60613 S60913	07/62-08/86	➲**207014**
1315	S60140 S60614 S60914	07/62-09/86	➲**207015**
1316	S60141 S60615 S60915	07/62-09/86	➲**207016**
1317	S60142 S60616 S60916	07/62-09/86	➲**207017**
1318	S60143 S60617 S60917	07/62-07/86	➲**207018**
1319	S60144 S60618 S60918	08/62-12/86	➲**207019**

Class 204

After the Class 206 'Tadpole' units were disbanded in 1979, their EMU trailers were reformed in class 205 2H units to form three-car units to work on non-electrified lines in Berkshire, Hampshire and Wiltshire.

Class 204 BR Eastleigh

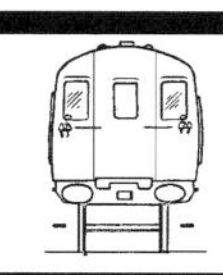

3T units
Three-car units
DMBSO-DTSso-DTCsoL

1401	S60107 S77500 S60807	07/79-07/86	➲**204001**
1402	S60121 S77508 S60821	02/80-05/86	➲**204002**
1403	S60102 S77507 S60802	03/80-05/86	➲**204003**
1404	S60103 S77503 S60803	09/79-06/86	➲**204004**

Class 201/202 BR Eastleigh

Preserved 'Hastings Line' unit
Five-car unit
DMBSO-TSOL-TSOL-TSOL-DMBSO

This preserved unit was formed to run on the main line. It is owned by Hastings Diesels Ltd. An EMU buffet 69337 was purchased in March 1998 to be added to the set.

60000 is named "Hastings" and 60118 is named "Tunbridge Wells". 60116 (ex 60016) was acquired in December 2002 and is named "Mountfield". Reformations in preservation are not shown.

Unit						Dates
201001	60000	60501	70262	60529	60118	05/96-

Class 202 BR Eastleigh

6L 'Hastings Line' unit
Six-car unit
DMBSO-TSOL-TFK-TSOL-TSOL-DMBSO

Unit							Dates	Notes
202001	60018	60529	60709	60528	60527	60019	07/86-12/87	➲ *203101*

Class 203 BR Eastleigh

6L 'Hastings Line' unit
Six-car unit
DMBSO-TSOL-TFK-TSOL-TSOL-DMBSO

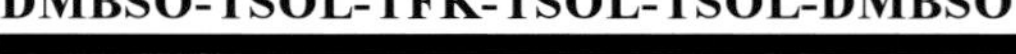

Unit							Dates	Notes
203001	60014	60523	60707	60522	60521	60015	08/86-06/89	
203001	*60152*	60523	60707	60522	60521	*60153*	06/89-05/90	*renumbering* ↻ ➲ *1067*

Class 203 BR Eastleigh

4L 'Hastings Line' unit
Four-car unit
DMBSO-TFK-TSOL-DMBSO

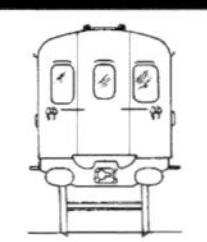

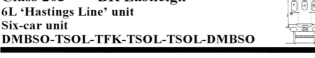

Unit					Dates
203101	60018	60709	60527	60019	12/87-03/88

Class 204 BR Eastleigh

3T units
Three-car units
DMBSO-DTSso-DTCsoL

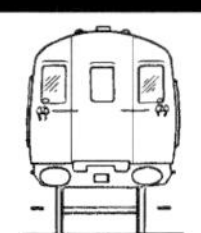

Unit				Dates	Notes
204001	60107	77500	60807	07/86-08/87	
204002	60121	77508	60821	05/86-11/87	
204003	60102	77507	60802	05/86-09/87	
204004	60103	77503	60803	06/86-08/87	
204004	60103	*77500*	60803	08/87-10/87	↻

Class 205 BR Eastleigh

3H (2H) units
Three (or two) car high density units
DMBSO-TSO-DTCsoL
DMBSO-DTCsoL

Unit				Dates	Notes
205001	60100	60650	60800	08/86-06/89	
205001	*60154*	60650	60800	06/89-11/99	*renumbering* ↻
205001	60154	60800		11/99-12/04	↻
205002	60101	60651	60801	08/86-06/89	
205002	*60155*	60651	60801	06/89-05/91	*renumbering* ↻
205005	60104	60654	60804	08/86-08/87	
205006	60105	60655	60805	08/86-09/87	
205007	60022	60656	60806	09/86-09/87	
205008	60120	60657	60820	09/86-05/91	
205008	60120	60657	*60814*	05/91-09/91	↻
205008	60120	60814		09/91-10/93	↻
205009	60108	60658	60808	06/86-12/04	
205010	60109	60659	60809	08/86-09/87	
205012	60111	60661	60811	08/86-07/03	
205012	60111	60811		07/03-02/04	↻
205014	60113	60663	60813	08/86-10/89	
205015	60114	60664	60814	08/86-05/91	
205015	60114	60664	*60801*	05/91-10/93	↻
205016	60115	60665	60815	09/86-08/94	
205017	60116	60666	60816	05/86-09/87	
205018	60117	60667	60817	07/86-01/95	
205018	60117	*60674*	*60828*	01/95-12/04	↻
205019	60118	60653	60818	08/86-08/87	
205020	60119	60652	60819	09/86-09/87	
205023	60122	60668	60822	09/86-01/99	
205024	60123	60669	60823	06/86-07/00	
205025	60124	60670	60824	10/86-10/03	
205025	60124	60824		10/03-02/04	↻
205026	60125	60671	60825	10/86-11/90	
205027	60145	60672	60826	08/86-09/94	
205028	60146	60673	60827	05/86-12/04	
205029	60147	60674	60828	05/86-01/95	➲ *205018*
205030	60148	60675	60829	09/86-11/92	
205031	60149	60676	60830	08/86-07/93	
205032	60150	60677	60831	06/86-12/04	
205033	60151	60678	60832	07/86-11/04	

Class 205/1 BR Eastleigh

3H (2H) refurbished unit
Three (or two) car high density unit
DMBSO-TSO-DTCsoL
DMBSO-DTCsoL
DMBSO-TSK-DTCsoL

Unit				Dates	Notes
205101	60110	60660	60810	08/86-01/93	
205101	60110	60810		01/93-06/95	➲ *205205* ↻
205205	60110	71634	60810	06/95-09/03	
205205	60110	60810		09/03-12/04	↻

Class 206/1 BR Eastleigh

3R unit
Three-car unit
DMBSO-TSOL-DTCsoL

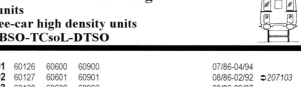

Unit				Dates
206101	60044	60561	60812	04/86-09/87

Class 207 BR Eastleigh

3D units
Three-car high density units
DMBSO-TCsoL-DTSO

Unit				Dates	Notes
207001	60126	60600	60900	07/86-04/94	
207002	60127	60601	60901	08/86-02/92	➲ *207103*
207003	60128	60602	60902	08/86-09/87	
207004	60129	60603	60903	08/86-07/91	➲ *207101*
207005	60130	60604	60904	06/86-07/91	➲ *207102*
207006	60131	60605	60905	10/86-09/87	
207007	60132	60606	60906	06/86-09/87	
207008	60133	60607	60907	07/86-05/88	
207009	60045	60608	60908	07/86-09/87	
207010	60135	60609	60909	06/86-09/93	
207011	60136	60610	60910	07/86-10/87	
207011	*60139*	60610	60910	10/87-05/90	➲ *1068* ↻
207012	60137	60611	60911	10/86-09/87	
207013	60138	60612	60912	08/86-09/93	
207014	60139	60613	60913	08/86-10/87	
207015	60140	60614	60914	09/86-09/87	
207016	60141	60615	60915	09/86-09/87	
207017	60142	60616	60916	09/86-02/04	
207018	60143	60617	60917	07/86-09/87	
207019	60144	60618	60918	12/86-05/88	

Class 207/1 BR Eastleigh
2D units
Two-car high density units
DMBSO-DTSO

207101	60129	60903	09/91-05/95	➲*207201*
207102	60130	60904	09/91-05/95	➲*207202*
207103	60127	60901	03/92-05/95	➲*207203*

Class 207/2 BR Eastleigh
3D units
Three-car high density units
DMBSO-TSK-DTSO

207201	60129	70549	60903	05/95-10/03
207202	60130	70547	60904	05/95-12/04
207203	60127	70286	60901	05/95-01/05

Departmental units

066/1066	ADB977376	ADB977379	ADB977377	05/86-03/94	
1067	ADB977698	ADB977697	ADB977699	09/90-06/93	
1067	ADB977698	*ADB977870*	ADB977699	06/93-10/94	
1068	60139	ADB977696	60910	09/90-04/92	
951068	ADB977700	ADB977696	ADB977701	04/92-05/92	*renumbering*
951069	ADB977939	ADB977870	ADB977940	10/94-11/97	
951070	*977906*	*977907*		09/93-09/93	*not formed*
930301	ADB977939	ADB977870	ADB977940	11/97-11/05	

Blue Pullman units

Class 251 Blue Pullman

These Blue Pullmans were totally unlike anything that had been built before. They were intended to provide competition with the quality of service that was being introduced on UK domestic airline services. They were fitted with double glazing for sound insulation and they were fitted with air-conditioning.

The trains were designed for two areas of service. Two six-car units were built for the Midland Pullman from London St. Pancras to Manchester, and three eight-car units were designed for the Birmingham Pullman and the Bristol Pullman services out of Paddington.

The electrification of the LMR main line eventually led to both the Midland and Birmingham Pullmans being superseded by electric services.

All the units then worked on the Western Region to Bristol and Cardiff and they were repainted in reversed blue and grey livery for their final years of service. On the Western Region the six-car units were fitted with multiple-unit jumper cables to enable them to work as a twelve coach train. Some seating was downgraded to second class and the units worked the busy morning and evening "Bristol Pullman" services.

A poor ride, combined with upgrading of competing services with Mk II hauled coaches led to these distinctive units being withdrawn from service in the early seventies. Unfortunately none survived to be preserved.

Class 251 Metropolitan-Cammell
'Blue Pullman'
Six-car units
DMBFL-MFLRK-TPFL-TPFL-MFLRK-DMBFL

M60090	**M60730**	**M60740**	**M60741**	**M60731**	**M60091**	11/59	Reddish
M60092	**M60732**	**M60742**	**M60743**	**M60733**	**M60093**	11/59	Reddish

Class 251 Metropolitan-Cammell
'Blue Pullman'
Eight-car units
DMBS-MPSL-TFLRK-TPFL-TPFL-TFLRK-MPSL-DMBS

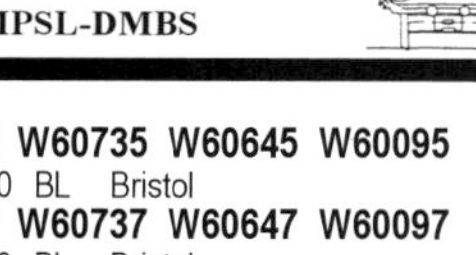

W60094	**W60644**	**W60734**	**W60744**	**W60745**	**W60735**	**W60645**	**W60095**	02/60	BL	Bristol
W60096	**W60646**	**W60736**	**W60746**	**W60747**	**W60737**	**W60647**	**W60097**	04/60	BL	Bristol
W60098	**W60648**	**W60738**	**W60748**	**W60749**	**W60739**	**W60649**	**W60099**	05/60	BL	Bristol

Part 3. DEMU coaches showing units.

This section shows the Southern Region DEMU carriages listed numerically. Each individual carriage is listed together with the dates when it ran in each unit. This allows you to follow the unit reformations of individual carriages.

Coach	Unit	Dates	Unit	Dates	Unit	Dates	Unit	Dates
S60000	**1001**	01/57-05/86	**201001**	05/96-				
S60001	**1001**	01/57-05/86						
S60002	**1002**	02/57-01/65	**1201**	01/65-05/79	**1002**	05/79-05/86		
S60003	**1002**	02/57-01/65	**1202**	01/65-05/79	**1002**	05/79-05/86		
S60004	**1003**	02/57-11/64	**1203**	01/65-05/79	**1003**	04/86-04/86		
S60005	**1003**	02/57-11/64	**1204**	01/65-05/79	**1003**	04/86-04/86		
S60006	**1004**	02/57-01/65	**1205**	01/65-01/81	**1004**	01/81-04/86		
S60007	**1004**	02/57-01/65	**1206**	01/65-11/80	**1004**	01/81-04/86		
S60008	**1005**	03/57-04/86						
S60009	**1005**	03/57-04/86						
S60010	**1006**	03/57-04/86						
S60011	**1006**	03/57-04/86						
S60012	**1007**	04/57-01/64	**1007**	11/64-01/68	**1007**	10/69-04/86		
S60013	**1007**	04/57-01/64	**1007**	11/64-01/68	**1007**	10/69-04/86		
S60014	**1011**	05/57-08/86	**203001**	08/86-06/89				
S60015	**1011**	05/57-08/86	**203001**	08/86-06/89				
S60016	**1012**	05/57-05/86						
S60017	**1012**	05/57-05/86						
S60018	**1013**	06/57-07/86	**202001**	07/86-12/87	**203101**	12/87-03/88		
S60019	**1013**	06/57-07/86	**202001**	07/86-12/87	**203101**	12/87-03/88		
S60020	**1014**	12/57-04/86						
S60021	**1014**	12/57-03/85						
S60022	**1015**	12/57-04/86	**1107**	04/86-09/86	**205007**	09/86-09/87		
S60023	**1015**	12/57-04/86						
S60024	**1016**	01/58-05/86						
S60025	**1016**	01/58-05/86						
S60026	**1017**	02/58-05/86						
S60027	**1017**	02/58-05/86						
S60028	**1018**	02/58-05/86						
S60029	**1018**	02/58-05/86						
S60030	**1019**	03/58-10/84						
S60031	**1019**	03/58-10/84	**1014**	03/85-04/86				
S60032	**1031**	03/58-04/86						
S60033	**1031**	03/58-04/86						
S60034	**1032**	04/58-11/80	**1032**	01/81-05/86				
S60035	**1032**	04/58-11/80	**1032**	01/81-05/86				
S60036	**1033**	04/58-03/80						
S60037	**1033**	04/58-03/80	**1206**	11/80-04/83	**1107**	07/85-04/86		
S60038	**1034**	04/58-04/86						
S60039	**1034**	04/58-04/86						
S60040	**1035**	05/58-10/80	**1035**	10/85-05/86				
S60041	**1035**	05/58-10/80	**1035**	10/85-05/86				
S60042	**1036**	05/58-10/85						
S60043	**1036**	05/58-10/80						
S60043	**1036**	10/80-10/85						
S60044	**1037**	05/58-11/85	**206101**	04/86-09/87				
S60045	**1037**	05/58-11/85	**1309**	11/85-07/86	**207009**	07/86-09/87		
S60100	**1101**	08/57-08/86	**205001**	08/86-06/89				
S60101	**1102**	08/57-08/86	**205002**	08/86-06/89				
S60102	**1103**	08/57-03/80	**1403**	03/80-05/86	**204003**	05/86-09/87		
S60103	**1104**	08/57-09/79	**1404**	09/79-06/86	**204004**	06/86-10/87		
S60104	**1105**	08/57-08/86	**205005**	08/86-08/87				
S60105	**1106**	08/57-08/86	**205006**	08/86-09/87				
S60106	**1107**	08/57-07/85						
S60107	**1108**	09/57-07/79	**1121**	05/74-07/79	**1401**	07/79-07/86	**204001**	07/86-08/87
S60108	**1109**	09/57-06/86	**205009**	06/86-12/04				
S60109	**1110**	09/57-08/86	**205010**	08/86-09/87				
S60110	**1111**	09/57-08/86	**205101**	08/86-06/95	**205205**	06/95-12/04		
S60111	**1112**	09/57-08/86	**205012**	08/86-02/04				
S60112	**1113**	09/57-04/86						
S60113	**1114**	10/57-08/86	**205014**	08/86-10/89				
S60114	**1115**	10/57-08/86	**205015**	08/86-10/93				
S60115	**1116**	10/57-09/86	**205016**	09/86-08/94				
S60116	**1117**	10/57-05/86	**205017**	05/86-09/87				
60116	**201001**	12/02-						
S60117	**1118**	10/57-07/86	**205018**	07/86-12/04				
S60118	**1119**	06/58-08/86	**205019**	08/86-08/87				
60118	**201001**	05/96-						
S60119	**1120**	06/58-09/86	**205020**	09/86-09/87				
S60120	**1121**	06/58-05/74	**1108**	05/74-09/86	**205008**	09/86-10/93		
S60121	**1122**	06/58-02/80	**1402**	02/80-05/86	**204002**	05/86-11/87		
S60122	**1123**	11/59-09/86	**205023**	09/86-01/99				
S60123	**1124**	11/59-06/86	**205024**	06/86-07/00				
S60124	**1125**	12/59-10/86	**205025**	10/86-02/04				
S60125	**1126**	12/59-10/86	**205026**	10/86-11/90				
S60126	**1301**	07/86-07/86	**207001**	07/86-04/94				
S60127	**1302**	08/86-08/86	**207002**	08/86-02/92	**207103**	03/92-05/95	**207203**	05/95-01/05
S60128	**1303**	05/62-08/86	**207003**	08/86-09/87				
S60129	**1304**	05/62-08/86	**207004**	08/86-07/91	**207101**	09/91-05/95	**207201**	05/95-10/03
S60130	**1305**	05/62-06/86	**207005**	06/86-07/91	**207102**	09/91-05/95	**207202**	05/95-12/04
S60131	**1306**	05/62-10/86	**207006**	10/86-09/87				
S60132	**1307**	05/62-06/86	**207007**	06/86-09/87				
S60133	**1308**	06/62-07/86	**207008**	07/86-05/88				
S60134	**1309**	06/62-11/85						
S60135	**1310**	06/62-06/86	**207010**	06/86-09/93				
S60136	**1311**	06/62-07/86	**207011**	07/86-10/87				
S60137	**1312**	07/62-10/86	**207012**	10/86-09/87				
S60138	**1313**	07/62-08/86	**207013**	08/86-09/93				
S60139	**1314**	07/62-08/86	**207014**	08/86-10/87	**207011**	10/87-05/90		
S60140	**1315**	07/62-09/86	**207015**	09/86-09/87				
S60141	**1316**	07/62-09/86	**207016**	09/86-09/87				
S60142	**1317**	07/62-09/86	**207017**	09/86-02/04				
S60143	**1318**	07/62-07/86	**207018**	07/86-09/87				
S60144	**1319**	08/62-12/86	**207019**	12/86-05/88				
S60145	**1127**	05/62-08/86	**205027**	08/86-09/94				
S60146	**1128**	05/62-05/86	**205028**	05/86-12/04				
S60147	**1129**	05/62-05/86	**205029**	05/86-01/95				
S60148	**1130**	06/62-09/86	**205030**	09/86-11/92				
S60149	**1131**	06/62-08/86	**205031**	08/86-07/93				
S60150	**1132**	06/62-06/86	**205032**	06/86-12/04				
S60151	**1133**	06/62-07/86	**205033**	07/86-11/04				
60152	**203001**	06/89-05/90						
60153	**203001**	06/89-05/90						
60154	**205001**	06/89-12/04						
60155	**205002**	06/89-05/91						
S60500	**1001**	01/57-05/86						
S60501	**1001**	01/57-05/86	**201001**	05/96-				
S60502	**1001**	01/57-05/86						
S60503	**1002**	02/57-01/65	**1201**	01/65-05/79	**1002**	05/79-05/86		
S60504	**1002**	02/57-01/65	**1202**	01/65-05/79	**1002**	05/79-05/86		
S60505	**1002**	02/57-01/65	**1203**	01/65-05/79	**1002**	05/79-05/86		
S60506	**1003**	02/57-11/64	**1204**	01/65-05/79	**1032**	05/79-11/80	**1004**	01/81-04/86
S60507	**1003**	02/57-11/64	**1007**	11/64-01/68				
S60508	**1003**	02/57-11/64	**1007**	11/64-01/68				
S60509	**1004**	02/57-01/65	**1205**	01/65-01/81	**1004**	01/81-03/83		
S60510	**1004**	02/57-01/65	**1206**	01/65-11/80	**1004**	01/81-04/86		
S60511	**1004**	02/57-01/65	**1007**	10/69-04/86				
S60512	**1005**	03/57-04/86						
S60513	**1005**	03/57-04/86						
S60514	**1005**	03/57-04/86						
S60515	**1006**	03/57-04/86						
S60516	**1006**	03/57-04/86						
S60517	**1006**	03/57-04/86						
S60518	**1007**	04/57-01/64	**1032**	01/64-10/69	**1007**	10/69-04/86		
S60519	**1007**	04/57-01/64	**1032**	01/64-10/69	**1007**	10/69-04/86		
S60520	**1007**	04/57-01/68						
S60521	**1011**	05/57-08/86	**203001**	08/86-05/90				
S60522	**1011**	05/57-08/86	**203001**	08/86-05/90				
S60523	**1011**	05/57-08/86	**203001**	08/86-05/90				
S60524	**1012**	05/57-05/86						
S60525	**1012**	05/57-05/86						
S60526	**1012**	05/57-05/86						
S60527	**1013**	06/57-07/86	**202001**	07/86-03/88				
S60528	**1013**	06/57-07/86	**202001**	07/86-12/87				
S60529	**1013**	06/57-07/86	**202001**	07/86-12/87	**201001**	05/96-		
S60530	**1014**	12/57-04/86						
S60531	**1014**	12/57-04/86						
S60532	**1014**	12/57-04/86						
S60533	**1015**	12/57-04/86	**1003**	04/86-04/86				
S60534	**1015**	12/57-04/86	**1003**	04/86-04/86				
S60535	**1015**	12/57-04/86	**1003**	04/86-04/86				
S60536	**1016**	01/58-05/86						
S60537	**1016**	01/58-05/86						
S60538	**1016**	01/58-05/86						
S60539	**1017**	02/58-05/86						
S60540	**1017**	02/58-05/86						
S60541	**1017**	02/58-05/86						
S60542	**1018**	02/58-05/86						
S60543	**1018**	02/58-05/86						
S60544	**1018**	02/58-05/86						
S60545	**1019**	03/58-10/84						
S60546	**1019**	03/58-10/84	**1004**	01/85-04/86				
S60547	**1019**	03/58-10/84						
S60548	**1031**	03/58-04/86						
S60549	**1031**	03/58-04/86						
S60550	**1034**	04/58-04/86						
S60551	**1032**	04/58-01/64	**1031**	01/64-04/86				
S60552	**1032**	04/58-11/80	**1032**	01/81-05/86				

S60553 1035 05/58-10/80 1035 10/85-05/86
S60554 1033 04/58-03/80 1032 01/81-05/86
S60555 1033 04/58-03/80 1032 01/81-05/86
S60556 1035 05/58-10/80 1035 10/85-05/86
S60557 1034 04/58-04/86
S60558 1036 05/58-10/85
S60559 1036 05/58-10/85 1035 10/85-05/86
S60560 1037 05/58-11/85 1034 11/85-04/86
S60561 1037 05/58-11/85 206101 04/86-09/87
S60600 1301 07/86-07/86 207001 07/86-04/94
S60601 1302 08/86-08/86 207002 08/86-02/92
S60602 1303 05/62-08/86 207003 08/86-09/87
S60603 1304 05/62-08/86 207004 08/86-07/91
S60604 1305 05/62-06/86 207005 06/86-07/91
S60605 1306 05/62-10/86 207006 10/86-09/87
S60606 1307 05/62-06/86 207007 06/86-09/87
S60607 1308 06/62-07/86 207008 07/86-05/88
S60608 1309 06/62-11/85 207009 07/86-09/87
S60609 1310 06/62-06/86 207010 06/86-09/93
S60610 1311 06/62-07/86 207011 07/86-05/90
S60611 1312 07/62-10/86 207012 10/86-09/87
S60612 1313 07/62-08/86 207013 08/86-09/93
S60613 1314 07/62-08/86 207014 08/86-10/87
S60614 1315 07/62-09/86 207015 09/86-09/87
S60615 1316 07/62-09/86 207016 09/86-09/87
S60616 1317 07/62-09/86 207017 09/86-02/04
S60617 1318 07/62-07/86 207018 07/86-09/87
S60618 1319 08/62-12/86 207019 12/86-05/88
S60650 1101 10/59-08/86 205001 08/86-11/99
S60651 1102 08/59-08/86 205002 08/86-05/91
S60652 1103 09/59-03/80 1120 03/80-09/86 205020 09/86-09/87
S60653 1104 09/59-09/79 1119 03/80-08/86 205019 08/86-08/87
S60654 1105 10/59-08/86 205005 08/86-08/87
S60655 1106 10/59-08/86 205006 08/86-09/87
S60656 1107 09/59-09/86 205007 09/86-09/87
S60657 1108 10/59-09/86 205008 09/86-09/91
S60658 1109 10/59-06/86 205009 06/86-12/04
S60659 1110 10/59-08/86 205010 08/86-09/87
S60660 1111 09/59-08/86 205101 08/86-01/93
S60661 1112 10/59-08/86 205012 08/86-07/03
S60662 1113 10/59-04/86
S60663 1114 10/59-08/86 205014 08/86-10/89
S60664 1115 08/59-05/91 205015 05/91-10/93
S60665 1116 10/59-09/86 205016 09/86-08/94
S60666 1117 10/59-05/86 205017 05/86-09/87
S60667 1118 08/59-07/86 205018 07/86-01/95
S60668 1123 11/59-09/86 205023 09/86-01/99
S60669 1124 11/59-06/86 205024 06/86-07/00
S60670 1125 12/59-10/86 205025 10/86-10/03
S60671 1126 12/59-10/86 205026 10/86-11/90
S60672 1127 05/62-08/86 205027 08/86-09/94
S60673 1128 05/62-05/86 205028 05/86-12/04
S60674 1129 05/62-05/86 205029 05/86-01/95 205018 01/95-12/04
S60675 1130 06/62-09/86 205030 09/86-11/92
S60676 1131 06/62-08/86 205031 08/86-07/93
S60677 1132 06/62-06/86 205032 06/86-12/04
S60678 1133 06/62-07/86 205033 07/86-11/04
S60700 1001 01/57-05/86
S60701 1002 02/57-01/65 1032 10/69-05/79 1002 05/79-05/86
S60702 1003 02/57-11/64 1032 10/69-11/80 1206 11/80-04/83 1004 04/83-01/85
S60703 1004 02/57-01/65 1007 10/69-04/86
S60704 1005 03/57-04/86
S60705 1006 03/57-04/86
S60706 1007 04/57-01/64 1007 11/64-01/68
S60707 1011 05/57-08/86 203001 08/86-05/90
S60708 1012 05/57-05/86
S60709 1013 06/57-07/86 202001 07/86-12/87 203101 12/87-03/88
S60710 1014 12/57-04/86
S60711 1015 12/57-04/86 1003 04/86-04/86
S60712 1016 01/58-05/86
S60713 1017 02/58-05/86
S60714 1018 02/58-05/86
S60715 1019 03/58-10/84
S60716 1031 03/58-04/86
S60717 1032 04/58-11/80 1032 01/81-05/86
S60718 1033 04/58-03/80 1004 01/81-04/86
S60719 1034 04/58-04/86
S60720 1035 05/58-10/80 1035 10/85-05/86
S60721 1036 05/58-10/85
S60722 1037 05/58-11/85
S60750 1032 04/58-01/64
S60751 1033 04/58-03/80
S60752 1035 05/58-10/80
S60753 1037 05/58-10/80
S60754 1034 04/58-10/80
S60755 1031 03/58-01/64
S60756 1036 05/58-10/80
S60800 1101 08/57-08/86 205001 08/86-12/04
S60801 1102 08/57-08/86 205002 08/86-05/91 205015 05/91-10/93
S60802 1103 08/57-03/80 1403 03/80-05/86 204003 05/86-09/87
S60803 1104 08/57-09/79 1404 09/79-06/86 204004 06/86-10/87
S60804 1105 08/57-08/86 205005 08/86-08/87
S60805 1106 08/57-08/86 205006 08/86-09/87
S60806 1107 08/57-09/86 205007 09/86-09/87
S60807 1108 09/57-05/74 1121 05/74-07/79 1401 07/79-07/86 204001 07/86-08/87
S60808 1109 09/57-06/86 205009 06/86-12/04
S60809 1110 09/57-08/86 205010 08/86-09/87
S60810 1111 09/57-08/86 205101 08/86-06/95 205205 06/95-12/04
S60811 1112 09/57-08/86 205012 08/86-02/04
S60812 1113 09/57-04/86 206101 04/86-09/87
S60813 1114 10/57-08/86 205014 08/86-10/89
S60814 1115 10/57-08/86 205015 08/86-05/91 205008 05/91-10/93
S60815 1116 10/57-09/86 205016 09/86-08/94
S60816 1117 10/57-05/86 205017 05/86-09/87
S60817 1118 10/57-07/86 205018 07/86-01/95
S60818 1119 06/58-08/86 205019 08/86-08/87
S60819 1120 06/58-09/86 205020 09/86-09/87
S60820 1121 06/58-05/74 1108 05/74-09/86 205008 09/86-05/91
S60821 1122 06/58-02/80 1402 02/80-05/86 204002 05/86-11/87
S60822 1123 11/59-09/86 205023 09/86-01/99
S60823 1124 11/59-06/86 205024 06/86-07/00
S60824 1125 12/59-10/86 205025 10/86-02/04
S60825 1126 12/59-10/86 205026 10/86-11/90
S60826 1127 05/62-08/86 205027 08/86-09/94
S60827 1128 05/62-05/86 205028 05/86-12/04
S60828 1129 05/62-05/86 205029 05/86-01/95 205018 01/95-12/04
S60829 1130 06/62-09/86 205030 09/86-11/92
S60830 1131 06/62-08/86 205031 08/86-07/93
S60831 1132 06/62-06/86 205032 06/86-12/04
S60832 1133 06/62-07/86 205033 07/86-11/04
S60900 1301 07/86-07/86 207001 07/86-04/94
S60901 1302 08/86-08/86 207002 08/86-02/92 207103 03/92-05/95 207203 05/95-01/05
S60902 1303 05/62-08/86 207003 08/86-09/87
S60903 1304 05/62-08/86 207004 08/86-07/91 207101 09/91-05/95 207201 05/95-10/03
S60904 1305 05/62-06/86 207005 06/86-07/91 207102 09/91-05/95 207202 05/95-12/04
S60905 1306 05/62-10/86 207006 10/86-09/87
S60906 1307 05/62-06/86 207007 06/86-09/87
S60907 1308 06/62-07/86 207008 07/86-05/88
S60908 1309 06/62-11/85 207009 07/86-09/87
S60909 1310 06/62-06/86 207010 06/86-09/93
S60910 1311 06/62-07/86 207011 07/86-05/90
S60911 1312 07/62-10/86 207012 10/86-09/87
S60912 1313 07/62-08/86 207013 08/86-09/93
S60913 1314 07/62-08/86 207014 08/86-10/87
S60914 1315 07/62-09/86 207015 09/86-09/87
S60915 1316 07/62-09/86 207016 09/86-09/87
S60916 1317 07/62-09/86 207017 09/86-02/04
S60917 1318 07/62-07/86 207018 07/86-09/87
S60918 1319 08/62-12/86 207019 12/86-05/88
69337 201001 03/98-
70262 201001 05/96-
70286 207203 05/95-01/05
70547 207202 05/95-12/04
70549 207201 05/95-10/03
71634 205205 06/95-09/03
S77500 1201 01/65-05/79 1401 07/79-07/86 204001 07/86-08/87 204004 08/87-10/87
S77503 1202 01/65-05/79 1404 09/79-06/86 204004 06/86-08/87
S77507 1203 01/65-05/79 1403 03/80-05/86 204003 05/86-09/87
S77508 1204 01/65-05/79 1402 02/80-05/86 204002 05/86-11/87
S77509 1205 01/65-01/81
S77510 1206 01/65-04/83

A brand new Birmingham RCW Class 110 three-car unit is seen at Darlington. Driving Motor Brake Composite E51811 is leading the train. *P J Sharpe*

Class 110 DMBC E52081 in BR blue livery is seen at Manchester Victoria on a Leeds service. *A H Bryant*

On 31st May 1983 a three-car Class 110 unit led by E52066 in blue and grey livery descends Miles Platting Bank towards Manchester Victoria on a Leeds to Blackpool North service. *M Howarth*

Rolls-Royce powered Class 111 Metropolitan-Cammell DMBS E51545 was displaying the Metrotrain logo incorporating the insignia of BR and West Yorkshire PTE when seen on 19th October 1982 at York. *C Boocock*

One of the short-lived Cravens Class 113 twin units heads a six-car train at Colne. It is in green livery with a small yellow warning panel. *P J Sharpe*

On 25th March 1967 the 12.10 Colne to Blackpool North service formed of a Class 113 and a Class 112 unit is seen west of Pleasington. *C T Gifford*

A blue liveried Class 112 unit is seen at Platform 12 at Manchester Victoria on the 07.50 train to Blackburn on the 4th August 1968. We should be grateful that the photographer spared some film for this shot because Sunday 4th August was the last normal day of working steam (not counting the very last train one week later), with a number of special trains running in the North West. *A McIntyre*

On 21st September 1976 the 11.55 Sheffield-Lincoln train rumbles across the High Street level crossing into Lincoln Station. E50036 is leading the blue Derby Class 114 two-car unit, while a Metropolitan-Cammell two-car unit follows with a spare motor coach bringing up the rear. *P Hawkins*

On the evening of 28th January 1980 refurbished Class 114 DTCL E56007 is seen at the head of a line of stabled DMUs at Sheffield. *C J Marsden*

Class 114 DMBS E50007 is about to depart from Brightside on the 16.21 service to New Mills on 21st April 1981. *J S Rinder*

This interior shot of Class 114 DTCL E56037 was taken at Derby between trips on the Matlock line on 18th May 1976. Note the very simple bus-type seats that many of these local and branch line units were fitted with. *P J Fowler*

During 1987 a number of Class 114 two-car units were converted for working Express Parcels services. E53027 and E54041 are seen at York with a parcels service for Cambridge on 2nd September 1987. *B Morrison*

Another Class 114 parcels unit, this time a power twin consisting of E53040 and E53004 is seen at Bradford Interchange on 10th July 1987. E53040 later underwent a more thorough conversion when it was fitted with roller-shutter doors and was renumbered 55931. *K Lane*

Two four-car Derby Class 115 sets form the 12.30pm Liverpool Central to Manchester Central express, approaching Cressington Station. This was before these services were diverted to run into Liverpool Lime Street.

This former Cheshire Lines Committee line was my local line when I was growing up. I lived a stone's throw from Mersey Road Station (now called Aigburth) which was the next station up the line.

This photograph was taken on the 19th January 1963, the year of the big freeze. I remember pushing through snow drifts that came up to my waist as I walked to school; but I *was* only six years old! I can also remember my Dad taking us to Sefton Park where it seemed like half of Liverpool was out enjoying walking on the frozen lake.

Cressington Station was in a conservation area and when the line was rebuilt in the late 1970s great care was taken to return the station to its Victorian splendour. My mate Rob Cruickshank who was a great lover of everything to do with the CLC lived down the road, on the riverfront. My parents later moved into one of the houses just seen on the left of this photograph. *I G Holt*

This shot captures the look and feel of Marylebone Station in the 1970s. M51900 is seen at the head of two four-car Class 115 sets leaving on a service to Aylesbury on 9th March 1978. Marylebone was always full of blue DMUs all of the same design. The diesel fumes rising as the train departs recalls the distinctive smell of the station, but judging from the plumes of smoke, are only six of the eight engines working on this train?

In August 1974 Grahame McCoyd and I spent a week spotting in London. We discovered Marylebone depot (which we did not know existed) just outside Marylebone, and spent a happy half-hour exploring this old steam-age depot which was filled with blue suburban units. They were exactly the same as our local Liverpool units, but we copped all of them! *B Morrison*

Right: Class 115 Trailer Second M59651 at Marylebone on 17th July 1970. The interior of these coaches was divided into three differently sized compartments with the centre one being non-smoking. The division points between the compartments can been seen from the outside as the points where two small windows are fitted between the doors, rather than one big window. *P R Foster*

Below: DMBS M51674 at Marylebone. Again notice how the external windows mark the interior layout of these units. *B G Loudwell*

In the later blue and grey livery M51655 leads the 16.40 Marylebone to Banbury train on 10th May 1987, as it runs down from Somerton Tunnel to Aynho Junction. *W A Sharman*

A Class 116 Derby three-car suburban unit led by W50854 is seen at Exeter St Davids on a Newton Abbott working. It is in the original non-corridor configuration and it is in blue livery with a small yellow warning panel. *J H Bird*

On 10th April 1982 M50119 is seen at Birmingham New Street as part of unit TS539. *J E Augustson*

A mixed parcels unit is seen at Crewe on 24th July 1987. Class 116 M53072 is coupled to Class 120 car M51785. Both are converted for parcels working with all their seats removed and they are carrying Red Star stickers. *S Widdowson*

Class 116 three-car unit 116388 is seen at Bridge of Weir on a Kilmacolm-Glasgow service in 1983. This unit was made up of SC50823, SC59354 and SC50876. *J Glover*

Pressed Steel Class 117 DMS W51397 is seen in original condition and livery on a Basingstoke-Woking train at Fleet. *J H Bird*

Part 4. Full listing of individual coaches.

This is a full listing of all DMU vehicles in numerical order.

For each vehicle the following information is shown:

1. Vehicle number with the regional prefix at the date of introduction.
2. New (➲) or previous (⊂) number in the general TOPS renumbering in 1983.
3. The period in service; introduction date to disposal date. The disposal date is when it was withdrawn, transferred to departmental service or renumbered on conversion (but not including the TOPS renumbering shown in column 2).
4. Disposal details: ⊗ scrapped (followed by date), Ⓟ preserved.
5. Detail difference (listed in the class header), including refurbishment ® followed by date.
6. Regional reallocations. Up until late 1986 each carriage carried a regional prefix which changed if it was reallocated to a different region. Regional prefix changes are shown by the date of the change, followed by ⇨ and then the new regional prefix. All units allocated to the North Eastern Region carried the E prefix until 1965 when they were recoded as NE. When the North Eastern Region was abolished and absorbed into the Eastern Region in 1968 they were all recoded as E again. A prefix is shown in italics if it is known that the new prefix was not carried on the coach in question.
7. Conversion details. If the carriage was converted and renumbered the new number is shown after ➲, with the date of conversion. In a few cases a carriage was withdrawn and reinstated again. This is shown in the lists as **⊠03/83-05/83**. In this example the carriage was withdrawn in March 1983 and reinstated in May the same year.

Here are some examples from the listings:

E50267 05/83➲**53267** 10/57-02/93 ⊗01/94 ®*10/76* 01/65⇨**NE** 01/68⇨**E**
E50268 03/83➲**53268** 10/57-01/01 Ⓟ⊗04/09 ®04/8301/65⇨**NE** 01/68⇨**E** 09/79⇨**SC**

E50267 was introduced in October 1957. In January 1965 it officially received its NE prefix as it was a North Eastern Region unit (note that for region changes, the date given is the official transfer date; it could take many months for the carriage concerned to actually receive its new prefix). In January 1968 it received an E prefix as the NER ceased to exist. It was refurbished around about October 1976 (dates in italics are approximate dates). In May 1983 it was renumbered to E53267 as part of the general TOPS renumbering. It was finally withdrawn in February 1993 and scrapped in January 1994.

E50268 followed a similar path until it was transferred to the Scottish Region in September 1979. It was refurbished in April 1983, withdrawn in January 2001 and was taken into preservation for a while before being scrapped in April 2009.

Any DMU which is renumbered is shown in two places in the lists; once under the old number and once under the new. Here are the second entries for these two coaches:

E53267 05/83⊂**50267** 10/57-02/93 ⊗01/94 ®*10/76*
SC53268 03/83⊂**50268** 10/57-01/01 Ⓟ⊗04/09 ®04/83

Note that the final disposal details and refurbishment details are repeated in both places (to save you flipping through the book all the time), but regional changes only refer to the specific number shown.

M50396 01/58-06/70 ⊗02/91 04/71➲**DB975089**
M50397 01/58-02/71 Ⓟ⊗09/09 02/71➲*DB975137*

In this example both of these carriages did not survive in capital stock long enough to be renumbered in the 53XXX series. M50396 was withdrawn from service in June 1970 and converted to departmental number DB975089 in April 1971. Its subsequent history will be found under that number. However it was finally scrapped in February 1991. M50397 was also converted for departmental service, but in this case it did not receive its allocated number of DB975137 (shown here in italics). More details will be found under the departmental number, but after spending some years in preservation it was scrapped in September 2009.

The symbol ↲ is used in a few places to show that the information on this line refers to the same carriage on the previous line, but at a later time in its life.

Modifications

There are some general types of change which are best described in this introduction.

Refurbishment

In July 1974 a three-car Metropolitan-Cammell Class 102 unit (51451, 59545, 51518) was given a trial refurbishment. It then set off on a three month tour around the country in its distinctive white livery with a blue band at waist level. The interiors were thoroughly refurbished with strip-lighting replacing the original tungsten bulbs. Three different levels of refurbishment were carried out in the three cars, (one with full refurbishment, one intermediate and one fairly basic car) allowing comparison of the different options. This unit did not carry regional prefixes at this time.

After its successful tour, BR started a programme of refurbishment on many of its classes, based on the refurbishment that required the least new materials. At first the refurbished units could be noted by their distinctive white livery, but later they were out-shopped in standard BR blue and grey livery, at the same time as other non-refurbished units were also being repainted in the same livery. The refurbishment programme finished in 1984.

Gangways

The Western Region chose to standardize on three-car high density non-gangwayed units for its suburban services. The London Midland Region used similar four-car units for its St Pancras and Marylebone suburban services in London. As designed the toilets in these units were only to be found in the trailer cars and passengers in the end cars could not access them. After complaints were received the Western Region started fitting through gangways to their units and these are shown in the class headings in the lists as ⑨. They were all complete by 1972. Other units were later fitted with through gangways in the mid 1980s and these are shown as *⑨*.

The opposite can be seen for some classes, for example the Class 126 Inter-city units and the Class 128 diesel parcels units, when later in their lives these vehicles had their external end gangways removed and plated over.

Buffets

Many units designed for long distance Inter-city or cross-country services included buffets when built. However it was not long before things changed as buffet facilities were no longer economical on many of these services. In some cases (for example the Trans-Pennine units) the buffet cars were completely removed from the sets. In other cases, many buffets were simply closed down, some being replaced by extra luggage shelving.

Downgrading of First Class accommodation

Another change which took place after the introduction of the new DMUs was the general reduction in demand for first class accommodation. This led to the downgrading of first class seating to second class in many units. Often a decision was made to withdraw first class seating in a whole area, and many units were downgraded in name only, sometimes to be upgraded again when transferred away. For this reason individual changes are not noted but the symbol ② in the header is used to show diagram number changes.

Engines

Two types of engine were adopted for the majority of diesel mechanical units. British United Traction (BUT) was an organization set up to co-ordinate the efforts of AEC and Leyland in their efforts in the railway field. Hence the BUT (AEC) and BUT (Leyland) 150hp 6-cylinder horizontal engines. Early on there was very little interchange of engines, but from about 1976 onwards many AEC engines were replaced with more reliable Leyland engines. These changes led directly to the merging of classes 101 and 102 and classes 105 and 106 which had only been distinguished by the different engine types.

Parcels

While some units were built specifically as parcels units, from the earliest days many units were commandeered for parcels service, particularly at Christmas, and had their seats removed. Later on, some conversions were more complex, for example the fitting of roller shutter doors. Some of these changes resulted in renumbering, but some retained their old numbers. In other cases, some units were reclassified and some retained their original class numbers. Many class 114 units were converted for parcels use, but they were only renumbered when they were fitted with roller shutter doors.

Liveries

It is not my intention to cover the subject of liveries in this book, but in broad terms the 1950s and early 1960s was the green era, using several different shades of green. From the late 1960s blue was the predominant colour; all-over blue for most units and blue and grey for long-distance units. From the mid 1970s on refurbished units appeared in all-over white. By the 1980s blue and grey had become the predominant livery. Units still surviving towards the end of the eighties were in the era when a wide range of different liveries started to appear on BR, depending on the operator.

Headcodes

The period of the introduction of the first generation DMUs was a period of changing policy on the carrying of headcodes. In the same way that many of the first generation diesel locomotives carried a variety of different headcodes or marker discs, the DMU fleet varied in the provision given to train identification, even within classes. The earliest DMUs were fitted with marker lights, and following this two-digit headcode boxes were fitted. Later still four-digit headcode boxes were fitted. These changes can be seen by looking at the drawings shown in each of the class headers. Then, when headcodes ceased to be displayed in the 1970s, the reverse process took place with headcodes being removed, sometimes just painted over or fitted with marker lights, other times by being completely plated over.

Half Motors

All the first generation DMUs (with the exception of Classes 112 and 113 which were spectacularly unsuccessful) were built with two engines. In 1982 Class 104 unit M50446 and M50521 was experimentally modified with only one engine per carriage. This modification was known as Half-motors (they only had half the number of engines that they used to have).

Later in 1982 the Class 111 three-car units working in the Leeds area were reduced to two cars due to changes in operating requirements. It was decided that the new units were overpowered and the same Half-motor modification was undertaken between 1982 and 1985. By removing one motor and one set of transmission from each car, the intention was to reduce maintenance costs.

All Half-motors were renumbered in the 78xxx number series.

Class 114 BR Derby
Driving Motor Brake Second
DMBS
E50000

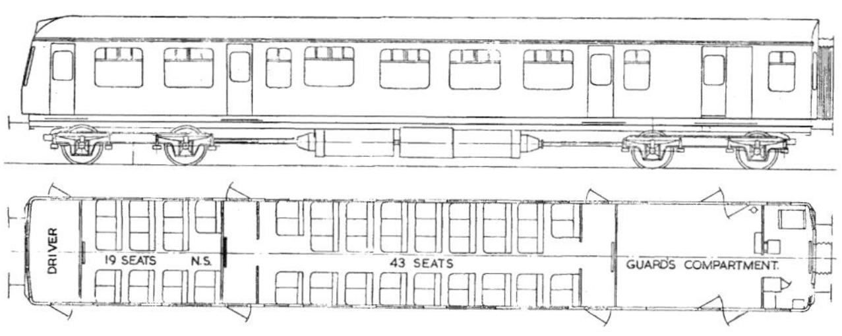

Coupling:	■ Blue square
Diagram:	632
Lot Number:	30341
Old class:	114
Engines:	Two Rolls-Royce 8-cyl horizontal type of 238 bhp.
Transmission:	Hydraulic. Twin-disc Torque Convertor
Body:	64' 6" × 9' 3"
Weight:	41t 3cwt
Seats:	62 second

E50000		03/57-10/67	⊗10/72	

Class 114 BR Derby
Driving Motor Brake Second
DMBS
E50001-E50048

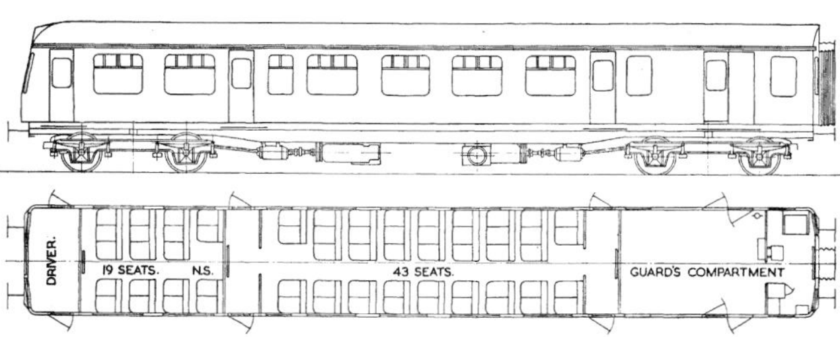

Coupling:	■ Blue square
Diagram:	516 DQ217
Lot Number:	30209
Old class:	114
Engines:	Two BUT (Leyland Albion) 6-cyl horizontal type of 230 bhp.
Transmission:	Mechanical. Standard
Body:	64' 6" × 9' 3"
Weight:	37t 10cwt
Seats:	62 second

E50001	06/83➲**53001**	10/56-06/88	⊗11/88	®11/78	
E50002	04/83➲**53002**	11/56-07/91	⊗11/91	®07/78	
E50003	05/83➲**53003**	11/56-02/88	⊗04/88	®02/81	
E50004	04/83➲**53004**	11/56-11/89	⊗04/90	®11/79	
E50005	04/83➲**53005**	11/56-10/91	⊗02/92	®01/81	
E50006	06/83➲**53006**	11/56-07/91	⊗11/91	® /81	
E50007	05/83➲**53007**	11/56-06/88	⊗12/88	®08/78	
E50008	/84➲**53008**	11/56-05/89	⊗02/91	® /81	
E50009	04/83➲**53009**	11/56-06/88	⊗01/89	®11/79	
E50010	02/83➲**53010**	12/56-08/87	⊗04/91	®05/83	08/87➲**55930**
E50011	04/83➲**53011**	11/56-06/88	⊗12/88	®01/78	
E50012	04/83➲**53012**	11/56-06/88	⊗11/88	®11/80	
E50013	05/83➲**53013**	12/56-06/88	⊗12/88	®01/78	
E50014	04/83➲**53014**	12/56-06/88	⊗11/88	®02/81	
E50015	04/83➲**53015**	02/57-07/89	℗	®07/78	07/89➲**55929**
E50016	04/83➲**53016**	02/57-09/86	⊗04/88	®03/78	
E50017	04/83➲**53017**	01/57-06/88	⊗12/88	®07/78	
E50018	11/83➲**53018**	01/57-07/89	⊗04/91	®10/77	07/89➲**55928**
E50019	06/83➲**53019**	01/57-06/92	℗	® /81	
E50020	06/83➲**53020**	01/57-05/90	⊗04/90	®07/79	
E50021	04/83➲**53021**	01/57-10/91	⊗11/91	® /82	
E50022	06/83➲**53022**	01/57-06/88	⊗12/88	®11/79	
E50023	04/83➲**53023**	01/57-02/88	⊗04/88	®07/79	
E50024	06/83➲**53024**	01/57-06/88	⊗12/88	®07/79	
E50025	/83➲**53025**	01/57-06/88	⊗12/88	®07/79	
E50026	08/83➲**53026**	01/57-03/89	⊗02/91	®11/79	
E50027	06/83➲**53027**	01/57-09/90	⊗04/91	®07/78	
E50028		01/57-08/62	⊗11/62		
E50029		01/57-12/71	⊗11/72		
E50030	05/83➲**53030**	01/57-12/90	⊗07/95	® /82	
E50031	04/83➲**53031**	01/57-06/88	⊗01/89	®11/79	
E50032	02/83➲**53032**	02/57-01/88	⊗04/91	®02/81	01/88➲**55932**
E50033	04/83➲**53033**	02/57-06/88	⊗11/88	®11/79	
E50034		02/57-12/71	⊗11/72		
E50035	04/83➲**53035**	03/57-11/89	⊗04/90	®03/78	
E50036	06/83➲**53036**	02/57-01/92	⊗07/93	®07/78	01/92➲**ADB977769**
E50037	04/83➲**53037**	02/57-03/89	⊗02/91	® /81	
E50038	06/83➲**53038**	02/57-03/89	⊗04/89	®11/77	
E50039	04/83➲**53039**	02/57-05/89	⊗02/91	® /82	
E50040	03/83➲**53040**	02/57-01/88	⊗04/91	®11/78	⊠09/86-10/86 01/88➲**55931**
E50041	10/83➲**53041**	03/57-06/88	⊗06/88	®02/81	
E50042	04/83➲**53042**	03/57-06/88	⊗11/88	®12/77	
E50043	08/83➲**53043**	03/57-06/88	⊗11/88	®04/78	
E50044	04/83➲**53044**	03/57-10/91	⊗11/91	®10/81	
E50045	06/83➲**53045**	03/57-06/88	⊗01/89	®11/78	
E50046	04/83➲**53046**	03/57-09/90	⊗04/91	®12/82	
E50047	06/83➲**53047**	04/57-06/88	⊗12/88	®07/80	
E50048		12/57-05/71	⊗06/73		

Class 114 BR Derby
Driving Motor Brake Second
DMBS
E50049

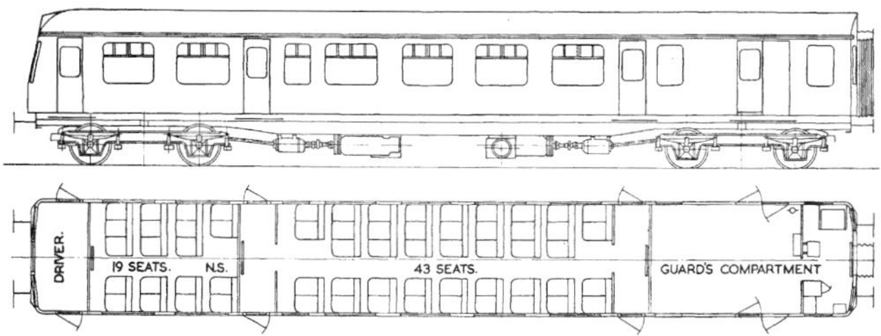

Coupling:	■ Blue square
Diagram:	516 DQ217
Lot Number:	30459
Old class:	114
Engines:	Two BUT (Leyland Albion) 6-cyl horizontal type of 230 bhp.
Transmission:	Mechanical. Standard. Fitted with Self-Changing Gears Ltd. automatic four-speed gearbox. This was replaced with a standard gearbox in 1976.
Body:	64' 6" × 9' 3"
Weight:	37t 10cwt
Seats:	62 second

E50049	06/83➲**53049**	08/57-01/84	⊗06/84	®11/78

Class 116 BR Derby
Driving Motor Brake Second
DMBS
W50050-W50091

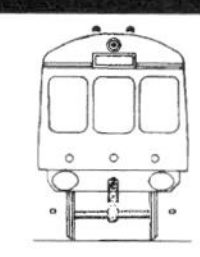

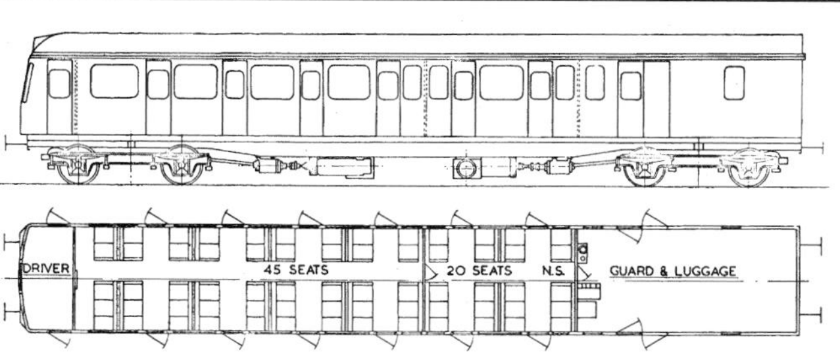

Diag. 553

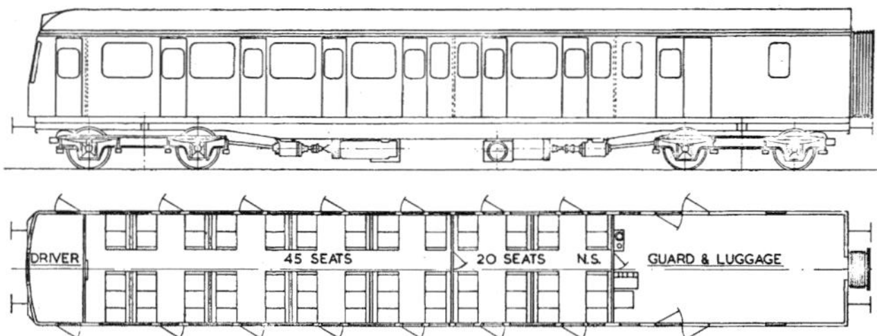

Diag. 853 ⓖ *Through gangway fitted* W50080-84/86-91 converted by 1972. Others (shown @) converted in the mid 1980s.

Coupling:	■ Blue square
Diagram:	553 DQ219 ⓖ 853 DQ230
Lot Number:	30211
Old class:	116/2
Engines:	Two BUT (Leyland) 6-cyl horizontal type of 150 bhp.
Transmission:	Mechanical. Standard
Body:	64' 0" × 9' 3" Suburban
Weight:	36t
Seats:	65 second

W50050	06/83➲**53050**	04/57-10/91	⊗03/92	@®03/79	01/63⇨**M**	
W50051	06/83➲**53051**	04/57-05/88	⊗09/88	®03/77	01/63⇨**M**	
W50052	04/83➲**53052**	05/57-01/88	⊗02/88	®04/77	01/63⇨**M**	
W50053	07/83➲**53053**	05/57-06/95	⊗06/95	@®06/82	01/63⇨**M**	
W50054	03/83➲**53054**	05/57-06/93	⊗06/93	@®05/83	01/63⇨**M**	
W50055	05/83➲**53055**	05/57-05/95	⊗08/95	@®09/83	01/63⇨**M**	
W50056	06/83➲**53056**	05/57-12/90	⊗05/91	@®01/81	01/63⇨**M**	
W50057	07/83➲**53057**	05/57-03/87	⊗04/87	®10/77	01/63⇨**M**	
W50058	06/83➲**53058**	05/57-10/91	⊗03/92	@®10/78	01/63⇨**M**	
W50059	04/83➲**53059**	08/57-11/88	⊗12/88	®01/80	01/63⇨**M**	
W50060	06/83➲**53060**	05/57-03/94	⊗03/94	@®02/84	01/63⇨**M**	
W50061	06/83➲**53061**	05/57-10/91	⊗11/91	@®05/76	01/63⇨**M**	
W50062	07/83➲**53062**	06/57-11/87	⊗11/87	®10/77	01/63⇨**M**	⊠03/83-05/83
W50063	06/83➲**53063**	06/57-03/88	⊗02/91		01/63⇨**M**	*08/88➲TDB977637*
W50064	07/83➲**53064**	06/57-04/87	⊗08/87	®09/77	01/63⇨**M**	
W50065	07/83➲**53065**	06/57-03/88	⊗03/88	®06/76	01/63⇨**M**	
W50066		08/57-07/82	⊗07/84		01/63⇨**M**	
W50067	06/83➲**53067**	05/57-10/87	⊗10/87	®07/78	01/63⇨**M**	
W50068	07/83➲**53068**	06/57-02/87	⊗02/87	®04/82	01/63⇨**M**	
W50069	06/83➲**53069**	06/57-05/87	⊗08/87	@®11/79	01/63⇨**M**	
W50070	08/83➲**53070**	08/57-03/88	⊗03/88	®06/77	01/63⇨**M**	
W50071	03/83➲**53071**	08/57-08/93	⊗09/93	@®07/83	01/63⇨**M**	⊠05/93-08/93
W50072	06/83➲**53072**	06/57-05/88	⊗09/88	®08/76	01/63⇨**M**	
W50073	07/83➲**53073**	06/57-10/92	⊗10/92	@®12/82	01/63⇨**M**	
W50074	07/83➲**53074**	08/57-08/87	⊗01/88	®01/78	01/63⇨**M**	
W50075	07/83➲**53075**	08/57-12/87	⊗01/88		01/63⇨**M**	
W50076	06/83➲**53076**	08/57-11/87	⊗10/87	®09/77	01/63⇨**M**	
W50077	06/83➲**53077**	08/57-03/88	⊗03/88	®11/76	01/63⇨**M**	
W50078	04/83➲**53078**	08/57-11/88	⊗12/88	®11/79	01/63⇨**M**	
W50079	07/83➲**53079**	09/57-04/92	⊗10/92	@®04/78	01/63⇨**M**	
W50080	04/83➲**53080**	10/57-10/89	⊗05/90	ⓖ®02/77		
W50081	04/83➲**53081**	10/57-10/88	⊗03/89	ⓖ®10/80	05/76⇨**M**	
W50082	05/85➲**53082**	08/57-11/90	⊗05/91	ⓖ®08/80	05/77⇨**M**	
W50083	04/83➲**53083**	08/57-09/92	⊗05/93	ⓖ®11/77		
W50084	03/83➲**53084**	08/57-12/86	⊗08/87	ⓖ®11/77		
W50085		08/57-07/75	⊗07/76		01/63⇨**M**	
W50086	04/83➲**53086**	09/57-10/89	⊗05/90	ⓖ®11/77		
W50087	04/83➲**53087**	09/57-12/88	⊗03/89	ⓖ®07/76		
W50088	04/83➲**53088**	09/57-04/87	⊗08/87	ⓖ®06/78		
W50089	04/83➲**53089**	09/57-06/89	⊗08/89	ⓖ®02/77		
W50090	03/83➲**53090**	09/57-05/93	⊗09/93	ⓖ®08/83	03/76⇨**M** 11/78⇨**SC**	
W50091	04/83➲**53091**	10/57-12/88	⊗03/89	ⓖ®06/78		

Class 116 BR Derby
Driving Motor Second
DMS
W50092-W50133

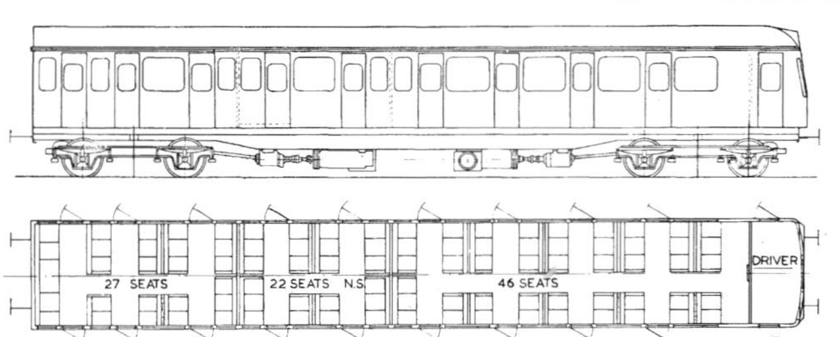

Diag. 554

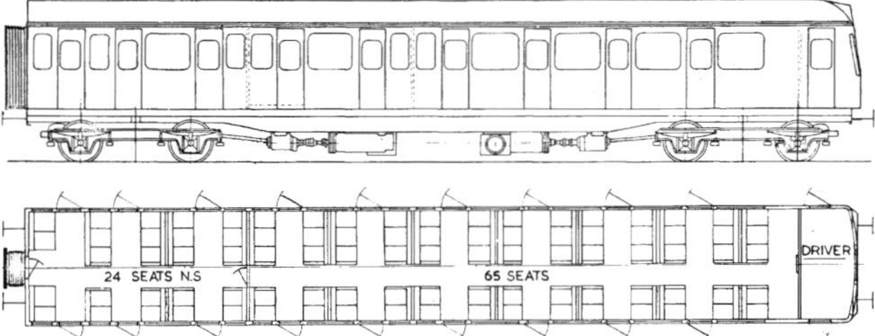

Diag. 854 ⓖ *Through gangway fitted* W50122-26/28-33 converted by 1972. Others (shown @) converted in the mid 1980s.

Coupling:	■ Blue square
Diagram:	554 DP201 ⓖ 854 DP220
Lot Number:	30213
Old class:	116/1
Engines:	Two BUT (Leyland) 6-cyl horizontal type of 150 bhp.
Transmission:	Mechanical. Standard
Body:	64' 0" × 9' 3" Suburban
Weight:	36t
Seats:	95 second ⓖ 89 second

W50092	06/83➲**53092**	04/57-10/92	⊗03/93	@®05/76	01/63⇨**M**	
W50093	06/83➲**53093**	04/57-10/92	⊗09/97	@®07/78	01/63⇨**M**	⊠06/92-09/92 10/92➲**TDB977829**
W50094	07/83➲**53094**	05/57-08/87	⊗05/88	®06/76	01/63⇨**M**	
W50095	08/83➲**53095**	05/57-03/88	⊗03/88	®06/77	01/63⇨**M**	
W50096		05/57-10/67	⊗		01/63⇨**M**	
W50097	07/83➲**53097**	05/57-11/87	⊗11/87	®10/77	01/63⇨**M**	
W50098	06/83➲**53098**	05/57-07/88	⊗02/88	®01/81	01/63⇨**M**	
W50099	06/83➲**53099**	05/57-05/87	⊗08/87	®07/78	01/63⇨**M**	
W50100	06/83➲**53100**	05/57-02/88	⊗02/88	®09/81	01/63⇨**M**	
W50101	03/83➲**53101**	08/57-01/94	⊗08/95	@®07/83	01/63⇨**M**	
W50102	03/83➲**53102**	05/57-05/93	⊗09/93	@®09/79	01/63⇨**M**	
W50103	07/83➲**53103**	05/57-11/87	⊗11/87		01/63⇨**M**	
W50104	04/83➲**53104**	06/57-02/87	⊗02/87	®01/80	01/63⇨**M**	
W50105	06/83➲**53105**	06/57-03/87	⊗02/87	®08/76	01/63⇨**M**	
W50106	03/83➲**53106**	06/57-01/94	⊗03/94	@®05/83	01/63⇨**M**	
W50107	03/83➲**53107**	06/57-12/85	⊗08/86	®04/77	01/63⇨**M**	
W50108	06/83➲**53108**	08/57-12/87	⊗05/88		01/63⇨**M**	
W50109	04/83➲**53109**	05/57-11/88	⊗12/88	®11/79	01/63⇨**M**	
W50110	07/83➲**53110**	06/57-11/87	⊗11/87	®01/78	01/63⇨**M**	
W50111	06/83➲**53111**	06/57-05/87	⊗08/87		01/63⇨**M**	
W50112	06/83➲**53112**	08/57-01/88	⊗12/87	®10/78	01/63⇨**M**	
W50113	06/83➲**53113**	07/57-12/85	⊗08/86	®03/77	01/63⇨**M**	
W50114	06/83➲**53114**	06/57-06/95	⊗06/95	@®10/83	01/63⇨**M**	
W50115		06/57-07/80	⊗09/82	®09/77	01/63⇨**M**	
W50116	05/83➲**53116**	08/57-06/95	⊗06/95	@®09/83	01/63⇨**M**	
W50117	06/83➲**53117**	08/57-11/88	⊗12/88	®10/77	01/63⇨**M**	
W50118	06/83➲**53118**	08/57-11/87	⊗11/87	®09/77	01/63⇨**M**	
W50119	06/83➲**53119**	08/57-03/88	⊗02/91		01/63⇨**M**	*08/88➲TDB977636*
W50120	06/83➲**53120**	08/57-03/88	⊗03/88	®11/76	01/63⇨**M**	
W50121	07/83➲**53121**	09/57-03/88	⊗03/88	®04/78	01/63⇨**M**	
W50122	04/83➲**53122**	10/57-10/89	⊗05/90	ⓖ®02/77		
W50123	04/83➲**53123**	10/57-04/88	⊗01/89	ⓖ®10/80	05/76⇨**M**	
W50124	06/83➲**53124**	08/57-05/95	⊗08/95	ⓖ®08/80	05/77⇨**M**	
W50125		08/57-08/61	⊗10/61			
W50126	03/83➲**53126**	08/57-12/86	⊗08/87	ⓖ®11/77		
W50127	06/83➲**53127**	08/57-11/87	⊗11/87		01/63⇨**M**	
W50128	04/83➲**53128**	09/57-10/89	⊗05/90	ⓖ®11/77		
W50129	04/83➲**53129**	09/57-06/88	⊗10/88	ⓖ®07/76		
W50130	04/83➲**53130**	09/57-04/87	⊗08/87	ⓖ®06/78		
W50131	04/83➲**53131**	09/57-08/89	⊗01/90	ⓖ®02/77		
W50132	03/83➲**53132**	09/57-06/95	⊗06/95	ⓖ®08/83	03/76⇨**M** 11/78⇨**SC**	⊠11/90-12/90
W50133	04/83➲**53133**	10/57-06/88	⊗06/88	ⓖ®06/78		

Class 111 Metropolitan-Cammell

Driving Motor Brake Second
DMBS
M50134-M50137

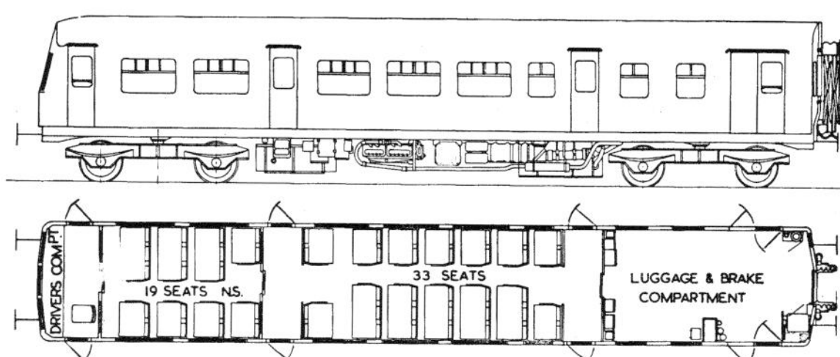

Coupling:	■ Blue square
Diagram:	520 DQ214
Lot Number:	30248
Old class:	111/2
Engines:	Two Rolls-Royce 6-cyl horizontal type of 180 bhp. s Two Rolls-Royce 6-cyl type supercharged to 230 bhp. until about 1967.
Transmission:	Mechanical. Standard
Body:	57' 6" × 9' 3"
Weight:	33t
Seats:	52 second

M50134	04/83➲**53134**	04/57-11/87	⊗08/89	®06/76	04/66⇨**NE**	01/68⇨**E** 11/87➲**TDB977538**
M50135	/83➲**53135**	04/57-11/87	⊗08/89	®07/76	04/66⇨**NE**	01/68⇨**E** 11/87➲**TDB977539**
M50136	05/83➲**53136**	04/57-02/87	⊗02/89 s	®03/78	04/66⇨**NE**	01/68⇨**E**
M50137	04/83➲**53137**	04/57-11/87	⊗08/89	®04/77	04/66⇨**NE**	01/68⇨**E** 11/87➲**TDB977540**

Class 101 Metropolitan-Cammell

Driving Motor Composite Lavatory
DMCL
E50138-E50151

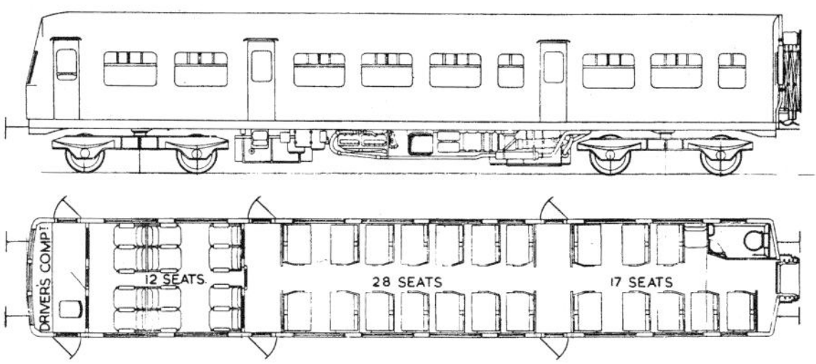

Coupling:	■ Blue square
Diagram:	618 DP301 ②DP212
Lot Number:	30249
Old class:	101/1
Engines:	Two BUT (AEC) 6-cyl horizontal type of 150 bhp.
Transmission:	Mechanical. Standard
Body:	57' 6" × 9' 3"
Weight:	32t
Seats:	12 first, 45 second

E50138	08/83➲**53138**	10/56-05/87	⊗01/88	®02/81	01/65⇨**NE**	01/68⇨**E**	02/78⇨**SC**
E50139	02/85➲**53139**	10/56-04/92	⊗10/92	® /82	01/65⇨**NE**	01/68⇨**E**	
E50140	08/83➲**53140**	10/56-01/87	⊗09/88	®*10/76*	01/65⇨**NE**	01/68⇨**E**	
E50141	08/83➲**53141**	10/56-05/89	⊗09/90	®08/79	01/65⇨**NE**	01/68⇨**E**	05/77⇨**SC**
E50142	03/83➲**53142**	10/56-09/86	⊗12/86	®02/81	01/65⇨**NE**	01/68⇨**E**	
E50143	08/83➲**53143**	10/56-05/87	⊗09/87		01/65⇨**NE**	01/68⇨**E**	05/77⇨**SC**
E50144	08/83➲**53144**	11/56-04/88	⊗06/90	®08/79	01/65⇨**NE**	01/68⇨**E**	04/77⇨**SC**
E50145		11/56-07/79	⊗12/81		01/65⇨**NE**	01/68⇨**E**	04/77⇨**SC**
E50146	08/83➲**53146**	11/56-10/91	⊗06/92	®08/82	01/65⇨**NE**	01/68⇨**E**	02/78⇨**SC**
E50147	01/84➲**53147**	11/56-07/87	⊗01/88	®10/80	01/65⇨**NE**	01/68⇨**E**	06/78⇨**SC**
E50148	08/83➲**53148**	11/56-03/87	⊗01/88	®10/80	01/65⇨**NE**	01/68⇨**E**	05/77⇨**SC**
E50149	06/83➲**53149**	11/56-03/92	⊗10/92	® /82	01/65⇨**NE**	01/68⇨**E**	
E50150	06/83➲**53150**	11/56-10/89	⊗03/92	®10/81	01/65⇨**NE**	01/68⇨**E**	
E50151	02/85➲**53151**	11/56-09/86	⊗02/87	®02/81	01/65⇨**NE**	01/68⇨**E**	

Class 101 Metropolitan-Cammell

Driving Motor Brake Second
DMBS
E50152-E50157

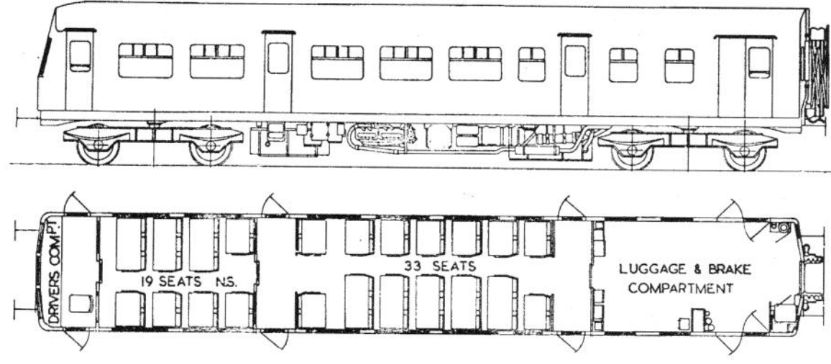

Coupling:	■ Blue square
Diagram:	523 DQ202
Lot Number:	30252
Old class:	101/2
Engines:	Two BUT (AEC) 6-cyl horizontal type of 150 bhp.
Transmission:	Mechanical. Standard
Body:	57' 6" × 9' 3"
Weight:	32t
Seats:	52 second

E50152		12/56-05/80	⊗02/82	®07/78	01/65⇨**NE**	03/66⇨**SC**	05/68⇨**E**
E50153	05/83➲**53153**	12/56-10/87	⊗11/87	®02/81	01/65⇨**NE**	03/66⇨**SC**	05/68⇨**E**
E50154	05/83➲**53154**	12/56-02/85	⊗03/85	®07/79	01/65⇨**NE**	01/68⇨**E**	
E50155	04/83➲**53155**	12/56-04/92	⊗02/93	®01/77	01/65⇨**NE**	01/68⇨**E**	
E50156	05/83➲**53156**	01/57-03/86	⊗10/86	®07/79	01/65⇨**NE**	01/68⇨**E**	
E50157	07/83➲**53157**	01/57-02/91	⊗02/91	®02/81	01/65⇨**NE**	01/68⇨**E**	

Class 101 Metropolitan-Cammell

Driving Motor Composite Lavatory
DMCL
E50158-E50163

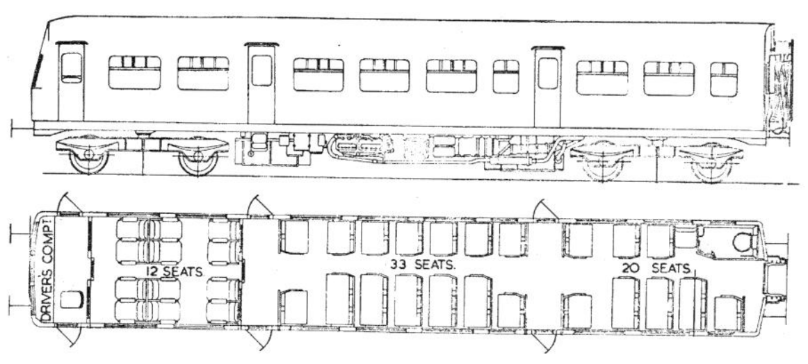

Coupling:	■ Blue square
Diagram:	620 DP303 ②DP214
Lot Number:	30253
Old class:	101/1
Engines:	Two BUT (AEC) 6-cyl horizontal type of 150 bhp.
Transmission:	Mechanical. Standard
Body:	57' 6" × 9' 3"
Weight:	32t
Seats:	12 first, 53 second

E50158	08/83➲**53158**	12/56-01/91	⊗02/91	®02/82	01/65⇨**NE**	03/66⇨**SC**	
E50159	08/83➲**53159**	12/56-05/89	⊗08/90	®10/80	01/65⇨**NE**	03/66⇨**SC**	
E50160	08/83➲**53160**	12/56-12/03	Ⓟ	®02/82	01/65⇨**NE**	01/68⇨**E**	09/79⇨**SC**
E50161	*/84*➲**53161**	12/56-10/88	⊗09/90	®05/76	01/65⇨**NE**	01/68⇨**E**	
E50162	05/83➲**53162**	01/57-09/89	⊗05/90	®08/78	01/65⇨**NE**	01/68⇨**E**	
E50163	08/83➲**53163**	01/57-08/02	⊗01/04	®04/83	01/65⇨**NE**	01/68⇨**E**	04/79⇨**SC**

Class 101 Metropolitan-Cammell
Driving Motor Brake Second
DMBS
E50164-E50167

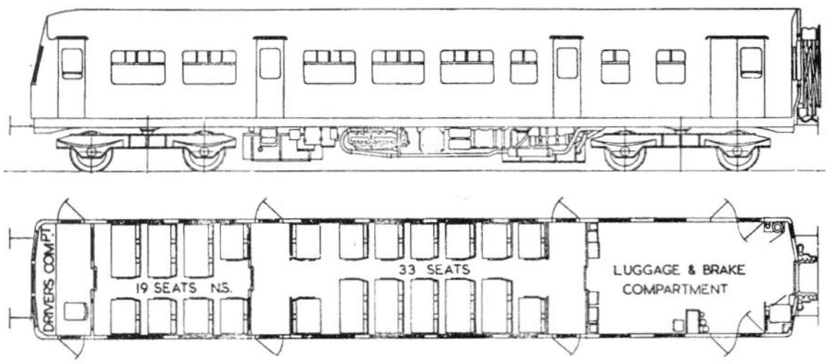

Coupling: ■ Blue square
Diagram: 523 DQ202
Lot Number: 30254
Old class: 101/2
Engines: Two BUT (AEC) 6-cyl horizontal type of 150 bhp.
Transmission: Mechanical. Standard
Body: 57' 6" × 9' 3"
Weight: 32t
Seats: 52 second

E50164 05/83➲**53164** 01/57-12/03 Ⓟ ® /82 01/65⇨**NE** 01/68⇨**E**

E50165 06/83➲**53165** 01/57-06/93 ⊗12/93 ® /81 01/65⇨**NE** 01/68⇨**E**

E50166 06/83➲**53166** 01/57-10/88 ⊗10/88 ®01/78 01/65⇨**NE** 01/68⇨**E**

E50167 05/83➲**53167** 01/57-02/87 Ⓟ ®07/79 01/65⇨**NE** 01/68⇨**E** 04/89➲DB977392

Class 101 Metropolitan-Cammell
Driving Motor Composite Lavatory
DMCL
E50168-E50171

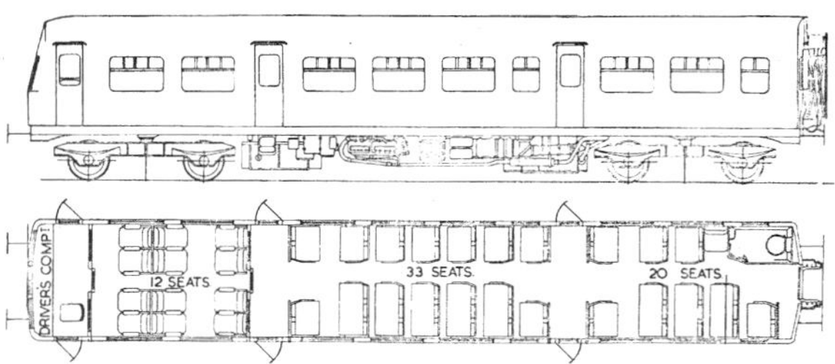

Coupling: ■ Blue square
Diagram: 620 DP303 ②DP214
Lot Number: 30255
Old class: 101/1
Engines: Two BUT (AEC) 6-cyl horizontal type of 150 bhp.
Transmission: Mechanical. Standard
Body: 57' 6" × 9' 3"
Weight: 32t
Seats: 12 first, 53 second

E50168 08/83➲**53168** 01/57-05/93 ⊗07/93 ® /81 01/65⇨**NE** 01/68⇨**E** 10/75⇨**W** 05/76⇨**E**

E50169 */84*➲**53169** 01/57-01/90 ⊗08/90 ®05/76 01/65⇨**NE** 01/68⇨**E** ☒09/89-10/89

E50170 06/83➲**53170** 01/57-12/03 Ⓟ ® /82 01/65⇨**NE** 01/68⇨**E**

E50171 06/83➲**53171** 01/57-12/01 ⊗12/03 ® /82 01/65⇨**NE** 01/68⇨**E**

Class 101 Metropolitan-Cammell
Driving Motor Composite Lavatory
DMCL
E50172-E50197

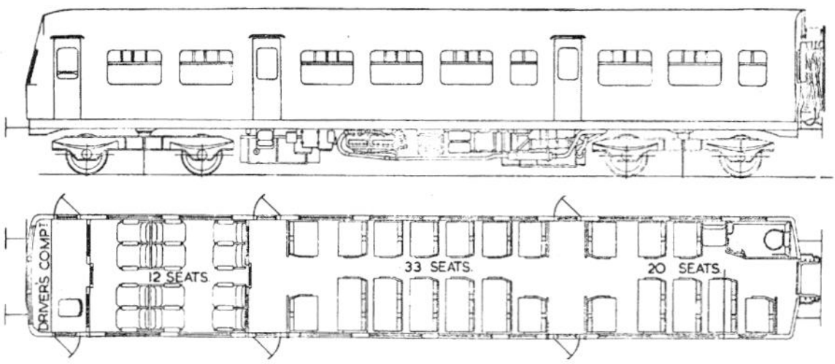

Coupling: ■ Blue square
Diagram: 620 DP303 ②DP214
Lot Number: 30256
Old class: 101/1
Engines: Two BUT (AEC) 6-cyl horizontal type of 150 bhp.
Transmission: Mechanical. Standard
Body: 57' 6" × 9' 3"
Weight: 32t
Seats: 12 first, 53 second

E50172 08/83➲**53172** 01/57-07/87 ⊗07/87 ®06/81 01/65⇨**NE** 01/68⇨**E** 04/78⇨**SC**

E50173 01/57-10/57 ⊗*11/57*

E50174 08/83➲**53174** 02/57-05/87 ⊗07/87 ®06/78 01/65⇨**NE** 03/66⇨**SC**

E50175 08/83➲**53175** 02/57-05/87 ⊗09/87 ®06/78 01/65⇨**NE** 03/66⇨**SC**

E50176 08/83➲**53176** 02/57-12/90 ⊗08/91 ®06/81 01/65⇨**NE** 01/68⇨**E** 05/77⇨**SC**

E50177 05/83➲**53177** 02/57-04/00 ⊗09/03 ® /81 01/65⇨**NE** 01/68⇨**E**

E50178 05/85➲**53178** 02/57-10/88 ⊗06/89 ®02/80 01/65⇨**NE** 01/68⇨**E**

E50179 02/85➲**53179** 02/57-10/87 ⊗06/91 ®02/81 01/65⇨**NE** 01/68⇨**E**

E50180 07/83➲**53180** 02/57-03/92 ⊗10/92 ® /81 01/65⇨**NE** 01/68⇨**E**

E50181 08/83➲**53181** 02/57-11/92 ⊗02/93 ®11/80 01/65⇨**NE** 01/68⇨**E**

E50182 05/85➲**53182** 03/57-09/89 ⊗09/90 ®11/79 01/65⇨**NE** 01/68⇨**E**

E50183 05/83➲**53183** 03/57-10/87 ⊗07/90 ®02/81 01/65⇨**NE** 01/68⇨**E**

E50184 08/83➲**53184** 02/57-11/85 ⊗10/87 ®06/80 01/65⇨**NE** 01/68⇨**E** 04/78⇨**SC**

E50185 08/83➲**53185** 02/57-02/91 ⊗04/91 ®06/81 01/65⇨**NE** 01/68⇨**E** 04/78⇨**SC**

E50186 08/83➲**53186** 03/57-10/89 ⊗05/91 ®*10/76* 01/65⇨**NE** 03/66⇨**SC**

E50187 08/83➲**53187** 03/57-12/89 ⊗08/91 ®02/77 01/65⇨**NE** 03/66⇨**SC**

E50188 07/83➲**53188** 03/57-06/89 ⊗09/90 ®11/79 01/65⇨**NE** 01/68⇨**E**

E50189 06/83➲**53189** 03/57-11/91 ⊗02/93 01/65⇨**NE** 01/68⇨**E** 03/77⇨**M** 04/79⇨**SC**

E50190 03/57-07/73 ⊗ */76* 01/65⇨**NE** 01/68⇨**E**

E50191 01/84➲**53191** 03/57-10/88 ⊗06/89 ® */80* 01/65⇨**NE** 01/68⇨**E**

E50192 */85*➲**53192** 03/57-10/87 ⊗06/90 ®10/80 01/65⇨**NE** 01/68⇨**E** 04/78⇨**SC**

E50193 04/83➲**53193** 03/57-06/93 Ⓟ ®*10/76* 01/65⇨**NE** 01/68⇨**E** 06/93➲**DB977898**

E50194 08/83➲**53194** 04/57-11/90 ⊗04/91 ®06/81 01/65⇨**NE** 01/68⇨**E** 08/77⇨**SC**

E50195 05/85➲**53195** 04/57-09/89 ⊗12/89 ® */80* 01/65⇨**NE** 01/68⇨**E**

E50196 06/83➲**53196** 04/57-11/89 ⊗04/90 ®05/78 01/65⇨**NE** 01/68⇨**E** ☒09/89-10/89

E50197 08/83➲**53197** 04/57-12/87 ⊗08/92 ®01/83 01/65⇨**NE** 01/68⇨**E** 03/77⇨**M** 04/79⇨**SC** 11/90➲**TDB977652**

Class 101 Metropolitan-Cammell
Driving Motor Brake Second
DMBS
E50198-E50209

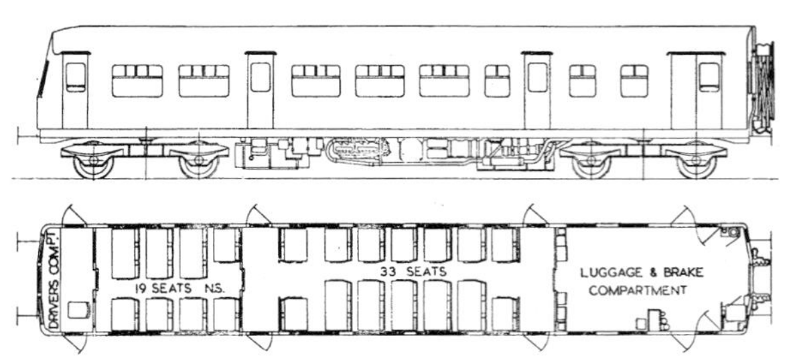

Coupling: ■ Blue square
Diagram: 523 DQ202
Lot Number: 30259
Old class: 101/2
Engines: Two BUT (AEC) 6-cyl horizontal type of 150 bhp.
Transmission: Mechanical. Standard
Body: 57' 6" × 9' 3"

Weight: 32t
Seats: 52 second

E50198	04/83➲**53198**	04/57-01/98	⊗01/98	®07/76	01/65⇨**NE**	01/68⇨**E**	
E50199	04/83➲**53199**	04/57-01/87	⊗06/89	®07/78	01/65⇨**NE**	01/68⇨**E**	
E50200	02/83➲**53200**	05/57-05/93	⊗04/03	®06/83	01/65⇨**NE**	01/68⇨**E**	
						05/93➲**DB977901**	
E50201	09/83➲**53201**	05/57-05/99	⊗05/99	®07/79	01/65⇨**NE**	01/68⇨**E**	
E50202	07/83➲**53202**	05/57-06/93	⊗12/95	®*10/76*	01/65⇨**NE**	01/68⇨**E**	
E50203	06/83➲**53203**	05/57-06/93	Ⓟ	®01/80	01/65⇨**NE**	04/66⇨**M**	
						06/93➲**DB977897**	
E50204	02/83➲**53204**	05/57-12/03	Ⓟ	®07/79	01/65⇨**NE**	01/68⇨**E**	
E50205	*/85*➲**53205**	04/57-10/88	⊗06/89	®02/81	01/65⇨**NE**	01/68⇨**E**	
E50206	04/83➲**53206**	04/57-11/87	⊗03/88	®10/77	01/65⇨**NE**	04/66⇨**M**	
E50207	05/84➲**53207**	05/57-12/91	⊗03/92	®04/77	01/65⇨**NE**	01/68⇨**E**	
E50208	06/83➲**53208**	05/57-06/93	⊗04/03	®10/76	01/65⇨**NE**	04/66⇨**M**	
						10/93➲**DB977903**	
E50209	*/84*➲**53209**	05/57-05/86	⊗02/88	®02/81	01/65⇨**NE**	01/68⇨**E**	08/69⇨**SC**
					08/77⇨**E**		

Class 101 Metropolitan-Cammell

Driving Motor Brake Second

DMBS

E50210-E50233

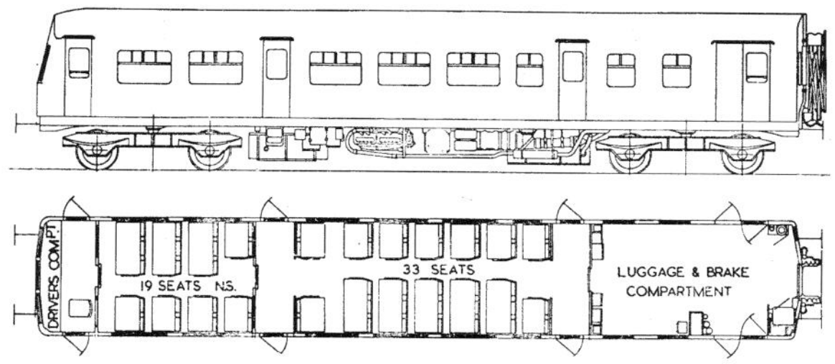

Coupling: ■ Blue square
Diagram: 523 DQ202
Lot Number: 30261
Old class: 101/2
Engines: Two BUT (AEC) 6-cyl horizontal type of 150 bhp.
Transmission: Mechanical. Standard
Body: 57' 6" × 9' 3"
Weight: 32t
Seats: 52 second

E50210	02/83➲**53210**	05/57-03/87	⊗01/88	®02/81	01/65⇨**NE**	01/68⇨**E**	
E50211	04/83➲**53211**	05/57-01/02	⊗12/03	® /82	01/65⇨**NE**	01/68⇨**E**	
E50212	05/83➲**53212**	06/57-11/90	⊗03/91	® /81	01/65⇨**NE**	01/68⇨**E**	
E50213		06/57-03/77	⊗01/82		01/65⇨**NE**	01/68⇨**E**	
E50214	04/83➲**53214**	06/57-02/89	⊗04/90	®01/78	01/65⇨**NE**	01/68⇨**E**	
E50215	04/83➲**53215**	07/57-10/89	⊗09/91	®11/79	01/65⇨**NE**	01/68⇨**E**	
E50216	04/83➲**53216**	07/57-05/93	⊗12/93	®04/77	01/65⇨**NE**	01/68⇨**E**	
E50217	05/83➲**53217**	07/57-10/88	⊗10/88	®04/77	01/65⇨**NE**	01/68⇨**E**	
E50218	05/83➲**53218**	07/57-05/89	⊗01/92	®11/79	01/65⇨**NE**	01/68⇨**E**	
						☒09/86-10/86	
E50219	04/83➲**53219**	07/57-10/89	⊗09/89	®07/79	01/65⇨**NE**	01/68⇨**E**	
E50220	04/83➲**53220**	07/57-10/88	⊗04/90	®07/78	01/65⇨**NE**	01/68⇨**E**	
E50221	06/83➲**53221**	08/57-07/89	⊗04/90	®07/78	01/65⇨**NE**	01/68⇨**E**	
						☒09/86-12/86	
E50222	06/83➲**53222**	06/57-08/90	Ⓟ	®05/80	01/65⇨**NE**	01/68⇨**E**	09/79⇨**M**
						04/91➲**RDB977693**	
E50223	08/83➲**53223**	06/57-02/91	⊗02/91	®06/81	01/65⇨**NE**	01/68⇨**E**	
E50224	05/83➲**53224**	06/57-11/90	⊗04/91	®06/76	01/65⇨**NE**	01/68⇨**E**	
E50225	08/83➲**53225**	06/57-07/86	⊗02/87	®07/79	01/65⇨**NE**	01/68⇨**E**	
E50226	05/83➲**53226**	07/57-05/87	⊗08/88	®04/77	01/65⇨**NE**	01/68⇨**E**	
E50227	04/83➲**53227**	07/57-03/88	⊗01/89	®*10/76*	01/65⇨**NE**	01/68⇨**E**	
E50228	04/83➲**53228**	07/57-01/01	⊗03/04	® /82	01/65⇨**NE**	04/66⇨**M**	
E50229	04/83➲**53229**	07/57-03/89	⊗04/90	®11/79	01/65⇨**NE**	01/68⇨**E**	
E50230	06/83➲**53230**	08/57-05/89	⊗01/92	®07/79	01/65⇨**NE**	01/68⇨**E**	
						☒09/86-10/86	
E50231	05/83➲**53231**	08/57-05/93	⊗04/03	®02/81	01/65⇨**NE**	01/68⇨**E**	
						05/93➲**DB977902**	
E50232	05/83➲**53232**	08/57-02/85	⊗03/85	®02/78	01/65⇨**NE**	01/68⇨**E**	
E50233	04/84➲**53233**	09/57-07/89	⊗04/90	®07/78	01/65⇨**NE**	01/68⇨**E**	

Class 101 Metropolitan-Cammell

Driving Motor Composite Lavatory

DMCL

E50234-E50245

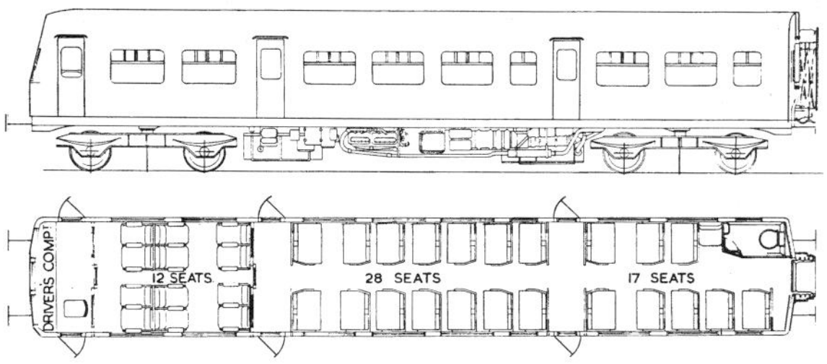

Coupling: ■ Blue square
Diagram: 619 DP302 ②DP213
Lot Number: 30263
Old class: 101/1
Engines: Two BUT (AEC) 6-cyl horizontal type of 150 bhp.
Transmission: Mechanical. Standard
Body: 57' 6" × 9' 3"
Weight: 32t
Seats: 12 first, 45 second

E50234	*/85*➲**53234**	09/57-07/88	⊗06/89	®05/80	01/65⇨**NE**	01/68⇨**E**	04/77⇨**SC**
E50235	02/85➲**53235**	09/57-02/90	⊗08/90	®02/80	01/65⇨**NE**	01/68⇨**E**	
E50236		09/57-09/65	⊗03/67		01/65⇨*NE*		
E50237	07/83➲**53237**	09/57-12/89	⊗08/90		01/65⇨**NE**	01/68⇨**E**	09/79⇨**M**
E50238	05/84➲**53238**	10/57-04/92	⊗10/92	® /82	01/65⇨**NE**	01/68⇨**E**	
E50239	08/83➲**53239**	10/57-12/90	⊗08/91	® /82	01/65⇨**NE**	01/68⇨**E**	06/78⇨**SC**
E50240	02/85➲**53240**	10/57-10/89	⊗05/90	®02/80	01/65⇨**NE**	01/68⇨**E**	10/75⇨**W**
					05/76⇨**E**		
E50241	08/83➲**53241**	10/57-02/92	⊗01/94	® /82	01/65⇨**NE**	01/68⇨**E**	04/79⇨**SC**
E50242	03/83➲**53242**	10/57-11/92	⊗10/92	®04/83	01/65⇨**NE**	01/68⇨**E**	04/77⇨**SC**
E50243	08/83➲**53243**	10/57-10/92	⊗01/94	®06/81	01/65⇨**NE**	01/68⇨**E**	04/77⇨**SC**
E50244	03/83➲**53244**	10/57-10/90	⊗11/90	® /81	01/65⇨**NE**	01/68⇨**E**	
E50245	08/83➲**53245**	10/57-07/93	⊗08/93	® /82	01/65⇨**NE**	01/68⇨**E**	10/75⇨**W**
					05/76⇨**E**	08/77⇨**SC**	

Class 101 Metropolitan-Cammell

Driving Motor Brake Second

DMBS

E50246-E50248

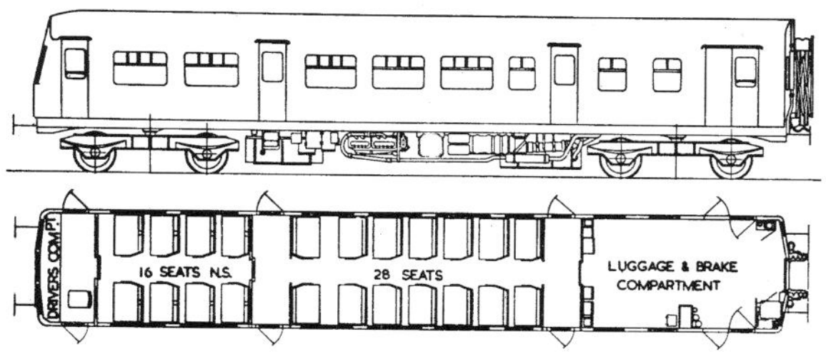

Coupling: ■ Blue square
Diagram: 522 DQ203
Lot Number: 30339
Old class: 101/2
Engines: Two BUT (AEC) 6-cyl horizontal type of 150 bhp.
Transmission: Mechanical. Standard
Body: 57' 6" × 9' 3"
Weight: 32t
Seats: 44 second

E50246	07/83➲**53246**	09/57-02/87	⊗06/93	®11/78	01/65⇨**NE**	01/68⇨**E**	
						07/89➲**DB977393**	
E50247	05/83➲**53247**	09/57-11/90	⊗02/91	® */81*	01/65⇨**NE**	01/68⇨**E**	
E50248	07/83➲**53248**	09/57-02/91	⊗03/91	® */82*	01/65⇨**NE**	01/68⇨**E**	

Class 105 Cravens

Driving Motor Brake Second
DMBS
E50249

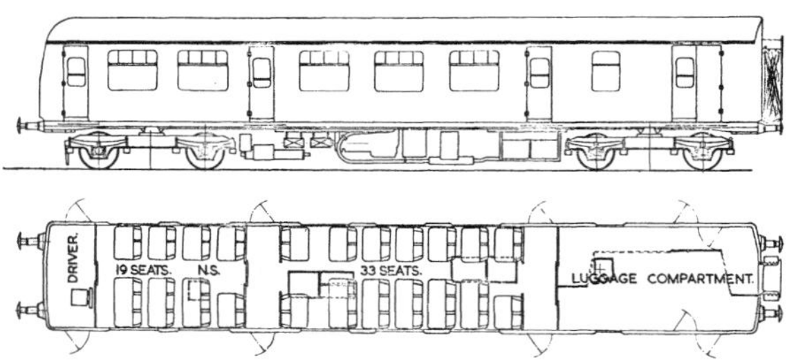

Coupling: ■ Blue square
Diagram: 548
Lot Number: 30505
Old class: 105/2
Engines: Two BUT (AEC) 6-cyl horizontal type of 150 bhp.
Transmission: Mechanical. Standard
Body: 57' 6" × 9' 3"
Weight: 30t 10cwt
Seats: 52 second

E50249		09/59-04/78	⊗06/80		01/65⇨**NE**	01/68⇨**E**

Class 102⇨101 Metropolitan-Cammell

Driving Motor Brake Second
DMBS
E50250-E50259

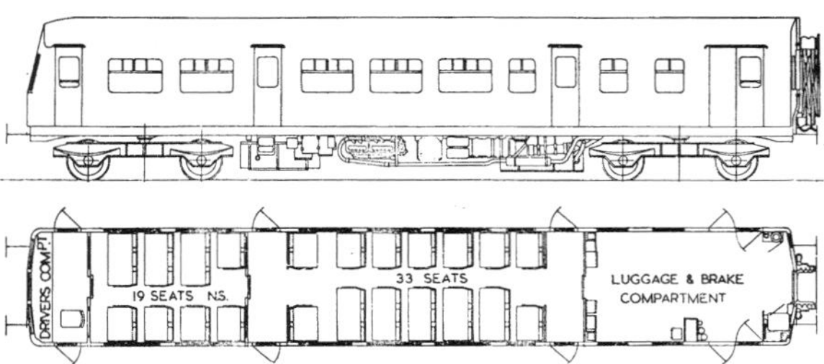

Coupling: ■ Blue square
Diagram: 523 DQ202
Lot Number: 30266
Old class: 102/2
Engines: Two BUT (AEC) 6-cyl horizontal type of 150 bhp.
Transmission: Mechanical. Standard
Body: 57' 6" × 9' 3"
Weight: 32t
Seats: 52 second

E50250	07/83➲**53250**	06/57-10/92	⊗02/93	®07/79	01/65⇨**NE**	01/68⇨**E**	
E50251	05/83➲**53251**	06/57-02/89	⊗03/89	®11/79	01/65⇨**NE**	01/68⇨**E**	
E50252	05/83➲**53252**	07/57-12/88	⊗04/90	®03/80	01/65⇨**NE**	01/68⇨**E**	
E50253	04/83➲**53253**	07/57-12/03	Ⓟ	® /82	01/65⇨**NE**	01/68⇨**E**	
E50254	08/83➲**53254**	08/57-12/87	⊗09/88	®08/79	01/65⇨**NE**	01/68⇨**E**	08/69⇨**SC**
E50255	05/83➲**53255**	09/57-07/89	⊗04/90	®07/78	01/65⇨**NE**	01/68⇨**E**	
E50256	05/83➲**53256**	10/57-06/01	Ⓟ	®11/80	01/65⇨**NE**	01/68⇨**E**	
E50257	04/83➲**53257**	10/57-09/89	⊗09/90	®01/78	01/65⇨**NE**	01/68⇨**E**	
E50258	04/83➲**53258**	10/57-08/88	⊗11/89	®07/79	01/65⇨**NE**	01/68⇨**E**	
E50259	08/83➲**53259**	10/57-11/87	⊗02/93	®07/79	01/65⇨**NE**	01/68⇨**E** 11/87➲**TDB977535**	

Class 102⇨101 Metropolitan-Cammell

Driving Motor Composite Lavatory
DMCL
E50260-E50269

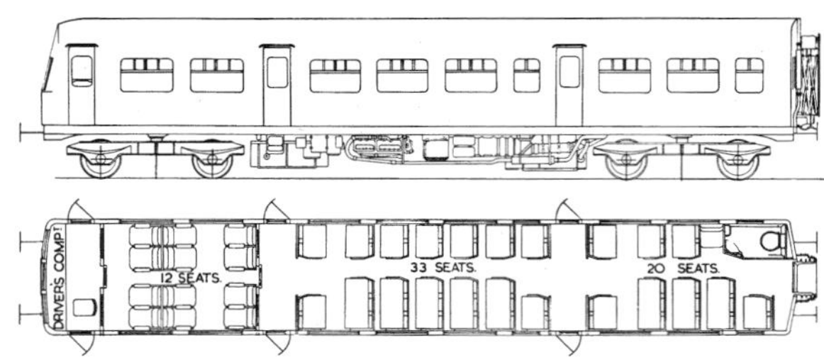

Coupling: ■ Blue square
Diagram: 621 DP304 ②DP210
Lot Number: 30267
Old class: 102/1
Engines: Two BUT (AEC) 6-cyl horizontal type of 150 bhp.
Transmission: Mechanical. Standard
Body: 57' 6" × 9' 3"
Weight: 32t
Seats: 12 first, 53 second

E50260	08/83➲**53260**	06/57-11/90	⊗03/91	®06/81	01/65⇨**NE**	01/68⇨**E**	04/78⇨**SC**
E50261	09/84➲**53261**	06/57-06/89	⊗06/89	® */80*	01/65⇨**NE**	01/68⇨**E**	
E50262	07/83➲**53262**	07/57-11/87	⊗09/88	®07/79	01/65⇨**NE**	01/68⇨**E**	
E50263	06/83➲**53263**	07/57-10/89	⊗12/89	®11/79	01/65⇨**NE**	01/68⇨**E**	
E50264	08/83➲**53264**	08/57-08/89	⊗09/89	®08/79	01/65⇨**NE**	01/68⇨**E**	08/69⇨**SC**
E50265	06/83➲**53265**	09/57-07/93	⊗02/94	®09/82	01/65⇨**NE**	01/68⇨**E**	
E50266	03/83➲**53266**	10/57-12/03	Ⓟ	® /81	01/65⇨**NE** 05/76⇨**E**	01/68⇨**E**	10/75⇨**W**
E50267	05/83➲**53267**	10/57-02/93	⊗01/94	®*10/76*	01/65⇨**NE**	01/68⇨**E**	
E50268	03/83➲**53268**	10/57-01/01	Ⓟ⊗04/09	®04/83	01/65⇨**NE**	01/68⇨**E**	09/79⇨**SC**
E50269	03/83➲**53269**	10/57-06/01	⊗12/03	®05/83	01/65⇨**NE**	01/68⇨**E**	08/69⇨**SC**

Class 111 Metropolitan-Cammell

Driving Motor Composite Lavatory
DMCL
E50270-E50279

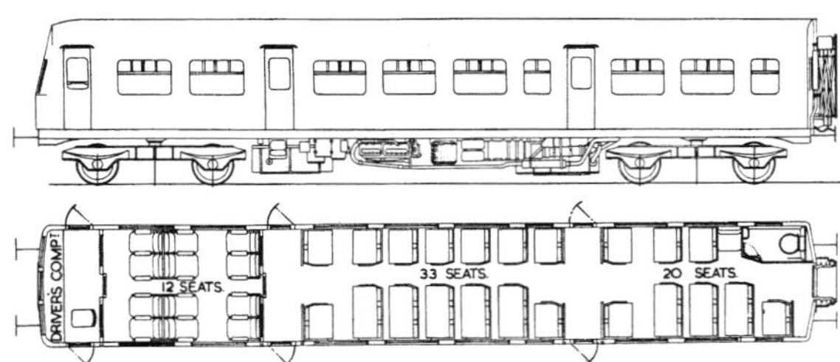

Coupling: ■ Blue square
Diagram: 616 DP314
Lot Number: 30268
Old class: 111/1
Engines: Two Rolls-Royce 6-cyl horizontal type of 180 bhp.
Transmission: Mechanical. Standard
Body: 57' 6" × 9' 3"
Weight: 33t
Seats: 12 first, 53 second

E50270		10/57-11/82	⊗11/84	®08/76	01/65⇨**NE**	01/68⇨**E**	
E50271		11/57-11/82	⊗09/88	®11/79	01/65⇨**NE**	01/68⇨**E**	➲**78708**
E50272	05/83➲**53272**	11/57-02/85	⊗04/90	® /82	01/65⇨**NE**	01/68⇨**E**	➲**78713**
E50273	/83➲**53273**	12/57-10/83	⊗05/90	®04/77	01/65⇨**NE**	01/68⇨**E**	➲**78709**
E50274		12/57-10/82	⊗02/88	®01/81	01/65⇨**NE**	01/68⇨**E**	➲**78707**
E50275	04/83➲**53275**	12/57-02/84	⊗04/90	® /81	01/65⇨**NE**	01/68⇨**E**	➲**78711**
E50276	04/83➲**53276**	12/57-10/83	⊗05/87	®04/77	01/65⇨**NE**	01/68⇨**E**	➲**78710**
E50277	04/83➲**53277**	01/58-08/85	⊗04/90	® /81	01/65⇨**NE**	01/68⇨**E**	➲**78714**
E50278	04/83➲**53278**	01/58-09/84	⊗07/90	® /82	01/65⇨**NE**	01/68⇨**E**	➲**78712**
E50279		01/58-08/82	⊗10/86	®11/79	01/65⇨**NE**	01/68⇨**E**	➲**78706**

Class 111 Metropolitan-Cammell
Driving Motor Brake Second
DMBS
E50280-E50289

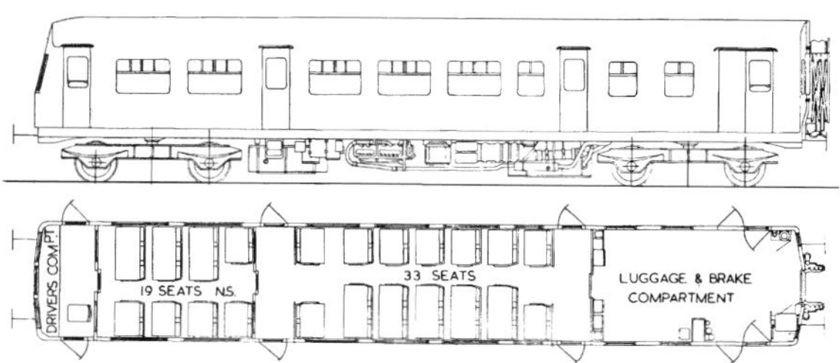

Coupling: ■ Blue square
Diagram: 524 DQ215
Lot Number: 30338
Old class: 111/2
Engines: Two Rolls-Royce 6-cyl horizontal type of 180 bhp.
Transmission: Mechanical. Standard
Body: 57' 6" × 9' 3"
Weight: 33t
Seats: 52 second

E50280	07/83➲**53280**	10/57-02/84	⊗04/90	® /81	01/65⇨**NE**	01/68⇨**E**	➲**78961**
E50281		11/57-11/82	⊗09/88	®11/79	01/65⇨**NE**	01/68⇨**E**	➲**78958**
E50282	/83➲**53282**	11/57-10/83	⊗07/90	® /82	01/65⇨**NE**	01/68⇨**E**	➲**78960**
E50283	04/83➲**53283**	12/57-09/84	⊗07/90	® /82	01/65⇨**NE**	01/68⇨**E**	➲**78962**
E50284	04/83➲**53284**	12/57-08/85	⊗04/90	®06/81	01/65⇨**NE**	01/68⇨**E**	➲**78964**
E50285		12/57-11/66	⊗09/67		01/65⇨**NE**		
E50286		12/57-08/82	⊗01/87	®11/79	01/65⇨**NE**	01/68⇨**E**	➲**78956**
E50287		01/58-10/82	⊗02/88	®01/81	01/65⇨**NE**	01/68⇨**E**	➲**78957**
E50288	/83➲**53288**	01/58-10/83	⊗05/90	®04/77	01/65⇨**NE**	01/68⇨**E**	➲**78959**
E50289	07/83➲**53289**	01/58-02/85	⊗02/88	®07/79	01/65⇨**NE**	01/68⇨**E**	➲**78963**

Class 101 Metropolitan-Cammell
Driving Motor Brake Second
DMBS
E50290-E50296

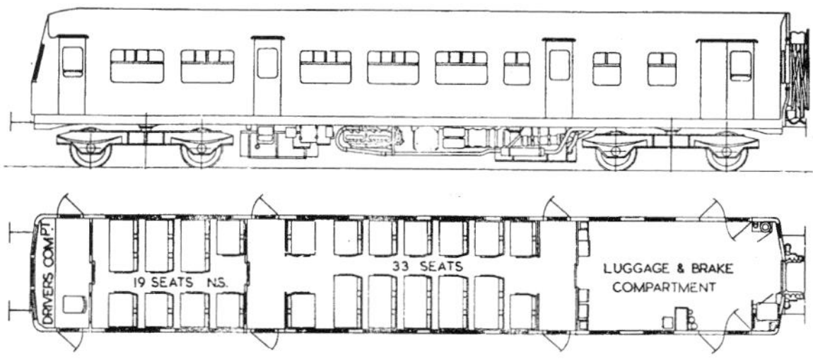

Coupling: ■ Blue square
Diagram: 523 DQ202
Lot Number: 30270
Old class: 101/2
Engines: Two BUT (AEC) 6-cyl horizontal type of 150 bhp.
Transmission: Mechanical. Standard
Body: 57' 6" × 9' 3"
Weight: 32t
Seats: 52 second

E50290	08/83➲**53290**	11/57-12/87	⊗02/93	®01/83	01/65⇨**NE**	03/66⇨**SC**	
							11/90➲**TDB977651**
E50291	07/83➲**53291**	11/57-06/93	⊗04/03	® /81	01/65⇨**NE**	03/66⇨**SC**	08/77⇨**E**
							10/93➲**DB977904**
E50292	08/83➲**53292**	11/57-12/87	⊗03/89	®06/80	01/65⇨**NE**	03/66⇨**SC**	
E50293	02/83➲**53293**	12/57-12/92	⊗01/94	®07/78	01/65⇨**NE**	01/68⇨**E**	
E50294	05/83➲**53294**	12/57-10/92	⊗02/94	®11/79	01/65⇨**NE**	01/68⇨**E**	
E50295	04/83➲**53295**	12/57-11/87	⊗02/93	®07/79	01/65⇨**NE**	01/68⇨**E**	
							11/87➲**TDB977536**
E50296	04/83➲**53296**	12/57-12/91	⊗03/92	®04/77	01/65⇨**NE**	01/68⇨**E**	

Class 101 Metropolitan-Cammell
Driving Motor Brake Second
DMBS
M50303-M50320

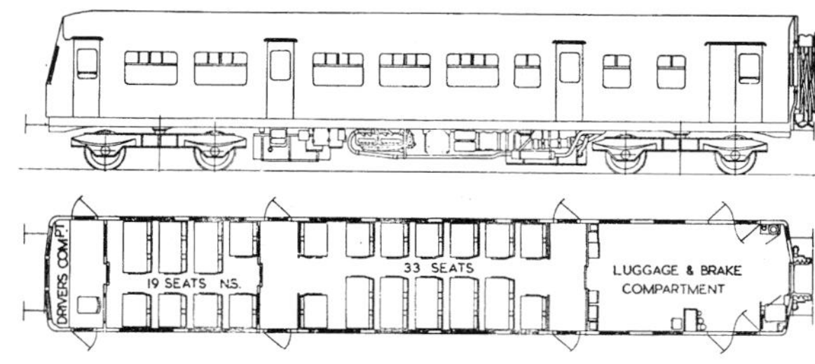

Coupling: ■ Blue square
Diagram: 523 DQ202
Lot Number: 30275
Old class: 101/2
Engines: Two BUT (AEC) 6-cyl horizontal type of 150 bhp.
Transmission: Mechanical. Standard
Body: 57' 6" × 9' 3"
Weight: 32t
Seats: 52 second

M50303	04/83➲**53303**	02/58-10/89	⊗08/90	®11/78		
M50304	07/83➲**53304**	02/58-07/87	⊗08/88	®11/76	05/79⇨**W**	
M50305	06/83➲**53305**	02/58-05/95	⊗09/95	®*09/76*		
M50306	04/83➲**53306**	02/58-09/89	⊗12/89	®05/80		
M50307	04/83➲**53307**	02/58-05/89	⊗05/89	®09/81		
M50308	07/83➲**53308**	03/58-09/93	⊗09/03	® /82		09/93➲**DB977895**
M50309	06/83➲**53309**	03/58-05/89	⊗05/89	®*10/76*		
M50310	06/83➲**53310**	02/58-01/94	⊗09/95			
M50311	04/83➲**53311**	02/58-09/00	⊗12/03	®02/81		
M50312	04/83➲**53312**	03/58-09/96	⊗09/96	® /81		
M50313	07/83➲**53313**	03/58-05/86	⊗03/87			
M50314	07/83➲**53314**	03/58-03/97	⊗07/02	®01/83		
M50315	05/83➲**53315**	03/58-11/93	⊗03/94	®09/81		
M50316	06/83➲**53316**	03/58-07/86	⊗12/86			
M50317	04/83➲**53317**	04/58-10/89	⊗07/90	®07/76		
M50318	06/83➲**53318**	04/58-05/89	⊗05/89	®10/78		
M50319	04/83➲**53319**	04/58-10/89	⊗06/91	®*10/76*	05/79⇨**W**	
M50320	07/83➲**53320**	04/58-11/87	⊗08/89			11/87➲**TDB977537**

Class 101 Metropolitan-Cammell
Driving Motor Composite Lavatory
DMCL
M50321-M50338

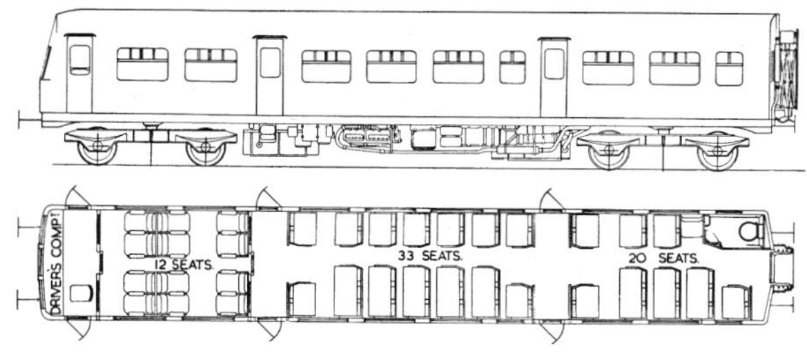

Coupling: ■ Blue square
Diagram: 621 DP304 ②DP210
Lot Number: 30276
Old class: 101/1
Engines: Two BUT (AEC) 6-cyl horizontal type of 150 bhp.
Transmission: Mechanical. Standard
Body: 57' 6" × 9' 3"
Weight: 32t
Seats: 12 first, 53 second

M50321	06/83➲**53321**	02/58-05/93	Ⓟ	®10/78		05/93➲**977900**
M50322	04/83➲**53322**	02/58-09/00	⊗12/03	®02/81		
M50323	04/83➲**53323**	02/58-05/89	⊗05/89	®03/77		
M50324	04/83➲**53324**	02/58-10/89	⊗06/90	®01/80		
M50325	04/83➲**53325**	02/58-10/89	⊗07/90			
M50326	04/83➲**53326**	03/58-01/94	⊗09/95	®10/79		
M50327	07/83➲**53327**	03/58-03/97	⊗07/02	®07/76		
M50328	06/83➲**53328**	02/58-08/87	⊗01/88	®09/78		
M50329	06/83➲**53329**	02/58-02/88	⊗08/88	®06/77	05/79⇨**W**	

M50330	07/83➲**53330**	03/58-11/93	⊗03/94	®02/81		
M50331	07/83➲**53331**	03/58-09/93	⊗09/03	® /82		09/93➲**DB977896**
M50332	05/83➲**53332**	03/58-09/96	⊗09/96	® /81		
M50333	05/83➲**53333**	03/58-03/93	⊗08/93	®09/81		
M50334	06/83➲**53334**	03/58-07/89	⊗08/90			
M50335	04/83➲**53335**	04/58-03/89	⊗04/90	®03/77	05/79⇨**W**	
M50336	05/83➲**53336**	04/58-05/89	⊗05/89	®06/78		
M50337	06/83➲**53337**	04/58-05/89	⊗05/89			
M50338	06/83➲**53338**	04/58-08/90	Ⓟ	®*09/76*		04/91➲**RDB977694**

Class 100 Gloucester RC&W

Driving Motor Brake Second

DMBS

SC50339-M50358

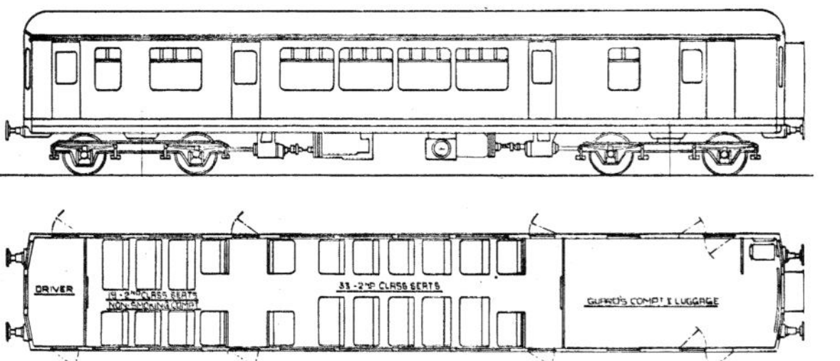

Coupling: ■ Blue square
Diagram: 536 DQ201
Lot Number: 30278
Old class: 100
Engines: Two BUT (AEC) 6-cyl horizontal type of 150 bhp.
Transmission: Mechanical. Standard
s Fitted with CAV automatic gear change equipment
Body: 57' 6" × 9' 3"
Weight: 30t
Seats: 52 second

SC50339		05/57-02/72	⊗11/73		05/68⇨**E**		
SC50340		05/57-02/81	⊗07/84		05/75⇨**M**		⊠10/72-01/73
SC50341		06/57-02/72	Ⓟ⊗05/91		05/68⇨**E**		
SC50342		06/57-08/82	⊗09/84		05/75⇨**M**		⊠10/72-01/73
SC50343		07/57-09/81	⊗05/85		05/75⇨**M**		⊠10/72-12/72
SC50344		07/57-10/71	⊗03/73		05/68⇨**E**		
SC50345		07/57-05/71	⊗04/74				
SC50346		07/57-09/82	⊗04/84		05/68⇨**E**	11/80⇨**M**	
							⊠10/72-03/75
SC50347		08/57-01/72	⊗12/72		05/68⇨**E**		
M50348		08/57-07/82	⊗04/84				
M50349		09/57-07/83	⊗05/84				
M50350		09/57-11/81	⊗11/82				
M50351		09/57-07/83	⊗12/84				
M50352		09/57-05/81	⊗11/82				
M50353		09/57-07/83	⊗06/84				
M50354		09/57-07/83	⊗04/84				
M50355	07/83➲**53355**	09/57-06/89	⊗10/90				⊠10/85-11/85
M50356		10/57-07/83	⊗09/84				
M50357		10/57-06/78	⊗11/79				
M50358		10/57-07/83	⊗09/84	s			

Class 106⇨105 Cravens

Driving Motor Brake Second

DMBS

E50359-E50372

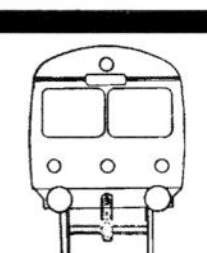

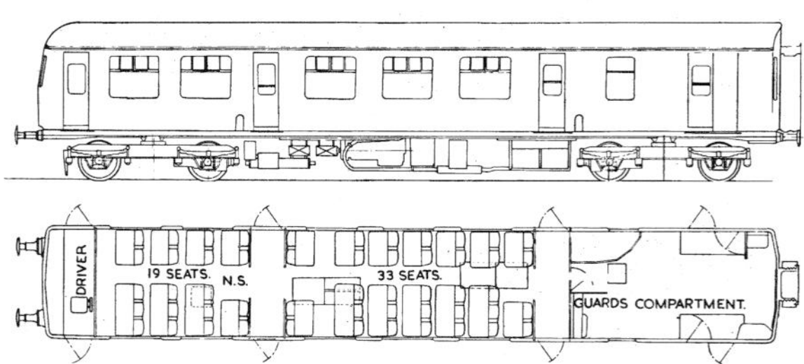

Coupling: ■ Blue square
Diagram: 525 DQ207
Lot Number: 30280
Old class: 106/2
Engines: Two BUT (Leyland) 6-cyl horizontal type of 150 bhp.
Transmission: Mechanical. Standard
Body: 57' 6" × 9' 2"
Weight: 29t
Seats: 52 second

E50359	03/83➲**53359**	08/56-10/88	⊗02/89	01/65⇨**NE**	01/68⇨**E**	
E50360	05/83➲**53360**	10/56-07/85	⊗05/86	01/65⇨**NE**	09/65⇨**E**	
E50361	04/83➲**53361**	11/56-03/89	⊗04/89	01/65⇨**NE**	01/68⇨**E**	
					⊠09/86-10/86	
E50362	05/83➲**53362**	11/56-03/87	⊗03/88	01/65⇨**NE**	09/65⇨**E**	
					03/87➲**55945**	
E50363	04/83➲**53363**	12/56-07/86	⊗03/88	01/65⇨**NE**	01/68⇨**E**	
E50364	04/83➲**53364**	12/56-03/89	⊗04/90	01/65⇨**NE**	01/68⇨**E**	
E50365	04/83➲**53365**	01/57-03/89	⊗04/89	01/65⇨**NE**	01/68⇨**E**	
					⊠11/86-12/86	
E50366	05/83➲**53366**	01/57-10/86	⊗06/87	01/65⇨**NE**	09/65⇨**E**	
E50367	05/83➲**53367**	01/57-03/89	⊗04/90	01/65⇨**NE**	01/68⇨**E**	
E50368	04/83➲**53368**	01/57-03/89	⊗04/89	01/65⇨**NE**	01/68⇨**E**	
E50369	04/83➲**53369**	02/57-09/88	⊗12/88	01/65⇨**NE**	01/68⇨**E**	
E50370		02/57-10/83	⊗08/84	01/65⇨**NE**	01/68⇨**E**	
E50371		02/57-09/83	⊗06/84	01/65⇨**NE**	01/68⇨**E**	
E50372		02/57-12/82	⊗09/84	01/65⇨**NE**	01/68⇨**E**	03/77⇨**M**

Class 105 Cravens

Driving Motor Brake Second

DMBS

E50373-E50389

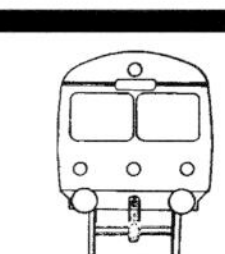

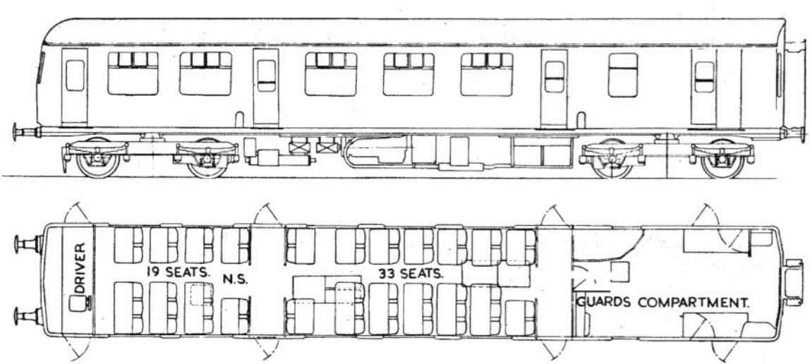

Coupling: ■ Blue square
Diagram: 525 DQ207
Lot Number: 30282
Old class: 105/2
Engines: Two BUT (AEC) 6-cyl horizontal type of 150 bhp.
Transmission: Mechanical. Standard
Body: 57' 6" × 9' 2"
Weight: 29t
Seats: 52 second

E50373	*/84*➲**53373**	02/57-03/89	⊗04/89	01/65⇨**NE**	01/68⇨**E**	
E50374		03/57-12/82	⊗05/84	01/65⇨**NE**	01/68⇨**E**	02/77⇨**M**
E50375	*/84*➲**53375**	03/57-05/87	⊗11/87	01/65⇨**NE**	01/68⇨**E**	
E50376		03/57-11/83	⊗01/84	11/82⇨**SC**		
E50377	*/85*➲**53377**	03/57-09/86	⊗01/87			
E50378		04/57-06/81	⊗06/82	01/65⇨**NE**	01/68⇨**E**	
E50379	03/83➲**53379**	04/57-07/84	⊗10/84	01/65⇨**NE**	01/68⇨**E**	
E50380	09/83➲**53380**	04/57-09/86	⊗11/87	01/65⇨**NE**	01/68⇨**E**	
E50381	11/84➲**53381**	05/57-05/87	⊗10/87	01/65⇨**NE**	01/68⇨**E**	
E50382		05/57-06/81	⊗09/83	01/65⇨**NE**	01/68⇨**E**	
E50383		05/57-07/81	⊗09/83			
E50384		05/57-10/83	⊗06/84	11/82⇨**SC**		
E50385		05/57-12/82	⊗03/84	01/65⇨**NE**	01/68⇨**E**	02/77⇨**M**
E50386		05/57-10/83	⊗06/84	01/65⇨**NE**	01/68⇨**E**	11/82⇨**SC**
E50387		06/57-11/81	⊗01/83	01/65⇨**NE**	01/68⇨**E**	12/76⇨**M**
E50388		07/57-09/81	⊗01/83	01/65⇨**NE**	01/68⇨**E**	01/77⇨**M**
E50389		07/57-09/82	⊗10/82	01/65⇨**NE**	01/68⇨**E**	01/77⇨**M**

Class 105 Cravens

Driving Motor Brake Second
DMBS
M50390-M50394

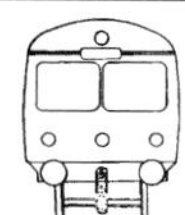

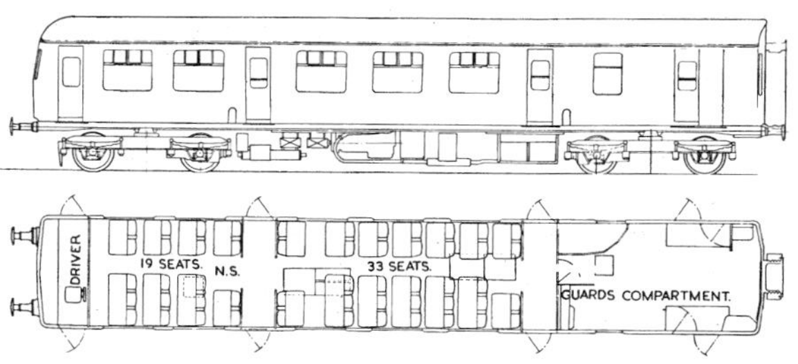

Coupling:	■ Blue square
Diagram:	525 DQ207
Lot Number:	30284
Old class:	105/2
Engines:	Two BUT (AEC) 6-cyl horizontal type of 150 bhp.
Transmission:	Mechanical. Standard
Body:	57' 6" × 9' 2"
Weight:	29t
Seats:	52 second

M50390	07/57-11/81	⊗03/83
M50391	07/57-11/81	⊗03/83
M50392	07/57-01/81	⊗01/83
M50393	08/57-09/82	⊗03/83
M50394	08/57-09/76	⊗09/85

Class 103 Park Royal

Driving Motor Brake Second
DMBS
M50395-M50414

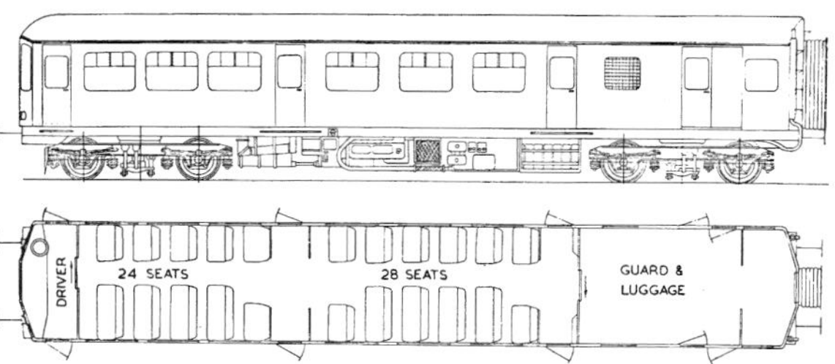

Coupling:	■ Blue square
Diagram:	635 DQ204
Lot Number:	30286
Old class:	103
Engines:	Two BUT (AEC) 6-cyl horizontal type of 150 bhp.
Transmission:	Mechanical. Standard
Body:	57' 6" × 9' 3"
Weight:	33t 10cwt
Seats:	52 second

M50395	11/57-04/82	⊗08/84		
M50396	01/58-06/70	⊗02/91		04/71⊃**DB975089**
M50397	01/58-02/71	Ⓟ⊗09/09		02/71⊃*DB975137*
M50398	02/58-12/82	⊗09/84		
M50399	03/58-07/82	⊗04/85		
M50400	04/58-11/82	⊗12/84		
M50401	04/58-11/80	⊗04/85		
M50402	05/58-12/82	⊗04/85		
M50403	05/58-09/82	⊗09/84		
M50404	05/58-06/82	⊗09/84		
M50405	06/58-12/82	⊗09/84		
M50406	06/58-11/75	⊗07/76		
M50407	07/58-06/72	⊗12/72		
M50408	07/58-02/81	⊗12/84		
M50409	08/58-02/83	⊗12/84		
M50410	09/58-11/71	⊗03/73		
M50411	09/58-05/72	⊗09/73	10/70⇦**W**	
M50412	09/58-05/72	⊗08/73	10/70⇦**W**	
M50413	10/58-12/72	Ⓟ	05/70⇦**W**	
M50414	10/58-12/72	Ⓟ⊗05/91	05/70⇦**W**	

Class 109 Wickham

Driving Motor Brake Second
DMBS
E50415-E50419

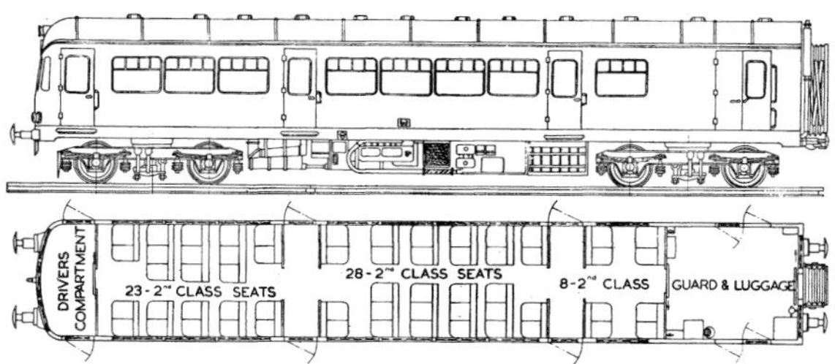

Coupling:	■ Blue square
Diagram:	606
Lot Number:	30288
Old class:	109
Engines:	Two BUT (Leyland) 6-cyl horizontal type of 150 bhp.
Transmission:	Mechanical. Standard
Body:	57' 0" × 9' 3"
Weight:	27t
Seats:	59 second

E50416 was converted to the ER General Manager's saloon in June 1966. E50415 and E50419 were returned to the manufacturer in 1961 to fulfil an export order to Trinidad.

E50415	08/57-09/61	⊗ /98	Exported
E50416	10/57-10/67	Ⓟ	10/67⊃**DB975005**
E50417	11/57-05/71	⊗12/72	
E50418	04/58-10/71	⊗03/73	
E50419	08/58-09/61	⊗ /98	Exported

Class 104 Birmingham RC&W

Driving Motor Brake Second
DMBS
M50420-M50423

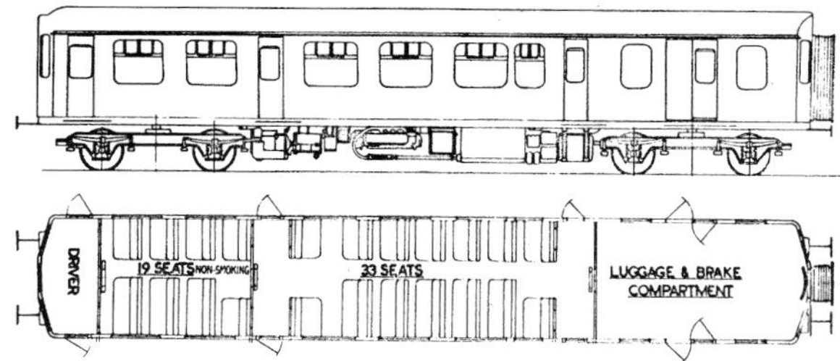

Coupling:	■ Blue square
Diagram:	556 DQ205
Lot Number:	30290
Old class:	104/2
Engines:	Two BUT (Leyland) 6-cyl horizontal type of 150 bhp.
Transmission:	Mechanical. Standard
Body:	57' 6" × 9' 3"
Weight:	31t
Seats:	52 second

M50420	/83⊃**53420**	04/57-05/86	⊗12/86	
M50421	/83⊃**53421**	04/57-08/89	⊗10/90	☒05/89-08/89
M50422	10/83⊃**53422**	05/57-11/85	⊗05/87	11/85⊃**ADB977344**
M50423	05/83⊃**53423**	05/57-01/84	⊗05/84	

Class 104 Birmingham RC&W
Driving Motor Composite Lavatory
DMCL
M50424-M50427

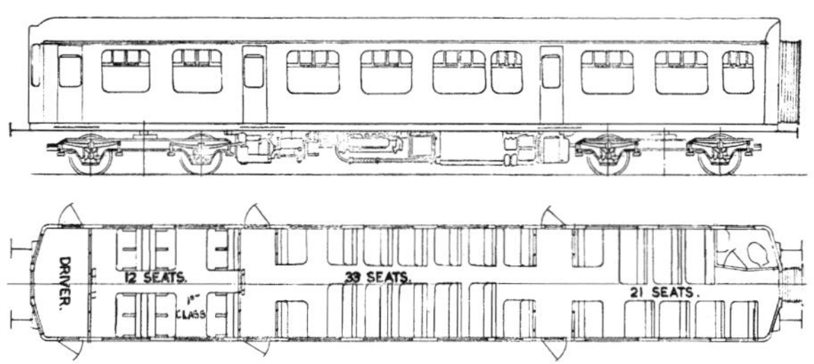

Coupling: ■ Blue square
Diagram: 558 DP305 ②DP209
Lot Number: 30291
Old class: 104/1
Engines: Two BUT (Leyland) 6-cyl horizontal type of 150 bhp.
Transmission: Mechanical. Standard
Body: 57' 6" × 9' 3"
Weight: 31t
Seats: 12 first, 54 second

M50424	/83➲**53424**	04/57-12/87	⊗06/91		
M50425	01/85➲**53425**	04/57-10/89	⊗01/90		
M50426	/83➲**53426**	05/57-12/84	⊗01/85		
M50427	08/83➲**53427**	05/57-03/89	⊗03/89		

Class 104 Birmingham RC&W
Driving Motor Brake Second
DMBS
M50428-M50479

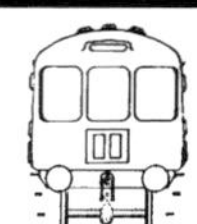

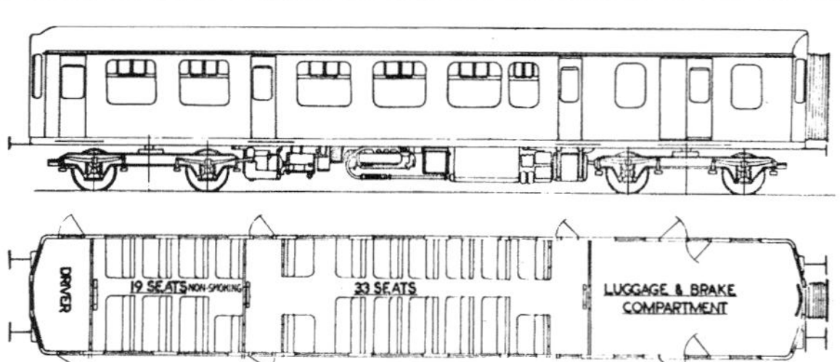

Coupling: ■ Blue square
Diagram: 556 DQ205
Lot Number: 30293
Old class: 104/2
Engines: Two BUT (Leyland) 6-cyl horizontal type of 150 bhp.
Transmission: Mechanical. Standard
Body: 57' 6" × 9' 3"
Weight: 31t
Seats: 52 second

M50428	/83➲**53428**	05/57-01/86	⊗12/86		
M50429	03/83➲**53429**	05/57-12/91	⊗12/93		
M50430	/83➲**53430**	06/57-07/86	⊗05/88		
M50431	05/83➲**53431**	06/57-03/90	⊗06/91		
M50432	07/83➲**53432**	06/57-07/84	⊗11/85		
M50433	/83➲**53433**	06/57-03/86	⊗08/86		
M50434	/83➲**53434**	06/57-12/87	⊗06/91		
M50435	/83➲**53435**	07/57-02/84	⊗11/85		
M50436	02/83➲**53436**	07/57-08/85	⊗05/86		
M50437	03/83➲**53437**	07/57-02/92	Ⓟ		
M50438		07/57-07/74	⊗10/74		
M50439	01/85➲**53439**	07/57-01/90	⊗01/90		
M50440		07/57-08/82	⊗02/83		
M50441		08/57-05/69	⊗10/69		
M50442	/84➲**53442**	08/57-05/90	⊗06/91		
M50443	09/83➲**53443**	08/57-08/89	⊗10/90		⊠05/89-08/89
M50444	06/84➲**53444**	09/57-05/89	⊗10/90		
M50445	/83➲**53445**	09/57-10/85	⊗03/86		
M50446		09/57-09/82	⊗09/86		09/82➲**78851**
M50447	06/84➲**53447**	09/57-03/92	Ⓟ		
M50448	/83➲**53448**	09/57-03/86	⊗03/86		
M50449	/83➲**53449**	10/57-07/84	⊗04/85		
M50450	09/83➲**53450**	10/57-03/86	⊗03/86		
M50451	04/83➲**53451**	10/57-06/90	⊗02/91		
M50452	01/84➲**53452**	10/57-07/86	⊗07/86	01/84⇨**SC**	
M50453	10/83➲**53453**	10/57-05/87	⊗09/90		
M50454	03/83➲**53454**	10/57-03/92	Ⓟ		
M50455	03/83➲**53455**	10/57-09/92	Ⓟ		
M50456	/83➲**53456**	11/57-10/87	⊗03/88		⊠11/86-*02/87*
M50457	04/83➲**53457**	11/57-07/85	⊗03/86		
M50458	04/83➲**53458**	11/57-02/84	⊗11/85		
M50459	/83➲**53459**	11/57-04/86	⊗05/86		
M50460	/83➲**53460**	11/57-03/89	⊗03/89		
M50461	01/84➲**53461**	11/57-03/87	⊗06/87	01/84⇨**SC**	
M50462		12/57-01/81	⊗02/86	06/68⇨**E** 01/78⇨**M**	
M50463	10/83➲**53463**	12/57-05/86	⊗07/86		
M50464	10/83➲**53464**	12/57-08/89	⊗10/90		⊠05/89-08/89
M50465	10/83➲**53465**	12/57-08/89	⊗09/89		
M50466	10/83➲**53466**	12/57-01/90	⊗01/90		
M50467	07/83➲**53467**	01/58-04/85	⊗07/85		
M50468	05/83➲**53468**	01/58-09/89	⊗12/89 ®12/80		
M50469	10/83➲**53469**	01/58-03/86	⊗03/86		
M50470	08/83➲**53470**	01/58-12/91	⊗03/93		
M50471	08/83➲**53471**	01/58-03/86	⊗05/86		
M50472	03/83➲**53472**	01/58-09/89	⊗12/89		
M50473	01/84➲**53473**	02/58-03/87	⊗11/87	01/84⇨**SC**	
M50474	/83➲**53474**	02/58-03/89	⊗03/89		
M50475	10/83➲**53475**	02/58-11/85	⊗12/88		11/85➲**ADB977342**
M50476	08/83➲**53476**	02/58-10/89	⊗12/89		
M50477	08/83➲**53477**	02/58-02/93	⊗10/95		
M50478	07/83➲**53478**	03/58-06/89	⊗09/89		
M50479	03/83➲**53479**	03/58-02/92	Ⓟ		

Class 104 Birmingham RC&W
Driving Motor Composite Lavatory
DMCL
M50480-M50531

Coupling: ■ Blue square
Diagram: 558 DP305 ②DP209
Lot Number: 30294
Old class: 104/1
Engines: Two BUT (Leyland) 6-cyl horizontal type of 150 bhp.
Transmission: Mechanical. Standard
Body: 57' 6" × 9' 3"
Weight: 31t
Seats: 12 first, 54 second

M50480	03/83➲**53480**	05/57-07/84	⊗09/85 ®04/81		
M50481	/83➲**53481**	05/57-08/83	⊗05/84		
M50482	06/84➲**53482**	06/57-02/86	⊗07/86		
M50483	/83➲**53483**	06/57-01/84	⊗05/84		
M50484	07/83➲**53484**	06/57-12/84	⊗11/85		
M50485	/83➲**53485**	06/57-12/84	⊗02/86		
M50486		06/57-02/79	⊗11/79		
M50487	/83➲**53487**	07/57-08/89	⊗12/90		⊠05/89-08/89
M50488	10/83➲**53488**	07/57-08/85	⊗05/86		
M50489		07/57-10/76	⊗11/79		
M50490	/83➲**53490**	07/57-05/84	⊗02/86		
M50491	/83➲**53491**	07/57-12/86	⊗03/87		
M50492	03/83➲**53492**	07/57-08/89	⊗09/89		
M50493	09/83➲**53493**	08/57-05/89	⊗10/90		
M50494	06/84➲**53494**	08/57-06/90	Ⓟ		
M50495		08/57-03/77	⊗11/79		
M50496	05/83➲**53496**	09/57-03/89	⊗03/89		
M50497	/83➲**53497**	09/57-07/84	⊗12/84		
M50498	/83➲**53498**	09/57-07/84	⊗04/85		
M50499	08/83➲**53499**	09/57-09/89	⊗04/91		
M50500	06/84➲**53500**	10/57-06/89	⊗10/90		
M50501	/83➲**53501**	10/57-03/89	⊗03/89		
M50502	/83➲**53502**	10/57-07/84	⊗12/84		
M50503	/83➲**53503**	10/57-08/85	⊗12/86		
M50504	12/83➲**53504**	10/57-09/89	⊗12/89		
M50505	01/84➲**53505**	10/57-03/87	⊗01/88	01/84⇨**SC**	
M50506	/83➲**53506**	10/57-11/85	⊗05/87		11/85➲**ADB977343**
M50507	03/83➲**53507**	10/57-09/89	⊗12/89		

M50508	/83➲**53508**	11/57-07/85	⊗03/86			
M50509	04/83➲**53509**	11/57-07/85	⊗03/86			
M50510	01/84➲**53510**	11/57-05/86	⊗07/86		01/84⇨**SC**	
M50511	/83➲**53511**	11/57-08/89	⊗10/90			☒05/89-08/89
M50512	/83➲**53512**	11/57-06/90	⊗06/91			
M50513		11/57-11/63	⊗11/63			
M50514	04/83➲**53514**	12/57-10/87	⊗01/88			☒11/86-*02/87*
M50515	05/85➲**53515**	12/57-07/84	⊗01/86			
M50516	05/83➲**53516**	12/57-05/90	⊗06/91			
M50517	06/84➲**53517**	12/57-05/90	Ⓟ			
M50518	10/83➲**53518**	12/57-05/89	⊗10/90			
M50519	10/83➲**53519**	01/58-04/85	⊗07/85			
M50520	10/83➲**53520**	01/58-09/89	⊗12/89			
M50521		01/58-09/82	⊗09/86			09/82➲**78601**
M50522	/83➲**53522**	01/58-08/89	⊗09/89			
M50523	/83➲**53523**	01/58-03/86	⊗05/86			
M50524	06/84➲**53524**	01/58-02/86	⊗02/86	®03/81		
M50525	01/84➲**53525**	02/58-02/87	⊗06/87		01/84⇨**SC**	
M50526		02/58-11/80	⊗10/83			
M50527	10/83➲**53527**	02/58-01/86	⊗02/86			
M50528	04/83➲**53528**	02/58-03/92	Ⓟ			
M50529	08/83➲**53529**	02/58-06/90	⊗02/91			
M50530	10/83➲**53530**	03/58-06/89	⊗09/89			
M50531	10/83➲**53531**	03/58-03/92	Ⓟ			

Class 104 Birmingham RC&W
Driving Motor Brake Second
DMBS
M50532-M50541

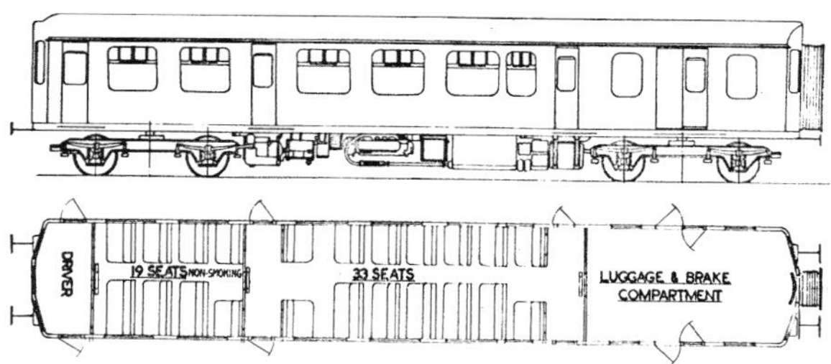

Coupling: ■ Blue square
Diagram: 556 DQ205
Lot Number: 30296
Old class: 104/2
Engines: Two BUT (Leyland) 6-cyl horizontal type of 150 bhp.
Transmission: Mechanical. Standard
Body: 57' 6" × 9' 3"
Weight: 31t
Seats: 52 second

M50532	/83➲**53532**	03/58-08/89	⊗12/90	☒05/89-08/89
M50533	08/83➲**53533**	03/58-02/86	⊗02/86	
M50534	03/83➲**53534**	04/58-06/90	⊗06/91	☒09/89-09/89
M50535	/83➲**53535**	04/58-02/86	⊗02/86	
M50536	/83➲**53536**	04/58-05/90	⊗06/91	
M50537	06/83➲**53537**	04/58-11/83	⊗05/84	
M50538	02/83➲**53538**	04/58-03/86	⊗03/86	
M50539	09/83➲**53539**	04/58-12/92	⊗12/95	
M50540	/84➲**53540**	04/58-10/93	⊗09/95	
M50541	07/83➲**53541**	05/58-09/89	⊗01/90	

Class 104 Birmingham RC&W
Driving Motor Composite Lavatory
DMCL
E50542-E50562

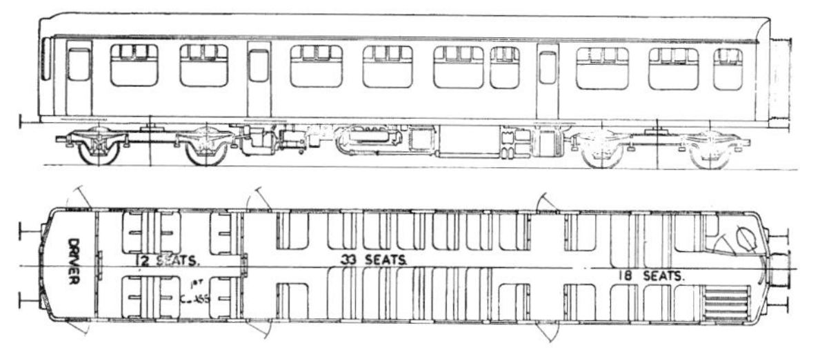

Coupling: ■ Blue square
Diagram: 580 DP307 ②DP217
Lot Number: 30298
Old class: 104/1
Engines: Two BUT (Leyland) 6-cyl horizontal type of 150 bhp.
Transmission: Mechanical. Standard
Body: 57' 6" × 9' 3"
Weight: 31t
Seats: 12 first, 51 second

E50542	/83➲**53542**	06/58-09/86	⊗11/87		01/65⇨**NE**	01/68⇨**E**	05/80⇨**M**
E50543		06/58-02/81	⊗10/83		01/65⇨**NE**	01/68⇨**E**	
E50544		06/58-06/82	⊗05/84		01/65⇨**NE**	01/68⇨**E**	
E50545		06/58-03/81	⊗08/81		01/65⇨**NE**	01/68⇨**E**	
E50546	/83➲**53546**	07/58-07/84	⊗11/85		01/65⇨**NE**	01/68⇨**E**	02/81⇨**M**
E50547		07/58-06/82	⊗03/84		01/65⇨**NE**	01/68⇨**E**	
E50548		07/58-02/81	⊗05/90		01/65⇨**NE**	01/68⇨**E**	
E50549		08/58-10/81	⊗07/82		01/65⇨**NE**	01/68⇨**E**	
E50550		08/58-06/81	⊗03/82		01/65⇨**NE**	01/68⇨**E**	
E50551		09/58-10/84	⊗12/84		01/65⇨**NE**	01/68⇨**E**	02/81⇨**M** ☒07/83-11/83
E50552		09/58-05/78	⊗03/81		01/65⇨**NE**	01/68⇨**E**	
E50553		09/58-05/82	⊗07/83		01/65⇨**NE**	01/68⇨**E**	
E50554		09/58-06/82	⊗07/83		01/65⇨**NE**	01/68⇨**E**	
E50555		10/58-05/82	⊗08/83		01/65⇨**NE**	01/68⇨**E**	
E50556	12/83➲**53556**	10/58-05/89	Ⓟ		01/65⇨**NE**	01/68⇨**E**	02/81⇨**M**
E50557		10/58-06/81	⊗08/81		01/65⇨**NE**	01/68⇨**E**	
E50558		10/58-07/67	⊗12/67		01/65⇨**NE**		
E50559		11/58-09/77	⊗01/78		01/65⇨**NE**	01/68⇨**E**	
E50560		11/58-04/82	⊗10/83		01/65⇨**NE**	01/68⇨**E**	
E50561	/83➲**53561**	11/58-02/82	⊗12/84	®02/81	01/65⇨**NE**	01/68⇨**E**	11/80⇨**M**
E50562	/83➲**53562**	12/58-07/84	⊗11/85		01/65⇨**NE**	01/68⇨**E**	11/80⇨**M**

Class 104 Birmingham RC&W
Driving Motor Composite Lavatory
DMCL
E50563-E50583

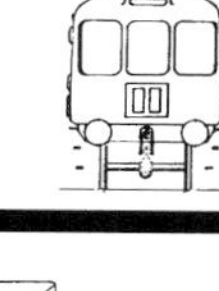

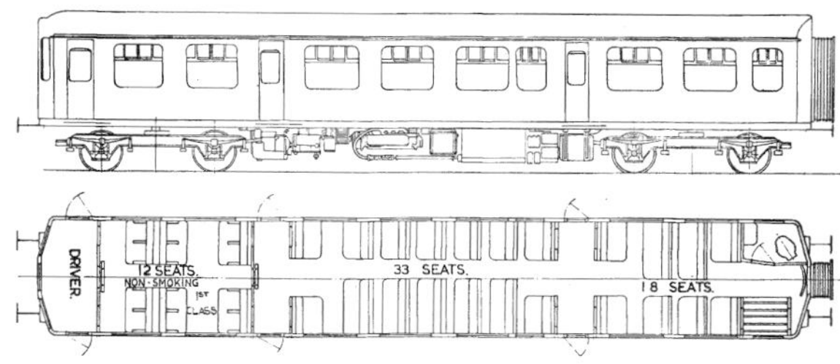

Coupling: ■ Blue square
Diagram: 559 DP307 ②DP217
Lot Number: 30298
Old class: 104/1
Engines: Two BUT (Leyland) 6-cyl horizontal type of 150 bhp.
Transmission: Mechanical. Standard
Body: 57' 6" × 9' 3"
Weight: 31t
Seats: 12 first, 51 second

E50563		06/58-06/82	⊗05/84		01/65⇨**NE**	01/68⇨**E**	
E50564		06/58-02/81	⊗06/89	®02/81	01/65⇨**NE**	01/68⇨**E**	
E50565	/83➲**53565**	06/58-05/86	⊗07/86		01/65⇨**NE**	01/68⇨**E**	
E50566		06/58-06/82	⊗02/84		01/65⇨**NE**	01/68⇨**E**	
E50567		07/58-06/82	⊗02/84		01/65⇨**NE**	01/68⇨**E**	
E50568		07/58-11/80	⊗09/81		01/65⇨**NE**	01/68⇨**E**	
E50569		07/58-08/69	⊗10/69		01/65⇨**NE**	01/68⇨**E**	
E50570		08/58-06/82	⊗03/83		01/65⇨**NE**	01/68⇨**E**	
E50571	/83➲**53571**	08/58-02/84	⊗12/84		01/65⇨**NE**	01/68⇨**E**	
E50572		09/58-07/83	⊗12/84		01/65⇨**NE**	01/68⇨**E**	02/81⇨**M**
E50573		09/58-02/82	⊗06/83		01/65⇨**NE**	01/68⇨**E**	
E50574		09/58-10/81	⊗03/82		01/65⇨**NE**	01/68⇨**E**	
E50575		09/58-06/82	⊗07/83		01/65⇨**NE**	01/68⇨**E**	
E50576		10/58-06/82	⊗09/85		01/65⇨**NE**	01/68⇨**E**	
E50577	/83➲**53577**	10/58-09/86	⊗04/87		01/65⇨**NE**	01/68⇨**E**	
E50578		10/58-06/82	⊗10/83		01/65⇨**NE**	01/68⇨**E**	
E50579		10/58-01/82	⊗11/82		01/65⇨**NE**	01/68⇨**E**	
E50580		11/58-06/81	⊗06/83		01/65⇨**NE**	01/68⇨**E**	
E50581		11/58-08/82	⊗01/82		01/65⇨**NE**	01/68⇨**E**	
E50582		11/58-06/81	⊗02/84		01/65⇨**NE**	01/68⇨**E**	
E50583		12/58-05/82	⊗07/83		01/65⇨**NE**	01/68⇨**E**	

Class 104 Birmingham RC&W

Driving Motor Composite Lavatory

DMCL

E50584-E50588

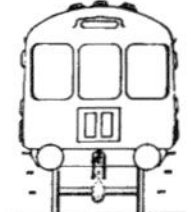

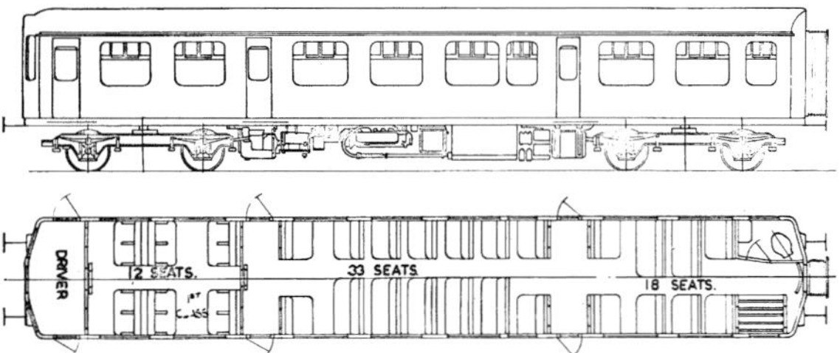

Coupling: ■ Blue square
Diagram: 580 DP307 ⓩDP217
Lot Number: 30301
Old class: 104/1
Engines: Two BUT (Leyland) 6-cyl horizontal type of 150 bhp.
Transmission: Mechanical. Standard
Body: 57' 6" × 9' 3"
Weight: 31t
Seats: 12 first, 51 second

E50584		01/59-02/82	⊗03/83		01/65⇨**NE**	01/68⇨**E**	02/81⇨**M**
E50585		12/58-02/81	⊗10/83		01/65⇨**NE**	01/68⇨**E**	
E50586		01/59-05/82	⊗03/83		01/65⇨**NE**	01/68⇨**E**	
E50587		01/59-06/82	⊗09/84		01/65⇨**NE**	01/68⇨**E**	
E50588		03/59-03/82	⊗06/83		01/65⇨**NE**	01/68⇨**E**	

Class 104 Birmingham RC&W

Driving Motor Composite Lavatory

DMCL

E50589-E50593

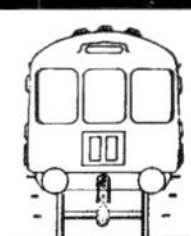

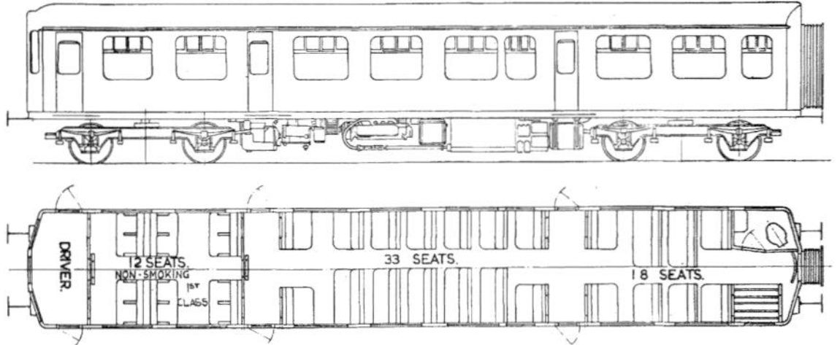

Coupling: ■ Blue square
Diagram: 559 DP307 ⓩDP217
Lot Number: 30301
Old class: 104/1
Engines: Two BUT (Leyland) 6-cyl horizontal type of 150 bhp.
Transmission: Mechanical. Standard
Body: 57' 6" × 9' 3"
Weight: 31t
Seats: 12 first, 51 second

E50589		01/59-05/83	⊗10/83		01/65⇨**NE**	01/68⇨**E**	
E50590	/83➲**53590**	12/58-07/84	⊗11/85		01/65⇨**NE**	01/68⇨**E**	11/80⇨**M**
E50591		01/59-03/81	⊗02/84		01/65⇨**NE**	01/68⇨**E**	
E50592		01/59-07/67	⊗02/68		01/65⇨**NE**		
E50593	/83➲**53593**	03/59-10/84	⊗11/85		01/65⇨**NE**	01/68⇨**E**	02/81⇨**M**

Class 104 Birmingham RC&W

Driving Motor Brake Second

DMBS

E50594-E50598

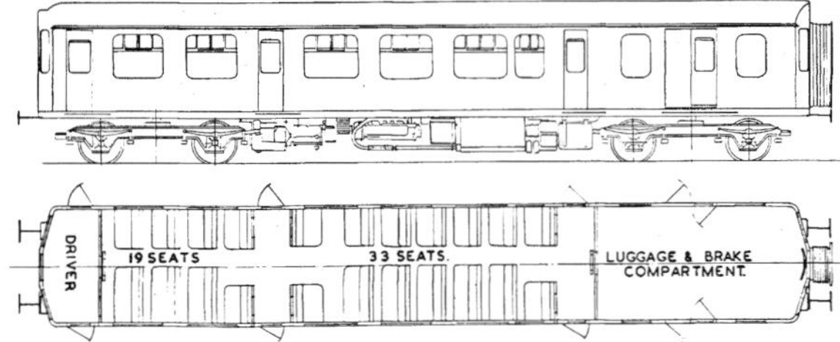

Coupling: ■ Blue square
Diagram: 557 DQ206
Lot Number: 30404
Old class: 104/2
Engines: Two BUT (Leyland) 6-cyl horizontal type of 160 bhp.
Transmission: Mechanical. Standard
Body: 57' 6" × 9' 3"
Weight: 31t
Seats: 52 second

E50594	06/83➲**53594**	05/58-07/85	⊗03/86		01/65⇨**NE**	01/68⇨**E**	06/82⇨**M**
E50595	/83➲**53595**	05/58-02/84	⊗08/84		01/65⇨**NE**	01/68⇨**E**	05/82⇨**M**
E50596		05/58-07/81	⊗10/82		01/65⇨**NE**	01/68⇨**E**	
E50597		05/58-02/82	⊗10/82		01/65⇨**NE**	01/68⇨**E**	
E50598	/83➲**53598**	05/58-12/86	⊗01/88		01/65⇨**NE**	01/68⇨**E**	04/82⇨**M**

Class 108 BR Derby

Driving Motor Brake Second

DMBS

E50599-E50624

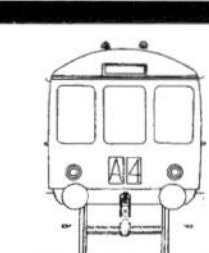

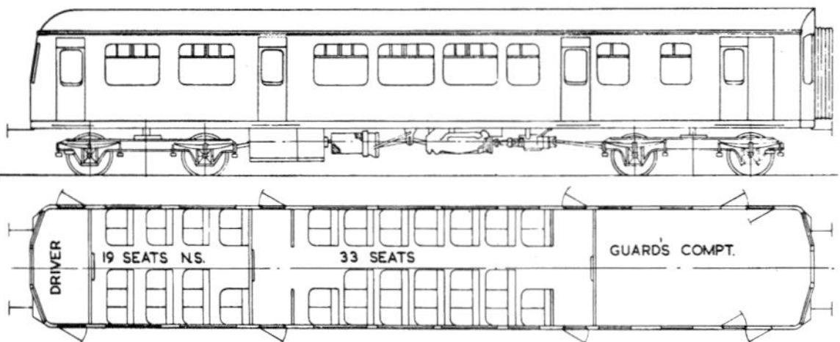

Coupling: ■ Blue square
Diagram: 543 DQ212
Lot Number: 30406
Old class: 108/2
Engines: Two BUT (Leyland) 6-cyl horizontal type of 150 bhp.
Transmission: Mechanical. Standard
Body: 58' 1" × 9' 2"
Weight: 29t
Seats: 52 second

E50599	04/83➲**53599**	07/58-01/93	℗	® /81	01/65⇨**NE**	01/68⇨**E**	
E50600		05/58-08/70	⊗07/70		01/65⇨**NE**	01/68⇨**E**	
E50601	04/83➲**53601**	05/58-07/89	⊗08/90	®06/75	01/65⇨**NE**	01/68⇨**E**	
E50602	02/83➲**53602**	05/58-05/92	⊗08/95	®03/83	01/65⇨**NE**	01/68⇨**E**	
E50603	04/83➲**53603**	07/58-02/87	⊗06/88	®12/76	01/65⇨**NE**	01/68⇨**E**	
E50604	05/83➲**53604**	07/58-05/88	⊗06/88	®12/76	01/65⇨**NE**	01/68⇨**E**	
E50605	04/83➲**53605**	06/58-03/85	⊗03/85	®02/77	01/65⇨**NE**	01/68⇨**E**	
E50606	05/83➲**53606**	07/58-10/89	⊗08/90	®11/77	01/65⇨**NE**	01/68⇨**E**	
E50607	04/83➲**53607**	06/58-03/90	⊗08/90	®02/81	01/65⇨**NE**	01/68⇨**E**	
E50608	04/83➲**53608**	07/58-03/92	⊗08/95	®08/76	01/65⇨**NE**	01/68⇨**E**	
E50609		08/58-10/82	⊗06/83	®02/81	01/65⇨**NE**	01/68⇨**E**	
E50610	05/83➲**53610**	08/58-05/88	⊗06/88	®10/77	01/65⇨**NE**	03/66⇨**SC**	01/68⇨**E**
E50611		08/58-10/66	⊗02/68		01/65⇨**NE**	03/66⇨**SC**	
E50612	04/83➲**53612**	08/58-01/92	⊗03/92	®06/75	01/65⇨**NE**	01/68⇨**E**	
E50613	04/83➲**53613**	08/58-11/88	⊗10/89	®06/75	01/65⇨**NE**	01/68⇨**E**	
E50614	08/84➲**53614**	07/58-01/91	⊗07/91	®05/75	01/65⇨**NE**	01/68⇨**E**	
E50615		09/58-09/68	⊗01/70		01/65⇨**NE**	01/68⇨**E**	
E50616	07/83➲**53616**	09/58-05/91	⊗11/91	®05/75	01/65⇨**NE**	01/68⇨**E**	
E50617	05/83➲**53617**	08/58-04/92	⊗05/92	®10/80	01/65⇨**NE**	01/68⇨**E**	
E50618	04/83➲**53618**	08/58-02/92	⊗01/92	®07/79	01/65⇨**NE**	01/68⇨**E**	
E50619	04/83➲**53619**	08/58-05/91	℗	®*10/76*	01/65⇨**NE**	01/68⇨**E**	

E50620 04/83➲**53620** 10/58-11/92 ⊗10/92 ®01/78 01/65⇨**NE** 03/66⇨**SC** 06/67⇨**NE** 01/68⇨**E**
E50621 04/83➲**53621** 10/58-02/92 ⊗02/92 ®01/78 01/65⇨**NE** 03/66⇨**SC** 06/68⇨**E**
E50622 05/83➲**53622** 11/58-03/92 ⊗05/92 ®08/76 01/65⇨**NE** 03/66⇨**SC** 06/67⇨**NE** 01/68⇨**E**
E50623 04/83➲**53623** 11/58-06/87 ⊗06/89 ®07/76 01/65⇨**NE** 03/66⇨**SC** 06/67⇨**NE** 01/68⇨**E**
E50624 05/83➲**53624** 11/58-06/92 ⊗06/92 ®08/76 01/65⇨**NE** 03/66⇨**SC** 06/67⇨**NE** 01/68⇨**E**

Class 108 BR Derby
Driving Motor Brake Second
DMBS
M50625-M50629

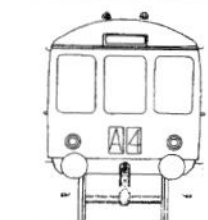

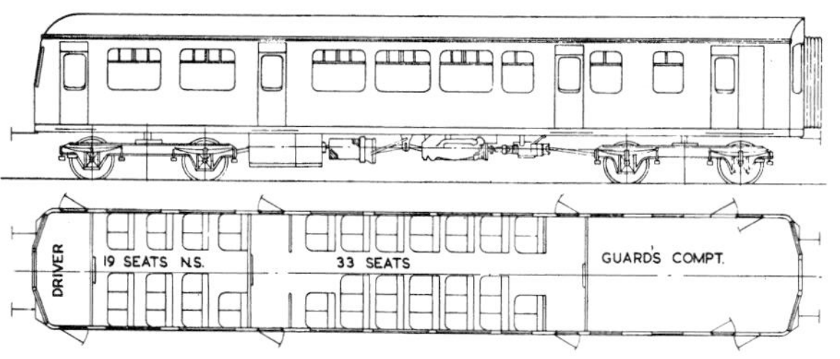

Coupling: ■ Blue square
Diagram: 543 DQ212
Lot Number: 30407
Old class: 108/2
Engines: Two BUT (Leyland) 6-cyl horizontal type of 150 bhp.
Transmission: Mechanical. Standard
Body: 58' 1" × 9' 2"
Weight: 29t
Seats: 52 second

M50625 09/83➲**53625** 12/58-01/92 ⊗10/91 ®01/83
M50626 05/83➲**53626** 12/58-10/91 ⊗01/93 ® /82 05/79⇨**E** 10/91➲**ADB977745**
M50627 07/83➲**53627** 12/58-02/93 ℗ ®09/81 02/93➲**ADB977853**
M50628 07/83➲**53628** 12/58-10/93 ℗ ® /81
M50629 /83➲**53629** 02/59-10/92 ⊗08/94 ®10/76 ⊠06/92-09/92 10/92➲**TDB977820**

Class 108 BR Derby
Driving Motor Composite Lavatory
DMCL
E50630-E50641

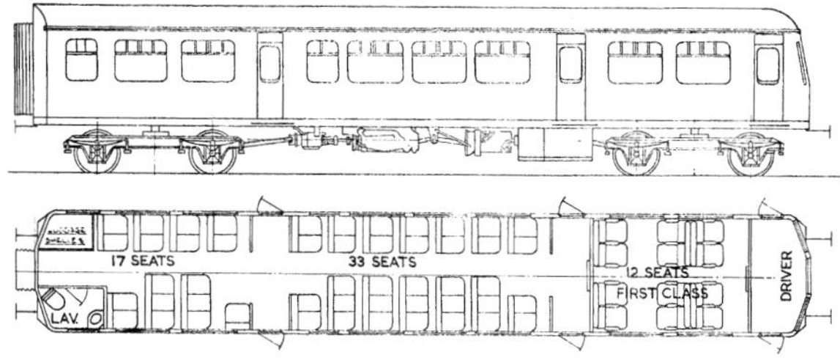

Coupling: ■ Blue square
Diagram: 544 DP310 ②DP219
Lot Number: 30408
Old class: 108/1
Engines: Two BUT (Leyland) 6-cyl horizontal type of 150 bhp.
Transmission: Mechanical. Standard
Body: 58' 1" × 9' 2"
Weight: 28t
Seats: 12 first, 50 second

E50630 11/84➲**53630** 10/58-09/91 ⊗10/91 ®08/76 01/65⇨**NE** 01/68⇨**E**
E50631 05/83➲**53631** 10/58-11/91 ⊗11/91 ®01/78 01/65⇨**NE** 01/68⇨**E**
E50632 04/83➲**53632** 10/58-02/93 ℗ ®01/77 01/65⇨**NE** 03/66⇨**SC** 06/67⇨**NE** 01/68⇨**E**
E50633 05/83➲**53633** 10/58-06/92 ⊗12/92 ®10/80 01/65⇨**NE** 03/66⇨**SC** 06/67⇨**NE** 01/68⇨**E**
E50634 02/83➲**53634** 10/58-11/92 ⊗11/92 01/65⇨**NE** 01/68⇨**E** 11/82⇨**M**
E50635 04/83➲**53635** 10/58-01/92 ⊗02/92 ® /81 01/65⇨**NE** 01/68⇨**E**
E50636 05/83➲**53636** 10/58-01/92 ⊗02/92 01/65⇨**NE** 01/68⇨**E**
E50637 /83➲**53637** 10/58-06/92 ⊗10/92 ®*09/76* 01/65⇨**NE** 01/68⇨**E**
E50638 07/83➲**53638** 10/58-02/91 ⊗02/91 ®*09/76* 01/65⇨**NE** 01/68⇨**E**
E50639 04/83➲**53639** 10/58-11/90 ⊗03/91 ®05/78 01/65⇨**NE** 01/68⇨**E**
E50640 10/58-11/75 ⊗05/77 01/65⇨**NE** 01/68⇨**E**
E50641 07/83➲**53641** 10/58-06/92 ⊗09/92 ®01/77 01/65⇨**NE** 01/68⇨**E**

Class 108 BR Derby
Driving Motor Composite Lavatory
DMCL
E50642-E50646

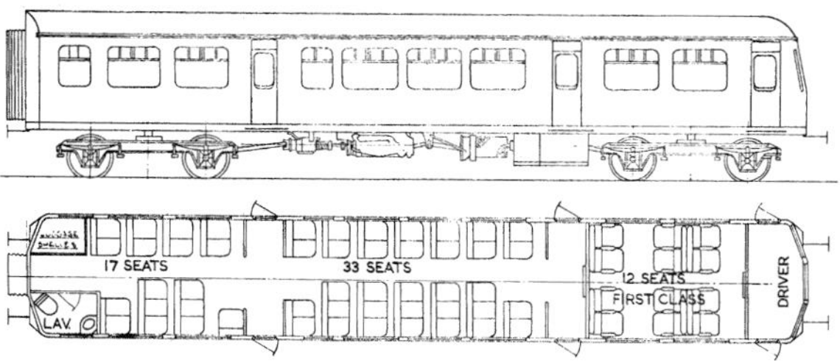

Coupling: ■ Blue square
Diagram: 544 DP310 ②DP219
Lot Number: 30408
Old class: 108/1
Engines: Two BUT (Leyland) 6-cyl horizontal type of 150 bhp.
Transmission: Mechanical. Standard
Body: 58' 1" × 9' 2"
Weight: 28t
Seats: 12 first, 50 second

E50642 05/83➲**53642** 10/58-10/92 ⊗11/93 ®01/78 01/65⇨**NE** 03/66⇨**SC** 06/67⇨**NE** 01/68⇨**E** ⊠06/92-07/92 10/92➲**ADB977839**
E50643 04/83➲**53643** 10/58-02/92 ⊗02/92 ®01/77 01/65⇨**NE** 03/66⇨**SC** 06/67⇨**NE** 01/68⇨**E**
E50644 04/83➲**53644** 11/58-01/92 ⊗01/92 ®04/77 01/65⇨**NE** 03/66⇨**SC** 06/67⇨**NE** 01/68⇨**E**
E50645 04/83➲**53645** 11/58-02/93 ℗ ®04/77 01/65⇨**NE** 03/66⇨**SC** 06/68⇨**E**
E50646 04/83➲**53646** 11/58-06/92 ⊗05/92 ®01/78 01/65⇨**NE** 03/66⇨**SC** 06/67⇨**NE** 01/68⇨**E**

Class 120 BR Swindon
Driving Motor Second Lavatory
DMSL
W50647-W50695

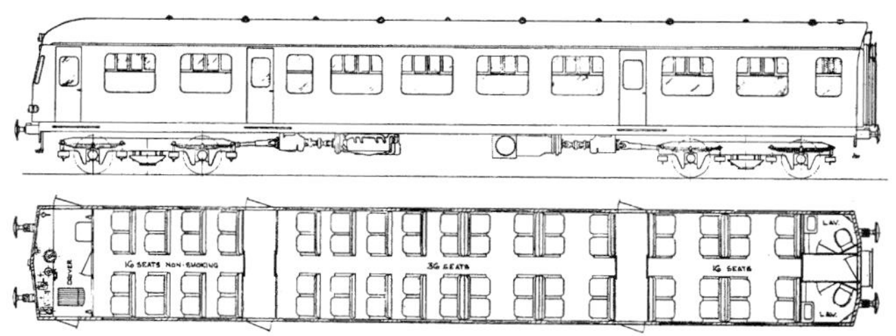

Coupling: ■ Blue square
Diagram: 586 DP204
Lot Number: 30334
Old class: 120/2
Engines: Two BUT (AEC) 6-cyl horizontal type of 150 bhp.
Transmission: Mechanical. Standard
Body: 64' 6" × 9' 3" Cross Country
Weight: 36t 10cwt
Seats: 68 second

W50647 05/83➲**53647** 12/57-03/87 ⊗05/87 11/80⇨**M**
W50648 09/83➲**53648** 12/57-03/87 ⊗09/87 10/79⇨**M**
W50649 04/83➲**53649** 01/58-12/86 ⊗03/87 06/82⇨**M**
W50650 /83➲**53650** 01/58-12/86 ⊗08/87 05/69⇨**M**
W50651 07/83➲**53651** 01/58-03/87 ⊗01/88 ®11/79 01/63⇨**M** 12/63⇨**W** 05/69⇨**M**
W50652 07/83➲**53652** 01/58-02/87 ⊗08/87 06/69⇨**M**
W50653 06/83➲**53653** 01/58-12/86 ⊗06/87 02/81⇨**M**
W50654 /83➲**53654** 01/58-02/88 ⊗08/91 ®07/78 05/69⇨**M**
W50655 04/83➲**53655** 02/58-12/86 ⊗03/87 05/69⇨**M**
W50656 07/83➲**53656** 02/58-07/86 ⊗07/86 05/69⇨**M**
W50657 02/83➲**53657** 02/58-03/86 ⊗10/86 05/69⇨**M**
W50658 05/84➲**53658** 02/58-10/89 ⊗08/91 12/80⇨**M**
W50659 /84➲**53659** 02/58-12/86 ⊗09/87 12/80⇨**M**
W50660 08/83➲**53660** 02/58-03/86 ⊗06/86 10/77⇨**M**
W50661 07/83➲**53661** 03/58-06/85 ⊗05/86 01/63⇨**M** 12/63⇨**W** 12/80⇨**M**

W50662	/85➲**53662**	03/58-08/85	⊗05/86		12/80⇨**M**		
W50663	/83➲**53663**	03/58-12/84	⊗04/85		05/69⇨**M**		
W50664	09/83➲**53664**	03/58-12/86	⊗06/87		06/82⇨**M**		
W50665	09/83➲**53665**	04/58-03/86	⊗06/86		12/80⇨**M**		
W50666	06/84➲**53666**	05/58-04/86	⊗04/86		06/82⇨**M**		
W50667	03/83➲**53667**	05/58-03/86	⊗10/86		05/69⇨**M**		
W50668	08/83➲**53668**	05/58-10/85	⊗12/86		02/79⇨**M**		
W50669	/83➲**53669**	05/58-12/86	⊗06/87		05/69⇨**M**		
W50670	/83➲**53670**	05/58-12/86	⊗08/87		05/69⇨**M**		
W50671	/83➲**53671**	05/58-11/84	⊗04/85		06/69⇨**M**		
W50672	09/83➲**53672**	05/58-08/87	⊗05/89		11/81⇨**M**		
W50673	07/83➲**53673**	05/58-12/86	⊗01/87		01/82⇨**M**		
W50674	04/83➲**53674**	05/58-04/86	⊗04/86	®02/77	12/80⇨**M**		
W50675	04/83➲**53675**	05/58-03/86	⊗08/86		02/79⇨**M**		
W50676	09/83➲**53676**	06/58-06/84	⊗04/85		06/69⇨**M**		
W50677	/83➲**53677**	09/58-06/86	⊗01/87		01/63⇨**M**	12/63⇨**W**	05/69⇨**M**
W50678	07/83➲**53678**	09/58-03/86	⊗06/86		05/69⇨**M**		
W50679	07/83➲**53679**	09/58-12/86	⊗06/87		10/77⇨**M**		
W50680	05/83➲**53680**	09/58-05/86	⊗07/86		01/63⇨**M**	12/63⇨**W**	05/69⇨**M**
W50681	05/83➲**53681**	09/58-04/86	⊗05/86		06/82⇨**M**		
W50682	/84➲**53682**	09/58-09/89	⊗05/91		10/77⇨**M**		
W50683	/83➲**53683**	10/58-02/84	⊗04/85		10/77⇨**M**		
W50684	08/83➲**53684**	10/58-01/86	⊗10/86		05/69⇨**M**		
W50685	06/83➲**53685**	10/58-03/86	⊗10/86		05/69⇨**M**		
W50686	08/84➲**53686**	10/58-10/89	⊗05/91		06/82⇨**M**		⊠05/69-11/69
W50687	05/83➲**53687**	10/58-03/87	⊗04/87		05/69⇨**M**		
W50688	08/83➲**53688**	10/58-12/86	⊗04/87		01/63⇨**M**	12/63⇨**W**	05/69⇨**M**
W50689	/83➲**53689**	01/59-03/86	⊗06/86	®11/79	05/69⇨**M**		
W50690		01/59-09/68	⊗02/69				
W50691	04/83➲**53691**	01/59-11/85	⊗08/87		12/80⇨**M**		
W50692	/83➲**53692**	02/59-03/86	⊗06/86	®10/77	01/63⇨**M**	12/63⇨**W**	05/69⇨**M**
W50693	09/83➲**53693**	02/59-03/87	⊗11/87		01/63⇨**M**	12/63⇨**W**	10/77⇨**M**
W50694	09/83➲**53694**	03/59-02/86	⊗03/86		10/77⇨**M**		
W50695	/83➲**53695**	03/59-05/86	⊗05/91		10/77⇨**M**		

Class 120 BR Swindon

Driving Motor Brake Composite
DMBC
W50696-W50744

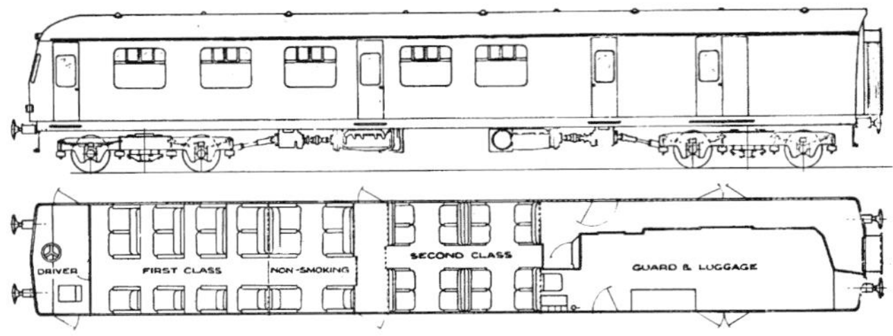

Coupling: ■ Blue square
Diagram: 587 DQ303
Lot Number: 30335
Old class: 120/1
Engines: Two BUT (AEC) 6-cyl horizontal type of 150 bhp.
Transmission: Mechanical. Standard
Body: 64' 6" × 9' 3" Cross Country
Weight: 36t
Seats: 18 first, 16 second

W50696	06/83➲**53696**	10/57-09/86	⊗01/87		06/69⇨**M**		
W50697	04/83➲**53697**	10/57-07/87	⊗04/87		05/69⇨**M**		
W50698	04/83➲**53698**	10/57-03/87	⊗07/87		06/82⇨**M**		
W50699	05/84➲**53699**	10/57-10/89	⊗08/91		12/80⇨**M**		
W50700	/85➲**53700**	10/57-09/89	⊗08/91		12/80⇨**M**		
W50701	05/83➲**53701**	10/57-11/85	⊗08/87		01/63⇨**M**	12/63⇨**W**	06/82⇨**M**
W50702	09/83➲**53702**	11/57-03/86	⊗03/86		06/82⇨**M**		
W50703	06/83➲**53703**	11/57-05/88	⊗12/88		05/69⇨**M**		
W50704	/84➲**53704**	11/57-04/87	⊗08/87	®11/79	05/69⇨**M**		
W50705	05/83➲**53705**	11/57-12/86	⊗04/87		11/80⇨**M**		
W50706	09/83➲**53706**	11/57-12/86	⊗06/87		10/79⇨**M**		
W50707	08/83➲**53707**	11/57-10/84	⊗04/85		02/81⇨**M**		
W50708	/83➲**53708**	12/57-08/87	⊗03/89	®10/77	05/69⇨**M**		
W50709	/83➲**53709**	12/57-06/86	⊗09/87		06/69⇨**M**		
W50710	07/83➲**53710**	12/57-08/85	⊗01/86		01/63⇨**M**	12/63⇨**W**	12/80⇨**M**
W50711	/84➲**53711**	12/57-12/86	⊗06/87		12/80⇨**M**		
W50712	09/83➲**53712**	01/58-01/86	⊗06/86		06/82⇨**M**		
W50713	02/83➲**53713**	01/58-05/88	⊗12/88		05/69⇨**M**		
W50714	07/83➲**53714**	03/58-04/87	⊗08/87		05/69⇨**M**		
W50715	06/83➲**53715**	03/58-09/86	⊗01/87		12/80⇨**M**		
W50716	04/83➲**53716**	03/58-03/86	⊗08/86		02/79⇨**M**		
W50717	06/83➲**53717**	04/58-09/86	⊗01/87		05/69⇨**M**		
W50718	/83➲**53718**	04/58-01/86	⊗04/87		05/69⇨**M**		
W50719	/83➲**53719**	04/58-10/85	⊗06/86		05/69⇨**M**		
W50720	09/83➲**53720**	06/58-06/86	⊗07/86		05/69⇨**M**		
W50721	09/83➲**53721**	06/58-10/85	⊗07/86		02/79⇨**M**		
W50722	07/83➲**53722**	07/58-03/87	⊗06/87		11/81⇨**M**		
W50723	04/83➲**53723**	07/58-04/86	⊗04/86		12/80⇨**M**		
W50724	07/83➲**53724**	08/58-12/86	⊗03/87		01/82⇨**M**		
W50725	07/83➲**53725**	08/58-03/87	⊗02/89		01/63⇨**M**	12/63⇨**W**	05/69⇨**M**
					⊠04/86-05/86		03/87➲**55948**
W50726	/85➲**53726**	08/58-03/87	⊗06/87		10/77⇨**M**		03/87➲**55938**
W50727	07/83➲**53727**	08/58-07/86	⊗01/87		10/77⇨**M**		
W50728	04/83➲**53728**	08/58-05/86	⊗05/86		12/80⇨**M**		
W50729	05/83➲**53729**	08/58-03/87	⊗06/87		10/77⇨**M**		⊠04/86-05/86
W50730	06/83➲**53730**	08/58-12/86	⊗04/87		01/63⇨**M**	12/63⇨**W**	05/69⇨**M**
W50731	05/83➲**53731**	08/58-12/85	⊗10/86		05/69⇨**M**		
W50732	08/84➲**53732**	11/58-10/89	⊗05/91		10/77⇨**M**		⊠11/81-08/82
W50733	/85➲**53733**	11/58-10/89	⊗05/91		06/82⇨**M**		⊠05/69-11/69
W50734	09/83➲**53734**	11/58-01/85	⊗04/85		06/69⇨**M**		
W50735	/83➲**53735**	11/58-05/86	⊗12/86		10/77⇨**M**		
W50736	07/83➲**53736**	11/58-03/87	⊗06/87	®11/79	05/69⇨**M**		
W50737	08/83➲**53737**	12/58-03/87	⊗06/87		05/69⇨**M**		
W50738	/84➲**53738**	12/58-03/87	⊗09/87		01/63⇨**M**	12/63⇨**W**	10/77⇨**M**
W50739	04/83➲**53739**	12/58-08/87	⊗05/88		10/77⇨**M**		⊠05/86-07/86
W50740		12/58-06/68	⊗01/69				
W50741	07/83➲**53741**	12/58-12/86	⊗01/88		01/63⇨**M**	12/63⇨**W**	05/69⇨**M**
W50742	/83➲**53742**	12/58-09/86	⊗03/87		05/69⇨**M**		
W50743	09/83➲**53743**	12/58-07/86	⊗07/86		01/63⇨**M**	12/63⇨**W**	05/69⇨**M**
W50744	08/83➲**53744**	12/58-03/87	⊗01/88		05/69⇨**M**		

Class 101 Metropolitan-Cammell

Driving Motor Composite Lavatory
DMCL
E50745-E50751

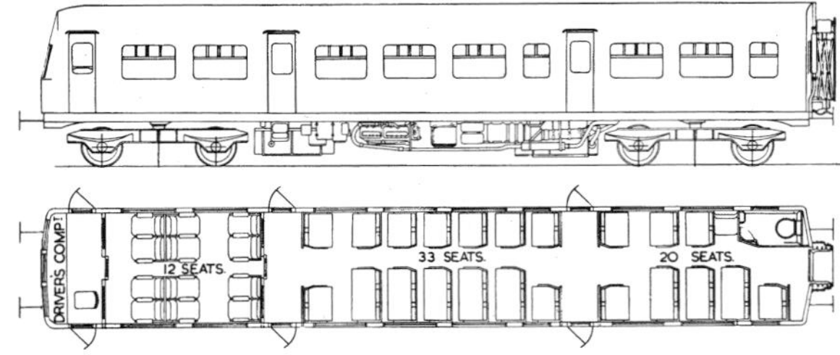

Coupling: ■ Blue square
Diagram: 621 DP304 ②DP210
Lot Number: 30271
Old class: 101/1
Engines: Two BUT (AEC) 6-cyl horizontal type of 150 bhp.
Transmission: Mechanical. Standard
Body: 57' 6" × 9' 3"
Weight: 32t
Seats: 12 first, 53 second

E50745		11/57-02/76	⊗09/87		01/65⇨**NE**	03/66⇨**SC**	
E50746	08/83➲**53746**	11/57-12/03	Ⓟ	®02/82	01/65⇨**NE**	03/66⇨**SC**	
E50747	08/83➲**53747**	11/57-11/88	⊗03/90	®08/79	01/65⇨**NE**	03/66⇨**SC**	
E50748	08/83➲**53748**	11/57-05/87	⊗11/87		01/65⇨**NE**	01/68⇨**E**	08/69⇨**SC**
E50749	08/83➲**53749**	11/57-11/88	⊗04/90	®11/78	01/65⇨**NE**	01/68⇨**E**	08/69⇨**SC**
E50750	02/85➲**53750**	11/57-11/88	⊗05/89	®02/80	01/65⇨**NE**	01/68⇨**E**	
E50751	07/83➲**53751**	11/57-09/92	⊗02/93	® /82	01/65⇨**NE**	01/68⇨**E**	

Class 105 Cravens

Driving Motor Brake Second
DMBS
M50752-M50784

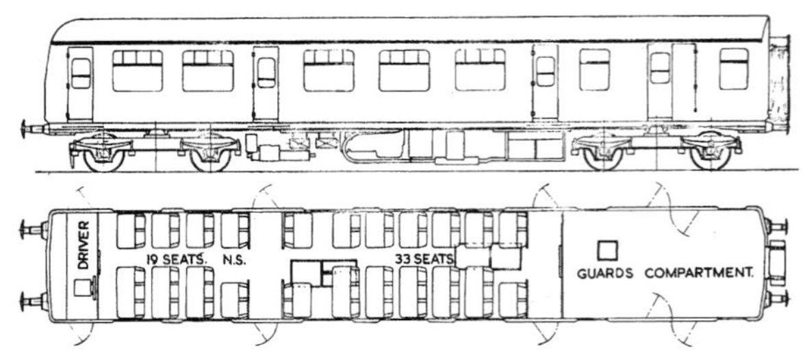

Coupling: ■ Blue square
Diagram: 528 DQ208
Lot Number: 30352

Old class:	105/2
Engines:	Two BUT (Leyland) 6-cyl horizontal type of 150 bhp.
Transmission:	Mechanical. Standard
Body:	57' 6" × 9' 3"
Weight:	30t
Seats:	52 second

M50752	09/57-11/81	⊗01/82	
M50753	09/57-10/73	⊗03/74	
M50754	10/57-06/82	⊗03/83	
M50755	10/57-09/81	⊗01/83	
M50756	10/57-12/81	⊗02/82	
M50757	10/57-02/83	⊗05/84	
M50758	11/57-12/81	⊗05/82	
M50759	11/57-09/81	⊗12/84	
M50760	11/57-07/80	⊗03/81	
M50761	11/57-07/83	⊗05/84 ®12/80	
M50762	12/57-09/81	⊗01/82	
M50763	01/58-11/81	⊗03/83	
M50764	01/58-09/82	⊗06/84	
M50765	01/58-09/82	⊗05/83	
M50766	01/58-08/82	⊗10/82	04/76⇨**SC** 04/77⇨**E** 01/78⇨**M**
M50767	01/58-09/81	⊗01/82	
M50768	02/58-04/82	⊗03/82	
M50769	02/58-09/82	⊗03/83	
M50770	03/58-06/81	⊗03/83	02/81⇨**SC**
M50771	02/58-09/81	⊗01/82	
M50772	02/58-09/82	⊗03/83	
M50773	03/58-09/81	⊗06/82	
M50774	03/58-02/69	⊗05/69	
M50775	03/58-05/69	⊗02/73	11/68⇨*E*
M50776	03/58-12/81	⊗06/82	02/81⇨**SC** 03/81⇨**M**
M50777	03/58-07/82	⊗10/82 ®10/80	
M50778	04/58-06/81	⊗01/83	03/81⇨**SC**
M50779	04/58-08/82	⊗12/82	
M50780	04/58-05/69	⊗02/73	11/68⇨*E*
M50781	05/58-11/70	⊗04/71	
M50782	04/58-06/81	⊗08/82	02/81⇨**SC**
M50783	05/58-02/62	⊗03/62	
M50784	05/58-06/82	⊗04/84	

Class 105 Cravens

Driving Motor Composite Lavatory

DMCL

M50785-M50817

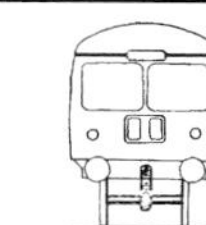

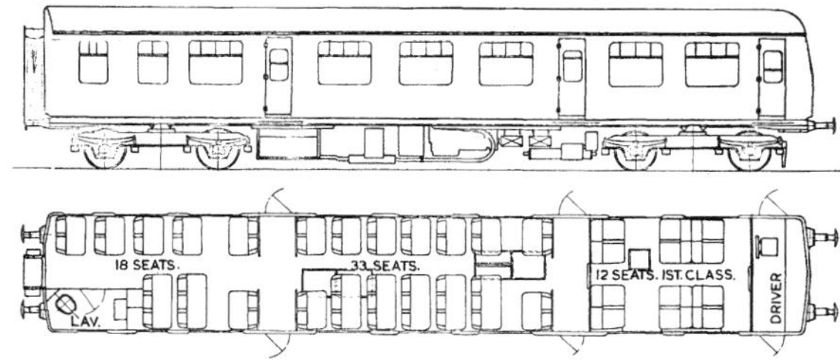

Coupling:	■ Blue square
Diagram:	529 DP308 ②DP211
Lot Number:	30353
Old class:	105/1
Engines:	Two BUT (Leyland) 6-cyl horizontal type of 150 bhp.
Transmission:	Mechanical. Standard
Body:	57' 6" × 9' 3"
Weight:	30t
Seats:	12 first, 51 second

M50785		09/57-07/80	⊗02/82	
M50786		09/57-11/81	⊗02/84	
M50787		10/57-09/82	⊗03/83	
M50788		10/57-12/80	⊗06/84	
M50789		10/57-06/81	⊗03/83	02/81⇨**SC**
M50790		10/57-12/81	⊗02/82	
M50791		11/57-12/81	⊗05/82	
M50792		11/57-09/81	⊗10/83	
M50793		11/57-09/82	⊗10/83	
M50794		11/57-07/83	⊗05/84 ®12/80	
M50795		12/57-09/81	⊗01/82	
M50796		01/58-12/82	⊗05/84	
M50797		01/58-11/81	⊗08/82	
M50798		01/58-09/82	⊗03/83	
M50799		01/58-02/69	⊗05/69	
M50800		01/58-09/81	⊗02/82	
M50801		02/58-06/82	⊗03/83	
M50802		02/58-07/82	⊗10/82	
M50803		03/58-06/81	⊗10/82	02/81⇨**SC**
M50804		02/58-08/82	⊗10/82 ®10/80	
M50805		02/58-06/81	⊗08/82	03/81⇨**SC**
M50806		03/58-09/81	⊗05/82	
M50807		03/58-07/82	⊗11/82	
M50808		03/58-10/61	⊗02/62	
M50809		03/58-09/81	⊗05/82	02/81⇨**SC** 03/81⇨**M**
M50810		03/58-08/82	⊗10/82	
M50811		04/58-04/69	⊗11/69	
M50812	07/83➲**53812**	04/58-05/89	⊗10/90	
M50813		04/58-05/69	⊗02/73	11/68⇨*E*
M50814		05/58-10/83	⊗10/83	
M50815		04/58-02/83	⊗04/84	
M50816		05/58-05/69	⊗02/73	11/68⇨*E*
M50817		05/58-01/70	⊗07/70	

Class 116 BR Derby

Driving Motor Brake Second

DMBS

W50818-W50870

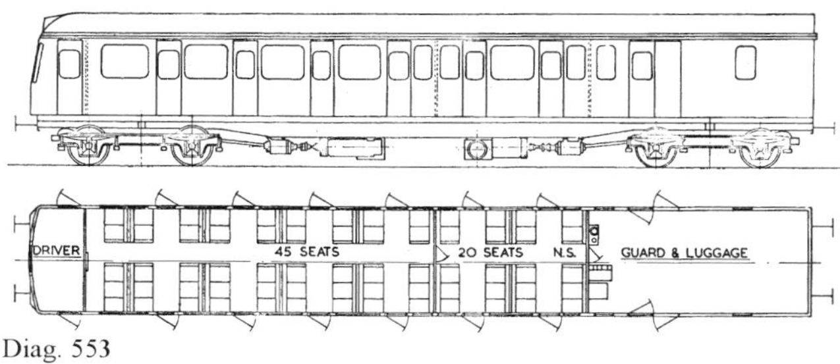

Diag. 553

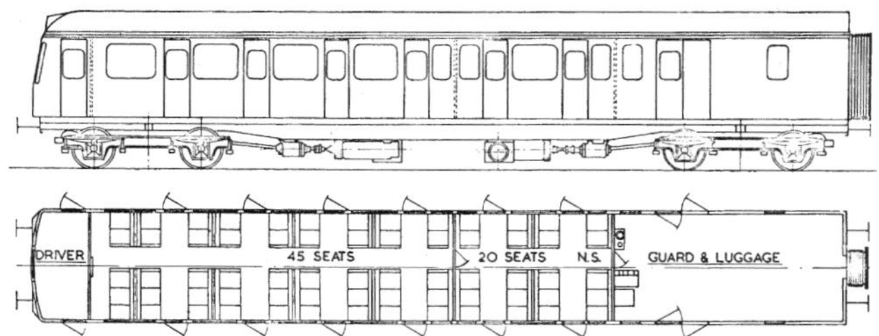

Diag. 853 ⓖ *Through gangway fitted* All WR examples fitted by 1972. Others (shown *ⓖ*) converted in the mid 1980s.

Coupling:	■ Blue square
Diagram:	553 DQ219 ⓖ 853 DQ230
Lot Number:	30363
Old class:	116/2
Engines:	Two BUT (Leyland) 6-cyl horizontal type of 150 bhp.
Transmission:	Mechanical. Standard
Body:	64' 0" × 9' 3" Suburban
Weight:	36t
Seats:	65 second

W50818	07/83➲**53818**	11/57-05/95	⊗08/95 *ⓖ*®02/79	11/66⇨**SC** 04/78⇨**M**
W50819	06/83➲**53819**	11/57-01/88	⊗03/88 ®01/78	10/77⇨**M** 09/66-10/77⇨Class 130 Parcels
W50820	07/83➲**53820**	11/57-07/92	⊗12/92 *ⓖ*®06/82	11/66⇨**SC** 03/82⇨**W**
W50821	06/83➲**53821**	11/57-03/87	⊗04/87 ®07/78	11/66⇨**SC** 04/78⇨**M**
W50822	10/83➲**53822**	11/57-06/93	⊗06/93 *ⓖ*®08/82	11/66⇨**SC**
W50823	01/84➲**53823**	12/57-12/87	⊗11/87 ®02/80	11/66⇨**SC**
W50824	07/83➲**53824**	12/57-04/88	⊗04/88 ®10/81	11/66⇨**NE** 01/68⇨**E** 02/78⇨**M**
W50825	10/83➲**53825**	11/57-06/88	⊗11/89 ®02/82	11/66⇨**SC**
W50826	08/83➲**53826**	12/57-06/91	⊗06/91 *ⓖ*®09/79	11/66⇨**SC** 04/78⇨**M**
W50827	05/83➲**53827**	11/57-11/90	⊗05/91 *ⓖ*®09/79	11/66⇨**NE** 01/68⇨**E** 02/78⇨**M** ⊠10/85-12/85
W50828	06/83➲**53828**	12/57-08/87	⊗05/88	11/66⇨**NE** 01/68⇨**E** 02/78⇨**M**
W50829	10/83➲**53829**	11/57-11/85	⊗09/86	11/66⇨**SC**
W50830	06/83➲**53830**	12/57-04/85	⊗08/86 ®06/78	11/66⇨**NE** 01/68⇨**E** 02/78⇨**M**
W50831	07/83➲**53831**	12/57-04/87	⊗04/87 ®10/77	01/63⇨**M**
W50832	06/83➲**53832**	01/58-06/88	⊗10/88 ®10/77	11/66⇨**M**
W50833	03/83➲**53833**	01/58-02/88	⊗02/88 ®04/77	01/63⇨**M**
W50834	08/83➲**53834**	01/58-10/85	⊗08/86ⓖ®06/77	10/78⇨**M**
W50835	/84➲**53835**	01/58-12/87	⊗01/88 ®10/77	11/66⇨**M**
W50836	/84➲**53836**	01/58-10/83	⊗07/84 ⓖ	06/72⇨**SC**
W50837	04/83➲**53837**	02/58-01/92	⊗02/92 *ⓖ*®11/82	11/66⇨**M**
W50838	07/83➲**53838**	01/58-05/93	⊗07/93 *ⓖ*®12/82	08/68⇨**M**
W50839	10/83➲**53839**	01/58-10/88	⊗12/90 ⓖ	06/72⇨**SC**
W50840	06/83➲**53840**	01/58-01/87	⊗02/87 ®09/81	08/68⇨**M**
W50841	01/84➲**53841**	01/58-09/86	⊗09/86	08/68⇨**E** 04/77⇨**SC**
W50842	07/83➲**53842**	02/58-07/88	⊗12/90ⓖ®02/76	10/78⇨**M**

W50843 04/83➲**53843** 01/58-09/89 ⊙07/90◎®11/76 ⊠08/89-08/89
W50844 02/83➲**53844** 02/58-12/90 ⊙05/91◎®03/83 06/72⇨SC 06/77⇨E
W50845 04/83➲**53845** 01/58-06/87 ⊙08/87◎®11/79 06/72⇨SC 04/77⇨E
W50846 10/83➲**53846** 01/58-12/87 ⊙11/87 04/68⇨E 06/77⇨SC
W50847 04/83➲**53847** 02/58-11/88 ⊙03/89◎®02/77
W50848 04/83➲**53848** 02/58-10/89 ⊙06/90◎®07/78
W50849 08/83➲**53849** 02/58-06/91 ⊙06/91@®09/84 07/68⇨M
W50850 03/83➲**53850** 02/58-03/92 ⊙03/92@®09/79 07/68⇨M
W50851 06/83➲**53851** 02/58-12/86 ⊙01/87◎®12/78 05/77⇨M
W50852 07/83➲**53852** 02/58-04/87 ⊙08/87 ®06/78 05/69⇨SC 02/78⇨M
W50853 04/83➲**53853** 03/58-10/92 ⊙10/92@® /82 08/68⇨E 06/77⇨SC 11/81⇨E
W50854 03/83➲**53854** 02/58-06/92 ⊙10/92◎®03/80 03/76⇨M ⊠11/90-12/90
W50855 04/83➲**53855** 03/58-11/89 ⊙04/90◎®02/77
W50856 04/83➲**53856** 03/58-10/88 ⊙09/88◎®09/76
W50857 07/83➲**53857** 03/58-01/89 ⊙03/89◎®10/78 04/76⇨M
W50858 04/83➲**53858** 04/58-10/89 ⊙05/90◎®01/76
W50859 10/83➲**53859** 04/58-03/86 ⊙10/87 12/63⇨M 11/78⇨SC
W50860 09/83➲**53860** 03/58-03/87 ⊙02/87 ®01/78 12/63⇨M
W50861 07/83➲**53861** 04/58-07/87 ⊙05/88 ®10/77 12/63⇨M
W50862 04/83➲**53862** 04/58-06/88 ⊙10/88 ®01/78 10/77⇨M
09/66-10/77⇨Class 130 Parcels
W50863 07/83➲**53863** 05/58-05/93 ⊙07/93◎®05/83 04/78⇨M
W50864 04/83➲**53864** 05/58-07/87 ⊙08/88◎®06/78
W50865 05/83➲**53865** 05/58-01/92 ⊙02/92◎®09/83 03/76⇨M 09/79⇨E
W50866 04/83➲**53866** 05/58-02/89 ⊙03/89◎®11/79 05/76⇨M
W50867 04/83➲**53867** 05/58-10/88 ⊙10/88◎®11/79 06/72⇨SC 06/77⇨E
W50868 04/83➲**53868** 06/58-03/87 ⊙08/87◎®11/78
W50869 04/83➲**53869** 07/58-02/89 ⊙03/89◎®09/76
W50870 09/83➲**53870** 07/58-11/88 ⊙12/88 07/68⇨M

Class 116 BR Derby
Driving Motor Second
DMS
W50871-W50923

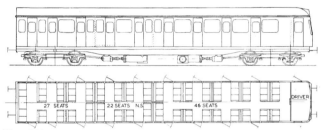

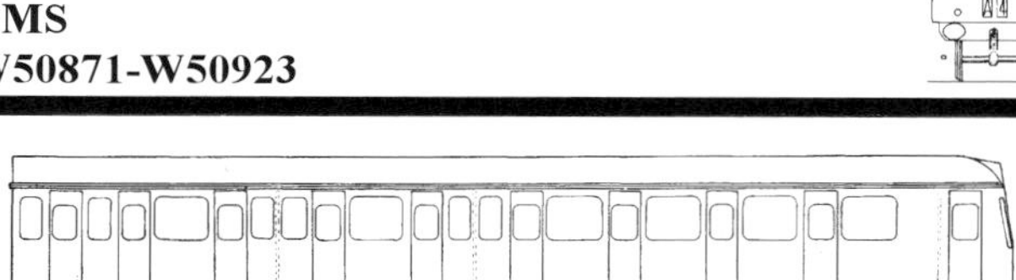

Diag. 554

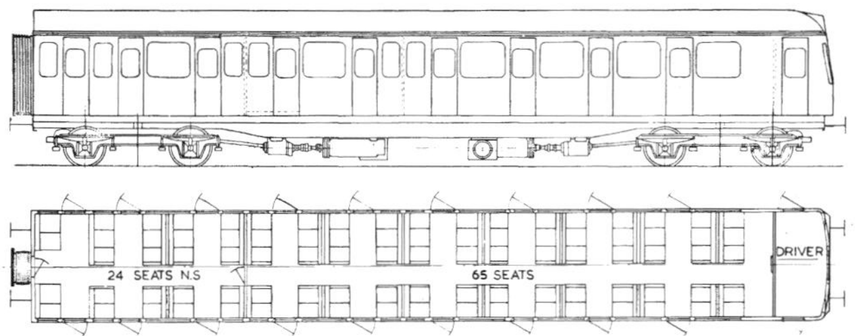

Diag. 854 ◎ *Through gangway fitted* All WR examples fitted by 1972. Others (shown @) converted in the mid 1980s.

Coupling: ■ Blue square
Diagram: 554 DP201 ◎ 854 DP220
Lot Number: 30364
Old class: 116/1
Engines: Two BUT (Leyland) 6-cyl horizontal type of 150 bhp.
Transmission: Mechanical. Standard
Body: 64' 0" × 9' 3" Suburban
Weight: 36t
Seats: 95 second ◎ 89 second

W50871 07/83➲**53871** 11/57-01/88 ⊙02/88 ®06/78 11/66⇨SC 02/78⇨M
W50872 04/83➲**53872** 11/57-06/88 ⊙10/88 ®01/78 10/77⇨M
09/66-10/77⇨Class 130 Parcels
W50873 10/83➲**53873** 11/57-04/92 ⊙10/92@®02/82 11/66⇨SC
W50874 11/57-02/76 ⊙10/78 11/66⇨SC
W50875 06/83➲**53875** 11/57-10/87 ⊙10/87 ®07/78 11/66⇨SC 04/78⇨M
W50876 01/84➲**53876** 12/57-12/87 ⊙11/87 ®02/80 11/66⇨SC
W50877 12/57-01/83 ⊙05/87 11/66⇨NE 01/68⇨E 02/78⇨M
11/78⇨SC
W50878 07/83➲**53878** 11/57-03/92 ⊙03/92@®02/79 11/66⇨SC 04/78⇨M
W50879 10/83➲**53879** 12/57-11/85 ⊙09/86 11/66⇨SC
W50880 05/83➲**53880** 11/57-11/90 ⊙05/91@®09/79 11/66⇨NE 01/68⇨E 02/78⇨M

W50881 10/83➲**53881** 11/57-09/92 ⊙09/97 @®08/82 08/68⇨E 06/77⇨SC
10/92➲**TDB977825**
W50882 /83➲**53882** 11/57-03/87 ⊙04/87 11/66⇨SC
W50883 06/83➲**53883** 12/57-06/87 ⊙08/87 ®06/78 11/66⇨NE 01/68⇨E 02/78⇨M
W50884 07/83➲**53884** 12/57-12/87 ⊙02/88 ®10/77 01/63⇨M
W50885 06/83➲**53885** 01/58-12/87 ⊙12/87 ®10/77 11/66⇨M
W50886 07/83➲**53886** 01/58-09/92 ⊙03/94 @®06/82 01/63⇨M 10/92➲**TDB977827**
W50887 08/83➲**53887** 01/58-10/89 ⊙06/90◎®06/77 10/78⇨M
W50888 /83➲**53888** 01/58-12/85 ⊙01/87 ®10/77 11/66⇨M
W50889 /84➲**53889** 01/58-10/83 ⊙07/84 ◎ 06/72⇨SC
W50890 04/83➲**53890** 02/58-03/92 ⊙03/92 @®11/82 11/66⇨M
W50891 07/83➲**53891** 01/58-01/93 ⊙03/93 @®01/83 08/68⇨M ⊠06/92-07/92
W50892 09/83➲**53892** 01/58-03/87 ⊙04/87 ◎ 06/72⇨SC
W50893 07/83➲**53893** 01/58-09/90 ⊙08/92 @ 08/68⇨M
W50894 04/83➲**53894** 01/58-10/92 ⊙10/92 @® /82 08/68⇨E 06/77⇨SC 11/81⇨E
W50895 07/83➲**53895** 02/58-10/88 ⊙10/88◎®02/76 10/78⇨M
W50896 04/83➲**53896** 01/58-06/88 ⊙06/88◎®11/76
W50897 02/83➲**53897** 02/58-08/94 ⊙08/94◎®03/83 06/72⇨SC 06/77⇨E
W50898 05/83➲**53898** 01/58-06/87 ⊙08/87 ◎ 06/72⇨SC 04/77⇨E
W50899 10/83➲**53899** 01/58-03/86 ⊙10/87 04/68⇨E 04/77⇨SC
W50900 04/83➲**53900** 02/58-04/88 ⊙01/89◎®02/77
W50901 04/83➲**53901** 02/58-05/88 ⊙09/88◎®07/78
W50902 06/83➲**53902** 02/58-09/93 ⊙03/94 @®10/80 07/68⇨M
W50903 06/83➲**53903** 02/58-06/87 ⊙08/87 07/68⇨M
W50904 06/83➲**53904** 02/58-11/88 ⊙03/89◎®12/78 05/77⇨M
W50905 08/83➲**53905** 02/58-12/87 ⊙11/87 ®09/79 05/69⇨SC 04/78⇨M
W50906 07/83➲**53906** 03/58-04/88 ⊙01/89 ®10/81 11/66⇨NE 01/68⇨E 02/78⇨M
W50907 03/83➲**53907** 02/58-06/92 ⊙03/93◎®03/80 03/76⇨M ⊠11/90-12/90
W50908 04/83➲**53908** 03/58-11/89 ⊙04/90◎®02/77
W50909 04/83➲**53909** 03/58-10/88 ⊙09/88◎®09/76
W50910 07/83➲**53910** 03/58-11/88 ⊙03/89◎®10/78 04/76⇨M
W50911 04/83➲**53911** 04/58-10/89 ⊙07/90◎®01/76
W50912 07/83➲**53912** 04/58-05/87 ⊙08/87 ®10/77 12/63⇨M
W50913 09/83➲**53913** 03/58-05/88 ⊙09/88 ®01/78 12/63⇨M
W50914 04/83➲**53914** 04/58-03/88 ⊙03/88 ®10/77 12/63⇨M
W50915 06/83➲**53915** 04/58-08/87 ⊙05/88 ®01/78 10/77⇨M
09/66-10/77⇨Class 130 Parcels
W50916 03/83➲**53916** 05/58-05/93 ⊙02/96◎®05/83 04/78⇨M
W50917 04/83➲**53917** 05/58-07/87 ⊙08/88◎®06/78
W50918 04/83➲**53918** 05/58-03/87 ⊙08/87◎®11/78
W50919 04/83➲**53919** 05/58-06/95 ⊙06/95◎®08/79 05/76⇨M
W50920 05/83➲**53920** 05/58-10/88 ⊙10/88 ◎ 06/72⇨SC 06/77⇨E
W50921 04/83➲**53921** 06/58-05/95 ⊙06/95◎®09/83 03/76⇨M 09/79⇨E
W50922 04/83➲**53922** 07/58-02/89 ⊙03/89◎®09/76
W50923 05/84➲**53923** 07/58-11/88 ⊙12/88 07/68⇨M

Class 108 BR Derby
Driving Motor Brake Second
DMBS
M50924-M50935

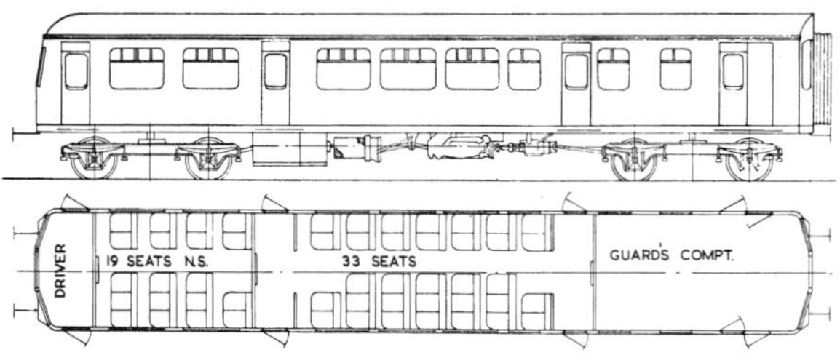

Coupling: ■ Blue square
Diagram: 543 DQ212
Lot Number: 30460
Old class: 108/2
Engines: Two BUT (AEC) 6-cyl horizontal type of 150 bhp.
Transmission: Mechanical. Standard
Body: 58' 1" × 9' 2"
Weight: 29t
Seats: 52 second

M50924 09/83➲**53924** 10/59-10/91 ⊙01/92 ®07/77 10/91➲**ADB977747**
M50925 /84➲**53925** 12/59-05/92 ⊙05/92
M50926 08/83➲**53926** 11/59-09/92 Ⓟ ®08/82 10/92➲**ADB977814**
M50927 /84➲**53927** 11/59-05/92 ⊙10/92 ®11/80
M50928 09/84➲**53928** 11/59-03/92 Ⓟ ®03/79
M50929 05/83➲**53929** 11/59-10/91 ⊙03/94 ®04/82 10/91➲**ADB977746**
M50930 05/83➲**53930** 12/59-02/92 ⊙02/92
M50931 /83➲**53931** 12/59-01/92 ⊙02/92
M50932 04/83➲**53932** 12/59-10/90 ⊙11/90 ®04/82
M50933 /83➲**53933** 01/60-11/92 Ⓟ
M50934 01/85➲**53934** 01/60-09/91 ⊙10/91 ®09/76
M50935 /85➲**53935** 01/60-11/92 ⊙01/93 ®10/76

Class 126 BR Swindon

Driving Motor Second Lavatory
DMSL
SC50936

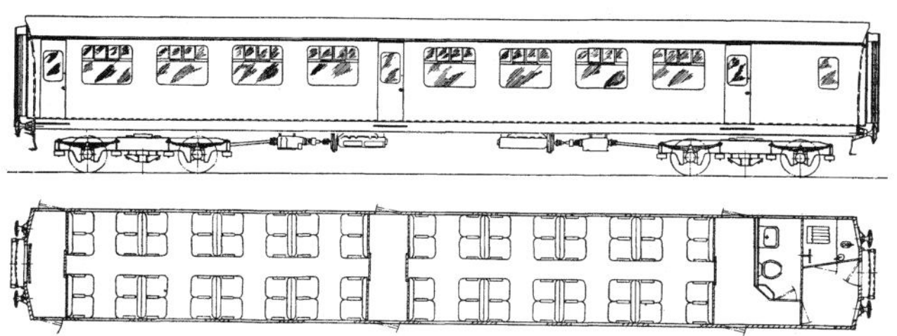

Coupling: ● White circle
Diagram: 551 DP208
Lot Number: 30413
Old class: 126/1
Engines: Two BUT (AEC) 6-cyl horizontal type of 150 bhp.
Transmission: Mechanical. Standard
Body: 64' 6" × 9' 3" Inter-City
Weight: 39t 3cwt
Seats: 64 second

SC50936		11/59-03/82	⊗10/82		

Class 108 BR Derby

Driving Motor Brake Second
DMBS
M50938-M50987

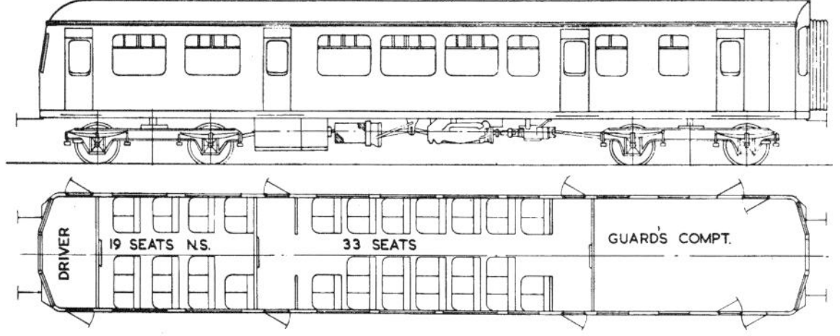

Coupling: ■ Blue square
Diagram: 543 DQ212
Lot Number: 30465
Old class: 108/2
Engines: Two BUT (Leyland) 6-cyl horizontal type of 150 bhp.
Transmission: Mechanical. Standard
Body: 58' 1" × 9' 2"
Weight: 28t 10cwt
Seats: 52 second

M50938	04/83➲**53938**	01/59-01/92	⊗03/92	®08/78	
M50939	04/83➲**53939**	01/59-09/92	⊗07/96	® /81	10/92➲**ADB977818**
M50940	09/83➲**53940**	01/59-06/92	⊗06/92	®11/80	
M50941	05/83➲**53941**	01/59-09/92	⊗10/96	®10/78	10/92➲**ADB977836**
M50942	02/83➲**53942**	01/59-07/91	⊗01/94	®06/78	
M50943	/85➲**53943**	01/59-07/92	⊗11/92	®07/77	
M50944	/84➲**53944**	01/59-01/92	⊗03/94	®04/82	01/92➲**ADB977766**
M50945	/83➲**53945**	01/59-06/92	⊗12/92	®10/77	
M50946		01/59-06/72	⊗12/72		
M50947	/83➲**53947**	02/59-06/92	⊗12/92	®11/77	
M50948	/83➲**53948**	02/59-02/92	⊗01/92	®01/78	
M50949	/83➲**53949**	02/59-04/91	⊗12/91	®01/78	
M50950	06/83➲**53950**	02/59-10/91	⊗03/94	®10/83	10/91➲**ADB977748**
M50951	05/83➲**53951**	02/59-06/92	⊗06/92		
M50952	06/83➲**53952**	02/59-12/90	⊗03/92		
M50953	06/83➲**53953**	02/59-07/91	⊗03/92		
M50954	06/83➲**53954**	03/59-07/91	⊗03/92		
M50955	06/83➲**53955**	03/59-04/91	⊗02/92		
M50956	06/83➲**53956**	03/59-09/92	⊗07/96		10/92➲**ADB977811**
M50957	06/83➲**53957**	03/59-10/91	⊗03/92	®10/77	10/91➲**ADB977751**
M50958	06/83➲**53958**	04/59-09/92	⊗02/96		10/92➲**ADB977809**
M50959	06/83➲**53959**	04/59-10/91	⊗03/92		10/91➲**ADB977749**
M50960	06/83➲**53960**	04/59-03/92	⊗02/92	®08/81	
M50961		04/59-01/74	⊗08/74		
M50962	06/83➲**53962**	04/59-12/90	⊗02/92		
M50963	06/83➲**53963**	06/59-10/91	⊗04/96		10/91➲**ADB977750**
M50964	04/83➲**53964**	05/59-06/92	⊗06/92		
M50965	06/83➲**53965**	05/59-02/91	⊗11/91		
M50966	06/83➲**53966**	05/59-06/92	⊗05/92		⊠12/90-01/91
M50967	06/83➲**53967**	06/59-05/88	⊗10/89		
M50968	06/83➲**53968**	05/59-07/92	⊗08/92		
M50969	06/83➲**53969**	06/59-10/91	⊗10/91	®08/80	
M50970	/83➲**53970**	07/59-04/92	⊗06/92	®01/78	
M50971	06/83➲**53971**	07/59-02/93	ⓟ	®07/79	
M50972		07/59-11/71	⊗05/72		
M50973	06/83➲**53973**	07/59-06/92	⊗06/92	®04/80	
M50974	02/83➲**53974**	07/59-06/92	⊗06/92	®08/78	
M50975	/83➲**53975**	08/59-05/91	⊗09/91	®01/78	
M50976	06/83➲**53976**	08/59-05/91	⊗11/91	®11/77	
M50977	06/83➲**53977**	08/59-06/91	⊗10/91	®09/76	
M50978	/83➲**53978**	08/59-06/92	⊗06/92	®07/78	
M50979		08/59-09/71	⊗05/72		
M50980	/83➲**53980**	09/59-01/93	ⓟ		
M50981	06/8➲**53981**	09/59-10/92	⊗08/95	®05/77	10/92➲**ADB977838**
M50982	06/83➲**53982**	09/59-09/92	ⓟ⊗ /02	®12/83	10/92➲**ADB977816**
M50983	/83➲**53983**	10/59-07/91	⊗08/91	®06/78	
M50984		10/59-11/69	⊗08/70	®06/78	
M50985	/83➲**53985**	10/59-10/87	⊗12/90	®01/78	
M50986	04/85➲**53986**	10/59-06/92	⊗06/92	®06/78	⊠11/90-12/90
M50987	06/83➲**53987**	10/59-01/93	ⓟ⊗02/98		

Class 125 BR Derby

Driving Motor Second
DMS
E50988-E51007

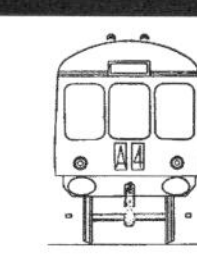

Coupling: ★ Orange star
Diagram: 596
Lot Number: 30462
Old class: 125/2
Engines: Two Rolls-Royce 8-cyl horizontal type of 238 bhp.
Transmission: Hydraulic. Twin-disc torque converter
Body: 64' 0" × 9' 3" Suburban
Weight: 39t 10cwt
Seats: 95 second

E50988	12/58-01/77	⊗03/81
E50989	01/59-10/76	⊗03/77
E50990	01/59-12/76	⊗06/79
E50991	01/59-01/77	⊗01/81
E50992	01/59-01/77	⊗11/81
E50993	01/59-01/77	⊗07/80
E50994	01/59-01/77	⊗03/81
E50995	02/59-02/77	⊗03/81
E50996	02/59-10/76	⊗03/77
E50997	02/59-01/77	⊗07/80
E50998	02/59-01/77	⊗07/78
E50999	02/59-10/76	⊗03/77
E51000	03/59-12/76	⊗07/80
E51001	05/59-01/77	⊗03/81
E51002	05/59-01/77	⊗12/77
E51003	05/59-12/76	⊗11/81
E51004	04/59-12/76	⊗03/81
E51005	04/59-01/77	⊗11/81
E51006	05/59-01/77	⊗07/81
E51007	09/59-01/77	⊗07/80

Class 126 BR Swindon

Driving Motor Second Lavatory

DMSL

SC51008-SC51029

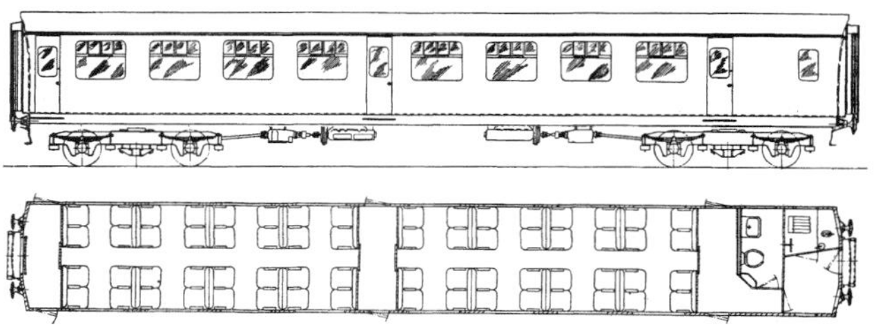

Coupling:	● White circle
Diagram:	551 DP208
Lot Number:	30413
Old class:	126/1
Engines:	Two BUT (AEC) 6-cyl horizontal type of 150 bhp.
Transmission:	Mechanical. Standard
Body:	64' 6" × 9' 3" Inter-City
Weight:	39t 3cwt
Seats:	64 second

SC51008	04/59-08/82	⊗12/82	
SC51009	04/59-11/81	⊗12/82	
SC51010	04/59-11/81	⊗03/83	
SC51011	04/59-09/73	⊗ /74	
SC51012	04/59-08/82	⊗10/82	
SC51013	04/59-08/82	⊗11/83	
SC51014	08/59-09/81	⊗10/81	
SC51015	08/59-08/82	⊗01/84	
SC51016	08/59-08/82	⊗11/83	
SC51017	08/59-01/83	Ⓟ	⊠08/82-08/82
SC51018	08/59-03/82	⊗10/82	
SC51019	08/59-07/81	⊗02/83	
SC51020	08/59-08/82	⊗03/83	
SC51021	08/59-11/81	⊗11/82	
SC51022	10/59-03/82	⊗11/82	
SC51023	10/59-11/81	⊗02/83	
SC51024	10/59-07/81	⊗10/81	
SC51025	10/59-08/82	⊗11/83	
SC51026	10/59-01/83	⊗01/84	⊠08/82-08/82
SC51027	11/59-11/81	⊗12/82	
SC51028	11/59-06/77	⊗11/78	
SC51029	11/59-08/82	⊗04/83	⊠08/82-08/82

Class 126 BR Swindon

Driving Motor Brake Second Lavatory

DMBSL

SC51030-SC51051

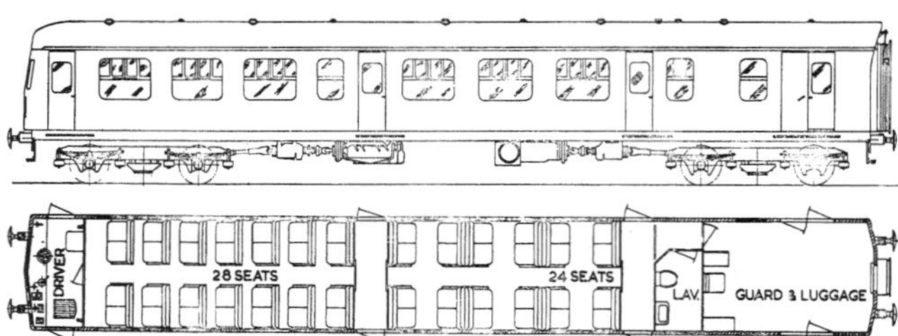

Coupling:	● White circle
Diagram:	608 DQ226
Lot Number:	30414
Old class:	126/2
Engines:	Two BUT (AEC) 6-cyl horizontal type of 150 bhp.
Transmission:	Mechanical. Standard
Body:	64' 6" × 9' 3" Inter-City
Weight:	37t 16cwt
Seats:	52 second

SC51030	05/59-11/81	⊗02/83	
SC51031	05/59-05/79	⊗07/79	
SC51032	05/59-03/82	⊗11/82	
SC51033	05/59-03/82	⊗01/84	
SC51034	05/59-08/82	⊗04/83	
SC51035	05/59-07/81	⊗10/81	
SC51036	06/59-01/83	⊗01/84	⊠08/82-08/82
SC51037	06/59-08/82	⊗02/83	
SC51038	06/59-08/82	⊗01/84	
SC51039	06/59-08/82	⊗01/83	
SC51040	06/59-08/82	⊗01/83	
SC51041	06/59-09/81	⊗10/81	
SC51042	06/59-08/82	⊗11/83	⊠08/82-08/82
SC51043	06/59-01/83	Ⓟ	
SC51044	09/59-08/82	⊗02/83	
SC51045	09/59-07/81	⊗02/83	
SC51046	09/59-03/82	⊗05/82	
SC51047	09/59-11/81	⊗02/83	
SC51048	09/59-08/82	⊗11/83	
SC51049	09/59-11/81	⊗12/82	
SC51050	09/59-11/81	⊗12/82	
SC51051	09/59-11/81	⊗05/82	

Class 119 Gloucester RC&W

Driving Motor Brake Composite

DMBC

W51052-W51079

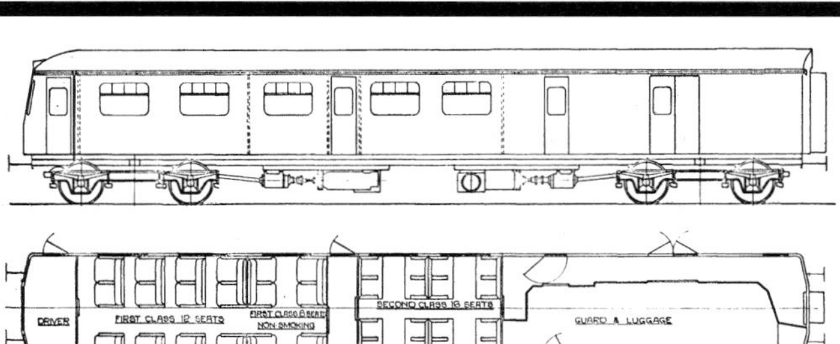

Coupling:	■ Blue square
Diagram:	540 DQ302
Lot Number:	30421
Old class:	119/1
Engines:	Two BUT (AEC) 6-cyl horizontal type of 150 bhp.
Transmission:	Mechanical. Standard
Body:	64' 6" × 9' 3" Cross Country
Weight:	37t
Seats:	18 first, 16 second

W51052	10/58-03/88	⊗09/90		
W51053	10/58-12/68	⊗09/70	04/68⇨**SC**	
W51054	10/58-03/88	⊗11/90		
W51055	10/58-05/88	⊗10/90		
W51056	11/58-03/88	⊗*09/90*		
W51057	11/58-05/89	⊗05/89	01/63⇨**M**	10/79⇨**W**
W51058	12/58-08/88	⊗10/88	01/63⇨**M**	10/77⇨**W**
W51059	12/58-03/88	⊗02/93	01/63⇨**M**	10/77⇨**W**
W51060	01/59-06/93	⊗06/93		
W51061	01/59-12/68	⊗09/70	*04/68⇨SC*	
W51062	02/59-10/90	⊗02/93		
W51063	02/59-07/88	⊗04/89		
W51064	03/59-06/86	⊗04/90		
W51065	03/59-03/92	⊗03/93		
W51066	04/59-07/92	⊗02/93		
W51067	06/59-08/87	⊗09/90		
W51068	06/59-07/87	⊗*09/90*		
W51069	06/59-10/87	⊗05/89		
W51070	06/59-05/86	⊗10/86		
W51071	07/59-10/89	⊗11/90	01/63⇨**M**	10/77⇨**W**
W51072	07/59-07/87	⊗09/90	01/63⇨**M**	10/77⇨**W**
W51073	08/59-06/95	Ⓟ	01/63⇨**M**	10/77⇨**W**
W51074	09/59-10/93	Ⓟ	01/63⇨**M**	10/77⇨**W**
W51075	10/59-12/87	⊗09/90		
W51076	10/59-09/93	⊗09/95	01/63⇨**M**	10/77⇨**W**
W51077	12/59-06/87	⊗04/90		
W51078	12/59-03/88	⊗09/90		
W51079	01/60-06/95	⊗08/95		

Class 119 Gloucester RC&W

Driving Motor Second Lavatory
DMSL
W51080-W51107

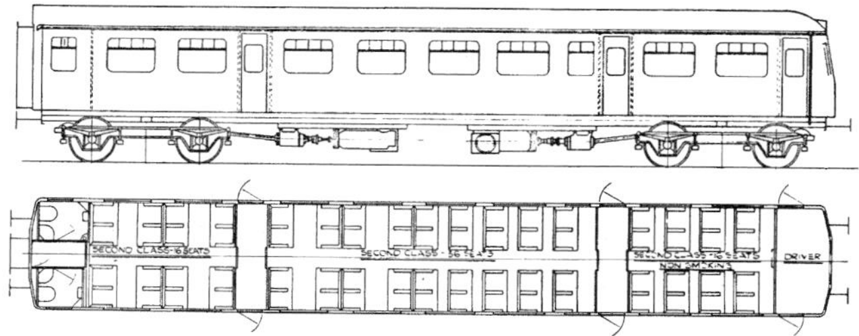

Coupling: ■ Blue square
Diagram: 541 DP203
Lot Number: 30422
Old class: 119/2
Engines: Two BUT (AEC) 6-cyl horizontal type of 150 bhp.
Transmission: Mechanical. Standard
Body: 64' 6" × 9' 3" Cross Country
Weight: 38t
Seats: 68 second

W51080	09/58-01/88	⊗05/93	
W51081	09/58-12/68	⊗09/70	04/68⇨SC
W51082	10/58-03/88	⊗09/90	
W51083	10/58-03/88	⊗*09/90*	
W51084	11/58-08/87	⊗09/90	
W51085	11/58-07/87	⊗10/90	01/63⇨M 10/77⇨W
W51086	12/58-10/93	⊗12/95	01/63⇨M 10/77⇨W
W51087	12/58-03/88	⊗10/88	01/63⇨M 10/77⇨W
W51088	01/59-06/93	⊗06/93	
W51089	01/59-12/68	⊗09/70	04/68⇨SC
W51090	02/59-02/92	⊗02/93	
W51091	02/59-10/88	⊗04/89	
W51092	03/59-12/87	⊗10/90	
W51093	03/59-01/85	⊗09/86	
W51094	04/59-07/92	⊗02/93	
W51095	06/59-05/89	⊗05/89	
W51096	06/59-02/87	⊗10/90	
W51097	06/59-10/87	⊗05/89	
W51098	06/59-07/87	⊗10/90	
W51099	07/59-09/93	⊗09/95	01/63⇨M 10/77⇨W
W51100	07/59-03/88	⊗09/90	01/63⇨M 10/79⇨W
W51101	08/59-10/89	⊗11/90	01/63⇨M 10/77⇨W
W51102	09/59-03/88	⊗01/89	01/63⇨M 10/77⇨W
W51103	10/59-02/92	⊗02/93	
W51104	10/59-06/95	Ⓟ	01/63⇨M 10/77⇨W
W51105	12/59-02/87	⊗09/87	
W51106	12/59-03/88	⊗10/90	
W51107	01/60-06/95	⊗08/95	

Class 100 Gloucester RC&W

Driving Motor Brake Second
DMBS
SC51108-SC51127

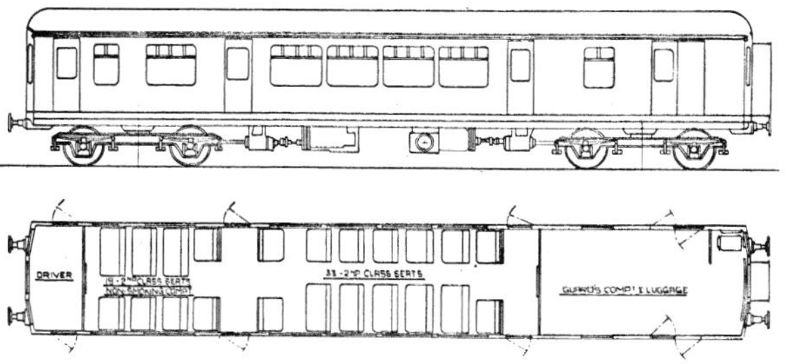

Coupling: ■ Blue square
Diagram: 536 DQ201
Lot Number: 30444
Old class: 100
Engines: Two BUT (AEC) 6-cyl horizontal type of 150 bhp.
Transmission: Mechanical. Standard
Body: 57' 6" × 9' 3"
Weight: 30t
Seats: 52 second

SC51108		10/57-05/72	⊗12/75		06/67⇨NE 01/68⇨E	
SC51109		10/57-08/72	⊗03/73			
SC51110		10/57-08/82	⊗06/84		05/75⇨M	⊠10/72-12/72
SC51111		11/57-09/73	⊗08/74		05/68⇨E	
SC51112		11/57-09/81	⊗05/85		05/75⇨M	
SC51113		11/57-11/66	⊗01/68			
SC51114		11/57-08/76	⊗03/81		06/67⇨NE 01/68⇨E	
SC51115		11/57-10/72			06/67⇨NE 01/68⇨E	05/74➲DB975348
E51115	➲TDB975348	03/76-12/82	⊗04/84		11/80⇨M	↺
SC51116		12/57-10/72	⊗07/93		05/68⇨E	05/74➲DB975349
SC51117		12/57-06/84	⊗10/83		05/75⇨M	⊠10/72-12/72
SC51118		12/57-10/72	Ⓟ		06/67⇨NE 01/68⇨E	
SC51119		01/58-08/82	⊗06/84		05/75⇨M	
SC51120		01/58-06/78	⊗05/81		06/67⇨NE 01/68⇨E	
SC51121		01/58-10/71	⊗03/73		06/67⇨NE 01/68⇨E	
SC51122		01/58-03/77	⊗08/90		05/75⇨E	⊠10/72-01/73 11/78-➲DB975664
SC51123		01/58-07/73	⊗08/74		05/68⇨E	
SC51124		02/58-07/82	⊗11/83	®11/79	05/75⇨E 11/80⇨M	⊠10/72-12/72
SC51125		02/58-10/77	⊗03/81		06/67⇨NE 01/68⇨E	
SC51126		02/58-12/77	⊗04/81		05/68⇨E	
SC51127		03/58-12/82	⊗05/84		05/75⇨E	⊠10/72-01/73

Class 116 BR Derby

Driving Motor Brake Second
DMBS
W51128-W51140

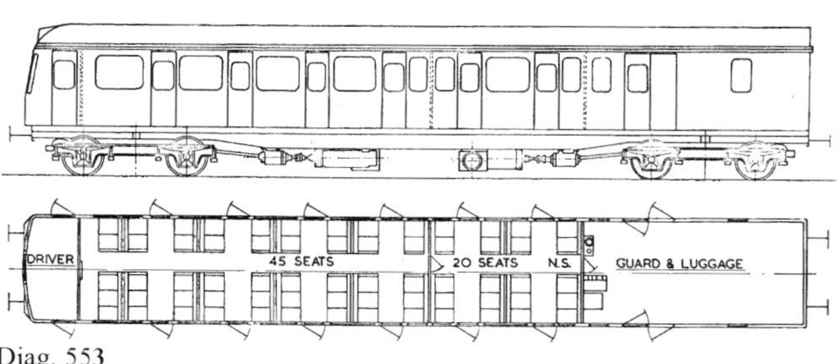

Diag. 553

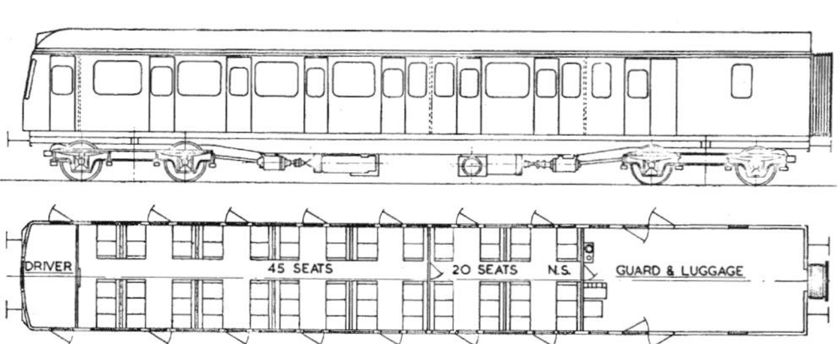

Diag. 853 ⓖ *Through gangway fitted* All WR examples fitted by 1972. Others (shown *ⓖ*) converted in the mid 1980s.

Coupling: ■ Blue square
Diagram: 553 DQ219 ⓖ 853 DQ230
Lot Number: 30446
Old class: 116/2
Engines: Two BUT (Leyland) 6-cyl horizontal type of 150 bhp.
Transmission: Mechanical. Standard
Body: 64' 0" × 9' 3" Suburban
Weight: 36t
Seats: 65 second

W51128	07/58-02/93	⊗06/94	ⓖ®10/76		
W51129	08/58-03/93	⊗03/93	*ⓖ*® /78	12/63⇨M	
W51130	08/58-01/92	⊗02/92	*ⓖ*	12/63⇨M	
W51131	08/58-09/93	Ⓟ	*ⓖ*®07/78	12/63⇨M	⊠12/90-01/91
W51132	08/58-11/92	⊗11/92	ⓖ®08/76		
W51133	08/58-03/92	⊗06/92	*ⓖ*	12/63⇨M	
W51134	09/58-05/93	Ⓟ⊗04/09	ⓖ®11/77		
W51135	09/58-04/92	Ⓟ⊗04/09	ⓖ®04/77		
W51136	09/58-03/92	⊗06/92	ⓖ®05/80	05/77⇨M	
W51137	10/58-10/72	⊗08/73		04/68⇨SC 07/69⇨W	12/65⇨Class 130 Parcels
W51138	10/58-11/93	Ⓟ	ⓖ®09/79	04/76⇨M	11/93➲*977921*
W51139	10/58-07/91	⊗06/92	ⓖ®11/76		
W51140	11/58-02/93	⊗06/95	ⓖ®06/78		

Class 116 BR Derby

Driving Motor Second

DMS

W51141-W51153

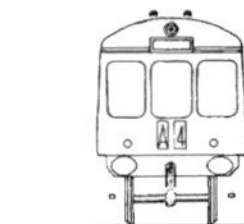

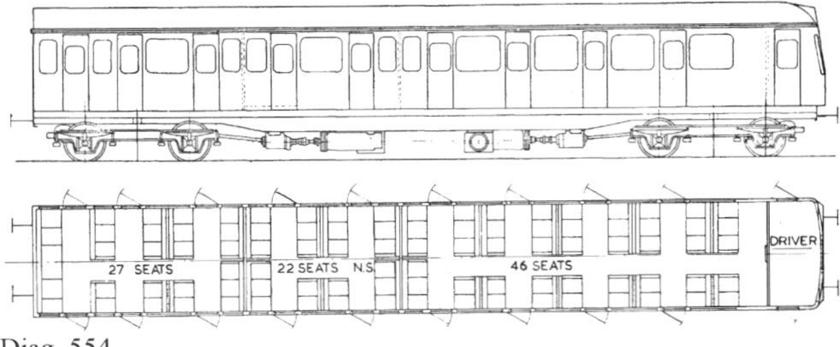

Diag. 554

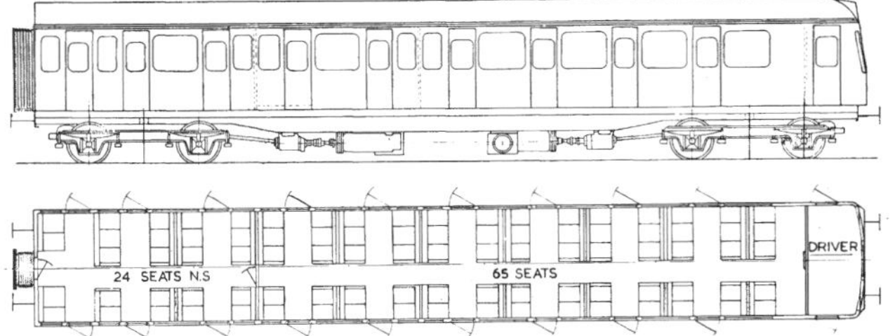

Diag. 854 ⓖ *Through gangway fitted* All WR examples fitted by 1972. Others (shown *ⓖ*) converted in the mid 1980s.

Coupling:	■ Blue square
Diagram:	554 DP201 ⓖ 854 DP220
Lot Number:	30447
Old class:	116/1
Engines:	Two BUT (Leyland) 6-cyl horizontal type of 150 bhp.
Transmission:	Mechanical. Standard
Body:	64' 0" × 9' 3" Suburban
Weight:	36t
Seats:	95 second ⓖ 89 second

W51141	07/58-08/93	⊗09/93	ⓖ®10/76		⊠05/93-08/93
W51142	08/58-01/94	⊗03/94	*ⓖ*®11/79	12/63⇨**M**	
W51143	08/58-11/92	⊗03/93	*ⓖ*®03/79	12/63⇨**M**	
W51144	08/58-06/95	⊗08/95	*ⓖ*®07/78	12/63⇨**M**	
W51145	08/58-11/92	⊗11/92	ⓖ®06/78		
W51146	08/58-03/94	⊗03/94	*ⓖ*	12/63⇨**M**	
W51147	09/58-05/93	ⓟ⊗04/09	ⓖ®11/77		
W51148	09/58-06/92	ⓟ	ⓖ®04/77		
W51149	09/58-01/94	⊗08/94	ⓖ®05/80	05/77⇨**M**	
W51150	10/58-10/72	⊗03/75		04/68⇨**SC** 07/69⇨**W**	
					12/65⇨Class 130 Parcels
W51151	10/58-11/94	ⓟ	ⓖ®10/78	04/76⇨**M**	
W51152	10/58-03/92	⊗06/92	ⓖ®11/76		
W51153	11/58-12/92	⊗03/94	ⓖ®06/78		⊠11/92-11/92
					10/92➲**ADB977843**

Class 125 BR Derby

Driving Motor Brake Second

DMBS

E51154-E51173

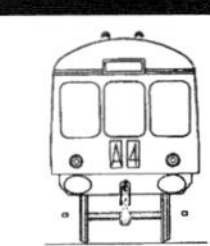

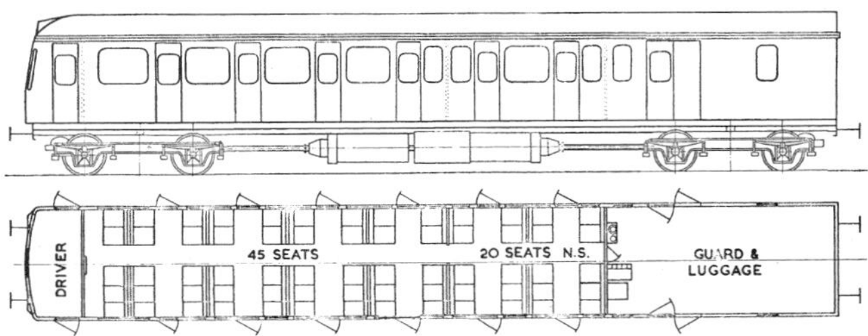

Coupling:	★ Orange star
Diagram:	595
Lot Number:	30464
Old class:	125/2
Engines:	Two Rolls-Royce 8-cyl horizontal type of 238 bhp.
Transmission:	Hydraulic. Twin-disc torque converter
Body:	64' 0" × 9' 3" Suburban
Weight:	39t
Seats:	65 second

E51154	12/58-01/77	⊗04/80
E51155	01/59-01/77	⊗05/82
E51156	01/59-12/76	⊗08/84
E51157	01/59-12/76	⊗02/81
E51158	01/59-01/77	⊗04/81
E51159	01/59-01/77	⊗11/80
E51160	01/59-01/77	⊗06/81
E51161	02/59-12/76	⊗05/82
E51162	02/59-01/77	⊗04/80
E51163	02/59-12/76	⊗09/81
E51164	02/59-01/77	⊗12/77
E51165	02/59-01/77	⊗11/80
E51166	03/59-12/76	⊗11/81
E51167	05/59-01/77	⊗07/78
E51168	05/59-01/77	⊗03/81
E51169	05/59-12/76	⊗09/81
E51170	04/59-05/71	⊗06/71
E51171	04/59-01/77	⊗07/80
E51172	05/59-01/77	⊗03/81
E51173	09/59-02/77	⊗09/81

Class 101 Metropolitan-Cammell

Driving Motor Brake Second

DMBS

M51174-SC51253

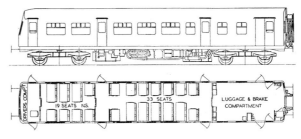

Coupling:	■ Blue square
Diagram:	523 DQ202
Lot Number:	30467
Old class:	101/2
Engines:	Two BUT (AEC) 6-cyl horizontal type of 150 bhp.
Transmission:	Mechanical. Standard
Body:	57' 6" × 9' 3"
Weight:	32t
Seats:	52 second

M51174	10/58-12/90	⊗05/91		11/85⇨**SC**	
M51175	11/58-07/02	⊗12/03	®04/83		
M51176	11/58-02/87	⊗09/88		11/85⇨**W** 02/86⇨**SC**	
M51177	11/58-06/01	⊗12/03	®03/79		
M51178	11/58-07/91	⊗03/92	®11/79		
M51179	11/58-01/01	⊗03/06	®03/77	10/86⇨**E**	
M51180	11/58-03/92	⊗02/93	®06/83		
M51181	11/58-07/91	⊗02/92	®11/79	09/86⇨**E**	⊠11/90-05/91
M51182	11/58-12/90	⊗08/91	®*09/76*	11/85⇨**W** 02/86⇨**SC**	
M51183	11/58-11/89	⊗04/90	®10/77	06/86⇨**E**	⊠09/89-10/89
M51184	11/58-03/93	⊗07/93	®10/77		
M51185	11/58-04/01	⊗01/04	® /82		
M51186	11/58-02/87	⊗01/88		11/85⇨**SC**	
M51187	12/58-10/00	ⓟ	®06/78	09/86⇨**E**	
M51188	12/58-01/01	ⓟ	®11/79		
M51189	12/58-01/01	ⓟ	®07/78	09/86⇨**E**	
M51190	12/58-03/93	⊗08/93			
M51191	12/58-04/91	⊗05/91		09/86⇨**E**	
M51192	12/58-12/03	ⓟ	® /82	09/86⇨**E**	
M51193	12/58-03/87	⊗08/87		11/85⇨**W** 02/86⇨**SC**	
M51194	12/58-11/90	⊗05/91	®08/80	11/86⇨**E**	
M51195	01/59-06/72	⊗12/72			
M51196	01/59-02/86	⊗05/86			
M51197	01/59-09/89	⊗09/89		03/86⇨**E**	
M51198	01/59-03/87	⊗07/87	®01/80	11/85⇨**W** 02/86⇨**SC**	
M51199	01/59-09/86	⊗03/88		03/86⇨**E**	
M51200	01/59-07/87	⊗*09/90*	®07/77	06/86⇨**E**	
M51201	01/59-01/01	⊗03/04	®09/76	05/86⇨**E**	
M51202	01/59-04/86	⊗02/87	®01/79	03/86⇨**E**	
M51203	01/59-09/89	ⓟ⊗10/96	®04/77	03/86⇨**E**	
E51204	07/58-11/88	⊗05/89	®02/81	01/65⇨**NE** 01/68⇨**E**	
E51205	07/58-12/03	ⓟ	® /82	01/65⇨**NE** 01/68⇨**E**	
E51206	08/58-08/89	⊗09/89	®07/79	01/65⇨**NE** 01/68⇨**E**	
E51207	08/58-09/92	⊗02/93	®10/82	01/65⇨**NE** 01/68⇨**E**	
E51208	08/58-11/95	⊗11/95	®07/79	01/65⇨**NE** 01/68⇨**E**	

No.	Dates	Details
E51209	08/58-10/88	⊗11/89 ®11/79 01/65⇨**NE** 01/68⇨**E**
E51210	09/58-12/03	Ⓟ ®05/78 01/65⇨**NE** 01/68⇨**E**
E51211	09/58-07/93	⊗02/94 ® /82 01/65⇨**NE** 01/68⇨**E**
E51212	09/58-12/91	⊗05/93 ®09/77 01/65⇨**NE** 01/68⇨**E** ⊠11/90-12/90
E51213	09/58-07/00	Ⓟ ® /82 01/65⇨**NE** 01/68⇨**E**
E51214	09/58-10/88	⊗06/89 ®11/79 01/65⇨**NE** 01/68⇨**E**
E51215	09/58-07/93	⊗03/94 ®01/78 01/65⇨**NE** 01/68⇨**E**
E51216	09/58-06/89	⊗09/90 ®11/79 01/65⇨**NE** 01/68⇨**E**
E51217	10/58-09/89	⊗09/90 ®10/80 01/65⇨**NE** 01/68⇨**E**
E51218	10/58-03/93	⊗05/95 ® /81 01/65⇨**NE** 01/68⇨**E**
E51219	10/58-02/91	⊗02/91 ® /81 01/65⇨**NE** 01/68⇨**E**
E51220	10/58-02/92	⊗05/93 ®10/77 01/65⇨**NE** 01/68⇨**E**
E51221	10/58-11/95	⊗11/95 ® /81 01/65⇨**NE** 01/68⇨**E**
E51222	10/58-09/94	⊗10/95 ®02/81 01/65⇨**NE** 01/68⇨**E** ⊠01/94-09/94
E51223	10/58-11/90	⊗03/91 ®07/78 01/65⇨**NE** 01/68⇨**E**
SC51224	05/58-06/01	⊗01/04 ® /82
SC51225	05/58-07/93	⊗02/94 ®01/78 09/69⇨**E**
SC51226	05/58-04/01	Ⓟ ® /81 10/69⇨**E** ⊠03/93-12/93
SC51227	05/58-09/89	⊗10/90 ®08/79 ⊠03/89-09/89
SC51228	05/58-03/01	Ⓟ ®06/81
SC51229	05/58-11/88	⊗12/91 ®06/80 10/69⇨**E**
SC51230	05/58-11/01	⊗12/03 ®01/77 10/69⇨**E**
SC51231	05/58-04/00	⊗06/09 ®11/83
SC51232	05/58-08/88	⊗04/90 ®11/79
SC51233	05/58-05/87	⊗11/87 ®06/81
SC51234	05/58-06/91	⊗06/92 ®04/83
SC51235	05/58-03/87	⊗09/87 ®06/78
SC51236	05/58-10/87	⊗06/90 ®02/81 09/69⇨**E** 04/86⇨**SC**
SC51237	05/58-03/87	⊗09/87 ®06/78
SC51238	06/58-12/76	⊗06/80 08/69⇨**E**
SC51239	06/58-05/87	⊗09/87
SC51240	06/58-05/87	⊗01/88 ®02/81
SC51241	06/58-11/90	⊗02/91 ®06/81
SC51242	06/58-03/88	⊗09/88 ®10/80
SC51243	06/58-05/89	⊗08/90 ®08/79
SC51244	06/58-12/90	⊗08/91 ®06/81
SC51245	06/58-03/93	⊗12/93 ®05/83
SC51246	07/58-05/95	⊗05/95 08/69⇨**E**
SC51247	07/58-02/01	Ⓟ ® /82 08/69⇨**E**
SC51248	07/58-02/88	⊗06/90 ®11/78
SC51249	07/58-10/91	⊗06/92 ®08/82
SC51250	07/58-10/88	⊗04/90 ®06/80
SC51251	07/58-02/88	⊗11/87 ®10/80
SC51252	07/58-09/93	⊗03/94 ®02/81 08/69⇨**E**
SC51253	07/58-12/01	⊗12/03 ®02/82

Class 105 Cravens
Driving Motor Brake Second
DMBS
E51254-E51301

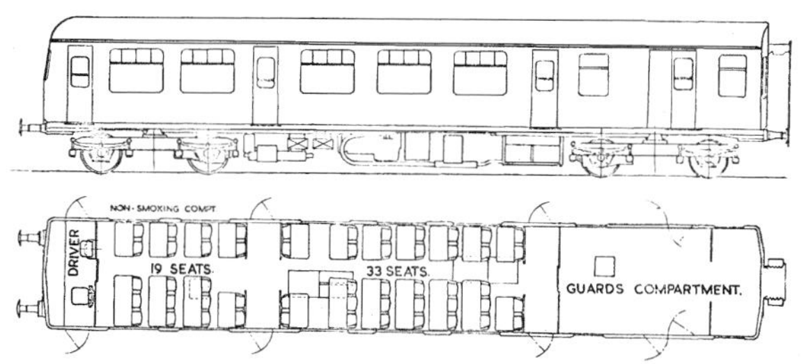

Coupling:	■ Blue square
Diagram:	532 DQ209
Lot Number:	30469
Old class:	105/2
Engines:	Two BUT (AEC) 6-cyl horizontal type of 150 bhp.
Transmission:	Mechanical. Standard
Body:	57' 6" × 9' 2"
Weight:	30t
Seats:	52 second

No.	Dates	Details
E51254	05/58-06/81	⊗09/83
E51255	05/58-10/84	⊗05/86
E51256	06/58-07/82	⊗10/84
E51257	06/58-11/82	⊗09/83
E51258	06/58-03/85	⊗05/85
E51259	06/58-03/86	⊗06/87
E51260	06/58-09/86	⊗12/88 09/86⊃**TDB977453**
E51261	06/58-04/84	⊗05/85
E51262	06/58-10/85	⊗01/86
E51263	07/58-09/86	⊗06/87
E51264	07/58-04/67	⊗11/67
E51265	07/58-01/86	⊗01/87 ⊠03/83-05/83
E51266	07/58-05/83	⊗09/84
E51267	07/58-09/83	⊗09/83
E51268	07/58-09/86	⊗11/87 06/86⇨**SC**
E51269	08/58-03/87	⊗11/87 06/86⇨**SC**
E51270	08/58-02/83	⊗02/84
E51271	08/58-09/86	⊗06/87
E51272	09/58-06/86	⊗02/87
E51273	09/58-11/84	⊗05/86
E51274	09/58-07/81	⊗09/83
E51275	09/58-12/82	⊗07/84
E51276	09/58-06/86	⊗06/87
E51277	09/58-05/85	⊗08/85
E51278	09/58-08/86	⊗09/86
E51279	09/58-05/85	⊗08/85
E51280	09/58-08/84	⊗10/84
E51281	10/58-04/81	⊗06/84
E51282	10/58-11/83	⊗05/84 01/78⇨**M** 05/79⇨**E**
E51283	10/58-06/81	⊗05/82 02/78⇨**M** 05/79⇨**E**
E51284	10/58-05/87	⊗02/88
E51285	10/58-09/83	⊗06/84
E51286	11/58-11/82	⊗08/90 11/82⊃**TDB977123**
E51287	11/58-02/83	⊗01/84
E51288	11/58-09/84	⊗12/84
E51289	11/58-09/85	⊗02/89
E51290	11/58-01/85	⊗10/84
E51291	11/58-01/85	⊗10/84
E51292	12/58-03/86	⊗02/89
E51293	12/58-03/87	⊗12/91 07/86⇨Parcels 03/87⊃**55944**
E51294	12/58-09/86	⊗01/87
E51295	12/58-07/83	⊗09/84
E51296	12/58-11/82	⊗08/90 11/82⊃**TDB977124**
E51297	01/59-10/84	⊗05/86
E51298	01/59-09/86	⊗08/88
E51299	01/59-05/87	⊗02/88
E51300	01/59-04/72	⊗03/73
E51301	01/59-09/83	⊗01/84 11/82⇨**SC**

Class 118 Birmingham RC&W
Driving Motor Brake Second
DMBS
W51302-W51316

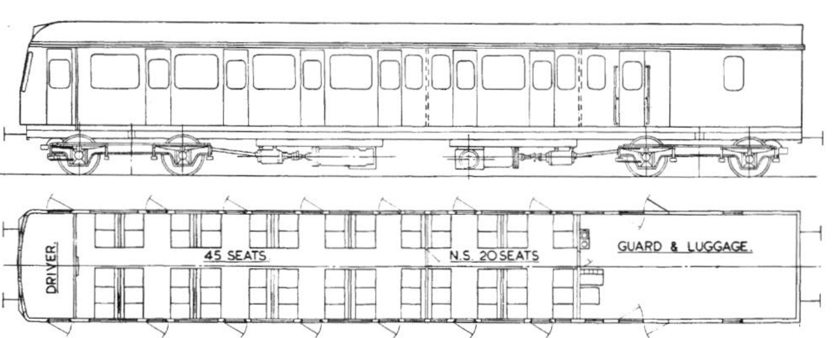

Diag. 534

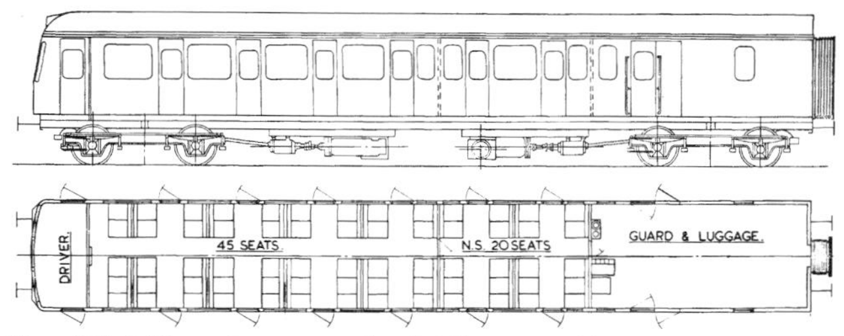

Diag. 850 ⓖ *Through gangway fitted* All converted by 1972.

Coupling:	■ Blue square
Diagram:	534 ⓖ 850 DQ220
Lot Number:	30543
Old class:	118/2
Engines:	Two BUT (Leyland) 6-cyl horizontal type of 150 bhp.
Transmission:	Mechanical. Standard
Body:	64' 0" × 9' 3" Suburban
Weight:	36t
Seats:	65 second

No.	Dates	Details
W51302	04/60-07/88	⊗04/89 ⓖ
W51303	04/60-03/88	⊗04/90 ⓖ®01/80
W51304	04/60-07/85	⊗02/86 ⓖ
W51305	04/60-08/89	⊗12/89 ⓖ
W51306	05/60-10/91	⊗03/94 ⓖ®02/84 02/92⊃**ADB977752**
W51307	05/60-05/89	⊗08/89 ⓖ

W51308	05/60-03/88	⊗03/88	⑨	05/86⇨**M**	
W51309	05/60-03/88	⊗03/88	⑨	05/86⇨**M**	
W51310	06/60-06/89	⊗08/89	⑨		
W51311	06/60-06/87	⊗08/90	⑨		
W51312	06/60-10/89	⊗06/92	⑨®07/78		
W51313	07/60-08/87	⊗08/88	⑨		
W51314	07/60-08/95	⊗08/95	⑨		
W51315	07/60-06/90	⊗06/92	⑨		
W51316	07/60-07/93	⊗08/93	⑨®02/84		

Class 118 Birmingham RC&W

Driving Motor Second

DMS

W51317-W51331

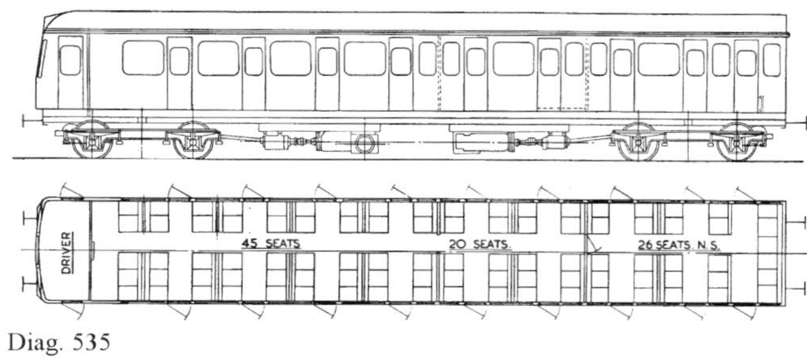

Diag. 535

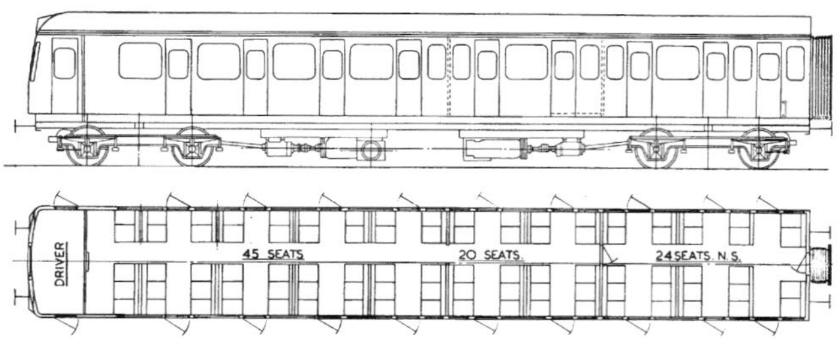

Diag. 852 ⑨ *Through gangway fitted* All converted by 1972.

Coupling:	■ Blue square
Diagram:	535 ⑨ 852 DP221
Lot Number:	30545
Old class:	118/1
Engines:	Two BUT (Leyland) 6-cyl horizontal type of 150 bhp.
Transmission:	Mechanical. Standard
Body:	64' 0" × 9' 3" Suburban
Weight:	36t
Seats:	91 second ⑨ 89 second

W51317	04/60-07/88	⊗04/89	⑨		
W51318	04/60-03/88	⊗03/89	⑨®01/80		
W51319	04/60-07/92	⊗04/93	⑨		
W51320	04/60-08/89	⊗12/89	⑨		
W51321	05/60-10/91	℗	⑨®02/84		02/92➲**ADB977753**
W51322	05/60-07/88	⊗12/89	⑨		
W51323	05/60-03/88	⊗03/88	⑨	05/86⇨**M**	
W51324	05/60-03/88	⊗05/88	⑨	05/86⇨**M**	
W51325	06/60-05/89	⊗08/89	⑨		
W51326	06/60-06/87	⊗08/90	⑨		
W51327	06/60-10/89	⊗08/90	⑨		
W51328	07/60-08/87	⊗08/88	⑨		
W51329	07/60-08/95	⊗08/95	⑨		
W51330	07/60-06/90	⊗06/92	⑨		
W51331	07/60-07/93	⊗08/93	⑨®02/84		

Class 117 Pressed Steel

Driving Motor Brake Second

DMBS

W51332-W51373

Diag. 534

Diag. 850 ⑨ *Through gangway fitted* All converted by 1972.

Coupling:	■ Blue square
Diagram:	534 ⑨ 850 DQ220
Lot Number:	30546
Old class:	117/2
Engines:	Two BUT (Leyland) 6-cyl horizontal type of 150 bhp.
Transmission:	Mechanical. Standard
Body:	64' 0" × 9' 3" Suburban
Weight:	36t
Seats:	65 second

51332 was named "Marston Vale" in 1997.
51358 was named "LESLIE CRABBE" in 1997.

W51332	11/59-04/99	⊗04/99	⑨®03/79	
W51333	01/60-05/99	⊗05/99	⑨®03/79	
W51334	02/60-04/98	⊗04/98	⑨®04/77	
W51335	02/60-05/98	⊗05/04	⑨®03/78	
W51336	02/60-04/99	⊗04/99	⑨®05/79	
W51337	03/60-10/90	⊗05/92	⑨®02/77	
W51338	03/60-12/92	⊗01/94	⑨®04/78	
W51339	04/60-11/99	℗	⑨®11/77	
W51340	03/60-01/98	⊗01/98	⑨®09/79	
W51341	04/60-03/00	℗	⑨®06/78	
W51342	04/60-12/93	℗	⑨®11/78	
W51343	04/60-12/93	⊗08/94	⑨®10/78	
W51344	04/60-04/99	⊗04/99	⑨®03/79	
W51345	04/60-10/96	⊗10/96	⑨®06/77	
W51346	05/60-07/93	℗	⑨®04/80	⊠01/93-02/93
W51347	05/60-12/93	℗	⑨®01/79	
W51348	05/60-02/92	⊗01/92	⑨®11/77	
W51349	05/60-06/95	⊗06/95	⑨®01/79	
W51350	06/60-09/99	⊗06/09	⑨®10/77	
W51351	06/60-12/93	℗	⑨®09/78	⊠01/93-02/93
W51352	06/60-11/99	℗	⑨®10/78	⊠08/97-11/97
W51353	06/60-11/99	℗	⑨®04/77	
W51354	06/60-09/99	℗	⑨®11/79	
W51355	06/60-02/93	⊗10/94	⑨®07/78	
W51356	07/60-11/00	℗	⑨®04/78	
W51357	07/60-04/68	⊗08/68		
W51358	07/60-11/98	⊗05/04	⑨®11/79	
W51359	07/60-02/97	℗	⑨®10/78	
W51360	07/60-09/93	℗	⑨®01/79	
W51361	07/60-04/99	⊗04/99	⑨®03/79	
W51362	07/60-07/93	⊗01/96	⑨®01/80	
W51363	07/60-10/99	℗	⑨®03/79	
W51364	08/60-03/94	⊗09/96	⑨®02/79	
W51365	08/60-08/95	℗	⑨®03/79	
W51366	09/60-03/00	⊗05/09	⑨®02/79	
W51367	09/60-02/93	℗	⑨®05/79	
W51368	09/60-04/99	⊗04/99	⑨®05/75	
W51369	09/60-11/99	⊗05/02	⑨®06/78	
W51370	09/60-01/94	℗	⑨®09/79	
W51371	10/60-11/99		⑨®02/78	10/03➲**977987**

W51372	10/60-01/94	Ⓟ ⑨®06/78	
W51373	10/60-09/99	⊗10/03 ⑨®04/79	

Class 117 Pressed Steel

Driving Motor Second
DMS
W51374-W51415

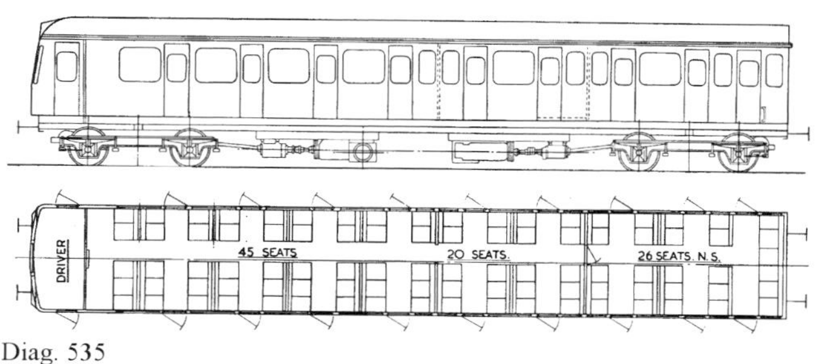

Diag. 535

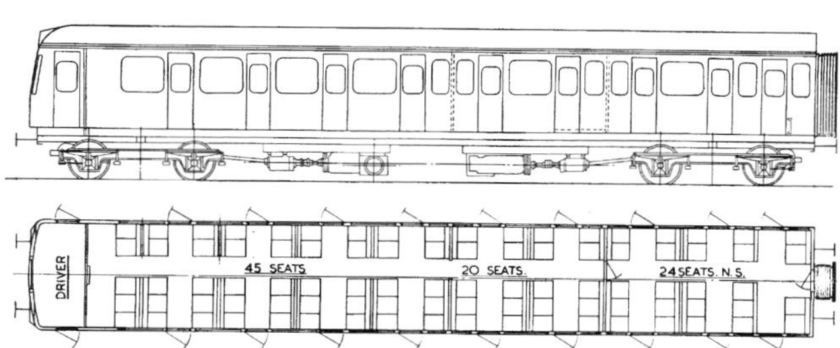

Diag. 852 ⑨ *Through gangway fitted* All converted by 1972.

Coupling:	■ Blue square
Diagram:	535 ⑨ 852 DP221
Lot Number:	30548
Old class:	117/1
Engines:	Two BUT (Leyland) 6-cyl horizontal type of 150 bhp.
Transmission:	Mechanical. Standard
Body:	64' 0" × 9' 3" Suburban
Weight:	36t
Seats:	91 second ⑨ 89 second

W51374	11/59-04/99	⊗04/99 ⑨®03/79	
W51375	01/60-04/99	⑨®03/79	⊠08/98-11/98 Ⓟ then 08/04➲**977992**
W51376	02/60-11/99	Ⓟ ⑨®04/77	
W51377	02/60-05/98	⊗05/04 ⑨®03/78	
W51378	02/60-04/99	⊗04/99 ⑨®05/79	
W51379	03/60-03/92	⊗10/94 ⑨®02/77	
W51380	03/60-12/92	⊗01/94 ⑨®04/78	
W51381	03/60-09/99	Ⓟ ⑨®09/79	
W51382	04/60-11/99	Ⓟ ⑨®11/77	
W51383	04/60-03/00	⊗06/09 ⑨®06/78	
W51384	04/60-12/93	Ⓟ ⑨®11/78	
W51385	04/60-02/93	⊗03/94 ⑨®11/78	
W51386	04/60-04/99	Ⓟ⊗04/04⑨®03/79	
W51387	04/60-11/95	⊗11/95 ⑨®06/77	
W51388	05/60-07/93	Ⓟ ⑨®04/80	⊠01/93-02/93
W51389	05/60-12/93	⊗01/96 ⑨®10/78	
W51390	05/60-02/92	⊗01/92 ⑨®11/77	
W51391	05/60-06/95	⊗06/95 ⑨®01/79	
W51392	06/60-09/99	Ⓟ ⑨®10/77	
W51393	06/60-12/93	⊗08/94 ⑨®09/78	⊠01/93-02/93
W51394	06/60-04/98	⊗04/98 ⑨®10/78	
W51395	06/60-11/99	Ⓟ ⑨®04/77	
W51396	06/60-09/99	Ⓟ ⑨®11/79	
W51397	06/60-12/93	Ⓟ ⑨®01/79	
W51398	07/60-11/00	Ⓟ ⑨®04/78	
W51399	07/60-11/95	⊗11/95 ⑨®11/77	
W51400	07/60-03/00	Ⓟ ⑨®11/79	
W51401	07/60-02/97	Ⓟ ⑨® */80*	
W51402	07/60-09/93	Ⓟ ⑨®01/79	
W51403	07/60-04/82	⊗04/82 ⑨®03/79	
W51404	07/60-07/93	⊗08/94 ⑨®01/80	
W51405	07/60-10/99	Ⓟ ⑨®03/79	
W51406	08/60-01/94	⊗09/96 ⑨®02/79	
W51407	08/60-06/95	Ⓟ ⑨®03/79	
W51408	09/60-08/98	⊗06/09 ⑨®02/79	
W51409	09/60-01/93	⊗01/96 ⑨®05/79	
W51410	09/60-09/96	⊗09/96 ⑨®05/75	
W51411	09/60-11/99	⊗09/09 ⑨®06/78	
W51412	09/60-01/94	Ⓟ ⑨®09/79	
W51413	10/60-11/99	⑨®02/78	10/03➲**977988**
W51414	10/60-01/94	⊗01/96 ⑨®06/78	
W51415	10/60-10/96	⊗10/96 ⑨®04/79	

Class 108 BR Derby

Driving Motor Brake Second
DMBS
M51416-M51424

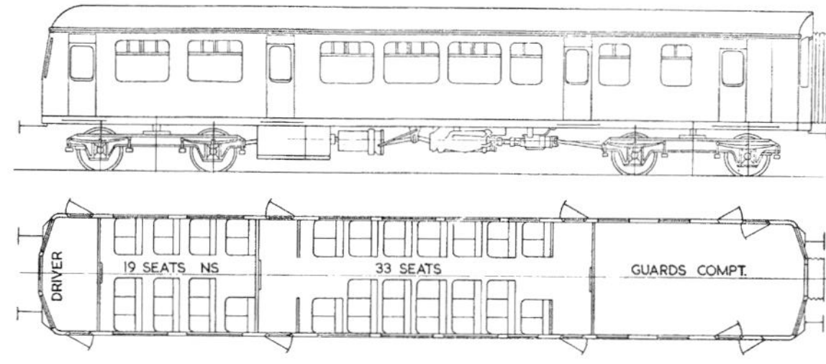

Coupling:	■ Blue square
Diagram:	634 DQ213
Lot Number:	30498
Old class:	108/2
Engines:	Two BUT (AEC) 6-cyl horizontal type of 150 bhp.
Transmission:	Mechanical. Standard
Body:	58' 1" × 9' 3"
Weight:	29t
Seats:	52 second

M51416	02/60-05/92	⊗05/92 ® /82
M51417	02/60-03/92	⊗02/92 ®08/82
M51418	02/60-09/90	⊗05/92 ®08/80
M51419	02/60-02/92	⊗01/92
M51420	02/60-07/91	⊗11/91 ®05/79
M51421	03/60-07/92	⊗07/92 ®03/80
M51422	03/60-01/91	⊗09/91 ®11/78
M51423	03/60-07/71	⊗02/74
M51424	03/60-07/92	⊗07/92 ®05/79

Class 102⇨101 Metropolitan-Cammell

Driving Motor Brake Second
DMBS
E51425-SC51470

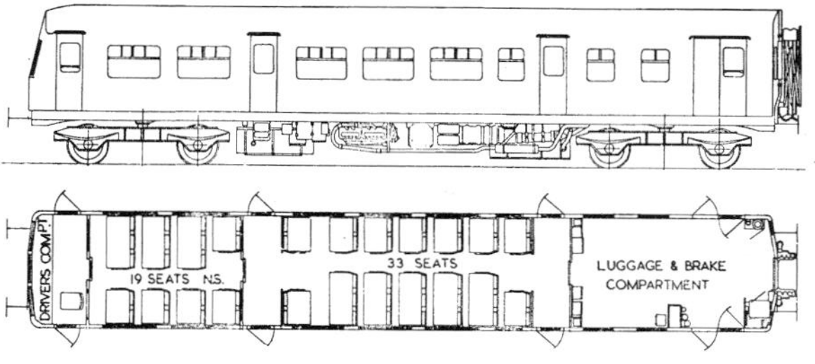

Coupling:	■ Blue square
Diagram:	523 DQ202
Lot Number:	30500
Old class:	102/2
Engines:	Two BUT (Leyland) 6-cyl horizontal type of 150 bhp.
Transmission:	Mechanical. Standard
Body:	57' 6" × 9' 3"
Weight:	32t
Seats:	52 second

E51425	02/59-09/92	⊗12/92	®06/83	01/65⇨**NE**	01/68⇨**E**
E51426	02/59-01/01	⊗03/04	®*10/76*	01/65⇨**NE**	01/68⇨**E**
E51427	02/59-05/93	Ⓟ	® */83*	01/65⇨**NE**	01/68⇨**E** 05/93➲**DB977899**
E51428	03/59-09/01	⊗01/04	® /82	01/65⇨**NE**	01/68⇨**E**
E51429	03/59-10/99	⊗04/04	® */83*	01/65⇨**NE**	01/68⇨**E**
E51430	03/59-07/89	⊗04/90	®02/81	01/65⇨**NE**	01/68⇨**E** 07/86⇨Parcels ➲*55943*
E51431	04/59-11/99	⊗08/00	® /81	01/65⇨**NE**	01/68⇨**E**
E51432	04/59-04/00		®12/82	01/65⇨**NE**	01/68⇨**E**
E51433	04/59-02/87	Ⓟ	®02/79	01/65⇨**NE**	01/68⇨**E** 04/89➲**DB977391**
E51434	05/59-08/96	Ⓟ	® /82	01/65⇨**NE**	01/68⇨**E**
E51435	02/59-04/00	⊗01/07	®02/81	01/65⇨**NE**	01/68⇨**E**

E51436	02/59-01/90	⊙05/90	®02/81	01/65⇨**NE**	01/68⇨**E**
					⊠09/89-10/89
E51437	03/59-09/92	⊙02/93	®*10/76*	01/65⇨**NE**	01/68⇨**E**
E51438	03/59-09/92	⊙12/92	® /81	01/65⇨**NE**	01/68⇨**E**
E51439	03/59-07/89	⊙04/90	®11/80	01/65⇨**NE**	01/68⇨**E**
					06/86⇨Parcels ➲*55941*
E51440	03/59-11/86	⊙01/89	®02/81	01/65⇨**NE**	01/68⇨**E**
E51441	04/59-07/89	⊙04/90	® */81*	01/65⇨**NE**	01/68⇨**E**
				⊠07/86-07/86	07/86⇨Parcels ➲*55942*
E51442	04/59-03/01	⊙04/03	®*10/76*	01/65⇨**NE**	01/68⇨**E**
E51443	04/59-02/92	⊙02/93	®09/77	01/65⇨**NE**	01/68⇨**E**
E51444	05/59-05/95	⊙06/95	®04/77	01/65⇨**NE**	01/68⇨**E**
SC51445	05/59-02/93	⊙02/93	®11/79	05/74⇨**W**	⊠03/89-05/89
SC51446	05/59-09/89	⊙07/90	®10/78	05/74⇨**W**	
SC51447	05/59-09/77	⊙09/79	®06/77		
SC51448	05/59-10/84	⊙02/86	®*10/76*		
SC51449	05/59-10/89	⊙05/90	®04/78	05/74⇨**W**	
SC51450	06/59-09/89	⊙01/90	®09/78	05/74⇨**W**	
SC51451	06/59-10/87	⊙11/87	®07/74		
SC51452	06/59-08/87	⊙08/88	®04/77	05/74⇨**W**	
SC51453	06/59-10/87	⊙06/91	®07/76		
SC51454	06/59-05/89	⊙08/90	®02/77		
SC51455	06/59-09/89	⊙09/90	®08/79		
SC51456	07/59-10/89	⊙07/90	®05/78		
SC51457	07/59-06/88	⊙01/89	®*10/76*		
SC51458	07/59-09/89	⊙05/90	®*10/76*		
SC51459	07/59-10/87	⊙01/88	®06/78		
SC51460	07/59-11/83	⊙07/84	®10/77		
SC51461	08/59-05/81	⊙09/87	®02/77		
SC51462	08/59-03/91	⊙04/91	® /82	04/79⇨**W**	⊠10/89-*11/89*
SC51463	08/59-10/00	⊙04/03	®01/83	04/79⇨**W**	
SC51464	08/59-06/88	⊙02/93	®06/77		12/88➲**TDB977607**
SC51465	08/59-03/89	⊙04/90	®06/77		
SC51466	09/59-10/87	⊙01/88	®*10/76*		
SC51467	09/59-09/89	⊙09/90	®*03/77*		
SC51468	09/59-10/92	⊙12/95	®10/77		
SC51469	09/59-02/87	⊙07/88	®04/78		
SC51470	09/59-04/88	⊙10/89	®12/76		

Class 105 Cravens

Driving Motor Brake Second
DMBS
E51471-SC51494

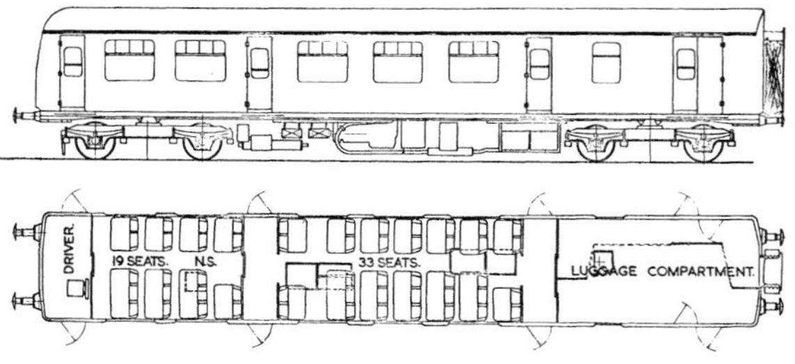

Coupling:	■ Blue square
Diagram:	548 DQ210
Lot Number:	30503
Old class:	105/2
Engines:	Two BUT (AEC) 6-cyl horizontal type of 150 bhp.
Transmission:	Mechanical. Standard
Body:	57' 6" × 9' 3"
Weight:	30t
Seats:	52 second

E51471	02/59-02/81	⊙05/90		
E51472	02/59-09/86	⊙09/88		⊠07/86-08/86
SC51473	02/59-11/81	⊙06/82		
SC51474	02/59-11/81	⊙10/82		
SC51475	02/59-11/81	⊙06/82		
SC51476	03/59-11/81	⊙10/82		
SC51477	03/59-11/81	⊙05/82		
SC51478	03/59-04/87	⊙11/87	04/74⇨**E**	
SC51479	03/59-11/81	⊙10/82		
SC51480	03/59-11/81	⊙12/82		
SC51481	03/59-11/81	⊙10/82		
SC51482	04/59-11/81	⊙09/83	05/75⇨**E**	
SC51483	04/59-11/81	⊙05/82		
SC51484	04/59-04/81	⊙04/90	06/77⇨**E**	
SC51485	04/59-05/81	ⓟ	05/75⇨**E**	
SC51486	04/59-04/78	⊙03/81	04/77⇨**E**	
SC51487	04/59-04/78	⊙04/81	04/77⇨**E**	
SC51488	05/59-11/67	⊙06/68		
SC51489	05/59-06/81	⊙09/90	05/75⇨**E**	
SC51490	05/59-09/81	⊙10/82	05/75⇨**E**	02/78⇨**M**
SC51491	05/59-04/78	⊙11/79	05/75⇨**E**	
SC51492	05/59-04/82	⊙05/85	05/75⇨**E**	01/78⇨**M**
SC51493	06/59-11/83	⊙06/84	04/77⇨**E**	11/82⇨**SC**
SC51494	06/59-01/71	⊙01/73		

Class 102⇨101 Metropolitan-Cammell

Driving Motor Composite Lavatory
DMCL
E51495-SC51540

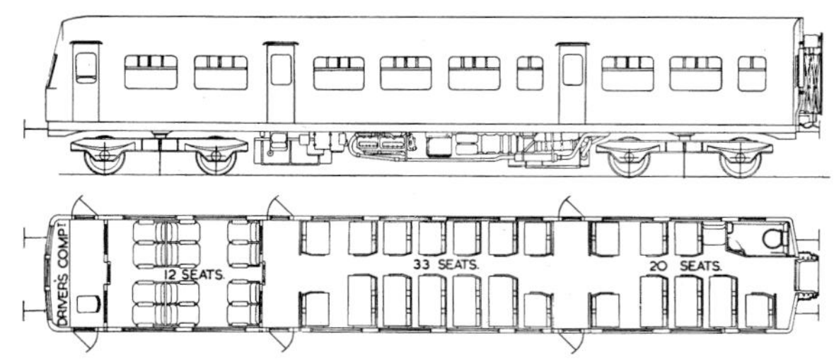

Coupling:	■ Blue square
Diagram:	621 DP304 ②DP210
Lot Number:	30501
Old class:	102/1
Engines:	Two BUT (Leyland) 6-cyl horizontal type of 150 bhp.
Transmission:	Mechanical. Standard
Body:	57' 6" × 9' 3"
Weight:	32t
Seats:	12 first, 53 second

E51495	02/59-03/90	⊙09/90		01/65⇨**NE**	01/68⇨**E**	05/79⇨**W**
E51496	02/59-01/01	⊙01/07	® /82	01/65⇨**NE**	01/68⇨**E**	
E51497	02/59-11/86	⊙01/89	®11/80	01/65⇨**NE**	01/68⇨**E**	
E51498	03/59-04/00		®03/83	01/65⇨**NE**	01/68⇨**E**	
E51499	03/59-04/01	ⓟ	® /81	01/65⇨**NE**	01/68⇨**E**	
						⊠03/93-12/93
E51500	03/59-04/00	⊙02/09	®02/84	01/65⇨**NE**	01/68⇨**E**	04/79⇨**W**
E51501	04/59-11/99	⊙08/00	® /81	01/65⇨**NE**	01/68⇨**E**	
E51502	04/59-03/87	⊙08/87	®01/81	01/65⇨**NE**	01/68⇨**E**	
E51503	04/59-08/96	ⓟ	® /82	01/65⇨**NE**	01/68⇨**E**	
E51504	05/59-09/92	⊙12/92	®05/83	01/65⇨**NE**	01/68⇨**E**	
E51505	02/59-06/01	ⓟ	®03/83	01/65⇨**NE**	01/68⇨**E**	04/79⇨**W**
E51506	02/59-01/01	⊙08/06	®*10/76*	01/65⇨**NE**	01/68⇨**E**	
E51507	03/59-08/75	⊙06/85		01/65⇨**NE**	01/68⇨**E**	
E51508	03/59-12/92	⊙03/93	®07/76	01/65⇨**NE**	01/68⇨**E**	
E51509	03/59-10/00	⊙04/03		01/65⇨**NE**	01/68⇨**E**	04/79⇨**W**
E51510	03/59-10/89	⊙05/90		01/65⇨**NE**	01/68⇨**E**	05/79⇨**W**
E51511	04/59-12/03	ⓟ	®03/83	01/65⇨**NE**	01/68⇨**E**	05/79⇨**W**
						⊠04/01-08/02
E51512	04/59-02/01	ⓟ	®02/84	01/65⇨**NE**	01/68⇨**E**	04/79⇨**W**
E51513	04/59-10/90	⊙11/90		01/65⇨**NE**	01/68⇨**E**	04/79⇨**W**
						⊠07/89-08/89
E51514	05/59-09/86	⊙12/86	®01/77	01/65⇨**NE**	01/68⇨**E**	
SC51515	05/59-09/89	⊙09/90	®11/79	05/74⇨**W**		
SC51516	05/59-09/89	⊙09/90	®06/77			
SC51517	05/59-10/89	⊙07/90	®11/78	05/74⇨**W**		
SC51518	05/59-10/87	⊙11/87	®07/74			
SC51519	05/59-06/89	⊙08/90	® /82	11/78⇨**W**		
SC51520	06/59-10/89	⊙05/90	®05/78			
SC51521	06/59-01/89	⊙09/90	®06/78	05/74⇨**W**		
SC51522	06/59-09/89	⊙07/90	®04/77	05/74⇨**W**		
SC51523	06/59-10/89	⊙09/89	®07/78	05/74⇨**W**		
SC51524	06/59-03/90	⊙09/90	®06/77			
SC51525	06/59-06/88	⊙02/93	®06/77			12/88➲**TDB977608**
SC51526	07/59-10/88	⊙07/90	®01/78			
SC51527	07/59-10/88	⊙10/88	®12/76			
SC51528	07/59-10/87	⊙11/87	®*10/76*			
SC51529	07/59-08/89	⊙01/90	®01/78			⊠07/89-08/89
SC51530	07/59-05/93	⊙12/93	® /82	04/79⇨**W**		
SC51531	08/59-03/92	⊙10/92	®02/84			
SC51532	08/59-08/89	⊙07/90	®05/78			⊠07/89-08/89
SC51533	08/59-06/01	⊙12/03	®01/83	04/79⇨**W**		
SC51534	08/59-10/87	⊙11/87	®10/77			
SC51535	08/59-10/87	⊙01/88	®08/79			
SC51536	09/59-03/87	⊙10/88	®04/78			
SC51537	09/59-08/88	⊙11/89	®04/78			
SC51538	09/59-10/89	⊙05/90	®06/80			
SC51539	09/59-10/87	⊙04/88	®01/78			
SC51540	09/59-01/77	⊙03/78				

Class 111 Metropolitan-Cammell

Driving Motor Brake Second
DMBS
E51541-E51550

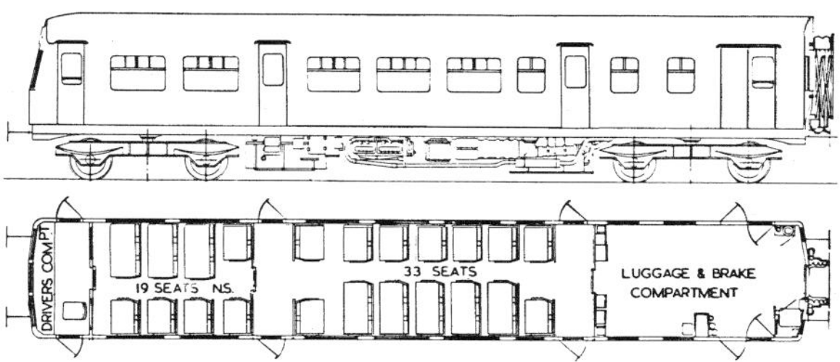

Coupling: ■ Blue square
Diagram: 615 DQ216
Lot Number: 30508
Old class: 111/2
Engines: Two Rolls-Royce 6-cyl horizontal type of 180 bhp.
Transmission: Mechanical. Standard
Body: 57' 6" × 9' 3"
Weight: 33t
Seats: 52 second

E51541	12/59-12/84	⊗05/87	®07/79	01/65⇨**NE**	01/68⇨**E**	➲**78970**
E51542	12/59-06/83	⊗08/89	® /81	01/65⇨**NE**	01/68⇨**E**	➲**78967**
E51543	12/59-08/83	⊗07/90	® /81	01/65⇨**NE**	01/68⇨**E**	➲**78968**
E51544	01/60-10/83	⊗04/90	® /81	01/65⇨**NE**	01/68⇨**E**	➲**78969**
E51545	01/60-11/84	⊗02/88	®11/79	01/65⇨**NE**	01/68⇨**E**	➲**78972**
E51546	01/60-12/82	⊗02/88	®03/80	01/65⇨**NE**	01/68⇨**E**	➲**78966**
E51547	01/60-07/70	⊗04/72		01/65⇨**NE**	01/68⇨**E**	
E51548	02/60-03/85	⊗06/87	®11/79	01/65⇨**NE**	01/68⇨**E**	➲**78973**
E51549	02/60-06/84	⊗05/90	® /81	01/65⇨**NE**	01/68⇨**E**	➲**78971**
E51550	03/60-05/85	⊗06/87	®11/80	01/65⇨**NE**	01/68⇨**E**	➲**78974**

Class 111 Metropolitan-Cammell

Driving Motor Composite Lavatory
DMCL
E51551-E51560

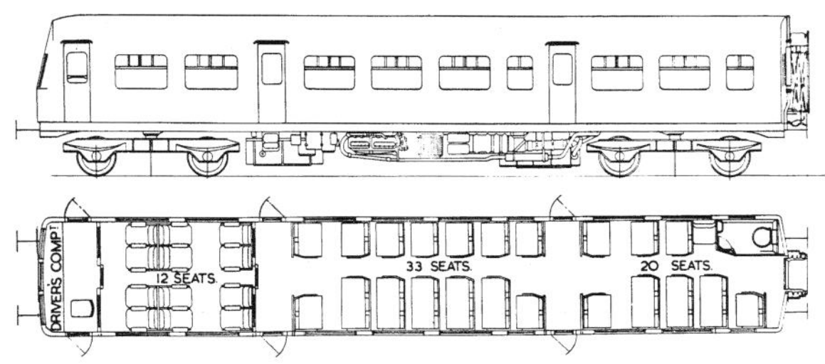

Coupling: ■ Blue square
Diagram: 617 DP315
Lot Number: 30509
Old class: 111/1
Engines: Two Rolls-Royce 6-cyl horizontal type of 180 bhp.
Transmission: Mechanical. Standard
Body: 57' 6" × 9' 3"
Weight: 33t
Seats: 12 first, 53 second

E51551	12/59-12/83	⊗05/87	®07/79	01/65⇨**NE**	01/68⇨**E**	➲**78720**
E51552	12/59-06/83	⊗07/90	®10/81	01/65⇨**NE**	01/68⇨**E**	➲**78717**
E51553	12/59-10/83	⊗05/90	® /81	01/65⇨**NE**	01/68⇨**E**	➲**78719**
E51554	01/60-12/82	⊗02/88	®03/80	01/65⇨**NE**	01/68⇨**E**	➲**78716**
E51555	01/60-11/84	⊗07/89	®11/79	01/65⇨**NE**	01/68⇨**E**	➲**78722**
E51556	01/60-03/85	⊗05/88	®11/79	01/65⇨**NE**	01/68⇨**E**	➲**78723**
E51557	01/60-08/83	⊗07/90	®01/77	01/65⇨**NE**	01/68⇨**E**	➲**78718**
E51558	02/60-05/85	⊗06/87	®02/79	01/65⇨**NE**	01/68⇨**E**	➲**78724**
E51559	02/60-06/84	⊗02/88	®07/79	01/65⇨**NE**	01/68⇨**E**	➲**78721**
E51560	03/60-10/82	⊗12/82	® /81	01/65⇨**NE**	01/68⇨**E**	

Class 108 BR Derby

Driving Motor Composite Lavatory
DMCL
M51561-M51572

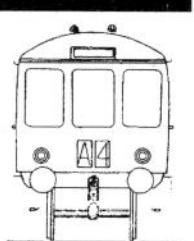

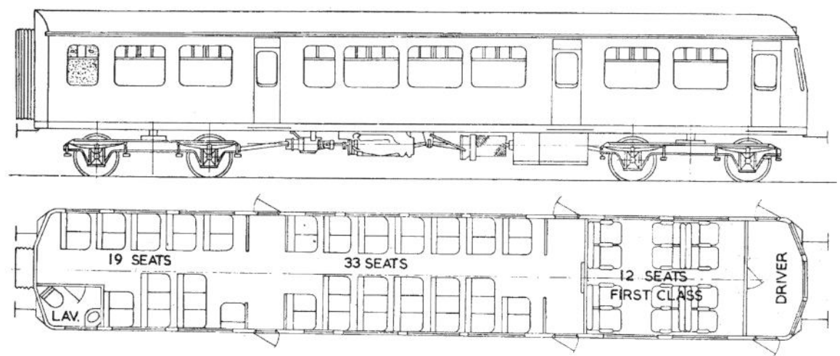

Coupling: ■ Blue square
Diagram: 609 DP311 ②DP226
Lot Number: 30461
Old class: 108/1
Engines: Two BUT (AEC) 6-cyl horizontal type of 150 bhp.
Transmission: Mechanical. Standard
Body: 58' 1" × 9' 2"
Weight: 28t
Seats: 12 first, 52 second

M51561	10/59-10/92	⊗08/94	®07/77	⊠05/92-09/92 10/92➲**TDB977823**
M51562	12/59-06/92	Ⓟ		
M51563	11/59-10/92	⊗08/94	®09/79	⊠05/92-09/92 10/92➲**TDB977822**
M51564	11/59-02/69	⊗09/69		
M51565	11/59-03/92	Ⓟ		
M51566	11/59-12/92	Ⓟ	® /82	
M51567	12/59-02/93	Ⓟ	®08/82	02/93➲**ADB977854**
M51568	12/59-02/93	Ⓟ	®03/79	
M51569	12/59-10/90	⊗11/90	®04/82	
M51570	01/60-01/92	⊗01/92	®07/77	
M51571	01/60-09/92	Ⓟ	®09/76	
M51572	01/60-01/93	Ⓟ	®10/76	

Class 120 BR Swindon

Driving Motor Brake Composite
DMBC
W51573-W51581

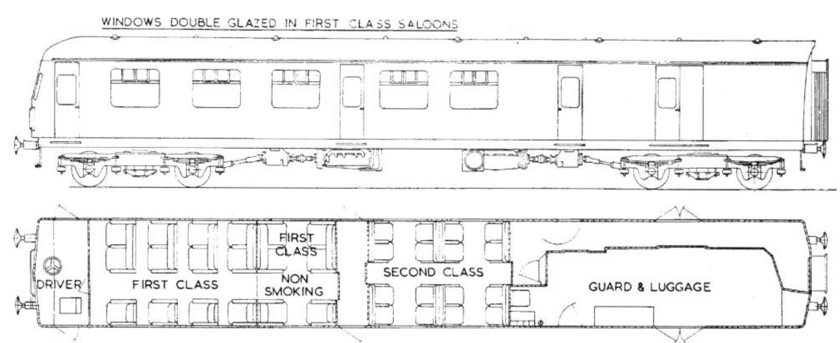

Coupling: ■ Blue square
Diagram: 636 DQ304
Lot Number: 30515
Old class: 120/1
Engines: Two BUT (AEC) 6-cyl horizontal type of 150 bhp.
Transmission: Mechanical. Standard
Body: 64' 7½" × 9' 3" Cross Country
Weight: 36t 19cwt
Seats: 18 first, 16 second

W51573	01/61-04/87	⊗07/88	11/81⇨**M** 04/86⇨**E** 05/86⇨Parcels 04/87➲**55934**
W51574	01/61-04/87	⊗08/87	06/82⇨**M** ⊠05/86-07/86 07/86⇨Parcels
W51575	01/61-08/87	⊗05/88	11/81⇨**M** 09/86⇨**E** ⊠05/86-07/86 07/86⇨Parcels
W51576	02/61-04/87	⊗06/87	06/82⇨**M** 06/86⇨**E** ⊠05/86-06/86 06/86⇨Parcels 04/87➲**55935**
W51577	02/61-02/86	⊗02/86	01/82⇨**M**
W51578	02/61-03/87	⊗09/88	01/82⇨**M** 04/86⇨**SC**

W51579	02/61-03/87	⊗06/87	06/82⇨**M** 05/86⇨**E** 07/86⇨Parcels 03/87➲**55936**
W51580	02/61-04/87	⊗08/87	06/82⇨**M** ⊠05/86-07/86 07/86⇨Parcels
W51581	02/61-03/87	⊗06/87	11/81⇨**M** 04/86⇨**E** 05/86⇨Parcels 03/87➲**55937**

Class 120 BR Swindon

Driving Motor Second Lavatory

DMSL

W51582-W51590

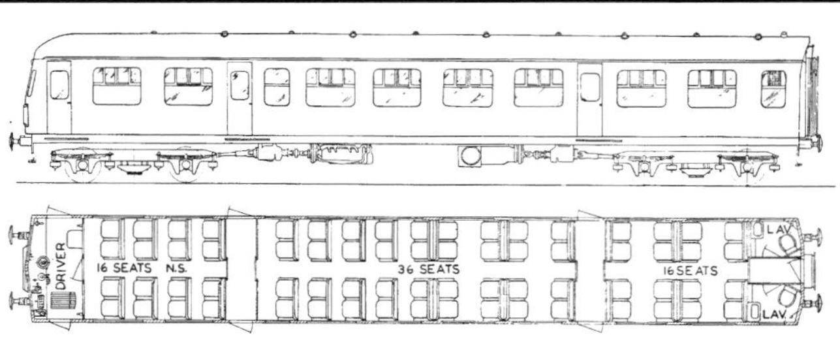

Coupling: ■ Blue square
Diagram: 637 DP205
Lot Number: 30516
Old class: 120/2
Engines: Two BUT (AEC) 6-cyl horizontal type of 150 bhp.
Transmission: Mechanical. Standard
Body: 64' 7½" × 9' 3" Cross Country
Weight: 37t 1cwt
Seats: 68 second

W51582	04/61-04/87	⊗07/88	11/81⇨**M** 04/86⇨**E** ⊠04/86-05/86 05/86⇨Parcels 04/87➲**55939**
W51583	04/61-02/87	⊗01/88	06/82⇨**M** *07/86*⇨**SC**
W51584	04/61-03/87	⊗01/88	11/81⇨**M** *07/86*⇨**SC**
W51585	04/61-04/87	⊗06/87	11/81⇨**M** 04/86⇨**E** ⊠04/86-05/86 05/86⇨Parcels 04/87➲**55940**
W51586	04/61-07/87	⊗06/87	01/82⇨**M**
W51587	04/61-06/88	⊗09/88	01/82⇨**M** 04/86⇨**SC**
W51588	05/61-05/86	⊗02/87	06/82⇨**M** 05/86⇨**E**
W51589	05/61-03/86	⊗03/86 ®11/78	06/82⇨**M**
W51590	05/61-11/86	⊗02/89	06/82⇨**M** 06/86⇨**E** ⊠05/86-06/86 06/86⇨Parcels

Class 127 BR Derby

Driving Motor Brake Second

DMBS

M51591-M51650

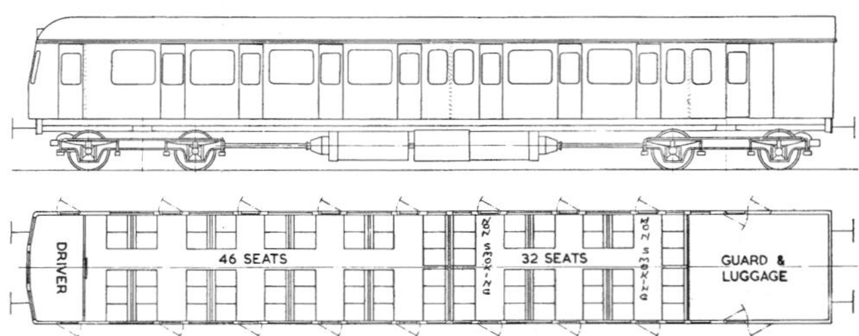

Coupling: ▲ Red triangle
Diagram: 588 DQ227
Lot Number: 30521
Old class: 127
Engines: Two Rolls-Royce 8-cyl horizontal type of 238 bhp.
Transmission: Hydraulic. Torque converter
Body: 64' 0" × 9' 3" Suburban
Weight: 40t
Seats: 78 second

M51591	05/59-12/83	ⓟ	⊠05/77-06/77 ⓟ then 02/86➲**55966**
M51592	05/59-01/84	ⓟ	
M51593	06/59-12/83	⊗07/85	
M51594	06/59-11/66	⊗12/66	
M51595	06/59-05/83	⊗08/84	
M51596	06/59-12/83	⊗03/91	05/85➲**55982**
M51597	06/59-01/84	⊗03/91	08/85➲**55971**
M51598	06/59-10/83	⊗08/84	
M51599	06/59-08/83	⊗07/85	
M51600	06/59-12/83	⊗02/92	08/85➲**55979**
M51601	07/59-12/77	⊗02/78	
M51602	07/59-07/76	⊗08/76	
M51603	07/59-08/83	⊗03/91	05/85➲**55977**
M51604	07/59-08/83	ⓟ	
M51605	08/59-01/84	⊗11/84	
M51606	08/59-08/83	⊗03/91	08/85➲**55989**
M51607	08/59-12/83	⊗09/84	
M51608	08/59-08/83	⊗02/92	08/85➲**55978**
M51609	08/59-04/64	⊗ /66	
M51610	08/59-12/83	ⓟ	02/86➲**55967**
M51611	08/59-12/83	⊗03/91	08/85➲**55972**
M51612	08/59-01/84	⊗06/91	05/85➲**55981**
M51613	08/59-08/83	⊗08/84	
M51614	08/59-05/83	⊗04/83	
M51615	08/59-08/83	⊗03/91	06/85➲**55975**
M51616	08/59-01/84	ⓟ	
M51617	09/59-12/82	⊗04/86	
M51618	09/59-12/83	ⓟ	
M51619	09/59-08/83	⊗03/91	06/85➲**55985**
M51620	09/59-06/83	⊗06/83	
M51621	09/59-12/82	⊗07/87	
M51622	09/59-01/84	ⓟ	
M51623	09/59-08/83	⊗07/84	
M51624	09/59-12/83	⊗03/91	08/85➲**55983**
M51625	09/59-08/83	ⓟ	06/85➲**55976**
M51626	09/59-12/83	⊗05/85	
M51627	09/59-12/83	ⓟ⊗04/94	06/85➲**55986**
M51628	09/59-12/83	⊗07/85	
M51629	10/59-01/75	⊗03/77	
M51630	10/59-05/83	⊗07/84	
M51631	10/59-09/79	⊗02/80	
M51632	10/59-07/76	⊗08/76	
M51633	10/59-08/83	⊗03/91	05/85➲**55980**
M51634	10/59-12/83	⊗05/85	
M51635	10/59-08/83	⊗03/91	08/85➲**55970**
M51636	10/59-08/83	⊗07/84	
M51637	11/59-08/83	⊗03/91	08/85➲**55988**
M51638	11/59-05/83	⊗07/84	
M51639	11/59-12/83	⊗03/91	05/85➲**55984**
M51640	11/59-12/83	⊗03/91	08/85➲**55973**
M51641	11/59-12/77	⊗11/78	
M51642	11/59-08/83	⊗07/87	08/85➲**55974**
M51643	11/59-12/82	⊗09/84	
M51644	11/59-12/83	⊗09/85	
M51645	12/59-12/83	⊗09/84	
M51646	12/59-12/83	⊗09/84	
M51647	12/59-01/84	⊗05/85	
M51648	12/59-12/83	⊗12/84	
M51649	12/59-08/83	⊗03/91	05/85➲**55987**
M51650	12/59-08/83	⊗12/84	

Class 115 BR Derby

Driving Motor Brake Second

DMBS

M51651-M51680

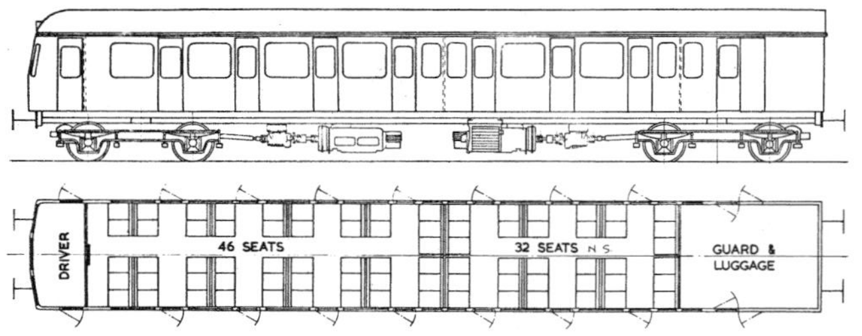

Coupling: ■ Blue square
Diagram: 598 DQ218
Lot Number: 30530
Old class: 115
Engines: Two BUT (Leyland Albion) 6-cyl horizontal type of 230 bhp.
Transmission: Mechanical. Standard
Body: 64' 0" × 9' 3" Suburban
Weight: 38t
Seats: 78 second

ⓖ Fitted with through gangways in the mid 1980s.

M51651	03/60-05/93	⊗02/95ⓖ	
M51652	03/60-02/93	⊗06/94	

M51653	03/60-08/92	⊗11/92 ®09/78
M51654	03/60-02/93	⊗06/95 @®11/79
M51655	03/60-08/92	℗ ®07/79
M51656	03/60-12/92	⊗06/95 @®10/79
M51657	04/60-12/92	⊗01/95 @
M51658	04/60-08/92	⊗09/93 ®11/79
M51659	04/60-11/92	⊗11/92 ®07/79
M51660	04/60-10/91	⊗04/93 ®10/83
M51661	06/60-05/93	⊗09/93
M51662	06/60-11/90	⊗01/92 @®05/83
M51663	05/60-08/92	℗ ® /82
M51664	05/60-12/91	⊗04/92 ®11/79
M51665	05/60-12/91	⊗04/92 ®02/81
M51666	05/60-12/91	⊗03/93 ®06/78
M51667	06/60-12/91	⊗08/92 ®08/83
M51668	06/60-12/91	⊗04/92
M51669	06/60-03/92	℗
M51670	06/60-12/91	⊗08/92 ®02/78
M51671	06/60-02/92	⊗08/92
M51672	06/60-04/82	⊗04/82
M51673	05/60-08/92	⊗01/95 ®04/83
M51674	05/60-08/92	⊗11/92
M51675	05/60-12/91	⊗04/92
M51676	05/60-04/93	⊗02/95 @
M51677	06/60-08/92	℗ ®08/78
M51678	06/60-12/91	⊗08/92 @®10/83
M51679	07/60-12/92	⊗02/95 @
M51680	07/60-12/91	⊗11/92 ®07/79

Class 112 Cravens

Driving Motor Brake Second

DMBS

M51681-M51705

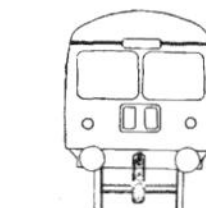

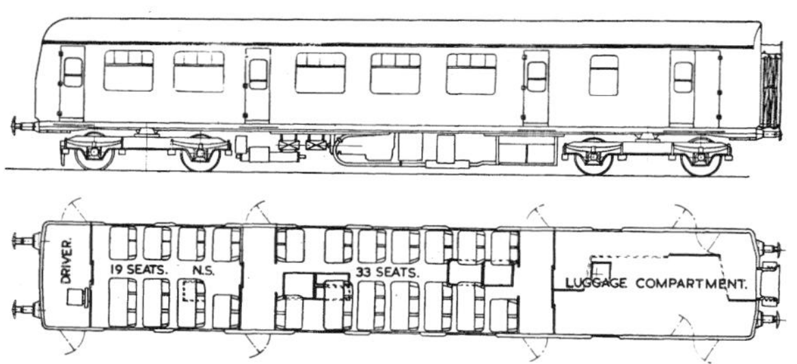

Coupling: ■ Blue square
Diagram: 602
Lot Number: 30533
Old class: 112/2
Engines: One Rolls-Royce 8-cyl horizontal type of 238 bhp.
Transmission: Mechanical. Standard
Body: 57' 6" × 9' 3"
Weight: 30t
Seats: 52 second

M51691 and M51692 were sold to Shotton Steel Works where they worked as permanent way vehicles until 1982.

M51681	10/59-11/68	⊗05/69	
M51682	09/59-11/68	⊗07/69	
M51683	11/59-11/69	⊗ /71	
M51684	08/59-11/68	⊗08/69	
M51685	08/59-11/68	⊗07/69	
M51686	08/59-11/68	⊗03/69	
M51687	08/59-11/68	⊗05/69	
M51688	08/59-11/69	⊗06/70	
M51689	08/59-11/68	⊗07/69	
M51690	08/59-11/68	⊗03/69	
M51691	08/59-11/69	⊗ /82	Shotton **PW1** 1971 to c 1982
M51692	09/59-11/69	⊗ /82	Shotton **PW2** 1971 to c 1982
M51693	09/59-11/68	⊗07/69	
M51694	09/59-11/68	⊗07/69	
M51695	09/59-11/68	⊗07/69	
M51696	09/59-11/68	⊗07/69	
M51697	10/59-11/69	⊗ /71	
M51698	10/59-11/68	⊗07/69	
M51699	10/59-11/68	⊗07/69	
M51700	10/59-11/69	⊗ /71	
M51701	10/59-11/69	⊗ /71	
M51702	10/59-11/69	⊗ /71	
M51703	10/59-11/69	⊗ /71	
M51704	10/59-11/68	⊗07/69	
M51705	11/59-12/67	⊗04/68	

Class 112 Cravens

Driving Motor Composite Lavatory

DMCL

M51706-M51730

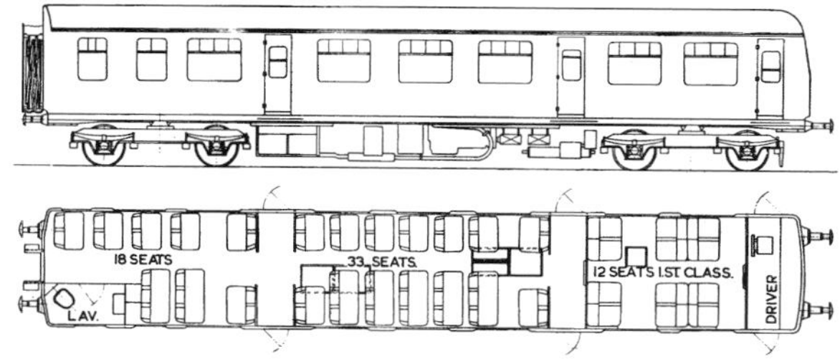

Coupling: ■ Blue square
Diagram: 603
Lot Number: 30534
Old class: 112/1
Engines: One Rolls-Royce 8-cyl horizontal type of 238 bhp.
Transmission: Mechanical. Standard
Body: 57' 6" × 9' 3"
Weight: 30t
Seats: 12 first, 51 second

M51706	10/59-11/69	⊗11/70	
M51707	09/59-11/68	⊗07/69	
M51708	11/59-11/68	⊗07/69	
M51709	08/59-03/69	⊗07/69	
M51710	08/59-11/69	⊗ /71	
M51711	08/59-11/68	⊗07/69	
M51712	08/59-11/68	⊗03/70	
M51713	08/59-11/69	⊗ /71	
M51714	08/59-11/68	⊗03/70	
M51715	08/59-11/68	⊗07/69	
M51716	08/59-11/68	⊗07/69	
M51717	09/59-11/69	⊗ /71	
M51718	09/59-11/68	⊗07/69	
M51719	09/59-11/69	⊗ /71	
M51720	09/59-11/69	⊗ /71	
M51721	09/59-11/68	⊗07/69	
M51722	10/59-11/68	⊗07/69	
M51723	10/59-11/68	⊗07/69	
M51724	10/59-12/67	⊗04/68	
M51725	10/59-11/68	⊗04/70	
M51726	10/59-11/68	⊗07/69	
M51727	10/59-11/69	⊗ /71	
M51728	10/59-11/69	⊗ /71	
M51729	10/59-11/68	⊗	Sold 07/69. Then to Yarmouth South Town
M51730	11/59-11/69	⊗ /71	⊠11/68-03/69

Class 113 Cravens

Driving Motor Brake Second

DMBS

M51731-M51755

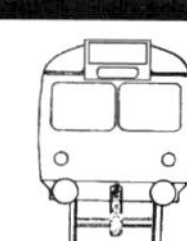

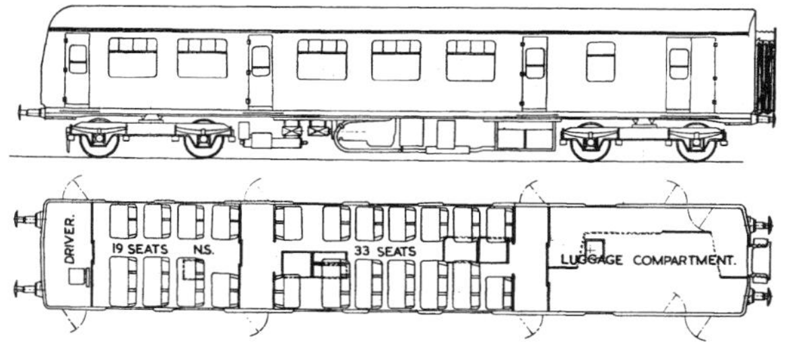

Coupling: ■ Blue square
Diagram: 604
Lot Number: 30535
Old class: 113/2
Engines: One Rolls-Royce 8-cyl horizontal type of 238 bhp.
Transmission: Hydraulic. Torque converter
Body: 57' 6" × 9' 3"
Weight: 30t
Seats: 52 second

M51731	11/59-07/69	⊗08/70
M51732	11/59-07/69	⊗06/70

M51733	11/59-02/69	⊗05/69
M51734	11/59-04/69	⊗08/69
M51735	12/59-07/69	⊗06/70
M51736	02/60-04/69	⊗08/69
M51737	12/59-07/69	⊗07/70
M51738	12/59-07/69	⊗08/70
M51739	12/59-05/69	⊗10/69
M51740	01/60-07/69	⊗08/70
M51741	01/60-04/69	⊗08/69
M51742	01/60-07/69	⊗08/70
M51743	01/60-04/69	⊗08/69
M51744	01/60-05/69	⊗10/69
M51745	01/60-07/69	⊗07/70
M51746	02/60-07/69	⊗07/70
M51747	02/60-07/69	⊗06/70
M51748	02/60-04/69	⊗08/69
M51749	02/60-07/69	⊗08/70
M51750	03/60-07/69	⊗07/70
M51751	03/60-07/69	⊗07/70
M51752	03/60-07/69	⊗08/70
M51753	04/60-07/69	⊗07/70
M51754	05/60-04/69	⊗08/69
M51755	07/60-07/69	⊗06/70

Class 113 Cravens

Driving Motor Composite Lavatory

DMCL

M51756-M51780

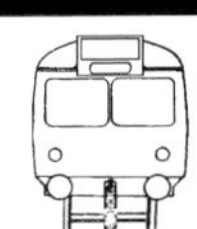

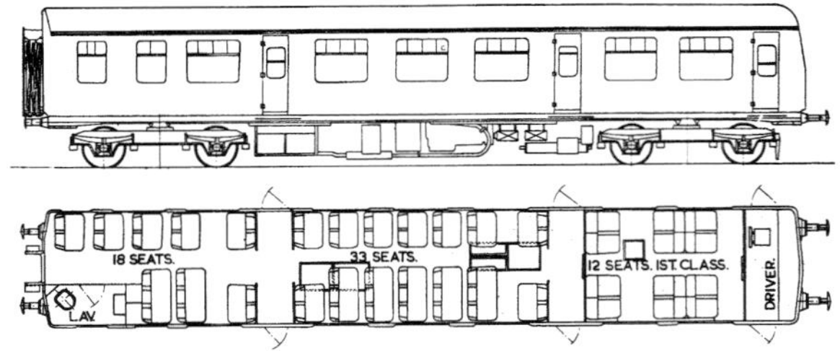

Coupling: ■ Blue square
Diagram: 605
Lot Number: 30536
Old class: 113/1
Engines: One Rolls-Royce 8-cyl horizontal type of 238 bhp.
Transmission: Hydraulic. Torque converter
Body: 57' 6" × 9' 3"
Weight: 30t
Seats: 12 first, 51 second

M51756	11/59-04/69	⊗08/69
M51757	11/59-07/69	⊗07/70
M51758	11/59-07/69	⊗08/70
M51759	11/59-07/69	⊗08/70
M51760	12/59-07/69	⊗06/70
M51761	02/60-05/69	⊗09/69
M51762	12/59-07/69	⊗07/70
M51763	12/59-12/66	⊗03/67
M51764	12/59-07/69	⊗08/70
M51765	01/60-07/69	⊗07/70
M51766	01/60-07/69	⊗06/70
M51767	01/60-07/69	⊗06/70
M51768	01/60-02/69	⊗09/69
M51769	01/60-05/69	⊗09/69
M51770	01/60-06/64	⊗05/64
M51771	02/60-07/69	⊗06/70
M51772	02/60-04/69	⊗08/69
M51773	02/60-07/69	⊗07/70
M51774	02/60-07/69	⊗06/70
M51775	03/60-07/69	⊗07/70
M51776	03/60-07/69	⊗06/70
M51777	03/60-07/69	⊗06/70
M51778	04/60-04/69	⊗08/69
M51779	05/60-07/69	⊗06/70
M51780	07/60-02/62	⊗09/62

Class 120 BR Swindon

Driving Motor Brake Composite

DMBC

SC51781-SC51787

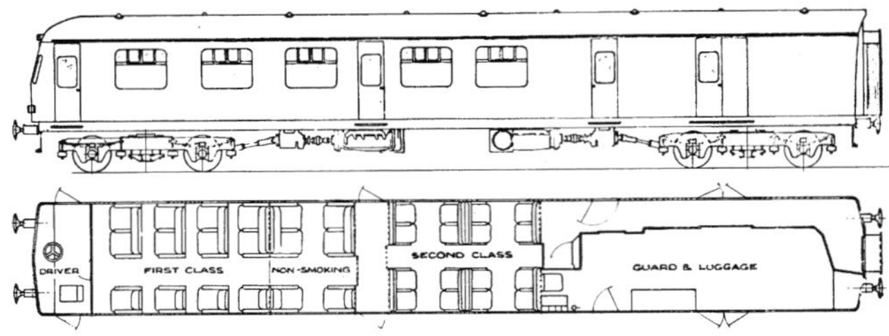

Coupling: ■ Blue square
Diagram: 587 DQ303 DQ101 ②DP204
Lot Number: 30559
Old class: 120/1
Engines: Two BUT (AEC) 6-cyl horizontal type of 150 bhp.
Transmission: Mechanical. Standard
Body: 64' 6" × 9' 3" Cross Country
Weight: 36t 7cwt
Seats: 18 first, 16 second

In 1985 51783/85/86/87 were converted to DMBF by conversion of the second class compartment to form an increased parcels area.

SC51781	11/59-03/87	⊗06/87	®10/77	03/80⇨**W**	05/86⇨**SC**	
SC51782	11/59-03/87	⊗07/87	®06/78	03/80⇨**W**	05/86⇨**SC**	
SC51783	11/59-08/87	⊗01/88	®06/77	03/80⇨**W**	10/82⇨**M**	12/85⇨Parcels
SC51784	12/59-12/80	⊗09/87	®11/78			
SC51785	12/59-10/87	⊗01/88	®11/79	03/80⇨**W**	10/82⇨**M**	12/85⇨Parcels
SC51786	12/59-09/87	⊗01/88	®05/78	03/80⇨**W**	06/82⇨**M**	12/85⇨Parcels
SC51787	12/59-09/87	⊗01/88	®10/77	10/81⇨**M**		12/85⇨Parcels

Class 120 BR Swindon

Driving Motor Second Lavatory

DMSL

SC51788-SC51794

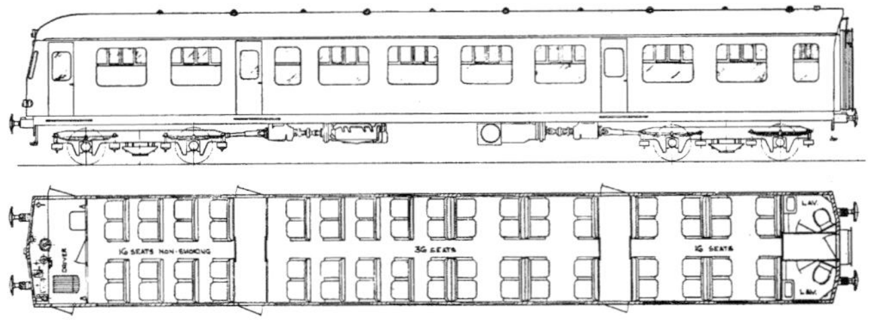

Coupling: ■ Blue square
Diagram: 586 DP202
Lot Number: 30560
Old class: 120/2
Engines: Two BUT (AEC) 6-cyl horizontal type of 150 bhp.
Transmission: Mechanical. Standard
Body: 64' 6" × 9' 3" Cross Country
Weight: 36t 10cwt
Seats: 68 second

SC51788	01/60-03/87	⊗07/87	®10/77	03/80⇨**W**	05/86⇨**SC**	
SC51789	01/60-04/86	⊗04/86	®10/77	10/81⇨**M**	10/85⇨**SC**	
SC51790	01/60-03/87	⊗06/87	®06/78	03/80⇨**W**	05/86⇨**SC**	
SC51791	01/60-04/86	⊗04/86	®05/78	03/80⇨**W**	06/82⇨**M**	
SC51792	02/60-04/86	⊗04/86	®06/77	03/80⇨**W**	10/82⇨**M**	10/85⇨**SC**
SC51793	02/60-04/86	⊗04/86	®11/78	03/80⇨**W**	10/82⇨**M**	10/85⇨**SC**
SC51794	02/60-06/86	⊗07/87	®02/81	10/81⇨**M**	04/86⇨**SC**	

Class 102⇨101 Metropolitan-Cammell
Driving Motor Brake Second
DMBS
SC51795-SC51801

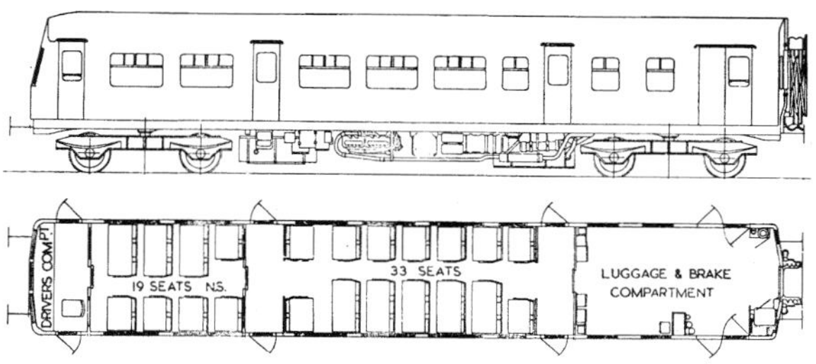

Coupling: ■ Blue square
Diagram: 523 DQ202
Lot Number: 30587
Old class: 102/2
Engines: Two BUT (AEC) 6-cyl horizontal type of 150 bhp.
Transmission: Mechanical. Standard
Body: 57' 6" × 9' 3"
Weight: 32t
Seats: 52 second

SC51795 10/59-10/89 ⊗07/90 ®01/78
SC51796 10/59-09/83 ⊗01/88 ®04/78
SC51797 11/59-10/87 ⊗05/88 ®01/78
SC51798 11/59-08/89 ⊗12/89 ®04/78
SC51799 11/59-12/90 ⊗05/91 ®04/82 11/78⇨**W**
SC51800 12/59-06/01 ⊗04/03 ®02/84 ⊠11/90-01/91, ⊠05/91-06/91
SC51801 12/59-03/89 ⊗04/90 ® /82 11/78⇨**W**

Class 102⇨101 Metropolitan-Cammell
Driving Motor Composite Lavatory
DMCL
SC51802-SC51808

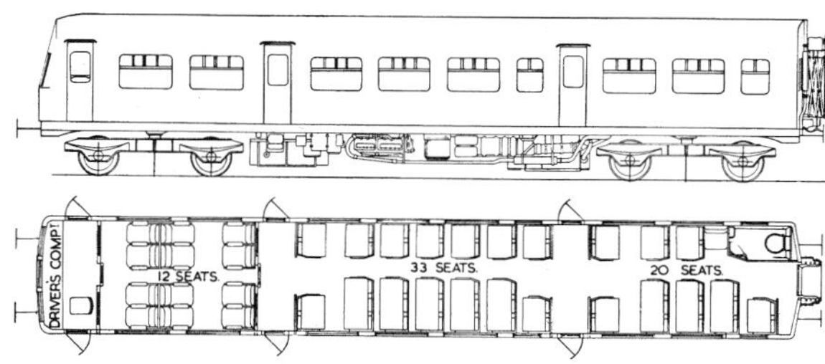

Coupling: ■ Blue square
Diagram: 621 DP210
Lot Number: 30588
Old class: 102/1
Engines: Two BUT (AEC) 6-cyl horizontal type of 150 bhp.
Transmission: Mechanical. Standard
Body: 57' 6" × 9' 3"
Weight: 32t
Seats: 12 first, 53 second

SC51802 10/59-06/88 ⊗01/89 ®*10/76*
SC51803 10/59-12/03 ℗ ®08/79
SC51804 11/59-01/90 ⊗01/90 ®03/77
SC51805 11/59-10/87 ⊗11/89 ®06/78
SC51806 11/59-02/84 ⊗09/84 ®*10/76*
SC51807 12/59-10/87 ⊗11/87 ®07/76
SC51808 12/59-06/93 ⊗06/93 ®04/82 11/78⇨**W**

Class 110 Birmingham RC&W
Driving Motor Brake Composite
DMBC
E51809-E51828

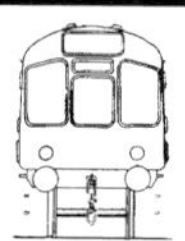

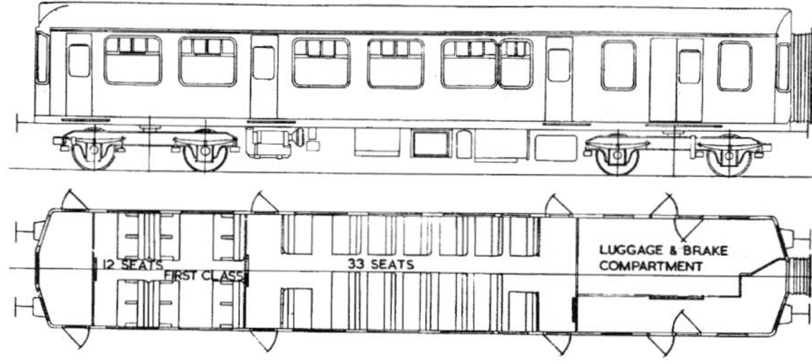

Coupling: ■ Blue square
Diagram: 564 DQ301
Lot Number: 30292
Old class: 110/2
Engines: Two Rolls-Royce series 130D of 180 bhp.
Transmission: Mechanical. Standard
Body: 57' 6" × 9' 3"
Weight: 32t
Seats: 12 first, 33 second

E51809 06/61-05/89 ⊗04/90 ®06/81 01/65⇨**NE** 01/68⇨**E**
E51810 06/61-01/87 ⊗03/87 ®11/79 01/65⇨**NE** 01/68⇨**E**
E51811 07/61-11/86 ⊗09/88 ®10/80 01/65⇨**NE** 01/68⇨**E**
E51812 07/61-09/89 ⊗05/90 ® /82 01/65⇨**NE** 01/68⇨**E**
E51813 07/61-03/90 ℗ ® /82 01/65⇨**NE** 01/68⇨**E**
E51814 07/61-03/87 ⊗06/87 ®10/81 01/65⇨**NE** 01/68⇨**E**
E51815 08/61-03/87 ⊗02/88 ® */82* 01/65⇨**NE** 01/68⇨**E**
E51816 08/61-08/87 ⊗01/89 ®11/78 01/65⇨**NE** 01/68⇨**E**
E51817 08/61-03/90 ⊗07/90 ® /81 01/65⇨**NE** 01/68⇨**E**
E51818 09/61-07/88 ⊗05/89 ®02/81 01/65⇨**NE** 01/68⇨**E**
E51819 09/61-07/87 ⊗02/89 ®07/79 01/65⇨**NE** 01/68⇨**E**
E51820 09/61-03/87 ⊗02/89 ®02/81 01/65⇨**NE** 01/68⇨**E**
E51821 09/61-11/63 ⊗11/63
E51822 10/61-07/87 ⊗09/88 ®02/81 01/65⇨**NE** 01/68⇨**E**
E51823 10/61-02/90 ⊗07/90 ®05/83 01/65⇨**NE** 01/68⇨**E**
E51824 10/61-12/88 ⊗09/90 ® */80* 01/65⇨**NE** 01/68⇨**E** 12/88⊃**ADB977611**
E51825 10/61-03/87 ⊗08/87 ®02/81 01/65⇨**NE** 01/68⇨**E**
E51826 11/61-12/88 ⊗09/90 ®02/81 01/65⇨**NE** 01/68⇨**E** 04/90⊃**ADB977613**
E51827 11/61-05/89 ⊗07/90 ® /82 01/65⇨**NE** 01/68⇨**E**
E51828 11/61-12/89 ⊗07/90 ®11/80 01/65⇨**NE** 01/68⇨**E**

Class 110 Birmingham RC&W
Driving Motor Composite Lavatory
DMCL
E51829-E51848

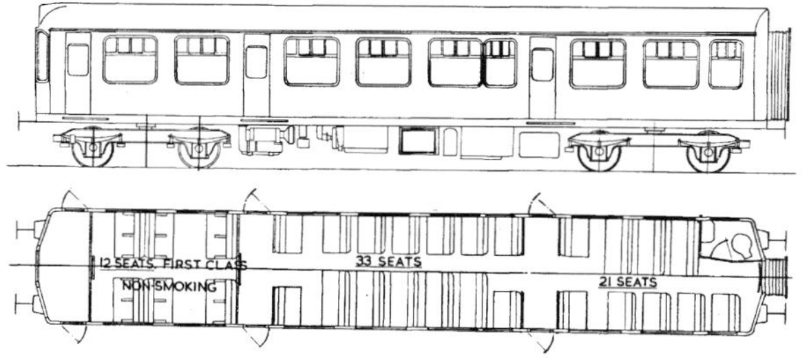

Coupling: ■ Blue square
Diagram: 563 DP313
Lot Number: 30593
Old class: 110/1
Engines: Two Rolls-Royce series 130D of 180 bhp.
Transmission: Mechanical. Standard
Body: 57' 6" × 9' 3"
Weight: 31t 10cwt
Seats: 12 first, 54 second

E51829 06/61-03/90 ⊗07/90 ®04/82 01/65⇨**NE** 01/68⇨**E**
E51830 06/61-03/90 ⊗07/90 ® */83* 01/65⇨**NE** 01/68⇨**E**
E51831 07/61-07/87 ⊗09/88 ®01/81 01/65⇨**NE** 01/68⇨**E**
E51832 07/61-07/87 ⊗09/88 ®07/79 01/65⇨**NE** 01/68⇨**E**

E51833	07/61-07/87	⊗02/89	®02/81	01/65⇨**NE**	01/68⇨**E**
E51834	07/61-02/90	⊗07/90	®03/83	01/65⇨**NE**	01/68⇨**E**
E51835	08/61-03/89	⊗03/90	® /82	01/65⇨**NE**	01/68⇨**E**
E51836	08/61-09/86	⊗05/87	®11/80	01/65⇨**NE**	01/68⇨**E**
E51837	09/61-11/63	⊗11/63			
E51838	09/61-12/88	⊗09/90	®10/80	01/65⇨**NE**	01/68⇨**E** 12/88➲**ADB977612**
E51839	09/61-02/87	⊗09/88	®11/79	01/65⇨**NE**	01/68⇨**E**
E51840	09/61-03/90	⊗08/90	® /81	01/65⇨**NE**	01/68⇨**E**
E51841	09/61-03/87	⊗07/88	®11/78	01/65⇨**NE**	01/68⇨**E**
E51842	10/61-02/90	Ⓟ	® /82	01/65⇨**NE**	01/68⇨**E**
E51843	10/61-03/90	⊗08/90	®11/78	01/65⇨**NE**	01/68⇨**E**
E51844	10/61-02/87	⊗08/87	®02/81	01/65⇨**NE**	01/68⇨**E**
E51845	10/61-07/88	⊗05/89	®11/79	01/65⇨**NE**	01/68⇨**E**
E51846	11/61-03/87	⊗02/89	®11/78	01/65⇨**NE**	01/68⇨**E**
E51847	11/61-03/90	⊗07/90	® /81	01/65⇨**NE**	01/68⇨**E**
E51848	11/61-07/81	⊗09/82		01/65⇨**NE**	01/68⇨**E**

Class 115 BR Derby

Driving Motor Brake Second
DMBS
M51849-M51860

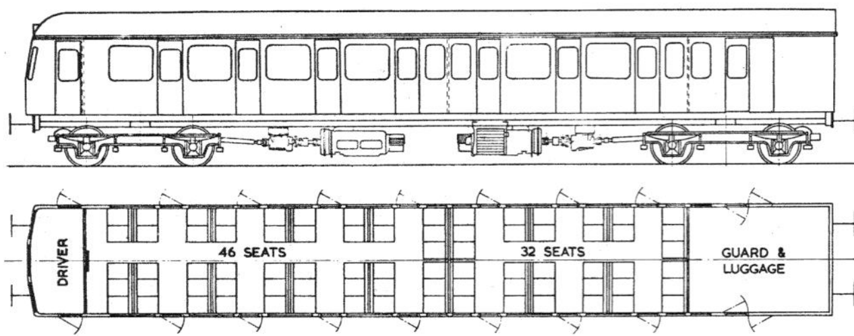

Coupling: ■ Blue square
Diagram: 598 DQ218
Lot Number: 30595
Old class: 115
Engines: Two BUT (Leyland Albion) 6-cyl horizontal type of 230 bhp.
Transmission: Mechanical. Standard
Body: 64' 0" × 9' 3" Suburban
Weight: 38t
Seats: 78 second

ⓖ Fitted with through gangways in the mid 1980s.

M51849	02/60-02/92	Ⓟ	ⓖ
M51850	02/60-01/85	⊗08/86	ⓖ
M51851	02/60-02/94	⊗03/94	ⓖ
M51852	02/60-09/93	Ⓟ	ⓖ®03/79
M51853	02/60-01/94	⊗03/94	ⓖ®04/82
M51854	02/60-07/92	⊗08/92	ⓖ®02/81
M51855	02/60-05/93	⊗09/93	ⓖ®11/80
M51856	02/60-11/91	⊗01/92	ⓖ®03/79
M51857	02/60-02/92	⊗08/92	®05/83
M51858	02/60-10/92	⊗09/92	ⓖ®02/79
M51859	03/60-07/95	Ⓟ	ⓖ® /82
M51860	03/60-07/96	⊗07/96	ⓖ®02/81

Class 115 BR Derby

Driving Motor Brake Second
DMBS
M51861-M51900

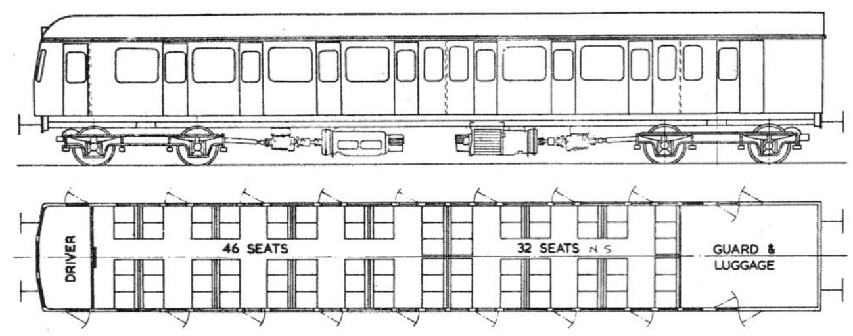

Coupling: ■ Blue square
Diagram: 598 DQ218
Lot Number: 30598
Old class: 115
Engines: Two BUT (Leyland Albion) 6-cyl horizontal type of 230 bhp.
Transmission: Mechanical. Standard
Body: 64' 0" × 9' 3" Suburban
Weight: 38t
Seats: 78 second

ⓖ Fitted with through gangways in the mid 1980s.

M51861	07/60-10/85	⊗08/86	® /82	
M51862	07/60-03/93	⊗03/93	ⓖ® /81	
M51863	07/60-08/92	⊗06/95	®04/82	
M51864	07/60-04/82	⊗02/86	®09/78	
M51865	08/60-06/92	⊗05/92	ⓖ	
M51866	08/60-12/92	⊗01/95	ⓖ	
M51867	08/60-06/92	⊗05/92	ⓖ	
M51868	08/60-06/93	⊗06/93	ⓖ®07/83	⊠12/90-12/90, ⊠06/92-06/92
M51869	08/60-05/93	⊗07/93	ⓖ® /82	
M51870	08/60-03/92	⊗08/92	ⓖ	
M51871	09/60-04/92	⊗09/92	® /81	
M51872	09/60-11/92	⊗11/92	® /82	
M51873	09/60-03/91	⊗09/92	®02/81	
M51874	09/60-08/92	⊗06/95	®02/81	
M51875	09/60-08/92	⊗01/95	® /82	
M51876	09/60-04/92	⊗08/92	ⓖ	
M51877	09/60-11/92	⊗03/93	ⓖ	
M51878	09/60-05/93	⊗06/94	ⓖ	
M51879	09/60-08/92	⊗09/93	®02/81	
M51880	09/60-07/95	Ⓟ	ⓖ® /82	
M51881	09/60-04/82	⊗02/86	® /81	
M51882	09/60-08/78	⊗04/80		
M51883	09/60-11/92	⊗11/92	® /81	
M51884	09/60-03/93	⊗03/93	ⓖ®11/78	
M51885	09/60-08/92	⊗11/94		
M51886	09/60-08/92	Ⓟ		
M51887	09/60-08/92	Ⓟ	®11/79	
M51888	09/60-07/92	⊗09/93		
M51889	10/60-10/91	⊗11/91	®07/79	
M51890	10/60-02/92	⊗11/92	®11/83	
M51891	10/60-03/92	⊗11/92	®07/79	
M51892	10/60-10/92	⊗09/92	ⓖ®07/78	
M51893	10/60-03/91	⊗09/92	ⓖ	
M51894	10/60-07/91	⊗11/91	® /82	
M51895	11/60-12/91	⊗01/93	ⓖ®02/81	
M51896	11/60-12/91	⊗04/92	®11/80	
M51897	11/60-05/93	⊗07/93		
M51898	11/60-03/90	⊗11/90	ⓖ	
M51899	12/60-08/92	Ⓟ	ⓖ®07/79	
M51900	12/60-02/92	⊗04/92	®07/79	

Class 108 BR Derby

Driving Motor Brake Second
DMBS
M51901-M51950

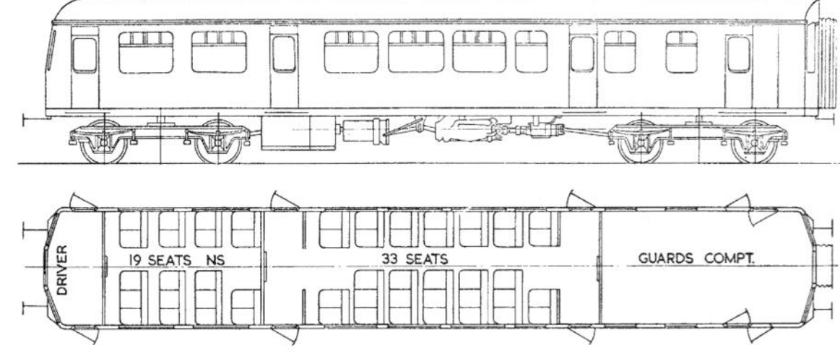

Coupling: ■ Blue square
Diagram: 634 DQ213
Lot Number: 30601
Old class: 108/2
Engines: Two BUT (AEC) 6-cyl horizontal type of 150 bhp.
Transmission: Mechanical. Standard
Body: 58' 1" × 9' 3"
Weight: 29t
Seats: 52 second

M51901	03/60-09/92	⊗07/96	®03/79	10/92➲**ADB977810**
M51902	03/60-11/90	⊗01/92	®12/76	
M51903	03/60-09/92	⊗08/95	®11/76	10/92➲**ADB977808**
M51904	03/60-07/91	⊗09/91	®06/77	
M51905	04/60-09/90	⊗06/92	®01/79	
M51906	04/60-10/91	⊗11/93	®01/78	10/91➲**ADB977744**
M51907	04/60-02/93	Ⓟ	®10/77	
M51908	04/60-07/91	⊗11/91	®04/78	

M51909	04/60-07/93	ⓟ	®02/79		
M51910	04/60-11/87	⊗08/88	®04/82	11/86⇨**W**	
M51911	04/60-01/92	⊗07/96	®03/78		01/92➲**ADB977768**
M51912	05/60-05/93	⊗08/94	®04/82		
M51913	05/60-06/91	⊗12/91	®04/80		
M51914	05/60-04/93	ⓟ	®06/78		
M51915	05/60-11/69	⊗04/70	®08/80		
M51916	06/60-05/93	⊗08/94			
M51917	06/60-06/92	⊗06/92	®03/79		
M51918	07/60-04/85	⊗02/86	®08/80		
M51919	06/60-02/93	ⓟ			
M51920	07/60-06/92	⊗09/92			
M51921	07/60-10/70	⊗04/71			
M51922	07/60-06/92	ⓟ		11/86⇨**W**	
M51923	07/60-10/79	⊗08/80	®07/77		
M51924	07/60-11/92	⊗01/93	®07/78		
M51925	08/60-11/91	⊗11/91	®09/77		
M51926	08/60-11/91	⊗11/91	®10/78		
M51927	08/60-06/92	⊗05/92			
M51928	10/60-11/92	⊗11/92	®07/78		
M51929	09/60-12/84	⊗06/87	®06/77		
M51930	09/60-10/92	⊗05/94	®10/78		☒05/92-09/92
M51931	09/60-10/92	⊗12/92	®10/77		
M51932	09/60-09/92	⊗02/95	®08/78		10/92➲**ADB977840**
M51933	10/60-02/93	ⓟ	®11/79		
M51934	10/60-12/87	⊗*05/88*	®11/79		
M51935	11/60-10/92	ⓟ	®04/80		
M51936	11/60-06/92	⊗05/92	®11/79		
M51937	10/60-09/92	ⓟ	®07/77		10/92➲**ADB977806**
M51938	02/61-01/92	⊗03/94	®07/79		01/92➲**ADB977765**
M51939	11/60-02/91	⊗02/91	®10/78		
M51940	11/60-10/92	⊗10/92	® /81		
M51941	11/60-11/90	ⓟ	®04/82		
M51942	01/61-06/93	ⓟ	®06/78		
M51943	12/60-02/93	⊗07/93	®08/82		
M51944	12/60-11/64	⊗05/65			
M51945	01/61-09/92	⊗06/96	®04/78		10/92➲**ADB977812**
M51946	01/61-01/74	⊗04/74			
M51947	02/61-02/93	ⓟ			
M51948	02/61-01/92	⊗01/92	®02/79		
M51949	03/61-02/77	⊗08/77			
M51950	06/61-06/91	ⓟ	®09/79		

Class 124 BR Swindon
Driving Motor Composite
DMC
E51951-E51967

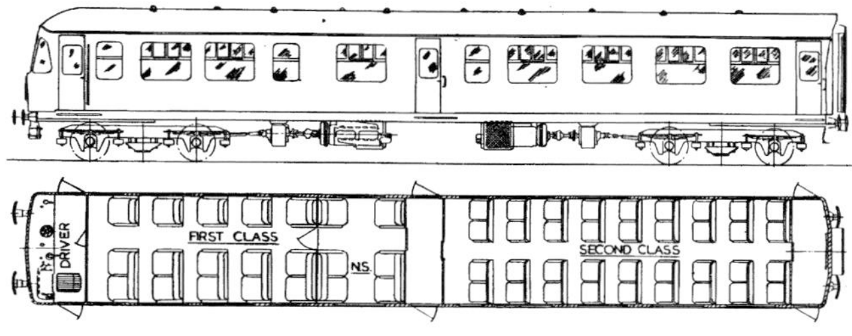

Coupling: ■ Blue square
Diagram: 577 DP316
Lot Number: 30603
Old class: 124/1
Engines: Two BUT (Leyland Albion) 6-cyl horizontal type of 230 bhp.
Transmission: Mechanical. Standard
Body: 64' 9" × 9' 3" Trans-Pennine
Weight: 40t
Seats: 21 first, 36 second

E51951	07/60-08/84	⊗03/85	01/65⇨**NE**	01/68⇨**E**
E51952	07/60-05/84	⊗03/85	01/65⇨**NE**	01/68⇨**E**
E51953	08/60-08/84	⊗10/84	01/65⇨**NE**	01/68⇨**E**
E51954	08/60-04/84	⊗09/84	01/65⇨**NE**	01/68⇨**E**
E51955	08/60-08/84	⊗11/84	01/65⇨**NE**	01/68⇨**E**
E51956	08/60-05/84	⊗02/85	01/65⇨**NE**	01/68⇨**E**
E51957	09/60-04/84	⊗07/84	01/65⇨**NE**	01/68⇨**E**
E51958	09/60-05/84	⊗12/84	01/65⇨**NE**	01/68⇨**E**
E51959	09/60-04/77	⊗12/77	01/65⇨**NE**	01/68⇨**E**
E51960	09/60-08/84	⊗05/85	01/65⇨**NE**	01/68⇨**E**
E51961	10/60-04/84	⊗07/84	01/65⇨**NE**	01/68⇨**E**
E51962	10/60-11/83	⊗07/84	01/65⇨**NE**	01/68⇨**E**
E51963	11/60-08/84	⊗05/85	01/65⇨**NE**	01/68⇨**E**
E51964	11/60-08/84	⊗10/84	01/65⇨**NE**	01/68⇨**E**
E51965	12/60-02/84	⊗09/84	01/65⇨**NE**	01/68⇨**E**
E51966	12/60-08/84	⊗05/85	01/65⇨**NE**	01/68⇨**E**
E51967	01/61-08/84	⊗03/85	01/65⇨**NE**	01/68⇨**E**

Class 124 BR Swindon
Motor Brake Side-Corridor with Lavatory
MBSK
E51968-E51984

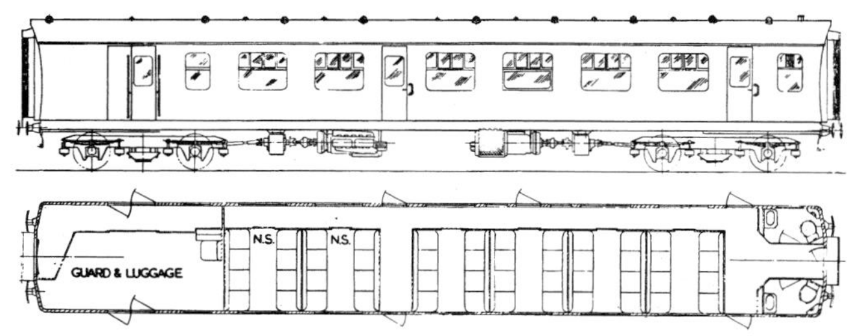

Coupling: ■ Blue square
Diagram: 579 DR201
Lot Number: 30604
Old class: 124/2
Engines: Two BUT (Leyland Albion) 6-cyl horizontal type of 230 bhp.
Transmission: Mechanical. Standard
Body: 64' 6" × 9' 3" Trans-Pennine
Weight: 41t
Seats: 48 second

E51968	07/60-10/80	⊗02/82	01/65⇨**NE**	01/68⇨**E**	
E51969	07/60-04/81	⊗08/84	01/65⇨**NE**	01/68⇨**E**	➲**E59834**
E51970	08/60-10/80	⊗02/84	01/65⇨**NE**	01/68⇨**E**	
E51971	08/60-03/80	⊗10/84	01/65⇨**NE**	01/68⇨**E**	
E51972	08/60-08/80	⊗10/83	01/65⇨**NE**	01/68⇨**E**	
E51973	08/60-11/81	⊗09/84	01/65⇨**NE**	01/68⇨**E**	➲**E59841**
E51974	09/60-05/81	⊗08/84	01/65⇨**NE**	01/68⇨**E**	➲**E59835**
E51975	09/60-08/81	⊗09/84	01/65⇨**NE**	01/68⇨**E**	➲**E59839**
E51976	09/60-07/81	⊗08/84	01/65⇨**NE**	01/68⇨**E**	➲**E59838**
E51977	09/60-06/80	⊗07/85	01/65⇨**NE**	01/68⇨**E**	
E51978	10/60-05/81	⊗09/84	01/65⇨**NE**	01/68⇨**E**	➲**E59836**
E51979	10/60-10/81	⊗07/84	01/65⇨**NE**	01/68⇨**E**	
E51980	11/60-11/81	⊗02/85	01/65⇨**NE**	01/68⇨**E**	➲**E59842**
E51981	11/60-03/81	⊗07/84	01/65⇨**NE**	01/68⇨**E**	➲**E59833**
E51982	12/60-06/81	⊗03/82	01/65⇨**NE**	01/68⇨**E**	
E51983	12/60-11/81	⊗07/84	01/65⇨**NE**	01/68⇨**E**	➲**E59840**
E51984	01/61-06/81	⊗09/84	01/65⇨**NE**	01/68⇨**E**	➲**E59837**

Class 107 BR Derby
Driving Motor Brake Second
DMBS
SC51985-SC52010

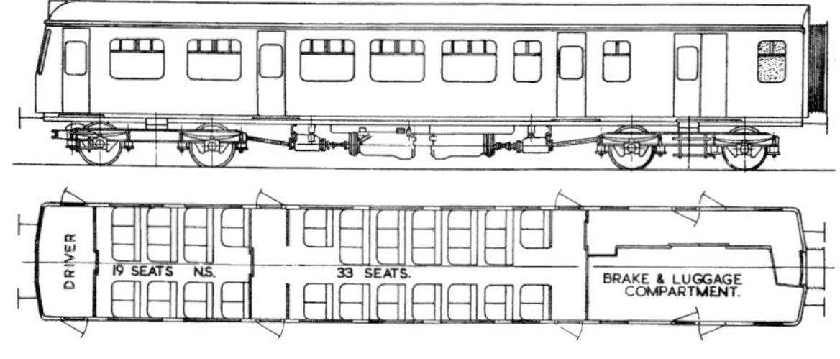

Coupling: ■ Blue square
Diagram: 639 DQ211
Lot Number: 30611
Old class: 107/2
Engines: Two BUT (AEC) 6-cyl horizontal type of 150 bhp.
Transmission: Mechanical. Standard
Body: 58' 1" × 9' 3"
Weight: 34t 10cwt
Seats: 52 second

SC51985	12/60-07/91	⊗02/93	®06/81	☒05/91-06/91 12/91➲**ADB977756**
SC51986	12/60-11/91	⊗01/92	®10/80	
SC51987	12/60-11/91	⊗01/92	®06/80	
SC51988	12/60-07/91	⊗08/91	®11/78	
SC51989	12/60-07/91	⊗01/92	®05/79	

SC51990	12/60-09/92	℗	®11/79	09/92➲**ADB977830**
SC51991	12/60-01/90	⊗08/92	®11/79	
SC51992	12/60-07/91	⊗02/93	® /81	⊠05/91-06/91 12/91➲**ADB977758**
SC51993	01/61-09/92	℗	®02/81	09/92➲**ADB977834**
SC51994	01/61-10/92	⊗03/94	®11/78	
SC51995	01/61-01/73	⊗04/73		
SC51996	01/61-03/90	⊗11/90	®06/80	
SC51997	02/61-11/91	⊗03/92	®06/80	
SC51998	02/61-07/91	⊗08/91	®02/81	
SC51999	02/61-05/91	⊗08/91	®06/81	
SC52000	02/61-07/91	⊗01/92	®06/81	
SC52001	02/61-11/91	⊗03/92	®06/80	
SC52002	02/61-02/86	⊗09/87	®11/79	
SC52003	02/61-08/84	⊗09/84		
SC52004	03/61-01/92	⊗01/92	®11/78	
SC52005	03/61-09/92	℗	®11/78	09/92➲**ADB977832**
SC52006	03/61-10/92	℗	®10/80	
SC52007	04/61-01/92	⊗01/92	®08/79	
SC52008	04/61-10/92	℗	®10/80	
SC52009	04/61-02/84	⊗09/84	®11/79	
SC52010	06/61-11/91	⊗01/92	®08/79	

Class 107 BR Derby

Driving Motor Composite Lavatory
DMCL
SC52011-SC52036

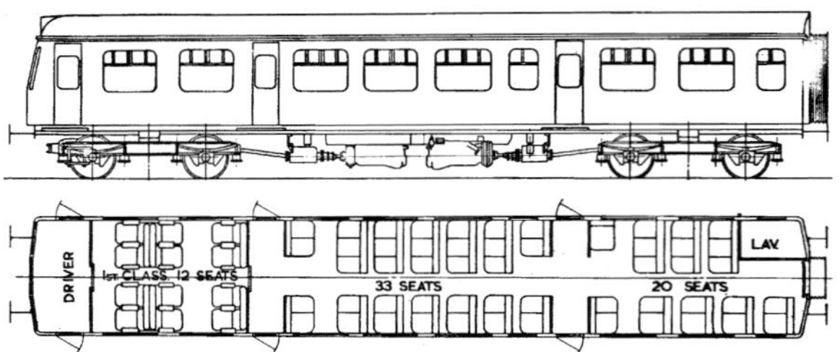

Coupling: ■ Blue square
Diagram: 649 DP215
Lot Number: 30612
Old class: 107/1
Engines: Two BUT (AEC) 6-cyl horizontal type of 150 bhp.
Transmission: Mechanical. Standard
Body: 58' 1" × 9' 3"
Weight: 35t
Seats: 12 first, 53 second

SC52011	12/60-10/92	⊗03/94	®11/78	
SC52012	12/60-09/92	℗	®02/82	09/92➲**ADB977835**
SC52013	12/60-07/91	⊗08/91	®11/78	
SC52014	12/60-02/84	⊗12/87	®06/80	05/84➲**RDB977225**
SC52015	12/60-03/92	⊗02/93	®10/80	
SC52016	12/60-01/92	⊗01/92	®11/79	
SC52017	12/60-08/84	⊗09/84	®11/79	
SC52018	12/60-11/91	⊗01/92	®06/80	
SC52019	01/61-03/90	⊗11/90	®06/80	
SC52020	01/61-11/91	⊗01/92	®06/80	
SC52021	01/61-07/91	⊗08/91	®02/81	
SC52022	01/61-11/83	⊗08/84	®02/81	
SC52023	02/61-07/91	⊗02/93	®08/79	12/91➲**ADB977762**
SC52024	02/61-11/91	⊗03/92	®06/80	
SC52025	02/61-09/92	℗		⊠11/91-01/92, ⊠04/92-09/92 09/92➲**ADB977833**
SC52026	02/61-07/91	⊗01/92	® /81	⊠05/91-06/91
SC52027	02/61-11/85	⊗02/86	®11/79	
SC52028	02/61-07/91	⊗02/93	®06/81	⊠05/91-06/91 12/91➲**ADB977757**
SC52029	02/61-10/92	℗	®06/80	
SC52030	03/61-09/92	℗	®06/81	09/92➲**ADB977831**
SC52031	03/61-10/92	℗	®11/78	
SC52032	03/61-02/84	⊗12/87	®11/78	05/84➲**RDB977227**
SC52033	04/61-01/92	⊗01/92	®08/79	
SC52034	04/61-11/91	⊗01/92	®08/79	
SC52035	04/61-11/90	⊗08/92	®11/79	
SC52036	06/61-07/91	⊗01/92	®06/81	

Class 108 BR Derby

Driving Motor Composite Lavatory
DMCL
M52037-M52065

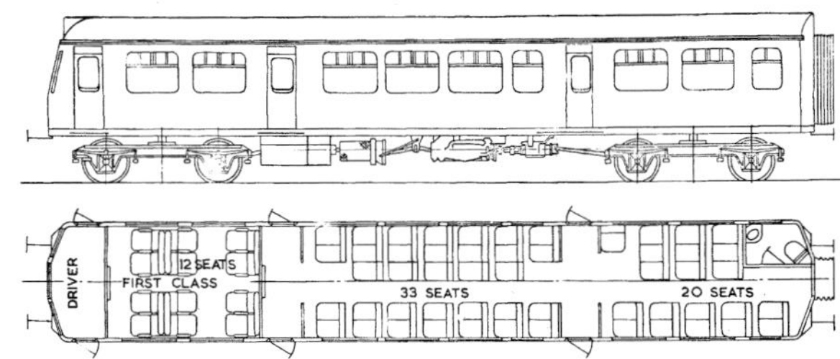

Coupling: ■ Blue square
Diagram: 638 DP312
Lot Number: 30660
Old class: 108/1
Engines: Two BUT (AEC) 6-cyl horizontal type of 150 bhp.
Transmission: Mechanical. Standard
Body: 58' 1" × 9' 3"
Weight: 28t
Seats: 12 first, 53 second

M52037	07/60-11/87	⊗08/88	®09/77	
M52038	07/60-11/92	⊗11/92	®07/78	
M52039	07/60-06/92	⊗05/92	®10/77	
M52040	08/60-03/84	⊗05/84	® /82	
M52041	08/60-11/92	⊗01/93	®10/78	
M52042	08/60-10/92	⊗11/92	®10/77	
M52043	10/60-08/89	⊗03/93	®07/77	
M52044	09/60-02/93	℗	®04/80	
M52045	09/60-11/91	⊗11/91	®04/78	
M52046	09/60-09/92	⊗09/95		10/92➲**TDB977819**
M52047	09/60-09/92	⊗02/95	®09/78	10/92➲**ADB977841**
M52048	10/60-02/93	℗	®04/78	
M52049	10/60-10/91	⊗01/92	® /82	
M52050	11/60-10/91	⊗10/92	®04/80	
M52051	11/60-02/91	⊗08/91	®11/79	
M52052	10/60-12/80	⊗02/85		
M52053	02/61-09/92	℗	®07/78	10/92➲**ADB977807**
M52054	11/60-02/93	℗	®10/78	
M52055	11/60-11/92	⊗08/93	®03/79	
M52056	11/60-02/92	⊗02/92	®04/82	
M52057	01/61-04/92	⊗05/92	®06/83	
M52058	12/60-10/92	⊗08/94	®08/82	⊠05/92-09/92 10/92➲**TDB977821**
M52059	12/60-09/92	⊗10/96	® /81	10/92➲**ADB977815**
M52060	01/61-09/92	℗⊗04/04	®06/78	10/92➲**ADB977813**
M52061	01/61-09/92	℗⊗ /02	® /82	⊠08/89-08/89 10/92➲**ADB977817**
M52062	02/61-06/91	℗		
M52063	02/61-02/91	⊗02/91	®02/79	
M52064	03/61-11/90	℗	®07/77	
M52065	06/61-03/92	⊗05/92	® /82	

Class 110 Birmingham RC&W

Driving Motor Brake Composite
DMBC
M52066-M52075

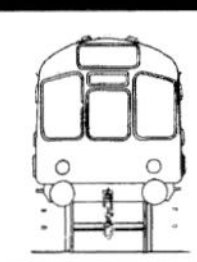

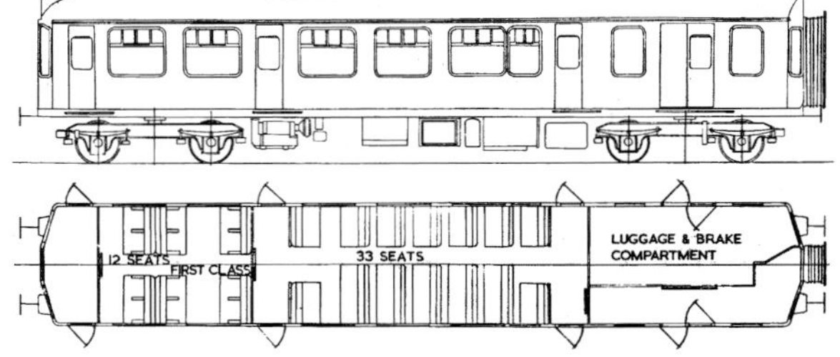

Coupling: ■ Blue square
Diagram: 564 DQ301
Lot Number: 30691
Old class: 110/2
Engines: Two Rolls-Royce series 130D of 180 bhp.
Transmission: Mechanical. Standard

Body: 57' 6" × 9' 3"
Weight: 32t
Seats: 12 first, 33 second

M52066	11/61-03/90	⊗08/90	® /81	05/67⇨**NE**	01/68⇨**E**
M52067	11/61-09/89	⊗04/90	® /81	05/67⇨**NE**	01/68⇨**E**
M52068	12/61-02/87	⊗02/88	®11/80	05/67⇨**NE**	01/68⇨**E**
M52069	12/61-03/90	⊗07/90	®12/82	05/67⇨**NE**	01/68⇨**E**
M52070	12/61-09/86	⊗05/87	®11/80	05/67⇨**NE**	01/68⇨**E**
M52071	01/62-03/90	Ⓟ	®01/83	05/67⇨**NE**	01/68⇨**E**
M52072	01/62-02/90	⊗08/90	® /83	05/67⇨**NE**	01/68⇨**E**
M52073	01/62-02/88	⊗09/88	®07/79	05/67⇨**NE**	01/68⇨**E**
M52074	01/62-06/71	⊗07/72		05/67⇨**NE**	01/68⇨**E**
M52075	01/62-02/90	⊗08/90	® /81	05/67⇨**NE**	01/68⇨**E**

Class 110 Birmingham RC&W

Driving Motor Composite Lavatory
DMCL
M52076-M52085

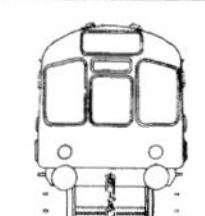

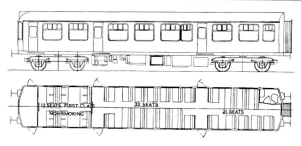

Coupling: ■ Blue square
Diagram: 563 DP313
Lot Number: 30692
Old class: 110/1
Engines: Two Rolls-Royce series 130D of 180 bhp.
Transmission: Mechanical. Standard
Body: 57' 6" × 9' 3"
Weight: 31t 10cwt
Seats: 12 first, 54 second

M52076	11/61-12/88	⊗09/90	®02/81	05/67⇨**NE**	01/68⇨**E** 11/89⊃**DB977614**
M52077	11/61-03/90	Ⓟ	® /82	05/67⇨**NE**	01/68⇨**E**
M52078	12/61-01/87	⊗03/87	®02/81	05/67⇨**NE**	01/68⇨**E**
M52079	12/61-03/87	⊗07/88	®02/81	05/67⇨**NE**	01/68⇨**E**
M52080	12/61-03/90	⊗07/90	®04/82	05/67⇨**NE**	01/68⇨**E**
M52081	01/62-08/89	⊗03/90	® /83	05/67⇨**NE**	01/68⇨**E** ⊠08/89-08/89
M52082	01/62-03/90	⊗08/90		05/67⇨**NE**	01/68⇨**E**
M52083	01/62-03/87	⊗02/88	®02/81	05/67⇨**NE**	01/68⇨**E**
M52084	01/62-02/89	⊗04/90	® /82	05/67⇨**NE**	01/68⇨**E**
M52085	01/62-03/90	⊗08/90	® /82	05/67⇨**NE**	01/68⇨**E**

Class 123 BR Swindon

Driving Motor Brake Second Lavatory
DMBSL
W52086-W52095

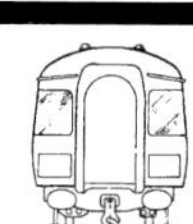

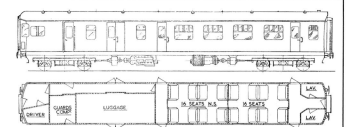

Coupling: ■ Blue square
Diagram: 566 DQ223
Lot Number: 30703
Old class: 123/2
Engines: Two BUT (AEC) 6-cyl horizontal type of 150 bhp.
Transmission: Mechanical. Standard
Body: 64' 11⅛" × 9' 3" Inter-City
Weight: 41t 14cwt
Seats: 32 second

W52086	02/63-04/79	⊗06/81	04/78⇨**E**
W52087	02/63-03/84	⊗08/84	04/78⇨**E**
W52088	02/63-08/84	⊗03/85	04/78⇨**E**
W52089	03/63-08/84	⊗11/84	04/78⇨**E**
W52090	04/63-08/84	⊗11/84	01/78⇨**E**
W52091	05/63-08/84	⊗03/85	06/77⇨**E**
W52092	05/63-08/84	⊗03/85	06/77⇨**E**
W52093	06/63-08/84	⊗03/85	06/77⇨**E**
W52094	06/63-08/84	⊗03/85	04/78⇨**E**
W52095	06/63-08/84	⊗11/84	04/78⇨**E**

Class 123 BR Swindon

Driving Motor Side-Corridor with Lavatory
DMSK
W52096-W52105

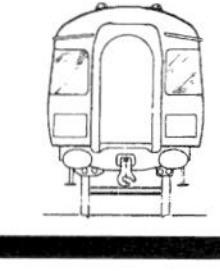

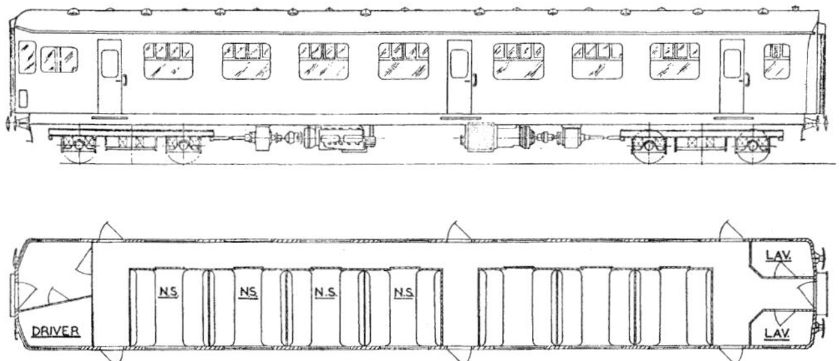

Coupling: ■ Blue square
Diagram: 574 DP206
Lot Number: 30704
Old class: 123/1
Engines: Two BUT (AEC) 6-cyl horizontal type of 150 bhp.
Transmission: Mechanical. Standard
Body: 64' 11⅛" × 9' 3" Inter-City
Weight: 41t 9cwt
Seats: 56 second

W52096	02/63-05/84	⊗11/84	04/78⇨**E**
W52097	02/63-05/84	⊗11/84	06/77⇨**E**
W52098	02/63-05/84	⊗01/85	06/77⇨**E**
W52099	03/63-02/84	⊗08/84	04/78⇨**E**
W52100	04/63-05/84	⊗12/84	01/78⇨**E**
W52101	05/63-04/77	⊗02/85	
W52102	05/63-05/84	⊗11/84	04/78⇨**E**
W52103	06/63-05/84	⊗11/84	04/78⇨**E**
W52104	06/63-05/84	⊗11/84	04/78⇨**E**
W52105	06/63-03/84	⊗07/84	06/77⇨**E**

Class 114 BR Derby

Driving Motor Brake Second
DMBS
E53001-E53047

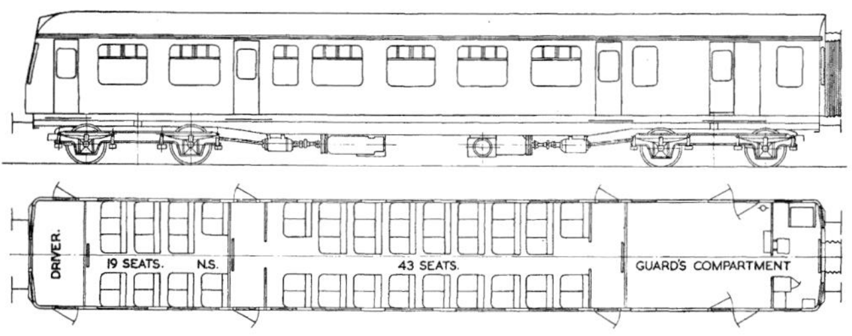

Coupling: ■ Blue square
Diagram: 516 DQ217
Lot Number: 30209
Old class: 114
Engines: Two BUT (Leyland Albion) 6-cyl horizontal type of 230 bhp.
Transmission: Mechanical. Standard
Body: 64' 6" × 9' 3"
Weight: 37t 10cwt
Seats: 62 second

E53001	06/83⊂**50001**	10/56-06/88	⊗11/88	®11/78
E53002	04/83⊂**50002**	11/56-07/91	⊗11/91	®07/78
E53003	05/83⊂**50003**	11/56-02/88	⊗04/88	®02/81

E53004	04/83⊂**50004**	11/56-11/89	⊗04/90	®11/79	06/87⇨Parcels
E53005	04/83⊂**50005**	11/56-10/91	⊗02/92	®01/81	
E53006	06/83⊂**50006**	11/56-07/91	⊗11/91	® /81	
E53007	05/83⊂**50007**	11/56-06/88	⊗12/88	®08/78	
E53008	/84⊂**50008**	11/56-05/89	⊗02/91	® /81	
E53009	04/83⊂**50009**	11/56-06/88	⊗01/89	®11/79	
E53010	02/83⊂**50010**	12/56-08/87	⊗04/91	®05/83	11/86⇨Parcels 08/87⊃**55930**
E53011	04/83⊂**50011**	11/56-06/88	⊗12/88	®01/78	
E53012	04/83⊂**50012**	11/56-06/88	⊗11/88	®11/80	
E53013	05/83⊂**50013**	12/56-06/88	⊗12/88	®01/78	
E53014	04/83⊂**50014**	12/56-06/88	⊗11/88	®02/81	
E53015	04/83⊂**50015**	02/57-07/89	℗	®07/78	07/89⊃**55929**
E53016	04/83⊂**50016**	02/57-09/86	⊗04/88	®03/78	
E53017	04/83⊂**50017**	01/57-06/88	⊗12/88	®07/78	06/87⇨Parcels
E53018	11/83⊂**50018**	01/57-07/89	⊗04/91	®10/77	07/89⊃**55928**
E53019	06/83⊂**50019**	01/57-06/92	℗	® /81	
E53020	06/83⊂**50020**	01/57-05/90	⊗04/90	®07/79	10/87⇨Parcels
E53021	04/83⊂**50021**	01/57-10/91	⊗11/91	® /82	
E53022	06/83⊂**50022**	01/57-06/88	⊗12/88	®11/79	
E53023	04/83⊂**50023**	01/57-02/88	⊗04/88	®07/79	04/87⇨Parcels
E53024	06/83⊂**50024**	01/57-06/88	⊗12/88	®07/79	04/87⇨Parcels
E53025	/83⊂**50025**	01/57-06/88	⊗12/88	®07/79	
E53026	08/83⊂**50026**	01/57-03/89	⊗02/91	®11/79	
E53027	06/83⊂**50027**	01/57-09/90	⊗04/91	®07/78	03/87⇨Parcels
E53030	05/83⊂**50030**	01/57-12/90	⊗07/95	® /82	
E53031	04/83⊂**50031**	01/57-06/88	⊗01/89	®11/79	
E53032	02/83⊂**50032**	02/57-01/88	⊗04/91	®02/81	01/88⇨Parcels 01/88⊃**55932**
E53033	04/83⊂**50033**	02/57-06/88	⊗11/88	®11/79	
E53035	04/83⊂**50035**	03/57-11/89	⊗04/90	®03/78	
E53036	06/83⊂**50036**	02/57-01/92	⊗07/93	®07/78	01/92⊃**ADB977769**
E53037	04/83⊂**50037**	02/57-03/89	⊗02/91	® /81	
E53038	06/83⊂**50038**	02/57-03/89	⊗04/89	®11/77	
E53039	04/83⊂**50039**	02/57-05/89	⊗02/91	® /82	
E53040	03/83⊂**50040**	02/57-01/88	⊗04/91	®11/78	☒09/86-10/86 10/86⇨Parcels 01/88⊃**55931**
E53041	10/83⊂**50041**	03/57-06/88	⊗06/88	®02/81	
E53042	04/83⊂**50042**	03/57-06/88	⊗11/88	®12/77	
E53043	08/83⊂**50043**	03/57-06/88	⊗11/88	®04/78	
E53044	04/83⊂**50044**	03/57-10/91	⊗11/91	®10/81	
E53045	06/83⊂**50045**	03/57-06/88	⊗01/89	®11/78	
E53046	04/83⊂**50046**	03/57-09/90	⊗04/91	®12/82	10/87⇨Parcels
E53047	06/83⊂**50047**	04/57-06/88	⊗12/88	®07/80	

Class 114 BR Derby

Driving Motor Brake Second
DMBS
E53049

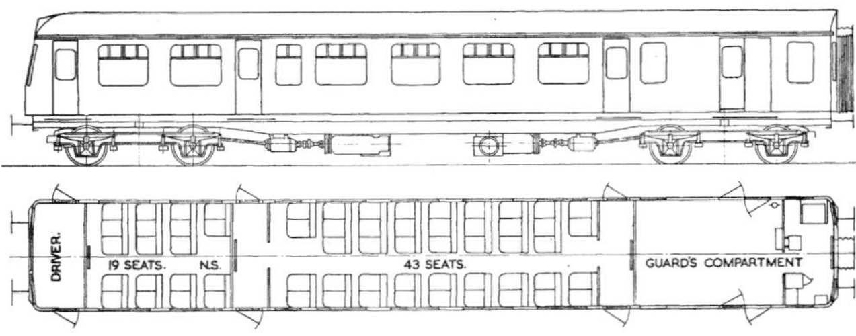

Coupling: ■ Blue square
Diagram: 516 DQ217
Lot Number: 30459
Old class: 114
Engines: Two BUT (Leyland Albion) 6-cyl horizontal type of 230 bhp.
Transmission: Mechanical. Standard.
Body: 64' 6" × 9' 3"
Weight: 37t 10cwt
Seats: 62 second

E53049	06/83⊂**50049**	08/57-01/84	⊗06/84	®11/78	

Class 116 BR Derby

Driving Motor Brake Second
DMBS
M53050-W53091

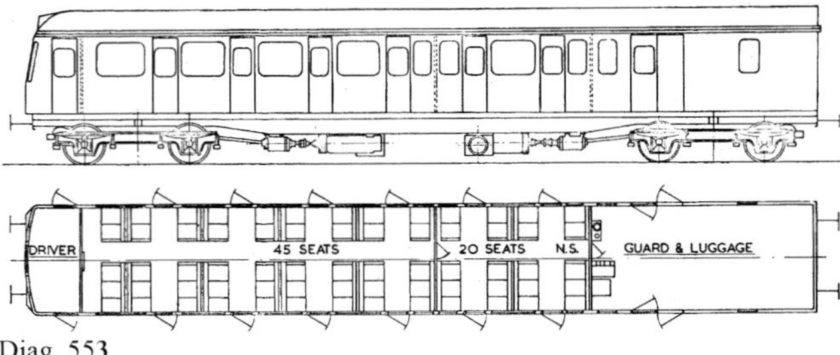

Diag. 553

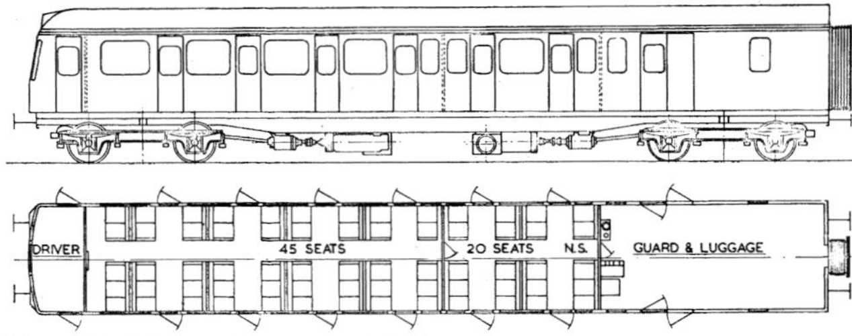

Diag. 853 ⓖ *Through gangway fitted*

Coupling: ■ Blue square
Diagram: 553 DQ219 ⓖ 853 DQ230
Lot Number: 30211
Old class: 116/2
Engines: Two BUT (Leyland) 6-cyl horizontal type of 150 bhp.
Transmission: Mechanical. Standard
Body: 64' 0" × 9' 3" Suburban
Weight: 36t
Seats: 65 second

M53050	06/83⊂**50050**	04/57-10/91	⊗03/92	*ⓖ*®03/79	
M53051	06/83⊂**50051**	04/57-05/88	⊗09/88	®03/77	10/85⇨Parcels
M53052	04/83⊂**50052**	05/57-01/88	⊗02/88	®04/77	
M53053	07/83⊂**50053**	05/57-06/95	⊗06/95	*ⓖ*®06/82	
M53054	03/83⊂**50054**	05/57-06/93	⊗06/93	*ⓖ*®05/83	
M53055	05/83⊂**50055**	05/57-05/95	⊗08/95	*ⓖ*®09/83	
M53056	06/83⊂**50056**	05/57-12/90	⊗05/91	*ⓖ*®01/81	
M53057	07/83⊂**50057**	05/57-03/87	⊗04/87	®10/77	
M53058	06/83⊂**50058**	05/57-10/91	⊗03/92	*ⓖ*®10/78	
M53059	04/83⊂**50059**	08/57-11/88	⊗12/88	®01/80	
M53060	06/83⊂**50060**	05/57-03/94	⊗03/94	*ⓖ*®02/84	
M53061	06/83⊂**50061**	05/57-10/91	⊗11/91	*ⓖ*®05/76	
M53062	07/83⊂**50062**	06/57-11/87	⊗11/87	®10/77	☒03/83-05/83
M53063	06/83⊂**50063**	06/57-03/88	⊗02/91		*08/88⊃TDB977637*
M53064	07/83⊂**50064**	06/57-04/87	⊗08/87	®09/77	
M53065	07/83⊂**50065**	06/57-03/88	⊗03/88	®06/76	
M53067	06/83⊂**50067**	05/57-10/87	⊗10/87	®07/78	
M53068	07/83⊂**50068**	06/57-02/87	⊗02/87	®04/82	
M53069	06/83⊂**50069**	06/57-05/87	⊗08/87	*ⓖ*®11/79	10/85⇨Parcels
M53070	08/83⊂**50070**	08/57-03/88	⊗03/88	®06/77	
M53071	03/83⊂**50071**	08/57-08/93	⊗09/93	*ⓖ*®07/83	☒05/93-08/93
M53072	06/83⊂**50072**	06/57-05/88	⊗09/88	®08/76	10/85⇨Parcels
M53073	07/83⊂**50073**	06/57-10/92	⊗10/92	*ⓖ*®12/82	
M53074	07/83⊂**50074**	08/57-08/87	⊗01/88	®01/78	
M53075	07/83⊂**50075**	08/57-12/87	⊗01/88		
M53076	06/83⊂**50076**	08/57-11/87	⊗10/87	®09/77	
M53077	06/83⊂**50077**	08/57-03/88	⊗03/88	®11/76	
M53078	04/83⊂**50078**	08/57-11/88	⊗12/88	®11/79	
M53079	07/83⊂**50079**	09/57-04/92	⊗10/92	*ⓖ*®04/78	
W53080	04/83⊂**50080**	10/57-10/89	⊗05/90	ⓖ®02/77	
M53081	04/83⊂**50081**	10/57-10/88	⊗03/89	ⓖ®10/80	
M53082	05/85⊂**50082**	08/57-11/90	⊗05/91	ⓖ®08/80	
W53083	04/83⊂**50083**	08/57-09/92	⊗05/93	ⓖ®11/77	
W53084	03/83⊂**50084**	08/57-12/86	⊗08/87	ⓖ®11/77	
W53086	04/83⊂**50086**	09/57-10/89	⊗05/90	ⓖ®11/77	
W53087	04/83⊂**50087**	09/57-12/88	⊗03/89	ⓖ®07/76	
W53088	04/83⊂**50088**	09/57-04/87	⊗08/87	ⓖ®06/78	
W53089	04/83⊂**50089**	09/57-06/89	⊗08/89	ⓖ®02/77	
SC53090	03/83⊂**50090**	09/57-05/93	⊗09/93	ⓖ®08/83	
W53091	04/83⊂**50091**	10/57-12/88	⊗03/89	ⓖ®06/78	

A side view of Class 117 DMBS W51350 in blue livery leaving Acton Main Line Station on a Slough-Paddington local service on 17th March 1977. *B Morrison*

Refurbished Class 117 unit number L404 (W51337, W59489 and W41379) is seen on 3rd July 1977 leaving Maidenhead with the 13.59 Paddington-Oxford service. *L Bertram*

Class 117 DMBS W51366 of unit B428 is seen outside the paint shop at BREL Doncaster Works on 12th February 1987 after having been repainted into Network South East Livery. *C J Marsden*

On 22nd July 1977 Birmingham RCW Class 118 twin unit P480 (W51327 and W51312) is seen at Gunnislake on the 12.05 service for Plymouth.

In June 1974, after we had finished our 'O' levels and while we waiting for the results, Rob Cruickshank and I set off to chase Westerns with a Western Region Rail Rover. In the middle of the week Rob persuaded me to take a side trip on the Gunnislake Branch, which he had read about. On a glorious summer's day P480 (which then comprised W51326 and W51311) took us up the branch. There is a reversal halfway up the line at Bere Alston, and we got to know the almost empty two-car unit very well as we followed the driver from end to end every time we reversed. *B Morrison*

The driver and guard of Class 118 three-car unit L469 have stopped to discuss something while working a Paddington service at Cholsey and Moulsford on 6th February 1979. L469 is my old Gunnislake acquaintance W51311 and W51326, now augmented with Class 117 trailer W59490.
D Kimber

It was rare in BR days for trains to carry all-over advertising liveries. One exception was this three-car Class 118 unit P460 (51302, 59469 and 51317). In February 1982 it was painted bright yellow to advertise British Telecom and it ran in this form until its withdrawal in 1988.
C J Court

On 3rd November 1962 a down empty stock service formed of a Gloucester RCW Class 119 three-car Cross-Country unit is seen at Knowle and Dorridge. This unit was based at Tyseley in Birmingham just before the boundary changes in 1963 brought it into the London Midland Region. It carries the unit number 509 on stickers in the front window, but these units' formations were not fixed at this point. Viewing the original print under a magnifying glass shows that the leading carriage is possibly DMBC W51073. *M Mensing*

Above: Class 119 DMSL W51083 is seen in original green livery. *P J Sharpe*

Right: Class 119 three-car unit L573 is working the 10.27 Gatwick-Reading on 21st March 1987 at Hook, diverted via Woking and Basingstoke. L573 (51055, 59417 and 51083) was one of the units fitted out with extra luggage space to work this service. *D E Canning*

On 27th November 1974 three-car blue and grey Class 119 unit P588 led by W51079 is leaving Truro on the 14.48 Truro-Falmouth service. *B Morrison*

Swindon Class 120 Cross-Country DMBC number W50696 is seen in its original green livery. *A Swain*

This 1958 interior view of W59255 shows the Formica covered buffet originally fitted to these cross-country units. *BR*

W51574 is one of the later Class 120 Cross-Country units which was fitted with a four-character headcode box. It is seen at Birmingham Snow Hill station on 11th May 1961. *D Kingston*

On 30th January 1980 a blue and grey liveried Class 120 three-car set waits at Derby ready to form the 19.50 Derby-Lincoln service. *C J Marsden*

On 30th December 1980 Class 120 unit C621 is running temporarily as a two-car set (51785 and 51793 with no prefix) having just been transferred from Scotland. It is seen at Shrewsbury having worked in on the 05.44 Swansea-Shrewsbury service. Next to it can be seen a Class 128 DPU (with its gangway connection removed) waiting to work the 09.40 parcels service to Newtown. *T Clift*

Left: This view of Chester depot on 20th September 1986 shows several Class 120 units, with parcels units M53699 + M53713 on the right and M53658 + M53714 on the left. *S Turner*

Below: Brand new Pressed Steel Class 121 single unit W55020 is seen on delivery. *P J Sharpe*

On a typical working for these units Class 121 W55031 (L131) is seen at Twyford Station on Sunday 29th July 1973 waiting to work the 16.50 service to Henley on Thames. *B Morrison*

Class 116 BR Derby

Driving Motor Second
DMS
M53092-W53133

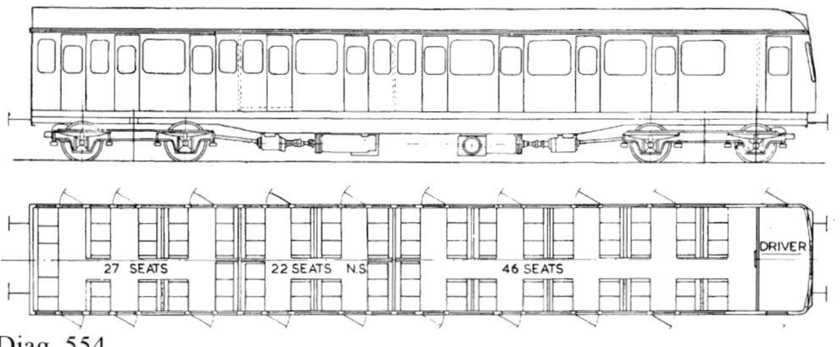

Diag. 554

Diag. 854 ⓖ *Through gangway fitted*

Coupling:	■ Blue square
Diagram:	554 DP201 ⓖ 854 DP220
Lot Number:	30213
Old class:	116/1
Engines:	Two BUT (Leyland) 6-cyl horizontal type of 150 bhp.
Transmission:	Mechanical. Standard
Body:	64' 0" × 9' 3" Suburban
Weight:	36t
Seats:	95 second ⓖ 89 second

M53092	06/83⊂**50092**	04/57-10/92	⊗03/93	*ⓖ*®05/76	
M53093	06/83⊂**50093**	04/57-10/92	⊗09/97	*ⓖ*®07/78	⊠06/92-09/92 10/92➲**TDB977829**
M53094	07/83⊂**50094**	05/57-08/87	⊗05/88	®06/76	
M53095	08/83⊂**50095**	05/57-03/88	⊗03/88	®06/77	
M53097	07/83⊂**50097**	05/57-11/87	⊗11/87	®10/77	
M53098	06/83⊂**50098**	05/57-07/88	⊗02/88	®01/81	
M53099	06/83⊂**50099**	05/57-05/87	⊗08/87	®*03/79*	10/85⇨Parcels
M53100	06/83⊂**50100**	05/57-02/88	⊗02/88	®09/81	
M53101	03/83⊂**50101**	08/57-01/94	⊗08/95	*ⓖ*®07/83	
M53102	03/83⊂**50102**	05/57-05/93	⊗09/93	*ⓖ*®09/79	
M53103	07/83⊂**50103**	05/57-11/87	⊗11/87		
M53104	04/83⊂**50104**	06/57-02/87	⊗02/87	®01/80	
M53105	06/83⊂**50105**	06/57-03/87	⊗02/87	®08/76	
M53106	03/83⊂**50106**	06/57-01/94	⊗03/94	*ⓖ*®05/83	
M53107	03/83⊂**50107**	06/57-12/85	⊗08/86	®04/77	
M53108	06/83⊂**50108**	08/57-12/87	⊗05/88		
M53109	04/83⊂**50109**	05/57-11/88	⊗12/88	®11/79	
M53110	07/83⊂**50110**	06/57-11/87	⊗11/87	®01/78	
M53111	06/83⊂**50111**	06/57-05/87	⊗08/87		
M53112	06/83⊂**50112**	08/57-01/88	⊗12/87	®10/78	
M53113	06/83⊂**50113**	07/57-12/85	⊗08/86	®03/77	
M53114	06/83⊂**50114**	06/57-06/95	⊗06/95	*ⓖ*®10/83	
M53116	05/83⊂**50116**	08/57-06/95	⊗06/95	*ⓖ*®09/83	
M53117	06/83⊂**50117**	08/57-11/88	⊗12/88	®10/77	
M53118	06/83⊂**50118**	08/57-11/87	⊗11/87	®09/77	
M53119	06/83⊂**50119**	08/57-03/88	⊗02/91		*08/88➲TDB977636*
M53120	06/83⊂**50120**	08/57-03/88	⊗03/88	®11/76	
M53121	07/83⊂**50121**	09/57-03/88	⊗03/88	®04/78	
W53122	04/83⊂**50122**	10/57-10/89	⊗05/90	ⓖ®02/77	
M53123	04/83⊂**50123**	10/57-04/88	⊗01/89	ⓖ®10/80	
M53124	06/83⊂**50124**	08/57-05/95	⊗08/95	ⓖ®08/80	
W53126	03/83⊂**50126**	08/57-12/86	⊗08/87	ⓖ®11/77	
M53127	06/83⊂**50127**	08/57-11/87	⊗11/87		
W53128	04/83⊂**50128**	09/57-10/89	⊗05/90	ⓖ®11/77	
W53129	04/83⊂**50129**	09/57-06/88	⊗10/88	ⓖ®07/76	
W53130	04/83⊂**50130**	09/57-04/87	⊗08/87	ⓖ®06/78	
W53131	04/83⊂**50131**	09/57-08/89	⊗01/90	ⓖ®02/77	
SC53132	03/83⊂**50132**	09/57-06/95	⊗06/95	ⓖ®08/83	⊠11/90-12/90
W53133	04/83⊂**50133**	10/57-06/88	⊗06/88	ⓖ®06/78	

Class 111 Metropolitan-Cammell

Driving Motor Brake Second
DMBS
E53134-E53137

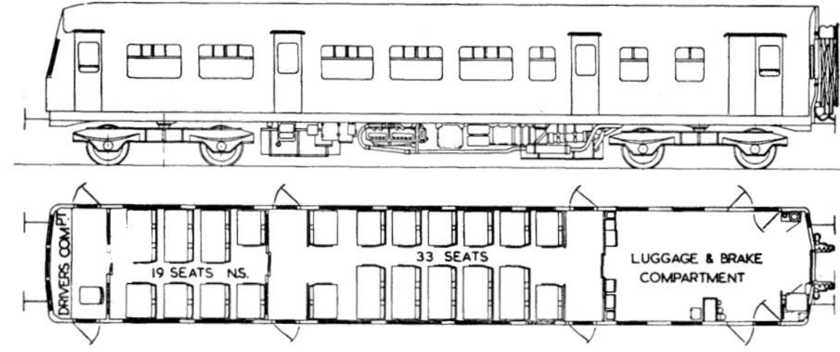

Coupling:	■ Blue square
Diagram:	520 DQ214
Lot Number:	30248
Old class:	111/2
Engines:	Two Rolls-Royce 6-cyl horizontal type of 180 bhp.
Transmission:	Mechanical. Standard
Body:	57' 6" × 9' 3"
Weight:	33t
Seats:	52 second

E53134	04/83⊂**50134**	04/57-11/87	⊗08/89	®06/76	11/87➲**TDB977538**
E53135	/83⊂**50135**	04/57-11/87	⊗08/89	®07/76	11/87➲**TDB977539**
E53136	05/83⊂**50136**	04/57-02/87	⊗02/89	®03/78	
E53137	04/83⊂**50137**	04/57-11/87	⊗08/89	®04/77	11/87➲**TDB977540**

Class 101 Metropolitan-Cammell

Driving Motor Composite Lavatory
DMCL
SC53138-E53151

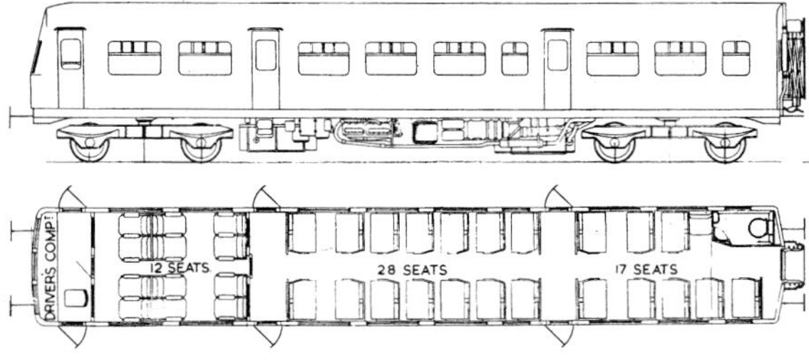

Coupling:	■ Blue square
Diagram:	618 DP301 ②DP212
Lot Number:	30249
Old class:	101/1
Engines:	Two BUT (AEC) 6-cyl horizontal type of 150 bhp.
Transmission:	Mechanical. Standard
Body:	57' 6" × 9' 3"
Weight:	32t
Seats:	12 first, 45 second

SC53138	08/83⊂**50138**	10/56-05/87	⊗01/88	®02/81
E53139	02/85⊂**50139**	10/56-04/92	⊗10/92	® /82
E53140	08/83⊂**50140**	10/56-01/87	⊗09/88	®*10/76*
SC53141	08/83⊂**50141**	10/56-05/89	⊗09/90	®08/79
E53142	03/83⊂**50142**	10/56-09/86	⊗12/86	®02/81
SC53143	08/83⊂**50143**	10/56-05/87	⊗09/87	
SC53144	08/83⊂**50144**	11/56-04/88	⊗06/90	®08/79
SC53146	08/83⊂**50146**	11/56-10/91	⊗06/92	®08/82
SC53147	01/84⊂**50147**	11/56-07/87	⊗01/88	®10/80
SC53148	08/83⊂**50148**	11/56-03/87	⊗01/88	®10/80
E53149	06/83⊂**50149**	11/56-03/92	⊗10/92	® /82
E53150	06/83⊂**50150**	11/56-10/89	⊗03/92	®10/81
E53151	02/85⊂**50151**	11/56-09/86	⊗02/87	®02/81

Class 101 Metropolitan-Cammell

Driving Motor Brake Second

DMBS

E53153-E53157

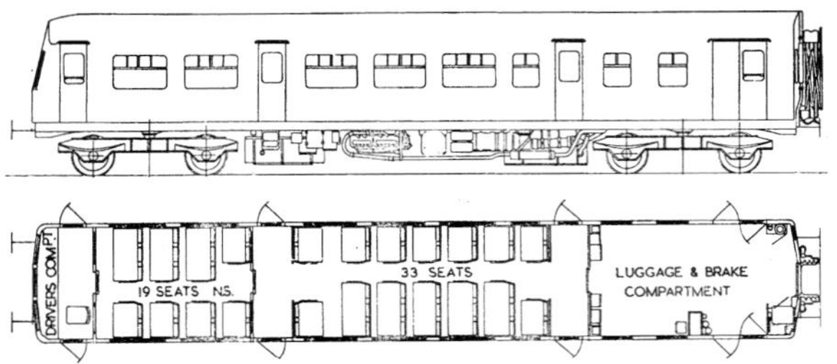

Coupling:	■ Blue square
Diagram:	523 DQ202
Lot Number:	30252
Old class:	101/2
Engines:	Two BUT (AEC) 6-cyl horizontal type of 150 bhp.
Transmission:	Mechanical. Standard
Body:	57' 6" × 9' 3"
Weight:	32t
Seats:	52 second

E53153	05/83⊂**50153**	12/56-10/87	⊗11/87	®02/81	04/86⇨**SC**
E53154	05/83⊂**50154**	12/56-02/85	⊗03/85	®07/79	
E53155	04/83⊂**50155**	12/56-04/92	⊗02/93	®01/77	
E53156	05/83⊂**50156**	01/57-03/86	⊗10/86	®07/79	
E53157	07/83⊂**50157**	01/57-02/91	⊗02/91	®02/81	

Class 101 Metropolitan-Cammell

Driving Motor Composite Lavatory

DMCL

SC53158-SC53163

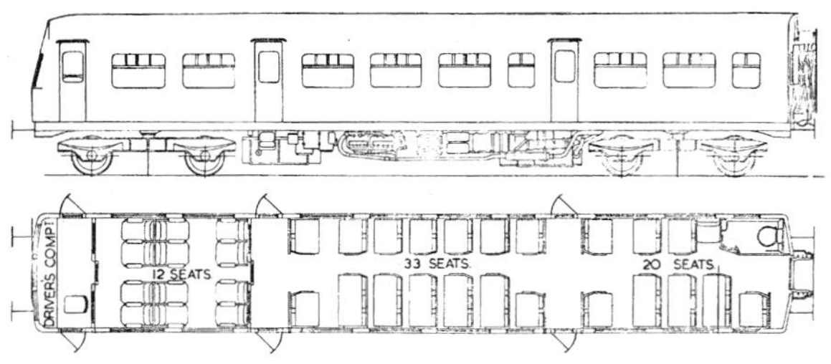

Coupling:	■ Blue square
Diagram:	620 DP303 ②DP214
Lot Number:	30253
Old class:	101/1
Engines:	Two BUT (AEC) 6-cyl horizontal type of 150 bhp.
Transmission:	Mechanical. Standard
Body:	57' 6" × 9' 3"
Weight:	32t
Seats:	12 first, 53 second

SC53158	08/83⊂**50158**	12/56-01/91	⊗02/91	®02/82
SC53159	08/83⊂**50159**	12/56-05/89	⊗08/90	®10/80
SC53160	08/83⊂**50160**	12/56-12/03	Ⓟ	®02/82
E53161	/84⊂**50161**	12/56-10/88	⊗09/90	®05/76
E53162	05/83⊂**50162**	01/57-09/89	⊗05/90	®08/78
SC53163	08/83⊂**50163**	01/57-08/02	⊗01/04	®04/83

Class 101 Metropolitan-Cammell

Driving Motor Brake Second

DMBS

E53164-E53167

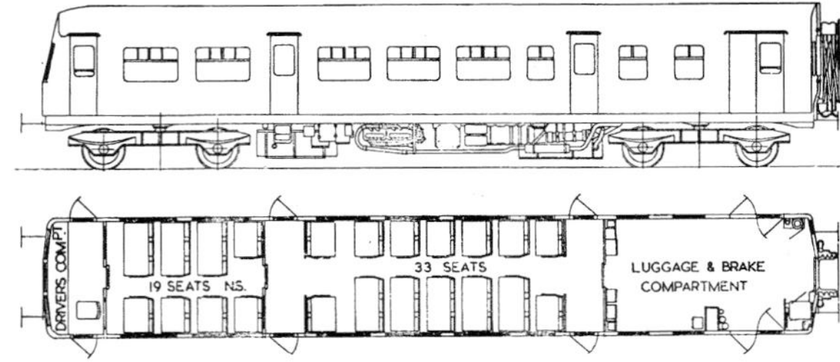

Coupling:	■ Blue square
Diagram:	523 DQ202
Lot Number:	30254
Old class:	101/2
Engines:	Two BUT (AEC) 6-cyl horizontal type of 150 bhp.
Transmission:	Mechanical. Standard
Body:	57' 6" × 9' 3"
Weight:	32t
Seats:	52 second

E53164	05/83⊂**50164**	01/57-12/03	Ⓟ	® /82	
E53165	06/83⊂**50165**	01/57-06/93	⊗12/93	® /81	
E53166	06/83⊂**50166**	01/57-10/88	⊗10/88	®01/78	
E53167	05/83⊂**50167**	01/57-02/87	Ⓟ	®07/79	04/89⊃**DB977392**

Class 101 Metropolitan-Cammell

Driving Motor Composite Lavatory

DMCL

E53168-E53171

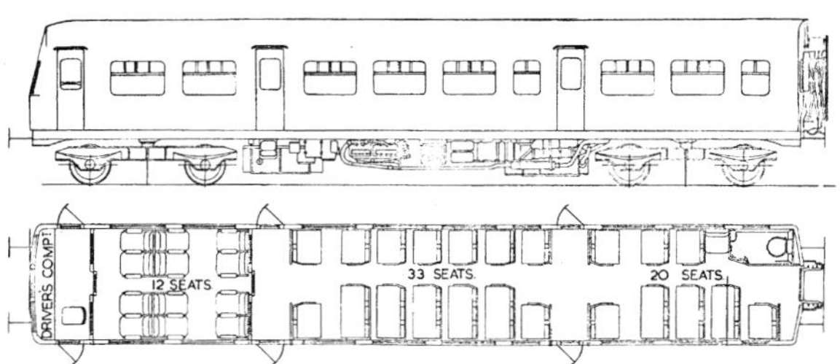

Coupling:	■ Blue square
Diagram:	620 DP303 ②DP214
Lot Number:	30255
Old class:	101/1
Engines:	Two BUT (AEC) 6-cyl horizontal type of 150 bhp.
Transmission:	Mechanical. Standard
Body:	57' 6" × 9' 3"
Weight:	32t
Seats:	12 first, 53 second

E53168	08/83⊂**50168**	01/57-05/93	⊗07/93	® /81	
E53169	/84⊂**50169**	01/57-01/90	⊗08/90	®05/76	⊠09/89-10/89
E53170	06/83⊂**50170**	01/57-12/03	Ⓟ	® /82	
E53171	06/83⊂**50171**	01/57-12/01	⊗12/03	® /82	

Class 101 Metropolitan-Cammell

Driving Motor Composite Lavatory
DMCL
SC53172-SC53197

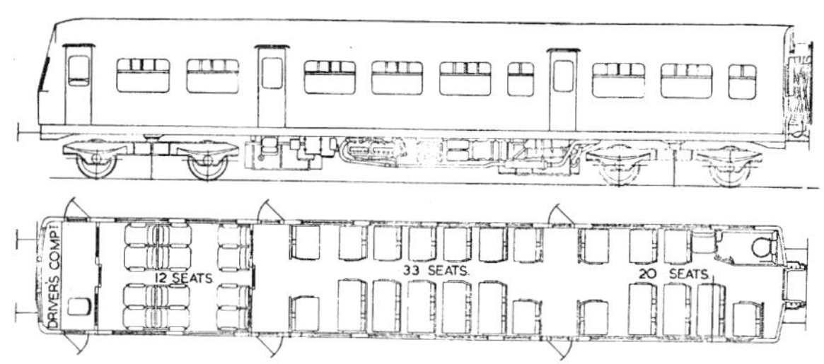

Coupling: ■ Blue square
Diagram: 620 DP303 ②DP214
Lot Number: 30256
Old class: 101/1
Engines: Two BUT (AEC) 6-cyl horizontal type of 150 bhp.
Transmission: Mechanical. Standard
Body: 57' 6" × 9' 3"
Weight: 32t
Seats: 12 first, 53 second

SC53172 08/83⊂**50172** 01/57-07/87 ⊗07/87 ®06/81
SC53174 08/83⊂**50174** 02/57-05/87 ⊗07/87 ®06/78
SC53175 08/83⊂**50175** 02/57-05/87 ⊗09/87 ®06/78
SC53176 08/83⊂**50176** 02/57-12/90 ⊗08/91 ®06/81
E53177 05/83⊂**50177** 02/57-04/00 ⊗09/03 ® /81
E53178 05/85⊂**50178** 02/57-10/88 ⊗06/89 ®02/80
E53179 02/85⊂**50179** 02/57-10/87 ⊗06/91 ®02/81 01/86⇨**SC**
E53180 07/83⊂**50180** 02/57-03/92 ⊗10/92 ® /81
E53181 08/83⊂**50181** 02/57-11/92 ⊗02/93 ®11/80
E53182 05/85⊂**50182** 03/57-09/89 ⊗09/90 ®11/79
E53183 05/83⊂**50183** 03/57-10/87 ⊗07/90 ®02/81 01/86⇨**SC**
SC53184 08/83⊂**50184** 02/57-11/85 ⊗10/87 ®06/80
SC53185 08/83⊂**50185** 02/57-02/91 ⊗04/91 ®06/81
SC53186 08/83⊂**50186** 03/57-10/89 ⊗05/91 ®*10/76*
SC53187 08/83⊂**50187** 03/57-12/89 ⊗08/91 ®02/77
E53188 07/83⊂**50188** 03/57-06/89 ⊗09/90 ®11/79
SC53189 06/83⊂**50189** 03/57-11/91 ⊗02/93
E53191 01/84⊂**50191** 03/57-10/88 ⊗06/89 ® */80*
SC53192 */85*⊂**50192** 03/57-10/87 ⊗06/90 ®10/80
E53193 04/83⊂**50193** 03/57-06/93 Ⓟ ®*10/76* 06/93➲**DB977898**
SC53194 08/83⊂**50194** 04/57-11/90 ⊗04/91 ®06/81
E53195 05/85⊂**50195** 04/57-09/89 ⊗12/89 ® */80*
E53196 06/83⊂**50196** 04/57-11/89 ⊗04/90 ®05/78 ⊠09/89-10/89
SC53197 08/83⊂**50197** 04/57-12/87 ⊗08/92 ®01/83 11/90➲**TDB977652**

Class 101 Metropolitan-Cammell

Driving Motor Brake Second
DMBS
E53198-E53209

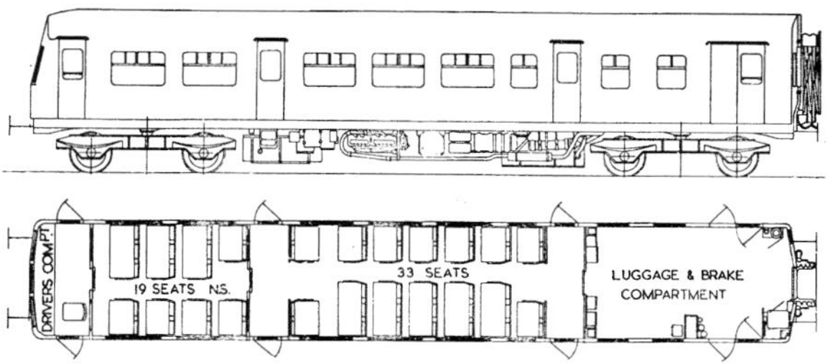

Coupling: ■ Blue square
Diagram: 523 DQ202
Lot Number: 30259
Old class: 101/2
Engines: Two BUT (AEC) 6-cyl horizontal type of 150 bhp.
Transmission: Mechanical. Standard
Body: 57' 6" × 9' 3"
Weight: 32t
Seats: 52 second

E53198 04/83⊂**50198** 04/57-01/98 ⊗01/98 ®07/76
E53199 04/83⊂**50199** 04/57-01/87 ⊗06/89 ®07/78
E53200 02/83⊂**50200** 05/57-05/93 ⊗04/03 ®06/83 05/93➲**DB977901**
E53201 09/83⊂**50201** 05/57-05/99 ⊗05/99 ®07/79
E53202 07/83⊂**50202** 05/57-06/93 ⊗12/95 ®*10/76*
M53203 06/83⊂**50203** 05/57-06/93 Ⓟ ®01/80 05/86⇨**E** 06/93➲**DB977897**
E53204 02/83⊂**50204** 05/57-12/03 Ⓟ ®07/79
E53205 */85*⊂**50205** 04/57-10/88 ⊗06/89 ®02/81
M53206 04/83⊂**50206** 04/57-11/87 ⊗03/88 ®10/77 05/86⇨**E**
E53207 05/84⊂**50207** 05/57-12/91 ⊗03/92 ®04/77
M53208 06/83⊂**50208** 05/57-06/93 ⊗04/03 ®10/76 05/86⇨**E** 10/93➲**DB977903**
E53209 */84*⊂**50209** 05/57-05/86 ⊗02/88 ®02/81 04/86⇨**E** 06/86⇨**SC**

Class 101 Metropolitan-Cammell

Driving Motor Brake Second
DMBS
E53210-E53233

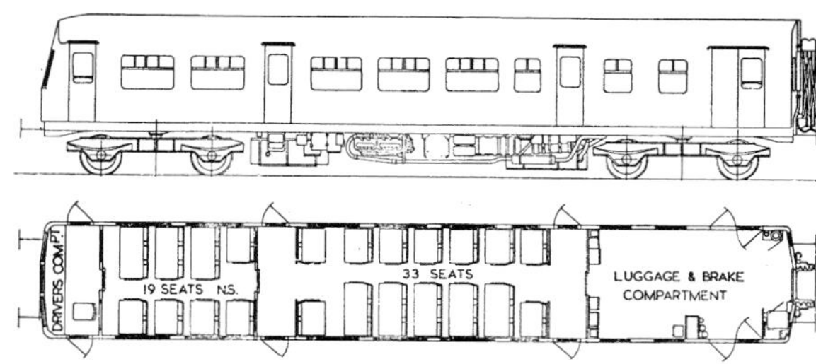

Coupling: ■ Blue square
Diagram: 523 DQ202
Lot Number: 30261
Old class: 101/2
Engines: Two BUT (AEC) 6-cyl horizontal type of 150 bhp.
Transmission: Mechanical. Standard
Body: 57' 6" × 9' 3"
Weight: 32t
Seats: 52 second

E53210 02/83⊂**50210** 05/57-03/87 ⊗01/88 ®02/81 04/86⇨**E** 06/86⇨**SC**
E53211 04/83⊂**50211** 05/57-01/02 ⊗12/03 ® /82
E53212 05/83⊂**50212** 06/57-11/90 ⊗03/91 ® /81
E53214 04/83⊂**50214** 06/57-02/89 ⊗04/90 ®01/78
E53215 04/83⊂**50215** 07/57-10/89 ⊗09/91 ®11/79
E53216 04/83⊂**50216** 07/57-05/93 ⊗12/93 ®04/77
E53217 05/83⊂**50217** 07/57-10/88 ⊗10/88 ®04/77
E53218 05/83⊂**50218** 07/57-05/89 ⊗01/92 ®11/79 ⊠09/86-10/86 10/86⇨Parcels
E53219 04/83⊂**50219** 07/57-10/89 ⊗09/89 ®07/79
E53220 04/83⊂**50220** 07/57-10/88 ⊗04/90 ®07/78
E53221 06/83⊂**50221** 08/57-07/89 ⊗04/90 ®07/78 ⊠09/86-12/86 12/86⇨Parcels
M53222 06/83⊂**50222** 06/57-08/90 Ⓟ ®05/80 04/91➲**RDB977693**
E53223 08/83⊂**50223** 06/57-02/91 ⊗02/91 ®07/79
E53224 05/83⊂**50224** 06/57-11/90 ⊗04/91 ®06/76
E53225 08/83⊂**50225** 06/57-07/86 ⊗02/87 ®01/80
E53226 05/83⊂**50226** 07/57-05/87 ⊗08/88 ®04/77
E53227 04/83⊂**50227** 07/57-03/88 ⊗01/89 ®*10/76*
M53228 04/83⊂**50228** 07/57-01/01 ⊗03/04 ® /82
E53229 04/83⊂**50229** 07/57-03/89 ⊗04/90 ®11/79
E53230 06/83⊂**50230** 08/57-05/89 ⊗01/92 ®07/79 ⊠09/86-10/86 10/86⇨Parcels
E53231 05/83⊂**50231** 08/57-05/93 ⊗04/03 ®02/81 05/93➲**DB977902**
E53232 05/83⊂**50232** 08/57-02/85 ⊗03/85 ®02/78
E53233 04/84⊂**50233** 09/57-07/89 ⊗04/90 ®07/78 11/86⇨Parcels

Class 101 Metropolitan-Cammell

Driving Motor Composite Lavatory
DMCL
SC53234-SC53245

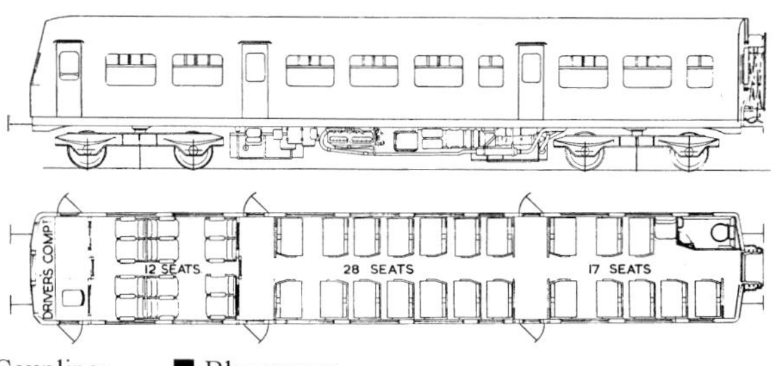

Coupling: ■ Blue square
Diagram: 619 DP302 ②DP213
Lot Number: 30263
Old class: 101/1
Engines: Two BUT (AEC) 6-cyl horizontal type of 150 bhp.

Transmission: Mechanical. Standard
Body: 57' 6" × 9' 3"
Weight: 32t
Seats: 12 first, 45 second

SC53234	/85⊂**50234**	09/57-07/88	⊗06/89	®05/80	
E53235	02/85⊂**50235**	09/57-02/90	⊗08/90	®02/80	
M53237	07/83⊂**50237**	09/57-12/89	⊗08/90		09/85⇨**E**
E53238	05/84⊂**50238**	10/57-04/92	⊗10/92	® /82	
SC53239	08/83⊂**50239**	10/57-12/90	⊗08/91	® /82	
E53240	02/85⊂**50240**	10/57-10/89	⊗05/90	®02/80	
SC53241	08/83⊂**50241**	10/57-02/92	⊗01/94	® /82	
SC53242	03/83⊂**50242**	10/57-11/92	⊗10/92	®04/83	
SC53243	08/83⊂**50243**	10/57-10/92	⊗01/94	®06/81	
E53244	03/83⊂**50244**	10/57-10/90	⊗11/90	® /81	
SC53245	08/83⊂**50245**	10/57-07/93	⊗08/93	® /82	

Class 101 Metropolitan-Cammell
Driving Motor Brake Second
DMBS
E53246-E53248

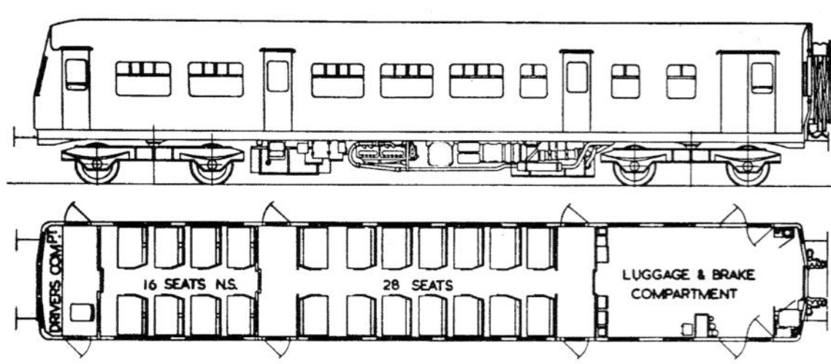

Coupling: ■ Blue square
Diagram: 522 DQ203
Lot Number: 30339
Old class: 101/2
Engines: Two BUT (AEC) 6-cyl horizontal type of 150 bhp.
Transmission: Mechanical. Standard
Body: 57' 6" × 9' 3"
Weight: 32t
Seats: 44 second

E53246	07/83⊂**50246**	09/57-02/87	⊗06/93	®11/78	07/89➲**DB977393**
E53247	05/83⊂**50247**	09/57-11/90	⊗02/91	® */81*	
E53248	07/83⊂**50248**	09/57-02/91	⊗03/91	® /82	

Class 101 Metropolitan-Cammell
Driving Motor Brake Second
DMBS
E53250-E53259

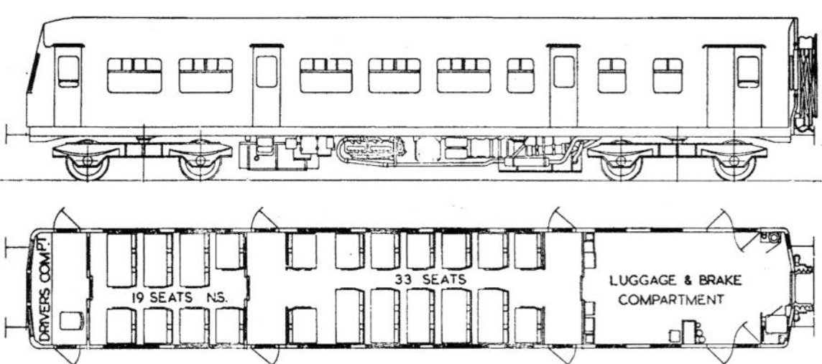

Coupling: ■ Blue square
Diagram: 523 DQ202
Lot Number: 30266
Old class: 102/2
Engines: Two BUT (AEC) 6-cyl horizontal type of 150 bhp.
Transmission: Mechanical. Standard
Body: 57' 6" × 9' 3"
Weight: 32t
Seats: 52 second

E53250	07/83⊂**50250**	06/57-10/92	⊗02/93	®07/79	
E53251	05/83⊂**50251**	06/57-02/89	⊗03/89	®11/79	
E53252	05/83⊂**50252**	07/57-12/88	⊗04/90	®03/80	
E53253	04/83⊂**50253**	07/57-12/03	Ⓟ	® /82	
SC53254	08/83⊂**50254**	08/57-12/87	⊗09/88	®08/79	
E53255	05/83⊂**50255**	09/57-07/89	⊗04/90	®07/78	11/86⇨Parcels
E53256	05/83⊂**50256**	10/57-06/01	Ⓟ	®11/80	
E53257	04/83⊂**50257**	10/57-09/89	⊗09/90	®01/78	
E53258	04/83⊂**50258**	10/57-08/88	⊗11/89	®07/79	
E53259	08/83⊂**50259**	10/57-11/87	⊗02/93	®07/79	11/87➲**TDB977535**

Class 101 Metropolitan-Cammell
Driving Motor Composite Lavatory
DMCL
SC53260-SC53269

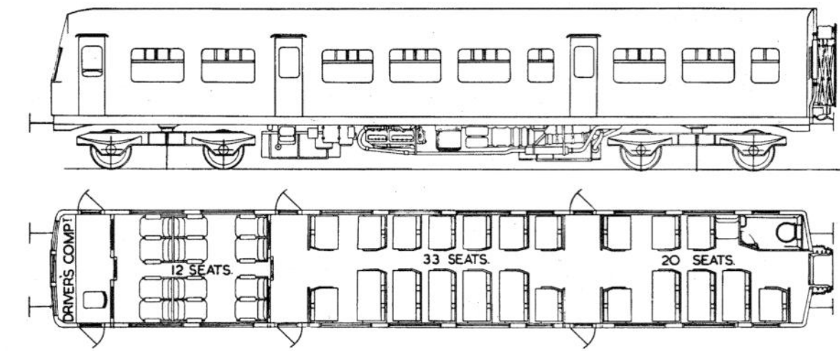

Coupling: ■ Blue square
Diagram: 621 DP304 ②DP210
Lot Number: 30267
Old class: 102/1
Engines: Two BUT (AEC) 6-cyl horizontal type of 150 bhp.
Transmission: Mechanical. Standard
Body: 57' 6" × 9' 3"
Weight: 32t
Seats: 12 first, 53 second

SC53260	08/83⊂**50260**	06/57-11/90	⊗03/91	®06/81
E53261	09/84⊂**50261**	06/57-06/89	⊗06/89	® */80*
E53262	07/83⊂**50262**	07/57-11/87	⊗09/88	®07/79
E53263	06/83⊂**50263**	07/57-10/89	⊗12/89	®11/79
SC53264	08/83⊂**50264**	08/57-08/89	⊗09/89	®08/79
E53265	06/83⊂**50265**	09/57-07/93	⊗02/94	®09/82
E53266	03/83⊂**50266**	10/57-12/03	Ⓟ	® /81
E53267	05/83⊂**50267**	10/57-02/93	⊗01/94	®*10/76*
SC53268	03/83⊂**50268**	10/57-01/01	Ⓟ⊗04/09	®04/83
SC53269	03/83⊂**50269**	10/57-06/01	⊗12/03	®05/83

Class 111 Metropolitan-Cammell
Driving Motor Composite Lavatory
DMCL
E53272-E53278

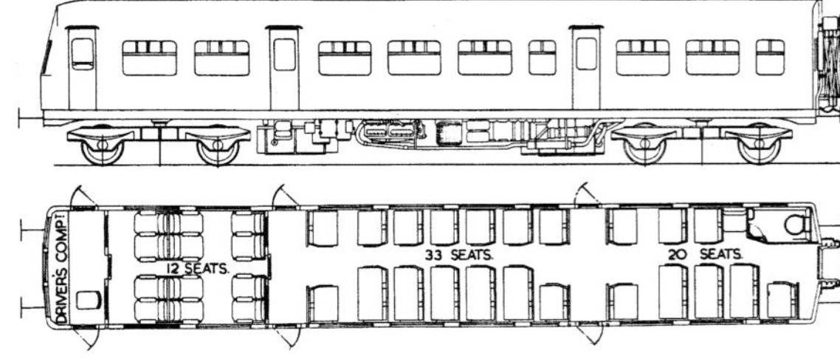

Coupling: ■ Blue square
Diagram: 616 DP314
Lot Number: 30268
Old class: 111/1
Engines: Two Rolls-Royce 6-cyl horizontal type of 180 bhp.
Transmission: Mechanical. Standard
Body: 57' 6" × 9' 3"
Weight: 33t
Seats: 12 first, 53 second

E53272	05/83⊂**50272**	11/57-02/85	⊗04/90	® /82	02/85➲**78713**
E53273	*/83*⊂**50273**	12/57-10/83	⊗05/90	®04/77	10/83➲**78709**
E53275	04/83⊂**50275**	12/57-02/84	⊗04/90	® /81	02/84➲**78711**
E53276	04/83⊂**50276**	12/57-10/83	⊗05/87	®04/77	10/83➲**78710**
E53277	04/83⊂**50277**	01/58-08/85	⊗04/90	® /81	08/85➲**78714**
E53278	04/83⊂**50278**	01/58-09/84	⊗07/90	® /82	09/84➲**78712**

Class 111 Metropolitan-Cammell
Driving Motor Brake Second
DMBS
E53280-E53289

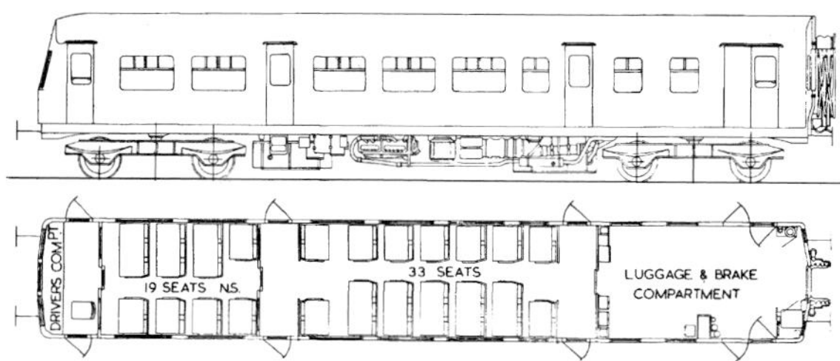

Coupling: ■ Blue square
Diagram: 524 DQ215
Lot Number: 30338
Old class: 111/2
Engines: Two Rolls-Royce 6-cyl horizontal type of 180 bhp.
Transmission: Mechanical. Standard
Body: 57' 6" × 9' 3"
Weight: 33t
Seats: 52 second

E53280	07/83⊂**50280**	10/57-02/84	⊗04/90	® /81	02/84⊃**78961**
E53282	/83⊂**50282**	11/57-10/83	⊗07/90	® /82	10/83⊃**78960**
E53283	04/83⊂**50283**	12/57-09/84	⊗07/90	® /82	09/84⊃**78962**
E53284	04/83⊂**50284**	12/57-08/85	⊗04/90	®06/81	08/85⊃**78964**
E53288	/83⊂**50288**	01/58-10/83	⊗05/90	®04/77	10/83⊃**78959**
E53289	07/83⊂**50289**	01/58-02/85	⊗02/88	®07/79	02/85⊃**78963**

Class 101 Metropolitan-Cammell
Driving Motor Brake Second
DMBS
SC53290-E53296

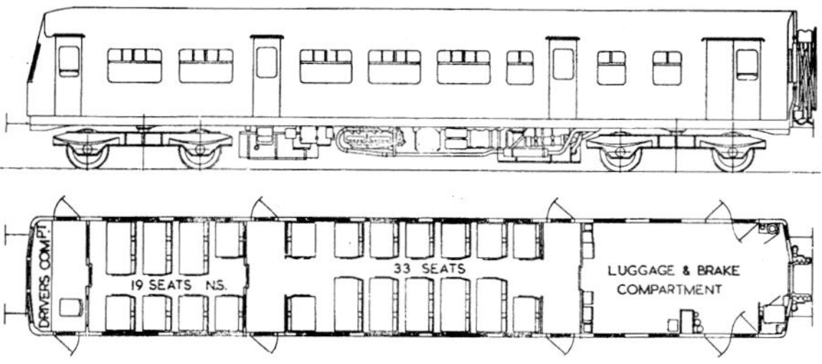

Coupling: ■ Blue square
Diagram: 523 DQ202
Lot Number: 30270
Old class: 101/2
Engines: Two BUT (AEC) 6-cyl horizontal type of 150 bhp.
Transmission: Mechanical. Standard
Body: 57' 6" × 9' 3"
Weight: 32t
Seats: 52 second

SC53290	08/83⊂**50290**	11/57-12/87	⊗02/93	®01/83	11/90⊃**TDB977651**
E53291	07/83⊂**50291**	11/57-06/93	⊗04/03	® /81	10/93⊃**DB977904**
SC53292	08/83⊂**50292**	11/57-12/87	⊗03/89	®06/80	
E53293	02/83⊂**50293**	12/57-12/92	⊗01/94	®07/78	
E53294	05/83⊂**50294**	12/57-10/92	⊗02/94	®11/79	
E53295	04/83⊂**50295**	12/57-11/87	⊗02/93	®07/79	11/87⊃**TDB977536**
E53296	04/83⊂**50296**	12/57-12/91	⊗03/92	®04/77	

Class 101 Metropolitan-Cammell
Driving Motor Brake Second
DMBS
M53303-M53320

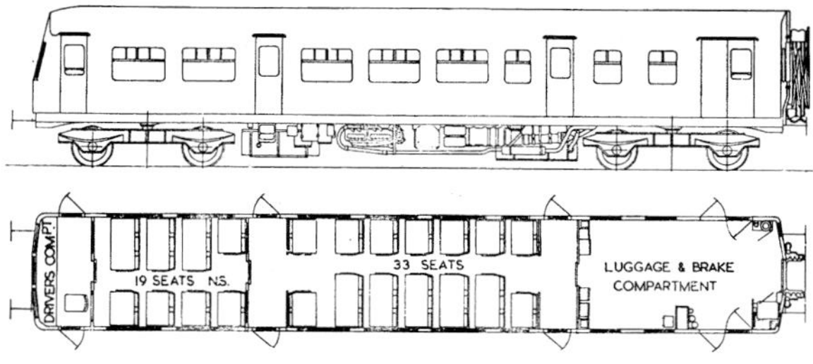

Coupling: ■ Blue square
Diagram: 523 DQ202
Lot Number: 30275
Old class: 101/2
Engines: Two BUT (AEC) 6-cyl horizontal type of 150 bhp.
Transmission: Mechanical. Standard
Body: 57' 6" × 9' 3"
Weight: 32t
Seats: 52 second

M53303	04/83⊂**50303**	02/58-10/89	⊗08/90	®11/78		
W53304	07/83⊂**50304**	02/58-07/87	⊗08/88	®11/76		
M53305	06/83⊂**50305**	02/58-05/95	⊗09/95	®*09/76*	03/85⇨**E**	
M53306	04/83⊂**50306**	02/58-09/89	⊗12/89	®05/80		
M53307	04/83⊂**50307**	02/58-05/89	⊗05/89	®09/81		
M53308	07/83⊂**50308**	03/58-09/93	⊗09/03	® /82		09/93⊃**DB977895**
M53309	06/83⊂**50309**	03/58-05/89	⊗05/89	®*10/76*	05/85⇨**W**	
M53310	06/83⊂**50310**	02/58-01/94	⊗09/95			
M53311	04/83⊂**50311**	02/58-09/00	⊗12/03	®02/81		
M53312	04/83⊂**50312**	03/58-09/96	⊗09/96	® /81		
M53313	07/83⊂**50313**	03/58-05/86	⊗03/87		04/86⇨**E**	
M53314	07/83⊂**50314**	03/58-03/97	⊗07/02	®01/83		03/97 to departmental
M53315	05/83⊂**50315**	03/58-11/93	⊗03/94	®09/81	03/85⇨**E**	
M53316	06/83⊂**50316**	03/58-07/86	⊗12/86			
M53317	04/83⊂**50317**	04/58-10/89	⊗07/90	®07/76		
M53318	06/83⊂**50318**	04/58-05/89	⊗05/89	®10/78		
W53319	04/83⊂**50319**	04/58-10/89	⊗06/91	®*10/76*		
M53320	07/83⊂**50320**	04/58-11/87	⊗08/89		09/85⇨**E**	11/87⊃**TDB977537**

Class 101 Metropolitan-Cammell
Driving Motor Composite Lavatory
DMCL
M53321-M53338

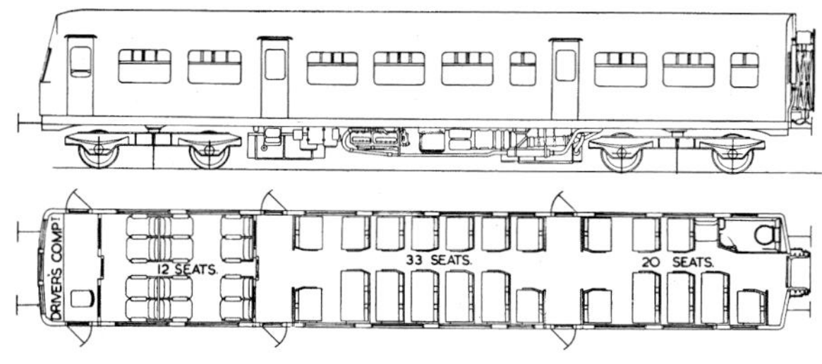

Coupling: ■ Blue square
Diagram: 621 DP304 ②DP210
Lot Number: 30276
Old class: 101/1
Engines: Two BUT (AEC) 6-cyl horizontal type of 150 bhp.
Transmission: Mechanical. Standard
Body: 57' 6" × 9' 3"
Weight: 32t
Seats: 12 first, 53 second

M53321	06/83⊂**50321**	02/58-05/93	Ⓟ	®10/78	03/85⇨**E**	05/93⊃**DB977900**
M53322	04/83⊂**50322**	02/58-09/00	⊗12/03	®02/81		
M53323	04/83⊂**50323**	02/58-05/89	⊗05/89	®03/77		
M53324	04/83⊂**50324**	02/58-10/89	⊗06/90	®01/80		
M53325	04/83⊂**50325**	02/58-10/89	⊗07/90			
M53326	04/83⊂**50326**	03/58-01/94	⊗09/95	®10/79		
M53327	07/83⊂**50327**	03/58-03/97	⊗07/02	®07/76		03/97 to departmental
M53328	06/83⊂**50328**	02/58-08/87	⊗01/88	®09/78		
W53329	06/83⊂**50329**	02/58-02/88	⊗08/88	®06/77		

M53330	07/83⊂**50330**	03/58-11/93	⊗03/94	®02/81	03/85⇨E	
M53331	07/83⊂**50331**	03/58-09/93	⊗09/03	® /82		09/93➲DB977896
M53332	05/83⊂**50332**	03/58-09/96	⊗09/96	® /81		
M53333	05/83⊂**50333**	03/58-03/93	⊗08/93	®09/81		
M53334	06/83⊂**50334**	03/58-07/89	⊗08/90			
W53335	04/83⊂**50335**	04/58-03/89	⊗04/90	®03/77		
M53336	05/83⊂**50336**	04/58-05/89	⊗05/89	®06/78		
M53337	06/83⊂**50337**	04/58-05/89	⊗05/89			
M53338	06/83⊂**50338**	04/58-08/90	Ⓟ	®*09/76*	05/85⇨W	04/91➲RDB977694

Class 100 Gloucester RC&W
Driving Motor Brake Second
DMBS
M53355

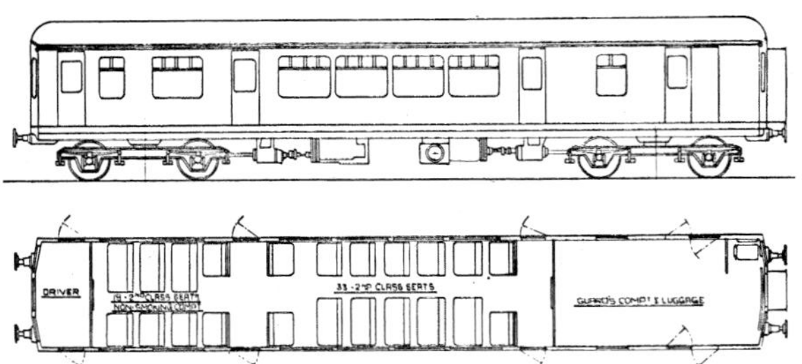

Coupling: ■ Blue square
Diagram: 536 DQ201
Lot Number: 30278
Old class: 100
Engines: Two BUT (AEC) 6-cyl horizontal type of 150 bhp.
Transmission: Mechanical. Standard
Body: 57' 6" × 9' 3"
Weight: 30t
Seats: 52 second

M53355	07/83⊂**50355**	09/57-06/89	⊗10/90	☒10/85-11/85

Class 105 Cravens
Driving Motor Brake Second
DMBS
E53359-E53369

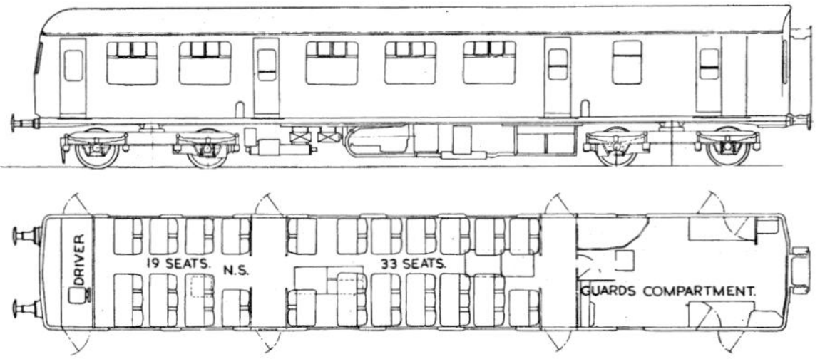

Coupling: ■ Blue square
Diagram: 525 DQ207
Lot Number: 30280
Old class: 106/2
Engines: Two BUT (Leyland) 6-cyl horizontal type of 150 bhp.
Transmission: Mechanical. Standard
Body: 57' 6" × 9' 2"
Weight: 29t
Seats: 52 second

E53359	03/83⊂**50359**	08/56-10/88	⊗02/89		
E53360	05/83⊂**50360**	10/56-07/85	⊗05/86		
E53361	04/83⊂**50361**	11/56-03/89	⊗04/89	☒09/86-10/86	10/86⇨Parcels
E53362	05/83⊂**50362**	11/56-03/87	⊗03/88	07/86⇨Parcels	03/87➲**55945**
E53363	04/83⊂**50363**	12/56-07/86	⊗03/88		
E53364	04/83⊂**50364**	12/56-03/89	⊗04/90	07/86⇨Parcels	➲*55946*
E53365	04/83⊂**50365**	01/57-03/89	⊗04/89	☒11/86-12/86	12/86⇨Parcels
E53366	05/83⊂**50366**	01/57-10/86	⊗06/87		
E53367	05/83⊂**50367**	01/57-03/89	⊗04/90		11/86⇨Parcels
E53368	04/83⊂**50368**	01/57-03/89	⊗04/89		11/86⇨Parcels
E53369	04/83⊂**50369**	02/57-09/88	⊗12/88		11/86⇨Parcels

Class 105 Cravens
Driving Motor Brake Second
DMBS
E53373-E53381

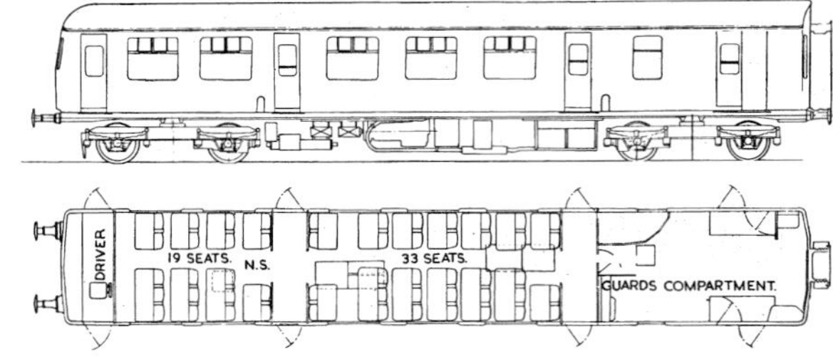

Coupling: ■ Blue square
Diagram: 525 DQ207
Lot Number: 30282
Old class: 105/2
Engines: Two BUT (AEC) 6-cyl horizontal type of 150 bhp.
Transmission: Mechanical. Standard
Body: 57' 6" × 9' 2"
Weight: 29t
Seats: 52 second

E53373	*/84*⊂**50373**	02/57-03/89	⊗04/89	07/86⇨Parcels	➲*55947*
E53375	*/84*⊂**50375**	03/57-05/87	⊗11/87		
E53377	*/85*⊂**50377**	03/57-09/86	⊗01/87	06/86⇨**SC**	
E53379	03/83⊂**50379**	04/57-07/84	⊗10/84		
E53380	09/83⊂**50380**	04/57-09/86	⊗11/87	06/86⇨**SC**	
E53381	11/84⊂**50381**	05/57-05/87	⊗10/87		

Class 104 Birmingham RC&W
Driving Motor Brake Second
DMBS
M53420-M53423

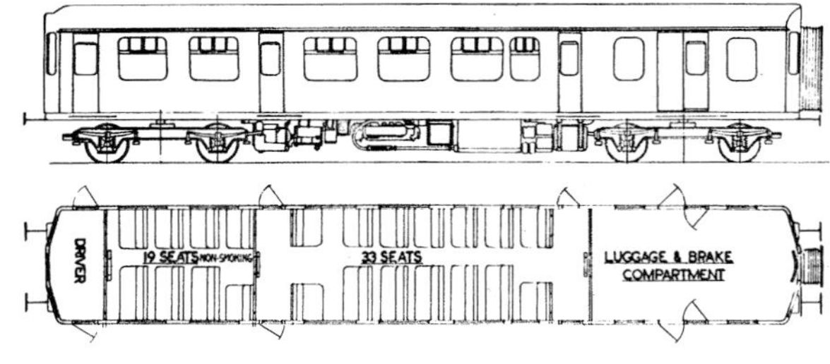

Coupling: ■ Blue square
Diagram: 556 DQ205
Lot Number: 30290
Old class: 104/2
Engines: Two BUT (Leyland) 6-cyl horizontal type of 150 bhp.
Transmission: Mechanical. Standard
Body: 57' 6" × 9' 3"
Weight: 31t
Seats: 52 second

M53420	/83⊂**50420**	04/57-05/86	⊗12/86	
M53421	/83⊂**50421**	04/57-08/89	⊗10/90	☒05/89-08/89
M53422	10/83⊂**50422**	05/57-11/85	⊗05/87	11/85➲**ADB977344**
M53423	05/83⊂**50423**	05/57-01/84	⊗05/84	

Class 104 Birmingham RC&W

Driving Motor Composite Lavatory
DMCL
M53424-M53427

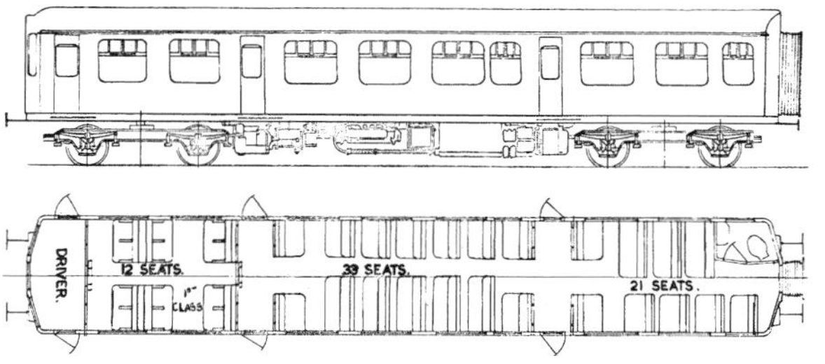

Coupling:	■ Blue square
Diagram:	558 DP305 ②DP209
Lot Number:	30291
Old class:	104/1
Engines:	Two BUT (Leyland) 6-cyl horizontal type of 150 bhp.
Transmission:	Mechanical. Standard
Body:	57' 6" × 9' 3"
Weight:	31t
Seats:	12 first, 54 second

M53424	/83⊂50424	04/57-12/87	⊗06/91	02/85⇨SC	
M53425	01/85⊂50425	04/57-10/89	⊗01/90		
M53426	/83⊂50426	05/57-12/84	⊗01/85		
M53427	08/83⊂50427	05/57-03/89	⊗03/89		

Class 104 Birmingham RC&W

Driving Motor Brake Second
DMBS
M53428-M53479

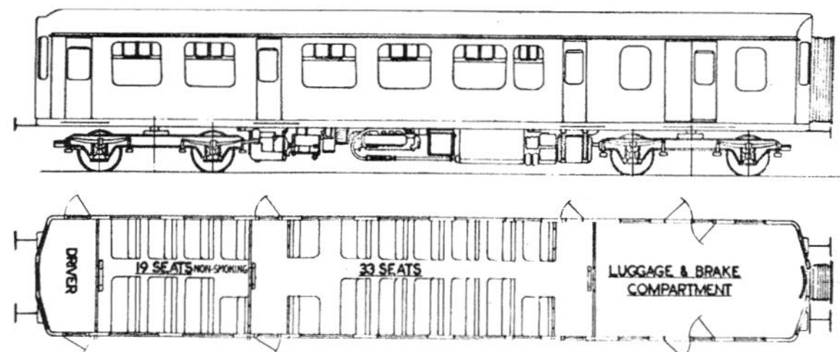

Coupling:	■ Blue square
Diagram:	556 DQ205
Lot Number:	30293
Old class:	104/2
Engines:	Two BUT (Leyland) 6-cyl horizontal type of 150 bhp.
Transmission:	Mechanical. Standard
Body:	57' 6" × 9' 3"
Weight:	31t
Seats:	52 second

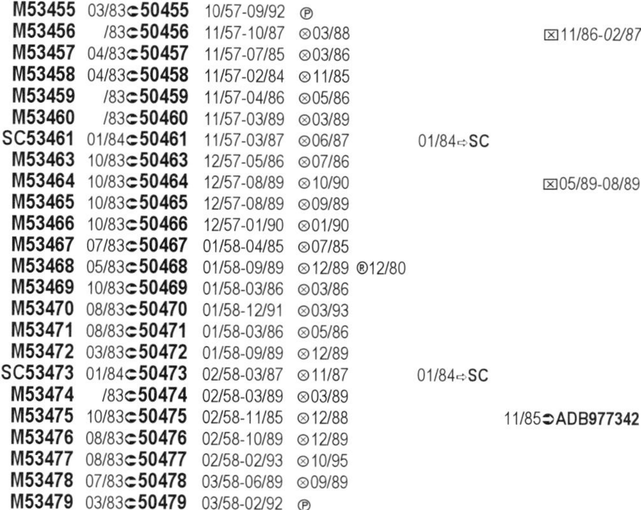

M53428	/83⊂50428	05/57-01/86	⊗12/86		
M53429	03/83⊂50429	05/57-12/91	⊗12/93		
M53430	/83⊂50430	06/57-07/86	⊗05/88		
M53431	05/83⊂50431	06/57-03/90	⊗06/91		
M53432	07/83⊂50432	06/57-07/84	⊗11/85		
M53433	/83⊂50433	06/57-03/86	⊗08/86		
M53434	/83⊂50434	06/57-12/87	⊗06/91	02/85⇨SC	
M53435	/83⊂50435	07/57-02/84	⊗11/85		
M53436	02/83⊂50436	07/57-08/85	⊗05/86		
M53437	03/83⊂50437	07/57-02/92	℗		
M53439	01/85⊂50439	07/57-01/90	⊗01/90		
M53442	/84⊂50442	08/57-05/90	⊗06/91		
M53443	09/83⊂50443	08/57-08/89	⊗10/90		⊠05/89-08/89
M53444	06/84⊂50444	09/57-05/89	⊗10/90		
M53445	/83⊂50445	09/57-10/85	⊗03/86		
M53447	06/84⊂50447	09/57-03/92	℗		
M53448	/83⊂50448	09/57-03/86	⊗03/86		
M53449	/83⊂50449	10/57-07/84	⊗04/85		
M53450	09/83⊂50450	10/57-03/86	⊗03/86		
M53451	04/83⊂50451	10/57-06/90	⊗02/91		
SC53452	01/84⊂50452	10/57-07/86	⊗07/86	01/84⇨SC	
M53453	10/83⊂50453	10/57-05/87	⊗09/90		
M53454	03/83⊂50454	10/57-03/92	℗		
M53455	03/83⊂50455	10/57-09/92	℗		
M53456	/83⊂50456	11/57-10/87	⊗03/88		⊠11/86-02/87
M53457	04/83⊂50457	11/57-07/85	⊗03/86		
M53458	04/83⊂50458	11/57-02/84	⊗11/85		
M53459	/83⊂50459	11/57-04/86	⊗05/86		
M53460	/83⊂50460	11/57-03/89	⊗03/89		
SC53461	01/84⊂50461	11/57-03/87	⊗06/87	01/84⇨SC	
M53463	10/83⊂50463	12/57-05/86	⊗07/86		
M53464	10/83⊂50464	12/57-08/89	⊗10/90		⊠05/89-08/89
M53465	10/83⊂50465	12/57-08/89	⊗09/89		
M53466	10/83⊂50466	12/57-01/90	⊗01/90		
M53467	07/83⊂50467	01/58-04/85	⊗07/85		
M53468	05/83⊂50468	01/58-09/89	⊗12/89 ®12/80		
M53469	10/83⊂50469	01/58-03/86	⊗03/86		
M53470	08/83⊂50470	01/58-12/91	⊗03/93		
M53471	08/83⊂50471	01/58-03/86	⊗05/86		
M53472	03/83⊂50472	01/58-09/89	⊗12/89		
SC53473	01/84⊂50473	02/58-03/87	⊗11/87	01/84⇨SC	
M53474	/83⊂50474	02/58-03/89	⊗03/89		
M53475	10/83⊂50475	02/58-11/85	⊗12/88		11/85⊃ADB977342
M53476	08/83⊂50476	02/58-10/89	⊗12/89		
M53477	08/83⊂50477	02/58-02/93	⊗10/95		
M53478	07/83⊂50478	03/58-06/89	⊗09/89		
M53479	03/83⊂50479	03/58-02/92	℗		

Class 104 Birmingham RC&W

Driving Motor Composite Lavatory
DMCL
M53480-M53531

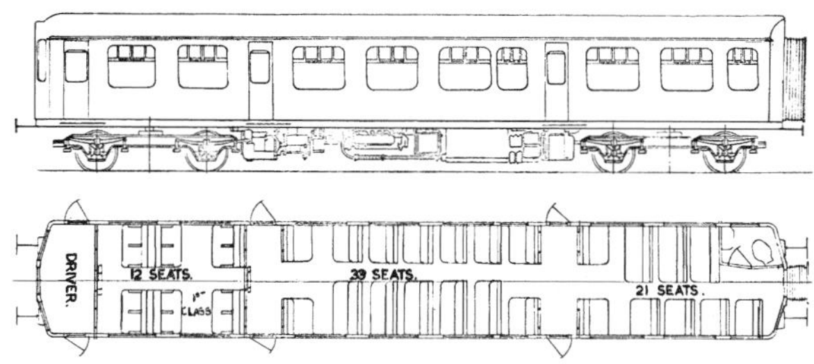

Coupling:	■ Blue square
Diagram:	558 DP305 ②DP209
Lot Number:	30294
Old class:	104/1
Engines:	Two BUT (Leyland) 6-cyl horizontal type of 150 bhp.
Transmission:	Mechanical. Standard
Body:	57' 6" × 9' 3"
Weight:	31t
Seats:	12 first, 54 second

M53480	03/83⊂50480	05/57-07/84	⊗09/85 ®04/81		
M53481	/83⊂50481	05/57-08/83	⊗05/84		
M53482	06/84⊂50482	06/57-02/86	⊗07/86		
M53483	/83⊂50483	06/57-01/84	⊗05/84		
M53484	07/83⊂50484	06/57-12/84	⊗11/85		
M53485	/83⊂50485	06/57-12/84	⊗02/86		
M53487	/83⊂50487	07/57-08/89	⊗12/90		⊠05/89-08/89
M53488	10/83⊂50488	07/57-08/85	⊗05/86		
M53490	/83⊂50490	07/57-05/84	⊗02/86		
M53491	/83⊂50491	07/57-12/86	⊗03/87	07/86⇨SC	
M53492	03/83⊂50492	07/57-08/89	⊗09/89		
M53493	09/83⊂50493	08/57-05/89	⊗10/90		
M53494	06/84⊂50494	08/57-06/90	℗		
M53496	05/83⊂50496	09/57-03/89	⊗03/89		
M53497	/83⊂50497	09/57-07/84	⊗12/84		
M53498	/83⊂50498	09/57-07/84	⊗04/85		
M53499	08/83⊂50499	09/57-09/89	⊗04/91		
M53500	06/84⊂50500	10/57-06/89	⊗10/90		
M53501	/83⊂50501	10/57-03/89	⊗03/89		
M53502	/83⊂50502	10/57-07/84	⊗12/84		
M53503	/83⊂50503	10/57-08/85	⊗12/86		
M53504	12/83⊂50504	10/57-09/89	⊗12/89		
SC53505	01/84⊂50505	10/57-03/87	⊗01/88	01/84⇨SC	
M53506	/83⊂50506	10/57-11/85	⊗05/87		11/85⊃ADB977343
M53507	03/83⊂50507	10/57-09/89	⊗12/89		
M53508	/83⊂50508	11/57-07/85	⊗03/86		
M53509	04/83⊂50509	11/57-07/85	⊗03/86		
SC53510	01/84⊂50510	11/57-05/86	⊗07/86	01/84⇨SC	
M53511	/83⊂50511	11/57-08/89	⊗10/90		⊠05/89-08/89
M53512	/83⊂50512	11/57-06/90	⊗06/91		
M53514	04/83⊂50514	12/57-10/87	⊗01/88		⊠11/86-02/87
M53515	05/85⊂50515	12/57-07/84	⊗01/86		
M53516	05/83⊂50516	12/57-05/90	⊗06/91		
M53517	06/84⊂50517	12/57-05/90	℗		

M53518 10/83⊂**50518** 12/57-05/89 ⊗10/90
M53519 10/83⊂**50519** 01/58-04/85 ⊗07/85
M53520 10/83⊂**50520** 01/58-09/89 ⊗12/89
M53522 /83⊂**50522** 01/58-08/89 ⊗09/89
M53523 /83⊂**50523** 01/58-03/86 ⊗05/86
M53524 06/84⊂**50524** 01/58-02/86 ⊗02/86 ®03/81
SC53525 01/84⊂**50525** 02/58-02/87 ⊗06/87 01/84⇐**SC**
M53527 10/83⊂**50527** 02/58-01/86 ⊗02/86
M53528 04/83⊂**50528** 02/58-03/92 Ⓟ
M53529 08/83⊂**50529** 02/58-06/90 ⊗02/91
M53530 10/83⊂**50530** 03/58-06/89 ⊗09/89
M53531 10/83⊂**50531** 03/58-03/92 Ⓟ

Class 104 Birmingham RC&W
Driving Motor Brake Second
DMBS
M53532-M53541

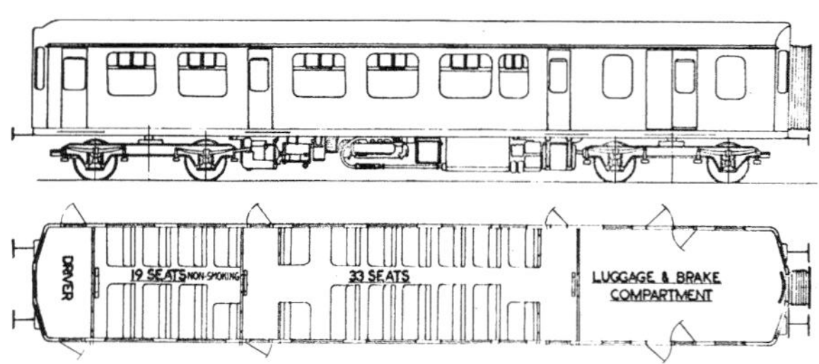

Coupling: ■ Blue square
Diagram: 556 DQ205
Lot Number: 30296
Old class: 104/2
Engines: Two BUT (Leyland) 6-cyl horizontal type of 150 bhp.
Transmission: Mechanical. Standard
Body: 57' 6" × 9' 3"
Weight: 31t
Seats: 52 second

M53532 /83⊂**50532** 03/58-08/89 ⊗12/90 ⊠05/89-08/89
M53533 08/83⊂**50533** 03/58-02/86 ⊗02/86
M53534 03/83⊂**50534** 04/58-06/90 ⊗06/91 ⊠09/89-09/89
M53535 /83⊂**50535** 04/58-02/86 ⊗02/86
M53536 /83⊂**50536** 04/58-05/90 ⊗06/91
M53537 06/83⊂**50537** 04/58-11/83 ⊗05/84
M53538 02/83⊂**50538** 04/58-03/86 ⊗03/86
M53539 09/83⊂**50539** 04/58-12/92 ⊗12/95
M53540 /84⊂**50540** 04/58-10/93 ⊗09/95
M53541 07/83⊂**50541** 05/58-09/89 ⊗01/90

Class 104 Birmingham RC&W
Driving Motor Composite Lavatory
DMCL
M53542-M53562

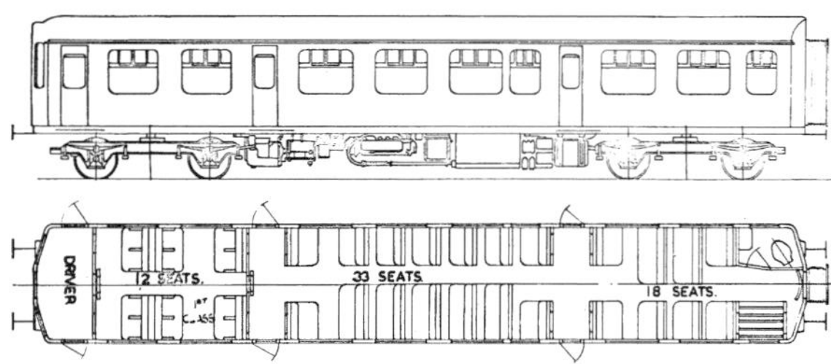

Coupling: ■ Blue square
Diagram: 580 DP307 ②DP217
Lot Number: 30298
Old class: 104/1
Engines: Two BUT (Leyland) 6-cyl horizontal type of 150 bhp.
Transmission: Mechanical. Standard
Body: 57' 6" × 9' 3"
Weight: 31t
Seats: 12 first, 51 second

M53542 /83⊂**50542** 06/58-09/86 ⊗11/87
M53546 /83⊂**50546** 07/58-07/84 ⊗11/85
M53556 12/83⊂**50556** 10/58-05/89 Ⓟ
M53561 /83⊂**50561** 11/58-02/82 ⊗12/84 ®06/81
M53562 /83⊂**50562** 12/58-07/84 ⊗11/85

Class 104 Birmingham RC&W
Driving Motor Composite Lavatory
DMCL
E53565-E53577

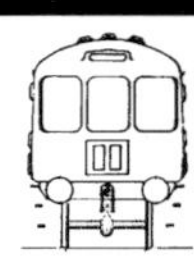

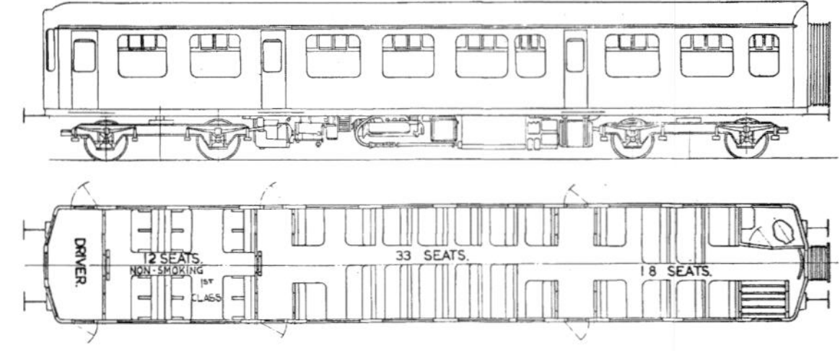

Coupling: ■ Blue square
Diagram: 559 DP307 ②DP217
Lot Number: 30298
Old class: 104/1
Engines: Two BUT (Leyland) 6-cyl horizontal type of 150 bhp.
Transmission: Mechanical. Standard
Body: 57' 6" × 9' 3"
Weight: 31t
Seats: 12 first, 51 second

E53565 /83⊂**50565** 06/58-05/86 ⊗07/86 05/84⇐**SC**
E53571 /83⊂**50571** 08/58-02/84 ⊗12/84
E53577 /83⊂**50577** 10/58-09/86 ⊗04/87 05/84⇐**SC**

Class 104 Birmingham RC&W
Driving Motor Composite Lavatory
DMCL
M53590-M53593

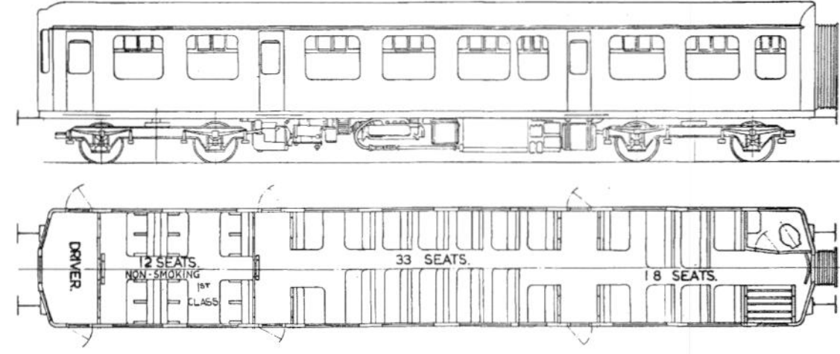

Coupling: ■ Blue square
Diagram: 559 DP307 ②DP217
Lot Number: 30301
Old class: 104/1
Engines: Two BUT (Leyland) 6-cyl horizontal type of 150 bhp.
Transmission: Mechanical. Standard
Body: 57' 6" × 9' 3"
Weight: 31t
Seats: 12 first, 51 second

M53590 /83⊂**50590** 12/58-07/84 ⊗11/85
M53593 /83⊂**50593** 03/59-10/84 ⊗11/85

Class 104 Birmingham RC&W

Driving Motor Brake Second
DMBS
M53594-M53598

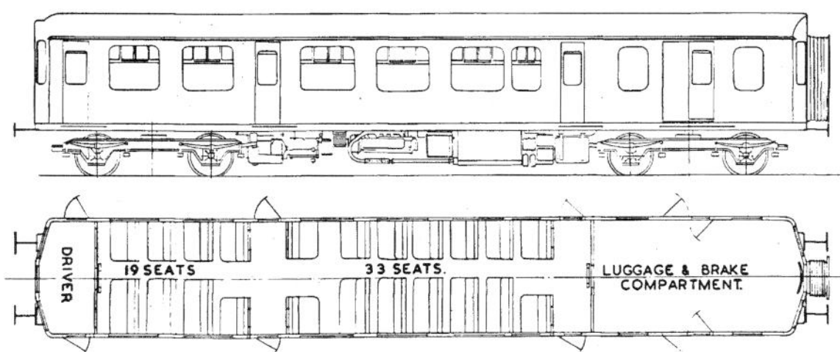

Coupling: ■ Blue square
Diagram: 557 DQ206
Lot Number: 30404
Old class: 104/2
Engines: Two BUT (Leyland) 6-cyl horizontal type of 160 bhp.
Transmission: Mechanical. Standard
Body: 57' 6" × 9' 3"
Weight: 31t
Seats: 52 second

M53594 06/83⊂**50594** 05/58-07/85 ⊗03/86
M53595 /83⊂**50595** 05/58-02/84 ⊗08/84
M53598 /83⊂**50598** 05/58-12/86 ⊗01/88 *07*/86⇨**SC**

Class 108 BR Derby

Driving Motor Brake Second
DMBS
E53599-E53624

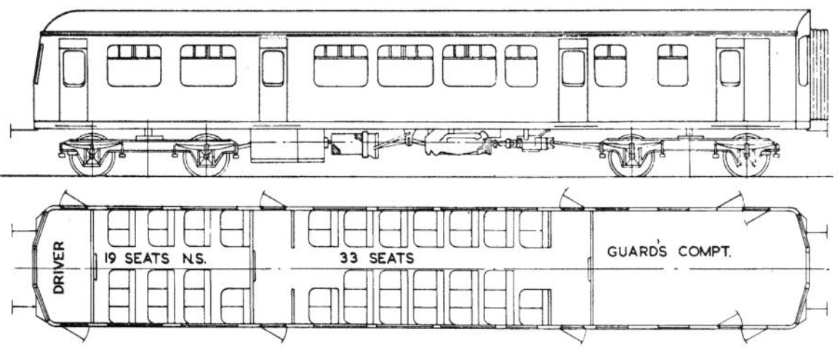

Coupling: ■ Blue square
Diagram: 543 DQ212
Lot Number: 30406
Old class: 108/2
Engines: Two BUT (Leyland) 6-cyl horizontal type of 150 bhp.
Transmission: Mechanical. Standard
Body: 58' 1" × 9' 2"
Weight: 29t
Seats: 52 second

E53599 04/83⊂**50599** 07/58-01/93 Ⓟ ® /81
E53601 04/83⊂**50601** 05/58-07/89 ⊗08/90 ®06/75
E53602 02/83⊂**50602** 05/58-05/92 ⊗08/95 ®03/83
E53603 04/83⊂**50603** 07/58-02/87 ⊗06/88 ®12/76
E53604 05/83⊂**50604** 07/58-05/88 ⊗06/88 ®12/76
E53605 04/83⊂**50605** 06/58-03/85 ⊗03/85 ®02/77
E53606 05/83⊂**50606** 07/58-10/89 ⊗08/90 ®11/77
E53607 04/83⊂**50607** 06/58-03/90 ⊗08/90 ®02/81
E53608 04/83⊂**50608** 07/58-03/92 ⊗08/95 ®08/76
E53610 05/83⊂**50610** 08/58-05/88 ⊗06/88 ®10/77
E53612 04/83⊂**50612** 08/58-01/92 ⊗03/92 ®06/75
E53613 04/83⊂**50613** 08/58-11/88 ⊗10/89 ®06/75
E53614 08/84⊂**50614** 07/58-01/91 ⊗07/91 ®05/75
E53616 07/83⊂**50616** 09/58-05/91 ⊗11/91 ®05/75
E53617 05/83⊂**50617** 08/58-04/92 ⊗05/92 ®10/80
E53618 04/83⊂**50618** 08/58-02/92 ⊗01/92 ®07/79
E53619 04/83⊂**50619** 08/58-05/91 Ⓟ ®*10/76*
E53620 04/83⊂**50620** 10/58-11/92 ⊗10/92 ®01/78
E53621 04/83⊂**50621** 10/58-02/92 ⊗02/92 ®01/78
E53622 05/83⊂**50622** 11/58-03/92 ⊗05/92 ®08/76
E53623 04/83⊂**50623** 11/58-06/87 ⊗06/89 ®07/76
E53624 05/83⊂**50624** 11/58-06/92 ⊗06/92 ®08/76

Class 108 BR Derby

Driving Motor Brake Second
DMBS
M53625-M53629

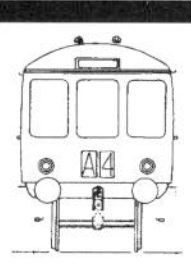

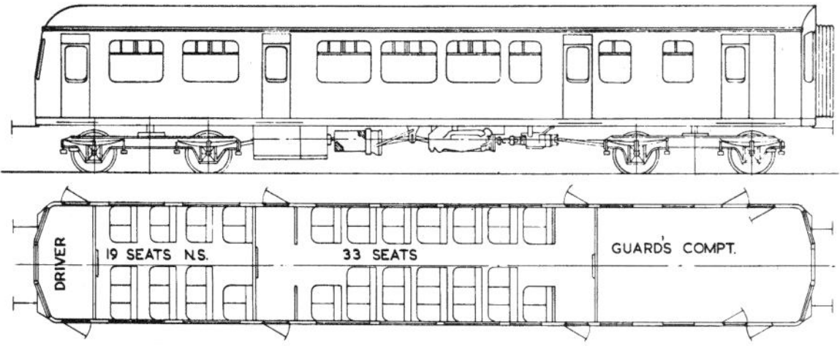

Coupling: ■ Blue square
Diagram: 543 DQ212
Lot Number: 30407
Old class: 108/2
Engines: Two BUT (Leyland) 6-cyl horizontal type of 150 bhp.
Transmission: Mechanical. Standard
Body: 58' 1" × 9' 2"
Weight: 29t
Seats: 52 second

M53625 09/83⊂**50625** 12/58-01/92 ⊗10/91 ®01/83 11/86⇨**W**
E53626 05/83⊂**50626** 12/58-10/91 ⊗01/93 ® /82 03/85⇨**M** 10/91⊃**ADB977745**
M53627 07/83⊂**50627** 12/58-02/93 Ⓟ ®09/81 02/93⊃**ADB977853**
M53628 07/83⊂**50628** 12/58-10/93 Ⓟ ® /81
M53629 /83⊂**50629** 02/59-10/92 ⊗08/94 ®10/76 ⊠06/92-09/92
10/92⊃**TDB977820**

Class 108 BR Derby

Driving Motor Composite Lavatory
DMCL
E53630-E53641

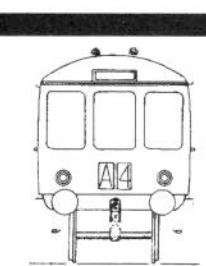

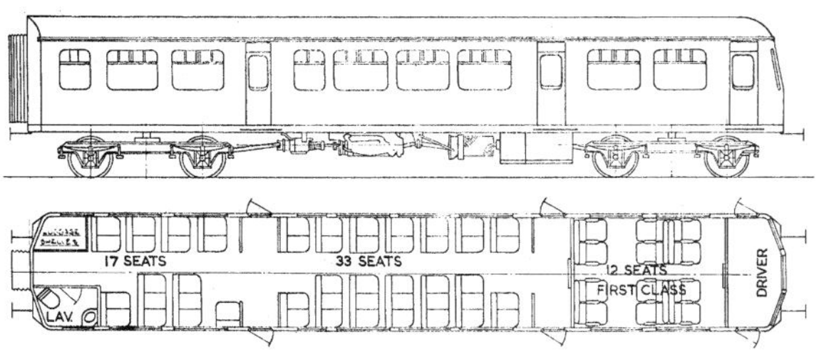

Coupling: ■ Blue square
Diagram: 544 DP310 ②DP219
Lot Number: 30408
Old class: 108/1
Engines: Two BUT (Leyland) 6-cyl horizontal type of 150 bhp.
Transmission: Mechanical. Standard
Body: 58' 1" × 9' 2"
Weight: 28t
Seats: 12 first, 50 second

E53630 11/84⊂**50630** 10/58-09/91 ⊗10/91 ®08/76
E53631 05/83⊂**50631** 10/58-11/91 ⊗11/91 ®01/78
E53632 04/83⊂**50632** 10/58-02/93 Ⓟ ®01/77
E53633 05/83⊂**50633** 10/58-06/92 ⊗12/92 ®10/80
M53634 02/83⊂**50634** 10/58-11/92 ⊗11/92
E53635 04/83⊂**50635** 10/58-01/92 ⊗02/92 ® /81
E53636 05/83⊂**50636** 10/58-01/92 ⊗02/92 ® /82 03/85⇨**M**
E53637 /83⊂**50637** 10/58-06/92 ⊗10/92 ®*09/76*
E53638 07/83⊂**50638** 10/58-02/91 ⊗02/91 ®*09/76*
E53639 04/83⊂**50639** 10/58-11/90 ⊗03/91 ®05/78
E53641 07/83⊂**50641** 10/58-06/92 ⊗09/92 ®01/77

Class 108 BR Derby
Driving Motor Composite Lavatory
DMCL
E53642-E53646

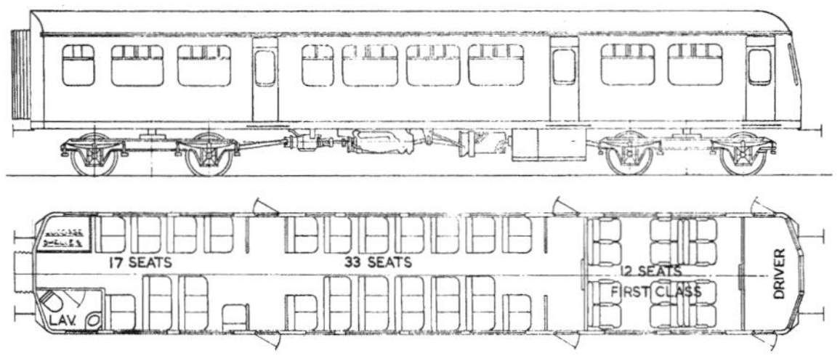

Coupling: ■ Blue square
Diagram: 544 DP310 ②DP219
Lot Number: 30408
Old class: 108/1
Engines: Two BUT (Leyland) 6-cyl horizontal type of 150 bhp.
Transmission: Mechanical. Standard
Body: 58' 1" × 9' 2"
Weight: 28t
Seats: 12 first, 50 second

E53642	05/83⊂**50642**	10/58-10/92	⊗11/93	®01/78	⊠06/92-07/92 10/92⊃ADB977839
E53643	04/83⊂**50643**	10/58-02/92	⊗02/92	®01/77	
E53644	04/83⊂**50644**	11/58-01/92	⊗01/92	®04/77	
E53645	04/83⊂**50645**	11/58-02/93	℗	®04/77	
E53646	04/83⊂**50646**	11/58-06/92	⊗05/92	®01/78	

Class 120 BR Swindon
Driving Motor Second Lavatory
DMSL
M53647-M53695

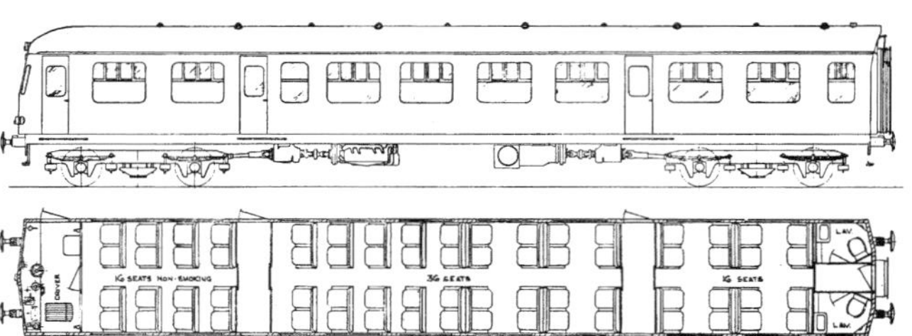

Coupling: ■ Blue square
Diagram: 586 DP204
Lot Number: 30334
Old class: 120/2
Engines: Two BUT (AEC) 6-cyl horizontal type of 150 bhp.
Transmission: Mechanical. Standard
Body: 64' 6" × 9' 3" Cross Country
Weight: 36t 10cwt
Seats: 68 second

M53647	05/83⊂**50647**	12/57-03/87	⊗05/87		02/86⇨**SC**	
M53648	09/83⊂**50648**	12/57-03/87	⊗09/87		03/86⇨**SC**	
M53649	04/83⊂**50649**	01/58-12/86	⊗03/87		03/86⇨**SC**	
M53650	/83⊂**50650**	01/58-12/86	⊗08/87		03/86⇨**SC**	
M53651	07/83⊂**50651**	01/58-03/87	⊗01/88	®11/79	03/86⇨**SC**	
M53652	07/83⊂**50652**	01/58-02/87	⊗08/87		03/86⇨**SC**	
M53653	06/83⊂**50653**	01/58-12/86	⊗06/87		02/86⇨**SC**	
M53654	/83⊂**50654**	01/58-02/88	⊗08/91	®07/78	02/86⇨**SC**	
M53655	04/83⊂**50655**	02/58-12/86	⊗03/87			
M53656	07/83⊂**50656**	02/58-07/86	⊗07/86		02/86⇨**SC**	
M53657	02/83⊂**50657**	02/58-03/86	⊗10/86			
M53658	05/84⊂**50658**	02/58-10/89	⊗08/91		09/86⇨**SC**	
M53659	/84⊂**50659**	02/58-12/86	⊗09/87		03/86⇨**SC**	
M53660	08/83⊂**50660**	02/58-03/86	⊗06/86			
M53661	07/83⊂**50661**	03/58-06/85	⊗05/86			
M53662	/85⊂**50662**	03/58-08/85	⊗05/86			
M53663	/83⊂**50663**	03/58-12/84	⊗04/85			
M53664	09/83⊂**50664**	03/58-12/86	⊗06/87			
M53665	09/83⊂**50665**	04/58-03/86	⊗06/86			
M53666	06/84⊂**50666**	05/58-04/86	⊗04/86		10/85⇨**SC**	
M53667	03/83⊂**50667**	05/58-03/86	⊗10/86			
M53668	08/83⊂**50668**	05/58-10/85	⊗12/86		09/85⇨**SC**	
M53669	/83⊂**50669**	05/58-12/86	⊗06/87		03/86⇨**SC**	
M53670	/83⊂**50670**	05/58-12/86	⊗08/87		03/86⇨**SC**	
M53671	/83⊂**50671**	05/58-11/84	⊗04/85			
M53672	09/83⊂**50672**	05/58-08/87	⊗05/89		03/86⇨**SC**	
M53673	07/83⊂**50673**	05/58-12/86	⊗01/87		03/86⇨**SC**	
M53674	04/83⊂**50674**	05/58-04/86	⊗04/86	®02/77	09/85⇨**SC**	
M53675	04/83⊂**50675**	05/58-03/86	⊗08/86			
M53676	09/83⊂**50676**	06/58-06/84	⊗04/85			
M53677	/83⊂**50677**	09/58-06/86	⊗01/87		02/86⇨**SC**	
M53678	07/83⊂**50678**	09/58-03/86	⊗06/86			
M53679	07/83⊂**50679**	09/58-12/86	⊗06/87		03/86⇨**SC**	
M53680	05/83⊂**50680**	09/58-05/86	⊗07/86			
M53681	05/83⊂**50681**	09/58-04/86	⊗05/86		05/86⇨**E**	
M53682	/84⊂**50682**	09/58-09/89	⊗05/91		09/86⇨**SC**	
M53683	/83⊂**50683**	10/58-02/84	⊗04/85			
M53684	08/83⊂**50684**	10/58-01/86	⊗10/86			
M53685	06/83⊂**50685**	10/58-03/86	⊗10/86			
M53686	08/84⊂**50686**	10/58-10/89	⊗05/91		11/86⇨**W**	⊠05/69-11/69
M53687	05/83⊂**50687**	10/58-03/87	⊗04/87		02/86⇨**SC**	
M53688	08/83⊂**50688**	10/58-12/86	⊗04/87		03/86⇨**SC**	
M53689	/83⊂**50689**	01/59-03/86	⊗06/86	®11/79		
M53691	04/83⊂**50691**	01/59-11/85	⊗08/87			
M53692	/83⊂**50692**	02/59-03/86	⊗06/86	®10/77		01/86⇨Parcels
M53693	09/83⊂**50693**	02/59-03/87	⊗11/87		02/86⇨**SC**	
M53694	09/83⊂**50694**	03/59-02/86	⊗03/86			
M53695	/83⊂**50695**	03/59-05/86	⊗05/91			

Class 120 BR Swindon
Driving Motor Brake Composite
DMBC
M53696-M53744

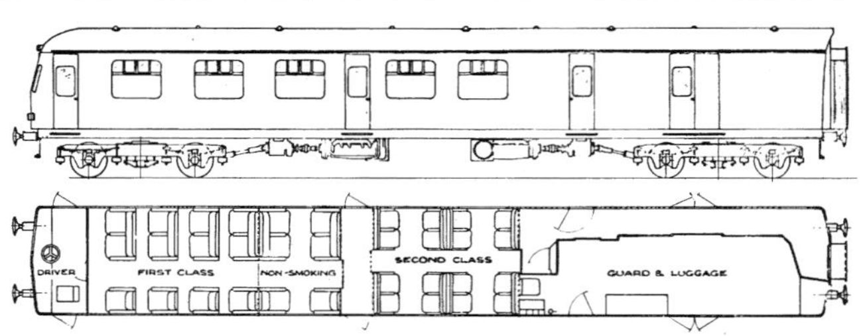

Coupling: ■ Blue square
Diagram: 587 DQ303
Lot Number: 30335
Old class: 120/1
Engines: Two BUT (AEC) 6-cyl horizontal type of 150 bhp.
Transmission: Mechanical. Standard
Body: 64' 6" × 9' 3" Cross Country
Weight: 36t
Seats: 18 first, 16 second

M53696	06/83⊂**50696**	10/57-09/86	⊗01/87		03/86⇨**SC**	
M53697	04/83⊂**50697**	10/57-07/87	⊗04/87			
M53698	04/83⊂**50698**	10/57-03/87	⊗07/87		03/86⇨**SC**	
M53699	05/84⊂**50699**	10/57-10/89	⊗08/91		09/86⇨**SC**	
M53700	/85⊂**50700**	10/57-09/89	⊗08/91		09/86⇨**SC**	
M53701	05/83⊂**50701**	10/57-11/85	⊗08/87			
M53702	09/83⊂**50702**	11/57-03/86	⊗03/86			
M53703	06/83⊂**50703**	11/57-05/88	⊗12/88			04/86⇨Parcels
M53704	/84⊂**50704**	11/57-04/87	⊗08/87	®11/79		01/86⇨Parcels
M53705	05/83⊂**50705**	11/57-12/86	⊗04/87		02/86⇨**SC**	
M53706	09/83⊂**50706**	11/57-12/86	⊗06/87		03/86⇨**SC**	
M53707	08/83⊂**50707**	11/57-10/84	⊗04/85			
M53708	/83⊂**50708**	12/57-08/87	⊗03/89	®10/77	02/86⇨**SC**	
M53709	/83⊂**50709**	12/57-06/86	⊗09/87		04/86⇨**SC**	
M53710	07/83⊂**50710**	12/57-08/85	⊗01/86			
M53711	/84⊂**50711**	12/57-12/86	⊗06/87		03/86⇨**SC**	
M53712	09/83⊂**50712**	01/58-01/86	⊗06/86			
M53713	02/83⊂**50713**	01/58-05/88	⊗12/88			07/86⇨Parcels
M53714	07/83⊂**50714**	03/58-04/87	⊗08/87			07/86⇨Parcels
M53715	06/83⊂**50715**	03/58-09/86	⊗01/87		03/86⇨**SC**	
M53716	04/83⊂**50716**	03/58-03/86	⊗08/86			
M53717	06/83⊂**50717**	04/58-09/86	⊗01/87		02/86⇨**SC**	
M53718	/83⊂**50718**	04/58-01/86	⊗04/87			
M53719	/83⊂**50719**	04/58-10/85	⊗06/86			
M53720	09/83⊂**50720**	06/58-06/86	⊗07/86		02/86⇨**SC**	
M53721	09/83⊂**50721**	06/58-10/85	⊗07/86			
M53722	07/83⊂**50722**	07/58-03/87	⊗06/87		03/86⇨**SC**	
M53723	04/83⊂**50723**	07/58-04/86	⊗04/86		10/85⇨**SC**	
M53724	07/83⊂**50724**	08/58-12/86	⊗03/87		03/86⇨**SC**	

M53725	07/83⊂**50725**	08/58-03/87	⊗02/89		05/86⇨**E**	⊠04/86-05/86
					07/86⇨Parcels	03/87⊃**55948**
M53726	/85⊂**50726**	08/58-03/87	⊗06/87		05/86⇨**E**	
					07/86⇨Parcels	03/87⊃**55938**
M53727	07/83⊂**50727**	08/58-07/86	⊗01/87		10/85⇨**SC** 09/86⇨**M**	
M53728	04/83⊂**50728**	08/58-05/86	⊗05/86		05/86⇨**E**	
M53729	05/83⊂**50729**	08/58-03/87	⊗06/87		05/86⇨**E**	⊠04/86-05/86
					07/86⇨Parcels	03/87⊃**55949**
M53730	06/83⊂**50730**	08/58-12/86	⊗04/87		03/86⇨**SC**	
M53731	05/83⊂**50731**	08/58-12/85	⊗10/86			
M53732	08/84⊂**50732**	11/58-10/89	⊗05/91			
M53733	/85⊂**50733**	11/58-10/89	⊗05/91		09/86⇨**SC**	⊠05/69-11/69
M53734	09/83⊂**50734**	11/58-01/85	⊗04/85			
M53735	/83⊂**50735**	11/58-05/86	⊗12/86			
M53736	07/83⊂**50736**	11/58-03/87	⊗06/87	®11/79	03/86⇨**SC**	
M53737	08/83⊂**50737**	12/58-03/87	⊗06/87		03/86⇨**SC** 09/86⇨**M**	
M53738	/84⊂**50738**	12/58-03/87	⊗09/87		02/86⇨**SC**	
M53739	04/83⊂**50739**	12/58-08/87	⊗05/88		09/86⇨**E**	⊠05/86-07/86
						07/86⇨Parcels
M53741	07/83⊂**50741**	12/58-12/86	⊗01/88		03/86⇨**SC**	
M53742	/83⊂**50742**	12/58-09/86	⊗03/87		02/86⇨**SC**	
M53743	09/83⊂**50743**	12/58-07/86	⊗07/86		02/86⇨**SC**	
M53744	08/83⊂**50744**	12/58-03/87	⊗01/88		03/86⇨**SC**	

Class 101 Metropolitan-Cammell

Driving Motor Composite Lavatory
DMCL
SC53746-E53751

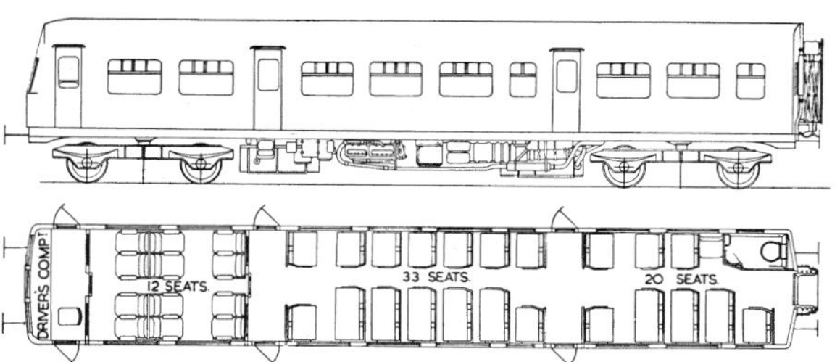

Coupling: ■ Blue square
Diagram: 621 DP304 ②DP210
Lot Number: 30271
Old class: 101/1
Engines: Two BUT (AEC) 6-cyl horizontal type of 150 bhp.
Transmission: Mechanical. Standard
Body: 57' 6" × 9' 3"
Weight: 32t
Seats: 12 first, 53 second

SC53746	08/83⊂**50746**	11/57-12/03	Ⓟ	®02/82
SC53747	08/83⊂**50747**	11/57-11/88	⊗03/90	®08/79
SC53748	08/83⊂**50748**	11/57-05/87	⊗11/87	
SC53749	08/83⊂**50749**	11/57-11/88	⊗04/90	®11/78
E53750	02/85⊂**50750**	11/57-11/88	⊗05/89	®02/80
E53751	07/83⊂**50751**	11/57-09/92	⊗02/93	® /82

Class 105 Cravens

Driving Motor Composite Lavatory
DMCL
M53812

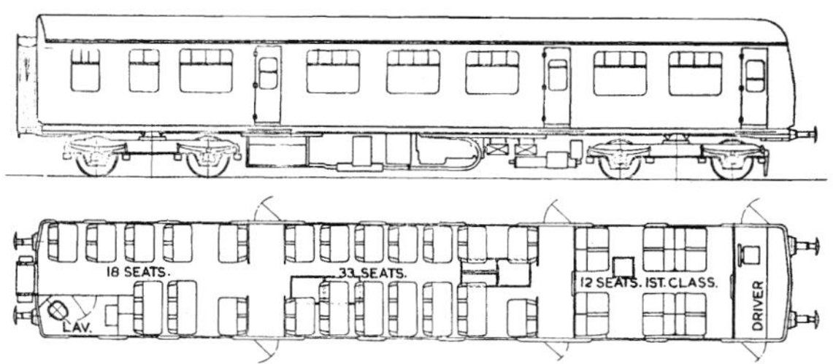

Coupling: ■ Blue square
Diagram: 529 DP308 ②DP211
Lot Number: 30353
Old class: 105/1
Engines: Two BUT (AEC) 6-cyl horizontal type of 150 bhp.
Transmission: Mechanical. Standard
Body: 57' 6" × 9' 3"
Weight: 30t
Seats: 12 first, 51 second

M53812	07/83⊂**50812**	04/58-05/89	⊗10/90

Class 116 BR Derby

Driving Motor Brake Second
DMBS
M53818-M53870

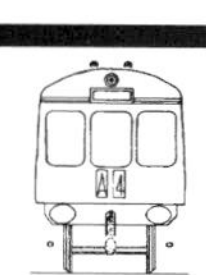

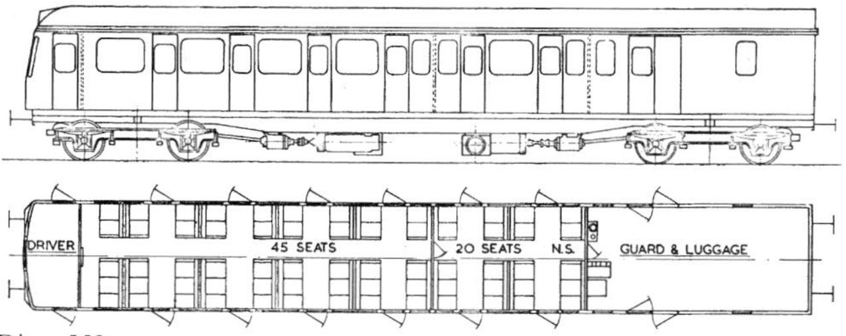

Diag. 553

Diag. 853 ⓖ *Through gangway fitted*

Coupling: ■ Blue square
Diagram: 553 DQ219 ⓖ 853 DP230
Lot Number: 30363
Old class: 116/2
Engines: Two BUT (Leyland) 6-cyl horizontal type of 150 bhp.
Transmission: Mechanical. Standard
Body: 64' 0" × 9' 3" Suburban
Weight: 36t
Seats: 65 second

M53818	07/83⊂**50818**	11/57-05/95	⊗08/95	ⓖ®02/79		
M53819	06/83⊂**50819**	11/57-01/88	⊗03/88	®01/78		
W53820	07/83⊂**50820**	11/57-07/92	⊗12/92	ⓖ®06/82		
M53821	06/83⊂**50821**	11/57-03/87	⊗04/87	®07/78		
SC53822	10/83⊂**50822**	11/57-06/93	⊗06/93	ⓖ®08/82		
SC53823	01/84⊂**50823**	12/57-12/87	⊗11/87	®02/80		
M53824	07/83⊂**50824**	12/57-04/88	⊗04/88	®10/81		
SC53825	10/83⊂**50825**	11/57-06/88	⊗11/89	®02/82		
M53826	08/83⊂**50826**	12/57-06/91	⊗06/91	ⓖ®09/79		
M53827	05/83⊂**50827**	11/57-11/90	⊗05/91	ⓖ®09/79		⊠10/85-12/85
M53828	06/83⊂**50828**	12/57-08/87	⊗05/88			
SC53829	10/83⊂**50829**	11/57-11/85	⊗09/86			
M53830	06/83⊂**50830**	12/57-04/85	⊗08/86	®06/78		
M53831	07/83⊂**50831**	12/57-04/87	⊗04/87	®10/77		
M53832	06/83⊂**50832**	01/58-06/88	⊗10/88	®10/77		
M53833	03/83⊂**50833**	01/58-02/88	⊗02/88	®04/77		
M53834	08/83⊂**50834**	01/58-10/85	⊗08/86	ⓖ®06/77		
M53835	/84⊂**50835**	01/58-12/87	⊗01/88	®10/77		
SC53836	/84⊂**50836**	01/58-10/83	⊗07/84	ⓖ		
M53837	04/83⊂**50837**	02/58-01/92	⊗02/92	ⓖ®11/82		
M53838	07/83⊂**50838**	01/58-05/93	⊗07/93	ⓖ®12/82		
SC53839	10/83⊂**50839**	01/58-10/88	⊗12/90	ⓖ® /82		
M53840	06/83⊂**50840**	01/58-01/87	⊗02/87	®09/81		
SC53841	01/84⊂**50841**	01/58-09/86	⊗09/86			
M53842	07/83⊂**50842**	02/58-07/88	⊗12/90	ⓖ®02/76		
W53843	04/83⊂**50843**	01/58-09/89	⊗07/90	ⓖ®11/76		⊠08/89-08/89
E53844	02/83⊂**50844**	02/58-12/90	⊗05/91	ⓖ®03/83	05/86⇨**M**	
E53845	04/83⊂**50845**	01/58-06/87	⊗08/87	ⓖ®11/79	05/86⇨**SC**	
SC53846	10/83⊂**50846**	01/58-12/87	⊗11/87			
W53847	04/83⊂**50847**	02/58-11/88	⊗03/89	ⓖ®02/77		
W53848	04/83⊂**50848**	02/58-10/89	⊗06/90	ⓖ®07/78		
M53849	08/83⊂**50849**	02/58-06/91	⊗06/91	ⓖ®09/84		
M53850	03/83⊂**50850**	02/58-03/92	⊗03/92	ⓖ®09/79		
M53851	06/83⊂**50851**	02/58-12/86	⊗01/87	ⓖ®12/78		
M53852	07/83⊂**50852**	02/58-04/87	⊗08/87	®06/78		
E53853	04/83⊂**50853**	03/58-10/92	⊗10/92	ⓖ® /82	05/86⇨**M**	
M53854	03/83⊂**50854**	02/58-06/92	⊗10/92	ⓖ®03/80		⊠11/90-12/90
W53855	04/83⊂**50855**	03/58-11/89	⊗04/90	ⓖ®02/77		

W53856 04/83⊂**50856** 03/58-10/88 ⊗09/88 ⓖ®*09/76*
M53857 07/83⊂**50857** 03/58-01/89 ⊗03/89 ⓖ®10/78
W53858 04/83⊂**50858** 04/58-10/89 ⊗05/90 ⓖ®01/76
SC53859 10/83⊂**50859** 04/58-03/86 ⊗10/87
M53860 09/83⊂**50860** 03/58-03/87 ⊗02/87 ®01/78
M53861 07/83⊂**50861** 04/58-07/87 ⊗05/88 ®10/77
M53862 04/83⊂**50862** 04/58-06/88 ⊗10/88 ®01/78
M53863 07/83⊂**50863** 05/58-05/93 ⊗07/93 ⓖ®05/83
W53864 04/83⊂**50864** 05/58-07/87 ⊗08/88 ⓖ®06/78
E53865 05/83⊂**50865** 05/58-01/92 ⊗02/92 ⓖ®09/83 05/86⇨**M**
M53866 04/83⊂**50866** 05/58-02/89 ⊗03/89 ⓖ®11/79
E53867 04/83⊂**50867** 05/58-10/88 ⊗10/88 ⓖ®11/79 05/86⇨**M**
W53868 04/83⊂**50868** 06/58-03/87 ⊗08/87 ⓖ®11/78
W53869 04/83⊂**50869** 07/58-02/89 ⊗03/89 ⓖ®*09/76*
M53870 09/83⊂**50870** 07/58-11/88 ⊗12/88

Class 116 BR Derby
Driving Motor Second
DMS
M53871-M53923

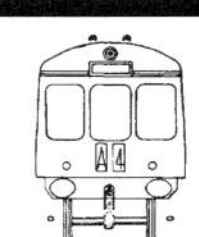

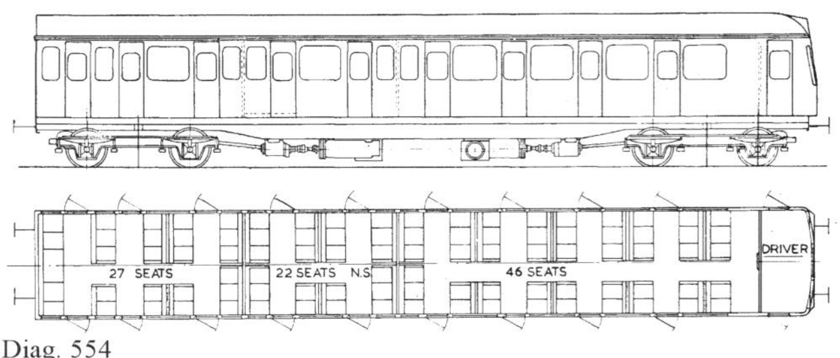

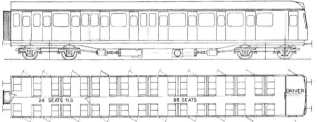

Diag. 554

Diag. 854 ⓖ *Through gangway fitted*

Coupling: ■ Blue square
Diagram: 554 DP201 ⓖ 854 DP220
Lot Number: 30364
Old class: 116/1
Engines: Two BUT (Leyland) 6-cyl horizontal type of 150 bhp.
Transmission: Mechanical. Standard
Body: 64' 0" × 9' 3" Suburban
Weight: 36t
Seats: 95 second ⓖ 89 second

M53871 07/83⊂**50871** 11/57-01/88 ⊗02/88 ®06/78
M53872 04/83⊂**50872** 11/57-06/88 ⊗10/88 ®01/78
SC53873 10/83⊂**50873** 11/57-04/92 ⊗10/92 *ⓖ*®02/82
M53875 06/83⊂**50875** 11/57-10/87 ⊗10/87 ®07/78
SC53876 01/84⊂**50876** 12/57-12/87 ⊗11/87 ®02/80
M53878 07/83⊂**50878** 11/57-03/92 ⊗03/92 *ⓖ*®02/79
SC53879 10/83⊂**50879** 12/57-11/85 ⊗09/86
M53880 05/83⊂**50880** 11/57-11/90 ⊗05/91 *ⓖ*®09/79
SC53881 10/83⊂**50881** 11/57-09/92 ⊗09/97 *ⓖ*®08/82 10/92➲**TDB977825**
SC53882 /83⊂**50882** 11/57-03/87 ⊗04/87
M53883 06/83⊂**50883** 12/57-06/87 ⊗08/87 ®06/78
M53884 07/83⊂**50884** 12/57-12/87 ⊗02/88 ®10/77
M53885 06/83⊂**50885** 01/58-12/87 ⊗12/87 ®10/77
M53886 07/83⊂**50886** 01/58-09/92 ⊗03/94 *ⓖ*®06/82 10/92➲**TDB977827**
M53887 08/83⊂**50887** 01/58-10/89 ⊗06/90 ⓖ®06/77
M53888 /83⊂**50888** 01/58-12/85 ⊗01/87 ®10/77
SC53889 /84⊂**50889** 01/58-10/83 ⊗07/84 ⓖ
M53890 04/83⊂**50890** 02/58-03/92 ⊗03/92 *ⓖ*®11/82
M53891 07/83⊂**50891** 01/58-01/93 ⊗03/93 *ⓖ*®01/83 ⊠06/92-07/92
SC53892 09/83⊂**50892** 01/58-03/87 ⊗04/87 ⓖ
M53893 07/83⊂**50893** 01/58-09/90 ⊗08/92 *ⓖ*
E53894 04/83⊂**50894** 01/58-10/92 ⊗10/92 *ⓖ*® /82 05/86⇨**M**
M53895 07/83⊂**50895** 02/58-10/88 ⊗10/88 ⓖ®02/76
W53896 04/83⊂**50896** 01/58-06/88 ⊗06/88 ⓖ®11/76
E53897 02/83⊂**50897** 02/58-08/94 ⊗08/94 ⓖ®03/83 05/86⇨**M**
E53898 05/83⊂**50898** 01/58-06/87 ⊗08/87 ⓖ 05/86⇨**SC**
SC53899 10/83⊂**50899** 01/58-03/86 ⊗10/87
W53900 04/83⊂**50900** 02/58-04/88 ⊗01/89 ⓖ®02/77
W53901 04/83⊂**50901** 02/58-05/88 ⊗09/88 ⓖ®07/78
M53902 06/83⊂**50902** 02/58-09/93 ⊗03/94 *ⓖ*®10/80
M53903 06/83⊂**50903** 02/58-06/87 ⊗08/87
M53904 06/83⊂**50904** 02/58-11/88 ⊗03/89 ⓖ®12/78
M53905 08/83⊂**50905** 02/58-12/87 ⊗11/87 ®09/79
M53906 07/83⊂**50906** 03/58-04/88 ⊗01/89 ®10/81
M53907 03/83⊂**50907** 02/58-06/92 ⊗03/93 ⓖ®03/80 ⊠11/90-12/90
W53908 04/83⊂**50908** 03/58-11/89 ⊗04/90 ⓖ®02/77
W53909 04/83⊂**50909** 03/58-10/88 ⊗09/88 ⓖ®*09/76*
M53910 07/83⊂**50910** 03/58-11/88 ⊗03/89 ⓖ®10/78
W53911 04/83⊂**50911** 04/58-10/89 ⊗07/90 ⓖ®01/76
M53912 07/83⊂**50912** 04/58-05/87 ⊗08/87 ®10/77
M53913 09/83⊂**50913** 03/58-05/88 ⊗09/88 ®01/78
M53914 04/83⊂**50914** 04/58-03/88 ⊗03/88 ®10/77
M53915 06/83⊂**50915** 04/58-08/87 ⊗05/88 ®01/78
M53916 03/83⊂**50916** 05/58-05/93 ⊗02/96 ⓖ®05/83
W53917 04/83⊂**50917** 05/58-07/87 ⊗08/88 ⓖ®06/78
W53918 04/83⊂**50918** 05/58-03/87 ⊗08/87 ⓖ®11/78
M53919 04/83⊂**50919** 05/58-06/95 ⊗06/95 ⓖ®08/79
E53920 05/83⊂**50920** 05/58-10/88 ⊗10/88 ⓖ 05/86⇨**M**
E53921 04/83⊂**50921** 06/58-05/95 ⊗06/95 ⓖ®09/83 05/86⇨**M**
W53922 04/83⊂**50922** 07/58-02/89 ⊗03/89 ⓖ®*09/76*
M53923 05/84⊂**50923** 07/58-11/88 ⊗12/88

Class 108 BR Derby
Driving Motor Brake Second
DMBS
M53924-M53935

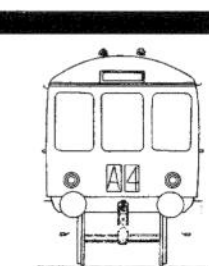

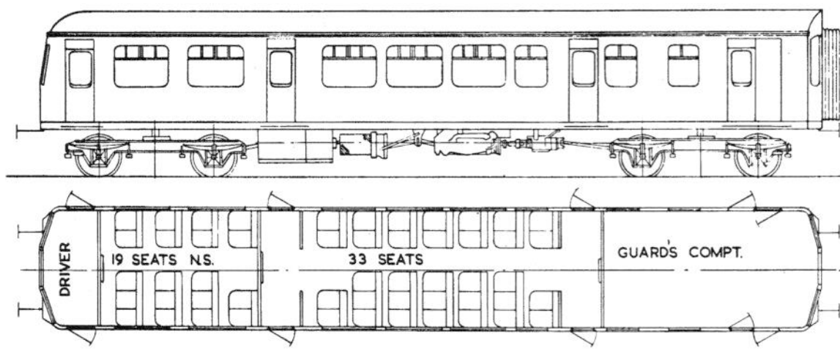

Coupling: ■ Blue square
Diagram: 543 DQ212
Lot Number: 30460
Old class: 108/2
Engines: Two BUT (AEC) 6-cyl horizontal type of 150 bhp.
Transmission: Mechanical. Standard
Body: 58' 1" × 9' 2"
Weight: 29t
Seats: 52 second

M53924 09/83⊂**50924** 10/59-10/91 ⊗01/92 ®07/77 10/91➲**ADB977747**
M53925 */84*⊂**50925** 12/59-05/92 ⊗05/92
M53926 08/83⊂**50926** 11/59-09/92 Ⓟ ®08/82 10/92➲**ADB977814**
M53927 */84*⊂**50927** 11/59-05/92 ⊗10/92 ®11/80
M53928 09/84⊂**50928** 11/59-03/92 Ⓟ ®03/79
M53929 05/83⊂**50929** 11/59-10/91 ⊗03/94 ®04/82 10/91➲**ADB977746**
M53930 05/83⊂**50930** 12/59-02/92 ⊗02/92
M53931 /83⊂**50931** 12/59-01/92 ⊗02/92
M53932 04/83⊂**50932** 12/59-10/90 ⊗11/90 ®04/82
M53933 /83⊂**50933** 01/60-11/92 Ⓟ
M53934 01/85⊂**50934** 01/60-09/91 ⊗10/91 ®09/76
M53935 */85*⊂**50935** 01/60-11/92 ⊗01/93 ®10/76

Class 108 BR Derby
Driving Motor Brake Second
DMBS
M53938-M53987

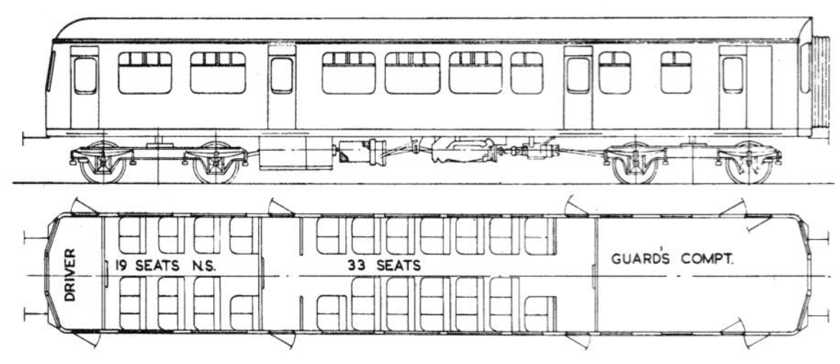

Coupling: ■ Blue square

Diagram: 543 DQ212
Lot Number: 30465
Old class: 108/2
Engines: Two BUT (Leyland) 6-cyl horizontal type of 150 bhp.
Transmission: Mechanical. Standard
Body: 58' 1" × 9' 2"
Weight: 29t
Seats: 52 second

M53938 04/83⊂**50938** 01/59-01/92 ⊗03/92 Ⓡ08/78
M53939 04/83⊂**50939** 01/59-09/92 ⊗07/96 Ⓡ /81 10/92➲**ADB977818**
M53940 09/83⊂**50940** 01/59-06/92 ⊗06/92 Ⓡ11/80
M53941 05/83⊂**50941** 01/59-09/92 ⊗10/96 Ⓡ10/78 11/86⇨W 10/92➲**ADB977836**
M53942 02/83⊂**50942** 01/59-07/91 ⊗01/94 Ⓡ06/78
M53943 /85⊂**50943** 01/59-07/92 ⊗11/92 Ⓡ07/77
M53944 /84⊂**50944** 01/59-01/92 ⊗03/94 Ⓡ04/82 01/92➲**ADB977766**
M53945 /83⊂**50945** 01/59-06/92 ⊗12/92 Ⓡ10/77
M53947 /83⊂**50947** 02/59-06/92 ⊗12/92 Ⓡ11/77
M53948 /83⊂**50948** 02/59-02/92 ⊗01/92 Ⓡ01/78
M53949 /83⊂**50949** 02/59-04/91 ⊗12/91 Ⓡ01/78
M53950 06/83⊂**50950** 02/59-10/91 ⊗03/94 Ⓡ10/83 10/91➲**ADB977748**
M53951 05/83⊂**50951** 02/59-06/92 ⊗06/92
M53952 06/83⊂**50952** 02/59-12/90 ⊗03/92
M53953 06/83⊂**50953** 02/59-07/91 ⊗03/92
M53954 06/83⊂**50954** 03/59-07/91 ⊗03/92
M53955 06/83⊂**50955** 03/59-04/91 ⊗02/92
M53956 06/83⊂**50956** 03/59-09/92 ⊗07/96 10/92➲**ADB977811**
M53957 06/83⊂**50957** 03/59-10/91 ⊗03/92 Ⓡ10/77 10/91➲**ADB977751**
M53958 06/83⊂**50958** 04/59-09/92 ⊗02/96 10/92➲**ADB977809**
M53959 06/83⊂**50959** 04/59-10/91 ⊗03/92 10/91➲**ADB977749**
M53960 06/83⊂**50960** 04/59-03/92 ⊗02/92 Ⓡ08/81
M53962 06/83⊂**50962** 04/59-12/90 ⊗02/92
M53963 06/83⊂**50963** 06/59-10/91 ⊗04/96 10/91➲**ADB977750**
M53964 04/83⊂**50964** 05/59-06/92 ⊗06/92
M53965 06/83⊂**50965** 05/59-02/91 ⊗11/91
M53966 06/83⊂**50966** 05/59-06/92 ⊗05/92 ⊠12/90-01/91
M53967 06/83⊂**50967** 06/59-05/88 ⊗10/89
M53968 06/83⊂**50968** 05/59-07/92 ⊗08/92
M53969 06/83⊂**50969** 06/59-10/91 ⊗10/91 Ⓡ08/80
M53970 /83⊂**50970** 07/59-04/92 ⊗06/92 Ⓡ01/78
M53971 06/83⊂**50971** 07/59-02/93 Ⓟ Ⓡ07/79
M53973 06/83⊂**50973** 07/59-06/92 ⊗06/92 Ⓡ04/80
M53974 02/83⊂**50974** 07/59-06/92 ⊗06/92 Ⓡ08/78
M53975 /83⊂**50975** 08/59-05/91 ⊗09/91 Ⓡ01/78
M53976 06/83⊂**50976** 08/59-05/91 ⊗11/91 Ⓡ11/77
M53977 06/83⊂**50977** 08/59-06/91 ⊗10/91 Ⓡ09/76
M53978 /83⊂**50978** 08/59-06/92 ⊗06/92 Ⓡ07/78
M53980 /83⊂**50980** 09/59-01/93 Ⓟ
M53981 06/83⊂**50981** 09/59-10/92 ⊗08/95 Ⓡ05/77 10/92➲**ADB977838**
M53982 06/83⊂**50982** 09/59-09/92 Ⓟ⊗ /02 Ⓡ12/83 10/92➲**ADB977816**
M53983 /83⊂**50983** 10/59-07/91 ⊗08/91 Ⓡ06/78
M53985 /83⊂**50985** 10/59-10/87 ⊗12/90 Ⓡ01/78
M53986 04/85⊂**50986** 10/59-06/92 ⊗06/92 Ⓡ06/78 ⊠11/90-12/90
M53987 06/83⊂**50987** 10/59-01/93 Ⓟ⊗01/98

Class 114 BR Derby
Driving Trailer Composite Lavatory
DTCL
E54001-E54049

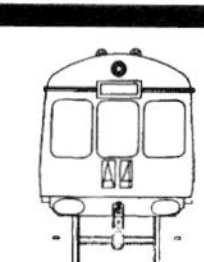

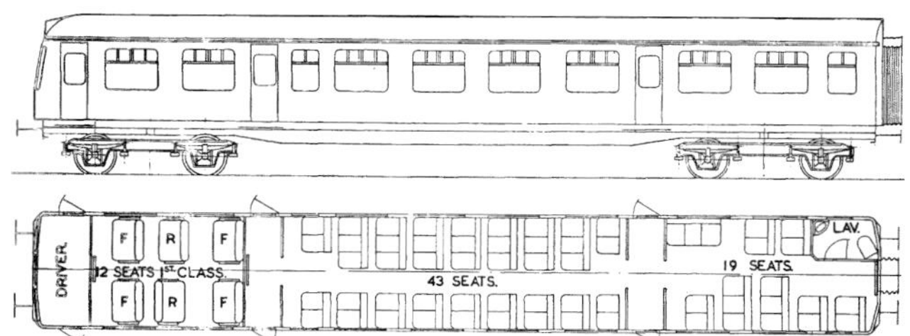

Coupling: ■ Blue square
Diagram: 641 DS313
Lot Number: 30210
Old class: 148
Body: 64' 6" × 9' 3"
Weight: 29t 10cwt
Seats: 12 first, 62 second

E54001 05/83⊂**56001** 10/56-02/88 ⊗04/88 Ⓡ11/80
E54002 07/83⊂**56002** 11/56-06/88 ⊗11/88 Ⓡ09/80
E54003 08/83⊂**56003** 11/56-06/88 ⊗11/88 Ⓡ01/78
E54004 /83⊂**56004** 11/56-06/88 ⊗12/88 Ⓡ07/79
E54005 04/83⊂**56005** 11/56-01/88 ⊗02/88 Ⓡ06/78
E54006 04/83⊂**56006** 11/56-03/92 Ⓟ Ⓡ /81
E54007 04/83⊂**56007** 11/56-06/88 ⊗12/88 Ⓡ02/78
E54008 03/83⊂**56008** 11/56-05/89 ⊗02/92 Ⓡ02/78
E54009 02/83⊂**56009** 11/56-07/89 ⊗04/91 Ⓡ05/83 07/89➲**54903**
E54010 04/83⊂**56010** 12/56-09/91 ⊗11/91 Ⓡ10/81
E54011 06/83⊂**56011** 11/56-05/89 ⊗02/92 Ⓡ /82
E54012 06/83⊂**56012** 11/56-10/91 ⊗11/91 Ⓡ11/78
E54013 08/83⊂**56013** 12/56-03/89 ⊗06/91 Ⓡ /82
E54014 05/83⊂**56014** 12/56-06/88 ⊗12/88 Ⓡ02/81 11/86⇨Parcels
E54015 06/83⊂**56015** 02/57-07/89 Ⓟ Ⓡ07/78 07/89➲**54904**
E54016 02/83⊂**56016** 12/56-01/88 ⊗04/91 Ⓡ01/78 01/88➲**54901**
E54017 /83⊂**56017** 01/57-06/88 ⊗01/89 Ⓡ07/78
E54018 04/83⊂**56018** 01/57-06/88 ⊗11/88 Ⓡ08/77
E54019 /84⊂**56019** 01/57-03/89 ⊗06/91 Ⓡ /81
E54021 04/83⊂**56021** 01/57-06/88 ⊗12/88 Ⓡ11/79
E54022 04/83⊂**56022** 01/57-02/88 ⊗04/88 Ⓡ07/79
E54023 06/83⊂**56023** 01/57-06/88 ⊗12/88 Ⓡ07/79
E54024 06/83⊂**56024** 01/57-05/89 ⊗02/91 Ⓡ /81
E54025 04/83⊂**56025** 01/57-06/88 ⊗12/88 Ⓡ07/79
E54026 04/83⊂**56026** 01/57-11/89 ⊗04/90 Ⓡ11/78
E54027 04/83⊂**56027** 01/57-01/92 ⊗07/93 Ⓡ07/78 01/92➲**ADB977770**
E54028 06/83⊂**56028** 01/57-05/90 ⊗08/90 Ⓡ11/78 08/87⇨Parcels
E54029 04/83⊂**56029** 01/57-02/88 ⊗04/88 Ⓡ02/81
E54030 06/83⊂**56030** 01/57-02/87 ⊗09/90 Ⓡ11/79
E54032 06/83⊂**56032** 02/57-05/87 ⊗04/88 Ⓡ03/78
E54033 04/83⊂**56033** 02/57-09/88 ⊗12/88 Ⓡ07/79 ⊠09/86-04/87 04/87⇨Parcels
E54034 04/83⊂**56034** 02/57-01/88 ⊗04/91 Ⓡ07/80 01/88➲**55933** 01/88➲**54900**
E54035 04/83⊂**56035** 03/57-05/87 ⊗11/88 Ⓡ03/80
E54036 04/83⊂**56036** 02/57-01/88 ⊗04/91 Ⓡ01/81 08/87⇨Parcels 01/88➲**55932** 01/88➲**54902**
E54037 04/83⊂**56037** 02/57-06/88 ⊗01/89 Ⓡ /81
E54038 04/83⊂**56038** 02/57-06/88 ⊗12/88 Ⓡ10/77
E54039 /83⊂**56039** 02/57-10/91 ⊗02/92 Ⓡ /80
E54040 10/83⊂**56040** 02/57-06/88 ⊗12/88 Ⓡ02/81
E54041 04/83⊂**56041** 03/57-05/90 ⊗08/90 Ⓡ01/78 10/86⇨Parcels
E54042 04/83⊂**56042** 03/57-03/89 ⊗04/89 Ⓡ12/77
E54043 04/83⊂**56043** 03/57-10/91 ⊗11/91 Ⓡ04/78
E54044 03/84⊂**56044** 03/57-06/88 ⊗12/88 Ⓡ04/79
E54045 06/83⊂**56045** 03/57-06/88 ⊗01/89 Ⓡ03/79
E54047 05/83⊂**56047** 04/57-10/91 Ⓟ Ⓡ /82
E54049 04/83⊂**56049** 08/57-02/84 ⊗12/84 Ⓡ11/79

Class 101 Metropolitan-Cammell
Driving Trailer Composite Lavatory
DTCL
E54050-E54061

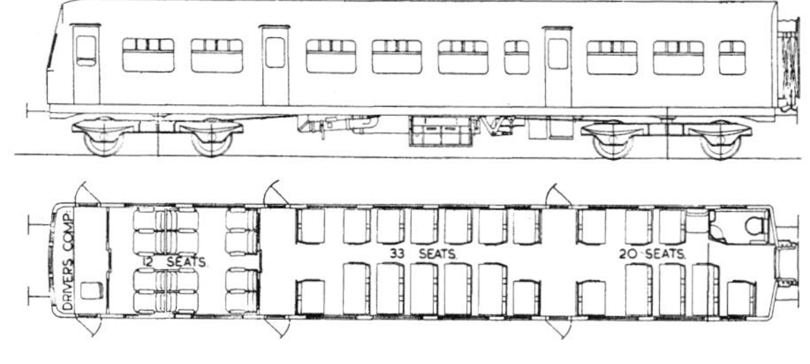

Coupling: ■ Blue square
Diagram: 630 DS302 ⊘DS206
Lot Number: 30260
Old class: 144
Body: 57' 6" × 9' 3"
Weight: 25t
Seats: 12 first, 53 second

E54050 06/83⊂**56050** 04/57-05/93 ⊗12/95 Ⓡ01/79
E54051 04/83⊂**56051** 04/57-06/87 ⊗06/88 Ⓡ01/78
E54052 04/83⊂**56052** 05/57-05/86 ⊗12/86 Ⓡ07/78 03/85⇨**M**
E54053 04/83⊂**56053** 05/57-06/87 ⊗10/88 Ⓡ07/79
E54054 07/83⊂**56054** 05/57-05/89 ⊗04/91 Ⓡ /81
M54055 04/83⊂**56055** 05/57-06/00 Ⓟ Ⓡ /82 05/86⇨**E**
E54056 05/83⊂**56056** 05/57-11/01 ⊗07/06 Ⓡ09/82
E54057 09/83⊂**56057** 04/57-09/86 ⊗07/88 Ⓡ11/76
M54058 04/83⊂**56058** 04/57-06/87 ⊗02/89 Ⓡ10/77 06/86⇨**E**
E54059 04/83⊂**56059** 05/57-06/87 ⊗01/89 Ⓡ07/79
M54060 06/83⊂**56060** 05/57-06/93 ⊗12/93 Ⓡ06/76 05/86⇨**E**
E54061 05/83⊂**56061** 05/57-06/00 ⊗01/07 Ⓡ07/79

Class 101 Metropolitan-Cammell
Driving Trailer Composite Lavatory
DTCL
E54062-E54085

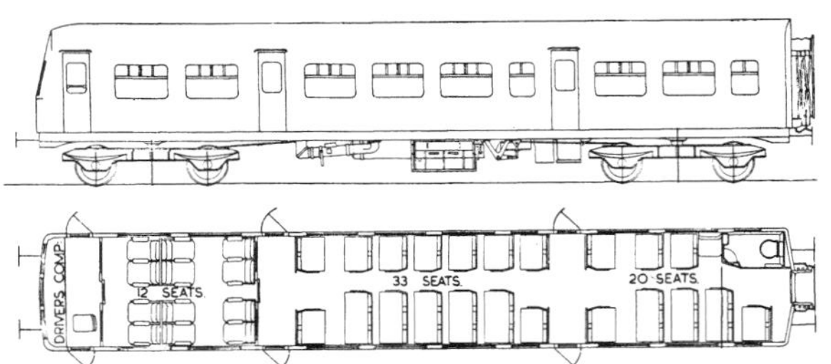

Coupling: ■ Blue square
Diagram: 630 DS302 ②DS206
Lot Number: 30262
Old class: 144
Body: 57' 6" × 9' 3"
Weight: 25t
Seats: 12 first, 53 second

E54062 09/83⊂56062 05/57-03/01 ⓟ ®11/79 ⊠09/90-06/91
E54063 04/83⊂56063 05/57-10/87 ⊗09/88 ®*09/76*
E54064 04/83⊂56064 06/57-06/87 ⊗01/88 ®01/78
E54065 03/83⊂56065 06/57-12/92 ⊗01/94 ®02/81
E54066 04/83⊂56066 06/57-02/87 ⊗01/89 ®01/78
E54067 05/83⊂56067 07/57-06/87 ⊗07/88 ®04/77
E54068 09/83⊂56068 07/57-05/95 ⊗06/95 ®01/77
E54069 05/83⊂56069 07/57-03/88 ⊗06/89 ®07/79
E54070 04/83⊂56070 07/57-12/91 ⊗04/93 ®*10/76* ⊠11/90-12/90
E54071 10/83⊂56071 07/57-05/89 ⊗04/91 ® /81
E54072 02/83⊂56072 07/57-09/86 ⊗09/86 ®02/81 06/86⇨SC
E54073 08/83⊂56073 08/57-10/92 ⊗01/94 ®*10/76*
E54074 04/83⊂56074 06/57-02/88 ⊗01/89 ®02/81
E54075 04/83⊂56075 06/57-05/89 ⊗10/90 ®*10/76*
E54076 05/83⊂56076 06/57-02/87 ⊗01/89 ®05/78
E54077 */84*⊂56077 06/57-02/88 ⊗10/88 ®07/78
E54078 */84*⊂56078 07/57-08/88 ⊗04/89 ®11/79
E54079 05/83⊂56079 07/57-09/86 ⊗05/87 ®07/79
M54080 07/83⊂56080 07/57-10/89 ⊗08/90 ®02/81 05/86⇨E
E54081 09/83⊂56081 07/57-10/93 ⊗02/94 ® /82 ⊠07/93-08/93
E54082 05/83⊂56082 08/57-06/87 ⊗06/88 ®11/79
E54083 05/83⊂56083 08/57-03/88 ⊗03/88 ®11/79
E54084 04/83⊂56084 08/57-07/86 ⊗02/93 ®11/79
E54085 /83⊂56085 09/57-01/02 ⊗12/03 ® /81

Class 101 Metropolitan-Cammell
Driving Trailer Composite Lavatory
DTCL
E54086-E54089

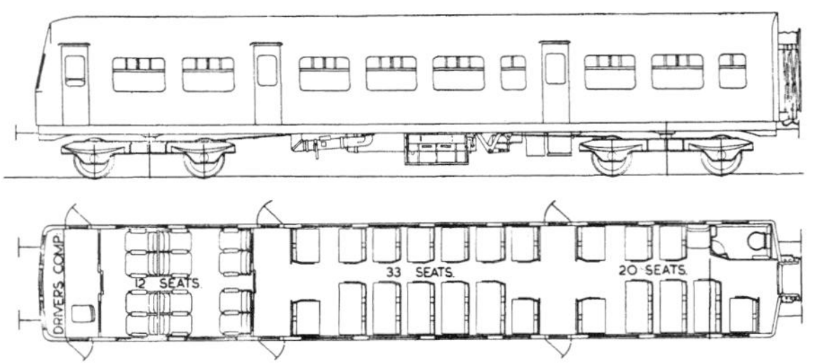

Coupling: ■ Blue square
Diagram: 630 DS302 ②DS206
Lot Number: 30272
Old class: 144
Body: 57' 6" × 9' 3"
Weight: 25t
Seats: 12 first, 53 second

E54086 02/83⊂56086 12/57-07/86 ⊗10/88 ®11/79
E54087 10/83⊂56087 12/57-09/86 ⊗05/87 ®07/78
E54088 05/84⊂56088 12/57-06/87 ⊗*09/90* ®04/77
E54089 */85*⊂56089 12/57-03/88 ⊗03/88 ®11/79

Class 111 Metropolitan-Cammell
Driving Trailer Composite Lavatory
DTCL
E54090-E54093

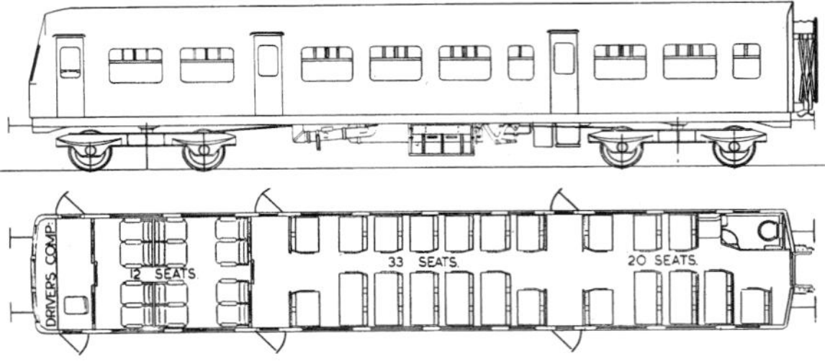

Coupling: ■ Blue square
Diagram: 628 DS312
Lot Number: 30337
Old class: 147
Body: 57' 6" × 9' 3"
Weight: 25t
Seats: 12 first, 53 second

E54090 04/83⊂56090 04/57-08/88 ⊗04/89 ®08/77
E54091 02/83⊂56091 04/57-10/00 ⊗12/03 ®05/83 ⊠09/89-09/90
E54092 05/85⊂56092 04/57-06/87 ⊗06/88 ®01/78
E54093 04/83⊂56093 04/57-07/86 ⊗01/89 ®02/81

Class 105 Cravens
Driving Trailer Composite Lavatory
DTCL
E54114-E54126

Coupling: ■ Blue square
Diagram: 526 DS307 ②DS204
Lot Number: 30281
Old class: 141
Body: 57' 6" × 9' 2"
Weight: 23t
Seats: 12 first, 51 second

E54114 06/83⊂56114 08/56-05/86 ⊗02/89
E54115 05/84⊂56115 10/56-05/87 ⊗11/87
E54119 */85*⊂56119 12/56-04/87 ⊗11/87
E54122 05/83⊂56122 01/57-10/88 ⊗02/89
E54125 /83⊂56125 02/57-09/86 ⊗07/88
E54126 03/83⊂56126 02/57-06/86 ⊗02/89

Class 105 Cravens

Driving Trailer Composite Lavatory
DTCL
E54130-E54143

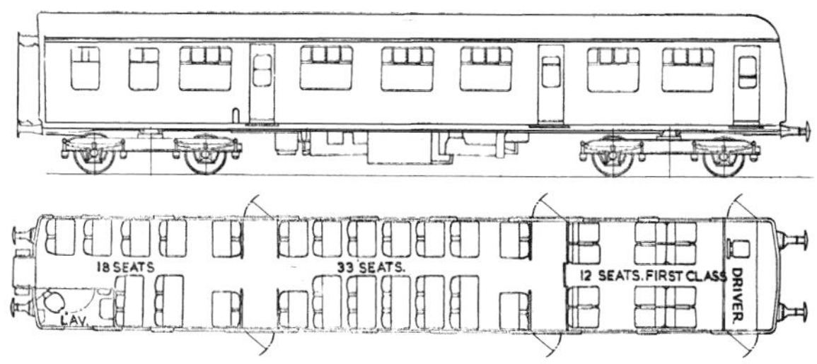

Coupling:	■ Blue square		
Diagram:	526	DS307	②DS204
Lot Number:	30283		
Old class:	141		
Body:	57' 6" × 9' 2"		
Weight:	23t		
Seats:	12 first, 51 second		

E54130	05/84⊂**56130**	03/57-05/84	⊗10/84	
E54131	02/83⊂**56131**	03/57-06/86	⊗07/88	
E54132	04/83⊂**56132**	03/57-06/86	⊗02/87	
E54133	05/83⊂**56133**	04/57-05/87	⊗11/87	
E54134	05/84⊂**56134**	04/57-09/85	⊗05/86	
E54136	02/83⊂**56136**	04/57-09/86	⊗01/87	06/86⇨**SC**
E54139	05/84⊂**56139**	05/57-05/85	⊗08/85	
E54143	04/83⊂**56143**	07/57-05/87	⊗11/87	

Class 104 Birmingham RC&W

Driving Trailer Composite Lavatory
DTCL
M54175-M54184

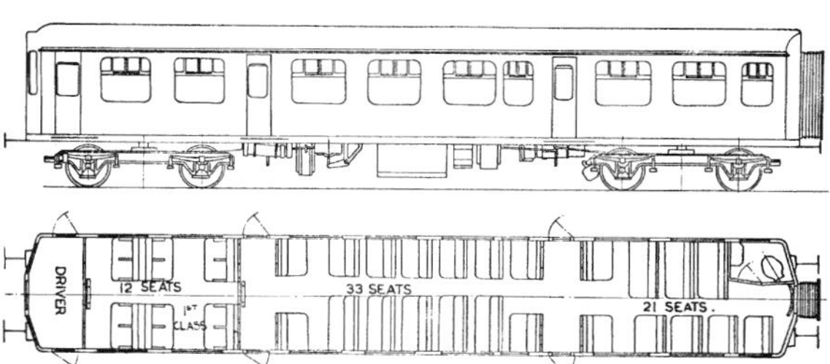

Coupling:	■ Blue square		
Diagram:	585	DS306	②DS205
Lot Number:	30297		
Old class:	140		
Body:	57' 6" × 9' 3"		
Weight:	24t		
Seats:	12 first, 54 second		

M54175	10/83⊂**56175**	03/58-03/86	⊗03/86		
M54176	/83⊂**56176**	03/58-03/86	⊗03/86		
M54177	03/83⊂**56177**	04/58-03/88	⊗03/88		
M54178	08/83⊂**56178**	04/58-02/86	⊗02/86		
M54179	09/83⊂**56179**	04/58-06/88	⊗10/90		
M54180	06/83⊂**56180**	04/58-02/86	⊗02/86		
M54181	/83⊂**56181**	04/58-11/86	⊗02/92		
M54182	08/83⊂**56182**	04/58-05/87	℗	09/86⇨**W**	11/86⇨**M** 07/89➲**ADB977554**
M54183	07/83⊂**56183**	04/58-05/87	⊗02/94		04/88➲**ADB977555**
M54184	/83⊂**56184**	05/58-08/88	⊗10/90		

Class 104 Birmingham RC&W

Driving Trailer Composite Lavatory
DTCL
M54186-M54187

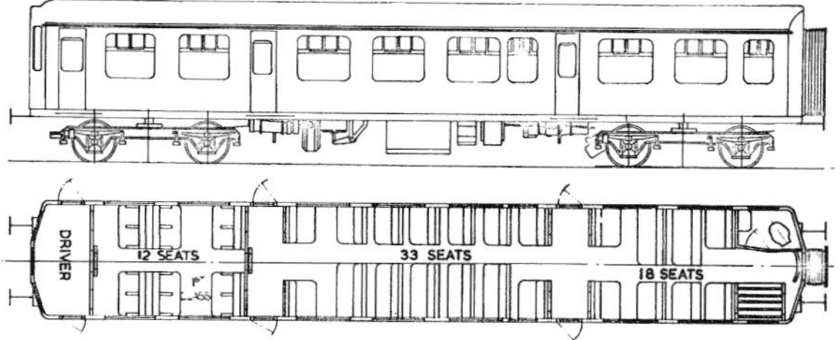

Coupling:	■ Blue square		
Diagram:	581	DS306	
Lot Number:	30405		
Old class:	140		
Body:	57' 6" × 9' 3"		
Weight:	24t		
Seats:	12 first, 54 second		

M54186	06/83⊂**56186**	05/58-02/84	⊗02/86
M54187	/83⊂**56187**	05/58-10/84	⊗08/84

Class 108 BR Derby

Driving Trailer Composite Lavatory
DTCL
E54190-E54210

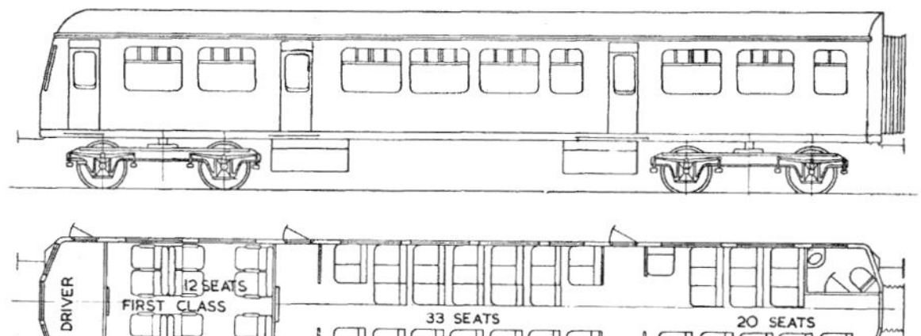

Coupling:	■ Blue square		
Diagram:	640	DS310	②DS207
Lot Number:	30409		
Old class:	142		
Body:	58' 1" × 9' 2"		
Weight:	21t		
Seats:	12 first, 53 second		

E54190	04/83⊂**56190**	07/58-02/87	⊗06/88	®07/79		
E54191	04/83⊂**56191**	05/58-01/92	⊗03/92	®05/75		⊠02/90-07/90
E54192	04/84⊂**56192**	05/58-06/87	⊗06/88	®06/75		
E54193	04/83⊂**56193**	05/58-06/87	⊗07/88	®02/81		
E54194	04/83⊂**56194**	07/58-06/93	⊗02/94	®01/77		
E54195	04/83⊂**56195**	07/58-05/87	⊗07/87	®01/78		⊠03/87-05/87
E54196	05/83⊂**56196**	06/58-07/89	⊗08/90	®*10/76*		
E54197	05/83⊂**56197**	07/58-05/92	⊗05/92	®*10/76*		
E54198	04/83⊂**56198**	06/58-05/87	⊗09/88	®01/77		⊠03/87-05/87
E54199	04/83⊂**56199**	07/58-06/87	⊗06/88	®11/77		
E54200	05/83⊂**56200**	08/58-05/86	⊗12/86	®11/77	08/84⇨**M**	
E54201	05/83⊂**56201**	08/58-11/90	⊗05/92	®01/78		
E54202	05/83⊂**56202**	08/58-02/90	⊗12/93	®06/76		
E54203	05/83⊂**56203**	08/58-06/93	⊗05/94	®01/77		
E54204	08/84⊂**56204**	08/58-03/92	⊗02/92	®05/75		⊠05/91-06/91
E54205	04/83⊂**56205**	07/58-08/91	⊗09/91	®06/75		
E54207	04/83⊂**56207**	09/58-06/91	℗	®02/81		
E54208	04/83⊂**56208**	08/58-03/93	℗	®05/76		
E54209	07/83⊂**56209**	08/58-05/91	⊗06/91	®06/75		
E54210	04/83⊂**56210**	08/58-09/91	⊗09/91	®01/78		

Class 108 BR Derby

Driving Trailer Composite Lavatory

DTCL

M54212-M54214

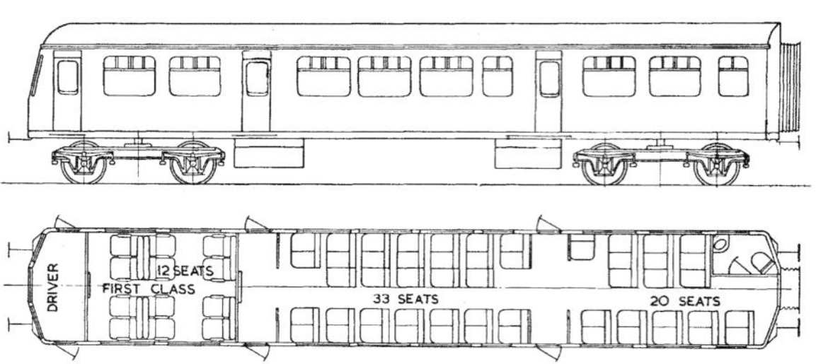

Coupling: ■ Blue square
Diagram: 640 DS310 ②DS207
Lot Number: 30410
Old class: 142
Body: 58' 1" × 9' 2"
Weight: 21t
Seats: 12 first, 53 second

M54212	08/83⊂**56212**	12/58-03/92	⊗03/92	® /82	
M54213	07/83⊂**56213**	12/58-10/89	⊗*04/90*	®01/83	
M54214	/83⊂**56214**	12/58-06/92	⊗10/92	®11/80	

Class 101 Metropolitan-Cammell

Driving Trailer Composite Lavatory

DTCL

E54218-E54220

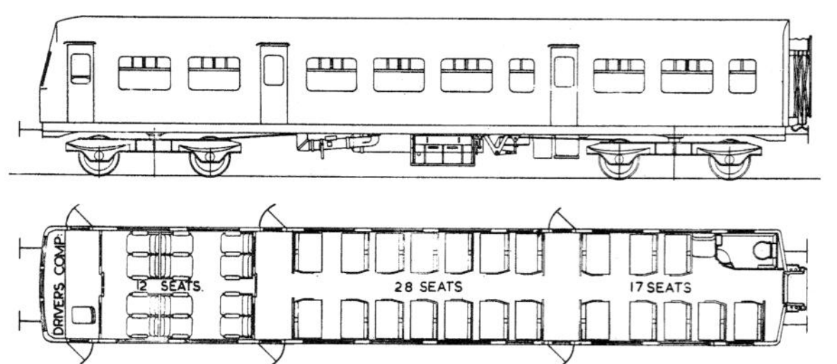

Coupling: ■ Blue square
Diagram: 629 DS303 ②DS210
Lot Number: 30340
Old class: 144
Body: 57' 6" × 9' 3"
Weight: 25t
Seats: 12 first, 45 second

E54218	04/83⊂**56218**	09/57-03/92	⊗06/92	® /81	
E54219	06/83⊂**56219**	09/57-07/89	⊗05/91	®07/78	
E54220	04/83⊂**56220**	09/57-09/94	⊗10/95	®07/76	⊠01/94-09/94

Class 108 BR Derby

Driving Trailer Composite Lavatory

DTCL

M54221-M54270

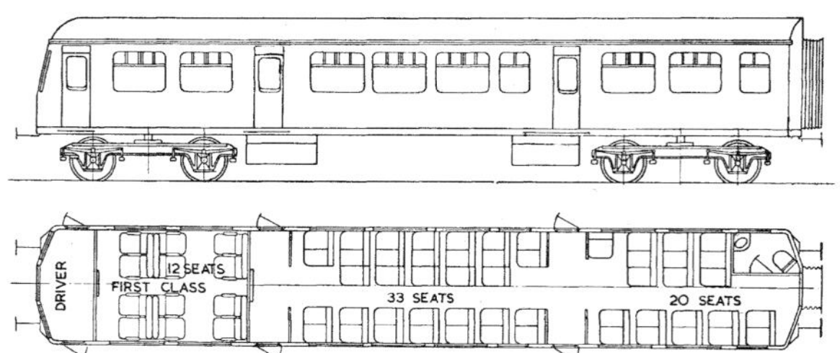

Coupling: ■ Blue square
Diagram: 640 DS310 ②DS207
Lot Number: 30466
Old class: 142
Body: 58' 1" × 9' 2"
Weight: 21t
Seats: 12 first, 53 second

M54221	06/83⊂**56221**	01/59-06/92	⊗06/92	®06/78	⊠11/90-12/90
M54222	/83⊂**56222**	01/59-07/91	⊗10/91	®03/80	
M54223	07/83⊂**56223**	01/59-06/93	Ⓟ	®02/81	
M54224	06/84⊂**56224**	01/59-09/92	Ⓟ	®08/81	
M54225	03/83⊂**56225**	01/59-05/91	⊗11/91	®06/78	
M54227	06/83⊂**56227**	01/59-01/92	⊗12/91	®10/83	
M54228	07/83⊂**56228**	01/59-04/93	⊗05/93	®10/77	
M54230	/83⊂**56230**	02/59-11/92	⊗11/92	®10/77	
M54231	/83⊂**56231**	02/59-05/91	⊗10/91	®01/78	
M54232	/83⊂**56232**	02/59-07/92	⊗07/92	®01/78	
M54234	03/83⊂**56234**	02/59-11/83	⊗02/84		
M54235	06/83⊂**56235**	02/59-06/92	⊗06/92		
M54236	06/83⊂**56236**	02/59-10/91	⊗10/91		
M54238	06/83⊂**56238**	03/59-09/92	⊗09/92		
M54239	06/83⊂**56239**	03/59-09/92	⊗09/92		
M54240	06/83⊂**56240**	03/59-01/92	⊗12/91		
M54241	06/83⊂**56241**	04/59-03/92	⊗03/92	®08/81	
M54242	06/83⊂**56242**	04/59-06/92	⊗06/92		
M54243	06/83⊂**56243**	04/59-12/91	⊗11/91		
M54244	06/83⊂**56244**	04/59-12/90	⊗03/92		
M54245	06/83⊂**56245**	04/59-04/91	⊗11/91		⊠*02/91*-04/91
M54246	06/83⊂**56246**	06/59-07/92	⊗09/92	®12/83	
M54247	04/83⊂**56247**	05/59-06/92	⊗06/92		
M54248	06/83⊂**56248**	05/59-07/91	⊗11/91		
M54249	06/83⊂**56249**	05/59-04/92	⊗06/92	®11/79	⊠12/90-01/91
M54250	06/83⊂**56250**	06/59-02/88	⊗01/90		
M54251	06/83⊂**56251**	05/59-04/91	⊗03/92		
M54252	06/83⊂**56252**	06/59-04/91	⊗12/91	®08/80	
M54253	/83⊂**56253**	07/59-10/92	⊗11/92	®05/77	
M54256	06/83⊂**56256**	07/59-06/93	⊗11/93		
M54257	06/84⊂**56257**	07/59-04/93	⊗08/94	®08/78	
M54258	/83⊂**56258**	08/59-05/91	⊗09/91	®11/77	
M54259	05/83⊂**56259**	08/59-12/91	⊗10/93	®11/78	
M54260	06/83⊂**56260**	08/59-06/92	⊗10/92	®09/76	
M54261	07/83⊂**56261**	08/59-10/91	⊗10/91	®07/78	
M54262	08/83⊂**56262**	08/59-06/92	⊗01/92	®07/78	
M54263	/83⊂**56263**	09/59-01/92	⊗12/91	®11/79	
M54264	/83⊂**56264**	09/59-04/92	⊗06/92	®01/78	
M54265	06/83⊂**56265**	09/59-07/91	⊗03/92		
M54266	/83⊂**56266**	10/59-07/91	⊗08/91	®06/78	
M54267	10/83⊂**56267**	10/59-06/92	⊗06/92		
M54268	/83⊂**56268**	10/59-01/92	⊗01/92	®01/78	
M54269	04/83⊂**56269**	10/59-01/92	⊗12/91	®04/82	
M54270	06/83⊂**56270**	10/59-06/93	Ⓟ		

Class 108 BR Derby

Driving Trailer Composite Lavatory

DTCL

M54271-M54279

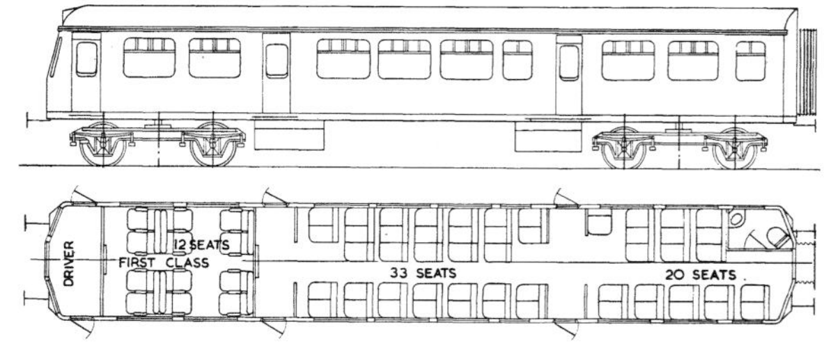

Coupling: ■ Blue square
Diagram: 646 DS310 ②DS207
Lot Number: 30499
Old class: 142
Body: 58' 1" × 9' 3"
Weight: 22t
Seats: 12 first, 53 second

M54271	08/83⊂**56271**	02/60-07/93	Ⓟ	
M54272	*/85*⊂**56272**	02/60-06/92	⊗06/92	
M54273	07/83⊂**56273**	02/60-02/92	⊗01/92	®09/79
M54274	06/83⊂**56274**	02/60-02/92	Ⓟ	®08/80
M54275	07/83⊂**56275**	02/60-07/92	⊗07/92	
M54276	10/83⊂**56276**	03/60-09/92	⊗09/92	®03/80
M54277	07/83⊂**56277**	03/60-01/91	⊗09/91	®03/79
M54278	08/83⊂**56278**	03/60-12/91	⊗11/91	®06/78
M54279	07/83⊂**56279**	03/60-08/93	Ⓟ	®02/79

Class 121 Pressed Steel

Driving Trailer Second
DTS
W54280-W54289

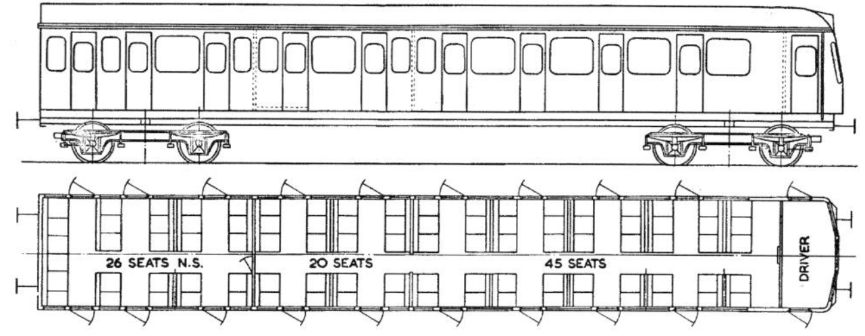

Coupling: ■ Blue square
Diagram: 513 DS201
Lot Number: 30519
Old class: 149
Body: 64' 0" × 9' 3"
Weight: 29t 7cwt
Seats: 95 second

W54280	04/83⊂**56280**	09/60-03/91	⊗11/92	®12/80		
W54281	08/83⊂**56281**	01/61-03/88	⊗11/90	®10/80	05/86⇨**M**	03/88⊃**ADB977615**
W54283	08/83⊂**56283**	01/61-04/91	⊗11/92	®05/79		
W54284	07/83⊂**56284**	02/61-02/92	⊗02/94	®02/81	05/86⇨**M**	
W54285	03/83⊂**56285**	02/61-12/86	Ⓟ	®08/80		12/86⊃**TDB977486**
W54286	05/83⊂**56286**	02/61-10/86	⊗10/96	®01/80		10/86⊃**TDB977466**
W54287	07/83⊂**56287**	02/61-04/92	Ⓟ	®01/80		
W54289	05/83⊂**56289**	02/61-12/92	Ⓟ	®09/79		

Class 101 Metropolitan-Cammell

Driving Trailer Composite Lavatory
DTCL
M54332-M54411

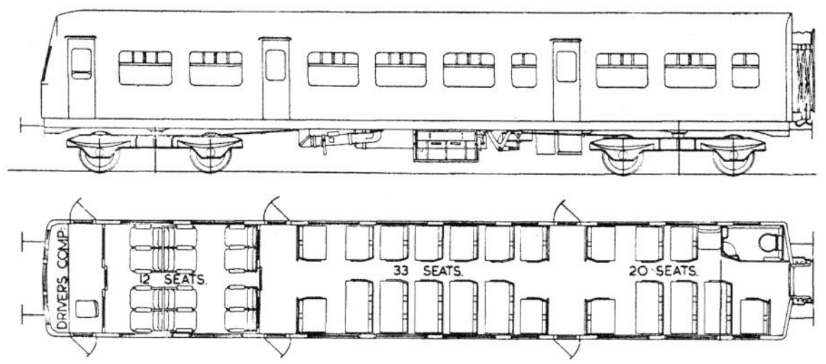

Coupling: ■ Blue square
Diagram: 630 DS302 ②DS206
Lot Number: 30468
Old class: 144
Body: 57' 6" × 9' 3"
Weight: 25t
Seats: 12 first, 53 second

M54332	03/83⊂**56332**	10/58-05/92	⊗10/92	®06/78	09/86⇨**E**	
M54333	08/83⊂**56333**	11/58-04/85	⊗07/86	®10/77		
M54334	07/83⊂**56334**	11/58-09/86	⊗08/88	®08/80	03/86⇨**E**	
M54335	03/83⊂**56335**	11/58-10/89	⊗07/90	®11/79		
M54336	07/83⊂**56336**	11/58-03/88	⊗10/88		03/86⇨**E**	
M54337	04/83⊂**56337**	11/58-09/86	⊗05/88	®01/80	11/85⇨**W** 02/86⇨**SC**	
M54339	04/83⊂**56339**	11/58-06/87	⊗06/89	®11/76	03/86⇨**E**	
M54340	04/83⊂**56340**	11/58-04/91	⊗05/91	®11/83	09/86⇨**E**	
M54341	11/83⊂**56341**	11/58-09/86	⊗12/95	®*10/76*	11/85⇨**W** 02/86⇨**SC**	
M54342	04/83⊂**56342**	11/58-12/90	Ⓟ	®05/76		12/90⊃**042222**
M54343	03/83⊂**56343**	11/58-07/00	Ⓟ	®08/78	09/86⇨**E**	
M54344	09/83⊂**56344**	11/58-02/87	⊗06/89	®03/77	06/86⇨**E**	
M54345	04/83⊂**56345**	12/58-10/89	⊗11/90	®11/83	09/86⇨**E**	
M54346	/83⊂**56346**	12/58-01/98	⊗01/98	®08/78	11/86⇨**E**	
M54347	04/83⊂**56347**	12/58-01/01	Ⓟ	®03/79	05/86⇨**E**	
M54348	04/83⊂**56348**	12/58-12/89	⊗07/90	®06/76		
M54349	04/83⊂**56349**	12/58-10/87	⊗09/88	®01/79	03/86⇨**E**	
M54350	03/83⊂**56350**	12/58-05/89	⊗03/04	®04/83		
M54351	04/83⊂**56351**	12/58-09/89	⊗09/90	®04/77		
M54352	09/83⊂**56352**	12/58-06/00	Ⓟ	® /82		
M54353	09/83⊂**56353**	01/59-09/86	⊗07/88		04/86⇨**E**	
M54354	04/83⊂**56354**	01/59-05/92	⊗01/94	® /82	09/86⇨**E**	
M54355	04/83⊂**56355**	01/59-10/89	⊗08/90			
M54356	04/83⊂**56356**	01/59-09/86	Ⓟ	® /82	11/85⇨**W** 02/86⇨**SC**	09/86⊃**6300**
M54357	04/83⊂**56357**	01/59-05/86	⊗07/86		11/85⇨**SC**	
M54358	04/83⊂**56358**	01/59-01/01	Ⓟ	® */84*	06/86⇨**E**	☒03/91-04/91
M54359	04/83⊂**56359**	01/59-07/87	⊗10/90	®08/78	06/86⇨**E**	
M54360	09/83⊂**56360**	01/59-09/86	⊗07/88		11/85⇨**W** 02/86⇨**SC**	
M54361	09/83⊂**56361**	01/59-05/86	⊗02/87			
E54362	04/83⊂**56362**	07/58-02/93	⊗02/93	®02/81		
E54363	06/83⊂**56363**	07/58-12/91	⊗04/92	®07/79		
E54364	07/83⊂**56364**	08/58-08/88	⊗10/88	®10/80		
E54365	05/83⊂**56365**	08/58-06/00	Ⓟ	® /82		
E54366	05/83⊂**56366**	08/58-06/87	⊗06/88	®02/81		
E54367	10/83⊂**56367**	08/58-09/89	⊗02/97	®11/79		
E54368	04/83⊂**56368**	09/58-05/93	⊗03/94	®11/79		
E54369	02/83⊂**56369**	09/58-07/92	⊗08/92	®01/77		
E54370	11/83⊂**56370**	09/58-04/90	⊗09/90	® /81		
E54371	09/83⊂**56371**	09/58-02/92	⊗05/93	®01/78		
E54372	09/83⊂**56372**	09/58-07/93	⊗03/94	®04/77		
E54373	09/83⊂**56373**	09/58-06/87	⊗03/88	®09/77		
E54374	04/83⊂**56374**	09/58-09/86	⊗02/88	®07/79		
E54375	05/83⊂**56375**	10/58-02/89	⊗03/89	® /81		
E54376	04/83⊂**56376**	10/58-06/87	⊗03/88	®02/81		
E54377	*/84*⊂**56377**	10/58-05/86	⊗05/88	®10/77		
E54378	06/83⊂**56378**	10/58-09/86	⊗05/87	®11/79		
E54379	04/83⊂**56379**	10/58-05/99	⊗05/99	® /82		
E54380	04/83⊂**56380**	10/58-05/93	⊗12/93	®08/83		
E54381	07/83⊂**56381**	10/58-09/92	⊗12/92	®11/78		☒05/89-07/89
E54382	11/83⊂**56382**	05/58-09/92	⊗12/92	®01/77		
E54383	05/83⊂**56383**	05/58-06/87	⊗07/88	®04/77		
E54384	03/84⊂**56384**	05/58-09/86	⊗07/88	®11/79		
E54385	07/83⊂**56385**	05/58-04/93	⊗03/94	®01/77		
E54386	05/83⊂**56386**	05/58-09/86	⊗02/88	®11/79		
E54387	05/83⊂**56387**	05/58-10/92	⊗10/92	® /82		
E54388	11/83⊂**56388**	05/58-05/93	⊗12/93	® /81		
E54389	/83⊂**56389**	05/58-09/86	⊗02/89	®07/79		
E54390	05/83⊂**56390**	05/58-06/87	⊗07/88	®11/79		
E54391	04/83⊂**56391**	05/58-09/89	⊗11/90	® /82		
E54392	06/83⊂**56392**	05/58-06/87	⊗07/88	®11/78		☒09/86-11/86
E54393	02/83⊂**56393**	05/58-10/99	⊗09/06	® */83*		☒03/93-03/93
E54394	04/83⊂**56394**	05/58-03/87	⊗02/89	®01/77		
E54396	02/85⊂**56396**	06/58-10/93	⊗02/94	® /81		
E54397	05/83⊂**56397**	06/58-09/86	⊗02/87	®07/78		
E54398	04/83⊂**56398**	06/58-03/89	⊗03/89	® /82		
E54399	04/83⊂**56399**	06/58-03/93	⊗05/95	®06/78		
E54400	05/83⊂**56400**	06/58-07/86	⊗02/87	®02/81		
E54401	08/83⊂**56401**	06/58-05/89	⊗02/92	®07/76		
E54402	09/83⊂**56402**	06/58-10/93	⊗02/94	®04/77		
E54403	04/83⊂**56403**	06/58-05/86	⊗07/86	®02/81	03/85⇨**M** 11/85⇨**SC**	
E54404	04/83⊂**56404**	07/58-03/88	⊗02/89	®11/79		
E54405	04/83⊂**56405**	07/58-09/92	⊗02/93	®10/82		
E54406	04/83⊂**56406**	07/58-03/88	⊗10/88	®02/81		
E54407	10/83⊂**56407**	07/58-09/86	⊗02/89	®04/79		
E54408	05/83⊂**56408**	07/58-06/01	Ⓟ	®07/78		
E54409	04/83⊂**56409**	07/58-06/87	⊗02/89	®11/79		
E54410	02/83⊂**56410**	07/58-07/86	⊗10/86	®10/80		
M54411	04/83⊂**56411**	07/58-03/87	⊗04/87			

Class 105 Cravens

Driving Trailer Composite Lavatory
DTCL
E54413-E54458

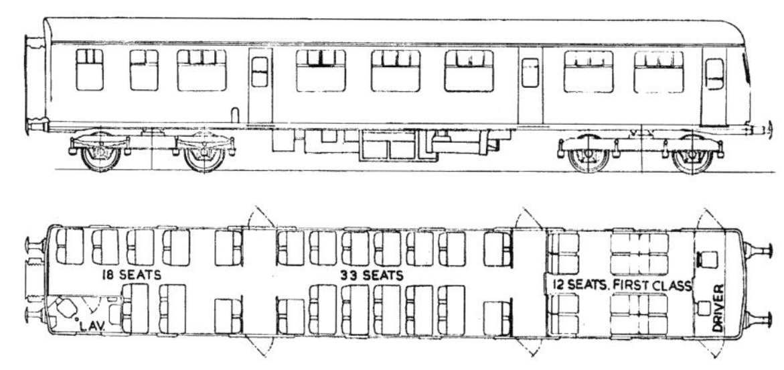

Coupling: ■ Blue square
Diagram: 533 DS308 ②DS208
Lot Number: 30470
Old class: 141
Body: 57' 6" × 9' 2"
Weight: 24t
Seats: 12 first, 51 second

E54413	05/84⊂**56413**	05/58-05/84	⊗10/84	
E54415	04/83⊂**56415**	06/58-06/83	⊗01/84	
E54416	04/83⊂**56416**	06/58-09/86	⊗07/88	
E54417	03/83⊂**56417**	06/58-09/86	⊗01/87	06/86⇨**SC**

E54419	03/84⊂**56419**	06/58-10/85	⊗01/86		
E54420	04/83⊂**56420**	06/58-05/87	⊗10/87		
E54421	04/83⊂**56421**	07/58-02/87	⊗10/87		
E54422	06/83⊂**56422**	07/58-09/86	⊗09/86	06/86⇨**SC**	
E54423	04/83⊂**56423**	07/58-07/86	⊗07/88		
E54424	/83⊂**56424**	07/58-11/83	⊗09/84		
E54426	05/85⊂**56426**	07/58-05/85	⊗08/85		
E54429	01/85⊂**56429**	08/58-10/86	⊗10/87		
E54431	/83⊂**56431**	09/58-09/84	⊗12/84		
E54433	05/83⊂**56433**	09/58-02/86	⊗12/86		
E54434	06/84⊂**56434**	09/58-08/86	⊗09/86		
E54435	*/84*⊂**56435**	09/58-05/84	⊗10/84		
E54436	08/83⊂**56436**	09/58-09/86	⊗08/88		⊠07/86-08/86
E54438	*/84*⊂**56438**	09/58-05/83	⊗09/84		
E54439	11/84⊂**56439**	10/58-10/86	⊗11/87		
E54440	05/84⊂**56440**	10/58-09/86	⊗12/88		09/86➲**TDB977454**
E54442	06/83⊂**56442**	10/58-10/86	⊗10/87		
E54443	*/85*⊂**56443**	10/58-06/86	⊗01/89		
E54446	07/83⊂**56446**	11/58-10/84	⊗11/84		
E54447	03/83⊂**56447**	11/58-09/86	⊗09/86	06/86⇨**SC**	
E54449	04/83⊂**56449**	11/58-07/85	⊗05/86		
E54450	05/83⊂**56450**	12/58-03/85	⊗05/85		
M54453	10/83⊂**56453**	12/58-10/84	⊗07/84		
E54454	06/83⊂**56454**	12/58-09/86	⊗07/88		
E54455	04/83⊂**56455**	01/59-07/86	⊗07/88		
E54458	01/85⊂**56458**	01/59-09/86	⊗01/89		

Class 105 Cravens
Driving Trailer Composite Lavatory
DTCL
E54463-E54472

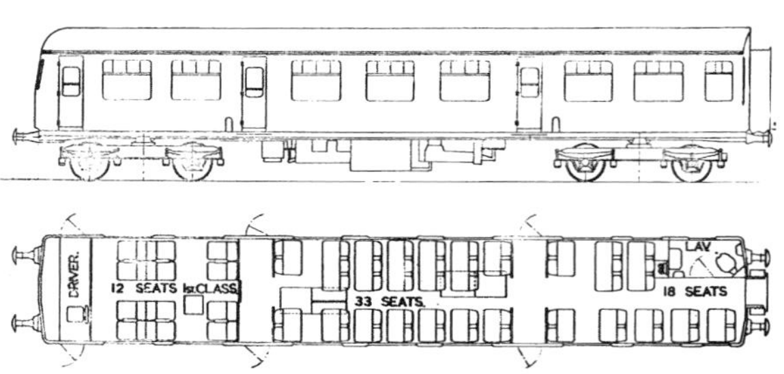

Coupling: ■ Blue square
Diagram: 549 DS309 ②DS209
Lot Number: 30504
Old class: 141
Body: 57' 6" × 9' 3"
Weight: 23t
Seats: 12 first, 51 second

E54463	*/85*⊂**56463**	02/59-07/86	⊗01/87	
E54467	04/83⊂**56467**	03/59-09/86	⊗09/86	06/86⇨**SC**
E54468	05/85⊂**56468**	03/59-10/86	⊗08/88	
E54470	02/83⊂**56470**	03/59-05/84	⊗10/84	
E54472	/83⊂**56472**	04/59-06/86	⊗07/87	

Class 108 BR Derby
Driving Trailer Composite Lavatory
DTCL
M54484-M54504

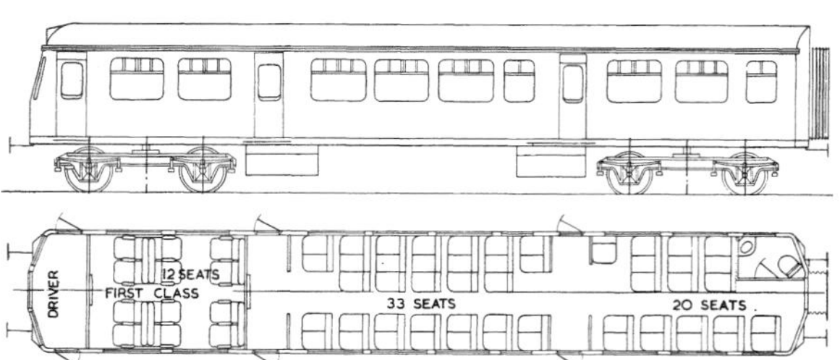

Coupling: ■ Blue square
Diagram: 646 DS311 ②DS207
Lot Number: 30602
Old class: 142
Body: 58' 1" × 9' 3"
Weight: 22t
Seats: 12 first, 53 second

M54484	04/83⊂**56484**	03/60-10/92	Ⓟ	®04/80
M54485	/83⊂**56485**	03/60-06/92	⊗06/92	®12/76
M54486	/83⊂**56486**	03/60-04/90	⊗02/93	®11/76
M54487	*/84*⊂**56487**	03/60-05/91	⊗09/91	®06/77
M54488	/83⊂**56488**	04/60-02/92	⊗01/92	®01/79
M54489	/83⊂**56489**	04/60-05/91	⊗10/91	®01/78
M54490	/83⊂**56490**	04/60-02/93	Ⓟ	®10/77
M54491	06/83⊂**56491**	04/60-12/92	Ⓟ	®03/78
M54492	/83⊂**56492**	04/60-05/91	Ⓟ	®03/80
M54493	08/83⊂**56493**	04/60-12/91	⊗08/94	
M54494	03/83⊂**56494**	04/60-05/91	⊗07/91	®08/78
M54495	07/83⊂**56495**	05/60-10/93	Ⓟ	®04/82
M54496	08/83⊂**56496**	05/60-02/92	⊗01/92	®09/81
M54497	06/83⊂**56497**	05/60-06/91	⊗12/91	® /81
M54498	07/83⊂**56498**	05/60-07/91	⊗11/91	®11/79
M54499	10/83⊂**56499**	06/60-09/92	⊗11/93	®11/79
M54500	08/83⊂**56500**	06/60-09/92	⊗11/93	®04/82
M54501	07/83⊂**56501**	07/60-07/91	⊗11/91	®10/76
M54502	04/83⊂**56502**	06/60-08/85	⊗05/86	®01/78
M54503	05/83⊂**56503**	07/60-06/92	⊗06/92	®05/83
M54504	/83⊂**56504**	07/60-02/93	Ⓟ	

Class 114/1 BR Derby
Driving Trailer Parcels Van
DTLV
54900-54904

Coupling: ■ Blue square
Diagram: DS502
Lot Number: 30210
Body: 64' 6" × 9' 3"
Weight: 31t

54900	01/88⊂**55933**	01/88-11/90	⊗04/91	
54901	01/88⊂**54016**	01/88-11/90	⊗04/91	
54902	01/88⊂**55932**	01/88-11/90	⊗04/91	
54903	07/89⊂**54009**	07/89-11/90	⊗04/91	
54904	07/89⊂**54015**	07/89-11/90	Ⓟ	03/92➲**TDB977776**

Class 122 Gloucester RC&W
Driving Motor Brake Second
DMBS
W55000-W55019

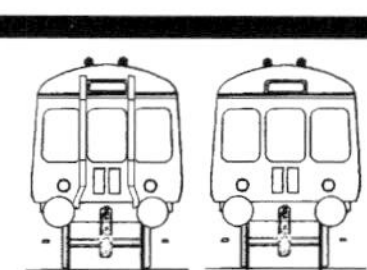

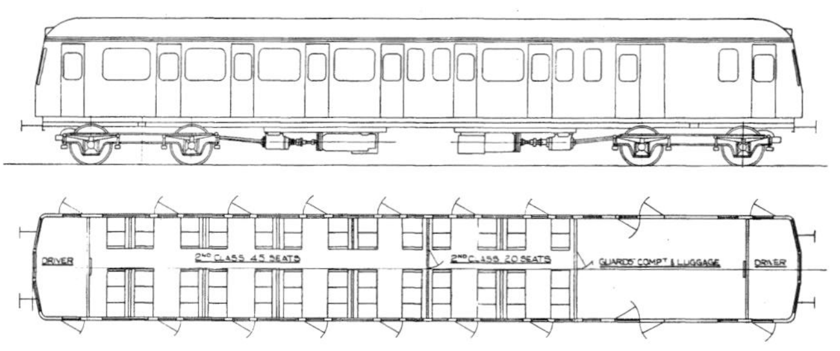

Coupling: ■ Blue square
Diagram: 539 DQ222 131 DX505
Lot Number: 30419
Old class: 122
Engines: Two BUT (AEC) 6-cyl horizontal type of 150 bhp.
Transmission: Mechanical. Standard
Body: 64' 6" × 9' 3"
Weight: 36t
Seats: 65 second

W55000	05/58-01/94	Ⓟ	®10/80	01/67⇨**SC** 08/84⇨**M**
W55001	05/58-06/69	Ⓟ		06/69➲**DB975023**
W55002	05/58-12/86	⊗01/87		01/63⇨**M** 06/68⇨**SC** 08/84⇨**M**
W55003	05/58-09/93	Ⓟ		01/63⇨**M** 09/85⇨Parcels
W55004	05/58-10/90	⊗11/90		01/63⇨**M**
W55005	05/58-10/92	Ⓟ		01/63⇨**M** 06/68⇨**SC** 03/81⇨**M**
W55006	05/58-09/93	Ⓟ		01/63⇨**M**
W55007	05/58-12/83	⊗06/91	®08/78	01/63⇨**M** 06/68⇨**SC** 12/83➲**TDB977223**
W55008	05/58-07/72	⊗12/84		01/63⇨**M** 04/72⇨*E* 05/74➲**DB975309**
W55009	05/58-09/93	Ⓟ		01/63⇨**M**

W55010	05/58-07/72	⊗08/84	01/63⇨**M**	04/72⇨*E*	
					07/74⊃**DB975310**
W55011	05/58-10/90	⊗11/90	04/68⇨**SC**	08/84⇨**M**	
W55012	05/58-*04/04*	Ⓟ	01/63⇨**M**		*04/04⊃977941*
W55013	05/58-12/80	⊗03/82	04/68⇨**SC**		
		09/71⇨Class 131 Parcels			12/80⊃**TDB975998**
W55014	05/58-10/80	⊗10/88	04/68⇨**SC**		10/80⇨*E*
		09/71⇨Class 131 Parcels			10/80⊃**TDB975994**
W55015	07/58-09/83	⊗07/90	04/68⇨**SC**		
		09/71⇨Class 131 Parcels			09/83⊃**TDB977177**
W55016	07/58-11/75	⊗07/93			11/75⊃**TDB975540**
W55017	07/58-06/72	⊗02/89	07/68⇨**M**		06/72⊃**DB975227**
W55018	07/58-07/76	⊗03/79	01/63⇨**M**	08/70⇨**W**	
W55019	07/58-11/69		07/68⇨**M**		11/69⊃**DB975042**

Class 121 Pressed Steel
Driving Motor Brake Second
DMBS
W55020-W55035

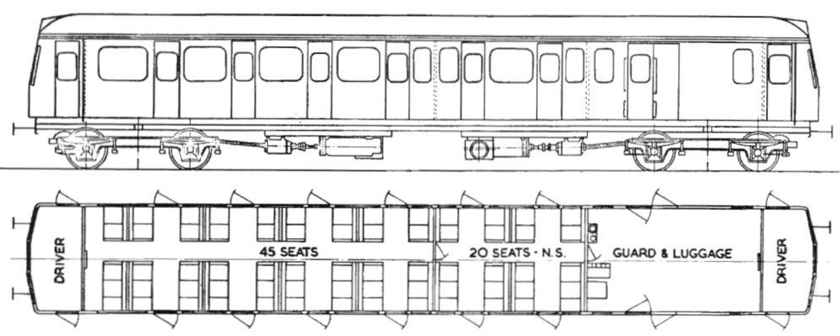

Coupling:	■ Blue square
Diagram:	512 DQ221
Lot Number:	30518
Old class:	121
Engines:	Two BUT (AEC) 6-cyl horizontal type of 150 bhp.
Transmission:	Mechanical. Standard
Body:	64' 6" × 9' 3"
Weight:	37t 8cwt
Seats:	65 second

55029 was named "Marston Vale" in 1998.

W55020		09/60-01/92		®08/80		01/92⊃**ADB977722**
55020	⊂**ADB977722**	09/02-				☜
W55021		10/60-01/92		®09/80		11/91⊃**ADB977723**
W55022		10/60-06/93		®01/80		09/93⊃**DB977873**
W55023		10/60-02/97	Ⓟ	®10/80		
W55024		10/60-09/93		® /81		09/93⊃**ADB977858**
W55025		10/60-09/93		®02/81		09/93⊃**ADB977859**
W55026		10/60-09/92	Ⓟ⊗04/09	® /81		10/92⊃**TDB977824**
W55027		10/60-12/02		®12/80		12/02⊃**977975**
W55028		12/60-09/93	Ⓟ	®11/79		09/93⊃**ADB977860**
W55029		12/60-02/02		®01/80		02/02⊃**977968**
W55030		12/60-09/93		®10/80		09/93⊃**ADB977866**
W55031		12/60-12/02		®08/80		12/02⊃**977976**
W55032		12/60-12/92	Ⓟ	®09/81	05/86⇨**M**	12/92⊃**ADB977842**
55032	⊂**ADB977842**	04/06-				☜
W55033		12/60-09/92	Ⓟ	®08/80	05/86⇨**M**	10/92⊃**TDB977826**
W55034		01/61-09/92	Ⓟ	®03/79	05/86⇨**M**	10/92⊃**DB977828**
W55035		02/61-07/78	⊗04/92			07/78⊃**TDB975659**

Class 114/1 BR Derby
Driving Motor Parcels Van
DMLV
55928-55933

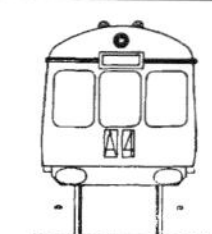

Coupling:	■ Blue square
Diagram:	DQ502
Lot Number:	30209
Engines:	Two BUT (Leyland Albion) 6-cyl horizontal type of 230 bhp. p Several were fitted with a TL11 Pacer type engine
Transmission:	Mechanical. Standard
Body:	64' 6" × 9' 3"
Weight:	37t 10cwt

54036 and 54034 were at first numbered in this series until it was realised that as they were trailers they should be numbered in a separate series.

55928	07/89⊂**53018**	07/89-11/90	⊗04/91	p	
55929	07/89⊂**53015**	07/89-11/90	Ⓟ	p	03/92⊃**TDB977775**
55930	08/87⊂**53010**	08/87-11/90	⊗04/91		
55931	01/88⊂**53040**	01/88-11/90	⊗04/91		
55932	01/88⊂**54036**	01/88-01/88	⊗04/91		01/88⊃**54902**
55932	01/88⊂**53032**	01/88-11/90	⊗04/91	p	*2nd to carry this number*
55933	01/88⊂**54034**	01/88-01/88	⊗04/91		01/88⊃**54900**

Class 120 BR Swindon
Driving Motor Parcels Van
DMLV
55934-55940

Coupling:	■ Blue square
Diagram:	
Lot Number:	30335 30515
Engines:	Two BUT (AEC) 6-cyl horizontal type of 150 bhp.
Transmission:	Mechanical. Standard
Body:	64' 6" × 9' 3"
Weight:	36t 7cwt

55934	04/87⊂**51573**	04/87-05/87	⊗07/88
55935	04/87⊂**51576**	04/87-05/87	⊗06/87
55936	03/87⊂**51579**	03/87-05/87	⊗06/87
55937	03/87⊂**51581**	03/87-05/87	⊗06/87
55938	03/87⊂**53726**	03/87-05/87	⊗06/87
55939	04/87⊂**51582**	04/87-05/87	⊗07/88
55940	04/87⊂**51585**	04/87-05/87	⊗06/87

Class 101 Metropolitan-Cammell
Driving Motor Brake Second
DMLV
55941-55943

Coupling:	■ Blue square
Diagram:	
Lot Number:	30500
Engines:	Two BUT (Leyland) 6-cyl horizontal type of 150 bhp.
Transmission:	Mechanical. Standard
Body:	57' 6" × 9' 3"
Weight:	32t

Allocated numbers not carried.

55941	⊂**51439**	*/87-07/89*	⊗04/90
55942	⊂**51441**	*/87-07/89*	⊗04/90
55943	⊂**51430**	*/87-07/89*	⊗04/90

Class 105 Cravens
Driving Motor Parcels Van
DMLV
55944-55947

Coupling:	■ Blue square
Diagram:	
Lot Numbers:	30280 30282 30469
Engines:	Two BUT (AEC) 6-cyl horizontal type of 150 bhp.
Transmission:	Mechanical. Standard
Body:	57' 6" × 9' 2"
Weight:	30t

55946 & 55947 did not carry their allocated numbers.

55944	03/87⊂**51293**	03/87-05/87	⊗12/91
55945	03/87⊂**53362**	03/87-09/87	⊗03/88
55946	⊂**53364**	*/87-03/89*	⊗04/90
55947	⊂**53373**	*/87-03/89*	⊗04/89

Class 120 BR Swindon
Driving Motor Parcels Van
DMLV
55948-55949

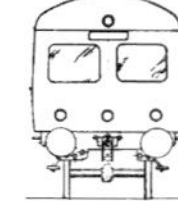

Coupling:	■ Blue square
Diagram:	
Lot Number:	30335
Engines:	Two BUT (AEC) 6-cyl horizontal type of 150 bhp.
Transmission:	Mechanical. Standard

Body: 64' 6" × 9' 3"
Weight: 36t

55948	04/87⊂**53725**	04/87-05/87	⊗02/89	
55949	04/87⊂**53729**	04/87-05/87	⊗06/87	

Class 127 BR Derby
Driving Motor Parcels Van
DMLV
55966-M55987

Coupling: ▲ Red triangle
Diagram: DX501
Lot Number: 30521
Engines: Two Rolls-Royce 8-cyl horizontal type of 238 bhp.
Transmission: Hydraulic. Torque converter
Body: 64' 0" × 9' 3"
Weight: 40t

M55968 and M55969 were at first numbered M55988 and M55989 until October 1985. Twenty-one vehicles were available for conversion, so to create an eleventh 2-car set M51591 from the National Railway Museum was used. This had previously been acquired for preservation as part of the National Collection and was painted green. M55967 was painted green to match it.

M55966	02/86⊂**51591**	02/86-05/89	Ⓟ	
M55967	02/86⊂**51610**	02/86-05/89	Ⓟ	
M55968	10/85⊂**55988**	10/85-05/89	⊗03/91	
M55969	10/85⊂**55989**	10/85-05/89	⊗03/91	
M55970	08/85⊂**51635**	08/85-05/89	⊗03/91	
M55971	08/85⊂**51597**	08/85-05/89	⊗03/91	
M55972	08/85⊂**51611**	08/85-05/89	⊗03/91	
M55973	08/85⊂**51640**	08/85-05/89	⊗03/91	
M55974	08/85⊂**51642**	08/85-11/86	⊗07/87	
M55975	06/85⊂**51615**	06/85-05/89	⊗03/91	
M55976	06/85⊂**51625**	06/85-05/89	Ⓟ	
M55977	05/85⊂**51603**	05/85-05/89	⊗03/91	
M55978	08/85⊂**51608**	08/85-05/89	⊗02/92	
M55979	08/85⊂**51600**	08/85-05/89	⊗02/92	
M55980	05/85⊂**51633**	05/85-05/89	⊗03/91	
M55981	05/85⊂**51612**	05/85-05/89	⊗06/91	
M55982	05/85⊂**51596**	05/85-05/89	⊗03/91	
M55983	08/85⊂**51624**	08/85-05/89	⊗03/91	
M55984	05/85⊂**51639**	05/85-05/89	⊗03/91	
M55985	06/85⊂**51619**	06/85-05/89	⊗03/91	
M55986	06/85⊂**51627**	06/85-05/89	Ⓟ⊗04/94	
M55987	05/85⊂**51649**	05/85-05/89	⊗03/91	*2nd to carry this number*
M55988	08/85⊂**51637**	08/85-10/85	⊗03/91	*2nd to carry this number* 10/85⊃**55968**
M55989	08/85⊂**51606**	08/85-10/85	⊗03/91	*2nd to carry this number* 10/85⊃**55969**

Class 128 Gloucester RC&W
Driving Motor Parcels Van
DMPMV
M55987-M55990

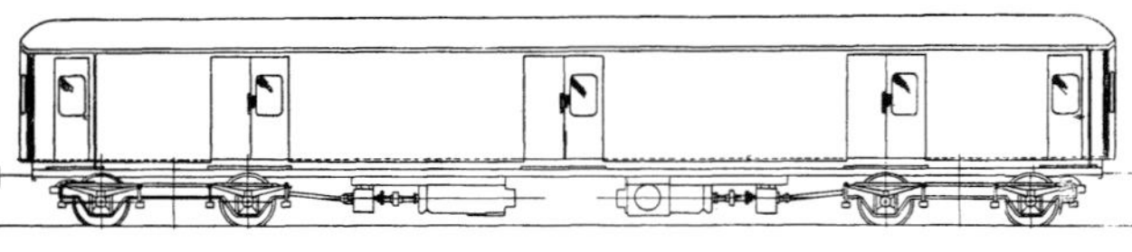

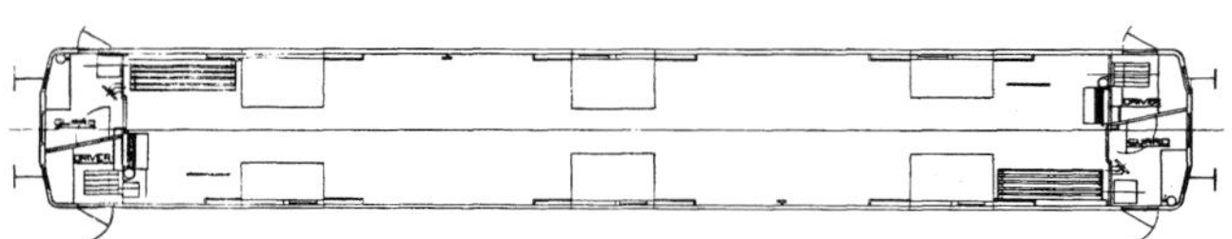

Coupling: ■ Blue square
Diagram: 644 DX502
Lot Number: 30552
Old class: 128
Engines: Two BUT (AEC) 6-cyl horizontal type of 238 bhp.
Transmission: Mechanical. Standard
Body: 64' 6" × 9' 3"
Weight: 40t

M55987	01/60-07/71	⊗07/73	02/70⇨**W**
M55988	01/60-10/80	⊗04/83	
M55989	01/60-09/82	⊗11/83	
M55990	01/60-04/82	⊗05/82	

Class 128 Gloucester RC&W
Driving Motor Parcels Van
DMPMV
W55991-W55996

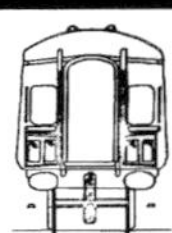

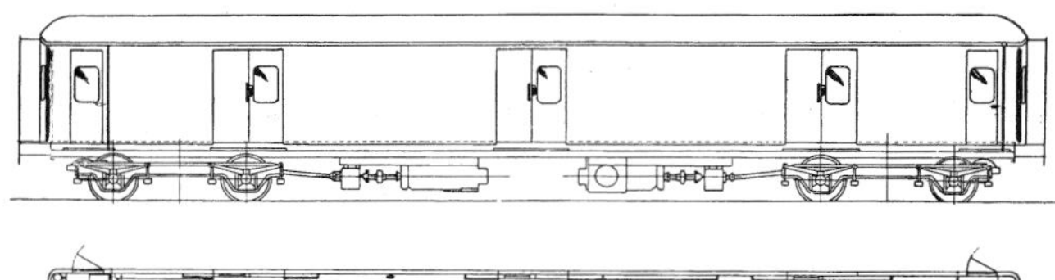

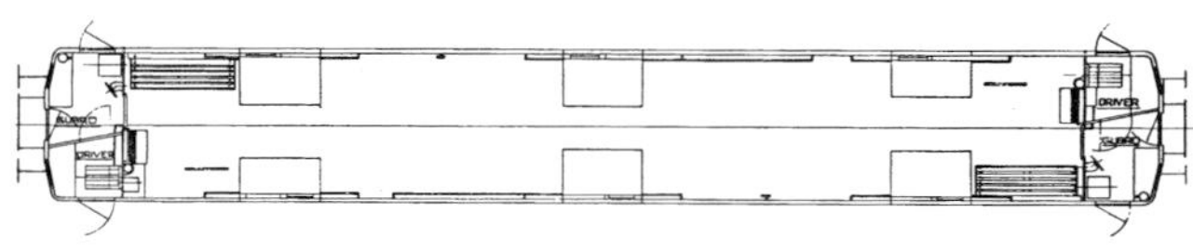

Coupling: ■ Blue square
Diagram: 643 DX501
Lot Number: 30551
Old class: 128
Engines: Two BUT (AEC) 6-cyl horizontal type of 238 bhp.
p Fitted with a TL11 Pacer type engine in 12/89
Transmission: Mechanical. Standard
Body: 64' 6" × 9' 3"
Weight: 41t

W55991	01/60-11/90	⊗04/91		
W55992	02/60-11/90	⊗04/91		
W55993	02/60-11/90	⊗04/91		01/63⇦**M**
W55994	03/60-11/90	⊗04/91		01/63⇦**M**
W55995	03/60-11/90	⊗04/91	p	01/63⇦**M**
W55996	04/60-02/79	⊗03/81		01/63⇦**M**

Class 129 Cravens
Driving Motor Parcels Van
DMPMV
M55997-M55999

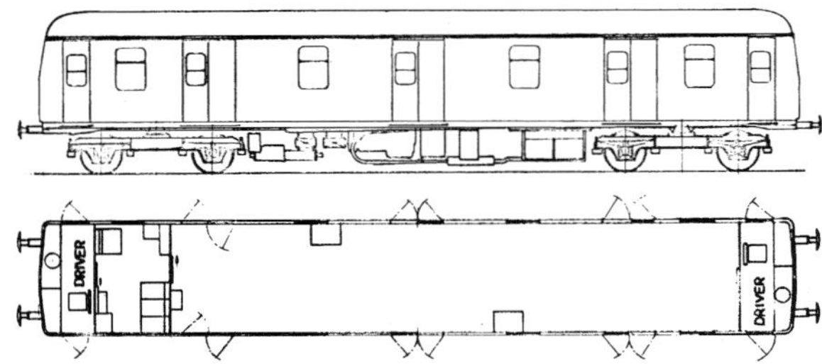

Coupling: ♦ Yellow diamond
Diagram: 531
Lot Number: 30418
Old class: 129
Engines: Two BUT (AEC) 6-cyl horizontal type of 150 bhp.
Transmission: Mechanical. Standard
Body: 57' 6" × 9' 3"
Weight: 30t

M55997	07/58-10/73	⊗05/86	04/75⊃**RDB975385**
M55998	07/58-12/72	⊗07/80	
M55999	08/58-10/73	⊗01/75	

Class 114 BR Derby

Driving Trailer Composite Lavatory

DTCL

E56000

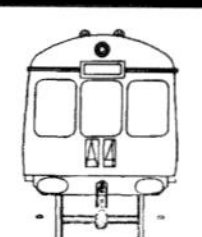

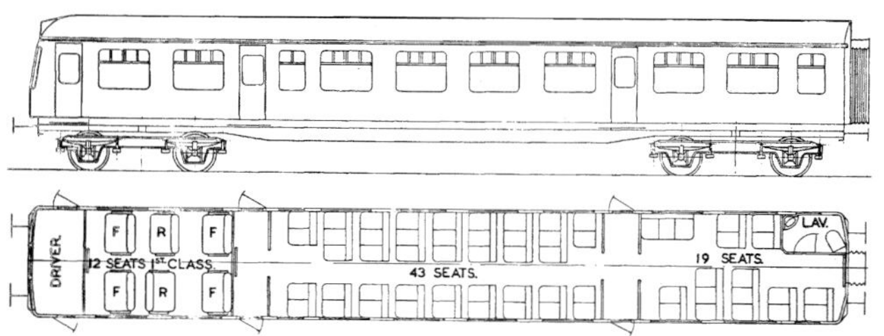

Coupling:	■ Blue square
Diagram:	641
Lot Number:	30342
Old class:	148
Body:	64' 6" × 9' 3"
Weight:	31t 3cwt
Seats:	12 first, 62 second

E56000	03/57-10/67	⊗10/72	

Class 114 BR Derby

Driving Trailer Composite Lavatory

DTCL

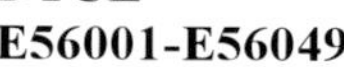

E56001-E56049

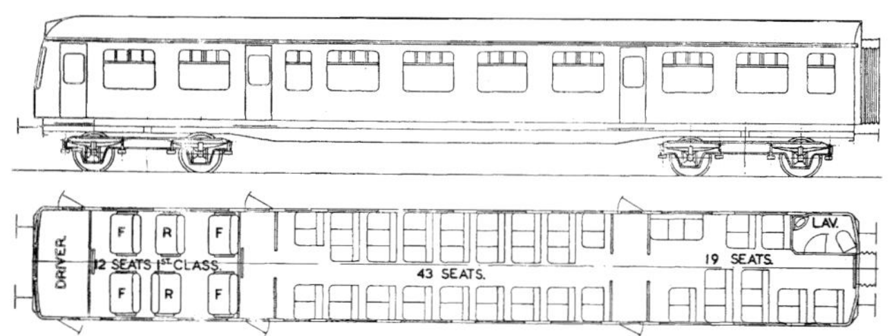

Coupling:	■ Blue square	
Diagram:	641	DS313
Lot Number:	30210	
Old class:	148	
Body:	64' 6" × 9' 3"	
Weight:	29t 10cwt	
Seats:	12 first, 62 second	

E56001	05/83➲**54001**	10/56-02/88	⊗04/88	®11/80		
E56002	07/83➲**54002**	11/56-06/88	⊗11/88	®09/80		
E56003	08/83➲**54003**	11/56-06/88	⊗11/88	®01/78		
E56004	/83➲**54004**	11/56-06/88	⊗12/88	®07/79		
E56005	04/83➲**54005**	11/56-01/88	⊗02/88	®06/78		
E56006	04/83➲**54006**	11/56-03/92	Ⓟ	® /81		
E56007	04/83➲**54007**	11/56-06/88	⊗12/88	®02/78		
E56008	03/83➲**54008**	11/56-05/89	⊗02/92	®02/78		
E56009	02/83➲**54009**	11/56-07/89	⊗04/91	®05/83		07/89➲**54903**
E56010	04/83➲**54010**	12/56-09/91	⊗11/91	®10/81		
E56011	06/83➲**54011**	11/56-05/89	⊗02/92	® /82		
E56012	06/83➲**54012**	11/56-10/91	⊗11/91	®11/78		
E56013	08/83➲**54013**	12/56-03/89	⊗06/91	® /82		
E56014	05/83➲**54014**	12/56-06/88	⊗12/88	®02/81		
E56015	06/83➲**54015**	02/57-07/89	Ⓟ	®07/78		07/89➲**54904**
E56016	02/83➲**54016**	12/56-01/88	⊗04/91	®01/78		01/88➲**54901**
E56017	/83➲**54017**	01/57-06/88	⊗01/89	®07/78		
E56018	04/83➲**54018**	01/57-06/88	⊗11/88	®08/77		
E56019	/84➲**54019**	01/57-03/89	⊗06/91	® /81		
E56020		01/57-05/70	⊗08/71			
E56021	04/83➲**54021**	01/57-06/88	⊗12/88	®11/79		
E56022	04/83➲**54022**	01/57-02/88	⊗04/88	®07/79		
E56023	06/83➲**54023**	01/57-06/88	⊗12/88	®07/79		
E56024	06/83➲**54024**	01/57-05/89	⊗02/91	® /81		
E56025	04/83➲**54025**	01/57-06/88	⊗12/88	®07/79		
E56026	04/83➲**54026**	01/57-11/89	⊗04/90	®11/78		
E56027	04/83➲**54027**	01/57-01/92	⊗07/93	®07/78		01/92➲**ADB977770**
E56028	06/83➲**54028**	01/57-05/90	⊗08/90	®11/78		
E56029	04/83➲**54029**	01/57-02/88	⊗04/88	®02/81		
E56030	06/83➲**54030**	01/57-02/87	⊗09/90	®11/79		
E56031		01/57-01/70	⊗07/70			
E56032	06/83➲**54032**	02/57-05/87	⊗04/88	®03/78		
E56033	04/83➲**54033**	02/57-09/88	⊗12/88	®07/79		☒09/86-04/87
E56034	04/83➲**54034**	02/57-01/88	⊗04/91	®07/80	01/88➲**55933**	01/88➲**54900**
E56035	04/83➲**54035**	03/57-05/87	⊗11/88	®03/80		
E56036	04/83➲**54036**	02/57-01/88	⊗04/91	®01/81	01/88➲**55932**	01/88➲**54902**
E56037	04/83➲**54037**	02/57-06/88	⊗01/89	® /81		
E56038	04/83➲**54038**	02/57-06/88	⊗12/88	®10/77		
E56039	/83➲**54039**	02/57-10/91	⊗02/92	® /80		
E56040	10/83➲**54040**	02/57-06/88	⊗12/88	®02/81		
E56041	04/83➲**54041**	03/57-05/90	⊗08/90	®01/78		
E56042	04/83➲**54042**	03/57-03/89	⊗04/89	®12/77		
E56043	04/83➲**54043**	03/57-10/91	⊗11/91	®04/78		
E56044	03/84➲**54044**	03/57-06/88	⊗12/88	®04/79		
E56045	06/83➲**54045**	03/57-06/88	⊗01/89	®03/79		
E56046		03/57-04/65	⊗04/65			
E56047	05/83➲**54047**	04/57-10/91	Ⓟ	® /82		
E56048		12/57-05/71	⊗06/73			
E56049	04/83➲**54049**	08/57-02/84	⊗12/84	®11/79		

Class 101 Metropolitan-Cammell

Driving Trailer Composite Lavatory

DTCL

E56050-E56061

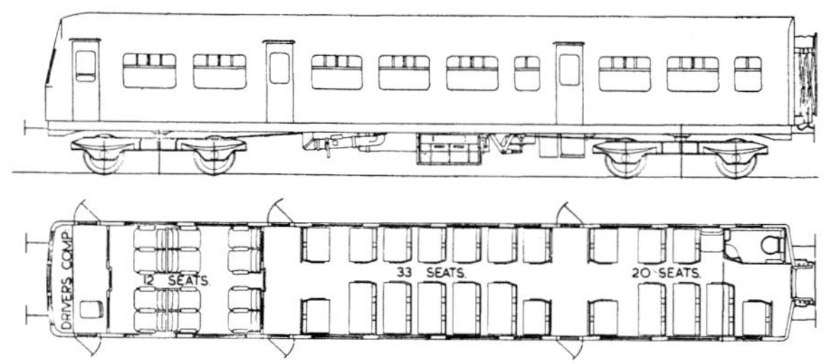

Coupling:	■ Blue square		
Diagram:	630	DS302	②DS206
Lot Number:	30260		
Old class:	144		
Body:	57' 6" × 9' 3"		
Weight:	25t		
Seats:	12 first, 53 second		

E56050	06/83➲**54050**	04/57-05/93	⊗12/95	®01/79	01/65⇨**NE**	01/68⇨**E**	
E56051	04/83➲**54051**	04/57-06/87	⊗06/88	®01/78	01/65⇨**NE**	01/68⇨**E**	
E56052	04/83➲**54052**	05/57-05/86	⊗12/86	®07/78	01/65⇨**NE**	01/68⇨**E**	
E56053	04/83➲**54053**	05/57-06/87	⊗10/88	®07/79	01/65⇨**NE**	01/68⇨**E**	
E56054	07/83➲**54054**	05/57-05/89	⊗04/91	® /81	01/65⇨**NE**	03/66⇨**SC**	05/68⇨**E**
E56055	04/83➲**54055**	05/57-06/00	Ⓟ	® /82	01/65⇨**NE**	04/66⇨**M**	
E56056	05/83➲**54056**	05/57-11/01	⊗07/06	®09/82	01/65⇨**NE**	01/68⇨**E**	
E56057	09/83➲**54057**	04/57-09/86	⊗07/88	®11/76	01/65⇨**NE**	01/68⇨**E**	
E56058	04/83➲**54058**	04/57-06/87	⊗02/89	®10/77	01/65⇨**NE**	04/66⇨**M**	
E56059	04/83➲**54059**	05/57-06/87	⊗01/89	®07/79	01/65⇨**NE**	01/68⇨**E**	
E56060	06/83➲**54060**	05/57-06/93	⊗12/93	®06/76	01/65⇨**NE**	04/66⇨**M**	
E56061	05/83➲**54061**	05/57-06/00	⊗01/07	®07/79	01/65⇨**NE**	01/68⇨**E**	

Class 101 Metropolitan-Cammell

Driving Trailer Composite Lavatory

DTCL

E56062-E56085

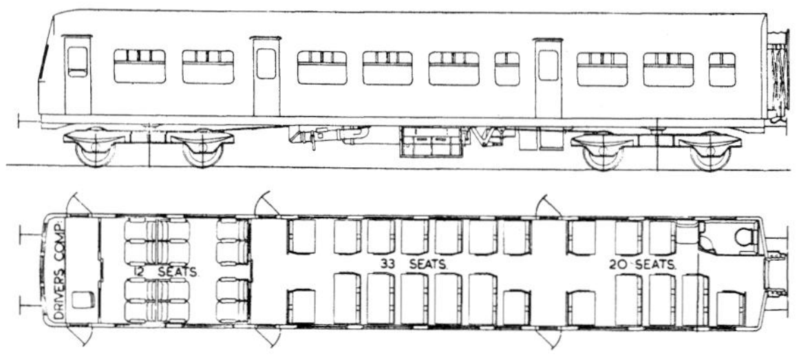

Coupling:	■ Blue square		
Diagram:	630	DS302	②DS206
Lot Number:	30262		
Old class:	144		
Body:	57' 6" × 9' 3"		

Weight: 25t
Seats: 12 first, 53 second

E56062	09/83➲**54062**	05/57-03/01	Ⓟ	®11/79	01/65⇨**NE**	01/68⇨**E**
						⊠09/90-06/91
E56063	04/83➲**54063**	05/57-10/87	⊗09/88	®*09/76*	01/65⇨**NE**	01/68⇨**E**
E56064	04/83➲**54064**	06/57-06/87	⊗01/88	®01/78	01/65⇨**NE**	01/68⇨**E**
E56065	03/83➲**54065**	06/57-12/92	⊗01/94	®02/81	01/65⇨**NE**	01/68⇨**E**
E56066	04/83➲**54066**	06/57-02/87	⊗01/89	®01/78	01/65⇨**NE**	01/68⇨**E**
E56067	05/83➲**54067**	07/57-06/87	⊗07/88	®04/77	01/65⇨**NE**	01/68⇨**E**
E56068	09/83➲**54068**	07/57-05/95	⊗06/95	®01/77	01/65⇨**NE**	01/68⇨**E**
E56069	05/83➲**54069**	07/57-03/88	⊗06/89	®07/79	01/65⇨**NE**	01/68⇨**E**
E56070	04/83➲**54070**	07/57-12/91	⊗04/93	®*10/76*	01/65⇨**NE**	01/68⇨**E**
						⊠11/90-12/90
E56071	10/83➲**54071**	07/57-05/89	⊗04/91	® /81	01/65⇨**NE**	01/68⇨**E**
E56072	02/83➲**54072**	07/57-09/86	⊗09/86	®02/81	01/65⇨**NE**	01/68⇨**E**
E56073	08/83➲**54073**	08/57-10/92	⊗01/94	®*10/76*	01/65⇨**NE**	01/68⇨**E**
E56074	04/83➲**54074**	06/57-02/88	⊗01/89	®02/81	01/65⇨**NE**	01/68⇨**E**
E56075	04/83➲**54075**	06/57-05/89	⊗10/90	®*10/76*	01/65⇨**NE**	01/68⇨**E**
E56076	05/83➲**54076**	06/57-02/87	⊗01/89	®11/79	01/65⇨**NE**	01/68⇨**E**
E56077	*/84*➲**54077**	06/57-02/88	⊗10/88	®07/78	01/65⇨**NE**	01/68⇨**E**
E56078	*/84*➲**54078**	07/57-08/88	⊗04/89	®11/79	01/65⇨**NE**	01/68⇨**E**
E56079	05/83➲**54079**	07/57-09/86	⊗05/87	®07/79	01/65⇨**NE**	01/68⇨**E**
E56080	07/83➲**54080**	07/57-10/89	⊗08/90	®02/81	01/65⇨**NE**	04/66⇨**M**
E56081	09/83➲**54081**	07/57-10/93	⊗02/94	® /82	01/65⇨**NE**	01/68⇨**E**
						⊠07/93-08/93
E56082	05/83➲**54082**	08/57-06/87	⊗06/88	®11/79	01/65⇨**NE**	01/68⇨**E**
E56083	05/83➲**54083**	08/57-03/88	⊗03/88	®11/79	01/65⇨**NE**	01/68⇨**E**
E56084	04/83➲**54084**	08/57-07/86	⊗02/93	®11/79	01/65⇨**NE**	01/68⇨**E**
E56085	*/83*➲**54085**	09/57-01/02	⊗12/03	® /81	01/65⇨**NE**	01/68⇨**E**

Class 101 Metropolitan-Cammell
Driving Trailer Composite Lavatory
DTCL
E56086-E56089

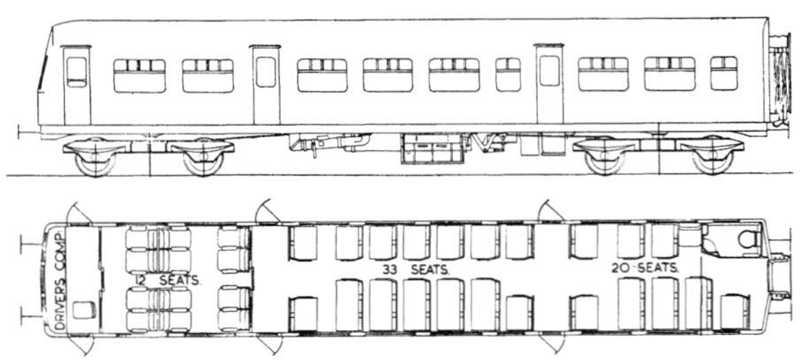

Coupling: ■ Blue square
Diagram: 630 DS302 ②DS206
Lot Number: 30272
Old class: 144
Body: 57' 6" × 9' 3"
Weight: 25t
Seats: 12 first, 53 second

E56086	02/83➲**54086**	12/57-07/86	⊗10/88	®11/79	01/65⇨**NE**	01/68⇨**E**
E56087	10/83➲**54087**	12/57-09/86	⊗05/87	®07/78	01/65⇨**NE**	01/68⇨**E**
E56088	05/84➲**54088**	12/57-06/87	⊗*09/90*	®04/77	01/65⇨**NE**	01/68⇨**E**
E56089	*/85*➲**54089**	12/57-03/88	⊗03/88	®11/79	01/65⇨**NE**	01/68⇨**E**

Class 111 Metropolitan-Cammell
Driving Trailer Composite Lavatory
DTCL
M56090-M56093

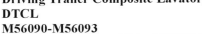

Coupling: ■ Blue square
Diagram: 628 DS312
Lot Number: 30337
Old class: 147
Body: 57' 6" × 9' 3"
Weight: 25t
Seats: 12 first, 53 second

M56090	04/83➲**54090**	04/57-08/88	⊗04/89	®08/77	04/66⇨**NE**	01/68⇨**E**
M56091	02/83➲**54091**	04/57-10/00	⊗12/03	®05/83	04/66⇨**NE**	01/68⇨**E**
						⊠09/89-09/90
M56092	05/85➲**54092**	04/57-06/87	⊗06/88	®01/78	04/66⇨**NE**	01/68⇨**E**
M56093	04/83➲**54093**	04/57-07/86	⊗01/89	®02/81	04/66⇨**NE**	01/68⇨**E**

Class 100 Gloucester RC&W
Driving Trailer Composite Lavatory
DTCL
SC56094-M56113

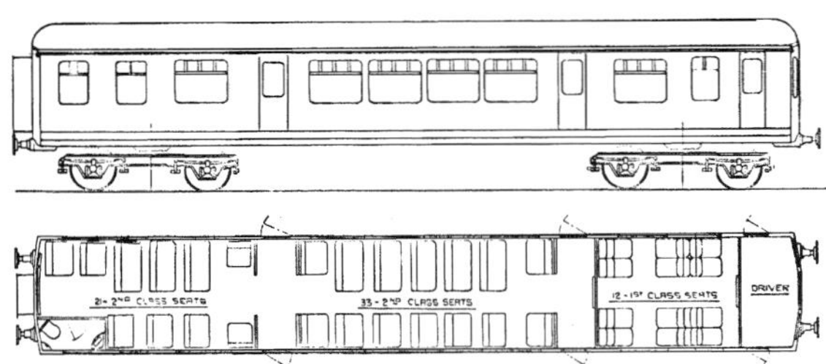

Coupling: ■ Blue square
Diagram: 537 DS203
Lot Number: 30279
Old class: 143
Body: 57' 6" × 9' 3"
Weight: 25t
Seats: 12 first, 54 second

SC56094	05/57-10/72	⊗06/80	05/68⇨**E**		
SC56095	05/57-10/72	⊗04/74			
SC56096	06/57-02/72	⊗04/73	05/68⇨**E**		
SC56097	06/57-10/72	Ⓟ			
SC56098	07/57-02/71	⊗07/73	05/68⇨**E**		
SC56099	07/57-02/72	Ⓟ⊗05/91	06/67⇨**NE**	01/68⇨**E**	
SC56100	07/57-02/78	⊗03/81	05/68⇨**E**		
SC56101	07/57-10/72	⊗07/93	05/68⇨**E**		03/76➲**DB975539**
SC56102	08/57-10/72	⊗12/73			
M56103	08/57-12/82	⊗04/84			
M56104	09/57-07/83	⊗005/84			
M56105	09/57-07/83	⊗05/84			
M56106	09/57-07/83	⊗ /02			07/83➲**TDB977191**
M56107	09/57-05/81	⊗11/82			
M56108	09/57-07/83	⊗06/84			
M56109	09/57-07/83	⊗04/84			
M56110	09/57-07/80	⊗07/87			
M56111	10/57-07/83	⊗07/85			07/83➲**TDB977196**
M56112	10/57-06/78	⊗11/79			
M56113	10/57-07/83	⊗12/84			

Class 106⇨105 Cravens
Driving Trailer Composite Lavatory
DTCL
E56114-E56127

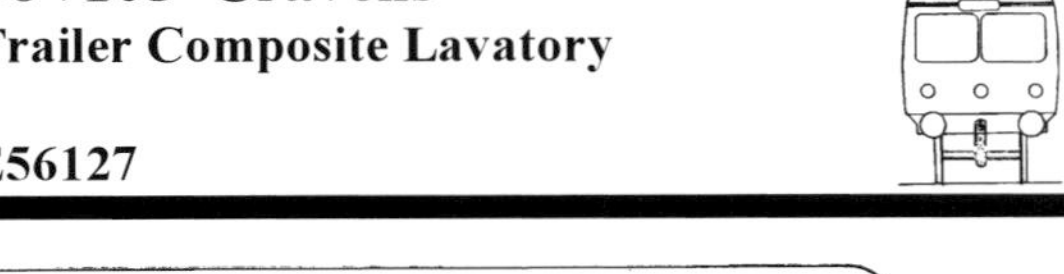

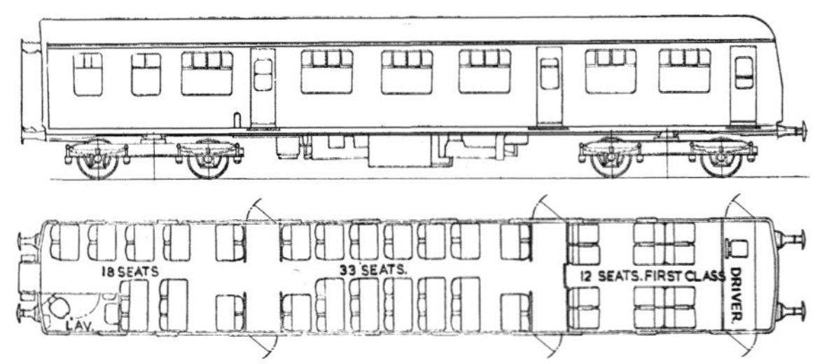

Coupling: ■ Blue square
Diagram: 526 DS307 ②DS204
Lot Number: 30281
Old class: 141
Body: 57' 6" × 9' 2"
Weight: 23t
Seats: 12 first, 51 second

E56114	06/83➲**54114**	08/56-05/86	⊗02/89	01/65⇨**NE**	01/68⇨**E**	
E56115	05/84➲**54115**	10/56-05/87	⊗11/87	01/65⇨**NE**	09/65⇨**E**	
E56116		11/56-11/82	⊗04/84	01/65⇨**NE**	01/68⇨**E**	10/80⇨**M**
E56117		11/56-01/72	⊗11/72	01/65⇨**NE**	09/65⇨**E**	
E56118		12/56-12/82	⊗02/84	01/65⇨**NE**	01/68⇨**E**	02/77⇨**M**
E56119	/85➲**54119**	12/56-04/87	⊗11/87	01/65⇨**NE**	01/68⇨**E**	
E56120		01/57-03/82	⊗01/91	01/65⇨**NE**	01/68⇨**E**	01/77⇨**M**
E56121		01/57-05/81	Ⓟ	01/65⇨**NE**	09/65⇨**E**	
E56122	05/83➲**54122**	01/57-10/88	⊗02/89	01/65⇨**NE**	01/68⇨**E**	
E56123		01/57-09/83	⊗10/83	01/65⇨**NE**	01/68⇨**E**	
E56124		02/57-04/81	⊗08/81	01/65⇨**NE**	01/68⇨**E**	
E56125	/83➲**54125**	02/57-09/86	⊗07/88	01/65⇨**NE**	01/68⇨**E**	
E56126	03/83➲**54126**	02/57-06/86	⊗02/89	01/65⇨**NE**	01/68⇨**E**	
E56127		02/57-12/82	⊗11/83	01/65⇨**NE**	01/68⇨**E**	02/77⇨**M**

Class 105 Cravens
Driving Trailer Composite Lavatory
DTCL
E56128-E56144

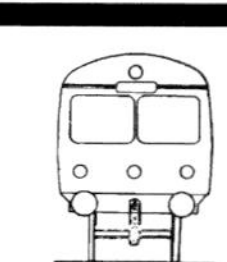

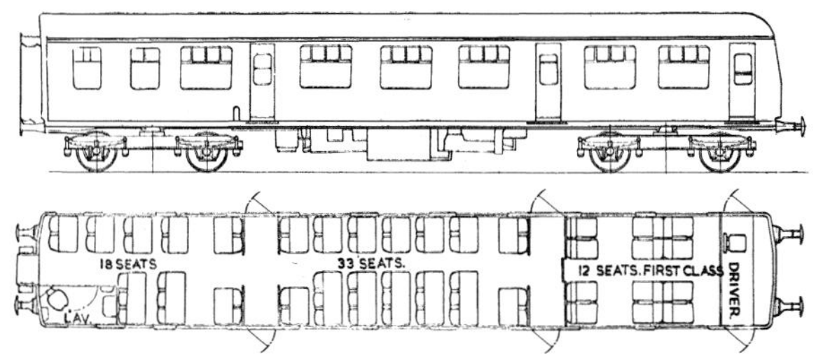

Coupling: ■ Blue square
Diagram: 526 DS307 ②DS204
Lot Number: 30283
Old class: 141
Body: 57' 6" × 9' 2"
Weight: 23t
Seats: 12 first, 51 second

E56128		02/57-07/78	⊗05/81	01/65⇨**NE**	01/68⇨**E**	
E56129		03/57-07/82	⊗04/87	01/65⇨**NE**	01/68⇨**E** 07/82➲**ADB977114**	03/77⇨**M**
E56130	05/84➲**54130**	03/57-05/84	⊗10/84	01/65⇨**NE**	01/68⇨**E**	
E56131	02/83➲**54131**	03/57-06/86	⊗07/88			
E56132	04/83➲**54132**	03/57-06/86	⊗02/87			
E56133	05/83➲**54133**	04/57-05/87	⊗11/87	01/65⇨**NE**	01/68⇨**E**	
E56134	05/84➲**54134**	04/57-09/85	⊗05/86	01/65⇨**NE**	01/68⇨**E**	
E56135		04/57-04/84	⊗06/85	01/65⇨**NE**	01/68⇨**E**	
E56136	02/83➲**54136**	04/57-09/86	⊗01/87	01/65⇨**NE** 12/82⇨**E**	01/68⇨**E**	11/82⇨**SC**
E56137		05/57-07/83	⊗01/84	01/65⇨**NE**	01/68⇨**E**	
E56138		05/57-07/82	⊗01/85			
E56139	05/84➲**54139**	05/57-05/85	⊗08/85			
E56140		05/57-05/84	⊗05/86	01/65⇨**NE**	01/68⇨**E**	
E56141		05/57-04/81	⊗10/81	01/65⇨**NE**	01/68⇨**E**	
E56142		06/57-07/81	⊗10/91	01/65⇨**NE**	01/68⇨**E** 12/81➲**ADB977048**	
E56143	04/83➲**54143**	07/57-05/87	⊗11/87	01/65⇨**NE**	01/68⇨**E**	
E56144		07/57-01/82	⊗09/83	01/65⇨**NE**	01/68⇨**E**	

Class 105 Cravens
Driving Trailer Composite Lavatory
DTCL
M56145-M56149

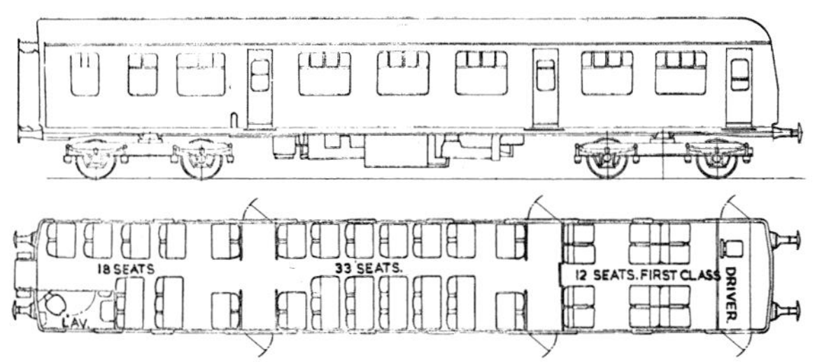

Coupling: ■ Blue square
Diagram: 526 DS307 ②DS204
Lot Number: 30285
Old class: 141
Body: 57' 6" × 9' 2"
Weight: 23t
Seats: 12 first, 51 second

M56145	07/57-09/81	⊗10/91	01/82➲**ADB977052**
M56146	07/57-08/82	⊗03/83	
M56147	07/57-06/76	⊗07/76	
M56148	08/57-09/81	⊗12/84	
M56149	08/57-07/82	⊗01/91	

Class 103 Park Royal
Driving Trailer Composite Lavatory
DTCL
M56150-M56169

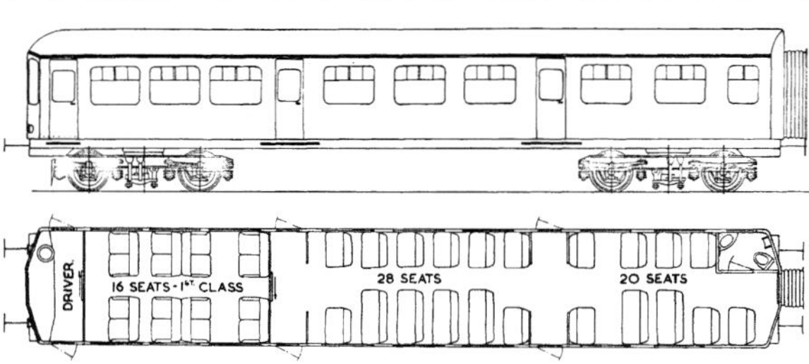

Coupling: ■ Blue square
Diagram: 645 DS304
Lot Number: 30287
Old class: 145
Body: 57' 6" × 9' 3"
Weight: 26t 10cwt
Seats: 16 first, 48 second

M56150	11/57-09/82	⊗09/84		
M56151	01/58-11/82	⊗07/84		
M56152	01/58-02/83	⊗12/84		
M56153	02/58-01/76	⊗03/79		
M56154	03/58-10/73	⊗02/74		
M56155	04/58-09/82	⊗01/86		
M56156	04/58-02/81	⊗08/86		12/81➲**ADB977047**
M56157	05/58-11/80	⊗06/84		
M56158	05/58-11/82	⊗09/84		
M56159	05/58-07/82	⊗06/84		
M56160	06/58-02/71	Ⓟ		02/71➲**DB975228**
M56161	06/58-06/82	⊗09/84		
M56162	07/58-06/70	⊗02/91		04/71➲**DB975090**
M56163	07/58-07/82	⊗06/84		
M56164	08/58-11/82	⊗01/86		
M56165	09/58-04/82	⊗06/84		
M56166	09/58-05/72	⊗08/73	10/70⇨**W**	
M56167	09/58-05/72	⊗09/73	10/70⇨**W**	
M56168	10/58-12/72	Ⓟ⊗05/91	05/70⇨**W**	
M56169	10/58-12/72	Ⓟ	05/70⇨**W**	

Class 109 Wickham
Driving Trailer Composite Lavatory
DTCL
E56170-E56174

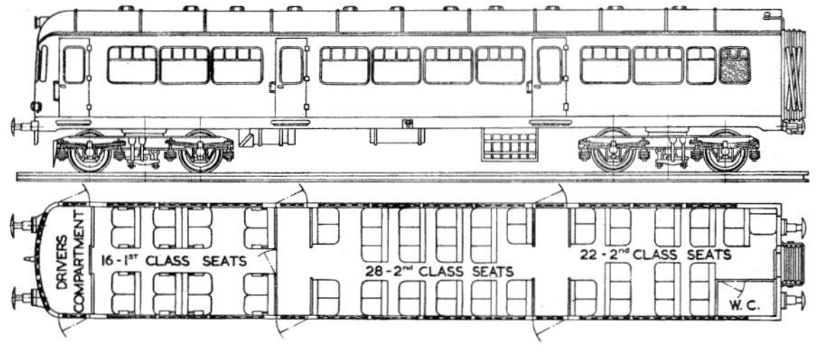

Coupling: ■ Blue square
Diagram: 607
Lot Number: 30289
Body: 57' 0" × 9' 3"
Weight: 22t 10cwt
Seats: 16 first, 50 second

E56171 was converted to the ER General Manager's saloon in June 1966.

E56170 and E56174 were returned to the manufacturer in 1961 to fulfil an export order to Trinidad.

E56170	08/57-09/61	⊗ /98	Exported
E56171	10/57-10/67	℗	10/67➲**DB975006**
E56172	11/57-10/71	⊗*10/74*	
E56173	04/58-10/71	⊗*11/74*	
E56174	08/58-09/61	⊗ /98	Exported

Class 104 Birmingham RC&W

Driving Trailer Composite Lavatory
DTCL
M56175-M56184

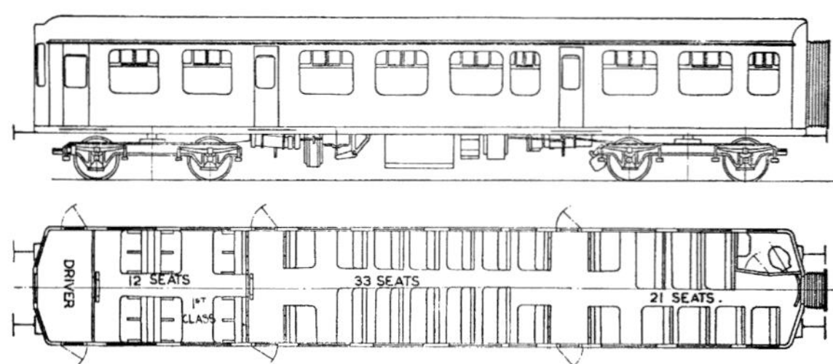

Coupling: ■ Blue square
Diagram: 585 DS306 ②DS205
Lot Number: 30297
Old class: 140
Body: 57' 6" × 9' 3"
Weight: 24t
Seats: 12 first, 54 second

M56175	10/83➲**54175**	03/58-03/86	⊗03/86	
M56176	/83➲**54176**	03/58-03/86	⊗03/86	
M56177	03/83➲**54177**	04/58-03/88	⊗03/88	
M56178	08/83➲**54178**	04/58-02/86	⊗02/86	
M56179	09/83➲**54179**	04/58-06/88	⊗10/90	
M56180	06/83➲**54180**	04/58-02/86	⊗02/86	
M56181	/83➲**54181**	04/58-11/86	⊗02/92	
M56182	08/83➲**54182**	04/58-05/87	℗	07/89➲**ADB977554**
M56183	07/83➲**54183**	04/58-05/87	⊗02/94	04/88➲**ADB977555**
M56184	/83➲**54184**	05/58-08/88	⊗10/90	

Class 104 Birmingham RC&W

Driving Trailer Composite Lavatory
DTCL
E56185-E56189

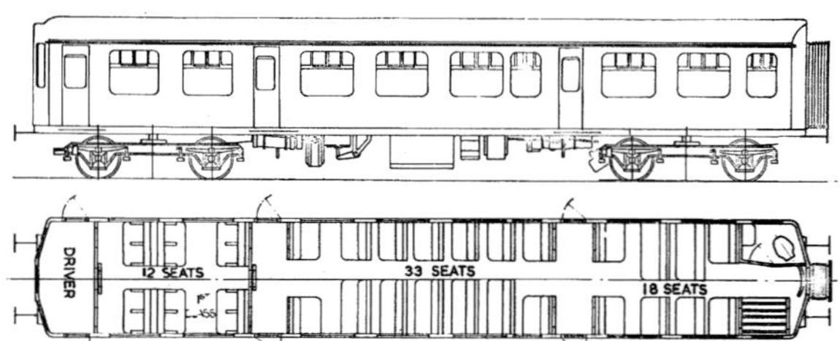

Coupling: ■ Blue square
Diagram: 581 DS205
Lot Number: 30405
Old class: 140
Body: 57' 6" × 9' 3"
Weight: 24t
Seats: 12 first, 51 second

E56185		05/58-05/81	⊗08/81	01/65⇨**NE**	01/68⇨**E**	
E56186	06/83➲**54186**	05/58-02/84	⊗02/86	01/65⇨**NE**	01/68⇨**E**	06/82⇨**M**
E56187	/83➲**54187**	05/58-10/84	⊗08/84	01/65⇨**NE**	01/68⇨**E**	04/82⇨**M**
E56188		05/58-02/82	⊗11/82	01/65⇨**NE**	01/68⇨**E**	
E56189		05/58-10/84	⊗08/84	01/65⇨**NE**	01/68⇨**E**	05/82⇨**M**

Class 108 BR Derby

Driving Trailer Composite Lavatory
DTCL
E56190-E56210

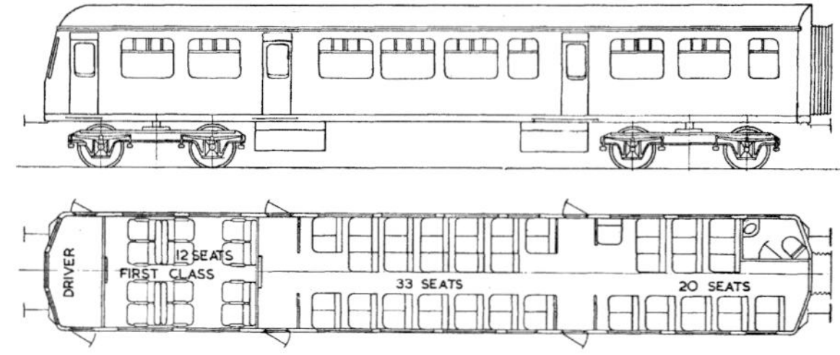

Coupling: ■ Blue square
Diagram: 640 DS310 ②DS207
Lot Number: 30409
Old class: 142
Body: 58' 1" × 9' 2"
Weight: 21t
Seats: 12 first, 53 second

E56190	04/83➲**54190**	07/58-02/87	⊗06/88	®07/79	01/65⇨**NE**	01/68⇨**E**	
E56191	04/83➲**54191**	05/58-01/92	⊗03/92	®05/75	01/65⇨**NE**	01/68⇨**E**	
						⊠02/90-07/90	
E56192	04/84➲**54192**	05/58-06/87	⊗06/88	®06/75	01/65⇨**NE**	01/68⇨**E**	
E56193	04/83➲**54193**	05/58-06/87	⊗07/88	®02/81	01/65⇨**NE**	01/68⇨**E**	
E56194	04/83➲**54194**	07/58-06/93	⊗02/94	®01/77	01/65⇨**NE**	01/68⇨**E**	
E56195	04/83➲**54195**	07/58-05/87	⊗07/87	®01/78	01/65⇨**NE**	01/68⇨**E**	
						⊠03/87-05/87	
E56196	05/83➲**54196**	06/58-07/89	⊗08/90	®*10/76*	01/65⇨**NE**	01/68⇨**E**	
E56197	05/83➲**54197**	07/58-05/92	⊗05/92	®*10/76*	01/65⇨**NE**	01/68⇨**E**	
E56198	04/83➲**54198**	06/58-05/87	⊗09/88	®01/77	01/65⇨**NE**	01/68⇨**E**	
						⊠03/87-05/87	
E56199	04/83➲**54199**	07/58-06/87	⊗06/88	®11/77	01/65⇨**NE**	01/68⇨**E**	
E56200	05/83➲**54200**	08/58-05/86	⊗12/86	®11/77	01/65⇨**NE**	01/68⇨**E**	
E56201	05/83➲**54201**	08/58-11/90	⊗05/92	®01/78	01/65⇨**NE**	03/66⇨**SC**	01/68⇨**E**
E56202	05/83➲**54202**	08/58-02/90	⊗12/93	®06/76	01/65⇨**NE**	03/66⇨**SC**	01/68⇨**E**
E56203	05/83➲**54203**	08/58-06/93	⊗05/94	®01/77	01/65⇨**NE**	01/68⇨**E**	
E56204	08/84➲**54204**	08/58-03/92	⊗02/92	®05/75	01/65⇨**NE**	01/68⇨**E**	
						⊠05/91-06/91	
E56205	04/83➲**54205**	07/58-08/91	⊗09/91	®06/75	01/65⇨**NE**	01/68⇨**E**	
E56206		09/58-11/72	⊗09/73		01/65⇨**NE**	01/68⇨**E**	
E56207	04/83➲**54207**	09/58-06/91	℗	®02/81	01/65⇨**NE**	01/68⇨**E**	
E56208	04/83➲**54208**	08/58-03/93	℗	®05/76	01/65⇨**NE**	01/68⇨**E**	
E56209	07/83➲**54209**	08/58-05/91	⊗06/91	®06/75	01/65⇨**NE**	01/68⇨**E**	
E56210	04/83➲**54210**	08/58-09/91	⊗09/91	®01/78	01/65⇨**NE**	01/68⇨**E**	

Class 108 BR Derby

Driving Trailer Composite Lavatory
DTCL
M56211-M56215

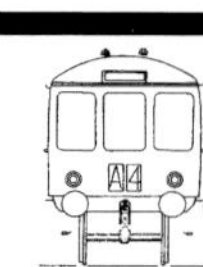

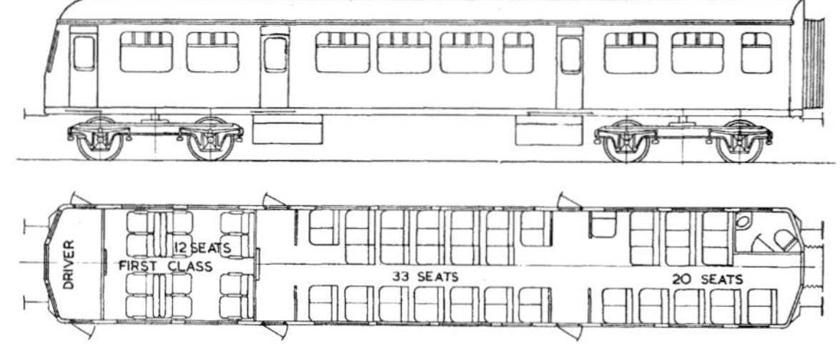

Coupling: ■ Blue square
Diagram: 640 DS310 ②DS207
Lot Number: 30410
Old class: 142
Body: 58' 1" × 9' 2"
Weight: 21t
Seats: 12 first, 53 second

M56211		12/58-11/69	⊗10/70	
M56212	08/83➲**54212**	12/58-03/92	⊗03/92	® /82
M56213	07/83➲**54213**	12/58-10/89	⊗*04/90*	®01/83
M56214	/83➲**54214**	12/58-06/92	⊗10/92	®11/80
M56215		02/59-09/71	⊗05/72	

Class 101 Metropolitan-Cammell

Driving Trailer Composite Lavatory
DTCL
E56218-E56220

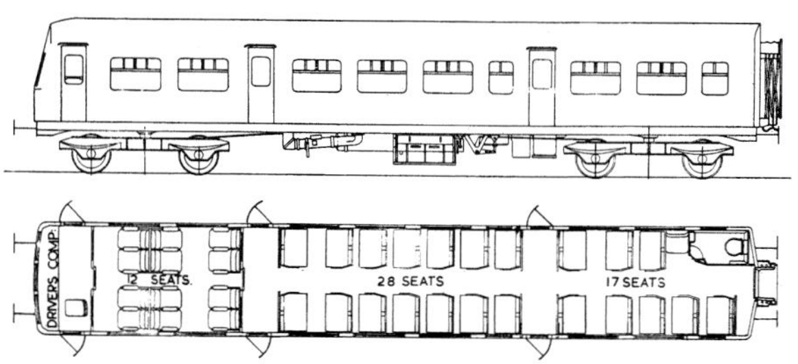

Coupling:	■ Blue square
Diagram:	629 DS303 ②DS210
Lot Number:	30340
Old class:	144
Body:	57' 6" × 9' 3"
Weight:	25t
Seats:	12 first, 45 second

E56218	04/83➲**54218**	09/57-03/92	⊗06/92	® /81	01/65⇨**NE**	01/68⇨**E**	
E56219	06/83➲**54219**	09/57-07/89	⊗05/91	®07/78	01/65⇨**NE**	01/68⇨**E**	
E56220	04/83➲**54220**	09/57-09/94	⊗10/95	®07/76	01/65⇨**NE**	01/68⇨**E**	⊠01/94-09/94

Class 108 BR Derby

Driving Trailer Composite Lavatory
DTCL
M56221-M56270

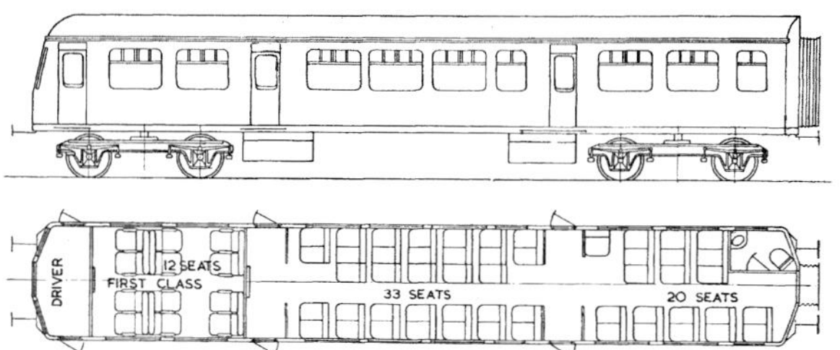

Coupling:	■ Blue square
Diagram:	640 DS310 ②DS207
Lot Number:	30466
Old class:	142
Body:	58' 1" × 9' 2"
Weight:	21t
Seats:	12 first, 53 second

M56221	06/83➲**54221**	01/59-06/92	⊗06/92	®06/78	⊠11/90-12/90
M56222	/83➲**54222**	01/59-07/91	⊗10/91	®03/80	
M56223	07/83➲**54223**	01/59-06/93	Ⓟ	®02/81	
M56224	06/84➲**54224**	01/59-09/92	Ⓟ	®08/81	
M56225	03/83➲**54225**	01/59-05/91	⊗11/91	®06/78	
M56226		01/59-09/66	⊗08/66		
M56227	06/83➲**54227**	01/59-01/92	⊗12/91	®10/83	
M56228	07/83➲**54228**	01/59-04/93	⊗05/93	®10/77	
M56229		01/59-06/72	⊗12/72		
M56230	/83➲**54230**	02/59-11/92	⊗11/92	®10/77	
M56231	/83➲**54231**	02/59-05/91	⊗10/91	®01/78	
M56232	/83➲**54232**	02/59-07/92	⊗07/92		
M56233		02/59-09/79	⊗06/80		
M56234	03/83➲**54234**	02/59-11/83	⊗02/84		
M56235	06/83➲**54235**	02/59-06/92	⊗06/92		
M56236	06/83➲**54236**	02/59-10/91	⊗10/91		
M56237		03/59-10/75	⊗01/76		
M56238	06/83➲**54238**	03/59-09/92	⊗09/92		
M56239	06/83➲**54239**	03/59-09/92	⊗09/92		
M56240	06/83➲**54240**	03/59-01/92	⊗12/91		
M56241	06/83➲**54241**	04/59-03/92	⊗03/92	®08/81	
M56242	06/83➲**54242**	04/59-06/92	⊗06/92		
M56243	06/83➲**54243**	04/59-12/91	⊗11/91		
M56244	06/83➲**54244**	04/59-12/90	⊗03/92		
M56245	06/83➲**54245**	04/59-04/91	⊗11/91		⊠02/91-04/91
M56246	06/83➲**54246**	06/59-07/92	⊗09/92	®12/83	
M56247	04/83➲**54247**	05/59-06/92	⊗06/92		
M56248	06/83➲**54248**	05/59-07/91	⊗11/91		
M56249	06/83➲**54249**	05/59-04/92	⊗06/92	®11/79	⊠12/90-01/91
M56250	06/83➲**54250**	06/59-02/88	⊗01/90		
M56251	06/83➲**54251**	05/59-04/91	⊗03/92		
M56252	06/83➲**54252**	06/59-04/91	⊗12/91	®08/80	
M56253	/83➲**54253**	07/59-10/92	⊗11/92	®05/77	
M56254		07/59-11/71	⊗05/72		
M56255		07/59-11/69	⊗08/70		
M56256	06/83➲**54256**	07/59-06/93	⊗11/93		
M56257	/84➲**54257**	07/59-04/93	⊗08/94	®08/78	
M56258	/83➲**54258**	08/59-05/91	⊗09/91	®11/77	
M56259	05/83➲**54259**	08/59-12/91	⊗10/93	®11/78	
M56260	06/83➲**54260**	08/59-06/92	⊗10/92	®09/76	
M56261	07/83➲**54261**	08/59-10/91	⊗10/91	®07/78	
M56262	08/83➲**54262**	08/59-06/92	⊗01/92	®07/78	
M56263	/83➲**54263**	09/59-01/92	⊗12/91	®11/79	
M56264	/83➲**54264**	09/59-04/92	⊗06/92		
M56265	06/83➲**54265**	09/59-07/91	⊗03/92		
M56266	/83➲**54266**	10/59-07/91	⊗08/91	®06/78	
M56267	10/83➲**54267**	10/59-06/92	⊗06/92		
M56268	/83➲**54268**	10/59-01/92	⊗01/92		
M56269	04/83➲**54269**	10/59-01/92	⊗12/91	®04/82	
M56270	06/83➲**54270**	10/59-06/93	Ⓟ		

Class 108 BR Derby

Driving Trailer Composite Lavatory
DTCL
M56271-M56279

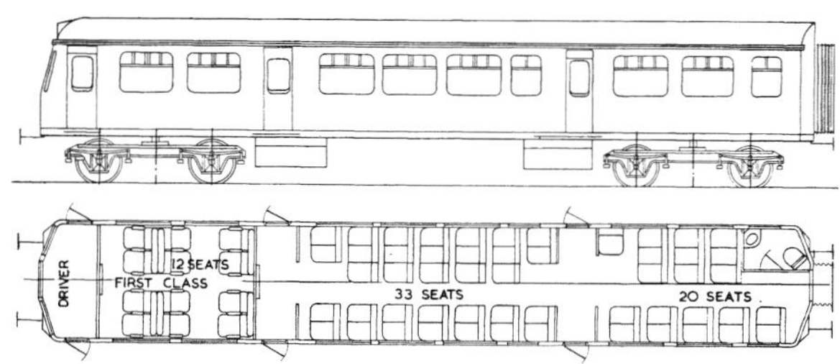

Coupling:	■ Blue square
Diagram:	646 DS311 ②DS207
Lot Number:	30499
Old class:	142
Body:	58' 1" × 9' 3"
Weight:	22t
Seats:	12 first, 53 second

M56271	08/83➲**54271**	02/60-07/93	Ⓟ	
M56272	/85➲**54272**	02/60-06/92	⊗06/92	
M56273	07/83➲**54273**	02/60-02/92	⊗01/92	®09/79
M56274	06/83➲**54274**	02/60-02/92	Ⓟ	®08/80
M56275	07/83➲**54275**	02/60-07/92	⊗07/92	
M56276	10/83➲**54276**	03/60-09/92	⊗09/92	®03/80
M56277	07/83➲**54277**	03/60-01/91	⊗09/91	®03/79
M56278	08/83➲**54278**	03/60-12/91	⊗11/91	®06/78
M56279	07/83➲**54279**	03/60-08/93	Ⓟ	®02/79

Class 121 Pressed Steel

Driving Trailer Second
DTS
W56280-W56289

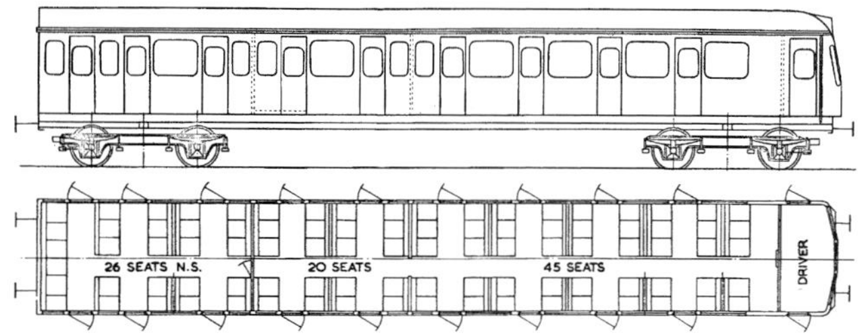

Coupling:	■ Blue square
Diagram:	513 DS201
Lot Number:	30519
Old class:	149
Body:	64' 0" × 9' 3"

Weight: 29t 7cwt
Seats: 95 second

W56280	04/83➲**54280**	09/60-03/91	⊗11/92	®12/80	
W56281	08/83➲**54281**	01/61-03/88	⊗11/90	®10/80	03/88➲**TDB977615**
W56282		01/61-12/72	⊗09/73		
W56283	08/83➲**54283**	01/61-04/91	⊗11/92	®05/79	
W56284	07/83➲**54284**	02/61-02/92	⊗02/94	®02/81	
W56285	03/83➲**54285**	02/61-12/86	Ⓟ	®08/80	12/86➲**TDB977486**
W56286	05/83➲**54286**	02/61-10/86	⊗10/96	®01/80	10/86➲**TDB977466**
W56287	07/83➲**54287**	02/61-04/92	Ⓟ	®01/80	
W56288		02/61-02/69	⊗06/69		
W56289	05/83➲**54289**	02/61-12/92	Ⓟ	®09/79	

Class 122 Gloucester RC&W

Driving Trailer Second
DTS
W56291-W56299

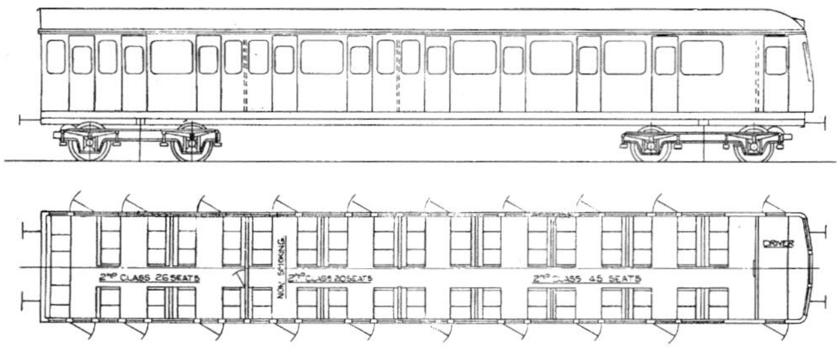

Coupling: ■ Blue square
Diagram: 538 DS202
Lot Number: 30420
Old class: 150
Body: 64' 0" × 9' 3"
Weight: 27t
Seats: 91 second

W56291	06/58-08/77	⊗04/82	01/63⇨**M** 06/68⇨**SC**
W56292	06/58-06/72	⊗11/72	07/68⇨**M**
W56293	06/58-10/72	⊗08/73	01/63⇨**M** 11/70⇨**W**
W56294	06/58-11/82	⊗*11/74*	07/68⇨**M**
W56295	07/58-11/82	⊗07/84	01/63⇨**M**
W56296	07/58-11/82	⊗10/83	01/63⇨**M**
W56297	07/58-08/77	⊗02/82	05/68⇨**SC**
W56298	07/58-06/72	⊗11/72	07/68⇨**M**
W56299	07/58-08/77	⊗01/82	01/63⇨**M** 06/68⇨**SC**

Class 100 Gloucester RC&W

Driving Trailer Composite Lavatory
DTCL
SC56300-SC56319

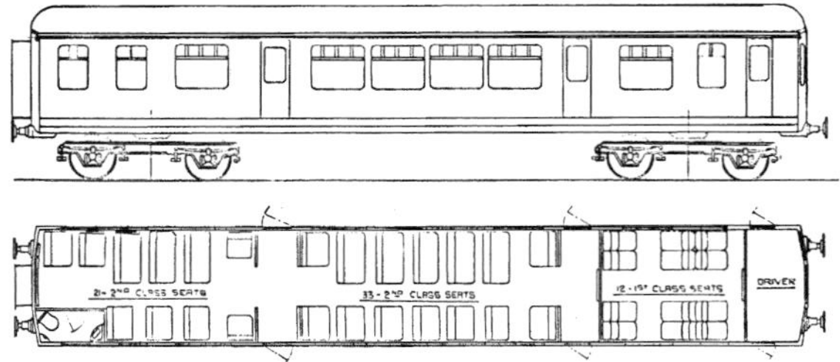

Coupling: ■ Blue square
Diagram: 537 DS203
Lot Number: 30445
Old class: 143
Body: 57' 6" × 9' 3"
Weight: 25t
Seats: 12 first, 54 second

SC56300	10/57-04/77	⊗08/90	06/67⇨**NE**	01/68⇨**E**	
			☒10/72-01/73		11/78-➲**DB975637**
SC56301	10/57-02/72	Ⓟ	05/68⇨**E**		
SC56302	10/57-08/72	⊗03/73			
SC56303	11/57-12/75	⊗01/80	06/67⇨**NE**	01/68⇨**E**	
SC56304	11/57-03/66	⊗11/66			
SC56305	11/57-11/66	⊗01/68			
SC56306	11/57-01/73	⊗12/73			
SC56307	11/57-03/79	⊗05/82	06/67⇨**NE**	01/68⇨**E**	
SC56308	12/57-10/72	⊗12/73			
SC56309	12/57-06/72	⊗12/73			
SC56310	12/57-10/72	⊗07/80	06/67⇨**NE**	01/68⇨**E**	04/77⇨**E**
SC56311	01/58-10/72	⊗12/73			
SC56312	01/58-01/73	⊗12/73			
SC56313	01/58-05/72	⊗11/73	06/67⇨**NE**	01/68⇨**E**	
SC56314	01/58-10/72	⊗12/73			
SC56315	01/58-01/74	⊗03/90	05/68⇨**E**		☒10/73-12/73
					03/75➲**FA99900**
SC56316	02/58-04/78	⊗04/81	05/68⇨**E**		
SC56317	02/58-04/74	Ⓟ	06/67⇨**NE**	01/68⇨**E**	
					☒10/73-12/73
SC56318	02/58-10/71	⊗*07/74*	05/68⇨**E**		
SC56319	03/58-10/72	⊗12/73			

Class 101 Metropolitan-Cammell

Driving Trailer Composite Lavatory
DTCL
M56332-SC56411

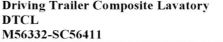

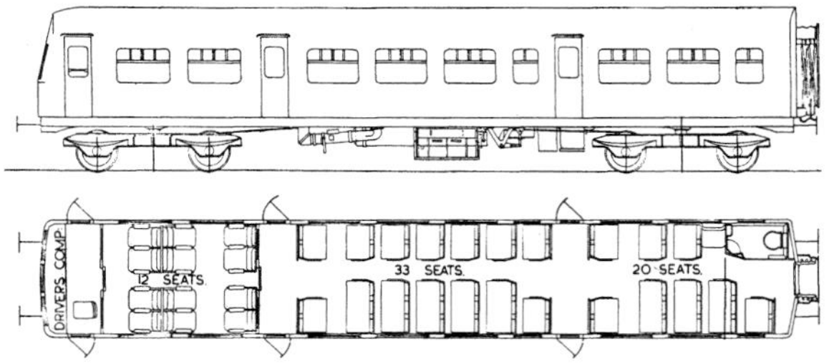

Coupling: ■ Blue square
Diagram: 630 DS302 ②DS206
Lot Number: 30468
Old class: 144
Body: 57' 6" × 9' 3"
Weight: 25t
Seats: 12 first, 53 second

M56332	03/83➲**54332**	10/58-05/92	⊗10/92	®06/78			
M56333	08/83➲**54333**	11/58-04/85	⊗07/86	®10/77			
M56334	07/83➲**54334**	11/58-09/86	⊗08/88	®08/80			
M56335	03/83➲**54335**	11/58-10/89	⊗07/90	®11/79			
M56336	07/83➲**54336**	11/58-03/88	⊗10/88				
M56337	04/83➲**54337**	11/58-09/86	⊗05/88	®01/80			
M56338		11/58-06/72	⊗12/72				
M56339	04/83➲**54339**	11/58-06/87	⊗06/89	®11/76			
M56340	04/83➲**54340**	11/58-04/91	⊗05/91	®11/83			
M56341	11/83➲**54341**	11/58-09/86	⊗12/95	®*10/76*			
M56342	04/83➲**54342**	11/58-12/90	Ⓟ	®05/76			12/90➲**042222**
M56343	03/83➲**54343**	11/58-07/00	Ⓟ	®08/78			
M56344	09/83➲**54344**	11/58-02/87	⊗06/89	®03/77			
M56345	04/83➲**54345**	12/58-10/89	⊗11/90	®11/83			
M56346	/83➲**54346**	12/58-01/98	⊗01/98	®08/78			
M56347	04/83➲**54347**	12/58-01/01	Ⓟ	®03/79			
M56348	04/83➲**54348**	12/58-12/89	⊗07/90	®06/76			
M56349	04/83➲**54349**	12/58-10/87	⊗09/88	®01/79			
M56350	03/83➲**54350**	12/58-05/89	⊗03/04	®04/83			
M56351	04/83➲**54351**	12/58-09/89	⊗09/90	®04/77			
M56352	09/83➲**54352**	12/58-06/00	Ⓟ	® /82			
M56353	09/83➲**54353**	01/59-09/86	⊗07/88				
M56354	04/83➲**54354**	01/59-05/92	⊗01/94	® /82			
M56355	04/83➲**54355**	01/59-10/89	⊗08/90				
M56356	04/83➲**54356**	01/59-09/86	Ⓟ	® /82			09/86➲**6300**
M56357	04/83➲**54357**	01/59-05/86	⊗07/86				
M56358	04/83➲**54358**	01/59-01/01	Ⓟ	® */84*			☒03/91-04/91
M56359	04/83➲**54359**	01/59-07/87	⊗10/90	®08/78			
M56360	09/83➲**54360**	01/59-09/86	⊗07/88				
M56361	09/83➲**54361**	01/59-05/86	⊗02/87				
E56362	04/83➲**54362**	07/58-02/93	⊗02/93	®02/81	01/65⇨**NE**	01/68⇨**E**	
E56363	06/83➲**54363**	07/58-12/91	⊗04/92	®07/79	01/65⇨**NE**	01/68⇨**E**	
E56364	07/83➲**54364**	08/58-08/88	⊗10/88	®10/80	01/65⇨**NE**	01/68⇨**E**	
E56365	05/83➲**54365**	08/58-06/00	Ⓟ	® /82	01/65⇨**NE**	01/68⇨**E**	
E56366	05/83➲**54366**	08/58-06/87	⊗06/88	®02/81	01/65⇨**NE**	01/68⇨**E**	
E56367	10/83➲**54367**	08/58-09/89	⊗02/97	®11/79	01/65⇨**NE**	01/68⇨**E**	
E56368	04/83➲**54368**	09/58-05/93	⊗03/94	®11/79	01/65⇨**NE**	01/68⇨**E**	
E56369	02/83➲**54369**	09/58-07/92	⊗08/92	®01/77	01/65⇨**NE**	01/68⇨**E**	
E56370	11/83➲**54370**	09/58-04/90	⊗09/90	® /81	01/65⇨**NE**	01/68⇨**E**	
E56371	09/83➲**54371**	09/58-02/92	⊗05/93		01/65⇨**NE**	01/68⇨**E**	
E56372	09/83➲**54372**	09/58-07/93	⊗03/94	®04/77	01/65⇨**NE**	01/68⇨**E**	
E56373	09/83➲**54373**	09/58-06/87	⊗03/88	®09/77	01/65⇨**NE**	01/68⇨**E**	
E56374	04/83➲**54374**	09/58-09/86	⊗02/88	®07/79	01/65⇨**NE**	01/68⇨**E**	

E56375	05/83➲**54375**	10/58-02/89	⊗03/89	® /81	01/65⇨**NE**	01/68⇨**E**	
E56376	04/83➲**54376**	10/58-06/87	⊗03/88	®02/81	01/65⇨**NE**	01/68⇨**E**	
E56377	/84➲**54377**	10/58-05/86	⊗05/88	®10/77	01/65⇨**NE**	01/68⇨**E**	
E56378	06/83➲**54378**	10/58-09/86	⊗05/87	®11/79	01/65⇨**NE**	01/68⇨**E**	
E56379	04/83➲**54379**	10/58-05/99	⊗05/99	® /82	01/65⇨**NE**	01/68⇨**E**	
E56380	04/83➲**54380**	10/58-05/93	⊗12/93	®08/83	01/65⇨**NE**	01/68⇨**E**	
E56381	07/83➲**54381**	10/58-09/92	⊗12/92	®11/78	01/65⇨**NE**	01/68⇨**E**	
							☒05/89-07/89
SC56382	11/83➲**54382**	05/58-09/92	⊗12/92	®01/77	07/74⇨**E**		
SC56383	05/83➲**54383**	05/58-06/87	⊗07/88	®04/77	05/68⇨**E**		
SC56384	03/84➲**54384**	05/58-09/86	⊗07/88	®11/79	10/69⇨**E**		
SC56385	07/83➲**54385**	05/58-04/93	⊗03/94	®01/77	10/69⇨**E**		
SC56386	05/83➲**54386**	05/58-09/86	⊗02/88	®11/79	12/77⇨**E**		
SC56387	05/83➲**54387**	05/58-10/92	⊗10/92	® /82	08/69⇨**E**		
SC56388	11/83➲**54388**	05/58-05/93	⊗12/93	® /81	11/78⇨**E**		
SC56389	/83➲**54389**	05/58-09/86	⊗02/89	®07/79	11/78⇨**E**		
SC56390	05/83➲**54390**	05/58-06/87	⊗07/88	®11/79	10/79⇨**E**		
SC56391	04/83➲**54391**	05/58-09/89	⊗11/90	® /82	10/79⇨**E**		
SC56392	06/83➲**54392**	05/58-06/87	⊗07/88	®11/78	05/77⇨**E**		☒09/86-11/86
SC56393	02/83➲**54393**	05/58-10/99	⊗09/06	® /83	10/69⇨**E**		☒03/93-03/93
SC56394	04/83➲**54394**	05/58-03/87	⊗02/89	®01/77	08/69⇨**E**		
SC56395		05/58-03/74	⊗01/84				
SC56396	02/85➲**54396**	06/58-10/93	⊗02/94	® /81	09/69⇨**E**		
SC56397	05/83➲**54397**	06/58-09/86	⊗02/87	®07/78	05/77⇨**E**		
SC56398	04/83➲**54398**	06/58-03/89	⊗03/89	® /82	08/69⇨**E**		
SC56399	04/83➲**54399**	06/58-03/93	⊗05/95	®06/78	05/77⇨**E**		
SC56400	05/83➲**54400**	06/58-07/86	⊗02/87	®02/81	05/77⇨**E**		
SC56401	08/83➲**54401**	06/58-05/89	⊗02/92	®07/76	05/75⇨**E**		
SC56402	09/83➲**54402**	06/58-10/93	⊗02/94	®04/77	08/69⇨**E**		
SC56403	04/83➲**54403**	06/58-05/86	⊗07/86	®02/81	12/77⇨**E**		
SC56404	04/83➲**54404**	07/58-03/88	⊗02/89	®11/79	12/77⇨**E**		
SC56405	04/83➲**54405**	07/58-09/92	⊗02/93	®10/82	09/69⇨**E**		
SC56406	04/83➲**54406**	07/58-03/88	⊗10/88	®02/81	12/77⇨**E**		
SC56407	10/83➲**54407**	07/58-09/86	⊗02/89	®04/79	12/77⇨**E**		
SC56408	05/83➲**54408**	07/58-06/01	℗	®07/78	12/77⇨**E**		
SC56409	04/83➲**54409**	07/58-06/87	⊗02/89	®11/79	08/77⇨**E**		
SC56410	02/83➲**54410**	07/58-07/86	⊗10/86	®10/80	08/77⇨**E**		
SC56411	04/83➲**54411**	07/58-03/87	⊗04/87		05/75⇨**M**		

Class 105 Cravens

Driving Trailer Composite Lavatory
DTCL
E56412-E56459

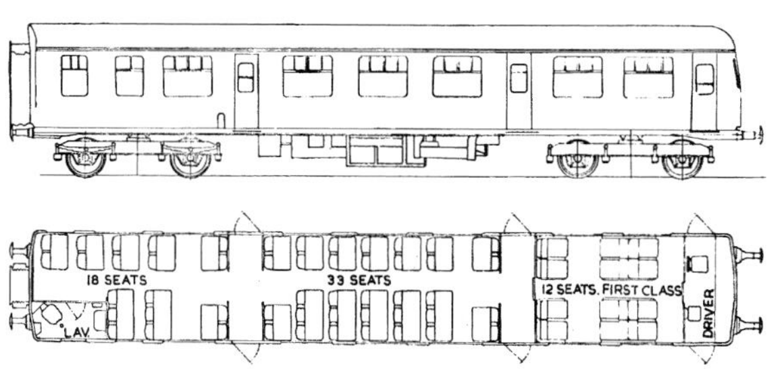

Coupling: ■ Blue square
Diagram: 533 DS308 ②DS208
Lot Number: 30470
Old class: 141
Body: 57' 6" × 9' 2"
Weight: 24t
Seats: 12 first, 51 second

E56412		05/58-12/75	⊗03/81		
E56413	05/84➲**54413**	05/58-05/84	⊗10/84		
E56414		06/58-11/82	⊗10/83		
E56415	04/83➲**54415**	06/58-06/83	⊗01/84		
E56416	04/83➲**54416**	06/58-09/86	⊗07/88		
E56417	03/83➲**54417**	06/58-09/86	⊗01/87		
E56418		06/58-04/83	⊗07/84		
E56419	03/84➲**54419**	06/58-10/85	⊗01/86		
E56420	04/83➲**54420**	06/58-05/87	⊗10/87		
E56421	04/83➲**54421**	07/58-02/87	⊗10/87		
E56422	06/83➲**54422**	07/58-09/86	⊗09/86		
E56423	04/83➲**54423**	07/58-07/86	⊗07/88		
E56424	/83➲**54424**	07/58-11/83	⊗09/84		
E56425		07/58-06/81	⊗01/89		
E56426	05/85➲**54426**	07/58-05/85	⊗08/85		
E56427		08/58-07/81	⊗04/87		12/81➲**ADB977051**
E56428		08/58-12/77	⊗10/81		
E56429	01/85➲**54429**	08/58-10/86	⊗10/87		
E56430		09/58-09/78	⊗06/80		
E56431	/83➲**54431**	09/58-09/84	⊗12/84		
E56432		09/58-11/82	⊗04/84	11/80⇨**M**	
E56433	05/83➲**54433**	09/58-02/86	⊗12/86		☒03/83-05/83
E56434	06/84➲**54434**	09/58-08/86	⊗09/86		
E56435	/84➲**54435**	09/58-05/84	⊗10/84		
E56436	08/83➲**54436**	09/58-09/86	⊗08/88		☒07/86-08/86
E56437		09/58-10/83	⊗06/84	11/82⇨**SC**	
E56438	/84➲**54438**	09/58-05/83	⊗09/84		
E56439	11/84➲**54439**	10/58-10/86	⊗11/87		
E56440	05/84➲**54440**	10/58-09/86	⊗12/88		09/86➲**TDB977454**
E56441		10/58-09/83	⊗11/83	11/82⇨**SC**	12/82⇨**E**
E56442	06/83➲**54442**	10/58-10/86	⊗10/87		
E56443	/85➲**54443**	10/58-06/86	⊗01/89		
E56444		11/58-11/82	⊗08/90		11/82➲**TDB977125**
E56445		11/58-11/82	⊗08/90		11/82➲**TDB977126**
E56446	07/83➲**54446**	11/58-10/84	⊗11/84		
E56447	03/83➲**54447**	11/58-09/86	⊗09/86		
E56448		11/58-07/81	⊗01/89		12/81➲**ADB977050**
E56449	04/83➲**54449**	11/58-07/85	⊗05/86		
E56450	05/83➲**54450**	12/58-03/85	⊗05/85		
E56451		12/58-05/84	⊗11/84		
E56452		12/58-12/82	⊗05/84	12/76⇨**M**	
E56453	10/83➲**54453**	12/58-10/84	⊗07/84	10/80⇨**M**	
E56454	06/83➲**54454**	12/58-09/86	⊗07/88		
E56455	04/83➲**54455**	01/59-07/86	⊗07/88		
E56456		01/59-07/83	℗	01/77⇨**M**	
E56457		01/59-01/83	⊗11/83		
E56458	01/85➲**54458**	01/59-09/86	⊗01/89		☒06/81-06/81
E56459		01/59-02/81	⊗01/89		

Class 105 Cravens

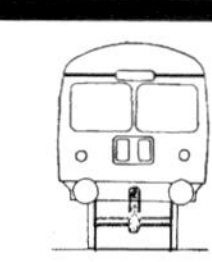

Driving Trailer Composite Lavatory
DTCL

E56460-SC56483

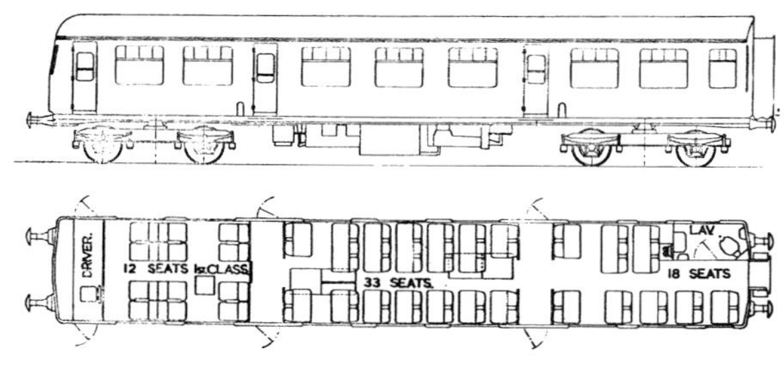

Coupling: ■ Blue square
Diagram: 549 DS309 ②DS209
Lot Number: 30504
Old class: 141
Body: 57' 6" × 9' 3"
Weight: 23t
Seats: 12 first, 51 second

E56460		02/59-11/80	⊗09/81			
E56461		02/59-03/83	⊗05/84			
SC56462		02/59-09/83	⊗11/83	05/75⇨**E**		
SC56463	/85➲**54463**	02/59-07/86	⊗01/87	05/75⇨**E**		
SC56464		02/59-10/83	⊗06/84	11/75⇨**E**	11/82⇨**SC**	
						☒06/75-11/75
SC56465		03/59-12/82	⊗04/84	05/75⇨**E**	11/80⇨**M**	
SC56466		03/59-02/83	⊗01/84	05/75⇨**E**		
SC56467	04/83➲**54467**	03/59-09/86	⊗09/86	05/75⇨**E**		
SC56468	05/85➲**54468**	03/59-10/86	⊗08/88	05/75⇨**E**		
SC56469		03/59-11/83	⊗06/84	04/74⇨**E**	11/82⇨**SC**	
SC56470	02/83➲**54470**	03/59-05/84	⊗10/84	05/75⇨**M**	03/76⇨**SC**	04/77⇨**E**
SC56471		04/59-03/83	⊗05/84	05/75⇨**E**		
SC56472	/83➲**54472**	04/59-06/86	⊗07/87	05/75⇨**E**		
SC56473		04/59-06/81	⊗09/83	05/75⇨**E**		
SC56474		04/59-07/81	⊗04/88	07/75⇨**E**	12/81➲**ADB977049**	
SC56475		04/59-09/82	⊗05/84	06/75⇨**M**		
SC56476		04/59-04/78	⊗06/80	04/77⇨**E**		
SC56477		05/59-04/78	⊗05/81	04/77⇨**E**		
SC56478		05/59-04/78	⊗07/84	04/77⇨**E**		
SC56479		05/59-04/78	⊗06/80			
SC56480		05/59-05/81	⊗08/81	06/77⇨**E**		
SC56481		05/59- /73	⊗04/74			
SC56482		06/59-08/82	⊗03/83	06/75⇨**M**		
SC56483		06/59-01/71	⊗01/73			

Class 108 BR Derby

Driving Trailer Composite Lavatory
DTCL
M56484-M56504

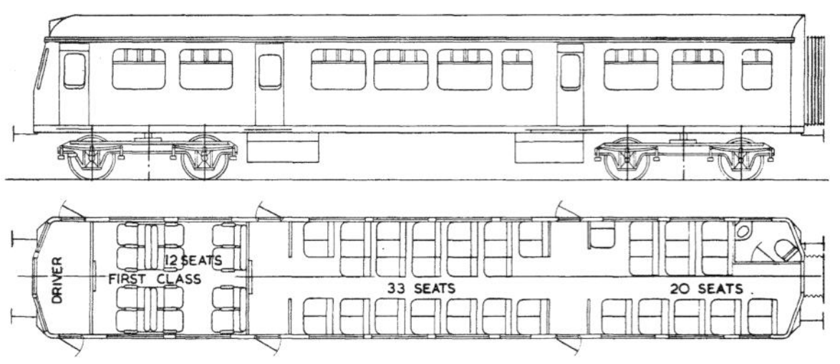

Coupling: ■ Blue square
Diagram: 646 DS311 ②DS207
Lot Number: 30602
Old class: 142
Body: 58' 1" × 9' 3"
Weight: 22t
Seats: 12 first, 53 second

M56484	04/83➲**54484**	03/60-10/92	Ⓟ	®04/80
M56485	/83➲**54485**	03/60-06/92	⊗06/92	®12/76
M56486	/83➲**54486**	03/60-04/90	⊗02/93	®11/76
M56487	*/84*➲**54487**	03/60-05/91	⊗09/91	®06/77
M56488	/83➲**54488**	04/60-02/92	⊗01/92	®01/79
M56489	/83➲**54489**	04/60-05/91	⊗10/91	®01/78
M56490	/83➲**54490**	04/60-02/93	Ⓟ	®10/77
M56491	06/83➲**54491**	04/60-12/92	Ⓟ	®03/78
M56492	/83➲**54492**	04/60-05/91	Ⓟ	®03/80
M56493	08/83➲**54493**	04/60-12/91	⊗08/94	
M56494	03/83➲**54494**	04/60-05/91	⊗07/91	®08/78
M56495	07/83➲**54495**	05/60-10/93	Ⓟ	®04/82
M56496	08/83➲**54496**	05/60-02/92	⊗01/92	®09/81
M56497	06/83➲**54497**	05/60-06/91	⊗12/91	® /81
M56498	07/83➲**54498**	05/60-07/91	⊗11/91	®11/79
M56499	10/83➲**54499**	06/60-09/92	⊗11/93	®11/79
M56500	08/83➲**54500**	06/60-09/92	⊗11/93	®04/82
M56501	07/83➲**54501**	07/60-07/91	⊗11/91	®10/76
M56502	04/83➲**54502**	06/60-08/85	⊗05/86	®01/78
M56503	05/83➲**54503**	07/60-06/92	⊗06/92	®05/83
M56504	/83➲**54504**	07/60-02/93	Ⓟ	

Class 116 BR Derby
Trailer Composite
TC
M59000-M59031

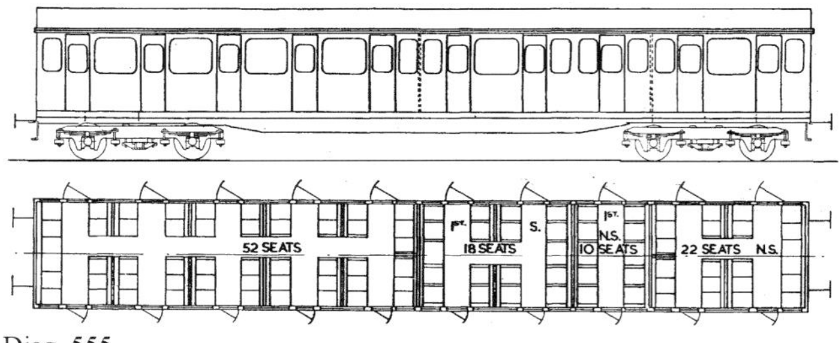

Diag. 555

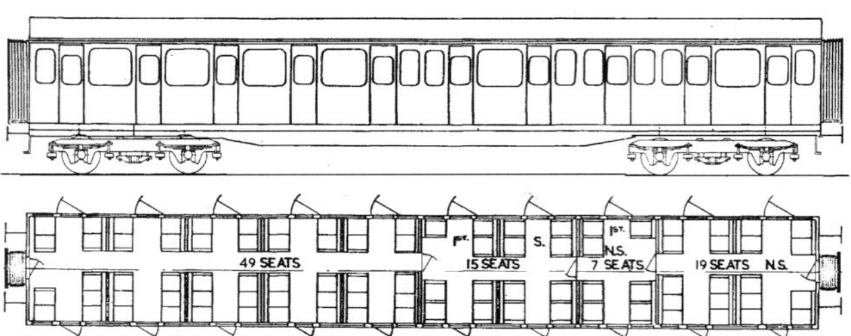

Diag. 855 ⓖ *Through gangway fitted* W59030-31 converted by 1972.

Coupling: ■ Blue square
Diagram: 555 DT215 ⓖ 855 DT219
Lot Number: 30212
Old class: 175
Body: 63' 8¾" × 9' 3" Suburban
Weight: 28t 10cwt
Seats: 28 first, 74 second ⓖ 22 first, 68 second

W59000	04/57-12/82	⊗03/83	®05/76	01/63⇨**M**	
W59001	04/57-12/83	⊗07/84	®10/77	01/63⇨**M**	
W59002	05/57-12/83	⊗07/84	®10/77	01/63⇨**M**	
W59003	05/57-11/83	Ⓟ	®09/77	01/63⇨**M**	
W59004	05/57-11/83	Ⓟ	®01/80	01/63⇨**M**	
W59005	05/57-12/83	⊗07/84	®06/76	01/63⇨**M**	
W59006	05/57-05/83	⊗10/83	®10/78	01/63⇨**M**	
W59007	05/57-10/83	⊗11/83	®11/79	01/63⇨**M**	
W59008	05/57-08/82	⊗09/85		01/63⇨**M**	
W59009	08/57-10/83	⊗11/83	®08/76	01/63⇨**M**	
W59010	05/57-10/83	⊗06/84	®07/78	01/63⇨**M**	
W59011	05/57-05/83	⊗10/83		01/63⇨**M**	
W59012	06/57-12/83	⊗07/84	®03/77	01/63⇨**M**	
W59013	06/57-10/83	⊗07/84	®11/76	01/63⇨**M**	
W59014	06/57-10/83	⊗06/84	®06/78	01/63⇨**M**	Stored 02/70-09/77
W59015	06/57-10/83	⊗11/83	®03/79	01/63⇨**M**	
W59016	08/57-10/84	⊗06/84	®01/78	01/63⇨**M**	
W59017	05/57-08/82	⊗01/83		01/63⇨**M**	
W59018	06/57-10/83	⊗11/83	®01/81	01/63⇨**M**	
W59019	06/57-10/83	⊗11/83	®10/77	01/63⇨**M**	
W59020	08/57-05/83	⊗10/83	®09/79	01/63⇨**M**	
W59021	07/57-10/83	⊗02/84		01/63⇨**M**	
W59022	06/57-05/83	⊗10/83	®11/79	01/63⇨**M**	
W59023	06/57-06/82	⊗01/83		01/63⇨**M**	
W59024	08/57-07/82	⊗07/84		01/63⇨**M**	
W59025	08/57-10/67	⊗12/67		01/63⇨**M**	
W59026	08/57-10/83	⊗06/84	®06/77	01/63⇨**M**	
W59027	08/57-11/83	⊗06/91		01/63⇨**M**	11/78⇨**SC**
W59028	09/57-05/83	⊗10/83	®10/77	01/63⇨**M**	
W59029	09/57-12/83	⊗06/84	®10/77	11/66⇨**M**	
W59030	10/57-10/87	⊗01/89	ⓖ®02/77		
W59031	10/57-05/85	⊗01/86	ⓖ®04/77		

Class 116 BR Derby
Trailer Second
TS
W59032-W59041

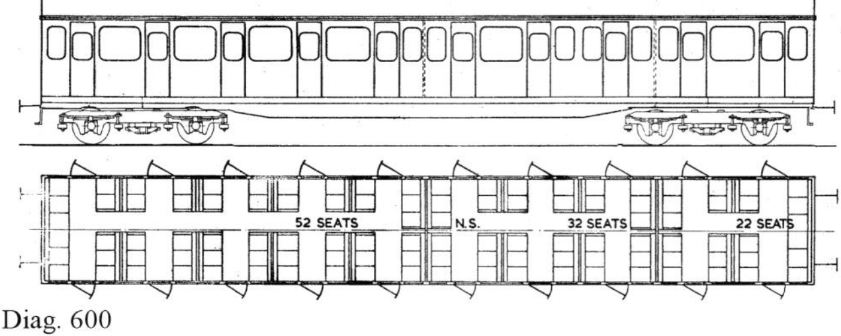

Diag. 600

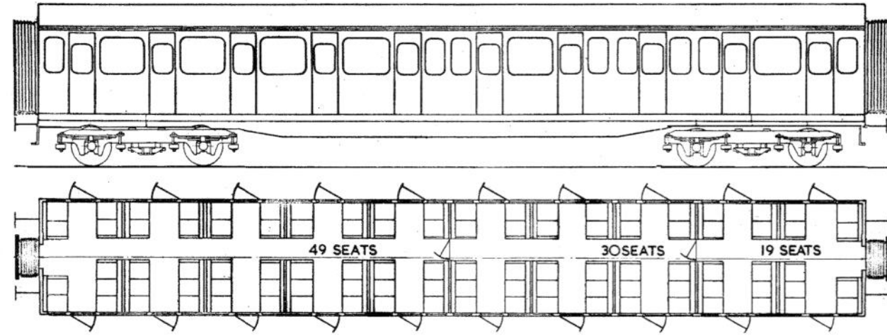

Diag. 856 ⓖ *Through gangway fitted* All converted by 1972.

Coupling: ■ Blue square
Diagram: 600 ⓖ 856 DT209
Lot Number: 30385
Old class: 172
Body: 63' 8¾" × 9' 3" Suburban
Weight: 29t
Seats: 106 second ⓖ 98 second

W59032	08/57-07/93	⊗08/93	ⓖ®06/78			
W59033	08/57-10/87	⊗01/88	ⓖ®11/76			
W59034	08/57-10/87	⊗08/88	ⓖ®06/78			
W59035	08/57-05/88	⊗06/88	ⓖ®*09/76*	01/63⇨**M**	12/63⇨**W**	☒10/87-01/88
W59036	09/57-10/87	⊗01/89	ⓖ®11/77			
W59037	09/57-05/88	⊗06/88	ⓖ®07/76			☒10/87-01/88
W59038	09/57-07/83	⊗11/83	ⓖ®06/77	10/78⇨**M**		

On another of the London Division Branch lines, this Class 121 single unit has been augmented with Class 121 trailer W56289 (L289) on a branch line service from Windsor arriving at Slough in 1975. *J G Glover*

Another common use for Class 121 units was to add extra carriages to main line suburban services. On 28th March 1981 L285 W56285 leads the 09.22 Reading to Paddington service leaving Ealing Broadway. The complete formation is Class 121 DTS, Class 121 DMBS, and Class 117 three-car unit. *J E Oxley*

On 15th August 1987 Class 121 55033 is seen in Midline livery with its sister unit 55034 in blue and grey livery, leaving Tamworth on the 14.56 Stafford-Coventry service. *C Morrison*

Above: With the introduction of second generation DMUs (which had disc brakes rather than tread brakes which could clean the wheel's surface), combined with a new policy of letting trees grow on railway embankments, it was found that the railway became like an ice-rink every autumn. One way of dealing with this problem was to spread a sticky gritty compound known as Sandite on the rails every night during the leaf fall season. Many redundant DMU vehicles found a new lease of life in departmental service as Sandite vehicles. Former Class 121 Sandite car TDB977486 (ex W54285) is seen at Plymouth Laira on 17th November 1987. *B Morrison*

Right: Brand new Gloucester RCW Class 122 single unit W55000 is seen outside Swindon Stock Shed on 4th May 1958. *A Swain*

Below: Ready for delivery, new Class 122 DTS W56295 is seen in 1958. *P J Sharpe*

On 8th January 1986 Tyseley base Class 122 M55002 is seen in the snow at Stourbridge Town ready to depart with the 13.11 service to Stourbridge Junction. *C J Tuffs*

Class 122 Route Learning Railcar TDB975309 (ex M55008) is seen at York on 23rd November 1975. These Class 121 and Class 122 "Bubble-cars" were very popular for conversions to departmental use. *B Morrison*

On 12th June 1963 a new Class 123 Inter-city set led by W52086 is seen running trials at Swindon. When new they were fitted with a bright yellow corridor cover. *A Swain*

By the mid 1970s the Class 123 Inter-city units had settled down to working outer suburban services from Paddington to Oxford and Newbury. On 21st May 1975 the 18.18 Paddington-Didcot service is seen approaching Royal Oak just outside Paddington. W52096 is leading the seven-car formation. *B Morrison*

By the end of the 1970s the Class 123 units had moved north to join the similar Class 124 units working on the southern Trans-Pennine services. This night view of a Hull-Sheffield service at Doncaster was taken on 28th October 1980.

The Class 124 Trans-Pennine units entered service in green livery. Here a unit is seen entering Huddersfield from Leeds on a train heading across the Pennines to Manchester. *P J Sharpe*

Class 124 DMC NE51960 newly repainted with a wrap-around yellow end on its blue and grey livery is seen at Liverpool Lime Street. *C R Whitfield*

On 26th March 1971 a Trans-Pennine DMU led by E51957 is waiting to leave Liverpool Lime Street on a service to Hull. By this time the buffet cars were starting to be taken out of use leaving five-car units. *J H Cooper-Smith*

Class 124 buffet E59776 was still in service when seen at Newton Heath on the 22nd September 1973, but within two years it was withdrawn from service. *D L Percival*

When first built the Trans-Pennine buffet cars (known as Griddle cars) were highly fashionable. This official BR interior shot shows the 1960s style decor. *BR*

By 1983 the Trans-Pennine DMUs were reduced to four cars, as seen by this shot of the 12.39 Morecambe to Leeds service leaving Skipton on 22nd February 1983. What would modern Health and Safety rules have to say about that platform surface? *G Scott-Lowe*

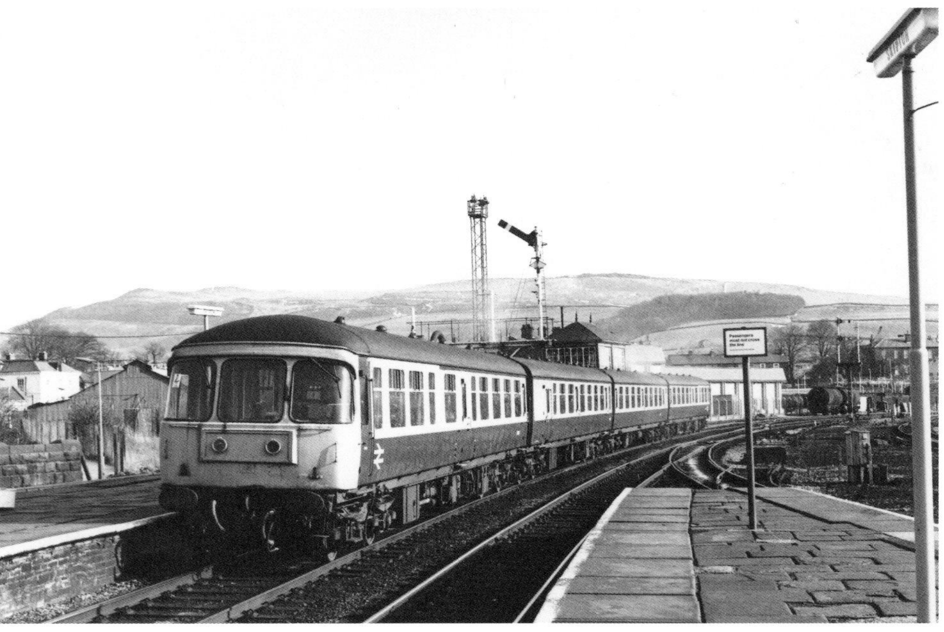

On 1st July 1978 a Trans-Pennine DMU is seen emerging from the Marsden end of a fume-filled Standedge Tunnel heading for Leeds. *M T Hemmings*

W59039 09/57-10/88 ⊗12/88 ⓖ®02/77
W59040 09/57-10/89 ⊗11/90 ⓖ®02/77
W59041 10/57-05/88 ⊗06/88 ⓖ®06/78 ⊠10/87-01/88

Class 101 Metropolitan-Cammell
Trailer Second Lavatory
TSL
E59042-E59048

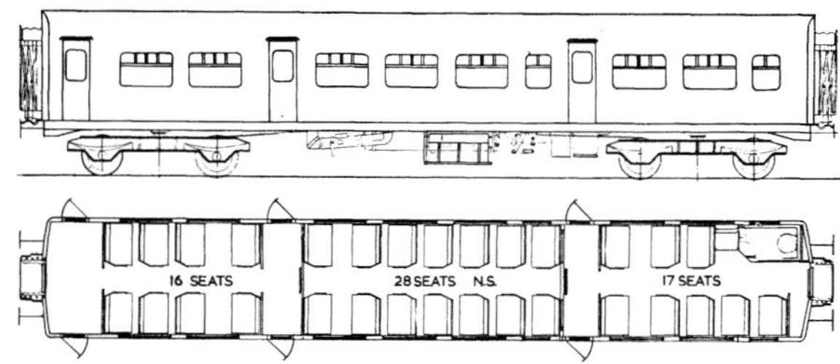

Coupling: ■ Blue square
Diagram: 622 DT201
Lot Number: 30250
Old class: 162
Body: 57' 6" × 9' 3"
Weight: 25t
Seats: 61 second

E59042 10/56-02/91 ⊗03/91 ®06/81 01/65⇨**NE** 01/68⇨**E** 04/78⇨**SC**
E59043 10/56-02/84 ⊗10/87 ®10/80 01/65⇨**NE** 01/68⇨**E** 08/77⇨**SC**
E59044 10/56-07/67 ⊗02/68 01/65⇨**NE**
E59045 11/56-05/88 ⊗12/88 ®08/79 01/65⇨**NE** 01/68⇨**E** 04/78⇨**SC**
E59046 11/56-02/88 ⊗06/90 ®11/78 01/65⇨**NE** 01/68⇨**E** 12/77⇨**SC**
E59047 11/56-05/87 ⊗08/87 01/65⇨**NE** 01/68⇨**E** 12/77⇨**SC**
E59048 11/56-04/88 ⊗09/88 ®08/79 01/65⇨**NE** 01/68⇨**E** 04/78⇨**SC**

Class 101 Metropolitan-Cammell
Trailer Brake Second Lavatory
TBSL
E59049-E59055

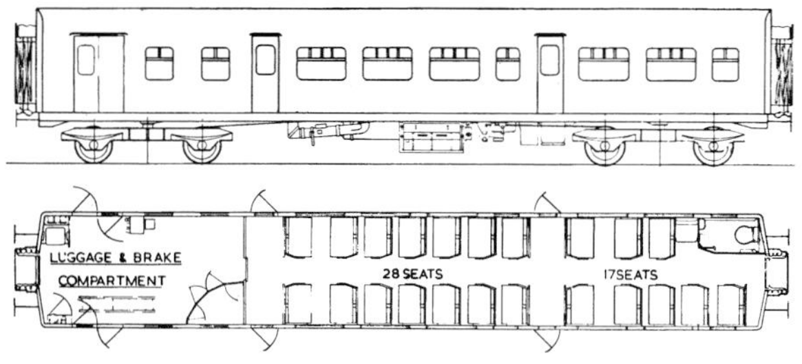

Coupling: ■ Blue square
Diagram: 626 DU202
Lot Number: 30251
Old class: 168
Body: 57' 6" × 9' 3"
Weight: 25t
Seats: 45 second

E59049 10/56-05/90 ⊗06/91 ®06/81 01/65⇨**NE** 01/68⇨**E** 09/79⇨**SC**
E59050 10/56-10/89 ⊗06/91 01/65⇨**NE** 01/68⇨**E** 04/79⇨**W**
E59051 10/56-06/68 ⊗07/69 01/65⇨**NE** 01/68⇨*E*
E59052 11/56-08/88 ⊗05/93 ®02/80 01/65⇨**NE** 01/68⇨**E**
E59053 11/56-04/88 ⊗03/89 ®10/80 01/65⇨**NE** 01/68⇨**E** 04/77⇨**SC**
E59054 11/56-03/88 ⊗04/88 ®07/76 01/65⇨**NE** 01/68⇨**E** 11/82⇨**M**
E59055 11/56-04/92 ⊗10/92 ®01/77 01/65⇨**NE** 01/68⇨**E**

Class 101 Metropolitan-Cammell
Trailer Second Lavatory
TSL
E59060-E59072

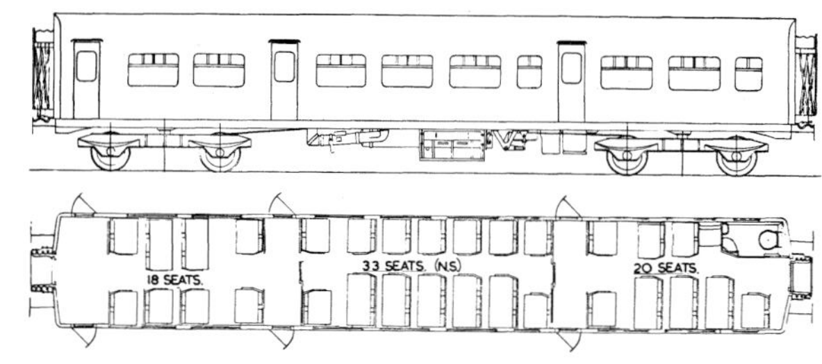

Coupling: ■ Blue square
Diagram: 623 DT202
Lot Number: 30257
Old class: 162
Body: 57' 6" × 9' 3"
Weight: 25t
Seats: 71 second

E59060 01/57-02/88 ⊗01/89 ®06/78 01/65⇨**NE** 01/68⇨**E** 05/77⇨**SC**
E59061 02/57-12/90 ⊗08/91 ®05/79 01/65⇨**NE** 03/66⇨**SC**
E59062 02/57-03/86 ⊗04/86 ®04/77 01/65⇨**NE** 01/68⇨**E** 01/83⇨**M**
E59063 02/57-03/87 ⊗11/87 ®08/78 01/65⇨**NE** 01/68⇨**E** 10/82⇨**M** 03/86⇨**SC**
E59064 02/57-12/85 ⊗03/86 ®07/79 01/65⇨**NE** 01/68⇨**E** 10/82⇨**M**
E59065 03/57-10/87 ⊗08/93 ®*10/76* 01/65⇨**NE** 01/68⇨**E** 01/83⇨**M**
E59066 02/57-03/87 ⊗09/88 ®11/79 01/65⇨**NE** 01/68⇨**E** 05/77⇨**SC**
E59067 03/57-05/87 ⊗11/87 ®02/81 01/65⇨**NE** 03/66⇨**SC**
E59068 03/57-11/83 ⊗08/84 01/65⇨**NE** 01/68⇨**E** 07/80⇨**SC**
E59069 03/57-11/88 ⊗05/89 ®02/81 01/65⇨**NE** 01/68⇨**E** 05/77⇨**SC**
E59070 03/57-03/86 ⊗05/87 ®07/76 01/65⇨**NE** 01/68⇨**E** 10/82⇨**M**
E59071 04/57-07/87 ⊗11/87 ®10/80 01/65⇨**NE** 01/68⇨**E** 12/77⇨**SC**
E59072 04/57-07/93 ⊗02/94 01/65⇨**NE** 01/68⇨**E** 07/80⇨**SC**

Class 101 Metropolitan-Cammell
Trailer Brake Second Lavatory
TBSL
E59073-E59085

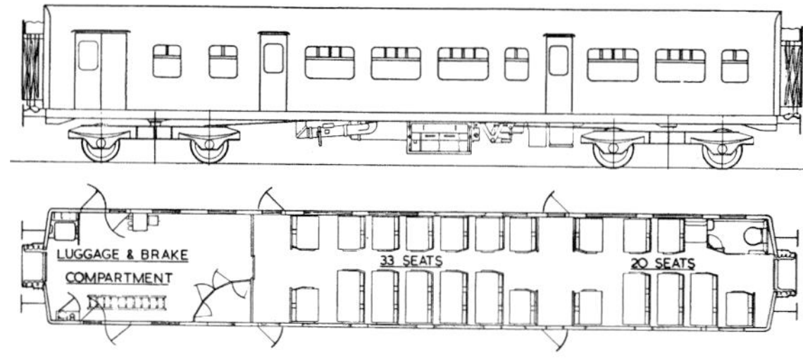

Coupling: ■ Blue square
Diagram: 627 DU203
Lot Number: 30258
Old class: 168
Body: 57' 6" × 9' 3"
Weight: 25t
Seats: 53 second

E59073 01/57-12/89 ⊗06/91 ® */80* 01/65⇨**NE** 01/68⇨**E** 04/79⇨**SC**
E59074 02/57-05/90 ⊗06/91 ®02/82 01/65⇨**NE** 03/66⇨**SC** ⊠05/90-05/90
E59075 02/57-08/88 ⊗10/88 ®02/76 01/65⇨**NE** 01/68⇨**E**
E59076 02/57-09/86 ⊗02/87 ® */80* 01/65⇨**NE** 01/68⇨**E**
E59077 02/57-03/92 ⊗01/94 ®12/82 01/65⇨**NE** 01/68⇨**E** 02/78⇨**SC** 07/80⇨**E**
E59078 03/57-03/89 ⊗05/89 ®11/79 01/65⇨**NE** 01/68⇨**E**
E59079 02/57-06/92 ⊗01/94 ®02/81 01/65⇨**NE** 01/68⇨**E**
E59080 03/57-06/92 ⊗01/94 ®04/83 01/65⇨**NE** 03/66⇨**SC**
E59081 03/57-05/81 ⊗10/86 01/65⇨**NE** 01/68⇨**E** 03/77⇨**M** 04/79⇨**SC**
E59082 03/57-05/90 ⊗04/91 ®04/83 01/65⇨**NE** 01/68⇨**E** 10/75⇨**W** 05/76⇨**E** 05/79⇨**W**
E59083 03/57-09/86 ⊗02/88 ®02/81 01/65⇨**NE** 01/68⇨**E**

E59084		04/57-04/92	⊗10/92	®*10/76*	01/65⇨**NE**	01/68⇨**E**	
E59085		04/57-10/89	⊗03/92	® */81*	01/65⇨**NE**	01/68⇨**E**	10/78⇨**SC**
					07/80⇨**E**		

Class 101 Metropolitan-Cammell
Trailer Second Lavatory
TSL
E59086-E59091

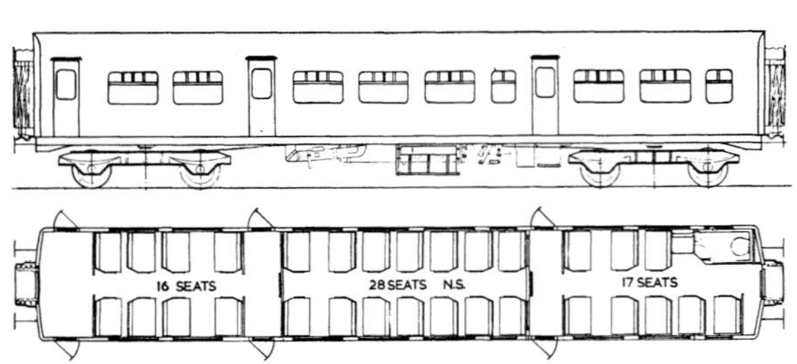

Coupling: ■ Blue square
Diagram: 622 DT201
Lot Number: 30264
Old class: 162
Body: 57' 6" × 9' 3"
Weight: 25t
Seats: 61 second

E59086		09/57-11/90	⊗05/91	®06/81	01/65⇨**NE**	01/68⇨**E**	12/77⇨**SC**
E59087		09/57-03/86	⊗05/87	®01/77	01/65⇨**NE**	01/68⇨**E**	01/83⇨**M**
E59088		10/57-09/87	⊗08/87	®09/78	01/65⇨**NE**	01/68⇨**E**	08/77⇨**SC**
E59089		10/57-04/86	⊗12/86	®01/77	01/65⇨**NE**	01/68⇨**E**	01/83⇨**M**
E59090		10/57-11/90	⊗05/91	® /82	01/65⇨**NE**	01/68⇨**E**	12/77⇨**SC**
E59091		10/57-12/93	⊗03/94	® /81	01/65⇨**NE**	01/68⇨**E**	05/83⇨**M**

Class 101 Metropolitan-Cammell
Trailer Brake Second Lavatory
TBSL
E59092-E59097

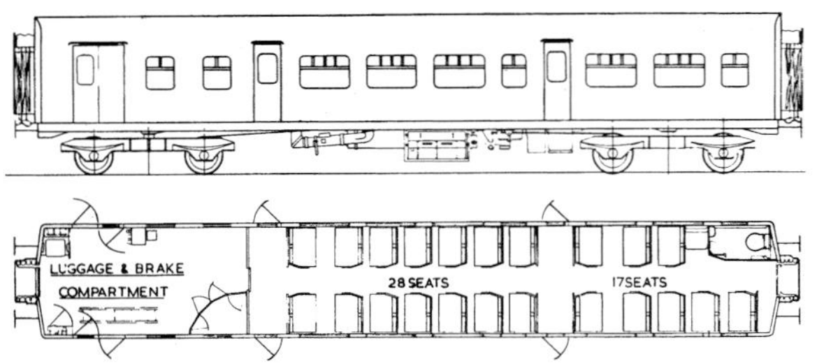

Coupling: ■ Blue square
Diagram: 626 DU202
Lot Number: 30265
Old class: 168
Body: 57' 6" × 9' 3"
Weight: 25t
Seats: 45 second

E59092		09/57-04/92	⊗10/92	® /82	01/65⇨**NE**	01/68⇨**E**	
E59093		09/57-06/92	⊗01/94		01/65⇨**NE**	01/68⇨**E**	04/79⇨**W**
E59094		10/57-09/86	⊗12/86	®01/77	01/65⇨**NE**	01/68⇨**E**	
E59095		10/57-01/92	⊗10/92	® /81	01/65⇨**NE**	01/68⇨**E**	10/75⇨**W**
					05/76⇨**E**		
E59096		10/57-03/88	⊗03/90		01/65⇨**NE**	01/68⇨**E**	05/79⇨**W**
E59097		10/57-10/87	⊗01/92	®02/80	01/65⇨**NE**	01/68⇨**E**	

Class 126 BR Swindon
Trailer Buffet First Side-Corridor with Lavatory
TFKRB
SC59098-SC59099

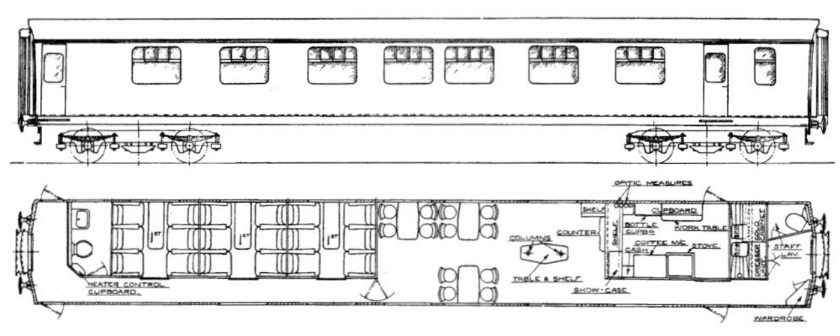

Coupling: ● White circle
Diagram: 560
Lot Number: 30537
Old class: 187
Body: 64' 6" × 9' 3" Inter-City
Weight: 35t 16cwt
Seats: 18 first, 12 buffet

SC59098	01/61-10/72	ⓟ⊗09/94
SC59099	02/61-10/72	ⓟ⊗09/94

Class 111 Metropolitan-Cammell
Trailer Second Lavatory
TSL
E59100-E59109, (59110-59111)

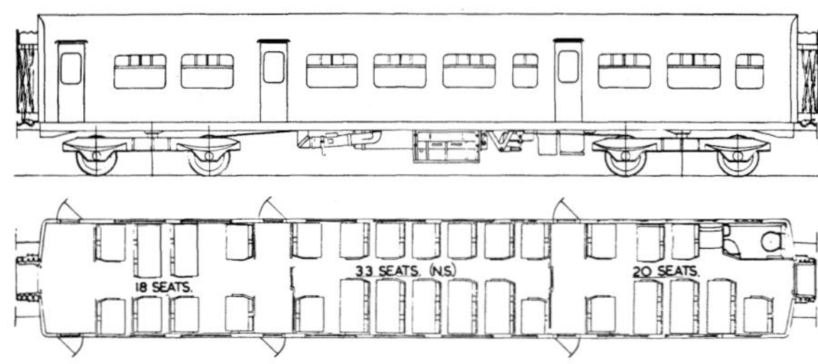

Coupling: ■ Blue square
Diagram: 623 DT202
Lot Number: 30269
Old class: 164
Body: 57' 6" × 9' 3"
Weight: 25t
Seats: 71 second

E59100		10/57-10/85	⊗07/86	®11/78	01/65⇨**NE**	01/68⇨**E**	10/82⇨**M**
E59101	04/90➲**59110**	11/57-04/90	⊗12/95	® /81	01/65⇨**NE**	01/68⇨**E**	10/83⇨**M**
E59102		11/57-02/87	⊗11/87	®11/79	01/65⇨**NE**	01/68⇨**E**	01/83⇨**M**
					03/86⇨**SC**		
E59103		12/57-08/69	⊗10/69		01/65⇨**NE**	01/68⇨**E**	
E59104		12/57-01/90	⊗02/92	® /82	01/65⇨**NE**	01/68⇨**E**	05/84⇨**M**
					03/86⇨**SC**		
E59105	04/90➲**59111**	12/57-04/90	⊗08/93	®01/81	01/65⇨**NE**	01/68⇨**E**	01/83⇨**M**
E59106		12/57-12/86	⊗01/87	®10/81	01/65⇨**NE**	01/68⇨**E**	05/83⇨**M**
E59107		01/58-02/91	⊗03/91	®10/81	01/65⇨**NE**	01/68⇨**E**	10/83⇨**M**
E59108		01/58-05/86	⊗07/88	®11/79	01/65⇨**NE**	01/68⇨**E**	05/83⇨**M**
					04/86⇨**E**		
E59109		01/58-05/79	⊗12/81		01/65⇨**NE**	01/68⇨**E**	04/77⇨**SC**
59110	04/90⊂**59101**	11/57-12/95	⊗12/95	® /81			
59111	04/90⊂**59105**	12/57-03/93	⊗08/93	®01/81			

Class 101 Metropolitan-Cammell
Trailer Brake Second Lavatory
TBSL
E59112-E59113

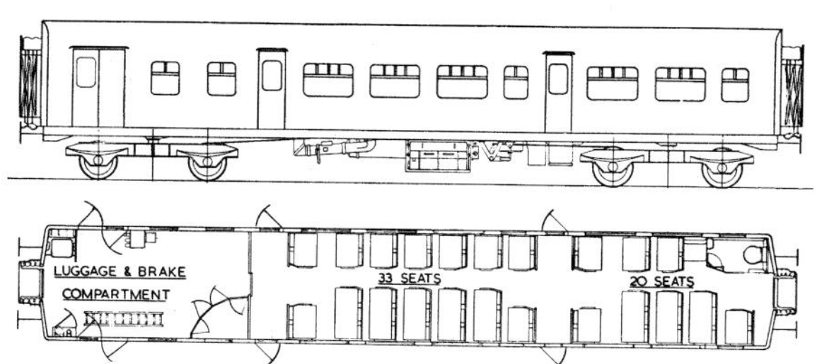

Coupling:	■ Blue square
Diagram:	627 DU203
Lot Number:	30274
Old class:	168
Body:	57' 6" × 9' 3"
Weight:	25t
Seats:	53 second

E59112	11/57-06/88	⊗06/90	®10/80	01/65⇨**NE**	01/68⇨**E**	08/69⇨**SC**
E59113	11/57-02/89	⊗06/91	® /83	01/65⇨**NE**	01/68⇨**E**	

Class 101 Metropolitan-Cammell
Trailer Composite Lavatory
TCL
M59114-M59131

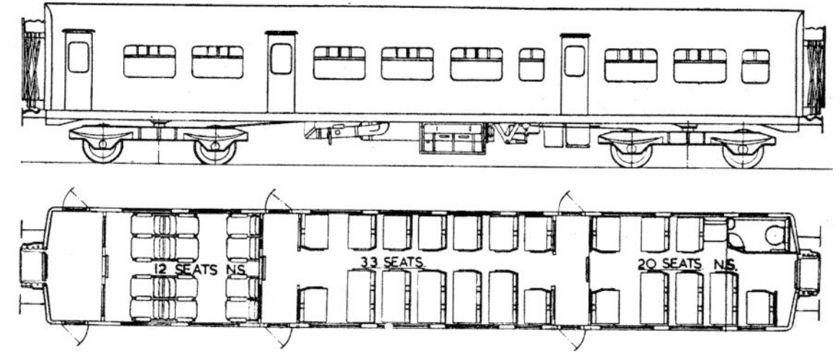

Coupling:	■ Blue square
Diagram:	624 DT301 ②DT220
Lot Number:	30277
Old class:	171
Body:	57' 6" × 9' 3"
Weight:	25t
Seats:	12 first, 53 second

M59114	02/58-09/88	⊗10/88	®11/78	
M59115	02/58-10/93	⊗08/94	®05/76	
M59116	02/58-10/89	⊗05/91	®09/81	
M59117	02/58-12/93	Ⓟ	®04/80	
M59118	02/58-07/93	⊗08/93	®05/83	03/85⇨**E**
M59119	03/58-02/88	⊗03/88	®02/77	
M59120	03/58-03/88	⊗04/88	®11/78	
M59121	02/58-03/87	⊗11/87	®06/78	03/86⇨**SC**
M59122	02/58-05/87	⊗11/90	®11/76	05/79⇨**W**
M59123	03/58-09/88	⊗03/90	®03/77	05/79⇨**W**
M59124	03/58-11/90	⊗08/91	® /81	03/86⇨**SC**
M59125	03/58-10/93	⊗08/94	® /82	
M59126	03/58-03/86	⊗10/86	®01/80	
M59127	03/58-12/86	⊗11/87		03/86⇨**SC**
M59128	04/58-09/92	⊗02/93		
M59129	04/58-12/85	⊗08/86	®10/81	
M59130	04/58-11/90	⊗03/91	®02/81	11/86⇨**W**
M59131	04/58-06/86	⊗08/86	®11/79	

Class 104 Birmingham RC&W
Trailer Composite Lavatory
TCL
M59132-M59135

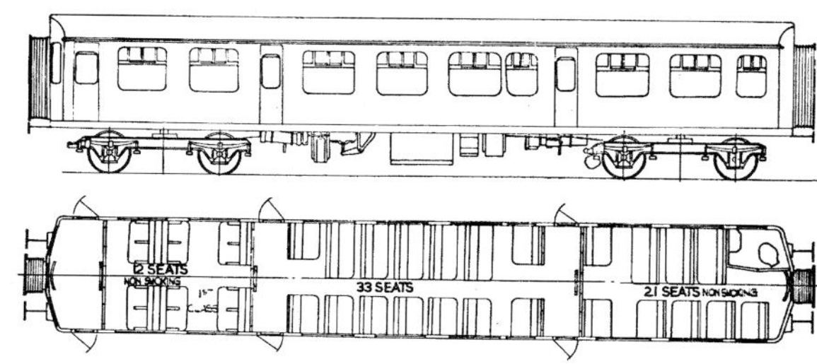

Coupling:	■ Blue square
Diagram:	582 DT302 ②DT218
Lot Number:	30292
Old class:	169
Body:	57' 6" × 9' 3"
Weight:	24t
Seats:	12 first, 54 second

M59132	04/57-03/83	⊗06/84	
M59133	04/57-03/83	⊗05/84	
M59134	05/57-12/81	⊗05/82	®04/81
M59135	05/57-05/81	⊗11/83	

Class 104 Birmingham RC&W
Trailer Composite Lavatory
TCL
M59136-M59187

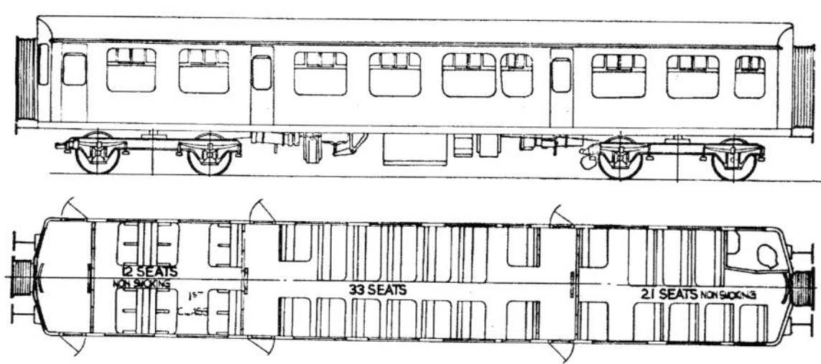

Coupling:	■ Blue square
Diagram:	582 DT302 ②DT218
Lot Number:	30295
Old class:	169
Body:	57' 0" × 9' 3"
Weight:	24t
Seats:	12 first, 54 second

M59136	05/57-05/81	⊗11/83			
M59137	05/57-10/89	Ⓟ			
M59138	06/57-12/81	⊗06/84			
M59139	06/57-10/80	⊗10/86			
M59140	06/57-12/82	⊗06/84			
M59141	06/57-03/83	⊗06/84			
M59142	06/57-09/81	⊗02/82			
M59143	07/57-03/83	⊗08/84			
M59144	07/57-08/89	⊗05/90			
M59145	07/57-03/83	⊗07/84			
M59146	07/57-11/81	⊗05/84	®05/80		
M59147	07/57-11/82	⊗03/84			
M59148	07/57-10/89	⊗01/90			
M59149	08/57-09/89	⊗09/89			
M59150	08/57-06/81	⊗08/82		02/81⇨**SC**	⊠01/81-02/81
M59151	08/57-11/81	⊗08/82			
M59152	09/57-09/89	⊗09/89			
M59153	09/57-10/89	⊗01/96	®06/81		
M59154	09/57-11/68	⊗07/69			
M59155	09/57-10/89	⊗12/89			
M59156	09/57-12/82	⊗12/84			
M59157	10/57-11/81	⊗04/82			
M59158	10/57-01/81	⊗01/84			
M59159	10/57-06/81	⊗08/82		02/81⇨**SC**	⊠01/81-02/81
M59160	10/57-12/82	⊗07/84			
M59161	10/57-06/81	⊗10/84		02/81⇨**SC**	⊠01/81-02/81
M59162	10/57-04/82	⊗06/84			

M59163	10/57-10/90	⊗03/92		
M59164	11/57-12/82	⊗04/84		
M59165	11/57-12/82	⊗05/84		
M59166	11/57-12/82	⊗05/84		
M59167	11/57-11/68	⊗03/69		
M59168	11/57-05/89	⊗08/90		
M59169	11/57-08/82	⊗07/84		
M59170	12/57-11/68	⊗07/69		
M59171	12/57-11/81	⊗08/82		
M59172	12/57-08/82	⊗08/84		
M59173	12/57-09/81	⊗08/82		
M59174	12/57-12/82	⊗09/84		
M59175	01/58-11/81	⊗05/82		
M59176	01/58-08/82	⊗05/84	®06/81	
M59177	01/58-11/81	⊗08/82		
M59178	01/58-11/81	⊗05/84		
M59179	01/58-12/82	⊗05/84		
M59180	01/58-12/82	⊗02/84		
M59181	02/58-12/82	⊗02/84		
M59182	02/58-11/80	⊗11/83		
M59183	02/58-10/89	⊗01/90		
M59184	02/58-11/81	⊗04/82		
M59185	02/58-09/81	⊗08/82		
M59186	03/58-12/84	⊗11/85		
M59187	03/58-02/90	⊗05/91		⊠05/89-08/89

Class 104 Birmingham RC&W

Trailer Second Lavatory

TSL

E59188-E59208

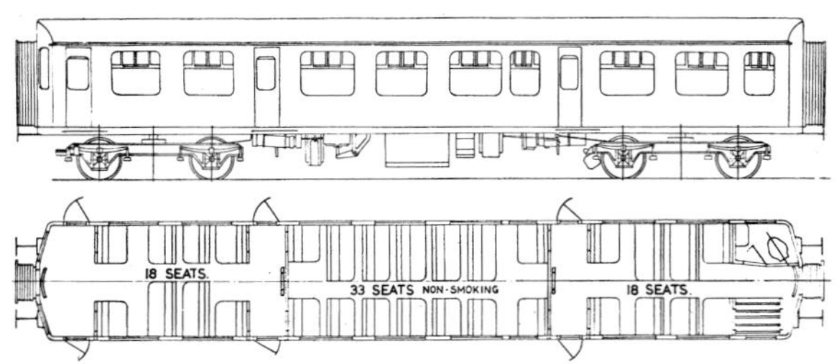

Coupling: ■ Blue square
Diagram: 583 DT203
Lot Number: 30299
Old class: 160
Body: 57' 6" × 9' 3"
Weight: 24t
Seats: 69 second

E59188	06/58-11/81	⊗03/82		01/65⇨**NE** 01/68⇨**E**
E59189	06/58-10/81	⊗03/82		01/65⇨**NE** 01/68⇨**E**
E59190	06/58-06/82	⊗05/84		01/65⇨**NE** 01/68⇨**E**
E59191	07/58-06/82	⊗02/84		01/65⇨**NE** 01/68⇨**E**
E59192	07/58-11/81	⊗02/83		01/65⇨**NE** 01/68⇨**E** 01/78⇨**M**
E59193	07/58-09/81	⊗08/85		01/65⇨**NE** 01/68⇨**E** 01/78⇨**M**
E59194	07/58-06/82	⊗02/84		01/65⇨**NE** 01/68⇨**E**
E59195	08/58-12/89	⊗05/91		01/65⇨**NE** 06/67⇨**M**
E59196	08/58-05/71	⊗11/72		01/65⇨**NE** 01/68⇨**E**
E59197	09/58-03/82	⊗09/83		01/65⇨**NE** 01/68⇨**E**
E59198	09/58-12/82	⊗03/84		01/65⇨**NE** 06/67⇨**M**
E59199	09/58-10/81	⊗07/82		01/65⇨**NE** 01/68⇨**E**
E59200	09/58-03/82	⊗09/83		01/65⇨**NE** 01/68⇨**E** 02/81⇨**M** 03/81⇨**E**
E59201	10/58-02/82	⊗05/82		01/65⇨**NE** 01/68⇨**E**
E59202	10/58-09/72	⊗07/73		01/65⇨**NE** 01/68⇨**E**
E59203	10/58-11/82	⊗11/83		01/65⇨**NE** 01/68⇨**E** 07/80⇨**M**
E59204	10/58-11/77	⊗09/82		01/65⇨**NE** 01/68⇨**E**
E59205	11/58-06/76	⊗10/81		01/65⇨**NE** 01/68⇨**E**
E59206	11/58-10/90	⊗10/91		01/65⇨**NE** 01/68⇨**E** 02/81⇨**M**
E59207	11/58-10/89	⊗01/90	®12/80	01/65⇨**NE** 01/68⇨**E** 07/80⇨**M**
E59208	12/58-06/82	⊗01/83		01/65⇨**NE** 01/68⇨**E**

Class 104 Birmingham RC&W

Trailer Brake Second Lavatory

TBSL

E59209-E59229

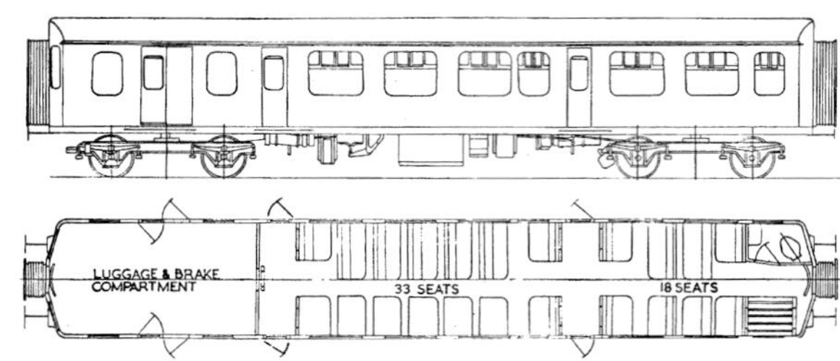

Coupling: ■ Blue square
Diagram: 584 DU204
Lot Number: 30300
Old class: 166
Body: 57' 6" × 9' 3"
Weight: 25t
Seats: 51 second

E59209	06/58-02/82	⊗05/82	01/65⇨**NE** 01/68⇨**E**
E59210	06/58-05/86	⊗07/86	01/65⇨**NE** 01/68⇨**E** 08/80⇨**M** 05/84⇨**SC**
E59211	06/58-06/82	⊗05/84	01/65⇨**NE** 01/68⇨**E**
E59212	07/58-10/84	⊗02/86	01/65⇨**NE** 01/68⇨**E** 02/81⇨**M**
E59213	07/58-06/82	⊗05/84	01/65⇨**NE** 01/68⇨**E**
E59214	07/58-02/81	⊗12/84	01/65⇨**NE** 01/68⇨**E**
E59215	07/58-12/87	⊗01/96	01/65⇨**NE** 01/68⇨**E** 05/82⇨**SC**
E59216	08/58-05/82	⊗09/83	01/65⇨**NE** 01/68⇨**E** 07/80⇨**M** 04/81⇨**E**
E59217	08/58-10/81	⊗07/82	01/65⇨**NE** 01/68⇨**E**
E59218	09/58-07/84	⊗12/84	01/65⇨**NE** 01/68⇨**E** 11/80⇨**M**
E59219	09/58-08/83	⊗04/85	01/65⇨**NE** 01/68⇨**E** 08/80⇨**M**
E59220	09/58-05/82	⊗03/83	01/65⇨**NE** 01/68⇨**E**
E59221	09/58-06/81	⊗08/81	01/65⇨**NE** 01/68⇨**E**
E59222	10/58-03/62	⊗12/63	
E59223	10/58-03/82	⊗10/83	01/65⇨**NE** 01/68⇨**E**
E59224	10/58-02/81	⊗10/88	01/65⇨**NE** 01/68⇨**E**
E59225	10/58-07/87	⊗11/87	01/65⇨**NE** 01/68⇨**E** 06/82⇨**M** 01/84⇨**SC**
E59226	11/58-07/83	⊗12/84	01/65⇨**NE** 01/68⇨**E** 02/81⇨**M**
E59227	11/58-03/85	⊗12/85	01/65⇨**NE** 01/68⇨**E** 11/80⇨**M**
E59228	11/58-10/88	℗	01/65⇨**NE** 01/68⇨**E** 08/80⇨**M**
E59229	12/58-10/83	⊗05/84	01/65⇨**NE** 01/68⇨**E** 06/82⇨**M**

Class 104 Birmingham RC&W

Trailer Second Lavatory

TSL

E59230-E59234

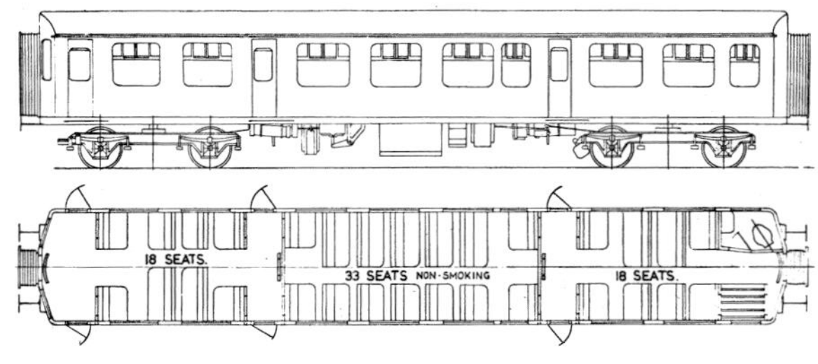

Coupling: ■ Blue square
Diagram: 583 DT203
Lot Number: 30302
Old class: 160
Body: 57' 6" × 9' 3"
Weight: 24t
Seats: 69 second

E59230	01/59-01/89	⊗04/89	01/65⇨**NE** 06/67⇨**M**
E59231	12/58-03/81	⊗02/82	01/65⇨**NE** 01/68⇨**E**
E59232	01/59-03/81	⊗08/81	01/65⇨**NE** 01/68⇨**E**
E59233	01/59-05/82	⊗07/82	01/65⇨**NE** 01/68⇨**E**
E59234	03/59-06/82	⊗07/82	01/65⇨**NE** 01/68⇨**E**

Class 123 BR Swindon

Trailer Second Lavatory
TSL
W59235-W59239

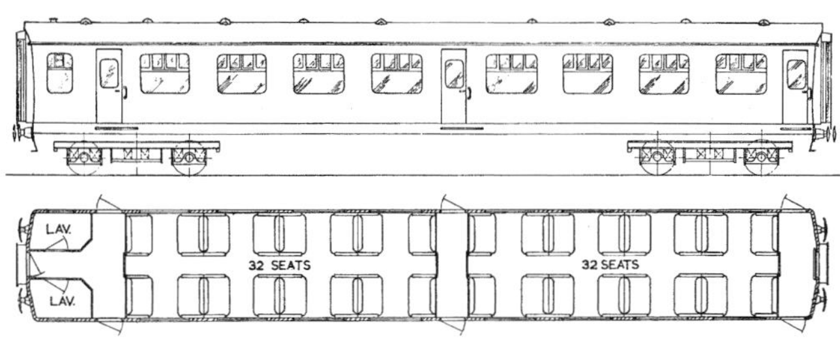

Coupling:	■ Blue square
Diagram:	568 DT211
Lot Number:	30706
Old class:	182
Body:	64' 6" × 9' 3" Inter-City
Weight:	31t 9cwt
Seats:	64 second

W59235	05/63-04/84	⊗11/84	06/77⇨**E**
W59236	05/63-05/84	⊗08/84	06/77⇨**E**
W59237	06/63-04/84	⊗07/84	06/77⇨**E**
W59238	06/63-05/84	⊗11/84	06/77⇨**E**
W59239	06/63-05/84	⊗08/84	06/77⇨**E**

Class 104 Birmingham RC&W

Trailer Brake Second Lavatory
TBSL
E59240-E59244

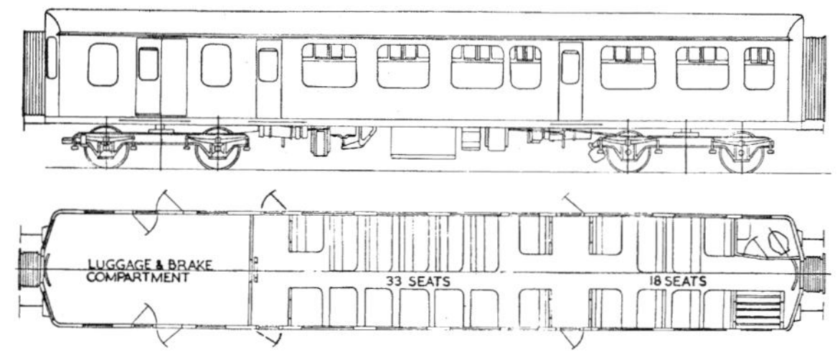

Coupling:	■ Blue square
Diagram:	584 DU204
Lot Number:	30303
Old class:	166
Body:	57' 6" × 9' 3"
Weight:	25t
Seats:	51 second

E59240	01/59-07/84	⊗12/85	®01/81	01/65⇨**NE**	01/68⇨**E**	02/81⇨**M**
E59241	12/58-06/81	⊗07/82		01/65⇨**NE**	01/68⇨**E**	
E59242	01/59-06/82	⊗02/84		01/65⇨**NE**	01/68⇨**E**	
E59243	01/59-05/82	⊗09/83		01/65⇨**NE**	01/68⇨**E**	
E59244	03/59-03/81	⊗07/85		01/65⇨**NE**	01/68⇨**E**	

Class 108 BR Derby

Trailer Brake Second Lavatory
TBSL
E59245-E59250

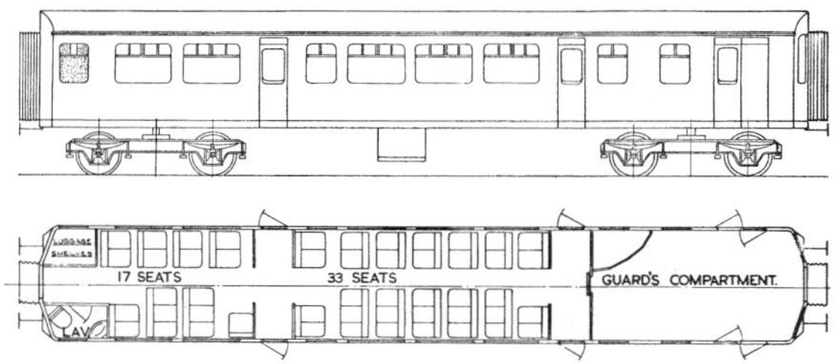

Coupling:	■ Blue square
Diagram:	546 DU201
Lot Number:	30412
Old class:	167
Body:	58' 1" × 9' 2"
Weight:	23t
Seats:	50 second

E59245	10/58-05/91	℗	®*09/76*	01/65⇨**NE**	01/68⇨**E**	
E59246	10/58-12/91	⊗11/91	®01/77	01/65⇨**NE**	03/66⇨**SC**	06/67⇨**NE**
				01/68⇨**E**		⊠11/90-01/91
E59247	10/58-02/85	⊗11/85	®04/77	01/65⇨**NE**	01/68⇨**E**	
E59248	10/58-03/92	⊗06/92	®02/78	01/65⇨**NE**	01/68⇨**E**	
E59249	10/58-11/90	⊗11/91	®01/77	01/65⇨**NE**	01/68⇨**E**	
E59250	10/58-11/90	℗	®01/78	01/65⇨**NE**	01/68⇨**E**	

Class 120 BR Swindon

Trailer Buffet Second Lavatory
TSLRB
W59255-W59301

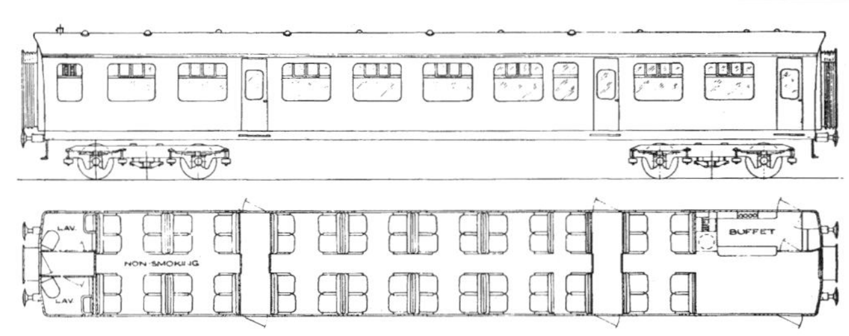

Coupling:	■ Blue square
Diagram:	561 DT217
Lot Number:	30336
Old class:	179
Body:	64' 6" × 9' 3" Cross Country
Weight:	31t
Seats:	60 second

W59255	03/58-02/83	⊗08/85	05/69⇨**M**			
W59256	03/58-07/85	⊗03/86	05/69⇨**M**			⊠01/84-03/85
W59257	03/58-11/83	⊗09/85	05/69⇨**M**			
W59258	03/58-03/86	⊗10/86	05/69⇨**M**			⊠01/84-03/85
W59259	03/58-01/84	⊗02/86	05/69⇨**M**			
W59260	03/58-05/83	⊗02/86	12/80⇨**M**			
W59261	03/58-05/86	⊗07/86	10/77⇨**M**			
W59262	03/58-12/87	⊗11/89	02/79⇨**M**	02/86⇨**SC**		
W59263	03/58-05/86	⊗07/86	06/69⇨**M**			
W59264	03/58-03/87	⊗11/87	12/80⇨**M**	02/86⇨**SC**		
W59265	03/58-05/83	⊗09/85	11/80⇨**M**			
W59266	03/58-11/82	⊗09/84	10/77⇨**M**			
W59267	03/58-11/83	⊗09/85	06/69⇨**M**			
W59268	03/58-03/87	⊗08/87	02/81⇨**M**	02/86⇨**SC**		
W59269	03/58-06/83	⊗04/85	01/63⇨**M**	12/63⇨**W**	12/80⇨**M**	
W59270	03/58-12/67	⊗12/68				
W59271	03/58-12/67	⊗12/68				
W59272	03/58-03/85	⊗09/85	05/69⇨**M**			
W59273	05/58-02/83	⊗09/85	05/69⇨**M**			
W59274	05/58-03/86	⊗05/87	05/69⇨**M**			
W59275	05/58-06/83	⊗09/84	02/79⇨**M**			
W59276	05/58-11/83	℗	05/69⇨**M**			
W59277	05/58-06/83	⊗12/84	12/80⇨**M**			
W59278	05/58-11/82	⊗12/84	12/80⇨**M**			

W59279	05/58-03/83	⊗12/84		10/77⇨M
W59280	05/58-11/83	⊗08/85		05/69⇨M
W59281	07/58-10/87	⊗09/88		01/63⇨M 12/63⇨W 05/69⇨M 02/86⇨SC ⊠05/83-03/85
W59282	07/58-06/88	⊗10/90		12/80⇨M 05/81⇨W
W59283	08/58-03/83	⊗02/86		05/69⇨M
W59284	08/58-05/86	⊗07/86		06/82⇨M
W59285	09/58-03/87	⊗07/87		11/81⇨M 02/86⇨SC
W59286	09/58-10/85	⊗03/86		06/82⇨M
W59287	09/58-03/86	⊗05/87		05/69⇨M
W59288	09/58-11/82	⊗11/83		10/77⇨M
W59289	09/58-10/87	⊗09/88		01/63⇨M 12/63⇨W 05/69⇨M 02/86⇨SC
W59290	10/58-01/84	⊗09/85		01/63⇨M 12/63⇨W 05/69⇨M
W59291	10/58-11/82	⊗12/84		10/77⇨M
W59292	10/58-11/83	⊗02/86		12/80⇨M
W59293	10/58-03/85	⊗09/85		05/69⇨M ⊠01/84-03/85
W59294	10/58-01/84	⊗09/85		10/77⇨M
W59295	01/59-03/86	⊗05/87	®11/79	05/69⇨M
W59296	01/59-11/82	⊗12/84		10/79⇨M
W59297	01/59-08/87	⊗03/89		01/63⇨M 04/86⇨SC
W59298	02/59-09/68	⊗01/69		
W59299	02/59-03/83	⊗04/85		01/63⇨M 12/63⇨W 10/77⇨M
W59300	03/59-03/86	⊗06/86	®11/79	01/63⇨M 12/63⇨W 05/69⇨M
W59301	03/59-03/86	⊗06/86	®10/77	05/69⇨M 01/86⇨Parcels

Class 101 Metropolitan-Cammell

Trailer Second Lavatory
TSL
E59302-E59306

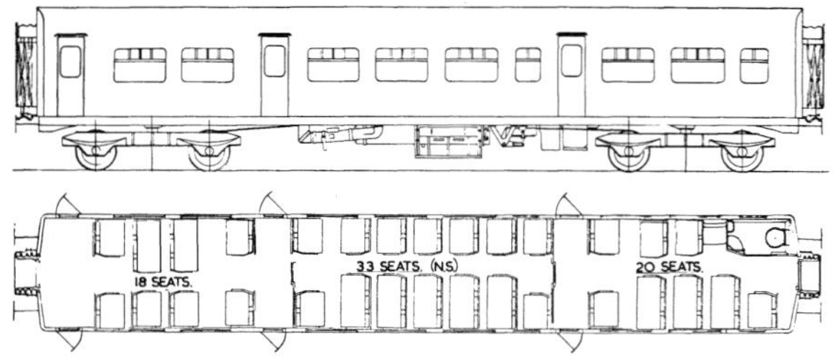

Coupling: ■ Blue square
Diagram: 623 DT202
Lot Number: 30273
Old class: 162
Body: 57' 6" × 9' 3"
Weight: 25t
Seats: 71 second

E59302	11/57-01/95	⊗12/94	®04/83	01/65⇨NE 03/66⇨SC ⊠11/90-01/91
E59303	11/57-08/00	Ⓟ	®01/83	01/65⇨NE 03/66⇨SC
E59304	11/57-09/91	⊗02/92	®02/82	01/65⇨NE 03/66⇨SC
E59305	11/57-02/89	⊗08/91	®11/79	01/65⇨NE 01/68⇨E 08/69⇨SC
E59306	11/57-12/93	⊗02/94	®06/76	01/65⇨NE 01/68⇨E 01/83⇨M

Class 105 Cravens

Trailer Composite Lavatory
TCL
M59307-M59325

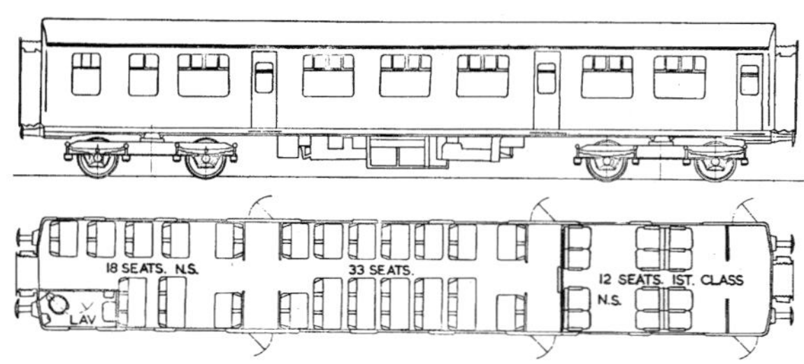

Coupling: ■ Blue square
Diagram: 30354
Lot Number: 530
Body: 57' 6" × 9' 2"
Weight: 23t
Seats: 12 first, 51 second

M59307	09/57-11/68	⊗08/69
M59308	09/57-07/69	⊗10/69
M59309	10/57-07/69	⊗10/69
M59310	10/57-07/69	⊗10/69
M59311	10/57-07/69	⊗10/69
M59312	10/57-07/69	⊗10/69
M59313	11/57-07/69	⊗10/69
M59314	11/57-05/70	⊗08/70
M59315	11/57-05/70	⊗08/70
M59316	11/57-07/69	⊗10/69
M59317	12/57-07/69	⊗10/69
M59318	01/58-07/69	⊗10/69
M59319	01/58-07/69	⊗10/69
M59320	01/58-11/69	⊗05/70
M59321	01/58-11/69	⊗05/70
M59322	01/58-02/69	⊗05/69
M59323	02/58-07/69	⊗10/69
M59324	02/58-07/69	⊗10/69
M59325	02/58-07/69	⊗10/69

Class 116 BR Derby

Trailer Composite
TC
W59326-W59376

Diag. 555

Diag. 855 ⑨ *Through gangway fitted* All WR examples fitted by 1972. Others (shown ⑨) converted in the mid 1980s.

Coupling: ■ Blue square
Diagram: 555 DT215 ⑨ 855 DT219
Lot Number: 30365
Old class: 175
Body: 63' 8¾" × 9' 3" Suburban
Weight: 28t 10cwt
Seats: 28 first, 74 second ⑨ 22 first, 68 second

W59326	11/57-01/87	⊗11/89	®02/79	11/66⇨SC 04/78⇨M
W59327	11/57-12/67	⊗11/68		
W59328	11/57-10/83	⊗06/84	®06/78	11/66⇨SC 02/78⇨M
W59329	11/57-12/87	⊗11/87	®02/82	11/66⇨SC
W59330	11/57-03/89	⊗03/89	⑨®08/82	11/66⇨SC
W59331	12/57-09/86	⊗09/86	®07/78	11/66⇨SC
W59332	12/57-10/83	⊗06/84	®06/78	11/66⇨NE 01/68⇨E 02/78⇨M
W59333	11/57-01/85	⊗02/86	®07/78	11/66⇨SC 04/78⇨M
W59334	12/57-12/83	⊗07/85	®10/77	11/66⇨M
W59335	11/57-02/93	⊗07/93	⑨®03/83	06/72⇨SC 06/77⇨E 05/86⇨M
W59336	12/57-07/83	⊗10/83	®03/80	11/66⇨NE 01/68⇨E 02/78⇨M
W59337	11/57-11/85	⊗09/86		11/66⇨SC
W59338	12/57-06/82	⊗02/83		01/63⇨M
W59339	12/57-12/83	⊗07/85	®10/77	01/63⇨M
W59340	01/58-05/85	⊗01/86	⑨®11/77	
W59341	01/58-12/83	⊗07/85	®10/77	01/63⇨M
W59342	01/58-01/87	⊗05/88	®06/82	01/63⇨M
W59343	01/58-12/83	⊗07/84		11/66⇨NE 01/68⇨E 02/78⇨M
W59344	01/58-10/92	⊗03/93	⑨®08/83	06/72⇨SC
W59345	02/58-01/88	⊗02/88		11/66⇨SC
W59346	01/58-10/84	⊗02/86	⑨®01/78	03/76⇨M
W59347	01/58-10/83	⊗07/84	⑨	06/72⇨SC
W59348	01/58-11/81	⊗01/83		08/68⇨M
W59349	01/58-03/86	⊗10/87		08/68⇨E 06/77⇨SC
W59350	02/58-07/85	⊗07/85	⑨®02/76	10/78⇨M

W59351 01/58-10/83 ⊗02/84 ®04/78 01/63⇨M
W59352 02/58-07/85 ⊗07/85⑨®08/79 03/76⇨M
W59353 01/58-10/92 ⊗03/93⑨®09/83 06/72⇨SC 04/77⇨E 05/86⇨M
W59354 01/58-11/87 ⊗11/87 ®02/80 01/68⇨E 04/77⇨SC
W59355 02/58-10/87 ⊗01/88⑨®11/76
W59356 02/58-02/87 ⊗06/87⑨®07/78
W59357 02/58-02/88 ⊗08/88⑨®10/76
W59358 02/58-06/82 ⊗01/83 11/66⇨M
W59359 02/58-05/85 ⊗08/90⑨®10/78
W59360 02/58-12/83 ⊗07/84 ®09/79 05/69⇨SC 04/78⇨M
W59361 03/58-12/83 ⊗07/84 ®02/79 11/66⇨NE 01/68⇨E 02/78⇨M
W59362 02/58-06/87 ⊗08/87⑨®06/78
W59363 03/58-10/87 ⊗01/89⑨®02/77
W59364 03/58-03/88 ⊗04/88⑨®*09/76*
W59365 03/58-12/83 ⊗06/84⑨ 11/78⇨M ⊠08/82-12/82
W59366 04/58-07/85 ⊗07/85⑨®09/76 11/78⇨M
W59367 04/58-10/92 ⊗10/92 ® /82 08/68⇨E 06/77⇨SC 11/81⇨E 05/86⇨M
W59368 03/58-07/85 ⊗07/85⑨®10/78 04/76⇨M
W59369 04/58-07/87 ⊗08/88⑨®06/78
W59370 04/58-12/67 ⊗11/68
W59371 05/58-03/87 ⊗08/87⑨®04/78
W59372 05/58-05/88 ⊗06/88⑨ 03/76⇨M 09/79⇨E 05/86⇨M
W59373 05/58-12/86 ⊗08/87⑨®11/77
W59374 05/58-03/88 ⊗03/88⑨ 05/76⇨M 11/78⇨SC
W59375 05/58-06/88 ⊗12/88⑨ 06/72⇨SC 06/77⇨E 05/86⇨SC
W59376 06/58-12/83 ⊗07/84 ®01/78 08/68⇨M

Class 108 BR Derby

Trailer Second Lavatory
TSL
E59380-E59385

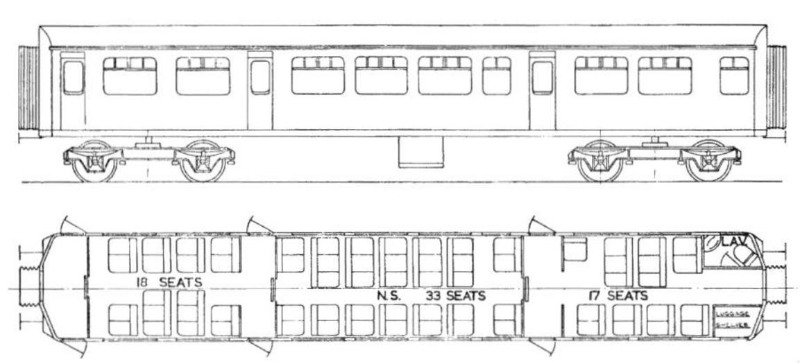

Coupling: ■ Blue square
Diagram: 547 DT205
Lot Number: 30411
Old class: 161
Body: 58' 1" × 9' 2"
Weight: 22t
Seats: 68 second

E59380 10/58-06/92 ⊗05/92 ®02/81 01/65⇨NE 01/68⇨E ⊠08/89-08/89
E59381 10/58-11/90 ⊗06/91 ®04/77 01/65⇨NE 01/68⇨E
E59382 10/58-06/92 ⊗05/92 ®01/78 01/65⇨NE 01/68⇨E
E59383 10/58-03/92 ⊗06/92 ®10/81 01/65⇨NE 01/68⇨E ⊠07/89-08/89
E59384 10/58-05/92 ⊗05/92 ® /82 01/65⇨NE 01/68⇨E
E59385 10/58-11/90 ⊗06/92 ® /81 01/65⇨NE 01/68⇨E

Class 108 BR Derby

Trailer Second Lavatory
TSL
E59386-E59390

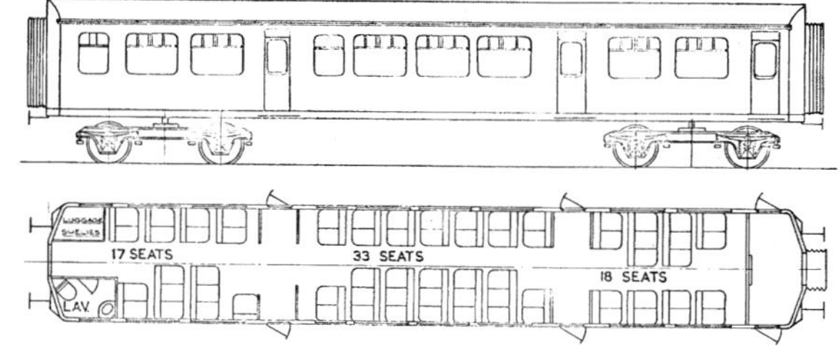

Coupling: ■ Blue square
Diagram: 545 DT206
Lot Number: 30493
Old class: 161
Body: 58' 1" × 9' 2"
Weight: 23t
Seats: 68 second

E59386 10/58-05/92 ⊗05/92 ®01/79 01/65⇨NE 03/66⇨SC 06/67⇨NE 01/68⇨E 08/82⇨M
E59387 10/58-11/92 Ⓟ ®01/77 01/65⇨NE 03/66⇨SC 07/68⇨E 08/82⇨M
E59388 11/58-05/91 ⊗11/92 01/65⇨NE 03/66⇨SC 06/67⇨NE 01/68⇨E 08/82⇨M
E59389 11/58-11/90 Ⓟ⊗03/98 ®*09/76* 01/65⇨NE 03/66⇨SC 06/67⇨NE 01/68⇨E 08/82⇨M 10/91➲**024949**
E59390 11/58-07/91 ⊗10/91 ®01/77 01/65⇨NE 03/66⇨SC 06/67⇨NE 01/68⇨E 08/82⇨M

Class 126 BR Swindon

Trailer First Side-Corridor with Lavatory
TFK
SC59391-SC59400

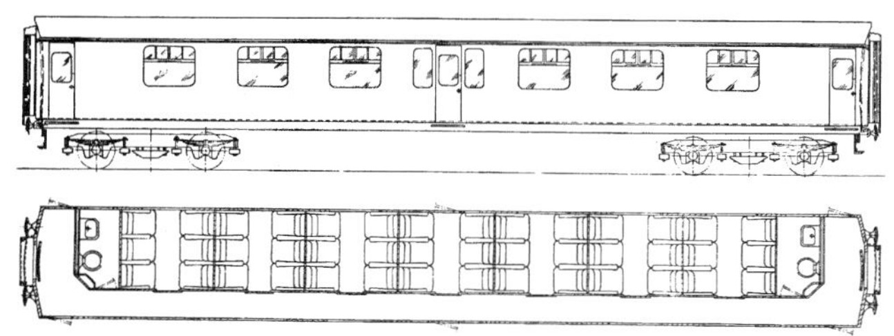

Coupling: ● White circle
Diagram: 570 DT223
Lot Number: 30415
Old class: 188
Body: 64' 6" × 9' 3" Inter-City
Weight: 33t 8cwt
Seats: 42 second

SC59391 04/59-11/81 ⊗12/83
SC59392 04/59-03/82 ⊗10/82
SC59393 04/59-11/81 ⊗10/82
SC59394 04/59-11/81 ⊗10/82
SC59395 06/59-11/81 ⊗10/82
SC59396 06/59-07/81 ⊗10/81
SC59397 07/59-08/82 ⊗01/84
SC59398 07/59-08/82 ⊗01/84
SC59399 09/59-09/81 ⊗11/81
SC59400 09/59-08/82 ⊗10/82

Class 126 BR Swindon

Trailer Composite Lavatory
TCL
SC59402-SC59412

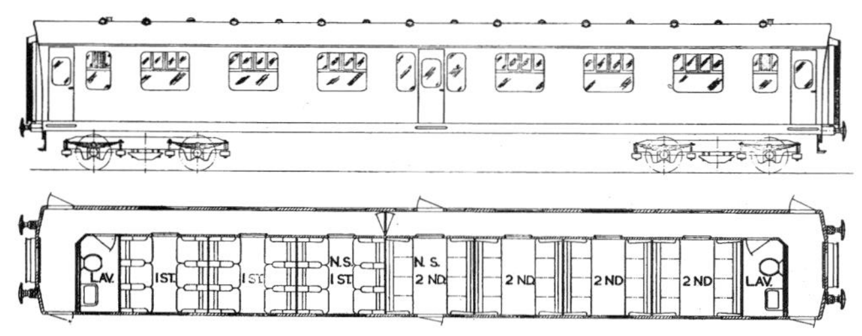

Coupling: ● White circle
Diagram: 571 ②DT223
Lot Number: 30416
Old class: 189
Body: 64' 6" × 9' 3" Inter-City
Weight: 31t 16cwt
Seats: 18 first, 32 second

SC59402 04/59-08/82 ⊗01/84
SC59403 04/59-11/81 ⊗02/83
SC59404 05/59-01/83 Ⓟ ⊠08/82-08/82
SC59405 05/59-07/81 ⊗02/84
SC59406 07/59-03/82 ⊗02/83
SC59407 07/59-08/82 ⊗01/84

SC59408	08/59-08/82	⊗02/83	
SC59409	08/59-11/81	⊗02/83	
SC59410	10/59-08/82	⊗04/83	
SC59411	10/59-01/83	⊗11/83	⊠08/82-08/82
SC59412	10/59-08/82	⊗04/83	

Class 119 Gloucester RC&W

Trailer Buffet Second Lavatory

TSLRB

W59413-W59437

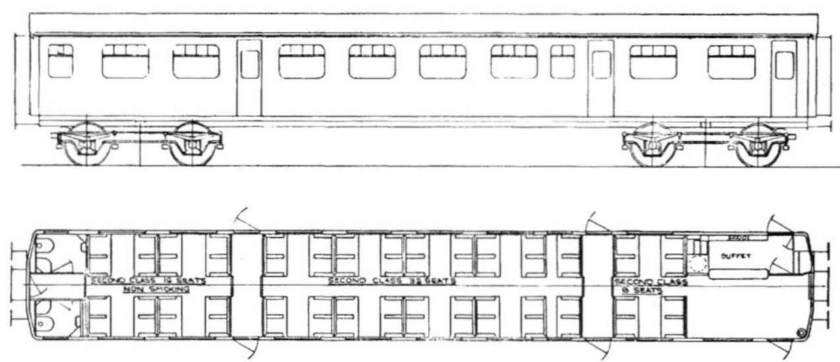

Coupling: ■ Blue square
Diagram: 542 DT216
Lot Number: 30423
Old class: 178
Body: 64' 6" × 9' 3" Cross Country
Weight: 31t
Seats: 60 second

W59413	11/58-07/87	⊗10/90	
W59414	11/58-06/88	⊗09/90	01/63⇨**M** 10/77⇨**W**
W59415	12/58-02/88	⊗09/90	
W59416	12/58-09/93	⊗09/95	01/63⇨**M** 10/79⇨**W**
W59417	12/58-11/88	⊗02/92	
W59418	12/58-08/88	⊗07/89	01/63⇨**M** 10/77⇨**W**
W59419	01/59-06/93	⊗06/93	
W59420	01/59-02/87	⊗06/87	
W59421	02/59-11/90	⊗02/92	
W59422	02/59-10/88	⊗12/88	
W59423	03/59-02/88	⊗01/89	
W59424	03/59-11/90	⊗02/92	
W59425	04/59-07/92	⊗02/93	
W59426	06/59-02/88	⊗09/90	
W59427	06/59-09/86	⊗10/86	
W59428	06/59-07/88	⊗04/90	
W59429	06/59-07/87	⊗01/89	
W59430	07/59-10/93	⊗08/95	01/63⇨**M** 10/77⇨**W**
W59431	07/59-07/87	⊗01/89	01/63⇨**M** 10/77⇨**W**
W59432	08/59-12/87	⊗09/90	01/63⇨**M** 10/77⇨**W**
W59433	09/59-10/88	⊗10/88	01/63⇨**M** 10/77⇨**W**
W59434	10/59-10/87	⊗01/89	
W59435	10/59-05/95	⊗08/95	01/63⇨**M** 10/77⇨**W**
W59436	12/59-07/87	⊗10/90	
W59437	12/59-05/95	⊗08/95	

Class 116 BR Derby

Trailer Composite

TC

W59438-W59448

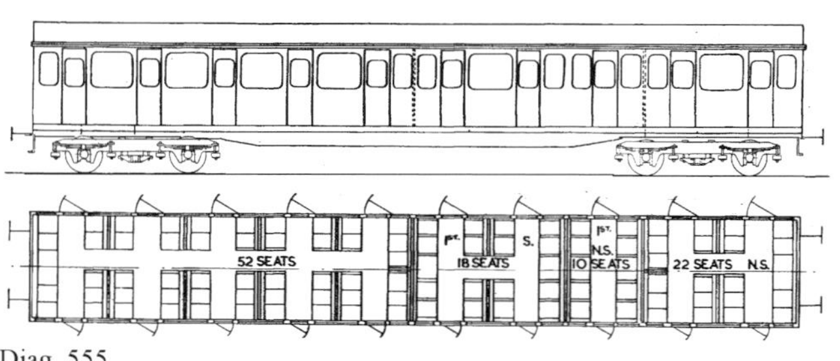

Diag. 555

Diag. 855 ⓖ *Through gangway fitted* All WR examples fitted by 1972. Others (shown *ⓖ*) converted in the mid 1980s.

Coupling: ■ Blue square
Diagram: 555 DT215 ⓖ 555 DT219
Lot Number: 30448
Old class: 175
Body: 63' 8¾" × 9' 3" Suburban
Weight: 28t 10cwt
Seats: 28 first, 74 second ⓖ 22 first, 68 second

W59438	07/58-12/87	⊗08/88	®01/78	12/63⇨**M**	02/86⇨**W**
W59439	08/58-12/87	⊗08/88	®11/79	12/63⇨**M**	02/86⇨**W**
W59440	08/58-01/87	⊗07/87		12/63⇨**M**	
W59441	08/58-01/87	⊗07/87	®07/78	12/63⇨**M**	
W59442	08/58-11/91	⊗02/92	*ⓖ*®04/77	12/63⇨**M**	02/86⇨**W**
W59443	08/58-12/87	⊗08/88		12/63⇨**M**	02/86⇨**W**
W59444	09/58-07/90	Ⓟ	ⓖ®11/77		
W59445	09/58-10/92	Ⓟ⊗04/09ⓖ®04/77			
W59446	09/58-06/93	⊗06/93	ⓖ®11/77		
W59447	10/58-09/71	⊗08/73		04/68⇨**SC**	07/69⇨**W**
					12/65⇨Class 130 Parcels
W59448	10/58-06/90	⊗10/92	ⓖ®10/78	04/76⇨**M**	

Class 125 BR Derby

Trailer Second

TS

E59449-E59468

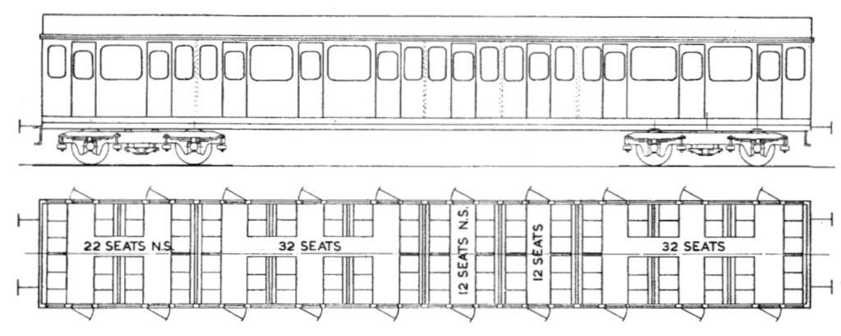

Coupling: ★ Orange star
Diagram: 597
Lot Number: 30463
Old class: 185
Body: 63' 10" × 9' 3" Suburban
Weight: 29t
Seats: 110 second

E59449	12/58-12/76	⊗11/81	
E59450	01/59-01/77	⊗03/82	
E59451	01/59-01/77	⊗11/80	
E59452	01/59-01/77	⊗07/81	
E59453	01/59-01/77	⊗11/80	
E59454	01/59-01/77	⊗05/82	
E59455	01/59-01/77	⊗03/82	
E59456	02/59-12/76	⊗11/81	
E59457	02/59-12/76	⊗11/81	
E59458	02/59-12/76	⊗02/86	03/84➲**RDB975993**
E59459	02/59-02/77	⊗07/80	
E59460	02/59-01/77	⊗07/80	
E59461	03/59-01/77	⊗11/81	
E59462	05/59-01/77	⊗07/78	
E59463	05/59-12/76	⊗07/80	
E59464	05/59-01/77	⊗12/77	
E59465	04/59-12/76	⊗07/80	
E59466	04/59-12/76	⊗07/88	03/84➲**DB975964**
E59467	05/59-01/77	⊗07/80	
E59468	09/59-01/77	⊗05/82	

Class 118 Birmingham RC&W
Trailer Composite Lavatory
TCL
W59469-W59483

Diag. 601

Diag. 851 ⓖ *Through gangway fitted* All converted by 1972.

Coupling:	■ Blue square
Diagram:	601 ⓖ 851 DT305
Lot Number:	30544
Old class:	174
Body:	63' 10" × 9' 3" Suburban
Weight:	30t
Seats:	24 first, 50 second ⓖ 22 first, 48 second

W59469	04/60-10/88	⊗12/88 ⓖ	
W59470	04/60-10/87	⊗07/91 ⓖⓇ01/80	
W59471	04/60-03/88	⊗03/88 ⓖ	
W59472	04/60-09/87	⊗08/88 ⓖ	
W59473	05/60-10/91	⊗11/91 ⓖⓇ02/84	
W59474	05/60-02/87	⊗01/89 ⓖ	
W59475	05/60-11/88	⊗06/89 ⓖ	05/86⇨**M**
W59476	05/60-04/87	⊗05/87 ⓖ	05/86⇨**M**
W59477	06/60-03/88	⊗04/90 ⓖ	
W59478	06/60-12/88	⊗12/88 ⓖⓇ02/78	
W59479	06/60-10/88	⊗12/88 ⓖⓇ06/78	
W59480	07/60-06/87	⊗08/90 ⓖⓇ11/78	
W59481	07/60-07/93	⊗08/93 ⓖ	
W59482	07/60-08/89	⊗12/89 ⓖ	
W59483	07/60-07/93	⊗08/93 ⓖⓇ02/84	

Class 117 Pressed Steel
Trailer Composite Lavatory
TCL
W59484-W59522

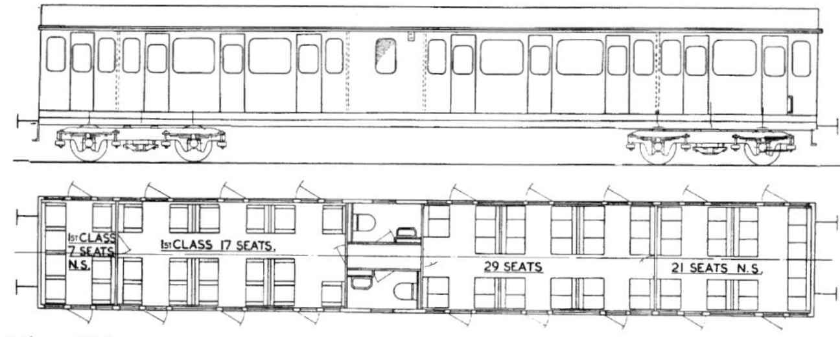

Diag. 601

Diag. 851 ⓖ *Through gangway fitted* All converted by 1972.

Coupling:	■ Blue square
Diagram:	601 ⓖ 851 DT305
Lot Number:	30547
Old class:	176
Body:	63' 10" × 9' 3" Suburban
Weight:	30t
Seats:	24 first, 50 second ⓖ 22 first, 48 second

W59484	11/59-05/95	⊗09/95 ⓖⓇ03/79		
W59485	01/60-05/95	⊗09/95 ⓖⓇ03/79		
W59486	02/60-09/99	Ⓟ ⓖⓇ03/79	05/76⇨**M** 07/78⇨**W**	
W59487	02/60-05/95	⊗09/95 ⓖⓇ03/78		
W59488	02/60-10/93	Ⓟ ⓖⓇ05/79		
W59489	03/60-04/98	⊗04/98 ⓖⓇ02/77		
W59490	03/60-01/94	Ⓟ⊗04/09ⓖⓇ */81*		
W59491	03/60-05/95	⊗09/95 ⓖⓇ09/79		
W59492	04/60-09/99	Ⓟ ⓖⓇ02/79	05/77⇨**M** 11/78⇨**W**	
W59493	04/60-09/95	Ⓟ ⓖⓇ06/78		
W59494	04/60-07/93	Ⓟ ⓖⓇ11/78		
W59495	04/60-08/93	⊗08/93 ⓖⓇ11/78		⊠01/93-02/93
W59496	04/60-03/94	Ⓟ⊗03/09ⓖⓇ03/79		
W59497	04/60-09/95	⊗09/97 ⓖⓇ06/77		
W59498	05/60-05/93	⊗07/93 ⓖⓇ04/80		⊠01/93-02/93
W59499	05/60-07/93	⊗08/93 ⓖⓇ09/78		
W59500	05/60-09/99	Ⓟ ⓖⓇ11/77		
W59501	05/60-03/94	Ⓟ ⓖⓇ10/78		
W59502	06/60-09/92	⊗03/93 ⓖⓇ10/77		
W59503	06/60-01/93	Ⓟ ⓖⓇ09/78		
W59504	06/60-12/92	⊗01/94 ⓖⓇ11/78	05/77⇨**M** 11/78⇨**W**	
W59505	06/60-09/99	Ⓟ ⓖⓇ04/77		
W59506	06/60-09/95	Ⓟ ⓖⓇ11/79		
W59507	06/60-03/94	Ⓟ ⓖⓇ07/78		
W59508	07/60-04/93	Ⓟ ⓖⓇ04/78		
W59509	07/60-09/99	Ⓟ ⓖⓇ11/80		
W59510	07/60-08/94	Ⓟ ⓖⓇ05/79		
W59511	07/60-10/93	Ⓟ ⓖⓇ02/81		
W59512	07/60-07/93	⊗08/93 ⓖⓇ01/79		
W59513	07/60-03/94	Ⓟ ⓖⓇ03/79		
W59514	07/60-07/93	Ⓟ ⓖⓇ01/80		
W59515	07/60-09/95	Ⓟ ⓖⓇ03/79		
W59516	08/60-01/94	Ⓟ ⓖⓇ02/79		
W59517	08/60-09/93	Ⓟ ⓖⓇ03/79		
W59518	09/60-09/93	Ⓟ ⓖⓇ02/79		
W59519	09/60-09/92	⊗05/93 ⓖⓇ05/79		
W59520	09/60-12/95	Ⓟ ⓖⓇ05/75		
W59521	09/60-09/99	Ⓟ ⓖⓇ06/78		
W59522	09/60-09/93	Ⓟ ⓖⓇ09/79		

Class 102⇨101 Metropolitan-Cammell
Trailer Composite Lavatory
TCL
E59523- SC59568

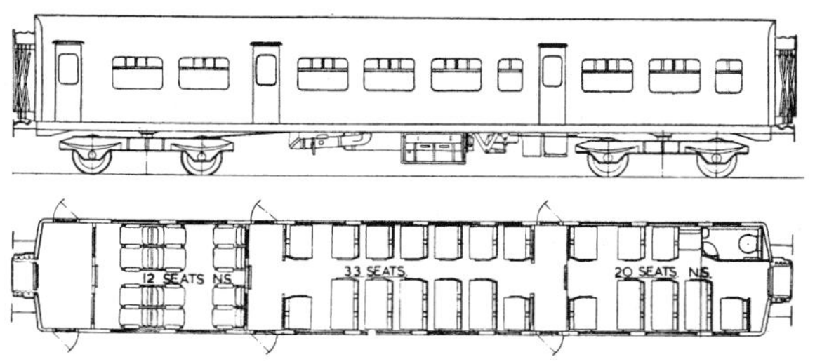

Coupling:	■ Blue square
Diagram:	624 DT301 ②DT220
Lot Number:	30502
Old class:	171
Body:	57' 6" × 9' 3"
Weight:	25t
Seats:	12 first, 53 second

E59523	02/59-06/86	⊗08/86	®04/77	01/65⇨**NE** 01/68⇨**E** 08/82⇨**M**
E59524	02/59-03/88	⊗03/88	®01/77	01/65⇨**NE** 01/68⇨**E** 01/83⇨**M** 03/86⇨**SC**
E59525	02/59-11/90	⊗08/93	®05/83	01/65⇨**NE** 01/68⇨**E** 09/79⇨**SC**
E59526	02/59-11/92	⊗01/94	® /81	01/65⇨**NE** 01/68⇨**E** 10/82⇨**M**
E59527	03/59-12/87	⊗12/87	®11/80	01/65⇨**NE** 01/68⇨**E** 05/83⇨**M**
E59528	03/59-07/88	⊗10/88	®05/80	01/65⇨**NE** 01/67⇨**W** 05/77⇨**M** ⊠05/86-06/86
E59529	03/59-12/86	⊗01/87	®03/80	01/65⇨**NE** 01/68⇨**E** 01/83⇨**M**
E59530	03/59-12/93	⊗02/94	® /82	01/65⇨**NE** 01/68⇨**E** 12/77⇨**SC** 04/79⇨**W** 09/82⇨**M**
E59531	03/59-03/87	⊗11/87	®07/79	01/65⇨**NE** 01/68⇨**E** 01/83⇨**M** 02/86⇨**SC**
E59532	03/59-04/90	⊗05/91	® /81	01/65⇨**NE** 01/68⇨**E** 05/83⇨**M**
E59533	03/59-11/87	⊗11/87	®11/79	01/65⇨**NE** 01/68⇨**E** 01/83⇨**M**
E59534	03/59-01/86	⊗05/87	®11/79	01/65⇨**NE** 01/68⇨**E** 01/83⇨**M**
E59535	04/59-07/86	⊗07/86	®07/79	01/65⇨**NE** 01/68⇨**E** 08/82⇨**M** 03/86⇨**SC**
E59536	04/59-01/95	⊗12/94	®02/84	01/65⇨**NE** 01/68⇨**E** 09/79⇨**M** 03/85⇨**E**
E59537	04/59-07/67	⊗01/68		01/65⇨**NE**
E59538	04/59-03/85	⊗09/85		01/65⇨**NE** 01/67⇨**W** 04/78⇨**M**
E59539	04/59-08/00	℗	®04/82	01/65⇨**NE** 01/68⇨**E** 05/77⇨**SC** 11/78⇨**W**
E59540	04/59-12/93	⊗03/94	® /81	01/65⇨**NE** 01/68⇨**E** 05/83⇨**M**
E59541	05/59-02/88	⊗03/88	®06/78	01/65⇨**NE** 01/68⇨**E** 08/69⇨**SC**
E59542	05/59-11/90	⊗05/91	®08/82	01/65⇨**NE** 01/68⇨**E** 09/79⇨**SC**
SC59543	05/59-09/92	⊗12/92	® /81	01/67⇨**W** 07/78⇨**M**
SC59544	05/59-10/83	⊗10/87		
SC59545	05/59-04/88	⊗07/88	®07/74	
SC59546	05/59-03/86	⊗06/87	®11/79	05/74⇨**W**
SC59547	05/59-05/85	⊗06/87	®11/78	05/74⇨**W**
SC59548	06/59-07/87	⊗06/87		11/78⇨**W**
SC59549	06/59-05/85	⊗01/86	®11/79	05/74⇨**W**
SC59550	06/59-10/85	⊗06/87	®04/78	05/74⇨**W**
SC59551	06/59-02/87	⊗06/87	®11/79	05/74⇨**W**
SC59552	06/59-02/88	⊗03/88	®07/76	
SC59553	06/59-10/89	⊗05/91	®*10/76*	
SC59554	07/59-10/88	⊗10/88	®05/78	
SC59555	07/59-06/88	⊗06/90	®05/78	
SC59556	07/59-05/88	⊗10/89	®06/77	
SC59557	07/59-10/87	⊗11/87	®04/78	
SC59558	07/59-12/86	⊗11/87	®*10/76*	
SC59559	08/59-02/87	⊗08/87	®06/80	
SC59560	08/59-01/88	⊗03/88	®04/78	
SC59561	08/59-11/90	⊗02/91	®12/82	04/79⇨**W**
SC59562	08/59-06/89	⊗08/89	®06/77	
SC59563	08/59-03/88	⊗09/88	®12/76	
SC59564	09/59-08/88	⊗01/89	®10/77	
SC59565	09/59-03/89	⊗08/89	®02/77	
SC59566	09/59-01/88	⊗11/87	®06/81	
SC59567	09/59-03/87	⊗11/87		
SC59568	09/59-01/88	⊗03/88	®*10/76*	

Class 111 Metropolitan-Cammell
Trailer Second Lavatory
TSL
E59569-E59572

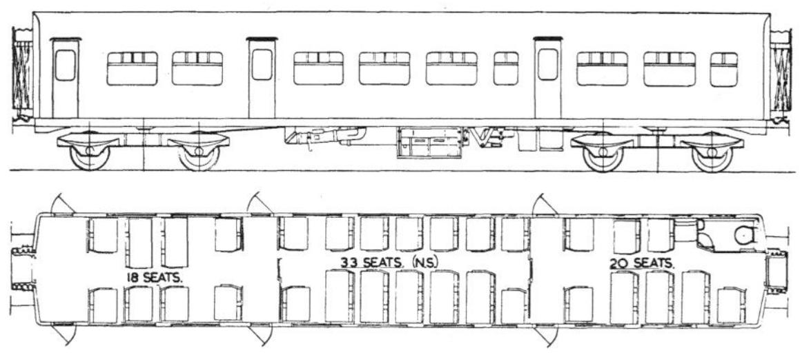

Coupling: ■ Blue square
Diagram: 623 DT202
Lot Number: 30510
Old class: 164
Body: 57' 6" × 9' 3"
Weight: 25t
Seats: 71 second

E59569	12/59-04/88	⊗01/88	®04/77	01/65⇨**NE** 01/68⇨**E** 10/82⇨**M** 03/86⇨**SC**
E59570	12/59-03/93	⊗08/93	® /82	01/65⇨**NE** 01/68⇨**E** 10/83⇨**M** 11/86⇨**W**
E59571	12/59-10/89	⊗01/92	® /82	01/65⇨**NE** 01/68⇨**E** 05/84⇨**M** 03/86⇨**SC**
E59572	12/59-01/86	⊗10/86	®11/80	01/65⇨**NE** 01/68⇨**E** 05/84⇨**M** 10/84⇨**SC**

Class 101 Metropolitan-Cammell
Trailer Buffet Second Lavatory
TSLRB
E59573-E59578

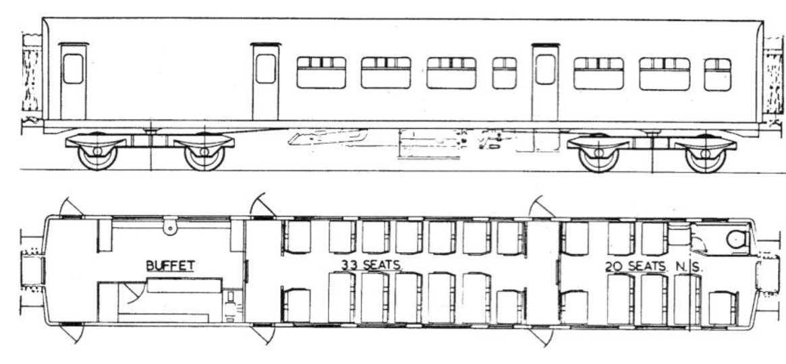

Coupling: ■ Blue square
Diagram: 625 DT221
Lot Number: 30615
Old class: 165
Body: 57' 6" × 9' 3"
Weight: 25t
Seats: 53 second

E59573	05/60-09/75	⊗03/84		01/65⇨**NE** 01/68⇨**E**
E59574	05/60-11/81	⊗02/83	®09/78	01/65⇨**NE** 01/68⇨**E** 07/78⇨**SC**
E59575	05/60-07/73	℗		01/65⇨**NE** 01/68⇨**E**
E59576	05/60-09/75	⊗03/81		01/65⇨**NE** 01/68⇨**E**
E59577	05/60-11/81	⊗03/83		01/65⇨**NE** 01/68⇨**E** 10/78⇨**SC**
E59578	05/60-11/81	⊗02/83		01/65⇨**NE** 01/68⇨**E** 06/79⇨**SC**

Class 120 BR Swindon
Trailer Second Lavatory
TSL
W59579-W59588

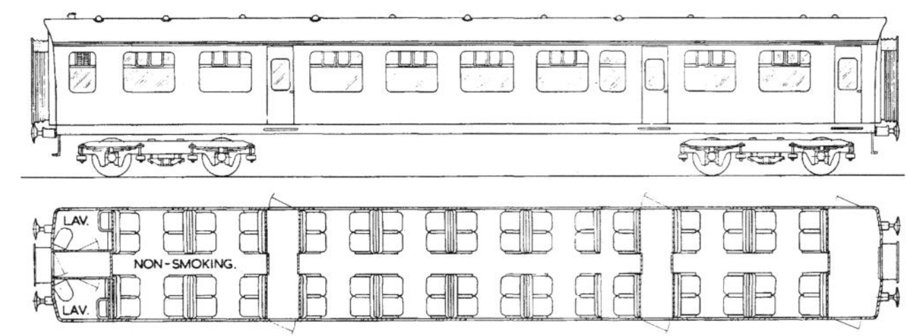

Coupling: ■ Blue square
Diagram: 572 DT210
Lot Number: 30517
Old class: 179
Body: 64' 6" × 9' 3" Cross Country
Weight: 30t 3cwt
Seats: 68 second

W59579	12/60-12/67	⊗12/68	
W59580	12/60-03/87	⊗08/87	01/82⇨**M** 04/86⇨**SC**
W59581	12/60-05/86	⊗07/86	11/81⇨**M**
W59582	01/61-05/86	⊗05/86	06/82⇨**M**
W59583	01/61-05/86	⊗05/86	01/82⇨**M**
W59584	03/61-12/67	⊗12/68	
W59585	03/61-12/67	⊗12/68	
W59586	03/61-05/86	⊗07/86	06/82⇨**M**
W59587	03/61-05/86	⊗09/88	11/81⇨**M** 04/86⇨**E**
W59588	03/61-10/85	⊗03/86	06/82⇨**M**

Class 127 BR Derby
Trailer Second Lavatory
TSL
M59589-M59618

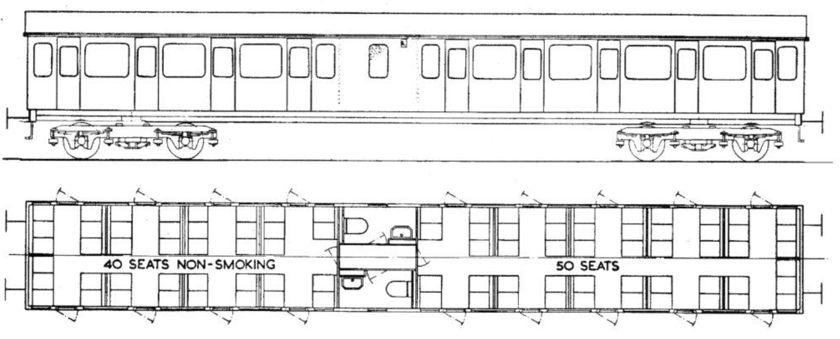

Coupling: ▲ Red triangle
Diagram: 589 DT214
Lot Number: 30522
Old class: 186
Body: 63' 7½" × 9' 3" Suburban
Weight: 30t
Seats: 90 second

M59589	05/59-11/92	⊗11/92	®08/83	
M59590	06/59-10/92	⊗10/92		
M59591	06/59-06/93	⊗06/93	®11/83	
M59592	06/59-09/93	⊗11/93	®05/83	
M59593	06/59-11/90	⊗09/91	®02/84	
M59594	07/59-10/92	⊗09/92	®05/83	
M59595	07/59-01/92	⊗05/92		
M59596	08/59-11/90	⊗09/91		
M59597	08/59-10/92	⊗09/92	®10/83	
M59598	08/59-07/92	⊗08/92		
M59599	08/59-12/72	⊗03/73		
M59600	08/59-10/93	⊗10/94		
M59601	08/59-06/68	⊗01/69		
M59602	09/59-03/93	⊗07/93	®02/84	⊠12/84-12/84
M59603	09/59-10/93	Ⓟ		⊠12/84-12/84
M59604	09/59-10/93	⊗10/94	®10/83	⊠12/84-12/84
M59605	09/59-06/83	⊗06/83		
M59606	09/59-11/90	⊗09/91	®04/83	
M59607	09/59-10/93	⊗10/94		⊠12/84-12/84
M59608	10/59-02/92	⊗02/92	®11/83	⊠12/84-12/84
M59609	10/59-09/93	Ⓟ		
M59610	10/59-11/90	⊗09/91		
M59611	10/59-07/93	⊗08/93		
M59612	11/59-11/90	⊗11/91		
M59613	11/59-11/90	⊗11/91		
M59614	11/59-10/93	⊗10/94		
M59615	11/59-07/92	⊗08/92		
M59616	11/59-11/90	⊗11/91	® /83	
M59617	11/59-10/92	⊗09/92		
M59618	12/59-07/76	⊗08/76		

Class 127 BR Derby
Trailer Second
TS
M59619-M59648

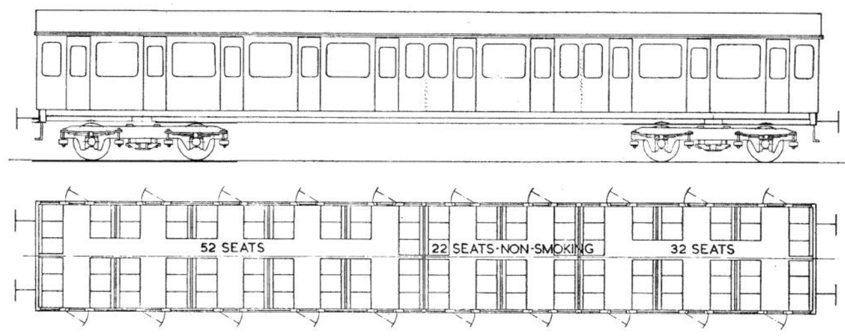

Coupling: ▲ Red triangle
Diagram: 590 DT208
Lot Number: 30523
Old class: 186
Body: 63' 7½" × 9' 3" Suburban
Weight: 29t
Seats: 106 second

ⓖ Fitted with through gangways in the mid 1980s.

M59619	05/59-06/84	⊗12/90	
M59620	06/59-06/84	⊗05/90	
M59621	06/59-07/90	⊗02/92	®07/83
M59622	06/59-07/90	⊗02/92	
M59623	06/59-01/87	⊗07/87	
M59624	07/59-07/76	⊗08/76	
M59625	07/59-10/92	⊗02/92	ⓖ®11/83
M59626	08/59-03/88	⊗03/88	
M59627	08/59-07/90	⊗02/92	
M59628	08/59-06/84	⊗12/90	
M59629	08/59-07/92	⊗08/92	ⓖ®02/84
M59630	08/59-07/76	⊗08/76	
M59631	08/59-07/90	⊗02/92	
M59632	09/59-04/92	⊗05/92	ⓖ®10/83
M59633	09/59-06/84	⊗12/90	
M59634	09/59-12/87	⊗10/92	
M59635	09/59-12/66	⊗12/66	
M59636	09/59-03/88	⊗03/88	®07/83
M59637	09/59-06/84	⊗12/90	
M59638	10/59-03/88	⊗03/88	®02/84
M59639	10/59-06/84	⊗12/90	
M59640	10/59-12/87	⊗04/88	
M59641	10/59-09/93	⊗11/93	ⓖ®11/83
M59642	11/59-03/88	⊗03/88	
M59643	11/59-04/92	⊗05/92	ⓖ®02/84
M59644	11/59-06/84	⊗12/90	
M59645	11/59-06/84	⊗12/90	
M59646	12/59-06/84	⊗12/90	
M59647	11/59-03/88	⊗03/88	
M59648	12/59-10/92	⊗09/92	®02/84

Class 115 BR Derby
Trailer Second
TS
M59649-M59663

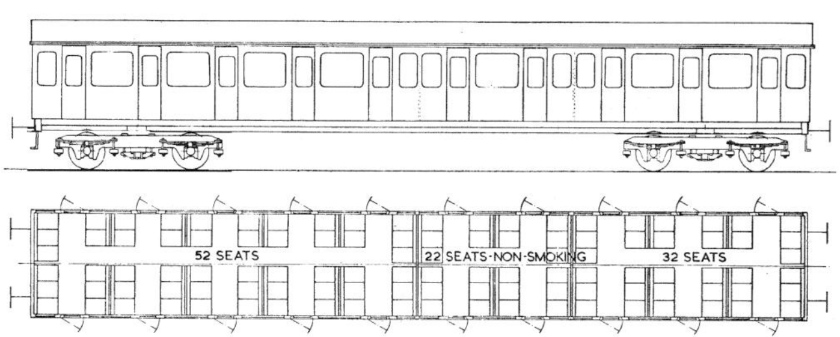

Coupling: ■ Blue square
Diagram: 590 DT208
Lot Number: 30531
Old class: 173
Body: 63' 7½" × 9' 3" Suburban
Weight: 29t
Seats: 106 second

ⓖ Fitted with through gangways in the mid 1980s.

M59649	03/60-06/88	⊗06/88	
M59650	03/60-03/88	⊗11/89	
M59651	03/60-08/92	⊗08/92	®07/79
M59652	04/60-12/91	⊗08/92	®08/78
M59653	04/60-07/90	⊗02/92	
M59654	06/60-12/91	⊗08/92	®02/81
M59655	05/60-03/92	⊗08/92	
M59656	05/60-12/91	⊗08/92	® /82
M59657	06/60-08/92	⊗09/92	®04/82
M59658	06/60-07/93	⊗08/93 ⓖ	
M59659	06/60-08/92	Ⓟ	®07/79
M59660	05/60-03/91	⊗08/92	®07/79
M59661	05/60-10/92	⊗10/92	ⓖ®07/83
M59662	06/60-08/92	⊗08/92	®10/83
M59663	07/60-08/92	⊗08/92	®07/79

Class 115 BR Derby
Trailer Composite Lavatory
TCL
M59664-M59678

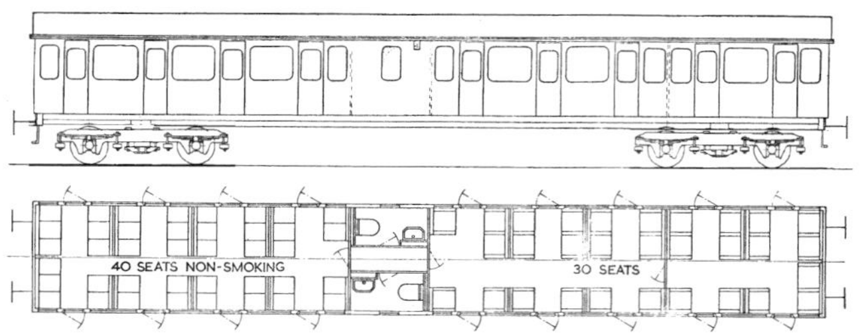

Coupling: ■ Blue square
Diagram: 599 DT303 ②DT227
Lot Number: 30532
Old class: 177
Body: 63' 7½" × 9' 3" Suburban
Weight: 30t
Seats: 30 first, 40 second

ⓖ Fitted with through gangways in the mid 1980s.

M59664	03/60-08/92	Ⓟ	®10/83
M59665	03/60-12/91	⊗09/92	® /82
M59666	03/60-05/89	⊗11/89	® /82
M59667	04/60-08/92	⊗09/92	®07/79
M59668	04/60-10/92	⊗03/93 ⓖ	
M59669	06/60-04/92	⊗08/92	®09/78
M59670	05/60-10/92	⊗10/92 ⓖ	
M59671	05/60-04/92	⊗09/92	®07/79
M59672	06/60-06/92	⊗08/92 ⓖ	® /81
M59673	06/60-02/92	⊗02/92 ⓖ	®10/79
M59674	06/60-07/92	⊗08/92 ⓖ	
M59675	05/60-03/91	⊗11/91	® /82
M59676	05/60-02/92	⊗08/92	®11/80
M59677	06/60-02/92	⊗01/92 ⓖ	
M59678	07/60-08/92	Ⓟ	®07/79

Class 120 BR Swindon
Trailer Buffet Second Lavatory
TSLRB
SC59679-SC59685

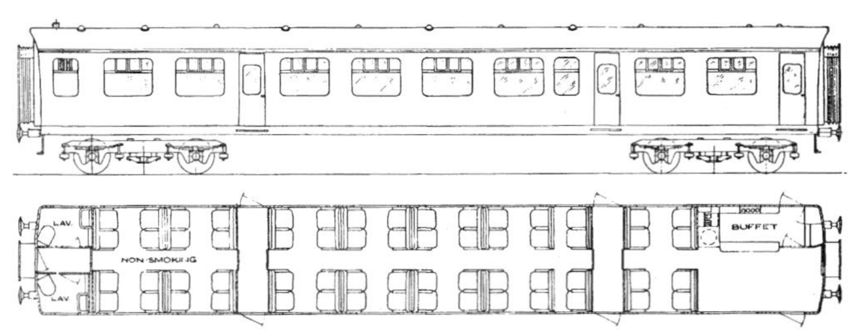

Coupling: ■ Blue square
Diagram: 561 DT217
Lot Number: 30561
Old class: 179
Body: 64' 6" × 9' 3" Cross Country
Weight: 30t 12cwt
Seats: 60 second

SC59679	12/59-10/85	⊗03/86	®05/78	03/80⇨**W**	06/82⇨**M**
SC59680	12/59-11/83	⊗09/85	®02/81	10/81⇨**M**	
SC59681	12/59-03/87	⊗08/87	®06/78	03/80⇨**W**	05/86⇨**SC**
SC59682	12/59-03/87	⊗07/87	®10/77	03/80⇨**W**	05/86⇨**SC**
SC59683	01/60-10/85	⊗03/86	®06/77	03/80⇨**W**	10/82⇨**M**
SC59684	01/60-10/85	⊗03/86	®11/78	03/80⇨**W**	10/82⇨**M**
SC59685	01/60-03/86	⊗03/86	®10/77	10/81⇨**M**	

Class 102⇨101 Metropolitan-Cammell
Trailer Composite Lavatory
TCL
SC59686-SC59692

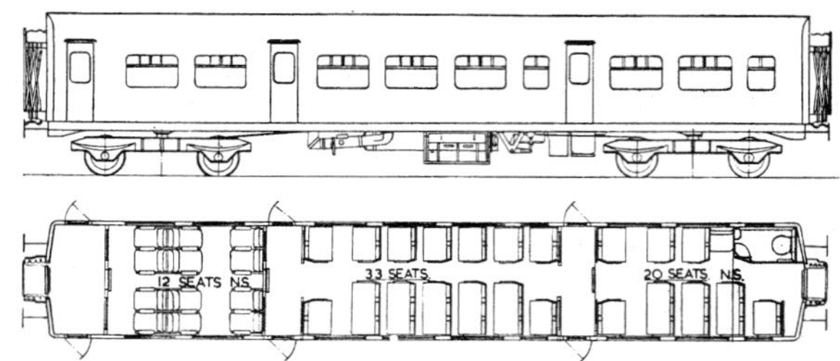

Coupling: ■ Blue square
Diagram: 624 DT220
Lot Number: 30589
Old class: 171
Body: 57' 6" × 9' 3"
Weight: 25t
Seats: 12 first, 53 second

SC59686	10/59-05/88	⊗06/89	®01/78
SC59687	10/59-05/88	⊗09/88	®*10/76*
SC59688	11/59-10/92	⊗03/94	®10/83
SC59689	11/59-05/88	⊗12/88	®12/76
SC59690	11/59-03/89	⊗08/90	®06/77
SC59691	12/59-09/88	⊗08/88	®01/78
SC59692	12/59-05/88	⊗11/89	®02/77

Class 110 Birmingham RC&W
Trailer Second Lavatory
TSL
E59693-E59712

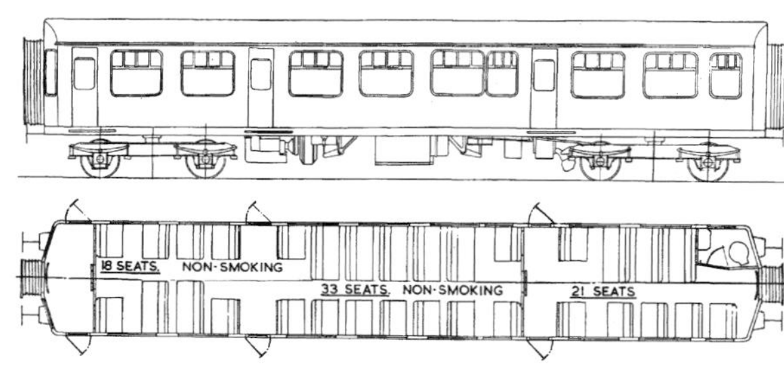

Coupling: ■ Blue square
Diagram: 648 DT207
Lot Number: 30594
Old class: 171
Body: 57' 6" × 9' 3"
Weight: 24t
Seats: 72 second

E59693	06/61-10/83	⊗09/84	®11/79	01/65⇨**NE**	01/68⇨**E**
E59694	06/61-12/90	⊗09/93	® /82	01/65⇨**NE**	01/68⇨**E**
E59695	07/61-01/83	⊗09/84		01/65⇨**NE**	01/68⇨**E**
E59696	07/61-01/90	⊗01/90	® /81	01/65⇨**NE**	01/68⇨**E**
E59697	07/61-10/89	⊗06/91	®10/81	01/65⇨**NE**	01/68⇨**E**
E59698	08/61-10/83	⊗09/84	®02/81	01/65⇨**NE**	01/68⇨**E**
E59699	08/61-10/83	⊗05/84	®02/81	01/65⇨**NE**	01/68⇨**E**
E59700	09/61-10/83	⊗05/84	®02/81	01/65⇨**NE**	01/68⇨**E**
E59701	09/61-04/91	Ⓟ	® /82	01/65⇨**NE**	01/68⇨**E**
E59702	09/61-01/83	⊗06/83		01/65⇨**NE**	01/68⇨**E**
E59703	09/61-10/83	⊗05/84	®01/81	01/65⇨**NE**	01/68⇨**E**
E59704	09/61-10/83	⊗05/84	® /82	01/65⇨**NE**	01/68⇨**E**
E59705	09/61-06/71	⊗07/72		01/65⇨**NE**	01/68⇨**E**
E59706	10/61-11/63	⊗11/63			
E59707	10/61-10/83	⊗05/84	®07/79	01/65⇨**NE**	01/68⇨**E**
E59708	10/61-10/83	⊗05/84	®10/80	01/65⇨**NE**	01/68⇨**E**
E59709	10/61-07/89	⊗08/89	®12/82	01/65⇨**NE**	01/68⇨**E**
E59710	11/61-09/89	⊗06/91	® /81	01/65⇨**NE**	01/68⇨**E**
E59711	11/61-10/83	⊗09/84	®11/80	01/65⇨**NE**	01/68⇨**E**
E59712	11/61-10/83	⊗09/84	®02/81	01/65⇨**NE**	01/68⇨**E**

Class 115 BR Derby
Trailer Second
TS
M59713-M59718

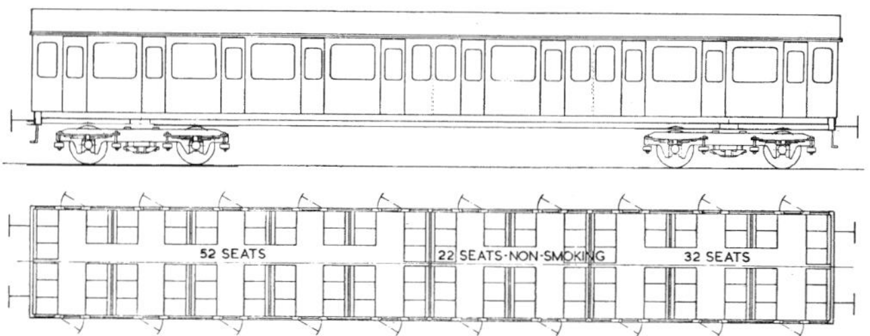

Coupling:	■ Blue square
Diagram:	590 DT208
Lot Number:	30596
Old class:	173
Body:	63' 7½" × 9' 3" Suburban
Weight:	29t
Seats:	106 second

⑨ Fitted with through gangways in the mid 1980s.

M59713	02/60-05/93	⊗09/93 ⑨	
M59714	02/60-02/88	⊗02/88	®11/79
M59715	02/60-04/90	⊗02/92	®11/79
M59716	02/60-04/90	⊗02/92	® /80
M59717	02/60-04/90	⊗02/92	
M59718	03/60-05/84	⊗07/85	

Class 115 BR Derby
Trailer Composite Lavatory
TCL
M59719-M59724

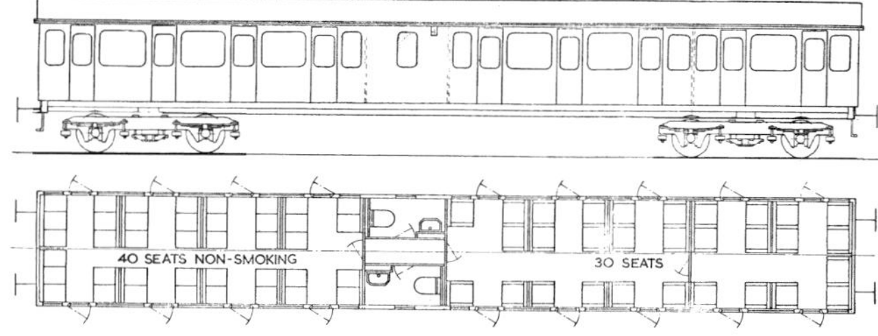

Coupling:	■ Blue square
Diagram:	599 DT303 ②DT227
Lot Number:	30597
Old class:	177
Body:	63' 8¾" × 9' 3" Suburban
Weight:	30t
Seats:	30 first, 40 second

⑨ Fitted with through gangways in the mid 1980s.

M59719	02/60-11/90	Ⓟ	⑨®01/79
M59720	02/60-10/92	⊗09/92 ⑨	
M59721	02/60-02/92	⊗10/92 ⑨	
M59722	02/60-11/90	⊗09/91 ⑨	
M59723	02/60-11/90	⊗09/91 ⑨	
M59724	03/60-06/92	⊗05/92 ⑨	

Class 115 BR Derby
Trailer Second
TS
M59725-M59744

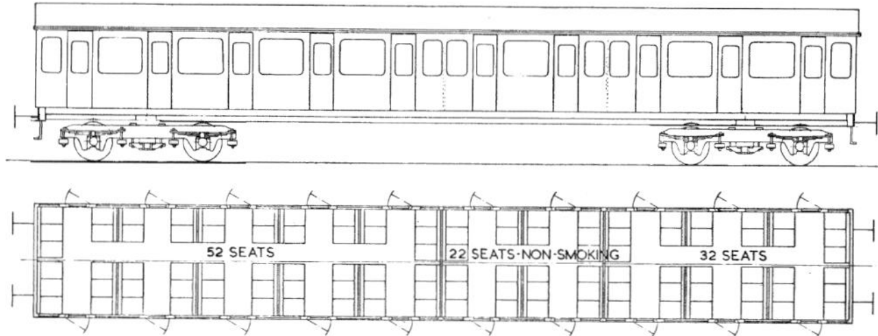

Coupling:	■ Blue square
Diagram:	590 DT208
Lot Number:	30599
Old class:	173
Body:	63' 7½" × 9' 3" Suburban
Weight:	29t
Seats:	106 second

⑨ Fitted with through gangways in the mid 1980s.

M59725	07/60-04/90	⊗02/92	®05/83
M59726	07/60-02/92	⊗02/92	⑨® /81
M59727	08/60-12/91	⊗08/92	®06/78
M59728	08/60-11/92	⊗11/92	® /81
M59729	08/60-05/91	⊗08/92	®04/82
M59730	09/60-05/87	⊗05/88	
M59731	09/60-11/92	⊗11/92	®11/82
M59732	09/60-03/91	⊗04/92	®04/82
M59733	09/60-08/92	⊗08/92	® /81
M59734	09/60-05/93	⊗06/93 ⑨	
M59735	09/60-07/93	⊗08/93 ⑨	
M59736	09/60-02/92	⊗04/92	®07/79
M59737	09/60-08/92	⊗08/92	®11/79
M59738	09/60-12/91	⊗03/93	
M59739	10/60-11/89	⊗ /91	
M59740	10/60-08/92	Ⓟ	®11/82
M59741	10/60-02/92	⊗02/92	⑨®07/78
M59742	11/60-09/71	⊗03/80	
M59743	11/60-07/92	⊗08/92	⑨® /81
M59744	11/60-04/90	⊗02/92	

Class 115 BR Derby
Trailer Composite Lavatory
TCL
M59745-M59764

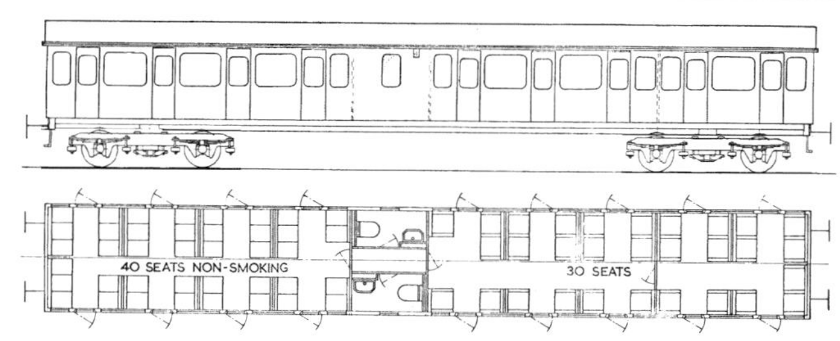

Coupling:	■ Blue square
Diagram:	599 DT303 ②DT227
Lot Number:	30600
Old class:	177
Body:	63' 8¾" × 9' 3" Suburban
Weight:	30t
Seats:	30 first, 40 second

⑨ Fitted with through gangways in the mid 1980s.

M59745	07/60-01/94	⊗11/95 ⑨	
M59746	07/60-03/91	⊗10/91	®02/78
M59747	08/60-08/92	⊗08/92	®02/81
M59748	08/60-05/89	⊗06/91	
M59749	08/60-08/92	⊗08/92	®10/83
M59750	09/60-08/92	⊗08/92	®07/79

M59751	09/60-09/93	⊗11/93 @		07/86⇨W
M59752	09/60-12/91	⊗04/92		
M59753	09/60-01/94	⊗11/95 @		
M59754	09/60-08/92	⊗08/92		
M59755	09/60-10/91	⊗10/91	®02/81	
M59756	09/60-06/92	⊗05/92 @		
M59757	09/60-06/92	⊗05/92 @		
M59758	09/60-11/92	⊗11/92		
M59759	10/60-08/92	⊗09/92	®07/79	
M59760	10/60-11/90	⊗09/91 @®	/82	
M59761	10/60-08/92	Ⓟ	®08/78	
M59762	11/60-10/91	⊗04/92		
M59763	11/60-10/91	⊗11/91	®02/81	
M59764	12/60-08/92	⊗08/92	® /81	

Class 124 BR Swindon

Trailer Second Lavatory
TSL
E59765-E59773

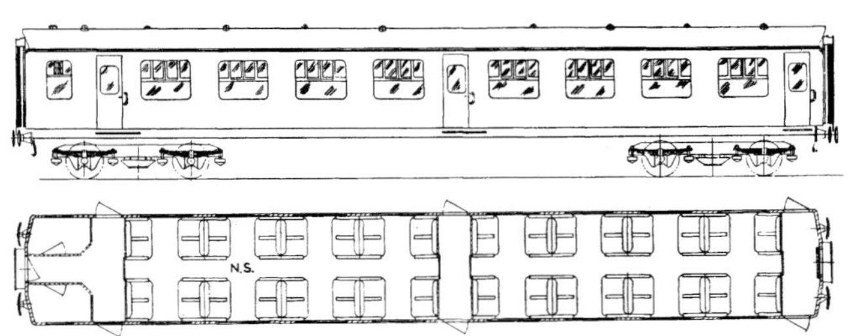

Coupling: ■ Blue square
Diagram: 573 DT212
Lot Number: 30605
Old class: 180
Body: 64' 6" × 9' 3" Trans-Pennine
Weight: 32t
Seats: 64 second

E59765	07/60-05/84	⊗08/84	01/65⇨**NE**	01/68⇨**E**
E59766	08/60-12/83	⊗07/84	01/65⇨**NE**	01/68⇨**E**
E59767	08/60-05/84	⊗08/84	01/65⇨**NE**	01/68⇨**E**
E59768	09/60-05/84	⊗09/84	01/65⇨**NE**	01/68⇨**E**
E59769	09/60-05/84	⊗09/84	01/65⇨**NE**	01/68⇨**E**
E59770	10/60-05/84	⊗08/84	01/65⇨**NE**	01/68⇨**E**
E59771	11/60-05/84	⊗08/84	01/65⇨**NE**	01/68⇨**E**
E59772	12/60-05/84	⊗08/84	01/65⇨**NE**	01/68⇨**E**
E59773	12/60-05/84	⊗09/84	01/65⇨**NE**	01/68⇨**E**

Class 124 BR Swindon

Trailer Buffet First Lavatory
TFLRB
E59774-E59781

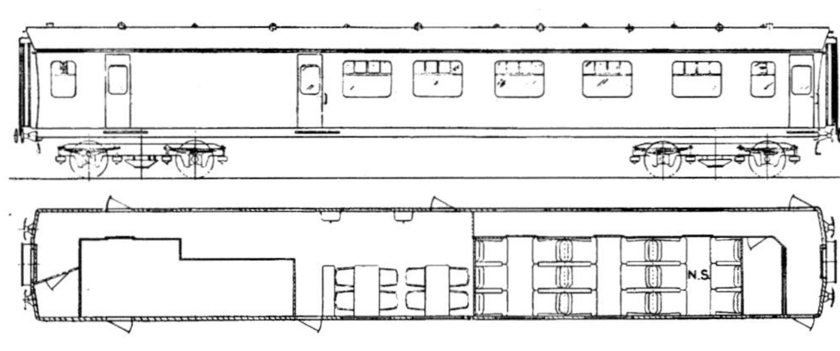

Coupling: ■ Blue square
Diagram: 562
Lot Number: 30606
Old class: 181
Body: 64' 6" × 9' 3" Trans-Pennine
Weight: 34t
Seats: 18 first, 8 buffet

E59774	07/60-08/72	⊗02/73	01/65⇨**NE**	01/68⇨**E**
E59775	08/60-10/75	⊗04/81	01/65⇨**NE**	01/68⇨**E**
E59776	08/60-10/75	⊗04/81	01/65⇨**NE**	01/68⇨**E**
E59777	09/60-10/75	⊗03/81	01/65⇨**NE**	01/68⇨**E**
E59778	09/60-10/75	⊗03/81	01/65⇨**NE**	01/68⇨**E**
E59779	10/60-10/75	⊗04/81	01/65⇨**NE**	01/68⇨**E**
E59780	11/60-08/72	⊗02/73	01/65⇨**NE**	01/68⇨**E**
E59781	12/60-08/72	⊗02/73	01/65⇨**NE**	01/68⇨**E**

Class 107 BR Derby

Trailer Second Lavatory
TSL
SC59782-SC59807

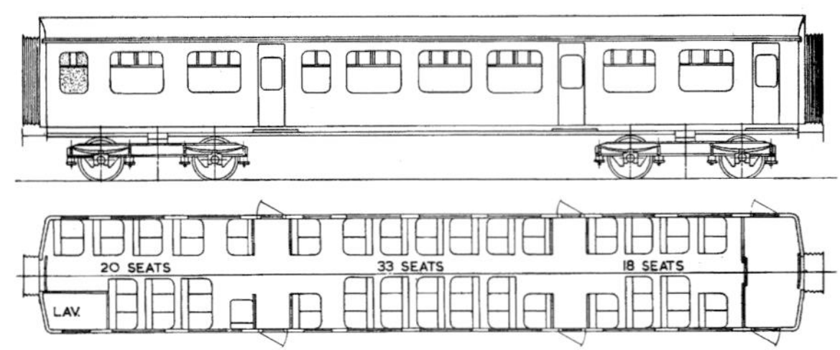

Coupling: ■ Blue square
Diagram: 647 DT204
Lot Number: 30613
Old class: 161
Body: 58' 1" × 9' 3"
Weight: 28t
Seats: 71 second

SC59782	12/60-07/91	⊗08/91	®02/81		
SC59783	12/60-11/91	⊗03/92	®11/79		
SC59784	12/60-04/92	⊗08/94	®06/80		⊠11/91-01/92
SC59785	12/60-07/91	⊗01/92	®06/81		
SC59786	12/60-07/91	⊗08/91	®11/78		
SC59787	12/60-02/84	⊗12/87	®06/80		05/84➲**RDB977226**
SC59788	12/60-02/84	⊗09/84	®06/80		
SC59789	12/60-11/90	⊗08/92	®11/79		
SC59790	01/61-10/92	⊗10/92	®07/79		
SC59791	01/61-10/92	Ⓟ	®11/78		
SC59792	01/61-10/92	⊗01/94			
SC59793	01/61-03/90	⊗09/90	®06/80		
SC59794	02/61-07/91	⊗07/91		03/81⇨**M**	
SC59795	02/61-07/91	⊗01/92	®05/79		
SC59796	02/61-10/92	⊗03/94	®06/81		
SC59797	02/61-07/91	⊗01/92	®06/81		⊠05/91-06/91
SC59798	02/61-03/90	⊗11/90	®06/80		
SC59799	02/61-02/84	⊗09/84	®11/79		
SC59800	02/61-07/91	⊗01/92	® /81		⊠05/91-06/91
SC59801	03/61-03/92	⊗10/92	®10/80		
SC59802	03/61-07/91	⊗01/92	®11/79		
SC59803	03/61-11/91	⊗03/92	®05/80		
SC59804	04/61-10/92	⊗08/93	®11/78		
SC59805	04/61-01/92	⊗01/92	®11/78		
SC59806	04/61-01/92	⊗01/92	®11/79		
SC59807	06/61-11/91	⊗01/92	®08/79		

Class 110 Birmingham RC&W

Trailer Second Lavatory
TSL
M59808-M59817

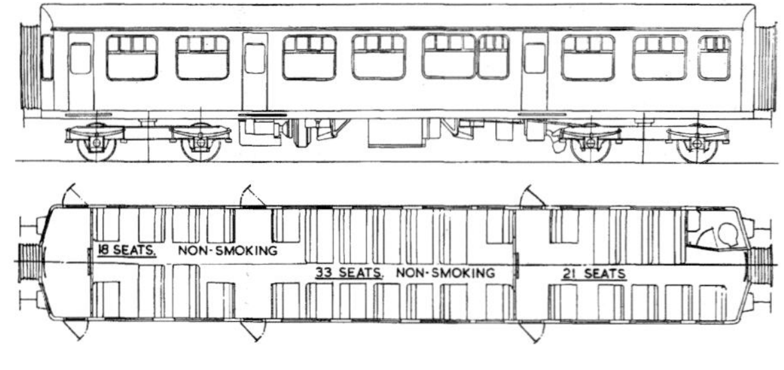

Coupling: ■ Blue square
Diagram: 648 DT207
Lot Number: 30693
Old class: 163
Body: 57' 6" × 9' 3"
Weight: 24t
Seats: 72 second

M59808	11/61-01/83	⊗02/84		05/67⇨**NE**	01/68⇨**E**
M59809	11/61-10/89	⊗09/91	®04/82	05/67⇨**NE**	01/68⇨**E**

M59810	12/61-05/89	⊗04/90		05/67⇨**NE**	01/68⇨**E**
M59811	12/61-10/83	⊗05/84	®07/79	05/67⇨**NE**	01/68⇨**E**
M59812	12/61-04/90	⊗06/91	® /82	05/67⇨**NE**	01/68⇨**E**
M59813	01/62-10/83	⊗05/84	®02/81	05/67⇨**NE**	01/68⇨**E**
M59814	01/62-10/83	⊗09/84	®02/81	05/67⇨**NE**	01/68⇨**E**
M59815	01/62-10/83	⊗05/84	®02/81	05/67⇨**NE**	01/68⇨**E**
M59816	01/62-10/83	⊗05/84	®07/79	05/67⇨**NE**	01/68⇨**E**
M59817	01/62-05/89	⊗08/90	® /82	05/67⇨**NE**	01/68⇨**E**

Class 123 BR Swindon

Trailer Composite Side-Corridor with Lavatory
TCK
W59818-W59827

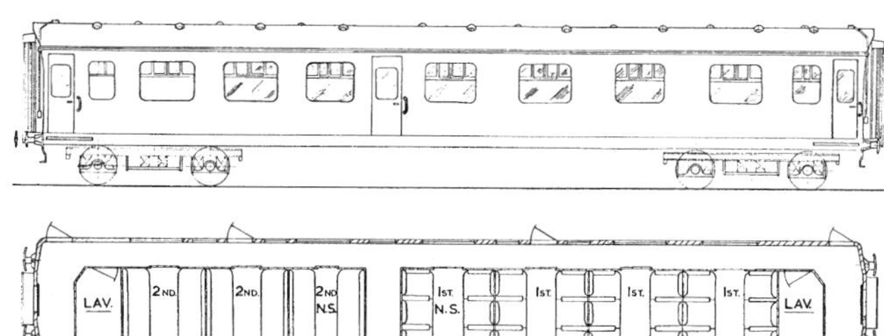

Coupling: ■ Blue square
Diagram: 567 DT306
Lot Number: 30705
Old class: 183
Body: 64' 6" × 9' 3" Inter-City
Weight: 32t 3cwt
Seats: 24 first, 24 second

W59818	02/63-05/84	⊗11/84	04/78⇨**E**
W59819	02/63-05/84	⊗08/84	04/78⇨**E**
W59820	02/63-05/84	⊗08/84	06/77⇨**E**
W59821	03/63-05/84	⊗11/84	06/77⇨**E**
W59822	04/63-05/84	⊗08/84	04/78⇨**E**
W59823	05/63-05/84	⊗08/84	06/77⇨**E**
W59824	05/63-05/84	⊗11/84	04/78⇨**E**
W59825	06/63-05/84	⊗08/84	01/78⇨**E**
W59826	06/63-04/84	⊗07/84	04/78⇨**E**
W59827	06/63-05/84	⊗11/84	04/78⇨**E**

Class 123 BR Swindon

Trailer Buffet Second Lavatory
TSLRB
W59828-W59832

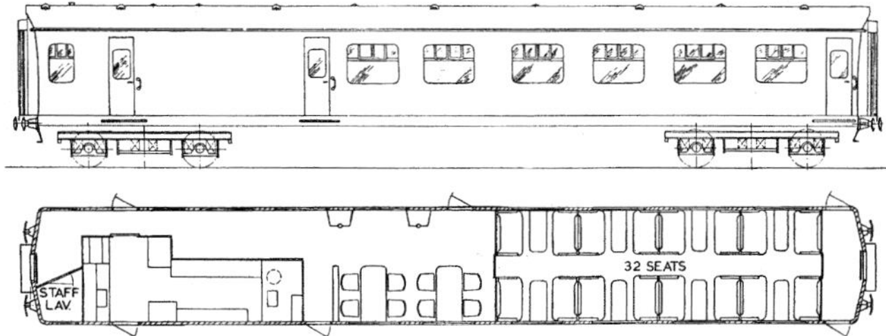

Coupling: ■ Blue square
Diagram: 569
Lot Number: 30707
Body: 64' 6" × 9' 3" Inter-City
Weight: 33t 5cwt
Seats: 32 second, 8 buffet

W59828	05/63-09/70	⊗11/87	/76⊃**DB975327**
W59829	05/63-09/70	⊗05/73	
W59830	06/63-09/70	⊗05/73	
W59831	06/63-09/70	⊗08/84	07/72⊃**E69108**
W59832	06/63-09/70	⊗04/73	

Class 124 BR Swindon

Trailer Brake Second Side-Corridor with Lavatory
TBSK
E59833-E59842

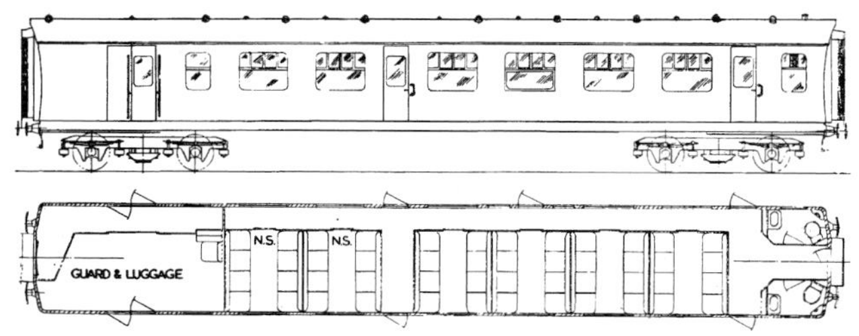

Coupling: ■ Blue square
Diagram: DU205
Lot Number: 30604
Body: 64' 6" × 9' 3" Trans-Pennine
Weight: 37t 10cwt
Seats: 48 second

E59833	03/81⊂**51981**	03/81-05/84	⊗07/84
E59834	04/81⊂**51969**	04/81-05/84	⊗08/84
E59835	05/81⊂**51974**	05/81-05/84	⊗08/84
E59836	05/81⊂**51978**	05/81-05/84	⊗09/84
E59837	06/81⊂**51984**	06/81-05/84	⊗09/84
E59838	07/81⊂**51976**	07/81-05/84	⊗08/84
E59839	08/81⊂**51975**	08/81-05/84	⊗09/84
E59840	11/81⊂**51983**	11/81-04/84	⊗07/84
E59841	11/81⊂**51973**	11/81-05/84	⊗09/84
E59842	11/81⊂**51980**	11/81-05/84	⊗02/85

Class 201 BR Eastleigh

Driving Motor Brake Second Open
DMBSO
S60000-S60013

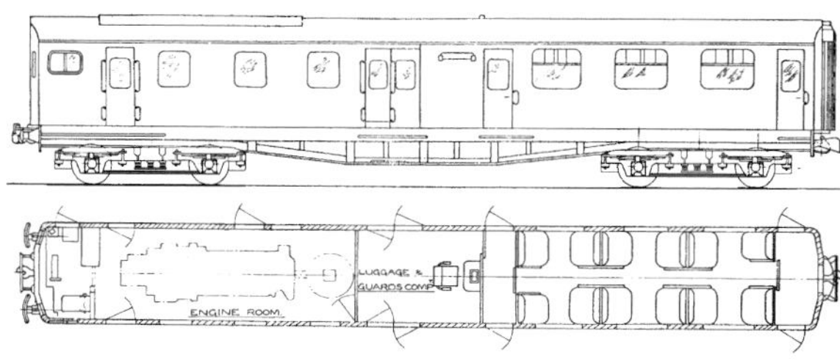

Diagram: 650 DB201
Lot Number: 30329
Engine: English Electric 4-cyl type 4SRKT Mark II of 500 bhp. at 1500 rpm.
Transmission: Electric. Two nose-suspended axle-hung traction motors
Body: 58' 0" × 8' 2½"/9' 0"
Weight: 54t
Seats: 22 second

60000 was named "HASTINGS" in 1996.

S60000	01/57-	Ⓟ	⊠05/86-05/96
S60001	01/57-05/86	Ⓟ	
S60002	02/57-05/86	⊗11/94	05/86⊃**ADB977376**
S60003	02/57-05/86	⊗11/94	05/86⊃**ADB977377**
S60004	02/57-04/86	⊗07/87	
S60005	02/57-04/86	⊗06/89	
S60006	02/57-04/86	⊗03/88	
S60007	02/57-04/86	⊗09/87	
S60008	03/57-04/86	⊗07/89	
S60009	03/57-04/86	⊗02/89	
S60010	03/57-04/86	⊗07/87	
S60011	03/57-04/86	⊗07/87	
S60012	04/57-04/86	⊗09/87	
S60013	04/57-04/86	⊗07/87	

Class 202 BR Eastleigh

Driving Motor Brake Second Open

DMBSO

S60014-S60019

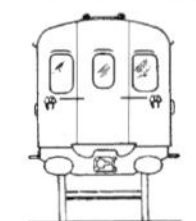

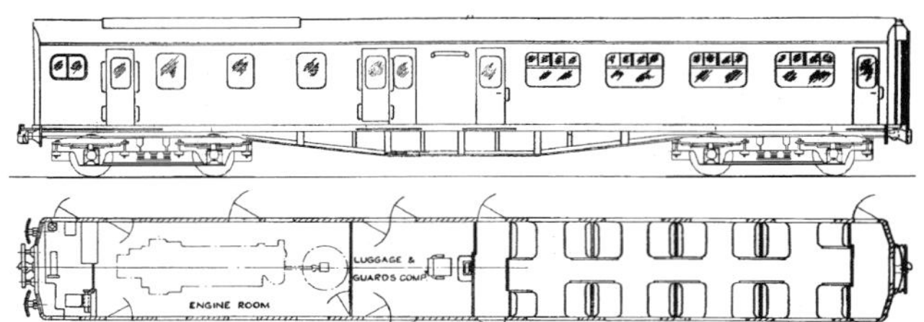

Diagram: 651 DB202
Lot Number: 30395
Engine: English Electric 4-cyl type 4SRKT Mark II of 500 bhp. at 1500 rpm.
Transmission: Electric. Two nose-suspended axle-hung traction motors
Body: 64' 6" × 8' 2½"/9' 0"
Weight: 55t
Seats: 30 second

S60014	06/89⊃**60152**	05/57-05/90	⊗*12/96*		09/90⊃**ADB977698**
S60015	06/89⊃**60153**	05/57-05/90	⊗*12/96*		09/90⊃**ADB977699**
S60016		05/57-	℗	☒05/86-12/02	12/02⊃**60116**
S60017		05/57-05/86	⊗04/89		
S60018		06/57-	℗	☒03/88-05/96	05/96⊃**60118**
S60019		06/57-03/88	℗		

Class 202 BR Eastleigh

Driving Motor Brake Second Open

DMBSO

S60020-S60031

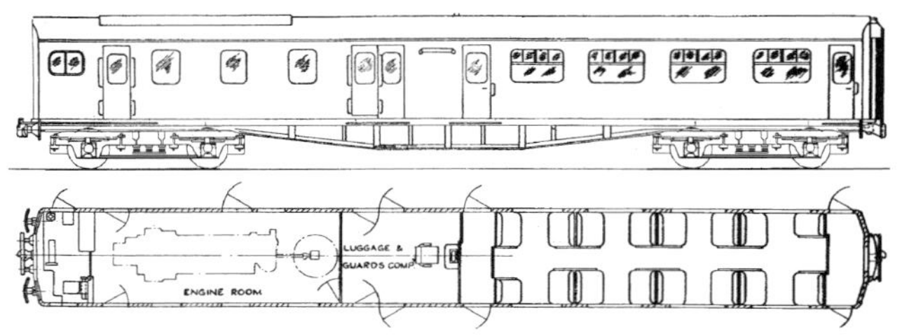

Diagram: 651 DB202
Lot Number: 30391
Engine: English Electric 4-cyl type 4SRKT Mark II of 500 bhp. at 1500 rpm.
Transmission: Electric. Two nose-suspended axle-hung traction motors
Body: 64' 6" × 8' 2½"/9' 0"
Weight: 55t
Seats: 30 second

S60020	12/57-04/86	⊗09/87
S60021	12/57-03/86	⊗03/88
S60022	12/57-02/88	⊗10/89
S60023	12/57-04/86	⊗03/88
S60024	01/58-05/86	⊗11/87
S60025	01/58-05/86	⊗07/87
S60026	02/58-05/86	⊗06/89
S60027	02/58-05/86	⊗10/88
S60028	02/58-05/86	⊗11/87
S60029	02/58-05/86	⊗04/89
S60030	03/58-10/84	⊗11/87
S60031	03/58-04/86	⊗09/87

Class 203 BR Eastleigh

Driving Motor Brake Second Open

DMBSO

S60032-S60045

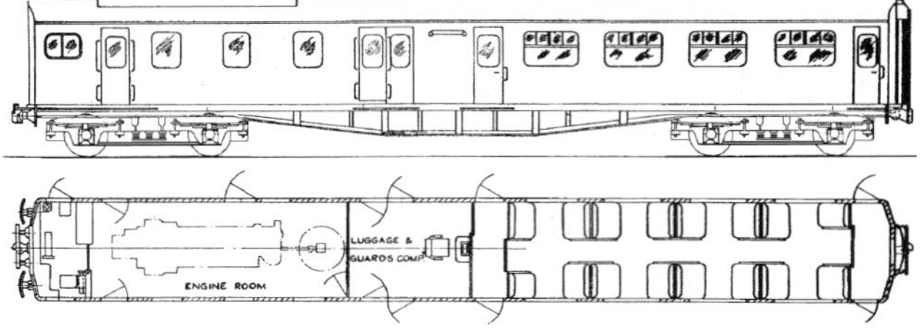

Diagram: 651 DB202
Lot Number: 30391
Engine: English Electric 4-cyl type 4SRKT Mark II of 500 bhp. at 1500 rpm.
Transmission: Electric. Two nose-suspended axle-hung traction motors
Body: 64' 6" × 8' 2½"/9' 0"
Weight: 55t
Seats: 30 second

S60032	03/58-04/86	⊗09/87
S60033	03/58-04/86	⊗04/89
S60034	04/58-05/86	⊗02/89
S60035	04/58-05/86	⊗10/88
S60036	04/58-03/80	⊗03/82
S60037	04/58-04/86	⊗11/89
S60038	04/58-04/86	⊗06/89
S60039	04/58-04/86	⊗06/89
S60040	05/58-05/86	⊗04/89
S60041	05/58-05/86	⊗04/89
S60042	05/58-04/86	⊗07/87
S60043	05/58-04/86	⊗11/87
S60044	05/58-09/87	⊗03/88
S60045	05/58-01/88	⊗01/89

Class 251 Metropolitan-Cammell

Driving Motor Brake First Lavatory

DMBFL

M60090-M60093

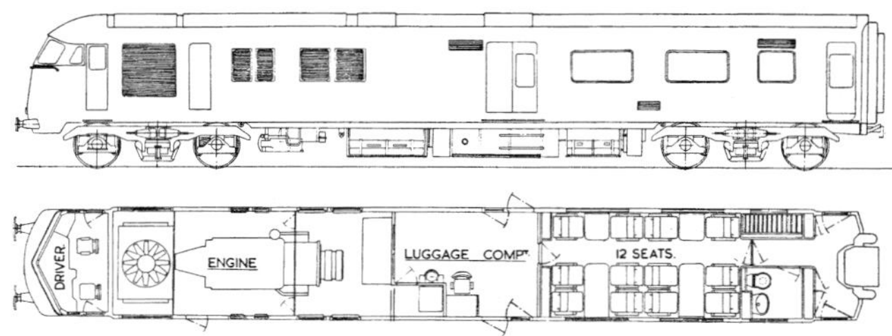

Diagram: 653
Lot Number: 30553
Engines: One North British/MAN 12 cyl. pressure charged V type LV12V18/21BS of 1000 bhp.
Transmission: Electric. Two 425 hp. GEC traction motors driving through Brown-Boveri spring drive
Body: 66' 5½" × 9' 3" Pullman
Weight: 67t
Seats: 12 first

M60090	11/59-05/73	⊗12/74	03/67⇨W
M60091	11/59-05/73	⊗12/74	03/67⇨W
M60092	11/59-05/73	⊗05/74	03/67⇨W
M60093	11/59-05/73	⊗05/74	03/67⇨W

Class 251 Metropolitan-Cammell

Driving Motor Brake Second
DMBS
W60094-W60099

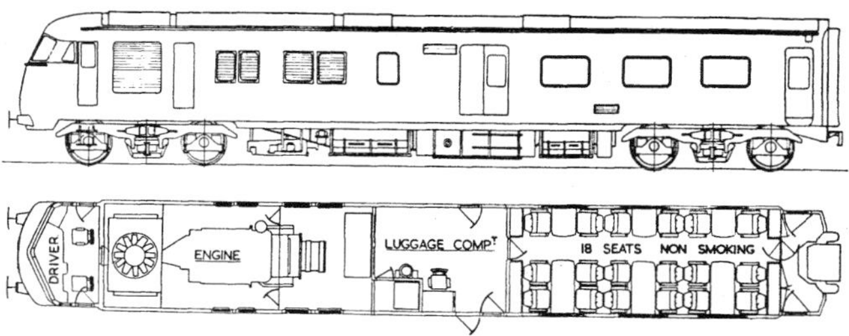

Diagram: 654
Lot Number: 30554
Engines: One North British/MAN 12 cyl. pressure charged V type LV12V18/21BS of 1000 bhp.
Transmission: Electric. Two 425 hp. GEC traction motors driving through Brown-Boveri spring drive
Body: 66' 5½" × 9' 3" Pullman
Weight: 67t 10cwt
Seats: 18 second

W60094	02/60-05/73	⊗07/74
W60095	02/60-05/73	⊗07/74
W60096	04/60-05/73	⊗05/74
W60097	04/60-05/73	⊗07/74
W60098	05/60-05/73	⊗05/74
W60099	05/60-05/73	⊗07/74

Class 205 BR Eastleigh

Driving Motor Brake Second Open
DMBSO
S60100-S60117

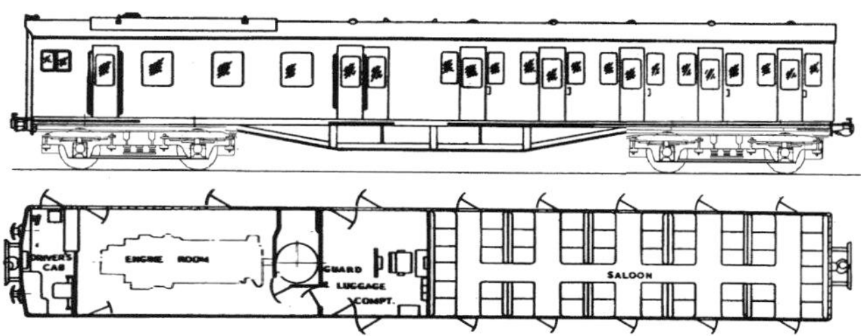

Diagram: 652 DB203
Lot Number: 30332
Engine: English Electric 4-cyl type 4SRKT Mark II of 600 bhp. at 1500 rpm.
Transmission: Electric. Two nose-suspended axle-hung traction motors
Body: 64' 0" × 9' 3"
Weight: 56t
Seats: 52 second

S60100	06/89➲**60154**	08/57-12/04	℗	
S60101	06/89➲**60155**	08/57-02/92	⊗01/92	
S60102		08/57-09/87	⊗12/88	
S60103		08/57-08/87	⊗01/89	
S60104		08/57-08/87	⊗03/90	
S60105		08/57-09/87	⊗04/90	
S60106		08/57-07/85	⊗07/87	
S60107		09/57-08/87	⊗12/89	
S60108		09/57-12/04	℗	
S60109		09/57-09/87	⊗04/90	
S60110		09/57-12/04	℗	®05/78
S60111		09/57-02/04	⊗09/05	
S60112		09/57-10/89	⊗11/87	
S60113		10/57-05/88	⊗10/89	
S60114		10/57-10/93	⊗03/94	
S60115		10/57-09/94	⊗08/95	
S60116		10/57-09/87	⊗03/90	
S60117		10/57-12/04	℗	

Class 202 BR Eastleigh

Driving Motor Brake Second Open
DMBSO
60116, 60118

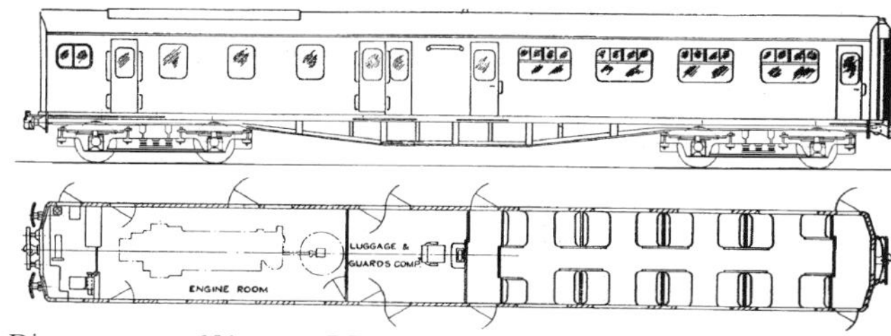

Diagram: 651 DB202
Lot Number: 30395
Engine: English Electric 4-cyl type 4SRKT Mark II of 500 bhp. at 1500 rpm.
Transmission: Electric. Two nose-suspended axle-hung traction motors
Body: 64' 6" × 8' 2½"/9' 0"
Weight: 55t
Seats: 30 second

Both were re-instated and returned to traffic to work with Hastings Diesel set 201001 (1001).

60118 was named "Tunbridge Wells" in 1998.
60116 was named "Mountfield" in 2003.

60116	12/02⊂**60016**	12/02	℗	⊠05/86-12/02
60118	05/96⊂**60018**	05/96-	℗	⊠03/88-05/96

Class 205 BR Eastleigh

Driving Motor Brake Second Open
DMBSO
S60118-S60121

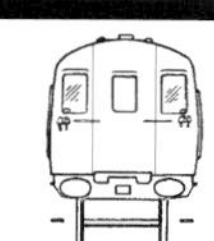

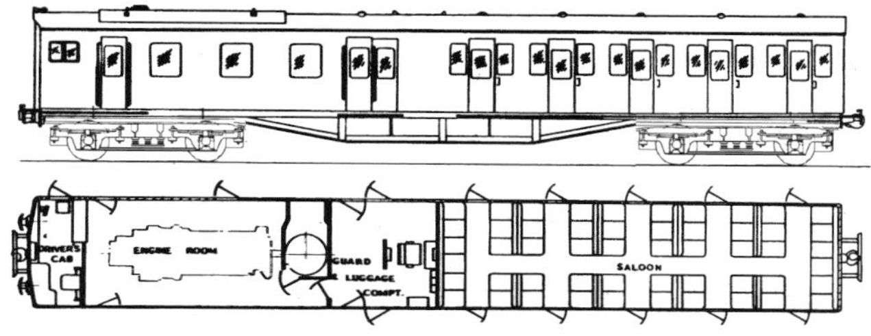

Diagram: 652 DB203
Lot Number: 30398
Engine: English Electric 4-cyl type 4SRKT Mark II of 600 bhp. at 1500 rpm.
Transmission: Electric. Two nose-suspended axle-hung traction motors
Body: 64' 0" × 9' 3"
Weight: 56t
Seats: 52 second

S60118	06/58-08/87	⊗02/89
S60119	06/58-09/87	⊗03/90
S60120	06/58-04/94	⊗08/95
S60121	06/58-11/87	⊗03/90

Class 205 BR Eastleigh
Driving Motor Brake Second Open
DMBSO
S60122-S60125

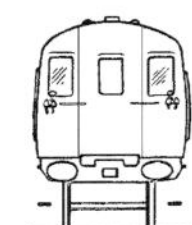

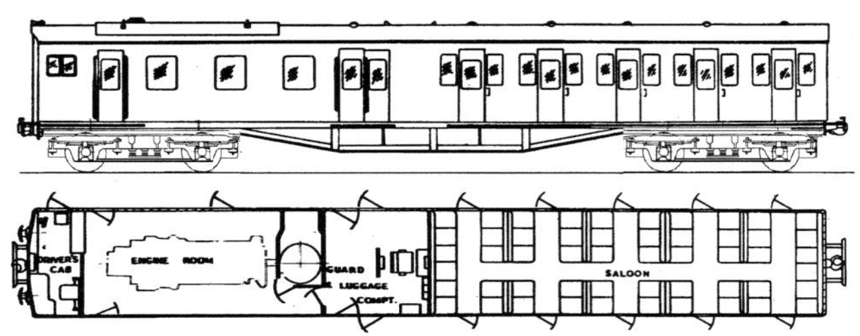

Diagram: 652 DB203
Lot Number: 30540
Engine: English Electric 4-cyl type 4SRKT Mark II of 600 bhp. at 1500 rpm.
Transmission: Electric. Two nose-suspended axle-hung traction motors
Body: 64' 0" × 9' 3"
Weight: 56t
Seats: 52 second

S60122	11/59-01/99	Ⓟ	
S60123	11/59-07/00	⊗09/03	
S60124	12/59-02/04	Ⓟ	
S60125	12/59-02/92	⊗01/92	⊠11/90-09/91

Class 207 BR Eastleigh
Driving Motor Brake Second Open
DMBSO
S60126-S60144

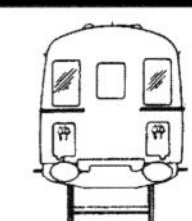

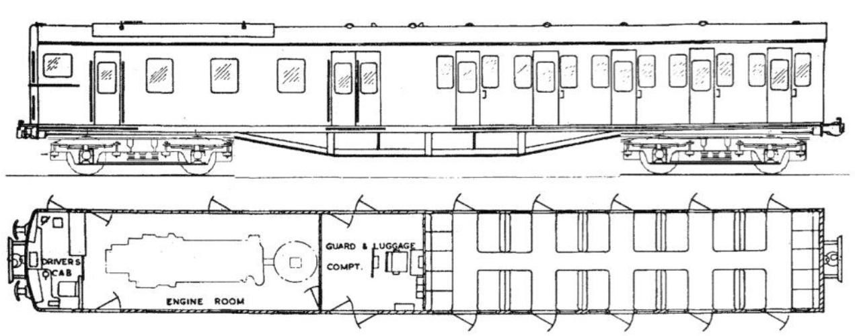

Diagram: 655 DB205
Lot Number: 30625
Engine: English Electric 4-cyl type 4SRKT Mark II of 600 bhp. at 1500 rpm.
Transmission: Electric. Two nose-suspended axle-hung traction motors
Body: 64' 0" × 8' 6"/9' 0"
Weight: 56t
Seats: 42 second

60129 was named "Ashford Fayre" and 60130 was named "Brighton Royal Pavilion" in 1995.

S60126	01/62-04/94	⊗05/94	
S60127	01/62-01/05	Ⓟ	
S60128	02/62-09/87	⊗01/89	
S60129	05/62-10/03	⊗10/04	
S60130	05/62-12/04	Ⓟ	
S60131	05/62-09/87	⊗12/88	
S60132	05/62-09/87	⊗12/88	
S60133	05/62-05/88	⊗02/89	
S60134	06/62-11/85	⊗09/87	
S60135	06/62-09/93	Ⓟ⊗*01/99*	09/93➲*977906*
S60136	06/62-12/87	⊗03/90	
S60137	07/62-09/87	⊗05/91	
S60138	07/62-09/93	Ⓟ	09/93➲*977907*
S60139	07/62-05/90	⊗05/92	04/92➲**ADB977700**
S60140	07/62-09/87	⊗06/88	
S60141	07/62-09/87	⊗06/88	
S60142	07/62-02/04	Ⓟ	⊠04/93-05/93
S60143	07/62-09/87	⊗04/90	
S60144	08/62-05/88	⊗10/89	

Class 205 BR Eastleigh
Driving Motor Brake Second Open
DMBSO
S60145-S60151

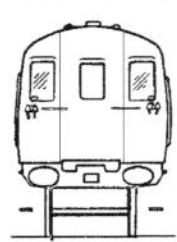

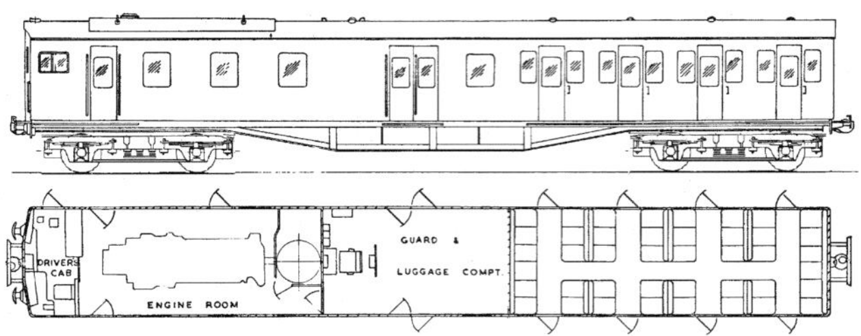

Diagram: 656 DB204
Lot Number: 30671
Engine: English Electric 4-cyl type 4SRKT Mark II of 600 bhp. at 1500 rpm.
d 60147 was fitted with a Dorman Engine in 1964-1971
Transmission: Electric. Two nose-suspended axle-hung traction motors
Body: 64' 0" × 9' 3"
Weight: 56t
Seats: 42 second

S60145	05/62-09/94		10/94➲**ADB977939**
S60146	05/62-12/04	Ⓟ	
S60147	05/62-01/95	⊗03/95 d	
S60148	06/62-11/92	⊗11/92	⊠08/92-09/92, ⊠10/92-11/92
S60149	06/62-07/93		10/94➲**ADB977940**
S60150	06/62-12/04	Ⓟ	
S60151	09/62-11/04	Ⓟ	

Class 202 BR Eastleigh
Driving Motor Brake Second Open
DMBSO
60152-60153

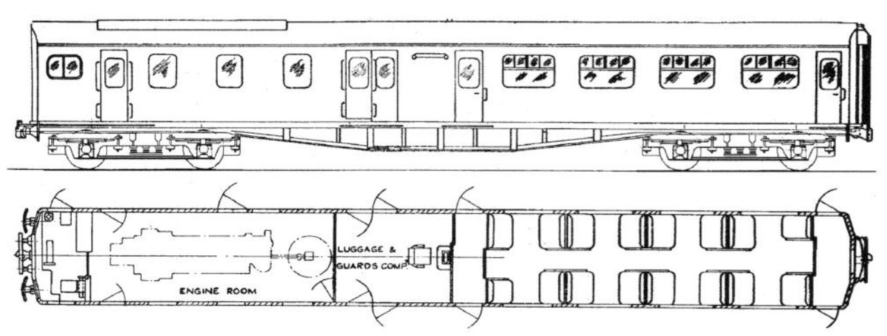

Diagram: 651 DB202
Lot Number: 30395
Engine: English Electric 4-cyl type 4SRKT Mark II of 500 bhp. at 1500 rpm.
Transmission: Electric. Two nose-suspended axle-hung traction motors
Body: 64' 6" × 8' 2½"/9' 0"
Weight: 55t
Seats: 30 second

60152	06/89➲**60014**	05/57-05/90	⊗*12/96*	09/90➲**ADB977698**
60153	06/89➲**60015**	05/57-05/90	⊗*12/96*	09/90➲**ADB977699**

Class 205 BR Eastleigh

Driving Motor Brake Second Open

DMBSO

60154-60155

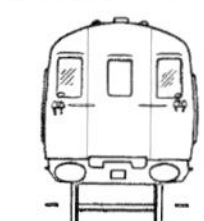

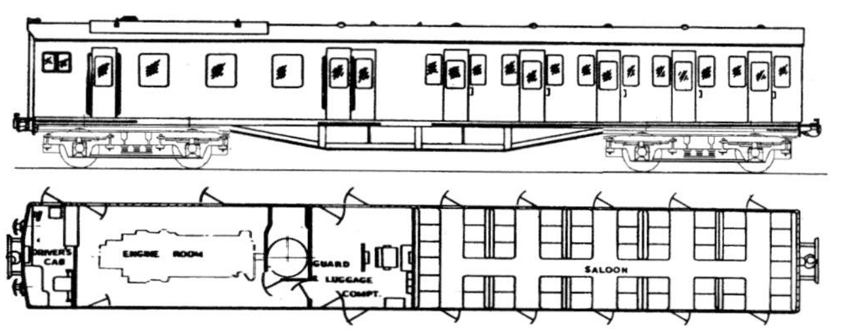

Diagram:	652	DB203
Lot Number:	30332	
Engine:	English Electric 4-cyl type 4SRKT Mark II of 500 bhp. at 1500 rpm.	
Transmission:	Electric. Two nose-suspended axle-hung traction motors	
Body:	64' 0" × 9' 3"	
Weight:	56t	
Seats:	52 second	

60154	06/89➲**60100**	08/57-12/04	Ⓟ	
60155	06/89➲**60101**	08/57-02/92	⊗01/92	⊠05/91-11/91

Class 201 BR Eastleigh

Trailer Second Open Lavatory

TSOL

S60500-S60520

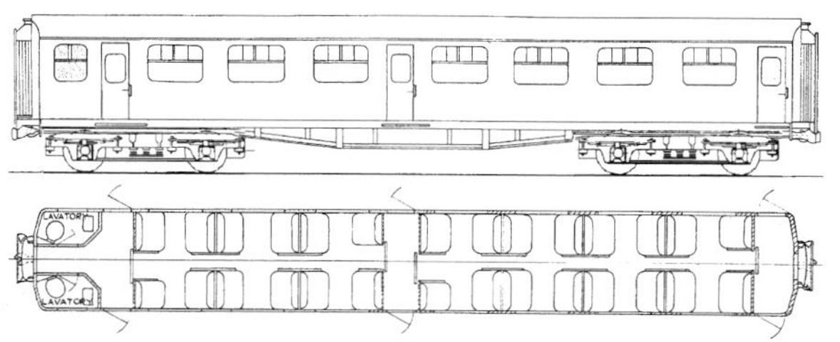

Diagram:	670	DH201
Lot Number:	30331	
Body:	58' 0" × 8' 2½"/9' 0"	
Weight:	29t	
Seats:	52 second	

S60500	01/57-05/86	Ⓟ	
S60501	01/57-	Ⓟ	⊠05/86-05/96
S60502	01/57-05/86	Ⓟ	
S60503	02/57-05/86	⊗10/89	*/86➲ADB977378*
S60504	02/57-05/86	⊗07/98	05/86➲**ADB977379**
S60505	02/57-05/86	⊗10/89	
S60506	02/57-04/86	⊗03/88	
S60507	02/57-01/68	⊗01/69	
S60508	02/57-01/68	⊗01/69	
S60509	03/57-03/83	⊗10/86	
S60510	03/57-04/86	⊗07/87	
S60511	03/57-04/86	⊗07/87	
S60512	03/57-04/86	⊗11/87	
S60513	03/57-04/86	⊗10/89	
S60514	03/57-04/86	⊗11/87	
S60515	03/57-04/86	⊗07/87	
S60516	03/57-04/86	⊗07/87	
S60517	03/57-04/86	⊗07/87	
S60518	04/57-04/86	⊗07/87	
S60519	04/57-04/86	⊗07/87	
S60520	04/57-01/69	⊗01/68	

Class 202 BR Eastleigh

Trailer Second Open Lavatory

TSOL

S60521-S60529

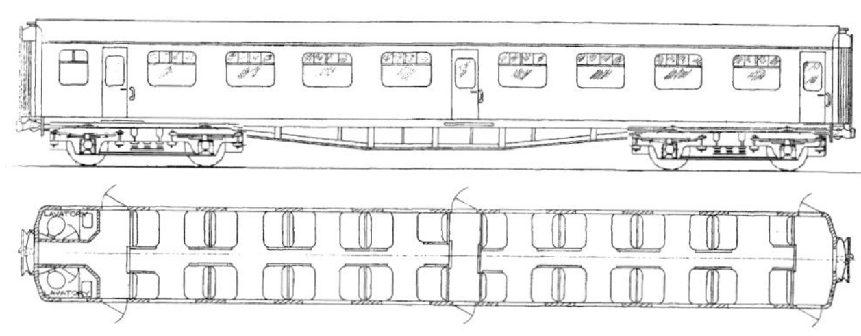

Diagram:	671	DH202
Lot Number:	30397	
Body:	64' 6" × 8' 2½"/9' 0"	
Weight:	30t	
Seats:	60 second	

S60521	05/57-04/86	⊗07/90	
S60522	05/57-05/90	⊗10/05	09/90➲**ADB977696**
S60523	05/57-05/90	⊗03/94	09/90➲**ADB977697**
S60524	05/57-05/86	⊗07/90	
S60525	05/57-05/86	⊗02/92	08/91➲**RDB977695**
S60526	05/57-05/86	⊗07/90	
S60527	05/57-03/88	Ⓟ	
S60528	05/57-03/88	Ⓟ	
S60529	05/57-	Ⓟ	⊠03/88-05/96

Class 202 BR Eastleigh

Trailer Second Open Lavatory

TSOL

S60530-S60547

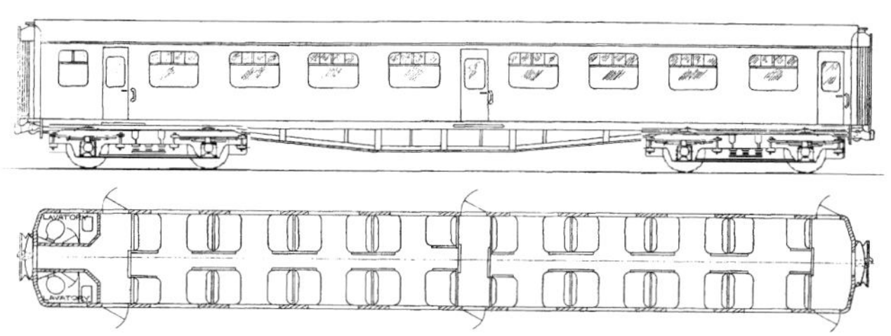

Diagram:	671	DH202
Lot Number:	30394	
Body:	64' 6" × 8' 2½"/9' 0"	
Weight:	30t	
Seats:	60 second	

S60530	01/58-04/86	⊗03/87
S60531	01/58-04/86	⊗03/87
S60532	01/58-04/86	⊗03/87
S60533	01/58-04/86	⊗07/87
S60534	01/58-04/86	⊗07/87
S60535	01/58-04/86	⊗07/87
S60536	01/58-05/86	⊗07/87
S60537	01/58-05/86	⊗07/87
S60538	01/58-05/86	⊗07/87
S60539	01/58-05/86	⊗06/89
S60540	02/58-05/86	⊗06/89
S60541	02/58-05/86	⊗06/89
S60542	02/58-05/86	⊗12/86
S60543	02/58-05/86	⊗12/86
S60544	02/58-05/86	⊗12/86
S60545	03/58-10/84	⊗11/85
S60546	03/58-04/86	⊗07/87
S60547	03/58-10/84	⊗11/85

Class 203 BR Eastleigh

Trailer Second Open Lavatory
TSOL
S60548-S60561

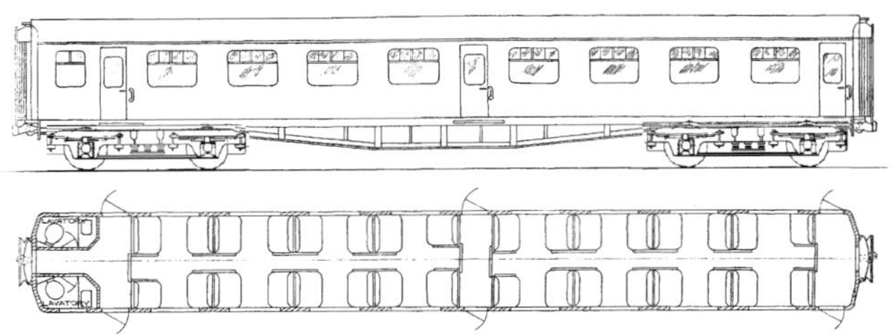

Diagram: 671 DH202
Lot Number: 30394
Body: 64' 6" × 8' 2½"/9' 0"
Weight: 30t
Seats: 60 second

S60548	03/58-04/86	⊗09/87
S60549	03/58-04/86	⊗09/87
S60550	03/58-04/86	⊗12/86
S60551	04/58-04/86	⊗09/87
S60552	04/58-05/86	⊗10/88
S60553	04/58-05/86	⊗07/89
S60554	04/58-05/86	⊗10/88
S60555	04/58-05/86	⊗10/88
S60556	04/58-05/86	⊗10/89
S60557	04/58-04/86	⊗12/86
S60558	04/58-04/86	⊗07/87
S60559	04/58-05/86	⊗10/89
S60560	05/58-04/86	⊗12/86
S60561	05/58-02/88	⊗03/88

Class 207 BR Eastleigh

Trailer Composite Semi-Open Lavatory
TCsoL
S60600-S60618

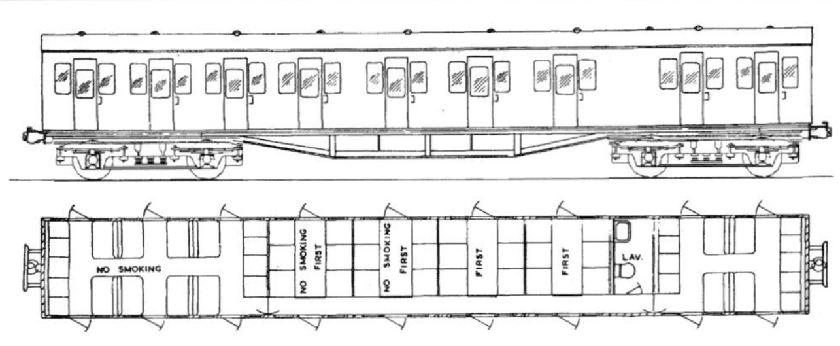

Diagram: 667 DH301
Lot Number: 30626
Body: 63' 6" × 8' 6"/9' 0"
Weight: 31t
Seats: 24 first, 42 second

S60600	01/62-04/94	⊗05/94	
S60601	01/62-02/92	⊗05/92	
S60602	02/62-09/87	⊗04/89	
S60603	05/62-07/91	⊗10/91	
S60604	05/62-07/91	⊗10/91	
S60605	05/62-09/87	⊗01/89	
S60606	05/62-09/87	⊗06/88	
S60607	05/62-05/88	⊗02/89	
S60608	06/62-09/87	⊗01/89	
S60609	06/62-09/93	⊗03/94	
S60610	06/62-05/90	⊗01/92	
S60611	07/62-09/87	⊗05/91	
S60612	07/62-09/93	⊗03/94	
S60613	07/62-12/87	⊗01/89	
S60614	07/62-09/87	⊗06/88	
S60615	07/62-09/87	⊗06/88	
S60616	07/62-07/99	℗	⊠04/93-05/93 then departmental
S60617	07/62-09/87	⊗04/89	
S60618	08/62-05/88	⊗10/89	

Class 251 Metropolitan-Cammell

Motor Parlour Second Lavatory
MPSL
W60644-W60649

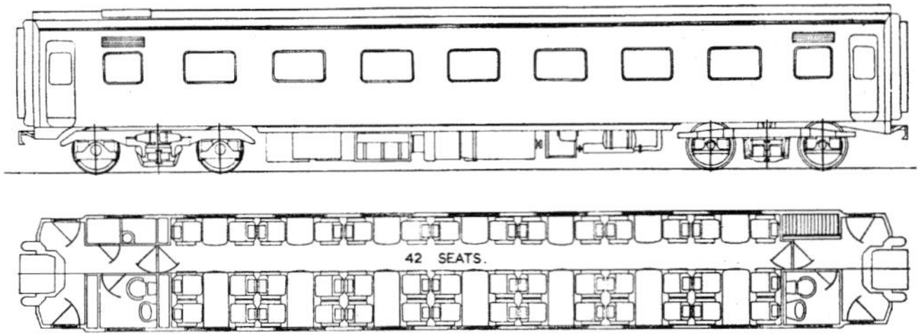

Diagram: 673
Lot Number: 30555
Transmission: Electric. Two 425 hp. GEC traction motors driving through Brown-Boveri spring drive
Body: 65' 6" × 9' 0" Pullman
Weight: 45t 10cwt
Seats: 42 second

W60644	02/60-05/73	⊗05/76
W60645	02/60-05/73	⊗05/76
W60646	04/60-05/73	⊗05/76
W60647	04/60-05/73	⊗07/75
W60648	05/60-05/73	⊗05/76
W60649	05/60-05/73	⊗05/76

Class 205 BR Eastleigh

Trailer Second Open
TSO
S60650-S60671

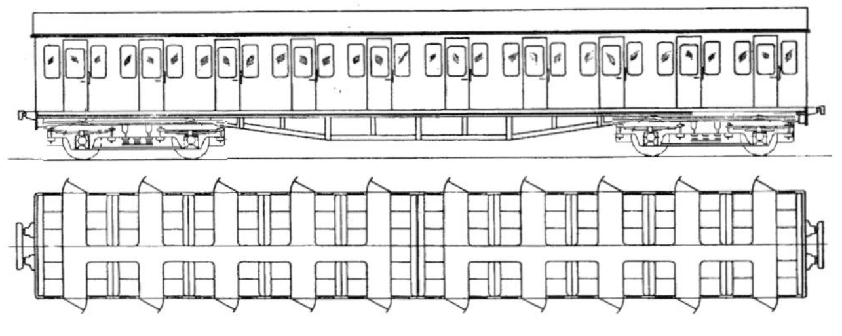

Diagram: 672 DH203
Lot Number: 30542
Body: 63' 6" × 9' 3"
Weight: 30t
Seats: 104 second

S60650	10/59-11/99	⊗10/05	
S60651	08/59-04/94	⊗04/94	
S60652	09/59-09/87	⊗10/89	
S60653	09/59-08/87	⊗04/89	
S60654	10/59-08/87	⊗02/89	
S60655	10/59-09/87	⊗02/88	
S60656	09/59-09/87	⊗12/89	
S60657	10/59-09/91	⊗01/92	
S60658	10/59-12/04	℗	
S60659	10/59-09/87	⊗06/88	
S60660	09/59-01/93	⊗08/09 ®05/78	06/93⊃**ADB977870**
S60661	10/59-07/03	⊗09/03	
S60662	10/59-02/88	⊗11/87	
S60663	10/59-10/89	⊗10/89	
S60664	08/59-08/96	℗⊗*01/98*	
S60665	10/59-08/96	℗⊗*02/98*	
S60666	10/59-09/87	⊗06/88	
S60667	08/59-01/95	⊗04/95	
S60668	11/59-01/99	℗⊗10/03	
S60669	11/59-07/00	℗	
S60670	12/59-10/03	⊗08/03	
S60671	12/59-11/90	⊗01/92	

Class 205 BR Eastleigh
Trailer Second Open
TSO
S60672-S60678

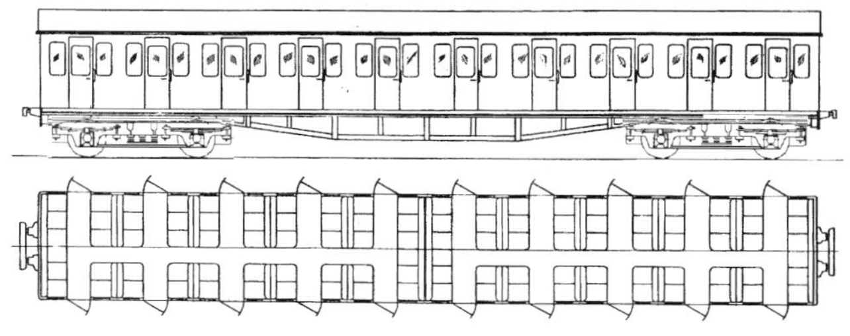

Diagram: 672 DH203
Lot Number: 30672
Body: 63' 6" × 9' 3"
Weight: 30t
Seats: 104 second

S60672	05/62-09/94	⊗08/94	
S60673	05/62-12/04	Ⓟ	
S60674	05/62-12/04	⊗06/05	
S60675	06/62-11/92	⊗11/92	⊠08/92-09/92, ⊠10/92-11/92
S60676	06/62-09/94	⊗08/94	
S60677	06/62-12/04	Ⓟ	
S60678	06/62-11/04	Ⓟ	

Class 201 BR Eastleigh
Trailer First Side-Corridor with Lavatory
TFK
S60700-S60706

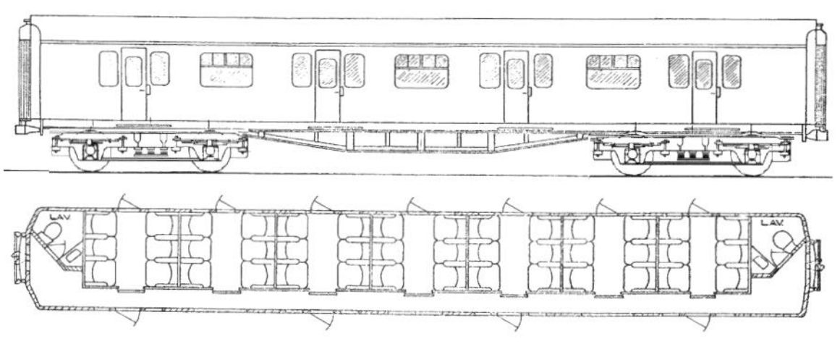

Diagram: 660 DH101
Lot Number: 30330
Body: 58' 0" × 8' 2½"/9' 0"
Weight: 30t
Seats: 42 first

S60700	01/57-05/86	Ⓟ
S60701	02/57-05/86	⊗10/89
S60702	02/57-09/86	⊗11/85
S60703	03/57-04/86	⊗07/87
S60704	03/57-04/86	⊗11/87
S60705	03/57-04/86	⊗07/87
S60706	04/57-01/68	⊗01/69

Class 202 BR Eastleigh
Trailer First Side-Corridor with Lavatory
TFK
S60707-S60709

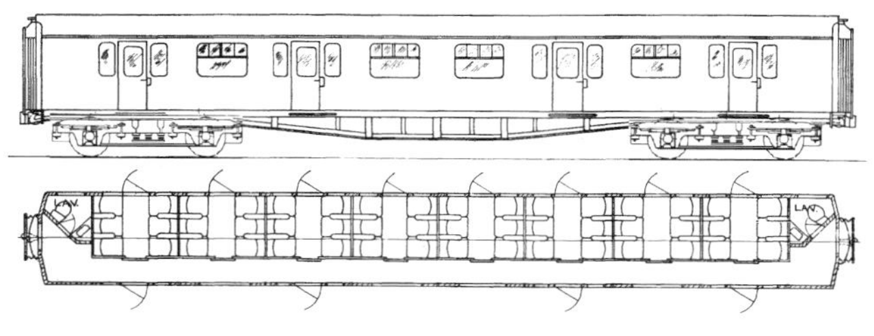

Diagram: 661 DH102
Lot Number: 30396
Body: 64' 6" × 8' 2½"/9' 0"
Weight: 31t
Seats: 48 first

S60707	05/57-04/86	⊗07/90
S60708	05/57-05/86	Ⓟ
S60709	05/57-03/88	Ⓟ

Class 202 BR Eastleigh
Trailer First Side-Corridor with Lavatory
TFK
S60710-S60715

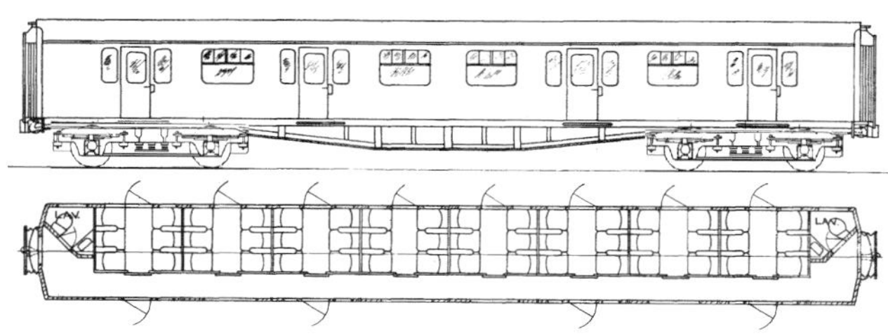

Diagram: 661 DH102
Lot Number: 30392
Body: 64' 6" × 8' 2½"/9' 0"
Weight: 31t
Seats: 48 first

S60710	12/57-04/86	⊗09/87
S60711	12/57-04/86	⊗07/87
S60712	01/58-05/86	⊗07/87
S60713	02/58-05/86	⊗10/88
S60714	02/58-05/86	⊗12/86
S60715	03/58-01/86	⊗11/85

Class 203 BR Eastleigh
Trailer First Side-Corridor with Lavatory
TFK
S60716-S60722

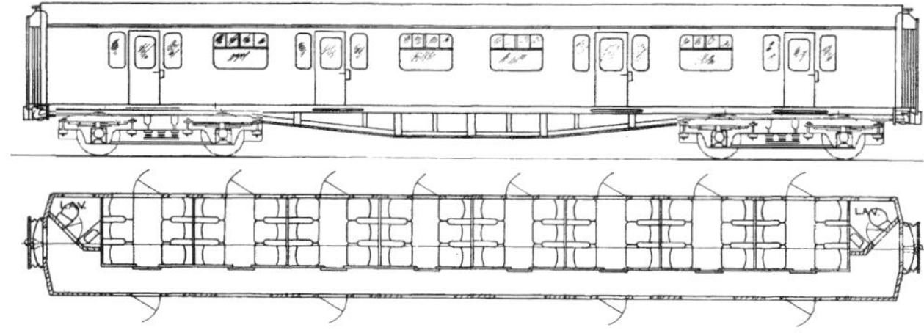

Diagram: 661 DH102
Lot Number: 30392
Body: 64' 6" × 8' 2½"/9' 0"
Weight: 31t
Seats: 48 first

S60716	03/58-04/86	⊗03/88
S60717	04/58-05/86	⊗10/88
S60718	04/58-04/86	⊗03/88
S60719	04/58-04/86	⊗11/87
S60720	05/58-05/86	⊗07/89
S60721	05/58-04/86	⊗07/87
S60722	05/58-04/86	⊗09/87

Class 251 Metropolitan-Cammell
Motor Kitchen First Lavatory
MFLRK
M60730-M60733

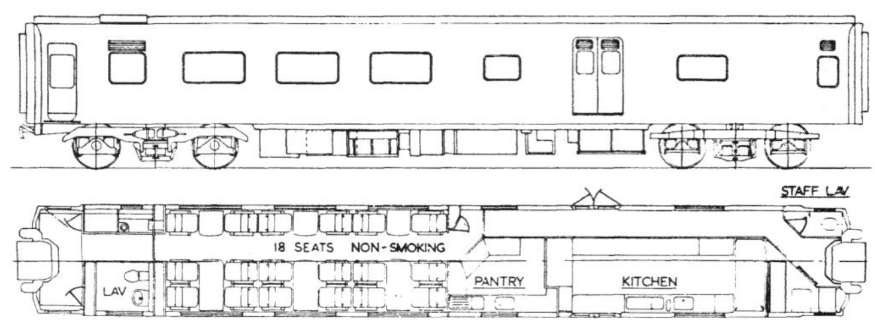

Diagram: 662
Lot Number: 30556
Transmission: Electric. Two 425 hp. GEC traction motors driving through Brown-Boveri spring drive
Body: 65' 6" × 9' 3" Pullman
Weight: 49t
Seats: 18 first

M60730	11/59-05/73	⊗07/74	03/67⇨W
M60731	11/59-05/73	⊗07/75	03/67⇨W
M60732	11/59-05/73	⊗07/74	03/67⇨W
M60733	11/59-05/73	⊗05/76	03/67⇨W

Class 251 Metropolitan-Cammell
Trailer Kitchen First Lavatory
TFLRK
W60734-W60739

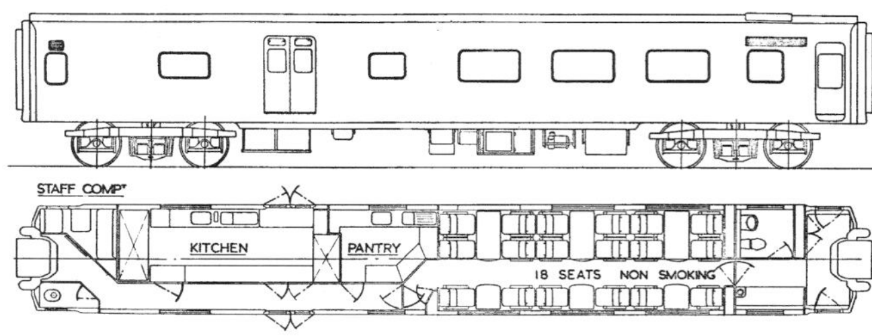

Diagram: 663
Lot Number: 30557
Body: 65' 6" × 9' 3" Pullman
Weight: 36t
Seats: 18 first

W60734	02/60-05/73	⊗07/74
W60735	02/60-05/73	⊗07/74
W60736	04/60-05/73	⊗07/74
W60737	04/60-05/73	⊗07/74
W60738	05/60-05/73	⊗05/74
W60739	05/60-05/73	⊗05/74

Class 251 Metropolitan-Cammell
Trailer Parlour First Lavatory
TPFL
M60740-W60749

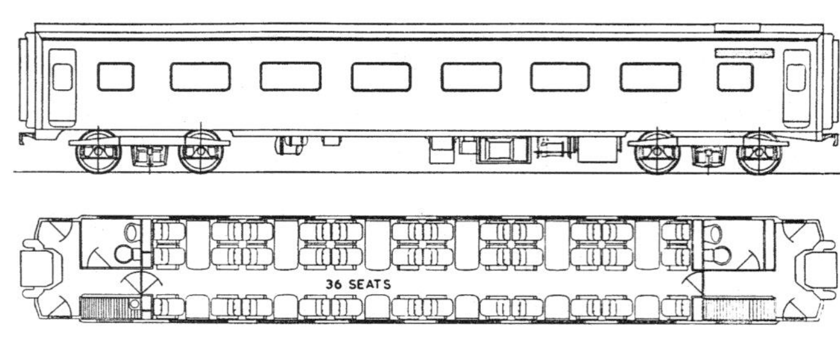

Diagram: 664
Lot Number: 30558
Body: 65' 6" × 9' 0" Pullman
Weight: 33t
Seats: 36 first

M60740	11/59-05/73	⊗07/74	03/67⇨W
M60741	11/59-05/73	⊗07/74	03/67⇨W
M60742	11/59-05/73	⊗07/74	03/67⇨W
M60743	11/59-05/73	⊗07/74	03/67⇨W
W60744	02/60-05/73	⊗07/74	
W60745	02/60-05/73	⊗07/74	
W60746	04/60-05/73	⊗07/74	
W60747	04/60-05/73	⊗05/74	
W60748	05/60-05/73	⊗05/74	
W60749	05/60-05/73	⊗05/74	

Class 203 BR Eastleigh
Trailer Buffet
TRB
S60750-S60756

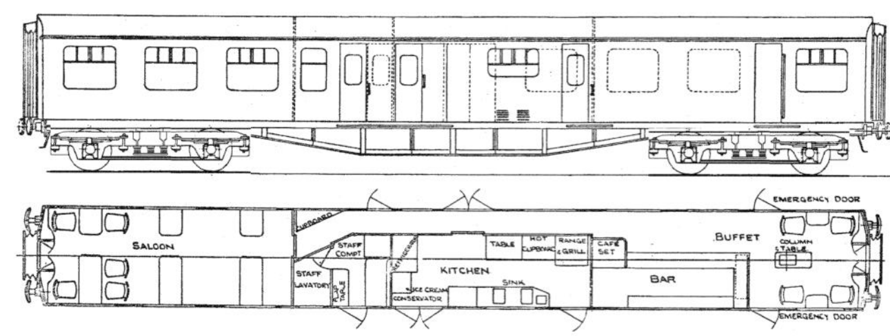

Diagram: 678 DN401
Lot Number: 30393
Body: 64' 6" × 8' 2½"/9' 0"
Weight: 35t
Seats: 17 Saloon, 4 buffet

S60750	04/58-01/64	Ⓟ	03/74➲**DB975386**
S60751	05/58-10/80	⊗08/82	
S60752	05/58-10/80	⊗08/82	
S60753	05/58-10/80	⊗08/82	
S60754	05/58-10/80	⊗08/82	
S60755	06/58-01/64		01/70-➲**DB975025**
S60756	06/58-10/80	⊗08/82	

Class 205 BR Eastleigh
Driving Trailer Composite Semi-Open Lavatory DTCsoL
S60800-S60817

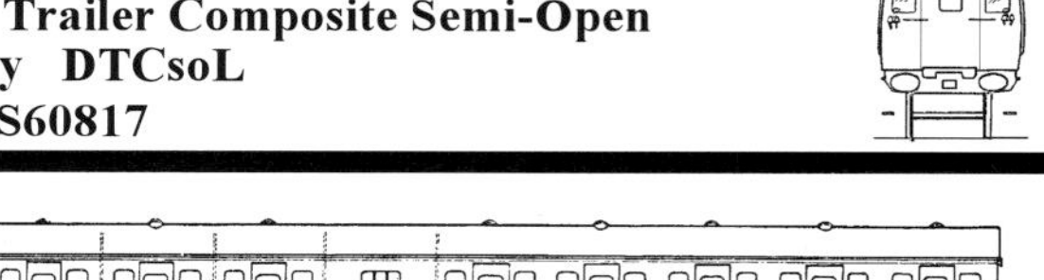

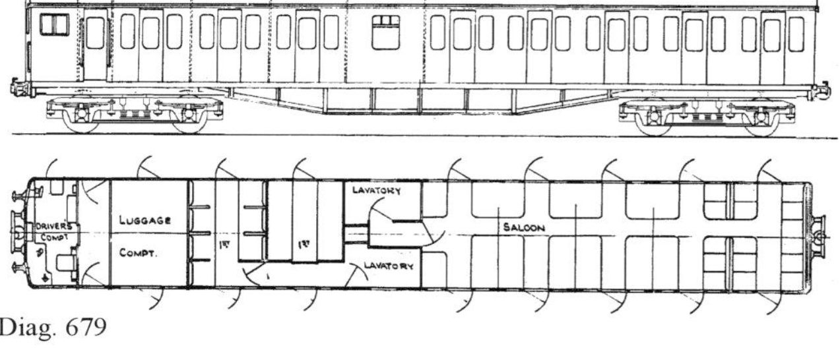

Diag. 679

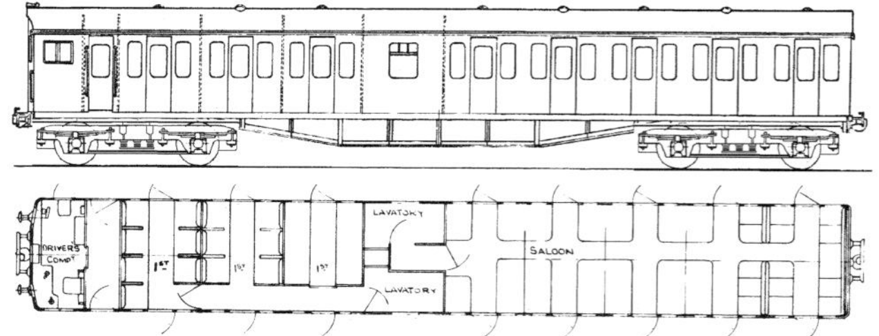

Diag. 683 f First class compartment fitted in former luggage area (converted c1976)

Diagram: 679 DE301 f 683 DE302 ② DE204
Lot Number: 30333
Body: 64' 0" × 9' 3"
Weight: 32t

Seats: 13 first, 50 second f 19 first, 50 second

S60800	08/57-12/04 ℗		
S60801	08/57-04/94 ⊗08/94		
S60802	08/57-08/87 ⊗02/88		
S60803	08/57-09/87 ⊗12/88		
S60804	08/57-08/87 ⊗02/89		
S60805	08/57-09/87 ⊗02/88		f
S60806	08/57-09/87 ⊗12/89		f
S60807	09/57-08/87 ⊗12/88		
S60808	09/57-12/04 ℗		f
S60809	09/57-09/87 ⊗06/88		
S60810	09/57-12/04 ℗	®05/78	
S60811	09/57-12/04 ℗		f
S60812	09/57-09/87 ⊗03/88		f
S60813	09/57-10/89 ⊗10/89		f
S60814	10/57-10/93 ⊗08/94		f
S60815	10/57-09/94 ⊗08/94		f
S60816	10/57-09/87 ⊗06/88		f
S60817	10/57-01/95 ⊗10/94		f

Class 205 BR Eastleigh
Driving Trailer Composite Semi-Open Lavatory DTCsoL
S60818-S60821

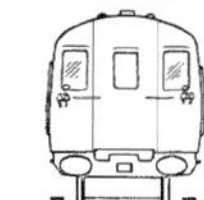

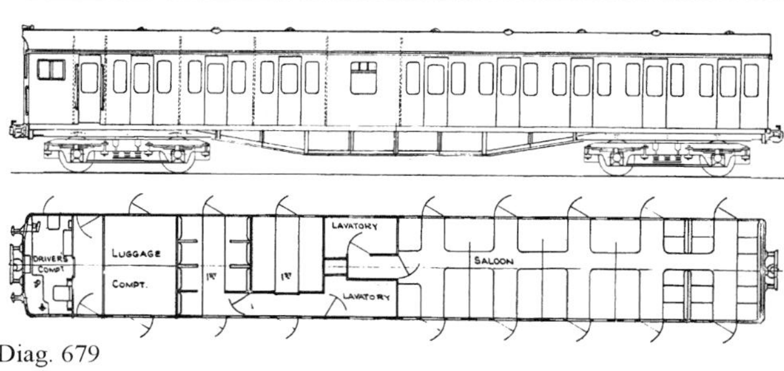

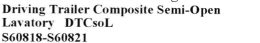

Diag. 679

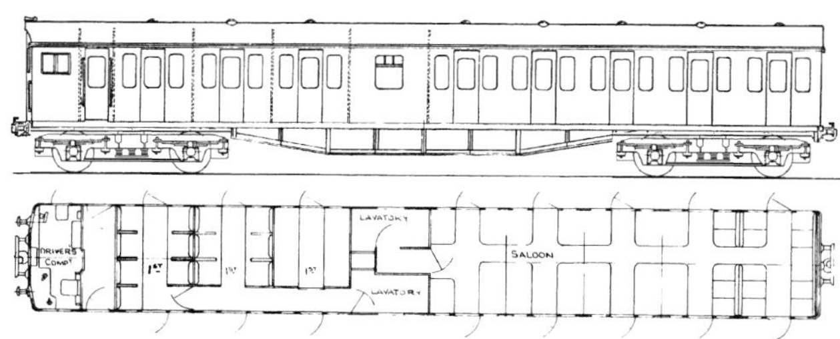

Diag. 683 f First class compartment fitted in former luggage area (converted c1976)

Diagram: 679 DE301 f 683 DE302
Lot Number: 30399
Body: 64' 0" × 9' 3"
Weight: 32t
Seats: 13 first, 50 second f 19 first, 50 second

S60818	06/58-08/87 ⊗04/89	
S60819	06/58-09/87 ⊗10/89	
S60820	06/58-09/91 ℗	f
S60821	06/58-11/87 ⊗12/88	

Class 205 BR Eastleigh
Driving Trailer Composite Semi-Open Lavatory DTCsoL
S60822-S60825

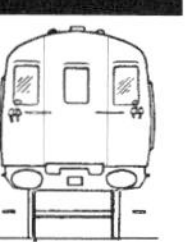

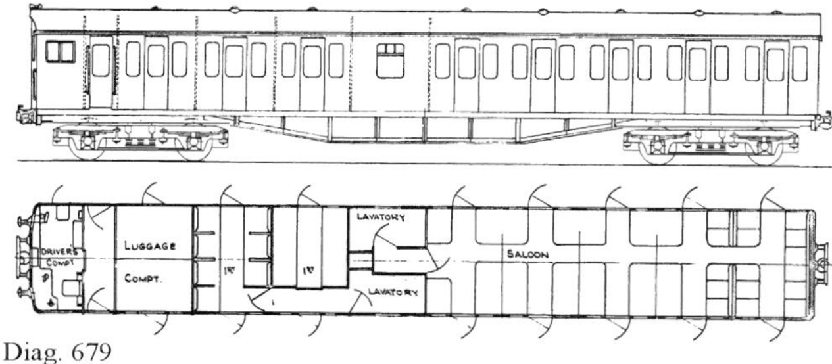

Diag. 679

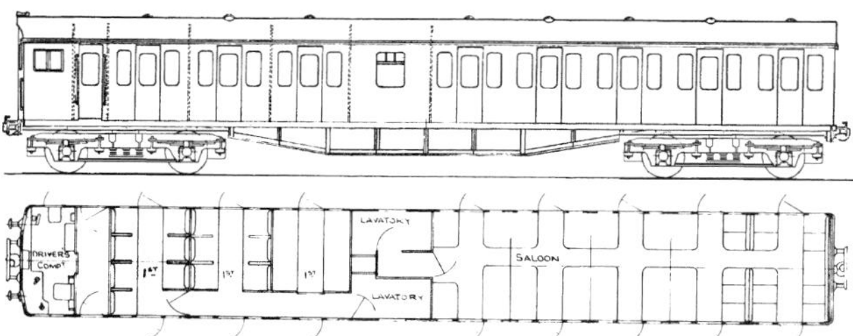

Diag. 683 f First class compartment fitted in former luggage area (converted c1976)

Diagram: 679 DE301 f 683 DE302
Lot Number: 30541
Body: 64' 0" × 9' 3"
Weight: 32t
Seats: 13 first, 50 second f 19 first, 50 second

S60822	11/59-01/99 ℗	f
S60823	11/59-07/00 ⊗08/03	
S60824	12/59-02/04 ℗	
S60825	12/59-11/90 ⊗01/92	

Class 205 BR Eastleigh
Driving Trailer Composite Semi-Open Lavatory DTCsoL
S60826-S60832

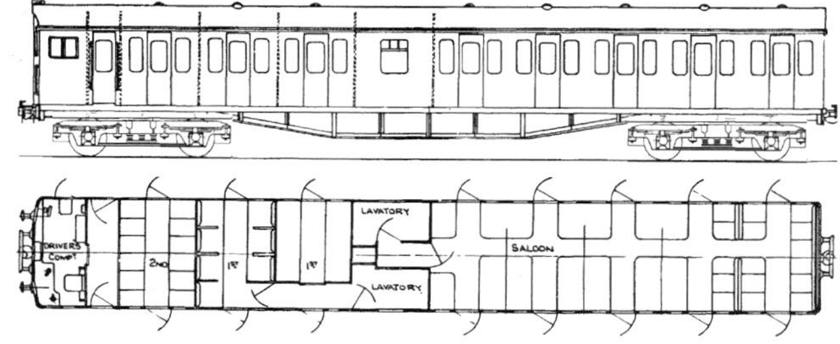

Diagram: 680 DE303
Lot Number: 30673
Body: 64' 0" × 9' 3"
Weight: 32t
Seats: 13 first, 62 second

S60826	05/62-09/94 ⊗08/94	
S60827	05/62-12/04 ℗	
S60828	05/62-12/04 ℗	
S60829	06/62-11/92 ⊗11/92	⊠08/92-09/92, ⊠10/92-11/92
S60830	06/62-09/94 ⊗08/94	
S60831	06/62-12/04 ℗	
S60832	06/62-11/04 ℗	

Class 207 BR Eastleigh

Driving Trailer Second Open
DTSO
S60900-S60918

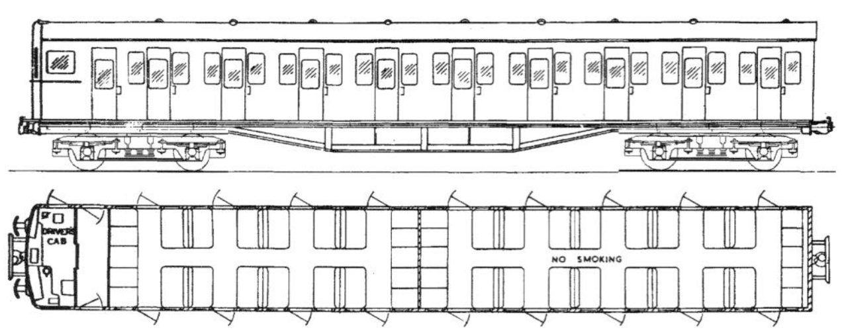

Diagram: 681 DE201
Lot Number: 30627
Body: 64' 2½" × 8' 6"/9' 0"
Weight: 32t
Seats: 76 second

S60900	01/62-04/94	⊗05/94	
S60901	01/62-01/05	Ⓟ	
S60902	02/62-09/87	⊗04/89	
S60903	05/62-10/03	⊗10/03	
S60904	05/62-12/04	Ⓟ	
S60905	05/62-09/87	⊗12/88	
S60906	05/62-09/87	⊗06/88	
S60907	05/62-05/88	⊗02/89	
S60908	06/62-09/87	⊗01/89	
S60909	06/62-09/93	⊗03/94	
S60910	06/62-05/90	⊗05/92	04/92⊃**ADB977701**
S60911	07/62-09/87	⊗05/91	
S60912	07/62-09/93	⊗03/94	
S60913	07/62-12/87	⊗12/88	
S60914	07/62-09/87	⊗06/88	
S60915	07/62-09/87	⊗06/88	
S60916	07/62-02/04	Ⓟ	⊠04/93-05/93
S60917	07/62-09/87	⊗04/89	
S60918	08/62-05/88	⊗12/88	

Class 104 Birmingham RC&W

Driving Half-Motor Second Lavatory
DHSL
M78601

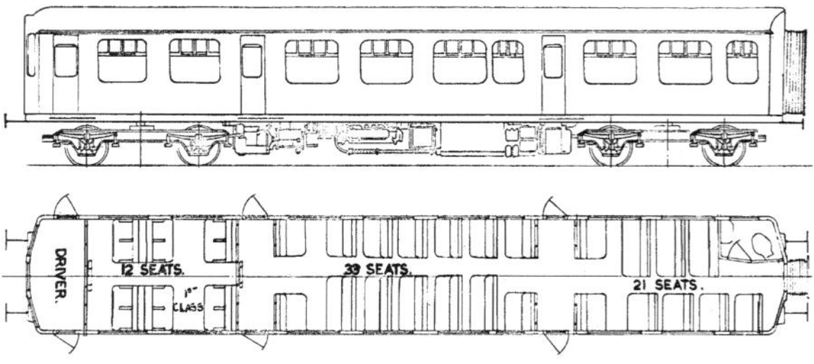

Coupling: ■ Blue square
Diagram:
Lot Number: 30294
Engines: One BUT (Leyland) 6-cyl horizontal type of 150 bhp.
Transmission: Mechanical. Standard
Body: 57' 6" × 9' 3"
Weight: 31t
Seats: 66 second

M78601	09/82⊂**50521**	09/82-11/85	⊗09/86

Class 111 Metropolitan-Cammell

Driving Half-Motor Composite Lavatory
DHCL
E78706-E78714

Coupling: ■ Blue square
Diagram: DW301
Lot Number: 30268
Engines: One Rolls-Royce 6-cyl horizontal type of 180 bhp.
Transmission: Mechanical. Standard
Body: 57' 6" × 9' 3"
Weight: 33t
Seats: 12 first, 53 second

E78706	08/82⊂**50279**	08/82-09/86	⊗10/86
E78707	10/82⊂**50274**	10/82-01/87	⊗02/88
E78708	11/82⊂**50271**	11/82-08/87	⊗09/88
E78709	10/83⊂**53273**	10/83-10/89	⊗05/90
E78710	10/83⊂**53276**	10/83-01/87	⊗05/87
E78711	02/84⊂**53275**	02/84-09/89	⊗04/90
E78712	09/84⊂**53278**	09/84-09/89	⊗07/90
E78713	02/85⊂**53272**	02/85-10/89	⊗04/90
E78714	08/85⊂**53277**	08/85-09/89	⊗04/90

Class 111 Metropolitan-Cammell

Driving Half-Motor Composite Lavatory
DHCL
E78716-E78724

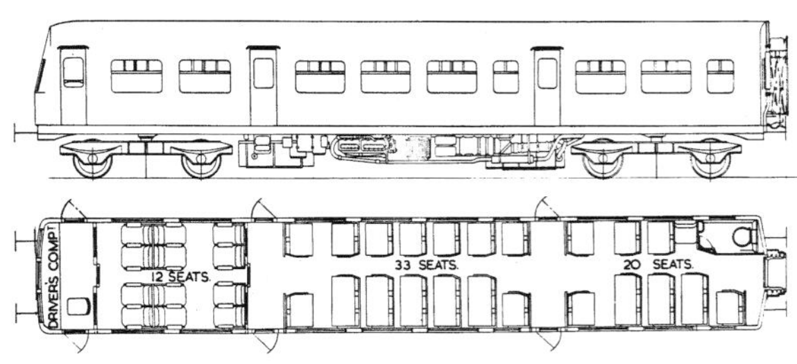

Coupling: ■ Blue square
Diagram: DW302
Lot Number: 30509
Engines: One Rolls-Royce 6-cyl horizontal type of 180 bhp.
Transmission: Mechanical. Standard
Body: 57' 6" × 9' 3"
Weight: 33t
Seats: 12 first, 53 second

E78716	12/82⊂**51554**	12/82-07/87	⊗02/88	
E78717	06/83⊂**51552**	06/83-09/89	⊗07/90	⊠05/86-06/86
E78718	08/83⊂**51557**	08/83-09/89	⊗07/90	
E78719	10/83⊂**51553**	10/83-10/89	⊗05/90	
E78720	12/83⊂**51551**	12/83-09/86	⊗05/87	
E78721	06/84⊂**51559**	06/84-07/87	⊗02/88	
E78722	11/84⊂**51555**	11/84-02/89	⊗07/89	
E78723	03/85⊂**51556**	03/85-07/87	⊗05/88	
E78724	05/85⊂**51558**	05/85-01/87	⊗06/87	

Class 104 Birmingham RC&W
Driving Half-Motor Brake Second
DHBS
M78851

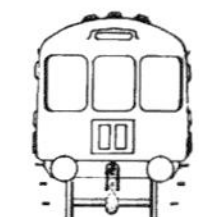

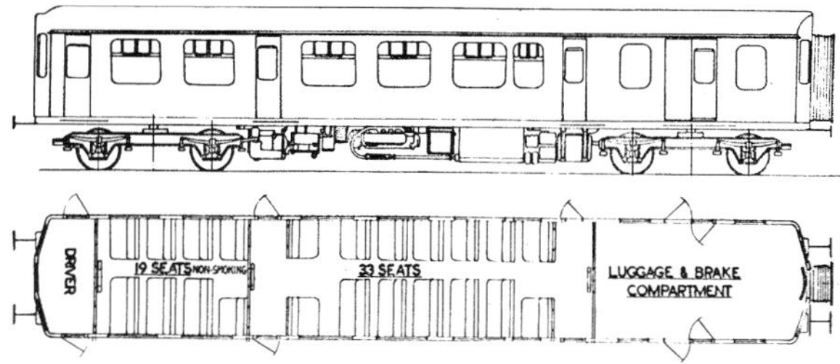

Coupling:	■ Blue square
Diagram:	
Lot Number:	30293
Engines:	One BUT (Leyland) 6-cyl horizontal type of 150 bhp.
Transmission:	Mechanical. Standard
Body:	57' 6" × 9' 3"
Weight:	31t
Seats:	52 second

M78851	09/82⊂**50446**	09/82-11/85	⊗09/86

Class 111 Metropolitan-Cammell
Driving Half-Motor Brake Second
DHBS
E78956-E78964

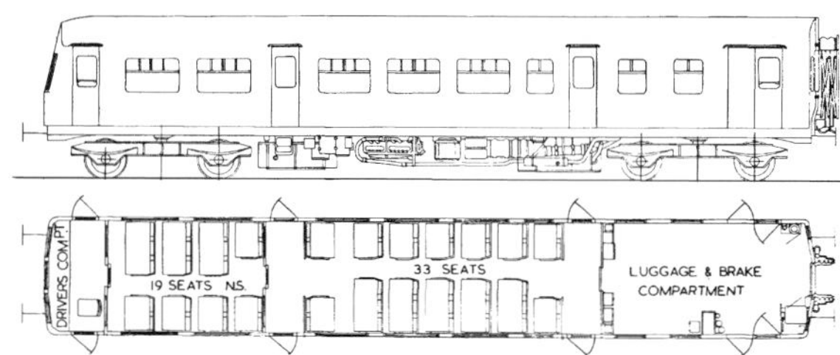

Coupling:	■ Blue square
Diagram:	DY202
Lot Number:	30338
Engines:	One Rolls-Royce 6-cyl horizontal type of 180 bhp.
Transmission:	Mechanical. Standard
Body:	57' 6" × 9' 3"
Weight:	33t
Seats:	52 second

E78956	08/82⊂**50286**	08/82-04/86	⊗01/87
E78957	10/82⊂**50287**	10/82-01/87	⊗02/88
E78958	11/82⊂**50281**	11/82-08/87	⊗09/88
E78959	10/83⊂**53288**	10/83-10/89	⊗05/90
E78960	10/83⊂**53282**	10/83-10/89	⊗07/90
E78961	02/84⊂**53280**	02/84-09/89	⊗04/90
E78962	09/84⊂**53283**	09/84-09/89	⊗07/90
E78963	02/85⊂**53289**	02/85-08/87	⊗02/88
E78964	08/85⊂**53284**	08/85-09/89	⊗04/90

Class 111 Metropolitan-Cammell
Driving Half-Motor Brake Second
DHBS
E78966-E78974

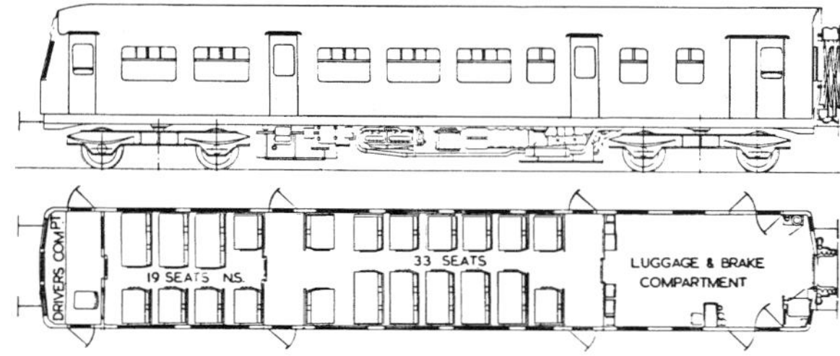

Coupling:	■ Blue square
Diagram:	DY203
Lot Number:	30508
Engines:	One Rolls-Royce 6-cyl horizontal type of 180 bhp.
Transmission:	Mechanical. Standard
Body:	57' 6" × 9' 3"
Weight:	33t
Seats:	52 second

E78966	12/82⊂**51546**	12/82-07/87	⊗02/88	
E78967	06/83⊂**51542**	06/83-06/89	⊗08/89	
E78968	08/83⊂**51543**	08/83-10/89	⊗07/90	
E78969	10/83⊂**51544**	10/83-09/89	⊗04/90	⊠09/89-09/89
E78970	12/84⊂**51541**	12/84-09/86	⊗05/87	
E78971	06/84⊂**51549**	06/84-10/89	⊗05/90	
E78972	11/84⊂**51545**	11/84-08/87	⊗02/88	
E78973	03/85⊂**51548**	03/85-01/87	⊗06/87	
E78974	05/85⊂**51550**	05/85-01/87	⊗06/87	

BR Derby
Driving Motor Brake Second
DMBS
E79000-E79007

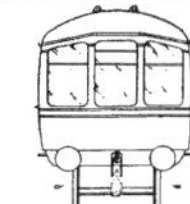

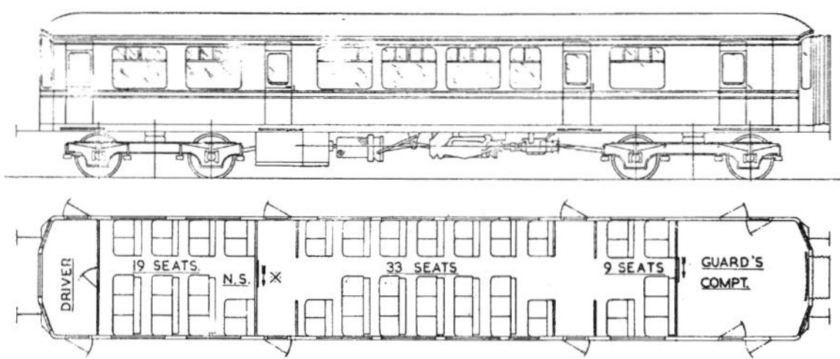

Coupling:	▲ Red triangle
Diagram:	501
Lot Number:	30084
Engines:	Two BUT (Leyland) 6-cyl horizontal type of 125 bhp.
Transmission:	Hydro-mechanical. Lysholm Smith (Leyland) torque convertor to final drive
Body:	57' 6" × 9' 2"
Weight:	26t
Seats:	61 second

E79000	04/54-02/64	⊗03/64
E79001	05/54-02/64	⊗03/64
E79002	05/54-02/64	⊗03/64
E79003	05/54-02/64	⊗03/64
E79004	05/54-02/64	⊗03/64
E79005	05/54-02/64	⊗03/64
E79006	08/54-02/64	⊗03/64
E79007	09/54-02/64	⊗03/64

BR Derby
Driving Motor Brake Second
DMBS
M79008-M79020

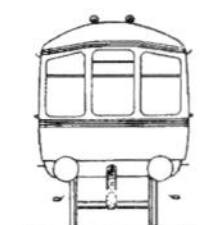

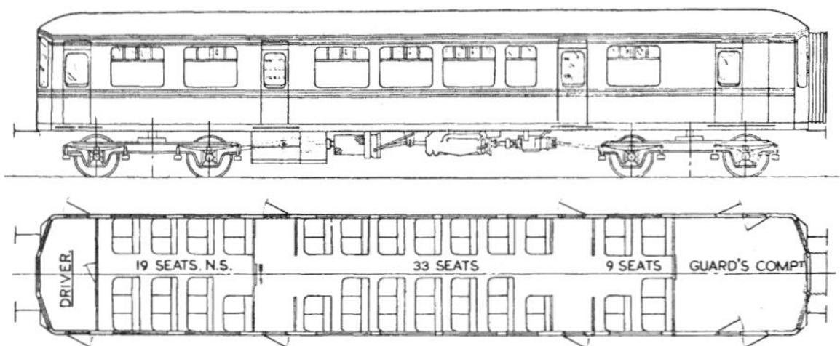

Coupling: ♦ Yellow diamond
Diagram: 503
Lot Number: 30123
Engines: Two BUT (AEC) 6-cyl horizontal type of 150 bhp.
Transmission: Mechanical. Standard
Body: 57' 6" × 9' 2"
Weight: 27t
Seats: 61 second

M79008	11/54-02/68	⊗02/69	
M79009	01/55-04/68	⊗08/69	
M79010	01/55-04/68	⊗08/69	
M79011	01/55-04/68	⊗06/69	
M79012	01/55-04/68	⊗08/69	
M79013	01/55-04/68	⊗06/69	
M79014	01/55-04/68	⊗06/69	
M79015	12/54-02/68	⊗06/69	
M79016	12/54-05/68	⊗06/69	
M79017	12/54-05/68	⊗06/69	
M79018	01/55-05/68	Ⓟ	11/70⊃**DB975007**
M79019	01/55-05/68	⊗06/69	
M79020	01/55-04/67	⊗04/68	

BR Derby
Driving Motor Brake Second
DMBS
E79021-E79033

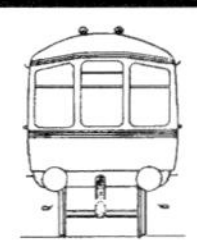

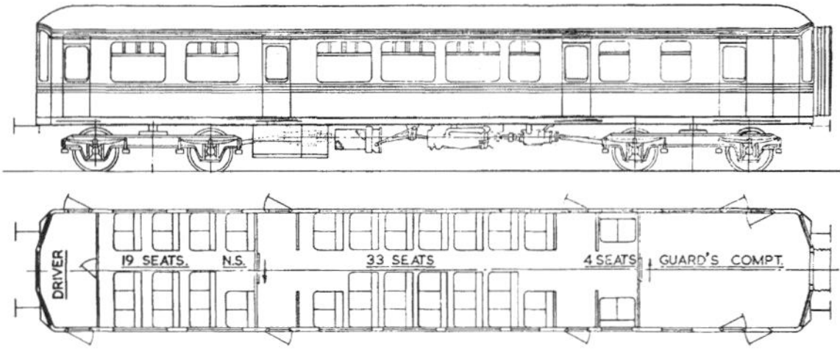

Coupling: ♦ Yellow diamond
Diagram: 504
Lot Number: 30126
Engines: Two BUT (AEC) 6-cyl horizontal type of 150 bhp.
Transmission: Mechanical. Standard
Body: 57' 6" × 9' 2"
Weight: 27t
Seats: 56 second

E79021	01/55-05/68	⊗03/69	
E79022	01/55-05/68	⊗03/69	
E79023	01/55-06/68	⊗06/69	
E79024	01/55-06/68	⊗05/69	
E79025	01/55-05/68	⊗06/69	
E79026	01/55-06/68	⊗04/69	
E79027	01/55-06/68	⊗06/69	
E79028	01/55-06/68	⊗06/69	
E79029	05/55-11/67	⊗06/69	
E79030	05/55-06/68	⊗04/69	
E79031	05/55-09/67	⊗06/69	
E79032	05/55-08/68	⊗05/69	
E79033	06/55-06/67	⊗02/68	11/66⇦**SC**

BR Derby
Driving Motor Brake Second
DMBS
E79034-E79046

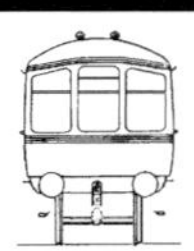

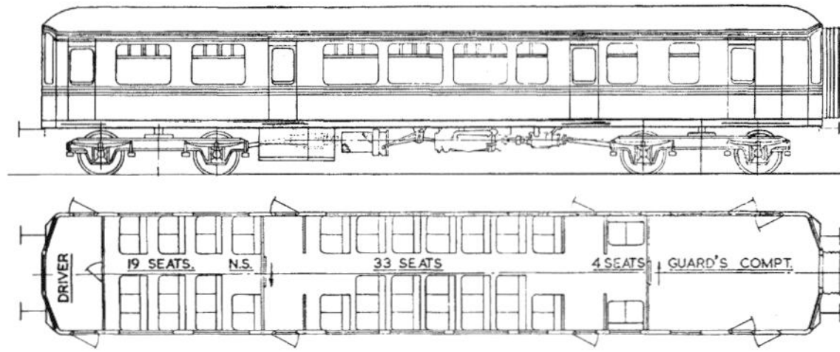

Coupling: ♦ Yellow diamond
Diagram: 504
Lot Number: 30177
Engines: Two BUT (AEC) 6-cyl horizontal type of 150 bhp.
Transmission: Mechanical. Standard
Body: 57' 6" × 9' 2"
Weight: 27t
Seats: 56 second

E79034	06/55-06/67	⊗02/68	11/66⇦**SC**
E79035	06/55-06/67	⊗02/68	11/66⇦**SC**
E79036	06/55-06/67	⊗02/71	10/66⇦**SC**
E79037	06/55-05/68	⊗03/69	
E79038	06/55-05/68	⊗04/69	
E79039	06/55-10/67	⊗08/68	
E79040	06/55-07/67	⊗04/69	
E79041	06/55-06/65	⊗08/65	
E79042	06/55-07/61	⊗10/61	
E79043	06/55-09/67	⊗08/68	
E79044	08/55-09/68	⊗08/69	
E79045	08/55-09/67	⊗06/69	
E79046	08/55-06/68	⊗04/69	

Metropolitan-Cammell
Driving Motor Brake Second
DMBS
E79047-E79075

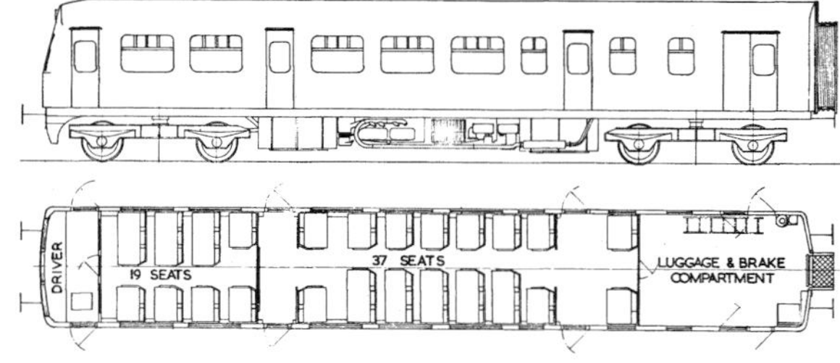

Coupling: ♦ Yellow diamond
Diagram: 591
Lot Number: 30190
Engines: Two BUT (AEC) 6-cyl horizontal type of 150 bhp.
Transmission: Mechanical. Standard
Body: 57' 6" × 9' 3"
Weight: 31t 10cwt
Seats: 56 second

E79047	01/56-09/68	⊗06/81	05/69⊃**DB975018**
E79048	01/56-09/68	⊗10/69	
E79049	01/56-08/68	⊗10/69	
E79050	01/56-09/68	⊗10/69	
E79051	01/56-09/68	⊗10/69	
E79052	01/56-09/68	⊗10/69	
E79053	02/56-11/68	⊗06/81	05/69⊃**DB975019**
E79054	02/56-01/69	⊗06/70	
E79055	02/56-06/69	⊗07/70	
E79056	02/56-11/68	⊗02/73	
E79057	03/56-06/69	⊗04/73	
E79058	03/56-06/69	⊗08/70	
E79059	03/56-11/68	⊗02/73	
E79060	03/56-11/68	⊗02/73	
E79061	04/56-11/68	⊗04/73	
E79062	04/56-11/68	⊗04/73	

E79063	04/56-04/69	⊗08/70	
E79064	05/56-04/69	⊗06/72	
E79065	05/56-01/69	⊗06/70	
E79066	05/56-06/69	⊗02/73	
E79067	05/56-11/68	⊗10/72	
E79068	05/56-01/69	⊗06/70	
E79069	06/56-10/68	⊗02/73	
E79070	06/56-10/68	⊗02/73	
E79071	06/56-10/68	⊗02/73	
E79072	06/56-01/69	⊗02/73	⊠10/68-11/68
E79073	06/56-01/69	⊗02/73	
E79074	07/56-10/68	⊗02/73	
E79075	08/56-01/69	⊗02/73	⊠10/68-11/68

Metropolitan-Cammell
Driving Motor Brake Second
DMBS
M79076-M79082

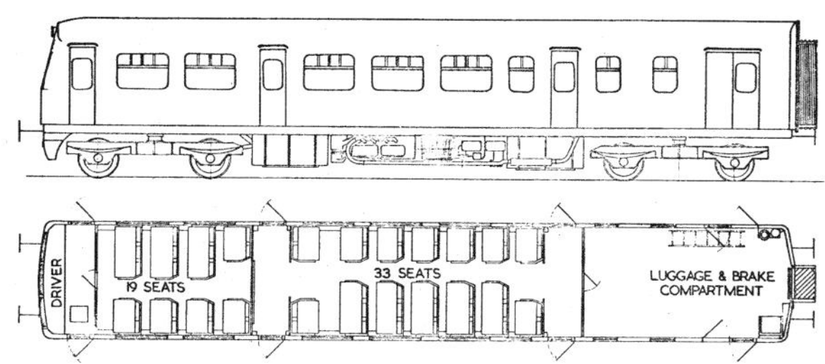

Coupling: ♦ Yellow diamond
Diagram: 592
Lot Number: 30190
Engines: Two BUT (AEC) 6-cyl horizontal type of 150 bhp.
Transmission: Mechanical. Standard
Body: 57' 6" × 9' 3"
Weight: 31t 10cwt
Seats: 52 second

M79076	09/55-10/64	⊗11/64
M79077	12/55-07/67	⊗02/68
M79078	12/55-07/67	⊗02/68
M79079	12/55-07/67	⊗02/68
M79080	12/55-07/67	⊗02/68
M79081	12/55-07/67	⊗02/68
M79082	12/55-07/67	⊗02/68

BR Swindon
Driving Motor Brake Second Lavatory
DMBSL
W79083-W79090

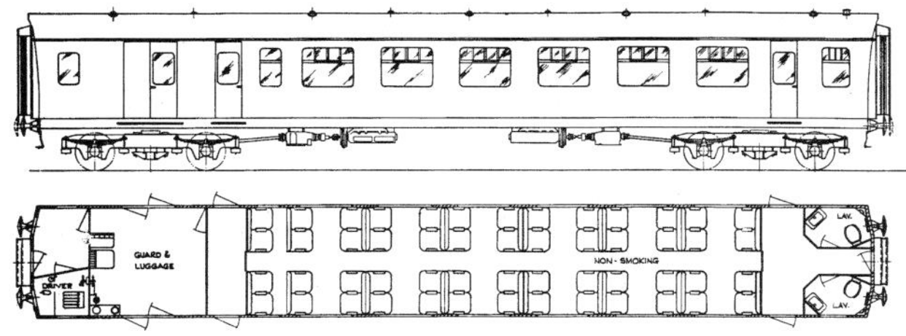

Coupling: ● White circle
Diagram: 550 DQ225
Lot Number: 30196
Engines: Two BUT (AEC) 6-cyl horizontal type of 150 bhp.
Transmission: Mechanical. Standard
Body: 64' 6" × 9' 3" Inter-City
Weight: 389t 13cwt
Seats: 52 second

W79083	09/56-10/72	⊗04/85	10/59⇨**SC**
W79084	09/56-10/72	⊗12/73	09/59⇨**SC**
W79085	09/56-10/72	⊗02/74	05/59⇨**SC**
W79086	10/56-10/72	⊗11/81	09/59⇨**SC**
W79087	10/56-10/72	⊗01/75	09/59⇨**SC**
W79088	12/56-07/81	⊗02/83	06/59⇨**SC**
W79089	11/56-10/72	⊗07/83	10/59⇨**SC**
W79090	11/56-10/72	⊗05/81	09/59⇨**SC**

BR Swindon
Driving Motor Brake Second Lavatory
DMBSL
W79091-W79094

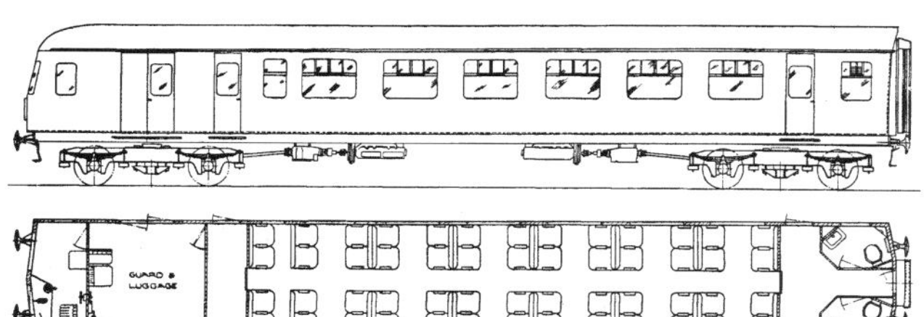

Coupling: ● White circle
Diagram: 552
Lot Number: 30200
Engines: Two BUT (AEC) 6-cyl horizontal type of 150 bhp.
Transmission: Mechanical. Standard
Body: 64' 6" × 9' 3" Inter-City
Weight: 38t
Seats: 52 second

W79091	06/57-10/72		05/59⇨**SC**	Exported
W79092	06/57-02/69	⊗04/72	09/59⇨**SC**	
W79093	06/57-10/72		09/59⇨**SC**	Exported
W79094	06/57-10/72		06/59⇨**SC**	Exported

BR Swindon
Driving Motor Brake Second Lavatory
DMBSL
SC79095

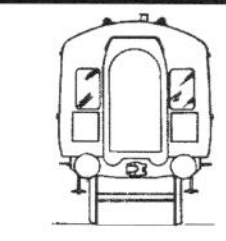

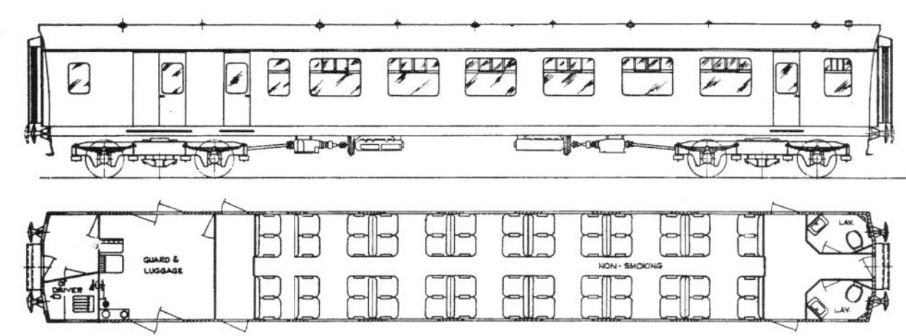

Coupling: ● White circle
Diagram: 550
Lot Number: 30196
Engines: Two BUT (AEC) 6-cyl horizontal type of 150 bhp.
Transmission: Mechanical. Standard
Body: 64' 6" × 9' 3" Inter-City
Weight: 39t 13cwt
Seats: 52 second

SC79095	08/56-10/72	⊗12/80

BR Swindon
Driving Motor Brake Second Lavatory
DMBSL
SC79096-SC79111

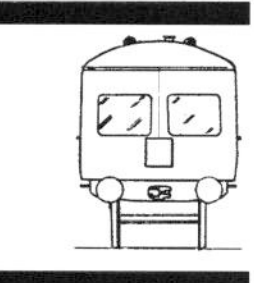

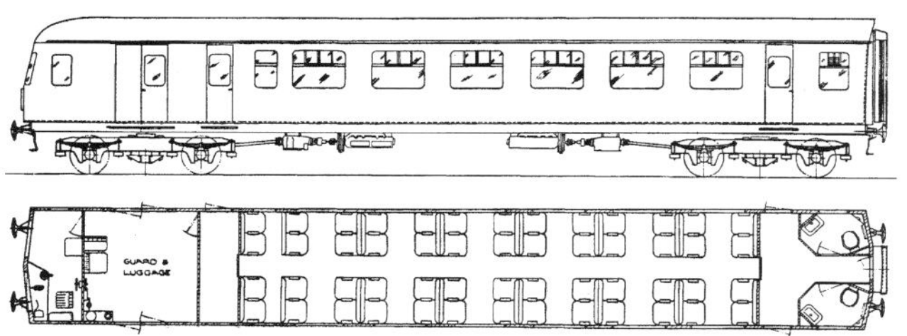

Coupling: ● White circle
Diagram: 552
Lot Number: 30200
Engines: Two BUT (AEC) 6-cyl horizontal type of 150 bhp.

Transmission: Mechanical. Standard
Body: 64' 6" × 9' 3" Inter-City
Weight: 38t
Seats: 52 second

SC79096	09/56-05/72		Exported
SC79097	09/56-10/72		Exported
SC79098	08/56-10/72	⊗05/82	07/76⊃DB975426
SC79099	08/56-10/72	⊗05/75	
SC79100	09/56-10/72	⊗08/83	
SC79101	09/56-10/72	⊗04/75	
SC79102	10/56-10/72	⊗09/75	
SC79103	10/56-10/72	⊗06/83	
SC79104	11/56-10/72	⊗06/83	
SC79105	11/56-10/72	⊗06/83	
SC79106	04/57-10/72	⊗09/75	
SC79107	04/57-10/72	⊗09/75	
SC79108	12/56-10/72	⊗09/75	
SC79109	12/56-10/72	⊗12/81	
SC79110	01/57-10/72	⊗12/81	
SC79111	01/57-10/72	⊗10/76	

BR Derby
Driving Motor Brake Second
DMBS
M79118-M79126

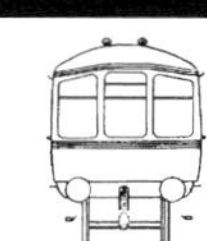

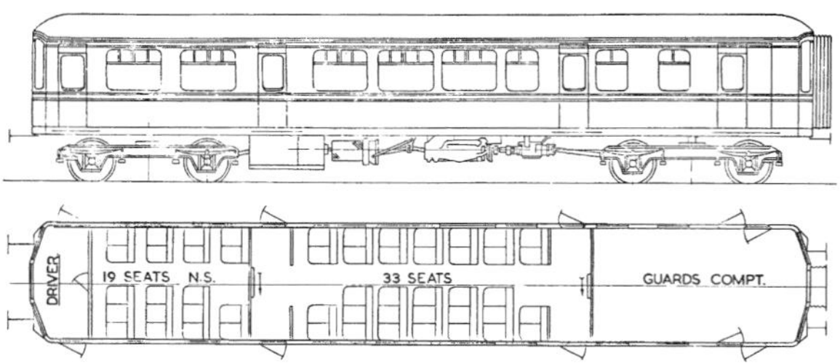

Coupling: ♦ Yellow diamond
Diagram: 633
Lot Number: 30235
Engines: Two BUT (AEC) 6-cyl horizontal type of 150 bhp.
Transmission: Mechanical. Standard
Body: 57' 6" × 9' 2"
Weight: 27t
Seats: 52 second

M79118	11/55-02/69	⊗08/69
M79119	12/55-04/69	⊗11/70
M79120	12/55-10/65	⊗05/68
M79121	12/55-04/69	⊗07/70
M79122	12/55-07/67	⊗12/68
M79123	12/55-04/69	⊗07/70
M79124	01/56-11/68	⊗06/69
M79125	01/56-04/69	⊗10/69
M79126	01/56-04/69	⊗10/69

BR Derby
Driving Motor Brake Second
DMBS
M79127-M79136

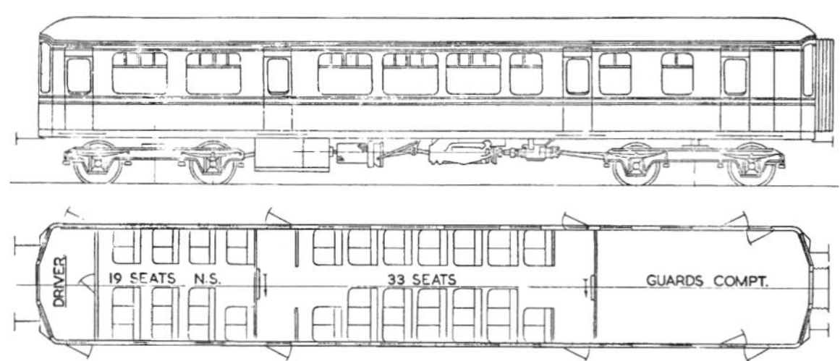

Coupling: ♦ Yellow diamond
Diagram: 633
Lot Number: 30240
Engines: Two BUT (AEC) 6-cyl horizontal type of 150 bhp.
Transmission: Mechanical. Standard
s Fitted with Self-Changing Gears automatic four-speed gearbox
Body: 57' 6" × 9' 2"
Weight: 27t
Seats: 52 second

M79127	02/56-04/69	⊗07/70	
M79128	02/56-04/69	⊗10/69	
M79129	02/56-04/69	⊗07/70	
M79130	03/56-04/67	⊗05/68	
M79131	03/56-01/68	⊗09/68	
M79132	03/56-10/67	⊗02/73	
M79133	03/56-10/67	⊗04/73	
M79134	03/56-04/68	⊗08/69	
M79135	03/56-04/69	⊗10/69	s
M79136	03/56-01/68	⊗05/68	

BR Derby
Driving Motor Brake Second
DMBS
E79137-E79140

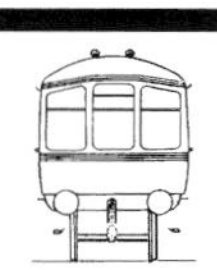

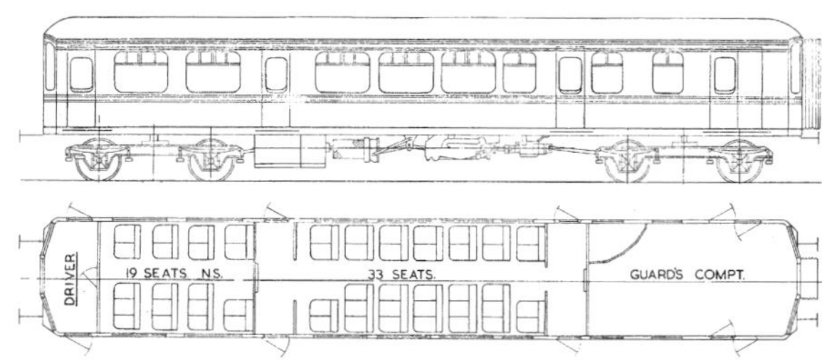

Coupling: ♦ Yellow diamond
Diagram: 527
Lot Number: 30240
Engines: Two BUT (AEC) 6-cyl horizontal type of 150 bhp.
Transmission: Mechanical. Standard
Body: 57' 6" × 9' 2"
Weight: 27t
Seats: 52 second

E79137	03/56-06/68	⊗06/69	01/65⇨NE	06/65⇨E
E79138	03/56-06/68	⊗06/69	01/65⇨NE	06/65⇨E
E79139	03/56-11/63	⊗05/65		
E79140	03/56-06/68	⊗06/69	01/65⇨NE	06/65⇨E

BR Derby
Driving Motor Brake Second
DMBS
M79141-M79142

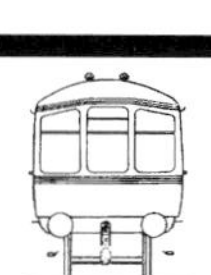

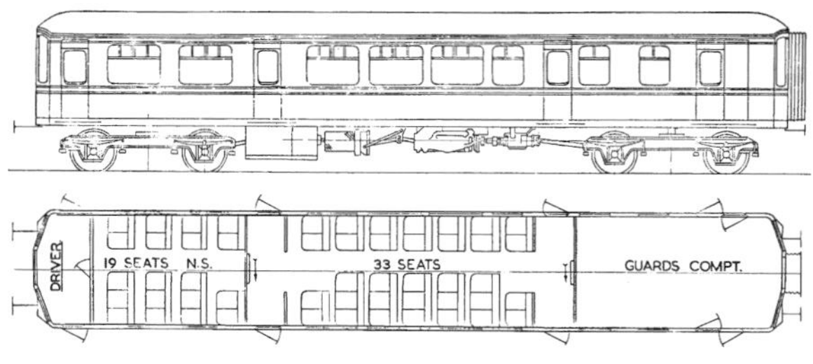

Coupling: ♦ Yellow diamond
Diagram: 633
Lot Number: 30246
Engines: Two BUT (AEC) 6-cyl horizontal type of 150 bhp.
Transmission: Mechanical. Standard
Body: 57' 6" × 9' 2"
Weight: 27t
Seats: 52 second

M79141	04/56-04/67	⊗04/68
M79142	07/56-04/69	⊗10/69

BR Derby
Driving Motor Brake Second
DMBS
M79143-M79149

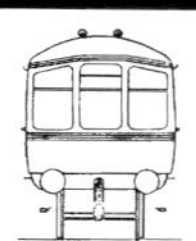

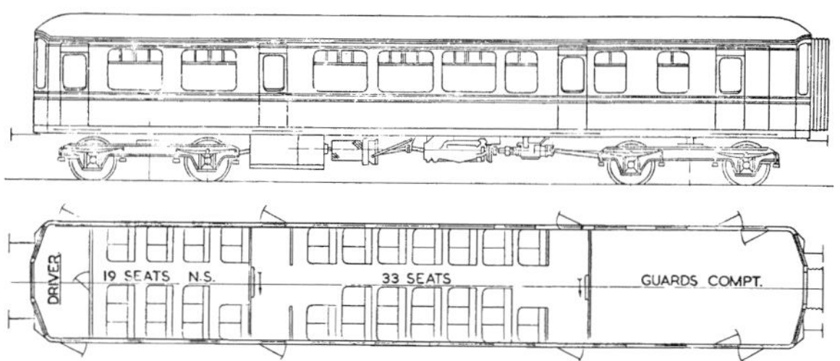

Coupling: ♦ Yellow diamond
Diagram: 633
Lot Number: 30201
Engines: Two BUT (AEC) 6-cyl horizontal type of 150 bhp.
Transmission: Mechanical. Standard
Body: 57' 6" × 9' 2"
Weight: 27t
Seats: 52 second

M79143	01/56-07/67	⊗11/67
M79144	01/56-04/69	⊗10/69
M79145	02/56-04/69	⊗10/70
M79146	02/56-02/68	⊗03/69
M79147	02/56-04/67	⊗04/68
M79148	02/56-04/68	⊗01/69
M79149	02/56-07/67	⊗04/68

BR Derby
Driving Motor Second
DMS
E79150-E79154

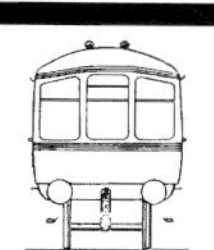

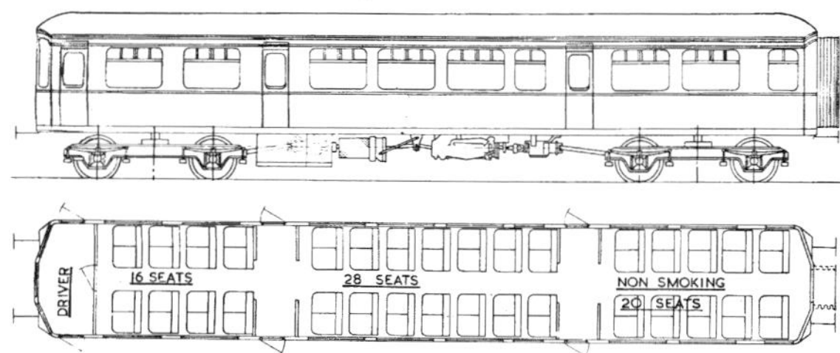

Coupling: ♦ Yellow diamond
Diagram: 518
Lot Number: 30193
Engines: Two BUT (AEC) 6-cyl horizontal type of 150 bhp.
Transmission: Mechanical. Standard
Body: 57' 6" × 9' 2"
Weight: 27t
Seats: 64 second

E79150	09/55-11/66	⊗07/71	01/65⇨*NE*
E79151	09/55-11/66	⊗02/73	01/65⇨*NE*
E79152	09/55-11/66	⊗02/71	01/65⇨*NE*
E79153	09/55-11/66	⊗02/71	01/65⇨*NE*
E79154	09/55-06/67	⊗02/71	01/65⇨*NE* 08/66⇨*SC*

BR Swindon
Driving Motor Second Lavatory
DMSL
SC79155-SC79168

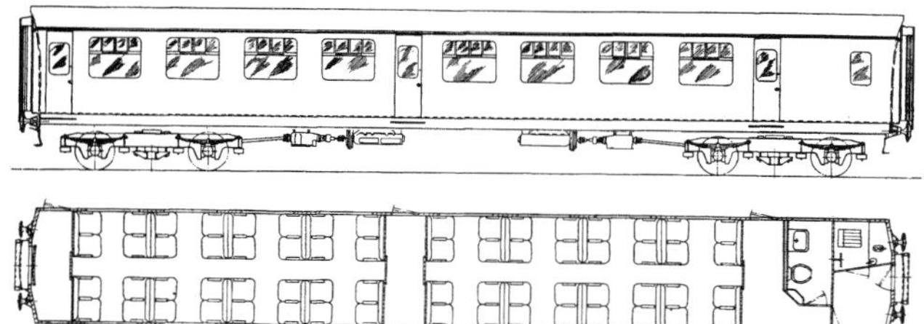

Coupling: ● White circle
Diagram: 551
Lot Number: 30199
Engines: Two BUT (AEC) 6-cyl horizontal type of 150 bhp.
Transmission: Mechanical. Standard
Body: 64' 6" × 9' 3" Inter-City
Weight: 39t 3cwt
Seats: 64 second

SC79155	01/57-10/72	⊗03/81	
SC79156	01/57-10/72	⊗08/83	
SC79157	02/57-10/72	⊗06/83	
SC79158	02/57-10/72	⊗03/80	
SC79159	02/57-10/72	⊗09/83	
SC79160	02/57-10/72	⊗01/75	
SC79161	03/57-10/72	⊗08/83	
SC79162	03/57-10/72	⊗03/80	
SC79163	03/57-10/72	⊗09/75	
SC79164	03/57-10/72	⊗12/81	
SC79165	04/57-01/74	⊗09/75	⊠10/72-10/73
SC79166	04/57-10/72	⊗04/83	
SC79167	04/57-10/72	⊗09/75	
SC79168	04/57-09/78	⊗11/81	⊠10/72-09/73

BR Derby
Driving Motor Brake Second
DMBS
M79169-M79181

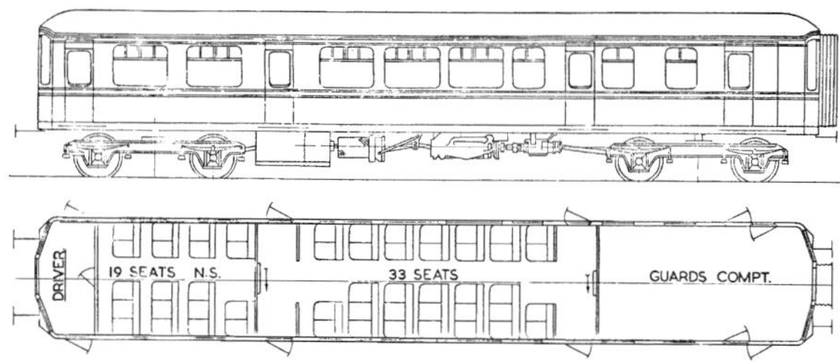

Coupling: ♦ Yellow diamond
Diagram: 633
Lot Number: 30321
Engines: Two BUT (AEC) 6-cyl horizontal type of 150 bhp.
Transmission: Mechanical. Standard
Body: 57' 6" × 9' 2"
Weight: 27t
Seats: 52 second

M79169	04/56-07/67	⊗02/68
M79170	05/56-09/61	⊗09/61
M79171	05/56-04/69	⊗10/69
M79172	05/56-04/67	⊗02/68
M79173	05/56-07/67	⊗02/68
M79174	05/56-07/67	⊗11/67
M79175	05/56-04/69	⊗10/69
M79176	06/56-07/67	⊗02/68
M79177	06/56-04/69	⊗10/69
M79178	06/56-07/67	⊗02/68
M79179	06/56-04/67	⊗08/68
M79180	06/56-04/69	⊗12/71
M79181	06/56-02/68	⊗08/70

BR Derby
Driving Motor Brake Second
DMBS
M79184-M79188

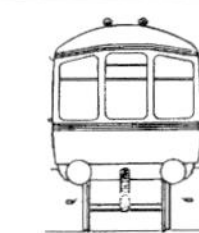

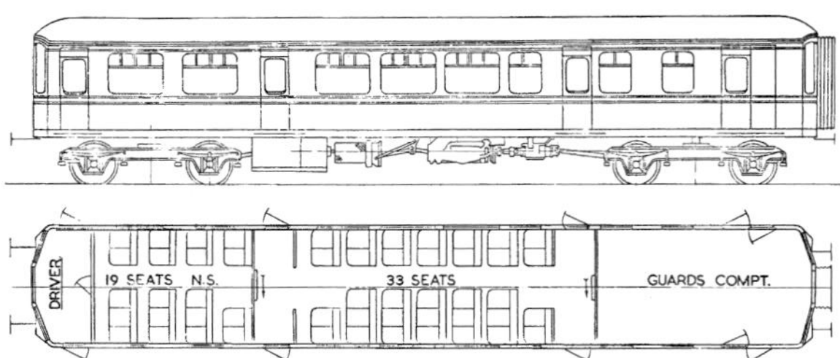

Coupling: ♦ Yellow diamond
Diagram: 633
Lot Number: 30324
Engines: Two BUT (AEC) 6-cyl horizontal type of 150 bhp.
Transmission: Mechanical. Standard
Body: 57' 6" × 9' 2"
Weight: 27t
Seats: 52 second

M79184	07/56-04/69	⊗04/70	
M79185	07/56-01/68	⊗07/70	01/68➲**DB975012**
M79186	07/56-04/69	⊗07/70	
M79187	08/56-04/68	⊗06/69	
M79188	07/56-12/64	⊗01/65	

BR Derby
Driving Motor Composite Lavatory
DMCL
M79189-M79193

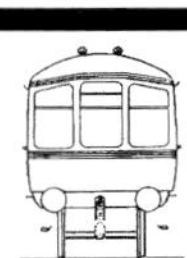

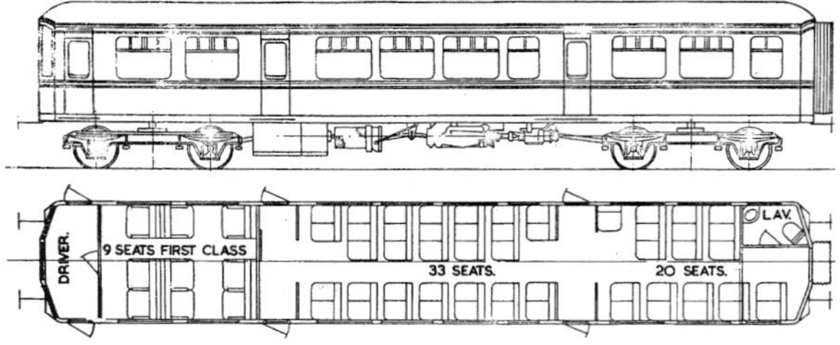

Coupling: ♦ Yellow diamond
Diagram: 510
Lot Number: 30325
Engines: Two BUT (AEC) 6-cyl horizontal type of 150 bhp.
Transmission: Mechanical. Standard
Body: 57' 6" × 9' 2"
Weight: 27t
Seats: 12 first, 53 second

Three of these were converted to trailers in 1962.

M79189	07/56-06/67	⊗02/73	09/66⇨**SC**	
M79190	07/56-06/67	⊗02/73	08/66⇨**SC**	
M79191	07/56-06/62	⊗10/70		06/62➲**79633**
M79192	08/56-08/62	⊗10/69		08/62➲**79634**
M79193	08/56-05/62	⊗		05/62➲**79635**

BR Derby
Driving Trailer Composite Lavatory
DTCL
E79250-E79262

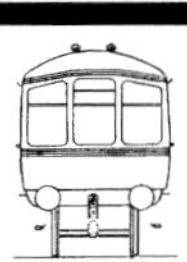

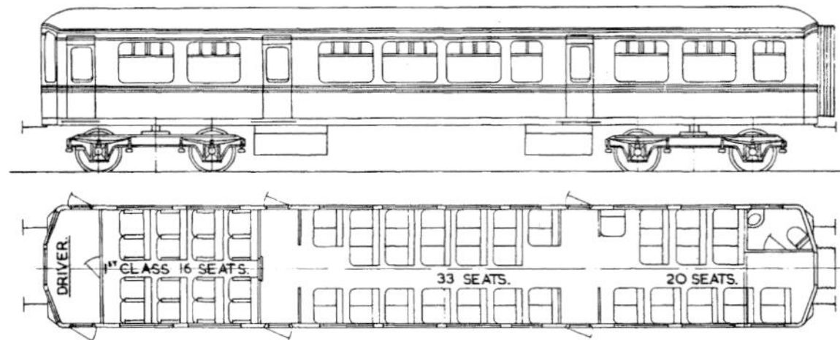

Coupling: ♦ Yellow diamond
Diagram: 505
Lot Number: 30178
Body: 57' 6" × 9' 2"
Weight: 20t
Seats: 16 first, 53 second

E79250	07/55-06/67	⊗02/78	11/66⇨**SC**	06/67➲**DB975013**
E79251	07/55-06/67	⊗02/68	11/66⇨**SC**	
E79252	06/55-06/67	⊗06/82	11/66⇨**SC**	06/67➲**DB975014**
E79253	07/55-06/68	⊗10/69		
E79254	07/55-06/68	⊗04/69		
E79255	07/55-06/68	⊗10/69		
E79256	07/55-07/67	⊗12/70		
E79257	07/55-06/68	⊗12/70		
E79258	07/55-11/67	⊗05/70		
E79259	07/55-09/67	⊗05/70		
E79260	08/55-09/68	⊗05/70		
E79261	08/55-09/67	⊗03/69		
E79262	08/55-09/67	⊗03/69		

Metropolitan-Cammell
Driving Trailer Second Lavatory
DTSL
E79263-E79291

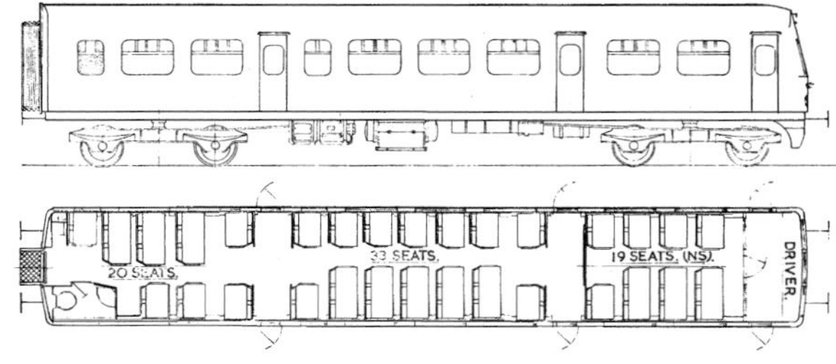

Coupling: ♦ Yellow diamond
Diagram: 593
Lot Number: 30191
Body: 57' 6" × 9' 3"
Weight: 25t
Seats: 72 second

E79263	01/56-09/68	⊗10/69
E79264	01/56-07/68	⊗10/69
E79265	01/56-09/68	⊗10/69
E79266	01/56-06/69	⊗02/73
E79267	01/56-09/68	⊗10/69
E79268	01/56-06/69	⊗02/73
E79269	02/56-11/68	⊗02/73
E79270	02/56-06/69	⊗02/73
E79271	02/56-11/68	⊗02/73
E79272	02/56-11/68	⊗02/73
E79273	03/56-06/69	⊗05/73
E79274	03/56-11/68	⊗02/73
E79275	03/56-01/69	⊗05/70
E79276	03/56-11/68	⊗04/73
E79277	04/56-06/69	⊗07/70
E79278	04/56-11/68	⊗05/70
E79279	04/56-01/69	⊗04/70
E79280	05/56-01/69	⊗02/73
E79281	05/56-01/69	⊗06/70
E79282	05/56-06/69	⊗04/73

E79283	05/56-11/68	⊗05/73	
E79284	05/56-01/69	⊗04/70	
E79285	06/56-10/68	⊗02/73	
E79286	06/56-10/68	⊗02/73	
E79287	06/56-10/68	⊗02/73	
E79288	06/56-10/68	⊗02/73	
E79289	06/56-01/69	⊗02/73	
E79290	07/56-10/68	⊗02/73	
E79291	07/56-01/69	⊗02/73	⊠10/68-11/68

BR Derby
Trailer Brake Second Lavatory
TBSL
E79325-E79329

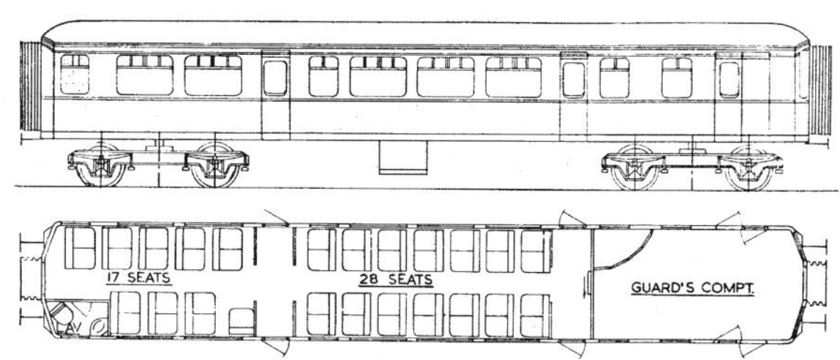

Coupling: ♦ Yellow diamond
Diagram: 508
Lot Number: 30194
Body: 57' 6" × 9' 2"
Weight: 21t
Seats: 45 second

E79325	09/55-06/67	⊗03/71	01/65⇨*NE* 08/66⇨*SC*
E79326	09/55-11/66	⊗02/71	01/65⇨*NE*
E79327	09/55-11/66	⊗02/71	01/65⇨*NE*
E79328	09/55-06/67	⊗08/69	01/65⇨*NE* 08/66⇨*SC*
E79329	09/55-06/67	⊗12/71	01/65⇨*NE* 08/66⇨*SC*

BR Derby
Trailer Second Lavatory
TSL
E79400-E79404

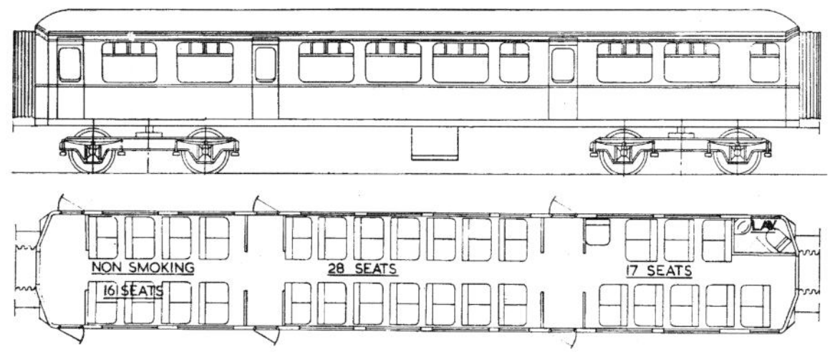

Coupling: ♦ Yellow diamond
Diagram: 517
Lot Number: 30195
Body: 57' 6" × 9' 2"
Weight: 21t
Seats: 61 second

E79400	09/55-06/67	⊗12/71	01/65⇨*NE* 08/66⇨*SC*
E79401	09/55-06/67	⊗12/71	01/65⇨*NE* 08/66⇨*SC*
E79402	09/55-11/66	⊗07/71	01/65⇨*NE*
E79403	09/55-06/67	⊗03/71	01/65⇨*NE* 08/66⇨*SC*
E79404	09/55-12/66	⊗02/71	01/65⇨*NE*

BR Swindon
Trailer Buffet First Side-Corridor with Lavatory
TFKRB
W79440-SC79447

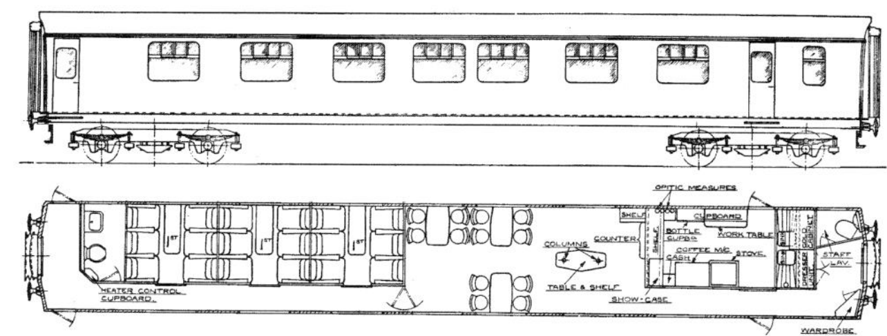

Coupling: ● White circle
Diagram: 560
Lot Number: 30197
Body: 64' 6" × 9' 3" Inter-City
Weight: 35t 16cwt
Seats: 18 first, 12 buffet

W79440	06/57-10/72	⊗03/73	06/59⇨**SC**
W79441	06/57-10/72	Ⓟ⊗*10/92*	09/59⇨**SC**
SC79442	02/57-10/72	⊗03/73	
SC79443	03/57-10/72	Ⓟ	
SC79444	03/57-10/72	⊗04/73	
SC79445	04/57-10/72	⊗04/73	
SC79446	04/57-10/72	⊗04/73	
SC79447	04/57-10/72	⊗04/73	

BR Swindon
Trailer First Side-Corridor with Lavatory
TFK
W79470-SC79482

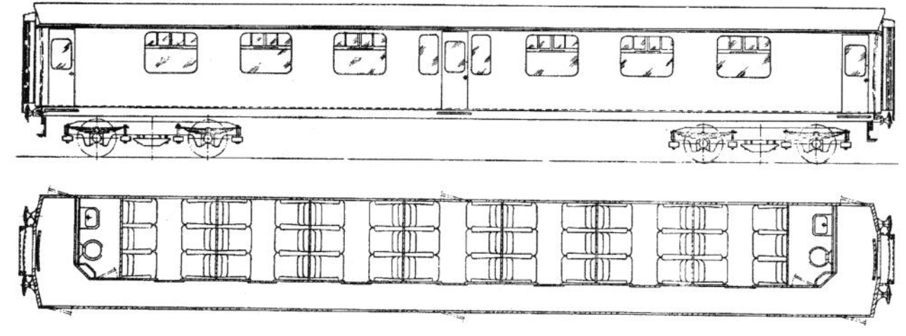

Coupling: ● White circle
Diagram: 570 DT224
Lot Number: 30198
Body: 64' 6" × 9' 3" Inter-City
Weight: 33t 9cwt
Seats: 42 first

W79470	08/56-07/81	⊗02/83	10/59⇨**SC**
W79471	05/56-10/72	⊗03/73	09/59⇨**SC**
W79472	05/56-10/72	⊗03/73	09/59⇨**SC**
W79473	05/56-10/72	⊗04/73	06/59⇨**SC**
SC79474	08/56-10/72	⊗04/73	
SC79475	09/56-10/72	⊗03/73	
SC79476	09/56-10/72	⊗03/73	
SC79477	09/56-10/72	⊗03/73	
SC79478	10/56-10/72	⊗04/73	
SC79479	10/56-09/78	⊗11/81	
SC79480	11/56-10/72	⊗03/73	
SC79481	11/56-10/72	⊗04/73	
SC79482	12/56-10/72	⊗04/73	

BR Derby

Driving Motor Composite Lavatory
DMCL
E79500-E79508

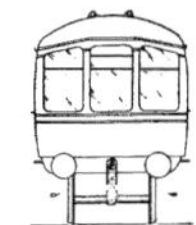

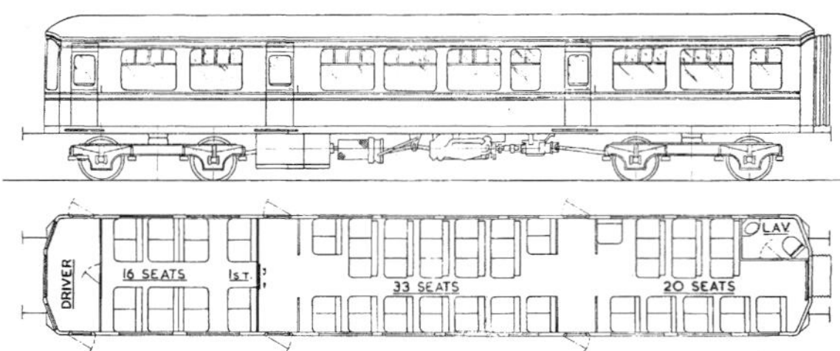

Coupling: ▲ Red triangle
Diagram: 507
Lot Number: 30085
Engines: Two BUT (Leyland) 6-cyl horizontal type of 125 bhp.
Transmission: Hydro-mechanical. Lysholm Smith (Leyland) torque convertor to final drive
Body: 57' 6" × 9' 2"
Weight: 27t
Seats: 16 first, 53 second

E79500	04/54-02/64	⊗03/64	
E79501	05/54-02/64	⊗03/64	
E79502	05/54-02/64	⊗03/64	
E79503	05/54-02/64	⊗03/64	
E79504	06/54-02/64	⊗03/64	
E79505	06/54-02/64	⊗03/64	
E79506	08/54-02/64	⊗03/64	
E79507	09/54-02/64	⊗03/64	

BR Derby

Driving Motor Composite
DMC
E79508-E79512

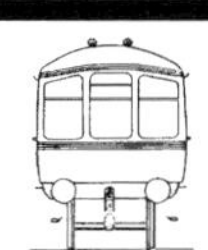

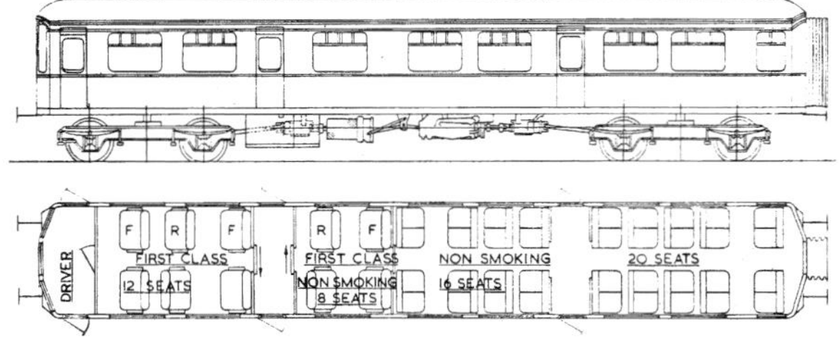

Coupling: ♦ Yellow diamond
Diagram: 502
Lot Number: 30192
Engines: Two BUT (AEC) 6-cyl horizontal type of 150 bhp.
Transmission: Mechanical. Standard
Body: 57' 6" × 9' 2"
Weight: 27t
Seats: 20 first, 36 second

E79508	09/55-06/67	⊗02/68	01/65⇨*NE* 08/66⇨*SC*
E79509	09/55-11/66	⊗02/71	01/65⇨*NE*
E79510	09/55-11/66	⊗02/71	01/65⇨*NE*
E79511	09/55-06/67	⊗02/68	01/65⇨*NE* 08/66⇨*SC*
E79512	09/55-06/67	⊗02/68	01/65⇨*NE* 08/66⇨*SC*

BR Derby

Driving Trailer Composite Lavatory
DTCL
M79600-M79612

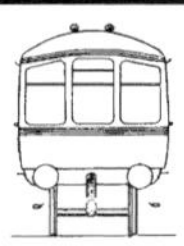

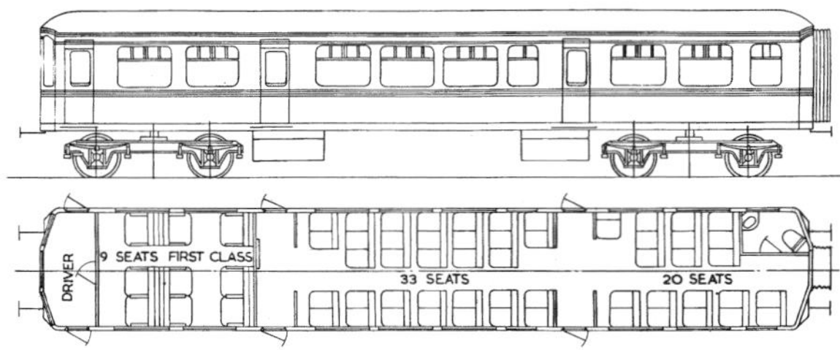

Coupling: ♦ Yellow diamond
Diagram: 509
Lot Number: 30124
Body: 57' 6" × 9' 2"
Weight: 21t
Seats: 9 first, 53 second

M79600	11/54-04/68	⊗06/69	
M79601	01/55-04/68	⊗06/69	
M79602	01/55-02/68	⊗06/69	
M79603	01/55-04/68	⊗06/69	
M79604	01/55-04/68	⊗06/69	
M79605	01/55-04/68	⊗06/69	
M79606	01/55-04/68	⊗06/69	
M79607	12/54-04/68	⊗06/69	
M79608	12/54-04/68	⊗06/69	
M79609	12/54-04/68	⊗06/69	
M79610	01/55-04/68	⊗06/71	
M79611	01/55-05/68	⊗06/69	
M79612	01/55-01/68	℗	11/70➲**DB975008**

BR Derby

Driving Trailer Composite Lavatory
DTCL
E79613-E79625

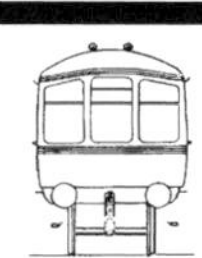

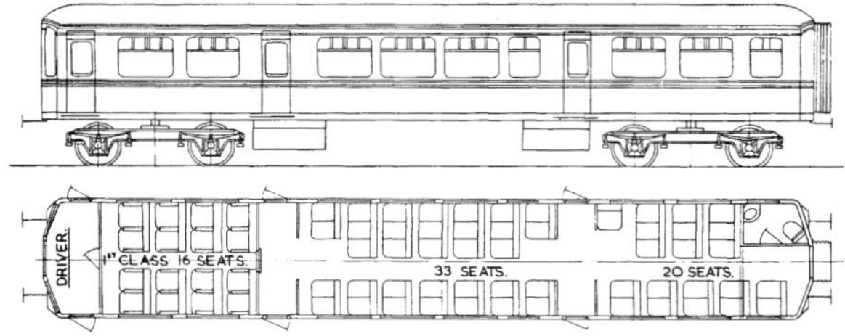

Coupling: ♦ Yellow diamond
Diagram: 505
Lot Number: 30127
Body: 57' 6" × 9' 2"
Weight: 21t
Seats: 16 first, 53 second

E79613	01/55-05/68	⊗03/69	
E79614	01/55-06/68	⊗05/69	
E79615	01/55-06/68	⊗06/69	
E79616	01/55-06/62	⊗03/63	
E79617	01/55-06/68	⊗05/69	
E79618	01/55-06/68	⊗06/69	
E79619	01/55-06/68	⊗04/69	
E79620	01/55-07/67	⊗08/72	
E79621	05/55-06/68	⊗04/69	
E79622	05/55-05/68	⊗04/69	
E79623	05/55-06/68	⊗04/69	
E79624	05/55-05/68	⊗03/69	
E79625	05/55-06/67	⊗05/70	11/66⇨**SC**

Metropolitan-Cammell

Driving Trailer Composite Lavatory
DTCL
M79626-M79632

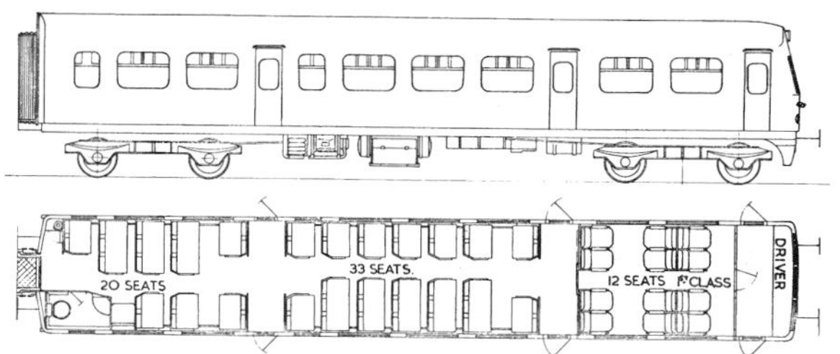

Coupling: ♦ Yellow diamond
Diagram: 594
Lot Number: 30191
Body: 57' 6" × 9' 3"
Weight: 25t
Seats: 12 first, 53 second

M79626 09/55-06/67 ⊗02/68
M79627 12/55-06/67 ⊗02/68
M79628 12/55-06/67 ⊗02/68
M79629 12/55-06/67 ⊗02/68
M79630 12/55-07/67 ⊗02/68
M79631 12/55-07/67 ⊗02/68
M79632 12/55-07/67 ⊗02/68

BR Derby

Driving Trailer Composite Lavatory
DTCL
M79633-M79635

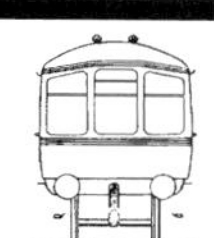

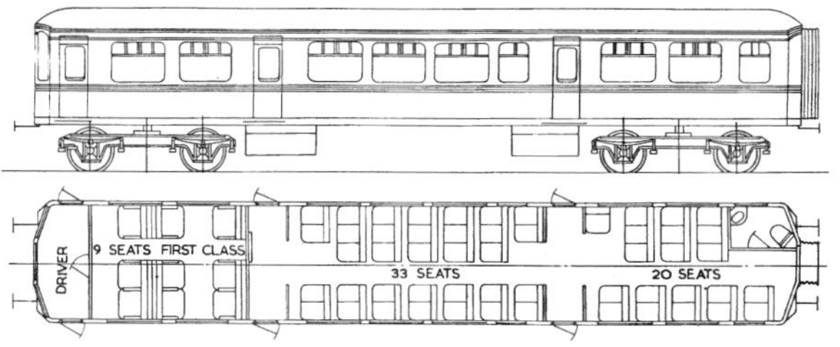

Coupling: ♦ Yellow diamond
Diagram: 509
Lot Number: 30325
Body: 57' 6" × 9' 2"
Weight: 21t
Seats: 9 first, 53 second

M79633 06/62⊂**79191** 06/62-04/69 ⊗10/70
M79634 08/62⊂**79192** 08/62-04/69 ⊗10/69
M79635 05/62⊂**79193** 05/62-04/69 ⊗

BR Derby

Driving Trailer Composite Lavatory
DTCL
M79639-M79647

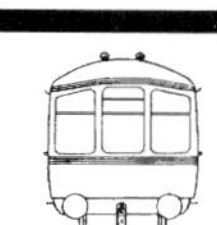

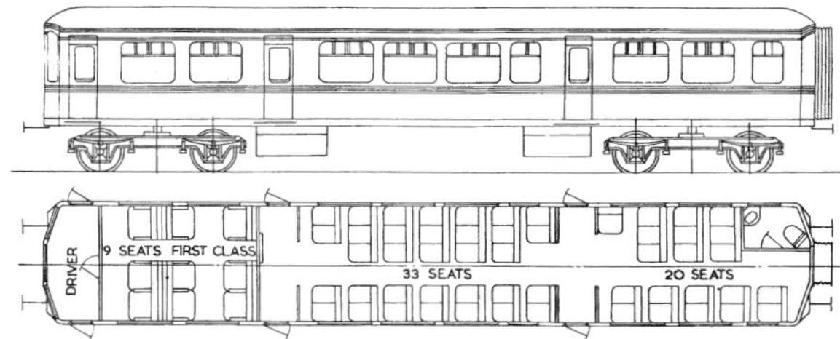

Coupling: ♦ Yellow diamond
Diagram: 509
Lot Number: 30236

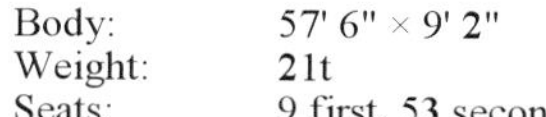

Body: 57' 6" × 9' 2"
Weight: 21t
Seats: 9 first, 53 second

M79639 11/55-04/69 ⊗10/69
M79640 12/55-04/69 ⊗10/70
M79641 12/55-04/69 ⊗10/69
M79642 12/55-04/69 ⊗10/69
M79643 01/56-04/69 ⊗10/69
M79644 01/56-04/69 ⊗10/69
M79645 01/56-04/69 ⊗10/69
M79646 01/56-04/69 ⊗10/69
M79647 01/56-02/68 ⊗10/69

BR Derby

Driving Trailer Composite Lavatory
DTCL
M79648-M79657

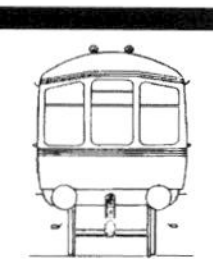

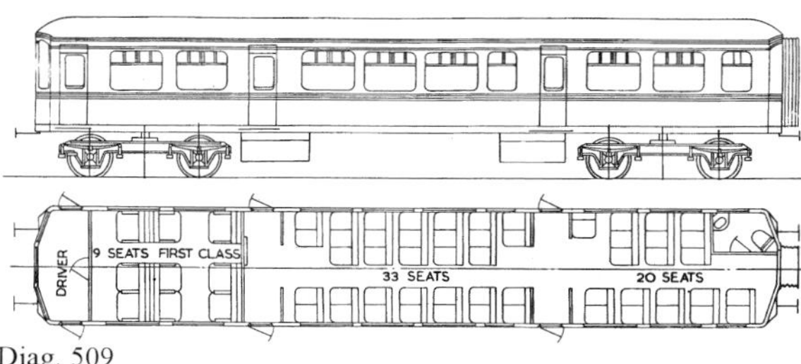

Diag. 509

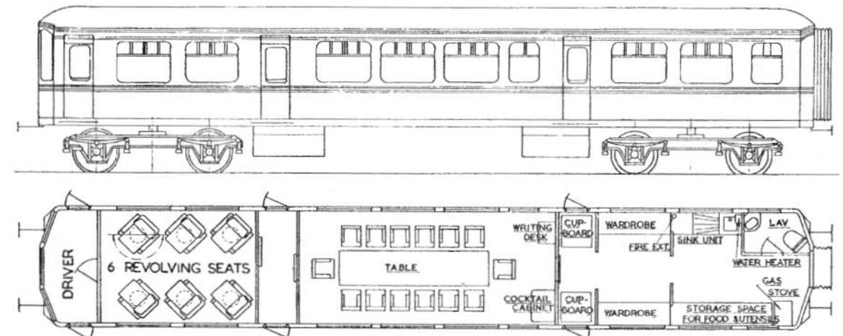

Diag. 565 Special Saloon M79649 (converted 1957)

Coupling: ♦ Yellow diamond s ■ Blue square (converted November 1960)
Diagram: 509 s 565
Lot Number: 30241
Body: 57' 6" × 9' 2"
Weight: 21t s 23t
Seats: 9 first, 53 second

M79648 02/56-07/67 ⊗06/68
M79649 02/56- /60 s /60⊃**DB999510**
M79650 02/56-06/67 ⊗02/68
M79651 03/56-07/67 ⊗02/68
M79652 03/56-07/67 ⊗07/69
M79653 03/56-04/68 ⊗06/69
M79654 03/56-04/69 ⊗10/69
M79655 03/56-06/67 ⊗07/67
M79656 03/56-10/67 ⊗02/73
M79657 03/56-04/69 ⊗09/70

BR Derby

Driving Trailer Composite Lavatory
DTCL
E79658-E79661

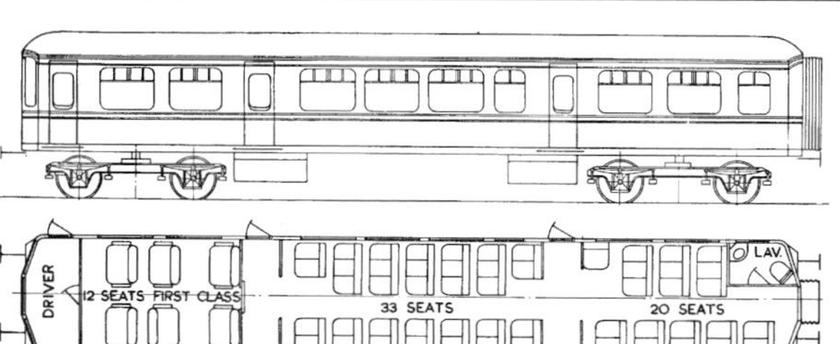

Coupling: ♦ Yellow diamond

Diagram: 631
Lot Number: 30241
Body: 57' 6" × 9' 2"
Weight: 21t
Seats: 12 first, 53 second

E79658	03/56-05/68	⊗03/69	01/65⇨**NE**	06/65⇨**E**
E79659	03/56-11/63	⊗05/65		
E79660	03/56-05/68	⊗03/69	01/65⇨**NE**	06/65⇨**E**
E79661	03/56-07/67	⊗08/72	01/65⇨**NE**	06/65⇨**E**

BR Derby
Driving Trailer Composite Lavatory
DTCL
M79662

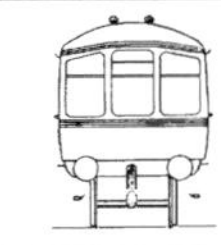

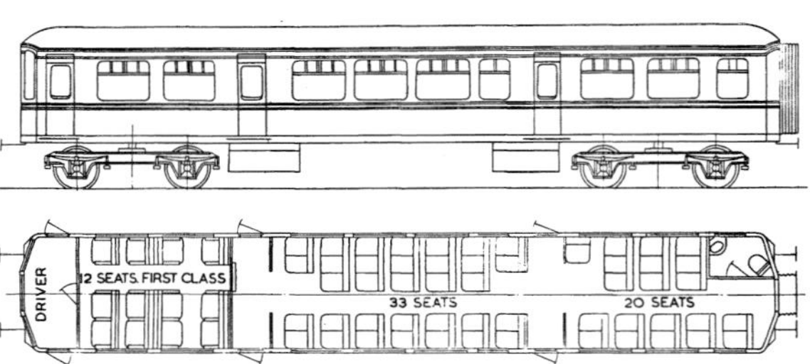

Coupling: ♦ Yellow diamond
Diagram: 642
Lot Number: 30247
Body: 57' 6" × 9' 2"
Weight: 21t
Seats: 12 first, 53 second

M79662	04/56-07/67	⊗04/68	09/67⇨*E*

BR Derby
Driving Trailer Composite Lavatory
DTCL
M79663-M79669

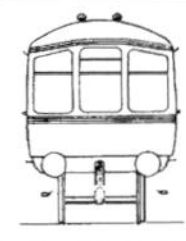

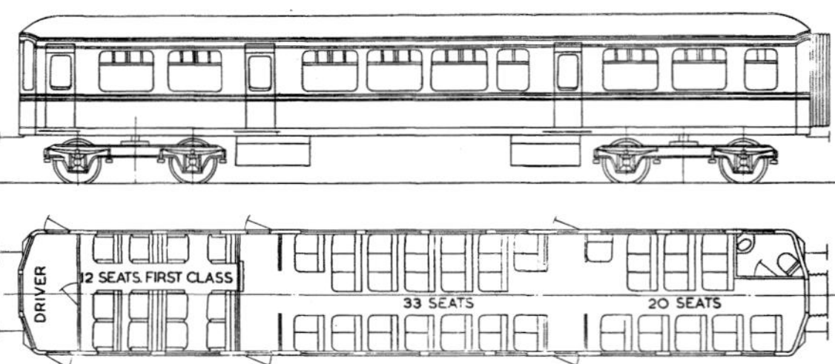

Coupling: ♦ Yellow diamond
Diagram: 642
Lot Number: 30202
Body: 57' 6" × 9' 2"
Weight: 21t
Seats: 12 first, 53 second

M79663	01/56-04/68	⊗08/69	02/60⇨*SC*
M79664	01/56-07/67	⊗02/68	02/60⇨*SC*
M79665	02/56-10/67	⊗02/73	02/60⇨*SC*
M79666	02/56-06/67	⊗03/68	01/66⇨*SC*
M79667	02/56-04/69	⊗10/69	01/66⇨*SC*
M79668	02/56-04/69	⊗07/70	01/66⇨*SC*
M79669	02/56-07/67	⊗02/68	01/66⇨*SC*

BR Derby
Driving Trailer Composite Lavatory
DTCL
M79670-M79682

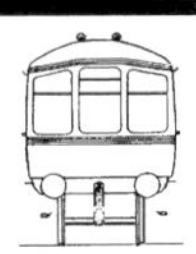

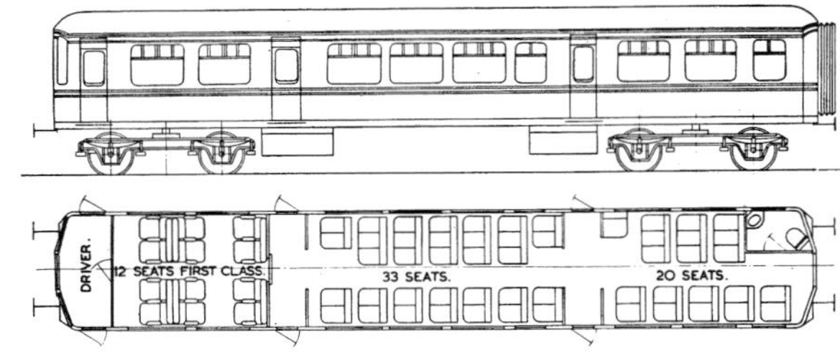

Coupling: ♦ Yellow diamond
Diagram: 511
Lot Number: 30322
Body: 57' 6" × 9' 2"
Weight: 21t
Seats: 12 first, 53 second

M79670	04/56-07/67	⊗02/68
M79671	04/56-07/67	⊗02/68
M79672	05/56-04/69	⊗08/70
M79673	05/56-04/69	⊗06/70
M79674	05/56-07/67	⊗02/68
M79675	05/56-04/69	⊗10/69
M79676	05/56-04/69	⊗10/69
M79677	06/56-07/67	⊗02/68
M79678	06/56-04/69	⊗07/70
M79679	06/56-04/68	⊗08/69
M79680	06/56-02/68	⊗06/69
M79681	06/56-07/67	⊗02/68
M79682	06/56-07/67	⊗02/68

BR Derby
Driving Trailer Composite Lavatory
DTCL
M79683

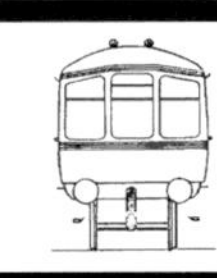

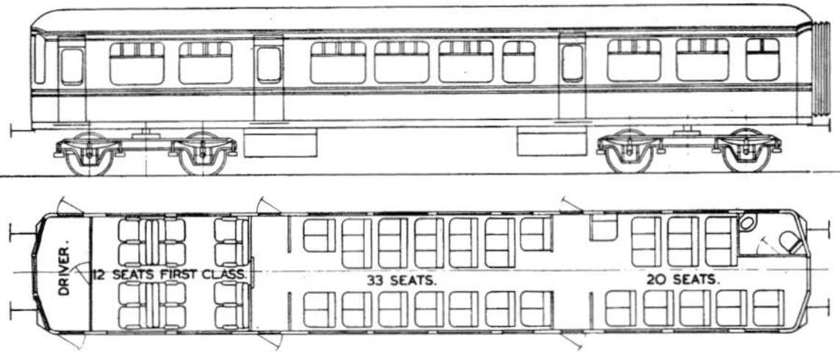

Coupling: ♦ Yellow diamond
Diagram: 511
Lot Number: 30322
Body: 57' 6" × 9' 2"
Weight: 21t
Seats: 12 first, 53 second

M79683	09/56-02/68	⊗08/69

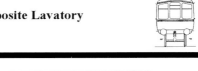

BR Derby
Driving Trailer Composite Lavatory
DTCL
M79684

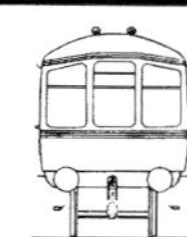

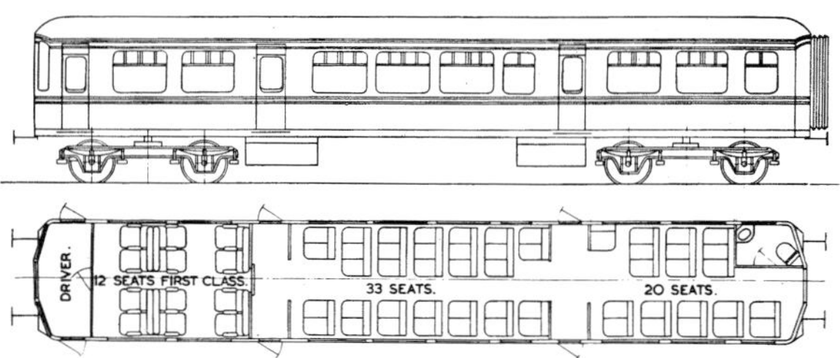

Coupling: ♦ Yellow diamond
Diagram: 511
Lot Number: 30322
Body: 57' 6" × 9' 2"
Weight: 21t
Seats: 12 first, 53 second

M79684 07/56-02/68 ⊗08/68

BUT
Four Wheel Unit
Diesel Railbus DRB
M79740

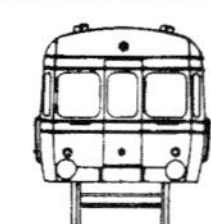

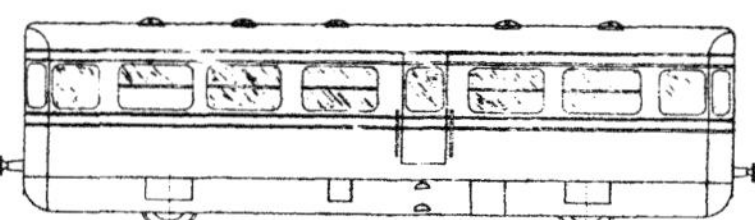

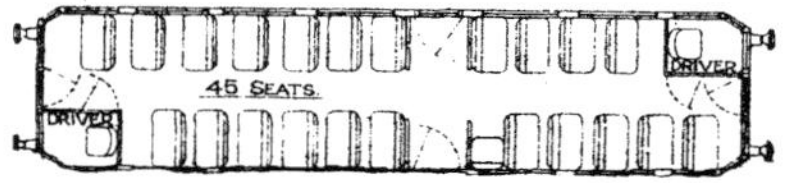

Diagram: 500
Lot Number: 30128
Engine: BUT (AEC) 6-cyl horizontal type of 125 bhp.
Transmission: Mechanical. Standard
Body: 37' 6" × 9' 0" Railcar
Weight: 14t 11cwt
Seats: 45 second

M79740 03/54-02/59 ⊗11/63

BUT
Four Wheel Unit
Railbus Trailer
M79741

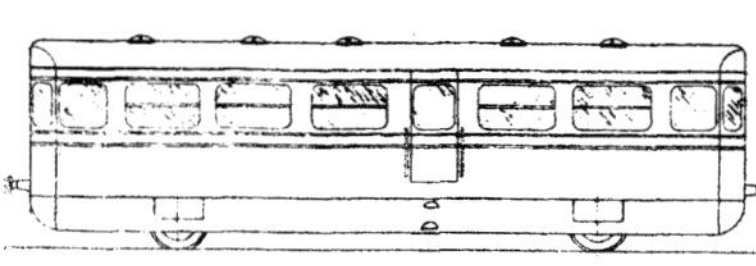

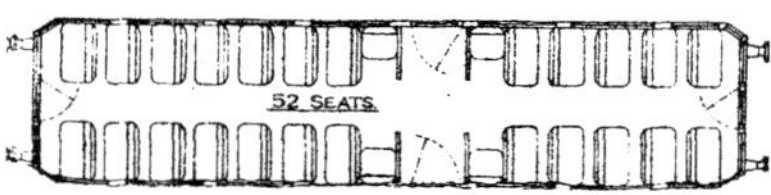

Diagram: 500
Lot Number: 30128
Body: 37' 6" × 9' 0" Railcar
Weight: 10t 10cwt
Seats: 52 second

M79741 03/54-02/59 ⊗11/63

BUT
Four Wheel Unit
Diesel Railbus DRB
M79742

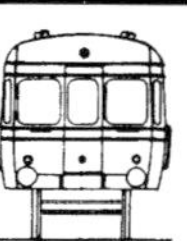

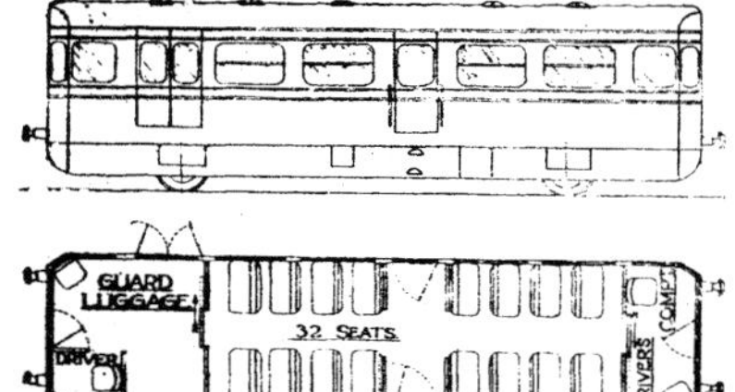

Diagram: 500
Lot Number: 30128
Engine: BUT (AEC) 6-cyl horizontal type of 125 bhp.
Transmission: Mechanical. Standard
Body: 37' 6" × 9' 0" Railcar
Weight: 14t 13cwt
Seats: 32 second

M79742 03/54-02/59 ⊗11/63

BUT
Four Wheel Unit
Diesel Railbus DRB
M79743-M79744

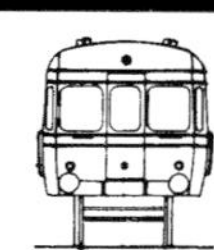

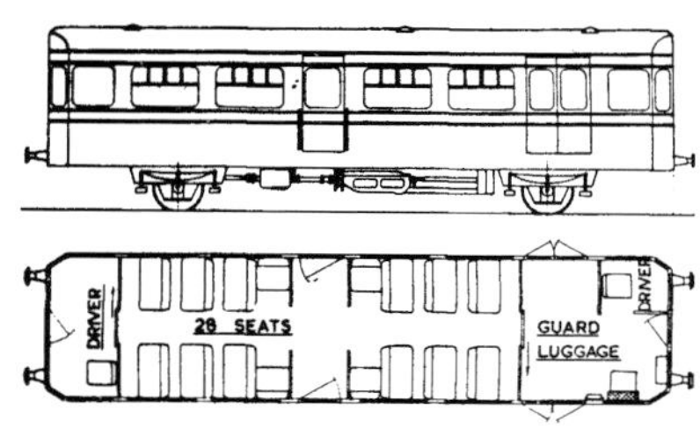

Diagram: 506
Lot Number: 30174
Engine: BUT (AEC) 6-cyl horizontal type of 125 bhp.
Transmission: Mechanical. Standard
Body: 37' 6" × 9' 0" Railcar
Weight: 15t
Seats: 28 second

M79743 07/55-02/59 ⊗11/63
M79744 07/55-02/59 ⊗11/63

BUT
Four Wheel Unit
Diesel Railbus DRB
M79745

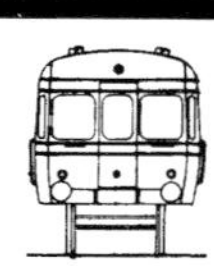

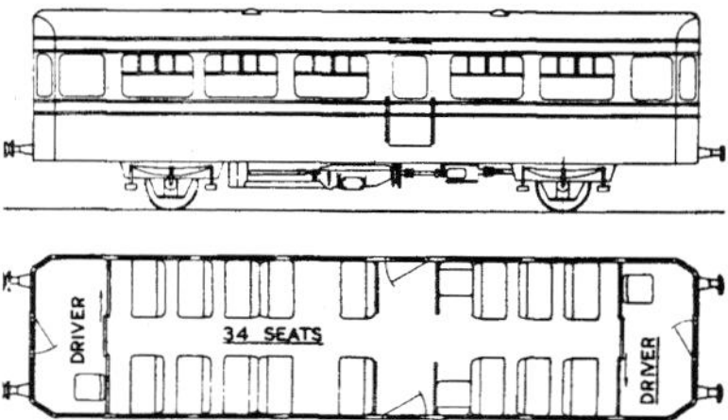

Diagram: 506
Lot Number: 30175
Engine: BUT (AEC) 6-cyl horizontal type of 125 bhp.
Transmission: Mechanical. Standard
Body: 37' 6" × 9' 0" Railcar
Weight: 15t
Seats: 34 second

M79745 07/55-02/59 ⊗11/63

BUT
Four Wheel Unit
Railbus Trailer
M79746-M79747

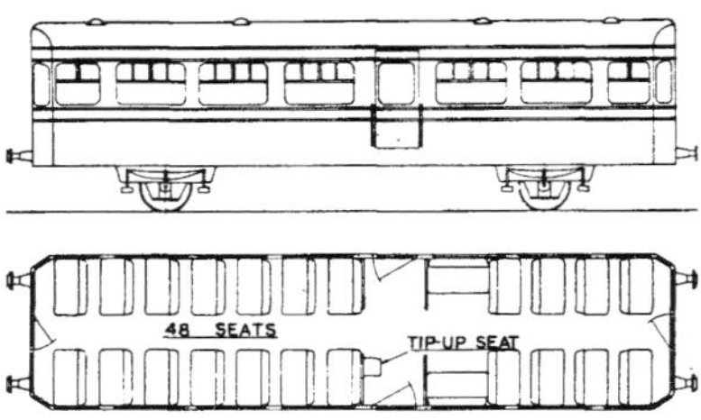

Diagram: 506
Lot Number: 30176
Body: 37' 6" × 9' 0" Railcar
Weight: 11t
Seats: 48 second

M79746	08/55-02/59	⊗11/63
M79747	08/55-02/59	⊗11/63

BUT
Four Wheel Unit
Diesel Railbus DRB
M79748

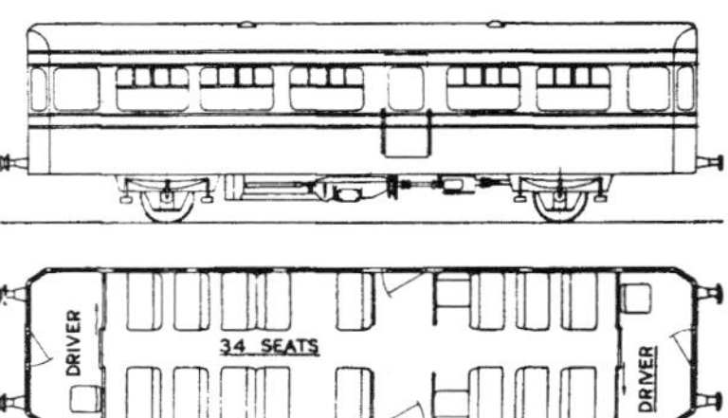

Diagram: 506
Lot Number: 30214
Engine: BUT (AEC) 6-cyl horizontal type of 125 bhp.
Transmission: Mechanical. Standard
Body: 37' 6" × 9' 0" Railcar
Weight: 15t
Seats: 34 second

M79748	08/57-02/59	⊗11/63

BUT
Four Wheel Unit
Railbus Trailer
M79749

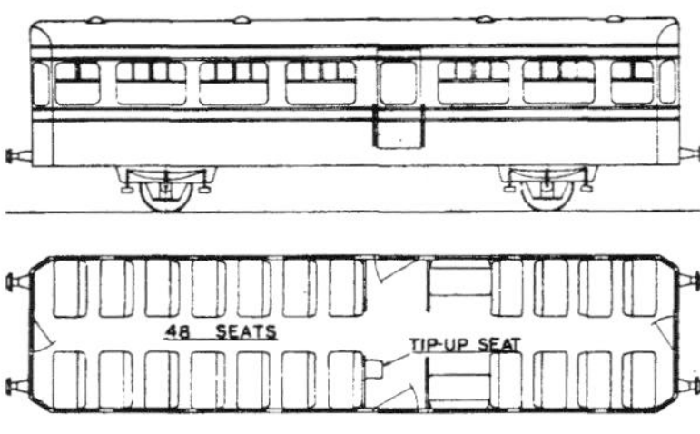

Diagram: 506
Lot Number: 30215
Body: 37' 6" × 9' 0" Railcar
Weight: 11t
Seats: 48 second

M79749	08/57-02/59	⊗11/63

BUT
Four Wheel Unit
Diesel Railbus DRB
M79750

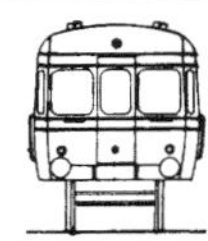

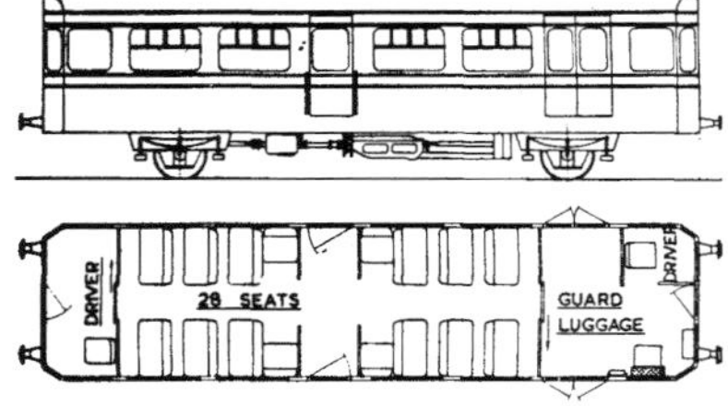

Diagram: 506
Lot Number: 30216
Engine: BUT (AEC) 6-cyl horizontal type of 125 bhp.
Transmission: Mechanical. Standard
Body: 37' 6" × 9' 0" Railcar
Weight: 15t
Seats: 28 second

M79750	08/57-02/59	⊗11/63

BR Derby
Driving Motor Brake Second
DMBS
M79900

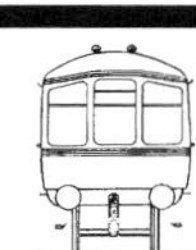

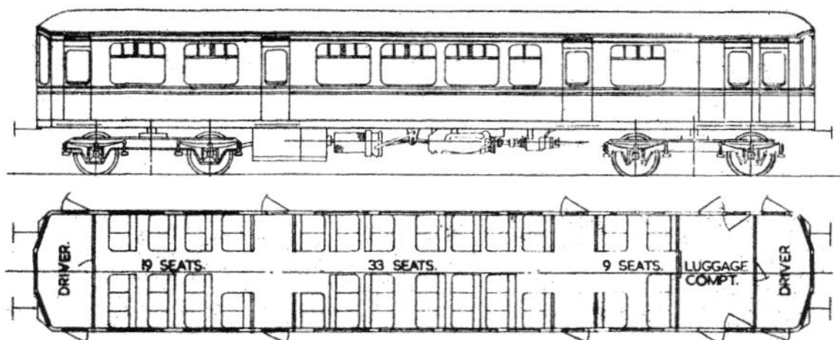

Coupling: ♦ Yellow diamond
Diagram: 514
Lot Number: 30380
Engines: Two BUT (AEC) 6-cyl horizontal type of 150 bhp.
Transmission: Mechanical. Standard
Body: 57' 6" × 9' 2"
Weight: 27t
Seats: 61 second

M79900	07/56-10/67 ℗	09/67⇦*NE*	10/67➲**DB975010**

BR Derby
Driving Motor Brake Second
DMBS
M79901

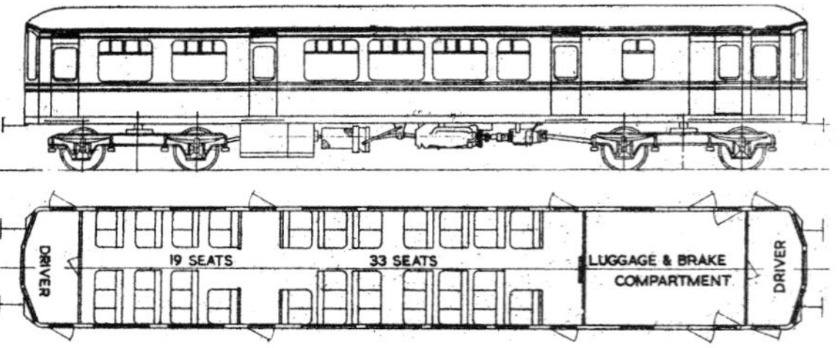

Coupling: ♦ Yellow diamond
Diagram: 515
Lot Number: 30387
Engines: Two BUT (AEC) 6-cyl horizontal type of 150 bhp.
Transmission: Mechanical. Standard
Body: 57' 6" × 9' 2"

Weight: 27t
Seats: 52 second

M79901	08/56-12/66	⊗04/67	

Bristol/Eastern Coach Works

Four Wheel Railbus

Diesel Railbus DRB

SC79958-SC79959

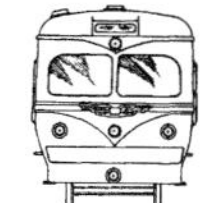

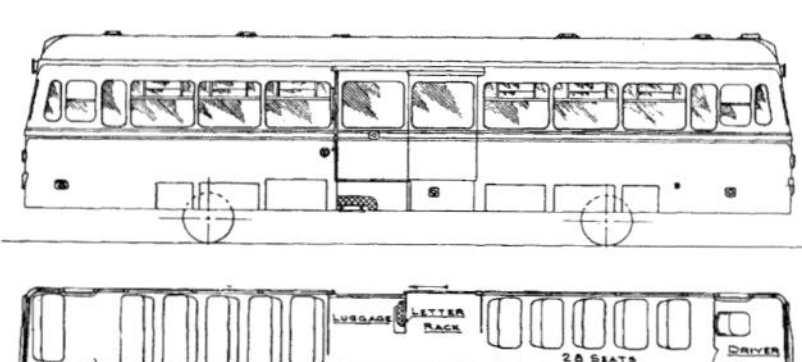

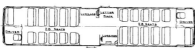

Diagram:	610
Lot Number:	30483
Engine:	Gardner 6HLW 6-cyl type of 112 bhp. at 1700 rpm.
Transmission:	Mechanical. Standard. Fitted with Self-Changing Gears five-speed epicyclic gearbox
Body:	42' 4" × 9' 3" Railcar
Weight:	13t 10cwt
Seats:	56 second

SC79958	09/58-10/66	⊗11/66
SC79959	11/58-10/66	⊗02/67

Waggon und Maschinenbau

Four Wheel Railbus

Diesel Railbus DRB

E79960-E79964

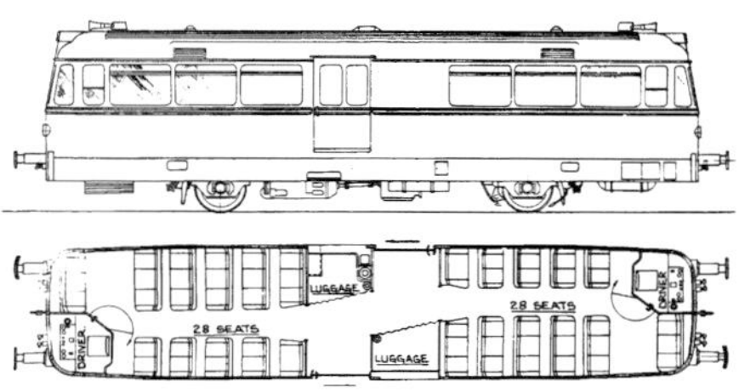

Diagram:	611
Lot Number:	30482
Engine:	Buessing 150 bhp. at 1900 rpm. a Fitted with an AEC 220X type engine 1962-63.
Transmission:	Mechanical. Cardan shaft to ZF electro-magnetic six-speed gearbox
Body:	41' 10" × 8' 8⅜" Railcar
Weight:	15t
Seats:	56 second

E79960	04/58-11/66	ⓟ		
E79961	04/58-02/67	⊗05/68	a	07/66⇨**M**
E79962	04/58-11/66	ⓟ		
E79963	04/58-11/66	ⓟ	a	
E79964	04/58-04/67	ⓟ	a	07/66⇨**M**

Wickham

Four Wheel Railbus

Diesel Railbus DRB

SC79965-SC79969

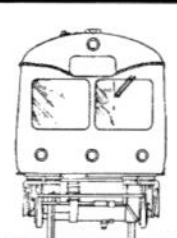

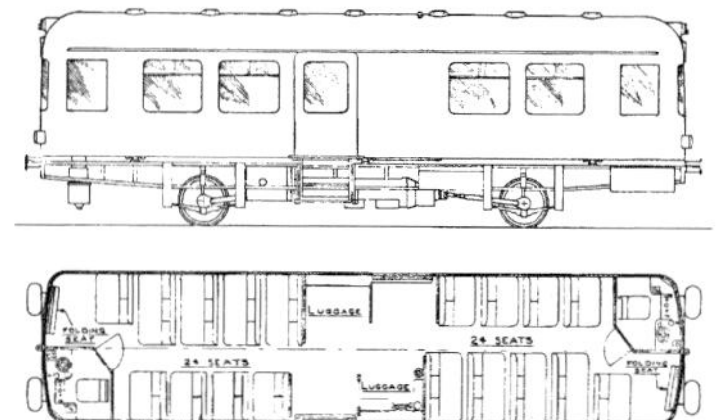

Diagram:	612
Lot Number:	30481
Engine:	Meadows 6-cyl type 6HDT500 of 105 bhp. at 1800 rpm.
Transmission:	Mechanical. Freeborn-Wickham disc-and-ring coupling driving Self-Changing Gears four speed epicyclic gearbox and cardan shaft to final drive
Body:	38' 0" × 9' 3" Railcar
Weight:	11t 10cwt
Seats:	48 second

M79965	09/58-06/64	⊗11/66	09/58⇨**SC**
M79966	01/59-06/64	⊗11/66	01/59⇨**SC**
SC79967	01/59-10/66	⊗11/66	
SC79968	05/59-10/66	⊗10/66	
SC79969	07/59-12/63	⊗11/66	

Park Royal

Four Wheel Railbus

Diesel Railbus DRB

SC79970-SC79974

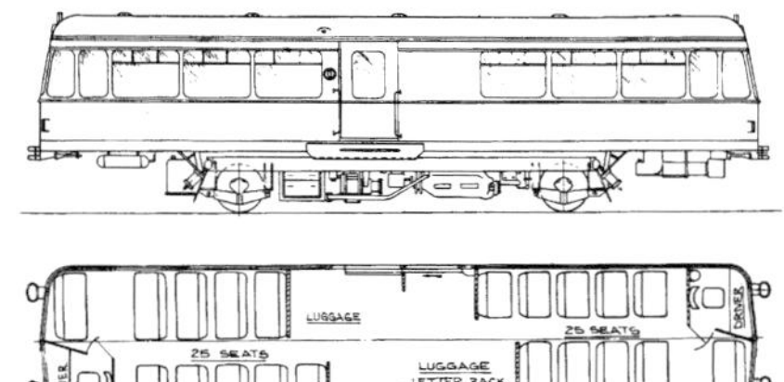

Diagram:	613
Lot Number:	30480
Engine:	BUT (AEC) 6-cyl horizontal type of 150 bhp.
Transmission:	Mechanical. Standard. Fitted with Self-Changing Gears four-speed epicyclic gearbox
Body:	42' 0" × 9' 3" Railcar
Weight:	15t
Seats:	50 second

SC79970	02/59-03/67	⊗09/67		
M79971	07/58-02/68	⊗07/84	02/60⇨*SC*	
M79972	07/58-11/66	⊗12/66	02/60⇨*SC*	12/65⇨**M**
M79973	07/58-11/66	⊗12/66	02/60⇨*SC*	12/65⇨**M**
SC79974	11/58-11/66	⊗12/68		

AC Cars
Four Wheel Railbus
Diesel Railbus DRB
W79975-SC79979

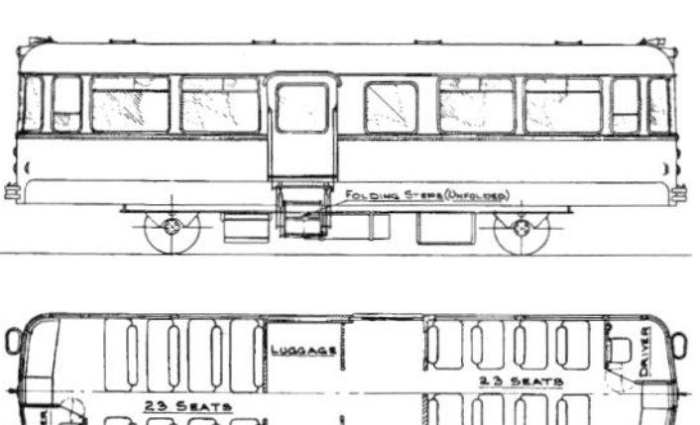

Diagram: 614
Lot Number: 30479
Engine: BUT (AEC) 6-cyl horizontal type of 150 bhp.
Transmission: Mechanical. Standard
Body: 36' 0" × 9' 3" Railcar
Weight: 11t
Seats: 46 second

W79975	08/58-12/67	⊗08/68	01/67⇐*SC*
W79976	09/58-02/68	Ⓟ	01/67⇐*SC*
W79977	10/58-02/68	⊗07/68	01/67⇐*SC*
W79978	11/58-02/68	Ⓟ	01/67⇐*SC*
SC79979	02/58-11/66	Ⓟ⊗*10/92*	

BR Derby
Battery Electric Railcar
Driving Motor Brake Second BDMBS
SC79998

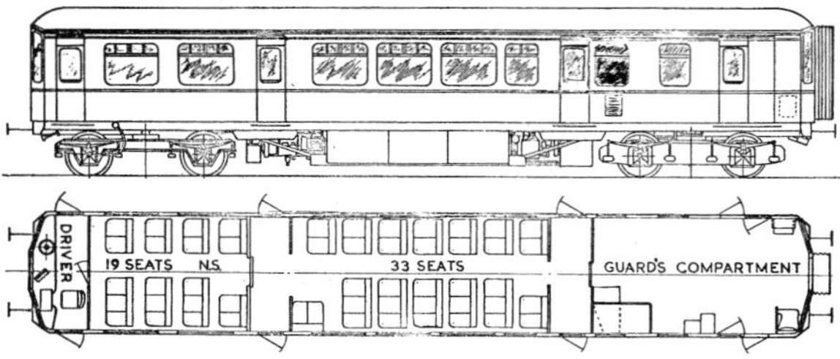

Diagram: 406
Lot Number: 30368
Equipment: Two 100 kW Siemens-Schuckert nose-suspended traction motors powered by 216 lead-acid cell batteries of 1070 amp/hour capacity
Body: 57' 6" × 9' 2"
Weight: 37t 10cwt
Seats: 52 second

SC79998	03/58-12/66	Ⓟ	10/67➲DB975003

BR Derby
Battery Electric Railcar
Driving Trailer Composite BDTCL
SC79999

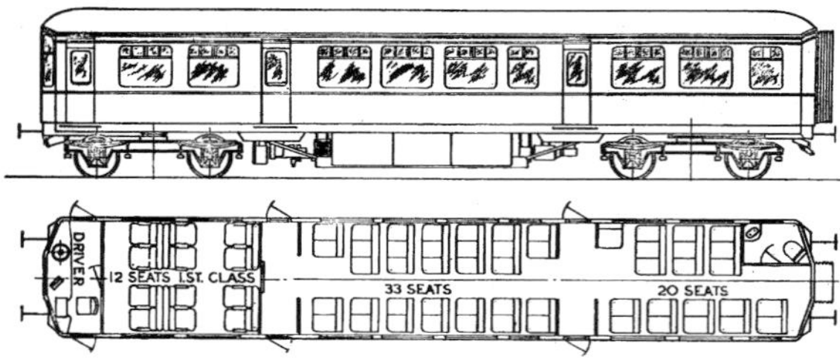

Diagram: 442
Lot Number: 30369
Body: 57' 6" × 9' 2"
Weight: 32t 10cwt
Seats: 12 first, 53 second

SC79999	03/58-12/66	Ⓟ	10/67➲DB975004

EMU coaches used in DMU sets

BR Ashford/Eastleigh
Trailer Second Corridor
TSK
S70262, S70286

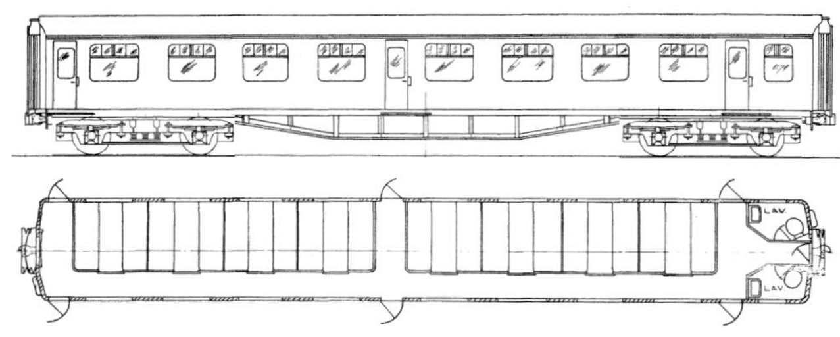

Diagram: 460 DH206
Lot Number: 30455
Body: 64' 6" × 9' 3"
Weight: 31t
Seats: 64 second

S70262	10/58-	Ⓟ
S70286	02/59-01/05	⊗09/03

BR Ashford/Eastleigh
Trailer Second Corridor
TSK
S70547, S70549

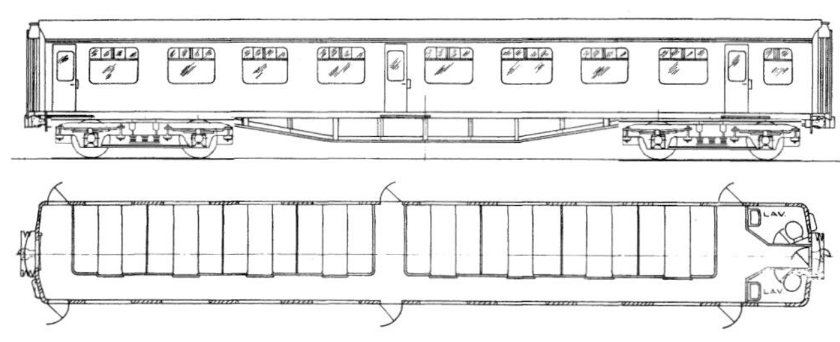

Diagram: 460 DH206
Lot Number: 30620
Body: 64' 6" × 9' 3"
Weight: 31t
Seats: 64 second

S70547	06/61-12/04	Ⓟ
S70549	07/61-10/03	Ⓟ

BR Swindon
Trailer Second Corridor
TSK
S71634

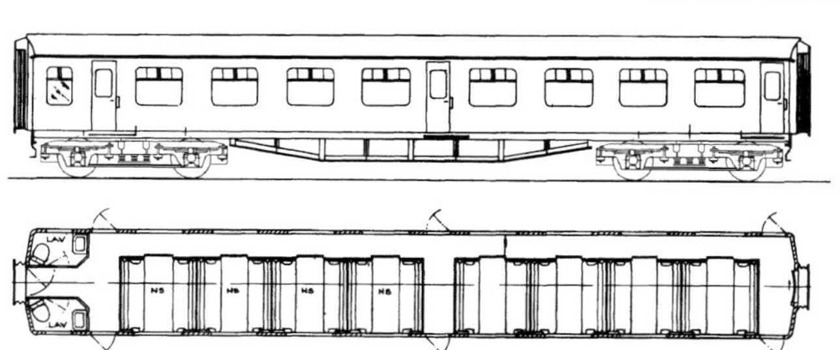

Diagram:	903	DH207
Lot Number:	30149	
Body:	64' 6" × 9' 3"	
Weight:	31t	
Seats:	64 second	

Originally built as Mark 1 hauled coach S4059 in 1956.

S71634	03/82-09/03 ⊗09/03

BR Ashford/Eastleigh
Driving Trailer Second Semi-open
DTSso
S77500-S77510

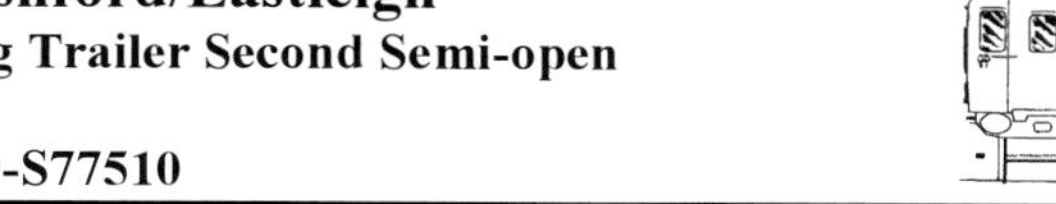

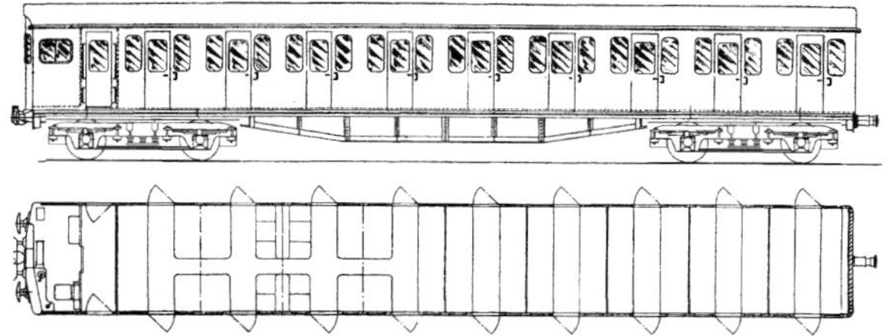

Diagram:	420	DE202
Lot Number:	30115	
Body:	57' 6" × 9' 3¼"	
Weight:	30t	
Seats:	102 second	

S77500	01/54-10/87 ⊗01/89
S77503	04/54-09/87 ⊗02/88
S77507	05/54-09/87 ⊗12/88
S77508	05/54-11/87 ⊗01/89
S77509	05/54-03/83 ⊗01/89
S77510	05/54-04/83 ⊗09/87

Parcels vehicles used with DMUs

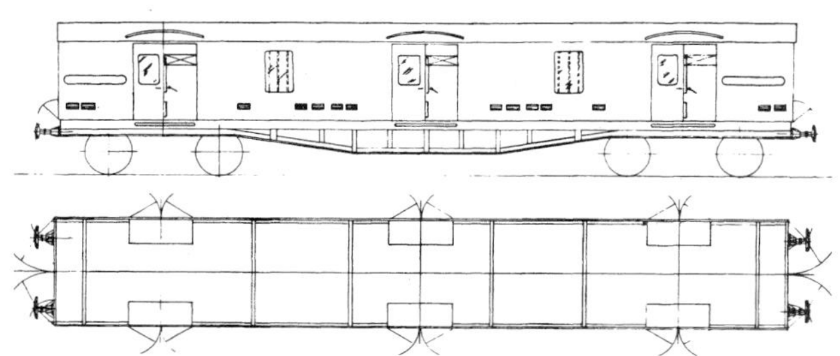

These were converted to work with Class 130 DMUs on London parcels services. In 1972 they worked with Class 128 units.

W86174	05/70-10/72 ⊗
W86572	05/70-10/72 ⊗

GWR Railcars

Strictly speaking these should not be included in this book, but as they were running at the same time as many of the first-generation units they are included for completeness. For a complete description of these vehicles look at the book *The History of Great Western A.E.C. Diesel Railcars* by Colin Judge.

GWR Railcar Park Royal
Driving Motor Brake Second
DMBS
W1W

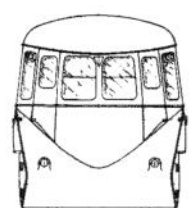

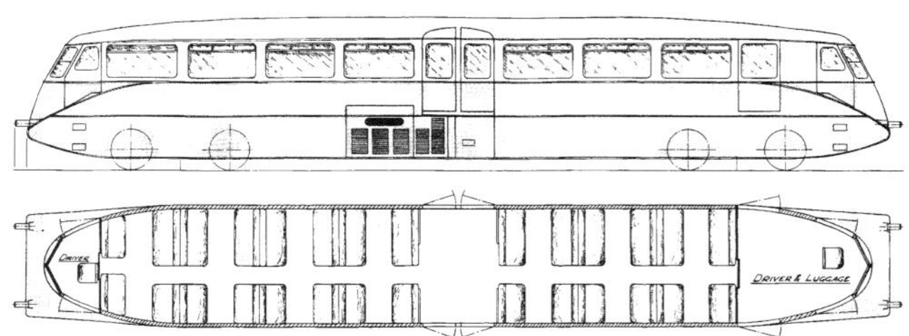

Engines:	One AEC 6-cyl engine of 130 bhp.
Transmission:	Mechanical Epicyclic Gearbox
Body:	63' 7" × 9' 0"
Weight:	34t 0cwt
Seats:	69 second

W1W	02/34-08/55	⊗01/63

GWR Railcar Park Royal
Driving Motor Brake Second Buffet
DMBSRB
W2W-W4W

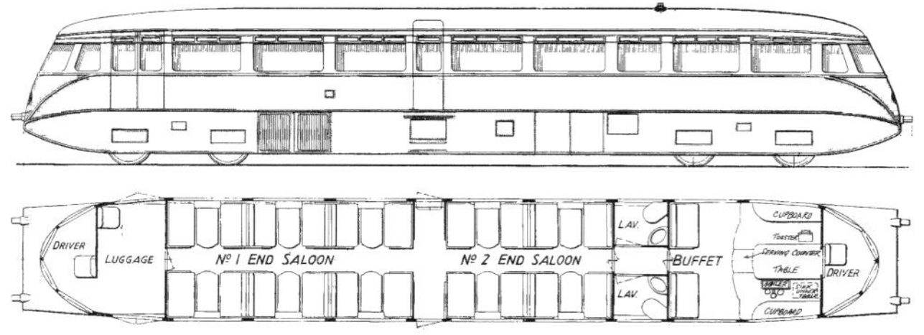

Engines:	Two AEC 6-cyl engines of 121 bhp.
Transmission:	Mechanical Epicyclic Gearbox
Body:	63' 7" × 9' 0"
Weight:	26t 4cwt
Seats:	44 second

W2W	07/34-02/54	⊗12/54
W3W	07/34-03/55	⊗12/55
W4W	09/34-07/58	Ⓟ

GWR Railcar Gloucester RC&W
Driving Motor Brake Second
DMBS
W5W-W9W, W13W-W16W

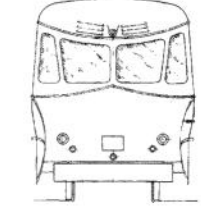

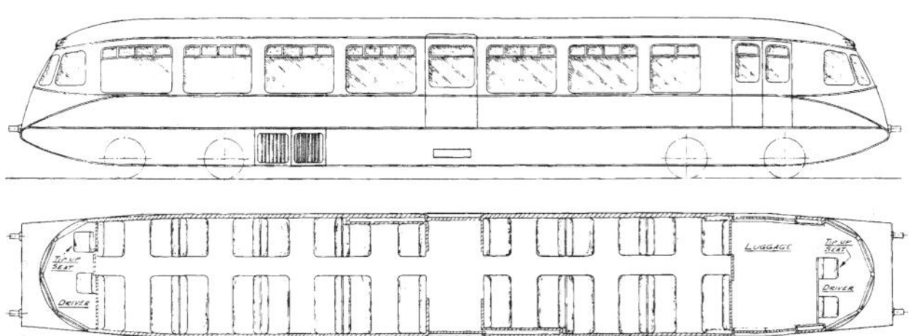

Engines:	Two AEC 6-cyl engines of 121 bhp.
Transmission:	Mechanical Epicyclic Gearbox
Body:	63' 7" × 9' 0"
Weight:	25t 6cwt h 29t 10cwt
Seats:	70 second

W5W	07/35-12/57	⊗*08/58*
W6W	08/35-04/58	⊗*08/58*
W7W	07/35-01/59	⊗12/59
W8W	03/36-01/59	⊗08/61 h
W9W	02/36-05/46	⊗*09/49* h

GWR Railcar Gloucester RC&W
Driving Motor Brake Second Lavatory
DMBSL
W10W-W12W

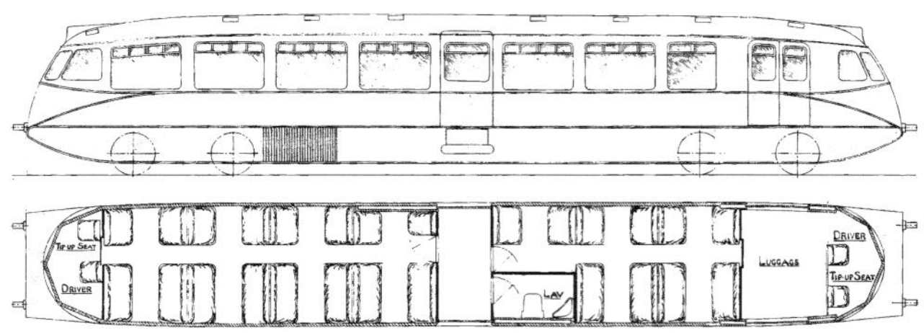

Engines:	Two AEC 6-cyl engines of 121 bhp.
Transmission:	Mechanical Epicyclic Gearbox
Body:	63' 7" × 9' 0"
Weight:	29t 18cwt
Seats:	63 second

W10W	02/36-04/56	⊗05/56
W11W	02/36-11/56	⊗*08/58*
W12W	02/36-06/57	⊗*08/58*

GWR Railcar Gloucester RC&W
Driving Motor Brake Second
DMBS
W5W-W9W, W13W-W16W

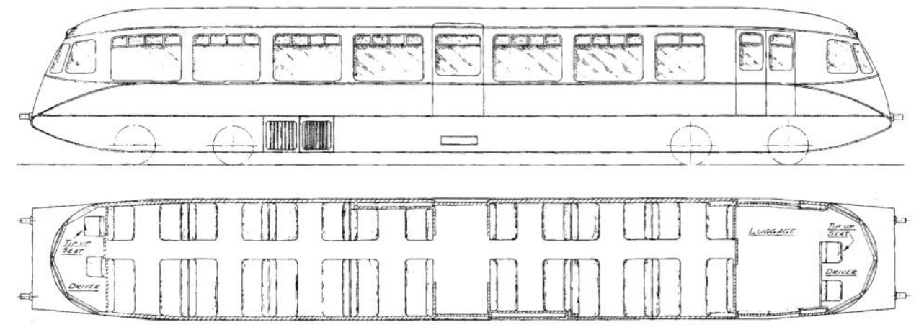

Engines:	Two AEC 6-cyl engines of 121 bhp.
Transmission:	Mechanical Epicyclic Gearbox
Body:	63' 7" × 9' 0"
Weight:	25t 6cwt h 29t 10cwt
Seats:	70 second

W13W	03/36-08/60	⊗ h	02/59⇨Parcels
W14W	03/36-08/60	⊗04/61 h	
W15W	04/36-01/59	⊗11/60 h	
W16W	04/36-10/57	⊗*08/58* h	

GWR Railcar Gloucester RC&W
Driving Motor Parcels
DMPMV
W17W

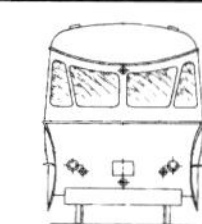

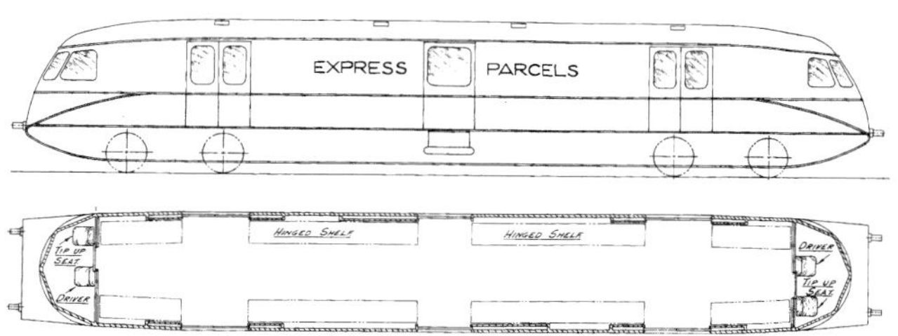

Engines: Two AEC 6-cyl engines of 121 bhp.
Transmission: Mechanical Epicyclic Gearbox
Body: 63' 7" × 9' 0"
Weight: 28t 17cwt

W17W 04/36-01/59 ⊗03/61

GWR Railcar Gloucester RC&W
Driving Motor Brake Second
DMBS
W18W

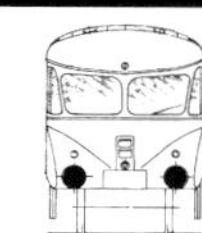

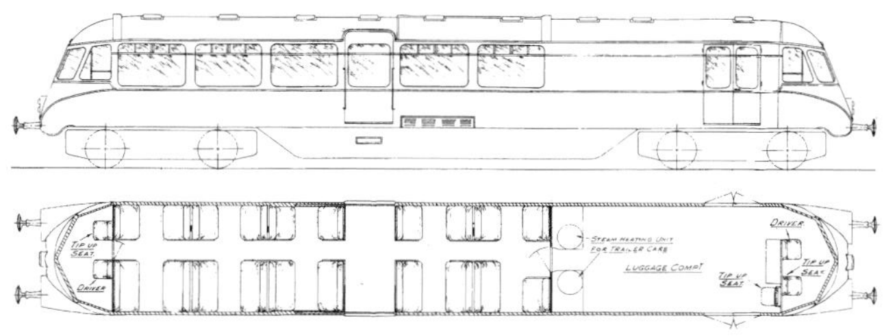

Engines: Two AEC 6-cyl engines of 130 bhp.
Transmission: Mechanical Epicyclic Gearbox
Body: 65' 8" × 9' 0½"
Weight: 34t 0cwt
Seats: 49 second

W18W 04/37-05/57 ⊗

GWR Railcar Swindon
Driving Motor Brake Second
DMBS
W19W-W32W

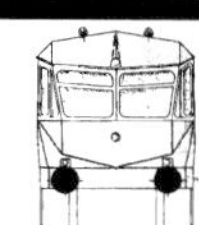

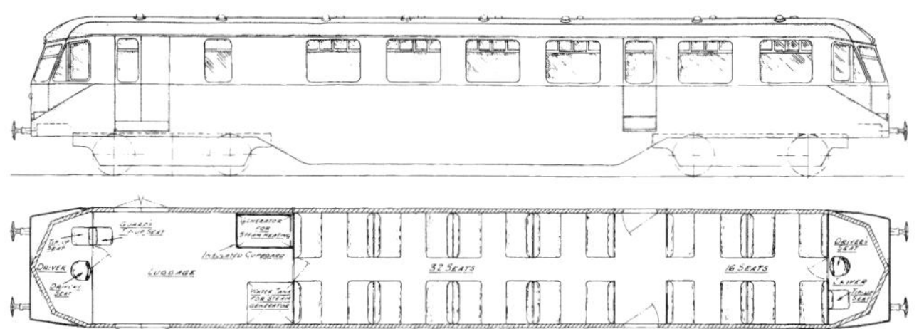

Engines: Two AEC 6-cyl engines of 105 bhp.
Transmission: Mechanical Epicyclic Gearbox
Body: 65' 8" × 9' 3"
Weight: 35t 13cwt
Seats: 48 second

W19W 07/40-02/60 ⊗11/60
W20W 06/40-10/62 Ⓟ
W21W 07/40-08/62 ⊗10/64
W22W 09/40-10/62 Ⓟ
W23W 09/40-10/62 ⊗07/64
W24W 09/40-10/62 ⊗10/64
W25W 09/40-08/62 ⊗11/62

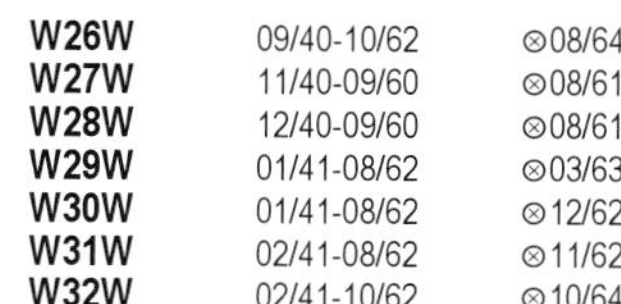

W26W 09/40-10/62 ⊗08/64
W27W 11/40-09/60 ⊗08/61
W28W 12/40-09/60 ⊗08/61
W29W 01/41-08/62 ⊗03/63
W30W 01/41-08/62 ⊗12/62
W31W 02/41-08/62 ⊗11/62
W32W 02/41-10/62 ⊗10/64

GWR Railcar Swindon Twin Unit
Driving Motor Brake Second
DMBS
W33W

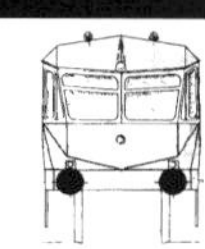

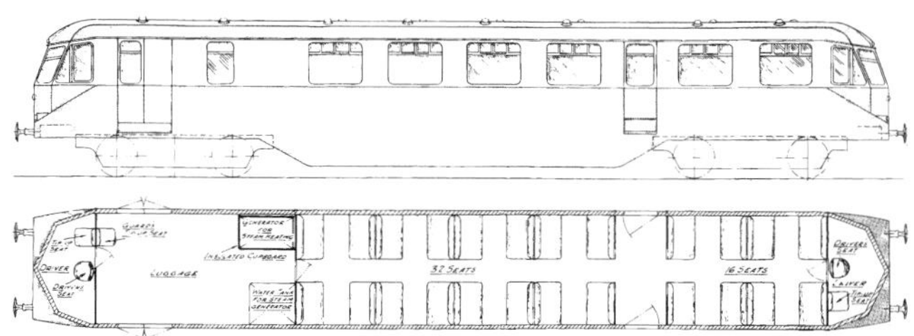

Original form

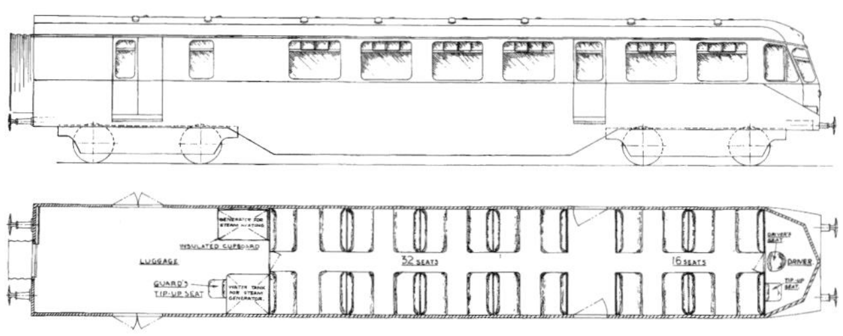

Rebuilt form

Engines: Two AEC 6-cyl engines of 105 bhp.
Transmission: Mechanical Epicyclic Gearbox
Body: 65' 8" × 9' 3"
Weight: 35t 13cwt
Seats: 48 second

This was rebuilt from a double ended railcar to replace No 37 which was destroyed by fire in 1947.

W33W 03/41-08/62 ⊗04/63

GWR Railcar Swindon
Driving Motor Parcels
DMPMV
W34W

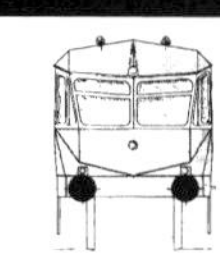

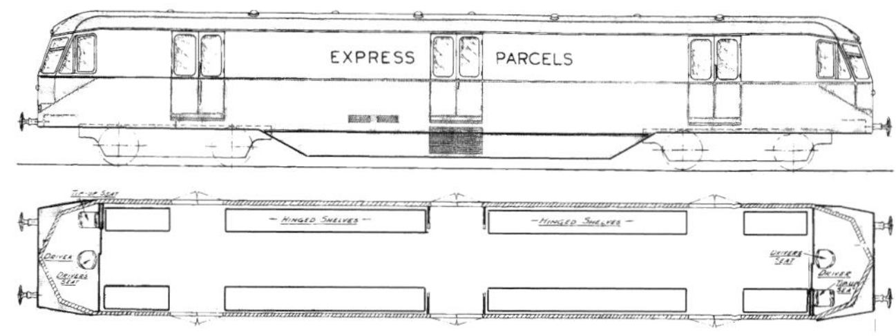

Engines: Two AEC 6-cyl engines of 105 bhp.
Transmission: Mechanical Epicyclic Gearbox
Body: 65' 8" × 9' 3"
Weight: 34t 0cwt

W34W 09/41-09/60 ⊗05/62

GWR Railcar Swindon Twin Unit
Driving Motor Brake Second Lavatory
DMBSL
W35W, W37W

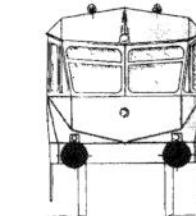

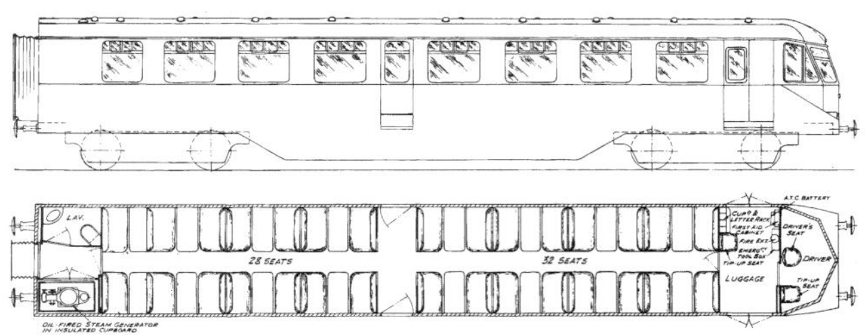

Engines: Two AEC 6-cyl engines of 105 bhp.
Transmission: Mechanical Epicyclic Gearbox
Body: 65' 8" × 9' 3"
Weight: 36t 14cwt
Seats: 60 second

W35W	11/41-04/57	⊗07/57

GWR Railcar Swindon Twin Unit
Driving Motor Brake Second Buffet
DMBSRB
W36W, W38W

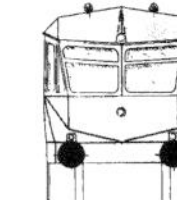

Engines: Two AEC 6-cyl engines of 105 bhp.
Transmission: Mechanical Epicyclic Gearbox
Body: 65' 8" × 9' 3"
Weight: 37t 12cwt
Seats: 44 second

W36W	11/41-04/57	⊗07/57

GWR Railcar Swindon Twin Unit
Driving Motor Brake Second Lavatory
DMBSL
W35W, W37W

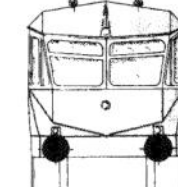

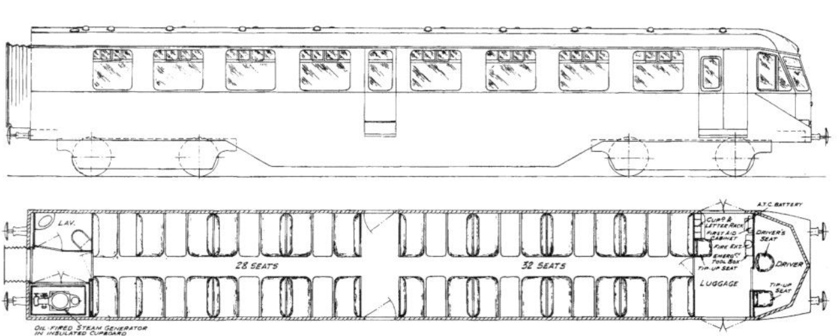

Engines: Two AEC 6-cyl engines of 105 bhp.
Transmission: Mechanical Epicyclic Gearbox
Body: 65' 8" × 9' 3"
Weight: 36t 14cwt
Seats: 60 second

W37W	02/42-09/49	⊗ /47

GWR Railcar Swindon Twin Unit
Driving Motor Brake Second Buffet
DMBSRB
W36W, W38W

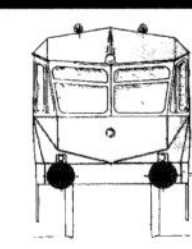

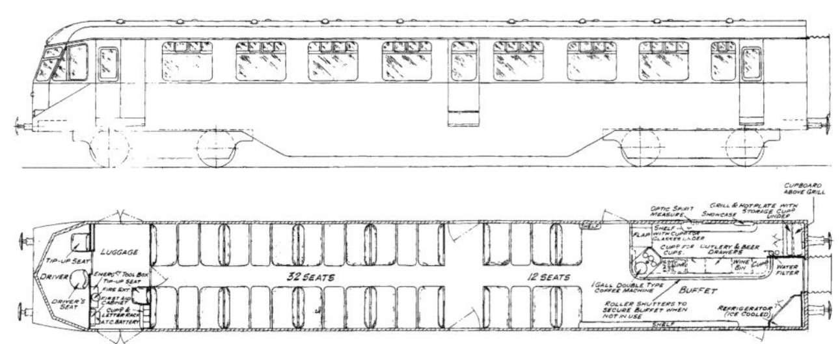

Body: 65' 8" × 9' 3"
Weight: 37t 12cwt
Seats: 44 second

W38W	02/42-08/62	⊗04/63

Unit formations

W33W W1096W W38W
W35W W36W

GWR
Hauled coaches used as DMU trailers

This coach was converted to work as a centre car with GWR railcars W33W and W38W.

W1096W	02/42-08/62	⊗04/63

These coaches were converted to work as centre cars with Class 119 Cross-country DMUs. They were converted from post-war Hawksworth CKs and were repainted in lined green livery. The units originally worked London-Oxford services. They also later worked in Class 117 units.

W7254W	01/62-12/66	⊗	Built 1948 Lot 1689
W7804W	08/61-12/66	⊗	Built 1949 Lot 1754
W7813W	01/62-12/66	⊗	Built 1949 Lot 1754

DMU coaches converted for Departmental or other further use

Number	Ex	Dates	Status	Use
RDB975003	⊂**SC79998**	10/67- /85	℗	Lab Coach 16 "Gemini"
RDB975004	⊂**SC79999**	10/67- /85	℗	Lab Coach 16 "Gemini"
TDB975005	⊂**E50416**	10/67-10/81	℗	ER General Manager's Saloon
TDB975006	⊂**E56171**	10/67-10/81	℗	ER General Manager's Saloon
DB975007	⊂**M79018**	11/70- /94	℗	Ultrasonic Test Car
DB975008	⊂**M79612**	11/70- /94	℗	Ultrasonic Test Car
RDB975010	⊂**M79900**	10/67-06/99	℗	Test Coach "Iris"
DB975012	⊂**M79185**	01/68-06/70	⊗07/70	Brake Trials Coach
TDB975013	⊂**SC79250**	06/67-*04/77*	⊗02/78	Staff Mess room
TDB975014	⊂**SC79252**	06/67-11/77	⊗06/82	Staff Mess room
RDB975018	⊂**E79047**	05/69- */81*	⊗06/81	Plasma Torch Train
RDB975019	⊂**E79053**	05/69- */81*	⊗06/81	Plasma Torch Train
TDB975023	⊂**W55001**	06/69-*05/98*	℗	Route Learning Car
				Numbered **DB975073** in error until 04/71
TDB975025	⊂**S60755**	01/70-		SR General Manager's Saloon
				Later Network Rail Inspection Saloon **975025** CAROLINE in 2005
TDB975042	⊂**M55019**	11/69-		Route Learning Car
				Later **ADB975042** Sandite Unit 960015 in 08/93
RDB975089	⊂**M50396**	04/71-03/90	⊗02/91	Lab Coach 5
RDB975090	⊂**M56162**	04/71-03/90	⊗02/91	Lab Coach 5
DB975137	⊂**M50397**	02/71-07/78	℗⊗09/09	CCE Universal Viaduct Inspection Unit 1
TDB975227	⊂**M55017**	06/72-02/89	⊗12/89	Route Learning Car
DB975228	⊂**M56160**	02/71-07/78	℗	Viaduct Inspection Unit
TDB975309	⊂**M55008**	05/74-08/82	⊗12/84	Route Learning Car
TDB975310	⊂**M55010**	07/74-08/82	⊗08/84	Route Learning Car
ADB975327	⊂**W59828**	/76- /87	⊗11/87	Staff & Dormitory Coach
				Later **DB975327** Stores Coach
TDB975348	⊂**E51115**	05/74-03/76	⊗04/84	Inspection Saloon 03/76⊃**E51115**
DB975349	⊂**E51116**	05/74-01/93	⊗07/93	Inspection Saloon
RDB975385	⊂**M55997**	04/75- /85	⊗05/86	Lab Coach 9 "Hydra"
RDB975386	⊂**S60750**	03/74-07/89	℗	Lab Coach 4 "Hastings"
ADB975426	⊂**SC79098**	07/76- /82	⊗05/82	Mess Coach
DB975539	⊂**E56101**	03/76-01/93	⊗07/93	Inspection Saloon
TDB975540	⊂**W55016**	11/75-05/93	⊗07/93	Inspection Saloon
DB975637	⊂**E56300**	11/78-05/90	⊗08/90	Inspection Saloon
TDB975659	⊂**W55035**	07/78-04/92	⊗04/92	Route Learning Car
DB975664	⊂**E51122**	11/78-05/90	⊗08/90	Inspection Saloon
RDB975964	⊂**E59466**	03/84- /88	⊗07/88	Stores Coach
RDB975993	⊂**E59458**	03/84- /85	⊗02/86	Test Coach for Fire Tests
TDB975994	⊂**SC55014**	10/80- /88	⊗10/88	Route Learning Car
TDB975998	⊂**SC55013**	12/80- /82	⊗03/82	Route Learning Car
ADB977047	⊂**M56156**	12/81- /85	⊗08/86	Sandite Coach
ADB977048	⊂**E56142**	12/81-07/89	⊗10/91	Sandite Coach
ADB977049	⊂**E56474**	12/81- /88	⊗04/88	Sandite Coach
ADB977050	⊂**E56448**	12/81- /88	⊗01/89	Sandite Coach
ADB977051	⊂**E56427**	12/81- /85	⊗04/87	Sandite Coach
ADB977052	⊂**M56145**	01/82-01/90	⊗10/91	Sandite Coach
ADB977114	⊂**M56129**	07/82- /85	⊗04/87	Sandite Coach
TDB977123	⊂**E51286**	11/82-05/90	⊗08/90	Route Learning Car
TDB977124	⊂**E51296**	11/82-05/90	⊗08/90	Route Learning Car
TDB977125	⊂**E56444**	11/82-05/90	⊗08/90	Route Learning Car
TDB977126	⊂**E56445**	11/82-05/90	⊗08/90	Route Learning Car
TDB977177	⊂**SC55015**	09/83-07/89	⊗07/90	Route Learning Car "Sandra"
ADB977191	⊂**M56106**	07/83- /88	⊗ /02	Crewe Works Test Train Coach
TDB977196	⊂**M56111**	07/83-02/85	⊗07/85	Instruction Coach
TDB977223	⊂**SC55007**	12/83- /89	⊗06/91	Route Learning Car
RDB977225	⊂**SC52014**	05/84- /87	⊗12/87	Laboratory Coach
RDB977226	⊂**SC59787**	05/84- /87	⊗12/87	Laboratory Coach
RDB977227	⊂**SC52032**	05/84- /87	⊗12/87	Laboratory Coach
ADB977342	⊂**M53475**	11/85- /88	⊗12/88	Carriage Washing Test Coach
ADB977343	⊂**M53506**	11/85-11/86	⊗05/87	Carriage Washing Test Coach
ADB977344	⊂**M53422**	11/85-11/86	⊗05/87	Carriage Washing Test Coach
ADB977376	⊂**S60002**	05/86-03/94	⊗11/94	Sandite Unit 066⊃1066
ADB977377	⊂**S60003**	05/86-03/94	⊗11/94	Sandite Unit 066⊃1066
ADB977378	⊂**S60503**	*/86- /89*	⊗10/89	Sandite Coach Not converted
ADB977379	⊂**S60504**	05/86-03/94	⊗07/98	Sandite Unit 066⊃1066
DB977391	⊂**E51433**	04/89-08/08	℗	Ultrasonic Test Coach
DB977392	⊂**E53167**	04/89-08/08	℗	Ultrasonic Test Coach
DB977393	⊂**E53246**	07/89-07/93	⊗06/93	Ultrasonic Test Coach
TDB977453	⊂**E51260**	09/86-05/88	⊗12/88	Route Learning Car
TDB977454	⊂**E54440**	09/86-05/88	⊗12/88	Route Learning Car
TDB977466	⊂**W54286**	10/86- /96	⊗10/96	Sandite Coach
TDB977486	⊂**W54285**	12/86- /96	℗	Sandite Coach 960006
TDB977535	⊂**E53259**	11/87-11/92	⊗02/93	Sandite Coach
TDB977536	⊂**E53295**	11/87-11/92	⊗02/93	Sandite Coach
TDB977537	⊂**E53320**	11/87-08/88	⊗08/89	Sandite Coach
TDB977538	⊂**E53134**	11/87-08/88	⊗08/89	Sandite Coach
TDB977539	⊂**E53135**	11/87-07/88	⊗08/89	Sandite Coach
TDB977540	⊂**E53137**	11/87-08/88	⊗08/89	Sandite Coach
ADB977554	⊂**M54182**	07/89-12/92	℗	Sandite Coach
ADB977555	⊂**M54183**	04/88-12/92	⊗02/94	Sandite Coach
TDB977607	⊂**SC51464**	12/88-02/93	⊗02/93	Route Learning & Sandite Coach
TDB977608	⊂**SC51525**	12/88-02/93	⊗02/93	Route Learning & Sandite Coach
ADB977611	⊂**E51824**	12/88-09/90	⊗09/90	Sandite Coach
ADB977612	⊂**E51838**	12/88-09/90	⊗09/90	Sandite Coach
ADB977613	⊂**E51826**	04/90-09/90	⊗09/90	Sandite Coach
ADB977614	⊂**E52076**	11/89-09/90	⊗09/90	Sandite Coach
ADB977615	⊂**W54281**	03/88-11/89	⊗11/90	Sandite Coach
RDB977636	⊂**53119**	*08/*88-05/90	⊗02/91	Conversion cancelled 05/90
RDB977637	⊂**53063**	*08/*88-05/90	⊗02/91	Conversion cancelled 05/90
ADB977651	⊂**SC53290**	11/90-02/92	⊗02/93	Route Learning & Sandite Coach
ADB977652	⊂**SC53197**	11/90-02/92	⊗08/92	Route Learning & Sandite Coach
RDB977693	⊂**53222**	04/91-04/08	℗	Lab Coach 19 Test Coach "Iris 2"
RDB977694	⊂**53338**	04/91-04/08	℗	Lab Coach 19 Test Coach "Iris 2"
RDB977695	⊂**60525**	08/91- */91*	⊗02/92	Rail Scrubber Coach Not Converted
ADB977696	⊂**60522**	09/90-12/96	⊗10/05	Sandite Coach Unit 1068
ADB977697	⊂**60523**	09/90-07/93	⊗03/94	Sandite Coach Unit 1067
ADB977698	⊂**60152**	09/90-12/96	⊗*12/96*	Sandite Coach Unit 1067 ex-S60014
ADB977699	⊂**60153**	09/90-12/96	⊗*12/96*	Sandite Coach Unit 1067 ex-S60015
ADB977700	⊂**60139**	04/92-05/92	⊗05/92	Sandite Coach Unit 1068
ADB977701	⊂**60910**	04/92-05/92	⊗05/92	Sandite Coach Unit 1068
ADB977722	⊂**55020**	01/92-08/99		Route Learning Car 960002 09/02⊃**55020**
ADB977723	⊂**55021**	11/91-		Route Learning Car 960021
ADB977744	⊂**51906**	10/91-08/93	⊗11/93	Route Learning Car 901
ADB977745	⊂**53626**	10/91-10/92	⊗01/93	Route Learning Car
ADB977746	⊂**53929**	10/91-08/93	⊗03/94	Route Learning Car 902
ADB977747	⊂**53924**	10/91-02/92	⊗01/92	Route Learning Car
ADB977748	⊂**53950**	10/91-08/93	⊗03/94	Route Learning Car 902
ADB977749	⊂**53959**	10/91-02/92	⊗03/92	Route Learning Car
ADB977750	⊂**53963**	10/91-10/95	⊗04/96	Route Learning Car 903
ADB977751	⊂**53957**	10/91-02/92	⊗03/92	Route Learning Car
ADB977752	⊂**51306**	02/92- /93	⊗03/94	Route Learning Car T007
ADB977753	⊂**51321**	02/92- /93	℗	Route Learning Car T007
ADB977756	⊂**51985**	12/91-11/92	⊗02/93	Sandite Coach
ADB977757	⊂**52028**	12/91-11/92	⊗02/93	Sandite Coach
ADB977758	⊂**51992**	12/91-11/92	⊗02/93	Sandite Coach
ADB977762	⊂**52023**	12/91-11/92	⊗02/93	Sandite Coach
ADB977765	⊂**51938**	01/92-08/93	⊗03/94	Sandite Coach 904
ADB977766	⊂**53944**	01/92-08/93	⊗03/94	Sandite Coach 904
ADB977768	⊂**51911**	01/92-02/94	⊗07/96	Sandite Coach 903
ADB977769	⊂**53036**	01/92-06/93	⊗07/93	Engine Testing Car
ADB977770	⊂**54027**	01/92-06/93	⊗07/93	Engine Testing Car
TDB977775	⊂**55929**	03/92-06/00	℗	ATP Test Train ex-53015
TDB977776	⊂**54904**	03/92-06/00	℗	ATP Test Train ex-54015
ADB977806	⊂**51937**	10/92-10/93	℗	Route Learning Car 905
ADB977807	⊂**52053**	10/92-10/93	℗	Route Learning Car 905
ADB977808	⊂**51903**	10/92-10/95	⊗08/95	Route Learning Car 906
ADB977809	⊂**53958**	10/92-10/95	⊗02/96	Route Learning Car 906
ADB977810	⊂**51901**	10/92-02/94	⊗07/96	Route Learning Car 907
ADB977811	⊂**53956**	10/92-10/95	⊗07/96	Route Learning Car 907
ADB977812	⊂**51945**	10/92-10/95	⊗06/96	Route Learning Car 908
ADB977813	⊂**52060**	10/92-02/94	℗⊗04/04	Route Learning Car 908
ADB977814	⊂**53926**	10/92-02/94	℗	Route Learning Car 909
ADB977815	⊂**52059**	10/92-11/94	⊗10/96	Route Learning Car 909
ADB977816	⊂**53982**	10/92-09/93	℗⊗ /02	Route Learning Car 921
ADB977817	⊂**52061**	10/92-09/93	℗⊗ /02	Route Learning Car 921
ADB977818	⊂**53939**	10/92-10/95	⊗07/96	Route Learning Car 922
TDB977819	⊂**52046**	10/92-10/95	⊗09/95	Route Learning Car 922
TDB977820	⊂**53629**	10/92-09/93	⊗12/94	Route Learning Car 923
TDB977821	⊂**52058**	10/92-09/93	⊗12/94	Route Learning Car 923
TDB977822	⊂**51563**	10/92-09/93	⊗12/94	Route Learning Car 924
TDB977823	⊂**51561**	10/92-09/93	⊗12/94	Route Learning Car 924
TDB977824	⊂**55026**	10/92-02/94	℗⊗04/09	Sandite Car T005
TDB977825	⊂**53881**	10/92-02/94	⊗09/97	Sandite Car T005
TDB977826	⊂**55033**	10/92-02/94	℗	Sandite Car T003
TDB977827	⊂**53886**	10/92-01/94	⊗03/94	Sandite Car T003
DB977828	⊂**55034**	10/92-*06/96*	℗	Sandite Car T004
TDB977829	⊂**53093**	10/92-02/94	⊗09/97	Sandite Car T004
ADB977830	⊂**51990**	09/92-02/95	℗	Sandite Unit 932 (carried S002)
ADB977831	⊂**52030**	09/92-02/95	℗	Sandite Unit 932 (carried S002)
ADB977832	⊂**52005**	09/92-02/95	℗	Sandite Unit 931 (carried S001)
ADB977833	⊂**52025**	09/92-02/95	℗	Sandite Unit 931 (carried S001)
ADB977834	⊂**51993**	09/92-02/95	℗	Sandite Unit 933 (carried S003)
ADB977835	⊂**52012**	09/92-02/95	℗	Sandite Unit 933 (carried S003)
ADB977836	⊂**53941**	10/92-10/95	⊗10/96	Sandite Unit 910
ADB977838	⊂**53981**	10/92-02/94	⊗08/95	Sandite Unit 910
ADB977839	⊂**53642**	10/92-08/93	⊗11/93	Sandite Coach 901
ADB977840	⊂**51932**	10/92-09/93	⊗02/95	Sandite Coach 925
ADB977841	⊂**52047**	10/92-09/93	⊗02/95	Sandite Coach 925
ADB977842	⊂**55032**	12/92-02/94	℗	Sandite Coach T009 04/06⊃**55032**
ADB977843	⊂**51153**	12/92-02/94	⊗03/94	Sandite Coach T009
ADB977853	⊂**53627**	02/93-01/94	℗	Route Learning Coach
ADB977854	⊂**51567**	02/93-01/94	℗	Route Learning Coach
ADB977858	⊂**55024**	09/93-		Sandite Unit 960010
ADB977859	⊂**55025**	09/93-05/00		Video-Survey Unit 960011
ADB977860	⊂**55028**	09/93-04/09	℗	Route Learning Unit 960012
ADB977866	⊂**55030**	09/93-		Sandite Unit 960013
ADB977870	⊂**60660**	06/93-11/05	⊗08/09	Sandite Coach 1067 / 951069⊃930301
DB977873	⊂**55022**	09/93-		Sandite Car 960014
DB977895	⊂**53308**	09/93-06/99	⊗09/03	Sandite Unit 991⊃960991
DB977896	⊂**53331**	09/93-06/99	⊗09/03	Sandite Unit 991⊃960991

DB977897	**⊂53203**	06/93-06/99	Ⓟ	Sandite Unit 992⊃960992
DB977898	**⊂53193**	06/93-06/99	Ⓟ	Sandite Unit 992⊃960992
DB977899	**⊂51427**	05/93-06/99	Ⓟ	Sandite Unit 993⊃960993
DB977900	**⊂53321**	05/93-06/99	Ⓟ	Sandite Unit 993⊃960993
DB977901	**⊂53200**	05/93-06/99	⊗04/03	Sandite Unit 994⊃960994
DB977902	**⊂53231**	05/93-06/99	⊗04/03	Sandite Unit 994⊃960994
DB977903	**⊂53208**	10/93-06/99	⊗04/03	Sandite Unit 995⊃960995
DB977904	**⊂53291**	10/93-06/99	⊗04/03	Sandite Unit 995⊃960995
977906	**⊂60135**	09/93-09/93	Ⓟ⊗*01/99*	Tractor unit Not converted 951070
977907	**⊂60138**	09/93-09/93	Ⓟ	Tractor unit Not converted 951070
977921	**⊂51138**	11/93-12/95	Ⓟ	Sandite Unit Not converted
ADB977939	**⊂60145**	10/94-11/05		Sandite Coach 951069⊃930301
ADB977940	**⊂60149**	10/94-11/05		Sandite Coach 951069⊃930301
977941	**⊂55012**	*04/04-04/04*	Ⓟ	Route Learning Unit
977968	**⊂55029**	02/02-		Video Survey Unit
977975	**⊂55027**	12/02-04/08		Severn Tunnel Emergency Train 960302
977976	**⊂55031**	12/02-04/08		Severn Tunnel Emergency Train 960303
977987	**⊂51371**	10/03-		Water-Cannon Unit 960301
977988	**⊂51413**	10/03-		Water-Cannon Unit 960301
977992	**⊂51375**	08/04-		Water-Cannon Unit 960301
DB999510	**⊂M79649**	/60- */81*	⊗03/81	Inspection Saloon
53314		03/97-06/99	⊗07/02	Test unit Iris 3 No departmental number
53327		03/97-06/99	⊗07/02	Test unit Iris 3 No departmental number
60616		05/93-07/99	Ⓟ	No departmental number
6300	**⊂56356**	09/86-	Ⓟ	Hauled Observation Car "Hebridean"
E69108	**⊂W59831**	07/72-08/84	⊗08/84	Class 309 EMU Coach Replacement
FA99900	**⊂SC56315**	03/75-	⊗03/90	Fisons Weed killing Train
024949	**⊂59389**	10/91- */95*	Ⓟ⊗03/98	Internal User Coach
042222	**⊂54342**	12/90-*09/05*	Ⓟ	Internal User Coach

A three-car high density Class 125 diesel-hydraulic unit is seen working the 16.20 Liverpool Street to Cheshunt on 20th April 1968. It is seen approaching Ponders End with Ponders End Gasworks in the background. *P Paye*

Swindon Class 126 DMSL SC51028 in rail blue livery is seen at Ayr Depot on 15th April 1973. This is one of the driving motors fitted with an end corridor connection and a narrow cab. *D L Percival*

A six-car Class 126 set led by unit 126420 (SC51050, SC59403 and SC51022) is seen passing Ayr Depot on 31st August 1981. This shows the non-corridor end of the units. *J C Hillmer*

In the stabling sidings at Ayr a three-car Class 126 unit consisting of SC51026, SC59404 and SC51043 is seen on 9th August 1982. *A O Wynn*

An eight-car Class 127 formation led by M51624 is seen approaching Elstree New Tunnel while forming the 2.15pm Bedford to St. Pancras service on 12th October 1963. The units are painted in green livery with yellow warning panels.
B Stephenson

A blue-liveried four-car Class 127 unit led by M51597 approaches Luton on the 12.27 St. Pancras to Bedford service on 30th September 1981.
J E Oxley

On the 7th October 1978 Class 127 Trailer Second M59632 is seen at Cricklewood Depot awaiting re-marshalling into a unit. *B Cresswell*

This photograph shows the interior of one of the London Midland Region's high density Trailer Seconds. *BR*

In 1985 a large number of redundant Class 127 motor vehicles were given a new lease of life as Diesel Parcels Units. On the evening of 30th January 1980 M55983, M55973, M55980 and M55970 are seen at Birmingham New Street waiting to work their next service. *M J Collins*

Left: Class 127 DMLV M55985 is seen in Express Parcels livery (blue with a red stripe) in Tyseley Yard on 4th May 1986. The roller-shutter doors were fitted to allow faster loading of parcels and also allowed access for BRUTE trolleys. *R C Jones*

Below: This official BR shot of Class 128 Diesel Parcels Van M55987 shows the carriage as built in green livery. This was one of the batch built for the London Midland Region without end corridors. *BR*

Left: On 22 September 1976 Class 128 M55988 heads west out of Manchester Victoria. By this time these units were painted blue with yellow ends.

In the 1970s Manchester Victoria was often a pick-up point for Dalescroft Railfans coach trips to various parts of the country. At Easter 1972 Grahame McCoyd and I waited under the North Eastern Railway tiled map until the small hours of the morning waiting for our coach-trip to Scottish depots. Manchester was the Newspaper centre of the North of England and Victoria Station was very busy at night.

I particularly remember several of these units being loaded up in one of the terminal platforms and disappearing off into the night. *B Morrison*

The Western Region version of Class 128 was fitted with end gangways, making them look very different to the London Midland units. W55993 is seen in early green livery. *R C Riley*

On 10th October 1985 55994 is seen unloading at Shrewsbury Station on its first day back at work after having been repainted into the new parcels livery. By this time the end-gangway had been removed, giving yet another new look for a Class 128 unit. *T R Moors*

55992 in Royal Mail red livery pulls away from Stratford on 25th March 1989. It is transferring mail from the 14.00 Norwich to Stratford Inter-city service during the temporary closure of Liverpool Street Station. This shot shows the opposite end of the unit to the other Class 128 photographs, without the engine exhaust pipes. *M McGowan*

Above: Cravens Class 129 Diesel Parcels Van M55997 is seen brand new in green livery.

Right: On 20th July 1969 Class 129 Parcels Van M55998 is seen in blue livery at Newton Heath. Note yellow diamond coupling code has had to be placed on a black patch on the yellow end in order to make it visible. *P R Foster*

Class 130 parcels unit W51137 and W51150 formed temporarily with both W86174 and W86572 when newly converted for parcels working. *BR*

Part 5. DMU allocations.

This is a full allocation list at several points in the lifetime of the first generation units. The allocations are given as at the beginning of 1960, 1970, 1980, 1990 and 2000. This gives an indication of the different geographical spread of the units over their lifetime. Note that the first depot at the date of introduction is shown in Part 1.

When first delivered the Western Region did not specify the depot allocations of its DMUs and these had to be ascertained by personal observation, which was recorded in the railway press of the time. Until the early 1960s the London Midland Region only notified re-allocations for power cars. An assumption has been made that the relevant trailers were re-allocated at the same time. When looking back, one should not always assume that the accuracy and availability of information in the 1950s and 1960s was as good as it became later.

1960	*1970*	*1980*	*1990*	*2000*
E50000 40A Lincoln				
E50001 40A Lincoln	**E50001** 40A Lincoln	**E50001** LN Lincoln		
E50002 40A Lincoln	**E50002** 40A Lincoln	**E50002** LN Lincoln	**53002** TS Tyseley	
E50003 40A Lincoln	**E50003** 40A Lincoln	**E50003** LN Lincoln		
E50004 40A Lincoln	**E50004** 40A Lincoln	**E50004** LN Lincoln		
E50005 40A Lincoln	**E50005** 40A Lincoln	**E50005** LN Lincoln	**53005** TS Tyseley	
E50006 40A Lincoln	**E50006** 40A Lincoln	**E50006** LN Lincoln	**53006** TS Tyseley	
E50007 40A Lincoln	**E50007** 40A Lincoln	**E50007** LN Lincoln		
E50008 40A Lincoln	**E50008** 40A Lincoln	**E50008** LN Lincoln		
E50009 40A Lincoln	**E50009** 40A Lincoln	**E50009** LN Lincoln		
E50010 40A Lincoln	**E50010** 40A Lincoln	**E50010** LN Lincoln		
E50011 40A Lincoln	**E50011** 40A Lincoln	**E50011** LN Lincoln		
E50012 40A Lincoln	**E50012** 40A Lincoln	**E50012** LN Lincoln		
E50013 40A Lincoln	**E50013** 40A Lincoln	**E50013** LN Lincoln		
E50014 40A Lincoln	**E50014** 40A Lincoln	**E50014** LN Lincoln		
E50015 41A Sheffield Darnall	**E50015** 40A Lincoln	**E50015** LN Lincoln		
E50016 40A Lincoln	**E50016** 40A Lincoln	**E50016** LN Lincoln		
E50017 40A Lincoln	**E50017** 40A Lincoln	**E50017** LN Lincoln		
E50018 40A Lincoln	**E50018** 40A Lincoln	**E50018** LN Lincoln		
E50019 40A Lincoln	**E50019** 40A Lincoln	**E50019** LN Lincoln	**53019** TS Tyseley	
E50020 40A Lincoln	**E50020** 40A Lincoln	**E50020** LN Lincoln	**53020** CA Cambridge	
E50021 40A Lincoln	**E50021** 40A Lincoln	**E50021** LN Lincoln	**53021** TS Tyseley	
E50022 41A Sheffield Darnall	**E50022** 40A Lincoln	**E50022** LN Lincoln		
E50023 40A Lincoln	**E50023** 40A Lincoln	**E50023** LN Lincoln		
E50024 41A Sheffield Darnall	**E50024** 40A Lincoln	**E50024** LN Lincoln		
E50025 40A Lincoln	**E50025** 40A Lincoln	**E50025** LN Lincoln		
E50026 41A Sheffield Darnall	**E50026** 40A Lincoln	**E50026** LN Lincoln		
E50027 41A Sheffield Darnall	**E50027** 40A Lincoln	**E50027** LN Lincoln	**53027** CA Cambridge	
E50028 41A Sheffield Darnall				
E50029 41A Sheffield Darnall	**E50029** 40A Lincoln			
E50030 41A Sheffield Darnall	**E50030** 40A Lincoln	**E50030** LN Lincoln	**53030** TS Tyseley (s)	
E50031 41A Sheffield Darnall	**E50031** 40A Lincoln	**E50031** LN Lincoln		
E50032 40A Lincoln	**E50032** 40A Lincoln	**E50032** LN Lincoln		
E50033 41A Sheffield Darnall	**E50033** 40A Lincoln	**E50033** LN Lincoln		
E50034 41A Sheffield Darnall	**E50034** 40A Lincoln			
E50035 41A Sheffield Darnall	**E50035** 40A Lincoln	**E50035** LN Lincoln		
E50036 41A Sheffield Darnall	**E50036** 40A Lincoln	**E50036** LN Lincoln	**53036** TS Tyseley	
E50037 40A Lincoln	**E50037** 40A Lincoln	**E50037** LN Lincoln		
E50038 40A Lincoln	**E50038** 40A Lincoln	**E50038** LN Lincoln		
E50039 40A Lincoln	**E50039** 40A Lincoln	**E50039** LN Lincoln		
E50040 40A Lincoln	**E50040** 40A Lincoln	**E50040** LN Lincoln		
E50041 40A Lincoln	**E50041** 40A Lincoln	**E50041** LN Lincoln		
E50042 40A Lincoln	**E50042** 40A Lincoln	**E50042** LN Lincoln		
E50043 40A Lincoln	**E50043** 40A Lincoln	**E50043** LN Lincoln		
E50044 40A Lincoln	**E50044** 40A Lincoln	**E50044** LN Lincoln	**53044** TS Tyseley	
E50045 40A Lincoln	**E50045** 40A Lincoln	**E50045** LN Lincoln		
E50046 40A Lincoln	**E50046** 40A Lincoln	**E50046** LN Lincoln	**53046** CA Cambridge	
E50047 40A Lincoln	**E50047** 40A Lincoln	**E50047** LN Lincoln		
E50048 40A Lincoln	**E50048** 40A Lincoln			
E50049 40A Lincoln	**E50049** 40A Lincoln	**E50049** LN Lincoln		
W50050 TYS Tyseley	**M50050** 2A Tyseley	**M50050** TS Tyseley	**53050** TS Tyseley	
W50051 TYS Tyseley	**M50051** 2A Tyseley	**M50051** TS Tyseley		
W50052 TYS Tyseley	**M50052** 2A Tyseley	**M50052** TS Tyseley		
W50053 TYS Tyseley	**M50053** 2A Tyseley	**M50053** TS Tyseley	**53053** TS Tyseley	
W50054 TYS Tyseley	**M50054** 14A Cricklewood	**M50054** CW Cricklewood	**53054** TS Tyseley	
W50055 TYS Tyseley	**M50055** 2A Tyseley	**M50055** TS Tyseley	**53055** TS Tyseley	
W50056 TYS Tyseley	**M50056** 2A Tyseley	**M50056** TS Tyseley	**53056** TS Tyseley	
W50057 TYS Tyseley	**M50057** 2A Tyseley	**M50057** TS Tyseley		
W50058 TYS Tyseley	**M50058** 2A Tyseley	**M50058** TS Tyseley	**53058** TS Tyseley	
W50059 TYS Tyseley	**M50059** 2A Tyseley	**M50059** TS Tyseley		
W50060 TYS Tyseley	**M50060** 14A Cricklewood	**M50060** CW Cricklewood	**53060** TS Tyseley	
W50061 TYS Tyseley	**M50061** 2A Tyseley	**M50061** TS Tyseley	**53061** TS Tyseley	
W50062 TYS Tyseley	**M50062** 2A Tyseley	**M50062** TS Tyseley		
W50063 TYS Tyseley	**M50063** 14A Cricklewood	**M50063** CW Cricklewood		
W50064 TYS Tyseley	**M50064** 2A Tyseley	**M50064** TS Tyseley		

1960	*1970*	*1980*	*1990*	*2000*
W50065 TYS Tyseley	**M50065** 2A Tyseley	**M50065** TS Tyseley		
W50066 TYS Tyseley	**M50066** 2A Tyseley	**M50066** TS Tyseley		
W50067 TYS Tyseley	**M50067** 2A Tyseley	**M50067** TS Tyseley		
W50068 TYS Tyseley	**M50068** 14A Cricklewood	**M50068** CW Cricklewood		
W50069 TYS Tyseley	**M50069** 2A Tyseley	**M50069** TS Tyseley		
W50070 TYS Tyseley	**M50070** 2A Tyseley	**M50070** TS Tyseley		
W50071 TYS Tyseley	**M50071** 14A Cricklewood	**M50071** CW Cricklewood	**53071** TS Tyseley	
W50072 TYS Tyseley	**M50072** 2A Tyseley	**M50072** TS Tyseley		
W50073 TYS Tyseley	**M50073** 2A Tyseley	**M50073** CW Cricklewood	**53073** TS Tyseley	
W50074 TYS Tyseley	**M50074** 14A Cricklewood	**M50074** TS Tyseley		
W50075 TYS Tyseley	**M50075** 14A Cricklewood	**M50075** CW Cricklewood		
W50076 TYS Tyseley	**M50076** 2A Tyseley	**M50076** TS Tyseley		
W50077 TYS Tyseley	**M50077** 2A Tyseley	**M50077** TS Tyseley		
W50078 TYS Tyseley	**M50078** 2A Tyseley	**M50078** TS Tyseley		
W50079 RDG Reading	**M50079** 2A Tyseley	**M50079** TS Tyseley	**53079** TS Tyseley	
W50080 CAT Cardiff Cathays	**W50080** 86A Cardiff Canton	**W50080** CF Cardiff Canton		
W50081 CAT Cardiff Cathays	**W50081** 86A Cardiff Canton	**M50081** TS Tyseley		
W50082 CAT Cardiff Cathays	**W50082** 86A Cardiff Canton	**M50082** TS Tyseley	**53082** TS Tyseley	
W50083 CAT Cardiff Cathays	**W50083** 81D Reading	**W50083** RG Reading	**53083** OO Old Oak Common	
W50084 CAT Cardiff Cathays	**W50084** 86A Cardiff Canton	**W50084** CF Cardiff Canton		
W50085 CDF Cardiff Canton	**M50085** 2A Tyseley			
W50086 CDF Cardiff Canton	**W50086** 86A Cardiff Canton	**W50086** CF Cardiff Canton		
W50087 CDF Cardiff Canton	**W50087** 86A Cardiff Canton	**W50087** CF Cardiff Canton		
W50088 CDF Cardiff Canton	**W50088** 86A Cardiff Canton	**W50088** CF Cardiff Canton		
W50089 CDF Cardiff Canton	**W50089** 86A Cardiff Canton	**W50089** CF Cardiff Canton		
W50090 CDF Cardiff Canton	**W50090** 86A Cardiff Canton	**SC50090** HN Hamilton	**53090** TS Tyseley	
W50091 CDF Cardiff Canton	**W50091** 86A Cardiff Canton	**W50091** CF Cardiff Canton		
W50092 TYS Tyseley	**M50092** 2A Tyseley	**M50092** TS Tyseley	**53092** TS Tyseley	
W50093 TYS Tyseley	**M50093** 2A Tyseley	**M50093** TS Tyseley	**53093** TS Tyseley	
W50094 TYS Tyseley	**M50094** 2A Tyseley	**M50094** TS Tyseley		
W50095 TYS Tyseley	**M50095** 2A Tyseley	**M50095** TS Tyseley		
W50096 TYS Tyseley				
W50097 TYS Tyseley	**M50097** 2A Tyseley	**M50097** TS Tyseley		
W50098 TYS Tyseley	**M50098** 2A Tyseley	**M50098** TS Tyseley		
W50099 TYS Tyseley	**M50099** 2A Tyseley	**M50099** TS Tyseley		
W50100 TYS Tyseley	**M50100** 2A Tyseley	**M50100** TS Tyseley		
W50101 TYS Tyseley	**M50101** 14A Cricklewood	**M50101** CW Cricklewood	**53101** TS Tyseley	
W50102 TYS Tyseley	**M50102** 14A Cricklewood	**M50102** TS Tyseley	**53102** TS Tyseley	
W50103 TYS Tyseley	**M50103** 2A Tyseley	**M50103** TS Tyseley		
W50104 TYS Tyseley	**M50104** 2A Tyseley	**M50104** TS Tyseley		
W50105 TYS Tyseley	**M50105** 2A Tyseley	**M50105** TS Tyseley		
W50106 TYS Tyseley	**M50106** 14A Cricklewood	**M50106** CW Cricklewood	**53106** TS Tyseley	
W50107 TYS Tyseley	**M50107** 2A Tyseley	**M50107** TS Tyseley		
W50108 TYS Tyseley	**M50108** 2A Tyseley	**M50108** TS Tyseley		
W50109 TYS Tyseley	**M50109** 2A Tyseley	**M50109** TS Tyseley		
W50110 TYS Tyseley	**M50110** 2A Tyseley	**M50110** TS Tyseley		
W50111 TYS Tyseley	**M50111** 14A Cricklewood	**M50111** CW Cricklewood		
W50112 TYS Tyseley	**M50112** 2A Tyseley	**M50112** TS Tyseley		
W50113 TYS Tyseley	**M50113** 2A Tyseley	**M50113** TS Tyseley		
W50114 TYS Tyseley	**M50114** 14A Cricklewood	**M50114** CW Cricklewood	**53114** TS Tyseley	
W50115 TYS Tyseley	**M50115** 2A Tyseley	**M50115** TS Tyseley		
W50116 TYS Tyseley	**M50116** 2A Tyseley	**M50116** TS Tyseley	**53116** TS Tyseley	
W50117 TYS Tyseley	**M50117** 2A Tyseley	**M50117** TS Tyseley		
W50118 TYS Tyseley	**M50118** 2A Tyseley	**M50118** TS Tyseley		
W50119 TYS Tyseley	**M50119** 2A Tyseley	**M50119** TS Tyseley		
W50120 TYS Tyseley	**M50120** 2A Tyseley	**M50120** TS Tyseley		
W50121 RDG Reading	**M50121** 2A Tyseley	**M50121** TS Tyseley		
W50122 CAT Cardiff Cathays	**W50122** 86A Cardiff Canton	**W50122** CF Cardiff Canton		
W50123 CAT Cardiff Cathays	**W50123** 86A Cardiff Canton	**M50123** TS Tyseley		
W50124 CAT Cardiff Cathays	**W50124** 86A Cardiff Canton	**M50124** TS Tyseley	**53124** TS Tyseley	
W50125 CAT Cardiff Cathays				
W50126 CAT Cardiff Cathays	**W50126** 86A Cardiff Canton	**W50126** CF Cardiff Canton		
W50127 CDF Cardiff Canton	**M50127** 2A Tyseley	**M50127** TS Tyseley		
W50128 CDF Cardiff Canton	**W50128** 86A Cardiff Canton	**W50128** CF Cardiff Canton		
W50129 CDF Cardiff Canton	**W50129** 86A Cardiff Canton	**W50129** CF Cardiff Canton		
W50130 CDF Cardiff Canton	**W50130** 86A Cardiff Canton	**W50130** CF Cardiff Canton		
W50131 CDF Cardiff Canton	**W50131** 86A Cardiff Canton	**W50131** CF Cardiff Canton		
W50132 CDF Cardiff Canton	**W50132** 86A Cardiff Canton	**SC50132** HN Hamilton	**53132** TS Tyseley	
W50133 CDF Cardiff Canton	**W50133** 86A Cardiff Canton	**W50133** CF Cardiff Canton		
M50134 9A Longsight	**E50134** 55H Neville Hill	**E50134** NL Neville Hill		
M50135 9A Longsight	**E50135** 55H Neville Hill	**E50135** NL Neville Hill		
M50136 9A Longsight	**E50136** 55H Neville Hill	**E50136** NL Neville Hill		
M50137 9A Longsight	**E50137** 55H Neville Hill	**E50137** NL Neville Hill		
E50138 South Gosforth	**E50138** 52J South Gosforth	**SC50138** DE Dundee		
E50139 South Gosforth	**E50139** 52J South Gosforth	**E50139** DN Darlington	**53139** NC Norwich Crown Point	
E50140 South Gosforth	**E50140** 52J South Gosforth	**E50140** NL Neville Hill		
E50141 South Gosforth	**E50141** 52J South Gosforth	**SC50141** DE Dundee		
E50142 South Gosforth	**E50142** 52J South Gosforth	**E50142** DN Darlington		
E50143 South Gosforth	**E50143** 52J South Gosforth	**SC50143** DE Dundee		
E50144 South Gosforth	**E50144** 52J South Gosforth	**SC50144** DE Dundee		
E50145 South Gosforth	**E50145** 52J South Gosforth			
E50146 South Gosforth	**E50146** 52J South Gosforth	**SC50146** DE Dundee	**53146** ED Eastfield	
E50147 South Gosforth	**E50147** 52J South Gosforth	**SC50147** DE Dundee		
E50148 South Gosforth	**E50148** 52J South Gosforth	**SC50148** DE Dundee		
E50149 South Gosforth	**E50149** 52J South Gosforth	**E50149** DN Darlington	**53149** NC Norwich Crown Point	
E50150 South Gosforth	**E50150** 55H Neville Hill	**E50150** DN Darlington		
E50151 South Gosforth	**E50151** 55H Neville Hill	**E50151** DN Darlington		

1960	*1970*	*1980*	*1990*	*2000*
E50152 56G Bradford Hammerton St	**E50152** 32A Norwich	**E50152** HT Heaton		
E50153 56G Bradford Hammerton St	**E50153** 32A Norwich	**E50153** DN Darlington		
E50154 56G Bradford Hammerton St	**E50154** 55H Neville Hill	**E50154** HT Heaton		
E50155 56G Bradford Hammerton St	**E50155** 51A Darlington	**E50155** NL Neville Hill	**53155** OO Old Oak Common	
E50156 56G Bradford Hammerton St	**E50156** 51A Darlington	**E50156** DN Darlington		
E50157 56G Bradford Hammerton St	**E50157** 55H Neville Hill	**E50157** DN Darlington	**53157** LA Laira	
E50158 56G Bradford Hammerton St	**SC50158** 62B Dundee	**SC50158** DE Dundee	**53158** ED Eastfield	
E50159 56G Bradford Hammerton St	**SC50159** 62B Dundee	**SC50159** DE Dundee		
E50160 56G Bradford Hammerton St	**E50160** 55H Neville Hill	**SC50160** DE Dundee	**53160** ED Eastfield	**53160** LO Longsight
E50161 56G Bradford Hammerton St	**E50161** 55H Neville Hill	**E50161** NL Neville Hill		
E50162 56G Bradford Hammerton St	**E50162** 55F Bradford Hammerton St	**E50162** BG Hull Botanic Gardens		
E50163 56G Bradford Hammerton St	**E50163** 55H Neville Hill	**SC50163** DE Dundee	**53163** HA Haymarket	**53163** LO Longsight
E50164 56G Bradford Hammerton St	**E50164** 55H Neville Hill	**E50164** DN Darlington	**53164** NL Neville Hill	**53164** LO Longsight
E50165 56G Bradford Hammerton St	**E50165** 51A Darlington	**E50165** DN Darlington	**53165** LA Laira	
E50166 56G Bradford Hammerton St	**E50166** 51A Darlington	**E50166** BG Hull Botanic Gardens		
E50167 56G Bradford Hammerton St	**E50167** 55H Neville Hill	**E50167** BG Hull Botanic Gardens		
E50168 56G Bradford Hammerton St	**E50168** 55H Neville Hill	**E50168** DN Darlington	**53168** NC Norwich Crown Point	
E50169 56G Bradford Hammerton St	**E50169** 55H Neville Hill	**E50169** NL Neville Hill	**53169** CF Cardiff Canton	
E50170 56G Bradford Hammerton St	**E50170** 52J South Gosforth	**E50170** DN Darlington	**53170** NC Norwich Crown Point	**53170** CK Corkerhill
E50171 56G Bradford Hammerton St	**E50171** 55H Neville Hill	**E50171** DN Darlington	**53171** CH Chester	**53171** CK Corkerhill
E50172 51A Darlington	**E50172** 52J South Gosforth	**SC50172** DE Dundee		
E50174 51A Darlington	**SC50174** 62B Dundee	**SC50174** HA Haymarket		
E50175 51A Darlington	**SC50175** 62B Dundee	**SC50175** HA Haymarket		
E50176 51A Darlington	**E50176** 51A Darlington	**SC50176** DE Dundee	**53176** HA Haymarket	
E50177 51A Darlington	**E50177** 51A Darlington	**E50177** DN Darlington	**53177** NC Norwich Crown Point	**53177** CK Corkerhill
E50178 51A Darlington	**E50178** 51A Darlington	**E50178** DN Darlington		
E50179 51A Darlington	**E50179** 52J South Gosforth	**E50179** DN Darlington		
E50180 51A Darlington	**E50180** 51A Darlington	**E50180** DN Darlington	**53180** NC Norwich Crown Point	
E50181 51A Darlington	**E50181** 51A Darlington	**E50181** DN Darlington	**53181** NC Norwich Crown Point	
E50182 51A Darlington	**E50182** 51A Darlington	**E50182** NR Norwich		
E50183 51A Darlington	**E50183** 51A Darlington	**E50183** DN Darlington		
E50184 51A Darlington	**E50184** 51A Darlington	**SC50184** DE Dundee		
E50185 51A Darlington	**E50185** 51A Darlington	**SC50185** DE Dundee	**53185** ED Eastfield	
E50186 51A Darlington	**SC50186** 66C Hamilton	**SC50186** DE Dundee		
E50187 51A Darlington	**SC50187** 66C Hamilton	**SC50187** DE Dundee		
E50188 51A Darlington	**E50188** 51A Darlington	**E50188** DN Darlington		
E50189 53B Hull Botanic Gardens (o/l)	**E50189** 51A Darlington	**SC50189** DE Dundee	**53189** HA Haymarket	
E50190 51A Darlington	**E50190** 55H Neville Hill			
E50191 51A Darlington	**E50191** 52J South Gosforth	**E50191** NR Norwich		
E50192 51A Darlington	**E50192** 51A Darlington	**SC50192** DE Dundee		
E50193 51A Darlington	**E50193** 51A Darlington	**E50193** NL Neville Hill	**53193** NC Norwich Crown Point	
E50194 51A Darlington	**E50194** 51A Darlington	**SC50194** DE Dundee	**53194** ED Eastfield	
E50195 51A Darlington	**E50195** 55H Neville Hill	**E50195** NR Norwich		
E50196 51A Darlington	**E50196** 52J South Gosforth	**E50196** DN Darlington		
E50197 51A Darlington	**E50197** 55H Neville Hill	**SC50197** DE Dundee		
E50198 51A Darlington	**E50198** 52J South Gosforth	**E50198** NL Neville Hill	**53198** CH Chester	
E50199 51A Darlington	**E50199** 52J South Gosforth	**E50199** HT Heaton		
E50200 51A Darlington	**E50200** 52J South Gosforth	**E50200** DN Darlington	**53200** LA Laira	
E50201 51A Darlington	**E50201** 52J South Gosforth	**E50201** BG Hull Botanic Gardens	**53201** NC Norwich Crown Point	
E50202 51A Darlington	**E50202** 32A Norwich	**E50202** NL Neville Hill	**53202** NC Norwich Crown Point	
E50203 51A Darlington	**M50203** 6A Chester	**M50203** CH Chester	**53203** NL Neville Hill	
E50204 51A Darlington	**E50204** 52J South Gosforth	**E50204** BG Hull Botanic Gardens	**53204** NL Neville Hill	**53204** LO Longsight
E50205 51A Darlington	**E50205** 52J South Gosforth	**E50205** HT Heaton		
E50206 51A Darlington	**M50206** 6A Chester	**M50206** CH Chester		
E50207 51A Darlington	**E50207** 52J South Gosforth	**E50207** NL Neville Hill	**53207** OO Old Oak Common	
E50208 51A Darlington	**M50208** 6A Chester	**M50208** CH Chester	**53208** NC Norwich Crown Point	
E50209 51A Darlington	**SC50209** 62B Dundee	**E50209** HT Heaton		
E50210 South Gosforth	**E50210** 52J South Gosforth	**E50210** HT Heaton		
E50211 51A Darlington (o/l)	**E50211** 51A Darlington	**E50211** HT Heaton	**53211** NL Neville Hill	**53211** LO Longsight
E50212 South Gosforth	**E50212** 51A Darlington	**E50212** DN Darlington	**53212** LA Laira	
E50213 South Gosforth	**E50213** 52J South Gosforth			
E50214 South Gosforth	**E50214** 51A Darlington	**E50214** BG Hull Botanic Gardens		
E50215 South Gosforth	**E50215** 51A Darlington	**E50215** BG Hull Botanic Gardens		
E50216 South Gosforth	**E50216** 52J South Gosforth	**E50216** NL Neville Hill	**53216** LO Longsight	
E50217 South Gosforth	**E50217** 51A Darlington	**E50217** BG Hull Botanic Gardens		
E50218 South Gosforth	**E50218** 52J South Gosforth	**E50218** BG Hull Botanic Gardens		
E50219 South Gosforth	**E50219** 52J South Gosforth	**E50219** DN Darlington		
E50220 South Gosforth	**E50220** 52J South Gosforth	**E50220** HT Heaton		
E50221 South Gosforth	**E50221** 52J South Gosforth	**E50221** DN Darlington		
E50222 South Gosforth	**E50222** 51A Darlington	**M50222** TS Tyseley	**53222** LA Laira	
E50223 South Gosforth	**E50223** 52J South Gosforth	**E50223** DN Darlington	**53223** LA Laira	
E50224 South Gosforth	**E50224** 51A Darlington	**E50224** NL Neville Hill	**53224** CH Chester	
E50225 South Gosforth	**E50225** 52J South Gosforth	**E50225** HT Heaton		
E50226 South Gosforth	**E50226** 52J South Gosforth	**E50226** BG Hull Botanic Gardens		
E50227 South Gosforth	**E50227** 52J South Gosforth	**E50227** NL Neville Hill		
E50228 South Gosforth	**M50228** 6A Chester	**M50228** CH Chester	**53228** NC Norwich Crown Point	**53228** LO Longsight
E50229 South Gosforth	**E50229** 52J South Gosforth	**E50229** HT Heaton		
E50230 South Gosforth	**E50230** 52J South Gosforth	**E50230** BG Hull Botanic Gardens		
E50231 South Gosforth	**E50231** 52J South Gosforth	**E50231** HT Heaton	**53231** NC Norwich Crown Point	
E50232 South Gosforth	**E50232** 52J South Gosforth	**E50232** HT Heaton		
E50233 South Gosforth	**E50233** 52J South Gosforth	**E50233** DN Darlington		
E50234 South Gosforth	**E50234** 52J South Gosforth	**SC50234** DE Dundee		
E50235 South Gosforth	**E50235** 55H Neville Hill	**E50235** DN Darlington	**53235** NH Newton Heath	
E50236 South Gosforth				
E50237 South Gosforth	**E50237** 55H Neville Hill	**M50237** TS Tyseley		
E50238 51A Darlington	**E50238** 52J South Gosforth	**E50238** DN Darlington	**53238** NC Norwich Crown Point	

1960	1970	1980	1990	2000
E50239 51A Darlington	**E50239** 52J South Gosforth	**SC50239** DE Dundee	**53239** HA Haymarket	
E50240 South Gosforth	**E50240** 55H Neville Hill	**E50240** DN Darlington		
E50241 South Gosforth	**E50241** 55H Neville Hill	**SC50241** DE Dundee	**53241** ED Eastfield	
E50242 South Gosforth	**E50242** 55H Neville Hill	**SC50242** DE Dundee	**53242** NL Neville Hill	
E50243 South Gosforth	**E50243** 52J South Gosforth	**SC50243** DE Dundee	**53243** HA Haymarket	
E50244 South Gosforth	**E50244** 55H Neville Hill	**E50244** DN Darlington	**53244** CH Chester	
E50245 South Gosforth	**E50245** 55H Neville Hill	**SC50245** HA Haymarket	**53245** NL Neville Hill	
E50246 South Gosforth	**E50246** 51A Darlington	**E50246** DN Darlington		
E50247 South Gosforth	**E50247** 52J South Gosforth	**E50247** HT Heaton	**53247** LA Laira	
E50248 South Gosforth	**E50248** 52J South Gosforth	**E50248** DN Darlington	**53248** LA Laira	
E50249 51A Darlington	**E50249** 51A Darlington			
E50250 51A Darlington	**E50250** 51A Darlington	**E50250** DN Darlington	**53250** NL Neville Hill	
E50251 51A Darlington	**E50251** 51A Darlington	**E50251** HT Heaton		
E50252 51A Darlington	**E50252** 51A Darlington	**E50252** DN Darlington		
E50253 51A Darlington	**E50253** 52J South Gosforth	**E50253** HT Heaton	**53253** LO Longsight	**53253** CK Corkerhill
E50254 51A Darlington	**SC50254** 66C Hamilton	**SC50254** DE Dundee		
E50255 51A Darlington	**E50255** 51A Darlington	**E50255** DN Darlington		
E50256 51A Darlington	**E50256** 55H Neville Hill	**E50256** DN Darlington	**53256** LA Laira	**53256** LO Longsight
E50257 51A Darlington	**E50257** 52J South Gosforth	**E50257** NL Neville Hill		
E50258 51A Darlington	**E50258** 52J South Gosforth	**E50258** BG Hull Botanic Gardens		
E50259 51A Darlington	**E50259** 51A Darlington	**E50259** DN Darlington		
E50260 51A Darlington	**E50260** 51A Darlington	**SC50260** DE Dundee	**53260** HA Haymarket	
E50261 51A Darlington	**E50261** 51A Darlington	**E50261** NR Norwich		
E50262 51A Darlington	**E50262** 51A Darlington	**E50262** DN Darlington		
E50263 51A Darlington	**E50263** 51A Darlington	**E50263** DN Darlington		
E50264 51A Darlington	**SC50264** 66C Hamilton	**SC50264** DE Dundee		
E50265 51A Darlington	**E50265** 51A Darlington	**E50265** DN Darlington	**53265** RG Reading	
E50266 51A Darlington	**E50266** 55H Neville Hill	**E50266** GF South Gosforth	**53266** NC Norwich Crown Point	**53266** CK Corkerhill
E50267 51A Darlington	**E50267** 52J South Gosforth	**E50267** NL Neville Hill	**53267** NC Norwich Crown Point	
E50268 51A Darlington	**E50268** 52J South Gosforth	**SC50268** DE Dundee	**53268** NL Neville Hill	**53268** CK Corkerhill
E50269 51A Darlington	**SC50269** 64H Leith Central	**SC50269** DE Dundee	**53269** CH Chester	**53269** LO Longsight
E50270 56G Bradford Hammerton St	**E50270** 30A Stratford	**E50270** NL Neville Hill		
E50271 56G Bradford Hammerton St	**E50271** 30A Stratford	**E50271** NL Neville Hill		
E50272 56G Bradford Hammerton St	**E50272** 30A Stratford	**E50272** NL Neville Hill		
E50273 56G Bradford Hammerton St	**E50273** 55H Neville Hill	**E50273** NL Neville Hill		
E50274 56G Bradford Hammerton St	**E50274** 55H Neville Hill	**E50274** NL Neville Hill		
E50275 56G Bradford Hammerton St	**E50275** 55H Neville Hill	**E50275** NL Neville Hill		
E50276 56G Bradford Hammerton St	**E50276** 55H Neville Hill	**E50276** NL Neville Hill		
E50277 56G Bradford Hammerton St	**E50277** 55H Neville Hill	**E50277** NL Neville Hill		
E50278 56G Bradford Hammerton St	**E50278** 55H Neville Hill	**E50278** NL Neville Hill		
E50279 56G Bradford Hammerton St	**E50279** 55H Neville Hill	**E50279** NL Neville Hill		
E50280 56G Bradford Hammerton St	**E50280** 30A Stratford	**E50280** NL Neville Hill		
E50281 56G Bradford Hammerton St	**E50281** 30A Stratford	**E50281** NL Neville Hill		
E50282 56G Bradford Hammerton St	**E50282** 30A Stratford	**E50282** NL Neville Hill		
E50283 56G Bradford Hammerton St	**E50283** 55H Neville Hill	**E50283** NL Neville Hill		
E50284 56G Bradford Hammerton St	**E50284** 55H Neville Hill	**E50284** NL Neville Hill		
E50285 56G Bradford Hammerton St				
E50286 56G Bradford Hammerton St	**E50286** 55H Neville Hill	**E50286** NL Neville Hill		
E50287 56G Bradford Hammerton St	**E50287** 55H Neville Hill	**E50287** NL Neville Hill		
E50288 56G Bradford Hammerton St	**E50288** 55H Neville Hill	**E50288** NL Neville Hill		
E50289 56G Bradford Hammerton St	**E50289** 55H Neville Hill	**E50289** NL Neville Hill		
E50290 51A Darlington	**SC50290** 62B Dundee	**SC50290** DE Dundee		
E50291 51A Darlington	**SC50291** 62B Dundee	**E50291** HT Heaton	**53291** NL Neville Hill	
E50292 51A Darlington	**SC50292** 62B Dundee	**SC50292** DE Dundee		
E50293 51A Darlington	**E50293** 51A Darlington	**E50293** BG Hull Botanic Gardens	**53293** NC Norwich Crown Point	
E50294 51A Darlington	**E50294** 51A Darlington	**E50294** HT Heaton	**53294** LO Longsight	
E50295 51A Darlington	**E50295** 51A Darlington	**E50295** DN Darlington		
E50296 51A Darlington	**E50296** 52J South Gosforth	**E50296** NL Neville Hill	**53296** OO Old Oak Common	
M50303 3E Monument Lane	**M50303** 2A Tyseley	**M50303** TS Tyseley		
M50304 3E Monument Lane	**M50304** 2A Tyseley	**W50304** BR Bristol Bath Road		
M50305 3E Monument Lane	**M50305** 2A Tyseley	**M50305** TS Tyseley	**53305** NC Norwich Crown Point	
M50306 3E Monument Lane	**M50306** 2A Tyseley	**M50306** TS Tyseley		
M50307 3E Monument Lane	**M50307** 2A Tyseley	**M50307** TS Tyseley		
M50308 3E Monument Lane	**M50308** 2A Tyseley	**M50308** TS Tyseley	**53308** RG Reading	
M50309 3E Monument Lane	**M50309** 2A Tyseley	**M50309** TS Tyseley		
M50310 3E Monument Lane	**M50310** 2A Tyseley	**M50310** TS Tyseley	**53310** RG Reading	
M50311 3E Monument Lane	**M50311** 2A Tyseley	**M50311** TS Tyseley	**53311** RG Reading	**53311** LO Longsight
M50312 3E Monument Lane	**M50312** 2A Tyseley	**M50312** TS Tyseley	**53312** RG Reading	
M50313 3E Monument Lane	**M50313** 2A Tyseley	**M50313** TS Tyseley		
M50314 3E Monument Lane	**M50314** 2A Tyseley	**M50314** TS Tyseley	**53314** RG Reading	
M50315 3E Monument Lane	**M50315** 6A Chester	**M50315** TS Tyseley	**53315** LA Laira	
M50316 3E Monument Lane	**M50316** 6A Chester	**M50316** CH Chester		
M50317 3E Monument Lane	**M50317** 6A Chester	**M50317** TS Tyseley		
M50318 3E Monument Lane	**M50318** 6A Chester	**M50318** TS Tyseley		
M50319 18A Toton (o/l)	**M50319** 6A Chester	**W50319** BR Bristol Bath Road		
M50320 3E Monument Lane	**M50320** 6A Chester	**M50320** CH Chester		
M50321 3E Monument Lane	**M50321** 2A Tyseley	**M50321** TS Tyseley	**53321** NC Norwich Crown Point	
M50322 3E Monument Lane	**M50322** 2A Tyseley	**M50322** TS Tyseley	**53322** RG Reading	**53322** LO Longsight
M50323 3E Monument Lane	**M50323** 2A Tyseley	**M50323** TS Tyseley		
M50324 3E Monument Lane	**M50324** 2A Tyseley	**M50324** TS Tyseley		
M50325 3E Monument Lane	**M50325** 2A Tyseley	**M50325** TS Tyseley		
M50326 3E Monument Lane	**M50326** 2A Tyseley	**M50326** TS Tyseley	**53326** RG Reading	
M50327 3E Monument Lane	**M50327** 2A Tyseley	**M50327** TS Tyseley	**53327** RG Reading	
M50328 3E Monument Lane	**M50328** 2A Tyseley	**M50328** TS Tyseley		
M50329 3E Monument Lane	**M50329** 2A Tyseley	**W50329** BR Bristol Bath Road		
M50330 3E Monument Lane	**M50330** 6A Chester	**M50330** CH Chester	**53330** LA Laira	
M50331 3E Monument Lane	**M50331** 2A Tyseley	**M50331** TS Tyseley	**53331** RG Reading	

1960	1970	1980	1990	2000
M50332 3E Monument Lane	**M50332** 2A Tyseley	**M50332** TS Tyseley	**53332** RG Reading	
M50333 3E Monument Lane	**M50333** 6A Chester	**M50333** TS Tyseley	**53333** RG Reading	
M50334 3E Monument Lane	**M50334** 6A Chester	**M50334** CH Chester		
M50335 3E Monument Lane	**M50335** 2A Tyseley	**W50335** BR Bristol Bath Road		
M50336 3E Monument Lane	**M50336** 6A Chester	**M50336** TS Tyseley		
M50337 18A Toton (o/l)	**M50337** 6A Chester	**M50337** TS Tyseley		
M50338 3E Monument Lane	**M50338** 2A Tyseley	**M50338** TS Tyseley	**53338** CH Chester	
SC50339 64H Leith Central	**E50339** 31A Cambridge			
SC50340 64H Leith Central	**SC50340** 64H Leith Central	**M50340** LO Longsight		
SC50341 64H Leith Central	**E50341** 31A Cambridge			
SC50342 64H Leith Central	**SC50342** 64H Leith Central	**M50342** LO Longsight		
SC50343 66C Hamilton (o/l)	**SC50343** 64H Leith Central	**M50343** TS Tyseley		
SC50344 64H Leith Central	**E50344** 31A Cambridge			
SC50345 64H Leith Central	**SC50345** 64H Leith Central			
SC50346 64H Leith Central	**E50346** 31A Cambridge	**E50346** NR Norwich		
SC50347 64H Leith Central	**E50347** 31A Cambridge			
M50348 3C Walsall Rycroft	**M50348** 9A Longsight	**M50348** LO Longsight		
M50349 3C Walsall Rycroft	**M50349** 9A Longsight	**M50349** LO Longsight		
M50350 3C Walsall Rycroft	**M50350** 9A Longsight	**M50350** LO Longsight		
M50351 3C Walsall Rycroft	**M50351** 9A Longsight	**M50351** LO Longsight		
M50352 2D Coventry (o/l)	**M50352** 9A Longsight	**M50352** LO Longsight		
M50353 3C Walsall Rycroft	**M50353** 9A Longsight	**M50353** LO Longsight		
M50354 3C Walsall Rycroft	**M50354** 9A Longsight	**M50354** LO Longsight		
M50355 3C Walsall Rycroft	**M50355** 9A Longsight	**M50355** LO Longsight		
M50356 3C Walsall Rycroft	**M50356** 9A Longsight	**M50356** LO Longsight		
M50357 3C Walsall Rycroft	**M50357** 9A Longsight			
M50358 9A Longsight	**M50358** 9A Longsight	**M50358** LO Longsight		
E50359 53B Hull Botanic Gardens	**E50359** 31A Cambridge	**E50359** SF Stratford		
E50360 53B Hull Botanic Gardens	**E50360** 34G Finsbury Park	**E50360** SF Stratford		
E50361 53B Hull Botanic Gardens	**E50361** 34G Finsbury Park	**E50361** SF Stratford		
E50362 53B Hull Botanic Gardens	**E50362** 34G Finsbury Park	**E50362** SF Stratford		
E50363 53B Hull Botanic Gardens	**E50363** 32A Norwich	**E50363** SF Stratford		
E50364 53B Hull Botanic Gardens	**E50364** 32A Norwich	**E50364** SF Stratford		
E50365 53B Hull Botanic Gardens	**E50365** 32A Norwich	**E50365** SF Stratford		
E50366 53B Hull Botanic Gardens	**E50366** 32A Norwich	**E50366** SF Stratford		
E50367 53B Hull Botanic Gardens	**E50367** 32A Norwich	**E50367** SF Stratford		
E50368 53B Hull Botanic Gardens	**E50368** 32A Norwich	**E50368** SF Stratford		
E50369 53B Hull Botanic Gardens	**E50369** 50C Hull Botanic Gardens	**E50369** SF Stratford		
E50370 53B Hull Botanic Gardens	**E50370** 50C Hull Botanic Gardens	**E50370** SF Stratford		
E50371 53B Hull Botanic Gardens	**E50371** 50C Hull Botanic Gardens	**E50371** NR Norwich		
E50372 53B Hull Botanic Gardens	**E50372** 50C Hull Botanic Gardens	**M50372** NH Newton Heath		
E50373 53B Hull Botanic Gardens	**E50373** 50C Hull Botanic Gardens	**E50373** HT Heaton		
E50374 53B Hull Botanic Gardens	**E50374** 50C Hull Botanic Gardens	**M50374** NH Newton Heath		
E50375 53B Hull Botanic Gardens	**E50375** 32A Norwich	**E50375** HT Heaton		
E50376 53B Hull Botanic Gardens	**E50376** 34G Finsbury Park	**E50376** NR Norwich		
E50377 53B Hull Botanic Gardens	**E50377** 34G Finsbury Park	**E50377** NR Norwich		
E50378 53B Hull Botanic Gardens	**E50378** 32A Norwich	**E50378** BG Hull Botanic Gardens		
E50379 53B Hull Botanic Gardens	**E50379** 50C Hull Botanic Gardens	**E50379** BG Hull Botanic Gardens		
E50380 53B Hull Botanic Gardens	**E50380** 50C Hull Botanic Gardens	**E50380** BG Hull Botanic Gardens		
E50381 53B Hull Botanic Gardens	**E50381** 50C Hull Botanic Gardens	**E50381** BG Hull Botanic Gardens		
E50382 53B Hull Botanic Gardens	**E50382** 50C Hull Botanic Gardens	**E50382** NR Norwich		
E50383 53B Hull Botanic Gardens	**E50383** 34G Finsbury Park	**E50383** NR Norwich		
E50384 53B Hull Botanic Gardens	**E50384** 34G Finsbury Park	**E50384** NR Norwich		
E50385 53B Hull Botanic Gardens	**E50385** 50C Hull Botanic Gardens	**M50385** NH Newton Heath		
E50386 53B Hull Botanic Gardens	**E50386** 50C Hull Botanic Gardens	**E50386** HT Heaton		
E50387 53B Hull Botanic Gardens	**E50387** 50C Hull Botanic Gardens	**M50387** BY Bletchley		
E50388 53B Hull Botanic Gardens	**E50388** 50C Hull Botanic Gardens	**M50388** BY Bletchley		
E50389 53B Hull Botanic Gardens	**E50389** 50C Hull Botanic Gardens	**M50389** NH Newton Heath		
M50390 18A Toton	**M50390** 1E Bletchley	**M50390** BY Bletchley		
M50391 18A Toton	**M50391** 1E Bletchley	**M50391** BY Bletchley		
M50392 18A Toton	**M50392** 1E Bletchley	**M50392** BY Bletchley		
M50393 18A Toton	**M50393** 1E Bletchley	**M50393** BY Bletchley		
M50394 18A Toton	**M50394** 1E Bletchley			
M50395 3C Walsall Rycroft	**M50395** 6A Chester	**M50395** CH Chester		
M50396 3C Walsall Rycroft	**M50396** 6A Chester			
M50397 3C Walsall Rycroft	**M50397** 6A Chester			
M50398 3C Walsall Rycroft	**M50398** 6A Chester	**M50398** CH Chester		
M50399 3C Walsall Rycroft	**M50399** 6A Chester	**M50399** CH Chester		
M50400 3C Walsall Rycroft	**M50400** 6A Chester	**M50400** CH Chester		
M50401 6G Llandudno Junction	**M50401** 6A Chester	**M50401** CH Chester		
M50402 3C Walsall Rycroft	**M50402** 6A Chester	**M50402** CH Chester		
M50403 3C Walsall Rycroft	**M50403** 6A Chester	**M50403** CH Chester		
M50404 3C Walsall Rycroft	**M50404** 6A Chester	**M50404** CH Chester		
M50405 3C Walsall Rycroft	**M50405** 6A Chester	**M50405** CH Chester		
M50406 3C Walsall Rycroft	**M50406** 6A Chester			
M50407 3C Walsall Rycroft	**M50407** 6A Chester			
M50408 3C Walsall Rycroft	**M50408** 6A Chester	**M50408** CH Chester		
M50409 3C Walsall Rycroft	**M50409** 6A Chester	**M50409** CH Chester		
M50410 3C Walsall Rycroft	**M50410** 6A Chester			
M50411 1C Watford Junction	**M50411** 6A Chester			
M50412 1C Watford Junction	**M50412** 6A Chester			
M50413 1C Watford Junction	**M50413** 6A Chester			
M50414 1C Watford Junction	**M50414** 6A Chester			
E50415 31A Cambridge				
E50416 31A Cambridge				
E50417 31A Cambridge	**E50417** 31A Cambridge			
E50418 31A Cambridge	**E50418** 31A Cambridge			

1960	1970	1980	1990	2000
E50419 31A Cambridge				
M50420 9D Buxton	**M50420** 9L Buxton	**M50420** BX Buxton		
M50421 9D Buxton	**M50421** 9L Buxton	**M50421** BX Buxton		
M50422 9D Buxton	**M50422** 9L Buxton	**M50422** BX Buxton		
M50423 9A Longsight	**M50423** 9L Buxton	**M50423** BX Buxton		
M50424 9D Buxton	**M50424** 9L Buxton	**M50424** BX Buxton		
M50425 9D Buxton	**M50425** 9L Buxton	**M50425** BX Buxton		
M50426 9D Buxton	**M50426** 9L Buxton	**M50426** BX Buxton		
M50427 9A Longsight	**M50427** 9L Buxton	**M50427** BX Buxton		
M50428 9D Buxton	**M50428** 9L Buxton	**M50428** BX Buxton		
M50429 9D Buxton	**M50429** 9L Buxton	**M50429** BX Buxton	**53429** OO Old Oak Common	
M50430 9D Buxton	**M50430** 9L Buxton	**M50430** BX Buxton		
M50431 9D Buxton	**M50431** 9L Buxton	**M50431** BX Buxton	**53431** CH Chester	
M50432 9D Buxton	**M50432** 9L Buxton	**M50432** BX Buxton		
M50433 9A Longsight	**M50433** 9L Buxton	**M50433** BX Buxton		
M50434 9A Longsight	**M50434** 9L Buxton	**M50434** BX Buxton		
M50435 9A Longsight	**M50435** 9L Buxton	**M50435** BX Buxton		
M50436 9A Longsight	**M50436** 9L Buxton	**M50436** BX Buxton		
M50437 9A Longsight	**M50437** 9D Newton Heath	**M50437** BX Buxton	**53437** OO Old Oak Common	
M50438 9A Longsight	**M50438** 9D Newton Heath			
M50439 9A Longsight	**M50439** 9D Newton Heath	**M50439** BX Buxton	**53439** CH Chester	
M50440 9A Longsight	**M50440** 9D Newton Heath	**M50440** BX Buxton		
M50441 9A Longsight				
M50442 9A Longsight	**M50442** 9D Newton Heath	**M50442** NH Newton Heath	**53442** NH Newton Heath	
M50443 9A Longsight	**M50443** 9D Newton Heath	**M50443** NH Newton Heath		
M50444 9A Longsight	**M50444** 16C Derby Etches Park	**M50444** DY Derby Etches Park		
M50445 9A Longsight	**M50445** 16C Derby Etches Park	**M50445** DY Derby Etches Park		
M50446 9A Longsight	**M50446** 16C Derby Etches Park	**M50446** NH Newton Heath		
M50447 5D Stoke-on-Trent	**M50447** 16C Derby Etches Park	**M50447** DY Derby Etches Park	**53447** CH Chester	
M50448 5D Stoke-on-Trent	**M50448** 16C Derby Etches Park	**M50448** DY Derby Etches Park		
M50449 5D Stoke-on-Trent	**M50449** 16C Derby Etches Park	**M50449** DY Derby Etches Park		
M50450 5D Stoke-on-Trent	**M50450** 16C Derby Etches Park	**M50450** DY Derby Etches Park		
M50451 5D Stoke-on-Trent	**M50451** 16C Derby Etches Park	**M50451** NH Newton Heath	**53451** CH Chester	
M50452 5D Stoke-on-Trent	**M50452** 6A Chester	**M50452** NH Newton Heath		
M50453 5D Stoke-on-Trent	**M50453** 9A Longsight	**M50453** NH Newton Heath		
M50454 5D Stoke-on-Trent	**M50454** 9A Longsight	**M50454** BX Buxton	**53454** NH Newton Heath	
M50455 5D Stoke-on-Trent	**M50455** 9A Longsight	**M50455** BX Buxton	**53455** OO Old Oak Common	
M50456 5D Stoke-on-Trent	**M50456** 9A Longsight	**M50456** NH Newton Heath		
M50457 5D Stoke-on-Trent	**M50457** 9A Longsight	**M50457** NH Newton Heath		
M50458 5D Stoke-on-Trent	**M50458** 9A Longsight	**M50458** NH Newton Heath		
M50459 5D Stoke-on-Trent	**M50459** 9A Longsight	**M50459** NH Newton Heath		
M50460 5D Stoke-on-Trent	**M50460** 9A Longsight	**M50460** NH Newton Heath		
M50461 5D Stoke-on-Trent	**M50461** 9D Newton Heath	**M50461** NH Newton Heath		
M50462 5B Crewe South	**E50462** 55H Neville Hill	**M50462** NH Newton Heath		
M50463 5B Crewe South	**M50463** 9A Longsight	**M50463** NH Newton Heath		
M50464 5B Crewe South	**M50464** 9A Longsight	**M50464** NH Newton Heath		
M50465 5B Crewe South	**M50465** 9A Longsight	**M50465** NH Newton Heath		
M50466 5B Crewe South	**M50466** 9A Longsight	**M50466** NH Newton Heath	**53466** NH Newton Heath	
M50467 5B Crewe South	**M50467** 9A Longsight	**M50467** NH Newton Heath		
M50468 5B Crewe South	**M50468** 9A Longsight	**M50468** NH Newton Heath		
M50469 5B Crewe South	**M50469** 9A Longsight	**M50469** NH Newton Heath		
M50470 5B Crewe South	**M50470** 9D Newton Heath	**M50470** NH Newton Heath	**53470** OO Old Oak Common	
M50471 5B Crewe South	**M50471** 9D Newton Heath	**M50471** NH Newton Heath		
M50472 5B Crewe South	**M50472** 9D Newton Heath	**M50472** NH Newton Heath		
M50473 5B Crewe South	**M50473** 9D Newton Heath	**M50473** NH Newton Heath		
M50474 5B Crewe South	**M50474** 9D Newton Heath	**M50474** NH Newton Heath		
M50475 18A Toton	**M50475** 9D Newton Heath	**M50475** NH Newton Heath		
M50476 18A Toton	**M50476** 9D Newton Heath	**M50476** NH Newton Heath		
M50477 18A Toton	**M50477** 9D Newton Heath	**M50477** NH Newton Heath	**53477** OO Old Oak Common	
M50478 18A Toton	**M50478** 9D Newton Heath	**M50478** NH Newton Heath		
M50479 18A Toton	**M50479** 9D Newton Heath	**M50479** NH Newton Heath	**53479** OO Old Oak Common	
M50480 9D Buxton	**M50480** 9L Buxton	**M50480** BX Buxton		
M50481 9D Buxton	**M50481** 9L Buxton	**M50481** BX Buxton		
M50482 9D Buxton	**M50482** 9L Buxton	**M50482** BX Buxton		
M50483 9D Buxton	**M50483** 9L Buxton	**M50483** BX Buxton		
M50484 9D Buxton	**M50484** 9L Buxton	**M50484** BX Buxton		
M50485 9A Longsight	**M50485** 9L Buxton	**M50485** BX Buxton		
M50486 9A Longsight	**M50486** 9L Buxton			
M50487 9A Longsight	**M50487** 9L Buxton	**M50487** BX Buxton		
M50488 9A Longsight	**M50488** 9L Buxton	**M50488** BX Buxton		
M50489 9A Longsight	**M50489** 9D Newton Heath			
M50490 9A Longsight	**M50490** 9D Newton Heath	**M50490** BX Buxton		
M50491 9A Longsight	**M50491** 9D Newton Heath	**M50491** BX Buxton		
M50492 9A Longsight	**M50492** 9D Newton Heath	**M50492** BX Buxton		
M50493 9A Longsight	**M50493** 9D Newton Heath	**M50493** NH Newton Heath		
M50494 9A Longsight	**M50494** 9D Newton Heath	**M50494** NH Newton Heath	**53494** CH Chester	
M50495 9A Longsight	**M50495** 16C Derby Etches Park			
M50496 9A Longsight	**M50496** 16C Derby Etches Park	**M50496** DY Derby Etches Park		
M50497 9A Longsight	**M50497** 9D Newton Heath	**M50497** DY Derby Etches Park		
M50498 9A Longsight	**M50498** 16C Derby Etches Park	**M50498** NH Newton Heath		
M50499 5D Stoke-on-Trent	**M50499** 16C Derby Etches Park	**M50499** NH Newton Heath		
M50500 5D Stoke-on-Trent	**M50500** 16C Derby Etches Park	**M50500** DY Derby Etches Park		
M50501 5D Stoke-on-Trent	**M50501** 16C Derby Etches Park	**M50501** DY Derby Etches Park		
M50502 5D Stoke-on-Trent	**M50502** 16C Derby Etches Park	**M50502** DY Derby Etches Park		
M50503 5D Stoke-on-Trent	**M50503** 16C Derby Etches Park	**M50503** DY Derby Etches Park		
M50504 5D Stoke-on-Trent	**M50504** 9D Newton Heath	**M50504** NH Newton Heath		
M50505 5D Stoke-on-Trent	**M50505** 9D Newton Heath	**M50505** NH Newton Heath		

1960	1970	1980	1990	2000
M50506 5D Stoke-on-Trent	**M50506** 9D Newton Heath	**M50506** BX Buxton		
M50507 5D Stoke-on-Trent	**M50507** 9D Newton Heath	**M50507** BX Buxton		
M50508 5D Stoke-on-Trent	**M50508** 9D Newton Heath	**M50508** NH Newton Heath		
M50509 5D Stoke-on-Trent	**M50509** 9D Newton Heath	**M50509** NH Newton Heath		
M50510 5D Stoke-on-Trent	**M50510** 9D Newton Heath	**M50510** NH Newton Heath		
M50511 5D Stoke-on-Trent	**M50511** 9D Newton Heath	**M50511** NH Newton Heath		
M50512 5D Stoke-on-Trent	**M50512** 9D Newton Heath	**M50512** NH Newton Heath	**53512** CH Chester	
M50513 5D Stoke-on-Trent				
M50514 5B Crewe South	**M50514** 9D Newton Heath	**M50514** NH Newton Heath		
M50515 5B Crewe South	**M50515** 9D Newton Heath	**M50515** NH Newton Heath		
M50516 5B Crewe South	**M50516** 9D Newton Heath	**M50516** NH Newton Heath	**53516** CH Chester	
M50517 5B Crewe South	**M50517** 9D Newton Heath	**M50517** NH Newton Heath	**53517** CH Chester	
M50518 5B Crewe South	**M50518** 9D Newton Heath	**M50518** NH Newton Heath		
M50519 5B Crewe South	**M50519** 9D Newton Heath	**M50519** NH Newton Heath		
M50520 5B Crewe South	**M50520** 9D Newton Heath	**M50520** NH Newton Heath		
M50521 5B Crewe South	**M50521** 9D Newton Heath	**M50521** NH Newton Heath		
M50522 5B Crewe South	**M50522** 9D Newton Heath	**M50522** NH Newton Heath		
M50523 5B Crewe South	**M50523** 9D Newton Heath	**M50523** NH Newton Heath		
M50524 5B Crewe South	**M50524** 9D Newton Heath	**M50524** NH Newton Heath		
M50525 5B Crewe South	**M50525** 9D Newton Heath	**M50525** NH Newton Heath		
M50526 5B Crewe South	**M50526** 9D Newton Heath	**M50526** NH Newton Heath		
M50527 18A Toton	**M50527** 9D Newton Heath	**M50527** NH Newton Heath		
M50528 18A Toton	**M50528** 9D Newton Heath	**M50528** NH Newton Heath	**53528** NH Newton Heath	
M50529 18A Toton	**M50529** 9D Newton Heath	**M50529** NH Newton Heath	**53529** CH Chester	
M50530 18A Toton	**M50530** 9D Newton Heath	**M50530** NH Newton Heath		
M50531 18A Toton	**M50531** 9D Newton Heath	**M50531** NH Newton Heath	**53531** CH Chester	
M50532 5D Stoke-on-Trent	**M50532** 9A Longsight	**M50532** LO Longsight		
M50533 5D Stoke-on-Trent	**M50533** 9A Longsight	**M50533** LO Longsight		
M50534 5D Stoke-on-Trent	**M50534** 9A Longsight	**M50534** LO Longsight	**53534** CH Chester	
M50535 5D Stoke-on-Trent	**M50535** 9A Longsight	**M50535** LO Longsight		
M50536 5B Crewe South	**M50536** 9A Longsight	**M50536** LO Longsight	**53536** NH Newton Heath	
M50537 5B Crewe South	**M50537** 9A Longsight	**M50537** LO Longsight		
M50538 5B Crewe South	**M50538** 9A Longsight	**M50538** LO Longsight		
M50539 5B Crewe South	**M50539** 9A Longsight	**M50539** LO Longsight	**53539** OO Old Oak Common	
M50540 5B Crewe South	**M50540** 9A Longsight	**M50540** LO Longsight	**53540** OO Old Oak Common	
M50541 5B Crewe South	**M50541** 9A Longsight	**M50541** LO Longsight		
E50542 51A Darlington	**E50542** 55H Neville Hill	**E50542** GF South Gosforth		
E50543 South Gosforth	**E50543** 30A Stratford	**E50543** GF South Gosforth		
E50544 51A Darlington	**E50544** 52J South Gosforth	**E50544** NL Neville Hill		
E50545 South Gosforth	**E50545** 55H Neville Hill	**E50545** NL Neville Hill		
E50546 50B Neville Hill	**E50546** 55H Neville Hill	**E50546** GF South Gosforth		
E50547 50B Neville Hill	**E50547** 55H Neville Hill	**E50547** NL Neville Hill		
E50548 50B Neville Hill	**E50548** 52J South Gosforth	**E50548** GF South Gosforth		
E50549 50B Neville Hill	**E50549** 55H Neville Hill	**E50549** NL Neville Hill		
E50550 53B Hull Botanic Gardens	**E50550** 50C Hull Botanic Gardens	**E50550** NL Neville Hill		
E50551 53B Hull Botanic Gardens	**E50551** 55H Neville Hill	**E50551** NR Norwich		
E50552 50A York	**E50552** 55H Neville Hill			
E50553 53B Hull Botanic Gardens	**E50553** 55H Neville Hill	**E50553** NL Neville Hill		
E50554 53B Hull Botanic Gardens	**E50554** 55H Neville Hill	**E50554** NL Neville Hill		
E50555 South Gosforth	**E50555** 30A Stratford	**E50555** GF South Gosforth		
E50556 South Gosforth	**E50556** 55H Neville Hill	**E50556** GF South Gosforth		
E50557 50B Neville Hill	**E50557** 50C Hull Botanic Gardens	**E50557** NR Norwich		
E50558 53B Hull Botanic Gardens				
E50559 53B Hull Botanic Gardens	**E50559** 50C Hull Botanic Gardens			
E50560 53B Hull Botanic Gardens	**E50560** 50C Hull Botanic Gardens	**E50560** NR Norwich		
E50561 53B Hull Botanic Gardens	**E50561** 50C Hull Botanic Gardens	**E50561** NR Norwich		
E50562 53B Hull Botanic Gardens	**E50562** 55H Neville Hill	**E50562** NR Norwich		
E50563 51A Darlington	**E50563** 55H Neville Hill	**E50563** NL Neville Hill		
E50564 South Gosforth	**E50564** 50C Hull Botanic Gardens	**E50564** GF South Gosforth		
E50565 51A Darlington	**E50565** 55H Neville Hill	**E50565** GF South Gosforth		
E50566 South Gosforth	**E50566** 55H Neville Hill	**E50566** NL Neville Hill		
E50567 50B Neville Hill	**E50567** 55H Neville Hill	**E50567** NL Neville Hill		
E50568 50B Neville Hill	**E50568** 55H Neville Hill	**E50568** GF South Gosforth		
E50569 50B Neville Hill				
E50570 50B Neville Hill	**E50570** 55H Neville Hill	**E50570** GF South Gosforth		
E50571 53B Hull Botanic Gardens	**E50571** 50C Hull Botanic Gardens	**E50571** NR Norwich		
E50572 53B Hull Botanic Gardens	**E50572** 55H Neville Hill	**E50572** NR Norwich		
E50573 50A York	**E50573** 55H Neville Hill	**E50573** NL Neville Hill		
E50574 53B Hull Botanic Gardens	**E50574** 55H Neville Hill	**E50574** GF South Gosforth		
E50575 53B Hull Botanic Gardens	**E50575** 55H Neville Hill	**E50575** NL Neville Hill		
E50576 South Gosforth	**E50576** 30A Stratford	**E50576** GF South Gosforth		
E50577 South Gosforth	**E50577** 30A Stratford	**E50577** GF South Gosforth		
E50578 50B Neville Hill	**E50578** 55H Neville Hill	**E50578** NR Norwich		
E50579 53B Hull Botanic Gardens	**E50579** 55H Neville Hill	**E50579** NR Norwich		
E50580 53B Hull Botanic Gardens	**E50580** 50C Hull Botanic Gardens	**E50580** NL Neville Hill		
E50581 53B Hull Botanic Gardens	**E50581** 50C Hull Botanic Gardens	**E50581** NR Norwich		
E50582 53B Hull Botanic Gardens	**E50582** 50C Hull Botanic Gardens	**E50582** NL Neville Hill		
E50583 53B Hull Botanic Gardens	**E50583** 55H Neville Hill	**E50583** NR Norwich		
E50584 50B Neville Hill	**E50584** 55H Neville Hill	**E50584** NL Neville Hill		
E50585 53B Hull Botanic Gardens	**E50585** 50C Hull Botanic Gardens	**E50585** NR Norwich		
E50586 South Gosforth	**E50586** 55H Neville Hill	**E50586** GF South Gosforth		
E50587 South Gosforth	**E50587** 55H Neville Hill	**E50587** NL Neville Hill		
E50588 South Gosforth	**E50588** 52J South Gosforth	**E50588** NR Norwich		
E50589 50B Neville Hill	**E50589** 50C Hull Botanic Gardens	**E50589** GF South Gosforth		
E50590 53B Hull Botanic Gardens	**E50590** 50C Hull Botanic Gardens	**E50590** NR Norwich		
E50591 South Gosforth	**E50591** 55H Neville Hill	**E50591** GF South Gosforth		
E50592 South Gosforth				

1960	1970	1980	1990	2000
E50593 South Gosforth	**E50593** 52J South Gosforth	**E50593** GF South Gosforth		
E50594 50A York	**E50594** 50C Hull Botanic Gardens	**E50594** NR Norwich		
E50595 South Gosforth	**E50595** 52J South Gosforth	**E50595** SF Stratford		
E50596 51A Darlington	**E50596** 55H Neville Hill	**E50596** NR Norwich		
E50597 South Gosforth	**E50597** 50C Hull Botanic Gardens	**E50597** NR Norwich		
E50598 South Gosforth	**E50598** 55H Neville Hill	**E50598** NR Norwich		
E50599 56G Bradford Hammerton St	**E50599** 52J South Gosforth	**E50599** NL Neville Hill	**53599** BY Bletchley	
E50600 56G Bradford Hammerton St	**E50600** 55H Neville Hill			
E50601 56G Bradford Hammerton St	**E50601** 55H Neville Hill	**E50601** NL Neville Hill		
E50602 56G Bradford Hammerton St	**E50602** 55H Neville Hill	**E50602** NL Neville Hill	**53602** BR Bristol Bath Road	
E50603 56G Bradford Hammerton St	**E50603** 55H Neville Hill	**E50603** NL Neville Hill		
E50604 56G Bradford Hammerton St	**E50604** 52J South Gosforth	**E50604** NL Neville Hill		
E50605 56G Bradford Hammerton St	**E50605** 52J South Gosforth	**E50605** NL Neville Hill		
E50606 56G Bradford Hammerton St	**E50606** 52J South Gosforth	**E50606** NL Neville Hill		
E50607 56G Bradford Hammerton St	**E50607** 55H Neville Hill	**E50607** NL Neville Hill	**53607** BR Bristol Bath Road	
E50608 53B Hull Botanic Gardens	**E50608** 55H Neville Hill	**E50608** NL Neville Hill	**53608** BR Bristol Bath Road	
E50609 56G Bradford Hammerton St	**E50609** 55H Neville Hill	**E50609** NL Neville Hill		
E50610 56G Bradford Hammerton St	**E50610** 32A Norwich	**E50610** NL Neville Hill		
E50611 56G Bradford Hammerton St				
E50612 56G Bradford Hammerton St	**E50612** 55H Neville Hill	**E50612** NL Neville Hill	**53612** BR Bristol Bath Road	
E50613 56G Bradford Hammerton St	**E50613** 55H Neville Hill	**E50613** NL Neville Hill		
E50614 56G Bradford Hammerton St	**E50614** 55H Neville Hill	**E50614** NL Neville Hill	**53614** BR Bristol Bath Road	
E50615 56G Bradford Hammerton St				
E50616 56G Bradford Hammerton St	**E50616** 55H Neville Hill	**E50616** NL Neville Hill	**53616** BR Bristol Bath Road	
E50617 56G Bradford Hammerton St	**E50617** 55H Neville Hill	**E50617** NL Neville Hill	**53617** CF Cardiff Canton	
E50618 56G Bradford Hammerton St	**E50618** 55H Neville Hill	**E50618** NL Neville Hill	**53618** BR Bristol Bath Road	
E50619 56G Bradford Hammerton St	**E50619** 55H Neville Hill	**E50619** NL Neville Hill	**53619** BR Bristol Bath Road	
E50620 56G Bradford Hammerton St	**E50620** 52J South Gosforth	**E50620** NL Neville Hill	**53620** BR Bristol Bath Road	
E50621 56G Bradford Hammerton St (o/l)	**E50621** 55H Neville Hill	**E50621** NL Neville Hill	**53621** BR Bristol Bath Road	
E50622 56G Bradford Hammerton St	**E50622** 52J South Gosforth	**E50622** NL Neville Hill	**53622** BR Bristol Bath Road	
E50623 56G Bradford Hammerton St (o/l)	**E50623** 52J South Gosforth	**E50623** NL Neville Hill		
E50624 56G Bradford Hammerton St (o/l)	**E50624** 52J South Gosforth	**E50624** NL Neville Hill	**53624** CF Cardiff Canton	
M50625 8C Speke Junction	**M50625** 8J Allerton	**M50625** CH Chester	**53625** LE Landore	
M50626 8C Speke Junction	**M50626** 8J Allerton	**E50626** NL Neville Hill	**53626** NL Neville Hill	
M50627 8C Speke Junction	**M50627** 8J Allerton	**M50627** AN Allerton	**53627** CF Cardiff Canton	
M50628 27F Brunswick	**M50628** 9A Longsight	**M50628** CH Chester	**53628** BY Bletchley	
M50629 27F Brunswick	**M50629** 8J Allerton	**M50629** LO Longsight	**53629** CF Cardiff Canton	
E50630 South Gosforth	**E50630** 52J South Gosforth	**E50630** NL Neville Hill	**53630** NL Neville Hill	
E50631 South Gosforth	**E50631** 52J South Gosforth	**E50631** NL Neville Hill	**53631** LE Landore	
E50632 53B Hull Botanic Gardens	**E50632** 52J South Gosforth	**E50632** NL Neville Hill	**53632** CF Cardiff Canton	
E50633 53B Hull Botanic Gardens	**E50633** 52J South Gosforth	**E50633** NL Neville Hill	**53633** LE Landore	
E50634 53B Hull Botanic Gardens	**E50634** 50C Hull Botanic Gardens	**E50634** NL Neville Hill	**53634** CH Chester	
E50635 53B Hull Botanic Gardens	**E50635** 50C Hull Botanic Gardens	**E50635** NL Neville Hill	**53635** CF Cardiff Canton	
E50636 South Gosforth	**E50636** 52J South Gosforth	**E50636** NL Neville Hill	**53636** NL Neville Hill	
E50637 South Gosforth	**E50637** 52J South Gosforth	**E50637** NL Neville Hill	**53637** LA Laira	
E50638 South Gosforth	**E50638** 52J South Gosforth	**E50638** NL Neville Hill	**53638** LA Laira	
E50639 South Gosforth	**E50639** 52J South Gosforth	**E50639** NL Neville Hill	**53639** LA Laira	
E50640 South Gosforth	**E50640** 52J South Gosforth			
E50641 South Gosforth	**E50641** 52J South Gosforth	**E50641** NL Neville Hill	**53641** NL Neville Hill	
E50642 56G Bradford Hammerton St	**E50642** 52J South Gosforth	**E50642** NL Neville Hill	**53642** CF Cardiff Canton	
E50643 56G Bradford Hammerton St (o/l)	**E50643** 52J South Gosforth	**E50643** NL Neville Hill	**53643** LE Landore	
E50644 56G Bradford Hammerton St	**E50644** 52J South Gosforth	**E50644** NL Neville Hill	**53644** NL Neville Hill	
E50645 56G Bradford Hammerton St (o/l)	**E50645** 55H Neville Hill	**E50645** NL Neville Hill	**53645** CH Chester	
E50646 56G Bradford Hammerton St (o/l)	**E50646** 52J South Gosforth	**E50646** NL Neville Hill	**53646** LA Laira	
W50647 CDF Cardiff Canton	**W50647** 86A Cardiff Canton	**W50647** CF Cardiff Canton		
W50648 CDF Cardiff Canton	**W50648** 86A Cardiff Canton	**M50648** CH Chester		
W50649 CDF Cardiff Canton	**W50649** 86A Cardiff Canton	**W50649** CF Cardiff Canton		
W50650 TYS Tyseley	**M50650** 16C Derby Etches Park	**M50650** DY Derby Etches Park		
W50651 TYS Tyseley	**M50651** 16C Derby Etches Park	**M50651** DY Derby Etches Park		
W50652 TYS Tyseley	**M50652** 16C Derby Etches Park	**M50652** DY Derby Etches Park		
W50653 CDF Cardiff Canton	**W50653** 86A Cardiff Canton	**W50653** CF Cardiff Canton		
W50654 TYS Tyseley	**M50654** 16C Derby Etches Park	**M50654** DY Derby Etches Park		
W50655 TYS Tyseley	**M50655** 16C Derby Etches Park	**M50655** CH Chester		
W50656 TYS Tyseley	**M50656** 16C Derby Etches Park	**M50656** DY Derby Etches Park		
W50657 CDF Cardiff Canton	**M50657** 16C Derby Etches Park	**M50657** DY Derby Etches Park		
W50658 CDF Cardiff Canton	**W50658** 82A Bristol	**W50658** CF Cardiff Canton		
W50659 CDF Cardiff Canton	**W50659** 82A Bristol	**W50659** CF Cardiff Canton		
W50660 CDF Cardiff Canton	**W50660** 86A Cardiff Canton	**M50660** CH Chester		
W50661 TYS Tyseley	**W50661** 82A Bristol	**W50661** CF Cardiff Canton		
W50662 CDF Cardiff Canton	**W50662** 86A Cardiff Canton	**W50662** CF Cardiff Canton		
W50663 CDF Cardiff Canton	**M50663** 16C Derby Etches Park	**M50663** DY Derby Etches Park		
W50664 CDF Cardiff Canton	**W50664** 86A Cardiff Canton	**W50664** CF Cardiff Canton		
W50665 CDF Cardiff Canton	**W50665** 82A Bristol	**W50665** CF Cardiff Canton		
W50666 CDF Cardiff Canton	**W50666** 82A Bristol	**W50666** CF Cardiff Canton		
W50667 CDF Cardiff Canton	**M50667** 16C Derby Etches Park	**M50667** DY Derby Etches Park		
W50668 CDF Cardiff Canton	**W50668** 86A Cardiff Canton	**M50668** CH Chester		
W50669 CDF Cardiff Canton	**M50669** 16C Derby Etches Park	**M50669** DY Derby Etches Park		
W50670 CDF Cardiff Canton	**M50670** 16C Derby Etches Park	**M50670** DY Derby Etches Park		
W50671 CDF Cardiff Canton	**M50671** 16C Derby Etches Park	**M50671** DY Derby Etches Park		
W50672 CDF Cardiff Canton	**W50672** 86A Cardiff Canton	**W50672** CF Cardiff Canton		
W50673 CDF Cardiff Canton	**W50673** 82A Bristol	**W50673** CF Cardiff Canton		
W50674 TYS Tyseley	**W50674** 86A Cardiff Canton	**W50674** CF Cardiff Canton		
W50675 CDF Cardiff Canton	**W50675** 86A Cardiff Canton	**M50675** CH Chester		
W50676 CDF Cardiff Canton	**M50676** 16C Derby Etches Park	**M50676** DY Derby Etches Park		
W50677 TYS Tyseley	**M50677** 16C Derby Etches Park	**M50677** DY Derby Etches Park		
W50678 TYS Tyseley	**M50678** 16C Derby Etches Park	**M50678** DY Derby Etches Park		
W50679 CDF Cardiff Canton	**W50679** 82A Bristol	**M50679** CH Chester		

1960	1970	1980	1990	2000
W50680 TYS Tyseley	**M50680** 16C Derby Etches Park	**M50680** DY Derby Etches Park		
W50681 CDF Cardiff Canton	**W50681** 82A Bristol	**W50681** CF Cardiff Canton		
W50682 CDF Cardiff Canton	**W50682** 86A Cardiff Canton	**M50682** CH Chester		
W50683 CDF Cardiff Canton	**W50683** 82A Bristol	**M50683** CH Chester		
W50684 CDF Cardiff Canton	**M50684** 16C Derby Etches Park	**M50684** DY Derby Etches Park		
W50685 CDF Cardiff Canton	**M50685** 16C Derby Etches Park	**M50685** DY Derby Etches Park		
W50686 CDF Cardiff Canton	**W50686** 86A Cardiff Canton	**W50686** CF Cardiff Canton		
W50687 BL Bristol	**M50687** 16C Derby Etches Park	**M50687** DY Derby Etches Park		
W50688 BL Bristol	**M50688** 16C Derby Etches Park	**M50688** DY Derby Etches Park		
W50689 BL Bristol	**M50689** 16C Derby Etches Park	**M50689** DY Derby Etches Park		
W50690 BL Bristol				
W50691 BL Bristol	**W50691** 86A Cardiff Canton	**W50691** CF Cardiff Canton		
W50692 BL Bristol	**M50692** 16C Derby Etches Park	**M50692** DY Derby Etches Park		
W50693 BL Bristol	**W50693** 82A Bristol	**M50693** CH Chester		
W50694 BL Bristol	**W50694** 86A Cardiff Canton	**M50694** CH Chester		
W50695 BL Bristol	**W50695** 82A Bristol	**M50695** CH Chester		
W50696 CDF Cardiff Canton	**M50696** 16C Derby Etches Park	**M50696** DY Derby Etches Park		
W50697 CDF Cardiff Canton	**M50697** 16C Derby Etches Park	**M50697** CH Chester		
W50698 CDF Cardiff Canton	**W50698** 86A Cardiff Canton	**W50698** CF Cardiff Canton		
W50699 CDF Cardiff Canton	**W50699** 86A Cardiff Canton	**W50699** CF Cardiff Canton		
W50700 TYS Tyseley	**W50700** 82A Bristol	**W50700** CF Cardiff Canton		
W50701 TYS Tyseley	**W50701** 82A Bristol	**W50701** CF Cardiff Canton		
W50702 CDF Cardiff Canton	**W50702** 86A Cardiff Canton	**W50702** CF Cardiff Canton		
W50703 TYS Tyseley	**M50703** 16C Derby Etches Park	**M50703** DY Derby Etches Park		
W50704 TYS Tyseley	**M50704** 16C Derby Etches Park	**M50704** DY Derby Etches Park		
W50705 CDF Cardiff Canton	**W50705** 86A Cardiff Canton	**W50705** CF Cardiff Canton		
W50706 CDF Cardiff Canton	**W50706** 86A Cardiff Canton	**M50706** CH Chester		
W50707 CDF Cardiff Canton	**W50707** 86A Cardiff Canton	**W50707** CF Cardiff Canton		
W50708 TYS Tyseley	**M50708** 16C Derby Etches Park	**M50708** DY Derby Etches Park		
W50709 TYS Tyseley	**M50709** 16C Derby Etches Park	**M50709** DY Derby Etches Park		
W50710 TYS Tyseley	**W50710** 82A Bristol	**W50710** CF Cardiff Canton		
W50711 CDF Cardiff Canton	**W50711** 82A Bristol	**W50711** CF Cardiff Canton		
W50712 CDF Cardiff Canton	**W50712** 82A Bristol	**W50712** CF Cardiff Canton		
W50713 CDF Cardiff Canton	**M50713** 16C Derby Etches Park	**M50713** DY Derby Etches Park		
W50714 CDF Cardiff Canton	**M50714** 16C Derby Etches Park	**M50714** DY Derby Etches Park		
W50715 CDF Cardiff Canton	**W50715** 82A Bristol	**W50715** CF Cardiff Canton		
W50716 CDF Cardiff Canton	**W50716** 86A Cardiff Canton	**M50716** CH Chester		
W50717 CDF Cardiff Canton	**M50717** 16C Derby Etches Park	**M50717** DY Derby Etches Park		
W50718 CDF Cardiff Canton	**M50718** 16C Derby Etches Park	**M50718** DY Derby Etches Park		
W50719 CDF Cardiff Canton	**M50719** 16C Derby Etches Park	**M50719** DY Derby Etches Park		
W50720 CDF Cardiff Canton	**M50720** 16C Derby Etches Park	**M50720** DY Derby Etches Park		
W50721 CDF Cardiff Canton	**W50721** 86A Cardiff Canton	**M50721** CH Chester		
W50722 CDF Cardiff Canton	**W50722** 86A Cardiff Canton	**W50722** CF Cardiff Canton		
W50723 CDF Cardiff Canton	**W50723** 86A Cardiff Canton	**W50723** CF Cardiff Canton		
W50724 CDF Cardiff Canton	**W50724** 82A Bristol	**W50724** CF Cardiff Canton		
W50725 TYS Tyseley	**M50725** 16C Derby Etches Park	**M50725** DY Derby Etches Park		
W50726 CDF Cardiff Canton	**W50726** 86A Cardiff Canton	**M50726** CH Chester		
W50727 CDF Cardiff Canton	**W50727** 82A Bristol	**M50727** CH Chester		
W50728 TYS Tyseley	**W50728** 86A Cardiff Canton	**W50728** CF Cardiff Canton		
W50729 CDF Cardiff Canton	**W50729** 86A Cardiff Canton	**M50729** CH Chester		
W50730 TYS Tyseley	**M50730** 16C Derby Etches Park	**M50730** DY Derby Etches Park		
W50731 TYS Tyseley	**M50731** 16C Derby Etches Park	**M50731** DY Derby Etches Park		
W50732 BL Bristol	**W50732** 86A Cardiff Canton	**M50732** CH Chester		
W50733 CDF Cardiff Canton	**W50733** 86A Cardiff Canton	**W50733** CF Cardiff Canton		
W50734 CDF Cardiff Canton	**M50734** 16C Derby Etches Park	**M50734** DY Derby Etches Park		
W50735 CDF Cardiff Canton	**W50735** 82A Bristol	**M50735** CH Chester		
W50736 CDF Cardiff Canton	**M50736** 16C Derby Etches Park	**M50736** DY Derby Etches Park		
W50737 BL Bristol	**M50737** 16C Derby Etches Park	**M50737** DY Derby Etches Park		
W50738 BL Bristol	**W50738** 82A Bristol	**M50738** CH Chester		
W50739 BL Bristol	**W50739** 82A Bristol	**M50739** CH Chester		
W50740 BL Bristol				
W50741 BL Bristol	**M50741** 16C Derby Etches Park	**M50741** DY Derby Etches Park		
W50742 BL Bristol	**M50742** 16C Derby Etches Park	**M50742** DY Derby Etches Park		
W50743 BL Bristol	**M50743** 16C Derby Etches Park	**M50743** DY Derby Etches Park		
W50744 BL Bristol	**M50744** 16C Derby Etches Park	**M50744** DY Derby Etches Park		
E50745 51A Darlington	**SC50745** 62B Dundee			
E50746 51A Darlington	**SC50746** 62B Dundee	**SC50746** DE Dundee	**53746** NL Neville Hill	**53746** LO Longsight
E50747 51A Darlington	**SC50747** 62B Dundee	**SC50747** DE Dundee		
E50748 51A Darlington	**SC50748** 66C Hamilton	**SC50748** DE Dundee		
E50749 51A Darlington	**SC50749** 66C Hamilton	**SC50749** HA Haymarket		
E50750 51A Darlington	**E50750** 55H Neville Hill	**E50750** GF South Gosforth		
E50751 51A Darlington	**E50751** 55H Neville Hill	**E50751** GF South Gosforth	**53751** RG Reading	
M50752 18A Toton	**M50752** 10E Accrington	**M50752** NH Newton Heath		
M50753 18A Toton	**M50753** 10E Accrington			
M50754 18A Toton	**M50754** 10E Accrington	**M50754** NH Newton Heath		
M50755 18A Toton	**M50755** 10E Accrington	**M50755** NH Newton Heath		
M50756 18A Toton	**M50756** 9D Newton Heath	**M50756** NH Newton Heath		
M50757 18A Toton	**M50757** 10E Accrington	**M50757** NH Newton Heath		
M50758 18A Toton	**M50758** 10E Accrington	**M50758** NH Newton Heath		
M50759 18A Toton	**M50759** 10E Accrington	**M50759** NH Newton Heath		
M50760 18A Toton	**M50760** 9D Newton Heath	**M50760** NH Newton Heath		
M50761 18A Toton	**M50761** 10E Accrington	**M50761** NH Newton Heath		
M50762 18A Toton	**M50762** 10E Accrington	**M50762** NH Newton Heath		
M50763 18A Toton	**M50763** 10E Accrington	**M50763** NH Newton Heath		
M50764 18A Toton	**M50764** 9D Newton Heath	**M50764** NH Newton Heath		
M50765 18A Toton	**M50765** 10E Accrington	**M50765** NH Newton Heath		
M50766 18A Toton	**M50766** 10E Accrington	**M50766** NH Newton Heath		

1960	1970	1980	1990	2000
M50767 18A Toton	**M50767** 10E Accrington	**M50767** NH Newton Heath		
M50768 18A Toton	**M50768** 10E Accrington	**M50768** NH Newton Heath		
M50769 18A Toton	**M50769** 10E Accrington	**M50769** NH Newton Heath		
M50770 18A Toton	**M50770** 10E Accrington	**M50770** NH Newton Heath		
M50771 26A Newton Heath	**M50771** 16C Derby Etches Park	**M50771** NH Newton Heath		
M50772 26A Newton Heath	**M50772** 10E Accrington	**M50772** NH Newton Heath		
M50773 26A Newton Heath	**M50773** 10E Accrington	**M50773** NH Newton Heath		
M50774 26A Newton Heath				
M50775 26A Newton Heath				
M50776 26A Newton Heath	**M50776** 9D Newton Heath	**M50776** NH Newton Heath		
M50777 26A Newton Heath	**M50777** 9D Newton Heath	**M50777** NH Newton Heath		
M50778 26A Newton Heath	**M50778** 9D Newton Heath	**M50778** NH Newton Heath		
M50779 26A Newton Heath	**M50779** 9D Newton Heath	**M50779** NH Newton Heath		
M50780 26A Newton Heath				
M50781 26A Newton Heath	**M50781** 9D Newton Heath			
M50782 26A Newton Heath	**M50782** 9D Newton Heath	**M50782** NH Newton Heath		
M50783 26A Newton Heath				
M50784 26A Newton Heath	**M50784** 9D Newton Heath	**M50784** NH Newton Heath		
M50785 18A Toton	**M50785** 10E Accrington	**M50785** NH Newton Heath		
M50786 18A Toton	**M50786** 10E Accrington	**M50786** TS Tyseley		
M50787 18A Toton	**M50787** 10E Accrington	**M50787** NH Newton Heath		
M50788 18A Toton	**M50788** 10E Accrington	**M50788** NH Newton Heath		
M50789 18A Toton	**M50789** 10E Accrington	**M50789** NH Newton Heath		
M50790 18A Toton	**M50790** 10E Accrington	**M50790** NH Newton Heath		
M50791 18A Toton	**M50791** 10E Accrington	**M50791** NH Newton Heath		
M50792 18A Toton	**M50792** 10E Accrington	**M50792** NH Newton Heath		
M50793 18A Toton	**M50793** 10E Accrington	**M50793** NH Newton Heath		
M50794 18A Toton	**M50794** 10E Accrington	**M50794** NH Newton Heath		
M50795 18A Toton	**M50795** 10E Accrington	**M50795** NH Newton Heath		
M50796 18A Toton	**M50796** 10E Accrington	**M50796** NH Newton Heath		
M50797 18A Toton	**M50797** 10E Accrington	**M50797** NH Newton Heath		
M50798 18A Toton	**M50798** 10E Accrington	**M50798** NH Newton Heath		
M50799 18A Toton				
M50800 18A Toton	**M50800** 10E Accrington	**M50800** NH Newton Heath		
M50801 18A Toton	**M50801** 10E Accrington	**M50801** NH Newton Heath		
M50802 18A Toton	**M50802** 10E Accrington	**M50802** NH Newton Heath		
M50803 18A Toton	**M50803** 10E Accrington	**M50803** NH Newton Heath		
M50804 26A Newton Heath	**M50804** 9D Newton Heath	**M50804** NH Newton Heath		
M50805 26A Newton Heath	**M50805** 9D Newton Heath	**M50805** NH Newton Heath		
M50806 26A Newton Heath	**M50806** 9D Newton Heath	**M50806** NH Newton Heath		
M50807 26A Newton Heath	**M50807** 9D Newton Heath	**M50807** NH Newton Heath		
M50808 26A Newton Heath				
M50809 26A Newton Heath	**M50809** 9D Newton Heath	**M50809** NH Newton Heath		
M50810 26A Newton Heath	**M50810** 9D Newton Heath	**M50810** NH Newton Heath		
M50811 26A Newton Heath				
M50812 26A Newton Heath	**M50812** 9D Newton Heath	**M50812** TS Tyseley		
M50813 26A Newton Heath				
M50814 26A Newton Heath	**M50814** 9D Newton Heath	**M50814** NH Newton Heath		
M50815 26A Newton Heath	**M50815** 9D Newton Heath	**M50815** NH Newton Heath		
M50816 26A Newton Heath				
M50817 26A Newton Heath	**M50817** 9D Newton Heath			
W50818 CAT Cardiff Cathays	**SC50818** 66C Hamilton	**M50818** TS Tyseley	**53818** TS Tyseley	
W50819 CAT Cardiff Cathays	**W50819** 81D Reading	**M50819** TS Tyseley		
W50820 CAT Cardiff Cathays	**SC50820** 66C Hamilton	**SC50820** HN Hamilton	**53820** OO Old Oak Common	
W50821 CAT Cardiff Cathays	**SC50821** 66C Hamilton	**M50821** TS Tyseley		
W50822 CAT Cardiff Cathays	**SC50822** 66C Hamilton	**SC50822** HN Hamilton	**53822** TS Tyseley	
W50823 CAT Cardiff Cathays	**SC50823** 66C Hamilton	**SC50823** HN Hamilton		
W50824 CAT Cardiff Cathays	**E50824** 34G Finsbury Park	**M50824** TS Tyseley		
W50825 CAT Cardiff Cathays	**SC50825** 66C Hamilton	**SC50825** HN Hamilton		
W50826 CAT Cardiff Cathays	**SC50826** 66C Hamilton	**M50826** TS Tyseley	**53826** TS Tyseley	
W50827 RDG Reading	**E50827** 34G Finsbury Park	**M50827** TS Tyseley	**53827** TS Tyseley	
W50828 CAT Cardiff Cathays	**E50828** 34G Finsbury Park	**M50828** TS Tyseley		
W50829 CAT Cardiff Cathays	**SC50829** 66C Hamilton	**SC50829** HN Hamilton		
W50830 CAT Cardiff Cathays	**E50830** 34G Finsbury Park	**M50830** TS Tyseley		
W50831 CAT Cardiff Cathays	**M50831** 2A Tyseley	**M50831** TS Tyseley		
W50832 CAT Cardiff Cathays	**M50832** 2A Tyseley	**M50832** TS Tyseley		
W50833 CAT Cardiff Cathays	**M50833** 2A Tyseley	**M50833** TS Tyseley		
W50834 CAT Cardiff Cathays	**W50834** 86A Cardiff Canton	**M50834** TS Tyseley		
W50835 CAT Cardiff Cathays	**M50835** 2A Tyseley	**M50835** TS Tyseley		
W50836 CAT Cardiff Cathays	**W50836** 86A Cardiff Canton	**SC50836** HN Hamilton		
W50837 CAT Cardiff Cathays	**M50837** 2A Tyseley	**M50837** TS Tyseley	**53837** TS Tyseley	
W50838 CAT Cardiff Cathays	**M50838** 14A Cricklewood	**M50838** CW Cricklewood	**53838** TS Tyseley	
W50839 CAT Cardiff Cathays	**W50839** 86A Cardiff Canton	**SC50839** HN Hamilton		
W50840 CAT Cardiff Cathays	**M50840** 2A Tyseley	**M50840** TS Tyseley		
W50841 RDG Reading	**E50841** 30A Stratford	**SC50841** HN Hamilton		
W50842 CAT Cardiff Cathays	**W50842** 86A Cardiff Canton	**M50842** TS Tyseley		
W50843 CAT Cardiff Cathays	**W50843** 86A Cardiff Canton	**W50843** CF Cardiff Canton		
W50844 CAT Cardiff Cathays	**W50844** 86A Cardiff Canton	**E50844** SF Stratford	**53844** TS Tyseley	
W50845 CAT Cardiff Cathays	**W50845** 86A Cardiff Canton	**E50845** SF Stratford		
W50846 CAT Cardiff Cathays	**E50846** 30A Stratford	**SC50846** HN Hamilton		
W50847 CAT Cardiff Cathays	**W50847** 84A Laira	**W50847** CF Cardiff Canton		
W50848 CAT Cardiff Cathays	**W50848** 86A Cardiff Canton	**W50848** CF Cardiff Canton		
W50849 SHL Southall	**M50849** 14A Cricklewood	**M50849** CW Cricklewood	**53849** TS Tyseley	
W50850 CAT Cardiff Cathays	**M50850** 14A Cricklewood	**M50850** TS Tyseley	**53850** TS Tyseley	
W50851 CAT Cardiff Cathays	**W50851** 86A Cardiff Canton	**M50851** TS Tyseley		
W50852 CAT Cardiff Cathays	**SC50852** 66C Hamilton	**M50852** TS Tyseley		
W50853 CAT Cardiff Cathays	**E50853** 30A Stratford	**SC50853** HN Hamilton	**53853** TS Tyseley	

1960	1970	1980	1990	2000
W50854 CAT Cardiff Cathays	**W50854** 84A Laira	**M50854** TS Tyseley	**53854** TS Tyseley	
W50855 CAT Cardiff Cathays	**W50855** 86A Cardiff Canton	**W50855** CF Cardiff Canton		
W50856 CAT Cardiff Cathays	**W50856** 86A Cardiff Canton	**W50856** CF Cardiff Canton		
W50857 CAT Cardiff Cathays	**W50857** 86A Cardiff Canton	**M50857** TS Tyseley		
W50858 CAT Cardiff Cathays	**W50858** 86A Cardiff Canton	**W50858** LA Laira		
W50859 CDF Cardiff Canton	**M50859** 2A Tyseley	**SC50859** HN Hamilton		
W50860 CDF Cardiff Canton	**M50860** 2A Tyseley	**M50860** TS Tyseley		
W50861 CDF Cardiff Canton	**M50861** 2A Tyseley	**M50861** TS Tyseley		
W50862 CAT Cardiff Cathays	**W50862** 81D Reading	**M50862** TS Tyseley		
W50863 CAT Cardiff Cathays	**W50863** 86A Cardiff Canton	**M50863** TS Tyseley	**53863** TS Tyseley	
W50864 CAT Cardiff Cathays	**W50864** 86A Cardiff Canton	**W50864** CF Cardiff Canton		
W50865 CAT Cardiff Cathays	**W50865** 84A Laira	**E50865** SF Stratford	**53865** TS Tyseley	
W50866 CAT Cardiff Cathays	**W50866** 86A Cardiff Canton	**M50866** TS Tyseley		
W50867 CAT Cardiff Cathays	**W50867** 86A Cardiff Canton	**E50867** SF Stratford		
W50868 CAT Cardiff Cathays	**W50868** 84A Laira	**W50868** LA Laira		
W50869 CAT Cardiff Cathays	**W50869** 86A Cardiff Canton	**W50869** CF Cardiff Canton		
W50870 CAT Cardiff Cathays	**M50870** 14A Cricklewood	**M50870** CW Cricklewood		
W50871 CAT Cardiff Cathays	**SC50871** 66C Hamilton	**M50871** TS Tyseley		
W50872 CAT Cardiff Cathays	**W50872** 81D Reading	**M50872** TS Tyseley		
W50873 CAT Cardiff Cathays	**SC50873** 66C Hamilton	**SC50873** HN Hamilton	**53873** TS Tyseley	
W50874 CAT Cardiff Cathays	**SC50874** 66C Hamilton			
W50875 CAT Cardiff Cathays	**SC50875** 66C Hamilton	**M50875** TS Tyseley		
W50876 CAT Cardiff Cathays	**SC50876** 66C Hamilton	**SC50876** HN Hamilton		
W50877 CAT Cardiff Cathays	**E50877** 34G Finsbury Park	**SC50877** HN Hamilton		
W50878 CAT Cardiff Cathays	**SC50878** 66C Hamilton	**M50878** TS Tyseley	**53878** TS Tyseley	
W50879 CAT Cardiff Cathays	**SC50879** 66C Hamilton	**SC50879** HN Hamilton		
W50880 RDG Reading	**E50880** 34G Finsbury Park	**M50880** TS Tyseley	**53880** TS Tyseley	
W50881 CAT Cardiff Cathays	**E50881** 30A Stratford	**SC50881** HN Hamilton	**53881** TS Tyseley	
W50882 CAT Cardiff Cathays	**SC50882** 66C Hamilton	**SC50882** HN Hamilton		
W50883 CAT Cardiff Cathays	**E50883** 34G Finsbury Park	**M50883** TS Tyseley		
W50884 CAT Cardiff Cathays	**M50884** 2A Tyseley	**M50884** TS Tyseley		
W50885 CAT Cardiff Cathays	**M50885** 2A Tyseley	**M50885** TS Tyseley		
W50886 CAT Cardiff Cathays	**M50886** 2A Tyseley	**M50886** TS Tyseley	**53886** TS Tyseley	
W50887 CAT Cardiff Cathays	**W50887** 86A Cardiff Canton	**M50887** TS Tyseley		
W50888 CAT Cardiff Cathays	**M50888** 2A Tyseley	**M50888** TS Tyseley		
W50889 CAT Cardiff Cathays	**W50889** 86A Cardiff Canton	**SC50889** HN Hamilton		
W50890 CAT Cardiff Cathays	**M50890** 2A Tyseley	**M50890** TS Tyseley	**53890** TS Tyseley	
W50891 CAT Cardiff Cathays	**M50891** 14A Cricklewood	**M50891** CW Cricklewood	**53891** TS Tyseley	
W50892 CAT Cardiff Cathays	**W50892** 86A Cardiff Canton	**SC50892** HN Hamilton		
W50893 CAT Cardiff Cathays	**M50893** 14A Cricklewood	**M50893** CW Cricklewood	**53893** TS Tyseley	
W50894 RDG Reading	**E50894** 30A Stratford	**SC50894** HN Hamilton	**53894** TS Tyseley	
W50895 CAT Cardiff Cathays	**W50895** 86A Cardiff Canton	**M50895** TS Tyseley		
W50896 CAT Cardiff Cathays	**W50896** 86A Cardiff Canton	**W50896** CF Cardiff Canton		
W50897 CAT Cardiff Cathays	**W50897** 86A Cardiff Canton	**E50897** SF Stratford	**53897** TS Tyseley	
W50898 CAT Cardiff Cathays	**W50898** 86A Cardiff Canton	**E50898** SF Stratford		
W50899 CAT Cardiff Cathays	**E50899** 30A Stratford	**SC50899** HN Hamilton		
W50900 CAT Cardiff Cathays	**W50900** 84A Laira	**W50900** CF Cardiff Canton		
W50901 CAT Cardiff Cathays	**W50901** 86A Cardiff Canton	**W50901** CF Cardiff Canton		
W50902 SHL Southall	**M50902** 14A Cricklewood	**M50902** CW Cricklewood	**53902** TS Tyseley	
W50903 CAT Cardiff Cathays	**M50903** 14A Cricklewood	**M50903** CW Cricklewood		
W50904 CAT Cardiff Cathays	**W50904** 86A Cardiff Canton	**M50904** TS Tyseley		
W50905 CAT Cardiff Cathays	**SC50905** 66C Hamilton	**M50905** TS Tyseley		
W50906 CAT Cardiff Cathays	**E50906** 34G Finsbury Park	**M50906** TS Tyseley		
W50907 CAT Cardiff Cathays	**W50907** 84A Laira	**M50907** TS Tyseley	**53907** TS Tyseley	
W50908 CAT Cardiff Cathays	**W50908** 86A Cardiff Canton	**W50908** CF Cardiff Canton		
W50909 CAT Cardiff Cathays	**W50909** 86A Cardiff Canton	**W50909** CF Cardiff Canton		
W50910 CAT Cardiff Cathays	**W50910** 86A Cardiff Canton	**M50910** TS Tyseley		
W50911 CAT Cardiff Cathays	**W50911** 86A Cardiff Canton	**W50911** LA Laira		
W50912 CDF Cardiff Canton	**M50912** 2A Tyseley	**M50912** TS Tyseley		
W50913 CDF Cardiff Canton	**M50913** 2A Tyseley	**M50913** TS Tyseley		
W50914 CDF Cardiff Canton	**M50914** 2A Tyseley	**M50914** TS Tyseley		
W50915 CAT Cardiff Cathays	**W50915** 81D Reading	**M50915** TS Tyseley		
W50916 CAT Cardiff Cathays	**W50916** 86A Cardiff Canton	**M50916** TS Tyseley	**53916** TS Tyseley	
W50917 CAT Cardiff Cathays	**W50917** 86A Cardiff Canton	**W50917** CF Cardiff Canton		
W50918 CAT Cardiff Cathays	**W50918** 84A Laira	**W50918** LA Laira		
W50919 CAT Cardiff Cathays	**W50919** 86A Cardiff Canton	**M50919** TS Tyseley	**53919** TS Tyseley	
W50920 CAT Cardiff Cathays	**W50920** 86A Cardiff Canton	**E50920** SF Stratford		
W50921 CAT Cardiff Cathays	**W50921** 84A Laira	**E50921** SF Stratford	**53921** TS Tyseley	
W50922 CAT Cardiff Cathays	**W50922** 86A Cardiff Canton	**W50922** CF Cardiff Canton		
W50923 CAT Cardiff Cathays	**M50923** 14A Cricklewood	**M50923** CW Cricklewood		
M50924 Wrexham Central	**M50924** 6A Chester	**M50924** AN Allerton	**53924** CH Chester	
M50925 6G Llandudno Junction	**M50925** 6A Chester	**M50925** CH Chester	**53925** CH Chester	
M50926 Wrexham Central (o/l)	**M50926** 6A Chester	**M50926** CH Chester	**53926** LE Landore	
M50927 6G Llandudno Junction	**M50927** 6A Chester	**M50927** CH Chester	**53927** CH Chester	
M50928 6G Llandudno Junction	**M50928** 6A Chester	**M50928** AN Allerton	**53928** LE Landore	
M50929 6G Llandudno Junction	**M50929** 6A Chester	**M50929** CH Chester	**53929** CH Chester	
M50930 6G Llandudno Junction	**M50930** 6A Chester	**M50930** CH Chester	**53930** CH Chester	
M50931 6G Llandudno Junction	**M50931** 6A Chester	**M50931** CH Chester	**53931** CH Chester	
M50932 6G Llandudno Junction	**M50932** 6A Chester	**M50932** CH Chester	**53932** CH Chester	
	M50933 8J Allerton	**M50933** CH Chester	**53933** CH Chester	
	M50934 8J Allerton	**M50934** CH Chester	**53934** CH Chester	
	M50935 8J Allerton	**M50935** CH Chester	**53935** LE Landore	
SC50936 67C Ayr	**SC50936** 67C Ayr	**SC50936** AY Ayr		
M50938 1E Bletchley	**M50938** 9A Longsight	**M50938** CH Chester	**53938** CH Chester	
M50939 1E Bletchley	**M50939** 9A Longsight	**M50939** CH Chester	**53939** LE Landore	
M50940 1E Bletchley	**M50940** 9A Longsight	**M50940** CH Chester	**53940** NL Neville Hill	
M50941 1E Bletchley	**M50941** 9A Longsight	**M50941** LO Longsight	**53941** BR Bristol Bath Road	

1960			1970			1980			1990			2000
M50942	1E	Bletchley	**M50942**	9A	Longsight	**M50942**	LO	Longsight	**53942**	LE	Landore	
M50943	1E	Bletchley	**M50943**	8J	Allerton	**M50943**	AN	Allerton	**53943**	NL	Neville Hill	
M50944	1E	Bletchley	**M50944**	9A	Longsight	**M50944**	NH	Newton Heath	**53944**	NL	Neville Hill	
M50945	1E	Bletchley	**M50945**	9A	Longsight	**M50945**	LO	Longsight	**53945**	LE	Landore	
M50946	1E	Bletchley	**M50946**	9A	Longsight							
M50947	27F	Brunswick	**M50947**	9A	Longsight	**M50947**	LO	Longsight	**53947**	LE	Landore	
M50948	9E	Trafford Park	**M50948**	9A	Longsight	**M50948**	LO	Longsight	**53948**	BR	Bristol Bath Road	
M50949	9E	Trafford Park	**M50949**	9A	Longsight	**M50949**	LO	Longsight	**53949**	NL	Neville Hill	
M50950	9E	Trafford Park	**M50950**	12A	Carlisle	**M50950**	KD	Carlisle Kingmoor	**53950**	HT	Heaton	
M50951		Reddish	**M50951**	12A	Carlisle	**M50951**	KD	Carlisle Kingmoor	**53951**	HT	Heaton	
M50952	9E	Trafford Park	**M50952**	12A	Carlisle	**M50952**	KD	Carlisle Kingmoor	**53952**	HT	Heaton	
M50953	9E	Trafford Park	**M50953**	12A	Carlisle	**M50953**	KD	Carlisle Kingmoor	**53953**	HT	Heaton	
M50954	9E	Trafford Park	**M50954**	12A	Carlisle	**M50954**	KD	Carlisle Kingmoor	**53954**	HT	Heaton	
M50955	9E	Trafford Park	**M50955**	12A	Carlisle	**M50955**	KD	Carlisle Kingmoor	**53955**	HT	Heaton	
M50956		Reddish	**M50956**	12A	Carlisle	**M50956**	KD	Carlisle Kingmoor	**53956**	HT	Heaton	
M50957	9E	Trafford Park	**M50957**	12A	Carlisle	**M50957**	KD	Carlisle Kingmoor	**53957**	HT	Heaton	
M50958	9E	Trafford Park	**M50958**	12A	Carlisle	**M50958**	KD	Carlisle Kingmoor	**53958**	HT	Heaton	
M50959		Reddish	**M50959**	12A	Carlisle	**M50959**	KD	Carlisle Kingmoor	**53959**	HT	Heaton	
M50960	9E	Trafford Park	**M50960**	12A	Carlisle	**M50960**	KD	Carlisle Kingmoor	**53960**	HT	Heaton	
M50961	9E	Trafford Park	**M50961**	12A	Carlisle							
M50962	24F	Fleetwood	**M50962**	12A	Carlisle	**M50962**	KD	Carlisle Kingmoor	**53962**	HT	Heaton	
M50963	24F	Fleetwood	**M50963**	12A	Carlisle	**M50963**	KD	Carlisle Kingmoor	**53963**	HT	Heaton	
M50964	24F	Fleetwood	**M50964**	12A	Carlisle	**M50964**	KD	Carlisle Kingmoor	**53964**	HT	Heaton	
M50965	24F	Fleetwood	**M50965**	10E	Accrington	**M50965**	NH	Newton Heath	**53965**	NL	Neville Hill	
M50966	24F	Fleetwood	**M50966**	10E	Accrington	**M50966**	NH	Newton Heath	**53966**	NL	Neville Hill	
M50967	24F	Fleetwood	**M50967**	10E	Accrington	**M50967**	NH	Newton Heath				
M50968	24F	Fleetwood	**M50968**	10E	Accrington	**M50968**	NH	Newton Heath	**53968**	NL	Neville Hill	
M50969	24F	Fleetwood	**M50969**	10E	Accrington	**M50969**	NH	Newton Heath	**53969**	NL	Neville Hill	
M50970	24F	Fleetwood	**M50970**	10E	Accrington	**M50970**	LO	Longsight	**53970**	CH	Chester	
M50971	24F	Fleetwood	**M50971**	10E	Accrington	**M50971**	NH	Newton Heath	**53971**	NL	Neville Hill	
M50972	24F	Fleetwood	**M50972**	10E	Accrington							
M50973	27F	Brunswick	**M50973**	10E	Accrington	**M50973**	NH	Newton Heath	**53973**	HT	Heaton	
M50974	27F	Brunswick	**M50974**	10E	Accrington	**M50974**	NH	Newton Heath	**53974**	NL	Neville Hill	
M50975	27F	Brunswick	**M50975**	10E	Accrington	**M50975**	LO	Longsight	**53975**	CH	Chester	
M50976	27F	Brunswick	**M50976**	10E	Accrington	**M50976**	NH	Newton Heath	**53976**	CH	Chester	
M50977	27F	Brunswick	**M50977**	10E	Accrington	**M50977**	LO	Longsight	**53977**	CH	Chester	
M50978	14E	Bedford	**M50978**	10E	Accrington	**M50978**	LO	Longsight	**53978**	CH	Chester	
M50979	26A	Newton Heath	**M50979**	10E	Accrington							
M50980	6G	Llandudno Junction	**M50980**	10E	Accrington	**M50980**	NH	Newton Heath	**53980**	CH	Chester	
M50981	6G	Llandudno Junction	**M50981**	10E	Accrington	**M50981**	LO	Longsight	**53981**	CH	Chester	
M50982	6G	Llandudno Junction	**M50982**	10E	Accrington	**M50982**	NH	Newton Heath	**53982**	CH	Chester	
M50983	6G	Llandudno Junction	**M50983**	10E	Accrington	**M50983**	NH	Longsight	**53983**	CH	Chester	
M50984	26A	Newton Heath										
M50985	26A	Newton Heath	**M50985**	10E	Accrington	**M50985**	LO	Longsight				
M50986	14E	Bedford (o/l)	**M50986**	10E	Accrington	**M50986**	LO	Longsight	**53986**	NL	Neville Hill	
M50987	14E	Bedford (o/l)	**M50987**	10E	Accrington	**M50987**	NH	Newton Heath	**53987**	NL	Neville Hill	
E50988	30A	Stratford	**E50988**	34G	Finsbury Park							
E50989	30A	Stratford	**E50989**	34G	Finsbury Park							
E50990	30A	Stratford	**E50990**	34G	Finsbury Park							
E50991	30A	Stratford	**E50991**	34G	Finsbury Park							
E50992	30A	Stratford	**E50992**	34G	Finsbury Park							
E50993	30A	Stratford	**E50993**	34G	Finsbury Park							
E50994	30A	Stratford	**E50994**	34G	Finsbury Park							
E50995	30A	Stratford	**E50995**	34G	Finsbury Park							
E50996	30A	Stratford	**E50996**	30A	Stratford							
E50997	30A	Stratford	**E50997**	34G	Finsbury Park							
E50998	30A	Stratford	**E50998**	30A	Stratford							
E50999	30A	Stratford	**E50999**	34G	Finsbury Park							
E51000	30A	Stratford	**E51000**	34G	Finsbury Park							
E51001	30A	Stratford	**E51001**	34G	Finsbury Park							
E51002	30A	Stratford	**E51002**	34G	Finsbury Park							
E51003	30A	Stratford	**E51003**	30A	Stratford							
E51004	30A	Stratford	**E51004**	34G	Finsbury Park							
E51005	30A	Stratford	**E51005**	34G	Finsbury Park							
E51006	30A	Stratford	**E51006**	34G	Finsbury Park							
E51007	30A	Stratford	**E51007**	34G	Finsbury Park							
SC51008	67C	Ayr	**SC51008**	67C	Ayr	**SC51008**	AY	Ayr				
SC51009	67C	Ayr	**SC51009**	67C	Ayr	**SC51009**	AY	Ayr				
SC51010	67C	Ayr	**SC51010**	67C	Ayr	**SC51010**	AY	Ayr				
SC51011	67C	Ayr	**SC51011**	67C	Ayr							
SC51012	67C	Ayr	**SC51012**	67C	Ayr	**SC51012**	AY	Ayr				
SC51013	67C	Ayr	**SC51013**	67C	Ayr	**SC51013**	AY	Ayr				
SC51014	67C	Ayr	**SC51014**	67C	Ayr	**SC51014**	AY	Ayr				
SC51015	67C	Ayr	**SC51015**	67C	Ayr	**SC51015**	AY	Ayr				
SC51016	67C	Ayr	**SC51016**	67C	Ayr	**SC51016**	AY	Ayr				
SC51017	67C	Ayr	**SC51017**	67C	Ayr	**SC51017**	AY	Ayr				
SC51018	67C	Ayr	**SC51018**	67C	Ayr	**SC51018**	AY	Ayr				
SC51019	67C	Ayr	**SC51019**	67C	Ayr	**SC51019**	AY	Ayr				
SC51020	67C	Ayr	**SC51020**	67C	Ayr	**SC51020**	AY	Ayr				
SC51021	67C	Ayr	**SC51021**	67C	Ayr	**SC51021**	AY	Ayr				
SC51022	67C	Ayr	**SC51022**	67C	Ayr	**SC51022**	AY	Ayr				
SC51023	67C	Ayr	**SC51023**	67C	Ayr	**SC51023**	AY	Ayr				
SC51024	67C	Ayr	**SC51024**	67C	Ayr	**SC51024**	AY	Ayr				
SC51025	67C	Ayr	**SC51025**	67C	Ayr	**SC51025**	AY	Ayr				
SC51026	67C	Ayr	**SC51026**	67C	Ayr	**SC51026**	AY	Ayr				
SC51027	67C	Ayr	**SC51027**	67C	Ayr	**SC51027**	AY	Ayr				
SC51028	67C	Ayr	**SC51028**	67C	Ayr							

1960	1970	1980	1990	2000
SC51029 67C Ayr	**SC51029** 67C Ayr	**SC51029** AY Ayr		
SC51030 67C Ayr	**SC51030** 67C Ayr	**SC51030** AY Ayr		
SC51031 67C Ayr	**SC51031** 67C Ayr			
SC51032 67C Ayr	**SC51032** 67C Ayr	**SC51032** AY Ayr		
SC51033 67C Ayr	**SC51033** 67C Ayr	**SC51033** AY Ayr		
SC51034 67C Ayr	**SC51034** 67C Ayr	**SC51034** AY Ayr		
SC51035 67C Ayr	**SC51035** 67C Ayr	**SC51035** AY Ayr		
SC51036 67C Ayr	**SC51036** 67C Ayr	**SC51036** AY Ayr		
SC51037 67C Ayr	**SC51037** 67C Ayr	**SC51037** AY Ayr		
SC51038 67C Ayr	**SC51038** 67C Ayr	**SC51038** AY Ayr		
SC51039 67C Ayr	**SC51039** 67C Ayr	**SC51039** AY Ayr		
SC51040 67C Ayr	**SC51040** 67C Ayr	**SC51040** AY Ayr		
SC51041 67C Ayr	**SC51041** 67C Ayr	**SC51041** AY Ayr		
SC51042 67C Ayr	**SC51042** 67C Ayr	**SC51042** AY Ayr		
SC51043 67C Ayr	**SC51043** 67C Ayr	**SC51043** AY Ayr		
SC51044 67C Ayr	**SC51044** 67C Ayr	**SC51044** AY Ayr		
SC51045 67C Ayr	**SC51045** 67C Ayr	**SC51045** AY Ayr		
SC51046 67C Ayr	**SC51046** 67C Ayr	**SC51046** AY Ayr		
SC51047 67C Ayr	**SC51047** 67C Ayr	**SC51047** AY Ayr		
SC51048 67C Ayr	**SC51048** 67C Ayr	**SC51048** AY Ayr		
SC51049 67C Ayr	**SC51049** 67C Ayr	**SC51049** AY Ayr		
SC51050 67C Ayr	**SC51050** 67C Ayr	**SC51050** AY Ayr		
SC51051 67C Ayr	**SC51051** 67C Ayr	**SC51051** AY Ayr		
W51052 BL Bristol	**W51052** 82A Bristol	**W51052** BR Bristol Bath Road		
W51053 BL Bristol				
W51054 CDF Cardiff Canton	**W51054** 82A Bristol	**W51054** CF Cardiff Canton		
W51055 CDF Cardiff Canton	**W51055** 82A Bristol	**W51055** RG Reading		
W51056 CDF Cardiff Canton	**W51056** 82A Bristol	**W51056** RG Reading		
W51057 CDF Cardiff Canton	**M51057** 6A Chester	**W51057** RG Reading		
W51058 CDF Cardiff Canton	**M51058** 6A Chester	**W51058** CF Cardiff Canton		
W51059 CDF Cardiff Canton	**M51059** 6A Chester	**W51059** CF Cardiff Canton		
W51060 BL Bristol	**W51060** 82A Bristol	**W51060** RG Reading	**51060** RG Reading	
W51061 BL Bristol				
W51062 BL Bristol	**W51062** 82A Bristol	**W51062** RG Reading	**51062** RG Reading	
W51063 BL Bristol	**W51063** 82A Bristol	**W51063** RG Reading		
W51064 BL Bristol	**W51064** 82A Bristol	**W51064** RG Reading		
W51065 BL Bristol	**W51065** 82A Bristol	**W51065** RG Reading	**51065** RG Reading	
W51066 BL Bristol	**W51066** 82A Bristol	**W51066** RG Reading	**51066** RG Reading	
W51067 BL Bristol	**W51067** 82A Bristol	**W51067** RG Reading		
W51068 BL Bristol	**W51068** 82A Bristol	**W51068** RG Reading		
W51069 BL Bristol	**W51069** 82A Bristol	**W51069** RG Reading		
W51070 BL Bristol	**W51070** 82A Bristol	**W51070** RG Reading		
W51071 TYS Tyseley	**M51071** 6A Chester	**W51071** CF Cardiff Canton		
W51072 TYS Tyseley	**M51072** 6A Chester	**W51072** CF Cardiff Canton		
W51073 CDF Cardiff Canton	**M51073** 6A Chester	**W51073** CF Cardiff Canton	**51073** RG Reading	
W51074 CDF Cardiff Canton	**M51074** 6A Chester	**W51074** CF Cardiff Canton	**51074** RG Reading	
W51075 RDG Reading	**W51075** 82A Bristol	**W51075** RG Reading		
W51076 TYS Tyseley	**M51076** 6A Chester	**W51076** CF Cardiff Canton	**51076** RG Reading	
W51077 BL Bristol	**W51077** 82A Bristol	**W51077** RG Reading		
W51078 CDF Cardiff Canton	**W51078** 82A Bristol	**W51078** RG Reading		
	W51079 82A Bristol	**W51079** RG Reading	**51079** RG Reading	
W51080 BL Bristol	**W51080** 82A Bristol	**W51080** BR Bristol Bath Road		
W51081 BL Bristol				
W51082 CDF Cardiff Canton	**W51082** 82A Bristol	**W51082** CF Cardiff Canton		
W51083 CDF Cardiff Canton	**W51083** 82A Bristol	**W51083** RG Reading		
W51084 CDF Cardiff Canton	**W51084** 82A Bristol	**W51084** RG Reading		
W51085 CDF Cardiff Canton	**M51085** 6A Chester	**W51085** CF Cardiff Canton		
W51086 CDF Cardiff Canton	**M51086** 6A Chester	**W51086** CF Cardiff Canton	**51086** RG Reading	
W51087 CDF Cardiff Canton	**M51087** 6A Chester	**W51087** CF Cardiff Canton		
W51088 BL Bristol	**W51088** 82A Bristol	**W51088** RG Reading	**51088** RG Reading	
W51089 BL Bristol				
W51090 BL Bristol	**W51090** 82A Bristol	**W51090** RG Reading	**51090** RG Reading	
W51091 BL Bristol	**W51091** 82A Bristol	**W51091** RG Reading		
W51092 BL Bristol	**W51092** 82A Bristol	**W51092** RG Reading		
W51093 BL Bristol	**W51093** 82A Bristol	**W51093** RG Reading		
W51094 BL Bristol	**W51094** 82A Bristol	**W51094** RG Reading	**51094** RG Reading	
W51095 BL Bristol	**W51095** 82A Bristol	**W51095** RG Reading		
W51096 BL Bristol	**W51096** 82A Bristol	**W51096** RG Reading		
W51097 BL Bristol	**W51097** 82A Bristol	**W51097** RG Reading		
W51098 BL Bristol	**W51098** 82A Bristol	**W51098** RG Reading		
W51099 TYS Tyseley	**M51099** 6A Chester	**W51099** CF Cardiff Canton	**51099** RG Reading	
W51100 TYS Tyseley	**M51100** 6A Chester	**W51100** RG Reading		
W51101 CDF Cardiff Canton	**M51101** 6A Chester	**W51101** CF Cardiff Canton		
W51102 CDF Cardiff Canton	**M51102** 6A Chester	**W51102** CF Cardiff Canton		
W51103 RDG Reading	**W51103** 82A Bristol	**W51103** RG Reading	**51103** RG Reading	
W51104 TYS Tyseley	**M51104** 6A Chester	**W51104** CF Cardiff Canton	**51104** RG Reading	
W51105 BL Bristol	**W51105** 82A Bristol	**W51105** RG Reading		
W51106 CDF Cardiff Canton	**W51106** 82A Bristol	**W51106** RG Reading		
	W51107 82A Bristol	**W51107** RG Reading	**51107** RG Reading	
SC51108 64H Leith Central	**E51108** 32A Norwich			
SC51109 64H Leith Central	**SC51109** 64H Leith Central			
SC51110 64H Leith Central	**SC51110** 64H Leith Central	**M51110** TS Tyseley		
SC51111 64H Leith Central	**E51111** 31A Cambridge			
SC51112 64H Leith Central	**SC51112** 64H Leith Central	**M51112** TS Tyseley		
SC51113 64H Leith Central				
SC51114 66C Hamilton	**E51114** 32A Norwich			
SC51115 64H Leith Central	**E51115** 32A Norwich	**E51115** NR Norwich		

1960	1970	1980	1990	2000
SC51116 64H Leith Central	**E51116** 31A Cambridge			
SC51117 66C Hamilton (o/l)	**SC51117** 64H Leith Central	**M51117** LO Longsight		
SC51118 64H Leith Central	**E51118** 52J South Gosforth			
SC51119 66C Hamilton	**SC51119** 64H Leith Central	**M51119** TS Tyseley		
SC51120 64H Leith Central	**E51120** 52J South Gosforth			
SC51121 64H Leith Central	**E51121** 32A Norwich			
SC51122 64H Leith Central	**SC51122** 64H Leith Central			
SC51123 66C Hamilton	**E51123** 31A Cambridge			
SC51124 64H Leith Central	**SC51124** 66C Hamilton	**E51124** NR Norwich		
SC51125 64H Leith Central	**E51125** 32A Norwich			
SC51126 66C Hamilton	**E51126** 31A Cambridge			
SC51127 64H Leith Central	**SC51127** 64H Leith Central	**E51127** NR Norwich		
W51128 BL Bristol	**W51128** 84A Laira	**W51128** CF Cardiff Canton	**51128** CF Cardiff Canton	
W51129 BL Bristol	**M51129** 2A Tyseley	**M51129** TS Tyseley	**51129** TS Tyseley	
W51130 BL Bristol	**M51130** 2A Tyseley	**M51130** TS Tyseley	**51130** TS Tyseley	
W51131 BL Bristol	**M51131** 2A Tyseley	**M51131** TS Tyseley	**51131** TS Tyseley	
W51132 BL Bristol	**W51132** 86A Cardiff Canton	**W51132** CF Cardiff Canton	**51132** CF Cardiff Canton	
W51133 BL Bristol	**M51133** 2A Tyseley	**M51133** TS Tyseley	**51133** CF Cardiff Canton	
W51134 BL Bristol	**W51134** 86A Cardiff Canton	**W51134** CF Cardiff Canton	**51134** CF Cardiff Canton	
W51135 BL Bristol	**W51135** 86A Cardiff Canton	**W51135** CF Cardiff Canton	**51135** CF Cardiff Canton	
W51136 BL Bristol	**W51136** 86A Cardiff Canton	**M51136** TS Tyseley	**51136** CF Cardiff Canton	
W51137 BL Bristol	**W51137** 82A Bristol			
W51138 BL Bristol	**W51138** 86A Cardiff Canton	**M51138** TS Tyseley	**51138** TS Tyseley	
W51139 BL Bristol	**W51139** 86A Cardiff Canton	**W51139** CF Cardiff Canton	**51139** CF Cardiff Canton	
W51140 BL Bristol	**W51140** 86A Cardiff Canton	**W51140** CF Cardiff Canton	**51140** CF Cardiff Canton	
W51141 BL Bristol	**W51141** 84A Laira	**W51141** CF Cardiff Canton	**51141** CF Cardiff Canton	
W51142 BL Bristol	**M51142** 2A Tyseley	**M51142** TS Tyseley	**51142** TS Tyseley	
W51143 BL Bristol	**M51143** 2A Tyseley	**M51143** TS Tyseley	**51143** TS Tyseley	
W51144 BL Bristol	**M51144** 2A Tyseley	**M51144** TS Tyseley	**51144** TS Tyseley	
W51145 BL Bristol	**W51145** 86A Cardiff Canton	**W51145** CF Cardiff Canton	**51145** CF Cardiff Canton	
W51146 BL Bristol	**M51146** 2A Tyseley	**M51146** TS Tyseley	**51146** TS Tyseley	
W51147 BL Bristol	**W51147** 86A Cardiff Canton	**W51147** CF Cardiff Canton	**51147** CF Cardiff Canton	
W51148 BL Bristol	**W51148** 86A Cardiff Canton	**W51148** CF Cardiff Canton	**51148** CF Cardiff Canton	
W51149 BL Bristol	**W51149** 86A Cardiff Canton	**M51149** TS Tyseley	**51149** TS Tyseley	
W51150 BL Bristol	**W51150** 82A Bristol			
W51151 BL Bristol	**W51151** 86A Cardiff Canton	**M51151** TS Tyseley	**51151** TS Tyseley	
W51152 BL Bristol	**W51152** 86A Cardiff Canton	**W51152** CF Cardiff Canton	**51152** CF Cardiff Canton	
W51153 BL Bristol	**W51153** 86A Cardiff Canton	**W51153** CF Cardiff Canton	**51153** CF Cardiff Canton	
E51154 30A Stratford	**E51154** 34G Finsbury Park			
E51155 30A Stratford	**E51155** 34G Finsbury Park			
E51156 30A Stratford	**E51156** 34G Finsbury Park			
E51157 30A Stratford	**E51157** 34G Finsbury Park			
E51158 30A Stratford	**E51158** 34G Finsbury Park			
E51159 30A Stratford	**E51159** 34G Finsbury Park			
E51160 30A Stratford	**E51160** 34G Finsbury Park			
E51161 30A Stratford	**E51161** 34G Finsbury Park			
E51162 30A Stratford	**E51162** 30A Stratford			
E51163 30A Stratford	**E51163** 34G Finsbury Park			
E51164 30A Stratford	**E51164** 30A Stratford			
E51165 30A Stratford	**E51165** 34G Finsbury Park			
E51166 30A Stratford	**E51166** 34G Finsbury Park			
E51167 30A Stratford	**E51167** 34G Finsbury Park			
E51168 30A Stratford	**E51168** 34G Finsbury Park			
E51169 30A Stratford	**E51169** 30A Stratford			
E51170 30A Stratford	**E51170** 34G Finsbury Park			
E51171 30A Stratford	**E51171** 34G Finsbury Park			
E51172 30A Stratford	**E51172** 34G Finsbury Park			
E51173 30A Stratford	**E51173** 34G Finsbury Park			
M51174 3E Monument Lane	**M51174** 6A Chester	**M51174** CH Chester	**51174** NL Neville Hill	
M51175 3E Monument Lane	**M51175** 6A Chester	**M51175** CH Chester	**51175** NL Neville Hill	**51175** LO Longsight
M51176 3E Monument Lane	**M51176** 6A Chester	**M51176** CH Chester		
M51177 3E Monument Lane	**M51177** 6A Chester	**M51177** CH Chester	**51177** NL Neville Hill	**51177** LO Longsight
M51178 3E Monument Lane	**M51178** 6A Chester	**M51178** CH Chester	**51178** NL Neville Hill	
M51179 3E Monument Lane	**M51179** 6A Chester	**M51179** CH Chester	**51179** LA Laira	**51179** LO Longsight
M51180 3E Monument Lane	**M51180** 6A Chester	**M51180** CH Chester	**51180** NL Neville Hill	
M51181 3E Monument Lane	**M51181** 6A Chester	**M51181** CH Chester	**51181** LA Laira	
M51182 3E Monument Lane	**M51182** 6A Chester	**M51182** CH Chester	**51182** HA Haymarket	
M51183 3E Monument Lane	**M51183** 6A Chester	**M51183** CH Chester		
M51184 3E Monument Lane	**M51184** 6A Chester	**M51184** CH Chester	**51184** NL Neville Hill	
M51185 3E Monument Lane	**M51185** 6A Chester	**M51185** CH Chester	**51185** NC Norwich Crown Point	**51185** CK Corkerhill
M51186 3E Monument Lane	**M51186** 6A Chester	**M51186** CH Chester		
M51187 3E Monument Lane	**M51187** 6A Chester	**M51187** CH Chester	**51187** NC Norwich Crown Point	**51187** CK Corkerhill
M51188 3E Monument Lane	**M51188** 6A Chester	**M51188** CH Chester	**51188** NL Neville Hill	**51188** CK Corkerhill
M51189 3C Walsall Rycroft	**M51189** 6A Chester	**M51189** CH Chester	**51189** NC Norwich Crown Point	**51189** LO Longsight
M51190 3C Walsall Rycroft	**M51190** 6A Chester	**M51190** CH Chester	**51190** RG Reading	
M51191 3C Walsall Rycroft	**M51191** 6A Chester	**M51191** CH Chester	**51191** NL Neville Hill	
M51192 3C Walsall Rycroft	**M51192** 6A Chester	**M51192** CH Chester	**51192** NC Norwich Crown Point	**51192** CK Corkerhill
M51193 24E Blackpool South	**M51193** 6A Chester	**M51193** CH Chester		
M51194 24E Blackpool South	**M51194** 6A Chester	**M51194** CH Chester	**51194** NL Neville Hill	
M51195 24E Blackpool South	**M51195** 6A Chester			
M51196 24E Blackpool South	**M51196** 6A Chester	**M51196** CH Chester		
M51197 24E Blackpool South	**M51197** 6A Chester	**M51197** CH Chester		
M51198 24E Blackpool South	**M51198** 6A Chester	**M51198** CH Chester		
M51199 24E Blackpool South	**M51199** 6A Chester	**M51199** CH Chester		
M51200 24E Blackpool South	**M51200** 6A Chester	**M51200** CH Chester		
M51201 24E Blackpool South	**M51201** 6A Chester	**M51201** CH Chester	**51201** NC Norwich Crown Point	**51201** LO Longsight
M51202 5D Stoke-on-Trent	**M51202** 6A Chester	**M51202** CH Chester		

1960	1970	1980	1990	2000
M51203 5D Stoke-on-Trent	**M51203** 6A Chester	**M51203** CH Chester		
E51204 50A York	**E51204** 32A Norwich	**E51204** HT Heaton		
E51205 50A York	**E51205** 52J South Gosforth	**E51205** DN Darlington	**51205** LA Laira	**51205** LO Longsight
E51206 56G Bradford Hammerton St	**E51206** 52J South Gosforth	**E51206** HT Heaton		
E51207 56G Bradford Hammerton St	**E51207** 32A Norwich	**E51207** DN Darlington	**51207** CA Cambridge	
E51208 53B Hull Botanic Gardens	**E51208** 52J South Gosforth	**E51208** NL Neville Hill	**51208** CA Cambridge	
E51209 53B Hull Botanic Gardens	**E51209** 52J South Gosforth	**E51209** HT Heaton		
E51210 56G Bradford Hammerton St	**E51210** 52J South Gosforth	**E51210** DN Darlington	**51210** LO Longsight	**51210** LO Longsight
E51211 56G Bradford Hammerton St	**E51211** 52J South Gosforth	**E51211** DN Darlington	**51211** RG Reading	
E51212 56G Bradford Hammerton St	**E51212** 51A Darlington	**E51212** CA Cambridge	**51212** OO Old Oak Common	
E51213 50A York	**E51213** 32A Norwich	**E51213** HT Heaton	**51213** NC Norwich Crown Point	**51213** LO Longsight
E51214 50A York	**E51214** 52J South Gosforth	**E51214** HT Heaton		
E51215 53B Hull Botanic Gardens	**E51215** 52J South Gosforth	**E51215** CA Cambridge	**51215** OO Old Oak Common	
E51216 53B Hull Botanic Gardens	**E51216** 51A Darlington	**E51216** HT Heaton		
E51217 South Gosforth	**E51217** 32A Norwich	**E51217** BG Hull Botanic Gardens		
E51218 50B Neville Hill	**E51218** 32A Norwich	**E51218** HT Heaton	**51218** NC Norwich Crown Point	
E51219 South Gosforth	**E51219** 51A Darlington	**E51219** DN Darlington	**51219** LA Laira	
E51220 South Gosforth	**E51220** 51A Darlington	**E51220** CA Cambridge	**51220** OO Old Oak Common	
E51221 South Gosforth	**E51221** 52J South Gosforth	**E51221** HT Heaton	**51221** OO Old Oak Common	
E51222 50B Neville Hill	**E51222** 32A Norwich	**E51222** HT Heaton	**51222** CH Chester	
E51223 50A York	**E51223** 32A Norwich	**E51223** DN Darlington	**51223** LA Laira	
SC51224 64H Leith Central	**SC51224** 62B Dundee	**SC51224** DE Dundee	**51224** ED Eastfield	**51224** LO Longsight
SC51225 66C Hamilton	**E51225** 50C Hull Botanic Gardens	**E51225** CA Cambridge	**51225** OO Old Oak Common	
SC51226 66C Hamilton	**E51226** 50C Hull Botanic Gardens	**E51226** DN Darlington	**51226** RG Reading	**51226** CK Corkerhill
SC51227 66C Hamilton	**SC51227** 64H Leith Central	**SC51227** DE Dundee		
SC51228 64H Leith Central	**SC51228** 62B Dundee	**SC51228** DE Dundee	**51228** HA Haymarket	**51228** LO Longsight
SC51229 66C Hamilton	**E51229** 50C Hull Botanic Gardens	**E51229** HT Heaton		
SC51230 66C Hamilton	**E51230** 50C Hull Botanic Gardens	**E51230** NL Neville Hill	**51230** NC Norwich Crown Point	**51230** LO Longsight
SC51231 64H Leith Central	**SC51231** 64H Leith Central	**SC51231** DE Dundee	**51231** HA Haymarket	**51231** CK Corkerhill (s)
SC51232 66C Hamilton	**SC51232** 64H Leith Central	**SC51232** DE Dundee		
SC51233 64H Leith Central	**SC51233** 64H Leith Central	**SC51233** DE Dundee		
SC51234 66C Hamilton	**SC51234** 66C Hamilton	**SC51234** DE Dundee	**51234** HA Haymarket	
SC51235 66C Hamilton	**SC51235** 64H Leith Central	**SC51235** HA Haymarket		
SC51236 66C Hamilton	**E51236** 50C Hull Botanic Gardens	**E51236** DN Darlington		
SC51237 66C Hamilton	**SC51237** 62B Dundee	**SC51237** HA Haymarket		
SC51238 62B Dundee	**E51238** 50C Hull Botanic Gardens			
SC51239 62B Dundee	**SC51239** 62B Dundee	**SC51239** DE Dundee		
SC51240 62B Dundee	**SC51240** 62B Dundee	**SC51240** DE Dundee		
SC51241 62B Dundee	**SC51241** 62B Dundee	**SC51241** DE Dundee	**51241** HA Haymarket	
SC51242 62B Dundee	**SC51242** 64H Leith Central	**SC51242** DE Dundee		
SC51243 62B Dundee	**SC51243** 64H Leith Central	**SC51243** IS Inverness		
SC51244 64H Leith Central	**SC51244** 66C Hamilton	**SC51244** DE Dundee	**51244** HA Haymarket	
SC51245 62B Dundee	**SC51245** 64H Leith Central	**SC51245** DE Dundee	**51245** CH Chester	
SC51246 62B Dundee	**E51246** 50C Hull Botanic Gardens	**E51246** DN Darlington	**51246** LA Laira	
SC51247 64H Leith Central	**E51247** 50C Hull Botanic Gardens	**E51247** DN Darlington	**51247** NC Norwich Crown Point	**51247** CK Corkerhill
SC51248 64H Leith Central	**SC51248** 66C Hamilton	**SC51248** HA Haymarket		
SC51249 62B Dundee	**SC51249** 62B Dundee	**SC51249** DE Dundee	**51249** ED Eastfield	
SC51250 62B Dundee	**SC51250** 66C Hamilton	**SC51250** DE Dundee		
SC51251 62B Dundee	**SC51251** 62B Dundee	**SC51251** DE Dundee		
SC51252 62B Dundee	**E51252** 50C Hull Botanic Gardens	**E51252** HT Heaton	**51252** NC Norwich Crown Point	
SC51253 62B Dundee	**SC51253** 64H Leith Central	**SC51253** DE Dundee	**51253** NL Neville Hill	**51253** CK Corkerhill
E51254 34B Hornsey	**E51254** 34G Finsbury Park	**E51254** NR Norwich		
E51255 34B Hornsey	**E51255** 34G Finsbury Park	**E51255** NR Norwich		
E51256 34B Hornsey	**E51256** 34G Finsbury Park	**E51256** NR Norwich		
E51257 34B Hornsey	**E51257** 34G Finsbury Park	**E51257** NR Norwich		
E51258 34B Hornsey	**E51258** 34G Finsbury Park	**E51258** NR Norwich		
E51259 34B Hornsey	**E51259** 34G Finsbury Park	**E51259** NR Norwich		
E51260 34B Hornsey	**E51260** 34G Finsbury Park	**E51260** NR Norwich		
E51261 34B Hornsey	**E51261** 34G Finsbury Park	**E51261** NR Norwich		
E51262 34B Hornsey	**E51262** 34G Finsbury Park	**E51262** NR Norwich		
E51263 34B Hornsey	**E51263** 34G Finsbury Park	**E51263** NR Norwich		
E51264 34B Hornsey				
E51265 34B Hornsey	**E51265** 40A Lincoln	**E51265** NR Norwich		
E51266 34B Hornsey	**E51266** 34G Finsbury Park	**E51266** NR Norwich		
E51267 34B Hornsey	**E51267** 34G Finsbury Park	**E51267** NR Norwich		
E51268 34B Hornsey	**E51268** 34G Finsbury Park	**E51268** NR Norwich		
E51269 34B Hornsey	**E51269** 34G Finsbury Park	**E51269** NR Norwich		
E51270 34B Hornsey	**E51270** 34G Finsbury Park	**E51270** NR Norwich		
E51271 34B Hornsey	**E51271** 34G Finsbury Park	**E51271** NR Norwich		
E51272 34B Hornsey	**E51272** 34G Finsbury Park	**E51272** NR Norwich		
E51273 34B Hornsey	**E51273** 34G Finsbury Park	**E51273** NR Norwich		
E51274 31A Cambridge	**E51274** 31A Cambridge	**E51274** HT Heaton		
E51275 31A Cambridge	**E51275** 34G Finsbury Park	**E51275** BG Hull Botanic Gardens		
E51276 31A Cambridge	**E51276** 31A Cambridge	**E51276** HT Heaton		
E51277 31A Cambridge	**E51277** 31A Cambridge	**E51277** NR Norwich		
E51278 31A Cambridge	**E51278** 31A Cambridge	**E51278** HT Heaton		
E51279 31A Cambridge	**E51279** 31A Cambridge	**E51279** HT Heaton		
E51280 31A Cambridge	**E51280** 34G Finsbury Park	**E51280** LN Lincoln		
E51281 31A Cambridge	**E51281** 34G Finsbury Park	**E51281** LN Lincoln		
E51282 31A Cambridge	**E51282** 31A Cambridge	**E51282** HT Heaton		
E51283 31A Cambridge	**E51283** 40A Lincoln	**E51283** HT Heaton		
E51284 31A Cambridge	**E51284** 40A Lincoln	**E51284** LN Lincoln		
E51285 31A Cambridge	**E51285** 40A Lincoln	**E51285** LN Lincoln		
E51286 31A Cambridge	**E51286** 40A Lincoln	**E51286** LN Lincoln		
E51287 31A Cambridge	**E51287** 40A Lincoln	**E51287** LN Lincoln		
E51288 31A Cambridge	**E51288** 40A Lincoln	**E51288** LN Lincoln		
E51289 34B Hornsey	**E51289** 34G Finsbury Park	**E51289** NR Norwich		

1960	1970	1980	1990	2000
E51290 34B Hornsey	**E51290** 34G Finsbury Park	**E51290** NR Norwich		
E51291 34B Hornsey	**E51291** 34G Finsbury Park	**E51291** NR Norwich		
E51292 34B Hornsey	**E51292** 34G Finsbury Park	**E51292** NR Norwich		
E51293 34B Hornsey	**E51293** 34G Finsbury Park	**E51293** NR Norwich		
E51294 34B Hornsey	**E51294** 34G Finsbury Park	**E51294** NR Norwich		
E51295 34B Hornsey	**E51295** 34G Finsbury Park	**E51295** NR Norwich		
E51296 34B Hornsey	**E51296** 30A Stratford	**E51296** LN Lincoln		
E51297 34B Hornsey	**E51297** 34G Finsbury Park	**E51297** NR Norwich		
E51298 34B Hornsey	**E51298** 34G Finsbury Park	**E51298** NR Norwich		
E51299 34B Hornsey	**E51299** 34G Finsbury Park	**E51299** HT Heaton		
E51300 40A Lincoln	**E51300** 34G Finsbury Park			
E51301 34B Hornsey	**E51301** 34G Finsbury Park	**E51301** HT Heaton		
	W51302 84A Laira	**W51302** BR Bristol Bath Road		
	W51303 84A Laira	**W51303** LA Laira		
	W51304 81D Reading	**W51304** BR Bristol Bath Road		
	W51305 81D Reading	**W51305** LA Laira		
	W51306 84A Laira	**W51306** LA Laira	**51306** TS Tyseley	
	W51307 84A Laira	**W51307** BR Bristol Bath Road		
	W51308 84A Laira	**W51308** BR Bristol Bath Road		
	W51309 81D Reading	**W51309** BR Bristol Bath Road		
	W51310 81D Reading	**W51310** BR Bristol Bath Road		
	W51311 84A Laira	**W51311** RG Reading		
	W51312 84A Laira	**W51312** LA Laira		
	W51313 84A Laira	**W51313** LA Laira		
	W51314 84A Laira	**W51314** BR Bristol Bath Road	**51314** TS Tyseley	
	W51315 81D Reading	**W51315** BR Bristol Bath Road	**51315** CF Cardiff Canton	
	W51316 81D Reading	**W51316** LA Laira	**51316** TS Tyseley	
	W51317 84A Laira	**W51317** BR Bristol Bath Road		
	W51318 84A Laira	**W51318** LA Laira		
	W51319 81D Reading	**W51319** BR Bristol Bath Road	**51319** OO Old Oak Common	
	W51320 81D Reading	**W51320** LA Laira		
	W51321 84A Laira	**W51321** LA Laira	**51321** TS Tyseley	
	W51322 84A Laira	**W51322** BR Bristol Bath Road		
	W51323 84A Laira	**W51323** BR Bristol Bath Road		
	W51324 81D Reading	**W51324** BR Bristol Bath Road		
	W51325 81D Reading	**W51325** BR Bristol Bath Road		
	W51326 84A Laira	**W51326** RG Reading		
	W51327 84A Laira	**W51327** LA Laira		
	W51328 84A Laira	**W51328** LA Laira		
	W51329 84A Laira	**W51329** BR Bristol Bath Road	**51329** TS Tyseley	
	W51330 81D Reading	**W51330** BR Bristol Bath Road	**51330** CF Cardiff Canton	
	W51331 81D Reading	**W51331** LA Laira	**51331** TS Tyseley	
W51332 RDG Reading	**W51332** 81D Reading	**W51332** RG Reading	**51332** RG Reading	
	W51333 81D Reading	**W51333** RG Reading	**51333** RG Reading	
	W51334 81D Reading	**W51334** CF Cardiff Canton	**51334** TS Tyseley	
	W51335 81D Reading	**W51335** RG Reading	**51335** RG Reading	
	W51336 81D Reading	**W51336** RG Reading	**51336** RG Reading	
	W51337 81D Reading	**W51337** RG Reading	**51337** RG Reading	
	W51338 81D Reading	**W51338** CF Cardiff Canton	**51338** TS Tyseley	
	W51339 81D Reading	**W51339** CF Cardiff Canton	**51339** TS Tyseley	
	W51340 81D Reading	**W51340** RG Reading	**51340** RG Reading	
	W51341 81D Reading	**W51341** RG Reading	**51341** RG Reading	**51341** Pigs Bay (s)
	W51342 81D Reading	**W51342** RG Reading	**51342** RG Reading	
	W51343 81D Reading	**W51343** RG Reading	**51343** RG Reading	
	W51344 81D Reading	**W51344** RG Reading	**51344** RG Reading	
	W51345 84A Laira	**W51345** RG Reading	**51345** RG Reading	
	W51346 84A Laira	**W51346** RG Reading	**51346** RG Reading	
	W51347 81D Reading	**W51347** RG Reading	**51347** RG Reading	
	W51348 81D Reading	**W51348** CF Cardiff Canton	**51348** TS Tyseley	
	W51349 81D Reading	**W51349** RG Reading	**51349** RG Reading	
	W51350 81D Reading	**W51350** RG Reading	**51350** RG Reading	
	W51351 81D Reading	**W51351** RG Reading	**51351** RG Reading	
	W51352 81D Reading	**W51352** CF Cardiff Canton	**51352** TS Tyseley	
	W51353 81D Reading	**W51353** RG Reading	**51353** TS Tyseley	
	W51354 81D Reading	**W51354** RG Reading	**51354** RG Reading	
	W51355 81D Reading	**W51355** RG Reading	**51355** RG Reading	
	W51356 81D Reading	**W51356** RG Reading	**51356** RG Reading	**51356** BY Bletchley
	W51358 81D Reading	**W51358** RG Reading	**51358** RG Reading	
	W51359 81D Reading	**W51359** RG Reading	**51359** RG Reading	
	W51360 81D Reading	**W51360** RG Reading	**51360** TS Tyseley	
	W51361 81D Reading	**W51361** RG Reading	**51361** RG Reading	
	W51362 81D Reading	**W51362** RG Reading	**51362** RG Reading	
	W51363 81D Reading	**W51363** RG Reading	**51363** RG Reading	
	W51364 81D Reading	**W51364** RG Reading	**51364** TS Tyseley	
	W51365 81D Reading	**W51365** RG Reading	**51365** TS Tyseley	
	W51366 81D Reading	**W51366** RG Reading	**51366** RG Reading	**51366** Pigs Bay (s)
	W51367 81D Reading	**W51367** RG Reading	**51367** RG Reading	
	W51368 81D Reading	**W51368** RG Reading	**51368** TS Tyseley	
	W51369 81D Reading	**W51369** RG Reading	**51369** TS Tyseley	
	W51370 81D Reading	**W51370** RG Reading	**51370** TS Tyseley	
	W51371 81D Reading	**W51371** RG Reading	**51371** TS Tyseley	
	W51372 81D Reading	**W51372** RG Reading	**51372** TS Tyseley	
	W51373 81D Reading	**W51373** RG Reading	**51373** TS Tyseley	
W51374 RDG Reading	**W51374** 81D Reading	**W51374** RG Reading	**51374** RG Reading	
	W51375 81D Reading	**W51375** RG Reading	**51375** RG Reading	
	W51376 81D Reading	**W51376** CF Cardiff Canton	**51376** TS Tyseley	
	W51377 81D Reading	**W51377** RG Reading	**51377** RG Reading	

1960	1970	1980	1990	2000
	W51378 81D Reading	**W51378** RG Reading	**51378** RG Reading	
	W51379 81D Reading	**W51379** RG Reading	**51379** RG Reading	
	W51380 81D Reading	**W51380** CF Cardiff Canton	**51380** TS Tyseley	
	W51381 81D Reading	**W51381** RG Reading	**51381** RG Reading	
	W51382 81D Reading	**W51382** CF Cardiff Canton	**51382** TS Tyseley	
	W51383 81D Reading	**W51383** RG Reading	**51383** RG Reading	**51383** Pigs Bay (s)
	W51384 81D Reading	**W51384** RG Reading	**51384** RG Reading	
	W51385 81D Reading	**W51385** RG Reading	**51385** RG Reading	
	W51386 81D Reading	**W51386** RG Reading	**51386** RG Reading	
	W51387 84A Laira	**W51387** RG Reading	**51387** RG Reading	
	W51388 84A Laira	**W51388** RG Reading	**51388** RG Reading	
	W51389 81D Reading	**W51389** RG Reading	**51389** RG Reading	
	W51390 81D Reading	**W51390** CF Cardiff Canton	**51390** TS Tyseley	
	W51391 81D Reading	**W51391** RG Reading	**51391** RG Reading	
	W51392 81D Reading	**W51392** RG Reading	**51392** RG Reading	
	W51393 81D Reading	**W51393** RG Reading	**51393** RG Reading	
	W51394 81D Reading	**W51394** CF Cardiff Canton	**51394** TS Tyseley	
	W51395 81D Reading	**W51395** RG Reading	**51395** TS Tyseley	
	W51396 81D Reading	**W51396** RG Reading	**51396** RG Reading	
	W51397 81D Reading	**W51397** RG Reading	**51397** RG Reading	
	W51398 81D Reading	**W51398** RG Reading	**51398** RG Reading	**51398** BY Bletchley
	W51399 81D Reading	**W51399** RG Reading	**51399** RG Reading	
	W51400 81D Reading	**W51400** RG Reading	**51400** RG Reading	**51400** Pigs Bay (s)
	W51401 81D Reading	**W51401** RG Reading	**51401** RG Reading	
	W51402 81D Reading	**W51402** RG Reading	**51402** TS Tyseley	
	W51403 81D Reading	**W51403** RG Reading		
	W51404 81D Reading	**W51404** RG Reading	**51404** RG Reading	
	W51405 81D Reading	**W51405** RG Reading	**51405** RG Reading	
	W51406 81D Reading	**W51406** RG Reading	**51406** TS Tyseley	
	W51407 81D Reading	**W51407** RG Reading	**51407** TS Tyseley	
	W51408 81D Reading	**W51408** RG Reading	**51408** RG Reading	
	W51409 81D Reading	**W51409** RG Reading	**51409** RG Reading	
	W51410 81D Reading	**W51410** RG Reading	**51410** TS Tyseley	
	W51411 81D Reading	**W51411** RG Reading	**51411** TS Tyseley	
	W51412 81D Reading	**W51412** RG Reading	**51412** TS Tyseley	
	W51413 81D Reading	**W51413** RG Reading	**51413** TS Tyseley	
	W51414 81D Reading	**W51414** RG Reading	**51414** TS Tyseley	
	W51415 81D Reading	**W51415** RG Reading	**51415** TS Tyseley	
	M51416 8J Allerton	**M51416** AN Allerton	**51416** CF Cardiff Canton	
	M51417 8J Allerton	**M51417** AN Allerton	**51417** CF Cardiff Canton	
	M51418 8J Allerton	**M51418** AN Allerton	**51418** CH Chester	
	M51419 8J Allerton	**M51419** AN Allerton	**51419** CF Cardiff Canton	
	M51420 8J Allerton	**M51420** AN Allerton	**51420** NL Neville Hill	
	M51421 8J Allerton	**M51421** AN Allerton	**51421** CH Chester	
	M51422 8J Allerton	**M51422** AN Allerton	**51422** CH Chester	
	M51423 8J Allerton			
	M51424 8J Allerton	**M51424** AN Allerton	**51424** CH Chester	
E51425 56G Bradford Hammerton St	**E51425** 55F Bradford Hammerton St	**E51425** HS Bradford Hammerton St	**51425** RG Reading	
E51426 56G Bradford Hammerton St	**E51426** 55F Bradford Hammerton St	**E51426** CA Cambridge	**51426** CH Chester	**51426** LO Longsight
E51427 56G Bradford Hammerton St	**E51427** 55F Bradford Hammerton St	**E51427** HT Heaton	**51427** NC Norwich Crown Point	
E51428 56G Bradford Hammerton St	**E51428** 55F Bradford Hammerton St	**E51428** HS Bradford Hammerton St	**51428** NC Norwich Crown Point	**51428** LO Longsight
E51429 56G Bradford Hammerton St	**E51429** 55F Bradford Hammerton St	**E51429** HT Heaton	**51429** NC Norwich Crown Point	
E51430 56G Bradford Hammerton St	**E51430** 55F Bradford Hammerton St	**E51430** HS Bradford Hammerton St		
E51431 56G Bradford Hammerton St	**E51431** 55F Bradford Hammerton St	**E51431** HS Bradford Hammerton St	**51431** RG Reading	
E51432 56G Bradford Hammerton St	**E51432** 55F Bradford Hammerton St	**E51432** HS Bradford Hammerton St	**51432** RG Reading	**51432** LO Longsight
E51433 56G Bradford Hammerton St	**E51433** 55F Bradford Hammerton St	**E51433** HS Bradford Hammerton St		
E51434 56G Bradford Hammerton St	**E51434** 55F Bradford Hammerton St	**E51434** HS Bradford Hammerton St	**51434** RG Reading	
E51435 53B Hull Botanic Gardens	**E51435** 52J South Gosforth	**E51435** NL Neville Hill	**51435** NL Neville Hill	**51435** CK Corkerhill
E51436 53B Hull Botanic Gardens	**E51436** 52J South Gosforth	**E51436** NL Neville Hill	**51436** CF Cardiff Canton	
E51437 50A York	**E51437** 52J South Gosforth	**E51437** CA Cambridge	**51437** RG Reading	
E51438 53B Hull Botanic Gardens	**E51438** 52J South Gosforth	**E51438** HT Heaton	**51438** CA Cambridge	
E51439 53B Hull Botanic Gardens	**E51439** 52J South Gosforth	**E51439** HT Heaton		
E51440 56G Bradford Hammerton St	**E51440** 52J South Gosforth	**E51440** HS Bradford Hammerton St		
E51441 53B Hull Botanic Gardens	**E51441** 52J South Gosforth	**E51441** HT Heaton		
E51442 South Gosforth	**E51442** 55H Neville Hill	**E51442** CA Cambridge	**51442** NC Norwich Crown Point	**51442** LO Longsight
E51443 51A Darlington	**E51443** 52J South Gosforth	**E51443** CA Cambridge	**51443** OO Old Oak Common	
E51444 51A Darlington	**E51444** 50C Hull Botanic Gardens	**E51444** CA Cambridge	**51444** CA Cambridge	
SC51445 62B Dundee	**SC51445** 66C Hamilton	**W51445** BR Bristol Bath Road	**51445** CA Cambridge	
SC51446 62B Dundee	**SC51446** 66C Hamilton	**W51446** BR Bristol Bath Road		
SC51447 62B Dundee	**SC51447** 66C Hamilton			
SC51448 62B Dundee	**SC51448** 66C Hamilton	**SC51448** ED Eastfield		
SC51449 62B Dundee	**SC51449** 66C Hamilton	**W51449** BR Bristol Bath Road		
SC51450 62B Dundee	**SC51450** 66C Hamilton	**W51450** BR Bristol Bath Road		
SC51451 62B Dundee	**SC51451** 66C Hamilton	**SC51451** ED Eastfield		
SC51452 62B Dundee	**SC51452** 66C Hamilton	**W51452** BR Bristol Bath Road		
SC51453 62B Dundee	**SC51453** 66C Hamilton	**SC51453** ED Eastfield		
SC51454 62B Dundee	**SC51454** 66C Hamilton	**SC51454** AY Ayr		
SC51455 62B Dundee	**SC51455** 66C Hamilton	**SC51455** ED Eastfield		
SC51456 62B Dundee	**SC51456** 66C Hamilton	**SC51456** AY Ayr		
SC51457 62B Dundee	**SC51457** 62B Dundee	**SC51457** ED Eastfield		
SC51458 61A Kittybrewster (o/l)	**SC51458** 62B Dundee	**SC51458** ED Eastfield		
SC51459 64H Leith Central	**SC51459** 62B Dundee	**SC51459** ED Eastfield		
SC51460 64H Leith Central	**SC51460** 62B Dundee	**SC51460** ED Eastfield		
SC51461 67C Ayr	**SC51461** 66C Hamilton	**SC51461** AY Ayr		
SC51462 67C Ayr	**SC51462** 66C Hamilton	**W51462** BR Bristol Bath Road	**51462** CH Chester	
SC51463 64H Leith Central	**SC51463** 66C Hamilton	**W51463** BR Bristol Bath Road	**51463** NL Neville Hill	**51463** LO Longsight
SC51464 67C Ayr	**SC51464** 60A Inverness	**SC51464** ED Eastfield		

1960	1970	1980	1990	2000
SC51465 67C Ayr	**SC51465** 67C Ayr	**SC51465** ED Eastfield		
SC51466 64H Leith Central	**SC51466** 64H Leith Central	**SC51466** ED Eastfield		
SC51467 64H Leith Central	**SC51467** 64H Leith Central	**SC51467** ED Eastfield		
SC51468 67C Ayr	**SC51468** 64H Leith Central	**SC51468** ED Eastfield	**51468** ED Eastfield	
SC51469 67C Ayr	**SC51469** 64H Leith Central	**SC51469** AY Ayr		
SC51470 64H Leith Central	**SC51470** 64H Leith Central	**SC51470** AY Ayr		
E51471 34B Hornsey	**E51471** 34G Finsbury Park	**E51471** HT Heaton		
E51472 34B Hornsey	**E51472** 34G Finsbury Park	**E51472** BG Hull Botanic Gardens		
SC51473 61A Kittybrewster	**SC51473** 66C Hamilton	**SC51473** HA Haymarket		
SC51474 61A Kittybrewster	**SC51474** 66C Hamilton	**SC51474** HA Haymarket		
SC51475 61A Kittybrewster	**SC51475** 66C Hamilton	**SC51475** HA Haymarket		
SC51476 61A Kittybrewster	**SC51476** 66C Hamilton	**SC51476** HA Haymarket		
SC51477 61A Kittybrewster	**SC51477** 66C Hamilton	**SC51477** HA Haymarket		
SC51478 61A Kittybrewster	**SC51478** 66C Hamilton	**E51478** HT Heaton		
SC51479 61A Kittybrewster	**SC51479** 66C Hamilton	**SC51479** HA Haymarket		
SC51480 61A Kittybrewster	**SC51480** 66C Hamilton	**SC51480** HA Haymarket		
SC51481 61A Kittybrewster	**SC51481** 66C Hamilton	**SC51481** HA Haymarket		
SC51482 66C Hamilton	**SC51482** 66C Hamilton	**E51482** HT Heaton		
SC51483 66C Hamilton	**SC51483** 66C Hamilton	**SC51483** HA Haymarket		
SC51484 66C Hamilton	**SC51484** 66C Hamilton	**E51484** LN Lincoln		
SC51485 66C Hamilton	**SC51485** 66C Hamilton	**E51485** HT Heaton		
SC51486 66C Hamilton	**SC51486** 66C Hamilton			
SC51487 66C Hamilton	**SC51487** 66C Hamilton			
SC51488 66C Hamilton				
SC51489 66C Hamilton	**SC51489** 66C Hamilton	**E51489** HT Heaton		
SC51490 66C Hamilton	**SC51490** 66C Hamilton	**M51490** TS Tyseley		
SC51491 66C Hamilton	**SC51491** 66C Hamilton			
SC51492 66C Hamilton	**SC51492** 66C Hamilton	**M51492** TS Tyseley		
SC51493 66C Hamilton	**SC51493** 66C Hamilton	**E51493** HT Heaton		
SC51494 66C Hamilton	**SC51494** 66C Hamilton			
E51495 56G Bradford Hammerton St	**E51495** 55F Bradford Hammerton St	**W51495** BR Bristol Bath Road	**51495** NL Neville Hill	
E51496 56G Bradford Hammerton St	**E51496** 55F Bradford Hammerton St	**E51496** HS Bradford Hammerton St	**51496** CH Chester	**51496** LO Longsight
E51497 56G Bradford Hammerton St	**E51497** 55F Bradford Hammerton St	**E51497** HS Bradford Hammerton St		
E51498 56G Bradford Hammerton St	**E51498** 55F Bradford Hammerton St	**E51498** HS Bradford Hammerton St	**51498** RG Reading	**51498** LO Longsight
E51499 56G Bradford Hammerton St	**E51499** 55F Bradford Hammerton St	**E51499** HS Bradford Hammerton St	**51499** RG Reading	**51499** CK Corkerhill
E51500 56G Bradford Hammerton St	**E51500** 55F Bradford Hammerton St	**W51500** BR Bristol Bath Road	**51500** LA Laira	**51500** CK Corkerhill (s)
E51501 56G Bradford Hammerton St	**E51501** 55F Bradford Hammerton St	**E51501** HS Bradford Hammerton St	**51501** RG Reading	**51501** CK Corkerhill
E51502 56G Bradford Hammerton St	**E51502** 55F Bradford Hammerton St	**E51502** HS Bradford Hammerton St		
E51503 56G Bradford Hammerton St	**E51503** 55F Bradford Hammerton St	**E51503** HS Bradford Hammerton St	**51503** RG Reading	
E51504 56G Bradford Hammerton St	**E51504** 55F Bradford Hammerton St	**E51504** HS Bradford Hammerton St	**51504** RG Reading	
E51505 53B Hull Botanic Gardens	**E51505** 52J South Gosforth	**W51505** BR Bristol Bath Road	**51505** CH Chester	
E51506 53B Hull Botanic Gardens	**E51506** 52J South Gosforth	**E51506** NL Neville Hill	**51506** NC Norwich Crown Point	**51506** LO Longsight
E51507 50A York	**E51507** 52J South Gosforth			
E51508 53B Hull Botanic Gardens	**E51508** 52J South Gosforth	**E51508** NL Neville Hill	**51508** NC Norwich Crown Point	
E51509 53B Hull Botanic Gardens	**E51509** 52J South Gosforth	**W51509** BR Bristol Bath Road	**51509** CH Chester	**51509** CK Corkerhill
E51510 56G Bradford Hammerton St	**E51510** 52J South Gosforth	**W51510** BR Bristol Bath Road		
E51511 53B Hull Botanic Gardens	**E51511** 52J South Gosforth	**W51511** BR Bristol Bath Road	**51511** CH Chester	**51511** CK Corkerhill
E51512 South Gosforth	**E51512** 55H Neville Hill	**W51512** BR Bristol Bath Road	**51512** LA Laira	**51512** CK Corkerhill
E51513 51A Darlington	**E51513** 52J South Gosforth	**W51513** BR Bristol Bath Road	**51513** CH Chester	
E51514 51A Darlington	**E51514** 52J South Gosforth	**E51514** NL Neville Hill		
SC51515 62A Thornton Junction	**SC51515** 66C Hamilton	**W51515** BR Bristol Bath Road		
SC51516 62A Thornton Junction	**SC51516** 66C Hamilton	**SC51516** ED Eastfield		
SC51517 62A Thornton Junction	**SC51517** 66C Hamilton	**W51517** BR Bristol Bath Road		
SC51518 62A Thornton Junction	**SC51518** 66C Hamilton	**SC51518** ED Eastfield		
SC51519 62A Thornton Junction	**SC51519** 66C Hamilton	**W51519** BR Bristol Bath Road		
SC51520 62A Thornton Junction	**SC51520** 66C Hamilton	**SC51520** AY Ayr		
SC51521 62A Thornton Junction	**SC51521** 66C Hamilton	**W51521** BR Bristol Bath Road		
SC51522 62B Dundee	**SC51522** 66C Hamilton	**W51522** BR Bristol Bath Road		
SC51523 62B Dundee	**SC51523** 66C Hamilton	**W51523** BR Bristol Bath Road		
SC51524 62B Dundee	**SC51524** 66C Hamilton	**SC51524** ED Eastfield	**51524** NL Neville Hill	
SC51525 62B Dundee	**SC51525** 66C Hamilton	**SC51525** ED Eastfield		
SC51526 62B Dundee	**SC51526** 66C Hamilton	**SC51526** ED Eastfield		
SC51527 62B Dundee	**SC51527** 62B Dundee	**SC51527** AY Ayr		
SC51528 61A Kittybrewster (o/l)	**SC51528** 62B Dundee	**SC51528** ED Eastfield		
SC51529 64H Leith Central	**SC51529** 64H Leith Central	**SC51529** AY Ayr		
SC51530 64H Leith Central	**SC51530** 64H Leith Central	**W51530** BR Bristol Bath Road	**51530** LA Laira	
SC51531 67C Ayr	**SC51531** 66C Hamilton	**SC51531** ED Eastfield	**51531** CH Chester	
SC51532 67C Ayr	**SC51532** 66C Hamilton	**SC51532** ED Eastfield		
SC51533 64H Leith Central	**SC51533** 66C Hamilton	**W51533** BR Bristol Bath Road	**51533** NL Neville Hill	**51533** LO Longsight
SC51534 67C Ayr	**SC51534** 60A Inverness	**SC51534** ED Eastfield		
SC51535 67C Ayr	**SC51535** 67C Ayr	**SC51535** ED Eastfield		
SC51536 64H Leith Central	**SC51536** 64H Leith Central	**SC51536** AY Ayr		
SC51537 64H Leith Central	**SC51537** 64H Leith Central	**SC51537** AY Ayr		
SC51538 67C Ayr	**SC51538** 64H Leith Central	**SC51538** ED Eastfield		
SC51539 67C Ayr	**SC51539** 64H Leith Central	**SC51539** AY Ayr		
SC51540 64H Leith Central	**SC51540** 64H Leith Central			
E51541 56G Bradford Hammerton St	**E51541** 30A Stratford	**E51541** NL Neville Hill		
E51542 56G Bradford Hammerton St	**E51542** 55H Neville Hill	**E51542** NL Neville Hill		
E51543 56G Bradford Hammerton St	**E51543** 55H Neville Hill	**E51543** NL Neville Hill		
	E51544 55H Neville Hill	**E51544** NL Neville Hill		
	E51545 55H Neville Hill	**E51545** NL Neville Hill		
	E51546 55H Neville Hill	**E51546** NL Neville Hill		
	E51547 55H Neville Hill			
	E51548 55H Neville Hill	**E51548** NL Neville Hill		
	E51549 55H Neville Hill	**E51549** NL Neville Hill		
	E51550 55H Neville Hill	**E51550** NL Neville Hill		
E51551 56G Bradford Hammerton St	**E51551** 30A Stratford	**E51551** NL Neville Hill		

1960	1970	1980	1990	2000
E51552 56G Bradford Hammerton St	**E51552** 55H Neville Hill	**E51552** NL Neville Hill		
E51553 56G Bradford Hammerton St	**E51553** 55H Neville Hill	**E51553** NL Neville Hill		
	E51554 55H Neville Hill	**E51554** NL Neville Hill		
	E51555 55H Neville Hill	**E51555** NL Neville Hill		
	E51556 55H Neville Hill	**E51556** NL Neville Hill		
	E51557 55H Neville Hill	**E51557** NL Neville Hill		
	E51558 55H Neville Hill	**E51558** NL Neville Hill		
	E51559 55H Neville Hill	**E51559** NL Neville Hill		
	E51560 55H Neville Hill	**E51560** NL Neville Hill		
M51561 Wrexham Central	**M51561** 6A Chester	**M51561** AN Allerton	**51561** LE Landore	
M51562 6G Llandudno Junction	**M51562** 6A Chester	**M51562** CH Chester	**51562** LE Landore	
M51563 Wrexham Central (o/l)	**M51563** 6A Chester	**M51563** CH Chester	**51563** LE Landore	
M51564 6G Llandudno Junction				
M51565 6G Llandudno Junction	**M51565** 6A Chester	**M51565** CH Chester	**51565** LE Landore	
M51566 6G Llandudno Junction	**M51566** 6A Chester	**M51566** CH Chester	**51566** CH Chester	
M51567 6G Llandudno Junction	**M51567** 6A Chester	**M51567** CH Chester	**51567** LE Landore	
M51568 6G Llandudno Junction	**M51568** 6A Chester	**M51568** AN Allerton	**51568** CH Chester	
M51569 6G Llandudno Junction	**M51569** 6A Chester	**M51569** CH Chester	**51569** CH Chester	
	M51570 8J Allerton	**M51570** AN Allerton	**51570** LA Laira	
	M51571 8J Allerton	**M51571** AN Allerton	**51571** BY Bletchley	
	M51572 8J Allerton	**M51572** AN Allerton	**51572** BY Bletchley	
	W51573 82A Bristol	**W51573** LA Laira		
	W51574 86A Cardiff Canton	**W51574** LA Laira		
	W51575 84A Laira	**W51575** LA Laira		
	W51576 82A Bristol	**W51576** LA Laira		
	W51577 82A Bristol	**W51577** LA Laira		
	W51578 84A Laira	**W51578** CF Cardiff Canton		
	W51579 86A Cardiff Canton	**W51579** CF Cardiff Canton		
	W51580 84A Laira	**W51580** CF Cardiff Canton		
	W51581 82A Bristol	**W51581** CF Cardiff Canton		
	W51582 82A Bristol	**W51582** LA Laira		
	W51583 86A Cardiff Canton	**W51583** LA Laira		
	W51584 84A Laira	**W51584** LA Laira		
	W51585 82A Bristol	**W51585** CF Cardiff Canton		
	W51586 82A Bristol	**W51586** LA Laira		
	W51587 84A Laira	**W51587** CF Cardiff Canton		
	W51588 86A Cardiff Canton	**W51588** CF Cardiff Canton		
	W51589 84A Laira	**W51589** CF Cardiff Canton		
	W51590 82A Bristol	**W51590** LA Laira		
M51591 14A Cricklewood	**M51591** 14A Cricklewood	**M51591** CW Cricklewood		
M51592 14A Cricklewood	**M51592** 14A Cricklewood	**M51592** CW Cricklewood		
M51593 14A Cricklewood	**M51593** 14A Cricklewood	**M51593** CW Cricklewood		
M51594 14A Cricklewood				
M51595 14A Cricklewood	**M51595** 14A Cricklewood	**M51595** CW Cricklewood		
M51596 14A Cricklewood	**M51596** 14A Cricklewood	**M51596** CW Cricklewood		
M51597 14A Cricklewood	**M51597** 14A Cricklewood	**M51597** CW Cricklewood		
M51598 14A Cricklewood	**M51598** 14A Cricklewood	**M51598** CW Cricklewood		
M51599 (s) Chaddesden	**M51599** 14A Cricklewood	**M51599** CW Cricklewood		
M51600 (s) Chaddesden	**M51600** 14A Cricklewood	**M51600** CW Cricklewood		
M51601 (s) Chaddesden	**M51601** 14A Cricklewood			
M51602 (s) Chaddesden	**M51602** 14A Cricklewood			
M51603 (s) Chaddesden	**M51603** 14A Cricklewood	**M51603** CW Cricklewood		
M51604 (s) Chaddesden	**M51604** 14A Cricklewood	**M51604** CW Cricklewood		
M51605 (s) Chaddesden	**M51605** 14A Cricklewood	**M51605** CW Cricklewood		
M51606 (s) Chaddesden	**M51606** 14A Cricklewood	**M51606** CW Cricklewood		
M51607 14A Cricklewood	**M51607** 14A Cricklewood	**M51607** CW Cricklewood		
M51608 14A Cricklewood	**M51608** 14A Cricklewood	**M51608** CW Cricklewood		
M51609 14A Cricklewood				
M51610 14A Cricklewood	**M51610** 14A Cricklewood	**M51610** CW Cricklewood		
M51611 14A Cricklewood	**M51611** 14A Cricklewood	**M51611** CW Cricklewood		
M51612 14A Cricklewood	**M51612** 14A Cricklewood	**M51612** CW Cricklewood		
M51613 14A Cricklewood	**M51613** 14A Cricklewood	**M51613** CW Cricklewood		
M51614 14A Cricklewood	**M51614** 14A Cricklewood	**M51614** CW Cricklewood		
M51615 14A Cricklewood	**M51615** 14A Cricklewood	**M51615** CW Cricklewood		
M51616 14A Cricklewood	**M51616** 14A Cricklewood	**M51616** CW Cricklewood		
M51617 (s) Chaddesden	**M51617** 14A Cricklewood	**M51617** CW Cricklewood		
M51618 (s) Chaddesden	**M51618** 14A Cricklewood	**M51618** CW Cricklewood		
M51619 14A Cricklewood	**M51619** 14A Cricklewood	**M51619** CW Cricklewood		
M51620 14A Cricklewood	**M51620** 14A Cricklewood	**M51620** CW Cricklewood		
M51621 14A Cricklewood	**M51621** 14A Cricklewood	**M51621** CW Cricklewood		
M51622 14A Cricklewood	**M51622** 14A Cricklewood	**M51622** CW Cricklewood		
M51623 14A Cricklewood	**M51623** 14A Cricklewood	**M51623** CW Cricklewood		
M51624 14A Cricklewood	**M51624** 14A Cricklewood	**M51624** CW Cricklewood		
M51625 14A Cricklewood	**M51625** 14A Cricklewood	**M51625** CW Cricklewood		
M51626 14A Cricklewood	**M51626** 14A Cricklewood	**M51626** CW Cricklewood		
M51627 14A Cricklewood	**M51627** 14A Cricklewood	**M51627** CW Cricklewood		
M51628 14A Cricklewood	**M51628** 14A Cricklewood	**M51628** CW Cricklewood		
M51629 14A Cricklewood	**M51629** 14A Cricklewood			
M51630 14A Cricklewood	**M51630** 14A Cricklewood	**M51630** CW Cricklewood		
M51631 14A Cricklewood	**M51631** 14A Cricklewood			
M51632 14A Cricklewood	**M51632** 14A Cricklewood			
M51633 14A Cricklewood	**M51633** 14A Cricklewood	**M51633** CW Cricklewood		
M51634 14A Cricklewood	**M51634** 14A Cricklewood	**M51634** CW Cricklewood		
M51635 (s) Derby Friargate	**M51635** 14A Cricklewood	**M51635** CW Cricklewood		
M51636 (s) Derby Friargate	**M51636** 14A Cricklewood	**M51636** CW Cricklewood		
M51637 14A Cricklewood	**M51637** 14A Cricklewood	**M51637** CW Cricklewood		
M51638 14A Cricklewood	**M51638** 14A Cricklewood	**M51638** CW Cricklewood		

1960	1970	1980	1990	2000
M51639 14A Cricklewood	**M51639** 14A Cricklewood	**M51639** CW Cricklewood		
M51640 14A Cricklewood	**M51640** 14A Cricklewood	**M51640** CW Cricklewood		
M51641 14A Cricklewood	**M51641** 14A Cricklewood			
M51642 14A Cricklewood	**M51642** 14A Cricklewood	**M51642** CW Cricklewood		
M51643 14A Cricklewood	**M51643** 14A Cricklewood	**M51643** CW Cricklewood		
M51644 14A Cricklewood	**M51644** 14A Cricklewood	**M51644** CW Cricklewood		
M51645 (s) Chaddesden	**M51645** 14A Cricklewood	**M51645** CW Cricklewood		
M51646 (s) Chaddesden	**M51646** 14A Cricklewood	**M51646** CW Cricklewood		
M51647 14A Cricklewood	**M51647** 14A Cricklewood	**M51647** CW Cricklewood		
M51648 14A Cricklewood	**M51648** 14A Cricklewood	**M51648** CW Cricklewood		
M51649 14A Cricklewood	**M51649** 14A Cricklewood	**M51649** CW Cricklewood		
M51650 14A Cricklewood	**M51650** 14A Cricklewood	**M51650** CW Cricklewood		
	M51651 1D Marylebone	**M51651** ME Marylebone	**51651** BY Bletchley	
	M51652 1D Marylebone	**M51652** ME Marylebone	**51652** BY Bletchley	
	M51653 1D Marylebone	**M51653** ME Marylebone	**51653** BY Bletchley	
	M51654 1D Marylebone	**M51654** AN Allerton	**51654** BY Bletchley	
	M51655 1D Marylebone	**M51655** ME Marylebone	**51655** BY Bletchley	
	M51656 1D Marylebone	**M51656** ME Marylebone	**51656** BY Bletchley	
	M51657 1D Marylebone	**M51657** ME Marylebone	**51657** BY Bletchley	
	M51658 1D Marylebone	**M51658** ME Marylebone	**51658** BY Bletchley	
	M51659 1D Marylebone	**M51659** ME Marylebone	**51659** BY Bletchley	
	M51660 1D Marylebone	**M51660** ME Marylebone	**51660** BY Bletchley	
	M51661 1D Marylebone	**M51661** ME Marylebone	**51661** BY Bletchley	
	M51662 1D Marylebone	**M51662** ME Marylebone	**51662** TS Tyseley	
	M51663 1D Marylebone	**M51663** ME Marylebone	**51663** BY Bletchley	
	M51664 1D Marylebone	**M51664** ME Marylebone	**51664** BY Bletchley	
	M51665 1D Marylebone	**M51665** ME Marylebone	**51665** BY Bletchley	
	M51666 1D Marylebone	**M51666** ME Marylebone	**51666** BY Bletchley	
	M51667 1D Marylebone	**M51667** ME Marylebone	**51667** BY Bletchley	
	M51668 1D Marylebone	**M51668** ME Marylebone	**51668** BY Bletchley	
	M51669 1D Marylebone	**M51669** ME Marylebone	**51669** BY Bletchley	
	M51670 1D Marylebone	**M51670** ME Marylebone	**51670** BY Bletchley	
	M51671 1D Marylebone	**M51671** ME Marylebone	**51671** BY Bletchley	
	M51672 1D Marylebone	**M51672** ME Marylebone		
	M51673 1D Marylebone	**M51673** ME Marylebone	**51673** BY Bletchley	
	M51674 1D Marylebone	**M51674** ME Marylebone	**51674** BY Bletchley	
	M51675 1D Marylebone	**M51675** ME Marylebone	**51675** BY Bletchley	
	M51676 1D Marylebone	**M51676** ME Marylebone	**51676** BY Bletchley	
	M51677 1D Marylebone	**M51677** ME Marylebone	**51677** BY Bletchley	
	M51678 1D Marylebone	**M51678** ME Marylebone	**51678** BY Bletchley	
	M51679 1D Marylebone	**M51679** ME Marylebone	**51679** BY Bletchley	
	M51680 1D Marylebone	**M51680** ME Marylebone	**51680** BY Bletchley	
M51681 26A Newton Heath				
M51682 26A Newton Heath				
M51683 26A Newton Heath				
M51684 26A Newton Heath				
M51685 26A Newton Heath				
M51686 26A Newton Heath				
M51687 26A Newton Heath				
M51688 26A Newton Heath				
M51689 26A Newton Heath				
M51690 26A Newton Heath				
M51691 8C Speke Junction				
M51692 8C Speke Junction				
M51693 8C Speke Junction				
M51694 8C Speke Junction				
M51695 8C Speke Junction				
M51696 8C Speke Junction				
M51697 8C Speke Junction				
M51698 8C Speke Junction				
M51699 24A Accrington				
M51700 24A Accrington				
M51701 24A Accrington				
M51702 24A Accrington				
M51703 24A Accrington				
M51704 24A Accrington				
M51705 24A Accrington				
M51706 26A Newton Heath				
M51707 26A Newton Heath				
M51708 26A Newton Heath				
M51709 26A Newton Heath				
M51710 26A Newton Heath				
M51711 26A Newton Heath				
M51712 26A Newton Heath				
M51713 26A Newton Heath				
M51714 26A Newton Heath				
M51715 26A Newton Heath				
M51716 8C Speke Junction				
M51717 8C Speke Junction				
M51718 8C Speke Junction				
M51719 8C Speke Junction				
M51720 8C Speke Junction				
M51721 8C Speke Junction				
M51722 8C Speke Junction				
M51723 8C Speke Junction				
M51724 24A Accrington				
M51725 24A Accrington				

1960	1970	1980	1990	2000
M51726 24A Accrington				
M51727 24A Accrington				
M51728 24A Accrington				
M51729 24A Accrington				
M51730 24A Accrington				
M51731 24A Accrington				
M51732 24A Accrington				
M51733 24A Accrington				
M51734 24A Accrington				
M51735 24A Accrington				
M51737 24A Accrington				
M51738 24A Accrington				
M51739 24A Accrington				
M51756 24A Accrington				
M51757 24A Accrington				
M51758 24A Accrington				
M51759 24A Accrington				
M51760 24A Accrington				
M51762 24A Accrington				
M51763 24A Accrington				
M51764 24A Accrington				
SC51781 61A Kittybrewster	**SC51781** 60A Inverness	**SC51781** IS Inverness		
SC51782 61A Kittybrewster	**SC51782** 60A Inverness	**SC51782** IS Inverness		
SC51783 61A Kittybrewster	**SC51783** 60A Inverness	**SC51783** IS Inverness		
SC51784 61A Kittybrewster	**SC51784** 60A Inverness	**SC51784** IS Inverness		
SC51785 61A Kittybrewster	**SC51785** 60A Inverness	**SC51785** IS Inverness		
SC51786 61A Kittybrewster	**SC51786** 60A Inverness	**SC51786** IS Inverness		
SC51787 61A Kittybrewster	**SC51787** 60A Inverness	**SC51787** IS Inverness		
	SC51788 60A Inverness	**SC51788** IS Inverness		
	SC51789 60A Inverness	**SC51789** IS Inverness		
	SC51790 60A Inverness	**SC51790** IS Inverness		
	SC51791 60A Inverness	**SC51791** IS Inverness		
	SC51792 60A Inverness	**SC51792** IS Inverness		
	SC51793 60A Inverness	**SC51793** IS Inverness		
	SC51794 60A Inverness	**SC51794** IS Inverness		
SC51795 64H Leith Central	**SC51795** 64H Leith Central	**SC51795** AY Ayr		
SC51796 64H Leith Central	**SC51796** 64H Leith Central	**SC51796** AY Ayr		
SC51797 64H Leith Central	**SC51797** 62B Dundee	**SC51797** AY Ayr		
SC51798 64H Leith Central	**SC51798** 64H Leith Central	**SC51798** ED Eastfield		
SC51799 64H Leith Central	**SC51799** 64H Leith Central	**W51799** BR Bristol Bath Road	**51799** NL Neville Hill	
SC51800 64H Leith Central	**SC51800** 64H Leith Central	**SC51800** ED Eastfield	**51800** CH Chester	**51800** LO Longsight
SC51801 64H Leith Central	**SC51801** 64H Leith Central	**W51801** BR Bristol Bath Road		
SC51802 64H Leith Central	**SC51802** 64H Leith Central	**SC51802** ED Eastfield		
SC51803 64H Leith Central	**SC51803** 64H Leith Central	**SC51803** ED Eastfield	**51803** ED Eastfield	**51803** LO Longsight
SC51804 64H Leith Central	**SC51804** 62B Dundee	**SC51804** AY Ayr	**51804** NL Neville Hill	
SC51805 64H Leith Central	**SC51805** 64H Leith Central	**SC51805** ED Eastfield		
SC51806 64H Leith Central	**SC51806** 64H Leith Central	**SC51806** ED Eastfield		
SC51807 64H Leith Central	**SC51807** 64H Leith Central	**SC51807** ED Eastfield		
SC51808 64H Leith Central	**SC51808** 64H Leith Central	**W51808** BR Bristol Bath Road	**51808** NL Neville Hill	
	E51809 55H Neville Hill	**E51809** HS Bradford Hammerton St		
	E51810 55H Neville Hill	**E51810** HS Bradford Hammerton St		
	E51811 55H Neville Hill	**E51811** HS Bradford Hammerton St		
	E51812 55F Bradford Hammerton St	**E51812** HS Bradford Hammerton St		
	E51813 55F Bradford Hammerton St	**E51813** NL Neville Hill	**51813** NL Neville Hill	
	E51814 55F Bradford Hammerton St	**E51814** HS Bradford Hammerton St		
	E51815 55F Bradford Hammerton St	**E51815** HS Bradford Hammerton St		
	E51816 55F Bradford Hammerton St	**E51816** HS Bradford Hammerton St		
	E51817 55F Bradford Hammerton St	**E51817** HS Bradford Hammerton St	**51817** NL Neville Hill	
	E51818 55F Bradford Hammerton St	**E51818** HS Bradford Hammerton St		
	E51819 55F Bradford Hammerton St	**E51819** HS Bradford Hammerton St		
	E51820 55F Bradford Hammerton St	**E51820** HS Bradford Hammerton St		
	E51822 55F Bradford Hammerton St	**E51822** HS Bradford Hammerton St		
	E51823 55F Bradford Hammerton St	**E51823** HS Bradford Hammerton St	**51823** NL Neville Hill	
	E51824 55H Neville Hill	**E51824** HS Bradford Hammerton St		
	E51825 55H Neville Hill	**E51825** HS Bradford Hammerton St		
	E51826 55H Neville Hill	**E51826** NL Neville Hill		
	E51827 55H Neville Hill	**E51827** HS Bradford Hammerton St		
	E51828 55H Neville Hill	**E51828** HS Bradford Hammerton St		
	E51829 55H Neville Hill	**E51829** HS Bradford Hammerton St	**51829** NL Neville Hill	
	E51830 55H Neville Hill	**E51830** NL Neville Hill	**51830** NL Neville Hill	
	E51831 55H Neville Hill	**E51831** HS Bradford Hammerton St		
	E51832 55F Bradford Hammerton St	**E51832** HS Bradford Hammerton St		
	E51833 55F Bradford Hammerton St	**E51833** HS Bradford Hammerton St		
	E51834 55F Bradford Hammerton St	**E51834** HS Bradford Hammerton St	**51834** NL Neville Hill	
	E51835 55F Bradford Hammerton St	**E51835** HS Bradford Hammerton St		
	E51836 55F Bradford Hammerton St	**E51836** HS Bradford Hammerton St		
	E51838 55F Bradford Hammerton St	**E51838** HS Bradford Hammerton St		
	E51839 55F Bradford Hammerton St	**E51839** HS Bradford Hammerton St		
	E51840 55F Bradford Hammerton St	**E51840** HS Bradford Hammerton St	**51840** NL Neville Hill	
	E51841 55F Bradford Hammerton St	**E51841** HS Bradford Hammerton St		
	E51842 55F Bradford Hammerton St	**E51842** HS Bradford Hammerton St	**51842** NL Neville Hill	
	E51843 55F Bradford Hammerton St	**E51843** HS Bradford Hammerton St	**51843** NL Neville Hill	

1960	1970	1980	1990	2000
	E51844 55H Neville Hill	**E51844** NL Neville Hill		
	E51845 55H Neville Hill	**E51845** HS Bradford Hammerton St		
	E51846 55H Neville Hill	**E51846** HS Bradford Hammerton St		
	E51847 55H Neville Hill	**E51847** HS Bradford Hammerton St	**51847** NL Neville Hill	
	E51848 55H Neville Hill	**E51848** HS Bradford Hammerton St		
	M51849 8J Allerton	**M51849** AN Allerton	**51849** BY Bletchley	
	M51850 8J Allerton	**M51850** AN Allerton		
	M51851 8J Allerton	**M51851** AN Allerton	**51851** TS Tyseley	
	M51852 8J Allerton	**M51852** AN Allerton	**51852** TS Tyseley	
	M51853 8J Allerton	**M51853** AN Allerton	**51853** TS Tyseley	
	M51854 8J Allerton	**M51854** AN Allerton	**51854** TS Tyseley	
	M51855 8J Allerton	**M51855** AN Allerton	**51855** BY Bletchley	
	M51856 8J Allerton	**M51856** AN Allerton	**51856** TS Tyseley	
	M51857 8J Allerton	**M51857** ME Marylebone	**51857** BY Bletchley	
	M51858 8J Allerton	**M51858** AN Allerton	**51858** TS Tyseley	
	M51859 8J Allerton	**M51859** AN Allerton	**51859** TS Tyseley	
	M51860 8J Allerton	**M51860** AN Allerton	**51860** TS Tyseley	
	M51861 1D Marylebone	**M51861** ME Marylebone		
	M51862 1D Marylebone	**M51862** ME Marylebone	**51862** TS Tyseley	
	M51863 1D Marylebone	**M51863** ME Marylebone	**51863** BY Bletchley	
	M51864 1D Marylebone	**M51864** ME Marylebone		
	M51865 1D Marylebone	**M51865** ME Marylebone	**51865** TS Tyseley	
	M51866 1D Marylebone	**M51866** ME Marylebone	**51866** BY Bletchley	
	M51867 1D Marylebone	**M51867** ME Marylebone	**51867** TS Tyseley	
	M51868 1D Marylebone	**M51868** ME Marylebone	**51868** TS Tyseley	
	M51869 1D Marylebone	**M51869** ME Marylebone	**51869** TS Tyseley	
	M51870 1D Marylebone	**M51870** ME Marylebone	**51870** TS Tyseley	
	M51871 1D Marylebone	**M51871** ME Marylebone	**51871** BY Bletchley	
	M51872 1D Marylebone	**M51872** ME Marylebone	**51872** BY Bletchley	
	M51873 1D Marylebone	**M51873** ME Marylebone	**51873** BY Bletchley	
	M51874 1D Marylebone	**M51874** ME Marylebone	**51874** BY Bletchley	
	M51875 1D Marylebone	**M51875** ME Marylebone	**51875** BY Bletchley	
	M51876 1D Marylebone	**M51876** ME Marylebone	**51876** TS Tyseley	
	M51877 1D Marylebone	**M51877** ME Marylebone	**51877** TS Tyseley	
	M51878 1D Marylebone	**M51878** ME Marylebone	**51878** BY Bletchley	
	M51879 1D Marylebone	**M51879** ME Marylebone	**51879** BY Bletchley	
	M51880 1D Marylebone	**M51880** ME Marylebone	**51880** TS Tyseley	
	M51881 1D Marylebone	**M51881** ME Marylebone		
	M51882 1D Marylebone			
	M51883 1D Marylebone	**M51883** ME Marylebone	**51883** BY Bletchley	
	M51884 1D Marylebone	**M51884** AN Allerton	**51884** TS Tyseley	
	M51885 1D Marylebone	**M51885** ME Marylebone	**51885** BY Bletchley	
	M51886 1D Marylebone	**M51886** ME Marylebone	**51886** BY Bletchley	
	M51887 1D Marylebone	**M51887** ME Marylebone	**51887** BY Bletchley	
	M51888 1D Marylebone	**M51888** ME Marylebone	**51888** BY Bletchley	
	M51889 1D Marylebone	**M51889** ME Marylebone	**51889** BY Bletchley	
	M51890 1D Marylebone	**M51890** ME Marylebone	**51890** BY Bletchley	
	M51891 1D Marylebone	**M51891** ME Marylebone	**51891** BY Bletchley	
	M51892 1D Marylebone	**M51892** AN Allerton	**51892** TS Tyseley	
	M51893 1D Marylebone	**M51893** ME Marylebone	**51893** BY Bletchley	
	M51894 1D Marylebone	**M51894** ME Marylebone	**51894** BY Bletchley	
	M51895 1D Marylebone	**M51895** ME Marylebone	**51895** BY Bletchley	
	M51896 1D Marylebone	**M51896** ME Marylebone	**51896** BY Bletchley	
	M51897 1D Marylebone	**M51897** ME Marylebone	**51897** TS Tyseley	
	M51898 1D Marylebone	**M51898** ME Marylebone	**51898** TS Tyseley	
	M51899 1D Marylebone	**M51899** ME Marylebone	**51899** BY Bletchley	
	M51900 1D Marylebone	**M51900** ME Marylebone	**51900** BY Bletchley	
	M51901 9A Longsight	**M51901** NH Newton Heath	**51901** CH Chester	
	M51902 9A Longsight	**M51902** LO Longsight	**51902** CH Chester	
	M51903 9A Longsight	**M51903** LO Longsight	**51903** CH Chester	
	M51904 9A Longsight	**M51904** LO Longsight	**51904** CH Chester	
	M51905 9A Longsight	**M51905** LO Longsight	**51905** CH Chester	
	M51906 9A Longsight	**M51906** LO Longsight	**51906** CH Chester	
	M51907 9A Longsight	**M51907** LO Longsight	**51907** CH Chester	
	M51908 8J Allerton	**M51908** AN Allerton	**51908** CH Chester	
	M51909 8J Allerton	**M51909** AN Allerton	**51909** BY Bletchley	
	M51910 8J Allerton	**M51910** AN Allerton		
	M51911 8J Allerton	**M51911** AN Allerton	**51911** CH Chester	
	M51912 8J Allerton	**M51912** AN Allerton	**51912** BY Bletchley	
	M51913 8J Allerton	**M51913** AN Allerton	**51913** CH Chester	
	M51914 8J Allerton	**M51914** AN Allerton	**51914** BY Bletchley	
	M51916 8J Allerton	**M51916** AN Allerton	**51916** BY Bletchley	
	M51917 8J Allerton	**M51917** AN Allerton	**51917** CH Chester	
	M51918 8J Allerton	**M51918** AN Allerton		
	M51919 8J Allerton	**M51919** CH Chester	**51919** LE Landore	
	M51920 6A Chester	**M51920** CH Chester	**51920** CH Chester	
	M51921 6A Chester			
	M51922 8J Allerton	**M51922** AN Allerton	**51922** LE Landore	
	M51923 8J Allerton			
	M51924 8J Allerton	**M51924** AN Allerton	**51924** LE Landore	
	M51925 8J Allerton	**M51925** AN Allerton	**51925** LE Landore	
	M51926 8J Allerton	**M51926** AN Allerton	**51926** LE Landore	
	M51927 8J Allerton	**M51927** NH Newton Heath	**51927** LO Longsight	
	M51928 8J Allerton	**M51928** AN Allerton	**51928** LE Landore	
	M51929 8J Allerton	**M51929** AN Allerton		
	M51930 8J Allerton	**M51930** AN Allerton	**51930** LE Landore	

1960	1970	1980	1990	2000
	M51931 8J Allerton	**M51931** AN Allerton	**51931** LE Landore	
	M51932 8J Allerton	**M51932** AN Allerton	**51932** LA Laira	
	M51933 8J Allerton	**M51933** NH Newton Heath	**51933** LA Laira	
	M51934 8J Allerton	**M51934** NH Newton Heath		
	M51935 8J Allerton	**M51935** NH Newton Heath	**51935** LO Longsight	
	M51936 8J Allerton	**M51936** NH Newton Heath	**51936** LA Laira	
	M51937 8J Allerton	**M51937** AN Allerton	**51937** CH Chester	
	M51938 8J Allerton	**M51938** NH Newton Heath	**51938** CH Chester	
	M51939 8J Allerton	**M51939** NH Newton Heath	**51939** LA Laira	
	M51940 8J Allerton	**M51940** NH Newton Heath	**51940** LA Laira	
	M51941 8J Allerton	**M51941** NH Newton Heath	**51941** CH Chester	
	M51942 8J Allerton	**M51942** AN Allerton	**51942** BY Bletchley	
	M51943 8J Allerton	**M51943** NH Newton Heath	**51943** CH Chester	
	M51945 9D Newton Heath	**M51945** NH Newton Heath	**51945** CH Chester	
	M51946 9D Newton Heath			
	M51947 9D Newton Heath	**M51947** CH Chester	**51947** CH Chester	
	M51948 9D Newton Heath	**M51948** NH Newton Heath	**51948** CH Chester	
	M51949 9D Newton Heath			
	M51950 9D Newton Heath	**M51950** CH Chester	**51950** CH Chester	
	E51951 50C Hull Botanic Gardens	**E51951** BG Hull Botanic Gardens		
	E51952 50C Hull Botanic Gardens	**E51952** BG Hull Botanic Gardens		
	E51953 50C Hull Botanic Gardens	**E51953** BG Hull Botanic Gardens		
	E51954 50C Hull Botanic Gardens	**E51954** BG Hull Botanic Gardens		
	E51955 50C Hull Botanic Gardens	**E51955** BG Hull Botanic Gardens		
	E51956 50C Hull Botanic Gardens	**E51956** BG Hull Botanic Gardens		
	E51957 50C Hull Botanic Gardens	**E51957** BG Hull Botanic Gardens		
	E51958 50C Hull Botanic Gardens	**E51958** BG Hull Botanic Gardens		
	E51959 50C Hull Botanic Gardens			
	E51960 50C Hull Botanic Gardens	**E51960** BG Hull Botanic Gardens		
	E51961 50C Hull Botanic Gardens	**E51961** BG Hull Botanic Gardens		
	E51962 50C Hull Botanic Gardens	**E51962** BG Hull Botanic Gardens		
	E51963 50C Hull Botanic Gardens	**E51963** BG Hull Botanic Gardens		
	E51964 50C Hull Botanic Gardens	**E51964** BG Hull Botanic Gardens		
	E51965 50C Hull Botanic Gardens	**E51965** BG Hull Botanic Gardens		
	E51966 50C Hull Botanic Gardens	**E51966** BG Hull Botanic Gardens		
	E51967 50C Hull Botanic Gardens	**E51967** BG Hull Botanic Gardens		
	E51968 50C Hull Botanic Gardens	**E51968** BG Hull Botanic Gardens		
	E51969 50C Hull Botanic Gardens	**E51969** BG Hull Botanic Gardens		
	E51970 50C Hull Botanic Gardens	**E51970** BG Hull Botanic Gardens		
	E51971 50C Hull Botanic Gardens	**E51971** BG Hull Botanic Gardens		
	E51972 50C Hull Botanic Gardens	**E51972** BG Hull Botanic Gardens		
	E51973 50C Hull Botanic Gardens	**E51973** BG Hull Botanic Gardens		
	E51974 50C Hull Botanic Gardens	**E51974** BG Hull Botanic Gardens		
	E51975 50C Hull Botanic Gardens	**E51975** BG Hull Botanic Gardens		
	E51976 50C Hull Botanic Gardens	**E51976** BG Hull Botanic Gardens		
	E51977 50C Hull Botanic Gardens	**E51977** BG Hull Botanic Gardens		
	E51978 50C Hull Botanic Gardens	**E51978** BG Hull Botanic Gardens		
	E51979 50C Hull Botanic Gardens	**E51979** BG Hull Botanic Gardens		
	E51980 50C Hull Botanic Gardens	**E51980** BG Hull Botanic Gardens		
	E51981 50C Hull Botanic Gardens	**E51981** BG Hull Botanic Gardens		
	E51982 50C Hull Botanic Gardens	**E51982** BG Hull Botanic Gardens		
	E51983 50C Hull Botanic Gardens	**E51983** BG Hull Botanic Gardens		
	E51984 50C Hull Botanic Gardens	**E51984** BG Hull Botanic Gardens		
	SC51985 66C Hamilton	**SC51985** HN Hamilton	**51985** ED Eastfield	
	SC51986 66C Hamilton	**SC51986** HN Hamilton	**51986** ED Eastfield	
	SC51987 66C Hamilton	**SC51987** HN Hamilton	**51987** ED Eastfield	
	SC51988 66C Hamilton	**SC51988** HN Hamilton	**51988** ED Eastfield	
	SC51989 66C Hamilton	**SC51989** HN Hamilton	**51989** ED Eastfield	
	SC51990 66C Hamilton	**SC51990** HN Hamilton	**51990** ED Eastfield	
	SC51991 66C Hamilton	**SC51991** HN Hamilton	**51991** HA Haymarket	
	SC51992 66C Hamilton	**SC51992** HN Hamilton	**51992** HA Haymarket	
	SC51993 66C Hamilton	**SC51993** HN Hamilton	**51993** ED Eastfield	
	SC51994 66C Hamilton	**SC51994** HN Hamilton	**51994** ED Eastfield	
	SC51995 66C Hamilton			
	SC51996 66C Hamilton	**SC51996** HN Hamilton	**51996** ED Eastfield	
	SC51997 66C Hamilton	**SC51997** HN Hamilton	**51997** ED Eastfield	
	SC51998 67A Corkerhill	**SC51998** HN Hamilton	**51998** ED Eastfield	
	SC51999 67A Corkerhill	**SC51999** HN Hamilton	**51999** ED Eastfield	
	SC52000 67A Corkerhill	**SC52000** HN Hamilton	**52000** HA Haymarket	
	SC52001 67A Corkerhill	**SC52001** HN Hamilton	**52001** ED Eastfield	
	SC52002 67A Corkerhill	**SC52002** HN Hamilton		
	SC52003 67A Corkerhill	**SC52003** HN Hamilton		
	SC52004 67A Corkerhill	**SC52004** HN Hamilton	**52004** ED Eastfield	
	SC52005 67A Corkerhill	**SC52005** HN Hamilton	**52005** ED Eastfield	
	SC52006 67A Corkerhill	**SC52006** HN Hamilton	**52006** ED Eastfield	
	SC52007 67A Corkerhill	**SC52007** HN Hamilton	**52007** ED Eastfield	
	SC52008 67A Corkerhill	**SC52008** HN Hamilton	**52008** ED Eastfield	
	SC52009 67A Corkerhill	**SC52009** HN Hamilton		
	SC52010 67A Corkerhill	**SC52010** HN Hamilton	**52010** ED Eastfield	
	SC52011 66C Hamilton	**SC52011** HN Hamilton	**52011** ED Eastfield	
	SC52012 66C Hamilton	**SC52012** HN Hamilton	**52012** ED Eastfield	
	SC52013 66C Hamilton	**SC52013** HN Hamilton	**52013** ED Eastfield	
	SC52014 66C Hamilton	**SC52014** HN Hamilton		
	SC52015 66C Hamilton	**SC52015** HN Hamilton	**52015** ED Eastfield	
	SC52016 66C Hamilton	**SC52016** HN Hamilton	**52016** ED Eastfield	
	SC52017 66C Hamilton	**SC52017** HN Hamilton		

1960	1970	1980	1990	2000
	SC52018 66C Hamilton	**SC52018** HN Hamilton	**52018** ED Eastfield	
	SC52019 66C Hamilton	**SC52019** HN Hamilton	**52019** ED Eastfield	
	SC52020 66C Hamilton	**SC52020** HN Hamilton	**52020** ED Eastfield	
	SC52021 66C Hamilton	**SC52021** HN Hamilton	**52021** ED Eastfield	
	SC52022 66C Hamilton	**SC52022** HN Hamilton		
	SC52023 66C Hamilton	**SC52023** HN Hamilton	**52023** ED Eastfield	
	SC52024 67A Corkerhill	**SC52024** HN Hamilton	**52024** ED Eastfield	
	SC52025 67A Corkerhill	**SC52025** HN Hamilton	**52025** ED Eastfield	
	SC52026 67A Corkerhill	**SC52026** HN Hamilton	**52026** HA Haymarket	
	SC52027 67A Corkerhill	**SC52027** HN Hamilton		
	SC52028 67A Corkerhill	**SC52028** HN Hamilton	**52028** ED Eastfield	
	SC52029 67A Corkerhill	**SC52029** HN Hamilton	**52029** ED Eastfield	
	SC52030 66C Hamilton	**SC52030** HN Hamilton	**52030** ED Eastfield	
	SC52031 67A Corkerhill	**SC52031** HN Hamilton	**52031** ED Eastfield	
	SC52032 67A Corkerhill	**SC52032** HN Hamilton		
	SC52033 67A Corkerhill	**SC52033** HN Hamilton	**52033** ED Eastfield	
	SC52034 67A Corkerhill	**SC52034** HN Hamilton	**52034** ED Eastfield	
	SC52035 67A Corkerhill	**SC52035** HN Hamilton	**52035** HA Haymarket	
	SC52036 67A Corkerhill	**SC52036** HN Hamilton	**52036** HA Haymarket	
	M52037 8J Allerton	**M52037** AN Allerton		
	M52038 8J Allerton	**M52038** AN Allerton	**52038** LE Landore	
	M52039 8J Allerton	**M52039** NH Newton Heath	**52039** CH Chester	
	M52040 8J Allerton	**M52040** NH Newton Heath		
	M52041 8J Allerton	**M52041** AN Allerton	**52041** LE Landore	
	M52042 8J Allerton	**M52042** AN Allerton	**52042** NL Neville Hill	
	M52043 8J Allerton	**M52043** AN Allerton		
	M52044 8J Allerton	**M52044** AN Allerton	**52044** LE Landore	
	M52045 8J Allerton	**M52045** AN Allerton	**52045** LE Landore	
	M52046 8J Allerton	**M52046** CH Chester	**52046** LE Landore	
	M52047 8J Allerton	**M52047** AN Allerton	**52047** LA Laira	
	M52048 8J Allerton	**M52048** AN Allerton	**52048** LE Landore	
	M52049 8J Allerton	**M52049** NH Newton Heath	**52049** CH Chester	
	M52050 8J Allerton	**M52050** NH Newton Heath	**52050** CH Chester	
	M52051 8J Allerton	**M52051** NH Newton Heath	**52051** LA Laira	
	M52052 8J Allerton	**M52052** NH Newton Heath		
	M52053 8J Allerton	**M52053** NH Newton Heath	**52053** CF Cardiff Canton	
	M52054 8J Allerton	**M52054** NH Newton Heath	**52054** LA Laira	
	M52055 8J Allerton	**M52055** NH Newton Heath	**52055** LE Landore	
	M52056 8J Allerton	**M52056** NH Newton Heath	**52056** CH Chester	
	M52057 8J Allerton	**M52057** NH Newton Heath	**52057** LA Laira	
	M52058 8J Allerton	**M52058** NH Newton Heath	**52058** CH Chester	
	M52059 8J Allerton	**M52059** NH Newton Heath	**52059** CF Cardiff Canton	
	M52060 9D Newton Heath	**M52060** NH Newton Heath	**52060** CH Chester	
	M52061 9D Newton Heath	**M52061** NH Newton Heath	**52061** LE Landore	
	M52062 9D Newton Heath	**M52062** CH Chester	**52062** CH Chester	
	M52063 9D Newton Heath	**M52063** NH Newton Heath	**52063** LA Laira	
	M52064 9D Newton Heath	**M52064** AN Allerton	**52064** CH Chester	
	M52065 9D Newton Heath	**M52065** CH Chester	**52065** CH Chester	
	E52066 55F Bradford Hammerton St	**E52066** HS Bradford Hammerton St	**52066** NL Neville Hill	
	E52067 55F Bradford Hammerton St	**E52067** HS Bradford Hammerton St		
	E52068 55F Bradford Hammerton St	**E52068** HS Bradford Hammerton St		
	E52069 55F Bradford Hammerton St	**E52069** HS Bradford Hammerton St	**52069** NL Neville Hill	
	E52070 55F Bradford Hammerton St	**E52070** HS Bradford Hammerton St		
	E52071 55F Bradford Hammerton St	**E52071** HS Bradford Hammerton St	**52071** NL Neville Hill	
	E52072 55F Bradford Hammerton St	**E52072** HS Bradford Hammerton St	**52072** NL Neville Hill	
	E52073 55F Bradford Hammerton St	**E52073** HS Bradford Hammerton St		
	E52074 55F Bradford Hammerton St			
	E52075 55F Bradford Hammerton St	**E52075** HS Bradford Hammerton St	**52075** NL Neville Hill	
	E52076 55F Bradford Hammerton St	**E52076** HS Bradford Hammerton St		
	E52077 55F Bradford Hammerton St	**E52077** HS Bradford Hammerton St	**52077** NL Neville Hill	
	E52078 55F Bradford Hammerton St	**E52078** HS Bradford Hammerton St		
	E52079 55F Bradford Hammerton St	**E52079** HS Bradford Hammerton St		
	E52080 55F Bradford Hammerton St	**E52080** HS Bradford Hammerton St	**52080** NL Neville Hill	
	E52081 55F Bradford Hammerton St	**E52081** HS Bradford Hammerton St		
	E52082 55F Bradford Hammerton St	**E52082** HS Bradford Hammerton St	**52082** NL Neville Hill	
	E52083 55F Bradford Hammerton St	**E52083** HS Bradford Hammerton St		
	E52084 55F Bradford Hammerton St	**E52084** HS Bradford Hammerton St		
	E52085 55F Bradford Hammerton St	**E52085** HS Bradford Hammerton St	**52085** NL Neville Hill	
	W52086 81D Reading			
	W52087 81D Reading	**E52087** BG Hull Botanic Gardens		
	W52088 81D Reading	**E52088** BG Hull Botanic Gardens		
	W52089 81D Reading	**E52089** BG Hull Botanic Gardens		
	W52090 81D Reading	**E52090** BG Hull Botanic Gardens		
	W52091 81D Reading	**E52091** BG Hull Botanic Gardens		
	W52092 81D Reading	**E52092** BG Hull Botanic Gardens		
	W52093 81D Reading	**E52093** BG Hull Botanic Gardens		
	W52094 81D Reading	**E52094** BG Hull Botanic Gardens		
	W52095 81D Reading	**E52095** BG Hull Botanic Gardens		
	W52096 81D Reading	**E52096** BG Hull Botanic Gardens		
	W52097 81D Reading	**E52097** BG Hull Botanic Gardens		
	W52098 81D Reading	**E52098** BG Hull Botanic Gardens		
	W52099 81D Reading	**E52099** BG Hull Botanic Gardens		
	W52100 81D Reading	**E52100** BG Hull Botanic Gardens		
	W52101 81D Reading			
	W52102 81D Reading	**E52102** BG Hull Botanic Gardens		
	W52103 81D Reading	**E52103** BG Hull Botanic Gardens		
	W52104 81D Reading	**E52104** BG Hull Botanic Gardens		

1960	*1970*	*1980*	*1990*	*2000*
	W52105 81D Reading	**E52105** BG Hull Botanic Gardens		
			54900 CA Cambridge	
			54901 CA Cambridge	
			54902 CA Cambridge	
			54903 CA Cambridge	
			54904 CA Cambridge	
W55000 RDG Reading	**SC55000** 66C Hamilton	**SC55000** DE Dundee	**55000** LA Laira	
W55001 RDG Reading				
W55002 TYS Tyseley	**SC55002** 66C Hamilton	**SC55002** IS Inverness		
W55003 TYS Tyseley	**M55003** 2A Tyseley	**M55003** TS Tyseley	**55003** LA Laira	
W55004 TYS Tyseley	**M55004** 2A Tyseley	**M55004** TS Tyseley	**55004** LA Laira	
W55005 TYS Tyseley	**SC55005** 66C Hamilton	**SC55005** DE Dundee	**55005** LA Laira	
W55006 TYS Tyseley	**M55006** 2A Tyseley	**M55006** TS Tyseley	**55006** LA Laira	
W55007 TYS Tyseley	**SC55007** 66C Hamilton	**SC55007** AB Aberdeen		
W55008 TYS Tyseley	**M55008** 2A Tyseley			
W55009 TYS Tyseley	**M55009** 2A Tyseley	**M55009** TS Tyseley	**55009** LA Laira	
W55010 SHL Southall	**M55010** 2A Tyseley			
W55011 SHL Southall	**SC55011** 60A Inverness	**SC55011** IS Inverness	**55011** LA Laira	
W55012 SHL Southall	**M55012** 2A Tyseley	**M55012** TS Tyseley	**55012** LA Laira	**55012** TE Thornaby
W55013 SHL Southall	**SC55013** 64H Leith Central	**SC55013** HA Haymarket		
W55014 SHL Southall	**SC55014** 64H Leith Central	**SC55014** HN Hamilton		
W55015 SHL Southall	**SC55015** 64H Leith Central	**SC55015** HN Hamilton		
W55016 LA Laira	**W55016** 84A Laira			
W55017 LA Laira	**M55017** 2A Tyseley			
W55018 TYS Tyseley	**M55018** 2A Tyseley			
W55019 RDG Reading				
	W55020 81D Reading	**W55020** RG Reading	**55020** OO Old Oak Common	
	W55021 81D Reading	**W55021** RG Reading	**55021** OO Old Oak Common	
	W55022 81D Reading	**W55022** RG Reading	**55022** OO Old Oak Common	
	W55023 81D Reading	**W55023** RG Reading	**55023** OO Old Oak Common	
	W55024 81D Reading	**W55024** LA Laira	**55024** OO Old Oak Common	
	W55025 86A Cardiff Canton	**W55025** LA Laira	**55025** OO Old Oak Common	
	W55026 86A Cardiff Canton	**W55026** LA Laira	**55026** LA Laira	
	W55027 84A Laira	**W55027** LA Laira	**55027** OO Old Oak Common	**55027** BY Bletchley
	W55028 82A Bristol	**W55028** RG Reading	**55028** OO Old Oak Common	
	W55029 84A Laira	**W55029** RG Reading	**55029** OO Old Oak Common	**55029** BY Bletchley
	W55030 81D Reading	**W55030** RG Reading	**55030** OO Old Oak Common	
	W55031 81D Reading	**W55031** RG Reading	**55031** OO Old Oak Common	**55031** BY Bletchley
	W55032 82A Bristol	**W55032** BR Bristol Bath Road	**55032** TS Tyseley	
	W55033 82A Bristol	**W55033** BR Bristol Bath Road	**55033** TS Tyseley	
	W55034 84A Laira	**W55034** RG Reading	**55034** TS Tyseley	
	W55035 82A Bristol			
			55928 CA Cambridge	
			55929 CA Cambridge	
			55930 CA Cambridge	
			55931 CA Cambridge	
			55932 CA Cambridge	
	M55987 9D Newton Heath			
	M55988 9D Newton Heath	**M55988** NH Newton Heath		
	M55989 2A Tyseley	**M55989** NH Newton Heath		
	M55990 6A Chester	**M55990** NH Newton Heath		
	W55991 81D Reading	**W55991** RG Reading	**55991** CA Cambridge	
	W55992 81D Reading	**W55992** RG Reading	**55992** CA Cambridge	
	M55993 2A Tyseley	**M55993** CH Chester	**55993** CA Cambridge	
	M55994 2A Tyseley	**M55994** CH Chester	**55994** CA Cambridge	
	M55995 2A Tyseley	**M55995** CH Chester	**55995** CA Cambridge	
	M55996 2A Tyseley			
M55997 12B Carlisle Upperby	**M55997** 9D Newton Heath			
M55998 3C Walsall Rycroft	**M55998** 9D Newton Heath			
M55999 5D Stoke-on-Trent	**M55999** 9D Newton Heath			
E56000 40A Lincoln				
E56001 40A Lincoln	**E56001** 40A Lincoln	**E56001** LN Lincoln		
E56002 40A Lincoln	**E56002** 40A Lincoln	**E56002** LN Lincoln		
E56003 40A Lincoln	**E56003** 40A Lincoln	**E56003** LN Lincoln		
E56004 40A Lincoln	**E56004** 40A Lincoln	**E56004** LN Lincoln		
E56005 40A Lincoln	**E56005** 40A Lincoln	**E56005** LN Lincoln		
E56006 40A Lincoln	**E56006** 40A Lincoln	**E56006** LN Lincoln	**54006** TS Tyseley	
E56007 40A Lincoln	**E56007** 40A Lincoln	**E56007** LN Lincoln		
E56008 40A Lincoln	**E56008** 40A Lincoln	**E56008** LN Lincoln		
E56009 40A Lincoln	**E56009** 40A Lincoln	**E56009** LN Lincoln		
E56010 40A Lincoln	**E56010** 40A Lincoln	**E56010** LN Lincoln	**54010** TS Tyseley	
E56011 40A Lincoln	**E56011** 40A Lincoln	**E56011** LN Lincoln		
E56012 40A Lincoln	**E56012** 40A Lincoln	**E56012** LN Lincoln	**54012** TS Tyseley	
E56013 40A Lincoln	**E56013** 40A Lincoln	**E56013** LN Lincoln		
E56014 40A Lincoln	**E56014** 40A Lincoln	**E56014** LN Lincoln		
E56015 41A Sheffield Darnall	**E56015** 40A Lincoln	**E56015** LN Lincoln		
E56016 40A Lincoln	**E56016** 40A Lincoln	**E56016** LN Lincoln		
E56017 40A Lincoln	**E56017** 40A Lincoln	**E56017** LN Lincoln		
E56018 40A Lincoln	**E56018** 40A Lincoln	**E56018** LN Lincoln		
E56019 40A Lincoln	**E56019** 40A Lincoln	**E56019** LN Lincoln		
E56020 40A Lincoln	**E56020** 40A Lincoln			
E56021 40A Lincoln	**E56021** 40A Lincoln	**E56021** LN Lincoln		
E56022 41A Sheffield Darnall	**E56022** 40A Lincoln	**E56022** LN Lincoln		
E56023 40A Lincoln	**E56023** 40A Lincoln	**E56023** LN Lincoln		
E56024 41A Sheffield Darnall	**E56024** 40A Lincoln	**E56024** LN Lincoln		
E56025 40A Lincoln	**E56025** 40A Lincoln	**E56025** LN Lincoln		

1960	1970	1980	1990	2000
E56026 41A Sheffield Darnall	**E56026** 40A Lincoln	**E56026** LN Lincoln		
E56027 41A Sheffield Darnall	**E56027** 40A Lincoln	**E56027** LN Lincoln	**54027** TS Tyseley	
E56028 41A Sheffield Darnall	**E56028** 40A Lincoln	**E56028** LN Lincoln	**54028** CA Cambridge	
E56029 41A Sheffield Darnall	**E56029** 40A Lincoln	**E56029** LN Lincoln		
E56030 41A Sheffield Darnall	**E56030** 40A Lincoln	**E56030** LN Lincoln		
E56031 41A Sheffield Darnall	**E56031** 40A Lincoln			
E56032 40A Lincoln	**E56032** 40A Lincoln	**E56032** LN Lincoln		
E56033 41A Sheffield Darnall	**E56033** 40A Lincoln	**E56033** LN Lincoln		
E56034 41A Sheffield Darnall	**E56034** 40A Lincoln	**E56034** LN Lincoln		
E56035 41A Sheffield Darnall	**E56035** 40A Lincoln	**E56035** LN Lincoln		
E56036 41A Sheffield Darnall	**E56036** 40A Lincoln	**E56036** LN Lincoln		
E56037 40A Lincoln	**E56037** 40A Lincoln	**E56037** LN Lincoln		
E56038 40A Lincoln	**E56038** 40A Lincoln	**E56038** LN Lincoln		
E56039 40A Lincoln	**E56039** 40A Lincoln	**E56039** LN Lincoln	**54039** TS Tyseley	
E56040 40A Lincoln	**E56040** 40A Lincoln	**E56040** LN Lincoln		
E56041 40A Lincoln	**E56041** 40A Lincoln	**E56041** LN Lincoln	**54041** CA Cambridge	
E56042 40A Lincoln	**E56042** 40A Lincoln	**E56042** LN Lincoln		
E56043 40A Lincoln	**E56043** 40A Lincoln	**E56043** LN Lincoln	**54043** TS Tyseley	
E56044 40A Lincoln	**E56044** 40A Lincoln	**E56044** LN Lincoln		
E56045 40A Lincoln	**E56045** 40A Lincoln	**E56045** LN Lincoln		
E56046 40A Lincoln				
E56047 40A Lincoln	**E56047** 40A Lincoln	**E56047** LN Lincoln	**54047** TS Tyseley	
E56048 40A Lincoln	**E56048** 40A Lincoln			
E56049 40A Lincoln	**E56049** 40A Lincoln	**E56049** LN Lincoln		
E56050 51A Darlington	**E56050** 52J South Gosforth	**E56050** HT Heaton	**54050** NC Norwich Crown Point	
E56051 51A Darlington	**E56051** 51A Darlington	**E56051** BG Hull Botanic Gardens		
E56052 51A Darlington	**E56052** 52J South Gosforth	**E56052** DN Darlington		
E56053 51A Darlington	**E56053** 52J South Gosforth	**E56053** BG Hull Botanic Gardens		
E56054 51A Darlington	**E56054** 32A Norwich	**E56054** DN Darlington		
E56055 51A Darlington	**M56055** 6A Chester	**M56055** CH Chester	**54055** NC Norwich Crown Point	**54055** LO Longsight
E56056 51A Darlington	**E56056** 52J South Gosforth	**E56056** DN Darlington	**54056** NL Neville Hill	**54056** LO Longsight
E56057 51A Darlington	**E56057** 51A Darlington	**E56057** CA Cambridge		
E56058 51A Darlington	**M56058** 6A Chester	**M56058** CH Chester		
E56059 51A Darlington	**E56059** 51A Darlington	**E56059** DN Darlington		
E56060 51A Darlington	**M56060** 6A Chester	**M56060** CH Chester	**54060** NC Norwich Crown Point	
E56061 51A Darlington	**E56061** 51A Darlington	**E56061** DN Darlington	**54061** NL Neville Hill	**54061** LO Longsight
E56062 South Gosforth	**E56062** 51A Darlington	**E56062** BG Hull Botanic Gardens	**54062** NC Norwich Crown Point	**54062** LO Longsight
E56063 South Gosforth	**E56063** 51A Darlington	**E56063** NL Neville Hill		
E56064 South Gosforth	**E56064** 52J South Gosforth	**E56064** NL Neville Hill		
E56065 South Gosforth	**E56065** 51A Darlington	**E56065** DN Darlington	**54065** NC Norwich Crown Point	
E56066 South Gosforth	**E56066** 52J South Gosforth	**E56066** BG Hull Botanic Gardens		
E56067 South Gosforth	**E56067** 51A Darlington	**E56067** BG Hull Botanic Gardens		
E56068 50B Neville Hill (o/l)	**E56068** 52J South Gosforth	**E56068** CA Cambridge	**54068** CA Cambridge	
E56069 South Gosforth	**E56069** 51A Darlington	**E56069** HT Heaton		
E56070 South Gosforth	**E56070** 52J South Gosforth	**E56070** NL Neville Hill	**54070** OO Old Oak Common	
E56071 South Gosforth	**E56071** 50C Hull Botanic Gardens	**E56071** DN Darlington		
E56072 South Gosforth	**E56072** 51A Darlington	**E56072** DN Darlington		
E56073 South Gosforth	**E56073** 52J South Gosforth	**E56073** CA Cambridge	**54073** NC Norwich Crown Point	
E56074 South Gosforth	**E56074** 32A Norwich	**E56074** NL Neville Hill		
E56075 South Gosforth	**E56075** 51A Darlington	**E56075** NL Neville Hill		
E56076 South Gosforth	**E56076** 51A Darlington	**E56076** NL Neville Hill		
E56077 South Gosforth	**E56077** 52J South Gosforth	**E56077** HT Heaton		
E56078 South Gosforth	**E56078** 52J South Gosforth	**E56078** HT Heaton		
E56079 South Gosforth	**E56079** 52J South Gosforth	**E56079** DN Darlington		
E56080 South Gosforth	**M56080** 6A Chester	**M56080** CH Chester		
E56081 South Gosforth	**E56081** 52J South Gosforth	**E56081** HT Heaton	**54081** OO Old Oak Common	
E56082 South Gosforth	**E56082** 52J South Gosforth	**E56082** HT Heaton		
E56083 51A Darlington (o/l)	**E56083** 52J South Gosforth	**E56083** HT Heaton		
E56084 South Gosforth	**E56084** 52J South Gosforth	**E56084** HT Heaton		
E56085 South Gosforth	**E56085** 52J South Gosforth	**E56085** HT Heaton	**54085** NL Neville Hill	**54085** LO Longsight
E56086 51A Darlington	**E56086** 51A Darlington	**E56086** HT Heaton		
E56087 51A Darlington	**E56087** 55H Neville Hill	**E56087** HT Heaton		
E56088 51A Darlington	**E56088** 51A Darlington	**E56088** NL Neville Hill		
E56089 51A Darlington	**E56089** 52J South Gosforth	**E56089** HT Heaton		
M56090 9A Longsight	**E56090** 55H Neville Hill	**E56090** NL Neville Hill		
M56091 9A Longsight	**E56091** 55H Neville Hill	**E56091** DN Darlington	**54091** NL Neville Hill	**54091** LO Longsight
M56092 9A Longsight	**E56092** 55H Neville Hill	**E56092** NL Neville Hill		
M56093 9A Longsight	**E56093** 55H Neville Hill	**E56093** DN Darlington		
SC56094 64H Leith Central	**E56094** 31A Cambridge			
SC56095 64H Leith Central	**SC56095** 64H Leith Central			
SC56096 64H Leith Central	**E56096** 31A Cambridge			
SC56097 64H Leith Central	**SC56097** 64H Leith Central			
SC56098 66C Hamilton (o/l)	**E56098** 31A Cambridge			
SC56099 66C Hamilton	**E56099** 52J South Gosforth			
SC56100 64H Leith Central	**E56100** 31A Cambridge			
SC56101 64H Leith Central	**E56101** 31A Cambridge			
SC56102 64H Leith Central	**SC56102** 64H Leith Central			
M56103 3C Walsall Rycroft	**M56103** 9A Longsight	**M56103** LO Longsight		
M56104 3C Walsall Rycroft	**M56104** 9A Longsight	**M56104** LO Longsight		
M56105 3C Walsall Rycroft	**M56105** 9A Longsight	**M56105** LO Longsight		
M56106 3C Walsall Rycroft	**M56106** 9A Longsight	**M56106** LO Longsight		
M56107 2D Coventry (o/l)	**M56107** 9A Longsight	**M56107** LO Longsight		
M56108 3C Walsall Rycroft	**M56108** 9A Longsight	**M56108** LO Longsight		
M56109 3C Walsall Rycroft	**M56109** 9A Longsight	**M56109** LO Longsight		
M56110 3C Walsall Rycroft	**M56110** 9A Longsight	**M56110** LO Longsight		
M56111 3C Walsall Rycroft	**M56111** 9A Longsight	**M56111** LO Longsight		
M56112 3C Walsall Rycroft	**M56112** 9A Longsight			

1960	1970	1980	1990	2000
M56113 9A Longsight	**M56113** 9A Longsight	**M56113** LO Longsight		
E56114 53B Hull Botanic Gardens	**E56114** 31A Cambridge	**E56114** NR Norwich		
E56115 53B Hull Botanic Gardens	**E56115** 34G Finsbury Park	**E56115** NR Norwich		
E56116 53B Hull Botanic Gardens	**E56116** 34G Finsbury Park	**E56116** NR Norwich		
E56117 53B Hull Botanic Gardens	**E56117** 34G Finsbury Park			
E56118 53B Hull Botanic Gardens	**E56118** 32A Norwich	**M56118** NH Newton Heath		
E56119 53B Hull Botanic Gardens	**E56119** 32A Norwich	**E56119** LN Lincoln		
E56120 53B Hull Botanic Gardens	**E56120** 32A Norwich	**M56120** BY Bletchley		
E56121 53B Hull Botanic Gardens	**E56121** 31A Cambridge	**E56121** HT Heaton		
E56122 53B Hull Botanic Gardens	**E56122** 32A Norwich	**E56122** SF Stratford		
E56123 53B Hull Botanic Gardens	**E56123** 32A Norwich	**E56123** NR Norwich		
E56124 53B Hull Botanic Gardens	**E56124** 50C Hull Botanic Gardens	**E56124** NR Norwich		
E56125 53B Hull Botanic Gardens	**E56125** 32A Norwich	**E56125** NR Norwich		
E56126 53B Hull Botanic Gardens	**E56126** 50C Hull Botanic Gardens	**E56126** SF Stratford		
E56127 53B Hull Botanic Gardens	**E56127** 50C Hull Botanic Gardens	**M56127** NH Newton Heath		
E56128 53B Hull Botanic Gardens	**E56128** 50C Hull Botanic Gardens			
E56129 53B Hull Botanic Gardens	**E56129** 50C Hull Botanic Gardens	**M56129** NH Newton Heath		
E56130 53B Hull Botanic Gardens	**E56130** 50C Hull Botanic Gardens	**E56130** NR Norwich		
E56131 53B Hull Botanic Gardens	**E56131** 34G Finsbury Park	**E56131** NR Norwich		
E56132 53B Hull Botanic Gardens	**E56132** 34G Finsbury Park	**E56132** NR Norwich		
E56133 53B Hull Botanic Gardens	**E56133** 50C Hull Botanic Gardens	**E56133** NR Norwich		
E56134 53B Hull Botanic Gardens	**E56134** 50C Hull Botanic Gardens	**E56134** NR Norwich		
E56135 53B Hull Botanic Gardens	**E56135** 50C Hull Botanic Gardens	**E56135** NR Norwich		
E56136 53B Hull Botanic Gardens	**E56136** 50C Hull Botanic Gardens	**E56136** HT Heaton		
E56137 53B Hull Botanic Gardens	**E56137** 50C Hull Botanic Gardens	**E56137** NR Norwich		
E56138 53B Hull Botanic Gardens	**E56138** 34G Finsbury Park	**E56138** SF Stratford		
E56139 53B Hull Botanic Gardens	**E56139** 34G Finsbury Park	**E56139** NR Norwich		
E56140 53B Hull Botanic Gardens	**E56140** 50C Hull Botanic Gardens	**E56140** NR Norwich		
E56141 53B Hull Botanic Gardens	**E56141** 50C Hull Botanic Gardens	**E56141** SF Stratford		
E56142 53B Hull Botanic Gardens	**E56142** 50C Hull Botanic Gardens	**E56142** NR Norwich		
E56143 53B Hull Botanic Gardens	**E56143** 32A Norwich	**E56143** SF Stratford		
E56144 53B Hull Botanic Gardens	**E56144** 50C Hull Botanic Gardens	**E56144** NR Norwich		
M56145 18A Toton	**M56145** 1E Bletchley	**M56145** BY Bletchley		
M56146 18A Toton	**M56146** 1E Bletchley	**M56146** BY Bletchley		
M56147 18A Toton	**M56147** 1E Bletchley			
M56148 18A Toton	**M56148** 1E Bletchley	**M56148** BY Bletchley		
M56149 18A Toton	**M56149** 1E Bletchley	**M56149** BY Bletchley		
M56150 3C Walsall Rycroft	**M56150** 6A Chester	**M56150** CH Chester		
M56151 3C Walsall Rycroft	**M56151** 6A Chester	**M56151** CH Chester		
M56152 3C Walsall Rycroft	**M56152** 6A Chester	**M56152** CH Chester		
M56153 3C Walsall Rycroft	**M56153** 6A Chester			
M56154 3C Walsall Rycroft	**M56154** 6A Chester			
M56155 3C Walsall Rycroft	**M56155** 6A Chester	**M56155** CH Chester		
M56156 6G Llandudno Junction	**M56156** 6A Chester	**M56156** CH Chester		
M56157 3C Walsall Rycroft	**M56157** 6A Chester	**M56157** CH Chester		
M56158 3C Walsall Rycroft	**M56158** 6A Chester	**M56158** CH Chester		
M56159 3C Walsall Rycroft	**M56159** 6A Chester	**M56159** CH Chester		
M56160 3C Walsall Rycroft	**M56160** 6A Chester			
M56161 3C Walsall Rycroft	**M56161** 6A Chester	**M56161** CH Chester		
M56162 3C Walsall Rycroft	**M56162** 6A Chester			
M56163 3C Walsall Rycroft	**M56163** 6A Chester	**M56163** CH Chester		
M56164 3C Walsall Rycroft	**M56164** 6A Chester	**M56164** CH Chester		
M56165 3C Walsall Rycroft	**M56165** 6A Chester	**M56165** CH Chester		
M56166 1C Watford Junction	**M56166** 6A Chester			
M56167 1C Watford Junction	**M56167** 6A Chester			
M56168 1C Watford Junction	**M56168** 6A Chester			
M56169 1C Watford Junction	**M56169** 6A Chester			
E56170 31A Cambridge				
E56171 31A Cambridge				
E56172 31A Cambridge	**E56172** 31A Cambridge			
E56173 31A Cambridge	**E56173** 31A Cambridge			
E56174 31A Cambridge				
M56175 5D Stoke-on-Trent	**M56175** 9A Longsight	**M56175** LO Longsight		
M56176 5D Stoke-on-Trent	**M56176** 9A Longsight	**M56176** LO Longsight		
M56177 5D Stoke-on-Trent	**M56177** 9A Longsight	**M56177** LO Longsight		
M56178 5D Stoke-on-Trent	**M56178** 9A Longsight	**M56178** LO Longsight		
M56179 5B Crewe South	**M56179** 9A Longsight	**M56179** LO Longsight		
M56180 5B Crewe South	**M56180** 9A Longsight	**M56180** LO Longsight		
M56181 5B Crewe South	**M56181** 9A Longsight	**M56181** LO Longsight		
M56182 5B Crewe South	**M56182** 9A Longsight	**M56182** LO Longsight		
M56183 5B Crewe South	**M56183** 9A Longsight	**M56183** LO Longsight		
M56184 5B Crewe South	**M56184** 9A Longsight	**M56184** LO Longsight		
E56185 50A York	**E56185** 52J South Gosforth	**E56185** NR Norwich		
E56186 South Gosforth	**E56186** 50C Hull Botanic Gardens	**E56186** SF Stratford		
E56187 51A Darlington	**E56187** 55H Neville Hill	**E56187** NR Norwich		
E56188 South Gosforth	**E56188** 50C Hull Botanic Gardens	**E56188** NR Norwich		
E56189 South Gosforth	**E56189** 55H Neville Hill	**E56189** NR Norwich		
E56190 56G Bradford Hammerton St (o/l)	**E56190** 52J South Gosforth	**E56190** NL Neville Hill		
E56191 56G Bradford Hammerton St	**E56191** 55H Neville Hill	**E56191** NL Neville Hill	**54191** BR Bristol Bath Road	
E56192 56G Bradford Hammerton St	**E56192** 55H Neville Hill	**E56192** NL Neville Hill		
E56193 56G Bradford Hammerton St	**E56193** 55H Neville Hill	**E56193** NL Neville Hill		
E56194 56G Bradford Hammerton St (o/l)	**E56194** 55H Neville Hill	**E56194** NL Neville Hill	**54194** BY Bletchley	
E56195 56G Bradford Hammerton St (o/l)	**E56195** 50C Hull Botanic Gardens	**E56195** NL Neville Hill		
E56196 56G Bradford Hammerton St (o/l)	**E56196** 52J South Gosforth	**E56196** NL Neville Hill		
E56197 56G Bradford Hammerton St (o/l)	**E56197** 55H Neville Hill	**E56197** NL Neville Hill	**54197** BR Bristol Bath Road	
E56198 56G Bradford Hammerton St	**E56198** 55H Neville Hill	**E56198** NL Neville Hill		
E56199 53B Hull Botanic Gardens	**E56199** 55H Neville Hill	**E56199** NL Neville Hill		

1960	*1970*	*1980*	*1990*	*2000*
E56200 56G Bradford Hammerton St	**E56200** 55H Neville Hill	**E56200** NL Neville Hill		
E56201 56G Bradford Hammerton St	**E56201** 32A Norwich	**E56201** NL Neville Hill	**54201** BR Bristol Bath Road	
E56202 56G Bradford Hammerton St	**E56202** 52J South Gosforth	**E56202** NL Neville Hill	**54202** BR Bristol Bath Road	
E56203 56G Bradford Hammerton St	**E56203** 32A Norwich	**E56203** NL Neville Hill	**54203** BR Bristol Bath Road	
E56204 56G Bradford Hammerton St	**E56204** 55H Neville Hill	**E56204** NL Neville Hill	**54204** BR Bristol Bath Road	
E56205 56G Bradford Hammerton St (o/l)	**E56205** 55H Neville Hill	**E56205** NL Neville Hill	**54205** BR Bristol Bath Road	
E56206 56G Bradford Hammerton St	**E56206** 55H Neville Hill			
E56207 56G Bradford Hammerton St	**E56207** 55H Neville Hill	**E56207** NL Neville Hill	**54207** BR Bristol Bath Road	
E56208 56G Bradford Hammerton St	**E56208** 55H Neville Hill	**E56208** NL Neville Hill	**54208** BR Bristol Bath Road	
E56209 56G Bradford Hammerton St	**E56209** 55H Neville Hill	**E56209** NL Neville Hill	**54209** BR Bristol Bath Road	
E56210 56G Bradford Hammerton St	**E56210** 32A Norwich	**E56210** NL Neville Hill	**54210** CF Cardiff Canton	
M56211 8C Speke Junction				
M56212 8C Speke Junction	**M56212** 8J Allerton	**M56212** AN Allerton	**54212** CF Cardiff Canton	
M56213 8C Speke Junction	**M56213** 8J Allerton	**M56213** CH Chester		
M56214 27F Brunswick	**M56214** 9A Longsight	**M56214** CH Chester	**54214** CH Chester	
M56215 27F Brunswick	**M56215** 8J Allerton			
E56218 South Gosforth	**E56218** 52J South Gosforth	**E56218** NL Neville Hill	**54218** NC Norwich Crown Point	
E56219 South Gosforth	**E56219** 52J South Gosforth	**E56219** DN Darlington		
E56220 South Gosforth	**E56220** 52J South Gosforth	**E56220** NL Neville Hill	**54220** CH Chester	
M56221 1E Bletchley	**M56221** 9A Longsight	**M56221** LO Longsight	**54221** NL Neville Hill	
M56222 1E Bletchley	**M56222** 9A Longsight	**M56222** AN Allerton	**54222** BY Bletchley	
M56223 1E Bletchley	**M56223** 9A Longsight	**M56223** CH Chester	**54223** BY Bletchley	
M56224 1E Bletchley	**M56224** 9A Longsight	**M56224** LO Longsight	**54224** BY Bletchley	
M56225 1E Bletchley	**M56225** 9A Longsight	**M56225** LO Longsight	**54225** CH Chester	
M56226 1E Bletchley				
M56227 1E Bletchley	**M56227** 9A Longsight	**M56227** NH Newton Heath	**54227** HT Heaton	
M56228 1E Bletchley	**M56228** 9A Longsight	**M56228** LO Longsight	**54228** BY Bletchley	
M56229 1E Bletchley	**M56229** 9A Longsight			
M56230 27F Brunswick	**M56230** 9A Longsight	**M56230** LO Longsight	**54230** BR Bristol Bath Road	
M56231 9E Trafford Park	**M56231** 9A Longsight	**M56231** LO Longsight	**54231** CH Chester	
M56232 9E Trafford Park	**M56232** 9A Longsight	**M56232** LO Longsight	**54232** CH Chester	
M56233 9E Trafford Park	**M56233** 12A Carlisle			
M56234 Reddish	**M56234** 12A Carlisle	**M56234** KD Carlisle Kingmoor		
M56235 9E Trafford Park	**M56235** 12A Carlisle	**M56235** KD Carlisle Kingmoor	**54235** HT Heaton	
M56236 9E Trafford Park	**M56236** 12A Carlisle	**M56236** KD Carlisle Kingmoor	**54236** HT Heaton	
M56237 9E Trafford Park	**M56237** 12A Carlisle			
M56238 9E Trafford Park	**M56238** 12A Carlisle	**M56238** KD Carlisle Kingmoor	**54238** HT Heaton	
M56239 Reddish	**M56239** 12A Carlisle	**M56239** KD Carlisle Kingmoor	**54239** HT Heaton	
M56240 9E Trafford Park	**M56240** 12A Carlisle	**M56240** KD Carlisle Kingmoor	**54240** HT Heaton	
M56241 9E Trafford Park	**M56241** 12A Carlisle	**M56241** KD Carlisle Kingmoor	**54241** HT Heaton	
M56242 Reddish	**M56242** 12A Carlisle	**M56242** KD Carlisle Kingmoor	**54242** HT Heaton	
M56243 9E Trafford Park	**M56243** 12A Carlisle	**M56243** KD Carlisle Kingmoor	**54243** HT Heaton	
M56244 9E Trafford Park	**M56244** 12A Carlisle	**M56244** KD Carlisle Kingmoor	**54244** HT Heaton	
M56245 24F Fleetwood	**M56245** 12A Carlisle	**M56245** KD Carlisle Kingmoor	**54245** HT Heaton	
M56246 24F Fleetwood	**M56246** 12A Carlisle	**M56246** KD Carlisle Kingmoor	**54246** CH Chester	
M56247 24F Fleetwood	**M56247** 12A Carlisle	**M56247** KD Carlisle Kingmoor	**54247** HT Heaton	
M56248 24F Fleetwood	**M56248** 10E Accrington	**M56248** NH Newton Heath	**54248** NL Neville Hill	
M56249 24F Fleetwood	**M56249** 10E Accrington	**M56249** NH Newton Heath	**54249** NL Neville Hill	
M56250 24F Fleetwood	**M56250** 10E Accrington	**M56250** NH Newton Heath		
M56251 24F Fleetwood	**M56251** 10E Accrington	**M56251** NH Newton Heath	**54251** NL Neville Hill	
M56252 24F Fleetwood	**M56252** 12A Carlisle	**M56252** NH Newton Heath	**54252** NL Neville Hill	
M56253 24F Fleetwood	**M56253** 10E Accrington	**M56253** LO Longsight	**54253** CH Chester	
M56254 24F Fleetwood	**M56254** 10E Accrington			
M56255 24F Fleetwood				
M56256 27F Brunswick	**M56256** 10E Accrington	**M56256** NH Newton Heath	**54256** CH Chester	
M56257 27F Brunswick	**M56257** 10E Accrington	**M56257** NH Newton Heath	**54257** BY Bletchley	
M56258 27F Brunswick	**M56258** 10E Accrington	**M56258** LO Longsight	**54258** CH Chester	
M56259 27F Brunswick	**M56259** 10E Accrington	**M56259** NH Newton Heath	**54259** BY Bletchley	
M56260 27F Brunswick	**M56260** 10E Accrington	**M56260** LO Longsight	**54260** CH Chester	
M56261 14E Bedford	**M56261** 10E Accrington	**M56261** LO Longsight	**54261** CH Chester	
M56262 26A Newton Heath	**M56262** 10E Accrington	**M56262** NH Newton Heath	**54262** HT Heaton	
M56263 6G Llandudno Junction	**M56263** 10E Accrington	**M56263** NH Newton Heath	**54263** HT Heaton	
M56264 6G Llandudno Junction	**M56264** 10E Accrington	**M56264** LO Longsight	**54264** CH Chester	
M56265 6G Llandudno Junction	**M56265** 10E Accrington	**M56265** NH Newton Heath	**54265** HT Heaton	
M56266 6G Llandudno Junction	**M56266** 10E Accrington	**M56266** NH Newton Heath	**54266** CH Chester	
M56267 26A Newton Heath	**M56267** 10E Accrington	**M56267** LO Longsight	**54267** CF Cardiff Canton	
M56268 26A Newton Heath	**M56268** 10E Accrington	**M56268** LO Longsight	**54268** BR Bristol Bath Road	
M56269 14E Bedford (o/l)	**M56269** 10E Accrington	**M56269** CH Chester	**54269** CH Chester	
M56270 14E Bedford (o/l)	**M56270** 10E Accrington	**M56270** NH Newton Heath	**54270** NL Neville Hill	
	M56271 8J Allerton	**M56271** AN Allerton	**54271** BY Bletchley	
	M56272 8J Allerton	**M56272** AN Allerton	**54272** CH Chester	
	M56273 8J Allerton	**M56273** CH Chester	**54273** CF Cardiff Canton	
	M56274 8J Allerton	**M56274** AN Allerton	**54274** BY Bletchley	
	M56275 8J Allerton	**M56275** AN Allerton	**54275** CH Chester	
	M56276 8J Allerton	**M56276** AN Allerton	**54276** CH Chester	
	M56277 8J Allerton	**M56277** AN Allerton	**54277** CH Chester	
	M56278 8J Allerton	**M56278** AN Allerton	**54278** CH Chester	
	M56279 8J Allerton	**M56279** AN Allerton	**54279** BY Bletchley	
	W56280 81D Reading	**W56280** RG Reading	**54280** OO Old Oak Common	
	W56281 81D Reading	**W56281** RG Reading		
	W56282 81D Reading			
	W56283 81D Reading	**W56283** RG Reading	**54283** OO Old Oak Common	
	W56284 81D Reading	**W56284** RG Reading	**54284** BY Bletchley	
	W56285 81D Reading	**W56285** RG Reading		
	W56286 81D Reading	**W56286** RG Reading		
	W56287 81D Reading	**W56287** RG Reading	**54287** OO Old Oak Common	

1960	1970	1980	1990	2000
	W56289 81D Reading	**W56289** RG Reading	**54289** OO Old Oak Common	
W56291 SHL Southall	**SC56291** 66C Hamilton			
W56292 SHL Southall	**M56292** 14A Cricklewood			
W56293 SHL Southall	**M56293** 2A Tyseley			
W56294 SHL Southall	**M56294** 14A Cricklewood	**W56294**		
W56295 TYS Tyseley	**M56295** 2A Tyseley	**M56295** TS Tyseley		
W56296 TYS Tyseley	**M56296** 2A Tyseley	**M56296** TS Tyseley		
W56297 SHL Southall	**SC56297** 66C Hamilton			
W56298 SHL Southall	**M56298** 14A Cricklewood			
W56299 TYS Tyseley	**SC56299** 66C Hamilton			
SC56300 64H Leith Central	**E56300** 32A Norwich			
SC56301 64H Leith Central	**E56301** 31A Cambridge			
SC56302 64H Leith Central	**SC56302** 64H Leith Central			
SC56303 64H Leith Central	**E56303** 32A Norwich			
SC56304 64H Leith Central				
SC56305 66C Hamilton				
SC56306 66C Hamilton	**SC56306** 64H Leith Central			
SC56307 64H Leith Central	**E56307** 32A Norwich			
SC56308 64H Leith Central	**SC56308** 64H Leith Central			
SC56309 66C Hamilton (o/l)	**SC56309** 64H Leith Central			
SC56310 64H Leith Central	**E56310** 52J South Gosforth			
SC56311 64H Leith Central	**SC56311** 64H Leith Central			
SC56312 64H Leith Central	**SC56312** 64H Leith Central			
SC56313 64H Leith Central	**E56313** 32A Norwich			
SC56314 64H Leith Central	**SC56314** 64H Leith Central			
SC56315 66C Hamilton	**E56315** 31A Cambridge			
SC56316 64H Leith Central	**E56316** 31A Cambridge			
SC56317 64H Leith Central	**E56317** 31A Cambridge			
SC56318 64H Leith Central	**E56318** 31A Cambridge			
SC56319 64H Leith Central	**SC56319** 64H Leith Central			
M56332 3E Monument Lane	**M56332** 6A Chester	**M56332** CH Chester	**54332** NC Norwich Crown Point	
M56333 3E Monument Lane	**M56333** 6A Chester	**M56333** CH Chester		
M56334 3E Monument Lane	**M56334** 6A Chester	**M56334** CH Chester		
M56335 3E Monument Lane	**M56335** 6A Chester	**M56335** CH Chester		
M56336 3E Monument Lane	**M56336** 6A Chester	**M56336** CH Chester		
M56337 3E Monument Lane	**M56337** 6A Chester	**M56337** CH Chester		
M56338 3E Monument Lane	**M56338** 6A Chester			
M56339 3E Monument Lane	**M56339** 6A Chester	**M56339** CH Chester		
M56340 3E Monument Lane	**M56340** 6A Chester	**M56340** CH Chester	**54340** NL Neville Hill	
M56341 3E Monument Lane	**M56341** 6A Chester	**M56341** CH Chester		
M56342 3E Monument Lane	**M56342** 6A Chester	**M56342** CH Chester	**54342** NL Neville Hill	
M56343 3E Monument Lane	**M56343** 6A Chester	**M56343** CH Chester	**54343** NC Norwich Crown Point	**54343** LO Longsight
M56344 3E Monument Lane	**M56344** 6A Chester	**M56344** CH Chester		
M56345 3E Monument Lane	**M56345** 6A Chester	**M56345** CH Chester		
M56346 3E Monument Lane	**M56346** 6A Chester	**M56346** CH Chester	**54346** NL Neville Hill	
M56347 3C Walsall Rycroft	**M56347** 6A Chester	**M56347** CH Chester	**54347** NC Norwich Crown Point	**54347** LO Longsight
M56348 3C Walsall Rycroft	**M56348** 6A Chester	**M56348** CH Chester		
M56349 3C Walsall Rycroft	**M56349** 6A Chester	**M56349** CH Chester		
M56350 3C Walsall Rycroft	**M56350** 6A Chester	**M56350** CH Chester		
M56351 24E Blackpool South	**M56351** 6A Chester	**M56351** CH Chester		
M56352 24E Blackpool South	**M56352** 6A Chester	**M56352** CH Chester	**54352** NC Norwich Crown Point	**54352** LO Longsight
M56353 24E Blackpool South	**M56353** 6A Chester	**M56353** CH Chester		
M56354 24E Blackpool South	**M56354** 6A Chester	**M56354** CH Chester	**54354** NC Norwich Crown Point	
M56355 24E Blackpool South	**M56355** 6A Chester	**M56355** CH Chester		
M56356 24E Blackpool South	**M56356** 6A Chester	**M56356** CH Chester		
M56357 24E Blackpool South	**M56357** 6A Chester	**M56357** CH Chester		
M56358 24E Blackpool South	**M56358** 6A Chester	**M56358** CH Chester	**54358** BY Bletchley	**54358** LO Longsight
M56359 24E Blackpool South	**M56359** 6A Chester	**M56359** CH Chester		
M56360 5D Stoke-on-Trent	**M56360** 6A Chester	**M56360** CH Chester		
M56361 5D Stoke-on-Trent	**M56361** 6A Chester	**M56361** CH Chester		
E56362 50A York	**E56362** 32A Norwich	**E56362** NL Neville Hill	**54362** CA Cambridge	
E56363 50A York	**E56363** 52J South Gosforth	**E56363** BG Hull Botanic Gardens	**54363** BY Bletchley	
E56364 56G Bradford Hammerton St	**E56364** 32A Norwich	**E56364** BG Hull Botanic Gardens		
E56365 56G Bradford Hammerton St	**E56365** 32A Norwich	**E56365** HT Heaton	**54365** NL Neville Hill	**54365** LO Longsight
E56366 53B Hull Botanic Gardens	**E56366** 55H Neville Hill	**E56366** DN Darlington		
E56367 53B Hull Botanic Gardens	**E56367** 52J South Gosforth	**E56367** HT Heaton		
E56368 56G Bradford Hammerton St	**E56368** 55H Neville Hill	**E56368** BG Hull Botanic Gardens	**54368** NC Norwich Crown Point	
E56369 56G Bradford Hammerton St	**E56369** 32A Norwich	**E56369** NL Neville Hill	**54369** NC Norwich Crown Point	
E56370 56G Bradford Hammerton St	**E56370** 55F Bradford Hammerton St	**E56370** DN Darlington	**54370** HT Heaton (s)	
E56371 50A York	**E56371** 32A Norwich	**E56371** CA Cambridge	**54371** OO Old Oak Common	
E56372 50A York	**E56372** 52J South Gosforth	**E56372** CA Cambridge	**54372** OO Old Oak Common	
E56373 53B Hull Botanic Gardens	**E56373** 52J South Gosforth	**E56373** CA Cambridge		
E56374 53B Hull Botanic Gardens	**E56374** 52J South Gosforth	**E56374** NL Neville Hill		
E56375 South Gosforth	**E56375** 52J South Gosforth	**E56375** HT Heaton		
E56376 50B Neville Hill	**E56376** 32A Norwich	**E56376** HT Heaton		
E56377 South Gosforth	**E56377** 51A Darlington	**E56377** CA Cambridge		
E56378 South Gosforth	**E56378** 51A Darlington	**E56378** DN Darlington		
E56379 South Gosforth	**E56379** 52J South Gosforth	**E56379** HT Heaton	**54379** NC Norwich Crown Point	
E56380 50B Neville Hill	**E56380** 32A Norwich	**E56380** HT Heaton	**54380** NC Norwich Crown Point	
E56381 50A York	**E56381** 52J South Gosforth	**E56381** DN Darlington	**54381** BY Bletchley	
SC56382 64H Leith Central	**SC56382** 62B Dundee	**E56382** CA Cambridge	**54382** CA Cambridge	
SC56383 66C Hamilton	**E56383** 32A Norwich	**E56383** BG Hull Botanic Gardens		
SC56384 66C Hamilton	**E56384** 50C Hull Botanic Gardens	**E56384** BG Hull Botanic Gardens		
SC56385 66C Hamilton	**E56385** 50C Hull Botanic Gardens	**E56385** NL Neville Hill	**54385** OO Old Oak Common	
SC56386 64H Leith Central	**SC56386** 64H Leith Central	**E56386** DN Darlington		
SC56387 62B Dundee	**E56387** 50C Hull Botanic Gardens	**E56387** HT Heaton	**54387** NC Norwich Crown Point	
SC56388 66C Hamilton	**SC56388** 64H Leith Central	**E56388** HT Heaton	**54388** NC Norwich Crown Point	

1960	1970	1980	1990	2000
SC56389 64H Leith Central	**SC56389** 64H Leith Central	**E56389** BG Hull Botanic Gardens		
SC56390 66C Hamilton	**SC56390** 64H Leith Central	**E56390** HT Heaton		
SC56391 64H Leith Central	**SC56391** 64H Leith Central	**E56391** HT Heaton		
SC56392 66C Hamilton	**SC56392** 66C Hamilton	**E56392** DN Darlington		
SC56393 66C Hamilton	**E56393** 50C Hull Botanic Gardens	**E56393** HT Heaton	**54393** NC Norwich Crown Point	
SC56394 66C Hamilton	**E56394** 50C Hull Botanic Gardens	**E56394** NL Neville Hill		
SC56395 66C Hamilton	**SC56395** 62B Dundee			
SC56396 62B Dundee	**E56396** 50C Hull Botanic Gardens	**E56396** DN Darlington	**54396** OO Old Oak Common	
SC56397 62B Dundee	**SC56397** 62B Dundee	**E56397** HT Heaton		
SC56398 62B Dundee	**E56398** 50C Hull Botanic Gardens	**E56398** DN Darlington		
SC56399 62B Dundee	**SC56399** 62B Dundee	**E56399** HT Heaton	**54399** NC Norwich Crown Point	
SC56400 62B Dundee	**SC56400** 62B Dundee	**E56400** HT Heaton		
SC56401 62B Dundee	**SC56401** 64H Leith Central	**E56401** NL Neville Hill		
SC56402 64H Leith Central	**E56402** 50C Hull Botanic Gardens	**E56402** CA Cambridge	**54402** CA Cambridge	
SC56403 62B Dundee	**SC56403** 62B Dundee	**E56403** HT Heaton		
SC56404 62B Dundee	**SC56404** 64H Leith Central	**E56404** HT Heaton		
SC56405 64H Leith Central	**E56405** 50C Hull Botanic Gardens	**E56405** DN Darlington	**54405** CA Cambridge	
SC56406 64H Leith Central	**SC56406** 66C Hamilton	**E56406** HT Heaton		
SC56407 62B Dundee	**SC56407** 64H Leith Central	**E56407** BG Hull Botanic Gardens		
SC56408 62B Dundee	**SC56408** 66C Hamilton	**E56408** HT Heaton	**54408** NL Neville Hill	**54408** LO Longsight
SC56409 66C Hamilton	**SC56409** 64H Leith Central	**E56409** HT Heaton		
SC56410 62B Dundee	**SC56410** 66C Hamilton	**E56410** HT Heaton		
SC56411 62B Dundee	**SC56411** 67A Corkerhill	**M56411** LO Longsight		
E56412 34B Hornsey	**E56412** 34G Finsbury Park			
E56413 34B Hornsey	**E56413** 34G Finsbury Park	**E56413** NR Norwich		
E56414 34B Hornsey	**E56414** 34G Finsbury Park	**E56414** NR Norwich		
E56415 34B Hornsey	**E56415** 34G Finsbury Park	**E56415** SF Stratford		
E56416 34B Hornsey	**E56416** 34G Finsbury Park	**E56416** SF Stratford		
E56417 34B Hornsey	**E56417** 34G Finsbury Park	**E56417** BG Hull Botanic Gardens		
E56418 34B Hornsey	**E56418** 34G Finsbury Park	**E56418** NR Norwich		
E56419 34B Hornsey	**E56419** 34G Finsbury Park	**E56419** NR Norwich		
E56420 34B Hornsey	**E56420** 34G Finsbury Park	**E56420** SF Stratford		
E56421 34B Hornsey	**E56421** 34G Finsbury Park	**E56421** SF Stratford		
E56422 34B Hornsey	**E56422** 34G Finsbury Park	**E56422** HT Heaton		
E56423 34B Hornsey	**E56423** 34G Finsbury Park	**E56423** HT Heaton		
E56424 34B Hornsey	**E56424** 34G Finsbury Park	**E56424** BG Hull Botanic Gardens		
E56425 34B Hornsey	**E56425** 34G Finsbury Park	**E56425** HT Heaton		
E56426 34B Hornsey	**E56426** 34G Finsbury Park	**E56426** HT Heaton		
E56427 34B Hornsey	**E56427** 34G Finsbury Park	**E56427** HT Heaton		
E56428 34B Hornsey	**E56428** 34G Finsbury Park			
E56429 34B Hornsey	**E56429** 34G Finsbury Park	**E56429** HT Heaton		
E56430 34B Hornsey	**E56430** 34G Finsbury Park			
E56431 34B Hornsey	**E56431** 34G Finsbury Park	**E56431** LN Lincoln		
E56432 31A Cambridge	**E56432** 31A Cambridge	**E56432** NR Norwich		
E56433 31A Cambridge	**E56433** 34G Finsbury Park	**E56433** BG Hull Botanic Gardens		
E56434 31A Cambridge	**E56434** 31A Cambridge	**E56434** NR Norwich		
E56435 31A Cambridge	**E56435** 31A Cambridge	**E56435** NR Norwich		
E56436 31A Cambridge	**E56436** 31A Cambridge	**E56436** NR Norwich		
E56437 31A Cambridge	**E56437** 31A Cambridge	**E56437** NR Norwich		
E56438 31A Cambridge	**E56438** 34G Finsbury Park	**E56438** LN Lincoln		
E56439 31A Cambridge	**E56439** 31A Cambridge	**E56439** NR Norwich		
E56440 31A Cambridge	**E56440** 31A Cambridge	**E56440** HT Heaton		
E56441 31A Cambridge	**E56441** 40A Lincoln	**E56441** NR Norwich		
E56442 31A Cambridge	**E56442** 40A Lincoln	**E56442** LN Lincoln		
E56443 31A Cambridge	**E56443** 40A Lincoln	**E56443** NR Norwich		
E56444 31A Cambridge	**E56444** 40A Lincoln	**E56444** LN Lincoln		
E56445 31A Cambridge	**E56445** 40A Lincoln	**E56445** LN Lincoln		
E56446 31A Cambridge	**E56446** 40A Lincoln	**E56446** LN Lincoln		
E56447 34B Hornsey	**E56447** 34G Finsbury Park	**E56447** NR Norwich		
E56448 34B Hornsey	**E56448** 34G Finsbury Park	**E56448** NR Norwich		
E56449 34B Hornsey	**E56449** 34G Finsbury Park	**E56449** SF Stratford		
E56450 34B Hornsey	**E56450** 34G Finsbury Park	**E56450** BG Hull Botanic Gardens		
E56451 34B Hornsey	**E56451** 34G Finsbury Park	**E56451** NR Norwich		
E56452 34B Hornsey	**E56452** 34G Finsbury Park	**M56452** TS Tyseley		
E56453 34B Hornsey	**E56453** 34G Finsbury Park	**E56453** HT Heaton		
E56454 34B Hornsey	**E56454** 34G Finsbury Park	**E56454** LN Lincoln		
E56455 34B Hornsey	**E56455** 34G Finsbury Park	**E56455** SF Stratford		
E56456 34B Hornsey	**E56456** 34G Finsbury Park	**M56456** LO Longsight		
E56457 34B Hornsey	**E56457** 34G Finsbury Park	**E56457** SF Stratford		
E56458 40A Lincoln	**E56458** 34G Finsbury Park	**E56458** NR Norwich		
E56459 34B Hornsey	**E56459** 34G Finsbury Park	**E56459** HT Heaton		
E56460 34B Hornsey	**E56460** 34G Finsbury Park	**E56460** HT Heaton		
E56461 34B Hornsey	**E56461** 34G Finsbury Park	**E56461** HT Heaton		
SC56462 61A Kittybrewster	**SC56462** 66C Hamilton	**E56462** NR Norwich		
SC56463 61A Kittybrewster	**SC56463** 66C Hamilton	**E56463** NR Norwich		
SC56464 61A Kittybrewster	**SC56464** 66C Hamilton	**E56464** HT Heaton		
SC56465 61A Kittybrewster	**SC56465** 66C Hamilton	**E56465** HT Heaton		
SC56466 61A Kittybrewster	**SC56466** 66C Hamilton	**E56466** HT Heaton		
SC56467 61A Kittybrewster	**SC56467** 66C Hamilton	**E56467** NR Norwich		
SC56468 61A Kittybrewster	**SC56468** 66C Hamilton	**E56468** NR Norwich		
SC56469 61A Kittybrewster	**SC56469** 66C Hamilton	**E56469** NR Norwich		
SC56470 61A Kittybrewster	**SC56470** 66C Hamilton	**E56470** HT Heaton		
SC56471 66C Hamilton	**SC56471** 66C Hamilton	**E56471** BG Hull Botanic Gardens		
SC56472 66C Hamilton	**SC56472** 66C Hamilton	**E56472** LN Lincoln		
SC56473 66C Hamilton	**SC56473** 66C Hamilton	**E56473** BG Hull Botanic Gardens		
SC56474 66C Hamilton	**SC56474** 66C Hamilton	**E56474** HT Heaton		
SC56475 66C Hamilton	**SC56475** 66C Hamilton	**M56475** NH Newton Heath		

1960	1970	1980	1990	2000
SC56476 66C Hamilton	**SC56476** 66C Hamilton			
SC56477 66C Hamilton	**SC56477** 66C Hamilton			
SC56478 66C Hamilton	**SC56478** 66C Hamilton			
SC56479 66C Hamilton	**SC56479** 66C Hamilton			
SC56480 66C Hamilton	**SC56480** 66C Hamilton	**E56480** NR Norwich		
SC56481 66C Hamilton	**SC56481** 66C Hamilton			
SC56482 66C Hamilton	**SC56482** 66C Hamilton	**M56482** BY Bletchley		
SC56483 66C Hamilton	**SC56483** 66C Hamilton			
	M56484 9A Longsight	**M56484** AN Allerton	**54484** CH Chester	
	M56485 9A Longsight	**M56485** LO Longsight	**54485** CH Chester	
	M56486 9A Longsight	**M56486** LO Longsight	**54486** CH Chester	
	M56487 9A Longsight	**M56487** LO Longsight	**54487** CH Chester	
	M56488 9A Longsight	**M56488** LO Longsight	**54488** CH Chester	
	M56489 9A Longsight	**M56489** LO Longsight	**54489** CH Chester	
	M56490 9A Longsight	**M56490** LO Longsight	**54490** CH Chester	
	M56491 8J Allerton	**M56491** AN Allerton	**54491** BY Bletchley	
	M56492 8J Allerton	**M56492** AN Allerton	**54492** BR Bristol Bath Road	
	M56493 8J Allerton	**M56493** AN Allerton	**54493** BY Bletchley	
	M56494 8J Allerton	**M56494** AN Allerton	**54494** CF Cardiff Canton	
	M56495 8J Allerton	**M56495** AN Allerton	**54495** BY Bletchley	
	M56496 8J Allerton	**M56496** AN Allerton	**54496** CH Chester	
	M56497 8J Allerton	**M56497** AN Allerton	**54497** CH Chester	
	M56498 8J Allerton	**M56498** AN Allerton	**54498** CF Cardiff Canton	
	M56499 8J Allerton	**M56499** AN Allerton	**54499** BY Bletchley	
	M56500 8J Allerton	**M56500** AN Allerton	**54500** BY Bletchley	
	M56501 8J Allerton	**M56501** LO Longsight	**54501** CH Chester	
	M56502 8J Allerton	**M56502** CH Chester		
	M56503 6A Chester	**M56503** CH Chester	**54503** NL Neville Hill	
	M56504 6A Chester	**M56504** CH Chester	**54504** NL Neville Hill	
W59000 TYS Tyseley	**M59000** 2A Tyseley	**M59000** TS Tyseley		
W59001 TYS Tyseley	**M59001** 2A Tyseley	**M59001** TS Tyseley		
W59002 TYS Tyseley	**M59002** 2A Tyseley	**M59002** TS Tyseley		
W59003 TYS Tyseley	**M59003** 2A Tyseley	**M59003** TS Tyseley		
W59004 TYS Tyseley	**M59004** 2A Tyseley	**M59004** TS Tyseley		
W59005 TYS Tyseley	**M59005** 2A Tyseley	**M59005** TS Tyseley		
W59006 TYS Tyseley	**M59006** 2A Tyseley	**M59006** TS Tyseley		
W59007 TYS Tyseley	**M59007** 2A Tyseley	**M59007** TS Tyseley		
W59008 TYS Tyseley	**M59008** 14A Cricklewood	**M59008** CW Cricklewood		
W59009 TYS Tyseley	**M59009** 2A Tyseley	**M59009** TS Tyseley		
W59010 TYS Tyseley	**M59010** 2A Tyseley	**M59010** TS Tyseley		
W59011 TYS Tyseley	**M59011** 14A Cricklewood	**M59011** CW Cricklewood		
W59012 TYS Tyseley	**M59012** 2A Tyseley	**M59012** TS Tyseley		
W59013 TYS Tyseley	**M59013** 2A Tyseley	**M59013** TS Tyseley		
W59014 TYS Tyseley	**M59014** 2A Tyseley	**M59014** TS Tyseley		
W59015 TYS Tyseley	**M59015** 2A Tyseley	**M59015** TS Tyseley		
W59016 TYS Tyseley	**M59016** 2A Tyseley	**M59016** TS Tyseley		
W59017 TYS Tyseley	**M59017** 14A Cricklewood	**M59017** CW Cricklewood		
W59018 TYS Tyseley	**M59018** 2A Tyseley	**M59018** TS Tyseley		
W59019 TYS Tyseley	**M59019** 2A Tyseley	**M59019** TS Tyseley		
W59020 TYS Tyseley	**M59020** 14A Cricklewood	**M59020** TS Tyseley		
W59021 TYS Tyseley	**M59021** 14A Cricklewood	**M59021** CW Cricklewood		
W59022 TYS Tyseley	**M59022** 2A Tyseley	**M59022** TS Tyseley		
W59023 TYS Tyseley	**M59023** 2A Tyseley	**M59023** TS Tyseley		
W59024 TYS Tyseley	**M59024** 2A Tyseley	**M59024** TS Tyseley		
W59025 TYS Tyseley				
W59026 TYS Tyseley	**M59026** 2A Tyseley	**M59026** TS Tyseley		
W59027 TYS Tyseley	**M59027** 2A Tyseley	**SC59027** HN Hamilton		
W59028 TYS Tyseley	**M59028** 2A Tyseley	**M59028** TS Tyseley		
W59029 CAT Cardiff Cathays	**M59029** 2A Tyseley	**M59029** TS Tyseley		
W59030 CAT Cardiff Cathays	**W59030** 86A Cardiff Canton	**W59030** CF Cardiff Canton		
W59031 CAT Cardiff Cathays	**W59031** 86A Cardiff Canton	**W59031** CF Cardiff Canton		
W59032 CDF Cardiff Canton	**W59032** 86A Cardiff Canton	**W59032** CF Cardiff Canton	**59032** TS Tyseley	
W59033 CDF Cardiff Canton	**W59033** 86A Cardiff Canton	**W59033** CF Cardiff Canton		
W59034 CDF Cardiff Canton	**W59034** 86A Cardiff Canton	**W59034** CF Cardiff Canton		
W59035 CDF Cardiff Canton	**W59035** 86A Cardiff Canton	**W59035** CF Cardiff Canton		
W59036 CDF Cardiff Canton	**W59036** 86A Cardiff Canton	**W59036** CF Cardiff Canton		
W59037 CDF Cardiff Canton	**W59037** 86A Cardiff Canton	**W59037** CF Cardiff Canton		
W59038 CDF Cardiff Canton	**W59038** 86A Cardiff Canton	**M59038** TS Tyseley		
W59039 CDF Cardiff Canton	**W59039** 86A Cardiff Canton	**W59039** CF Cardiff Canton		
W59040 CDF Cardiff Canton	**W59040** 86A Cardiff Canton	**W59040** CF Cardiff Canton		
W59041 CDF Cardiff Canton	**W59041** 86A Cardiff Canton	**W59041** CF Cardiff Canton		
E59042 South Gosforth	**E59042** 52J South Gosforth	**SC59042** DE Dundee	**59042** HA Haymarket	
E59043 South Gosforth	**E59043** 52J South Gosforth	**SC59043** HA Haymarket		
E59044 South Gosforth				
E59045 South Gosforth	**E59045** 52J South Gosforth	**SC59045** DE Dundee		
E59046 South Gosforth	**E59046** 52J South Gosforth	**SC59046** HA Haymarket		
E59047 South Gosforth	**E59047** 52J South Gosforth	**SC59047** HA Haymarket		
E59048 South Gosforth	**E59048** 55H Neville Hill	**SC59048** DE Dundee		
E59049 South Gosforth	**E59049** 52J South Gosforth	**SC59049** DE Dundee	**59049** ED Eastfield	
E59050 South Gosforth	**E59050** 52J South Gosforth	**W59050** BR Bristol Bath Road		
E59051 South Gosforth				
E59052 South Gosforth	**E59052** 52J South Gosforth	**E59052** DN Darlington		
E59053 South Gosforth	**E59053** 52J South Gosforth	**SC59053** DE Dundee		
E59054 South Gosforth	**E59054** 52J South Gosforth	**E59054** NL Neville Hill		
E59055 South Gosforth	**E59055** 55H Neville Hill	**E59055** NL Neville Hill	**59055** NC Norwich Crown Point	
E59060 51A Darlington	**E59060** 51A Darlington	**SC59060** HA Haymarket		
E59061 51A Darlington	**SC59061** 62B Dundee	**SC59061** DE Dundee	**59061** HA Haymarket	

1960	1970	1980	1990	2000
E59062 51A Darlington	**E59062** 52J South Gosforth	**E59062** NL Neville Hill		
E59063 51A Darlington	**E59063** 51A Darlington	**E59063** BG Hull Botanic Gardens		
E59064 51A Darlington	**E59064** 51A Darlington	**E59064** DN Darlington		
E59065 51A Darlington	**E59065** 55H Neville Hill	**E59065** NL Neville Hill		
E59066 51A Darlington	**E59066** 52J South Gosforth	**SC59066** DE Dundee		
E59067 51A Darlington	**SC59067** 62B Dundee	**SC59067** DE Dundee		
E59068 51A Darlington	**E59068** 51A Darlington	**E59068** DN Darlington		
E59069 51A Darlington	**E59069** 55H Neville Hill	**SC59069** DE Dundee		
E59070 51A Darlington	**E59070** 51A Darlington	**E59070** NL Neville Hill		
E59071 51A Darlington	**E59071** 52J South Gosforth	**SC59071** HA Haymarket		
E59072 51A Darlington	**E59072** 52J South Gosforth	**E59072** DN Darlington	**59072** NL Neville Hill	
E59073 51A Darlington	**E59073** 55H Neville Hill	**SC59073** DE Dundee		
E59074 51A Darlington	**SC59074** 62B Dundee	**SC59074** DE Dundee	**59074** ED Eastfield	
E59075 51A Darlington	**E59075** 51A Darlington	**E59075** NL Neville Hill		
E59076 51A Darlington	**E59076** 52J South Gosforth	**E59076** NR Norwich		
E59077 51A Darlington	**E59077** 52J South Gosforth	**SC59077** DE Dundee	**59077** NC Norwich Crown Point	
E59078 51A Darlington	**E59078** 51A Darlington	**E59078** NR Norwich		
E59079 51A Darlington	**E59079** 51A Darlington	**E59079** DN Darlington	**59079** NC Norwich Crown Point	
E59080 51A Darlington	**SC59080** 66C Hamilton	**SC59080** DE Dundee	**59080** ED Eastfield	
E59081 51A Darlington	**E59081** 51A Darlington	**SC59081** DE Dundee		
E59082 51A Darlington	**E59082** 55H Neville Hill	**W59082** BR Bristol Bath Road	**59082** ED Eastfield	
E59083 51A Darlington	**E59083** 51A Darlington	**E59083** DN Darlington		
E59084 51A Darlington	**E59084** 51A Darlington	**E59084** NL Neville Hill	**59084** NC Norwich Crown Point	
E59085 51A Darlington	**E59085** 52J South Gosforth	**SC59085** DE Dundee		
E59086 South Gosforth	**E59086** 55H Neville Hill	**SC59086** HA Haymarket	**59086** HA Haymarket	
E59087 South Gosforth	**E59087** 55H Neville Hill	**E59087** NL Neville Hill		
E59088 South Gosforth	**E59088** 52J South Gosforth	**SC59088** HA Haymarket		
E59089 South Gosforth	**E59089** 55H Neville Hill	**E59089** NL Neville Hill		
E59090 South Gosforth	**E59090** 52J South Gosforth	**SC59090** HA Haymarket	**59090** ED Eastfield	
E59091 South Gosforth	**E59091** 55H Neville Hill	**E59091** NL Neville Hill	**59091** RG Reading	
E59092 South Gosforth	**E59092** 55H Neville Hill	**E59092** DN Darlington	**59092** NC Norwich Crown Point	
E59093 South Gosforth	**E59093** 55H Neville Hill	**W59093** BR Bristol Bath Road	**59093** LA Laira	
E59094 South Gosforth	**E59094** 52J South Gosforth	**E59094** NL Neville Hill		
E59095 South Gosforth	**E59095** 55H Neville Hill	**E59095** DN Darlington	**59095** NC Norwich Crown Point	
E59096 South Gosforth	**E59096** 52J South Gosforth	**W59096** BR Bristol Bath Road		
E59097 South Gosforth	**E59097** 55H Neville Hill	**E59097** DN Darlington		
	SC59098 64H Leith Central			
	SC59099 64H Leith Central			
E59100 56G Bradford Hammerton St	**E59100** 30A Stratford	**E59100** DN Darlington		
E59101 56G Bradford Hammerton St	**E59101** 30A Stratford	**E59101** NL Neville Hill	**59101** RG Reading	
E59102 56G Bradford Hammerton St	**E59102** 30A Stratford	**E59102** NL Neville Hill		
E59103 56G Bradford Hammerton St				
E59104 56G Bradford Hammerton St	**E59104** 52J South Gosforth	**E59104** DN Darlington	**59104** HA Haymarket	
E59105 56G Bradford Hammerton St	**E59105** 55H Neville Hill	**E59105** NL Neville Hill	**59105** RG Reading	
E59106 56G Bradford Hammerton St	**E59106** 55H Neville Hill	**E59106** NL Neville Hill		
E59107 56G Bradford Hammerton St	**E59107** 55H Neville Hill	**E59107** DN Darlington	**59107** CH Chester (s)	
E59108 56G Bradford Hammerton St	**E59108** 55H Neville Hill	**E59108** NL Neville Hill		
E59109 56G Bradford Hammerton St	**E59109** 52J South Gosforth			
E59112 51A Darlington	**SC59112** 64H Leith Central	**SC59112** DE Dundee		
E59113 51A Darlington	**E59113** 55H Neville Hill	**E59113** DN Darlington		
M59114 3E Monument Lane	**M59114** 2A Tyseley	**M59114** TS Tyseley		
M59115 3E Monument Lane	**M59115** 2A Tyseley	**M59115** TS Tyseley	**59115** RG Reading	
M59116 3E Monument Lane	**M59116** 2A Tyseley	**M59116** TS Tyseley		
M59117 3E Monument Lane	**M59117** 2A Tyseley	**M59117** TS Tyseley	**59117** HA Haymarket	
M59118 3E Monument Lane	**M59118** 2A Tyseley	**M59118** TS Tyseley	**59118** RG Reading	
M59119 3E Monument Lane	**M59119** 2A Tyseley	**M59119** TS Tyseley		
M59120 3E Monument Lane	**M59120** 2A Tyseley	**M59120** TS Tyseley		
M59121 3E Monument Lane	**M59121** 2A Tyseley	**M59121** TS Tyseley		
M59122 3E Monument Lane	**M59122** 2A Tyseley	**W59122** BR Bristol Bath Road		
M59123 3E Monument Lane	**M59123** 2A Tyseley	**W59123** BR Bristol Bath Road		
M59124 3E Monument Lane	**M59124** 2A Tyseley	**M59124** TS Tyseley	**59124** HA Haymarket	
M59125 3E Monument Lane	**M59125** 2A Tyseley	**M59125** TS Tyseley	**59125** RG Reading	
M59126 3E Monument Lane	**M59126** 6A Chester	**M59126** TS Tyseley		
M59127 3E Monument Lane	**M59127** 6A Chester	**M59127** TS Tyseley		
M59128 3E Monument Lane	**M59128** 6A Chester	**M59128** TS Tyseley	**59128** RG Reading	
M59129 3E Monument Lane	**M59129** 6A Chester	**M59129** TS Tyseley		
M59130 18A Toton (o/l)	**M59130** 6A Chester	**M59130** CH Chester	**59130** LA Laira	
M59131 3E Monument Lane	**M59131** 6A Chester	**M59131** TS Tyseley		
M59132 9D Buxton	**M59132** 9L Buxton	**M59132** BX Buxton		
M59133 9D Buxton	**M59133** 9L Buxton	**M59133** BX Buxton		
M59134 9D Buxton	**M59134** 9L Buxton	**M59134** BX Buxton		
M59135 9A Longsight	**M59135** 9L Buxton	**M59135** BX Buxton		
M59136 9D Buxton	**M59136** 9L Buxton	**M59136** BX Buxton		
M59137 9D Buxton	**M59137** 9L Buxton	**M59137** BX Buxton		
M59138 9D Buxton	**M59138** 9L Buxton	**M59138** BX Buxton		
M59139 9D Buxton	**M59139** 9L Buxton	**M59139** BX Buxton		
M59140 9D Buxton	**M59140** 9L Buxton	**M59140** BX Buxton		
M59141 9A Longsight	**M59141** 9L Buxton	**M59141** BX Buxton		
M59142 9A Longsight	**M59142** 16C Derby Etches Park	**M59142** NH Newton Heath		
M59143 9A Longsight	**M59143** 9L Buxton	**M59143** NH Newton Heath		
M59144 9A Longsight	**M59144** 9L Buxton	**M59144** NH Newton Heath		
M59145 9A Longsight	**M59145** 9D Newton Heath	**M59145** BX Buxton		
M59146 9A Longsight	**M59146** 9D Newton Heath	**M59146** NH Newton Heath		
M59147 9A Longsight	**M59147** 9D Newton Heath	**M59147** BX Buxton		
M59148 9A Longsight	**M59148** 9D Newton Heath	**M59148** BX Buxton		
M59149 9A Longsight	**M59149** 9D Newton Heath	**M59149** NH Newton Heath		
M59150 9A Longsight	**M59150** 9D Newton Heath	**M59150** NH Newton Heath		

1960	1970	1980	1990	2000
M59151 9A Longsight	**M59151** 16C Derby Etches Park	**M59151** DY Derby Etches Park		
M59152 9A Longsight	**M59152** 16C Derby Etches Park	**M59152** DY Derby Etches Park		
M59153 9A Longsight	**M59153** 16C Derby Etches Park	**M59153** DY Derby Etches Park		
M59154 9A Longsight				
M59155 5D Stoke-on-Trent	**M59155** 16C Derby Etches Park	**M59155** DY Derby Etches Park		
M59156 5D Stoke-on-Trent	**M59156** 16C Derby Etches Park	**M59156** DY Derby Etches Park		
M59157 5D Stoke-on-Trent	**M59157** 16C Derby Etches Park	**M59157** DY Derby Etches Park		
M59158 5D Stoke-on-Trent	**M59158** 9D Newton Heath	**M59158** NH Newton Heath		
M59159 5D Stoke-on-Trent	**M59159** 16C Derby Etches Park	**M59159** NH Newton Heath		
M59160 5D Stoke-on-Trent	**M59160** 9D Newton Heath	**M59160** NH Newton Heath		
M59161 5D Stoke-on-Trent	**M59161** 9D Newton Heath	**M59161** NH Newton Heath		
M59162 5D Stoke-on-Trent	**M59162** 9D Newton Heath	**M59162** BX Buxton		
M59163 5D Stoke-on-Trent	**M59163** 9D Newton Heath	**M59163** BX Buxton	**59163** RG Reading	
M59164 5D Stoke-on-Trent	**M59164** 9D Newton Heath	**M59164** NH Newton Heath		
M59165 5D Stoke-on-Trent	**M59165** 16C Derby Etches Park	**M59165** NH Newton Heath		
M59166 5D Stoke-on-Trent	**M59166** 9D Newton Heath	**M59166** NH Newton Heath		
M59167 5D Stoke-on-Trent				
M59168 5D Stoke-on-Trent	**M59168** 9D Newton Heath	**M59168** NH Newton Heath		
M59169 5D Stoke-on-Trent	**M59169** 9D Newton Heath	**M59169** NH Newton Heath		
M59170 5B Crewe South				
M59171 5B Crewe South	**M59171** 9D Newton Heath	**M59171** NH Newton Heath		
M59172 5B Crewe South	**M59172** 9D Newton Heath	**M59172** CH Chester		
M59173 5B Crewe South	**M59173** 9D Newton Heath	**M59173** NH Newton Heath		
M59174 5B Crewe South	**M59174** 9D Newton Heath	**M59174** NH Newton Heath		
M59175 5B Crewe South	**M59175** 9D Newton Heath	**M59175** NH Newton Heath		
M59176 5B Crewe South	**M59176** 9D Newton Heath	**M59176** NH Newton Heath		
M59177 5B Crewe South	**M59177** 9D Newton Heath	**M59177** NH Newton Heath		
M59178 5B Crewe South	**M59178** 9D Newton Heath	**M59178** NH Newton Heath		
M59179 5B Crewe South	**M59179** 9D Newton Heath	**M59179** NH Newton Heath		
M59180 5B Crewe South	**M59180** 9D Newton Heath	**M59180** NH Newton Heath		
M59181 5B Crewe South	**M59181** 9D Newton Heath	**M59181** NH Newton Heath		
M59182 5B Crewe South	**M59182** 9D Newton Heath	**M59182** NH Newton Heath		
M59183 18A Toton	**M59183** 9D Newton Heath	**M59183** NH Newton Heath		
M59184 18A Toton	**M59184** 9D Newton Heath	**M59184** NH Newton Heath		
M59185 18A Toton	**M59185** 9D Newton Heath	**M59185** NH Newton Heath		
M59186 18A Toton	**M59186** 9D Newton Heath	**M59186** NH Newton Heath		
M59187 18A Toton	**M59187** 9D Newton Heath	**M59187** NH Newton Heath	**59187** NL Neville Hill	
E59188 51A Darlington	**E59188** 55H Neville Hill	**E59188** GF South Gosforth		
E59189 South Gosforth	**E59189** 55H Neville Hill	**E59189** NL Neville Hill		
E59190 51A Darlington	**E59190** 52J South Gosforth	**E59190** NL Neville Hill		
E59191 South Gosforth	**E59191** 55H Neville Hill	**E59191** NL Neville Hill		
E59192 50B Neville Hill	**E59192** 55H Neville Hill	**M59192** TS Tyseley		
E59193 50B Neville Hill	**E59193** 55H Neville Hill	**M59193** TS Tyseley		
E59194 50B Neville Hill	**E59194** 55H Neville Hill	**E59194** GF South Gosforth		
E59195 50B Neville Hill	**M59195** 9L Buxton	**M59195** BX Buxton		
E59196 53B Hull Botanic Gardens	**E59196** 50C Hull Botanic Gardens			
E59197 53B Hull Botanic Gardens	**E59197** 50C Hull Botanic Gardens	**E59197** GF South Gosforth		
E59198 50A York	**M59198** 9L Buxton	**M59198** BX Buxton		
E59199 53B Hull Botanic Gardens	**E59199** 55H Neville Hill	**E59199** NL Neville Hill		
E59200 53B Hull Botanic Gardens	**E59200** 50C Hull Botanic Gardens	**E59200** GF South Gosforth		
E59201 South Gosforth	**E59201** 55H Neville Hill	**E59201** NL Neville Hill		
E59202 South Gosforth	**E59202** 50C Hull Botanic Gardens			
E59203 50B Neville Hill	**E59203** 55H Neville Hill	**E59203** GF South Gosforth		
E59204 53B Hull Botanic Gardens	**E59204** 50C Hull Botanic Gardens			
E59205 53B Hull Botanic Gardens	**E59205** 50C Hull Botanic Gardens			
E59206 53B Hull Botanic Gardens	**E59206** 52J South Gosforth	**E59206** GF South Gosforth	**59206** BY Bletchley	
E59207 53B Hull Botanic Gardens	**E59207** 50C Hull Botanic Gardens	**E59207** GF South Gosforth		
E59208 53B Hull Botanic Gardens	**E59208** 50C Hull Botanic Gardens	**E59208** GF South Gosforth		
E59209 51A Darlington	**E59209** 55H Neville Hill	**E59209** NL Neville Hill		
E59210 South Gosforth	**E59210** 30A Stratford	**E59210** GF South Gosforth		
E59211 51A Darlington	**E59211** 55H Neville Hill	**E59211** NL Neville Hill		
E59212 South Gosforth	**E59212** 30A Stratford	**E59212** GF South Gosforth		
E59213 50B Neville Hill	**E59213** 55H Neville Hill	**E59213** NL Neville Hill		
E59214 50B Neville Hill	**E59214** 55H Neville Hill	**E59214** GF South Gosforth		
E59215 50A York	**E59215** 55H Neville Hill	**E59215** GF South Gosforth		
E59216 50B Neville Hill	**E59216** 55H Neville Hill	**E59216** GF South Gosforth		
E59217 53B Hull Botanic Gardens	**E59217** 50C Hull Botanic Gardens	**E59217** NL Neville Hill		
E59218 53B Hull Botanic Gardens	**E59218** 50C Hull Botanic Gardens	**E59218** NR Norwich		
E59219 53B Hull Botanic Gardens	**E59219** 52J South Gosforth	**E59219** GF South Gosforth		
E59220 53B Hull Botanic Gardens	**E59220** 55H Neville Hill	**E59220** GF South Gosforth		
E59221 53B Hull Botanic Gardens	**E59221** 50C Hull Botanic Gardens	**E59221** NR Norwich		
E59222 South Gosforth				
E59223 South Gosforth	**E59223** 50C Hull Botanic Gardens	**E59223** NR Norwich		
E59224 50B Neville Hill	**E59224** 50C Hull Botanic Gardens	**E59224** GF South Gosforth		
E59225 53B Hull Botanic Gardens	**E59225** 50C Hull Botanic Gardens	**E59225** NR Norwich		
E59226 53B Hull Botanic Gardens	**E59226** 50C Hull Botanic Gardens	**E59226** NR Norwich		
E59227 53B Hull Botanic Gardens	**E59227** 52J South Gosforth	**E59227** NR Norwich		
E59228 53B Hull Botanic Gardens	**E59228** 50C Hull Botanic Gardens	**E59228** NR Norwich		
E59229 53B Hull Botanic Gardens	**E59229** 50C Hull Botanic Gardens	**E59229** NL Neville Hill		
E59230 50B Neville Hill	**M59230** 9L Buxton	**M59230** BX Buxton		
E59231 53B Hull Botanic Gardens	**E59231** 50C Hull Botanic Gardens	**E59231** GF South Gosforth		
E59232 South Gosforth	**E59232** 55H Neville Hill	**E59232** NL Neville Hill		
E59233 South Gosforth	**E59233** 55H Neville Hill	**E59233** GF South Gosforth		
E59234 South Gosforth	**E59234** 52J South Gosforth	**E59234** NL Neville Hill		
	W59235 81D Reading	**E59235** BG Hull Botanic Gardens		
	W59236 81D Reading	**E59236** BG Hull Botanic Gardens		
	W59237 81D Reading	**E59237** BG Hull Botanic Gardens		

1960	1970	1980	1990	2000
	W59238 81D Reading	**E59238** BG Hull Botanic Gardens		
	W59239 81D Reading	**E59239** BG Hull Botanic Gardens		
E59240 50B Neville Hill	**E59240** 55H Neville Hill	**E59240** GF South Gosforth		
E59241 53B Hull Botanic Gardens	**E59241** 55H Neville Hill	**E59241** NL Neville Hill		
E59242 South Gosforth	**E59242** 55H Neville Hill	**E59242** NL Neville Hill		
E59243 South Gosforth	**E59243** 55H Neville Hill	**E59243** NL Neville Hill		
E59244 South Gosforth	**E59244** 52J South Gosforth	**E59244** GF South Gosforth		
E59245 South Gosforth	**E59245** 52J South Gosforth	**E59245** NL Neville Hill	**59245** CF Cardiff Canton	
E59246 53B Hull Botanic Gardens	**E59246** 52J South Gosforth	**E59246** NL Neville Hill	**59246** NL Neville Hill	
E59247 53B Hull Botanic Gardens	**E59247** 50C Hull Botanic Gardens	**E59247** NL Neville Hill		
E59248 South Gosforth	**E59248** 52J South Gosforth	**E59248** NL Neville Hill	**59248** CF Cardiff Canton	
E59249 South Gosforth	**E59249** 52J South Gosforth	**E59249** NL Neville Hill	**59249** NL Neville Hill	
E59250 South Gosforth	**E59250** 52J South Gosforth	**E59250** NL Neville Hill	**59250** NL Neville Hill	
W59255 TYS Tyseley	**M59255** 16C Derby Etches Park	**M59255** DY Derby Etches Park		
W59256 TYS Tyseley	**M59256** 16C Derby Etches Park	**M59256** DY Derby Etches Park		
W59257 CDF Cardiff Canton	**M59257** 16C Derby Etches Park	**M59257** DY Derby Etches Park		
W59258 TYS Tyseley	**M59258** 16C Derby Etches Park	**M59258** DY Derby Etches Park		
W59259 CDF Cardiff Canton	**M59259** 16C Derby Etches Park	**M59259** DY Derby Etches Park		
W59260 CDF Cardiff Canton	**W59260** 86A Cardiff Canton	**W59260** CF Cardiff Canton		
W59261 CDF Cardiff Canton	**W59261** 82A Bristol	**M59261** CH Chester		
W59262 CDF Cardiff Canton	**W59262** 86A Cardiff Canton	**M59262** CH Chester		
W59263 CDF Cardiff Canton	**M59263** 16C Derby Etches Park	**M59263** CH Chester		
W59264 CDF Cardiff Canton	**W59264** 82A Bristol	**W59264** CF Cardiff Canton		
W59265 CDF Cardiff Canton	**W59265** 86A Cardiff Canton	**W59265** CF Cardiff Canton		
W59266 CDF Cardiff Canton	**W59266** 86A Cardiff Canton	**M59266** CH Chester		
W59267 TYS Tyseley	**M59267** 16C Derby Etches Park	**M59267** DY Derby Etches Park		
W59268 CDF Cardiff Canton	**W59268** 86A Cardiff Canton	**W59268** CF Cardiff Canton		
W59269 TYS Tyseley	**W59269** 82A Bristol	**W59269** CF Cardiff Canton		
W59270 CDF Cardiff Canton				
W59271 CDF Cardiff Canton				
W59272 TYS Tyseley	**M59272** 16C Derby Etches Park	**M59272** DY Derby Etches Park		
W59273 CDF Cardiff Canton	**M59273** 16C Derby Etches Park	**M59273** DY Derby Etches Park		
W59274 CDF Cardiff Canton	**M59274** 16C Derby Etches Park	**M59274** DY Derby Etches Park		
W59275 CDF Cardiff Canton	**W59275** 86A Cardiff Canton	**M59275** CH Chester		
W59276 CDF Cardiff Canton	**M59276** 16C Derby Etches Park	**M59276** DY Derby Etches Park		
W59277 CDF Cardiff Canton	**W59277** 86A Cardiff Canton	**W59277** CF Cardiff Canton		
W59278 CDF Cardiff Canton	**W59278** 86A Cardiff Canton	**W59278** CF Cardiff Canton		
W59279 CDF Cardiff Canton	**W59279** 86A Cardiff Canton	**M59279** CH Chester		
W59280 CDF Cardiff Canton	**M59280** 16C Derby Etches Park	**M59280** DY Derby Etches Park		
W59281 TYS Tyseley	**M59281** 16C Derby Etches Park	**M59281** DY Derby Etches Park		
W59282 CDF Cardiff Canton	**W59282** 82A Bristol	**W59282** CF Cardiff Canton		
W59283 CDF Cardiff Canton	**M59283** 16C Derby Etches Park	**M59283** DY Derby Etches Park		
W59284 CDF Cardiff Canton	**W59284** 82A Bristol	**W59284** LA Laira		
W59285 CDF Cardiff Canton	**W59285** 86A Cardiff Canton	**W59285** LA Laira		
W59286 CDF Cardiff Canton	**W59286** 82A Bristol	**W59286** CF Cardiff Canton		
W59287 TYS Tyseley	**M59287** 16C Derby Etches Park	**M59287** DY Derby Etches Park		
W59288 CDF Cardiff Canton	**W59288** 86A Cardiff Canton	**M59288** CH Chester		
W59289 TYS Tyseley	**M59289** 16C Derby Etches Park	**M59289** DY Derby Etches Park		
W59290 TYS Tyseley	**M59290** 16C Derby Etches Park	**M59290** DY Derby Etches Park		
W59291 CDF Cardiff Canton	**W59291** 82A Bristol	**M59291** CH Chester		
W59292 CDF Cardiff Canton	**W59292** 82A Bristol	**W59292** BR Bristol Bath Road		
W59293 CDF Cardiff Canton	**M59293** 16C Derby Etches Park	**M59293** DY Derby Etches Park		
W59294 CDF Cardiff Canton	**W59294** 82A Bristol	**M59294** CH Chester		
W59295 BL Bristol	**M59295** 16C Derby Etches Park	**M59295** DY Derby Etches Park		
W59296 BL Bristol	**W59296** 82A Bristol	**M59296** CH Chester		
W59297 BL Bristol	**M59297** 16C Derby Etches Park	**M59297** DY Derby Etches Park		
W59298 BL Bristol				
W59299 BL Bristol	**W59299** 82A Bristol	**M59299** CH Chester		
W59300 BL Bristol	**M59300** 16C Derby Etches Park	**M59300** DY Derby Etches Park		
W59301 BL Bristol	**M59301** 16C Derby Etches Park	**M59301** DY Derby Etches Park		
E59302 51A Darlington	**SC59302** 62B Dundee	**SC59302** DE Dundee	**59302** HA Haymarket	
E59303 51A Darlington	**SC59303** 62B Dundee	**SC59303** DE Dundee	**59303** LO Longsight	**59303** Blackpool North (s)
E59304 51A Darlington	**SC59304** 62B Dundee	**SC59304** DE Dundee	**59304** HA Haymarket	
E59305 51A Darlington	**SC59305** 64H Leith Central	**SC59305** DE Dundee		
E59306 51A Darlington	**E59306** 55H Neville Hill	**E59306** NL Neville Hill	**59306** RG Reading	
M59307 18A Toton				
M59308 18A Toton				
M59309 18A Toton				
M59310 18A Toton				
M59311 18A Toton				
M59312 18A Toton				
M59313 18A Toton				
M59314 18A Toton	**M59314** 9D Newton Heath			
M59315 18A Toton	**M59315** 9D Newton Heath			
M59316 18A Toton				
M59317 18A Toton				
M59318 18A Toton				
M59319 18A Toton				
M59320 18A Toton				
M59321 18A Toton				
M59322 18A Toton				
M59323 18A Toton				
M59324 18A Toton				
M59325 18A Toton				
W59326 CAT Cardiff Cathays	**SC59326** 66C Hamilton	**M59326** TS Tyseley		
W59327 CAT Cardiff Cathays				
W59328 CAT Cardiff Cathays	**SC59328** 66C Hamilton	**M59328** TS Tyseley		

1960	1970	1980	1990	2000
W59329 CAT Cardiff Cathays	**SC59329** 66C Hamilton	**SC59329** HN Hamilton		
W59330 CAT Cardiff Cathays	**SC59330** 66C Hamilton	**SC59330** HN Hamilton		
W59331 TYS Tyseley	**SC59331** 66C Hamilton	**SC59331** HN Hamilton		
W59332 CAT Cardiff Cathays	**E59332** 34G Finsbury Park	**M59332** TS Tyseley		
W59333 CAT Cardiff Cathays	**SC59333** 66C Hamilton	**M59333** TS Tyseley		
W59334 CAT Cardiff Cathays	**M59334** 2A Tyseley	**M59334** TS Tyseley		
W59335 RDG Reading	**W59335** 86A Cardiff Canton	**E59335** SF Stratford	**59335** TS Tyseley	
W59336 CAT Cardiff Cathays	**E59336** 34G Finsbury Park	**M59336** TS Tyseley		
W59337 CAT Cardiff Cathays	**SC59337** 66C Hamilton	**SC59337** HN Hamilton		
W59338 CAT Cardiff Cathays	**M59338** 2A Tyseley	**M59338** TS Tyseley		
W59339 CAT Cardiff Cathays	**M59339** 2A Tyseley	**M59339** TS Tyseley		
W59340 CAT Cardiff Cathays	**W59340** 86A Cardiff Canton	**W59340** CF Cardiff Canton		
W59341 CAT Cardiff Cathays	**M59341** 2A Tyseley	**M59341** TS Tyseley		
W59342 CAT Cardiff Cathays	**M59342** 2A Tyseley	**M59342** TS Tyseley		
W59343 CAT Cardiff Cathays	**E59343** 34G Finsbury Park	**M59343** TS Tyseley		
W59344 CAT Cardiff Cathays	**W59344** 86A Cardiff Canton	**SC59344** HN Hamilton	**59344** TS Tyseley	
W59345 CAT Cardiff Cathays	**SC59345** 66C Hamilton	**SC59345** HN Hamilton		
W59346 CAT Cardiff Cathays	**W59346** 84A Laira	**M59346** TS Tyseley		
W59347 CAT Cardiff Cathays	**W59347** 86A Cardiff Canton	**SC59347** HN Hamilton		
W59348 CAT Cardiff Cathays	**M59348** 14A Cricklewood	**M59348** TS Tyseley		
W59349 RDG Reading	**E59349** 30A Stratford	**SC59349** HN Hamilton		
W59350 CAT Cardiff Cathays	**W59350** 86A Cardiff Canton	**M59350** TS Tyseley		
W59351 RDG Reading	**M59351** 2A Tyseley	**M59351** TS Tyseley		
W59352 CAT Cardiff Cathays	**W59352** 84A Laira	**M59352** TS Tyseley		
W59353 CAT Cardiff Cathays	**W59353** 86A Cardiff Canton	**E59353** SF Stratford	**59353** TS Tyseley	
W59354 CAT Cardiff Cathays	**E59354** 30A Stratford	**SC59354** HN Hamilton		
W59355 CAT Cardiff Cathays	**W59355** 86A Cardiff Canton	**W59355** CF Cardiff Canton		
W59356 CAT Cardiff Cathays	**W59356** 84A Laira	**W59356** CF Cardiff Canton		
W59357 SHL Southall	**W59357** 84A Laira	**W59357** CF Cardiff Canton		
W59358 CAT Cardiff Cathays	**M59358** 2A Tyseley	**M59358** TS Tyseley		
W59359 CAT Cardiff Cathays	**W59359** 86A Cardiff Canton	**W59359** CF Cardiff Canton		
W59360 CAT Cardiff Cathays	**SC59360** 66C Hamilton	**M59360** TS Tyseley		
W59361 CAT Cardiff Cathays	**E59361** 34G Finsbury Park	**M59361** TS Tyseley		
W59362 CAT Cardiff Cathays	**W59362** 86A Cardiff Canton	**W59362** CF Cardiff Canton		
W59363 CAT Cardiff Cathays	**W59363** 86A Cardiff Canton	**W59363** CF Cardiff Canton		
W59364 CAT Cardiff Cathays	**W59364** 86A Cardiff Canton	**W59364** CF Cardiff Canton		
W59365 CAT Cardiff Cathays	**W59365** 84A Laira	**M59365** CW Cricklewood		
W59366 CAT Cardiff Cathays	**W59366** 86A Cardiff Canton	**M59366** TS Tyseley		
W59367 CAT Cardiff Cathays	**E59367** 30A Stratford	**SC59367** HN Hamilton	**59367** TS Tyseley	
W59368 CAT Cardiff Cathays	**W59368** 86A Cardiff Canton	**M59368** TS Tyseley		
W59369 CAT Cardiff Cathays	**W59369** 86A Cardiff Canton	**W59369** CF Cardiff Canton		
W59370 CAT Cardiff Cathays				
W59371 CAT Cardiff Cathays	**W59371** 86A Cardiff Canton	**W59371** CF Cardiff Canton		
W59372 CAT Cardiff Cathays	**W59372** 84A Laira	**E59372** SF Stratford		
W59373 CAT Cardiff Cathays	**W59373** 86A Cardiff Canton	**W59373** CF Cardiff Canton		
W59374 CAT Cardiff Cathays	**W59374** 86A Cardiff Canton	**SC59374** HN Hamilton		
W59375 CAT Cardiff Cathays	**W59375** 86A Cardiff Canton	**E59375** SF Stratford		
W59376 CAT Cardiff Cathays	**M59376** 14A Cricklewood	**M59376** TS Tyseley		
E59380 South Gosforth	**E59380** 52J South Gosforth	**E59380** NL Neville Hill	**59380** LE Landore	
E59381 53B Hull Botanic Gardens	**E59381** 52J South Gosforth	**E59381** NL Neville Hill	**59381** LE Landore	
E59382 53B Hull Botanic Gardens	**E59382** 50C Hull Botanic Gardens	**E59382** NL Neville Hill	**59382** LE Landore	
E59383 South Gosforth	**E59383** 52J South Gosforth	**E59383** NL Neville Hill	**59383** LE Landore	
E59384 South Gosforth	**E59384** 52J South Gosforth	**E59384** NL Neville Hill	**59384** LE Landore	
E59385 South Gosforth	**E59385** 52J South Gosforth	**E59385** NL Neville Hill	**59385** CF Cardiff Canton	
E59386 56G Bradford Hammerton St	**E59386** 52J South Gosforth	**E59386** NL Neville Hill	**59386** LA Laira	
E59387 56G Bradford Hammerton St (o/l)	**E59387** 55H Neville Hill	**E59387** NL Neville Hill	**59387** NL Neville Hill	
E59388 56G Bradford Hammerton St	**E59388** 52J South Gosforth	**E59388** NL Neville Hill	**59388** LO Longsight	
E59389 56G Bradford Hammerton St (o/l)	**E59389** 52J South Gosforth	**E59389** NL Neville Hill	**59389** CH Chester	
E59390 56G Bradford Hammerton St (o/l)	**E59390** 52J South Gosforth	**E59390** NL Neville Hill	**59390** CH Chester	
SC59391 67C Ayr	**SC59391** 67C Ayr	**SC59391** AY Ayr		
SC59392 67C Ayr	**SC59392** 67C Ayr	**SC59392** AY Ayr		
SC59393 67C Ayr	**SC59393** 67C Ayr	**SC59393** AY Ayr		
SC59394 67C Ayr	**SC59394** 67C Ayr	**SC59394** AY Ayr		
SC59395 67C Ayr	**SC59395** 67C Ayr	**SC59395** AY Ayr		
SC59396 67C Ayr	**SC59396** 67C Ayr	**SC59396** AY Ayr		
SC59397 67C Ayr	**SC59397** 67C Ayr	**SC59397** AY Ayr		
SC59398 67C Ayr	**SC59398** 67C Ayr	**SC59398** AY Ayr		
SC59399 67C Ayr	**SC59399** 67C Ayr	**SC59399** AY Ayr		
SC59400 67C Ayr	**SC59400** 67C Ayr	**SC59400** AY Ayr		
SC59402 67C Ayr	**SC59402** 67C Ayr	**SC59402** AY Ayr		
SC59403 67C Ayr	**SC59403** 67C Ayr	**SC59403** AY Ayr		
SC59404 67C Ayr	**SC59404** 67C Ayr	**SC59404** AY Ayr		
SC59405 67C Ayr	**SC59405** 67C Ayr	**SC59405** AY Ayr		
SC59406 67C Ayr	**SC59406** 67C Ayr	**SC59406** AY Ayr		
SC59407 67C Ayr	**SC59407** 67C Ayr	**SC59407** AY Ayr		
SC59408 67C Ayr	**SC59408** 67C Ayr	**SC59408** AY Ayr		
SC59409 67C Ayr	**SC59409** 67C Ayr	**SC59409** AY Ayr		
SC59410 67C Ayr	**SC59410** 67C Ayr	**SC59410** AY Ayr		
SC59411 67C Ayr	**SC59411** 67C Ayr	**SC59411** AY Ayr		
SC59412 67C Ayr	**SC59412** 67C Ayr	**SC59412** AY Ayr		
W59413 CDF Cardiff Canton	**W59413** 82A Bristol	**W59413** CF Cardiff Canton		
W59414 CDF Cardiff Canton	**M59414** 6A Chester	**W59414** RG Reading		
W59415 CDF Cardiff Canton	**W59415** 82A Bristol	**W59415** RG Reading		
W59416 CDF Cardiff Canton	**M59416** 6A Chester	**W59416** CF Cardiff Canton	**59416** RG Reading	
W59417 CDF Cardiff Canton	**W59417** 82A Bristol	**W59417** RG Reading		
W59418 CDF Cardiff Canton	**M59418** 6A Chester	**W59418** CF Cardiff Canton		
W59419 BL Bristol	**W59419** 82A Bristol	**W59419** RG Reading	**59419** RG Reading	

1960	1970	1980	1990	2000
W59420 BL Bristol	**W59420** 82A Bristol	**W59420** RG Reading		
W59421 BL Bristol	**W59421** 82A Bristol	**W59421** RG Reading	**59421** RG Reading	
W59422 BL Bristol	**W59422** 82A Bristol	**W59422** RG Reading		
W59423 BL Bristol	**W59423** 82A Bristol	**W59423** RG Reading		
W59424 BL Bristol	**W59424** 82A Bristol	**W59424** RG Reading	**59424** RG Reading	
W59425 BL Bristol	**W59425** 82A Bristol	**W59425** RG Reading	**59425** RG Reading	
W59426 BL Bristol	**W59426** 82A Bristol	**W59426** RG Reading		
W59427 BL Bristol	**W59427** 82A Bristol	**W59427** RG Reading		
W59428 BL Bristol	**W59428** 82A Bristol	**W59428** RG Reading		
W59429 BL Bristol	**W59429** 82A Bristol	**W59429** RG Reading		
W59430 TYS Tyseley	**M59430** 6A Chester	**W59430** CF Cardiff Canton	**59430** RG Reading	
W59431 TYS Tyseley	**M59431** 6A Chester	**W59431** CF Cardiff Canton		
W59432 CDF Cardiff Canton	**M59432** 6A Chester	**W59432** CF Cardiff Canton		
W59433 CDF Cardiff Canton	**M59433** 6A Chester	**W59433** CF Cardiff Canton		
W59434 RDG Reading	**W59434** 82A Bristol	**W59434** RG Reading		
W59435 TYS Tyseley	**M59435** 6A Chester	**W59435** CF Cardiff Canton	**59435** RG Reading	
W59436 CDF Cardiff Canton	**W59436** 82A Bristol	**W59436** RG Reading		
W59437 BL Bristol	**W59437** 82A Bristol	**W59437** RG Reading	**59437** RG Reading	
W59438 BL Bristol	**M59438** 2A Tyseley	**M59438** TS Tyseley		
W59439 BL Bristol	**M59439** 2A Tyseley	**M59439** TS Tyseley		
W59440 BL Bristol	**M59440** 2A Tyseley	**M59440** TS Tyseley		
W59441 BL Bristol	**M59441** 2A Tyseley	**M59441** TS Tyseley		
W59442 BL Bristol	**M59442** 2A Tyseley	**M59442** TS Tyseley	**59442** TS Tyseley	
W59443 BL Bristol	**M59443** 2A Tyseley	**M59443** TS Tyseley		
W59444 BL Bristol	**W59444** 86A Cardiff Canton	**W59444** CF Cardiff Canton	**59444** TS Tyseley	
W59445 BL Bristol	**W59445** 86A Cardiff Canton	**W59445** CF Cardiff Canton	**59445** TS Tyseley	
W59446 BL Bristol	**W59446** 86A Cardiff Canton	**W59446** CF Cardiff Canton	**59446** TS Tyseley	
W59447 BL Bristol	**W59447** 82A Bristol			
W59448 BL Bristol	**W59448** 86A Cardiff Canton	**M59448** TS Tyseley	**59448** TS Tyseley	
E59449 30A Stratford	**E59449** 34G Finsbury Park			
E59450 30A Stratford	**E59450** 34G Finsbury Park			
E59451 30A Stratford	**E59451** 34G Finsbury Park			
E59452 30A Stratford	**E59452** 34G Finsbury Park			
E59453 30A Stratford	**E59453** 34G Finsbury Park			
E59454 30A Stratford	**E59454** 34G Finsbury Park			
E59455 30A Stratford	**E59455** 34G Finsbury Park			
E59456 30A Stratford	**E59456** 34G Finsbury Park			
E59457 30A Stratford	**E59457** 30A Stratford			
E59458 30A Stratford	**E59458** 34G Finsbury Park			
E59459 40A Lincoln	**E59459** 34G Finsbury Park			
E59460 40A Lincoln	**E59460** 34G Finsbury Park			
E59461 30A Stratford	**E59461** 34G Finsbury Park			
E59462 30A Stratford	**E59462** 34G Finsbury Park			
E59463 30A Stratford	**E59463** 34G Finsbury Park			
E59464 30A Stratford	**E59464** 30A Stratford			
E59465 30A Stratford	**E59465** 34G Finsbury Park			
E59466 30A Stratford	**E59466** 34G Finsbury Park			
E59467 30A Stratford	**E59467** 34G Finsbury Park			
E59468 30A Stratford	**E59468** 34G Finsbury Park			
	W59469 84A Laira	**W59469** BR Bristol Bath Road		
	W59470 84A Laira	**W59470** LA Laira		
	W59471 81D Reading	**W59471** BR Bristol Bath Road		
	W59472 81D Reading	**W59472** LA Laira		
	W59473 84A Laira	**W59473** LA Laira	**59473** TS Tyseley	
	W59474 84A Laira	**W59474** BR Bristol Bath Road		
	W59475 84A Laira	**W59475** BR Bristol Bath Road		
	W59476 81D Reading	**W59476** BR Bristol Bath Road		
	W59477 81D Reading	**W59477** BR Bristol Bath Road		
	W59478 81D Reading	**W59478** RG Reading		
	W59479 81D Reading	**W59479** RG Reading		
	W59480 81D Reading	**W59480** RG Reading		
	W59481 84A Laira	**W59481** BR Bristol Bath Road	**59481** TS Tyseley	
	W59482 81D Reading	**W59482** BR Bristol Bath Road		
	W59483 81D Reading	**W59483** LA Laira	**59483** TS Tyseley	
W59484 RDG Reading	**W59484** 81D Reading	**W59484** RG Reading	**59484** RG Reading	
	W59485 81D Reading	**W59485** RG Reading	**59485** RG Reading	
	W59486 81D Reading	**W59486** RG Reading	**59486** TS Tyseley	**59486** HA Haymarket (s)
	W59487 81D Reading	**W59487** RG Reading	**59487** RG Reading	
	W59488 81D Reading	**W59488** RG Reading	**59488** RG Reading	
	W59489 81D Reading	**W59489** RG Reading	**59489** RG Reading	
	W59490 81D Reading	**W59490** RG Reading	**59490** TS Tyseley	
	W59491 81D Reading	**W59491** RG Reading	**59491** RG Reading	
	W59492 81D Reading	**W59492** LA Laira	**59492** TS Tyseley	**59492** Pigs Bay (s)
	W59493 81D Reading	**W59493** RG Reading	**59493** RG Reading	
	W59494 81D Reading	**W59494** RG Reading	**59494** RG Reading	
	W59495 81D Reading	**W59495** RG Reading	**59495** RG Reading	
	W59496 81D Reading	**W59496** RG Reading	**59496** RG Reading	
	W59497 84A Laira	**W59497** RG Reading	**59497** RG Reading	
	W59498 84A Laira	**W59498** RG Reading	**59498** RG Reading	
	W59499 81D Reading	**W59499** RG Reading	**59499** RG Reading	
	W59500 81D Reading	**W59500** RG Reading	**59500** TS Tyseley	**59500** Pigs Bay (s)
	W59501 81D Reading	**W59501** RG Reading	**59501** RG Reading	
	W59502 81D Reading	**W59502** RG Reading	**59502** RG Reading	
	W59503 81D Reading	**W59503** RG Reading	**59503** RG Reading	
	W59504 81D Reading	**W59504** LA Laira	**59504** TS Tyseley	
	W59505 81D Reading	**W59505** RG Reading	**59505** TS Tyseley	**59505** Pigs Bay (s)
	W59506 81D Reading	**W59506** RG Reading	**59506** RG Reading	

1960	1970	1980	1990	2000
	W59507 81D Reading	**W59507** RG Reading	**59507** RG Reading	
	W59508 81D Reading	**W59508** RG Reading	**59508** RG Reading	
	W59509 81D Reading	**W59509** LA Laira	**59509** TS Tyseley	**59509** Pigs Bay (s)
	W59510 81D Reading	**W59510** RG Reading	**59510** RG Reading	
	W59511 81D Reading	**W59511** RG Reading	**59511** RG Reading	
	W59512 81D Reading	**W59512** RG Reading	**59512** TS Tyseley	
	W59513 81D Reading	**W59513** RG Reading	**59513** RG Reading	
	W59514 81D Reading	**W59514** RG Reading	**59514** RG Reading	
	W59515 81D Reading	**W59515** RG Reading	**59515** RG Reading	
	W59516 81D Reading	**W59516** RG Reading	**59516** TS Tyseley	
	W59517 81D Reading	**W59517** RG Reading	**59517** TS Tyseley	
	W59518 81D Reading	**W59518** RG Reading	**59518** RG Reading	
	W59519 81D Reading	**W59519** RG Reading	**59519** RG Reading	
	W59520 81D Reading	**W59520** RG Reading	**59520** TS Tyseley	
	W59521 81D Reading	**W59521** RG Reading	**59521** TS Tyseley	**59521** Pigs Bay (s)
	W59522 81D Reading	**W59522** RG Reading	**59522** TS Tyseley	
E59523 53B Hull Botanic Gardens	**E59523** 52J South Gosforth	**E59523** NL Neville Hill		
E59524 53B Hull Botanic Gardens	**E59524** 55H Neville Hill	**E59524** NL Neville Hill		
E59525 53B Hull Botanic Gardens	**E59525** 55H Neville Hill	**SC59525** DE Dundee	**59525** CH Chester (s)	
E59526 53B Hull Botanic Gardens	**E59526** 52J South Gosforth	**E59526** DN Darlington	**59526** RG Reading	
E59527 50A York	**E59527** 52J South Gosforth	**E59527** NL Neville Hill		
E59528 50A York	**W59528** 81D Reading	**M59528** TS Tyseley		
E59529 53B Hull Botanic Gardens	**E59529** 55H Neville Hill	**E59529** NL Neville Hill		
E59530 53B Hull Botanic Gardens	**E59530** 52J South Gosforth	**W59530** BR Bristol Bath Road	**59530** RG Reading	
E59531 53B Hull Botanic Gardens	**E59531** 52J South Gosforth	**E59531** NL Neville Hill		
E59532 53B Hull Botanic Gardens	**E59532** 55H Neville Hill	**E59532** NL Neville Hill	**59532** HA Haymarket	
E59533 56G Bradford Hammerton St	**E59533** 55H Neville Hill	**E59533** NL Neville Hill		
E59534 56G Bradford Hammerton St	**E59534** 55H Neville Hill	**E59534** NL Neville Hill		
E59535 53B Hull Botanic Gardens	**E59535** 52J South Gosforth	**E59535** NL Neville Hill		
E59536 53B Hull Botanic Gardens	**E59536** 50C Hull Botanic Gardens	**M59536** TS Tyseley	**59536** NC Norwich Crown Point	
E59537 South Gosforth				
E59538 South Gosforth	**W59538** 81D Reading	**M59538** CH Chester		
E59539 51A Darlington	**E59539** 52J South Gosforth	**W59539** BR Bristol Bath Road	**59539** LA Laira	**59539** Blackpool North (s)
E59540 51A Darlington	**E59540** 52J South Gosforth	**E59540** NL Neville Hill	**59540** RG Reading	
E59541 51A Darlington	**SC59541** 64H Leith Central	**SC59541** ED Eastfield		
E59542 51A Darlington	**E59542** 51A Darlington	**SC59542** DE Dundee	**59542** ED Eastfield	
SC59543 62B Dundee	**W59543** 81D Reading	**M59543** TS Tyseley	**59543** RG Reading	
SC59544 62B Dundee	**SC59544** 66C Hamilton	**SC59544** DE Dundee		
SC59545 62B Dundee	**SC59545** 66C Hamilton	**SC59545** ED Eastfield		
SC59546 62B Dundee	**SC59546** 66C Hamilton	**W59546** BR Bristol Bath Road		
SC59547 62B Dundee	**SC59547** 66C Hamilton	**W59547** BR Bristol Bath Road		
SC59548 62B Dundee	**SC59548** 66C Hamilton	**W59548** BR Bristol Bath Road		
SC59549 62B Dundee	**SC59549** 66C Hamilton	**W59549** BR Bristol Bath Road		
SC59550 62B Dundee	**SC59550** 66C Hamilton	**W59550** BR Bristol Bath Road		
SC59551 62B Dundee	**SC59551** 66C Hamilton	**W59551** BR Bristol Bath Road		
SC59552 62B Dundee	**SC59552** 66C Hamilton	**SC59552** ED Eastfield		
SC59553 62B Dundee	**SC59553** 66C Hamilton	**SC59553** AY Ayr		
SC59554 62B Dundee	**SC59554** 66C Hamilton	**SC59554** ED Eastfield		
SC59555 62B Dundee	**SC59555** 62B Dundee	**SC59555** AY Ayr		
SC59556 61A Kittybrewster (o/l)	**SC59556** 62B Dundee	**SC59556** ED Eastfield		
SC59557 64H Leith Central	**SC59557** 62B Dundee	**SC59557** AY Ayr		
SC59558 64H Leith Central	**SC59558** 62B Dundee	**SC59558** ED Eastfield		
SC59559 67C Ayr	**SC59559** 66C Hamilton	**SC59559** DE Dundee		
SC59560 67C Ayr	**SC59560** 66C Hamilton	**SC59560** AY Ayr		
SC59561 64H Leith Central	**SC59561** 66C Hamilton	**W59561** BR Bristol Bath Road	**59561** LA Laira	
SC59562 67C Ayr	**SC59562** 60A Inverness	**SC59562** ED Eastfield		
SC59563 67C Ayr	**SC59563** 64H Leith Central	**SC59563** ED Eastfield		
SC59564 64H Leith Central	**SC59564** 64H Leith Central	**SC59564** ED Eastfield		
SC59565 64H Leith Central	**SC59565** 64H Leith Central	**SC59565** ED Eastfield		
SC59566 67C Ayr	**SC59566** 64H Leith Central	**SC59566** ED Eastfield		
SC59567 67C Ayr	**SC59567** 64H Leith Central	**SC59567** DE Dundee		
SC59568 64H Leith Central	**SC59568** 64H Leith Central	**SC59568** ED Eastfield		
E59569 56G Bradford Hammerton St	**E59569** 30A Stratford	**E59569** NL Neville Hill		
E59570 56G Bradford Hammerton St	**E59570** 55H Neville Hill	**E59570** NL Neville Hill	**59570** RG Reading	
E59571 56G Bradford Hammerton St	**E59571** 55H Neville Hill	**E59571** NL Neville Hill		
E59572 56G Bradford Hammerton St	**E59572** 55H Neville Hill	**E59572** DN Darlington		
	E59573 52J South Gosforth			
	E59574 55F Bradford Hammerton St	**SC59574** IS Inverness		
	E59575 52J South Gosforth			
	E59576 52J South Gosforth			
	E59577 52J South Gosforth	**SC59577** DE Dundee		
	E59578 55H Neville Hill	**SC59578** DE Dundee		
	W59580 84A Laira	**W59580** CF Cardiff Canton		
	W59581 84A Laira	**W59581** CF Cardiff Canton		
	W59582 82A Bristol	**W59582** LA Laira		
	W59583 82A Bristol	**W59583** LA Laira		
	W59586 84A Laira	**W59586** CF Cardiff Canton		
	W59587 82A Bristol	**W59587** CF Cardiff Canton		
	W59588 82A Bristol	**W59588** CF Cardiff Canton		
M59589 14A Cricklewood	**M59589** 14A Cricklewood	**M59589** CW Cricklewood	**59589** TS Tyseley	
M59590 14A Cricklewood	**M59590** 14A Cricklewood	**M59590** CW Cricklewood	**59590** TS Tyseley	
M59591 14A Cricklewood	**M59591** 14A Cricklewood	**M59591** CW Cricklewood	**59591** TS Tyseley	
M59592 14A Cricklewood	**M59592** 14A Cricklewood	**M59592** CW Cricklewood	**59592** TS Tyseley	
M59593 (s) Chaddesden	**M59593** 14A Cricklewood	**M59593** CW Cricklewood	**59593** TS Tyseley	
M59594 (s) Chaddesden	**M59594** 14A Cricklewood	**M59594** CW Cricklewood	**59594** TS Tyseley	

1960	1970	1980	1990	2000
M59595 (s) Chaddesden	**M59595** 14A Cricklewood	**M59595** CW Cricklewood	**59595** TS Tyseley	
M59596 (s) Chaddesden	**M59596** 14A Cricklewood	**M59596** CW Cricklewood	**59596** TS Tyseley	
M59597 14A Cricklewood	**M59597** 14A Cricklewood	**M59597** CW Cricklewood	**59597** TS Tyseley	
M59598 14A Cricklewood	**M59598** 14A Cricklewood	**M59598** CW Cricklewood	**59598** TS Tyseley	
M59599 14A Cricklewood	**M59599** 14A Cricklewood			
M59600 14A Cricklewood	**M59600** 14A Cricklewood	**M59600** CW Cricklewood	**59600** TS Tyseley	
M59601 14A Cricklewood				
M59602 (s) Chaddesden	**M59602** 14A Cricklewood	**M59602** CW Cricklewood	**59602** TS Tyseley	
M59603 14A Cricklewood	**M59603** 14A Cricklewood	**M59603** CW Cricklewood	**59603** TS Tyseley	
M59604 14A Cricklewood	**M59604** 14A Cricklewood	**M59604** CW Cricklewood	**59604** TS Tyseley	
M59605 14A Cricklewood	**M59605** 14A Cricklewood	**M59605** CW Cricklewood		
M59606 14A Cricklewood	**M59606** 14A Cricklewood	**M59606** CW Cricklewood	**59606** TS Tyseley	
M59607 14A Cricklewood	**M59607** 14A Cricklewood	**M59607** CW Cricklewood	**59607** TS Tyseley	
M59608 14A Cricklewood	**M59608** 14A Cricklewood	**M59608** CW Cricklewood	**59608** TS Tyseley	
M59609 14A Cricklewood	**M59609** 14A Cricklewood	**M59609** CW Cricklewood	**59609** TS Tyseley	
M59610 14A Cricklewood	**M59610** 14A Cricklewood	**M59610** CW Cricklewood	**59610** TS Tyseley	
M59611 (s) Derby Friargate	**M59611** 14A Cricklewood	**M59611** CW Cricklewood	**59611** TS Tyseley	
M59612 14A Cricklewood	**M59612** 14A Cricklewood	**M59612** CW Cricklewood	**59612** TS Tyseley	
M59613 14A Cricklewood	**M59613** 14A Cricklewood	**M59613** CW Cricklewood	**59613** TS Tyseley	
M59614 14A Cricklewood	**M59614** 14A Cricklewood	**M59614** CW Cricklewood	**59614** TS Tyseley	
M59615 14A Cricklewood	**M59615** 14A Cricklewood	**M59615** CW Cricklewood	**59615** TS Tyseley	
M59616 (s) Chaddesden	**M59616** 14A Cricklewood	**M59616** CW Cricklewood	**59616** TS Tyseley	
M59617 14A Cricklewood	**M59617** 14A Cricklewood	**M59617** TS Tyseley	**59617** TS Tyseley	
M59618 14A Cricklewood	**M59618** 14A Cricklewood			
M59619 14A Cricklewood	**M59619** 14A Cricklewood	**M59619** CW Cricklewood		
M59620 14A Cricklewood	**M59620** 14A Cricklewood	**M59620** CW Cricklewood		
M59621 14A Cricklewood	**M59621** 14A Cricklewood	**M59621** CW Cricklewood	**59621** Crewe Carriage (s)	
M59622 14A Cricklewood	**M59622** 14A Cricklewood	**M59622** CW Cricklewood	**59622** Crewe Carriage (s)	
M59623 (s) Chaddesden	**M59623** 14A Cricklewood	**M59623** TS Tyseley		
M59624 (s) Chaddesden	**M59624** 14A Cricklewood			
M59625 (s) Chaddesden	**M59625** 14A Cricklewood	**M59625** CW Cricklewood	**59625** TS Tyseley	
M59626 (s) Chaddesden	**M59626** 14A Cricklewood	**M59626** CW Cricklewood		
M59627 14A Cricklewood	**M59627** 14A Cricklewood	**M59627** CW Cricklewood	**59627** Crewe Carriage (s)	
M59628 14A Cricklewood	**M59628** 14A Cricklewood	**M59628** CW Cricklewood		
M59629 14A Cricklewood	**M59629** 14A Cricklewood	**M59629** CW Cricklewood	**59629** TS Tyseley	
M59630 14A Cricklewood	**M59630** 14A Cricklewood			
M59631 14A Cricklewood	**M59631** 14A Cricklewood	**M59631** CW Cricklewood	**59631** Crewe Carriage (s)	
M59632 (s) Chaddesden	**M59632** 14A Cricklewood	**M59632** CW Cricklewood	**59632** TS Tyseley	
M59633 14A Cricklewood	**M59633** 14A Cricklewood	**M59633** CW Cricklewood		
M59634 14A Cricklewood	**M59634** 14A Cricklewood	**M59634** CW Cricklewood		
M59635 14A Cricklewood				
M59636 14A Cricklewood	**M59636** 14A Cricklewood	**M59636** CW Cricklewood		
M59637 14A Cricklewood	**M59637** 14A Cricklewood	**M59637** CW Cricklewood		
M59638 14A Cricklewood	**M59638** 14A Cricklewood	**M59638** CW Cricklewood		
M59639 14A Cricklewood	**M59639** 14A Cricklewood	**M59639** CW Cricklewood		
M59640 14A Cricklewood	**M59640** 14A Cricklewood	**M59640** CW Cricklewood		
M59641 (s) Derby Friargate	**M59641** 14A Cricklewood	**M59641** CW Cricklewood	**59641** TS Tyseley	
M59642 14A Cricklewood	**M59642** 14A Cricklewood	**M59642** CW Cricklewood		
M59643 14A Cricklewood	**M59643** 14A Cricklewood	**M59643** CW Cricklewood	**59643** TS Tyseley	
M59644 14A Cricklewood	**M59644** 14A Cricklewood	**M59644** CW Cricklewood		
M59645 14A Cricklewood	**M59645** 14A Cricklewood	**M59645** CW Cricklewood		
M59646 (s) Chaddesden	**M59646** 14A Cricklewood	**M59646** CW Cricklewood		
M59647 14A Cricklewood	**M59647** 14A Cricklewood	**M59647** CW Cricklewood		
M59648 14A Cricklewood	**M59648** 14A Cricklewood	**M59648** CW Cricklewood	**59648** TS Tyseley	
	M59649 1D Marylebone	**M59649** ME Marylebone		
	M59650 1D Marylebone	**M59650** ME Marylebone		
	M59651 1D Marylebone	**M59651** ME Marylebone	**59651** BY Bletchley	
	M59652 1D Marylebone	**M59652** ME Marylebone	**59652** BY Bletchley	
	M59653 1D Marylebone	**M59653** ME Marylebone	**59653** Crewe Carriage (s)	
	M59654 1D Marylebone	**M59654** ME Marylebone	**59654** BY Bletchley	
	M59655 1D Marylebone	**M59655** ME Marylebone	**59655** BY Bletchley	
	M59656 1D Marylebone	**M59656** ME Marylebone	**59656** BY Bletchley	
	M59657 1D Marylebone	**M59657** ME Marylebone	**59657** BY Bletchley	
	M59658 1D Marylebone	**M59658** ME Marylebone	**59658** TS Tyseley	
	M59659 1D Marylebone	**M59659** ME Marylebone	**59659** BY Bletchley	
	M59660 1D Marylebone	**M59660** ME Marylebone	**59660** BY Bletchley	
	M59661 1D Marylebone	**M59661** ME Marylebone	**59661** TS Tyseley	
	M59662 1D Marylebone	**M59662** ME Marylebone	**59662** BY Bletchley	
	M59663 1D Marylebone	**M59663** ME Marylebone	**59663** BY Bletchley	
	M59664 1D Marylebone	**M59664** ME Marylebone	**59664** BY Bletchley	
	M59665 1D Marylebone	**M59665** ME Marylebone	**59665** BY Bletchley	
	M59666 1D Marylebone	**M59666** ME Marylebone		
	M59667 1D Marylebone	**M59667** ME Marylebone	**59667** BY Bletchley	
	M59668 1D Marylebone	**M59668** ME Marylebone	**59668** TS Tyseley	
	M59669 1D Marylebone	**M59669** ME Marylebone	**59669** BY Bletchley	
	M59670 1D Marylebone	**M59670** ME Marylebone	**59670** TS Tyseley	
	M59671 1D Marylebone	**M59671** ME Marylebone	**59671** BY Bletchley	
	M59672 1D Marylebone	**M59672** ME Marylebone	**59672** TS Tyseley	
	M59673 1D Marylebone	**M59673** ME Marylebone	**59673** TS Tyseley	
	M59674 1D Marylebone	**M59674** ME Marylebone	**59674** TS Tyseley	
	M59675 1D Marylebone	**M59675** ME Marylebone	**59675** BY Bletchley	
	M59676 1D Marylebone	**M59676** ME Marylebone	**59676** BY Bletchley	
	M59677 1D Marylebone	**M59677** ME Marylebone	**59677** TS Tyseley	
	M59678 1D Marylebone	**M59678** ME Marylebone	**59678** BY Bletchley	
SC59679 61A Kittybrewster	**SC59679** 60A Inverness	**SC59679** IS Inverness		
SC59680 61A Kittybrewster	**SC59680** 60A Inverness	**SC59680** IS Inverness		
SC59681 61A Kittybrewster	**SC59681** 60A Inverness	**SC59681** IS Inverness		

1960	1970	1980	1990	2000
SC59682 61A Kittybrewster	**SC59682** 60A Inverness	**SC59682** IS Inverness		
	SC59683 60A Inverness	**SC59683** IS Inverness		
	SC59684 60A Inverness	**SC59684** IS Inverness		
	SC59685 60A Inverness	**SC59685** IS Inverness		
SC59686 64H Leith Central	**SC59686** 64H Leith Central	**SC59686** AY Ayr		
SC59687 64H Leith Central	**SC59687** 64H Leith Central	**SC59687** ED Eastfield		
SC59688 64H Leith Central	**SC59688** 64H Leith Central	**SC59688** DE Dundee	**59688** HA Haymarket	
SC59689 64H Leith Central	**SC59689** 64H Leith Central	**SC59689** ED Eastfield		
SC59690 64H Leith Central	**SC59690** 64H Leith Central	**SC59690** ED Eastfield		
SC59691 64H Leith Central	**SC59691** 64H Leith Central	**SC59691** AY Ayr		
SC59692 64H Leith Central	**SC59692** 64H Leith Central	**SC59692** AY Ayr		
	E59693 55F Bradford Hammerton St	**E59693** HS Bradford Hammerton St		
	E59694 55F Bradford Hammerton St	**E59694** HS Bradford Hammerton St	**59694** NL Neville Hill	
	E59695 55H Neville Hill	**E59695** NL Neville Hill		
	E59696 55H Neville Hill	**E59696** HS Bradford Hammerton St	**59696** HA Haymarket	
	E59697 55F Bradford Hammerton St	**E59697** HS Bradford Hammerton St		
	E59698 55F Bradford Hammerton St	**E59698** HS Bradford Hammerton St		
	E59699 55F Bradford Hammerton St	**E59699** HS Bradford Hammerton St		
	E59700 55F Bradford Hammerton St	**E59700** HS Bradford Hammerton St		
	E59701 55F Bradford Hammerton St	**E59701** HS Bradford Hammerton St	**59701** NL Neville Hill	
	E59702 55F Bradford Hammerton St	**E59702** HS Bradford Hammerton St		
	E59703 55F Bradford Hammerton St	**E59703** HS Bradford Hammerton St		
	E59704 55F Bradford Hammerton St	**E59704** HS Bradford Hammerton St		
	E59705 55F Bradford Hammerton St			
	E59707 55F Bradford Hammerton St	**E59707** HS Bradford Hammerton St		
	E59708 55H Neville Hill	**E59708** NL Neville Hill		
	E59709 55H Neville Hill	**E59709** HS Bradford Hammerton St		
	E59710 55H Neville Hill	**E59710** HS Bradford Hammerton St		
	E59711 55H Neville Hill	**E59711** HS Bradford Hammerton St		
	E59712 55H Neville Hill	**E59712** HS Bradford Hammerton St		
	M59713 8J Allerton	**M59713** AN Allerton	**59713** TS Tyseley	
	M59714 8J Allerton	**M59714** AN Allerton		
	M59715 8J Allerton	**M59715** AN Allerton	**59715** Crewe Carriage (s)	
	M59716 8J Allerton	**M59716** AN Allerton	**59716** Crewe Carriage (s)	
	M59717 8J Allerton	**M59717** AN Allerton	**59717** Crewe Carriage (s)	
	M59718 8J Allerton	**M59718** AN Allerton		
	M59719 8J Allerton	**M59719** AN Allerton	**59719** TS Tyseley	
	M59720 8J Allerton	**M59720** AN Allerton	**59720** TS Tyseley	
	M59721 8J Allerton	**M59721** AN Allerton	**59721** TS Tyseley	
	M59722 8J Allerton	**M59722** AN Allerton	**59722** TS Tyseley	
	M59723 8J Allerton	**M59723** AN Allerton	**59723** TS Tyseley	
	M59724 8J Allerton	**M59724** AN Allerton	**59724** TS Tyseley	
	M59725 1D Marylebone	**M59725** ME Marylebone	**59725** Crewe Carriage (s)	
	M59726 1D Marylebone	**M59726** ME Marylebone	**59726** TS Tyseley	
	M59727 1D Marylebone	**M59727** ME Marylebone	**59727** BY Bletchley	
	M59728 1D Marylebone	**M59728** ME Marylebone	**59728** BY Bletchley	
	M59729 1D Marylebone	**M59729** ME Marylebone	**59729** BY Bletchley	
	M59730 1D Marylebone	**M59730** ME Marylebone		
	M59731 1D Marylebone	**M59731** ME Marylebone	**59731** BY Bletchley	
	M59732 1D Marylebone	**M59732** ME Marylebone	**59732** BY Bletchley	
	M59733 1D Marylebone	**M59733** ME Marylebone	**59733** BY Bletchley	
	M59734 1D Marylebone	**M59734** ME Marylebone	**59734** BY Bletchley	
	M59735 1D Marylebone	**M59735** ME Marylebone	**59735** BY Bletchley	
	M59736 1D Marylebone	**M59736** ME Marylebone	**59736** BY Bletchley	
	M59737 1D Marylebone	**M59737** ME Marylebone	**59737** BY Bletchley	
	M59738 1D Marylebone	**M59738** ME Marylebone	**59738** BY Bletchley	
	M59739 1D Marylebone	**M59739** ME Marylebone		
	M59740 1D Marylebone	**M59740** ME Marylebone	**59740** BY Bletchley	
	M59741 1D Marylebone	**M59741** AN Allerton	**59741** TS Tyseley	
	M59742 1D Marylebone			
	M59743 1D Marylebone	**M59743** ME Marylebone	**59743** TS Tyseley	
	M59744 1D Marylebone	**M59744** ME Marylebone	**59744** Crewe Carriage (s)	
	M59745 1D Marylebone	**M59745** ME Marylebone	**59745** TS Tyseley	
	M59746 1D Marylebone	**M59746** ME Marylebone	**59746** BY Bletchley	
	M59747 1D Marylebone	**M59747** ME Marylebone	**59747** BY Bletchley	
	M59748 1D Marylebone	**M59748** ME Marylebone		
	M59749 1D Marylebone	**M59749** ME Marylebone	**59749** BY Bletchley	
	M59750 1D Marylebone	**M59750** ME Marylebone	**59750** BY Bletchley	
	M59751 1D Marylebone	**M59751** ME Marylebone	**59751** TS Tyseley	
	M59752 1D Marylebone	**M59752** ME Marylebone	**59752** BY Bletchley	
	M59753 1D Marylebone	**M59753** ME Marylebone	**59753** TS Tyseley	
	M59754 1D Marylebone	**M59754** ME Marylebone	**59754** BY Bletchley	
	M59755 1D Marylebone	**M59755** ME Marylebone	**59755** BY Bletchley	
	M59756 1D Marylebone	**M59756** ME Marylebone	**59756** TS Tyseley	
	M59757 1D Marylebone	**M59757** ME Marylebone	**59757** TS Tyseley	
	M59758 1D Marylebone	**M59758** ME Marylebone	**59758** BY Bletchley	
	M59759 1D Marylebone	**M59759** ME Marylebone	**59759** BY Bletchley	
	M59760 1D Marylebone	**M59760** AN Allerton	**59760** TS Tyseley	
	M59761 1D Marylebone	**M59761** ME Marylebone	**59761** BY Bletchley	
	M59762 1D Marylebone	**M59762** ME Marylebone	**59762** BY Bletchley	
	M59763 1D Marylebone	**M59763** ME Marylebone	**59763** BY Bletchley	
	M59764 1D Marylebone	**M59764** ME Marylebone	**59764** BY Bletchley	
	E59765 50C Hull Botanic Gardens	**E59765** BG Hull Botanic Gardens		
	E59766 50C Hull Botanic Gardens	**E59766** BG Hull Botanic Gardens		
	E59767 50C Hull Botanic Gardens	**E59767** BG Hull Botanic Gardens		
	E59768 50C Hull Botanic Gardens	**E59768** BG Hull Botanic Gardens		

1960	1970	1980	1990	2000
	E59769 50C Hull Botanic Gardens	**E59769** BG Hull Botanic Gardens		
	E59770 50C Hull Botanic Gardens	**E59770** BG Hull Botanic Gardens		
	E59771 50C Hull Botanic Gardens	**E59771** BG Hull Botanic Gardens		
	E59772 50C Hull Botanic Gardens	**E59772** BG Hull Botanic Gardens		
	E59773 50C Hull Botanic Gardens	**E59773** BG Hull Botanic Gardens		
	E59774 50C Hull Botanic Gardens (s)			
	E59775 50C Hull Botanic Gardens (s)			
	E59776 50C Hull Botanic Gardens (s)			
	E59777 50C Hull Botanic Gardens			
	E59778 50C Hull Botanic Gardens			
	E59779 50C Hull Botanic Gardens			
	E59780 50C Hull Botanic Gardens			
	E59781 50C Hull Botanic Gardens			
	SC59782 66C Hamilton	**SC59782** HN Hamilton	**59782** ED Eastfield	
	SC59783 66C Hamilton	**SC59783** HN Hamilton	**59783** ED Eastfield	
	SC59784 66C Hamilton	**SC59784** HN Hamilton	**59784** ED Eastfield	
	SC59785 66C Hamilton	**SC59785** HN Hamilton	**59785** HA Haymarket	
	SC59786 66C Hamilton	**SC59786** HN Hamilton	**59786** ED Eastfield	
	SC59787 66C Hamilton	**SC59787** HN Hamilton		
	SC59788 66C Hamilton	**SC59788** HN Hamilton		
	SC59789 66C Hamilton	**SC59789** HN Hamilton	**59789** HA Haymarket	
	SC59790 66C Hamilton	**SC59790** HN Hamilton	**59790** ED Eastfield	
	SC59791 66C Hamilton	**SC59791** HN Hamilton	**59791** ED Eastfield	
	SC59792 66C Hamilton	**SC59792** HN Hamilton	**59792** ED Eastfield	
	SC59793 66C Hamilton	**SC59793** HN Hamilton	**59793** ED Eastfield	
	SC59794 66C Hamilton	**SC59794** HN Hamilton	**59794** NL Neville Hill	
	SC59795 67A Corkerhill	**SC59795** HN Hamilton	**59795** ED Eastfield	
	SC59796 67A Corkerhill	**SC59796** HN Hamilton	**59796** ED Eastfield	
	SC59797 67A Corkerhill	**SC59797** HN Hamilton	**59797** ED Eastfield	
	SC59798 67A Corkerhill	**SC59798** HN Hamilton	**59798** ED Eastfield	
	SC59799 67A Corkerhill	**SC59799** HN Hamilton		
	SC59800 67A Corkerhill	**SC59800** HN Hamilton	**59800** HA Haymarket	
	SC59801 67A Corkerhill	**SC59801** HN Hamilton	**59801** ED Eastfield	
	SC59802 67A Corkerhill	**SC59802** HN Hamilton	**59802** ED Eastfield	
	SC59803 67A Corkerhill	**SC59803** HN Hamilton	**59803** ED Eastfield	
	SC59804 67A Corkerhill	**SC59804** HN Hamilton	**59804** ED Eastfield	
	SC59805 67A Corkerhill	**SC59805** HN Hamilton	**59805** ED Eastfield	
	SC59806 67A Corkerhill	**SC59806** HN Hamilton	**59806** ED Eastfield	
	SC59807 67A Corkerhill	**SC59807** HN Hamilton	**59807** ED Eastfield	
	E59808 55F Bradford Hammerton St	**E59808** HS Bradford Hammerton St		
	E59809 55F Bradford Hammerton St	**E59809** HS Bradford Hammerton St		
	E59810 55F Bradford Hammerton St	**E59810** HS Bradford Hammerton St		
	E59811 55F Bradford Hammerton St	**E59811** HS Bradford Hammerton St		
	E59812 55F Bradford Hammerton St	**E59812** HS Bradford Hammerton St	**59812** Crewe Carriage (s)	
	E59813 55F Bradford Hammerton St	**E59813** HS Bradford Hammerton St		
	E59814 55F Bradford Hammerton St	**E59814** HS Bradford Hammerton St		
	E59815 55F Bradford Hammerton St	**E59815** HS Bradford Hammerton St		
	E59816 55F Bradford Hammerton St	**E59816** HS Bradford Hammerton St		
	E59817 55F Bradford Hammerton St	**E59817** HS Bradford Hammerton St		
	W59818 81D Reading	**E59818** BG Hull Botanic Gardens		
	W59819 81D Reading	**E59819** BG Hull Botanic Gardens		
	W59820 81D Reading	**E59820** BG Hull Botanic Gardens		
	W59821 81D Reading	**E59821** BG Hull Botanic Gardens		
	W59822 81D Reading	**E59822** BG Hull Botanic Gardens		
	W59823 81D Reading	**E59823** BG Hull Botanic Gardens		
	W59824 81D Reading	**E59824** BG Hull Botanic Gardens		
	W59825 81D Reading	**E59825** BG Hull Botanic Gardens		
	W59826 81D Reading	**E59826** BG Hull Botanic Gardens		
	W59827 81D Reading	**E59827** BG Hull Botanic Gardens		
	W59828 81D Reading			
	W59829 81D Reading			
	W59830 81D Reading			
	W59831 81D Reading			
	W59832 81D Reading			
M60090 Reddish	**W60090** 82A Bristol			
M60091 Reddish	**W60091** 82A Bristol			
M60092 Reddish	**W60092** 82A Bristol			
M60093 Reddish	**W60093** 82A Bristol			
	W60094 81A Old Oak Common			
	W60095 81A Old Oak Common			
	W60096 81A Old Oak Common			
	W60097 81A Old Oak Common			
	W60098 86A Cardiff Canton			
	W60099 86A Cardiff Canton			
	W60644 81A Old Oak Common			
	W60645 81A Old Oak Common			
	W60646 81A Old Oak Common			
	W60647 81A Old Oak Common			
	W60648 86A Cardiff Canton			
	W60649 86A Cardiff Canton			
M60730 Reddish	**W60730** 82A Bristol			
M60731 Reddish	**W60731** 82A Bristol			
M60732 Reddish	**W60732** 82A Bristol			
M60733 Reddish	**W60733** 82A Bristol			
	W60734 81A Old Oak Common			
	W60735 81A Old Oak Common			

1960	1970	1980	1990	2000
	W60736 81A Old Oak Common			
	W60737 81A Old Oak Common			
	W60738 86A Cardiff Canton			
	W60739 86A Cardiff Canton			
M60740 Reddish	**W60740** 82A Bristol			
M60741 Reddish	**W60741** 82A Bristol			
M60742 Reddish	**W60742** 82A Bristol			
M60743 Reddish	**W60743** 82A Bristol			
	W60744 81A Old Oak Common			
	W60745 81A Old Oak Common			
	W60746 81A Old Oak Common			
	W60747 81A Old Oak Common			
	W60748 86A Cardiff Canton			
	W60749 86A Cardiff Canton			
E79000 56G Bradford Hammerton St				
E79001 56G Bradford Hammerton St				
E79002 56G Bradford Hammerton St				
E79003 56G Bradford Hammerton St				
E79004 56G Bradford Hammerton St				
E79005 56G Bradford Hammerton St				
E79006 56G Bradford Hammerton St				
E79007 56G Bradford Hammerton St				
M79008 12B Carlisle Upperby				
M79009 12B Carlisle Upperby				
M79010 Reddish				
M79011 12B Carlisle Upperby				
M79012 12B Carlisle Upperby				
M79013 12B Carlisle Upperby				
M79014 12B Carlisle Upperby				
M79015 12B Carlisle Upperby				
M79016 12B Carlisle Upperby				
M79017 12B Carlisle Upperby				
M79018 12B Carlisle Upperby				
M79019 12B Carlisle Upperby				
M79020 11B Workington				
E79021 31A Cambridge				
E79022 31A Cambridge				
E79023 31A Cambridge				
E79024 31A Cambridge				
E79025 31A Cambridge				
E79026 31A Cambridge				
E79027 31A Cambridge				
E79028 31A Cambridge				
E79029 31A Cambridge				
E79030 31A Cambridge				
E79031 31A Cambridge				
E79032 32A Norwich Thorpe				
E79033 32A Norwich Thorpe				
E79034 32A Norwich Thorpe				
E79035 32A Norwich Thorpe				
E79036 32A Norwich Thorpe				
E79037 32A Norwich Thorpe				
E79038 32A Norwich Thorpe				
E79039 32A Norwich Thorpe				
E79040 32A Norwich Thorpe				
E79041 32A Norwich Thorpe				
E79042 32A Norwich Thorpe				
E79043 32A Norwich Thorpe				
E79044 32A Norwich Thorpe				
E79045 32A Norwich Thorpe				
E79046 32A Norwich Thorpe				
E79047 30A Stratford				
E79048 30A Stratford				
E79049 32A Norwich Thorpe				
E79050 32A Norwich Thorpe				
E79051 30A Stratford				
E79052 30A Stratford				
E79053 32A Norwich Thorpe				
E79054 32A Norwich Thorpe				
E79055 32A Norwich Thorpe				
E79056 32A Norwich Thorpe				
E79057 32A Norwich Thorpe				
E79058 30A Stratford				
E79059 32A Norwich Thorpe				
E79060 32A Norwich Thorpe				
E79061 32A Norwich Thorpe				
E79062 32A Norwich Thorpe				
E79063 32A Norwich Thorpe				
E79064 32A Norwich Thorpe				
E79065 32A Norwich Thorpe				
E79066 32A Norwich Thorpe				
E79067 32A Norwich Thorpe				
E79068 32A Norwich Thorpe				
E79069 32A Norwich Thorpe				
E79070 32A Norwich Thorpe				
E79071 32A Norwich Thorpe				

1960	1970	1980	1990	2000
E79072 30A Stratford				
E79073 32A Norwich Thorpe				
E79074 30A Stratford				
E79075 32A Norwich Thorpe				
M79076 26A Newton Heath				
M79077 26A Newton Heath				
M79078 26A Newton Heath				
M79079 26A Newton Heath				
M79080 26A Newton Heath				
M79081 26A Newton Heath				
M79082 26A Newton Heath				
SC79083 67C Ayr	**SC79083** 67C Ayr			
SC79084 67C Ayr	**SC79084** 64H Leith Central			
SC79085 67C Ayr	**SC79085** 64H Leith Central			
SC79086 67C Ayr	**SC79086** 64H Leith Central			
SC79087 64H Leith Central	**SC79087** 64H Leith Central			
SC79088 64H Leith Central	**SC79088** 64H Leith Central	**SC79088** AY Ayr		
SC79089 64H Leith Central	**SC79089** 64H Leith Central			
SC79090 64H Leith Central	**SC79090** 64H Leith Central			
SC79091 64H Leith Central	**SC79091** 64H Leith Central			
SC79092 64H Leith Central				
SC79093 64H Leith Central	**SC79093** 64H Leith Central			
SC79094 64H Leith Central	**SC79094** 64H Leith Central			
SC79095 64H Leith Central	**SC79095** 64H Leith Central			
SC79096 64H Leith Central	**SC79096** 64H Leith Central			
SC79097 64H Leith Central	**SC79097** 64H Leith Central			
SC79098 64H Leith Central	**SC79098** 64H Leith Central			
SC79099 64H Leith Central	**SC79099** 64H Leith Central			
SC79100 64H Leith Central	**SC79100** 64H Leith Central			
SC79101 64H Leith Central	**SC79101** 64H Leith Central			
SC79102 64H Leith Central	**SC79102** 64H Leith Central			
SC79103 64H Leith Central	**SC79103** 64H Leith Central			
SC79104 64H Leith Central	**SC79104** 64H Leith Central			
SC79105 64H Leith Central	**SC79105** 64H Leith Central			
SC79106 64H Leith Central	**SC79106** 64H Leith Central			
SC79107 64H Leith Central	**SC79107** 64H Leith Central			
SC79108 64H Leith Central	**SC79108** 64H Leith Central			
SC79109 64H Leith Central	**SC79109** 64H Leith Central			
SC79110 64H Leith Central	**SC79110** 64H Leith Central			
SC79111 64H Leith Central	**SC79111** 64H Leith Central			
M79118 12B Carlisle Upperby				
M79119 12B Carlisle Upperby				
M79120 12B Carlisle Upperby				
M79121 Reddish				
M79122 Reddish				
M79123 Reddish				
M79124 12B Carlisle Upperby				
M79125 6G Llandudno Junction				
M79126 27F Brunswick				
M79127 Reddish				
M79128 6G Llandudno Junction				
M79129 6G Llandudno Junction				
M79130 6G Llandudno Junction				
M79131 6G Llandudno Junction				
M79132 6G Llandudno Junction				
M79133 6G Llandudno Junction				
M79134 6G Llandudno Junction				
M79135 6G Llandudno Junction				
M79136 6G Llandudno Junction				
E79137 South Gosforth (o/l to WR)				
E79138 South Gosforth				
E79139 South Gosforth (o/l to WR)				
E79140 South Gosforth (o/l to WR)				
M79141 Reddish				
M79142 26A Newton Heath				
M79143 Reddish				
M79144 Reddish				
M79145 Reddish				
M79146 Reddish				
M79147 27F Brunswick				
M79148 Reddish				
M79149 Reddish				
E79150 South Gosforth (o/l to WR)				
E79151 South Gosforth (o/l to WR)				
E79152 South Gosforth				
E79153 South Gosforth				
E79154 South Gosforth (o/l to WR)				
SC79155 64H Leith Central	**SC79155** 64H Leith Central			
SC79156 64H Leith Central	**SC79156** 64H Leith Central			
SC79157 64H Leith Central	**SC79157** 64H Leith Central			
SC79158 64H Leith Central	**SC79158** 64H Leith Central			
SC79159 64H Leith Central	**SC79159** 64H Leith Central			
SC79160 64H Leith Central	**SC79160** 64H Leith Central			
SC79161 64H Leith Central	**SC79161** 64H Leith Central			
SC79162 64H Leith Central	**SC79162** 64H Leith Central			
SC79163 64H Leith Central	**SC79163** 64H Leith Central			
SC79164 64H Leith Central	**SC79164** 64H Leith Central			

1960	1970	1980	1990	2000
SC79165 64H Leith Central	**SC79165** 64H Leith Central			
SC79166 64H Leith Central	**SC79166** 64H Leith Central			
SC79167 64H Leith Central	**SC79167** 64H Leith Central			
SC79168 64H Leith Central	**SC79168** 64H Leith Central			
M79169 9G Gorton				
M79170 9G Gorton				
M79171 9G Gorton				
M79172 9G Gorton				
M79173 9G Gorton				
M79174 9G Gorton				
M79175 9G Gorton				
M79176 9G Gorton				
M79177 9G Gorton				
M79178 9G Gorton				
M79179 9G Gorton				
M79180 Reddish				
M79181 Reddish				
M79184 8C Speke Junction				
M79185 8C Speke Junction				
M79186 8C Speke Junction				
M79187 6G Llandudno Junction				
M79188 8C Speke Junction				
M79189 6G Llandudno Junction				
M79190 8C Speke Junction				
M79191 8C Speke Junction				
M79192 6G Llandudno Junction				
M79193 8C Speke Junction				
E79250 32A Norwich Thorpe				
E79251 32A Norwich Thorpe				
E79252 31A Cambridge				
E79253 32A Norwich Thorpe				
E79254 32A Norwich Thorpe				
E79255 32A Norwich Thorpe				
E79256 32A Norwich Thorpe				
E79257 32A Norwich Thorpe				
E79258 32A Norwich Thorpe				
E79259 32A Norwich Thorpe				
E79260 32A Norwich Thorpe				
E79261 32A Norwich Thorpe				
E79262 32A Norwich Thorpe				
E79263 32A Norwich Thorpe				
E79264 30A Stratford				
E79265 32A Norwich Thorpe				
E79266 32A Norwich Thorpe				
E79267 30A Stratford				
E79268 30A Stratford				
E79269 32A Norwich Thorpe				
E79270 32A Norwich Thorpe				
E79271 32A Norwich Thorpe				
E79272 30A Stratford				
E79273 32A Norwich Thorpe				
E79274 30A Stratford				
E79275 32A Norwich Thorpe				
E79276 32A Norwich Thorpe				
E79277 32A Norwich Thorpe				
E79278 32A Norwich Thorpe				
E79279 32A Norwich Thorpe				
E79280 32A Norwich Thorpe				
E79281 32A Norwich Thorpe				
E79282 32A Norwich Thorpe				
E79283 32A Norwich Thorpe				
E79284 32A Norwich Thorpe				
E79285 32A Norwich Thorpe				
E79286 32A Norwich Thorpe				
E79287 32A Norwich Thorpe				
E79288 30A Stratford				
E79289 32A Norwich Thorpe				
E79290 30A Stratford				
E79291 32A Norwich Thorpe				
E79325 South Gosforth (o/l to WR)				
E79326 South Gosforth (o/l to WR)				
E79327 South Gosforth (o/l to WR)				
E79328 South Gosforth (o/l to WR)				
E79329 South Gosforth				
E79400 South Gosforth (o/l to WR)				
E79401 South Gosforth (o/l to WR)				
E79402 South Gosforth (o/l to WR)				
E79403 South Gosforth (o/l to WR)				
E79404 South Gosforth				
SC79440 67C Ayr	**SC79440** 64H Leith Central			
SC79441 67C Ayr	**SC79441** 64H Leith Central			
SC79442 64H Leith Central	**SC79442** 64H Leith Central			
SC79443 64H Leith Central	**SC79443** 64H Leith Central			
SC79444 64H Leith Central	**SC79444** 64H Leith Central			
SC79445 64H Leith Central	**SC79445** 64H Leith Central			
SC79446 64H Leith Central	**SC79446** 64H Leith Central			
SC79447 64H Leith Central	**SC79447** 64H Leith Central			

1960	1970	1980	1990	2000
SC79470 64H Leith Central	**SC79470** 67C Ayr	**SC79470** AY Ayr		
SC79471 64H Leith Central	**SC79471** 64H Leith Central			
SC79472 64H Leith Central	**SC79472** 64H Leith Central			
SC79473 64H Leith Central	**SC79473** 64H Leith Central			
SC79474 64H Leith Central	**SC79474** 64H Leith Central			
SC79475 64H Leith Central	**SC79475** 64H Leith Central			
SC79476 64H Leith Central	**SC79476** 64H Leith Central			
SC79477 64H Leith Central	**SC79477** 64H Leith Central			
SC79478 64H Leith Central	**SC79478** 64H Leith Central			
SC79479 64H Leith Central	**SC79479** 67C Ayr			
SC79480 64H Leith Central	**SC79480** 64H Leith Central			
SC79481 64H Leith Central	**SC79481** 64H Leith Central			
SC79482 64H Leith Central	**SC79482** 64H Leith Central			
E79500 56G Bradford Hammerton St				
E79501 56G Bradford Hammerton St				
E79502 56G Bradford Hammerton St				
E79503 56G Bradford Hammerton St				
E79504 56G Bradford Hammerton St				
E79505 56G Bradford Hammerton St				
E79506 56G Bradford Hammerton St				
E79507 56G Bradford Hammerton St				
E79508 South Gosforth (o/l to WR)				
E79509 South Gosforth (o/l to WR)				
E79510 South Gosforth (o/l to WR)				
E79511 South Gosforth (o/l to WR)				
E79512 South Gosforth (o/l to WR)				
M79600 12B Carlisle Upperby				
M79601 12B Carlisle Upperby				
M79602 Reddish				
M79603 12B Carlisle Upperby				
M79604 12B Carlisle Upperby				
M79605 12B Carlisle Upperby				
M79606 12B Carlisle Upperby				
M79607 12B Carlisle Upperby				
M79608 12B Carlisle Upperby				
M79609 12B Carlisle Upperby				
M79610 12B Carlisle Upperby				
M79611 12B Carlisle Upperby				
M79612 11B Workington				
E79613 31A Cambridge				
E79614 31A Cambridge				
E79615 31A Cambridge				
E79616 31A Cambridge				
E79617 31A Cambridge				
E79618 32A Norwich Thorpe				
E79619 31A Cambridge				
E79620 31A Cambridge				
E79621 30A Stratford				
E79622 31A Cambridge				
E79623 31A Cambridge				
E79624 32A Norwich Thorpe				
E79625 32A Norwich Thorpe				
M79626 26A Newton Heath				
M79627 26A Newton Heath				
M79628 26A Newton Heath				
M79629 26A Newton Heath				
M79630 26A Newton Heath				
M79631 26A Newton Heath				
M79632 26A Newton Heath				
M79639 12B Carlisle Upperby				
M79640 12B Carlisle Upperby				
M79641 12B Carlisle Upperby				
M79642 Reddish				
M79643 Reddish				
M79644 Reddish				
M79645 12B Carlisle Upperby				
M79646 6G Llandudno Junction				
M79647 27F Brunswick				
M79648 Reddish				
M79649 6G Llandudno Junction				
M79650 6G Llandudno Junction				
M79651 6G Llandudno Junction				
M79652 6G Llandudno Junction				
M79653 6G Llandudno Junction				
M79654 6G Llandudno Junction				
M79655 6G Llandudno Junction				
M79656 6G Llandudno Junction				
M79657 6G Llandudno Junction				
E79658 South Gosforth (o/l to WR)				
E79659 South Gosforth (o/l to WR)				
E79660 South Gosforth				
E79661 South Gosforth (o/l to WR)				
M79662 Reddish				
M79663 Reddish				
M79664 Reddish				
M79665 Reddish				

1960			1970	1980	1990	2000
M79666		Reddish				
M79667	27F	Brunswick				
M79668		Reddish				
M79669		Reddish				
M79670	9G	Gorton				
M79671	9G	Gorton				
M79672	9G	Gorton				
M79673	9G	Gorton				
M79674	9G	Gorton				
M79675	9G	Gorton				
M79676	9G	Gorton				
M79677	9G	Gorton				
M79678	9G	Gorton				
M79679	9G	Gorton				
M79680	9G	Gorton				
M79681		Reddish				
M79682		Reddish				
M79683	9A	Longsight				
M79684	26A	Newton Heath				
M79900	1E	Bletchley				
M79901	1E	Bletchley				
SC79958	66C	Hamilton				
SC79959	66C	Hamilton				
E79960	30A	Stratford				
E79961	31A	Cambridge				
E79962	31A	Cambridge				
E79963	31A	Cambridge				
E79964	31A	Cambridge				
SC79965	64H	Leith Central				
SC79966	60B	Aviemore				
SC79967	64H	Leith Central				
SC79968	64H	Leith Central				
SC79969	64H	Leith Central				
SC79970	64H	Leith Central				
M79971	14E	Bedford				
M79972	14E	Bedford				
M79973	14E	Bedford				
SC79974	64H	Leith Central				
W79975	SDN	Swindon				
W79976	SDN	Swindon				
W79977	SDN	Swindon				
W79978	SDN	Swindon				
SC79979	63A	Perth South				
SC79998	61A	Kittybrewster				
SC79999	61A	Kittybrewster				

Class 131 parcels van SC55013 is seen at Haymarket Depot on 18th August 1977. The windows on these parcels vans were painted over in white when converted for parcels working.
I Futers

Left: W7254W, one of the Hawksworth Corridor Composite coaches which was converted to work as a DMU trailer, is seen running in a three-car DMU set at Reading.
P J Sharpe

Below: Early Derby Lightweight DMBS E79035 is seen at Stratford on 17th April 1958.
P J Sharpe

Above: An early Derby lightweight two-car unit led by E79041 is seen working a local service in East Anglia. These units had to be fitted with a strengthening bar across the middle of the large front windscreens. *P J Sharpe*

Right: An early Derby lightweight unit M79018 and M79612 was converted in November 1970 to form the Ultrasonic Test Train unit DB975007 and DB975008. Its long life in departmental service has led to its survival in preservation. *C J Marsden*

Left: A four-car early Metropolitan-Cammell set led by E79047 is seen at Horsham on an excursion train from Southend and Tilbury to Brighton on 28th June 1959. *J Scrace*

Although of distinctly Metropolitan-Cammell appearance, these early units could be distinguished by their Yellow Diamond coupling-code and jumper cables, and by the valance fitted beneath the buffer beam. A two-car unit formed of E79281 and E79066 is seen at Norwich on 6th July 1967.
A Swain

This interior shot of the first class section of one of the Metropolitan-Cammell units for the Bury-Bacup service was taken on 14th March 1956. *BR*

SC79109 is one of the early Swindon Inter-city units which was put to work on the Edinburgh-Glasgow service.
P J Sharpe

Above: Several of the Swindon Inter-city units started their lives working Western Region services. W79087 is seen at Lydney Junction on 27th December 1957. *P J Sharpe*

Right: By the beginning of the 1970s the Swindon Inter-city units were near the end of their lives on the Glasgow-Edinburgh services. On 14th April 1971 SC79106 leads a six-car train on the Glasgow-Edinburgh Inter-city service at Cadder Yard. *D Cross*

Below: BUT railbus M79745 is seen at the end of a three-car formation at Watford. *P J Sharpe*

Above: BUT railbus is M79742 at Watford. This railbus carried a guard's and luggage compartment seen on the left in this photograph. *P J Sharpe*

Left: The BUT railbuses were taken out of service in February 1959. However they remained stored for many years before being scrapped. Here a sorry-looking line of railbuses formed of M79741, M79748, M79746, M79740, M79743, M79750, M79749 and M79744 is seen stored at Derby Friargate on the 22nd October 1961, still two years before final disposal. *P Mallaband*

Right: BUT railbus is M79742 at Watford. This railbus carried a guard's and luggage compartment seen on the left in this photograph. *P J Sharpe*
An early Derby Lightweight unit formed of single car M79900 and trailer M79190 is seen at Potton on 16th April 1966. *P R Foster*

Top: Waggon und Maschinenbau four-wheel railbus E79960 at Stratford on delivery on the 17th April 1958. The poster in the window declares it to be from Brown Boveri Switzerland, Mannheim. *P J Sharpe*

Above: Wickham four-wheel railbus SC79968 is seen at Gleneagles. *P J Sharpe*

Left: Park Royal four-wheel railbus SC79970 is at Craigellachie on a service for Aviemore. *P J Sharpe*

Part 6. DMU formations.

This is a listing of some of the more stable formations of units. The only region to consistently try to keep units in fixed formations was the Western Region. Some depots on other regions also tried to maintain units in formations, but not with the same consistency as the Western Region. In later years TOPS unit numbers were applied to many of the remaining units (particularly on the Scottish Region) and they were kept in more stable formations.

When presenting an overview like this it is noticeable how some depots tried to impose fixed unit formations, only to fall into a state of flux and then later trying to re-establish more stability. Even the Western Region had one major change to its unit numbering system (in 1972), one major renumbering (in 1976) and many other changes as necessary over the years. It must be assumed that while keeping fixed formations made operating sense, there were times (perhaps when having only just enough stock to cover the services or having trouble keeping old stock serviceable) when fixed formations were much less important than simply trying to keep the trains running. Some depots (notably Marylebone and Cricklewood) never kept fixed formations.

While I have tried to give as much information as possible it must be noted that changes often took place to fit in with operating requirements and DMU formations were never as stable as EMU formations. Having said that, these lists should give you good understanding of the way units were formed over the years, and the different types of unit numbering that were applied.

1965

Western Region

The Western Region attempted to keep its units in regular formation right from the start. Each unit was allocated a unit number prefixed by a depot code. These unit numbers were displayed on small rectangular plates fixed in clips to the sole bar of the power cars. By 1965 (this list is dated October 1965) most of the suburban units had settled down to stable formations. Tyseley depot had transferred to the London Midland Region in 1963 and is not listed here. It used the code TYS for its units but they did not settle down to stable formations before the transfer.

Bristol 82A

BL300 upwards Non-corridor two and three car sets
Not static formations
W50820 W59328 W50873
W50826 W59345 W50879
W50863 W59371 W50916
W50870 W50923
W51134 W59444 W51147
W51135 W59445 W51148
W51136 W59446 W51149
W51137 W59447 W51150
W51302 W59469 W51317
W51303 W59470 W51318
Spare W50083
W55013
W55032
W55033
W56292
W56294

BL500 upwards Cross-country sets
Formations varied regularly
W50650 W59255 W50696
W50651 W59256 W50697
W50658 W59261 W50701
W50667 W59274 W50708
W50670 W59280 W50711
W50673 W59281 W50720
W50674 W59286 W50724
W50677 W59287 W50725
W50678 W59288 W50730
W50680 W59289 W50731
W50681 W59290 W50735
W50683 W59294 W50737
W50687 W59295 W50739
W50690 W59298 W50740
W50692 W59300 W50743
W50695 W59588 W50744
W51054 W59413 W51082
W51055 W59415 W51083
W51056 W59417 W51084
W51060 W59420 W51088
W51062 W59421 W51090
W51063 W59422 W51091
W51064 W59423 W51092
W51065 W59424 W51093
W51066 W59425 W51094
W51067 W59426 W51095
W51068 W59427 W51096
W51069 W59428 W51097
W51070 W59429 W51098
W51075 W59434 W51103
W51078 W59436 W51106
W51079 W59437 W51107
W59419

Cardiff 86A

CDF was the code for Cardiff Canton. The CAT code was still used even though Cardiff Cathays had closed and its units were based at Canton.

CAT103 W55034
CAT104 W55035
CAT302 W50822 W59330 W50875
CAT303 W50080 W59030 W50122
CAT306 W50081 W59031 W50123
CAT307 W50823 W59331 W50876
CAT311 W50819 W59327 W50872
CAT312 W50821 W59329 W50874
CAT313 W50825 W59333 W50878
CAT314 W50827 W59361 W50880
CAT315 W50830 W59343 W50883
CAT316 W50832 W59029 W50885
CAT318 W50828 W59336 W50906
CAT319 W50839 W59347 W50892
CAT320 W50840 W59348 W50893
CAT323 W50843 W59355 W50896
CAT325 W50841 W59349 W50894
CAT326 W50846 W59354 W50899
CAT327 W50837 W59358 W50890
CAT328 W50842 W59350 W50895
CAT329 W50844 W59335 W50897
CAT331 W50851 W59359 W50904
CAT335 W50850 W59365 W50903
CAT337 W50836 W59344 W50889
CAT338 W50852 W59360 W50905
CAT341 W50853 W59367 W50881
CAT344 W50082 W59340 W50124
CAT345 W50862 W59370 W50915
CAT346 W50858 W59366 W50911
CAT347 W50084 W59373 W50126
CAT351 W50864 W59369 W50917
CAT353 W51138 W59448 W51151
CAT404 W50086 W59036 W50128
CAT406 W51140 W59032 W51153
CAT407 W50091 W59041 W50133
CAT408 W50834 W59038 W50887
CAT409 W50869 W59035 W50922
CAT410 W51132 W59034 W51145
CAT411 W50087 W59037 W50129
CAT412 W50089 W59039 W50131
CAT413 W51139 W59033 W51152
CAT414 W50090 W59040 W50132

CDF500 upwards Cross-country sets
Not static formations
W50647 W59257 W50698
W50648 W59258 W50699
W50649 W59259 W50700
W50652 W59260 W50702
W50653 W59262 W50703
W50654 W59263 W50704
W50655 W59264 W50705
W50656 W59265 W50706
W50657 W59266 W50707
W50659 W59267 W50709
W50660 W59268 W50712
W50662 W59270 W50713
W50663 W59271 W50714
W50664 W59272 W50715
W50665 W59273 W50716
W50666 W59275 W50717
W50668 W59276 W50718
W50669 W59277 W50719
W50671 W59278 W50721
W50672 W59279 W50722
W50675 W59282 W50723
W50676 W59283 W50726
W50679 W59284 W50727
W50682 W59285 W50728
W50684 W59291 W50729
W50685 W59292 W50732
W50686 W59293 W50733
W50689 W59296 W50734
W50691 W59297 W50736
W50694 W59301 W50742

CDF700-709 Inter-city sets
Not static formations
W52086 W59818 W59235 W52096
W52087 W59819 W59236 W52097
W52088 W59820 W59237 W52098
W52089 W59821 W59238 W52099
W52090 W59822 W59239 W52100

W52091	W59823	W59828	W52101
W52092	W59824	W59829	W52102
W52093	W59825	W59830	W52103
W52094	W59826	W59831	W52104
W52095	W59827	W59832	W52105

Laira (Plymouth) 84A

Unit			
LA100	W55000		
LA101	W55001		
LA102	W55011		
LA105	W55016		
LA106	W55017		
LA107	W55019		
LA108	W55014		
LA109	W55031		
LA110	W55025		
LA	W55015		
LA	W55026		
	W56289		
	W56297		
	W56298		
LA300	W50845	W59352	W50898
LA301	W50849	W59357	W50902
LA302	W50865	W59372	W50918
LA303	W51128	W59481	W51141
LA304	W51304	W59471	W51319
LA305	W51306	W59473	W51321
LA306	W51307	W59474	W51322
LA307	W51308	W59475	W51323
LA308	W51309	W59476	W51324
LA310	W50818	W59326	W50871
LA311	W50868	W59376	W50921
LA312	W50824	W59332	W50877
LA313	W50847	W59353	W50900
LA314	W50838	W59346	W50891
LA315	W50854	W59362	W50907
LA316	W50835	W59337	W50888
LA317	W50829	W59334	W50882
LA318	W50848	W59356	W50901
LA319	W50857	W59368	W50910
LA320	W50856	W59364	W50909
LA321	W50866	W59374	W50919
LA322	W50867	W59375	W50920
LA323	W50855	W59363	W50908
LA400	W51305	W51320	
LA401	W51311	W51326	
LA402	W51312	W51327	
LA403	W51313	W51328	
LA404	W51314	W51329	
LA405	W50088	W50130	

LA500 upwards
Variable formations

Unit			
LA500	W51573	W59579	W51582
LA501	W51574	W59580	W51583
LA502	W51581	W59587	W51590
LA503	W51575	W59581	W51584
LA504	W51576	W59582	W51585
LA505	W51577	W59583	W51586
LA506	W51580	W59586	W51589
LA507	W51579	W59585	W51588
LA508	W51578	W59584	W51587
LA509	W50661	W59269	W50710
LA510	W50693	W59299	W50738
	W79975	*based at Yeovil*	
	W79976	*based at Yeovil*	
	W79977	*based at St. Blazey*	
	W79978	*based at St. Blazey*	

Reading 81D

Unit			
RDG	W51053	W51081	
RDG	W51061	W59472	W51089
RDG300	W51332	W59484	W51374
RDG301	W51333	W59485	W51375
RDG302	W51335	W59487	W51377
RDG303	W51336	W59488	W51378
RDG304	W51337	W59489	W51379
RDG305	W51338	W59490	W51380
RDG306	W51343	W59495	W51385
RDG307	W51344	W59496	W51386
RDG308	W51345	W59497	W51387
RDG309	W51351	W59503	W51393
RDG310	W51352	W59504	W51394
RDG311	W51353	W59505	W51395
RDG312	W51354	W59506	W51396
RDG313	W51355	W59507	W51397
RDG314	W51358	W59510	W51400
RDG315	W51362	W59514	W51404
RDG316	W51363	W59515	W51405
RDG317	W51367	W59519	W51409
RDG318	W51368	W59520	W51410
RDG319	W51369	W59521	W51411
RDG320	W51370	W59522	W51412
RDG321	W51373	W59480	W51415
RDG322	W51310	W59477	W51325
RDG323	W51315	W59482	W51330
RDG328	W51316	W59483	W51331
	W55020		
	W55027		
	W55030		
		W7254W	
		W7804W	
		W7813W	

Southall 81C

Unit			
SHL300	W51334	W59486	W51376
SHL301	W51339	W59491	W51381
SHL302	W51340	W59492	W51382
SHL303	W51341	W59493	W51383
SHL304	W51342	W59494	W51384
SHL305	W51346	W59498	W51388
SHL306	W51347	W59499	W51389
SHL307	W51348	W59500	W51390
SHL308	W51349	W59501	W51391
SHL309	W51350	W59502	W51392
SHL310	W51356	W59508	W51398
SHL311	W51357	W59509	W51399
SHL312	W51359	W59511	W51401
SHL313	W51360	W59512	W51402
SHL314	W51361	W59513	W51403
SHL315	W51364	W59516	W51406
SHL316	W51365	W59517	W51407
SHL317	W51366	W59518	W51408
SHL318	W51371	W59478	W51413
SHL319	W51372	W59479	W51414
	W55021		
	W55022		
	W55023		
	W55024		
	W55028		
	W55029		
	W55991		
	W55992		
	W56280		
	W56281		
	W56282		
	W56283		
	W56284		
	W56285		
	W56286		
	W56287		
	W56288		

1967

Scottish Region

In late 1966 the Scottish Region allocated unit numbers to all its units. The situation at the beginning of 1967 was as follows:

11-20	Corkerhill	Class 100 Twin units
21-29	Hamilton	Class 100 Twin units
30-42	Hamilton	Class 101 Twin units
43-54	Hamilton	Class 105 Twin units
56-60	Kittybrewster	Class 105 Twin units
61-64	Dundee	Class 105 Twin units
65-74	Dundee	Class 101 Twin units
75-86	Leith	Class 100 Twin units
87-93	Leith	Class 101 Twin units
95	Leith	Class 108 Twin unit
96	Leith	Class 105 Twin unit
97-98	Leith	Yellow Diamond Twin
101-116	Hamilton	Class 102 Triple units
117-133	Corkerhill	Class 107 Triple units
134-142	Hamilton	Class 107 Triple units
143-144	Ayr	Class 107 Triple units
151-173	Ayr	Class 126 Inter-city units
201-205	Kittybrewster	Class 120 Triple units
206-218	Dundee	Class 102 Triple units
219-222	Leith	Class 108 Triple units
223-233	Leith	Class 102 Triple units
234-237	Leith	Yellow Diamond Triple
238-240	Leith	Class 116 Triple units
601-609	Leith	Swindon Inter-city units

1972

London Midland Region

London Midland Region introduced unit numbers early in 1969. Each unit carried its unit number on a card in the front window. Each was allocated a supposedly unique unit number with a depot prefix. The number ranges allocated in each category were based on ascending depot code order (with the exception of 10E Accrington which was due for early closure). That is, the range of numbers in each category were in the order 1D-1E-2A-6A-8J-9A-9D-9L-12A-14A-16C-10E.

The depot prefixes were two letter codes. Note that these were different from the depot codes allocated from 1974 onwards.

The categories were:

001-049 Motor Parcels Vans
050-089 Single MBS
100-199 Power Twins
200-399 Twins
400-499 Triples for medium distance work
500-550 Suburban Triples
551-560 Cross-Country Triples
561-639 Quads

There were some exceptions:

- Some suburban triples at Cricklewood took the numbers 561-565.
- Newly allocated Cross-country triples at Derby Etches Park took the numbers of old units they replaced.
- Some units transferred to Allerton from Newton Heath retained their old numbers with the new depot prefixes.

Although this was an all-encompassing scheme it did not in practice lead to more stable formations at most depots. 1972 is a good year to list the situation.

AC Accrington 10E

Closed 1st October 1972 and the units moved to Newton Heath.
Did not keep fixed formations

AC179-191	Class 105 Power Twins
AC336-358	Class 108 Twins

AN Allerton 8J

Did not keep fixed formations

AN114-123	Class 108 Twins

Class 108 Twins reallocated from NH and retaining old set number:

Unit		
AN140	M51930	M52045
AN141	M51931	M52046
AN143	M51933	M52048
AN145	M51935	M52050
AN146	M51936	M52051
AN146	M51938	M52053
AN150	M51940	M52059
AN155	M51945	M52060

AN263-287 Class 108 Power Twins
AN599-610 Class 115 Suburban Quads

BN Buxton 9L

Did not keep fixed formations

BN455 M50420 M59132 M50424
BN456 M50421 M59133 M50425
BN457 M50422 M59134 M50426
BN458 M50423 M59135 M50427
BN459 M50428 M59136 M50480
BN460 M50429 M59137 M50481
BN461 M50430 M59138 M50482
BN462 M50431 M59139 M50483
BN463 M50432 M59140 M50484
BN464 M50433 M59141 M50485
BN465 M50434 M59195 M50486
BN466 M50435 M59198 M50487
BN467 M50436 M59230 M50488

BY Bletchley 1E

BY385 M50390 M56145
BY386 M50391 M56146
BY387 M50392 M56147
BY388 M50393 M56148
BY389 M50394 M56149

CD Cricklewood 14A

Did not keep fixed formations

CD561-565 Class 116 Suburban Triples
CD611-639 Class 127 Suburban Quads

CE Carlisle Kingmoor 12A

Did not keep fixed formations

CE360-380 series Class 108 Twins
Very few carried set numbers

CR Chester 6A

Did not keep fixed formations

CR100-109 Class 108 Power Twins
CR200-255 Class 101 and Class 103 Twins
CR417-422 Class 101 Triples
CR551-558 Class 119 Cross-Country Triples

EP Derby (Etches Park) 16C

Did not keep fixed formations

EP471-499 Class 104 and Class 120 Triples

LT Longsight 9A

LT291 M50348 M56103
LT292 M50349 M56104
LT293 M50350 M56105
LT294 M50351 M56106
LT295 M50352 M56107
LT296 M50353 M56108
LT297 M50354 M56109
LT298 M50355 M56110
LT299 M50356 M56111
LT300 M50357 M56112
LT301 M50358 M56113
LT302 M50532 M56175
LT303 M50533 M56176
LT304 M50534 M56177
LT305 M50535 M56178
LT306 M50536 M56179
LT307 M50537 M56180
LT308 M50538 M56181
LT309 M50539 M56182
LT310 M50540 M56183
LT311 M50541 M56184
LT316 M50940 M56223
LT317 M50941 M56224
LT318 M50942 M56225
LT319 M50944 M56227
LT320 M50945 M56228
LT321 M50946 M56229
LT322 M50947 M56230
LT323 M50948 M56231
LT324 M50949 M56232
LT326 M51901 M56484
LT327 M51902 M56485
LT328 M51903 M56486
LT329 M51904 M56487
LT330 M51905 M56488
LT331 M51906 M56489
LT332 M51907 M56490

ME Marylebone 1D

Did not keep fixed formations
Unit numbers not carried

ME564-598 Class 115 Suburban Quads

NH Newton Heath 9D

NH017 M55988
NH018 M55989
NH019 M55990
NH020 M55996
NH126-139 Class 105 Power Twins
Not fixed formations
NH158 M51948 M52063
NH159 M51949 M52064
NH160 M51950 M52065
NH420 M50437 M59145 M50489
NH421 M50438 M59146 M50490
NH422 M50439 M59147 M50491
NH423 M50440 M59148 M50492
NH424 M50443 M59149 M50493
NH425 M50442 M59150 M50494
NH426 M50452 M59160 M50504
NH427 M50453 M59161 M50505
NH428 M50454 M59162 M50506
NH429 M50455 M59163 M50507
NH430 M50456 M59164 M50508
NH431 M50457 M59143 M50509
NH432 M50458 M59166 M50510
NH433 M50459 M59144 M50511
NH434 M50460 M59168 M50512
NH435 M50461 M59169 M50514
NH436 M50463 M59171 M50515
NH437 M50464 M59172 M50516
NH438 M50465 M59173 M50517
NH439 M50466 M59174 M50518
NH440 M50467 M59175 M50519
NH441 M50468 M59176 M50520
NH442 M50469 M59177 M50521
NH443 M50470 M59178 M50522
NH444 M50471 M59179 M50523
NH445 M50472 M59180 M50524
NH446 M50473 M59181 M50525
NH447 M50474 M59182 M50526
NH448 M50475 M59183 M50527
NH449 M50476 M59184 M50528
NH450 M50477 M59185 M50529
NH451 M50478 M59186 M50530
NH452 M50479 M59187 M50531
Spare M59142 M50497
Spare M59158

TY Tyseley 2A

TY001 M55993
TY002 M55994
TY003 M55995
TY050 M55003
TY051 M55004
TY052 M55006
TY053 M55008
TY054 M55009
TY055 M55010
TY056 M55012
TY057 M55017
TY400 M50303 M59114 M50321
TY401 M50304 M59115 M50338
TY402 M50305 M59116 M50323
TY403 M50306 M59125 M50326
TY404 M50307 M59118 M50325
TY405 M50308 M59119 M50324
TY406 M50309 M59120 M50327
TY407 M50310 M59121 M50328
TY408 M50311 M59122 M50329
TY409 M50312 M59123 M50335
TY410 M50313 M59124 M50331
TY411 M50314 M59117 M50332
TY500 M50061 M59000 M50092
TY501 M50057 M59001 M50097
TY502 M50861 M59002 M50912
TY503 M50076 M59003 M50118
TY504 M50059 M59004 M50104
TY505 M50065 M59005 M50094
TY506 M50058 M59006 M50112
TY507 M50069 M59007 M50099
TY509 M50072 M59009 M50105
TY510 M50067 M59010 M50093
TY512 M50051 M59012 M50113
TY513 M50077 M59013 M50120
TY515 M50050 M59015 M51143
TY516 M50074 M59016 M50110
TY518 M50056 M59018 M50098
TY519 M50064 M59019 M50115
TY520 M50066 M59020 M50103
TY523 M50055 M59023 M50116
TY524 M50078 M59024 M50109
TY526 M50070 M59026 M50095
TY527 M50859 M59027 M50119
TY528 M50062 M59028 M50117
TY529 M50085 M59338 M50127
TY530 M50831 M59339 M50884
TY531 M50052 M59341 M50886
TY532 M50079 M59351 M50121
TY533 M51129 M59439 M51142
TY534 M50053 M59342 M50914
TY535 M50860 M59438 M50913
TY536 M50833 M59442 M50107
TY537 M51130 M59440 M50108
TY538 M51131 M59441 M51144
TY539 M51133 M59443 M51146
TY540 M50832 M59029 M50885
TY541 M50835 M59334 M50888
TY542 M50837 M59358 M50890

Eastern Region

South Gosforth 52J
Darlington 51A

These two depots numbered their units in a common sequence prefixed "N".

South Gosforth

N100 E50198 E56363
N101 E50199 E56077
N102 E50200 E56084
N103 E50204 E56367
N104 E50205 E56381
N105 E50210 E56078
N106 E50211 E56379
N107 E50216 E56085
N108 E50219 E56079
N109 E50225 E56050
N110 E50226 E56372
N111 E50227 E56218
N112 E50231 E56068
N113 E50233 E56069
N114 E50248 E56082
N115 E50257 E56064
N116 E50259 E56070
N117 E50296 E56374
N118 E51206 E56053
N119 E51208 E56220
N120 E51209 E56083
N121 E51210 E56066
N122 E51212 E56373
N123 E51214 E56081
N124 E51221 E56073
N125 E51435 E56377
N126 E51437 E56375
N127 E51439 E56089
N128 E51441 E56370
N129 E51443 E56052
N140 E50605 E56203
N141 E50606 E56190
N142 E50620 E56195
N143 E50622 E56202
N144 E50623 E56196
N145 E50610 E56201

Darlington

N150 E50155 E56075
N151 E50166 E56051
N152 E50207 E56088
N153 E50212 E56065
N154 E50215 E56063
N155 E50220 E56072
N156 E50223 E56059
N157 E50246 E56061
N158 E50252 E56067
N159 E50293 E56087
N160 E50294 E56076
N161 E50295 E56056
N162 E51215 E56057
N163 E51216 E56086
N164 E51219 E56062
N165 E50250 E56219
N166 E51220 E56378

Darlington
N250 E50196 E50213
N251 E50262 E50255
N252 E50144 E51205
N253 E50139 E51211
N254 E50265 E50253
South Gosforth
N300 E50156 E59530 E50146
N301 E50165 E59062 E51509
N302 E50201 E59535 E51508
N303 E50214 E59071 E50138
N304 E50251 E59539 E50143
N310 E50624 E59389 E50641
N311 E50599 E59380 E50640
N312 E50604 E59390 E50646
N313 E50247 E59385 E50634
N314 E50232 E59386 E50645
South Gosforth
N402 E50176 E59088 E59093 E50194
N403 E50141 E59577 E59081 E50189
N404 E50145 E59531 E59053 E50148
N405 E51436 E59523 E59575 E51513
N406 E50229 E59090 E59576 E51510
N407 E50149 E59109 E59049 E50191
N408 E50147 E59043 E59050 E51511
N409 E50180 E59527 E59085 E50238
N410 E50234 E59104 E59052 E50243
N411 E50239 E59087 E59094 E51505
N412 E50267 E59526 E59054 E50177
N413 E51507 E59572 E59096 E50181
N414 E51438 E59046 E59573 E51506
N420 E50642 E59382 E59250 E50631
N421 E50632 E59387 E59246 E50643
N422 E50635 E59381 E59247 E50636
N423 E50637 E59384 E59248 E50638
N424 E50630 E59383 E59249 E50639
N425 E50633 E59388 E59245 E50644
Darlington
N450 E50142 E59060 E59084 E50193
N451 E50162 E59063 E59079 E50192
N452 E50170 E59045 E59078 E50184
N453 E50188 E59072 E59076 E50263
N454 E50182 E59064 E59083 E50179
N455 E50185 E59066 E59075 E50268

Neville Hill 55H
Bradford Hammerton Street 55F

These two depots numbered their units in a common sequence prefixed "L", with numbers carried on the sole bars.

Bradford
L101-109 Class 102 Power Twins *Not fixed formations*
Neville Hill
L120 E50602 E56193
L121 E50607 E56199
L122 E50603 E56198
L123 E50609 E56205
L124 E50612 E56200
L125 E50613 E56209
L126 E50614 E56204
L127 E50618 E56194
L128 E50601 E56192
L129 E50608 E56208
L130 E50616 E56210
L131 E50617 E56207
L132 E50619 E56206
L141 E50154 E51499
L142 E50164 E50163
L143 E50157 E56366
L144 E50152 E56371
L145 E50153 E56054
L146 E50202 E56376
L150 E51440 E51512
L151 E51426 E51496
L152 E51442 E50197
L153 E50134 E56091
L154 E50136 E56093
L155 E50137 E56090
L156 E50135 E56092
L157 E51432 E51502
L158 E50598 E56197
L159 E51431 E56368
L160 E50462 E56189
L161 E50596 E56187
L162 E50621 E56191
L170 E51542 E59106 E51552
L171 E50284 E59532 E50277
L172 E51544 E59536 E51553
L173 E50283 E59571 E50278
L174 E50289 E59107 E50276
L175 E51549 E59525 E51559
L176 E51545 E59534 E51555
L177 E51543 E59524 E51557
L178 E51546 E59529 E51554
L179 E51550 E59570 E51558
L180 E51548 E59533 E51556
L181 E50288 E59232 E50275
L182 E50286 E59108 E50279
L183 E50274 E59105 E50287
L190 E51541 E59569 E51551
L191 E50281 E59102 E50271
L192 E50282 E59101 E50272
L193 E50280 E59100 E50270
L194 E51809 E59696 E51829
L195 E51810 E59695 E51830
L196 E51811 E59709 E51831
Bradford
L205-226 Class 110 Triples *Not fixed formations*
Neville Hill
L235 E50150 E59069 E59073 E50237
L236 E50750 E59086 E59097 E50235
L237 E50242 E59089 E59055 E50241
L238 E50190 E59306 E59082 E50168
L239 E50244 E59091 E59092 E50151
L240 E50195 E59048 E59113 E50751
L241 E50240 E59065 E59095 E50245
L242 E50140 E59047 E59077 E51514
L250 E50566 E59191 E59242 E50545
L251 E50573 E59201 E59209 E50584
L252 E50591 E59194 E59219 E50586
L253 E50563 E59189 E59241 E50552
L254 E50575 E59234 E59211 E50554
L255 E50589 E59203 E59216 E50542
L256 E50593 E59206 E59244 E50548
L257 E50273 E59188 E59240 E51560
L260 E51846 E59192 E59711 E51828
L261 E51845 E59193 E59710 E51824
L262 E51848 E59233 E59712 E51825
L263 E51844 E59190 E59708 E51826

Norwich 32A

Fixed formations were not kept. The unit number was permanently associated with the power car and the rest of the sets were changed as circumstances required.
Unit numbers were carried on a card in the front window.

46 E50359 *E56116*
47 E50362 *E56117*
48 E50364 *E56119*
49 E50365 *E56121*
50 E50369 *E56439*
51 E50249 *E56440*
52 E50375 *E56125*
53 E50378 *E56143*
54 E51274 *E56432*
55 E51276 *E56434*
56 E51277 *E56435*
57 E51279 *E56436*
58 E51282 *E56437*
59 E50339 *E56094*
60 E50341 *E56096*
61 E50346 *E56099*
62 E50347 *E56100*
63 E51108 *E56300*
64 E51111 *E56301*
65 E51114 *E56307*
66 E51115 *E56313*
67 E51116 *E56315*
68 E51118 *E56310*
69 E51120 *E56303*
70 E51123 *E56316*
71 E51125 *E56317*
72 E51126 *E56318*
73 E51204 *E56362*
74 E51207 *E56364*
75 E51213 *E56074*
76 E51217 *E56365*
77 E51218 *E56380*
78 E51222 *E56383*
79 E51223 *E56369*
82 E50160 E50258
83 E50161 E50222
84 E50169 E50256
85 E50171 E50167
86 E50172 E50230

Scottish Region

Ayr 67C

Fixed formations were not kept. The unit number was permanently associated with the DMBSL (SC51030 upwards) and the rest of the sets were changed as circumstances required. The formations shown are as at August 1970.

151 SC51030 SC59394 SC51015
152 SC51031 SC59392 SC51009
153 SC51032 SC59400 SC51016
154 SC51033 SC59406 SC51017
155 SC51034 SC59411 SC51020
156 SC51035 SC59410 SC51010
157 SC51036 SC59399 SC51025
158 SC51037 SC59409 SC51019
159 SC51038 SC59412 SC51008
160 SC51039 SC59398 SC51022
161 SC51040 SC59405 SC51011
162 SC51041 SC59391 SC51012
163 SC51042 SC59396 SC51028
164 SC51043 SC59395 SC51029
165 SC51044 SC79470 SC51027
166 SC51045 SC59407 SC50936
167 SC51046 *SC59397* *SC51024*
168 SC51047 SC59408 SC51026
169 SC51048 SC59393 SC51021
170 SC51049 SC59404 SC51013
171 SC51050 SC59402 SC51023
172 SC51051 SC59403 SC51018
173 SC79088 *SC79479* *SC51014*

Corkerhill 67A

Fixed formations were not firmly kept. The unit number was permanently associated with the DMBS (SC51998 upwards) and the rest of the sets were changed as circumstances required. The formations shown are as at July 1970.

130 SC51998 SC59806 SC52027
131 SC51999 *SC59802* *SC52028*
132 SC52000 SC59805 SC52026
133 SC52001 *SC59803* *SC52030*
134 SC52002 SC59799 SC52034
135 SC52003 SC59796 SC52025
136 SC52004 SC59801 SC52024
137 SC52005 SC59807 SC52032
138 SC52006 SC59798 SC52031
139 SC52007 SC59797 SC52029
140 SC52008 SC59795 SC52033
141 SC52009 SC59804 SC52036
142 SC52010 SC59800 SC52035

Hamilton 66C

02 SC55002 SC56291
05 SC55005 SC56297
07 SC55007 SC56299
30 SC51234 SC56392
31 SC51242 SC56401
32 SC51248 SC56406
33 SC51250 SC56408
34 SC51473 SC56462
35 SC51474 SC56463
36 SC51475 SC56464
37 SC51476 SC56465
38 SC51477 SC56466
39 SC51478 SC56467
40 SC51479 SC56468
41 SC51480 SC56469
42 SC51481 SC56470
43 SC51482 SC56471
44 SC51483 SC56472
45 SC51484 SC56473
46 SC51485 SC56474
47 SC51486 SC56475
48 SC51487 SC56476
49 SC51489 SC56478
50 SC51490 SC56479
51 SC51491 SC56480
52 SC51492 SC56481
53 SC51493 SC56482
spare SC56477
101 SC50186 SC59080 SC50187
102 SC51445 SC51515
103 SC51446 SC59544 SC51516

104	SC51447	SC59545	SC51517
105	SC51448	SC59546	SC51518
106	SC51449	SC59547	SC51519
107	SC51450	SC59548	SC51520
108	SC51451	SC59549	SC51521
109	SC51452	SC59550	SC51522
110	SC51453	SC59551	SC51523
111	SC51454	SC59552	SC51524
112	SC51455	SC59553	SC51525
113	SC51456	SC59554	SC51526
114	SC51461	SC59559	SC51531
117	SC51985	SC59782	SC52011
118	SC51986	SC59783	SC52012
119	SC51987	SC59784	SC52013
120	SC51988	SC59785	SC52014
121	SC51989	SC59786	SC52015
122	SC51990	SC59787	SC52016
123	SC51991	SC59788	SC52017
124	SC51992	SC59789	SC52018
125	SC51993	SC59790	SC52019
126	SC51994	SC59791	SC52020
127	SC51995	SC59792	SC52021
128	SC51996	SC59793	SC52022
129	SC51997	SC59794	SC52023
143	SC50818	SC59326	SC50871
144	SC50820	SC59328	SC50873
145	SC50821	SC59329	SC50874
146	SC50822	SC59330	SC50875
147	SC50823	SC59331	SC50876
148	SC50825	SC59333	SC50878
149	SC50826	SC59345	SC50879
150	SC50829	SC59337	SC50882
150A	SC50852	SC59360	SC50905

Leith Central 67H

Fixed formations were not kept at this depot. The following is a list of the Inter-city formations operating on 10th June 1971

SC79099	SC79150	SC79480	SC79162	SC79096
SC79093	SC79163	SC79475	SC79160	SC79104
SC79109	SC79168	SC79478	SC79161	SC79100
SC79088	SC79157	SC79481	SC79164	SC79086
SC79085	SC79195	SC79482	SC79166	SC79087

Spare SC79094 SC79102

The remaining cars were stored at Millerhill.

Western Region

A new unit numbering scheme was started on the Western Region in January 1972. All units carried a painted unit number on the cab end. Each number was unique and each unit carried a prefix letter to show which division it was based in:

B	**Bristol Division**	**Bristol 82A**
C	**Cardiff Division**	**Cardiff 86A**
L	**London Division**	**Reading 81D**
P	**Plymouth Division**	**Laira 84A**

B101	DB975023	
L111	W50411	W56166
L112	W50412	W56167
P113	W50413	W56168
P114	W50414	W56169
P116	W55016	
P118	W55018	
L120	W55020	
L121	W55021	
L122	W55022	
L123	W55023	
P124	W55024	
P125	W55025	
C126	W55026	
P127	W55027	
L128	W55028	
P129	W55029	
L130	W55030	
L131	W55031	
B132	W55032	
B133	W55033	
B134	W55034	
B135	W55035	
L280	W56280	
L281	W56281	
L282	W56282	
L283	W56283	
L284	W56284	
L285	W56285	

L286	W56286		
L287	W56287		
L289	W56289		
C293	W56293		
C300	W51135	W59445	W51148
C301	W51136	W59446	W51149
C302	W50855	W59363	W50908
C303	W50080	W59030	W50122
C304	W51140	W59032	W51153
C305	W50857	W59368	W50910
C306	W50081	W59031	W50123
C307	W51134	W59444	W51147
C308	W50086	W59036	W50128
C309	W50869	W59035	W50922
C310	W50091	W59041	W50133
C311	W51132	W59034	W51145
C312	W51139	W59033	W51152
C313	W50863	W59371	W50916
C314	W50088	W59362	W50130
C315	W50845	W59353	W50898
C316	W50867	W59375	W50920
C317	W50087	W59037	W50129
C318	W50089	W59039	W50131
C319	W50839	W59347	W50892
C320	W50848	W59356	W50901
C321	W50834	W59038	W50887
C322	W50090		
C323	W50843	W59355	W50896
C324	W50132		
C327	W50866	W59374	W50919
C328	W50842	W59350	W50895
C329	W50844	W59335	W50897
C331	W50851	W59359	W50904
C337	W50836	W59344	W50889
C338	W50856	W59364	W50909
L340	W50819		
L341	W50862		
L342	W50872		
L343	W50915		
C344	W50082	W59340	W50124
C345	W50858	W59366	W50911
C347	W50084	W59373	W50126
C351	W50864	W59369	W50917
C353	W51138	W59448	W51151
P354	W50847	W59352	W50900
P355	W50854	W59346	W50907
P356	W50865	W59372	W50921
P357	W50868	W59365	W50918
P358	W51128	W59357	W51141
B390	W51137	W51150	
L400	W51334	W59486	W51376
L401	W51335	W59487	W51377
L402	W51337	W59489	W51379
L403	W51338	W59490	W51380
L404	W51340	W59491	W51381
B405	W51342	W59494	W51384
L406	W51343	W59495	W51385
B407	W51345	W59497	W51387
B408	W51346	W59498	W51388
L409	W51347	W59499	W51389
L410	W51351	W59503	W51393
L411	W51352	W59504	W51394
L412	W51353	W59505	W51395
L413	W51355	W59507	W51397
L414	W51356	W59508	W51398
L415	W51358	W59510	W51400
L416	W51361	W59513	W51403
L417	W51362	W59514	W51404
L418	W51364	W59516	W51406
L419	W51366	W59518	W51408
L420	W51367	W59519	W51409
L421	W51369	W59521	W51411
L422	W51371	W59478	W51413
L423	W51372	W59479	W51414
L424	W51373	W59480	W51415
L450	W51332	W59484	W51374
L451	W51333	W59485	W51375
L452	W51336	W59488	W51378
L453	W51339	W59492	W51382
L454	W51341	W59493	W51383
L455	W51344	W59496	W51386
L456	W51348	W59500	W51390
L457	W51349	W59501	W51391
L458	W51350	W59502	W51392
L459	W51354	W59506	W51396
L460	W50083	W59509	W51399
L461	W51359	W59511	W51401
B462	W51360	W59512	W51402

L463	W51363	W59515	W51405	
L464	W51365	W59517	W51407	
L465	W51368	W59520	W51410	
L466	W51370	W59522	W51412	
B467	W51302	W59469	W51317	
B468	W51303	W59470	W51318	
L469	W51304	W59471	W51319	
L470	W51305	W59472	W51320	
L471	W51309	W59476	W51324	
L472	W51310	W59477	W51325	
L473	W51315	W59482	W51330	
L474	W51316	W59483	W51331	
L475	W51308	W59475	W51323	
L476	W51314	W59481	W51329	
B477	W51306	W59473	W51321	
B478	W51307	W59474	W51322	
P480	W51311	W51326		
P481	W51312	W51327		
C482	W51313			
C483	W51328			
C500	W50647	W59265	W50705	
C501	W50683	W59294	W50735	
C502	W50693	W59299	W50738	
C503	W50653	W59268	W50707	
C504	W50679	W59291	W50727	
C505	W50666	W59264	W50712	
C506	W50659	W59282	W50700	
C507	W50661	W59269	W50710	
C508	W50658	W59581	W50711	
C509	W50665	W59040	W50715	
C510	W50668	W59275	W50721	
C511	W50675	W59262	W50716	
C512	W50648	W59296	W50706	
C513	W50660	W59266	W50729	
C520	W50674	W59278	W50723	
C524	W50662	W59260	W50699	
C526	W50682	W59288	W50726	
C530	W50691	W59277	W50728	
C533	W50694	W59279	W50732	
B551	W50695	W59588	W50739	
B552	W51573	W59285	W51582	
B553	W51574	W59284	W51583	
B554	W51575	W59261	W51584	
B555	W51576	W59582	W51590	
P556	W51577	W59583	W51586	
P557	W51578	W59580	W51587	
P558	W51579	W59286	W51588	
B559	W51580	W59586	W51589	
B560	W51581	W59587	W51585	
B571	W51052	W59292	W51080	
B572	W51054	W59413	W51082	
B573	W51055	W59417	W51083	
B574	W51056	W59415	W51084	
B575	W51060	W59419	W51088	
B576	W51062	W59421	W51090	
B577	W51063	W59422	W51091	
B578	W51064	W59423	W51092	
B579	W51065	W59424	W51093	
B580	W51066	W59425	W51094	
P581	W51067	W59426	W51095	
P582	W51068	W59427	W51096	
P583	W51069	W59428	W51097	
B584	W51070	W59429	W51098	
B585	W51075	W59434	W51103	
P586	W51077	W59420	W51105	
P587	W51078	W59436	W51106	
P588	W51079	W59437	W51107	
C600	W50664	W50702		
C601	W50672	W50722		
C602	W50649	W50698		
C603	W50673	W50724		
C604	W50681	W50701		
C605	W50686	W50733		
L706	W52086	W59236	W59818	W52101
L707	W52087	W59235	W59826	W52103
L708	W52088	W59819	W52099	
L709	W52089	W59827	W52104	
L710	W52090	W59239	W59825	W52100
L711	W52091	W59823	W52098	
L712	W52092	W59238	W59820	W52097
L713	W52093	W59237	W59821	W52105
L714	W52094	W59824	W52102	
L715	W52095	W59822	W52096	
	W55991			
	W55992			

1976

Western Region

A complete renumbering of the Western Region units was undertaken in 1976.

B	**Bristol Division**	**Bristol**	**BR**
C	**Cardiff Division**	**Cardiff**	**CF**
L	**London Division**	**Reading**	**RG**
P	**Plymouth Division**	**Laira**	**LA**

Unit			
L101	TDB975023		
L102	TDB975540		
P118	W55018		
L120	W55020		
L121	W55021		
L122	W55022		
L123	W55023		
L124	W55024		
P125	W55025		
P126	W55026		
L127	W55027		
L128	W55028		
L129	W55029		
L130	W55030		
L131	W55031		
B132	W55032		
B133	W55033		
B134	W55034		
B135	W55035		
L280	W56280		
L281	W56281		
B283	W56283		
L284	W56284		
L285	W56285		
L286	W56286		
L287	W56287		
L289	W56289		
C300	W50080	W59030	W50122
C301	W50084	W59373	W50126
C302	W50086	W59036	W50128
C303	W50087	W59037	W50129
C304	W50088	W59362	W50130
C305	W50089	W59039	W50131
C306	W50091	W59041	W50133
C310	W50834	W59038	W50887
C311	W50842	W59350	W50895
C312	W50843	W59355	W50896
C313	W50847	W59040	W50900
C314	W50848	W59356	W50901
C315	W50855	W59363	W50908
C316	W50856	W59364	W50909
C317	W50858	W59366	W50911
C318	W50864	W59369	W50917
C319	W50868	W59365	W50918
C320	W50869	W59035	W50922
C330	W51128	W59357	W51141
C331	W51132	W59034	W51145
C332	W51134	W59444	W51147
C333	W51135	W59445	W51148
C334	W51139	W59033	W51152
C335	W51140	W59032	W51153
L340	W50812		
L341	W50862		
L342	W50872		
L343	W50915		
L400	W51332	W59484	W51374
L401	W51333	W59485	W51375
L402	W51335	W59487	W51377
L403	W51336	W59488	W51378
L404	W51337	W59489	W51379
L405	W51340	W59491	W51381
L406	W51341	W59493	W51383
L407	W51342	W59494	W51384
L408	W51343	W59495	W51385
L409	W51344	W59496	W51386
L410	W51345	W59497	W51387
L411	W51346	W59498	W51388
L412	W51347	W59499	W51389
L413	W51349	W59501	W51391
L414	W51350	W59502	W51392
L415	W51351	W59503	W51393
L416	W51353	W59505	W51395
L417	W51354	W59506	W51396
L418	W51355	W59507	W51397
L419	W51356	W59508	W51398
L420	W51358	W59510	W51400
L421	W51359	W59511	W51401
L422	W51360	W59512	W51402
L423	W51361	W59513	W51403
L424	W51362	W59514	W51404
L425	W51363	W59515	W51405
L426	W51364	W59516	W51406
L427	W51365	W59517	W51407
L428	W51366	W59518	W51408
L429	W51367	W59519	W51409
L430	W51368	W59520	W51410
L431	W51369	W59521	W51411
L432	W51370	W59522	W51412
L433	W51371	W59478	W51413
L434	W51372	W59479	W51414
L435	W51373	W59480	W51415
L440	W50083	W59500	W51399
C450	W51334	W59031	W51376
C451	W51338	W59371	W51380
C452	W51339	W59446	W51382
C453	W51348	W59340	W51390
C454	W51352	W59359	W51394
B460	W51302	W59469	W51317
P461	W51303	W59470	W51318
B462	W51304	W59471	W51319
P463	W51305	W59472	W51320
P464	W51306	W59473	W51321
B465	W51307	W59474	W51322
B466	W51308	W59475	W51323
B467	W51309	W59476	W51324
B468	W51310	W59477	W51325
C469	W51311	W59538	W51326
P470	W51313	W59509	W51328
B471	W51314	W59481	W51329
B472	W51315	W59482	W51330
P473	W51316	W59483	W51331
P480	W51312	W51327	
C500	W50647	W59265	W50705
C501	W50648	W59296	W50706
C502	W50653	W59268	W50707
C503	W50658	W59581	W50711
C504	W50659	W59282	W50700
C505	W50660	W59266	W50729
C506	W50665	W59261	W50715
C507	W50668	W59275	W50721
C508	W50674	W59278	W50723
C509	W50675	W59262	W50716
C510	W50679	W59291	W50727
C511	W50682	W59288	W50726
C512	W50683	W59294	W50735
C513	W50693	W59299	W50738
C514	W50694	W59279	W50732
C515	W50695	W59588	W50739
C552	W51573	W59285	W51582
P553	W51574	W59284	W51583
P554	W51575	W51584	
P555	W51576	W59582	W51590
P556	W51577	W59583	W51586
P557	W51578	W59580	W51587
P558	W51579	W59264	W51588
C559	W51580	W59586	W51589
C560	W51581	W59587	W51585
B571	W51052	W59292	W51080
B572	W51054	W59413	W51082
B573	W51055	W59417	W51083
B574	W51056	W59415	W51084
B575	W51060	W59419	W51088
B576	W51062	W59421	W51090
B577	W51063	W59422	W51091
B578	W51064	W59423	W51092
B579	W51065	W59424	W51093
B580	W51066	W59425	W51094
B581	W51067	W59426	W51095
P582	W51068	W59427	W51096
P583	W51069	W59428	W51097
L584	W51070	W59429	W51098
B585	W51075	W59434	W51103
L586	W51077	W59420	W51105
L587	W51078	W59436	W51106
L588	W51079	W59437	W51107
C600	W50664	W50702	
C601	W50672	W50722	
C602	W50649	W50698	
C603	W50673	W50724	
C604	W50681	W50701	
C605	W50686	W50733	
C610	W50661	W59269	W50710
C611	W50662	W59260	W50699
C612	W50666	W59286	W50712
C613	W50691	W59277	W50728
C706	W52086	W59818	W52101
C707	W52087	W59826	W52103
C708	W52088	W59819	W52099
C709	W52089	W59827	W52104
C710	W52090	W59825	W52100
C711	W52091	W59823	W52098
C712	W52092	W59820	W52097
C713	W52093	W59821	W52105
C714	W52094	W59824	W52102
C715	W52095	W59822	W52096
B800	W51445	W59549	W51515
B801	W51446	W59547	W51517
B802	W51449	W59550	W51521
B803	W51450	W59546	W51522
B804	W51452	W59551	W51523
	W55991		W55992
Spare	W59543		
Stored	W59235 W59236 W59237 W59238 W59239		

1980

London Midland Region

Carlisle Kingmoor KD

M50951	M56235
M50952	M56244
M50953	M56242
M50954	M56238
M50955	M56234
M50956	M56246
M50957	M56236
M50958	M56239
M50959	M56243
M50960	M56241
M50962	M56245
M50963	M56240
M50964	M56247
M50965	M56248

Tyseley TS

Unit			
TS050	M55003		
TS051	M55004		
TS052	M55006		
TS059	M55009		
TS056	M55012		
	M56295		
TS400	M50303	M59114	M50321
TS402	M50315	M59116	M50333
TS403	M50222	M59536	M50237
TS405	M50314	M59127	M50337
TS406	M50307	M59118	M50326
TS407	M50309	M59121	M50336
TS408	M50305	M59119	M50338
TS409	M50308	M59126	M50324
TS410	M50313	M59125	M50331
TS411	M51492	M59124	M50332
TS412	M50325	M59131	M50317
TS413	M51119	M59129	M50312
TS416	M51110	M59193	M51490
TS417	M50306	M59117	M50323
TS418	M50310	M59128	M50343
TS419	M50318	M59120	M50328
TS500	M50061	M59000	M50092
TS501	M50057	M59001	M50097
TS502	M50861	M59002	M50912
TS503	M50076	M59003	M50118
TS504	M50059	M59004	M50104
TS505	M50065	M59005	M50094
TS506	M50058	M59006	M50112
TS507	M50069	M59007	M50099
TS508	M50851	M59376	M50904

TS509	M50072	M59009	M50105
TS510	M50067	M59010	M50093
TS511	M50819	M59346	M50915
TS512	M50051	M59012	M50113
TS513	M50077	M59013	M50120
TS514	M50862	M59014	M50872
TS515	M50050	M59015	M51143
TS516	M50074	M59016	M50316
TS517	M50824	M59343	M50906
TS518	M50056	M59018	M50098
TS519	M50064	M59019	M50115
TS520	M50827	M59361	M50880
TS521	M51112	M59336	M51146
TS522	M50078	M59022	M50109
TS523	M50055	M59023	M50116
TS524	M50066	M59024	M50103
TS525	M50830	M59332	M50883
TS526	M50070	M59026	M50095
TS527	M50834	M59038	M50887
TS528	M50062	M59028	M50117
TS529	M50828	M59338	M50127
TS530	M50831	M59339	M50884
TS531	M50052	M59341	M50914
TS532	M50079	M59351	M50121
TS533	M51129	M59439	M51142
TS534	M50053	M59342	M50886
TS535	M50860	M59438	M50913
TS536	M50107	M59442	M50833
TS537	M50108	M59440	M51130
TS538	M51131	M59441	M51144
TS539	M50119	M59443	M51133
TS540	M50832	M59029	M50885
TS541	M50835	M59334	M50888
TS542	M50837	M59358	M50890
TS543	M50842	M59350	M50895
TS544	M50854	M59192	M50907
TS546	M51138	M59448	M51151
TS547	M50857	M59368	M50910
TS548	M50866	M59352	M50919
TS549	M51136	M59528	M51149
TS550	M50082	M59366	M50124
TS551	M50852	M59328	M50871
TS552	M50081	M59543	M50123
TS553	M50818	M59326	M50878
TS554	M50821	M59333	M50875
TS555	M50826	M59360	M50905
TS556	M50863	M59623	M50916
TS557	M50100	M59115	M50840
TS558	M50102	M59020	M50850
	M50812	M50786	
Spare	M59617	M59348	
	M50322	M50327	
	M50110		

Eastern Region

Stratford SF

Stratford depot allocated its units to permanent sets, but these formations were rarely adhered to.

E50359	E56457	
E50360	E56420	
E50361	E56122	
E50362	E56126	
E50363	E56449	
E50364	E56455	
E50365	E56141	
E50366	E56421	
E50367	E56138	
E50368	E56416	
E50369	E56143	
E50370	E56415	
E50551	E59226	E50572
E50844	E59335	E50897
E50845	E59353	E50898
E50865	E59372	E50921
E50867	E59375	E50920

Western Region

B	**Bristol Division**	**Bristol BR**
C	**Cardiff Division**	**Cardiff CF**
L	**London Division**	**Reading RG**
P	**Plymouth Division**	**Laira LA**

L101	TDB975023		
L102	TDB975540		
L103	TDB975659		
L120	W55020		
L121	W55021		
L122	W55022		
L123	W55023		
P124	W55024		
P125	W55025		
P126	W55026		
P127	W55027		
L128	W55028		
L129	W55029		
L130	W55030		
L131	W55031		
B132	W55032		
B133	W55033		
L134	W55034		
L280	W56280		
L281	W56281		
L283	W56283		
L284	W56284		
L285	W56285		
L286	W56286		
L287	W56287		
L289	W56289		
C300	W50080	W59030	W50122
C301	W50084	W59373	W50126
C302	W50086	W59036	W50128
C303	W50087	W59037	W50129
C304	W50088	W59362	W50130
C305	W50089	W59039	W50131
C306	W50091	W59041	W50133
C312	W50843	W59355	W50896
C313	W50847	W59040	W50900
C314	W50848	W59356	W50901
C315	W50855	W59363	W50908
C316	W50856	W59364	W50909
P317	W50858	W59492	W50911
C318	W50864	W59369	W50917
P319	W50868	W59504	W50918
C320	W50869	W59035	W50922
C330	W51128	W59357	W51141
C331	W51132	W59034	W51145
C332	W51134	W59444	W51147
C333	W51135	W59445	W51148
C334	W51139	W59033	W51152
C335	W51140	W59032	W51153
L400	W51332	W59484	W51374
L401	W51333	W59485	W51375
L402	W51335	W59487	W51377
L403	W51336	W59488	W51378
L404	W51337	W59489	W51379
L405	W51340	W59491	W51381
L406	W51341	W59493	W51383
L407	W51342	W59494	W51384
L408	W51343	W59495	W51385
L409	W51344	W59496	W51386
L410	W51345	W59497	W51387
L411	W51346	W59498	W51388
L412	W51347	W59499	W51389
L413	W51349	W59501	W51391
L414	W51350	W59502	W51392
L415	W51351	W59503	W51393
L416	W51353	W59505	W51395
L417	W51354	W59506	W51396
L418	W51355	W59507	W51397
L419	W51356	W59508	W51398
L420	W51358	W59510	W51400
L421	W51359	W59511	W51401
L422	W51360	W59512	W51402
L423	W51361	W59513	W51403
L424	W51362	W59514	W51404
L425	W51363	W59515	W51405
L426	W51364	W59516	W51406
L427	W51365	W59517	W51407
L428	W51366	W59518	W51408
L429	W51367	W59519	W51409
L430	W51368	W59520	W51410
L431	W51369	W59521	W51411
L432	W51370	W59522	W51412
L433	W51371	W59478	W51413
L434	W51372	W59479	W51414
L435	W51373	W59480	W51415
L440	W50083	W59500	W51399
C450	W51334	W59031	W51376
C451	W51338	W59371	W51380
C452	W51339	W59446	W51382
C453	W51348	W59340	W51390
C454	W51352	W59359	W51394
B460	W51302	W59469	W51317
P461	W51303	W59470	W51318
B462	W51304	W59477	W51319
P463	W51305	W59472	W51320
P464	W51306	W59473	W51321
B465	W51307	W59474	W51322
B466	W51308	W59475	W51323
B467	W51309	W59476	W51324
B468	W51310	W59471	W51325
L469	W51311	W59490	W51326
P470	W51313	W59509	W51328
B471	W51314	W59481	W51329
B472	W51315	W59482	W51330
P473	W51316	W59483	W51331
P480	W51312	W51327	
C500	W50647	W59265	W50705
C501	W50653	W59268	W50707
C502	W50658	W59282	W50711
C503	W50659	W59581	W50700
C504	W50665	W59588	W50715
C505	W50674	W59278	W50723
P552	W51573	W59285	W51582
P553	W51574	W59284	W51583
P554	W51575	W51584	
P555	W51576	W59582	W51590
P556	W51577	W59583	W51586
C557	W51578	W59580	W51587
C558	W51579	W59264	W51588
C559	W51580	W59586	W51589
C560	W51581	W59587	W51585
B571	W51052	W59292	W51080
C572	W51054	W59413	W51082
L573	W51055	W59417	W51083
L574	W51056	W59415	W51084
L575	W51060	W59419	W51088
L576	W51062	W59421	W51090
L577	W51063	W59422	W51091
L578	W51064	W59423	W51092
L579	W51065	W59424	W51093
L580	W51066	W59425	W51094
L581	W51067	W59426	W51095
L582	W51068	W59427	W51096
L583	W51069	W59428	W51097
L584	W51070	W59429	W51098
L585	W51075	W59434	W51103
L586	W51077	W59420	W51105
L587	W51078	W59436	W51106
L588	W51079	W59437	W51107
L589	W51057	W59414	W51100
C590	W51058	W59418	W51087
C591	W51059	W59433	W51102
C592	W51071	W59432	W51101
C593	W51072	W59431	W51085
C594	W51073	W59435	W51104
C595	W51074	W59430	W51086
C596	W51076	W59416	W51099
C600	W50664	W50702	
C601	W50672	W50722	
C602	W50649	W50698	
C603	W50673	W50724	
C604	W50681	W50701	
C605	W50686	W50733	
C610	W50661	W59269	W50710
C611	W50662	W59260	W50699
C612	W50666	W59286	W50712
C613	W50691	W59277	W50728
B800	W51445	W59549	W51515
B801	W51446	W59547	W51517
B802	W51449	W59550	W51521
B803	W51450	W59546	W51522
B804	W51452	W59551	W51523
B805	W50304	W59122	W50329
B806	W50319	W59123	W50335
B810	W51799	W59539	W51808
B811	W51801	W59548	W51519
B812	W51462	W59530	W51530
B813	W51463	W59561	W51533
B820	W51500	W59093	W51512
B821	W51509	W59050	W51513
B822	W51495	W59096	W51510
B823	W51505	W59082	W51511

1981

Scottish Region

A comprehensive scheme was undertaken on the Scottish Region in 1981. All units were formed into fixed formations. They initially carried a three digit unit number, but this was soon changed by the addition of the class number.

Ayr AY
Dundee DE
Eastfield ED
Haymarket HA
Hamilton HN

101301	SC50254	SC59305	SC50144	DE
101302	SC50290	SC59303	SC50197	DE
101303	SC50292	SC59053	SC50184	DE
101304	SC51224	SC59090	SC50241	DE
101305	SC51227	SC59045	SC50264	DE
101306	SC51228	SC59086	SC50243	DE
101307	SC51231	SC59688	SC50189	DE
101308	SC51232	SC59066	SC50141	DE
101309	SC51233	SC59566	SC50172	DE
101310	SC51234	SC59302	SC50163	DE
101311	SC51235	SC59060	SC50174	DE
101312	SC51237	SC59088	SC50175	HA
101313	SC51239	SC59047	SC50143	DE
101314	SC51240	SC59067	SC50138	DE
101315	SC51241	SC59042	SC50260	DE
101316	SC51242	SC59071	SC50147	DE
101317	SC51243	SC59048	SC50747	DE
101318	SC51244	SC59061	SC50176	DE
101319	SC51245	SC59525	SC50269	DE
101320	SC51248	SC59046	SC50749	HA
101321	SC51249	SC59542	SC50146	DE
101322	SC51250	SC59069	SC50159	AY
101323	SC51251	SC59043	SC50148	DE
101324	SC51253	SC59304	SC50746	DE
101325	SC51448	SC59558	SC51528	ED
101326	SC51451	SC59545	SC51518	ED
101327	SC51453	SC59552	SC51807	ED
101328	SC51454	SC59562	SC51524	ED
101329	SC51455	SC59559	SC51538	ED
101330	SC51456	SC59555	SC51520	AY
101331	SC51457	SC59689	SC51802	ED
101332	SC51458	SC59687	SC51527	ED
101333	SC51459	SC59541	SC51805	ED
101334	SC51460	SC59564	SC51534	ED
101335	SC51461	SC59565	SC51804	AY
101336	SC51464	SC59556	SC51525	ED
101337	SC51465	SC59563	SC51526	ED
101338	SC51466	SC59568	SC51535	ED
101339	SC51467	SC59690	SC51516	ED
101340	SC51468	SC59692	SC51537	AY
101341	SC51469	SC59557	SC51536	AY
101342		SC59553	SC51806	HA
101343	SC51795	SC59686	SC51529	AY
101344	SC51796	SC59560	SC51803	HA
101345	SC51797	SC59691	SC51539	AY
101346	SC51798	SC59554	SC51532	ED
101347	SC51800	SC59578	SC51531	ED
101360	SC50158	SC59074	SC50160	DE
101361	SC50192	SC59112	SC50234	DE
101362	SC50187	SC59073	SC50186	DE
101363	SC50185	SC59049	SC50194	DE
101364	SC50242	SC59080	SC50268	DE
101365	SC50239	SC59577	SC50245	DE
105375	SC51473	SC59567	SC51477	HA
105376	SC51474	SC59574	SC51481	HA
105377	SC51476	SC59072	SC51480	HA
105378	SC51479	SC59068	SC51483	HA
105379	SC51475	SC59544	SC50748	HA
107425	SC51985	SC59797	SC52028	HN
107426	SC51986	SC59803	SC52018	HN
107427	SC51987	SC59793	SC52020	HN
107428	SC51988	SC59786	SC52013	HN
107429	SC51989	SC59795	SC52023	HN
107430	SC51990	SC59799	SC52016	HN
107431	SC51991	SC59789	SC52017	HN
107432	SC51992	SC59800	SC52026	HN
107433	SC51993	SC59790	SC52022	HN
107434	SC51994	SC59791	SC52011	HN
107435	SC51996	SC59798	SC52019	HN
107436	SC51997	SC59784	SC52024	HN
107437	SC51998	SC59782	SC52021	HN
107438	SC51999	SC59796	SC52030	HN
107439	SC52000	SC59785	SC52036	HN
107440	SC52001	SC59787	SC52014	HN
107441	SC52002	SC59783	SC52027	HN
107442	SC52003	SC59792	SC52025	HN
107443	SC52004	SC59805	SC52032	HN
107444	SC52005	SC59804	SC52031	HN
107445	SC52006	SC59801	SC52015	HN
107446	SC52007	SC59806	SC52033	HN
107447	SC52008	SC59788	SC52029	HN
107448	SC52009	SC59802	SC52035	HN
107449	SC52010	SC59807	SC52034	HN
116385	SC50090	SC59344	SC50132	HN
116386	SC50820	SC59027	SC52012	HN
116387	SC50822	SC59330	SC50881	HN
116388	SC50823	SC59354	SC50876	HN
116389	SC50825	SC59329	SC50873	HN
116390	SC50829	SC59337	SC50879	HN
116391	SC50836	SC59347	SC50889	HN
116392	SC50839	SC59374	SC50892	HN
116393	SC50841	SC59331	SC50877	HN
116394	SC50846	SC59345	SC50882	HN
116395	SC50853	SC59367	SC50894	HN
116396	SC50859	SC59349	SC50899	HN
120398	SC51787	SC59685	SC51789	AY
120399	SC51470	SC59680	SC51794	AY
126401	SC51030	SC59394	SC51027	AY
126402	SC51032	SC59408	SC51023	AY
126403	SC51033	SC59396	SC51012	AY
126404	SC51034	SC59411	SC51016	AY
126405	SC51035	SC59407	SC51015	AY
126406	SC51036	SC59412	SC51019	AY
126407	SC51037	SC59397	SC51026	AY
126408	SC51038	SC59400	SC51020	AY
126409	SC51039	SC59406	SC51029	AY
126410	SC51040	SC59402	SC51013	AY
126411	SC51041	SC59393	SC51018	AY
126412	SC51042	SC59395	SC51021	AY
126413	SC51043	SC59391	SC50936	AY
126414	SC51044	SC59398	SC51014	AY
126415	SC51045	SC59392	SC51008	AY
126416	SC51046	SC59410	SC51017	AY
126417	SC51047	SC59405	SC51009	AY
126418	SC51048	SC59404	SC51025	AY
126419	SC51049	SC59399	SC51024	AY
126420	SC51050	SC59403	SC51022	AY
126421	SC51051	SC59409	SC51010	AY
126422	SC79088	SC79470		AY

1982

London Midland Region

In 1982 the London Midland Region began (again) to allocate set numbers to units.

Derby Etches Park EP

Unit			
EP500	M50647	M59265	M50705
EP501	M50669	M59256	M50718
EP502	M50663	M59297	M50709
EP504	M51787	M59685	M51789
EP505	M50680	M59264	M50715
EP506	M50692	M59301	M50708
EP507	M50658	M59260	M50699
EP508	M50650	M59255	M50704
EP509	M50657	M59273	M50731
EP510	M50667	M59257	M50713
EP511	M50665	M59259	M50725
EP512	M50684	M59272	M50707
EP513	M50652	M59276	M50741
EP514	M50687	M59280	M50696
EP515	M50670	M59258	M50744
EP516	M50656	M59283	M50730
EP517	M50654	M59268	M50742
EP518	M50688	M59274	M50737
EP519	M50651	M59290	M50736
EP520	M50659	M59292	M50711
EP521	M50677	M59267	M50720
EP522	M50678	M59293	M50714
EP523	M50671	M59287	M50734
EP524	M50689	M59295	M50719
EP525	M50662	M59680	M50700
EP526	M51794	M59300	M50743
EP527	M50685	M59281	M50703
EP528	M50653	M59289	M50717
EP529	M50390	M56462	

Manchester Area

Allocated unit numbers in one common series

Buxton BX
Longsight LO
Newton Heath NH

Unit		
NH131	M50423	M50483
NH132	M50428	M50485
NH133	M50443	M50493
NH134	M50447	M52050
NH135	M50449	M50503
NH136	M50450	M50517
NH137	M50451	M50528
NH138	M50453	M50520
NH139	M50465	M50531
NH140	M50466	M50518
NH141	M50467	M50519
NH142	M50468	M50516
NH143	M50474	M50556
NH144	M50476	M52053
NH145	M50478	M50530
NH147	M50757	M50815
NH148	M50761	M50794
NH149	M50763	M50796
NH150	M50764	M50810
NH151	M50765	M50804
NH152	M50769	M50798
NH153	M50772	M50787
NH154	M50777	M50802
NH155	M51901	M52055
NH156	M51927	M52049
NH157	M51933	M52063
NH158	M51934	M52061
NH159	M51935	M52060
NH160	M51936	M52051
NH161	M51938	M52039
NH162	M51939	M52054
NH163	M51940	M52057
NH164	M51943	M52058
NH165	M51945	M52059
NH166	M51948	M52040
NH	M51941	M52056
NH	M50470	M52064
LO291	M50348	M56103
LO292	M50349	M56104
LO293	M50351	M56106
LO294	M50353	M56108
LO295	M50354	M56109
LO296	M50355	M56105
LO297	M50356	M56111
LO298	M50358	M56113
LO299	M50629	M56267
LO300	M50941	M56259
LO301	M50942	M56225
LO302	M50945	M56228
LO303	M50947	M56230
LO304	M50949	M56232
LO305	M51115	M56465
LO306	M51124	M56116
LO307	M50970	M56264
LO308	M50975	M56258
LO309	M50978	M56261
LO310	M50981	M56253
LO311	M50985	M56268
LO312	M50986	M56221
LO313	M51902	M56485
LO314	M51903	M56486
LO315	M51904	M56487
LO316	M51905	M56488
LO317	M51906	M56489

LO318	M51907	M56490	
LO319	M50977	M56260	
LO323	M51929	M52041	
LO324	M51930	M52045	
LO	M50948	M56231	
NH336	M50372	M56127	
NH337	M50374	M56452	
NH338	M50385	M56118	
NH340	M50533	M56178	
NH341	M50535	M56176	
NH342	M50537	M56180	
NH343	M50538	M56175	
NH344	M50944	M56501	
NH345	M50971	M56456	
NH346	M50974	M56257	
NH347	M50976	M56224	
NH348	M50983	M56266	
NH349	M51127	M56453	
NH350	M50446	M50521	
NH441	M50442	M59160	M50494
NH442	M50444	M59212	M50500
NH443	M50445	M59155	M50504
NH444	M50448	M59156	M50501
NH445	M50452	M59186	M50505
NH446	M50461	M59152	M50510
NH447	M50463	M59153	M50515
NH448	M50464	M59176	M50498
NH449	M50469	M59174	M50499
NH450	M50471	M59179	M50523
NH451	M50472	M59206	M50522
NH452	M50473	M59181	M50525
NH453	M50475	M59149	M50527
NH454	M50477	M59183	M50529
NH455	M50479	M59180	M50524
NH456	M50496	M59219	M50571
NH457	M50497	M59228	M50502
NH458	M50551	M59226	M50572
NH459	M50561	M59218	M50589
NH460	M50565	M59210	M50577
NH461	M51573	M59285	M51582
NH462	M51575	M59581	M51584
NH463	M51577	M59583	M51586
NH464	M51578	M59580	M51587
NH465	M51581	M59587	M51585
NH466	M50460	M59168	M50512
NH467	M50546	M59240	M50593
NH	M50562	M59227	M50590
NH	M50666	M59286	M50712
NH	M51574	M59284	M51583
NH	M51576	M59282	M51590
NH	M51579	M59588	M51588
NH	M51580	M59586	M51589
BX480	M50421	M59148	M50487
BX481	M50422	M59198	M50506
BX482	M50429	M59195	M50542
BX483	M50430	M59143	M50491
BX484	M50431	M59137	M50507
BX485	M50432	M59162	M50484
BX487	M50434	M59132	M50424
BX488	M50435	M59145	M50427
BX489	M50436	M59141	M50488
BX490	M50437	M59147	M50490
BX491	M50439	M59187	M50425
BX492	M50440	M59203	M50481
BX493	M50454	M59140	M50480
BX494	M50455	M59230	M50492
BX	M50420	M59163	M50426
LO525	M50456	M59164	M50508
LO526	M50457	M59165	M50509
LO527	M50458	M59166	M50514
LO528	M50459	M59144	M50511

Marylebone ME
Set numbers from **ME750** upwards allocated

1985

London Midland Region

Buxton BX

BX480	M53420	M59152	M53474
BX481	M53421	M59148	M53487
BX482	M53429	M59195	M53507
BX483	M53430	M59187	M53491
BX484	M53431	M59137	M53496
BX485	M53456	M59230	M53504
BX486	M53459	M59183	M53427
BX487	M53514	M59228	M53556
BX488	M53598	M59144	M53542
BX489	M53932	M59207	M51569
BX490	M51927	M59390	M52049
BX491	M51934	M59387	M53634
BX492	M51935	M59389	M52050
BX493	M51936	M59794	M52051
BX494	M51938	M59386	M52039
BX495	M51943	M59388	M52058
BX496	M51947	M59155	M52062
BX497	M51950	M59149	M52065

Carlisle KD

M53950	M54227
M53951	M54235
M53952	M54244
M53953	M54242
M53954	M54265
M53955	M54262
M53956	M54238
M53957	M54236
M53958	M54239
M53959	M54243
M53960	M54241
M53962	M54245
M53963	M54240
M53964	M54247
M53965	M54248
M53966	M54249
M53967	M54250
M53968	M54251
M53969	M54252
M53973	M54263
M53980	M54256
M53982	M54246
M53987	M54270

Longsight LO

M53629	M54267
M53941	M54259
M53942	M54225
M53945	M54228
M53947	M54230
M53948	M54231
M53949	M54232
M53970	M54264
M53975	M54258
M53977	M54260
M53978	M54261
M53981	M54253
M53985	M54268
M53986	M54221
M51902	M54485
M51903	M54486
M51904	M54487
M51905	M54488
M51906	M54489
M51907	M54490
M51912	M54500
M51913	M54497
M51914	M54484
M51916	M54499
M51922	M54493
M51942	M54491
M51930	M52045
M53926	M51567
M78601	M78851
M55005	
M55006	

Tyseley TS

TS050	M55000		
TS052	M55002		
TS053	M55003		
TS054	M55004		
TS059	M55009		
TS061	M55011		
TS062	M55012		
TS400	M53315	M59118	M53330
TS408	M53305	M59536	M53321
TS412	M53317	M59131	M53324
TS417	M53307	M59129	M53323
TS418	M53310	M59128	M53326
TS419	M53318	M59114	M53328
TS500	M53061	M59442	M53092
TS501	M53057	M59725	M53097
TS502	M53861	M59597	M53912
TS503	M53076	M59631	M53118
TS504	M53059	M59610	M53104
TS505	M53065	M59638	M53094
TS506	M53100	M59612	M53840
TS507	M53069	M59714	M53099
TS508	M53852	M59741	M53871
TS509	M53072	M59648	M53105
TS510	M53056	M59448	M53093
TS511	M53054	M59626	M53106
TS512	M53051	M59608	M53113
TS513	M53077	M59735	M53120
TS514	M53870	M59614	M53923
TS515	M53067	M59615	M53103
TS516	M53074	M59595	M53110
TS517	M53824	M59640	M53906
TS518	M53050	M59642	M53121
TS519	M53064	M59589	M53111
TS520	M53071	M59616	M53101
TS521	M53838	M59634	M53893
TS522	M53078	M59613	M53109
TS523	M53075	M59643	M53903
TS524	M53068	M59622	M53112
TS525	M53830	M59443	M53883
TS526	M53070	M59441	M53095
TS527	M53058	M59632	M53108
TS528	M53062	M59715	M53117
TS529	M53828	M59716	M53127
TS530	M53831	M59713	M53884
TS531	M53052	M59757	M53914
TS532	M53818		M53098
TS534	M53053	M59629	M53886
TS535	M53860	M59438	M53913
TS536	M53833	M59621	M53107
TS537	M51130	M59627	M51143
TS539	M53063	M59717	M53119
TS540	M53832	M59625	M53885
TS541	M53835	M59641	M53888
TS543	M53079	M59439	M53114
TS545	M53819	M59647	M53915
TS554	M53821	M59674	M53875
TS555	M53826	M59617	M53905
TS600	M53857	M59130	M53910
TS601	M53081	M59543	M53123
TS602	M51133	M59570	M51146
TS603	M51136	M59106	M51149
TS604	M51129	M59101	M51142
TS605	M53851	M59527	M53904
TS606	M53082	M59602	M53124
TS607	M53862	M59600	M53872
TS608	M51131	M59596	M51144
TS609	M53827	M59533	M53880
TS610	M53837	M59603	M53890
TS611	M53055	M59611	M53116
TS612	M53060	M59593	M53902
TS613	M53863	M59594	M53916
TS614	M53842	M59609	M53895
TS615	M53850	M59591	M53102
TS616	M53834	M59607	M53887
TS617	M51138	M59107	M51151
TS618	M53073	M59592	M53891
TS619	M53854	M59598	M53907
TS620	M53849	M59606	M53878
TS621	M53866	M59604	M53919

Eastern Region

Cambridge CA

E51207	E54382
E51208	E54388
E51212	E54057
E51215	E54377
E51218	E54399
E51220	E54371
E51221	E54396
E51225	E54373
E51247	E54387

E51426	E54402
E51427	E54380
E51429	E54393
E51435	E54362
E51436	E54074
E51437	E54405
E51438	E54065
E51439	E54087
E51441	E54384
E51442	E54073
E51443	E54372
E51444	E54068
E53204	E54363

Neville Hill NL

E78956	E78706
E78957	E78707
E78958	E78708
E78959	E78709
E78960	E78710
E78961	E78711
E78962	E78712
E78966	E78716
E78967	E78717
E78968	E78718
E78969	E78719
E78970	E78720
E78971	E78721
E78972	E78722
E51230	E54369
E53134	E54063
E53135	E54092
E53136	E54076
E53137	E54218
E53155	E54294
E53198	E54220
E53202	E54385
E53207	E54088
E53216	E54075
E53224	E54401
E53227	E54070
E53257	E54090
E53296	E54064
E51425	E51503
E51428	E51496
E51430	E51504
E51431	E51501
E51432	E51498
E51433	E51499
E51434	E51502
E51440	E51497
E51548	E51556
E51550	E51558
E53277	E53284
E53289	E53272
E53599	E53635
E53617	E53633
E53626	E53636

Class 110 not kept in fixed formations

Norwich Crown Point NC

30	E53373	E54125
31	E53375	E54468
33	E53377	E54427
34	E53366	E54421
35	E53364	E54423
38	E51292	E54115
39	E51294	E54436
40	E51293	E54131
42	E51272	E54443
45	E53365	E54417
46	E53369	E54133
49	E51271	E54463
51	E51269	E54136
52	E51299	E54429
55	E51265	E54433
56	E51472	E54420
57	E51263	E54132
58	E53367	E54143
59	E53368	E54416
63	E51268	E54422
69	E51478	E54119
70	E53380	E54467
71	E53381	E54439
74	E53215	E54368
75	E51217	E54364
76	E51252	E54400
78	E53201	E54062
81	E53231	E54050
89	E51229	E54089

90	E53178	E59052	E53195
92	E53139	E59092	E53238
94	E53267	E59095	E53266
95	E53168	E59079	E53177
100	E53305	E59536	E53150
101	E53315	E59118	E53330
102	E53180	E59055	E53193
103	E53149	E59077	E53170
104	E51508	E59084	E51506
105	E53321	E59085	E53181
spare	E53182	E53191	

Scottish Region

Formations quite fluid at this time.

Ayr AY
Eastfield ED
Haymarket HA

101301	SC53144	SC59305	SC53254	HA
101302	SC53290	SC59071	SC53147	HA
101303	SC53292	SC59688	SC53184	HA
101304	SC51224	SC59066	SC53146	HA
101305	SC51227		SC53264	HA
101306	SC51228	SC59086	SC53260	HA
101307	SC51231	SC59542	SC53189	HA
101308	SC51232	SC59304	SC53194	HA
101309	SC51233	SC59566	SC53197	HA
101310	SC51234	SC59806	SC53163	HA
101311	SC51235	SC59042	SC53186	HA
101312	SC51237	SC59088	SC53175	HA
101313	SC51239	SC59047	SC53143	HA
101314	SC51240	SC59303	SC53187	HA
101315	SC51241			HA
101316	SC51242	SC59067	SC53172	HA
101317	SC51243	SC59060	SC53174	HA
101318	SC51244	SC59045	SC53176	HA
101319	SC51245	SC59090	SC53141	HA
101320	SC51248	SC59046	SC53749	HA
101321	SC51249	SC59048	SC53138	HA
101322	SC51250	SC59567	SC53159	AY
101323	SC51251	SC59210	SC52018	HA
101324	SC51253	SC59553	SC53269	HA
101325		SC59687	SC51516	ED
101326	SC51451	SC59558	SC51527	ED
101327	SC51453	SC59552	SC51807	ED
101328	SC51454	SC59562	SC51524	ED
101329	SC51455	SC59690	SC51537	ED
101330	SC51456	SC59555	SC51520	ED
101331	SC51457	SC59689	SC51804	ED
101332	SC51458	SC59692	SC51538	ED
101333	SC51459	SC59541	SC51805	ED
101335	SC51470	SC59565	SC53748	ED
101336	SC51464	SC59556	SC51525	ED
101337	SC51465	SC59563	SC51535	ED
101338	SC51466	SC59545	SC51529	ED
101339	SC51467	SC59564	SC51528	ED
101340	SC51468			ED
101341	SC51469	SC59557	SC51536	ED
101343	SC51795	SC59686	SC51526	ED
101345	SC51797	SC59691	SC51539	ED
101346	SC51798	SC59554	SC51532	ED
101347	SC51800	SC59072	SC51531	ED
101360	SC53158	SC59074	SC53192	HA
101361	SC53747	SC59112	SC53234	HA
101362		SC59073		HA
101363	SC53241	SC59049	SC53746	HA
101365	SC53239	SC59053	SC52028	HA
101366	SC53577	SC59215	SC52012	AY
104450	SC53452	SC59784	SC53505	AY
104451	SC53473	SC59559	SC53525	AY
104453	SC53461	SC59798	SC53245	AY
107425	SC51985	SC59797	SC52023	AY
107426	SC51986	SC59225	SC52030	AY
107427	SC51987	SC59792	SC52021	AY
107428	SC51988	SC59786	SC52013	AY
107429	SC51989	SC59783	SC52033	AY
107430	SC51990	SC59802	SC51803	AY
107431	SC51991	SC59789	SC52034	AY
107432	SC51992	SC59800	SC53565	AY
107433	SC51993	SC59080	SC53242	AY
107434	SC51994	SC59791	SC52011	AY
107435	SC51996	SC59807	SC53185	AY
107436	SC51997	SC59302	SC52024	AY
107437	SC51998	SC59782	SC52029	AY
107438	SC51999	SC59796	SC52020	AY
107439	SC52000	SC59785	SC52015	AY
107440	SC52001	SC59560	SC52025	AY
107441	SC52002	SC59069	SC52019	AY
107443	SC52004	SC59805	SC52016	AY
107444	SC52005	SC59804	SC52031	AY
107445	SC52006	SC59790	SC52036	AY
107446	SC52007	SC59795	SC53268	AY
107447	SC52008	SC59793	SC52027	AY
107449	SC52010	SC59801	SC53510	AY
116385	SC53090	SC59344	SC53132	AY
116387	SC53822	SC59330	SC53881	AY
116388	SC53823	SC59354	SC53876	AY
116389	SC53825	SC59329	SC53873	AY
116390	SC53829	SC59568	SC51518	AY
116392	SC53839	SC59374	SC53892	AY
116393	SC53841	SC59337	SC53879	AY
116394	SC53846	SC59345	SC53882	AY
116396	SC53859	SC59349	SC53899	AY

Western Region

B	**Bristol Division**	**Bristol BR**
C	**Cardiff Division**	**Cardiff CF**
L	**London Division**	**Reading RG**
P	**Plymouth Division**	**Laira LA**

L120	W55020		
L121	W55021		
L122	W55022		
L123	W55023		
L124	W55024		
P125	W55025		
P126	W55026		
L127	W55027		
L128	W55028		
L129	W55029		
L130	W55030		
L131	W55031		
C132	W55032		
C133	W55033		
L134	W55034		
L280	W54280		
L281	W54281		
L283	W54283		
L284	W54284		
L285	W54285		
L286	W54286		
L287	W54287		
L289	W54289		
C300	W53080	W59030	W53122
C301	W53084	W59373	W53126
C302	W53086	W59036	W53128
C303	W53087	W59037	W53129
C304	W53088	W59362	W53130
C305	W53089	W59039	W53131
C306	W53091	W59041	W53133
C307	W53083	W59550	W53820
C312	W53843	W59355	W53896
C313	W53847	W59040	W53900
C314	W53848	W59356	W53901
C315	W53855	W59363	W53908
C316	W53856	W59364	W53909
C317	W53858	W59446	W53911
C318	W53864	W59369	W53917
C319	W53868	W59371	W53918
C320	W53869	W59035	W53922
C330	W51128	W59357	W51141
C331	W51132	W59034	W51145
C332	W51134	W59444	W51147
C333	W51135	W59445	W51148
C334	W51139	W59033	W51152
C335	W51140	W59032	W51153
L400	W51332	W59484	W51374
L401	W51333	W59485	W51375
L402	W51335	W59487	W51377
L403	W51336	W59488	W51378
L404	W51337	W59489	W51379
L405	W51340	W59491	W51381
L406	W51341	W59493	W51383
L407	W51342	W59494	W51384
L408	W51343	W59495	W51385
L409	W51344	W59496	W51386
L410	W51345	W59497	W51387
L411	W51346	W59498	W51388
L412	W51347	W59499	W51389
L413	W51349	W59501	W51391
L414	W51350	W59502	W51392

L415	W51351	W59503	W51393
L416	W51353	W59505	W51395
L417	W51354	W59506	W51396
L418	W51355	W59507	W51397
L419	W51356	W59508	W51398
L420	W51358	W59510	W51400
L421	W51359	W59511	W51401
L422	W51360	W59512	W51402
L423	W51361	W59513	W51399
L424	W51362	W59514	W51404
B425	W51363	W59515	W51405
B426	W51364	W59516	W51406
B427	W51365	W59517	W51407
B428	W51366	W59518	W51408
B429	W51367	W59519	W51409
B430	W51368	W59520	W51410
B431	W51369	W59521	W51411
B432	W51370	W59522	W51412
B433	W51371	W59509	W51413
B434	W51372	W59490	W51414
B435	W51373	W59486	W51415
B436	W51376	W59500	W51334
B437	W51338	W59504	W51380
B438	W51339	W59492	W51382
B439	W51348	W59479	W51390
B450	W51352	W59539	W51394
P460	W51302	W59469	W51317
P461	W51303	W59470	W51318
P462	W51304	W59477	W51319
P463	W51305	W59472	W51320
P464	W51306	W59473	W51321
P465	W51307	W59474	W51322
P466	W51308	W59475	W51323
P467	W51309	W59476	W51324
P468	W51310	W59471	W51325
P469	W51311	W59480	W51326
P470	W51313	W59478	W51328
P471	W51314	W59481	W51329
B472	W51315	W59482	W51330
B473	W51316	W59483	W51331
P480	W51312	W51327	
L571	W51052	W59282	W51080
L572	W51054	W59413	W51082
L573	W51055	W59417	W51083
L574	W51056	W59415	W51084
L575	W51060	W59419	W51088
L576	W51062	W59421	W51090
B577	W51063	W59422	W51091
L578	W51064	W59423	W51092
L579	W51065	W59424	
L580	W51066	W59425	W51094
L581	W51067	W59426	W51095
L582	W51068	W59427	W51096
B583	W51069	W59428	W51097
L584	W51070	W59429	W51098
L585	W51075	W59434	W51103
B586	W51077	W59420	W51105
L587	W51078	W59436	W51106
L588	W51079	W59437	W51107
L589	W51057	W59414	W51100
B590	W51058	W59418	W51087
B591	W51059	W59433	W51102
L592	W51071	W59432	W51101
L593	W51072	W59431	W51085
L594	W51073	W59435	W51104
B595	W51074	W59430	W51086
B596	W51076	W59416	W51099
L615	W51781	W59682	W51788
L616	W51782	W59681	W51790
C800	W51445	W51515	
C801	W51446	W51517	
C802	W51449	W51521	
C803	W51450	W51522	
C804	W51452	W51523	
C805	W51462	W51530	
C806	W51799	W51808	
C811	W51519	W59548	W51801
C812	W51463	W59561	W51533
C813	W53304	W59122	W53329
C814	W53319	W59123	W53335
C820	W51500	W59093	W51512
C821	W51509	W59050	W51513
C822	W51495	W59096	W51510
C823	W51505	W59082	W51511

1988

1988 is a useful date to look at unit formations. During 1987 all units had been allocated to the new BR sectors. By 1988 the deliveries of second generation DMUs was increasing and it marks the beginning of the end for most of the first generation DMUs. It is also a useful point to view the large number of parcels units that had been created.

BR was at this time aspiring to run as many units as possible in fixed formations, and it issued an official list of these formations from which this is taken. This is, therefore, the only *complete* list of formations in this section; the only depots not attempting to maintain fixed formations were Bletchley and Marylebone, but their allocations are included for completeness.

London Midland Region

Bletchley BY

Not fixed formations

55004	*51570*	*54271*	*59163*
55011	*51571*	*54279*	*59206*
	51572	*54493*	*59367*
	51909		*59734*
	51912		*59735*
	51914		
	51942		
	53628		

Buxton BX

BX370	53626	59144	53636
BX371	53925		52039
BX372	53930	59148	52056
BX373	53932	59207	51569
BX374	51935	59183	51568
BX375	51938	59137	52065
BX376	51941	59388	52064
BX377	51943	59390	52049
BX378	51945	59149	52060
BX379	51947	59389	52050
BX380	51948	59187	53634
BX381	51950	59155	52062
Spare	52058	59152	

Chester CH

51417 54212
51418 54498
51419 54494
51421 54275
51422 54276
51424 54278
51901 54231
51902 54485
51903 54486
51904 54487
51905 54488
51906 54489
51907 54490
51908 54501
51911 54496
51913 54497
51917 54272
51920 54277
51931 52055
53924 54232
53927 54214
53929 54269
53931 54350
53938 54484
53939 52046
53940 54273
53222 53337
53303 53336
53306 53325
53307 53323
53309 53338
53317 53324
53318 53334
53824 59640 53906
53081 59120 53123
53904 59054 53910
Spare 51523 54260

Parcels units
53051 53072
53703 53713

Kingmoor KM

53606 54196
53950 54227
53951 54235
53952 54244
53953 54242
53954 54265
53955 54262
53956 54238
53957 54236
53958 54239
53959 54243
53960 54241
53962 54245
53963 54240
53964 54247
53965 54248
53966 54249
53967 54250
53968 54251
53969 54252
53973 54263

Longsight LO

910	55970	55980
911	55971	55981
912	55972	55982
913	55973	55983
914		55984
915	55975	55985
916	55976	55986
917	55977	55987
918	55978	55968
919	55979	55969
920	55966	55967

Newton Heath NH

51420 54085
53949 54056
53970 54264
53971 54504
53974 54503
53975 54258
53976 54225
53977 54268
53978 54261
53980 54256
53981 54253
53982 54246
53983 54266
53986 54221
53987 54270
53532 53487
53536 53520
53948 54177
53059 53117
53078 53109
53843 53896
53848 53901
53870 53923
53355 53812
53421 53529
53431 53512
53439 53492
53442 53516
53444 53493
53447 53531
53451 53518
53454 53528
53460 53496
53465 53499
53466 53511
53468 53494
53474 53427
53476 53425

	53534 53507
	53541 53522
	53934 53501
	53944 53500
	53087 59037 53129
	53091 59041 53133
	53839 59433 53857
	53862 59528 53872
	53867 59372 53920
	53869 59035 53922
Spare	53443 54071 59119
	54179 59374
	54184 59524
	54367 59541
	59552

Tyseley

T003	55993
T004	55994
T005	55995
T021	53038 54042
T022	53027 54041
T055	55005
T062	55012
T132	55032
T133	55033
T134	55034
T201	51927 53943
T207	53842 53895
T211	51937 54081
T221	53002 54047
T222	53005 54039
T223	53006 54009
T224	53008 54008
T225	53015 54015
T226	53018 54010
T227	53019 54027
T228	53021 54012
T229	53026 54013
T230	53030 54011
T231	53036 54006
T232	53037 54019
T233	53039 54024
T234	53044 54043
T301	51353 59505 51395
T302	51360 59512 51402
T303	51364 59516 51406
T304	51365 59517 51407
T306	51369 59521 53873
T307	51370 59522 51412
T308	51371 59509 51413
T311	51334 59500 51376
T312	51338 59504 51380
T313	51339 59492 51382
T314	51348 51390
T315	51352 59677 51394
T317	51314 59481 51329
T318	51316 59483 51331
T319	51129 59756 51149
T320	51138 59720 53890
T321	53854 59723 53907
T322	53071 59760 53880
T323	53818 59724 53093
T324	53053 59672 53101
T325	53060 59757 51142
T326	53822 59668 53881
T331	53090 59595 51133
T332	53865 59598 53073
T333	53082 59617 51131
T334	53054 59596 51136
T335	53844 59674 53827
T336	53849 59721 51130
T337	53853 59751 53838
T338	53058 59722 53050
T339	53863 59597 53850
T340	53837 59719 53826
T341	53061 59753 53079
T349	53866 59114 53887
T401	51662 59743 59610 53886
T402	51851 59658 59614 51146
T403	51852 59641 59616 53106
T404	51853 59604 59445 53919
T405	51854 59726 59615 51143
T406	51856 59606 59344 53132
T407	51858 59442 59594 53916
T408	51859 59448 59592 53114
T409	51860 59600 59375 53894
T410	51862 59602 59713 53124
T412	51867 59446 59591 53102
T413	51868 59632 59593 53902
T414	51869 59661 59613 51144
T415	51870 59589 59353 53921
T416	51876 59609 59648 53891
T417	51877 59444 59603 53893
T418	51880
T419	51884 59629 59590 51151
T420	51892 59607 59032 53092
T421	51897
T505	53065 59638 53121
T511	53832 59649 53913
T512	53063 59642 53119
T513	53077 59650 53120
T522	53833 59714 53100
T526	53070 59626 53095
T611	53055 59611 53116
T620	53056 59612 53878
T802	51865 59748 59636 53914
Spare	53825 59625 59643 59670
	59673 59741

On loan to BY	59666
Works	59745

Stored (at Crewe)

54061 59330 59621 59622
54091 59627 59631 59653
54375 59715 59716 59717
54381 59725 59744

Eastern Region

Cambridge CA

02	51208 54402
16	51438 54382
21	51444 54068

Diesel Parcels units

001	53361
701	51430 51441
702	51439 53221
703	53218 53230
704	53233 53255
705	53365 53368
706	53364 53373
707	53367 53369
708	55930 54900
709	55931 54901
710	53020 53046
711	53004 54028
713	53017 54014
714	53024 54033

Departmental Service units

301	DB975664	DB975637
302	DB975349	DB975539
303	TDB977123	TDB977125
304	TDB977124	TDB977126
305	TDB977453	TDB977454

Norwich NC

01	51207 54405
02	51221 54396
30	53359 54122
51	51218 54399
53	51247 54387
54	51230 54369
55	51427 54380
56	51429 54393
57	51435 54362
58	51213 54065
59	51442 54073
60	53204 54363
61	51178 54351
62	51194 54346
63	51428 54218
64	51191 54340
65	51189 54343
66	51192 54354
67	51187 54332
68	53293 54379
69	51179 54358
70	53202 54385
71	53219 54090
72	51201 54347
73	53252 54404
75	51206 54078
76	51252 54083
77	51177 54335
78	53201 54062
79	51184 54342
80	51180 54355
81	53231 54050
82	51188 54348
84	51209 54083
85	51185 54352
86	53228 54055
87	53203 54080
88	53208 54060
89	51229 54089
100	51506 59079 53181
101	51508 59055 53266
102	53193 59084 53168
104	53305 59085 53150
105	53180 59536 53321
106	53139 59092 53238
107	53177 59095 53267
108	53149 59077 53170
spare	54368 54388

Neville Hill NL

201	78709 78959
202	78711 78960
203	78722 78961
204	78712 78962
205	78714 78964
206	78717 78967
207	78718 78968
208	78719 78969
209	78713 78971
401	51809 51838
406	51823 52081
409	51827 51835
410	51828 51847
411	52066 51829
413	52069 52080
414	52071 52082
415	52072 51834
416	52073 51843
417	52075 52084
451	51204 53159
454	51215 53162
456	51425 51504
457	51431 51503
458	51434
459	51436 53750
463	51175 51501
464	53601
465	53607
502	51812 59069 51842
503	51813 59565 51830
505	51818 59246 52077
507	51824 59078 51845
508	51826 59250 52076
512	52067 59687 51840
566	59113
567	53633 59249
568	51455 59690 51538
569	51232 59060 53141
570	51465 59563 51526
571	51795 59686 51529

Sandite units

306	TDB977537	TDB977538
307	TDB977539	TDB977540

Heaton HT

402	53217 53237
405	53220 53240
410	51250 53161
413	51214 53235
414	51449 51521
418	53205 53191
425	51450 51522
429	51217 53178
432	53214 53261
433	51445 51515
442	53229 53182
443	53166 53196
480	51197
481	51203
486	53251 53258
500	51183 59052 53188
501	53227 59075 53263

504	51216 59123 53169	
505	53257 59477 53195	
515	53856 59418 53909	
516	53847 59471 53900	
518	51058 59364 51087	
519	51059 59040 51102	
	51308 59475 51323	
	51309 59415 51324	
	51458 51527	
Spare	51805 54054 54069 54074	
	51804 54075 54077 54219	
	54220 54345 54364	
	54365 54370 54391	
	54401 54406 54408	
Sandite unit		
308	TDB977535 TDB977536	

ScotRail

Ayr AY
Eastfield ED
Haymarket HA

101304	51224 59090 53241	AY
101305	51227 59045 53264	AY
101306	51228 59086 53243	HA
101307	51231 59688 53189	HA
101310	51234 59302 53163	HA
101315	51241 59042 53260	HA
101317	51243 59048 51587	HA
101318	51244 59061 53176	HA
101319	51245 59525 53269	HA
101320	51248 59046 53749	AY
101321	51249 59542 53146	AY
101324	51253 59304 53746	HA
101328	51454 59562 51524	ED
101330	51456 59555 51520	ED
101331	51457 59689 51802	ED
101336	51464 59556 51525	ED
101339	51467 59564 51516	ED
101340	51468 59692	ED
101346	51798 59554 51532	ED
101347	51800 59072 51531	ED
101350	51182 59124 53239	HA
101355	51174 59104 53245	HA
101356	53253 59696 51496	HA
101357	53198 59107 53244	ED
101358	51426 59809 53171	ED
101359	51210 59116 53164	HA
101360	53158 59074 53160	AY
101361	53654 59112 53234	AY
101362	53187 59073 53186	HA
101363	53194 59049 53185	AY
101364	53242 59080 53268	HA
101390	53250 59810 53645	ED
101393	53216 59794 53632	ED
101394	53294 53644	ED
104456	53464 59168 53517	ED
104457	53556 59228 53504	ED
104458	53478 59230 53530	ED
104459	53472 59195 52042	ED
107425	51985 59797 52028	ED
107426	51986 59803 52018	AY
107427	51987 59793 52020	AY
107428	51988 59786 52013	ED
107429	51989 59795 52023	AY
107430	51990 59802 51803	AY
107431	51991 59789 52035	ED
107432	51992 59800 52026	ED
107433	51993 59790 52012	AY
107434	51994 59791 52011	ED
107435	51996 59798 52019	AY
107436	51997 59784 52024	AY
107437	51998 59782 52021	AY
107438	51999 59796 52030	AY
107439	52000 59785 52036	AY
107440	52001 59783 52025	AY
107443	52004 59805 52016	AY
107444	52005 59804 52031	AY
107445	52006 59801 52015	AY
107446	52007 59806 52033	AY
107447	52008 59792 52029	AY
107449	52010 59807 52034	AY
108380	52053 59245 52059	ED
108381	52043 59248 53630	ED
108383	53933 59387 51566	ED
108384	51936 59386 52051	ED
108385	51925 59710 53643	ED
108386	51926 59697 53631	ED
108391	53291 59701 53641	ED
108392	53211 59817 53642	ED
120532	53699 59571 53658	HA
120533	53700 59532 53682	HA
120534	53732 59303 53686	HA
120535	53733 59065 53215	HA

Western Region

B	**Bristol Division**	**Bristol BR**
C	**Cardiff Division**	**Cardiff CF**
L	**London Division**	**Reading RG**
		Old Oak Common OO
P	**Plymouth Division**	**Laira LA**
S	**Swansea Division**	**Landore LE**

	55991		OO
	55992		OO
P100	55000		
L101	TDB975023	Route Learning car	OO
P103	55003		
P106	55006		
P109	55009		
L116	TDB975540	Route Learning car	OO
L120	55020		OO
L121	55021		OO
L122	55022		OO
L123	55023		OO
L124	55024		OO
L125	55025		OO
P126	55026		
L127	55027		OO
L128	55028		OO
L129	55029		OO
L130	55030		OO
L131	55031		OO
L135	TDB975659	Route Learning car	OO
L201	51212 54070		OO
L202	51225 54372		OO
L203	53207 53296		OO
L204	51220 54371		OO
L205	51443 53155		OO
L280	54280		OO
P281	54281		
L283	54283		OO
P284	54284		
L287	54287		OO
L289	54289		OO
C300	53080 53122		
C302	53086 53128		
C305	53089 53131		
L307	53083 53820	Parcels unit	OO
C315	53855 59381 53908		
C317	53858 59539 53911		
C330	51128 51141		
C331	51132 51145		
C332	51134 51147		
C333	51135 51148		
C334	51139 51152		
C335	51140 51153		
L400	51332 59484 51374		RG
L401	51333 59485 51375		RG
L402	51335 59487 51377		RG
L403	51336 59488 51378		RG
L404	51337 59489 51379		RG
L405	51340 59491 51381		RG
L406	51341 59493 51383		RG
L407	51342 59494 51384		RG
L408	51343 59495 51385		RG
L409	51344 59496 51386		RG
L410	51345 59497 51387		RG
L411	51346 59498 51388		RG
L412	51347 59499 51389		RG
L413	51349 59501 51391		RG
L414	51350 59502 51392		RG
L415	51351 59503 51393		RG
L417	51354 59506 51396		RG
L418	51355 59507 51397		RG
L419	51356 59508 51398		RG
L420	51358 59510 51400		RG
L421	51359 59511 51401		RG
L423	51361 59513 51399		RG
L424	51362 59514 51404		RG
L425	51363 59515 51405		RG
L428	51366 59518 51408		RG
L429	51367 59519 51409		RG
B430	51368 59520 51410		

B434	51372 59490 51414	
B435	51373 59486 51415	
P460	51302 59469 51317	
P461	51303 51318	
P463	51305 51320	
B464	51306 59473 51321	
C465	51307 51322	
P468	51310 51325	
P472	51315 59482 51330	
B480	51312 59479 51327	
L571	51052 59128 51080	RG
L572	51054 59540 51082	RG
L573	51055 59417 51083	RG
L574	51056 51095	RG
L575	51060 59419 51088	RG
L576	51062 59421 51090	RG
S577	51063 59422 51091	
L579	51065 59424 51103	RG
L580	51066 59425 51094	RG
L587	51078 59543 51106	RG
L588	51079 59437 51107	RG
L589	51057 59414 51100	RG
L592	51071 59530 51101	RG
L594	51073 59435 51104	RG
L595	51074 59430 51086	RG
L596	51076 59416 51099	RG
L701	53437 53479	OO
L702	53455 53539	OO
L703	53429 53470	OO
L704	53477 53540	OO
S801	51446 51517	
C808	51801 51519	
S809	53319 53335	
C820	51500 59093 51512	
C821	51509 59050 51513	
S822	51495 59096 51510	
L830	51190 59105 53333	RG
L831	51211 59526 53265	RG
L832	51226 59570 51499	RG
L835	51432 51498	RG
L837	51437 59115 53751	RG
L838	53308 59125 53331	RG
L839	53310 59306 53326	RG
L840	53311 59117 53322	RG
L841	53312 59091 53332	RG
L842	53314 59101 53327	RG
C851	51462 59382 51530	
C852	51463 59812 51533	
C853	51799 59694 51808	
P860	51181 51222	
P861	51205 53157	
P862	51223 53212	
P863	51246 53165	
P870	53200 53638	
P871	53256 53639	
P872	53247 53646	
P873	53248 53637	
P874	53315 53330	
C900	53224 59709 52048	
B920	53599	
B930	51416 59385 51511	
B931	53617 59130 53635	
B933	53941 59380 51505	
S940	51919	
S941	51922 51562	
S942	51928 52044	
S943	51930 51561	
S947	53942 51567	
S948	53926 51565	
S949	53945 51563	
S950	53928 52061	
S951	53935 52041	
S952	53625 52045	
P954	51932 52047	
P955	51933 52054	
P956	51939 52063	
P957	51940 52057	
S958	51924 52038	
B960	53602 54197	
B961	53608 54208	
B962	53612 54205	
B963	53613 54191	
B964	53614 54204	
B965	53616 54209	
B966	53618 54202	
B967	53619 54492	
B968	53620 54201	
B969	53621 54203	

B970 53622 54207
B971 53624 54194
B972 53627 54210
B973 53629 54267
B974 53947 54230
Spare (BR) 59383 59384
Spare (CF) 59561
Spare (LA) 51219 53223 59118
Spare (RG) 51319 59282

Ultrasonic Test Train (RG)
DB975007 DB975008
Sandite Vehicle (LA)
TDB977486
Sandite Vehicle (CF)
TDB977466

Marylebone ME

Marylebone depot transferred to the Western Region early in 1988. In October 1988 all Marylebone units were reallocated to Bletchley bringing them back within the London Midland Region.

Four-car units. Not fixed formations
51652 59651 59731 51680
51653 59652 59732 51857
51655 59654 59733 51863
51658 59655 59736 51871
51659 59656 59737 51872
51660 59657 59738 51873
51661 59659 59739 51874
51663 59660 59740 51875
51664 59662 59746 51879
51665 59663 59747 51883
51666 59664 59749 51885
51667 59665 59750 51886
51668 59667 59752 51887
51669 59669 59754 51888
51670 59671 59755 51889
51671 59675 59758 51890
51673 59676 59759 51891
51674 59678 59761 51894
51675 59727 59762 51896
51677 59728 59763 51899
51678 59729 59764 51900

Two-car units. Not fixed formations.
⑨ All Class 115 DMBS gangway fitted.
51651 54213
51654 54222
51656 54499
51657 54495
51676 54224
51679 54257
51849 54274
51855 54491
51866 54228
51878 54259
51893 54223
51895 54500

1990

London Midland Region

Chester CH

CH250 51418 54485
CH252 53975 54258
CH253 51421 54275
CH254 51422 54277
CH255 51424 54232
CH256 51901 54231
CH257 53970 54264
CH258 51903 54486
CH260 51905 54488
CH261 51906 54489
CH263 51908 54501
CH264 51911 54496
CH265 51913 54497
CH267 51920 54276
CH268 53924 54278
CH269 53927 54214
CH270 53929 54269
CH271 53931 54260
CH272 53938 54484
CH273 53976 54225
CH274 53978 54261
CH275 53980 54256
CH276 53981 54253
CH277 53982 54246
CH278 53983 54266
CH351 51937 59390 51943
CH610 53447 53531
CH611 53451 53517
CH615 53534 51505
CH620 51948 51568
CH621 51902 52049
CH622 51904 52050
CH623 51907 52058
CH624 51917 53516
CH625 51938 52065
CH626 51941 52064
CH627 51945 52060
CH628 51947 53634
CH629 51950 52062
CH631 53925 52039
CH632 53930 52056
CH633 53932 51569
CH634 53933 51566
CH635 53934 53512
CH637 53977 53645
CH640 51800 51513
CH641 51245 53269
CH642 51426 53171
CH643 51462 51511
CH645 53224 51509
CH646 53198 53244

Longsight LO

LO347 53216 59303 53294
LO348 51210 59065 53253
LO350 51927 59388 51935

Tyseley TS

The unit numbers were painted on the cab ends in the style of WR units.

T012 55032
T013 55033
T014 55034
T021 53021 54012
T022 53002 54047
T023 53036 54006
T024 53044 54043
T025 53005 54039
T026 53006 54010
T027 53019 54027
T301 51353 59505 51395
T302 51360 59512 51402
T303 51364 59516 51406
T304 51365 59517 51407
T305 51368 59520 51410
T306 51369 59521 51411
T307 51370 59522 51412
T308 51371 59509 51413
T309 51372 59490 51414
T310 51373 59486 51415
T311 51334 59500 51376
T312 51338 59504 51380
T313 51339 59492 51382
T314 51348 59677 51390
T315 51352 59745 51394
T316 51306 59473 51321
T317 51314 59481 51329
T318 51316 59483 51331
T319 51129 59756 51149
T320 51138 59720 53890
T321 53854 59723 53907
T322 53071 59760 53880
T323 53818 53093
T324 53053 59672 53101
T325 53060 59757 51142
T326 53822 59444 53881
T332 53865 59598 53073
T333 53082 59617 51131
T334 53054 59596 53850
T335 53844 59674 53827
T336 53849 59721 51130
T337 53853 59751 53838
T338 53050 59722 53058
T339 53090 59724 53863
T340 53826 59719 53837
T341 53061 59753 53079
T342 53055 59673 53056
T401 51662 59610 59743 53886
T402 51851 59658 59614 51146
T403 51852 59641 59616 53106
T404 51853 59604 59445 53919
T405 51854 59615 59335 51143
T406 51856 59606 59344 53893
T407 51858 59594 59442 53916
T408 51859 59448 59592 53114
T409 51860 59600 59367 53894
T410 51862 59602 59713 53124
T411 51898 59625 59597 53873
T412 51867 59446 59591 53116
T413 51868 59632 59593 53902
T414 51869 59661 59613 51144
T415 51870 59589 59353 53921
T416 51876 59609 59648 53891
T417 51877 59603 59726 53897
T419 51884 59629 59668 51151
T420 51892 59607 59032 53092
T421 51897 59741 59612 53878

Eastern Region

Heaton HT

Set numbers not carried. Only class 108s maintained fixed formations at Heaton

HT001 53950 54227
HT002 53951 54235
HT003 53952 54244
HT004 53953 54242
HT005 53954 54265
HT006 53955 54262
HT007 53956 54238
HT008 53957 54236
HT009 53958 54239
HT010 53959 54243
HT011 53960 54241
HT012 53962 54245
HT013 53963 54240
HT014 53964 54247
HT015 53973 54263

Anglia Region

Cambridge CA

Set numbers not carried

220 51207 54405
221 51208 54402
222 51438 54382
223 51444 54068
224 51445 54028
902 53027 54041
911 53020 53046
928 55928 54903
929 55929 54904
930 55930 54900
931 55931 54901
932 55932 54902

Norwich Crown Point NC

51 51218 54399
53 51247 54387
54 51230 54369
55 51427 54368
56 51429 54393
58 51213 54380
59 51442 54073
63 51428 54218
65 51189 54343
66 51192 54354
67 51187 54332
68 53293 54062
70 53202 54388

72	51201 54347	
76	51252 54352	
78	53201 54379	
81	53231 54050	
85	51185 54065	
86	53228 54055	
88	53208 54060	
100	51508 59095 53181	
101	51506 59055 53266	
102	53149 59084 53193	
103	53305 59536 53180	
106	53139 59092 53238	
107	53177 59079 53267	
108	53168 59077 53170	

ScotRail

Eastfield ED
Haymarket HA

101304	51224 59090 53241	ED
101306	51228 59086 53243	HA
101307	51231 59688 53189	HA
101310	51234 59302 53163	HA
101315	51241 59042 53260	HA
101318	51244 59061 53176	HA
101321	51249 59542 53146	ED
101350	51182 59124 53239	HA
101360	53158 59074 53160	ED
101363	53185 59049 53194	ED
107725	51985 59797 52028	ED
107726	51986 59803 52018	ED
107727	51987 52020	ED
107728	51988 59786 52013	ED
107729	51989 59795 52023	ED
107730	51990 59802 51803	ED
107731	51991 59789 52035	HA
107732	51992 59800 52026	HA
107733	51993 59790 52012	ED
107734	51994 59791 52011	ED
107735	51996 52019	ED
107736	51997 59784 52025	ED
107737	51998 59782 52021	ED
107738	51999 59796 52030	ED
107739	52000 59785 52036	HA
107740	52001 59783 52024	ED
107743	52004 59805 52016	ED
107744	52005 59804 52031	ED
107745	52006 59801 52015	ED
107746	52007 59806 52033	ED
107747	52008 59792 52029	ED
107749	52010 59807 52034	ED

Western Region

B	**Bristol Division**	**Bristol BR**
C	**Cardiff Division**	**Cardiff CF**
L	**London Division**	**Reading RG**
		Old Oak Common OO
P	**Plymouth Division**	**Laira LA**
S	**Swansea Division**	**Landore LE**

P100	55000	
P103	55003	
P104	55004	
P105	55005	
P106	55006	
P109	55009	
P111	55011	
P112	55012	
L120	55020	OO
L121	55021	OO
L122	55022	OO
L123	55023	OO
L124	55024	OO
L125	55025	OO
P126	55026	
L127	55027	OO
L128	55028	OO
L129	55029	OO
L130	55030	OO
L131	55031	OO
L201	51212 54070	OO
L202	51225 54372	OO
L204	51220 54371	OO
L205	51443 54385	OO
L206	51215 54081	OO
L207	51221 54396	OO
L210	53083 54289	OO
L211	53155 54287	OO
L280	54280	OO
L283	54283	OO
C362	53086 53128	
C393	51135 51148	
C394	51139 51152	
C395	51140 51153	
L400	51332 59484 51374	RG
L401	51333 59485 51375	RG
L402	51335 59487 51377	RG
L403	51336 59488 51378	RG
L404	51337 59489 51379	RG
L405	51340 59491 51381	RG
L406	51341 59493 51383	RG
L407	51342 59494 51384	RG
L408	51343 59495 51385	RG
L409	51344 59496 51386	RG
L410	51345 59497 51387	RG
L411	51346 59498 51388	RG
L412	51347 59499 51389	RG
L413	51349 59501 51391	RG
L414	51350 59502 51392	RG
L415	51351 59503 51393	RG
L417	51354 59506 51396	RG
L418	51355 59507 51397	RG
L419	51356 59508 51398	RG
L420	51358 59510 51400	RG
L421	51359 59511 51401	RG
L423	51361 59513 51399	RG
L424	51362 59514 51404	RG
L425	51363 59515 51405	RG
L428	51366 59518 51408	RG
L429	51367 59519 51409	RG
C472	51315 51327	
C480	51312 51330	
L575	51060 59419 51088	RG
L576	51062 59421 51090	RG
L579	51065 59424 51103	RG
L580	51066 59425 51094	RG
L588	51079 59437 51107	RG
L594	51073 59435 51104	RG
L595	51074 59430 51086	RG
L596	51076 59416 51099	RG
L700	53207 53296	OO
L701	53437 53479	OO
L702	53455 53539	OO
L703	53429 53470	OO
L704	53477 53540	OO
L705	51319 53820	OO
P825	53165 59118 51246	
P826	53223 59561 51219	
P827	53212 59130 51223	
P828	51936 59386 52051	
P829	51500 59093 53157	
L830	51190 59105 53333	RG
L831	51211 59115 53265	RG
L832	51226 59570 51499	RG
L833	51425 59543 51504	RG
L834	51431 59526 51501	RG
L835	51432 59530 51498	RG
L836	51434 59540 51503	RG
L837	51437 59128 53751	RG
L838	53308 59125 53331	RG
L839	53310 59306 53326	RG
L840	53311 59117 53322	RG
L841	53312 59091 53332	RG
L842	53314 59101 53327	RG
P860	51181 51530	
P861	51205 51512	
P862	51179 51570	
P870	53200 53638	
P871	53256 53639	
P872	53247 53646	
P873	53248 53637	
P874	53313 53330	
C901	51128 53632 51141	
C902	53642 51132 51145	
C903	51134 52053 51147	
C904	51133 52059 51136	
S939	51926 53631	
S940	51919 52048	
S941	51922 51562	
S942	51928 59382 52044	
S943	51930 51561	
S944	51931 52055	
S945	51925 59380 53643	
S946	53939 52046	
S947	53942 51567	
S948	53928 51565	
S949	53945 51563	
S950	53926 52061	
S951	53935 52041	
S952	53625 52045	
P954	51932 52047	
P955	51933 52054	
P956	51939 52063	
P957	51940 52057	
S958	51924 59384 52038	
S959	53947 53633	
B960	53602 54197	
B961	53608 54208	
B962	53612 54492	
B963	53948 54268	
B964	53614 54204	
B965	53616 54209	
B966	53618 54202	
B967	53619 54230	
B968	53620 54203	
B969	53621 54201	
B970	53622 54207	
B971	53941 54205	
C972	53627 54210	
C973	53692 54267	
C974	51416 54498	
C975	53624 54273	
C976	51417 54212	
C977	51419 54494	
C983	53617 53635	
C995	51436 53169	

1995

Bletchley BY
Corkerhill CK
Haymarket HA
Heaton HT
Longsight LO
Norwich NC
Old Oak Common OM
Penzance PZ
Reading RG
Salisbury SA
Tyseley TS
Derby Technical Centre ZA

101651	53201 54379	LO
101652	53198 54346	LO
101653	51426 54358	LO
101654	51800 54408	LO
101655	51428 54062	LO
101656	51230 54056	LO
101657	53211 54085	LO
101658	51175 54091	LO
101659	51213 54352	LO
101660	51189 54343	LO
101661	51463 54365	LO
101662	53228 54055	LO
101663	51201 54347	LO
101664	51442 54061	LO
101665	51429 54393	LO
101676	51205 51803	LO
101677	51179 51496	LO
101678	51210 53746	LO
101679	51224 51533	LO
101680	53204 53163	LO
101681	51228 51506	LO
101682	53256 51505	LO
101683	51177 59303 53269	LO
101684	51187 51509	CK
101685	53164 59539 53160	LO
101686	51231 51500	CK

101687 51247 51512 CK
101688 51431 51501 CK
101689 51185 51511 CK
101690 51435 53177 CK
101691 51253 53171 CK
101692 53253 53170 CK
101693 51192 53266 CK
101694 51188 53268 CK
101695 51226 51499 CK
101835 51432 51498 LO
101836 51434 51503 TS
101840 53311 53322 LO
101841 53312 53332 LO
101842 53314 59110 53327 PZ
117301 51353 59505 51395 HA
117304 51365 51407 PZ
117305 51368 59520 51410 PZ
117306 51369 59521 51411 HA
117308 51371 59509 51413 HA
117310 51373 59486 51415 HA
117311 51334 59500 51376 HA
117313 51339 59492 51382 HA
117314 51352 59489 51394 HA
117700 51332 51374 carried **L700** BY
117701 51350 51392 carried **L701** BY
117702 51356 51398 carried **L702** BY
117703 51359 51401 carried **L703** BY
117704 51341 51383 carried **L704** BY
117705 51358 51400 carried **L705** BY
117706 51366 51408 carried **L706** BY
117707 51335 51377 carried **L707** BY
117708 51336 51378 PZ
117709 51344 51386 PZ
117720 51354 51396 carried **L720** BY
117721 51363 51405 carried **L721** BY
117722 51345 51387 carried **L722** BY
117723 51361 51399 PZ
121123 55023 carried **L123** BY
121127 55027 carried **L127** BY
121129 55029 carried **L129** BY
121131 55031 carried **L131** BY

T021 51073 51104 TS
T022 51079 53921 TS
T023 53053 53132 TS
T024 53055 51375 TS
T025 51381 51333 TS

Departmental

977391 999602 977392 ZA
977693 977694 ZA
977775 977776 ZA
T003 51151 977826 53124 TS
T004 977828 51144 TS
T005 977824 977825 TS
T006 51314 53818 TS
T007 51349 51391 TS
L119 ADB975042 BY
L120 ADB977722 OM
L121 ADB977723 BY
L122 977873 SA
L124 977858 AL
L125 977859 SA
L128 977860 RG
L130 977866 SA
906 977808 977809 HT
907 977811 977812 HT
909 977750 977815 HT
910 977836 977921 HT
922 977818 977819 HT
931 977832 977833 carried **S001** HA
932 977830 977831 carried **S002** HA
933 977834 977835 carried **S003** HA
991 977895 977896 LO
992 977897 977898 LO
993 977899 977900 LO
994 977901 977902 LO
995 977903 977904 LO
977932 977933 NC

2000

Bletchley BY
Corkerhill CK
Longsight LO

101653 51426 54358 LO
101654 51800 54408 LO
101655 51428 54062 LO
101656 51230 54056 LO
101657 53211 54085 LO
101658 51175 54091 LO
101659 51213 54352 LO
101660 51189 54343 LO
101661 51463 54365 LO
101662 53228 54055 LO
101663 51201 54347 LO
101664 51442 54061 LO
101676 51205 51803 LO
101677 51179 51496 LO
101678 51210 53746 LO
101679 51224 51533 LO
101680 53204 53163 LO
101681 51228 51506 LO
101682 53256 51505 LO
101683 51177 53269 LO
101684 51187 51509 CK
101685 53164 53160 LO
101686 51231 51500 CK
101687 51247 51512 CK
101689 51185 51511 CK
101690 51435 53177 CK
101691 51253 53171 CK
101692 53253 53170 CK
101693 51192 53266 CK
101694 51188 53268 CK
101695 51226 51499 CK
101835 51432 51498 LO
101840 53311 53322 CK
117702 51356 51398 BY
121027 55027 BY
121029 55029 BY
121031 55031 BY

2010

To bring the picture right up-to-date, here are the remaining first generation units still on the National Railway at the beginning of 2010.

Aylesbury AY
Cardiff Canton CF
Derby RTC Business Park ZA
Rugby Rail Plant RU
St. Leonards SE
Tyseley Locomotive Works TS

121020 55020 AL
121032 55032 CF
201001 60116 60529 70262 69337 60501 60118 SE
Spare 60000 SE
960010 977858 AL
960013 977866 AL
960014 977873 AL
960015 975042 AL
960021 977723 AL
960301 977987 977992 977988 AL
975025 CAROLINE ZA
977968 RU

Awaiting disposal
51432 51498 Shoeburyness
960011 977859 TM
960302 977975 CF
960303 977976 CF

AC Cars four-wheel railbus W79975 is seen at Swindon Shed on 27th September 1959. *P H Groom*

Left: On 14th May 1966 two four-wheel railbuses are stored at 67C Ayr. The dumb-buffers formed of metal bands on Wickham SC79968 do not seem to have performed well as it has been shunted into a siding with Park Royal SC79974. *P Foster*

Below: The two-car Battery Railcar unit which was built for the for Aberdeen-Ballater service, SC79998 and SC79999, is seen in this official photograph on 10th March 1958. *BR*

Hastings Line Class 201 6S unit 1002 is seen at the rear of a 12-car formation at Hither Green.
P J Sharpe

The 10.45 Charing Cross to Hastings service on 31 December 1983 was formed of Class 202 6L unit 1011 and Class 203 unit 1035 (out of view at the rear). The formation is seen approaching Tonbridge with S60014 leading.
A Dasi-Sutton

On 14th September 1977 Class 203 6B unit 1037 is seen at Charing Cross ready to form the 11.46 train to Hastings.
B Morrison

Class 205 2H Hampshire unit 1114 is seen at Eastleigh on an Alton line service. It was reformed as a three-car unit in October 1959. *P J Sharpe*

On 26th June 1976 Class 205 3H unit 1124 in blue livery is seen working the 14.55 Southampton-Portsmouth service at Netley. This photograph shows clearly just how much of the DMBSO was taken up by the engine room. *J Scrace*

Class 205 3H unit 1110 at seen on 18th January 1969 at Reading General with DTCsoL S60809 leading. *J H Bird*

Class 205 unit 205029 is working the 11.40 Salisbury to Portsmouth Harbour at Dunbridge on 7th April 1988. The black triangle painted on the front shows platform staff which end of the unit the luggage compartment is located. *J Scrace*

Newly converted Class 206 "Tadpole" unit 1204 (with S60005 leading) is seen leaving Redhill on the 13.04 service to Tonbridge on 12th March 1965. *J Scrace*

Now in blue livery Class 206 unit 1206 (with S60007 leading) is arriving at Guildford with the 13.26 Reading to Tonbridge service on 16th June 1977. The difference in width between the Hastings line carriages and the converted EMU DrivingTrailer can be seen clearly in this shot. *D Maxey*

This view of 1206 in blue and grey livery on the Hastings- Ashford working at Ham Street and Orlestone on 27th July 1982 shows the former EMU DTSso S77510 leading. *B Morrison*

Above: New Class 207 3D East Sussex unit 1301 is seen at Eastleigh on 10th March 1962. *L Elsey*

Right: Now painted in BR blue livery Class 207 1306 (with S60925 leading) is seen at Redhill on 27th March 1973. *J Scrace*

Appendix: Year End Totals

	1954	1955	1956	1957	1958	1959	1960	1961	1962	1963	1964	1965	1966	1967	1968	1969	1970	1971	1972
Class 100				**62**	**80**	**80**	**80**	**80**	**80**	**80**	**80**	**80**	**77**	**77**	**77**	**77**	**77**	**72**	**42**
Class 100 DMBS				31	40	40	40	40	40	40	40	40	39	39	39	39	39	36	23
Class 100 DTCL				31	40	40	40	40	40	40	40	40	38	38	38	38	38	36	19
Class 101			**36**	**226**	**422**	**440**	**446**	**446**	**446**	**446**	**446**	**445**	**445**	**444**	**443**	**443**	**443**	**443**	**441**
Class 101 DMBS			4	56	145	154	154	154	154	154	154	154	154	154	154	154	154	154	153
Class 101 DMCL			18	68	86	86	86	86	86	86	86	85	85	85	85	85	85	85	85
Class 101 DMLV																			
Class 101 DTCL				43	114	123	123	123	123	123	123	123	123	123	123	123	123	123	122
Class 101 TBSL			7	28	28	28	28	28	28	28	28	28	28	28	27	27	27	27	27
Class 101 TCL					18	18	18	18	18	18	18	18	18	18	18	18	18	18	18
Class 101 TSL			7	31	31	31	31	31	31	31	31	31	31	30	30	30	30	30	30
Class 101 TSLRB							6	6	6	6	6	6	6	6	6	6	6	6	6
Class 102				**20**	**20**	**179**	**179**	**179**	**179**	**179**	**179**	**179**	**179**	**178**	**178**	**178**	**178**	**178**	**178**
Class 102 DMBS				10	10	63	63	63	63	63	63	63	63	63	63	63	63	63	63
Class 102 DMCL				10	10	63	63	63	63	63	63	63	63	63	63	63	63	63	63
Class 102 TCL						53	53	53	53	53	53	53	53	52	52	52	52	52	52
Class 103				**2**	**40**	**40**	**40**	**40**	**40**	**40**	**40**	**40**	**40**	**40**	**40**	**40**	**38**	**35**	**26**
Class 103 DMBS				1	20	20	20	20	20	20	20	20	20	20	20	20	19	17	12
Class 103 DTCL				1	20	20	20	20	20	20	20	20	20	20	20	20	19	18	14
Class 104				**129**	**286**	**302**	**302**	**302**	**301**	**300**	**300**	**300**	**300**	**298**	**295**	**293**	**293**	**292**	**291**
Class 104 DMBS				43	71	71	71	71	71	71	71	71	71	71	71	70	70	70	70
Class 104 DMCL				43	100	108	108	108	108	107	107	107	107	105	105	104	104	104	104
Class 104 DTCL					15	15	15	15	15	15	15	15	15	15	15	15	15	15	15
Class 104 TBSL					22	26	26	26	25	25	25	25	25	25	25	25	25	25	25
Class 104 TCL				43	56	56	56	56	56	56	56	56	56	56	53	53	53	53	53
Class 104 TSL					22	26	26	26	26	26	26	26	26	26	26	26	26	25	24
Class 104 DHBS																			
Class 104 DHSL																			
Class 105				**77**	**215**	**274**	**274**	**273**	**272**	**272**	**272**	**272**	**272**	**270**	**269**	**246**	**242**	**240**	**239**
Class 105 DMBS				33	98	128	128	128	127	127	127	127	127	125	125	122	121	120	119
Class 105 DMCL				11	33	33	33	32	32	32	32	32	32	32	32	28	27	27	27
Class 105 DMLV																			
Class 105 DTCL				22	65	94	94	94	94	94	94	94	94	94	94	94	94	93	93
Class 105 TCL				11	19	19	19	19	19	19	19	19	19	19	18	2			
Class 106			**12**	**28**	**28**	**28**	**28**	**28**	**28**	**28**	**28**	**28**	**28**	**28**	**28**	**28**	**28**	**28**	**27**
Class 106 DMBS			6	14	14	14	14	14	14	14	14	14	14	14	14	14	14	14	14
Class 106 DTCL			6	14	14	14	14	14	14	14	14	14	14	14	14	14	14	14	13
Class 107							**24**	**78**	**78**	**78**	**78**	**78**	**78**	**78**	**78**	**78**	**78**	**78**	**78**
Class 107 DMBS							8	26	26	26	26	26	26	26	26	26	26	26	26
Class 107 DMCL							8	26	26	26	26	26	26	26	26	26	26	26	26
Class 107 TSL							8	26	26	26	26	26	26	26	26	26	26	26	26
Class 108					**89**	**209**	**317**	**333**	**333**	**333**	**332**	**332**	**330**	**330**	**329**	**324**	**322**	**317**	**314**
Class 108 DMBS					30	90	144	152	152	152	151	151	150	150	149	147	145	142	141
Class 108 DMCL					17	26	50	58	58	58	58	58	58	58	58	57	57	57	57
Class 108 DTCL					25	76	106	106	106	106	106	106	105	105	105	103	103	101	99
Class 108 TBSL					6	6	6	6	6	6	6	6	6	6	6	6	6	6	6
Class 108 TSL					11	11	11	11	11	11	11	11	11	11	11	11	11	11	11
Class 109				**6**	**10**	**10**	**10**	**6**	**6**	**6**	**6**	**6**	**6**	**4**	**4**	**4**	**4**		
Class 109 DMBS				3	5	5	5	3	3	3	3	3	3	2	2	2	2		
Class 109 DTCL				3	5	5	5	3	3	3	3	3	3	2	2	2	2		
Class 110								**75**	**90**	**87**	**87**	**87**	**87**	**87**	**87**	**87**	**87**	**85**	**85**
Class 110 DMBC								25	30	29	29	29	29	29	29	29	29	28	28
Class 110 DMCL								25	30	29	29	29	29	29	29	29	29	29	29
Class 110 TSL								25	30	29	29	29	29	29	29	29	29	28	28

	1973	1974	1975	1976	1977	1978	1979	1980	1981	1982	1983	1984	1985	1986	1987	1988	1989	1990	1991
Class 100	**43**	**41**	**41**	**41**	**37**	**32**	**31**	**30**	**24**	**15**	**2**	**1**	**1**	**1**	**1**	**1**			
Class 100 DMBS	25	25	26	26	23	21	21	21	16	8	2	1	1	1	1	1			
Class 100 DTCL	18	16	15	15	14	11	10	9	8	7									
Class 101	**439**	**438**	**436**	**611**	**608**	**608**	**607**	**606**	**601**	**601**	**597**	**594**	**584**	**529**	**430**	**354**	**252**	**211**	**192**
Class 101 DMBS	153	153	153	215	213	213	213	212	211	211	209	208	206	189	156	137	104	91	79
Class 101 DMCL	84	84	84	145	144	144	143	143	143	143	143	142	141	137	113	99	65	53	49
Class 101 DMLV														8	8	8			
Class 101 DTCL	122	121	121	121	121	121	121	121	121	121	121	121	120	94	70	60	44	41	39
Class 101 TBSL	27	27	27	27	27	27	27	27	26	26	26	26	26	23	22	16	11	8	8
Class 101 TCL	18	18	18	70	70	70	70	70	70	70	69	69	64	55	45	23	18	12	12
Class 101 TSL	30	30	30	30	30	30	30	30	30	30	29	28	27	23	16	11	10	6	5
Class 101 TSLRB	5	5	3	3	3	3	3	3											
Class 102	**178**	**178**	**177**																
Class 102 DMBS	63	63	63																
Class 102 DMCL	63	63	62																
Class 102 TCL	52	52	52																
Class 103	**25**	**25**	**24**	**23**	**23**	**23**	**23**	**21**	**19**	**2**									
Class 103 DMBS	12	12	11	11	11	11	11	10	9	1									
Class 103 DTCL	13	13	13	12	12	12	12	11	10	1									
Class 104	**291**	**290**	**290**	**288**	**285**	**284**	**283**	**279**	**232**	**173**	**161**	**132**	**116**	**84**	**73**	**69**	**27**	**12**	**10**
Class 104 DMBS	70	69	69	69	69	69	69	69	67	64	63	57	50	34	30	30	17	10	8
Class 104 DMCL	104	104	104	103	101	100	99	97	85	62	59	43	37	27	24	24	7	2	2
Class 104 DTCL	15	15	15	15	15	15	15	15	14	13	13	10	10	5	3				
Class 104 TBSL	25	25	25	25	25	25	25	25	19	11	8	5	4	3	1				
Class 104 TCL	53	53	53	53	53	53	53	51	32	17	12	11	11	11	11	11	2		
Class 104 TSL	24	24	24	23	22	22	22	22	15	4	4	4	4	4	4	4	1		
Class 104 DHBS										1	1	1							
Class 104 DHSL										1	1	1							
Class 105	**237**	**237**	**236**	**261**	**260**	**250**	**250**	**246**	**180**	**133**	**98**	**81**	**67**	**24**	**10**	**7**			
Class 105 DMBS	118	118	118	131	131	127	127	126	85	64	48	41	33	7	1				
Class 105 DMCL	27	27	27	27	27	27	27	25	13	4	1	1	1	1	1	1			
Class 105 DMLV														9	7	6			
Class 105 DTCL	92	92	91	103	102	96	96	95	82	65	49	39	33	7	1				
Class 105 TCL																			
Class 106	**27**	**27**	**27**																
Class 106 DMBS	14	14	14																
Class 106 DTCL	13	13	13																
Class 107	**77**	**77**	**77**	**77**	**77**	**77**	**77**	**77**	**77**	**77**	**76**	**68**	**67**	**66**	**66**	**66**	**66**	**59**	**24**
Class 107 DMBS	25	25	25	25	25	25	25	25	25	25	25	23	23	22	22	22	22	20	8
Class 107 DMCL	26	26	26	26	26	26	26	26	26	26	25	22	21	21	21	21	21	19	8
Class 107 TSL	26	26	26	26	26	26	26	26	26	26	26	23	23	23	23	23	23	20	8
Class 108	**314**	**312**	**310**	**310**	**309**	**309**	**307**	**306**	**306**	**305**	**304**	**302**	**298**	**297**	**285**	**280**	**275**	**252**	**182**
Class 108 DMBS	141	139	139	139	138	138	137	137	137	136	136	135	133	133	128	124	122	113	82
Class 108 DMCL	57	57	56	56	56	56	56	55	55	55	55	54	54	54	53	53	52	49	40
Class 108 DTCL	99	99	98	98	98	98	97	97	97	97	96	96	95	94	88	87	85	80	53
Class 108 TBSL	6	6	6	6	6	6	6	6	6	6	6	6	5	5	5	5	5	2	1
Class 108 TSL	11	11	11	11	11	11	11	11	11	11	11	11	11	11	11	11	11	8	6
Class 109																			
Class 109 DMBS																			
Class 109 DTCL																			
Class 110	**85**	**85**	**85**	**85**	**85**	**85**	**85**	**85**	**84**	**84**	**66**	**66**	**66**	**63**	**44**	**37**	**23**	**1**	
Class 110 DMBC	28	28	28	28	28	28	28	28	28	28	28	28	28	26	17	13	8		
Class 110 DMCL	29	29	29	29	29	29	29	29	28	28	28	28	28	27	17	14	11		
Class 110 TSL	28	28	28	28	28	28	28	28	28	28	10	10	10	10	10	10	4	1	

	1992	1993	1994	1995	1996	1997	1998	1999	2000	2001	2002	2003	2004	2005	2006	2007	2008
Class 100																	
Class 100 DMBS																	
Class 100 DTCL																	
Class 101	**145**	**93**	**89**	**81**	**77**	**75**	**73**	**67**	**48**	**15**	**12**						
Class 101 DMBS	67	47	45	40	38	37	36	33	26	8	6						
Class 101 DMCL	37	26	25	25	23	22	22	21	16	6	6						
Class 101 DMLV																	
Class 101 DTCL	28	16	15	14	14	14	13	11	6	1							
Class 101 TBSL																	
Class 101 TCL	8	2	2	1	1	1	1	1									
Class 101 TSL	5	2	2	1	1	1	1	1									
Class 101 TSLRB																	
Class 102																	
Class 102 DMBS																	
Class 102 DMCL																	
Class 102 TCL																	
Class 103																	
Class 103 DMBS																	
Class 103 DTCL																	
Class 104	**2**																
Class 104 DMBS	2																
Class 104 DMCL																	
Class 104 DTCL																	
Class 104 TBSL																	
Class 104 TCL																	
Class 104 TSL																	
Class 104 DHBS																	
Class 104 DHSL																	
Class 105																	
Class 105 DMBS																	
Class 105 DMCL																	
Class 105 DMLV																	
Class 105 DTCL																	
Class 105 TCL																	
Class 106																	
Class 106 DMBS																	
Class 106 DTCL																	
Class 107																	
Class 107 DMBS																	
Class 107 DMCL																	
Class 107 TSL																	
Class 108	**37**																
Class 108 DMBS	16																
Class 108 DMCL	8																
Class 108 DTCL	13																
Class 108 TBSL																	
Class 108 TSL																	
Class 109																	
Class 109 DMBS																	
Class 109 DTCL																	
Class 110																	
Class 110 DMBC																	
Class 110 DMCL																	
Class 110 TSL																	

1954 1955 1956 1957 1958 1959 1960 1961 1962 1963 1964 1965 1966 1967 1968 1969 1970 1971 1972 1973 1974 1975 1976 1977 1978 1979 1980 1981 1982 1983 1984 1985 1986 1987 1988 1989 1990 1991 1992 1993 1994 1995 1996 1997 1998 1999 2000 2001 2002 2003 2004 2005 2006 2007 2008

	1954	1955	1956	1957	1958	1959	1960	1961	1962	1963	1964	1965	1966	1967	1968	1969	1970	1971	1972	1973	1974	1975	1976	1977	1978	1979	1980	1981
Class 111				**29**	**38**	**48**	**62**	**62**	**62**	**62**	**62**	**62**	**61**	**61**	**61**	**60**	**59**	**59**	**59**	**59**	**59**	**59**	**59**	**59**	**59**	**58**	**58**	**58**
Class 111 DMBS				11	14	17	24	24	24	24	24	24	23	23	23	23	22	22	22	22	22	22	22	22	22	22	22	22
Class 111 DMCL				7	10	13	20	20	20	20	20	20	20	20	20	20	20	20	20	20	20	20	20	20	20	20	20	20
Class 111 DTCL				4	4	4	4	4	4	4	4	4	4	4	4	4	4	4	4	4	4	4	4	4	4	4	4	4
Class 111 TSL				7	10	14	14	14	14	14	14	14	14	14	14	13	13	13	13	13	13	13	13	13	13	12	12	12
Class 111 DHBS																												
Class 111 DHCL																												
Class 112						**50**	**50**	**50**	**50**	**50**	**50**	**50**	**50**	**48**	**18**													
Class 112 DMBS						25	25	25	25	25	25	25	25	24	9													
Class 112 DMCL						25	25	25	25	25	25	25	25	24	9													
Class 113						**16**	**50**	**50**	**49**	**49**	**48**	**48**	**47**	**47**	**47**													
Class 113 DMBS						8	25	25	25	25	25	25	25	25	25													
Class 113 DMCL						8	25	25	24	24	23	23	22	22	22													
Class 114			**29**	**100**	**100**	**100**	**100**	**100**	**99**	**99**	**99**	**98**	**98**	**96**	**96**	**96**	**94**	**90**	**90**	**90**	**90**	**90**	**90**	**90**	**90**	**90**	**90**	**90**
Class 114 DMBS			14	50	50	50	50	50	49	49	49	49	49	48	48	48	48	45	45	45	45	45	45	45	45	45	45	45
Class 114 DTCL			15	50	50	50	50	50	50	50	50	49	49	48	48	48	46	45	45	45	45	45	45	45	45	45	45	45
Class 114 DMLV																												
Class 114 DTLV																												
Class 114/1 DMLV																												
Class 114/1 DTLV																												
Class 115							**164**	**164**	**164**	**164**	**164**	**164**	**164**	**164**	**164**	**164**	**164**	**163**	**163**	**163**	**163**	**163**	**163**	**163**	**162**	**162**	**162**	**162**
Class 115 DMBS							82	82	82	82	82	82	82	82	82	82	82	82	82	82	82	82	82	82	81	81	81	81
Class 115 TCL							41	41	41	41	41	41	41	41	41	41	41	41	41	41	41	41	41	41	41	41	41	41
Class 115 TS							41	41	41	41	41	41	41	41	41	41	41	40	40	40	40	40	40	40	40	40	40	40
Class 116				**168**	**320**	**320**	**320**	**319**	**319**	**319**	**319**	**316**	**312**	**308**	**308**	**308**	**308**	**308**	**308**	**308**	**308**	**307**	**306**	**310**	**310**	**310**	**309**	**308**
Class 116 DMBS				56	108	108	108	108	108	108	108	107	105	105	105	105	105	105	105	105	105	104	104	106	106	106	106	106
Class 116 DMS				56	108	108	108	107	107	107	107	106	104	103	103	103	103	103	103	103	103	103	102	104	104	104	103	103
Class 116 TC				46	94	94	94	94	94	94	94	93	93	90	90	90	90	90	90	90	90	90	90	90	90	90	90	89
Class 116 TS				10	10	10	10	10	10	10	10	10	10	10	10	10	10	10	10	10	10	10	10	10	10	10	10	10
Class 116 DMLV																												
Class 117						**3**	**123**	**123**	**123**	**123**	**123**	**123**	**123**	**123**	**122**	**122**	**122**	**122**	**122**	**122**	**122**	**122**	**122**	**122**	**122**	**122**	**122**	**122**
Class 117 DMBS						1	42	42	42	42	42	42	42	42	41	41	41	41	41	41	41	41	41	41	41	41	41	41
Class 117 DMS						1	42	42	42	42	42	42	42	42	42	42	42	42	42	42	42	42	42	42	42	42	42	42
Class 117 TCL						1	39	39	39	39	39	39	39	39	39	39	39	39	39	39	39	39	39	39	39	39	39	39
Class 118							**45**	**45**	**45**	**45**	**45**	**45**	**45**	**45**	**45**	**45**	**45**	**45**	**45**	**45**	**45**	**45**	**45**	**45**	**45**	**45**	**45**	**45**
Class 118 DMBS							15	15	15	15	15	15	15	15	15	15	15	15	15	15	15	15	15	15	15	15	15	15
Class 118 DMS							15	15	15	15	15	15	15	15	15	15	15	15	15	15	15	15	15	15	15	15	15	15
Class 118 TCL							15	15	15	15	15	15	15	15	15	15	15	15	15	15	15	15	15	15	15	15	15	15
Class 119					**22**	**79**	**81**	**81**	**81**	**81**	**81**	**81**	**81**	**81**	**77**	**77**	**77**	**77**	**77**	**77**	**77**	**77**	**77**	**77**	**77**	**77**	**77**	**77**
Class 119 DMBC					8	27	28	28	28	28	28	28	28	28	26	26	26	26	26	26	26	26	26	26	26	26	26	26
Class 119 DMSL					8	27	28	28	28	28	28	28	28	28	26	26	26	26	26	26	26	26	26	26	26	26	26	26
Class 119 TSLRB					6	25	25	25	25	25	25	25	25	25	25	25	25	25	25	25	25	25	25	25	25	25	25	25
Class 120				**18**	**131**	**156**	**169**	**194**	**194**	**194**	**194**	**194**	**194**	**189**	**186**	**186**	**186**	**186**	**186**	**186**	**186**	**186**	**186**	**186**	**186**	**186**	**185**	**184**
Class 120 DMBC				16	49	56	56	65	65	65	65	65	65	65	64	64	64	64	64	64	64	64	64	64	64	64	63	62
Class 120 DMSL				2	42	49	56	65	65	65	65	65	65	65	64	64	64	64	64	64	64	64	64	64	64	64	64	64
Class 120 TSL							3	10	10	10	10	10	10	7	7	7	7	7	7	7	7	7	7	7	7	7	7	7
Class 120 TSLRB					40	51	54	54	54	54	54	54	54	52	51	51	51	51	51	51	51	51	51	51	51	51	51	51
Class 120 DMLV																												
Class 121							**15**	**26**	**26**	**26**	**26**	**26**	**26**	**26**	**26**	**25**	**25**	**25**	**24**	**24**	**24**	**24**	**24**	**24**	**23**	**23**	**23**	**23**
Class 121 DMBS							14	16	16	16	16	16	16	16	16	16	16	16	16	16	16	16	16	16	15	15	15	15
Class 121 DTS							1	10	10	10	10	10	10	10	10	9	9	9	8	8	8	8	8	8	8	8	8	8
Class 122					**29**	**29**	**29**	**29**	**29**	**29**	**29**	**29**	**29**	**29**	**29**	**27**	**27**	**24**	**18**	**18**	**18**	**17**	**16**	**13**	**13**	**13**	**13**	**13**
Class 122 DMBS					20	20	20	20	20	20	20	20	20	20	20	18	18	15	12	12	12	11	10	10	10	10	10	10
Class 122 DTS					9	9	9	9	9	9	9	9	9	9	9	9	9	9	6	6	6	6	6	3	3	3	3	3
Class 122 DMLV																												

	1982	1983	1984	1985	1986	1987	1988	1989	1990	1991	1992	1993	1994	1995	1996	1997	1998	1999	2000	2001	2002	2003	2004	2005	2006	2007	2008
Class 111	**56**	**56**	**56**	**55**	**47**	**27**	**25**	**5**	**5**	**5**	**4**	**2**	**2**	**1**	**1**	**1**	**1**	**1**									
Class 111 DMBS	18	13	8	4	4																						
Class 111 DMCL	14	8	4																								
Class 111 DTCL	4	4	4	4	3	2	1		1	2	1	1	1	1	1	1	1	1									
Class 111 TSL	12	12	12	11	8	7	6	5	4	3	3	1	1														
Class 111 DHBS	4	9	14	18	16	9	9																				
Class 111 DHCL	4	10	14	18	16	9	9																				
Class 112																											
Class 112 DMBS																											
Class 112 DMCL																											
Class 113																											
Class 113 DMBS																											
Class 113 DMCL																											
Class 114	**90**	**90**	**88**	**88**	**86**	**84**	**44**	**30**	**14**	**4**																	
Class 114 DMBS	45	45	44	44	42	35	16	8	7	2																	
Class 114 DTCL	45	45	44	44	41	36	16	7	7	2																	
Class 114 DMLV					1	7	4	3																			
Class 114 DTLV					2	5	2	2																			
Class 114/1 DMLV						1	3	5																			
Class 114/1 DTLV							3	5																			
Class 115	**159**	**159**	**158**	**156**	**156**	**155**	**152**	**149**	**137**	**105**	**25**	**7**	**3**	**1**													
Class 115 DMBS	78	78	78	76	76	76	76	76	74	57	18	5	3	1													
Class 115 TCL	41	41	41	41	41	41	41	39	35	28	3	2															
Class 115 TS	40	40	39	39	39	38	35	34	28	20	4																
Class 116	**300**	**260**	**258**	**242**	**233**	**162**	**105**	**86**	**77**	**71**	**39**	**18**	**10**														
Class 116 DMBS	105	104	104	98	94	72	50	40	35	30	16	4	3														
Class 116 DMS	103	101	101	96	94	69	43	36	34	34	20	14	7														
Class 116 TC	82	46	44	35	32	16	10	9	7	6	2																
Class 116 TS	10	9	9	9	9	3	2	1	1	1	1																
Class 116 DMLV				4	4	2																					
Class 117	**121**	**121**	**121**	**121**	**121**	**121**	**121**	**121**	**120**	**120**	**112**	**81**	**68**	**53**	**50**	**48**	**40**	**6**									
Class 117 DMBS	41	41	41	41	41	41	41	41	40	40	38	29	26	24	23	22	18	3									
Class 117 DMS	41	41	41	41	41	41	41	41	41	41	38	29	26	22	20	19	16	3									
Class 117 TCL	39	39	39	39	39	39	39	39	39	39	36	23	16	7	7	7	6										
Class 118	**45**	**45**	**45**	**44**	**44**	**35**	**20**	**12**	**10**	**7**	**6**	**2**	**2**														
Class 118 DMBS	15	15	15	14	14	12	8	4	3	2	2	1	1														
Class 118 DMS	15	15	15	15	15	13	8	5	4	3	2	1	1														
Class 118 TCL	15	15	15	15	15	10	4	3	3	2	2																
Class 119	**77**	**77**	**77**	**76**	**73**	**53**	**28**	**24**	**21**	**21**	**15**	**6**	**6**														
Class 119 DMBC	26	26	26	26	24	18	10	8	7	7	5	2	2														
Class 119 DMSL	26	26	26	25	25	18	10	8	8	8	5	2	2														
Class 119 TSLRB	25	25	25	25	24	17	8	8	6	6	5	2	2														
Class 120	**180**	**164**	**153**	**138**	**64**	**12**	**7**																				
Class 120 DMBC	63	63	62	52	22	6	4																				
Class 120 DMSL	64	64	60	56	17	5	3																				
Class 120 TSL	7	7	7	6	1																						
Class 120 TSLRB	46	30	24	20	10	1																					
Class 120 DMLV				4	14																						
Class 121	**23**	**23**	**23**	**23**	**21**	**21**	**20**	**20**	**20**	**18**	**9**	**4**	**4**	**4**	**4**	**3**	**3**	**3**	**3**	**3**	**1**	**1**	**1**	**1**	**2**	**2**	**2**
Class 121 DMBS	15	15	15	15	15	15	15	15	15	15	9	4	4	4	4	3	3	3	3	3	1	1	1	1	2	2	2
Class 121 DTS	8	8	8	8	6	6	5	5	5	3																	
Class 122	**10**	**9**	**9**	**9**	**8**	**8**	**8**	**8**	**6**	**6**	**5**	**2**	**1**	**1**	**1**	**1**	**1**	**1**	**1**	**1**	**1**	**1**					
Class 122 DMBS	10	9	9	8	7	7	7	7	5	5	4	2	1	1	1	1	1	1	1	1	1	1					
Class 122 DTS																											
Class 122 DMLV				1	1	1	1	1	1	1	1																

	1954	1955	1956	1957	1958	1959	1960	1961	1962	1963	1964	1965	1966	1967	1968	1969	1970	1971	1972
Class 123										**40**	**40**	**40**	**40**	**40**	**40**	**40**	**35**	**35**	**35**
Class 123 DMBSL										10	10	10	10	10	10	10	10	10	10
Class 123 DMSK										10	10	10	10	10	10	10	10	10	10
Class 123 TCK										10	10	10	10	10	10	10	10	10	10
Class 123 TSL										5	5	5	5	5	5	5	5	5	5
Class 123 TSLRB										5	5	5	5	5	5	5			
Class 124							**49**	**51**	**51**	**51**	**51**	**51**	**51**	**51**	**51**	**51**	**51**	**51**	**48**
Class 124 DMC							16	17	17	17	17	17	17	17	17	17	17	17	17
Class 124 MBSK							16	17	17	17	17	17	17	17	17	17	17	17	17
Class 124 TFLRB							8	8	8	8	8	8	8	8	8	8	8	8	5
Class 124 TSL							9	9	9	9	9	9	9	9	9	9	9	9	9
Class 124 TBSK																			
Class 125					**3**	**60**	**60**	**60**	**60**	**60**	**60**	**60**	**60**	**60**	**60**	**60**	**60**	**59**	**59**
Class 125 DMBS					1	20	20	20	20	20	20	20	20	20	20	20	20	19	19
Class 125 DMS					1	20	20	20	20	20	20	20	20	20	20	20	20	20	20
Class 125 TS					1	20	20	20	20	20	20	20	20	20	20	20	20	20	20
Class 126						**66**	**66**	**68**	**68**	**68**	**68**	**68**	**68**	**68**	**68**	**68**	**68**	**68**	**66**
Class 126 DMBSL						22	22	22	22	22	22	22	22	22	22	22	22	22	22
Class 126 DMSL						23	23	23	23	23	23	23	23	23	23	23	23	23	23
Class 126 TCL						11	11	11	11	11	11	11	11	11	11	11	11	11	11
Class 126 TFK						10	10	10	10	10	10	10	10	10	10	10	10	10	10
Class 126 TFKRB								2	2	2	2	2	2	2	2	2	2	2	
Class 127						**120**	**120**	**120**	**120**	**120**	**119**	**119**	**117**	**117**	**116**	**116**	**116**	**116**	**115**
Class 127 DMBS						60	60	60	60	60	59	59	58	58	58	58	58	58	58
Class 127 TS						30	30	30	30	30	30	30	29	29	29	29	29	29	29
Class 127 TSL						30	30	30	30	30	30	30	30	30	29	29	29	29	28
Class 127 DMLV																			
Class 128							**10**	**10**	**10**	**10**	**10**	**10**	**10**	**10**	**10**	**10**	**10**	**9**	**9**
Class 128 DMPMV							10	10	10	10	10	10	10	10	10	10	10	9	9
Class 129					**3**	**3**	**3**	**3**	**3**	**3**	**3**	**3**	**3**	**3**	**3**	**3**	**3**	**3**	**2**
Class 129 DMPMV					3	3	3	3	3	3	3	3	3	3	3	3	3	3	2
Class 130												**3**	**7**	**7**	**7**	**7**	**7**	**6**	**4**
Class 130 DPMV												2	6	6	6	6	6	6	4
Class 130 TPMV												1	1	1	1	1	1		
Class 131																		**3**	**3**
Class 131 DPMV																		3	3
Class 201				**42**	**42**	**42**	**42**	**42**	**42**	**42**	**42**	**42**	**42**	**42**	**39**	**38**	**38**	**38**	**38**
Class 201 DMBSO				14	14	14	14	14	14	14	14	14	14	14	14	14	14	14	14
Class 201 TFK				7	7	7	7	7	7	7	7	7	7	7	6	6	6	6	6
Class 201 TSOL				21	21	21	21	21	21	21	21	21	21	21	19	18	18	18	18
Class 202				**24**	**54**	**54**	**54**	**54**	**54**	**54**	**54**	**54**	**54**	**54**	**54**	**54**	**54**	**54**	**54**
Class 202 DMBSO				10	18	18	18	18	18	18	18	18	18	18	18	18	18	18	18
Class 202 TFK				5	9	9	9	9	9	9	9	9	9	9	9	9	9	9	9
Class 202 TSOL				9	27	27	27	27	27	27	27	27	27	27	27	27	27	27	27
Class 203					**42**	**42**	**42**	**42**	**42**	**42**	**40**	**40**	**40**	**40**	**40**	**40**	**40**	**40**	**40**
Class 203 DMBSO					14	14	14	14	14	14	14	14	14	14	14	14	14	14	14
Class 203 TFK					7	7	7	7	7	7	7	7	7	7	7	7	7	7	7
Class 203 TRB					7	7	7	7	7	7	5	5	5	5	5	5	5	5	5
Class 203 TSOL					14	14	14	14	14	14	14	14	14	14	14	14	14	14	14
Class 205				**36**	**44**	**74**	**74**	**74**	**95**	**95**	**95**	**95**	**95**	**95**	**95**	**95**	**95**	**95**	**95**
Class 205 DMBSO				18	22	26	26	26	33	33	33	33	33	33	33	33	33	33	33
Class 205 DTCsoL				18	22	26	26	26	33	33	33	33	33	33	33	33	33	33	33
Class 205 TSO						22	22	22	29	29	29	29	29	29	29	29	29	29	29
Class 207									**57**	**57**	**57**	**57**	**57**	**57**	**57**	**57**	**57**	**57**	**57**
Class 207 DMBSO									19	19	19	19	19	19	19	19	19	19	19
Class 207 DTSO									19	19	19	19	19	19	19	19	19	19	19
Class 207 TCsoL									19	19	19	19	19	19	19	19	19	19	19

	1973	1974	1975	1976	1977	1978	1979	1980	1981	1982	1983	1984	1985	1986	1987	1988	1989	1990
Class 123	**35**	**35**	**35**	**35**	**34**	**34**	**33**	**33**	**33**	**33**	**33**							
Class 123 DMBSL	10	10	10	10	10	10	9	9	9	9	9							
Class 123 DMSK	10	10	10	10	9	9	9	9	9	9	9							
Class 123 TCK	10	10	10	10	10	10	10	10	10	10	10							
Class 123 TSL	5	5	5	5	5	5	5	5	5	5	5							
Class 123 TSLRB																		
Class 124	**48**	**48**	**43**	**43**	**42**	**42**	**42**	**37**	**35**	**35**	**33**							
Class 124 DMC	17	17	17	17	16	16	16	16	16	16	15							
Class 124 MBSK	17	17	17	17	17	17	17	12										
Class 124 TFLRB	5	5																
Class 124 TSL	9	9	9	9	9	9	9	9	9	9	8							
Class 124 TBSK									10	10	10							
Class 125	**59**	**59**	**59**	**39**														
Class 125 DMBS	19	19	19	13														
Class 125 DMS	20	20	20	13														
Class 125 TS	20	20	20	13														
Class 126	**65**	**65**	**65**	**65**	**64**	**64**	**63**	**63**	**38**	**6**								
Class 126 DMBSL	22	22	22	22	22	22	21	21	13	2								
Class 126 DMSL	22	22	22	22	21	21	21	21	13	2								
Class 126 TCL	11	11	11	11	11	11	11	11	8	2								
Class 126 TFK	10	10	10	10	10	10	10	10	4									
Class 126 TFKRB																		
Class 127	**115**	**115**	**114**	**109**	**107**	**107**	**106**	**106**	**106**	**103**	**60**	**44**	**64**	**65**	**62**	**57**	**36**	**25**
Class 127 DMBS	58	58	57	55	53	53	52	52	52	49	7							
Class 127 TS	29	29	29	27	27	27	27	27	27	27	27	18	18	18	15	10	10	6
Class 127 TSL	28	28	28	27	27	27	27	27	27	27	26	26	26	26	26	26	26	19
Class 127 DMLV													20	21	21	21		
Class 128	**9**	**9**	**9**	**9**	**9**	**9**	**8**	**7**	**7**	**5**	**5**	**5**	**5**	**5**	**5**	**5**	**5**	
Class 128 DMPMV	9	9	9	9	9	9	8	7	7	5	5	5	5	5	5	5	5	
Class 129																		
Class 129 DMPMV																		
Class 130	**4**	**4**	**4**	**4**														
Class 130 DPMV	4	4	4	4														
Class 130 TPMV																		
Class 131	**3**	**3**	**3**	**3**	**3**	**3**	**3**	**1**	**1**	**1**								
Class 131 DPMV	3	3	3	3	3	3	3	1	1	1								
Class 201	**38**	**38**	**38**	**38**	**38**	**38**	**38**	**38**	**38**	**38**	**37**	**37**	**37**					
Class 201 DMBSO	14	14	14	14	14	14	14	14	14	14	14	14	14					
Class 201 TFK	6	6	6	6	6	6	6	6	6	6	6	6	6					
Class 201 TSOL	18	18	18	18	18	18	18	18	18	18	17	17	17					
Class 202	**54**	**54**	**54**	**54**	**54**	**54**	**54**	**54**	**54**	**54**	**54**	**51**	**51**	**11**	**11**	**4**	**4**	
Class 202 DMBSO	18	18	18	18	18	18	18	18	18	18	18	17	17	5	5	2	2	
Class 202 TFK	9	9	9	9	9	9	9	9	9	9	9	9	9	1	1			
Class 202 TSOL	27	27	27	27	27	27	27	27	27	27	27	25	25	5	5	2	2	
Class 203	**40**	**40**	**40**	**40**	**40**	**40**	**40**	**34**	**34**	**34**	**34**	**34**	**34**	**3**	**2**			
Class 203 DMBSO	14	14	14	14	14	14	14	13	13	13	13	13	13	2	1			
Class 203 TFK	7	7	7	7	7	7	7	7	7	7	7	7	7					
Class 203 TRB	5	5	5	5	5	5	5											
Class 203 TSOL	14	14	14	14	14	14	14	14	14	14	14	14	14	1	1			
Class 205	**95**	**95**	**95**	**95**	**95**	**95**	**95**	**95**	**95**	**95**	**95**	**95**	**94**	**94**	**65**	**63**	**60**	**57**
Class 205 DMBSO	33	33	33	33	33	33	33	33	33	33	33	33	32	32	22	21	20	19
Class 205 DTCsoL	33	33	33	33	33	33	33	33	33	33	33	33	33	33	21	21	20	19
Class 205 TSO	29	29	29	29	29	29	29	29	29	29	29	29	29	29	22	21	20	19
Class 207	**57**	**57**	**57**	**57**	**57**	**57**	**57**	**57**	**57**	**57**	**57**	**57**	**56**	**56**	**30**	**24**	**24**	**21**
Class 207 DMBSO	19	19	19	19	19	19	19	19	19	19	19	19	18	18	10	8	8	7
Class 207 DTSO	19	19	19	19	19	19	19	19	19	19	19	19	19	19	10	8	8	7
Class 207 TCsoL	19	19	19	19	19	19	19	19	19	19	19	19	19	19	10	8	8	7

	1991	1992	1993	1994	1995	1996	1997	1998	1999	2000	2001	2002	2003	2004	2005	2006	2007	2008
Class 123																		
Class 123 DMBSL																		
Class 123 DMSK																		
Class 123 TCK																		
Class 123 TSL																		
Class 123 TSLRB																		
Class 124																		
Class 124 DMC																		
Class 124 MBSK																		
Class 124 TFLRB																		
Class 124 TSL																		
Class 124 TBSK																		
Class 125																		
Class 125 DMBS																		
Class 125 DMS																		
Class 125 TS																		
Class 126																		
Class 126 DMBSL																		
Class 126 DMSL																		
Class 126 TCL																		
Class 126 TFK																		
Class 126 TFKRB																		
Class 127	**25**	**11**																
Class 127 DMBS																		
Class 127 TS	6	1																
Class 127 TSL	19	10																
Class 127 DMLV																		
Class 128																		
Class 128 DMPMV																		
Class 129																		
Class 129 DMPMV																		
Class 130																		
Class 130 DPMV																		
Class 130 TPMV																		
Class 131																		
Class 131 DPMV																		
Class 201						**2**	**2**	**2**	**2**	**2**	**2**	**2**	**2**	**2**	**2**	**2**	**2**	**2**
Class 201 DMBSO						1	1	1	1	1	1	1	1	1	1	1	1	1
Class 201 TFK																		
Class 201 TSOL						1	1	1	1	1	1	1	1	1	1	1	1	1
Class 202						**2**	**2**	**2**	**2**	**2**	**2**	**3**	**3**	**3**	**3**	**3**	**3**	**3**
Class 202 DMBSO						1	1	1	1	1	1	2	2	2	2	2	2	2
Class 202 TFK																		
Class 202 TSOL						1	1	1	1	1	1	1	1	1	1	1	1	1
Class 203																		
Class 203 DMBSO																		
Class 203 TFK																		
Class 203 TRB																		
Class 203 TSOL																		
Class 205	**55**	**51**	**47**	**37**	**34**	**32**	**32**	**32**	**28**	**25**	**25**	**24**	**22**					
Class 205 DMBSO	19	17	15	12	11	11	11	11	10	9	9	8	8					
Class 205 DTCsoL	18	17	16	12	11	11	11	11	10	9	9	9	9					
Class 205 TSO	18	17	16	13	12	10	10	10	8	7	7	7	5					
Class 207	**19**	**18**	**12**	**9**	**9**	**9**	**9**	**9**	**8**	**8**	**8**	**8**	**6**	**2**				
Class 207 DMBSO	7	7	5	4	4	4	4	4	4	4	4	4	3	1				
Class 207 DTSO	7	7	5	4	4	4	4	4	4	4	4	4	3	1				
Class 207 TCsoL	5	4	2	1	1	1	1	1										

	1954	1955	1956	1957	1958	1959	1960	1961	1962	1963	1964	1965	1966	1967	1968	1969	1970	1971	1972
Class 251						**12**	**36**	**36**	**36**	**36**	**36**	**36**	**36**	**36**	**36**	**36**	**36**	**36**	**36**
Class 251 DMBFL						4	4	4	4	4	4	4	4	4	4	4	4	4	4
Class 251 DMBS							6	6	6	6	6	6	6	6	6	6	6	6	6
Class 251 MFLRK						4	4	4	4	4	4	4	4	4	4	4	4	4	4
Class 251 MPSL							6	6	6	6	6	6	6	6	6	6	6	6	6
Class 251 TFLRK							6	6	6	6	6	6	6	6	6	6	6	6	6
Class 251 TPFL						4	10	10	10	10	10	10	10	10	10	10	10	10	10
Derby Hydro-mech	**16**	**16**	**16**	**16**	**16**	**16**	**16**	**16**	**16**	**16**									
Derby Hydro-mech DMBS	8	8	8	8	8	8	8	8	8	8									
Derby Hydro-mech DMCL	8	8	8	8	8	8	8	8	8	8									
Derby Early Lightweight	**8**	**108**	**201**	**201**	**201**	**201**	**200**	**198**	**197**	**195**	**194**	**192**	**181**	**114**	**39**				
Derby DMBS	4	45	91	91	91	91	91	89	89	88	87	85	84	57	19				
Derby DMC		5	5	5	5	5	5	5	5	5	5	5	3						
Derby DMCL			5	5	5	5	5	5	2	2	2	2	2						
Derby DMS		5	5	5	5	5	5	5	5	5	5	5	1						
Derby DTCL	4	30	72	72	72	72	71	71	73	72	72	72	72	52	20				
Derby DTSL		13	13	13	13	13	13	13	13	13	13	13	13	5					
Derby TBSL		5	5	5	5	5	5	5	5	5	5	5	3						
Derby TSL		5	5	5	5	5	5	5	5	5	5	5	3						
Early Metropolitan-Cammell		**14**	**72**	**72**	**72**	**72**	**72**	**72**	**72**	**72**	**71**	**71**	**71**	**58**	**25**				
Metropolitan-Cammell DMBS		7	36	36	36	36	36	36	36	36	35	35	35	29	12				
Metropolitan-Cammell DTCL		7	7	7	7	7	7	7	7	7	7	7	7						
Metropolitan-Cammell DTSL			29	29	29	29	29	29	29	29	29	29	29	29	13				
Swindon Inter-city			**34**	**64**	**64**	**64**	**64**	**64**	**64**	**64**	**64**	**64**	**64**	**64**	**64**	**63**	**63**	**63**	**3**
Swindon DMBSL			21	29	29	29	29	29	29	29	29	29	29	29	29	28	28	28	1
Swindon DMSL				14	14	14	14	14	14	14	14	14	14	14	14	14	14	14	
Swindon TFK			13	13	13	13	13	13	13	13	13	13	13	13	13	13	13	13	2
Swindon TFKRB				8	8	8	8	8	8	8	8	8	8	8	8	8	8	8	
Diesel Railbuses	**3**	**8**	**8**	**11**	**28**	**22**	**22**	**22**	**22**	**21**	**19**	**19**	**8**	**4**					
AC Cars					5	5	5	5	5	5	5	5	4	3					
Bristol/Eastern Coach Works					2	2	2	2	2	2	2	2							
BUT	3	8	8	11	11														
Park Royal					4	5	5	5	5	5	5	5	2	1					
Waggon und Maschinenbau					5	5	5	5	5	5	5	5	2						
Wickham					1	5	5	5	5	4	2	2							
Battery Electric					**2**	**2**	**2**	**2**	**2**	**2**	**2**	**2**							
Battery Electric Railcar BDMBS					1	1	1	1	1	1	1	1							
Battery Electric Railcar BDTCL					1	1	1	1	1	1	1	1							
Grand Total	**27**	**146**	**408**	**1331**	**2401**	**3213**	**3840**	**4017**	**4105**	**4138**	**4113**	**4109**	**4076**	**3971**	**3811**	**3646**	**3630**	**3600**	**3477**
	1954	1955	1956	1957	1958	1959	1960	1961	1962	1963	1964	1965	1966	1967	1968	1969	1970	1971	1972

	1973	1974	1975	1976	1977	1978	1979	1980	1981	1982	1983	1984	1985	1986	1987	1988	1989	1990
Swindon Inter-city	**5**	**4**	**4**	**4**	**4**	**2**	**2**	**2**										
Swindon DMBSL	1	1	1	1	1	1	1	1										
Swindon DMSL	2	1	1	1	1													
Swindon TFK	2	2	2	2	2	1	1	1										
Grand Total	**3435**	**3428**	**3413**	**3379**	**3320**	**3300**	**3290**	**3261**	**3103**	**2912**	**2716**	**2555**	**2492**	**2151**	**1762**	**1497**	**1227**	**1048**
	1973	1974	1975	1976	1977	1978	1979	1980	1981	1982	1983	1984	1985	1986	1987	1988	1989	1990

	1991	1992	1993	1994	1995	1996	1997	1998	1999	2000	2001	2002	2003	2004	2005	2006	2007	2008
Grand Total	**864**	**479**	**274**	**231**	**184**	**178**	**173**	**163**	**118**	**89**	**56**	**51**	**35**	**8**	**6**	**7**	**7**	**7**
	1991	1992	1993	1994	1995	1996	1997	1998	1999	2000	2001	2002	2003	2004	2005	2006	2007	2008

Appendix 2: BR Lot Numbers

Lot	Type	Numbers	Builder	Year
30001	CK	15000	Eastleigh	1952
30002	SK	24000-24179	Derby	1951
30003	BSK	34000-34094	Derby	1951-52
30004	CK	15001-15020	Derby	1952
30005	CK	15065-15270	Metro-Cammell	1952-53
30006	BCK	21000-21019	Metro-Cammell	1954
30007	SK	24332-24396	BRCW	1953
30008	FO	3003-3019	BRCW	1954
30009	BG	80500-80529	Derby	1952-53
30010	FO	3000-3002	York	1951
30011	TSO	3700-3705	York	1951
30012	RFO	1-11	York	1951
30013	RF	301-305	Doncaster	1952
30014	RSO	1000-1013	York	1951
30015	SK	24180-24219	Doncaster	1951-52
30016	CK	15271-15310	Cravens	1952-53
30017	TSO	3706-3720	Cravens	1952
30018	RK	80000-80009	Doncaster	1951
30019	FK	13000-13032	Swindon	1951-52
30019	FK	13036-13059	Swindon	1951-52
30020	SK	24302-24331	Ashford/Eastleigh	1951-52
30021	BSK	34225-34284	Ashford/Eastleigh	1952
30022	CK	15021-15064	Ashford/Eastleigh	1952
30023	BG	80530-80535	Eastleigh	1951
30025	BSK	34096-34224	Wolverton	1951-52
30026	SK	24220-24301	York	1951-52
30027	FK	13060-13064	Swindon	1953
30028	S	46000-46018	Swindon	1954
30030	SK	24397-24436	Derby	1953
30031	SO	3721-3735	Derby	1954
30032	BSK	34285-34289	Wolverton	1952
30032	BSK	34372-34388	Wolverton	1952
30032	BSK	34410-34412	Wolverton	1952
30033	CK	15311-15349	Derby	1953
30034	BCK	21020-21024	Derby	1954
30035	SLF	2000-2009	Wolverton	1957-58
30036	SLSTP	2500-2521	Doncaster	1957
30037	S	46019-46062	Swindon	1955
30038	S	46109-46198	Wolverton	1954
30039	BG	80536-80566	Derby	1954
30040	BG	80567-80596	Wolverton	1954-55
30042	FO	3020-3039	Doncaster	1953-53
30043	TSO	3736-3753	Doncaster	1953
30043	TSO	3773-3788	Doncaster	1953
30044	SK	24557-24568	York	1952
30045	BS	43100-43161	York	1954-55
30046	BG	80597-80671	York	1954
30047	BS	43162-43170 ex-53036-53051	Swindon	1955
30047	BS	43260-43266	Swindon	1955
30051	S	46063-46108	Derby	1954
30052	FK	13033-13035	Eastleigh	1951
30053	SO	3500-3514	Eastleigh	1953
30054	TSO	3824-3849	Ashford/Eastleigh	1953-54
30054	TSO	3886-3903	Eastleigh	1954
30057	SK	24576-24675	BRCW	1953-54
30058	SK	24676-24700	Cravens	1953
30059	SK	24701-24720	Cravens	1953
30060	BSK	34451-34500	Gloucester	1953-54
30061	BSK	34501-34520	Charles Roberts	1954
30062	CK	15443-15532	Metro-Cammell	1953-54
30063	CK	15533-15542	Metro-Cammell	1954
30064	BSK	34413-34450	Wolverton	1953
30065	BSK	34290-34301	Wolverton	1953
30066	FK	13065-13076	Swindon	1953
30067	TSO	4358-4362	Eastleigh	1955
30068	SK	24539-24548	York	1952
30070	SK	24469-24538	York	1954
30070	SK	24549-24556	York	1954
30070	SK	24569-24575	York	1954
30071	C	41000-41022	Wolverton	1954
30072	SK	24437-24446	Wolverton	1953
30073	SK	24721-24745	Wolverton	1953
30074	BSK	34316-34371	Wolverton	1953
30074	BSK	34389-34409	Wolverton	1954
30075	CK	15350-15424	Derby	1954
30076	CK	15425-15435	Derby	1953
30077	SK	24746-24753	Swindon	1953-54
30078	SK	24754-24795	Swindon	1954
30079	TSO	3754-3772	York	1953
30079	TSO	3789-3823	York	1953
30080	TSO	3850-3885	York	1953-54
30081	CK	15436-15442	Derby	1954
30082	BSK	34302-34315	Wolverton	1954
30083	FK	13077-13084	Swindon	1953
30084	**DMBS**	**79000-79007**	**Derby**	**1954**
30085	**DMCL**	**79500-79507**	**Derby**	**1954**
30086	TSO	3904-3969	Eastleigh	1954-55
30087	BS	43267-43359 ex-53078-53170	York	1955
30088	SK	24447-24468	Swindon	1954
30089	FK	13085-13107	Swindon	1954
30090	TSO	3970-3997	York	1954
30091	FO	3040-3057	Doncaster	1954
30092	SLO	48000-48027	Doncaster	1955
30093	BS	43171-43259 ex-53171-53259	Doncaster	1954
30094	CL	43000-43049	Doncaster	1954-55
30095	BSK	34521-34584	Wolverton	1955
30096	SLC	2400-2401	Wolverton	1957
30098	S	46199-46266	Derby	1955
30099	SO[NG]	48035-48042	Derby	1955
30100	BS	43360-43367	Derby	1955
30101	S	46299-46306	Derby	1955
30102	C	41023-41042	Wolverton	1955
30102	C	41049-41059	Wolverton	1955
30103	C	41043-41048	Swindon	1955
30104	S	46267-46279	Swindon	1954-55
30105	SO[NG]	48043-48053	Swindon	1955
30106	BS	43368-43373 ex-53268-53273	Swindon	1955
30107	FK	13108-13125	Swindon	1954
30108	DMBSO	61033-61040	Ashford/Eastleigh	1956
30109	TSK	70033-70036	Ashford/Eastleigh	1956
30110	TCK	70037-70040	Ashford/Eastleigh	1956
30111	DMBSO	61041-61044	Ashford/Eastleigh	1956
30112	TCK	70041-70042	Ashford/Eastleigh	1956
30113	TRB	69000-69001	Ashford/Eastleigh	1957
30114	DMBSO	65300-65310	Ashford/Eastleigh	1954
30115	DTSso	77500-77510	Ashford/Eastleigh	1954
30116	DMBSO	65311-65325	Eastleigh	1954-55
30117	DTSso	77100-77114	Eastleigh	1955
30118	DMLV	68000	Eastleigh	1955
30119	DMBSO	65326-65341	Ashford/Eastleigh	1954
30120	DTSso	77511-77526	Ashford/Eastleigh	1954
30121	SO	4363-4372	Eastleigh	1955
30123	**DMBS**	**79008-79020**	**Derby**	**1955**
30124	**DTCL**	**79600-79612**	**Derby**	**1955**
30125	Fish	87000-87499	Faverdale	1954-55
30126	**DMBS**	**79021-79033**	**Derby**	**1955**
30127	**DTCL**	**79613-79625**	**Derby**	**1955**
30128	**DMS**	**79740**	**BUT**	**1953**
30128	**TS**	**79741**	**BUT**	**1953**
30128	**DMBS**	**79742**	**BUT**	**1953**
30129	ROY	499	Wolverton	1956
30130	ROY	2900	Wolverton	1955
30131	ROY	2901	Wolverton	1957
30132	BCK	21025-21059	Metro-Cammell	1954-55
30133	BCK	21060-21091	Metro-Cammell	1955
30134	CK	15543-15562	Metro-Cammell	1955
30135	CK	15563-15584	Metro-Cammell	1955
30136	BG	80672-80724	Metro-Cammell	1955
30137	SK	24796-24818	BRCW	1955
30138	CK	15585-15596	BRCW	1955
30139	CK	15597-15624	BRCW	1955
30140	BG	80725-80802	BRCW	1955-56
30141	BSK	34585-34612	Gloucester	1955
30142	BSK	34613-34630	Gloucester	1955
30143	BSK	34631-34654	Charles Roberts	1954-55
30144	BG	80803-80854	Cravens	1955
30145	SO[NG]	48028-48034	Doncaster	1955
30146	HB	96300-96414	Earlestown	1958
30147	FK	13126-13184	Swindon	1955
30148	BFK	14000-14001	Ashford/Swindon	1959
30149	TSO	3998-4097	Ashford/Swindon	1956-57
30150	S	46280-46298	Swindon	1955
30151	BS	43374-43383	Swindon	1956
30152	C	41060-41064	Swindon	1956
30153	SK	24819-24944	Derby	1955-56
30154	SK	24945-24974	Derby	1956
30155	SK	25045-25164	Wolverton	1955-56
30156	BSK	34655-34748	Wolverton	1955
30157	BSK	34749-34808	Wolverton	1955
30158	CK	15625-15694	Wolverton	1956
30159	SLF	2010-2019	Wolverton	1958
30160	SLSTP	2522-2526	York/Doncaster	1957
30161	SLC	2402-2403	Wolverton	1957
30162	BG	80855-80964	Pressed Steel	1956-57
30163	BG	81205-81265	Pressed Steel	1957
30167	DMBSO	65342-65366	Ashford/Eastleigh	1955
30168	DTSso	77527-77551	Ashford/Eastleigh	1955
30169	FO	3058-3070	Doncaster	1955
30170	BSO	9200-9276	Doncaster	1955-56
30171	TSO	4098-4197	York	1955-56
30172	TSO	4198-4257	York	1956
30173	BG	80965-81014	York	1956
30174	**DMBS**	**79743-79744**	**BUT**	**1955**
30175	**DMS**	**79745**	**BUT**	**1955**
30176	**TS**	**79746-79747**	**BUT**	**1955**
30177	**DMBS**	**79034-79046**	**Derby**	**1955**
30178	**DTCL**	**79250-79262**	**Derby**	**1955**
30179	CK	15695-15770	Metro-Cammell	1955-56
30180	CK	15771-15820	Metro-Cammell	1955-56
30185	BCK	21092-21118	Metro-Cammell	1956
30186	BCK	21119-21133	Metro-Cammell	1956
30187	BCK	21134-21168	Charles Roberts	1955-56
30188	GUV	86500	York	1956
30189	CCT	94100	Doncaster	1955
30190	**DMBS**	**79047-79075**	**Metro-Cammell**	**1956**
30190	**DMBS**	**79076-79082**	**Metro-Cammell**	**1955**
30191	**DTSL**	**79263-79291**	**Metro-Cammell**	**1956**
30191	**DTCL**	**79626-79632**	**Metro-Cammell**	**1955**
30192	**DMC**	**79508-79512**	**Derby**	**1955**
30193	**DMS**	**79150-79154**	**Derby**	**1955**
30194	**TBSL**	**79325-79329**	**Derby**	**1955**
30195	**TSL**	**79400-79404**	**Derby**	**1955**
30196	**DMBSL**	**79083-79090**	**Swindon**	**1956**
30196	**DMBSL**	**79095**	**Swindon**	**1956**
30197	**TFKRB**	**79440-79447**	**Swindon**	**1957**
30198	**TFK**	**79470-79482**	**Swindon**	**1957**
30199	**DMSL**	**79155-79168**	**Swindon**	**1957**
30200	**DMBSL**	**79091-79094**	**Swindon**	**1957**
30200	**DMBSL**	**79096-79111**	**Swindon**	**1957**
30201	**DMBSL**	**79143-79149**	**Derby**	**1956**
30202	**DTCL**	**79663-79669**	**Derby**	**1956**
30203	MS	61001-61032	Ashford/Eastleigh	1956
30204	TCsoL	70001-70032	Ashford/Eastleigh	1956
30205	DTBS	75001-75032	Ashford/Eastleigh	1956
30206	DTCOL	75101-75132	Ashford/Eastleigh	1956
30207	TSO	4258-4357	BRCW	1956
30208	SK	24975-25044	Derby	1956
30209	**DMBS**	**50001-50048**	**Derby**	**1958**
30210	**DTCL**	**56001-56049**	**Derby**	**1958**
30211	**DMBS**	**50050-50091**	**Derby**	**1957**
30212	**TC**	**59000-59031**	**Derby**	**1957**
30213	**DMS**	**50092-50133**	**Derby**	**1957**
30214	**DMS**	**79748**	**BUT**	**1957**
30215	**TS**	**79749**	**BUT**	**1957**
30216	**DMBS**	**79750**	**BUT**	**1957**
30217	FK	13185-13219	Ashford/Swindon	1957-59
30218	BFK	14002-14006	Ashford/Swindon	1959-60
30219	TSO	4373-4412	Ashford/Swindon	1957
30220	BSK	34809-34868	Gloucester	1956
30221	CK	15821-15860	Metro-Cammell	1956
30222	CK	15861-15915	Metro-Cammell	1956
30223	BSK	34869-34880	Charles Roberts	1956
30224	BG	81015-81054	Cravens	1956
30225	BSK	34881-34930	Charles Roberts	1957
30226	TSO	4413-4472	BRCW	1956-57
30227	SO	4473-4487	BRCW	1957
30228	BG	81055-81179	Metro-Cammell	1957-58
30229	BSK	34931-35023	Metro-Cammell	1957
30230	SK	25165-25247	Metro-Cammell	1957
30231	SK	25248-25279	Metro-Cammell	1957-58
30232	BSK	35024-35038	Gloucester	1956
30233	BSK	35039-35113	Gloucester	1957
30234	BG	81180-81204	Cravens	1956-57
30235	**DMBSL**	**79118-79126**	**Derby**	**1956**
30236	**DTCL**	**79639-79647**	**Derby**	**1956**
30240	**DMBSL**	**79127-79136**	**Derby**	**1956**
30240	**DMBSL**	**79137-79140**	**Derby**	**1956**
30241	**DTCL**	**79648-79657**	**Derby**	**1956**
30241	**DTCL**	**79658-79661**	**Derby**	**1956**
30242	FO	3071-3080	York/Doncaster	1956
30243	TSO	4488-4636	York	1956-57
30244	BSO	9277-9321	Doncaster	1956
30245	SLSTP	2527-2536	York/Doncaster	1957
30246	**DMBSL**	**79141-79142**	**Derby**	**1956**
30247	**DTCL**	**79662**	**Derby**	**1956**
30248	**DMBS**	**50134-50137**	**Metro-Cammell**	**1957**
30249	**DMCL**	**50138-50151**	**Metro-Cammell**	**1956**
30250	**TSL**	**59042-59048**	**Metro-Cammell**	**1956**
30251	**TBSL**	**59049-59055**	**Metro-Cammell**	**1956**
30252	**DMBS**	**50152-50157**	**Metro-Cammell**	**1956**
30253	**DMCL**	**50158-50163**	**Metro-Cammell**	**1956**
30254	**DMBS**	**50164-50167**	**Metro-Cammell**	**1957**
30255	**DMCL**	**50168-50171**	**Metro-Cammell**	**1957**
30256	**DMCL**	**50172-50197**	**Metro-Cammell**	**1957**
30257	**TSL**	**59060-59072**	**Metro-Cammell**	**1957**
30258	**TBSL**	**59073-59085**	**Metro-Cammell**	**1957**
30259	**DMBS**	**50198-50209**	**Metro-Cammell**	**1957**
30260	**DTCL**	**56050-56061**	**Metro-Cammell**	**1957**
30261	**DMBS**	**50210-50233**	**Metro-Cammell**	**1957**
30262	**DTCL**	**56062-56085**	**Metro-Cammell**	**1957**
30263	**DMCL**	**50234-50245**	**Metro-Cammell**	**1957**
30264	**TSL**	**59086-59091**	**Metro-Cammell**	**1957**
30265	**TBSL**	**59092-59097**	**Metro-Cammell**	**1957**
30266	**DMBS**	**50250-50259**	**Metro-Cammell**	**1957**
30267	**DMCL**	**50260-50269**	**Metro-Cammell**	**1957**
30268	**DMCL**	**50270-50279**	**Metro-Cammell**	**1957-58**
30269	**TSL**	**59100-59109**	**Metro-Cammell**	**1957-58**
30270	**DMBS**	**50290-50296**	**Metro-Cammell**	**1957**
30271	**DMCL**	**50745-50751**	**Metro-Cammell**	**1957**
30272	**DTCL**	**56086-56089**	**Metro-Cammell**	**1957**
30273	**TSL**	**59302-59306**	**Metro-Cammell**	**1957**
30274	**TBSL**	**59112-59113**	**Metro-Cammell**	**1957**
30275	**DMBS**	**50303-50320**	**Metro-Cammell**	**1958**
30276	**DMCL**	**50321-50338**	**Metro-Cammell**	**1958**
30277	**TCL**	**59114-59131**	**Metro-Cammell**	**1958**
30278	**DMBS**	**50339-50358**	**Gloucester**	**1957**
30279	**DTCL**	**56094-56113**	**Gloucester**	**1957**
30280	**DMBS**	**50359-50372**	**Cravens**	**1956-58**
30281	**DTCL**	**56114-56127**	**Cravens**	**1956-57**
30282	**DMBS**	**50373-50389**	**Cravens**	**1957**
30283	**DTCL**	**56128-56144**	**Cravens**	**1957**
30284	**DMBS**	**50390-50394**	**Cravens**	**1957**
30285	**DTCL**	**56145-56149**	**Cravens**	**1957**
30286	**DMBS**	**50395-50414**	**Park Royal**	**1957-58**
30287	**DTCL**	**56150-56169**	**Park Royal**	**1957-58**
30288	**DMBS**	**50415-50419**	**Wickham**	**1958**
30289	**DTCL**	**56170-56174**	**Wickham**	**1958**
30290	**DMBS**	**50420-50423**	**BRCW**	**1957**
30291	**DMCL**	**50424-50427**	**BRCW**	**1957**
30292	**TCL**	**59132-59135**	**BRCW**	**1957**
30293	**DMBS**	**50428-50479**	**BRCW**	**1957-58**
30294	**DMCL**	**50480-50531**	**BRCW**	**1957-58**
30295	**TCL**	**59136-59187**	**BRCW**	**1957-58**
30296	**DMBS**	**50532-50541**	**BRCW**	**1958**
30297	**DTCL**	**56175-56184**	**BRCW**	**1958**
30298	**DMCL**	**50542-50583**	**BRCW**	**1958**
30299	**TSL**	**59188-59208**	**BRCW**	**1958**
30300	**TBSL**	**59209-59229**	**BRCW**	**1958**
30301	**DMCL**	**50584-50593**	**BRCW**	**1959**
30302	**TSL**	**59230-59234**	**BRCW**	**1959**
30303	**TBSL**	**59240-59244**	**BRCW**	**1959**
30314	DMBSO	65367-65396	Ashford/Eastleigh	1956-57
30315	DTSso	77552-77577	Ashford/Eastleigh	1956
30316	DTCsoL	77115-77118	Ashford/Eastleigh	1957
30317	CK	15916-15985	Wolverton	1956-57
30318	SLF	2020-2029	York	1958
30319	DMBSO	65397-65403	Ashford/Eastleigh	1957
30320	DTCsoL	77119-77125	Ashford/Eastleigh	1957
30321	**DMBSL**	**79169-79181**	**Derby**	**1956**
30322	**DTCL**	**79670-79684**	**Derby**	**1956**
30323	BG	81266-81312	Pressed Steel	1957
30324	**DMBS**	**79184-79188**	**Derby**	**1956**
30325	**DMCL**	**79189-79193**	**Derby**	**1956**
30326	DMBSO	61133-61189	Ashford/Eastleigh	1957-58
30327	TS	70133-70189	Ashford/Eastleigh	1957-58
30328	DTBSO	75133-75189	Ashford/Eastleigh	1957-58
30329	**DMBS**	**60000-60013**	**Ashford/Eastleigh**	**1957**
30330	**TFK**	**60700-60706**	**Ashford/Eastleigh**	**1957**
30331	**TSOL**	**60500-60520**	**Ashford/Eastleigh**	**1957**
30332	**DMBSO**	**60100-60117**	**Ashford/Eastleigh**	**1957**
30333	**DTCsoL**	**60800-60817**	**Ashford/Eastleigh**	**1957**
30334	**DMSL**	**50647-50695**	**Swindon**	**1958-59**
30335	**DMBC**	**50696-50744**	**Swindon**	**1958-59**
30336	**TSLRB**	**59255-59301**	**Swindon**	**1958-59**
30337	**DTCL**	**56090-56093**	**Metro-Cammell**	**1957**
30338	**DMBS**	**50280-50289**	**Metro-Cammell**	**1957-58**
30339	**DMBS**	**50246-50248**	**Metro-Cammell**	**1957**
30340	**DTCL**	**56218-56220**	**Metro-Cammell**	**1957**
30341	**DMBS**	**50000**	**Derby**	**1956**
30342	**DTCL**	**56000**	**Derby**	**1956**
30343	GUV	86501-86520	Doncaster	1957
30344	Fish	87500-87692	Faverdale	1960

Lot	Type	Numbers	Builder	Year
30345	FRUIT D	92000-92064	Swindon	1957-58
30346	RKB	1546	Ashford/Eastleigh	1956
30347	RB	1700	Eastleigh	1956
30348	RU	1900	Eastleigh	1956
30349	SK	25283-25402	Wolverton	1957
30350	SK	25403-25454	Wolverton	1957
30351	CK	15986-16057	Wolverton	1956-57
30352	DMBS	50752-50784	Cravens	1957-58
30353	DMCL	50785-50817	Cravens	1957-58
30354	TCL	59307-59325	Cravens	1957-58
30355	FK	13220	Metro-Cammell	1957
30356	SK	25455	Metro-Cammell	1957
30357	FK	13221	Gloucester	1957
30358	SK	25456	Gloucester	1957
30359	FO	3081	BRCW	1957
30360	SO	4637	BRCW	1957
30361	FO	3082	Cravens	1957
30362	TSO	4638	Cravens	1957
30363	DMBS	50818-50870	Derby	1957-58
30364	DMS	50871-50923	Derby	1957-58
30365	TC	59326-59376	Derby	1957-58
30368	BDMBS	79998	Derby/Cowlairs	1958
30368	BDTCL	79999	Derby/Cowlairs	1958
30370	FK	13222	Doncaster	1957
30371	SK	25457	Doncaster	1957
30372	FO	3083	Doncaster	1957
30373	FO	3084	Doncaster	1957
30374	SK	25458-25507	York	1958
30375	TSO	4639-4726	York	1957
30375	TSO	4739-4778	York	1957
30376	SO	4779-4809	York	1957
30377	SLF	2030-2063	York	1959
30379	SLSTP	2537-2573	York/Doncaster	1957-58
30380	DMBS	79900	Derby	1956
30381	FK	13223-13238	Ashford/Swindon	1959
30382	BFK	14007-14012	Ashford/Swindon	1960
30383	FRUIT D	92065-92114	Swindon	1958-59
30384	Fish	87693-87957	Faverdale	1960-61
30385	TS	59032-59041	Derby	1957
30386	BSK	35114-35175	Charles Roberts	1958
30387	DMBS	79901	Derby	1956
30388	DMBSO	65404-65435	Ashford/Eastleigh	1958
30389	DTCsoL	77126-77156	Ashford/Eastleigh	1958
30390	DTSso	77578	Ashford/Eastleigh	1958
30391	DMBSO	60020-60045	Ashford/Eastleigh	1957-58
30392	TFK	60710-60722	Ashford/Eastleigh	1957-58
30393	TRB	60750-60756	Ashford/Eastleigh	1958
30394	TSOL	60530-60561	Ashford/Eastleigh	1957-58
30395	DMBSO	60014-60019	Ashford/Eastleigh	1957
30396	TFK	60707-60709	Ashford/Eastleigh	1957
30397	TSOL	60521-60529	Ashford/Eastleigh	1957
30398	DMBSO	60118-60121	Ashford/Eastleigh	1958
30399	DTCsoL	60818-60821	Ashford/Eastleigh	1958
30400	BG	81313-81497	Pressed Steel	1957-58
30401	RU	1901-1912	Ashford/Swindon	1957
30402	GUV	86521-86654	York/Glasgow	1958-60
30404	DMBS	50594-50598	BRCW	1958
30405	DTCL	56185-56189	BRCW	1958
30406	DMBS	50599-50624	Derby	1958
30407	DMBS	50625-50629	Derby	1958
30408	DMCL	50630-50646	Derby	1958
30409	DTCL	56190-56210	Derby	1958
30410	DTCL	56211-56215	Derby	1959
30411	TSL	59380-59385	Derby	1959
30412	TBSL	59245-59250	Derby	1958
30413	DMSL	50936	Swindon	1959
30413	DMSL	51008-51029	Swindon	1959
30414	DMBSL	51030-51051	Swindon	1959
30415	TFK	59391-59400	Swindon	1959
30416	TCL	59402-59412	Swindon	1959
30417	GUV	86078-86499	Pressed Steel	1958-59
30418	DMPMV	55997-55999	Cravens	1958
30419	DMBS	55000-55019	Gloucester	1958
30420	DTS	56291-56299	Gloucester	1958
30421	DMBC	51052-51079	Gloucester	1958-59
30422	DMSL	51080-51107	Gloucester	1958-59
30423	TSLRB	59413-59437	Gloucester	1958-59
30424	BCK	21169-21194	Charles Roberts	1958-59
30425	BCK	21195-21224	Metro-Cammell	1958
30426	SK	25558-25703	Wolverton	1957-58
30427	BSK	35176-35273	Wolverton	1959
30428	MBS	61045-61059	Wolverton	1960
30429	DTSOL	75045-75059	Wolverton	1960
30430	DTBSO	75645-75659	Wolverton	1960
30431	TCsoL	70045-70059	Wolverton	1960
30432	FK	13239-13251	Ashford/Swindon	1959
30434	MBS	61060-61096	York	1958-59
30435	DTS	75033-75044	York	1958-59
30435	DTS	75060-75084	York	1959
30436	DTSOL	75085-75100	York/Doncaster	1958-59
30436	DTSOL	75190-75210	York/Doncaster	1959
30437	TCsoL	70060-70096	York/Doncaster	1958-59
30438	MBS	61097-61132	York	1959
30438	MBS	61190-61228	York	1959-60
30439	DTS	75211-75285	York	1959-60
30440	DTSOL	75286-75360	York/Doncaster	1959
30441	TCsoL	70097-70132	York	1959
30441	TCsoL	70190-70228	York	1959-61
30442	Fish	87958-88057	Faverdale	1961
30443	BSO	9322-9362	Gloucester	1959-60
30444	DMBS	51108-51127	Gloucester	1957-58
30445	DTCL	56300-56319	Gloucester	1957-58
30446	DMBS	51128-51140	Derby	1958
30447	DMS	51141-51153	Derby	1958
30448	TC	59438-59448	Derby	1958
30449	DMBSO	61229-61240	Ashford/Eastleigh	1958
30450	TSK	70229-70234	Ashford/Eastleigh	1958
30451	TCK	70235-70240	Ashford/Eastleigh	1958
30452	DMBSO	61241-61303	Ashford/Eastleigh	1958-59
30453	DTCsoL	75361-75423	Ashford/Eastleigh	1958-59
30454	DMBSO	61304-61409	Ashford/Eastleigh	1958-59
30455	TSK	70260-70302	Ashford/Eastleigh	1958-59
30456	TCK	70303-70355	Ashford/Eastleigh	1958-59
30457	TRB	69002-69011	Ashford/Eastleigh	1959
30458	DMLV	68001-68002	Ashford/Eastleigh	1959
30459	DMBS	50049	Derby	1957
30460	DMBS	50924-50935	Derby	1959-60
30461	DMCL	51561-51572	Derby	1959-60
30462	DMS	50988-51007	Derby	1958-59
30463	TS	59449-59468	Derby	1958-59
30464	DMBS	51154-51173	Derby	1958-59
30465	DMBS	50938-50987	Derby	1959
30466	DTCL	56221-56270	Derby	1959
30467	DMBS	51174-51253	Metro-Cammell	1958-59
30468	DTCL	56332-56411	Metro-Cammell	1958-59
30469	DMBS	51254-51301	Cravens	1958-59
30470	DTCL	56412-56459	Cravens	1958-59
30471	CK	16058-16092	Metro-Cammell	1958-59
30472	FO	3085-3094	BRCW	1959
30473	SO	4810-4829	BRCW	1959
30474	BCK	21225-21230	Charles Roberts	1959
30475	CK	16093-16107	Charles Roberts	1959
30476	RU	1913-1924	Ashford/Swindon	1958
30477	DMBSO	65436-65461	Wolverton	1959
30478	DTSO	77157-77182	Wolverton	1959
30479	DMBS	79975-79979	AC Cars	1958
30480	DMBS	79970-79974	Park Royal	1958
30481	DMBS	79965-79969	Wickham	1959
30482	DMBS	79960-79964	Waggon & Masch.	1958
30483	DMBS	79958-79959	BRCW	1958
30484	BG	81498-81572	Pressed Steel	1958
30485	RMB	1801-1812	York	1957-58
30486	POS	80300-80305	Wolverton	1959
30487	POS	80306-80308	Wolverton	1959
30488	POT	80400-80402	Wolverton	1959
30489	BPOT	80450-80455	Wolverton	1959
30490	SLF	2064-2104	Metro-Cammell	1959
30491	SLSTP	2574-2578	Metro-Cammell	1959
30492	SLC	2404-2426	Metro-Cammell	1959-60
30493	TSL	59386-59390	Derby	1958
30494	SK	25280-25282	Metro-Cammell	1958
30498	DMBS	51416-51424	Derby	1960
30499	DTCL	56271-56279	Derby	1960
30500	DMBS	51425-51470	Metro-Cammell	1959
30501	DMCL	51495-51540	Metro-Cammell	1959
30502	TCL	59523-59568	Metro-Cammell	1959
30503	DMBS	51471-51494	Cravens	1959
30504	DTCL	56460-56483	Cravens	1959
30505	DMBS	50249	Cravens	1959
30506	TSO	4830-4839	Wolverton	1959
30507	RMB	1838-1852	Wolverton	1960
30508	DMBS	51541-51550	Metro-Cammell	1959-60
30509	DMCL	51551-51560	Metro-Cammell	1959-60
30510	TSL	59569-59572	Metro-Cammell	1959
30511	RF	306-309	BRCW	1961
30512	RB	1701-1738	BRCW	1960
30513	RU	1925-1943	BRCW	1959-60
30514	RKB	1500-1526	Cravens	1959-60
30515	DMBCL	51573-51581	Swindon	1961
30516	DMSL	51582-51590	Swindon	1961
30517	TSL	59579-59588	Swindon	1961
30518	DMBS	55020-55035	Pressed Steel	1960-61
30519	DTS	56280-56289	Pressed Steel	1960-61
30520	RMB	1813-1837	Wolverton	1960
30521	DMBS	51591-51650	Derby	1959
30522	TSL	59589-59618	Derby	1959
30523	TS	59619-59648	Derby	1959
30524	RK	80010-80021	Charles Roberts	1962
30525	TSO	4840-4899	Wolverton	1959-60
30526	RSO	1014-1017	Wolverton	1960
30527	RB	1739-1754	BRCW	1961
30528	SLF	2105-2106	Wolverton	1959
30529	SLSTP	2579-2606	Wolverton	1959-60
30530	DMBS	51651-51680	Derby	1960
30531	TS	59649-59663	Derby	1960
30532	TCL	59664-59678	Derby	1960
30533	DMBS	51681-51705	Cravens	1959
30534	DMCOL	51706-51730	Cravens	1959
30535	DMBS	51731-51755	Cravens	1960
30536	DMCOL	51756-51780	Cravens	1960
30537	TFKRB	59098-59099	Swindon	1961
30538	SLC	2427	Metro-Cammell	1960
30539	RK	80022-80027	Charles Roberts	1962
30540	DMBSO	60122-60125	Ashford/Eastleigh	1959
30541	DTCsoL	60822-60825	Ashford/Eastleigh	1959
30542	TSO	60650-60671	Ashford/Eastleigh	1959
30543	DMBS	51302-51316	BRCW	1960
30544	TCL	59469-59483	BRCW	1960
30545	DMS	51317-51331	BRCW	1960
30546	DMBS	51332-51373	Pressed Steel	1959-60
30547	TCL	59484-59522	Pressed Steel	1959-60
30548	DMS	51374-51415	Pressed Steel	1959-60
30549	CCT	94101-94300	Earlestown	1959-60
30550	FK	13252	Swindon	1963
30551	DMPMV	55991-55996	Gloucester	1960
30552	DMPMV	55987-55990	Gloucester	1959
30553	DMBFL	60090-60093	Metro-Cammell	1960
30554	DMBS	60094-60099	Metro-Cammell	1960
30555	MPSL	60644-60649	Metro-Cammell	1960
30556	MFLRK	60730-60733	Metro-Cammell	1960
30557	TFLRK	60734-60739	Metro-Cammell	1960
30558	TPFL	60740-60749	Metro-Cammell	1960
30559	DMBC	51781-51787	Swindon	1959-60
30560	DMSL	51788-51794	Swindon	1959-60
30561	TSLRB	59679-59685	Swindon	1959-60
30562	CCT	94301-94454	Earlestown	1960
30563	CCT	94455-94595	Earlestown	1960
30564	CCT	94596-94692	Earlestown	1960-61
30565	GUV	86655-86834	Pressed Steel	1959
30566	DTSOL	75424-75442	York/Doncaster	1960
30567	MBS	61410-61428	York/Doncaster	1959-60
30568	TCsoL	70356-70374	York/Doncaster	1960
30569	DTS	75443-75461	York/Doncaster	1960
30570	DTSO	75462-75513	York	1960
30571	MBSO	61429-61480	York	1960
30572	DTSO	75514-75565	York	1960
30573	BSK	35274-35293	Gloucester	1960
30574	BCK	21231-21235	Gloucester	1960
30575	RU	1944-1958	Ashford/Swindon	1960
30576	FO	3095-3100	BRCW	1959
30577	CK	16108-16152	Metro-Cammell	1959-60
30578	FK	13253-13302	Metro-Cammell	1960
30579	DTSO	75566-75600	Pressed Steel	1959-61
30580	MBSO	61481-61515	Pressed Steel	1959-61
30581	DTBSO	75601-75635	Pressed Steel	1959-61
30582	DMBS	61516-61627	Eastleigh	1960-61
30583	TSso	70375-70482	Eastleigh	1960-61
30584	DTSso	75636	Eastleigh	1960
30585	RK	80028-80039	Charles Roberts	1962-63
30586	SLSTP	2607-2658	Wolverton	1960-61
30587	DMBS	51795-51801	Metro-Cammell	1959
30588	DMCL	51802-51808	Metro-Cammell	1959
30589	TCL	59686-59692	Metro-Cammell	1959
30590	SLF	2107-2120	Metro-Cammell	1960
30591	SLC	2428-2437	Metro-Cammell	1960
30592	DMBC	51809-51828	BRCW	1961
30593	DMCL	51829-51848	BRCW	1961
30594	TSL	59693-59712	BRCW	1961
30595	DMBS	51849-51860	Derby	1960
30596	TS	59713-59718	Derby	1960
30597	TCL	59719-59724	Derby	1960
30598	DMBS	51861-51900	Derby	1960
30599	TS	59725-59744	Derby	1960
30600	TCL	59745-59764	Derby	1960
30601	DMBS	51901-51950	Derby	1960-61
30602	DTCL	56484-56504	Derby	1960
30603	DMC	51951-51967	Swindon	1960
30604	MBSK	51968-51984	Swindon	1960
30605	TSL	59765-59773	Swindon	1960
30606	TFLRB	59774-59781	Swindon	1960
30607	MBSO	61628-61647	Wolverton	1960-61
30608	DTBSO	75660-75679	Wolverton	1960-61
30609	TCsoL	70483-70502	Wolverton	1960-61
30610	DTSOL	75680-75699	Wolverton	1960-61
30611	DMBS	51985-52010	Derby	1960-61
30612	DMCL	52011-52036	Derby	1960-61
30613	TSL	59782-59807	Derby	1960-61
30614	CCT	94693-94892	Earlestown	1960-61
30615	TSLRB	59573-59578	Metro-Cammell	1960
30616	GUV	86835-86984	Pressed Steel	1959-60
30617	DMBSO	61648-61688	Eastleigh	1961
30618	DTCsoL	75700-75740	Ashford/Eastleigh	1961
30619	DMBSO	61694-61811	Ashford/Eastleigh	1960-61
30620	TSK	70503-70551	Ashford/Eastleigh	1960-61
30621	TCK	70552-70610	Ashford/Eastleigh	1960-61
30622	TRB	69012-69021	Ashford/Eastleigh	1961
30623	DMLV	68003-68010	Ashford/Eastleigh	1960-61
30624	RKB	1547-1569	Cravens	1961
30625	DMBSO	60126-60144	Ashford/Eastleigh	1962
30626	TCsoL	60600-60618	Ashford/Eastleigh	1961
30627	DTSO	60900-60918	Ashford/Eastleigh	1962
30628	RB	1644-1699	Pressed Steel	1960-61
30629	DTSO	75746-75801	Pressed Steel	1960-61
30630	MBSO	61812-61867	Pressed Steel	1960-61
30631	DTBSO	75802-75857	Pressed Steel	1960-61
30632	RU	1959-1991	Ashford/Swindon	1960-61
30633	RF	310-342	Ashford/Swindon	1962
30634	RK	80040	Charles Roberts	1963
30635	RKB	1527-1529	Cravens	1961
30636	RB	1755-1772	Pressed Steel	1961-62
30637	RG	1100-1102	Ashford/Eastleigh	1960
30638	DMBSO	61868-61871	Ashford/Eastleigh	1961
30639	TCK	70043-70044	Ashford/Eastleigh	1961
30640	TSK	70241-70242	Ashford/Eastleigh	1961
30641	DMBSO	61872	Ashford/Eastleigh	1961
30642	MBSO	61873-61882	Wolverton	1961
30643	DTBSO	75858-75867	Wolverton	1961
30644	TCsoL	70243-70252	Wolverton	1961
30645	DTSOL	75868-75877	Wolverton	1961
30646	TSO	4900-4917	Wolverton	1961
30647	RUO	1018-1057	Wolverton	1961
30648	FO	3101-3103	Wolverton	1961
30649	SLC	2438	Wolverton	1961
30650	SLF	2121-2125	Wolverton	1961
30651	CCT	94893-94922	Earlestown	1961
30652	DTSOL	75878-75886	York	1961
30653	MBS	61883-61891	York	1961
30654	TCsoL	70611-70619	York	1961
30655	DTS	75887-75895	York	1961
30656	DTSOL	75896-75928	York	1961
30657	MBS	61892-61915	York	1961
30658	TCsoL	70620-70652	York	1961
30659	DTS	75929-75961	York	1961
30660	DMCL	52037-52065	Derby	1961
30661	POS	80309-80314	Wolverton	1961
30662	POS	80315-80317	Wolverton	1961
30663	POS	80318	Wolverton	1961
30664	TCV	96286-96299	Newton Chambers	1961-62
30665	CK	16153-16197	Derby	1961
30666	CK	16198-16225	Derby	1961
30667	FK	13303-13360	Swindon	1962
30668	BFK	14013-14022	Swindon	1961
30669	BCK	21236-21251	Swindon	1961-62
30670	RMB	1853-1864	Wolverton	1961-62
30671	DMBSO	60145-60151	Ashford/Eastleigh	1962
30672	TSO	60672-60678	Ashford/Eastleigh	1962
30673	DTCsoL	60826-60832	Ashford/Eastleigh	1962
30674	CCT	96200-96203	Doncaster	1960
30675	DTCsoL	75962-75968	York	1962
30676	MBSK	61925-61931	York	1962
30677	TSOL	70253-70259	York	1962
30678	DTCsoL	75969-75975	York	1962
30679	DTCsoL	75637-75644	York	1962
30680	MBSK	61932-61939	York	1962
30681	TRB	69100-69107	York	1962-63
30682	DTCOL	75976-75983	York	1962-63
30683	DTSOL	75984-75991	York	1962
30684	DMBSK	61940-61947	York	1962-63
30685	SK	25704-25905	Derby	1961-62
30686	SK	25906-25972	Derby	1962
30687	SLF	2126-2130	Wolverton	1961
30688	SLC	2439-2442	Wolverton	1961
30689	SLSTP	2659-2666	Wolverton	1961
30690	TSO	4918-5044	Wolverton	1961-62
30691	DMBC	52066-52075	BRCW	1961-62
30692	DMCL	52076-52085	BRCW	1961-62
30693	TSL	59808-59817	BRCW	1961-62
30694	DTSO	75741-75743	York	1961
30695	MBSO	61689-61691	York	1961
30696	DTSO	75992-75994	York	1961
30697	FO	3104-3129	Swindon	1962-63

Lot	Type	Numbers	Builder	Date
30698	BSO	9363-9380	Wolverton	1963
30699	BSK	35294-35400	Wolverton	1963
30700	BSK	35401-35406	Wolverton	1963
30701	MLV	68011-68019	York	1961
30702	RMB	1865-1882	Wolverton	1962
30703	**DMBSL**	**52086-52095**	**Swindon**	**1963**
30704	**DMSK**	**52096-52105**	**Swindon**	**1963**
30705	**TCK**	**59818-59827**	**Swindon**	**1963**
30706	**TSL**	**59235-59239**	**Swindon**	**1963**
30707	**TSLRB**	**59828-59832**	**Swindon**	**1963**
30708	DMBSO	61948-61961	Ashford/Eastleigh	1963
30709	TCK	70653-70659	Ashford/Eastleigh	1963
30710	TSK	70660-70666	Ashford/Eastleigh	1963
30711	DMBSO	61962-61988	Ashford/Eastleigh	1963
30712	DTCsoL	75995-76021	Ashford/Eastleigh	1963
30713	DMBSO	61989-62016	Ashford/Eastleigh	1962-63
30714	TSso	70667-70694	Ashford/Eastleigh	1962-63
30715	BG	81573-81592	Gloucester	1962
30716	BG	81593-81612	Gloucester	1962
30717	FO	3130-3151	Swindon	1963
30718	BFK	14023-14027	Swindon	1963
30719	SK	25973-26059	Derby	1962
30720	SK	26060-26137	Derby	1962-63
30721	BSK	35407-35446	Wolverton	1963
30721	BSK	35450-35499	Wolverton	1963
30722	SLF	2131-2132	Wolverton	1962
30723	SLSTP	2667-2681	Wolverton	1962
30724	TSO	5045-5069	York	1963
30725	BG	81613-81628	Gloucester	1963
30726	SK	26138-26217	York	1962-63
30727	SLC	2443-2445	Wolverton	1962-63
30728	BSK	35447-35449	Wolverton	1963
30729	CK	16226-16240	Derby	1963
30730	CK	16241-16267	Derby	1963
30731	BCK	21252-21262	Derby	1963
30732	BCK	21263-21275	Derby	1964
30733	FK	13361-13378	Derby	1964
30734	FK	13379-13406	Derby	1964
30735	SLSTP	2682-2691	Wolverton	1963
30736	SLC	2446-2454	Wolverton	1963-64
30737	SK	25508-25509	Derby	1964
30738	FK	13407-13409	Derby	1964
30739	TSO	4727-4729	Derby	1964
30740	DTCsoL	76022-76075	York	1964-66
30741	DTCsoL	76076-76129	York	1964-66
30742	MBSO	62017-62070	York	1964-66
30743	TSO	70695-70730	York	1964-66
30744	TSORB	69301-69318	York	1965-66
30745	DTSOL	76130-76179	Derby	1965-67
30746	MBSO	62071-62120	Derby	1965-67
30747	TSO	70731-70780	Derby	1965-67
30748	DTCOL	76180-76229	Derby	1965-67
30749	FK	13410-13431	Derby	1964
30750	FK	13432-13433	Derby	1964
30751	TSO	5070-5228	Derby	1965-67
30752	SO	5229-5256	Derby	1966
30753	PB	580-586	Derby	1966
30754	PC	540-553	Derby	1966
30755	PK	500-507	Derby	1966
30756	BFK	14028-14055	Derby	1966
30757	BSO	9381-9416	Derby	1966
30758	DTCsoL	76230-76269	York	1967
30759	TSO	70781-70800	Derby	1967
30760	MBSO	62121-62140	Derby	1967
30761	DMSO	62141-62162	York	1967
30762	TBFK	70801-70811	York	1967
30763	TRB	69319-69329	York	1967
30764	DTSO	76270-76332	York	1966-67
30765	TBSK	70812-70843	York	1966-67
30766	TFK	70844-70871	York	1966-67
30767	DTSO	76403-76421	Cravens	1967
30768	MBSO	62163-62181	Cravens	1967
30769	DTSO	76422-76440	Cravens	1967
30770	CARTIC-4	95001-95016	Rootes/Pressed Steel	1966-67
30770	CARTIC-4	95051-95066	Rootes/Pressed Steel	1966-67
30771	DTCsoL	76333-76402	York	1967-68
30772	TSO	70872-70906	York	1967-68
30773	MBSO	62182-62216	York	1967-68
30774	FK	13434-13463	Derby	1968
30775	BFK	14056-14077	Derby	1967-68
30776	TSO	5257-5345	Derby	1967-68
30777	BSO	9417-9425	Derby	1967
30778	POS	80319-80327	York	1968-69
30779	POS	80328-80338	York	1968-69
30780	POS	80339-80355	York	1968-69
30781	POT	80415-80424	York	1968
30782	BPOT	80456-80458	York	1968
30783	RG	1106	Derby	1968
30784	Bar	1883	Derby	1968
30785	FK	13464-13475	Derby	1968
30786	BFK	14078-14103	Derby	1968
30787	TSO	5346-5433	Derby	1968
30788	BSO	9426-9438	Derby	1968
30789	FK	13476-13513	Derby	1969
30790	BFK	14104-14112	Derby	1969
30791	TSO	5434-5497	Derby	1969
30792	DTCsoL	76441-76540	York	1968-69
30793	TSO	70907-70956	York	1968-69
30794	MBSO	62217-62266	York	1968-69
30795	TSO	5498-5615	Derby	1969-70
30796	BFK	14113-14138	Derby	1969-70
30797	FK	13514-13561	Derby	1969-70
30798	BSO	9439-9448	Derby	1970
30799	DTCsoL	76541-76560	York	1970
30800	MBSO	62267-62276	York	1970
30801	TSO	70957-70966	York	1970
30802	TCK	76561-76570	York	1970
30803	TCK	76571-76580	York	1970
30804	MBSO	62277-62286	York	1970-71
30805	TSORB	69330-69339	York	1970
30806	DTCsoL	76581-76610	York	1970-71
30807	DTCsoL	76611-76640	York	1970-71
30808	MBSO	62287-62316	York	1970-71
30809	TSO	70967-70996	York	1971
30810	FO	3152-3169	Derby	1970
30811	DTCsoL	76641-76716	York	1973
30812	TSO	70997-71034	York	1972-73
30813	MBSO	62317-62354	York	1972-73
30814	DTCsoL	76717-76787	York	1970-72
30815	DTCsoL	76788-76858	York	1970-72
30816	MBSO	62355-62425	York	1970-72
30817	TSO	71035-71105	York	1970-72
30818	DMBSO	64300-64305	York	1971
30819	MSO	62426-62429	York	1971-72
30820	BSO	9449-9478	Derby	1970
30821	FO	3170-3216	Derby	1971-72
30822	TSO	5616-5743	Derby	1971-72
30823	BFK	14139-14172	Derby	1971-72
30824	BSO	9479-9495	Derby	1971
30825	FK	13562-13610	Derby	1971-72
30826	BCV	85000	Derby	1970
30827	DTCsoL	76859	York	1972
30828	DTCsoL	76860	York	1972
30829	MBSO	62430	York	1972
30830	TSO	71106	York	1972
30831	BFB	99500-99503	Derby	1971
30832	TSO	12003	Derby	1972
30833	FO	11003	Derby	1972
30837	TSO	5744-5804	Derby	1972
30838	BSO	9496-9509	Derby	1972
30839	POS	80356-80380	York	1973
30840	POT	80425-80430	York	1973
30841	ExhibVan	99602-99613	Swindon (conversion)	1973
30842	ExhibVan	99614	Swindon (conversion)	1976
30842	ExhibVan	99620-99625	Swindon (conversion)	1976
30843	FO	3221-3275	Derby	1973
30844	TSO	5809-5907	Derby	1973
30845	FO	3276-3320	Derby	1973
30846	TSO	5908-5958	Derby	1973
30847	TSO	12000-12002	Derby	1972
30848	FO	11000-11002	Derby	1972
30849	RUB	10000	Derby	1973
30850	RUK	10100	Derby	1973
30851	MBSO	62435-62475	York	1974
30852	TSO	71115-71155	York	1974
30853	DTCsoL	76861-76942	York	1974
30854	TBFK	71156-71159	York	1974
30855	TBSK	71160-71161	York	1974
30856	TFK	71162-71167	York	1974
30857	DTSO	76943-76948	York	1974
30858	TRB	69022-69025	York	1974
30859	FO	3321-3428	Derby	1974
30860	TSO	5959-6170	Derby	1974
30861	BSO	9510-9539	Derby	1974
30862	DMSO	62476-62483	York	1974
30863	DTSOL	76949-76974	York	1977-78
30864	MBSO	62484-62509	York	1977-78
30865	TSO	71168-71193	York	1977-78
30866	DTCOL	78000-78025	York	1977-78
30867	DTSOL	76975-76993	York	1975-76
30868	MBSO	62510-62528	York	1975-76
30869	TSO	71194-71212	York	1975-76
30870	DTCOL	78026-78044	York	1975-76
30871	TSK	71107-71110	Wolverton	1974
30872	TCK	71111-71114	Wolverton	1974
30873	FO	3429-3439	Derby	1975
30874	TSO	6171-6184	Derby	1975
30875	DMB	43000-43001	Crewe	1974
30876	DMB	43002-43055	Crewe	1977
30877	TSO	12004-12168	Derby	1977
30878	FO	11004-11063	Derby	1976
30879	DMSO	62529-62592	York	1976-77
30880	TSO	71213-71276	York	1976-77
30881	TF	41003-41056	Derby	1977
30882	TS	42003-42090	Derby	1977
30883	TRSB	40001-40027	Derby	1977
30884	TRUK	40501-40520	Derby	1977
30885	BDMSO	62593-62656	York	1976-77
30886	ROY	2903	Wolverton	1977
30887	ROY	2904	Wolverton	1977
30888	ROY	2905	Wolverton	1977
30889	ROY	2906	Wolverton	1977
30890	RFB	10001-10028	Derby	1980
30891	DTSOL	76994-76997	York	1976
30892	MBSO	62657-62660	York	1976
30893	TSO	71277-71280	York	1976
30894	DTCOL	78045-78048	York	1976
30895	DMB	43056-43123	Crewe	1979
30896	TF	41057-41120	Derby	1978
30897	TS	42091-42250	Derby	1979
30899	TRSB	40028-40037	Derby	1977
30900	POS	80381-80395	York	1977
30901	POT	80431-80439	York	1976
30902	DMSO	64461-64582	York	1980-81
30903	PTSO	71389-71449	York	1980-81
30904	TSO	71281-71341	York	1980-81
30906	BDMSO	64367-64399	York	1978-80
30907	TSO	71342-71374	York	1978-80
30908	DMSO	64405-64437	York	1978-80
30912	DMSO	64583-64614	York	1979
30913	TSO	71450-71465	York	1979
30921	TRUB	40300-40321	Derby	1979
30922	PVG	85500-85507	Wolverton	1978
30922	PVG	85508-85534	Doncaster	1978
30923	DTS	48101-48107	Derby	1980
30924	TS	48201-48206	Derby	1980
30925	TRSB	48401-48406	Derby	1980
30926	TF	48501-48506	Derby	1980
30927	TBF	48601-48607	Derby	1980
30928	M	49001-49006	Derby	1980
30930	DMBSO	53001	Derby	1980
30931	DMSO	53000	Derby	1980
30932	TSO	57000-57001	Derby	1980
30933	TCOL	58000	Derby	1980
30934	DTSO	54000-54001	Derby	1980
30938	TF	41121-41148	Derby	1980
30939	TS	42251-42305	Derby	1980
30940	TRUB	40322-40335	Derby	1980
30941	DMB	43124-43152	Crewe	1981
30942	DMSO	64649-64687	York	1979-80
30943	TSO	71483-71520	York	1979-80
30944	TSO	71526-71568	York	1977-80
30945	BDMSO	64692-64729	York	1980
30946	DM	43153-43190	Crewe	1981
30947	TF	41149-41166	Derby	1980
30948	TRUB	40336-40353	Derby	1981
30949	TGS	44001-44090	Derby	1982
30950	ExhibVan	99629	Stewarts Lane (conv.)	1979
30951	ExhibVan	99630	Stewarts Lane (conv.)	1979
30952	ExhibVan	99631	Stewarts Lane (conv.)	1979
30953	TGS	44000	Derby	1980
30954	TSOL	71569-71572	Wolverton	1981
30954	TCsoL	71573-71576	Wolverton	1981
30955	DTSO	77000-77047	York	1981-82
30956	DTSO	77048-77095	York	1981-82
30957	TCOL	71577-71624	Derby	1981-82
30958	MSO	62661-62708	York	1981-82
30959	TU	48301-48306	Derby	1980
30960	SLEP	10500-10619	Derby	1983
30961	SLE	10646-10733	Derby	1984
30962	DMS	55500	Derby/Leyland Bus	1983
30962	DMSL	55501	Derby/Leyland Bus	1980
30963	TF	41167-41169	Derby	1982
30964	TGS	44091-44094	Derby	1982
30966	TRUB	40354-40357	Derby	1982
30967	TF	41170-41174	Derby	1982
30968	DM	43191-43198	Crewe	1982
30969	TS	42306-42322	Derby	1982
30970	TGS	44095-44101	Derby	1982
30971	ExhibVan	99641-99642	Stewarts Lane (conv.)	1981
30972	DTSO	77579-77726	York	1982-84
30973	MSO	62709-62782	York	1984-85
30974	TSO	71637-71710	York	1982-84
30975	MSO	62783-62825	York	1985
30976	DTSO	77727-77812	York	1984-85
30977	DMS	55502-55521	Derby/Leyland Bus	1984
30978	DMSL	55522-55541	Derby/Leyland Bus	1984
30979	DMSO	64688-64691	York	1979-80
30980	TSO	71521-71525	York	1980
30981	BDMSO	64730-64734	York	1980
30982	FO	11064-11101	Derby	1985
30983	TS	42323-42341	Derby	1985
30984	DMSL	55200-55201	York	1984
30985	DMS	55300-55301	York	1984
30986	MS	55400	York	1984
30986	MS	55401	York	1984
30987	DMSL	55202-55203	Metro-Cammell	1985
30988	DMS	55302-55303	Metro-Cammell	1985
30989	MS	55402-55403	Metro-Cammell	1985
30990	BFO	17173-17175	Derby	1986
30991	DTSO	77813-77852	York	1985
30992	MSO	62826-62845	York	1985
30993	TSO	71714-71733	York	1985
30994	DTSO	77200-77219	York	1985-86
30995	DTSO	77220-77239	York	1985-86
30996	MSO	62846-62865	York	1985-86
30997	TCOL	71734-71753	York	1985-86
30998	MSOL	62866-62885	York	1985-86
30999	DTSOL	77240-77259	York	1985-86
31000	DTSO	77260-77279	York	1985-86
31001	TSO	71754-71761	Wolverton	1981
31002	ROY	2914-2915	Derby/Wolverton	1985
31003	DMS	55542-55591	Derby/Leyland Bus	1985-86
31004	DMSL	55592-55641	Derby/Leyland Bus	1985-86
31005	DMS	55642-55666	Alexander/Barclay	1985-86
31006	DMSL	55667-55691	Alexander/Barclay	1985-86
31007	DTSO	77280-77283	York	1987
31008	DTSO	77284-77287	York	1987
31009	MSO	62886-62889	York	1987
31010	TCOL	71762-71765	York	1981
31011	DMSL	52101-52150	York	1985-86
31012	DMS	57101-57150	York	1985-86
31013	DMS	55701-55746	Derby/Leyland Bus	1987
31014	DMSL	55747-55792	Derby/Leyland Bus	1987
31015	DMS	55801-55823	Derby/Alexander	1986-87
31016	DMSL	55824-55846	Derby/Alexander	1986-87
31017	DMSL	52201-52285	York	1986-87
31018	DMS	57201-57285	York	1986-87
31019	MSO	62890	York	1987
31020	DTSL	77288	York	1987
31021	DTS	77289	York	1987
31022	DTS(A)	77291-77381 *odds*	York	1987-88
31023	MSO	62891-62936	York	1987-88
31024	TSOL	71772-71817	York	1987-88
31025	DTSL	77290-77380 *evens*	York	1987-88
31026	DMSL	52301-52335	Leyland Bus	1987-88
31027	DMS	57301-57335	Leyland Bus	1987-88
31028	DMSL	52401-52514	Metro-Cammell	1988-89
31029	DMS	57401-57514	Metro-Cammell	1988-89
31030	DTCsoL	77382-77405	Derby	1988-89
31031	DTSOL	77406-77429	Derby	1988-89
31032	TSOL(A)	71818-71841	Derby	1988-89
31033	TSOL(B)	71842-71865	Derby	1988-89
31034	MBRSM	62937-62960	Derby	1988-89
31035	ROY	2922	Derby/Wolverton	1989
31036	ROY	2923	Derby/Wolverton	1989
31037	MS	55850-55859	Derby/Alexander	1987
31038	DTSO	77431-77457 *odds*	York	1988
31039	MSO	62961-62974	York	1988
31040	TSOL	71866-71879	York	1988
31041	DTSOL	77430-77456 *evens*	York	1988
31042	DVT	82101-82152	Derby	1988
31043	DVT	82200-82231	Metro-Cammell	1988
31044	ROY	2920	Derby/Wolverton	1988
31045	RFB	10300-10333	Metro-Cammell	1989
31046	FO	11200-11271	Metro-Cammell	1989-92
31047	TSOEnd	12200-12231	Metro-Cammell	1989-91
31048	TSOD	12300-12330	Metro-Cammell	1989-91
31049	TSO	12400-12512	Metro-Cammell	1989-92
31050	MS	58701-58739	Derby	1991-92
31051	DMSO(A)	52701-52894	Derby	1989-93
31051	DMSO(A)	52901-52910	Derby	1990-92
31052	DMSO(B)	57701-57894	Derby	1989-92
31052	DMSO(B)	57901-57910	Derby	1990-92
31053	DTCO	78049-78094	York	1988-90
31053	DTCO	78131-78150	York	1988-90
31054	MSO	62975-63020	York	1988-90

31054	MSO	63105-63124	York	1988-90
31055	TSOL	71880-71925	York	1988-90
31055	TSOL	71991-72010	York	1988-90
31056	DTSO	77853-77898	York	1988-90
31056	DTSO	78280-78299	York	1988-90
31057	DMS(A)	52341-52347	Leyland Bus	1988
31058	DMS(B)	57341-57347	Leyland Bus	1988
31059	ROY	2916	Derby/Wolverton	1988
31060	DTSO(A)	77899-77920	York	1990
31061	DTSO(B)	77921-77942	York	1990
31062	MSO	63021-63042	York	1990
31063	DTCO	77459-77497	York	1990
		odds		
31063	DTCO	77973-77983	York	1990
		odds		
31064	MSO	63043-63062	York	1990
31064	MSO	63093-63098	York	1990
31065	TSOL	71929-71948	York	1990
31065	TSOL	71979-71984	York	1990
31066	DTSO	77458-77496	York	1990
		evens		
31066	DTSO	77974-77984	York	1990
		evens		
31067	DTCO	78095-78130	York	1989-90
31067	DTCO	78151-78162	York	1989-90
31068	MSO	63063-63092	York	1989-90
31068	MSO	63099-63104	York	1989-90
31068	MSO	63125-63136	York	1989-90
31069	TSOL	71949-71978	York	1989-90
31069	TSOL	71985-71990	York	1989-90
31069	TSOL	72011-72022	York	1989-90
31070	DTSO	77943-77972	York	1989-90
31070	DTSO	78274-78279	York	1989-90
31070	DTSO	78300-78311	York	1989-90
31071	DMSO(A)	121-129	Metro-Cammell (conv.)	1989-90
31072	DMSO(B)	221-229	Metro-Cammell (conv.)	1989-90
31073	DMSO	64735-64758	York	1990-91
31074	DTSO	78250-78273	York	1990-91
31083	ROY	2918	Wolverton	1990
31084	ROY	2917	Wolverton	1990
31085	ROY	2919	Wolverton	1990
31086	ROY	2920	Wolverton	1990
31087	DMCL	58801-58822	York	1991-92
31087	DMCL	58873-58878	York	1991-92
31088	DMS	58834-58872	York	1991-92
31089	DMCL	58823-58833	York	1991-92
31090	MS	55404-55414	York	1991-92
31091	DTSO	77985-77989	York	1990
31092	TSOL	72023-72027	York	1990
31093	MSO	63137-63141	York	1990
31094	DTCO	78163-78167	York	1990
31096	DMCL	58879-58898	York	1992
31097	DMS	58916-58952	York	1992
31098	DMCL	58953-58969	York	1992
31099	MS	55415-55431	York	1992
31100	DMSO(A)	64759-64808	York	1991-93
31100	DMSO(B)	64809-64858	York	1991-93
31101	TSOL	72029-72127	York	1991-93
		odds		
31101	TSOL	72901-72993	York	1993-94
		odds		
31102	TSO	72028-72126	York	1991-93
		evens		
31102	TSO	72900-72992	York	1993-94
		evens		
31103	DMSO(A)	65700-65749	Metro-Cammell	1991-93
31103	DMSO(B)	65750-65799	Metro-Cammell	1991-93
31104	TSOL	72719-72817	Metro-Cammell	1991-92
		odds		
31105	TSO	72720-72818	Metro-Cammell	1991-92
		evens		
31108	DTSO(A)	77990-77992	York	1991
31109	MSO	63153-63155	York	1991
31109	TSOL	72128-72130	York	1991
31111	DTSO(B)	77993-77995	York	1991
31112	DMSO(A)	64001-64043	Hunslet	1992-93
31113	TSOL	72201-72239	Hunslet	1992-93
31113	TSOL	72340-72343	Hunslet	1992-93
31114	DMSO(B)	65001-65043	Hunslet	1992-93
31115	DMSL	52301-52335	Rebuilt	1991-92
31115	DMSL	57351-57385	Rebuilt	1991-92
31116	DMCL(A)	58101-58121	York	1992-93
31116	DMCL(B)	58122-58142	York	1992-93
31117	MS	58601-58621	York	1992-93
31118	DM	3730010-3730220	*every 10th*	1992-95
31118	DM	3731010-3731080	*every 10th*	1992-95
31118	DM	3732010-3732320	*every 10th*	1992-95
31118	DM	3733010-3733140	*every 10th*	1992-95
31118	DM	3739990		1992-95
31119	MS	3730011-3730221	*every 10th*	1992-95
31119	MS	3731011-3731081	*every 10th*	1992-95
31119	MS	3732011-3732321	*every 10th*	1992-95
31119	MS	3733011-3733141	*every 10th*	1992-95
31120	TS	3730012-3730222	*every 10th*	1992-95
31120	TS	3731012-3731082	*every 10th*	1992-95
31120	TS	3732012-3732322	*every 10th*	1992-95
31120	TS	3733012-3733142	*every 10th*	1992-95
31121	TS	3730013-3730223	*every 10th*	1992-95
31121	TS	3731013-3731083	*every 10th*	1992-95
31121	TS	3732013-3732323	*every 10th*	1992-95
31121	TS	3733013-3733143	*every 10th*	1992-95
31122	TS	3730014-3730224	*every 10th*	1992-95
31122	TS	3731014-3731084	*every 10th*	1992-95
31122	TS	3732014-3732324	*every 10th*	1992-95
31123	TS	3730015-3730225	*every 10th*	1992-95
31123	TS	3731015-3731085	*every 10th*	1992-95
31123	TS	3732015-3732325	*every 10th*	1992-95
31123	TS	3733015-3733145	*every 10th*	1992-95
31124	RB	3730016-3730226	*every 10th*	1992-95
31124	RB	3731016-3731086	*every 10th*	1992-95
31124	RB	3732016-3732326	*every 10th*	1992-95
31124	RB	3733016-3733146	*every 10th*	1992-95
31125	TFOH	3730017-3730227	*every 10th*	1992-95
31125	TFOH	3731017-3731087	*every 10th*	1992-95
31125	TFOH	3732017-3732327	*every 10th*	1992-95
31125	TFOH	3733017-3733147	*every 10th*	1992-95
31126	TFOH	3730018-3730228	*every 10th*	1992-95
31126	TFOH	3731018-3731088	*every 10th*	1992-95
31126	TFOH	3732018-3732328	*every 10th*	1992-95
31127	TBF	3730019-3730229	*every 10th*	1992-95
31127	TBF	3731019-3731089	*every 10th*	1992-95
31127	TBF	3732019-3732329	*every 10th*	1992-95
31127	TBF	3733019-3733149	*every 10th*	1992-95
31128	DMSO	64860-64902	GEC/Alsthom	1993-94
31129	DTSO	78312-78354	GEC/Alsthom	1993-94
31130	DMSO(A)	65800-65846	York	1993-94
31130	DMSO(B)	65847-65893	York	1993-94
31133	DMCO(A)	65894-65934	York	1994-95
31134	TSOL	72241-72321	York	1994-95
		odds		
31135	PTSOL	72240-72320	York	1994-95
		evens		
31136	DMCO(B)	65935-65975	York	1994-95
31144	DTPMV	68300-68331	Derby	1995
31145	MPMV	68340-68355	Derby	1995
31146	TPMV	68360-68375	Derby	1995

Having been transferred to the Western Region a six-car Class 251 Blue Pullman is forming the down morning Bristol Pullman at Keynsham, near Bristol on 5th April 1968. This unit shows the intermediate livery; still in Nanking Blue, but with full yellow ends. *P J Fowler*

Appendix 3: DMU Diagram Numbers

406	30368	79998	BDMBS	Derby/Cowlairs
442	30368	79999	BDTCL	Derby/Cowlairs
500	30128	79740	DMS	BUT
500	30128	79741	TS	BUT
500	30128	79742	DMBS	BUT
501	30084	79000-79007	DMBS	Derby
502	30192	79508-79512	DMC	Derby
503	30123	79008-79020	DMBS	Derby
504	30126	79021-79033	DMBS	Derby
504	30177	79034-79046	DMBS	Derby
505	30127	79613-79625	DTCL	Derby
505	30178	79250-79262	DTCL	Derby
506	30174	79743-79744	DMBS	BUT
506	30175	79745	DMS	BUT
506	30176	79746-79747	TS	BUT
506	30214	79748	DMS	BUT
506	30215	79749	TS	BUT
506	30216	79750	DMBS	BUT
507	30085	79500-79507	DMCL	Derby
508	30194	79325-79329	TBSL	Derby
509	30124	79600-79612	DTCL	Derby
509	30236	79639-79647	DTCL	Derby
509	30241	79648-79657	DTCL	Derby
509	30325	79189-79193	DMCL	Derby
511	30322	79670-79684	DTCL	Derby
512	30518	55020-55035	DMBS	Pressed Steel
513	30519	56280-56289	DTS	Pressed Steel
514	30380	79900	DMBS	Derby
515	30387	79901	DMBS	Derby
516	30209	50001-50048	DMBS	Derby
516	30459	50049	DMBS	Derby
517	30195	79400-79404	TSL	Derby
518	30193	79150-79154	DMS	Derby
520	30248	50134-50137	DMBS	Metro-Cammell
522	30339	50246-50248	DMBS	Metro-Cammell
523	30252	50152-50157	DMBS	Metro-Cammell
523	30254	50164-50167	DMBS	Metro-Cammell
523	30259	50198-50209	DMBS	Metro-Cammell
523	30261	50210-50233	DMBS	Metro-Cammell
523	30266	50250-50259	DMBS	Metro-Cammell
523	30270	50290-50296	DMBS	Metro-Cammell
523	30275	50303-50320	DMBS	Metro-Cammell
523	30467	51174-51253	DMBS	Metro-Cammell
523	30500	51425-51470	DMBS	Metro-Cammell
523	30587	51795-51801	DMBS	Metro-Cammell
524	30296	50532-50541	DMBS	BRCW
524	30338	50280-50289	DMBS	Metro-Cammell
525	30280	50359-50372	DMBS	Cravens
525	30282	50373-50389	DMBS	Cravens
525	30284	50390-50394	DMBS	Cravens
526	30281	56114-56127	DTCL	Cravens
526	30283	56128-56144	DTCL	Cravens
526	30285	56145-56149	DTCL	Cravens
527	30240	79137-79140	DMBSL	Derby
528	30352	50752-50784	DMBS	Cravens
529	30353	50785-50817	DMCL	Cravens
530	30354	59307-59325	TCL	Cravens
531	30418	55997-55999	DMPMV	Cravens
532	30469	51254-51301	DMBS	Cravens
533	30470	56412-56459	DTCL	Cravens
534	30543	51302-51316	DMBS	BRCW
534	30546	51332-51373	DMBS	Pressed Steel
535	30545	51317-51331	DMS	BRCW
535	30548	51374-51415	DMS	Pressed Steel
536	30278	50339-50358	DMBS	Gloucester
536	30444	51108-51127	DMBS	Gloucester
537	30279	56094-56113	DTCL	Gloucester
537	30445	56300-56319	DTCL	Gloucester
538	30420	56291-56299	DTS	Gloucester
539	30419	55000-55019	DMBS	Gloucester
540	30421	51052-51079	DMBC	Gloucester
541	30422	51080-51107	DMSL	Gloucester
542	30423	59413-59437	TSLRB	Gloucester
543	30406	50599-50624	DMBS	Derby
543	30407	50625-50629	DMBS	Derby
543	30460	50924-50935	DMBS	Derby
543	30465	50938-50987	DMBS	Derby
544	30408	50630-50646	DMCL	Derby
545	30493	59386-59390	TSL	Derby
546	30412	59245-59250	TBSL	Derby
547	30411	59380-59385	TSL	Derby
548	30503	51471-51494	DMBS	Cravens
548	30505	50249	DMBS	Cravens
549	30504	56460-56483	DTCL	Cravens
550	30196	79083-79090	DMBSL	Swindon
550	30196	79095	DMBSL	Swindon
551	30199	79155-79168	DMSL	Swindon
551	30413	50936	DMSL	Swindon
551	30413	51008-51029	DMSL	Swindon
552	30200	79091-79094	DMBSL	Swindon
552	30200	79096-79111	DMBSL	Swindon
553	30211	50050-50091	DMBS	Derby
553	30363	50818-50870	DMBS	Derby
553	30446	51128-51140	DMBS	Derby
554	30213	50092-50133	DMS	Derby
554	30364	50871-50923	DMS	Derby
554	30447	51141-51153	DMS	Derby
555	30212	59000-59031	TC	Derby
555	30365	59326-59376	TC	Derby
555	30448	59438-59448	TC	Derby
556	30290	50420-50423	DMBS	BRCW
556	30293	50428-50479	DMBS	BRCW
557	30404	50594-50598	DMBS	BRCW
558	30291	50424-50427	DMCL	BRCW
558	30294	50480-50531	DMCL	BRCW
560	30197	79440-79447	TFKRB	Swindon
560	30537	59098-59099	TFKRB	Swindon
561	30336	59255-59301	TSLRB	Swindon
561	30561	59679-59685	TSLRB	Swindon
562	30606	59774-59781	TFLRB	Swindon
563	30593	51829-51848	DMCL	BRCW
563	30692	52076-52085	DMCL	BRCW
564	30592	51809-51828	DMBC	BRCW
564	30691	52066-52075	DMBC	BRCW
566	30703	52086-52095	DMBSL	Swindon
567	30705	59818-59827	TCK	Swindon
568	30706	59235-59239	TSL	Swindon
569	30707	59828-59832	TSLRB	Swindon
570	30198	79470-79482	TFK	Swindon
570	30415	59391-59400	TFK	Swindon
571	30416	59402-59412	TCL	Swindon
572	30517	59579-59588	TSL	Swindon
573	30605	59765-59773	TSL	Swindon
574	30704	52096-52105	DMSK	Swindon
577	30603	51951-51967	DMC	Swindon
579	30604	51968-51984	MBSK	Swindon
580	30298	50542-50583	DMCL	BRCW
580	30301	50584-50593	DMCL	BRCW
581	30405	56185-56189	DTCL	BRCW
582	30292	59132-59135	TCL	BRCW
582	30295	59136-59187	TCL	BRCW
583	30299	59188-59208	TSL	BRCW
583	30302	59230-59234	TSL	BRCW
584	30300	59209-59229	TBSL	BRCW
584	30303	59240-59244	TBSL	BRCW
585	30297	56175-56184	DTCL	BRCW
586	30334	50647-50695	DMSL	Swindon
586	30560	51788-51794	DMSL	Swindon
587	30335	50696-50744	DMBC	Swindon
587	30559	51781-51787	DMBC	Swindon
588	30521	51591-51650	DMBS	Derby
589	30522	59589-59618	TSL	Derby
590	30523	59619-59648	TS	Derby
590	30531	59649-59663	TS	Derby
590	30596	59713-59718	TS	Derby
590	30599	59725-59744	TS	Derby
591	30190	79047-79075	DMBS	Metro-Cammell
592	30190	79076-79082	DMBS	Metro-Cammell
593	30191	79263-79291	DTSL	Metro-Cammell
594	30191	79626-79632	DTCL	Metro-Cammell
595	30464	51154-51173	DMBS	Derby
596	30462	50988-51007	DMS	Derby
597	30463	59449-59468	TS	Derby
598	30530	51651-51680	DMBS	Derby
598	30595	51849-51860	DMBS	Derby
598	30598	51861-51900	DMBS	Derby
599	30532	59664-59678	TCL	Derby
599	30597	59719-59724	TCL	Derby
599	30600	59745-59764	TCL	Derby
600	30385	59032-59041	TS	Derby
601	30544	59469-59483	TCL	BRCW
601	30547	59484-59522	TCL	Pressed Steel
602	30533	51681-51705	DMBS	Cravens
603	30534	51706-51730	DMCOL	Cravens
604	30535	51731-51755	DMBS	Cravens
605	30536	51756-51780	DMCOL	Cravens
606	30288	50415-50419	DMBS	Wickham
607	30289	56170-56174	DTCL	Wickham
608	30414	51030-51051	DMBSL	Swindon
609	30461	51561-51572	DMCL	Derby
610	30483	79958-79959	DMBS	BRCW
611	30482	79960-79964	DMBS	Waggon & Masch.
612	30481	79965-79969	DMBS	Wickham
613	30480	79970-79974	DMBS	Park Royal
614	30479	79975-79979	DMBS	AC Cars
615	30508	51541-51550	DMBS	Metro-Cammell
616	30268	50270-50279	DMCL	Metro-Cammell
617	30509	51551-51560	DMCL	Metro-Cammell
618	30249	50138-50151	DMCL	Metro-Cammell
619	30263	50234-50245	DMCL	Metro-Cammell
620	30253	50158-50163	DMCL	Metro-Cammell
620	30255	50168-50171	DMCL	Metro-Cammell
620	30256	50172-50197	DMCL	Metro-Cammell
621	30267	50260-50269	DMCL	Metro-Cammell
621	30271	50745-50751	DMCL	Metro-Cammell
621	30276	50321-50338	DMCL	Metro-Cammell
621	30501	51495-51540	DMCL	Metro-Cammell
621	30588	51802-51808	DMCL	Metro-Cammell
622	30250	59042-59048	TSL	Metro-Cammell
622	30264	59086-59091	TSL	Metro-Cammell
623	30257	59060-59072	TSL	Metro-Cammell
623	30269	59100-59109	TSL	Metro-Cammell
623	30273	59302-59306	TSL	Metro-Cammell
623	30510	59569-59572	TSL	Metro-Cammell
624	30277	59114-59131	TCL	Metro-Cammell
624	30502	59523-59568	TCL	Metro-Cammell
624	30589	59686-59692	TCL	Metro-Cammell
625	30615	59573-59578	TSLRB	Metro-Cammell
626	30251	59049-59055	TBSL	Metro-Cammell
626	30265	59092-59097	TBSL	Metro-Cammell
627	30258	59073-59085	TBSL	Metro-Cammell
627	30274	59112-59113	TBSL	Metro-Cammell
628	30337	56090-56093	DTCL	Metro-Cammell
629	30340	56218-56220	DTCL	Metro-Cammell
630	30260	56050-56061	DTCL	Metro-Cammell
630	30262	56062-56085	DTCL	Metro-Cammell
630	30272	56086-56089	DTCL	Metro-Cammell
630	30468	56332-56411	DTCL	Metro-Cammell
631	30241	79658-79661	DTCL	Derby
632	30341	50000	DMBS	Derby
633	30201	79143-79149	DMBSL	Derby
633	30235	79118-79126	DMBSL	Derby
633	30240	79127-79136	DMBSL	Derby
633	30246	79141-79142	DMBSL	Derby
633	30321	79169-79181	DMBSL	Derby
633	30324	79184-79188	DMBS	Derby
634	30498	51416-51424	DMBS	Derby
634	30601	51901-51950	DMBS	Derby
635	30286	50395-50414	DMBS	Park Royal
636	30515	51573-51581	DMBCL	Swindon
637	30516	51582-51590	DMSL	Swindon
638	30660	52037-52065	DMCL	Derby
639	30611	51985-52010	DMBS	Derby
640	30409	56190-56210	DTCL	Derby
640	30410	56211-56215	DTCL	Derby
640	30466	56221-56270	DTCL	Derby
641	30210	56001-56049	DTCL	Derby
641	30342	56000	DTCL	Derby
642	30202	79663-79669	DTCL	Derby
642	30247	79662	DTCL	Derby
643	30551	55991-55996	DMPMV	Gloucester
644	30552	55987-55990	DMPMV	Gloucester
645	30287	56150-56169	DTCL	Park Royal
646	30499	56271-56279	DTCL	Derby
646	30602	56484-56504	DTCL	Derby
647	30613	59782-59807	TSL	Derby
648	30594	59693-59712	TSL	BRCW
648	30693	59808-59817	TSL	BRCW
649	30612	52011-52036	DMCL	Derby
650	30329	60000-60013	DMBS	Ashford/Eastleigh
651	30391	60020-60045	DMBSO	Ashford/Eastleigh
651	30395	60014-60019	DMBSO	Ashford/Eastleigh
652	30332	60100-60117	DMBSO	Ashford/Eastleigh
652	30398	60118-60121	DMBSO	Ashford/Eastleigh
652	30540	60122-60125	DMBSO	Ashford/Eastleigh
653	30553	60090-60093	DMBFL	Metro-Cammell
654	30554	60094-60099	DMBS	Metro-Cammell
655	30625	60126-60144	DMBSO	Ashford/Eastleigh
656	30671	60145-60151	DMBSO	Ashford/Eastleigh
660	30330	60700-60706	TFK	Ashford/Eastleigh
661	30392	60710-60722	TFK	Ashford/Eastleigh
661	30396	60707-60709	TFK	Ashford/Eastleigh
662	30556	60730-60733	MFLRK	Metro-Cammell
663	30557	60734-60739	TFLRK	Metro-Cammell
664	30558	60740-60749	TPFL	Metro-Cammell
667	30626	60600-60618	TCsoL	Ashford/Eastleigh
670	30331	60500-60520	TSOL	Ashford/Eastleigh
671	30394	60530-60561	TSOL	Ashford/Eastleigh
671	30397	60521-60529	TSOL	Ashford/Eastleigh
672	30542	60650-60671	TSO	Ashford/Eastleigh
672	30672	60672-60678	TSO	Ashford/Eastleigh
673	30555	60644-60649	MPSL	Metro-Cammell
678	30393	60750-60756	TRB	Ashford/Eastleigh
679	30333	60800-60817	DTCsoL	Ashford/Eastleigh
679	30399	60818-60821	DTCsoL	Ashford/Eastleigh
680	30673	60826-60832	DTCsoL	Ashford/Eastleigh
681	30627	60900-60918	DTSO	Ashford/Eastleigh
683	30541	60822-60825	DTCsoL	Ashford/Eastleigh
850	30543	51302-51316	DMBS	BRCW
850	30546	51332-51373	DMBS	Pressed Steel
851	30544	59469-59483	TCL	BRCW
851	30547	59484-59522	TCL	Pressed Steel
852	30545	51317-51331	DMS	BRCW
852	30548	51374-51415	DMS	Pressed Steel
853	30211	50050-50091	DMBS	Derby
853	30363	50818-50870	DMBS	Derby
853	30446	51128-51140	DMBS	Derby
854	30213	50092-50133	DMS	Derby
854	30364	50871-50923	DMS	Derby
854	30447	51141-51153	DMS	Derby
855	30212	59000-59031	TC	Derby
855	30365	59326-59376	TC	Derby
855	30448	59438-59448	TC	Derby
856	30385	59032-59041	TS	Derby

On the 14th October 2009 while visiting Marylebone Station to see the Class 67s working on the Wrexham and Shropshire service I heard the unmistakeable sound of a first generation DMU pulling in to the station. It was Chiltern's Water-Jetting unit 960301 (977987, 977992 and 977988) out and about on its Autumn leaf-clearing duties. It is seen here waiting at Marylebone in its BR green livery complete with early BR emblems, before heading north again.

The unit proudly displays its blue square coupling code (although there are not a lot of other units around for it to couple to these days). The middle carriage is unique in being a non-driving motor vehicle, the cab being removed when it was converted. The only other first-generation non-driving motors were included in the Class 124 Trans-Pennine units, now long gone.

Who would have thought when the first generation units were being built in the 1950s that it would still be possible to see one earning its keep on the National Railway ten years into the new millennium? *H Longworth*